# American Odyssey

## The United States in the Twentieth Century

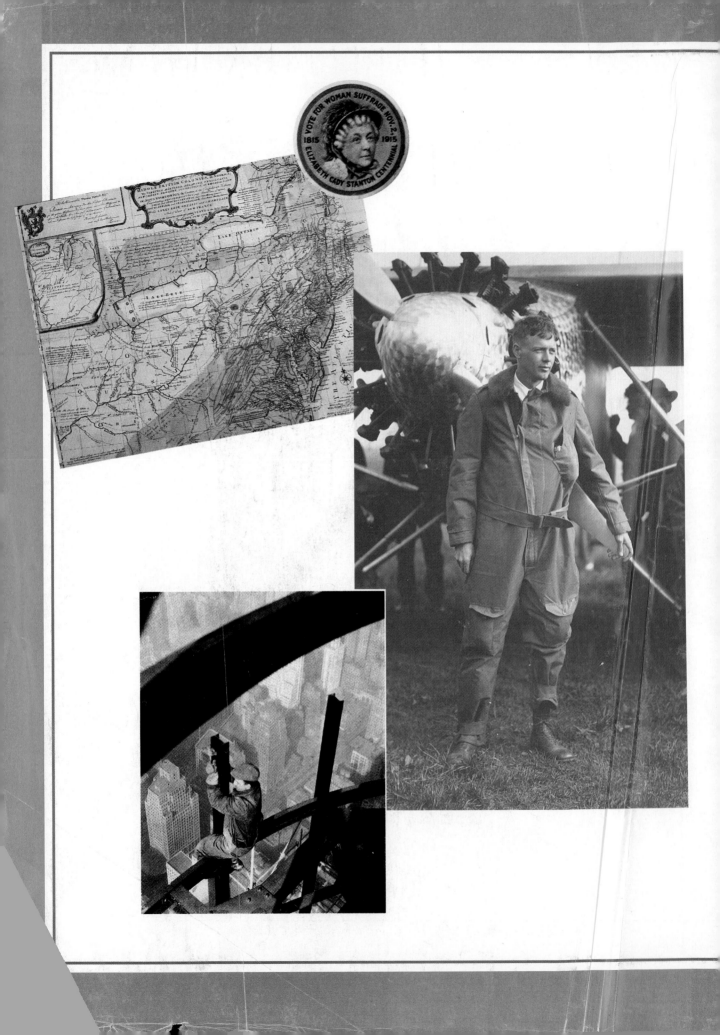

# American Odyssey

## The United States in the Twentieth Century

### Gary B. Nash

*Professor of History*
*University of California at Los Angeles*

## GLENCOE
McGraw-Hill

New York, New York   Columbus, Ohio   Mission Hills, California   Peoria, Illinois

# Author

**Gary B. Nash** is Professor of History at the University of California at Los Ang~es and Associate Director of the National Center for History in the Schools. He is au~or of *Red, White, and Black: The People of Early America* (Prentice-Hall, 1982) and *Forgi~ Press, 1988), Formation of Philadelphia's Black Community, 1720–1840* (Harvard Universi~*Freedom: The* among other publications.

# Consultants

## Program Consultants

### Geography Consultant
Christopher L. Salter
Professor and Chair
Department of Geography
University of Missouri
Columbia, Missouri

### ~nal Consultant
*Edu~*. Scholl
~Aldary Social Science Specialist
~ice of Instruction
~os Angeles Unified School District
Los Angeles, California

## ~g Consultants

### Multicultural Education
Gloria Contreras
Professor of Secondary Education
University of North Texas
Denton, Texas

### American West Frontiers
Albert L. Hurtado
Associate Professor of Hi~
Arizona State Universi~~ation
Tempe, Arizona

### Reading and Bi~ucation
Eileen Morter~sity
Assistant Pr~
National ~
Evanst~

### Con~~tudies and ~American History
~Johnson Odim
~tant Professor of History
~yola University
~hicago, Illinois

### Asian Studies
Gary Okihiro
Associate Professor of History
Cornell University
Ithaca, New York

### African American History
Julius S. Scott
Assistant Professor of History
Duke University
Durham, North Carolina

### Mexican American Women's History
Vicki L. Ruiz
Associate Professor of History
University of California
Davis, California

### Native American History
John Waukechan, M.A.
Member, American Indian Resource
    and Education Coalition
Austin, Texas

Y. Elaine Childers, Ph.D.
Member, Creek Nation
Austin, Texas

~all inquiries to:
~ncoe/McGraw-Hill
~36 Eastwind Drive
Westerville, Ohio 43081

Development by Ligature, Inc.

ISBN 0-02-822723-9 (teacher's wraparound edition)
ISBN 0-02-822722-0 (student text)

5 6 7 8 9 10 VH/LP 00 99 98 97 96 95

Cover: This DC-3, the first airplane model to carry passengers profitably, is on display at the National Air and Space Museum's Hall of Air Transportation in Washington, D.C.

iv

# Reviewers

## Content Reviewers

David Anderson
Department of History and
  Political Science
University of Indianapolis
Indianapolis, Indiana

D'Ann Campbell
Department of History
U.S. Military Academy
West Point, New York

Lynn Dumenil
History Department
Claremont-McKenna College
Claremont, California

Paula Fass
Department of History
University of California
Berkeley, California

Otis Graham
Department of History
University of California
Santa Barbara, California

James R. Grossman
Director, Family and
  Community History Center
Newberry Library
Chicago, Illinois

Warren F. Kimball
Department of History
Rutgers University
Newark, New Jersey

John Martz
Department of Political Science
Pennsylvania State University
University Park, Pennsylvania

Allen J. Matusow
School of Humanities
Rice University
Houston, Texas

David Oshinsky
Department of History
Rutgers University
New Brunswick, New Jersey

Herbert Parmet
Department of History
Queensborough Community
  College
Bayside, New York

Richard Polenberg
Department of History
Cornell University
Ithaca, New York

Athan Theoharis
Department of History
Marquette University
Milwaukee, Wisconsin

## Educational Reviewers

David Bardos
Carmel High School
Carmel, Indiana

Thomas H. Bond
Harper High School
Chicago, Illinois

Edward Brickner
Woodbury High School
Woodbury, Minnesota

Ralph Childs
Lane Technical High School
Chicago, Illinois

Carolyn Conner
Westbury High School
Houston Independent School
  District
Houston, Texas

Bruce Eddy
Evanston Township High
  School
Evanston, Illinois

Roy Erickson
San Juan Unified School
  District
Carmichael, California

Brook A. Goddard
Miami Norland Senior High
  School
Dade County Public Schools
Miami, Florida

Robert Griesing
Toms River Regional School
  District
Toms River, New Jersey

Clinton P. Hartmann
Principal, Lydia Patterson
  Institute
El Paso, Texas

Sonya Heckman
Greencastle-Antrim Middle
  School
Greencastle, Pennsylvania

Merle Knight
Lewis S. Mills High School
Burlington, Connecticut

Tom Laiches
Crossroads School
Santa Monica, California

Halston Lewis
Bromfield School (retired)
Harvard, Massachusetts

John McDonough
Shaler Area Senior High School
Shaler School District
Shaler, Pennsylvania

Sheldon Obelsky
Arlington High School
Arlington, Massachusetts

Judy Parsons
Columbia Public Schools
Columbia, Missouri

Denny Schillings
Homewood-Flossmoor High
  School
Flossmoor, Illinois

Gloria Sesso
Half Hollow Hills School
  District
Dix Hills, New York

Shirley Simmons
Fuquay-Varina High School
Fuquay-Varina, North Carolina

Jim Snopko
Springfield Southeast High
  School
Springfield, Illinois

Louise Stricklin
Redondo Union High School
Redondo Beach, California

Larry Sutton
Madison High School
San Diego Unified School
  District
San Diego, California

Darla Weissenberg
Lincoln Park High School
Chicago, Illinois

# American Odyssey

# CONTENTS

# *Features*

## Evidence of the Past

*Evidence of the past comes to light once per unit in detailed examinations of the ways historians use artifacts and documents.*

## One Day in History

*Reminiscent of a daily newspaper, these "front pages" recall the dramatic—and the ordinary—events of nine special days in history.*

## Culture of the Time

*Visual and verbal displays appearing once per unit bring the popular culture of the time to life.*

## Geography: Impact on History

*Geographic themes are explored through six pivotal developments in U.S. history.*

## Social Studies Skills

*Social Studies Skills provide learning and practice in the context of historical and geographic topics.*

# CONTENTS

## Charts and Graphs

*Charts and graphs in easy-to-read formats present information in a clear and focused way.*

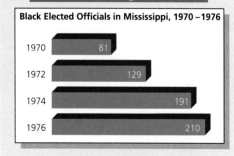

**Black Voting Power**

Black Elected Officials in Mississippi, 1970–1976

1970   81
1972   129
1974   191
1976   210

## Diagraphics

*Lively combinations of diagrams, statistical information, and "talking" annotations convey complex situations accurately and concisely.*

# Understanding the Section

*Just as each unit is organized into chapters, each chapter is organized into sections to make learning manageable. The basic plan of the section is easy to follow and includes a built-in Study Guide at the bottom of each page to help you monitor your progress.*

> Main **headings** in red and **subheadings** in green help you keep the story organized as you read.

> Just as a journalist opens a story with a compelling "hook," each section of this book opens with a retelling of a dramatic moment in U.S. history. The **dateline** anchors the moment in time.

---

**SECTION 1**

# The Cold War Begins

### April 25, 1945: GIs Meet Soviet Troops

LILACS BLOOMED AND THE SUN SHONE ON APRIL 25, 1945, AS AMERICAN SOLDIERS BATTLING THE GERMANS FROM THE WEST APPROACHED THEIR SOVIET ALLIES fighting from the east. Victory was in the air, and as the armies neared the Elbe River south of Berlin, small patrols of Americans drove out in jeeps to meet their Soviet comrades in arms. Throughout the day Soviet and American soldiers embraced for the first time. Andy Rooney, staff writer for the armed forces newspaper, *Stars & Stripes*, caught the moment:

ARMED WORLD PHOTOS

*There was a mad scene of jubilation on the east and west banks of the Elbe at Torgau as infantrymen of Lieutenant General Courtney H. Hodges . . . swapped K rations for a vodka with soldiers of Marshal Kornian's Ukrainian Army, congratulating each other . . . on the linkup.*

*Men of the 69th Division sat on the banks of the Elbe in warm sunshine today with no enemy in front of them or behind them and . . . watched their new Russian friends and listened to them as they played accordions and sang Russian songs.*

*The Russian soldiers are the most carefree bunch . . . that ever came together in an army. They would best be described as exactly like Americans, only twice as much. . . . You get the feeling of exuberance, a great new world opening up.*

Andy Rooney, "Good Soldiers Meet," *Stars & Stripes*, April 28, 1945

## An Iron Curtain Starts to Fall

The possibility of the opening of that "great new world" evaporated quickly. The war had left the United States and the Soviet Union as the world's dominant powers. Cautious allies during the struggle, the two nations emerged from the war with misgivings about one another. Each viewed the other with deep mistrust. Each had special interests to protect. And each carried the weight of its own history to the moment.

**An Uneasy Alliance** During the war Britain, the Soviet Union, the United States, and 23 other nations had joined forces in the Grand Alliance. Pooling their military might, the 26 set out to crush the Axis powers in Europe and Asia.

The organization was a strong, but uneasy, alliance. Among its members were nations with old hatreds and misunderstandings of one another, bound together by a common enemy. At the heart of the alliance stood the United States and the Soviet Union.

While the Soviets praised the courage of American fighting men and the leadership of President Roosevelt, old hostilities simmered beneath the surface. The Soviets resented the fact that American troops, along with British and French forces, tried to undo their revolution of 1917. When that attempt failed, the United States still refused to recognize the Soviet government until 1933. Furthermore, Soviet propaganda stirred up popular fears of American capitalism with its divisions between rich and poor and its swings between prosperity and depression.

The Allies' de[...]
made Stalin sus[...]
vasion of France[...]
from his countr[...]
two-year delay [...]
secretly wanted a[...]

Americans a[...]
Union. Commun[...]
olution, had alw[...]
more, past Sovie[...]
Americans. In 1[...]
peace with Germ[...]
many without S[...]
short-lived nonag[...]
American fears w[...]
tacks on his inter[...]

During the w[...]
Allies focused [...]
problem—and o[...]
war came to an e[...]
Union faced their[...]

**Two Views of** [...]
the western Sov[...]
struction. More [...]
the struggle. Gr[...]
destroyed more t[...]
towns, and 70,[...]

**Comparing an**[...]
The Soviets feared [...]
it is essentially a fr[...]
system in which in[...]
operate privately fi[...]
In a socialist econo[...]

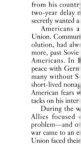

---

**STUDY GUIDE**

**As You Read**
Identify the events that led to Soviet dominance in eastern Europe, the Truman Doctrine, and the cold war. Also, think about the following concepts and skills.

**Central Concepts**
- understanding how differing ideologies shaped postwar Europe and fueled the **cold war**
- understanding the main elements of the **Truman Doctrine**

**Thinking Skills**
- comparing and contrasting
- recognizing points of view
- analyzing behavior

460     Chapter 14

> The first element of the Study Guide in each section, **As You Read,** helps you focus your attention on the main point of the section.

> The second element of the Study Guide lists the **Central Concepts** of the section and helps you see their significance.

> The **Thinking Skills** listed in the Study Guide on the first page of each section are exemplified on subsequent pages, giving you the opportunity to further develop your understanding.

Boldface type within the text highlights the central concepts of the section as well as other key **vocabulary terms.**

Some of the most exciting aspects of the story are told through **visuals.** Photos and fine art enhance your sense of "being on the scene" as history happens; maps and graphs interpret the setting and the statistics of history.

Serving as a link between visuals and text, **captions** use boldface type to identify the visual and italic type to guide you in thinking about what you see.

Replacing the Study Guide on the last page of each section, the Section Review gives you the chance to demonstrate your understanding of the section, think about the material in a new and critical way, and relate this period in history to today or to another time.

**Questions** footnoted to specific passages of the text allow you to check your understanding of the material you have just read.

---

worked. Congress approved the request about one month later.

This view, which came to be known as the **Truman Doctrine,** defined American foreign policy for the next 20 years. From this moment on, most Americans would view communism as a worldwide threat to democracy that they had a duty to resist. The cold war would become not just a struggle for territory but a fight between two opposing views of the world.

[While military aid could help] [Trum]an and his advisers knew it [...]er. In June 1947 Secretary of [...]ggested another way to bol[...]elping Europe rebuild.

[...]r for two years, but Euro[...]ng to survive. Cities and [...]nto ruin. Roads and canals [...]all, millions of people were [...]ry. In May 1947 Churchill ["a rubble heap . . . a breed-] [disease] and hate."

[...]vere not only heartbreaking [...]terrible suffering provided [...]unism to grow, and already [...]athering strength in France [...]ed, starving Europe would [...]omy—and American busi[...]ed on European markets. [...]d spending billions of dol[...]cluding the USSR, back on [...] aid, nations had to agree to [...]s from the United States. At [...]n Congress disagreed with [...]stern Europe soon changed [...] refused to take part in the [...]ica's way of taking over Eu[...]he Communist party seized [...]ia, completing the Soviet [...]ope.

GEORGE C. MARSHALL FOUNDATION

**The slogan on this poster—"For the lifting up of self and a better life"—tells the benefits of the European Recovery Program, also called the Marshall Plan.**

Two months later Truman approved Congress's bill for $17 billion in aid to Europe over five years. Sixteen nations participated in the plan, and by 1952 they were more successful than anyone had dreamed. The Communist party in western Europe was severely weakened. Western European industries had increased their output by 64 percent, and American prosperity was ensured. At the same time, however, tensions with the Soviet Union continued to grow.

---

**After World War II, victory celebrations took place in both American and Soviet cities.** *What effects of the war are evident in the picture on the right?*

[...]also [...]in[...]ces [...]in's [...]ans

[...]viet [...]ev[...]er[...]led [...]ate [...]er[...]d a [...]g to [...]at-

[...]the [...]ion [...]the [...]viet

[...]var, [...]de[...]d in [...]had [...]000 [...]ins

wandered the hungry and homeless—25 million of them—seeking a place to settle.

Nothing was more important to Soviet leaders than protecting themselves from a rearmed Germany and rebuilding their shattered economy. One key to their security, they believed, was a permanently weakened Germany. Another was a ring of pro-Soviet nations protecting their western border. From Napoleon's attack on Moscow in 1812 through the German invasions of World Wars I and II, enemy armies had always swept in from the west.

Unlike the Soviets, the Americans emerged from the war more powerful than when they entered it. American casualties of 405,000 were tragic, but small, compared with the millions of Soviet dead. A booming American economy controlled nearly 50 percent of the world's wealth, and most Americans felt proud of their successful fight for democracy.[1]

American leaders envisioned a future of international peace and prosperity. They imagined a world patterned after the United States—democratic, open to business expansion and free trade. In this world free nations would solve their differences by talking, not by fighting. Like the Puritans and believers in Manifest Destiny before them, many Americans felt

---

**[STU]DY GUIDE**

[...]vored, the state (the gov[...] and operates businesses [...] of society at large. Strict [...]not allow for private

1 How did America's position at the end of the war compare with the Soviet Union's?

The Uneasy Peace    461

---

## SECTION REVIEW

[...]e Grand
[...]Soviets
[...]icans?
[...]fear the

[...]in Russian
[...]World

[...]uropean
[...]nd control

4. How was Germany divided at the Potsdam conference?
5. Describe the U.S. commitment to rebuild Europe as part of the Marshall Plan.

**Thinking Critically**
6. **Analyzing Behavior** Why might the United States have waited 16 years after the Russian Revolution to officially recognize the Soviet government?

7. **Comparing and Contrasting** Why did the Soviets prefer Roosevelt's style of diplomacy to Truman's?

**Linking Across Time**
8. What was the political status of eastern Europe at the start of the cold war? How has that status changed today?

SOVFOTO

POUR SE SOULEVER ET VIVRE MIEUX

xiii

# Going Beyond the Section

*The Case Study is a special kind of section designed to give you an in-depth look at a pivotal situation in U.S. history. What factors persuaded President Truman to drop the atomic bomb? How did the Cherokee respond when ordered off their land? Nine Case Studies—one in each unit—take you behind the scenes to understand the decision-making process.*

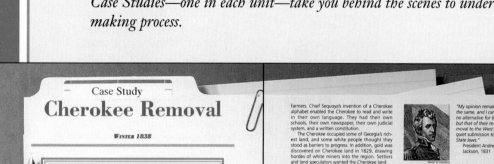

Case Study

## Cherokee Removal

**WINTER 1838**

> The Cherokee nation, then, is a distinct community, occupying its own territory, with boundaries accurately described, in which the laws of Georgia can have no force, and which the citizens of Georgia have no right to enter, but with the assent of the Cherokees themselves. . . .
>
> It is the opinion of this court that the judgment of the superior court . . . of Georgia, condemning Samuel A. Worcester to hard labour, . . . was pronounced by that court under . . . a law which is void . . . and ought, therefore, to be reversed and nullified.
>
> John Marshall, Chief Justice, Supreme Court, 1832

### The Case

The news was a cause for great celebration. The Cherokee and their supporters were jubilant. The case of *Worcester v. The State of Georgia* was over, and the Supreme Court of the United States had ruled in favor of Samuel Worcester, reversing the state's earlier judgment against him.

Worcester, a missionary who had lived among the Cherokee for years, had broken a Georgia state law. This law stated that non-Cherokee people living on Cherokee lands could either sign an oath of allegiance to Georgia or leave the Cherokee land. Worcester refused to do either. Instead, he chose a prison sentence of four years, but appealed his case to the U.S. Supreme Court.

The Supreme Court ruling in *Worcester v. Georgia* was an important victory, one that promised far more than just freedom for Worcester. Chief Justice John Marshall's words appeared to say that the Cherokee would be free to control their own fate, without interference from the state of Georgia. No one would enter the Cherokee Nation without the permission of the Cherokee, and the Cherokee could invite whomever they wanted to live on their land. The U.S. government would protect their lands.

But the victory in *Worcester v. Georgia* proved to be an empty one. President Andrew Jackson is said to have remarked, "John Marshall has made his decision; let him enforce it now if he can." Indeed, the decision could not be enforced. Jackson did nothing to see that the ruling was obeyed, and Worcester stayed in prison.

### The Background

The Cherokee had held their land long before European settlers arrived. Through treaties with the U.S. government, the Cherokee became a sovereign nation within Georgia. By the early 1800s, the Cherokee were principally an agricultural people, having adopted many of the customs and life styles of neighboring white

farmers. Chief Sequoya's invention of a Cherokee alphabet enabled the Cherokee to read and write in their own language. They had their own schools, their own newspaper, their own judicial system, and a written constitution.

The Cherokee occupied some of Georgia's richest land, and some white people thought they stood as barriers to progress. In addition, gold was discovered on Cherokee land in 1829, drawing hordes of white miners into the region. Settlers and land speculators wanted the Cherokee land.

By the time of *Worcester v. Georgia* in 1832, federal and state laws had opened the door for Cherokee removal. In 1830 Congress had passed the Indian Removal Act, allowing Jackson to pursue his goal of relocating eastern Native Americans to lands west of the Mississippi River.

That same year, Georgia lawmakers had decreed that all Cherokee lands were under state jurisdiction, erasing Cherokee claims to sovereignty. Further, the Cherokee could not testify against a white person or dig for the gold discovered in their own nation. Their laws were nullified. Finally, in December of 1830, Georgia restricted the presence of white settlers on Cherokee lands, a law that led to the *Worcester v. Georgia* case.

In 1832, with the Supreme Court's ruling, the Cherokee scored a short-lived triumph. When Jackson ignored the ruling, the Cherokee realized their hopes for federal protection were in vain.

Jackson recognized the Cherokee had not been treated fairly. Nevertheless, he believed that the eastern Native Americans would have to be relocated, since a separate nation could not continue to exist within a U.S. state. Long before *Worcester v. Georgia*, Jackson had warned Congress against "encroachments upon the legitimate sphere of State sovereignty." It was no surprise that Jackson chose not to enforce the Supreme Court's ruling.

### The Opinions

Read the opinions of some of the people involved in the Cherokee drama. President Jackson and Georgia Governor Lumpkin favored removal, while Massachusetts Senator Everett sided with the Cherokee in opposing it.

The quotations show that the people involved in the dispute differed sharply on the issue of

> "My opinion remains the same, and I can see no alternative for them but that of their removal to the West or a quiet submission to the State laws."
> President Andrew Jackson, 1831

> "Any attempt to in- . . . of a state to . . . entire population within its territorial limits . . . would be the usurpation of a power never granted by the states."
> Wilson Lumpkin, Governor of Georgia, 1832

> "Whoever read of such a project? Ten or fifteen thousand families, to be rooted up . . .

**This painting depicts the Cherokee on their forced march to Oklahoma. One soldier noted that he**

their laws, to which we are unaccustomed, which harass our braves and make the children suffer and cry. . . . I know the Indians have an older title than theirs. We obtained the land from the living God above. . . . Yet they are strong and we are weak. We are few, they are many. We cannot remain here in safety and comfort. I know we love the graves of our fathers. . . . We can never forget these homes, I know, but an unbending, iron necessity tells us we must leave them."

Pressure to complete the Cherokee relocation intensified. The National party, representing about 16,000 Cherokee, adamantly resisted the move. Yet the Jackson administration dealt only with the Treaty party, which had about 1,000 members. Its leaders signed a relocation treaty, which was ratified by Congress in 1836.

Still, few of the Cherokee moved voluntarily. Most never understood nor shared the Ridges' viewpoint. In 1838, after the deadline set for removal had passed, soldiers with rifles and bayonets forced more than 18,000 Cherokee from their homes and marched them approximately 1,000 miles to what is now Oklahoma. During the relocation, nearly 4,000 Cherokee died from malnutrition, expo-

had seen as many as 22 Cherokee people die in a single night during the journey.

cholera, and harsh treatment. Their grueling trek earned the name the "Trail of Tears."

### Think About It

1. Jackson spoke of the Cherokee well as hunters who had no right to "tracts of country on which they have neither dwelt nor made improvements, merely because they have seen them from the mountain or passed them in the chase." Why do you think Jackson made this statement? What was he purposely ignoring?

2. Senator Theodore Frelinghuysen, in a speech on the Indian Removal Act, asked: "Do the obligations of justice change with the color of the skin?" Which views presented on page 69 would Frelinghuysen probably agree with?

3. Before the "Trail of Tears," the Ridges had decided that their people had no choice but to go west. What events had changed their minds? Could the *Worcester v. Georgia* case have been one of them? Why?

4. How was Major Ridge in sympathy with the Cherokee who continued to oppose removal? What were some of the values and assumptions he shared with them?

---

The **players** and the **opinions** on both sides of the issue are set forth within the Case Study. Seeing people's faces and reading their words gives you a unique insight into their thinking.

Each Case Study starts with a **primary source** quotation or visual that thrusts you into the center of the controversy.

Clear, crisp **headings** help you analyze every aspect of the case.

The last part of every Case Study, **Think About It,** gives you the opportunity to sort through the evidence yourself and hone your critical thinking skills.

# Wrapping Up

*Review pages at the end of each chapter and each unit allow you to complete your mastery of the material. Questions, activities, projects, and further resources help you set the story in a larger context.*

Each **Chapter Review** opens with a timeline that places the major events of the chapter in chronological sequence. You can use the **timeline** in connection with the **Summary** to review your understanding of the chapter.

## Chapter 14 Review

| 1946 "Iron Curtain" descends. War deepens. | June 1948 Soviets blockade Berlin | April 1949 NATO is formed. | June 1950 Korean War begins. | November 1952 Eisenhower is elected president. | July 1953 Korean War ends. | | July 1956 Nasser seizes Suez Canal. | October 1957 Soviets launch Sputnik | | November 1960 Kennedy is elected president. | |

1946 | 1947 | 1948 | 1949 | 1950 | 1951 | 1952 | 1953 | 1954 | 1955 | 1956 | 1957 | 1958 | 1959 | 1960 | 1961 | 1962 | 1963 | 1964

1945 ...velt dies suddenly. Truman becomes president. | April 1948 Marshall Plan begins aid to Europe. | October 1949 Mao declares People's Republic of China. | November 1952 United States tests hydrogen bomb. | November 1956 Soviets crush uprising in Budapest. | January 1959 Castro becomes dictator of Cuba. | April 1961 Bay of Pigs invasion fails. | October 1962 Soviets remove missiles from Cuba.

### Summary

Use the following outline as a tool for reviewing and summarizing the chapter. Copy the outline on your own paper, leaving spaces between headings to jot down notes about key events and concepts.

**I. The Cold War Begins**
  A. An Iron Curtain Starts to Fall
  B. Turning Point at Yalta
  C. Truman Comes to Power
  D. Cold War Is Declared
**II. The Cold War Deepens**
  A. Crisis in Berlin
  B. The Cold War Moves to Asia

4. Why did most Americans hope for a Nationalist victory in the Chinese civil war?
5. Why did Truman view the invasion of South Korea as an important test of containment?
6. What were some advantages and some dangers of Eisenhower's policy of massive retaliation?
7. Why didn't Khrushchev agree to Eisenhower's proposal to inspect each other's military sites?
8. What methods did the United States use to gain the friendship of third world countries? How was the CIA involved in that effort?
9. What conditions in Cuba helped to prepare the way for Castro's takeover?

### Social Studies Skills

**Analyzing Secondary Sources**
The photograph below, taken on September 20, 1960, is a primary source document that catches Castro and Khrushchev in a jovial moment. Write a paragraph that might appear in a secondary source about the 1960s. Explain how the friendship between the two men created a crisis for the world.

AP/WIDE WORLD PHOTOS

### Critical Thinking

1. **Comparing and Contrasting**
Compare and contrast the concerns that Roosevelt, Churchill, and Stalin brought to the conference at Yalta.
2. **Recognizing Cause and Effect**
What were some causes of the mistrust that grew up between Truman and Stalin?
3. **Analyzing Decisions**
How did the NSC-68 report and the Korean War cause Congress to vote massive increases in defense spending?
4. **Recognizing Assumptions**
In 1956 Khrushchev condemned Stalin's crimes and spoke of tolerating different kinds of communism. What did eastern European nations assume from such statements? How were such assumptions proven false in Hungary?
5. **Recognizing Points of View**
How might a nation's views on nuclear testing depend on whether it was a large or small power? On whether it was or was not a member of the "nuclear club"?

### Extension and Application

1. **Evidence of the Past**
In a library find information about the Yalta and Potsdam conferences. Write a short report explaining Roosevelt's and Truman's ideas about the postwar world.
2. **Community Connection**
Interview friends or family members who took part in World War II, the Korean War, or the war in Vietnam. Ask whether their opinions about the war have changed over the years and, if so, how. Discuss your findings with the class.

3. **Global Connection**
Research everyday life in China following the civil war and communist takeover. Focus on one aspect of the topic, such as how the commune system affected peasant life or how urban life changed under Mao Zedong.
4. **Linking Across Time**
George Washington said, "Liberty, when it begins to take root, is a plant of rapid growth." The 1990s might remind us of the era that followed World War II. Then, as now, a number of nations were in the midst of nationalist movements. Research a recent nationalist movement and write a news article or editorial about it.
5. **Cooperative Learning**
The Soviet launching of *Sputnik* resulted in intense efforts to improve America's educational system. Find out what the media are reporting about America's educational system today. Divide your class into groups of four. Have each group investigate one part of the topic, such as curriculum, teacher training, or textbooks. Have each group present the findings by a different means.

### Geography

1. How did the location of fighting in World War II influence the Soviet economy? The U.S. economy?
2. Identify the strategy used in waging the cold war. How was it different from strategy used in previous struggles? Where were the battlefields?
3. How did Berlin's location deep in East Germany work to the advantage of the United States?
4. During the height of the cold war what pressures might countries such as Spain, Yugoslavia, Austria, and Finland experience?
5. How does the spread of nuclear arms affect a country's ability to be neutral in a conflict?

The Uneasy Peace    493

## Unit 4 Review

*These unhappy times call for the building of plans . . . that build from the bottom up and not from the top down, that put their faith once more in the forgotten man at the bottom of the economic pyramid.*

Franklin D. Roosevelt,
Radio Address, April 7, 1932

*In the Presidents inaugural address . . . he made mention of The Forgotten Man, and I with thousands of others am wondering if the folk who was born here in America some 60 and 70 years ago are this Forgotten Man . . . if we are still Forgotten Man then we are still Forgotten.*

Mr. R. A., age 69, Letter to
Eleanor Roosevelt, Nebraska, May 1934

### Concepts and Themes

As the twenties roared to a close, more and more people had less cash to spend on products pouring off assembly lines. This combination of underconsumption and overproduction led to the devastating Depression of the 1930s. Millions milled about without jobs, food, homes, or hope. Then came Franklin D. Roosevelt's New Deal. Although it did not wipe away poverty, the New Deal did much to cure the nation's economic woes by means of work programs, relief, reform measures, and a promise for tomorrow. Never before had the United States government marched so boldly into individuals' lives.

1. Herbert Hoover advocated voluntary action and trickle-down measures to help the "forgotten man." Contrast his approach with Roosevelt's method of demanding legislation for direct help to the unemployed.
2. What were some of the effects of the CCC, WPA, and Wagner Act on "the forgotten man"?
3. Analyze why Mr. R. A., quoted above, might have been forgotten. What New Deal legislation eventually aided such people?

### History Projects

1. **Evidence of the Past**
Conduct an interview with a family member or friend who was an adult during the 1930s. Be prepared with written questions but also allow the interview to evolve spontaneously. Write a theme from the notes.
2. **Culture of the Time**
Create a collage contrasting today's pop culture with that of the 1930s.
3. **Geography**
Research the geography of the Tennessee Valley before the TVA project, right after it, and today. Make a chart explaining the geographical and technological changes.
4. **One Day in History**
Examine library microfiches of newspapers for Black Thursday, October 24, 1929. Create a feature following the format of One Day in History on page 384.
5. **Case Study**
Franklin D. Roosevelt's attempt in 1937 to increase the number of Supreme Court justices encountered opposition. Research Roosevelt's proposal and present the background. Check library sources to find quotations representing opposite views. In a written conclusion, tell the outcome.

### Writing Activities

1. Research the rich and poor of the 1930s. Write several paragraphs contrasting their shelter, clothing, food, and entertainment. (See the Writer's Guide, pages 825–827.)
2. Study Dorothea Lange's photo on page 338. Write a short imaginary narrative from the mother's viewpoint.

### The Arts

- *You Can't Take It with You* by George Kaufman and Moss Hart; a zany Broadway comedy.
- *Native Son* by Richard Wright; a novel depicting the frustrations of a black youth in Chicago during the Depression.
- *Number One* by John Dos Passos; a novel based on the life of Huey Long.
- *My Life and Hard Times* by James Thurber; humorous vignettes about the author's life.

388    Economic Crisis and the New Deal

**Skills-related** and **Critical Thinking Questions** review the skills you developed in the chapter.

**Extension and Application** activities and **Geography Questions** help you connect the material to the world beyond your textbook.

Various **projects** and **activities** related to the unit help you extend your understanding.

XV

# A Perspective on the Twentieth Century

Dear Students—

History is much more than facts and dates. History is about people and how they lived, thought, worked, voted, worshiped, raised families, and contributed to the changes that made their society different from that of their parents. It is not just about presidents, famous generals, and captains of industry.

These people were important, of course. But history is also about people like you and me, like our parents and grandparents. It is about people who came to this country a long time ago, a generation ago, or a few years ago. It is about all the people—women and men, adults and children, rich and poor. It is about people whose skins are different shades and whose beliefs vary, people from every section of the country. All of these people were history makers; not a single social movement or political reform could have happened in our society without the participation of masses of individuals.

Why should we bother to learn about the past? Because history helps us understand where we fit into the long stream of time. By studying the world of those who went before us, we gain perspective on our own world; we see better who we are, what we want, what is worth striving for and defending, what is in need of change. We learn how to tell what is important; how to detect bias, weigh evidence, separate anecdote from analysis, and distinguish between fact and conjecture. With these abilities we are equipped to change our world in ways that we understand are fitting.

In other words, history is a powerful tool. It empowers us by making us see the importance of becoming active participants in our society—in public as well as private ways. If we learn how ordinary individuals were often the source of mighty changes, we come to understand our own potential for contributing to the process by which the present becomes the future.

*Gary B. Nash*

# The American Land and People

T he drama of United States history is played out on a vast stage: the continent of North America. During the first act, the players moved on stage, from the hunter-gatherers who trekked across the Bering land bridge to the Europeans and Africans who sailed across the ocean.

Some came in search of food; some sought the wealth of gold and silver. For some this new home brought freedom and a better life; for others, enslavement and misery. The coming of all these peoples reshaped the land on which they lived, even as they were transformed by their new home. Their actions and interactions set in motion the story that continues to unfold in American life today.

DAVID MUENCH

People of many cultures have shaped North America. Native Americans fashioned this mask, left, from wood and cedar bark. Early European explorers used an astrolabe, right, to measure latitude by pointing one of its hands at the sun. Yet after millions of immigrants have arrived, parts of the Pacific Coast today, above, remain almost unchanged.

BURKE MUSEUM

THE BETTMANN ARCHIVE

1

# The First Americans

**D**uring the last great Ice Age, a land bridge connected northeastern Asia and northwestern North America. As early as 40,000 years ago small bands of people may have trudged across this span from Asia. Certainly by 12,000 years ago, according to archaeological research, they were living in North America. These people were the first Americans.

MUSEUM OF NEW MEXICO

**The Mimbres made this pottery bowl about 900 years ago.**

## Moving and Settling

Those who came to what is now Alaska followed the herds of animals that provided their food. Before them lay a grassy plain and mountain passes leading to the east and south.

A group settled where they found water, shelter, and good hunting. They remained months or even years until food grew scarce. Then it was time to move on to a better site for hunting. When a group grew too large, some members moved off on their own. Over the course of several thousand years the ancestors of these first Americans gradually populated all of the Western Hemisphere. As bands of people migrated, the languages and way of life of these Native Americans came to vary greatly from one area to the next. Many similarities among them remained, however.

The most recent migrants from Asia may have arrived just five to six thousand years ago. They caught whales, seals, fish, and walrus to provide themselves with food, clothing, and tools. They also made use of the bear, caribou, and birds they found in their new land. The descendants of these migrants live today in Alaska, northern Canada, and Greenland.

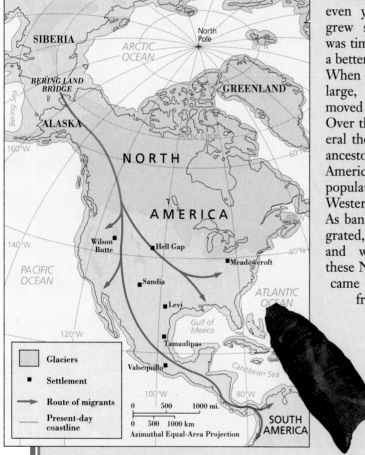

ASIA
EUROPE
SIBERIA
ARCTIC OCEAN
North Pole
80°N
BERING LAND BRIDGE
GREENLAND
Bering Sea
ALASKA
Arctic Circle
160°W
60°N
NORTH
AMERICA
60°N
Wilson Butte
Hell Gap
40°N
140°W
Meadowcroft
PACIFIC OCEAN
Sandia
Levi
ATLANTIC OCEAN
Gulf of Mexico
120°W
Tamaulipas
Valsequillo
Caribbean Sea

Glaciers
■ Settlement
→ Route of migrants
— Present-day coastline

0    500    1000 mi.
0   500  1000 km
Azimuthal Equal-Area Projection

100°W
80°W
SOUTH AMERICA

**Stone points used for hunting about 12,000 years ago are one clue to the routes Native Americans travelled in settling the continent.** *What physical barriers would they have encountered?*

LAURIE PLATT WINFREY, INC.

**40,000 B.C.**    10,000 B.C.    A.D. 500    700

As one generation followed another, the people continued this pattern of adaptation. They hunted wildlife and gathered the fruits of the land, settling for a time and then moving on.

## Passing on the Past

In addition to using the land for their physical needs, these Native Americans developed spiritual beliefs influenced by their environment. They passed on these beliefs orally from one generation to the next.

One kind of Native American belief takes the form of myths. These stories, based partly on actual people, wildlife, and events, and partly on imagined qualities and heroic deeds, often tell of the world's origins. One myth of the Haida, who live in Canada's British Columbia, says that the creator Raven caused tiny human beings to emerge from a cockle shell. These little humans, according to the myth, were the ancestors of all people. This story shows Native American reverence for the natural world and humankind's place in it.

The creation story of the Zuñi people of the American Southwest tells of the father of all Zuñi. He lived in the city of the Mists, where he was guarded by six animals of prey. The mountain lion guarded the north; the badger, the south; the wolf, the

**The Haida carved wood in the shape of a cockle shell to depict how humans originated.**

east; and the bear, the west. The mole guarded the lower regions and the eagle the upper regions. Each of these animals brought messages from humans to the gods and healed or punished people as the gods directed.

Some stories deal with the origin of other parts of the natural world. A legend of the Onondaga, who live in what is now New York, tells of eight dancing children. They asked their parents for food but were refused. Light-headed with hunger, they danced until they rose into the night sky, where they became stars. Seven of them formed the Pleiades constellation, but the eighth looked back and instead became a shooting star. This story illustrates the view of many Native Americans that people are eternally part of the rest of creation.

H. ARMSTRONG ROBERTS

**In the Southwest, the Anasazi built cities of cliffside dwellings such as this one at Mesa Verde, Colorado, around 1100.**

900    1100    1300    1500

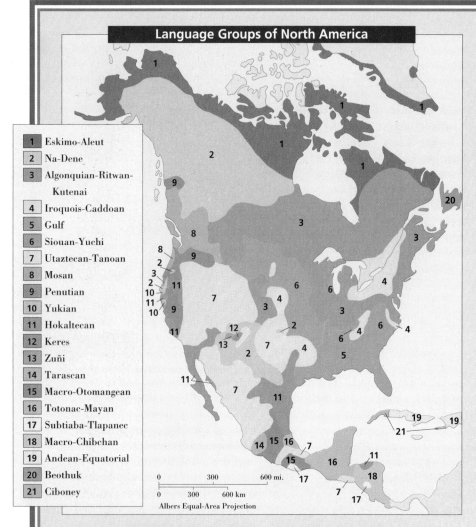

## Language Groups of North America

1. Eskimo-Aleut
2. Na-Dene
3. Algonquian-Ritwan-Kutenai
4. Iroquois-Caddoan
5. Gulf
6. Siouan-Yuchi
7. Utaztecan-Tanoan
8. Mosan
9. Penutian
10. Yukian
11. Hokaltecan
12. Keres
13. Zuñi
14. Tarascan
15. Macro-Otomangean
16. Totonac-Mayan
17. Subtiaba-Tlapanec
18. Macro-Chibchan
19. Andean-Equatorial
20. Beothuk
21. Ciboney

0    300    600 mi.
0    300    600 km
Albers Equal-Area Projection

**Native Americans on this continent spoke dozens of different languages. Groups in different regions developed separately.**

Louis, had perhaps 40,000 people and stretched for six miles along the Mississippi River.

The largest Native American civilizations arose much farther south. Huge pyramid-shaped temples marked Mayan cities in Central America around A.D. 700. By the year 1500 the Aztec capital city in the Valley of Mexico numbered 200,000 people or more. In the Andes Mountains of South America, the Inca built a remarkable civilization. Their empire stretched across 2,500 miles and included mountaintop temples and fortresses.

**Craftwork like this detail of a gold Inca knife handle declined after Europeans arrived in the Americas.**

## Living with the Land

As North America's climate became warmer and drier about 10,000 years ago, large game such as mammoths died off. Native Americans in the far north adapted by hunting smaller animals more often.

Groups who settled in regions with longer growing seasons and good soil learned in time to grow crops. Communities in central Mexico began to cultivate maize, known today as corn. As knowledge of agriculture spread to most of North and South America, people lived longer and their communities grew larger.

By farming and irrigating the land, some Native Americans transformed their environment. Some groups changed the lay of the land in even more dramatic ways. Probably the biggest Native American settlement in what is today the United States was a city built around 1300 by people now called the Cahokia. The city, near present-day St.

A.D. 500    600    700    800    900    1000

## Building Woodland Cultures

Many peoples lived in the eastern woodland region, the area roughly between the Atlantic Ocean and the Mississippi River. One culture, called the Mound Builders, flourished from about 2,700 to just 1,300 years ago. These people—including the Cahokia—constructed two kinds of earthen mounds. One was burial mounds—layers of graves for the dead and their belongings. The other was temple mounds, for worship in buildings at the top. Thousands of these mounds still stand in eastern North America. These cultural remnants are among the most dramatic Native American landmarks in North America.

The eastern woodlands were home to more than 40 Indian groups, among them the Shawnee, Iroquois, Potawatomi, and Lenni Lenape. Throughout the region people wore deerskin clothing, hunted with bows and arrows, and tended family or communal gardens. Climate permitting, the people grew tobacco and used a range of plant and mineral dyes on their clothes and skin. Those groups west of the Appalachian Mountains hunted buffalo to provide meat, hides for shelter, and horns for ceremonial dress. In the north, such groups as the Abenaki hunted during the winter on snowshoes and fished through ice.

People in the eastern woodlands benefited from what lay beneath the land, too. Near the Great Lakes as early as 5,000 years ago, Native Americans grew skilled at extracting copper ore from the earth and hammering it into tools. Ohio craftworkers 2,000 years ago used mica, another mineral, to fashion ornaments. Some resembled a hand, others a bird or a grinning face.

As eastern woodland societies became larger and more complex, some groups formed political blocs. The nations of the Iroquois Confederacy—comprising the Mohawk, Cayuga, Onondaga, Oneida, and Seneca —governed themselves by an unwritten constitution. Each nation had one vote, and a majority vote won. The exception to the rule was a declaration of war, which required a unanimous vote. The confederacy, also known as the Five Nations, enabled its members to enjoy long periods of peace among themselves while being respected, even feared, by their enemies.

In the lands that became the United States, Native Americans numbered roughly 4 to 7 million people by the year 1500. Yet life in the Americas, including the Caribbean islands, was soon to be drastically changed by the arrival of people from across the ocean.

An artist of the Hopewell culture carved this figure more than 1,200 years ago.

MILWAUKEE PUBLIC MUSEUM

THE GRANGER COLLECTION

The Great Serpent Mound near Locust Grove, Ohio, dates from sometime before A.D. 500.

1100    1200    1300    1400    ➤ *1500*

# Explorers from Europe

European navigators ventured farther west into the Atlantic Ocean as their technology improved. Around A.D. 1000, the Norse seafarer Leif Eriksson and 30 others sailed an open boat to what is now Newfoundland, Canada. They traded with the people there and built a small settlement that lasted only a few years. News of the Norse discovery did not reach most of Europe.

## Crossing the Atlantic

In 1492 an expedition led by Christopher Columbus for the crown of Spain verified what fishing crews had been saying for decades: land lay across the Atlantic. Columbus proved this point when his three ships landed in the Bahamas. He later called this place "a New World," realizing that he had landed on a new continent. Unlike Leif Eriksson, Columbus brought the Eastern and Western hemispheres into permanent contact.

Over the next century Spain, Portugal, England, France, and the Netherlands raced to explore and claim territory in this new world of the Americas. These kingdoms sought new lands to conquer and gold or silver for their treasuries. The rulers also wanted to convert native peoples to Christianity. In addition, they hoped to find a shorter trade route to Asia—the Northwest Passage.

Some expeditions concentrated on the Atlantic seaboard and the rivers leading from it. Henry VII of England sent a highly experienced sailor, John Cabot, to "seek out, discover and finde whatsoever isles, countreys regions or provinces" he could. In 1497 Cabot landed near where Leif Eriksson had, and Cabot soon claimed all of North America for England. Ponce de Leon skirted both coasts of Florida for Spain in 1513. A Frenchman, Jacques Cartier, sailed up a river

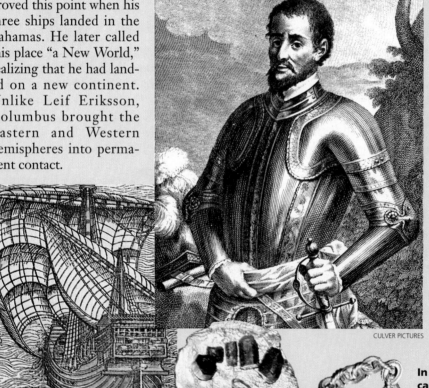

CULVER PICTURES

THE GRANGER COLLECTION

SYGMA

In 1492 Columbus sailed in a caravel, left, in search of gold and other riches. Hernando de Soto, above, like many Spanish explorers in the Americas, employed Africans on his crew.

*1000* ◄ 1450     1500     1550

in 1535 that he named the St. Lawrence. He wintered with the people of a Huron village, and the site eventually became the capital of New France. In 1609 Henry Hudson followed the river now bearing his name for 200 miles inland, claiming its banks for the Dutch.

Other explorers ventured into the interior of the continent. De Leon's countryman Hernando de Soto traveled north and west from Florida in the 1540s and crossed the Mississippi River. At this time Spain also laid claim to much of present-day California and New Mexico. Europe's mark on all of North America's shores was guaranteed when Vitus Bering, sailing for Russia, set foot in Alaska in 1741.

**The distance from England to Virginia, shown below, forced the first colonists at Jamestown, Virginia, to adapt to local conditions.** *Do their houses, right, suggest why so many early colonists died of disease?*

**Spanish missionaries in the Southwest tried to convert native peoples to Christianity.**

### Settling the Coasts

These voyagers found no Northwest Passage to Asia, but slowly the Europeans recognized that the land had riches of its own. The English in particular encouraged permanent colonists, who could ship the land's abundant raw materials to Europe.

Permanent settlements began to spring up. Spain founded St. Augustine, in Florida, in 1565 as a military outpost. This is the oldest European site in what is now the United States. In 1607 an English company founded Jamestown, in Virginia, and thanks to assistance from Powhatan Indians learned to cultivate the tobacco plant. A craze for smoking this "stinkingeweede," as some called it, swept Europe. Just 13 years later Virginia planters sold 40,000 pounds of tobacco to England.

The advance of Europeans onto Native American lands created hostility and warfare. Disease, however, took a much greater toll on both peoples, especially Native Americans. Millions died of bacterial and viral infections new to them. Smallpox, measles, typhus, and other diseases may have killed as many as 90 percent of the original Native American population over the next three centuries.

Harsh conditions, particularly in the heat of Southern tobacco fields, deterred English workers. As the 1600s progressed, tobacco planters turned to Africa for a new supply of laborers.

| 1600 | 1650 | 1700 | 1750 |

NATIONAL MARITIME MUSEUM

**Enslaved Africans endured deplorable conditions in the cargo holds of ships crossing the Atlantic.** *Who conducted the slave trade?*

## Coming from Africa

The first African to arrive in the New World was a member of Columbus's second expedition. Throughout the 1500s, Spanish and Portuguese voyages and overland expeditions included African sailors and soldiers. The vast majority of Africans arriving in the Americas each year, however, came as slaves because Europeans wanted them as laborers.

By 1525 Spanish trading ships were bringing slaves from Africa to work on sugar plantations in the West Indies. By about 1700 slaves also did much of the work in the Southern colonies of British North America.

Among the first Africans to reach North America was a group who landed in Virginia in 1619. These 20 men and women were taken from their homeland on a Spanish slave ship that was soon seized by a Dutch warship. They worked as servants in Virginia and a few of them eventually became free.

Although some Africans reached the colonies as free persons, mainly as sailors, most were enslaved in Africa and sold by Africans or Arabs to European traders. Only about 5 percent of some 12 million Africans caught up in the slave trade were brought to North America. The others found themselves laboring in the sugar, coffee, and tobacco plantations of the West Indies and South America.

A few European colonists, such as the Quakers, protested against the cruel practice of slavery. Yet by the early 1700s enslaved Africans lived throughout British North America. Most arrived in southern ports horribly packed into a ship's hold. Seaports in Rhode Island and Massachusetts also took in enslaved Africans for merchants to sell in the South.

In New England and the Middle colonies, enslaved persons worked as house servants, blacksmiths, cooks, shipbuilders, lumberjacks, tanners, and doctors' apprentices. In a few cases they were allowed to purchase their freedom.

Most enslaved Africans toiled in the Southern colonies to produce the crops—tobacco, rice, and indigo—vital to the economies of those colonies. The work Africans did was so vital that in 1662 the Virginia assembly declared that enslaved persons passed on their status to their children: "bond or freed according to the condition of the mother." By 1730 Africans made up about one third of the population of Maryland, Virginia, and the Carolinas.

Some slaves originally came from inland Africa, but the great

**Tobacco and sugarcane were the chief cash crops in the Southern colonies and in the Caribbean.**

| 1525 | 1550 | 1575 | 1600 | 1625 |

majority had lived in coastal West Africa. These people were familiar with farming such crops as rice, kola nuts, sesame, cotton, and yams. They had a strong sense of family and an elaborate web of religious beliefs involving the individual and the extended family. Enslavement broke up these family units. During the transatlantic voyages as many as 20 or 30 percent of the enslaved Africans died. After reaching the colonies, many Africans formed new families, but there was no guarantee that slaveholders would keep a family together.

### Increasing the Population

In 1630 only about 4,600 Europeans and Africans lived in England's American colonies,

**A woman operates a tobacco press in this print of life in Virginia about 1740.**

THE HUNTINGTON LIBRARY

but in 1660 there were 75,000 colonial subjects, among them about 3,000 Africans. The first settlers in eastern North America were mostly men. Gradually more women arrived.

In addition to immigration, high birthrates explain the leap in population. A couple who could not afford to hire servants or buy slaves would have many children to help run the farm. Families of 6 to 10 children were common, even after some infants—and mothers—had died in childbirth. Another spur to large families was the Bible's command, obeyed especially by New England Puritans, to people the earth.

Acquiring land was the core of most newcomers' dreams. Immigrants in the South could receive at least 50 acres from the colonial rulers, then hope to do well by farming tobacco. Some prospered, but many others failed and had to hire out to someone else.

In Virginia and Maryland many settlers paid the passage of other immigrants to receive more land from the colony. Samuel Matthews of Virginia amassed his estate in this way, receiving 50 acres for each servant whose passage across the Atlantic he paid. "He hath a fine house," Matthews's neighbor said. "He keeps Weavers . . . hath eight Shoemakers employed in their trade, hath forty negroe servants, brings them up to Trades in his house." Virtually all owners of large plantations in

WORCESTER ART MUSEUM

**By the late 1600s, colonists were rapidly populating the land.** *Why were Europeans attracted to North America?*

the 1600s started as small farmers. In 1663, moreover, 13 of the 30 members of Virginia's legislature, the House of Burgesses, had arrived in the colony as indentured servants.

Where land or profits beckoned, England's poor and middle classes were drawn as if by a magnet. Yet settlers did not recognize that much of the land was Native American hunting land. When Pilgrims came to Massachusetts Bay in 1620, they received much assistance from the Wampanoag. Within 50 years, however, as more settlers pushed Native Americans off their lands, warfare became common. This pattern was repeated to some degree everywhere Europeans settled.

1650    1675    1700    1725    *1741*

9

# Builders of New Societies

The settlers coming to North America brought with them just the few worldly possessions they could carry and a strong dedication to build a new life. By 1660, with England's monarchy restored after a 20-year revolution, England's colonies were sizable enough and profitable enough that their permanent existence was assured.

## The Three Regions

By the mid-1600s the English-controlled colonies stretched along the eastern coast from Maine to Georgia. Despite the many similarities in life throughout the colonies, three distinct regions developed: the New England colonies, the Middle colonies, and the Southern colonies.

The regions developed in response to the features of the landscape, the characteristics of the people who settled each area, and the economic and cultural activities these people pursued. Colonists from all three regions experienced separation from their homeland, isolation from other colonies, and the hardships of starting a new life in a new land.

## The New England Colonies

Immigrants from England comprised the largest number of

By the 1730s, the English colonies in North America displayed a variety of regional characteristics.

settlers in the northernmost colonies, New England. Most often the immigrants came in family groups; sometimes an entire family of three generations or a church group arrived

together. Townspeople worked together to construct public buildings such as churches, schools, and jails. Farm fields often circled the town, with each family working a modest-sized plot of about 50 acres.

New England's rocky terrain and cold climate made farming a struggle. Most families could raise enough crops for themselves and the town, but only a few could produce a surplus for export. To provide money to buy items they could not grow, build, or manufacture, the settlers turned to fishing, lumbering, wool production, crafts, and commerce.

The region's vast forests, not far from the Atlantic coast, encouraged the rise of a shipbuilding industry. By the early 1700s, New England turned out 150 vessels a year. Ships from New England sailed down the Atlantic

**1660**  1670  1680  1690  1700

coast, carrying cloth from England as well as nails, spun wool, and New England craft products to the Middle colonies. At Caribbean ports, the ships traded New England fish and wood for the islands' sugar, molasses, and indigo. The ships sailing to England brought the Royal Navy the best masts in the world, made from towering white pines with diameters of more than two feet. On the return trip the ships brought salt necessary for preserving New England fish; iron for use in manufacturing anchors, bolts, and pots; and luxury items such as linen and china.

The Puritans who settled New England were generally intolerant of religious views different from their own. For this reason, other European immigrants avoided settling in the New England colonies.

Native Americans living in the region also found themselves the target of Puritan intolerance. Puritans attempted to force them to follow the Puritan law that forbade any work on Sunday, including the hunting or fishing that provided native people their food. The settlers also took Native American farm and hunting lands. Tensions reached a boiling point in 1675 when the New Englanders arrested Metacomet, the leader of the Wampanoag. Metacomet, called King Philip by the colonists, was humiliated and forced to pay fines. The Wampanoag joined with the Narragansett and other

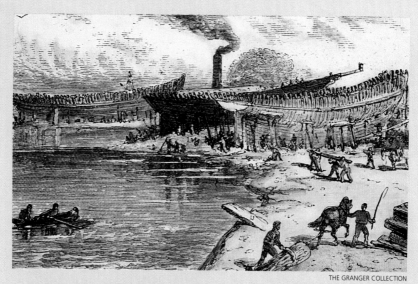

THE GRANGER COLLECTION

**Shipbuilding was vital to the New England colonies.** *What kinds of shipbuilding work are illustrated in this scene?*

Native American people in an effort to drive the settlers from the land. Over the next two years, settlers and native groups burned each other's settlements, captured and tortured prisoners, and destroyed each other's crops. The conflict ended with a series of treaties signed between 1676 and 1678.

Years before the conflict with Metacomet, the Puritans made strides in the field of education. New England law required any

town with more than 50 families to maintain a school. Families who could afford to pay tuition helped to subsidize the education of students who were unable to pay. In 1636, six years after the first Puritan settlers came to New England, they established Harvard College.

MASSACHUSETTS HISTORICAL SOCIETY

**Increase Mather, above, spent nearly 60 years preaching near Boston. A best-selling primer, left, taught reading and morals.**

NEW YORK PUBLIC LIBRARY

## The Middle Colonies

In contrast with New England, the Middle colonies drew early settlers from a variety of cultural and religious backgrounds. The Dutch established New Amsterdam (later named New York City) as a trading post in the early 1600s. Meanwhile, Swedish settlers landed along the Delaware River; New Jersey became a home for the Dutch, Swedes, and Finns as well as religious groups such as the Quakers and Puritans.

In 1660 events in England had a startling effect on the tiny settlements of the mid-Atlantic region. Charles II, reinstated as King of England, disregarded Dutch claims to land in North America. Charles granted New Amsterdam and the area surrounding it to his brother, the Duke of York. As proprietor, the Duke was allowed to sell, rent, or give away the land as he chose. The Duke divided the land, keeping the area he called New York for himself. He granted New Jersey to a group of friends.

In 1681, Charles II granted an expanse of land to William Penn. This grant, including land that is now Delaware, formed Penn's colony, Pennsylvania. Penn, a Quaker, wished to establish a colony that would offer religious freedom to all sects. To encourage settlement in his colony, Penn advertised. He printed pamphlets in a variety of languages and distributed them

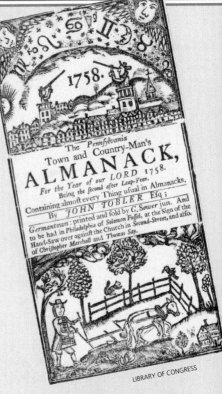

**This almanac of 1758 provided information about weather, planting times, and other advice to farmers and townspeople.**

throughout England and much of Europe. Penn made it easy for a settler to buy land: a hundred-acre plot sold for about five English pounds.

People from all over England, Ireland, and northern Europe responded. Pennsylvania's population eventually ranked among the most diverse of the colonies. Penn also advertised to attract skilled workers such as carpenters, glassmakers, tanners, and bakers as well as merchants who would invest money in the colony. These efforts helped Philadelphia, the capital, to grow more rapidly than any other city in the region.

Blessed with more fertile land than New Englanders, farmers in the Middle colonies

**William Penn's agents signed a treaty with the Lenni Lenape in 1681, a first step toward more peaceful relations in the Middle colonies.**

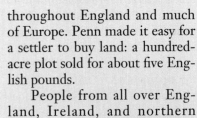

| 1660 | 1670 | 1680 | 1690 | 1700 |

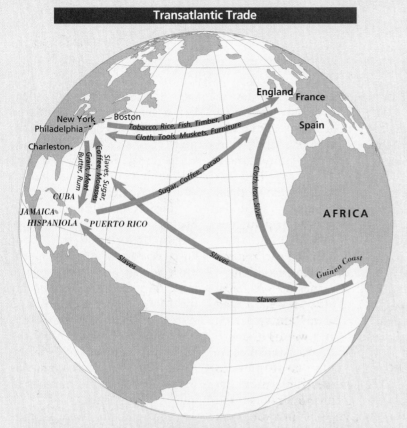

England France

New York • Boston
Philadelphia

*Tobacco, Rice, Fish, Timber, Tar*

Spain

Charleston •

*Cloth, Tools, Muskets, Furniture*

*Grain, Meat,* *Slaves, Sugar,*
*Butter, Rum* *Coffee, Molasses*

*Sugar, Coffee, Cacao*

*Cloth, Iron, Silver*

CUBA

JAMAICA
HISPANIOLA PUERTO RICO

AFRICA

*Slaves*

*Slaves*

*Guinea Coast*

*Slaves*

**Trade routes to and from North America helped coastal cities, particularly in the Middle colonies, to prosper.**

according to this eyewitness report from the docks:

*Many parents must sell and trade away their children like so many head of cattle . . . parents and children, after leaving the ship, do not see each other again for years, perhaps no more in all their lives.*

Gottfried Mittelberger,
*Journey to Pennsylvania*, 1756

Settlers in the Middle colonies were more tolerant toward Native Americans than the Puritans were in New England. Quakers, who vowed never to use violence in human affairs, promised to protect native peoples living in Pennsylvania. By offering this protection and paying for native lands, settlers in Pennsylvania had peace for most of the colonial period. The peace allowed the region to prosper.

raised a surplus of farm products that could be sold. The Middle colonies exported wheat, rye, beef, and pork to the other colonies and the West Indies. Mid-Atlantic settlements such as New York City, Philadelphia, and Lancaster prospered from the agricultural trade and became bustling commercial centers.

Many farmers and business owners in the Middle colonies needed additional workers for their thriving farms and businesses. These owners sent to Europe for indentured servants. Driven from their homelands by joblessness or hunger, poor people made the long voyage hoping to start a new life. Many agreed to serve for as long as seven years

before getting their freedom. The cruelty of servitude became apparent to some as they arrived,

NEW YORK HISTORICAL SOCIETY

**This painting, *A South-east Prospect of the City of New York,* shows that the harbor already bustled with international trade in the 1750s.**

| 1710 | 1720 | 1730 | 1740 | 1750 | 1760 |

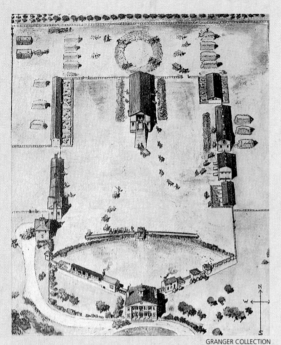

**Southern plantations reshaped the land to raise tobacco, crops, and livestock.**

## The Southern Colonies

While the Middle and New England colonies attracted people interested in religious freedom, commerce, and farming, the Southern colonies drew many fortune-seekers hoping to strike it rich. The South offered climate and soil particularly well suited to growing tobacco, which brought high prices in Europe.

By the mid-1600s, a plantation economy existed in Maryland, Virginia, and parts of the Carolinas. The plantation system made life in the Southern colonies very different from life in New England and the Middle colonies. Towns grew slowly in the Southern colonies because people remained relatively isolated on plantations or small farms. Power in these colonies was concentrated in the hands of a few wealthy landowners.

The plantation economy created a gap between the rich and the poor that was larger than in other regions. No matter what crop the plantation raised, the key to prosperity was a large number of unpaid, hard-working field hands.

Tobacco and other southern cash crops such as rice and indigo were labor intensive. At first, most southern planters relied on unskilled indentured servants, mainly from England and Ireland, to supply the necessary labor. Some were so miserable they fled, and others died

**William Buckland signed this contract for indenture, right, in 1755.** *How does the portrait indicate Buckland's unusual rise from indentured servitude to the middle class?*

from the grueling labor. Indentured servants who persisted earned their freedom and left the plantations to buy their own farms. In the 1700s, even among skilled servants, a later rise to wealth was rare.

Beginning in the early 1600s Spanish and Dutch trading ships began bringing a trickle of enslaved Africans to the Southern colonies. Some were able to trade their work for freedom. By the 1660s, however, slavery as a system of lifelong servitude was beginning to crystallize. By the 1690s the numbers of enslaved Africans in the tobacco and rice fields surpassed the number of indentured servants.

This epitaph, from a tombstone in Concord, Massachusetts, relates how one enslaved

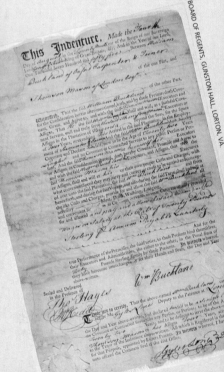

| 1660 | 1670 | 1680 | 1690 | 1700 |
|------|------|------|------|------|

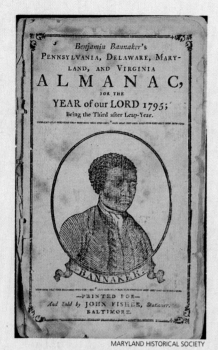

**Benjamin Banneker, a free black in Maryland, published this successful almanac.**

African felt about his life in America:

G od wills us free;
 man wills us slaves,
*I will as God wills,
God's will be done.
Here lies the body of John Jack.
A native of Africa,
who died March, 1773,
Aged about sixty years.
Tho' born in a land of slavery,
He was born free;
Tho' he lived in a land of liberty,
He lived a slave . . .
Tho' not long before Death,
 the grand Tyrant, Gave him
his final emancipation,
And set him on a footing with kings.*

Unlike New England, the South did not have laws requiring education: In fact, it was against the law in the South to teach a slave to read or write. White settlers' children who were needed to work in the fields of small family farms usually received no schooling. Nevertheless, the colonies' first tuition-free schools were established in Virginia before 1650. Children from wealthy families attended private schools, were tutored at home, or were sent to Europe to study.

## A People Emerge

The population of the thirteen colonies, excluding Native Americans, grew eightfold from 250,000 in 1700 to more than 2 million by 1770. The healthful conditions in the colonies contributed to this amazing growth. In general, colonists lived longer than their peers in Europe.

As word spread in England and Europe about religious tolerance, availability of land, and opportunity for wealth in North America, a more diverse group of immigrants arrived. Their diversity compounded the ways in which America was becoming less like England.

By the 1760s the colonies had established similar forms of government; each had a governor and a legislature, usually consisting of two houses. Colonial voters—only white men who owned land or had a certain amount of wealth—elected representatives to the lower house.

By the late 1700s the colonial governments and settlers had established an identity quite different from England.

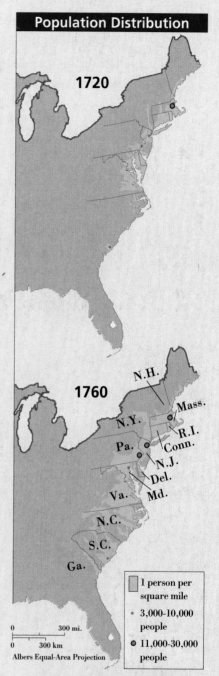

**Population Distribution**

1720

1760

N.H.
Mass.
N.Y.
R.I.
Pa.
Conn.
N.J.
Del.
Va.
Md.
N.C.
S.C.
Ga.

0 — 300 mi.
0 — 300 km
Albers Equal-Area Projection

| | 1 person per square mile |
| · | 3,000-10,000 people |
| ● | 11,000-30,000 people |

**By the mid-1700s, settlers were moving inland from the coast.** *How did sprawling settlement by Europeans affect Native Americans?*

# The Seeds of Conflict

During the first half of the eighteenth century a series of bitter wars between Britain and France overshadowed the lives of the colonists. The two powers often fought over rights to colonial lands around the world. When the conflicts reached North America, colonists joined in the fight. This longstanding conflict culminated in the Seven Years' War between 1756 and 1763.

BROWN UNIVERSITY

Rivalry between France and Britain for North America led to battles like this one by Lake George, in northern New York, in 1755. Different Native American groups fought on both sides during the war.

The Seven Years' War came to be known in the colonies as the French and Indian War. During this conflict, many native peoples in the northern regions sided with the French against the British. The Native Americans were familiar with the French fur traders, and relations between them were generally cordial. In contrast, many native peoples had lost lands to the British settlers during decades of wars in most of the colonies. The colonial and British forces won the Seven Years' War only with great difficulty.

The Treaty of 1763 gave French Canada as well as other land in North America to England, making the eastern half of North America British. The removal of the French threat made the colonists feel more secure than before. Victory in the Seven Years' War also brought a greater sense of independence and self-sufficiency in the colonies; the war had given colonists in all regions a common goal, and their victory gave them new confidence. The victory also brought new conflicts with the British crown. In the coming years the rapidly growing colonies would clash with the crown over issues such as westward expansion, the raising of armies, and the levying of taxes.

**1756** ← 1757  1758  1759  1760  1761  1762 → **1763**

# UNIT ONE

# A Nation of Nations

Union Pacific Museum Collection

Chapter 1: Forging a New Nation     Chapter 3: Rift and Reunion
Chapter 2: The Expanding Nation     Chapter 4: Farming and Industry

# Echoes of the Past

*Oral history, folklore, and tradition connect us to the past.
In* Roots, *author Alex Haley returns to the village of his ancestors to
learn the history of his people from a Mandinka* griot, *an elder who commits
history to memory and recites it to the next generation. Leslie Marmon Silko
connects her experience with that of her Native American ancestors in her poem
"Where Mountain Lion Lay Down with Deer." Finally, in "Ellis Island,"
Joseph Bruchac explores his Slovakian and Native American heritage.*

## from *Roots*

### *by Alex Haley*

There is an expression called "the peak experience"—that which emotionally, nothing in your life ever transcends. I've had mine, that first day in the back country of black West Africa.

When we got within sight of Juffure, the children who were playing outside gave the alert, and the people came flocking from their huts. It's a village of only about seventy people. Like most back-country villages, it was still very much as it was two hundred years ago, with its circular mud houses and their conical thatched roofs. Among the people as they gathered was a small man wearing an off-white robe, a pillbox hat over an aquiline-featured black face, and about him was an aura of "somebodiness" until I knew he was the man we had come to see and hear.

As the three interpreters left our party to converge upon him, the seventy-odd other villagers gathered closely around me, in a kind of horseshoe pattern, three or four deep all around; had I stuck out my arms, my fingers would have touched the nearest ones on either side. They were all staring at me. The eyes just raked me. Their foreheads were furrowed with their very intensity of staring. A kind of visceral surging or a churning sensation started up deep inside me; bewildered, I was wondering what on earth was this . . . then in a little while it was rather as if

some full-gale force of realization rolled in on me: Many times in my life I had been among crowds of people, but never where *every one was jet black!*

Rocked emotionally, my eyes dropped downward as we tend to do when we're uncertain, insecure, and my glance fell upon my own hands' brown complexion. This time more quickly than before, and even harder, another gale-force emotion hit me: I felt myself some variety of a hybrid . . . I felt somehow impure among the pure; it was a terribly shaming feeling. About then, abruptly the old man left the interpreters. The people immediately also left me now to go crowding about him.

One of my interpreters came up quickly and whispered in my ear, "They stare at you so much because they have never here seen a black American." When I grasped the significance, I believe that hit me harder than what had already happened. They hadn't been looking at me as an individual, but I represented in their eyes a symbol of the twenty-five millions of us black people whom they had never seen, who lived beyond an ocean.

The people were clustered thickly about the old man, all of them intermittently flicking glances toward me as they talked animatedly in their Mandinka tongue. After a while, the old man turned, walked briskly through the people, past my three interpreters,

**The story of our past is available to us through images as well as through words. This family's portrait was snapped twice, for viewing with a stereoscope.**

and right up to me. His eyes piercing into mine, seeming to feel I should understand his Mandinka, he expressed what they had all decided they *felt* concerning those unseen millions of us who lived in those places that had been slave ships' destinations—and the translation came: "We have been told by the forefathers that there are many of us from this place who are in exile in that place called America—and in other places."

The old man sat down, facing me, as the people hurriedly gathered behind him. Then he began to recite for me the ancestral history of the Kinte clan, as it had been passed along orally down across centuries from the forefathers' time. It was not merely conversational, but more as if a scroll were being read; for the still, silent villagers, it was clearly a formal occasion. The *griot* would speak, bending forward from the waist, his body rigid, his neck cords standing out, his words seeming almost physical objects. After a sentence or two, seeming to go limp, he would lean back, listening to an interpreter's translation. Spilling from the *griot's* head came an incredibly complex Kinte clan lineage that reached back across many generations: who married whom; who had what children; what children then married whom; then their offspring. It was all just unbelievable. I was struck not only by the profusion of details, but also by the narrative's biblical style, something like: "—and so-and-so took as a wife so-and-so, and begat . . . and begat . . .

and begat . . ." He would next name each begat's eventual spouse, or spouses, and their averagely numerous offspring, and so on. To date things the *griot* linked them to events, such as "—in the year of the big water"—a flood—"he slew a water buffalo." To determine the calendar date, you'd have to find out when that particular flood occurred.

Simplifying to its essence the encyclopedic saga that I was told, the *griot* said that the Kinte clan had begun in the country called Old Mali. Then the Kinte men traditionally were blacksmiths, "who had conquered fire," and the women mostly were potters and weavers. In time, one branch of the clan moved into the country called Mauretania; and it was from Mauretania that one son of this clan, whose name was Kairaba Kunta Kinte—a *marabout*, or holy man of the Moslem faith—journeyed down into the country called The Gambia. He went first to a village called Pakali N'Ding, stayed there for a while, then went to a village called Jiffarong, and then to the village of Juffure.

In Juffure, Kairaba Kunta Kinte took his first wife, a Mandinka maiden whose name was Sireng. And by her he begot two sons, whose names were Janneh and Saloum. Then he took a second wife; her name was Yaisa. And by Yaisa, he begot a son named Omoro.

Those three sons grew up in Juffure until they became of age. Then the elder two, Janneh and Saloum, went away and founded a new village called

**A Pomo woman of the early 1900s weaves in the tradition of her ancestors.** *How do arts and crafts such as weaving transmit the culture of a people?*

I sat as if I were carved of stone. My blood seemed to have congealed. This man whose lifetime had been in this back-country African village had no way in the world to know that he had just echoed what I had heard all through my boyhood years on my grandma's front porch in Henning, Tennessee . . . of an African who always had insisted that his name was "Kin-tay"; who had called a guitar a "*ko*," and a river within the state of Virginia, "Kamby Bolongo"; and who had been kidnaped into slavery while not far from his village, chopping wood, to make himself a drum.

I managed to fumble from my dufflebag my basic notebook, whose first pages containing grandma's story I showed to an interpreter. After briefly reading, clearly astounded, he spoke rapidly while showing it to the old *griot*, who became agitated; he got up, exclaiming to the people, gesturing at my notebook in the interpreter's hands, and *they* all got agitated.

I don't remember hearing anyone giving an order, I only recall becoming aware that those seventy-odd people had formed a wide human ring around me, moving counterclockwise, chanting softly, loudly, softly; their bodies close together, they were lifting their knees high, stamping up reddish puffs of the dust. . . .

Kinte-Kundah Janneh-Ya. The youngest son, Omoro, stayed on in Juffure village until he had thirty rains—years—of age, then he took as his wife a Mandinka maiden named Binta Kebba. And by Binta Kebba, roughly between the years 1750 and 1760, Omoro Kinte begat four sons, whose names were, in the order of their birth, Kunta, Lamin, Suwadu, and Madi.

The old *griot* had talked for nearly two hours up to then, and perhaps fifty times the narrative had included some detail about someone whom he had named. Now after he had just named those four sons, again he appended a detail, and the interpreter translated—

"About the time the King's soldiers came"—another of the *griot's* time-fixing references—"the eldest of these four sons, Kunta, went away from his village to chop wood . . . and he was never seen again. . . ." And the *griot* went on with his narrative.

The woman who broke from the moving circle was one of about a dozen whose infant children were within cloth slings across their backs. Her jet-black face deeply contorting, the woman came charging toward me, her bare feet slapping the earth, and snatching her baby free, she thrust it at me almost roughly, the gesture saying "Take it!" . . . and I did, clasping the baby to me. Then she snatched away her baby; and another woman was thrusting her baby, then another, and another . . . until I had embraced probably a dozen babies. I wouldn't learn until maybe a year later, from a Harvard University professor, Dr. Jerome Bruner, a scholar of such matters, "You didn't know you were participating in one of the oldest ceremonies of humankind, called 'The laying on of hands'! In their way, they were telling you 'Through this flesh, which is us, we are you, and you are us!'"

# Where Mountain Lion Lay Down with Deer

## by Leslie Marmon Silko

I climb the black rock mountain
  stepping from day to day
         silently.
I smell the wind for my ancestors
    pale blue leaves
    crushed wild mountain smell.
Returning
  up the gray stone cliff
  where I descended
        a thousand years ago.
Returning to faded black stone
  where mountain lion lay down with deer.
It is better to stay up here
       watching wind's reflection
       in tall yellow flowers.
The old ones who remember me are gone
     the old songs are all forgotten
and the story of my birth.
How I danced in snow-frost moonlight
   distant stars to the end of Earth,
How I swam away
     in freezing mountain water
     narrow mossy canyon tumbling down
        out of the mountain
        out of deep canyon stone
     down
       the memory
         spilling out
         into the world.

# Ellis Island

## by Joseph Bruchac

Beyond the red brick of Ellis Island
where the two Slovak children
who became my grandparents
waited the long days of quarantine,
after leaving the sickness,
the old Empires of Europe,
a Circle Line ship slips easily
on its way to the island
of the tall woman, green
as dreams of forests and meadows
waiting for those who'd worked
a thousand years
yet never owned their own.

Like millions of others,
I too come to this island,
nine decades the answerer
of dreams.

Yet only one part of my blood loves that memory.
Another voice speaks
of native lands
within this nation.
Lands invaded
when the earth became owned.
Lands of those who followed
the changing Moon,
knowledge of the seasons
in their veins.

## Responding to Literature

1. At the end of the *Roots* selection, Dr. Bruner defines the "laying on of hands" ceremony. Explain what he means in your own words.

2. Compare each narrator's reactions to information about the past. Why do you think each writer explores history? Why is it important?

*For Further Reading*
Fast, Howard: *April Morning*
Gaines, Ernest J.: *The Autobiography of Miss Jane Pittman*
Momaday, N. Scott: *The Way to Rainy Mountain*
Twain, Mark, and Warner, Charles Dudley: *The Gilded Age*

## CHAPTER 1

# Forging a New Nation

### October 19, 1781: British Surrender at Yorktown

A young slave named James gained permission from his owner, William Armistead, to join the Continental Army stationed nearby. It was March 1781.

The general commanding these American troops was a young Frenchman named Marie Joseph Lafayette, who had volunteered to serve with the American army. That spring Lafayette sent many spies to the nearby British camp, but no one was as important as James.

The secret information James gathered helped Lafayette and the Americans corner the British at Yorktown, Virginia, in October 1781. The British surrendered and Yorktown proved to be the final battle in the fight for independence. But at the end of the war, Lafayette went home a hero, and James went home a slave.

Yet, with Lafayette's help, James would be given his freedom. The Frenchman wrote a letter describing James's "essential services" during the war and urged that James be released by his owner. In 1786 the Virginia legislature finally freed James in thanks for his military efforts during the American Revolution.

James Armistead's story was exceptional, but the lives of many Americans—black and white, male and female, famous and unknown—changed during the revolutionary era. Americans tasted new freedoms as they faced new challenges after the Revolutionary War. People of all backgrounds struggled together to forge their new nation.

> *Americans tasted new freedoms as they faced new challenges after the Revolutionary War.*

VIRGINIA HISTORICAL SOCIETY

*James Armistead began calling himself "James Lafayette," in honor of the man who helped him win his freedom.*

*In this 1792 painting,* Liberty Displaying the Arts and Sciences, *liberty is personified as a young woman who upholds classical ideals.*

# Waging a Revolution

### August 14, 1765:  Boston Crowd Protests New Tax

THE SOUND OF SCUFFLING FEET AND SHOUT-ING VOICES SHATTERED THE QUIET SUMMER EVENING. HUNDREDS OF PEOPLE, LED BY A POOR, 28-YEAR-OLD SHOEMAKER NAMED Ebenezer MacIntosh, stormed up the street. Men walking at the head of the crowd carried an effigy—a rag-stuffed dummy.

The effigy represented Andrew Oliver, a wealthy Boston merchant. Oliver had recently been made Stamp Officer for Mas-sachusetts to help collect a British tax authorized by the Stamp Act from the American colonies. Many Bostonians hated the tax; MacIntosh was leading a group to protest it.

The crowd carried the effigy through the streets of Boston. Then, after burning Oliver's effigy on a nearby hill, they attacked Oliver's luxurious house.

Oliver heard the crash of glass, the splintering of wood, and hoarse shouts. When the noise died down, Oliver found his "garden torn in pieces, his house broken open, his furniture destroyed." Standing be-fore MacIntosh and his mob, Oliver "came to a sud-den resolution to resign his office" as Stamp Officer. The common people had scored a victory.

On that hot August night, Ebenezer MacIntosh, the poor Boston shoemaker, found himself at the forefront of a movement that strained the bonds be-tween Great Britain and its thirteen American colonies. Yet MacIntosh did not always oppose the British. Only a few years before, he had proudly fought for Britain's colonies in the French and Indian War (also known as the Seven Years' War). As re-cently as 1763, he had joined with other colonists in celebrating Britain's victory over France in that war.

## Paying for Security

Britain's leaders celebrated the end of the war in Eu-rope and North America as heartily as did the colonists. The British victory ended more than 70 years of fighting with France in North America. As a result of a treaty signed in February 1763, King George III took possession of all French territory east of the Mis-sissippi River, including lands in Canada. Yet the decades of fighting had left the British govern-ment struggling with a large national debt. Brit-ish politicians also faced the expense of paying for an army in North Amer-ica to secure the new borders and defend the enlarged territory.

THE METROPOLITAN MUSEUM OF ART

**The Proclamation of 1763** After the British vic-tory, settlers began moving into the newly acquired lands west of the Appalachians. What had been Na-tive American hunting grounds protected by the French were claimed by new settlers. In May 1763, Indian resentment erupted in a bloody uprising led by Pontiac, an Ottawa chief. Within a few months, Indi-ans captured or destroyed most of the British forts on the frontier and killed many settlers.

To prevent another war, which Britain could not afford, King George III issued the Proclamation of 1763. The document proclaimed that all lands west of the Appalachians were reserved for Native Americans and closed to colonial settlement. For the British, the proclamation preserved peace with the Native Ameri-cans and prevented colonists from moving westward, farther from Britain's control.

---

## STUDY GUIDE

**As You Read**
Examine the origins of the Revolution-ary War. Also think about the following concept and skills.

**Central Concept**
- understanding why colonialism in America ended in **revolution**

**Thinking Skills**
- recognizing points of view
- making inferences
- identifying cause and effect

Colonists, however, felt that Britain had slammed shut a door of opportunity. They deeply resented being forbidden to settle on lands they had helped Britain win from France. The colonists' resentment grew when Parliament demanded that they help pay for the army that was to defend the frontier.

**The Sugar Act** Beginning in 1764, Parliament tried to collect a series of taxes from the colonies to ease the war debt and strengthen the British empire. The colonists' reaction was strong; it was most violent in Boston. The Sugar Act hurt Boston especially, since that city depended heavily on shipping and trade. All duties, or taxes, on molasses and sugar imported to North America from places outside the British empire would now be strictly enforced. The act also placed new or higher duties on other foreign imports such as textiles, coffee, and wine.

These new duties caused an increase in the price of goods in the colonies, hurting businesses and customers alike. Just as important, the act also restricted smugglers by toughening the enforcement of customs laws. Smuggling formed a sizable part of colonial trade, in part because customs duties were high. The act had the overall effect of widening the division between Britain and the colonies. Americans resented having no representatives in Parliament to determine how their tax money would be spent by the British rulers.

Boston merchants protested the Sugar Act with orderly petitions. "If these taxes are laid upon us, in any shape," one petition read, "without our having a legal

**Eastern North America in 1763**

North America reflected many interests in 1763. Notice the cities in the English colonies, the lands claimed by other European powers, and the Indian lands.

representation where they are laid, are we not reduced . . . to the miserable status of tributary slaves?" Yet these petitions had little impact on Parliament, and the Sugar Act remained law.

**The Stamp Act** In 1765 Parliament passed a tax on all official documents and publications in the colonies. To be official, marriage licenses, mortgages, diplomas, bills of sale, and newspapers had to bear an official stamp, or seal, showing that a duty had been paid. The tax money was to pay for keeping British troops in North America.

The Stamp Act affected almost everyone, and most colonists hated it. Landowners and business owners despised it because the tax money raised went directly to the colonial governor. Colonists themselves had no say in how it was spent. Poorer people hated the tax because they had to pay extra for everyday items such as newspapers and playing cards.[1]

Opposition to the stamp tax focused not just on the cost of the stamps but also on the method of taxation. Colonists agreed that Parliament had the right to levy an **external tax,** one to regulate trade in goods that came into the colonies. The Stamp Act, however, was an **internal tax,** one levied on goods within the colonies, designed only to raise revenue. Colonists argued that only their elected representatives should have the right to levy internal taxes. Because colonists could not elect representatives to Parliament, they believed that the right to levy an internal tax should belong to their elected colonial assemblies.

Protests over the Stamp Act united the colonists. Daniel Dulany, an attorney from Maryland, wrote a pamphlet denying Britain's right to impose internal taxes on Americans. John Dickinson of Pennsylvania published a pamphlet that denied the authority of Parliament to tax the colonists in any form. It was James Otis, a Massachusetts lawyer, who gave the colonists their rallying cry with his statement, "Taxation without representation is tyranny!"

**Taxes imposed through the Stamp Act triggered an angry response among colonists.**

## The Coming of the Revolution

The taxation crisis of the 1760s heated the debate between Britain and its American colonies. Colonists argued that Parliament violated their cherished right as British subjects to consent to all taxes levied on them. Feelings of resentment grew. People had been asking, Who has the power to tax us? Now the question became, Who has the power to govern? A movement toward self-government began to take shape. Protests against British authority intensified and, in some cases, became violent.

**Sons of Liberty** Men like Samuel Adams of Boston felt that speeches and petitions against unjust British laws were not enough. A genial yet cagey politician, Samuel Adams came from a respected family and had attended Harvard College. He ran his own business, but after 20 years he was deep in debt. By the 1760s Adams was very involved in local politics and sought support for his ideas from the people of Boston.

Throughout 1765, Adams and leaders in other colonies formed a network of local groups called the Sons of Liberty to organize opposition to the Stamp Act. Often led by men of high position, these groups did not hesitate to resort to violence. They destroyed the homes of British officials and forced stamp agents to resign. To enforce a boycott of British goods, the Sons of Liberty threatened merchants. Anyone who imported or sold British goods risked being smeared with hot tar and covered with feathers.

In October 1765, delegates from nine colonies met in New York City and drafted a petition demanding repeal of the Stamp Act. This protest was effective, but the economic impact of the boycott was much stronger. The combination forced Parliament to repeal the Stamp Act in 1766. In its place, however, Parliament passed the Declaratory Act. This law flatly declared Parliament's right to make laws concerning the colonists without their consent.

**The Boston Massacre** Conflict over taxation prompted Britain to send troops to Boston to enforce laws and maintain order. The presence of British soldiers only raised tensions. Clashes between citizens and soldiers became common in Boston. On the evening of

March 5, 1770, the tensions exploded into violence in an event that came to be called the Boston Massacre.

Accounts of the incident vary, but most agree that it began when a mob of townspeople taunted a British sentry on duty. Other British soldiers, led by Captain Thomas Preston, came to the sentry's aid. Tempers flared. The crowd threw snowballs and rocks at the soldiers. In the confusion, shots rang out. Some reports say that one soldier's musket went off by mistake, and then other soldiers began to fire. Others say the soldiers were commanded to fire by an unidentified person. Three colonists, including Crispus Attucks, a sailor of African and Native American ancestry, lay dead. Two more colonists later died from their wounds. Captain Preston was put on trial and acquitted. Two of his men were convicted of manslaughter and were branded on the hand.

A period of uneasy calm followed the Boston Massacre. Samuel Adams continued to use the incident to stir up anti-British feelings, but no violent protests resulted.

New trouble began in 1773. Parliament passed the Tea Act to save the East India Company, a British trading company, from bankruptcy. According to this law, only the East India Company could sell tea to the colonies. Though the tea would sell for a lower price than Americans were used to paying, they would still have to pay the import tax on it. Most of all, colonists resented the East India Company's monopoly on selling tea. To protest the tea tax, Boston's Sons of Liberty disguised themselves as Mohawks and went to the pier one night. There they tossed 342 chests of newly arrived tea into the harbor.

As punishment for the so-called "Boston Tea Party," Parliament closed Boston Harbor to all shipping until the tea was paid for. General Thomas George Gage,

PAUL REVERE, *THE BLOODY MASSACRE*, 1770, METROPOLITAN MUSEUM OF ART

**In 1770, stung by colonists' taunts, British troops opened fire, killing five Bostonians. Colonists called the event the Boston Massacre.**

commander of British troops in North America, took over as governor of the colony to restore order to the rebellious city.[2]

### Committees of Correspondence

While Bostonians fought for their rights, people in other colonies also struggled against British control. Their struggle took different forms as tensions mounted. As early as the Stamp Act crisis in 1765, Virginia's assembly opposed Parliament with decrees worded so strongly that some colonists called them treason, or a betrayal of Britain.

In 1768 merchants up and down the coast boycotted British goods to protest the Townshend Acts of 1767. Five years later, patriots from New Hampshire to Virginia dumped or boycotted tea to protest the Tea Act. The "Boston Tea Party" was only the best known of these protests.

Most colonists, however, viewed the crisis with England as a local matter. A Philadelphia lawyer, a New England fisherman, and a Carolina planter might all oppose a tax on tea, but they felt little in common beyond that. Many colonists thought that Bostonians had brought trouble on themselves and felt no obligation to solve or share their problems.

A group in Boston tried to change that attitude in 1772 by forming what they called a "committee of correspondence." The committee would "state the rights of the colonists . . . and communicate and publish the same to the several towns and to the world." Within a year dozens of towns in Massachusetts and assemblies from nearly every colony had created similar letter-writing committees.

The letters carried along the muddy roads leading from colony to colony did much to bring North and South, town and country, closer together in the

**Identifying Cause and Effect**

Identifying cause and effect helps you see the relationship between events. Sometimes cause and effect are part of a series of events. A single cause, the passing of the Stamp Act, led to an effect—the Boston riots against the tax. Then the Boston riots became a cause resulting in a new effect—the repeal of the Stamp Act.

**2** How did the colonists respond to taxes levied on them by the British Parliament?

struggle for self-government. Farmers had been slow to join the protests against Britain, but now they, too, argued against unfair taxes. Many farmers organized against the British as city people had done earlier.

News in 1774 that the British had closed Boston Harbor circulated through the committees of correspondence and outraged Americans everywhere. This news especially distressed merchants and planters, for if Britain closed the main ports of their colonies, they would be ruined. So when Bostonians called for a meeting to discuss the crisis, 12 of the 13 colonies sent representatives.

**Continental Congress**  Fifty-six men from 12 colonies traveled to Philadelphia late in the summer of 1774 for the First Continental Congress. Most of them had served in colonial assemblies, but few knew any of the other representatives. John Adams of Massachusetts wrote, "We have numberless prejudices to remove here." Nobody knew what to expect of this unprecedented—and perhaps treasonable—meeting.

The First Continental Congress called for a halt in trade with England and resolved to meet again in the spring of 1775. In the process of discussing the crisis that had brought them together, the delegates had succeeded in removing some of their prejudices against one another and helped make Boston's crisis an American crisis.

By 1775 the machinery of the British empire —governors, councils, courts—had broken down. In its place grew a ramshackle system of local committees and congresses of men who ignored British authority.

General Gage, the governor of Massachusetts, received orders from London to arrest just such a group of men. On an April night in 1775, 700 British soldiers marched toward Concord, about 15 miles from Boston. At the town of Lexington, 70 American militiamen stood waiting. After a brief skirmish at dawn, the British left eight Americans dead on the village green and marched on to Concord.

At Concord, fighting again broke out. As the British began the return march to Boston, colonists hid behind rocks, trees, and fences all along the road and picked off scores of British troops. By the time the British forces reached Boston, they had suffered 273 casualties, and 88 Americans had fallen. The struggle to defend the colonists' rights had become a war.

## Fighting for Independence

When the Second Continental Congress met in May 1775 they found themselves leading 13 colonies against the greatest empire and strongest army on earth. The Congress attempted to deal with that awesome fact in two different ways. First, they called for the formation of a Continental army of 20,000 men. Second, they made an attempt to resolve the crisis with Britain. They sent King George III a petition blaming Parliament for the current problems and asking for the King's help in solving them. In December 1775 King George rejected the petition, declared the colonies in rebellion, and sent about 20,000 more British soldiers to America.

**Breaking the Bonds**  One month later, in January 1776, colonists began reading a pamphlet that helped prepare them for independence. *Common Sense* appeared first in Philadelphia where its author, Thomas Paine, lived. Paine grew up in England and for a time worked as a tax collector. After meeting Benjamin Franklin, then the most famous American alive, Paine decided to move to Philadelphia in 1774 and soon became involved in the colonists' fight for independence.

Unlike other revolutionary writers, Paine wrote in the direct, colorful language of America's farmers and city workers. Paine called King George "the Royal Brute of Britain." He asserted that "a government of our own is our own national right." *Common Sense* sold 120,000 copies in three months. Paine's arguments persuaded many Americans to join the cause.

Congress felt this popular push for independence. When it met in Philadelphia in June 1776, the Congress formed a committee to draft a declaration of America's independence. The committee, in turn,

**Trace the British attempts to control the colonists and the colonists' protests on the timeline below.**

### Major Events of the Revolutionary Era

**February 1763**
Treaty of Paris ends Seven Years' War.

**March 1765**
Parliament passes Stamp Act. Colonists react with petitions and violence.

**March 1770**
British troops kill colonists in Boston Massacre.

| 1763 | 1764 | 1765 | 1766 | 1767 | 1768 | 1769 | 1770 | 1771 | 1772 |

**April 1764**
Parliament passes Sugar Act.

**November 1767**
Townshend Acts go into effect. Colonists react with boycotts.

**November 1772**
Committees of Correspondence formed.

asked 33-year-old Thomas Jefferson, a lawyer from Virginia, to write it. He reluctantly agreed.

The tall, red-headed Jefferson owned a large plantation, and in the leisure hours of a planter's life, pursued a variety of interests: law, architecture, music, science, and politics. The document this cultured lawyer created consisted of three parts. The first part contained a statement of what the Congress believed a government should do. "All men are created equal," Jefferson wrote, "they are endowed by their Creator with certain unalienable rights; that among these are life, liberty, and the pursuit of happiness." Jefferson stated that governments existed to "secure these rights." The second part contained 27 "reasons for separation" from Britain. The document ended with a declaration of independence from Britain.

Congress discussed the declaration for several days before voting unanimously for independence on July 2, 1776. On July 4 the delegates adopted the Declaration of Independence. Congress now turned to the business of steering their new nation, the United States of America, through a **revolution,** a violent struggle to throw off British rule.

**Winning the War** Congress had made its most important decision about the war a year earlier when it called for a commander for the Continental Army. John Adams worried that the war would remain New England's war unless a southerner took command. A southern commander, reasoned Adams, would bring the whole nation—north, middle, and south—into the war together.

Adams had in mind for the job a Virginian named George Washington. Washington had fought in the French and Indian War, where he had been an able soldier and leader.

Delegates to the Congress approved of the aloof 43-year-old Virginian as the commander of their army. Washington had the qualities they admired in themselves and others: rank, wealth, and integrity.

Washington also had the discipline needed to turn a mass of poorly equipped, poorly trained men into an army that could survive the six long years of fighting. During those years Washington's army received little support from the Congress or the states, which

bickered throughout the war. Still, Washington maintained order through defeat, freezing winters, and starvation.

In the first years of the war, the British aimed to divide the rebellious colonies, cutting New England off from the rest of the nation. Only a surprise American victory at Saratoga, New York, in 1777 foiled their plan. The victory boosted the American spirits and persuaded the French to enter the war against their British rivals. After Saratoga, the British focused their energies in the South, where they hoped the

**Compare the number of British and American victories between 1775 and 1781.** *What geographic factors may have helped Americans win the war?*

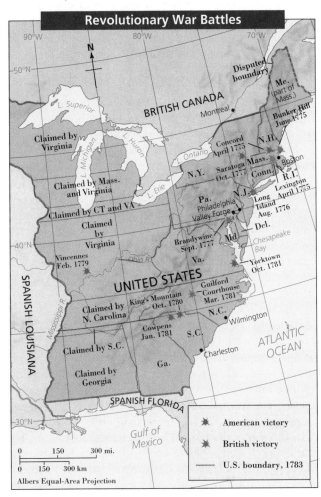

Revolutionary War Battles

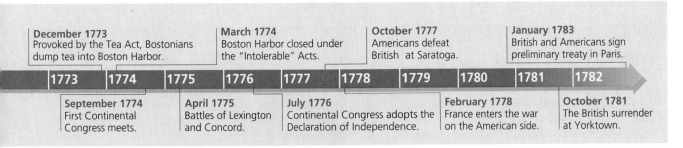

| December 1773 Provoked by the Tea Act, Bostonians dump tea into Boston Harbor. | March 1774 Boston Harbor closed under the "Intolerable" Acts. | October 1777 Americans defeat British at Saratoga. | January 1783 British and Americans sign preliminary treaty in Paris. |

1773  1774  1775  1776  1777  1778  1779  1780  1781  1782

| September 1774 First Continental Congress meets. | April 1775 Battles of Lexington and Concord. | July 1776 Continental Congress adopts the Declaration of Independence. | February 1778 France enters the war on the American side. | October 1781 The British surrender at Yorktown. |

many loyalists in the region might help them.

Washington learned valuable lessons during the first years of the war. The Americans, he knew, must avoid major battles with the better trained British troops. They learned to use surprise tactics and familiar terrain to their advantage. If the Americans could not defeat the British in open combat, at least they could drag the war on until the British no longer cared to fight. This strategy paid off when Washington, supported by French troops and the French navy, trapped a large British force at Chesapeake Bay in Yorktown, Virginia, in 1781. The British surrendered at Yorktown; it became clear that after six years and no conclusive victories, the British no longer cared to fight, nor could they afford to.[3]

The war finally ended in 1783, when Congress sent John Adams, Benjamin Franklin, and John Jay to negotiate a peace treaty with Britain. In the treaty, the British promised to remove their troops from America "with all convenient speed," officially recognized the independence of the United States of America, and agreed that the western border of the new nation lay at the Mississippi River.

## Surviving the War

It took the effort of over 250,000 American soldiers fighting for six years to break the back of British rule. During that time one out of every 10 Americans who fought died; the British captured and occupied most major cities, including Boston, New York, and Philadelphia; and many American lives were reshaped by the American Revolution.

**On the Battlefield** When America mobilized for war in 1775 and 1776 all levels of society became involved. Elite politicians designed state and national governments. Men with military experience volunteered for positions in the army. Some merchants loaned money to the army and to Congress, while

From the time he took command, Washington never had a full army. Poor conditions and farm duties caused many soldiers to abandon the war effort.

NEW YORK PUBLIC LIBRARY, PRINTS DIVISION

others made huge fortunes from wartime government contracts. Farmers provided food for armies.

These many groups contributed to the war effort, but most of the actual fighting was done by the poorest Americans: young city laborers, farm boys, indentured servants (people who had exchanged years of work for a passage to America), and sometimes slaves. A lack of money, food, and supplies made the usual wartime experiences—boredom, disease, bloodshed—worse for the men in the Continental Army. In 1778 one young American gave this nightmarish description of a soldier's life: "Poor food, hard lodging, cold weather, fatigue, nasty clothes, nasty cookery."

Boredom was relieved only by the horror of battle. Ranks of soldiers standing in open fields fired their muskets once, reloaded, and fired again. Orderly troop movements soon broke down into hand-to-hand combat; soldiers inflicted many wounds with bayonets and knives. Mud, smoke, blood, curses, and cannon shot flew about the battlefield. Medical treatment barely existed on or off the battlefield, and most wounds were fatal.

African Americans also stood and fell on the battlefields of the Revolutionary War. One slave named Jehu Grant escaped from his master and joined the colonists when he "saw liberty poles and people all engaged for the purpose of freedom." Yet only about 5,000 of the 500,000 blacks living in the colonies served in the Continental Army during the war. Many more sided with the British, who promised them freedom if they fought. As many as 20,000 slaves in the Carolinas and Georgia joined the British.

Many Native American tribes also sided with the British. The British represented a last hope for keeping land-hungry Americans out of Native American territories. During the war, colonists fought Native

**Artist Emanuel Leutze portrayed the plight of many American colonists during the Revolutionary War in** this 1852 painting, *Mrs. Schuyler Burning her Wheat Fields on the Approach of the British.*

Americans in bloody battles, and bitter feelings remained long after the war had ended.

**At Home** After the war, many soldiers returned to homes that had been forever changed by the deaths of fathers, brothers, and sons. Families were changed in other ways as well. Wives managed farms and businesses while husbands served in the army. Other women traveled with the army, working as cooks and nurses. These experiences gave satisfaction to many women who had never owned property nor voted. Women began to express their thoughts more freely on such subjects as politics. As Philadelphia's Anne Emlen wrote to her husband in 1777, "How shall I impose a silence upon myself when the subject is so very interesting, so much engrossing conversation—and what every member of the community is more or less concerned in?"

Women actively and openly participating in politics was a new phenomenon. In less than 20 years American society had changed in unpredictable and lasting ways. A group of colonies had challenged their mother country, fought the best army in the world, and won the right to be self-governing states. As the war ended, many Americans wondered how their experiment in self-government would turn out. "The answer to the question," said Thomas Paine, "can America be happy under a government of her own, is short and simple—as happy as she pleases; she hath a blank sheet to write upon."

## SECTION REVIEW

**Checking Facts**

1. What were the purposes of the Proclamation of 1763 from the British point of view?
2. What were the consequences of the Sugar Act?
3. Explain why colonists accepted the external taxes but resented the internal taxes that Parliament levied.
4. How did the Revolutionary War affect Americans on the battlefield and at home?

**Thinking Critically**

5. **Identifying Cause and Effect** Explain why the colonists resorted to crowd violence in dealing with the British.
6. **Making Inferences** What might the British government have done to prevent revolution?
7. **Recognizing Points of View** What was the British point of view about the American colonies at the end of the Revolutionary War?

**Linking Across Time**

8. Under what conditions might the people of a country feel justified in revolting against their government today?

# Reading a Map

Maps are visual tools that help communicate how places are related in terms of distance, direction, location, and other geographic features. The stronger your map decoding skills, the easier it will be for you to learn from maps.

## Learning the Skill

All maps share certain elements. Recognizing and understanding these common features is the key to interpreting maps quickly and accurately.

### Title

The title of a map explains the map's purpose. Knowing the intent of a map may help you to understand why certain features are included and allow you to interpret these features more easily. Read the title of the map on page 33. This map's purpose is to show ethnic diversity in the colonies in 1770. The title makes it clear that the map does not show where different ethnic groups live today.

### Scale and Distance

The scale of a map is the ratio between its size and the actual area of the earth's surface it represents. A small-scale map shows an area in a small space. Maps like the one on pages 830–831 show the location of a place in relation to the whole earth. The very small scale of such maps makes it impossible to use them to convey much other information. The larger a map's scale, the closer the map's size is to the actual area it represents, and the greater the amount of detail the map can convey.

A scale of miles shows the ratio between distance on the map and real distance on earth. For example, an inch on the map on page 33 represents 250 actual miles. The smallest-scale maps, used only to show general location, often do not include a scale of miles.

### Direction and Location

A directional arrow indicates which direction is north, usually toward the top of the map. South, then, is toward the bottom of the map, east is to the right, and west is to the left.

Lines of latitude and longitude also indicate direction on maps. These are the lines that form a grid, which mapmakers put on maps to show exact location.

Lines that run east and west are lines of latitude. The line of latitude halfway between the North and South poles is the Equator. It divides the earth into Northern and Southern hemispheres. Other lines of latitude measure distance from the Equator (0° latitude) to the North Pole (90° N) and to the South Pole (90° S) .

Lines of longitude run north and south and meet at the poles. These lines begin at the Prime Meridian (0° longitude), which runs through Greenwich, England. They are numbered both east and west, from 0° to 180°. New York City, at about 74° W 41° N, is located 74° *west* of the Prime Meridian and 41° *north* of the Equator.

### Keyed Symbols

You know that maps use symbols to represent various features related to the map's theme. Most maps include a legend, or key, to explain the use of symbols. Look at the map on page 33. The legend shows five different types of symbols: color, pattern, geometric shape, circled dot, and boundary line. Each type of symbol conveys a different category of information.

Different colors are used to identify areas with a high proportion of particular European ethnic groups. The culture and life style of these proportionately large groups generally had the greatest influence on the culture of everyone in the area.

A line pattern overlaying any color indicates where a significant number of African Americans, either slave or free, lived. In most of these areas, they probably made up less than half the population, and their presence would not be apparent without the overlay technique. Even where African Americans did comprise more than half the population, theirs was not the dominant culture.

The geometric shape denotes the location of other ethnic groups who contributed to the culture of an area, yet were not a dominant group numerically.

The circled dot is used to indicate areas with especially diverse populations, generally the largest cities. No circled dot is used for cities whose populations reflected the same ethnic makeup as that of the surrounding area.

The line showing the boundary of the thirteen colonies separates the subject area of the map theme from surrounding areas.

### Standard Uses of Color

Standard symbols are those that mapmakers do not explain but expect readers to interpret readily. To get as much information as possible from a map, you should become familiar with several standard map symbols. On the map here, the colors blue and beige are used without explanation. The key does not tell you that blue represents bodies of water, such as oceans, lakes, and rivers. Neither does it explain that areas shown in beige are outside the main subject area of the map. These areas help define the size, location, and shape of areas important to the map's theme.

Color is also frequently used to make boundaries easy to see. For example, each state or nation on a political map may be shown in a different color. This use of color generally will not be explained in the map legend.

### Boundaries

Many maps include two or more types of political division. The map on this page uses two different types of boundaries to indicate two levels of political division. The legend explains that a dark heavy line denotes the boundary of the thirteen colonies in 1770. The lightweight boundary line that separates individual colonies is not explained.

## Practicing the Skill

1. Use latitude and longitude to describe the location of Charleston, South Carolina, and of Philadelphia, Pennsylvania. How can you tell which city is farther north by comparing their latitudes?
2. Using the map on page 29, describe the distance and direction you would travel to go from the site where the

Revolutionary War began at Lexington to where the war ended, near Yorktown.
3. How do the symbols for American victory and British victory differ on the Revolutionary War map on page 29?
4. The eastern border of New

Hampshire was about 150 miles long. What is the measurement in inches for this border on the map below? What does it measure on the Revolutionary War map? Which map is drawn to a larger scale?

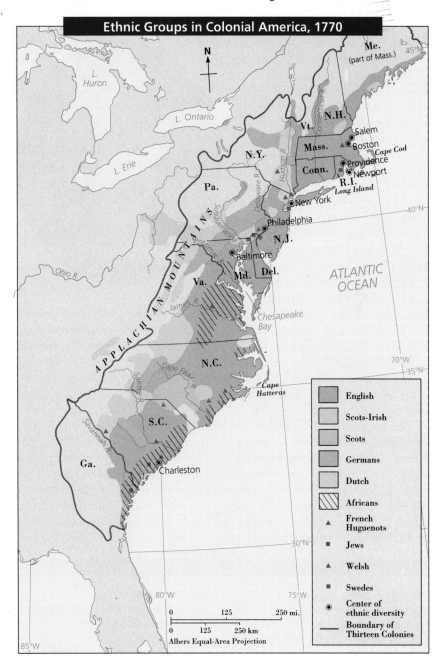

Ethnic Groups in Colonial America, 1770

Me. (part of Mass.)

L. Huron

L. Ontario

L. Erie

N.H.

Vt.

Salem

Mass.

Boston
Cape Cod

N.Y.

Conn.

Providence
Newport

R.I.
Long Island

Pa.

Philadelphia

New York

N.J.

Baltimore

Md.  Del.

Va.

ATLANTIC OCEAN

Chesapeake Bay

APPALACHIAN MOUNTAINS

Susquehanna R.

Potomac R.

James R.

Ohio R.

Santee R.

Savannah R.

N.C.

Cape Fear R.

Cape Hatteras

S.C.

Ga.

Charleston

Hudson R.

Delaware R.

Connecticut R.

45°N

40°N

70°W

35°N

30°N

80°W

75°W

85°W

| | English |
| | Scots-Irish |
| | Scots |
| | Germans |
| | Dutch |
| | Africans |
| ▲ | French Huguenots |
| ■ | Jews |
| ▲ | Welsh |
| ■ | Swedes |
| ◉ | Center of ethnic diversity |
| — | Boundary of Thirteen Colonies |

0       125       250 mi.

0    125    250 km

Albers Equal-Area Projection

# Framing the Constitution

---

### June 1788: Virginians Debate Proposed Constitution

---

THE WINDOWS OF THE STATE HOUSE IN RICHMOND, VIRGINIA, STOOD OPEN ON THE HOT SUMMER AFTERNOON. IMPASSIONED VOICES BOOMED FROM THE building's main hall. There, 168 Virginia representatives heard arguments for and against a plan for a new government of the United States.

Patrick Henry stood before his fellow Virginians; they knew him as a former governor of their state and a great public speaker. Henry explained his opposition to the proposed constitution. It stripped powers away from the states, he said. It increased the powers of federal government, and it had been written by men with no authority to do so. He twisted the first words of the document into an attack on those men. "What right had they to say *We, the People?*" he asked. "Who authorized them to speak the language of *We, the People*, instead of *We, the States?*"

COLONIAL WILLIAMSBURG

One of the men who helped design the new plan was at the convention. Edmund Randolph was as well known as Henry; he, too, had served as governor of the state and came from an old Virginia family. Randolph asked Virginia to accept the Constitution and unite the nation. Raising his right arm, Randolph exclaimed, "I will assent to the lopping of this limb before I assent to the dissolution of the Union."

The men debated the merits and faults of the Constitution through the rest of that warm June of 1788. Patrick Henry and his supporters argued for the rights of the states. Randolph and others urged unity under a strong federal government that the new Constitution offered. The differences between the two men summed up tensions that pulled at the fabric of life in the United States in the 1780s.

## A Firm League of Friendship

During the Revolution, 11 of the 13 states wrote new **constitutions,** or plans of government. In some of these states, the men who wrote the constitutions had served in colonial assemblies and in the Continental Congress: men such as Patrick Henry and Thomas Jefferson of Virginia, and John Adams of Massachusetts. Other state constitutions were drafted by men who had been denied political power under the colonial system. Some states sought only to correct the flaws of Britain's colonial governments, while others hoped to redistribute political power.

**In the States** One of the more radical groups wrote Pennsylvania's constitution. The men in this group replaced the governor with an executive committee which served the state's one-house legislature. Pennsylvania's constitution ended property requirements for officeholders and voters and allowed all taxpaying males to vote. More than any other state, Pennsylvania allowed the common people of the state to share political power.

In contrast, John Adams believed that society needed a strict order, with men of talent and experience—men like himself—in positions of power. The constitution he helped write in Massachusetts called for strict property requirements for voters and stricter ones for officeholders. The state assembly was "an exact portrait, in miniature," of the people, while a "natural aristocracy" of wealth and talent filled the state senate. The governor remained powerful.

State governments issued their own money, taxed

---

## STUDY GUIDE

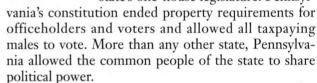

**As You Read**
Follow the struggle to write and to ratify the Constitution. Also, think about the following concepts and skills.

**Central Concepts**
- understanding how compromise and **representation** were crucial to drafting the Constitution
- examining the efforts at **ratification** of the Constitution

**Thinking Skills**
- analyzing decisions
- recognizing bias
- recognizing values

their own citizens, and competed with other states in trade and for land beyond the Appalachians. By the 1780s states acted more like 13 small independent nations—each with its own government, economy, and interests—than like parts of a larger nation.

Still, Americans realized that the states could not do everything on their own. By 1781 **ratification**, or the official acceptance of the new plan, joined the states in a "firm league of friendship."

**In Congress**   The Articles of Confederation, as this new plan was called, created a national government in the form of a one-house legislature, similar to the Continental Congress. Each state, regardless of its size, had one vote in the Confederation Congress. This body was given only those powers that individual states could not fulfill alone: declaring war, conducting foreign policy, and establishing a postal system were examples. The Articles denied Congress power to collect taxes, even for the support of an army, or to enforce its own laws and treaties. One rule firmly established the power of the states over Congress: only a unanimous vote of the states could change the Articles of Confederation. Many Americans believed that this new system avoided the evils of a strong government—such as Britain's government—but allowed the states to work together for their common good and protection.

When the states worked together, the Confederation Congress succeeded in passing laws of lasting value. The Northwest Ordinance of 1787, for example, established rules for the organization of the lush region west of the Appalachian Mountains. It also reached a compromise on slavery, allowing it in territory south of the Ohio River and prohibiting the im-

*ABIGAIL ADAMS*, B. BLYTHE, 1766, MASSACHUSETTS HISTORICAL SOCIETY

**Abigail Adams's letters to her husband, John Adams, reveal her commitment to equality for all people and provide vivid descriptions of daily life in the new American nation.**

portation of slaves north of the river. The Ordinance also provided rules for electing assemblies in the western territories and admitting territories "on an equal footing with the original states."

While effective in passing the Northwest Ordinance, Congress faced a variety of difficult problems after the war that states refused to help solve. The worst of these problems involved paying off war debts and stabilizing the American economy.

**In Debt**   Congress had borrowed nearly $60 million from American investors and European governments during the war. After the war Congress lacked cash to pay its old debts. Since Congress was not allowed to tax the states, the only way it could pay its debts was to print massive amounts of paper money.

At that time, paper money was nothing more than a promise that Congress would pay the holder of the bill in gold or silver, or **hard money**, at some time in the future. By the end of the war, the United States had a severe shortage of hard money. The more paper money Congress printed, therefore, the less it was worth. By the mid-1780s, Continental currency was worth only one-fortieth of its face value. With no hard money to back up the millions of dollars printed during the war, people's confidence in paper money fell. Many merchants refused to accept Continental currency, and few Americans had any hard money to spend.

Leaders in Congress desperately tried to convince the states that it needed a new way to raise money, but Congress never received the power to tax imports. Meanwhile, the money problems began to have dire effects on the lives of common Americans.

**In the Back Country**   One of those Americans was Daniel Shays. Shays had served as a captain in the Continental army during the Revolution. After the war, he returned to his small farm in western Massachusetts. In the best of times, Shays hardly had any extra money. Now he had none. In a time before banks, Shays and other farmers sometimes borrowed money from wealthy neighbors to buy food and supplies, or bought goods on credit from a store in town. When the wealthy neighbor or store owner asked the farmers to pay their debts—in hard money, of course—many could not pay.

For people who could not pay their debts, there were two alternatives. If they had property, a local court seized it and sold it to pay off the debt. If they had no property, they were sent to debtors' prison. In 1786 Shays and other farmers begged the Massachusetts legislature for extra time to pay their debts. The legislature ignored the requests and the county courts continued to seize farms.

Daniel Shays recalled the early days of the crisis with England when legal attempts to solve disputes with government failed. He knew what to do in the face of an arrogant legislature. In August and September 1786, disgruntled farmers marched on courthouses in Northampton and Worcester. Muskets in hand, they closed the courthouses and prevented the courts from seizing any more farms or throwing any more farmers into prison.[1]

After those successes, Shays and the farmers gathered near Springfield, where the state's Supreme Court was in session, and where the state arsenal also happened to be located. When wealthy New Englanders learned that angry farmers were massing near the arsenal, they feared open rebellion and attacks on their property. They called the farmers traitors and provided the money that induced 4,400 militiamen from eastern Massachusetts to march against the gathering farmers.

In January 1787 Shays and 1,200 farmers marched on the arsenal. When Shays's men advanced, the militia opened fire. Four farmers died and the rest scattered. The revolt broke up soon afterward.

While Shays and his farmers believed they were patriotic, other Americans were horrified. Men of wealth and power saw the rebellion as proof of social disorder. Congress sent Secretary of War Henry

**"Not worth a continental" became a popular saying after the war.** *What effect might devaluation of money have on people's faith in the young government?*

NATIONAL NUMISMATIC COLLECTION, SMITHSONIAN INSTITUTION

Knox to investigate. Knox reported that the farmers' uprising had "alarmed men of principle and property." He declared, "What is to afford our security against the violence of lawless men? Our government must be braced, changed, or altered to secure our lives and property."

## A More Perfect Union

By 1787 the flaws in the Articles of Confederation were obvious to many Americans, including most members of the Confederation Congress. A group of these men worried that the nation was headed for disaster unless the Articles were altered. They called on the states to send delegates to a convention where they might correct "such defects as may be discovered to exist" in the present government.

**Meeting in Philadelphia**   The group that gathered in Philadelphia in May 1787 contained some of the most distinguished men in America. Stern, proper George Washington, a delegate from Virginia, was mobbed by adoring crowds. Americans still hailed him as the hero of the American Revolution. Another Virginia delegate, the short and frail James Madison, had spent much of the previous year reading about governments in past history to prepare for the convention. Benjamin Franklin was the elder statesman of the convention. At age 81, Franklin tired easily and had other Pennsylvania delegates read his speeches

### STUDY GUIDE

**Recognizing Bias**

Recognizing bias helps you evaluate when a person's point of view is based on fear or self-interest. Knox's denouncement of the Shaysite rebels as "lawless men" shows a bias resulting

from his desire to maintain power, which was threatened by rebellion. He chose to squelch the rebellion rather than address Shays's complaints against the enforced laws.

1 What events led to Shays's Rebellion?

for him, but he enjoyed hosting the state delegates in his home city.

The other 52 delegates had experience drafting state constitutions and serving in state governments or the Confederation Congress. The delegates' average age was about 45, just past the prime of life in the 1700s. Many of them had attended college. All were white, male, and wealthy.

By May, 25 delegates from seven states had arrived and the meeting began. Delegates from three more states arrived late; Rhode Island never showed up. Sworn to secrecy, and meeting behind closed doors, the delegates began their work at green felt-covered tables in the Pennsylvania state house. The delegates quickly agreed that the Articles were beyond repair. The Virginia delegation, headed by Edmund Randolph, proposed an entirely new system of government, based on James Madison's studies. This new government would be larger and more powerful than the Confederation Congress.

That plan was the basis for the discussion in the convention throughout the long, hot summer of 1787. Working in the closed hall, the delegates suffered through sweltering heat. Six days a week, from May to September, they proposed and debated idea after idea. Angry delegates threatened to walk out of the convention and some did. But slowly, a plan for a new government emerged.

**Reshaping the Government**   Unlike the Confederation Congress, the new government was to consist of three equal but separate branches: an executive branch, a legislative branch, and a **judicial branch,** or system of federal courts. The job of the executive branch, headed by a president, was to enforce federal laws. The responsibility of the legislative branch, or Congress, as it was called, was to make laws. The

**Constitutional Convention delegates met at the Pennsylvania State House in Philadelphia, shown above.**
*What geographic factors may have figured into the delegates' decision to choose Philadelphia as their meeting place?*

judicial branch ruled on cases involving federal laws. The responsibilities of these branches overlapped and interlocked, creating **checks and balances** that prevented one branch from gaining too much power.

One major difference between the Confederation government and the new one lay in the executive branch. Under the new Constitution, the president held far-reaching powers: he was commander-in-chief of the army; he could veto acts of Congress, appoint judges, and put down rebellions. One delegate said that these powers might not have been so great "had not many of the members cast their eyes towards General Washington as president."

The greatest difficulty the convention faced centered on Congress. The delegates agreed early that Congress should consist of two houses, but the question of **representation,** or how many votes each state should have, nearly broke up the convention. Delegates from small states insisted that each state have an

STUDY GUIDE

**Analyzing Decisions**
The decision to have a strong executive branch may seem surprising considering that only eleven years before the colonists had rejected a monarchical system. However, the Confederation Congress had suffered from a lack of leadership, and the delegates knew they required a strong leader. Furthermore, the delegates realized with relief that the head of the executive branch would almost certainly be George Washington. Also the delegates knew that the legislative branch could impeach a president who acted against the Constitution.

equal vote in Congress. Those from larger states felt that was unfair: representation in Congress should be decided by population.

**Learning to Compromise**  After seven weeks of deadlock on this issue the two sides agreed to what historians call the **Great Compromise**. Both small and large states got part of what they wanted, but neither group got all they had hoped for. In the upper house, or Senate, each state would have two votes, regardless of its size. Representation in the lower house, called the House of Representatives, would be based on each state's population. Compromise was a vital skill to a convention juggling the interests of several diverse and independent states.

Another conflict erupted over the way to figure the number of representatives a state could have. Southern delegates insisted that slaves be counted in a state's population. Northern delegates objected to this proposal: some believed slavery was wrong; others realized that counting slaves would increase the power of southern states in Congress. To complicate matters, some northern delegates threatened to outlaw the slave trade.

The two sides finally agreed to a compromise over slavery. Representation in the House of Representatives would be based on all of the free inhabitants of a state, plus three-fifths of all slaves, even though they could not vote. The same formula would be used to figure the taxes each state owed to the federal government. The group also agreed that Congress could pass no laws abolishing the slave trade before 1808.[2]

The convention also decided at the very end of their meetings that the Constitution should be ratified in specially elected conventions of the people, rather than by the state legislatures. Delegates feared that their new plan, which strengthened the national government, would never be approved by state governments. In addition, the convention agreed that only nine of the 13 states had to ratify the Constitution before the new government went into effect.

When the delegates saw the final document, many felt disappointed. Many had compromised on issues of great importance to their states. "I confess there are several parts of this constitution which I do not at present approve," said Benjamin Franklin. He also said, however, that the new plan was better than their current government and encouraged the remaining delegates to sign it. All but three of them did so on September 17, 1787. (See pages 848–861 to read the Constitution.)

The next morning, Major William Jackson, secretary of the convention, left Philadelphia on a stagecoach. He carried a copy of the Constitution to the meeting of the Confederation Congress in New York. He also carried a letter from the convention explaining "the necessity of a different organization."

**The Constitution prevents any one group from having total power by making the three branches depend on each other for their authority. In the diagram below follow how each branch of the U.S. government checks the activities of the other two branches.**

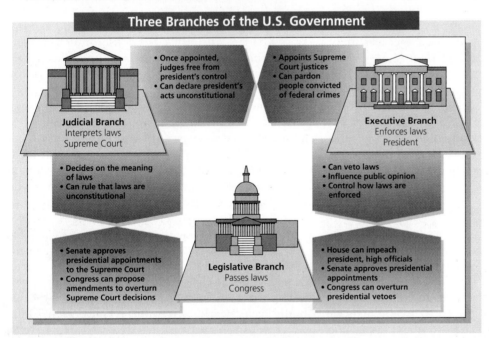

### Three Branches of the U.S. Government

**Judicial Branch**
Interprets laws
Supreme Court

- Once appointed, judges free from president's control
- Can declare president's acts unconstitutional

- Decides on the meaning of laws
- Can rule that laws are unconstitutional

**Executive Branch**
Enforces laws
President

- Appoints Supreme Court justices
- Can pardon people convicted of federal crimes

- Can veto laws
- Influence public opinion
- Control how laws are enforced

**Legislative Branch**
Passes laws
Congress

- Senate approves presidential appointments to the Supreme Court
- Congress can propose amendments to overturn Supreme Court decisions

- House can impeach president, high officials
- Senate approves presidential appointments
- Congress can overturn presidential vetoes

---

**STUDY GUIDE**

**Recognizing Values**
Recognizing other people's values helps you understand the framework from which they operate. Delegates to the Constitutional Convention operated out of a belief that they would serve best by representing the interests of their states. Each state wanted as much power as it could get, but only by compromising could the states work out a national constitution.

**2** Describe the role of compromise in the Constitutional Convention, citing two examples.

# We, the People

As soon as the convention in Philadelphia ended, the delegates rushed home to begin the campaign for ratification. That was a novel idea in itself. Never before had the nation's people at large been asked to ratify the laws under which they would live. The process of deciding for or against ratification produced perhaps the biggest and most informed political debate in American history.

News of the new Constitution spread rapidly through the states. Newspapers published the document and within days strongly worded pro and con arguments began to fill their pages. Those who favored the proposed Constitution called themselves **Federalists.** The Antifederalists opposed the new plan of government.

**The People Debate** The idea of a strong national government frightened some Americans. Many Antifederalists were small farmers who had learned to be self-sufficient and had found most of their contact with government unpleasant. The Antifederalist leaders, however, came from all classes and all regions. State politicians who saw the prospect of losing their power to the federal government were among the most active Antifederalist supporters.

The debate over the Constitution in newspapers, letters, and public discussions revealed divisions that remained in American society. One poor Antifederalist farmer mistrusted people of "wealth and talent" who had framed the Constitution:

**Study the arguments over ratification below.** *What type of person would tend to hold Federalist views? Antifederalist views? Why?*

REDEUNT SATURNIA REGNA.
On the erection of the Eleventh PILLAR of the great National DOME, we beg leave most sincerely to felicitate "OUR DEAR COUNTRY."

The FEDERAL EDIFICE.
COURTESY OF THE NEW-YORK HISTORICAL SOCIETY, NEW YORK CITY

**In this cartoon, 11 states (columns) have ratified the Constitution.** *Which two states have not yet ratified?*

*These lawyers, and men of learning, and moneyed men, that talk so finely, and gloss over matters so smoothly, to make us, poor illiterate people swallow down the pill, expect to get into Congress themselves; they expect to be managers of this Constitution, and get all the power and all the money into their own hands, and then they will swallow up all us little folks, like the great Leviathan, Mr. President; yes, just like the whale swallowed up Jonah.*

Amos Singletary, *Massachusetts Gazette,* January 25, 1788

Many Antifederalists feared that a strong central government would not preserve the essential rights of the people. Even Britain guaranteed certain rights to its citizens, they argued. Why was there no bill of basic American rights?

The leading Federalists, including George Washington, Benjamin Franklin, and James Madison, did not believe a bill of rights was necessary. All basic rights, they argued, were protected by the Constitution or by state constitutions.

The Federalists found support in the area where America's elite had always dominated, the Atlantic coast. Wealthy landowners in these areas wanted the protection a strong central government could provide. Merchants with overseas connections and artisans in America's large coastal cities also supported the proposed Constitution. These men had been hard hit by the inability of the Confederation Congress to control the nation's economy; they saw a strong government that would pass import taxes on foreign goods as their best chance to succeed in business.

As the ratifying conventions began to convene, the

## The Ratification Debate

| Antifederalist objections to the Constitution | Federalist defense of the Constitution |
|---|---|
| Articles of Confederation were a good plan for the government | Articles of Confederation were weak and ineffective |
| Constitution made national government too strong | National government needed to be strong in order to function |
| Strong national government threatened state power | Strong national government needed to protect against rebellious Indians and small farmers |
| Strong national government threatened rights of the common people | Men of experience and talent should govern the nation |
| Constitution favored wealthy men and preserved their power | National government would protect the rights of the people |
| Constitution lacked a bill of rights | Constitution and state governments protected individual freedoms without bill of rights |

In this print New Yorkers are shown celebrating the ratification of the Constitution in 1788. *Why was New York a key state in the campaign for ratification?*

CULVER PICTURES, INC.

Federalists knew they had clear majorities in some states. The vote was much closer in others, including large states like Massachusetts, Virginia, and New York. If any one of those states did not ratify, the Federalists risked total failure.

**The People Vote**   The first state conventions were held in December 1787 and January 1788. Delaware, New Jersey, Georgia, and Connecticut all ratified the Constitution without much dissent.

The first real test occurred in Massachusetts. Opponents of the Constitution, including Samuel Adams, held a clear majority when the convention met in January 1788. However, the state's urban craftsmen—still the source of Adams's political power—sided with the Federalists and persuaded Adams to vote for ratification. The Massachusetts convention agreed to the Constitution, but only if a bill of rights was added.

In June 1788 New Hampshire became the ninth state to ratify the Constitution. The Federalists had reached the minimum number required to make the new government legal. But Virginia and New York still had not yet ratified. Without these two large states the new government could hardly succeed.

George Washington and James Madison worked hard for ratification in Virginia, but Patrick Henry and other Antifederalists worked just as hard against it. Finally, at the urging of Thomas Jefferson, Madison compromised and agreed to add a bill of rights.

The contest was even closer in New York. Only a last-minute promise to add a bill of rights won ratification in New York. Once New York joined the other states, the Federalists' victory was made more secure.

**The Peoples' Rights**   Five states had ratified the Constitution with the understanding that Congress would add a bill of rights. Many Federalist leaders who had made this promise served in the new Congress. James Madison represented Virginia in the Congress, and in September 1789 he recommended that 12 amendments be added to the Constitution.

Over the next two years, state legislatures ratified ten of these 12 amendments. The Constitution now officially protected rights such as freedom of speech, religion, press, and assembly. In December 1791 these 10 amendments, known as the Bill of Rights, were added to the Constitution.

The Preamble to the Constitution states that it is designed to "promote the general welfare, and secure the blessings of liberty" of "the people of the United States." It did not, however, address the rights of many Americans. The Constitution protected slavery, ignored women, and did not acknowledge Native Americans' rights. It left to future generations problems that it could neither foresee nor solve.

Yet through the process of ratification and with the addition of the Bill of Rights, the Constitution was shaped by more people than the flawed Articles of Confederation. As they headed into the 1790s, the American people watched—with hopes and fears—to see how this latest experiment would turn out.

## SECTION REVIEW

### Checking Facts
1. What did the composition of the Massachusetts and Pennsylvania legislatures indicate about the differences between these states?
2. What was the Great Compromise and how did it satisfy all thirteen states?
3. Explain why the Bill of Rights was added to the Constitution.

### Thinking Critically
4. **Analyzing Decisions** Why did the delegates at the Constitutional Convention decide to compromise with each other?
5. **Recognizing Values** Discuss the political values of the Americans who wrote the Constitution.

### Linking Across Time
6. Give an example of a part of the Constitution that might be different if it were being written today for the first time. Explain your answer.

# Launching the New Government

## March 1801: A New President in a New Capital

JUST BEFORE NOON, THOMAS JEFFERSON LEFT HIS BOARDINGHOUSE AND WALKED THROUGH THE DUSTY STREETS OF WASHINGTON, D.C. AS HE STEPPED UP THE HILL TOWARD THE unfinished Capitol building, one observer noted that his clothing was "usual, that of a plain citizen, without any distinctive badge of office." Yet, that day Jefferson assumed the highest office in the nation: He became the third president of the United States.

Jefferson faced a number of firsts that day. He became the first president to be sworn into office in the nation's new capital city. He also became the first chief executive to succeed a political opponent in office. Jefferson had served as vice president under President John Adams, but by the time of the election the two men headed conflicting political parties: Adams led the Federalists, and Jefferson led the Democratic-Republicans.

When Jefferson won the presidential election, Americans feared that the transition from one political party to another might result in violence. Many Federalists worried that Jefferson would punish them as political enemies.

MUSEUM OF AMERICAN POLITICAL LIFE,
UNIVERSITY OF HARTFORD, WEST HARTFORD, CT

In his inaugural address, however, Jefferson asked all American people to "unite for the common good." "Every difference of opinion," he explained, "is not a difference of principle. We have called by different names brethren of the same principles. We are all Republicans—we are all Federalists."

After Jefferson's speech, many Americans breathed a sigh of relief. Yet their fears had been real. The struggles between the two parties threatened the stability of the nation. Even more disturbing, this political conflict had arisen in such a short time.

## Washington and the Government

Just 12 years earlier, in 1789, George Washington took the same oath after being unanimously elected president. While bonfires and parties marked the people's excitement, Washington himself had grave concerns. "I walk on untrodden ground," he said. As the first president, Washington had no examples to follow. Every move he made set a precedent. He also knew the nation faced dire problems.

Congress created several departments to help the president run the country. The heads of those departments made up the president's **cabinet**, or official advisers. Among others in his cabinet, Washington appointed fellow Virginian Thomas Jefferson as secretary of state, in charge of relations with foreign countries. He named 34-year-old Alexander Hamilton of New York as secretary of the treasury.

The brilliant and handsome Hamilton had served as Washington's assistant during the Revolution, and the two men remained close friends after the war. Both served at the Constitutional Convention, and both fought for ratification. Hamilton felt, however,

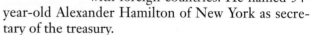

### STUDY GUIDE

**As You Read**

Trace the growth of the federal government's power during the first twenty-five years of the Constitution. Also, think about the following concepts and skills.

**Central Concepts**
- understanding why paying off the **national debt** became a source of conflict
- examining how and why **political parties** formed

**Thinking Skills**
- comparing and contrasting
- recognizing points of view
- making inferences

that the Constitution fell short of providing the type of government the United States needed.

As head of the Treasury Department, Hamilton hoped to increase the powers of the U.S. government. Under his guidance, he said, the government would work closely with "the rich, the well-born, and the good" to create wealth and stability in the young nation. Starting in 1790 he proposed a series of plans that helped to make this vision a reality.

**Hamilton's Plans** The **national debt**, money owed from the American Revolution, remained America's most serious economic problem. The U.S. government owed about $12 million to European countries and investors and about $40 million to American citizens. In addition, the state governments had war debts of nearly $21 million. Most of these debts took the form of bonds that the government had sold to investors to pay for the costs of the war. Like Continental currency, bonds were worth a fraction of their face value in 1790 because people doubted that bondholders would ever be paid. Hamilton worried that if the United States could not make good on its own bonds, it would never establish credit—or credibility—with other nations or its own citizens.

In 1790 Hamilton proposed to Congress that the government should pay off its bonds at full value and assume the debts of all the states as well. Congress agreed that foreign debts should be paid, but a storm of controversy arose over the rest of Hamilton's plan.

Some congressmen argued that paying off domestic bonds at full value was unfair. The people who originally bought the bonds had given up hope of ever collecting on them. Many of them—mostly farmers and others who lacked cash—had sold their bonds at a discount to **speculators**, people who bought the bonds in the hopes that their value would go up again. Under the plan, wealthy specula-

tors, not the common people who originally bought the bonds, would benefit. Hamilton believed that wealthy people were the key to the nation's economic development.

Other congressmen complained about paying off the states' debts. Some southern states had already paid their debts, while most New England states had not. Hamilton's plan favored the North, where most speculators lived. Southerners did not want to pay other states' debts after they had paid off their own.

Hamilton brushed these criticisms aside. He aimed to favor the commercial North over the agricultural South, and he hoped to ally the government with the wealthy men who had speculated in bonds. To get Congress to pass the plan, he struck a deal with southern leaders. Southerners agreed to support Hamilton's debt plan, while Hamilton and other northerners agreed to locate the proposed "Federal city" near Virginia, away from northern influence.

Hamilton then proposed the creation of a national bank. As a major stockholder, the government would have much influence running the Bank of the United States, as it would be called, but most of its stock would be owned by private citizens. The bank would issue money, regulate the nation's financial affairs, and loan money to American citizens.

Before signing the bank bill into law, Washington asked the members of his cabinet to give him a written opinion of the plan. Jefferson argued that the plan was illegal; the Constitution said nothing about the government having the power to create a bank. Hamilton argued that, in addition to powers spelled out, the Constitution gave the government "implied" powers to do anything "necessary and proper" to carry out its responsibilities. The Bank, he said, was necessary for the government to regulate the economy. Washington carefully considered both Jeffer-

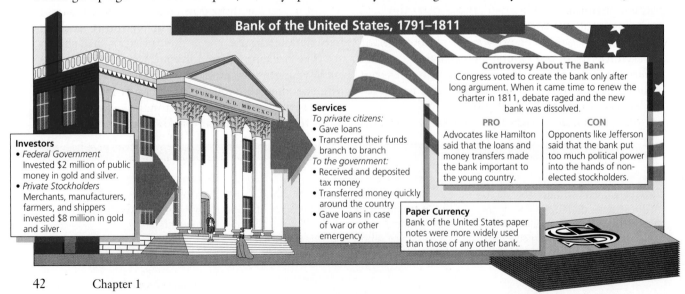

**Bank of the United States, 1791–1811**

**Investors**
- *Federal Government* Invested $2 million of public money in gold and silver.
- *Private Stockholders* Merchants, manufacturers, farmers, and shippers invested $8 million in gold and silver.

**Services**
*To private citizens:*
- Gave loans
- Transferred their funds branch to branch

*To the government:*
- Received and deposited tax money
- Transferred money quickly around the country
- Gave loans in case of war or other emergency

**Paper Currency**
Bank of the United States paper notes were more widely used than those of any other bank.

**Controversy About The Bank**
Congress voted to create the bank only after long argument. When it came time to renew the charter in 1811, debate raged and the new bank was dissolved.

| PRO | CON |
|---|---|
| Advocates like Hamilton said that the loans and money transfers made the bank important to the young country. | Opponents like Jefferson said that the bank put too much political power into the hands of non-elected stockholders. |

AMERICAN ANTIQUARIAN SOCIETY

**This political cartoon shows Robert Morris, a prominent Federalist, carrying the nation's capitol from New York City to his home city, Philadelphia.** *How does the cartoonist feel about moving the capitol? How can you tell?*

July 1794, 500 armed men surrounded the home of a local tax collector and demanded that he resign. When the farmers discovered soldiers in the house, they opened fire. In the violence that followed, several men were wounded and the tax collector's house was destroyed.

When the farmers ignored several orders to obey the law and pay their taxes, Washington and Hamilton reacted vigorously. In the fall of 1794, Henry Lee, accompanied by Hamilton, led a federal army to put down the rebels and demonstrate the power of the federal government. Threatened with this force, the "Whiskey Boys" dispersed and the Whiskey Rebellion ended. Two of the farmers were later convicted of treason, but Washington pardoned them both.

son's strict reading of the Constitution and Hamilton's loose interpretation. Though not entirely convinced by his argument, Washington sided with Hamilton and signed the bill in early 1791.

**Whiskey and Taxes** Later that year, Hamilton proposed a tax on distilled liquor. This tax would increase revenue and test the government's ability to tax—one of its most important powers, Hamilton thought. **1**

The liquor tax aroused strong opposition from farmers in the hills of western Pennsylvania. Most back country farmers made whiskey to sell in the eastern part of the state. This had always been the best way to transport processed corn, and whiskey proved to be a reliable source of extra cash. Hamilton's tax threatened to make this practice unprofitable.

For these farmers, the liquor tax brought back memories of the days before the American Revolution. At first the farmers simply refused to pay. Then they began to tar and feather tax collectors. Finally in

## Conflicts at Home and Abroad

The Whiskey Rebellion confirmed Hamilton's worst fears about the common people—"that great beast," as he called them. "How can you trust people who own no property?" he asked. The army had been needed, Hamilton argued, to enforce the laws of the land and put down a dangerous rebellion.

Thomas Jefferson, however, believed that "such an armament against people at their ploughs" had shown unnecessary force. The differences between the two men went beyond the Whiskey Rebellion, however. Both men had very different ideas of what the United States should be.

Hamilton envisioned a nation with bustling cities,

**STUDY GUIDE**

**Comparing and Contrasting**
Comparing and contrasting helps you to understand similarities and differences between events. At both the Boston Tea Party and Whiskey Rebellion, Americans revolted against taxes.

In 1773 Americans protested being taxed without direct representation in Parliament. In 1794 Americans who had elected representatives protested paying taxes that decreased their income.

**1** Why would Hamilton want to test the government's power to tax?

Forging a New Nation   43

EDWARD S. ELLIS, *YOUTH'S HISTORY OF THE US*, NY, 1887

**Angry Americans burn an effigy of John Jay upon his return from treaty negotiations in Britain.** *Why were Americans so upset by the terms of Jay's Treaty?*

Federalists continued to appeal to people with commercial interests, support for Jefferson and the Democratic-Republicans grew among common people. The parties not only differed on domestic issues; their conflicts over foreign policy nearly split the nation in the 1790s.

**France and Britain** In 1789 revolution erupted in France. What began as an effort to reform a corrupt monarchy turned into a violent, bloody battle that completely upset French society. Fearing the spread of revolt against monarchy and aristocracy, other nations, including Britain, declared war on France.

Jefferson, who had served as the United States's minister to France, supported the French. He and other Republicans believed the French Revolution continued the struggle for liberty that America had begun. They also remembered France's support during the American Revolution and argued that the alliance between the two countries remained intact.

To Federalists like Hamilton and Vice President John Adams, the French Revolution only showed the destructiveness of the common people. They sided with the British, admired the stability of the British government, and believed that American's economic livelihood depended on close ties with Britain.

Despite mounting pressure to enter the war on one side or the other, Washington chose to keep the United States **neutral**, or not allied with any side. Washington's decision did nothing to calm tensions in the United States or on the Atlantic Ocean. Both French and British ships seized American merchant vessels bound for Europe, and American trade suffered. The British navy **impressed**, or forced into service, American sailors (and·British deserters) and forced them to serve on British ships. In addition, the British had not removed all of their troops from forts in the western United States after the American Revolution. In 1794 war between the United States and either France or Britain seemed likely.

Fearing Britain's military power, Washington sent John Jay, a Federalist, to London to negotiate a treaty. When Jay returned home in 1795, however, it became clear that the new treaty was not very successful. The British agreed to remove their troops from the western United States, but not until 1796. To get this, Jay gave up American rights to ship cotton and sugar to

churning factories, big banks, and a powerful government. He found backers for his plans and ideas in large northern cities and New England—places where trade and manufacturing thrived.

The freedom of the common people thrived in Thomas Jefferson's America. "I know of no safe depository," Jefferson wrote, "of the ultimate powers of the society but the people themselves." Democracy worked best, he believed, in a society of small farmers, living in quiet, rural areas. Jefferson found support on plantations in the South, farms in the mid-Atlantic, and farms on the western frontier.

The people that these men attracted formed America's first political parties, groups that promoted ideas and supported candidates. As Hamilton and his

British colonies. In addition, he resolved nothing about the impressment of American sailors. The treaty seemed to please no one but those Federalists who wanted to maintain good relations with Britain at all costs. Democratic-Republicans called Jay's treaty "the death warrant of American liberty."

**Federalists and Republicans**  The political harmony of Washington's early years in office had long since disappeared, and Washington decided to leave office in 1797. In his farewell address, he urged the new nation to avoid conflicts with foreign nations and warned about the dangers of political parties.

In 1797 President John Adams ignored Washington's plea and sent three Americans to secure a treaty with France. In Paris the French foreign minister demanded a bribe of $240,000 from the Americans and hinted that if they refused to pay it France would declare war on the United States. This threat allowed Adams to sway American public opinion away from the French and the Democratic-Republicans.

Adams called for the formation of an army to defend against the expected French invasion in 1798; he also signed the Alien Act, giving him the power to expel any **aliens,** or foreign-born residents of the United States, who were "dangerous to the peace and safety of the United States." This act hit hardest the recent arrivals from Ireland who had been attracted to American democratic ideals.

Another law signed by Adams during the crisis—the Sedition Act—was aimed directly at the Republicans themselves. This law made it a crime for anyone to "write, print, utter, or publish . . . any false, scandalous, and malicious writing" about the president or the government. As a result, about ten Democratic-Republican editors, printers, and politicians—including the grandson of Benjamin Franklin—were jailed for publicly criticizing Federalist policies.

The Alien and Sedition Acts proved very unpopular, and public opinion turned against President Adams and the Federalists. When peaceful relations with France were restored in 1800, it appeared that the Federalists had manufactured the entire crisis. As a result, Adams and his party were in chaos as the presidential election of 1800 approached. Jefferson and his party were ready to challenge.

In 1800 the American people witnessed a hard fought and noisy presidential campaign. Democratic-Republicans spread rumors that President Adams would soon name himself King of America. New England Federalists whispered that Jefferson planned to burn every Bible in the nation. The final count of votes was close (see One Day in History, page 48), but Jefferson won.

Jefferson's ideas about government were so different from the Federalists' that many Americans feared a violent transfer of power. But people's fears were relieved on the day of Jefferson's inauguration.

Jefferson chose to let the nation heal rather than churn up old political conflicts. He quietly stopped enforcing the Alien and Sedition Acts and allowed them to expire. He reduced military spending. He even allowed the Bank of the United States to continue to exist. Some Federalist legacies, however, proved more troublesome than others.

## John Marshall and Judicial Power

After losing the election, John Adams sought ways to make Federalist ideas continue in a government dominated by Democratic-Republicans. He found his solution in the judiciary.

In the winter before their terms ran out, Adams and the Federalist Congress worked together to pass the Judiciary Act of 1801. This law added 21 positions to the roster of federal judges. The men filling them, Adams had determined, would all be Federalists. Adams also named John Marshall, a strong Federalist, Chief Justice of the Supreme Court.

Adams signed the appointments of the new Federalist judges the night before Jefferson's inauguration, leaving several appointments to be delivered by the new administration.[2] Yet Jefferson's Secretary of State James Madison refused to do this. When a Federalist named William Marbury did not receive his expected appointment, he appealed to the Supreme Court.

John Marshall found himself in a difficult position. As a Federalist, he would have liked to order Jefferson to make Marbury a federal judge. If he did, however, Jefferson and Madison would probably ignore the order; that would reduce the authority of the Supreme Court. Yet Marshall could not give in.

**Comparing and Contrasting**
At first, the Supreme Court heard cases about people accused of breaking federal law. Beginning with John Marshall's court, the justices continued to rule on cases concerning the breaking of federal law, but they also decided whether laws passed by the legislative branch were in accord with the Constitution. Marshall increased the responsibility of the Supreme Court.

**2** Why did Adams appoint Federalist judges on the night before he left office?

Marshall's solution bypassed short-term gains for the Federalists, but had long-term effects on the nation. In 1803 he ruled that Marbury was entitled to his appointment and that Madison had violated the law in not delivering it. Marshall ruled, however, that the Court could not require Madison to deliver the appointment because a part of the law giving the Court that right—the Judiciary Act of 1789—was **unconstitutional**, or violated the Constitution. Marshall had established the right of the Supreme Court to judge an act of Congress illegal. It is "the duty of the judicial department to say what the law is," he wrote. "A law repugnant to the Constitution is void."

What began as a petty political fight ended by strengthening the Supreme Court. John Marshall served as chief justice for 34 years, and during that time consistently supported the Federalist program of a strong federal government. In 1819, for example, Marshall defended the power of Congress to create the Bank of United States, using the same arguments Alexander Hamilton had used. In this way, Marshall remained the chief adversary of Democratic-Republican presidents for the next 16 years and helped Federalist policy endure long after the party ceased to exist.

## Foreign Policy and Local War

Along with the Federalist judiciary, conflicts with European nations troubled Thomas Jefferson's presidency. France and Britain continued to victimize the United States. Navies of the two nations seized nearly 1,500 American merchant ships during the 1790s and early 1800s. By 1807 the British had captured as many as 10,000 American sailors. The British fired on the American frigate Chesapeake, killing three Americans and wounding 18. Across the nation, Americans called for action against the British.

**The Embargo Act** Jefferson did not believe that the United States could fight a war against Britain. He also remembered the trouble that foreign conflicts had caused during the 1790s, and he hoped to avoid such conflicts now. Jefferson summed up this **isolationist** position, saying, "Peace, commerce, and honest friendship with other nations—entangling alliances with none."

Still, Jefferson knew that something had to be done. He believed that the European powers needed American food and materials. So in 1807 Jefferson signed the Embargo Act. The **embargo** stopped the export of all American goods and forbade American ships from sailing for foreign ports.

Jefferson thought that by depriving European countries of American products they would stop harassing the young nation. He was wrong. The Embargo Act had almost no effect on Britain and France. Instead, it proved to be a disaster for the United States, especially in the trading centers of New England. Depression and unemployment swept the country. Americans from South Carolina to New Hampshire openly defied the law.

Jefferson left office after two terms in 1809, but not before he convinced Congress to repeal the Embargo Act. James Madison won the presidency easily, but opposition to timid Democratic-Republican policies against the British grew. By 1811 a new breed of politician had swept into Congress.

**The War Hawks** These politicians came from the newly admitted states of the western frontier and were the first generation of politicians to come of age after the Revolution. They earned the name "War Hawks" for their calls for action against the British.

The British had heaped one insult after another on the American people, the War Hawks charged. They impressed American sailors, attacked American ships, and stirred up trouble between settlers and Native Americans. To westerners accustomed to action, the economic warfare of Jefferson and Madison seemed pathetic. "Is the rod of British power to be forever suspended over our heads?" asked War Hawk Henry Clay of Kentucky.[3]

Madison recognized the growing power of these new politicians, and in 1812 he made a deal with them. If they supported him for reelection as president, he would ask for a declaration of war. The War Hawks agreed, and by the summer of 1812 the United States and Britain were locked in combat.

American goals in the war were never very clear. The War Hawks had boasted of conquering Canada and Florida, but these plans were squelched when the British invaded the United States. Each side scored victories in battles around the Great Lakes, near

**Making Inferences**

Since the Embargo Act did not harm Britain and France economically, we can infer that they did not consider American goods a necessity and that they obtained goods from other countries.

Since economic hardship and unemployment in the United States increased after the act went into effect, we can also infer that most Americans must have initially honored the embargo.

**3** Over what issues did the "War Hawks" want to take action against the British?

**This print, *The Capture of the City of Washington*, shows the nation's capital after it was torched by British troops during the War of 1812. According to** **one story, British troops feasted on a dinner that had been prepared for President Madison and afterwards burned the White House.**

Washington, D.C., and on the Atlantic Ocean. By the end of 1814, British leaders, more concerned with European matters, had wearied of the American war and offered to make peace. The treaty, ratified in 1815, resolved few of the problems that had caused the conflict. It simply ended the fighting and restored everything as it had been before the war.

The United States had not won the war—no one had—but the War of 1812 became an important event for the young nation. The War Hawks hailed it as the "Second War for Independence." U.S. victories stimulated national pride and confidence. The war, which

had been urged by western politicians, also created a new western hero: General Andrew Jackson of Tennessee, who scored a sensational victory over the British near New Orleans. The War of 1812 also marked the end of U.S. involvement with European conflicts for over a century.

After the war, Americans looked eastward to Europe less and looked westward across their own continent more. At last, the United States put its colonial past behind and headed toward its future as a nation of lush prairies, growing cities, and restless and changing people.

## SECTION REVIEW

**Checking Facts**

1. Why did Alexander Hamilton feel it was crucial that the United States pay its war debts, especially to foreign nations?
2. What were the main conflicts at home and abroad during the Adams and Jefferson administrations?
3. Explain how the ruling on the Judiciary Act of 1789 changed the Supreme Court.

4. What were the War Hawks' objections to the Republican administration?

**Thinking Critically**

5. **Comparing and Contrasting** Did internal or external problems pose more of a threat to the nation during Washington's administration? Explain your answer.
6. **Making inferences** What can you infer from the fact that the

Constitution has survived for more than 200 years while the Articles of Confederation had to be abandoned so soon after they had been adopted?

**Linking Across Time**

7. National debt, internal unrest, and foreign policy were problems during the first four administrations. How do these problems affect the United States today?

## Jefferson Triumphs over Burr

*BOSTON—Splendid Intelligence! Thomas Jefferson is president, and Aaron Burr vice-president of the United States.*
*—Independent Chronicle, 1801*

### House Ends Stalemate

Wearily, members of the House of Representatives left their boarding houses on the morning of Tuesday, February 17, 1801, to gather at the unfinished Capitol. There, they would again try to break the deadlock between presidential contenders Thomas Jefferson and Aaron Burr.

For nearly a week, a battle of ballots had dragged on with late-night sessions, causing congressmen to catnap during lulls. Each state had one vote, and time after time Jefferson was one vote short of the required nine. After parleys and backroom politicking, members now braced themselves for another ballot—their 36th. On this one, Jefferson finally triumphed.

## Elsewhere in the News

### Northern Runaway Sought

BOSTON—The search was on. A local newspaper told of a "runaway Negro girl named Luce, about 13 years of age. Any person who will take her up . . . shall be rewarded for their trouble."

## King-Sized Quarters

Upon hearing of his victory, Thomas Jefferson made plans to move into the newly constructed "presidential palace," later known as the White House. Jefferson considered the mansion "big enough for two emperors, one Pope, and the Grand Lama."

### Related Stories
- 16-Cannon Salute in Baltimore
- Stray Cows on Capital Streets
- Library of Congress Planned
- Jefferson to Hire French Chef

## Bonaparte's New Home

PARIS—France's royal residence, the Tuileries Palace, was getting a final polish before the arrival of its new occupant—Napoleon Bonaparte. Napoleon ruled as France's First Consul.

## "No Smoking" Law

PROVIDENCE, R.I.—The town council tightened up on smoking laws. Pipes and cigars were banned on all streets, lanes, and alleys because of a recent blaze that gutted buildings.

# Chapter 1 Review

| 1763 | 1766 | 1769 | 1772 | 1775 | 1778 | 1781 | 1784 | 1787 | 1790 |

**1763**
Britain celebrates victory in French and Indian War.

**1773**
Bostonians dump tea in harbor to protest taxes.

**1781**
Articles of Confederation ratified.

**1787**
Constitution written in Philadelphia.

**1764**
Britain levies taxes on colonies to pay for the war.

**1776**
Colonists sign Declaration of Independence.

**1783**
Treaty of Paris ends Revolutionary War.

**1789**
George Washington elected first president.

## Summary

Use the following outline as a tool for reviewing and summarizing the chapter. Copy the outline on your own paper, leaving spaces between headings to jot down notes about key events and concepts.

I. **Waging a Revolution**
  A. Paying for Security
  B. The Coming of the Revolution
  C. Fighting for Independence
  D. Surviving the War
II. **Framing the Constitution**
  A. A Firm League of Friendship
  B. A More Perfect Union
  C. We, the People
III. **Launching the New Government**
  A. Washington and the Government
  B. Conflicts at Home and Abroad
  C. John Marshall and Judicial Power
  D. Foreign Policy and Local War

## Ideas, Events, and People

1. How did the French and Indian War contribute to the causes of the Revolutionary War?
2. How did the issue of taxation become linked to the issue of representation?
3. Who were the Sons of Liberty? What actions did they take?
4. Why did the Continental Congress meet? What actions did it take in 1774? In 1775?
5. What was the purpose of the Declaration of Independence? Who wrote it?
6. What was the difference between hard money and paper money? Which type of money did the Confederation Congress use? Why?
7. Why did the Constitution include a system of checks and balances for the new government?

8. Identify at least five rights guaranteed by the Bill of Rights.
9. What events caused the Whiskey Rebellion? What other rebellions did it resemble?
10. What were the basic differences between the Federalists and the Republicans?
11. What is an unconstitutional law? Which branch of government can declare a law unconstitutional? What events established its authority?
12. Why did the War Hawks call the War of 1812 the "Second War of Independence"?

## Social Studies Skills

**Map Study**
Use the map on page 33 to figure out how far a delegate to the Constitutional Convention in Philadelphia would have traveled from each of the following cities: Charleston, New York, and Boston. Give the approximate latitude and longitude of each of the four cities.

## Critical Thinking

1. **Comparing and Contrasting**
Compare and contrast external taxes and internal taxes. Were the colonists justified in feeling that Parliament had no right to levy internal taxes? Explain.
2. **Analyzing Decisions**
In 1775 the British decided to arrest a group of Americans in Concord. Do you think that was a wise decision? Why or why not? How else could the British have accomplished their goals?
3. **Recognizing Points of View**
What point of view did the wealthy people of Massachusetts have during Shays's Rebellion? What point of view did they have during the Revolution? What might explain any differences?

**1791**
Bill of Rights
ratified.

**1797**
John Adams
takes office.

**1808**
James Madison
elected president.

1793  1796  1799  1802  1805  1808  1811  1814  1817  1820

**1794**
Federal troops put
down Whiskey
Rebellion.

**1800**
Thomas Jefferson elected president
after bitter campaign between Federalists
and Democratic-Republicans.

**1812**
Britain and the United
States begin War of 1812.

**4. Identifying Cause and Effect**

What caused the War of 1812? What effects did it have on the United States?

# Extension and Application

### 1. Citizenship

Discuss the question of citizenship with your class. What do you think a good citizen is? Is it someone who follows the law? Or is it someone who breaks the law in order to stand up for an idea? Do you think that people like the Sons of Liberty act like good citizens? Are there groups like the Sons of Liberty today? Do you think they are good citizens? Write a persuasive paper explaining your views. Use the *Writer's Guide*, Unit 4 (pages 825–827), in developing your paper.

### 2. Community Connections

The Constitution gave Congress the power to tax its citizens. Today, U.S. citizens pay local, state, and federal taxes. What types of taxes are collected by your local government? What are these taxes used for?

### 3. Global Connections

Prepare a chart that compares and contrasts the American and French revolutions. What were the causes of each? How long did they last? What were the results of each? In what ways were they similar? Different?

### 4. Cooperative Learning

Working with a small group, read the Bill of Rights to the Constitution (pages 848–861). Rewrite the amendments in your own words. Use modern English and words that you can understand. Then compare the rewritings done by various groups of your classmates. How do they differ from the original amendments in the Bill of Rights?

# Geography

1. In which region of the colonies were most of the early battles of the Revolution fought? Why might war have broken out there first?

2. Why do you think British forces tended to win battles near seaports? What factors helped the American forces win in wilderness areas?

3. If British Canada had also rebelled against royal control, how might the American Revolution have been fought differently?

4. According to the map on page 33, which immigrant groups in the colonies settled mainly in or near urban areas? Which groups settled mainly in rural areas?

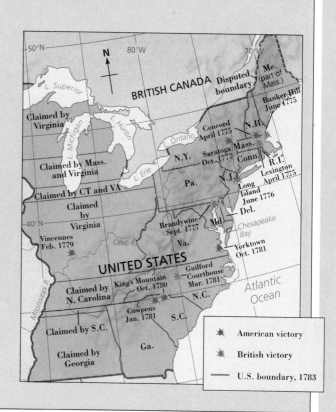

CHAPTER 2

# The Expanding Nation

## October 26, 1825: Erie Canal Opens

A large flatboat named *Seneca Chief*, strung with flowers, led "a grand aquatic procession" through New York Harbor on November 4, 1825. The fleet sailed to a spot near Sandy Hook, New Jersey, where the boats circled in a procession around the *Seneca Chief*.

On deck stood DeWitt Clinton, governor of New York. He raised a small wooden keg, pulled the cork and said: "May the God of the heavens and the earth smile on this work and render it subservient to the best interests of the human race." Then he emptied the small keg containing water from Lake Erie into the Atlantic Ocean.

> *Then he emptied the small keg containing water from Lake Erie into the Atlantic Ocean.*

The "Marriage of the Waters" concluded the official opening begun nine days earlier of the Erie Canal, the most important national waterway built in the United States. It stretched from the Hudson River to Lake Erie, connecting New York City with the fertile regions to the west.

The building and subsequent success of the Erie Canal changed the way Americans traveled, conducted business, and practiced politics. This vital link between the East Coast and the western frontier also changed how many Americans thought about their country. The canal served as a symbol of pride and economic determination.

MUNSON-WILLIAMS-PROCTOR INSTITUTE MUSEUM OF ART, UTICA, NY

*The Erie Canal was an achievement that inspired great pride in the United States.*

*The growing transportation network meant expanding markets for industry—and more jobs for mill girls and other factory workers.*

# Territorial Expansion

## November 7, 1805: Explorers Reach Pacific Ocean

A COLD RAIN FELL FROM THE GRAY SKY, DRENCHING THE MEN AS THEY PULLED THEIR CANOES ASHORE. GIANT PINES ROSE ABOVE THEM, GREEN AND FULL. DENSE forest lined the sides of the river that emptied into the Pacific Ocean.

One man climbed a muddy hill to get a better look at the vast sea. For a year and a half he had traveled by flatboat and horseback, on foot and by canoe, to reach this spot. To mark the journey's end, he chose a tall yellow pine tree, pulled a knife from his belt, and began carving. "William Clark," he cut into the bark, dating his entry. "By land from the U. States in 1804 and 1805."

Clark and his friend Meriwether Lewis had set out from St. Louis in May 1804 on orders from President Thomas Jefferson. The United States had just purchased much of the territory west of the Mississippi River, and Jefferson wanted it explored.

Lewis and Clark traveled through the lands of many Native American nations—land unknown to all but a few fur-trading white Americans. When they reached the Pacific, they had pushed the American frontier all the way to the continent's western edge.

THE GRANGER COLLECTION

## The Moving Frontier

O nly 40 years earlier, the **frontier,** the zone where land controlled by colonists met land controlled by Native Americans, began at the Appalachian Mountains. Over the next decades, white settlers steadily displaced Native Americans as they pushed this frontier westward. One of these white men, Daniel Boone, played a major part in this movement.

**The Wilderness Road** Daniel Boone first learned about the land west of the Appalachians during the French and Indian War. He had heard a soldier describe a hunter's paradise, a land with buffalo so large that the earth sagged beneath them. The soldier told of a mountain pass, the Cumberland Gap, that led to this paradise.

After the war Boone searched for a route to the West. In 1769 he found a Native American trail across the mountains. Warriors' Path, as it was called, led Boone through the Cumberland Gap to the gentle hills of a land that came to be called Kentucky. For two years, he explored the region's dense forests and lush meadows.

In 1775 Boone rounded up 30 skilled woodsmen to build a path so that pioneer families could take it west. Boone's crew widened the Warriors' Path, cleared rocks from the Cumberland Gap, cut down trees in Kentucky, and marked the trail. The new Wilderness Road, as it became known, became the main southern highway from the eastern states to the West. Over 100,000 people traveled it between 1775 and 1790.

Meanwhile Boone continued his wandering. In 1799 he crossed the Mississippi River into present-day Missouri, then controlled by Spain. The Spanish governor awarded Boone a large piece of land. However, Boone lost this land when this territory suddenly became the property of the United States in 1803.

## STUDY GUIDE

**As You Read**
Trace the events that led to the exploration and settlement of the West and the effects of settlement on white settlers and Native Americans.

**Central Concept**
- understanding how the American **frontier** moved westward from the Appalachians toward the Pacific Ocean

**Thinking Skills**
- assessing outcomes
- recognizing assumptions
- recognizing values

**The Louisiana Purchase**  Boone's land was part of the Louisiana Territory, a region that included about half the land between the Mississippi River and the Pacific. Louisiana had once belonged to France; but it came under Spain's control after the French and Indian War. Then, in 1800 French emperor Napoleon Bonaparte forced Spain to return ownership of Louisiana to France. Napoleon wanted Louisiana in order to expand France's American empire.

President Jefferson grew worried when he learned of this deal. He was anxious to ensure that New Orleans, a vital port, remain open to American trade. His fears turned out to be well founded, for the ruling official at New Orleans closed the port to American trade in 1802. Jefferson quickly planned his response.

Early in 1803 the president sent Virginian James Monroe to Paris with instructions to buy New Orleans. Congress had voted $2 million for the purchase, though Jefferson privately told Monroe to spend up to $10 million.

When Monroe reached Paris, Napoleon's situation had changed. A successful slave revolt in the French colony of Haiti had ended his hopes for an American empire. In addition, war between France and Britain again seemed likely, and Napoleon

**The settlement of the United States is a story of relentless westward movement.** *Why do you think settlers were willing to endure the hardships of frontier living rather than remain in the East?*

needed money. The French offered Monroe all of the Louisiana Territory for $15 million. Monroe agreed.

When news of the purchase reached the United States, some people grumbled that the president had no right to buy land without Congress's approval. Ultimately, however, Congress approved the purchase. The United States thus gained nearly 830,000 square miles of land—doubling the size of the country.

**Exploring the New Territory**  President Jefferson knew that this region had to be explored. He selected Meriwether Lewis, his personal secretary, and army officer William Clark to lead the expedition. Jefferson instructed the explorers to establish friendly relations with Native Americans and to study their habits and languages. Jefferson wanted descriptions of wildlife they saw along the way. He also wanted detailed maps of the region.

Lewis and Clark chose about 45 men for the expedition, including 20 soldiers accustomed to living in the woods. Others were specialists in Native American sign language, gun repair, and carpentry. The group left St. Louis in the spring of 1804, navigating the Missouri River on flatboats.

The explorers spent the winter of 1804–1805 near a friendly Mandan village in present-day North Dakota. There they met a French-Canadian trader named Toussaint Charbonneau, his Shoshone wife named Sacagawea, and their infant son. This family

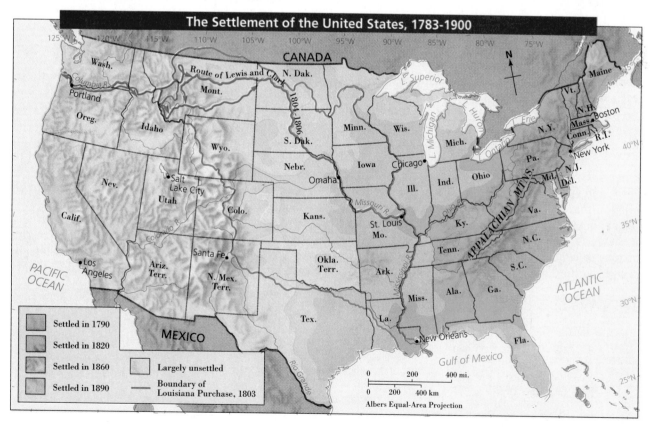

The Settlement of the United States, 1783-1900

| | |
|---|---|
| Settled in 1790 | |
| Settled in 1820 | |
| Settled in 1860 | Largely unsettled |
| Settled in 1890 | — Boundary of Louisiana Purchase, 1803 |

dinance, which Congress passed in 1787, each western territory was permitted limited self-government. When its population reached 60,000, a territory could draft a constitution. If Congress approved the document, the territory became a state.

Western territories quickly lined up to join the union. Kentucky became a state in 1792, Tennessee in 1796, Ohio in 1803, and Illinois in 1818. Meanwhile, more settlers flocked to territories farther west. By 1820 over 2 million Americans—about one-fourth of the population—lived west of the Appalachian Mountains.[1]

**Lewis and Clark helped open the West for fur trappers and established relationships with Native Americans living in the region.**

joined up as guides and translators when the expedition set out again in the spring of 1805.

That summer Lewis and Clark crossed the Rocky Mountains. Using horses and supplies provided by the Shoshone, they threaded their way through high mountain passes. After a month of climbing, the party reached the Pacific side of the range. From there they traveled quickly, arriving at the Pacific before the cold weather. The explorers built a fort and spent the winter at the ocean before returning to St. Louis in 1806.

**Westward Migration** The reports and maps Lewis and Clark brought back sparked the interest of a nation that was already looking to its western frontier. Thousands of families crossed the Appalachians in the early 1800s. These new western settlers were anxious to acquire the same political rights they had enjoyed in the East. According to the Northwest Or-

## Settling the West

In 1817 an English visitor to Ohio observed, "Old America seems to be breaking up and moving westward." The people who made this move were farmers, hunters, European immigrants, army veterans, artisans—a cross section of poor and middling people. The settlers brought their values and culture to their new homes in the West.

**Paths to the New Land** Pioneers by the thousands gathered their belongings and loaded them into wooden wagons called **Conestogas**. The 20-foot long, four-foot deep vehicles were short on comfort but long on durability. They were also versatile. A Conestoga could serve as a wagon on roads, a sled in the mud, and a boat in streams and rivers.

Conestogas were a common sight along the rough roads of America. One traveler in New York counted 500 wagons a day rolling west in 1797.

Rivers provided another important route to the West. Some settlers traveled overland to Pittsburgh, Pennsylvania, where they climbed aboard flatboats and floated down the Ohio River. After reaching the desired spot in Ohio or Kentucky or the Indiana Territory, the pioneers unloaded their belongings and headed inland.

When settlers reached a spot they liked, they built a home, often a small log cabin, and began clearing land for farming. One observer in western New York noted in 1805 that "the woods are full of new settlers. Axes are resounding, and the trees literally falling about us as we passed."

REYNOLDA HOUSE, MUSEUM OF AMERICAN ART, WINSTON-SALEM, NC

**Farms in the West**   The new frontier farms generally resembled farms in the East. A few southern settlers used slaves to plant and harvest cash crops like cotton. Most farmers on the southern frontier, however, owned no slaves, though many hoped to strike it rich and thus join the ranks of wealthy slaveholding planters. North of the Ohio River, where slavery was prohibited, farms were small and most produced only enough food to feed the families that worked them.

Northern and southern farmers raised crops of corn and wheat and hunted to provide their families with food. "My old daddy," recalled one pioneer woman, "caught rabbits, 'coons, and possums. He would work all day and hunt at night." Women did almost everything else. One farm journal reported that women "spun their own yarn . . . made and mended their own chairs, braided their own baskets, wove their own carpets . . . picked their own geese, milked their own cows. . . ." They also cooked meals, raised children, and cared for the sick.

Frontier farmers felt close bonds with their neighbors. Community activities—churchgoing and barn-raisings, weddings and funerals, barbecues and quilting bees—were necessary diversions from the rough life. Unlike the solitary explorers who first explored the frontiers, most settlers relied on the support of neighbors during good times and bad.

Bad times were an ever present threat. In the lawless wilderness of the early 1800s, conflicts were often settled with fists and guns. Frigid winters and steamy

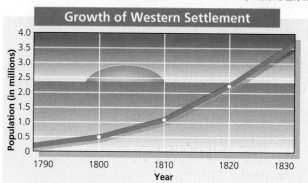

**As families moved west of the Appalachians, the population of the areas where they settled rose dramatically beginning in 1800.**

summers brought disease and death. The land was lush, but a bad harvest could spell disaster for a farm family. The threat pioneers feared most, however, was an attack from Native Americans.[2]

## Native Americans and the Settlers

The greatest threat to Native Americans, in turn, was white settlers. For over 150 years Native Americans had watched a tide of settlers stream west, threatening their ways of life. Usually, however, the conflicts between settlers and Native Americans arose over land.

In theory, the U.S. government insisted on respect

for Native American land claims. In 1787 the Northwest Ordinance declared:

> *The utmost good faith shall always be observed towards the Indians; their land and property shall never be taken from them without their consent; and, in their property, rights, and liberty, they shall never be invaded or disturbed.*
>
> The Northwest Ordinance, 1787

This well-intentioned promise proved flimsy, however, in the face of land-hungry settlers.

**Trouble in Ohio**   During the 1700s several Native American nations—the Shawnee, the Miami, the Wyandot—shared the land that is today Ohio. They settled in small villages and ate what they could hunt and grow in their small corn fields. But white settlers in this region pushed the Native Americans from their homes and hunting grounds. "Hear the lamentations of our women and children," cried one Shawnee leader, "Stop your people from killing our game."

When the U.S. government did nothing to stop this conflict, Native Americans in Ohio formed a con-

CHICAGO HISTORICAL SOCIETY

**The Treaty of Greenville marked another loss of Native American lands.** *What do you think happened to the Native American population during this time?*

federation to halt white settlement. In 1790 and 1791 warriors repeatedly attacked settlers, killing over 800 soldiers and handing the U.S. army several defeats.

In 1792 President Washington gave General Anthony Wayne command of an army in the Ohio country. After drilling some 3,000 soldiers for several months, Wayne led his army against the Ohio confederation. His troops fought about 2,000 warriors in the Battle of Fallen Timbers near Lake Erie in 1794. The Native Americans were soundly defeated. After the battle, Wayne torched their homes and fields. Under the Treaty of Greenville that ended the war, Native Americans gave up much of their land.

**The Shawnee Solution**   After the defeat, many Native Americans of the Ohio valley traveled west across the Mississippi, away from the settlers. Others tried to find new homes in Ohio.

One of those who remained in Ohio was a Shawnee named Tenskwatawa. Around 1805 Tenskwatawa began preaching a message of hope to the Shawnee. If the Shawnee returned to traditional ways, he said, he would lead them to "a rich, fertile country, abounding in game, fish, pleasant hunting grounds, and fine corn fields." Tenskwatawa told them to stop drinking the white man's whiskey, stop using his weapons, and stop eating "the food of the whites." Over time, Tenskwatawa's spiritual message turned into a political program, and his brother Tecumseh joined him as a leader of the Shawnee people.

The two brothers—the mystical prophet Tenskwatawa and the politically shrewd, militarily skillful Tecumseh—spoke of Native American pride, power, and unity. The brothers said they would reclaim lost land and draw a "boundary between Indians and white people." The magnetic presence and convincing speeches of the brothers attracted many impoverished Native Americans in Ohio and Indiana. In 1808 the two leaders established a community called Prophet's Town along Indiana's Tippecanoe River.

William Henry Harrison, governor of the Indiana Territory, grew alarmed at the power of the Shawnee leaders. In 1811 he gathered a force of 1,000 soldiers and attacked and destroyed Prophet's Town. Though Tecumseh and Tenskwatawa survived to continue their resistance, Tecumseh was eventually killed in 1813 while fighting for the British in the War of

1812. With his death came the decline of effective Native American resistance in the North. Soon more Native Americans were moving across the Mississippi River, away from white settlers.

**The Cherokee Solution**
Not all Native Americans spurned new ways and resisted white trespassers. The Cherokee of the southeastern United States, for example, tried to live in peace with whites.

In many ways Cherokee villages resembled white settlements in the South. The Cherokee built roads and collected taxes. Some adopted the Christian religion followed by most white settlers. One man named Sequoyah spent 12 years devising an alphabet for the Cherokee language. With this alphabet the Cherokee printed a newspaper called the *Cherokee Phoenix*.

The Cherokee learned that many conflicts between white settlers and Native Americans were resolved using the written laws of the state governments. In order to protect their interests, the Cherokee adopted their own legal code in 1808, combining Cherokee and American laws. In 1827 the Cherokee nation adopted a written constitution based on that of the United States.

These efforts, however, did not protect the Cherokee from southern whites who hungered to obtain Cherokee land to grow cotton. As the Case Study on pages 60–63 shows, the Cherokee were unable to

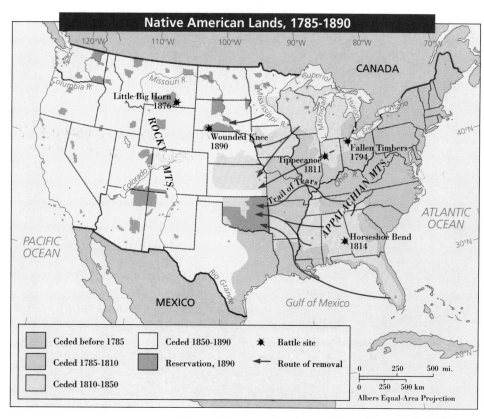

**Native American Lands, 1785-1890**

Ceded before 1785
Ceded 1785-1810
Ceded 1810-1850
Ceded 1850-1890
Reservation, 1890
★ Battle site
← Route of removal

Albers Equal-Area Projection

**Frontier settlers often came into conflict with Native Americans.** *Compare this map to the map on page 25. Describe the Cherokee lands of 1763.*

stop the relentless advance of white people in their move westward.

The Cherokee joined other Native Americans who had been expelled from the East and resettled in the "Great American Desert." Some Native Americans, however, remained in the East, the ancestors of today's eastern Native Americans. Yet far more common was the experience of those who, in the words of one Native American, were, "compelled to seek asylum [protection] from the craving desires of the white man, beyond the great river."

## SECTION REVIEW

**Checking Facts**

1. What was the American frontier? What were the main barriers that marked it in 1765 and in 1805?
2. What contribution did Daniel Boone make to the settlement of the West?
3. What geographic obstacles did the Lewis and Clark expedition face, and how did it overcome them?
4. Describe the life of a typical pioneer farm family.
5. What methods did Native Americans use in dealing with the threat of whites who wanted their lands?

**Thinking Critically**

6. **Assessing Outcomes** How did Monroe's 1803 trip to Paris bring benefits greater than Jefferson had in mind when he sent him there?
7. **Recognizing Values** Did pioneer families who traveled west have any purposes other than to "strike it rich"? Explain your answer.
8. **Recognizing Assumptions** Many settlers believed that Native Americans would benefit from white civilization. What is the assumption behind this belief?

**Linking Across Time**

9. Does the frontier as defined in this section still exist? Does any kind of frontier exist today? Explain your answers.

# Case Study

# Cherokee Removal

## *WINTER 1838*

> The Cherokee nation, then, is a distinct community, occupying its own territory, with boundaries accurately described, in which the laws of Georgia can have no force, and which the citizens of Georgia have no right to enter, but with the assent of the Cherokees themselves. . . .
>
> It is the opinion of this court that the judgment of the superior court . . . of Georgia, condemning Samuel A. Worcester to hard labour, . . . was pronounced by that court under . . . a law which is void . . . and ought, therefore, to be reversed and nullified.
>
> John Marshall, Chief Justice, Supreme Court, 1832

### The Case

The news was a cause for great celebration. The Cherokee and their supporters were jubilant. The case of *Worcester v. The State of Georgia* was over, and the Supreme Court of the United States had ruled in favor of Samuel Worcester, reversing the state's earlier judgment against him.

Worcester, a missionary who had lived among the Cherokee for years, had broken a Georgia state law. This law stated that non-Cherokee people living on Cherokee lands could either sign an oath of allegiance to Georgia or leave the Cherokee land. Worcester refused to do either. Instead, he chose a prison sentence of four years, but appealed his case to the U.S. Supreme Court.

The Supreme Court ruling in *Worcester v. Georgia* was an important victory, one that promised far more than just freedom for Worcester. Chief Justice John Marshall's words appeared to say that the Cherokee would be free to control their own fate, without interference from the state of Georgia. No one could enter the Cherokee Nation without the permission of the Cherokee, and the Cherokee could invite whomever they wanted to live on their land. The U.S. government would protect their lands.

But the victory in *Worcester v. Georgia* proved to be an empty one. President Andrew Jackson is said to have remarked, "John Marshall has made his decision; let him enforce it now if he can." Indeed, the decision could not be enforced. Jackson did nothing to see that the ruling was obeyed, and Worcester stayed in prison.

### The Background

The Cherokee had held their land long before European settlers arrived. Through treaties with the U.S. government, the Cherokee became a sovereign nation within Georgia.

By the early 1800s, the Cherokee were principally an agricultural people, having adopted many of the customs and life styles of neighboring white farmers. Chief Sequoya's invention of a Cherokee alphabet enabled the Cherokee to read and write in their own language. They had their own schools, their own newspaper, their own judicial system, and a written constitution.

The Cherokee occupied some of Georgia's richest land, and some white people thought they stood as barriers to progress. In addition, gold was discovered on Cherokee land in 1829, drawing hordes of white miners into the region. Settlers and land speculators wanted the Cherokee land.

By the time of *Worcester v. Georgia* in 1832, federal and state laws had opened the door for Cherokee removal. In 1830 Congress had passed the Indian Removal Act, allowing Jackson to pursue his goal of relocating eastern Native Americans to lands west of the Mississippi River.

That same year, Georgia lawmakers had decreed that all Cherokee lands were under state jurisdiction, erasing Cherokee claims to sovereignty. Further, the Cherokee could not testify against a white person or dig for the gold discovered in their own nation. Their laws were nullified. Finally, in December of 1830, Georgia restricted the presence of white settlers on Cherokee lands, a law that led to the *Worcester v. Georgia* case.

In 1832, with the Supreme Court's ruling, the Cherokee scored a short-lived triumph. When Jackson ignored the ruling, the Cherokee realized their hopes for federal protection were in vain.

Jackson recognized the Cherokee had not been treated fairly. Nevertheless, he believed that the eastern Native Americans would have to be relocated, since a separate nation could not continue to exist within a U.S. state. Long before *Worcester v. Georgia*, Jackson had warned Congress against "encroachments upon the legitimate sphere of State sovereignty." It was no surprise that Jackson chose not to enforce the Supreme Court's ruling.

## The Opinions

Read the opinions of some of the people involved in the Cherokee drama. President Jackson and Georgia Governor Lumpkin favored removal, while Massachusetts Senator Everett sided with the Cherokee in opposing it.

The quotations show that the people involved in the dispute differed sharply on the issue of

LIBRARY OF CONGRESS

*"My opinion remains the same, and I can see no alternative for them but that of their removal to the West or a quiet submission to the State laws."*
President Andrew Jackson, 1831

LIBRARY OF CONGRESS

*"Any attempt to infringe the evident right of a state to govern the entire population within its territorial limits . . . would be the usurpation of a power never granted by the states."*
Wilson Lumpkin, Governor of Georgia, 1832

MASSACHUSETTS HISTORICAL SOCIETY

*"Whoever read of such a project? Ten or fifteen thousand families, to be rooted up. . . . There is not . . . such a thing in the annals of mankind . . ."*
Senator Edward Everett, Massachusetts, 1830

*"The land on which we stand we have received as an inheritance from our fathers. . . . Permit us to ask, what better right can the people have to a country than the right of inheritance? . . ."*
The Cherokee, in a letter to Congress, 1829

removal. Like most opinions, theirs were formed partly on the basis of self-interest. Miners and expansionists wanted the land, rich in both soil and gold. Clearly, the government's removal policy would serve their interests. On the other hand, to most of the Cherokee, their best interest seemed to lie in staying on the land of their ancestors. Not only did they have a settled life on that land; they had also heard about the hardship and suffering of those who had already moved west.

## The Assumptions

Quotations like those you read reveal another basis for opinions—underlying assumptions. For example, President Jackson knew the Cherokee well, and he professed to have the "kindest feelings" toward them. Even so, his words and actions reveal that he believed that Native Americans could never be considered the equals of white people. On another occasion Jackson had said to them, "I tell you that you cannot remain where you now are. Circumstances that cannot be controlled, and which are beyond the reach of human laws, render it impossible that you can flourish in the midst of a civilized community." Notice the assumption that underlies Jackson's words in that last sentence.

Jackson based much of his argument for removal on his belief in state sovereignty. Governor Lumpkin had less sympathy for the Cherokee than Jackson, and far less knowledge of them. But like Jackson, he based much of his argument against the Supreme Court's ruling on his belief that the powers of the state took precedence over those of the federal government.

Everett's underlying assumptions caused him to speak passionately on behalf of the Cherokee. Unlike Jackson, Everett thought of them as "essentially a civilized people." This assumption led to his vehement expressions of indignation.

What about the Cherokee themselves? What were their assumptions? Their letter appeals to faith in "our common Father in Heaven" and the "right of inheritance and immemorial peaceable possession." The Cherokee believed that God had given the land to their ancestors, who then passed it on to them. The Cherokee placed special importance on the place where their ancestors were buried. Like many Native Americans, they revered their ancestors. Therefore, their land was sacred because it contained "the remains of our beloved men." The Cherokee assumed that their white audience would understand the importance of these values, implying a still more basic assumption on their part: that the white senators regarded Native Americans as equally human, with basic values and rights.

## The Outcome

For years, John Ross, the principal chief of the Cherokee, was able to maintain unity among his people in their opinions about removal. He and other Cherokee leaders—such as Major Ridge and his son John Ridge—all opposed the Cherokee Removal Act at first.

When news of the *Worcester v. Georgia* decision reached John Ridge, he was exuberant. He believed that the Supreme Court, and therefore the Cherokee, would prevail over Georgia. However, Ridge then spoke to Jackson himself and learned that the president had no intention of enforcing the decision. Jackson told him that the only hope for the Cherokee was in "abandoning their country and removing to the West."

By the mid-1830s, John Ridge, Major Ridge, and a few other Cherokee leaders had begun to believe that removal was inevitable. They became convinced it represented their only hope for survival. In this, the Ridges were joined by members of Congress who had once strongly opposed removal. The Cherokee leaders and their supporters realized that the U.S. government would never protect the Cherokee lands in Georgia. Also, they believed the government was making the Cherokee a better offer in terms of land and assistance than ever before.

The two factions that developed among the Cherokee were the Treaty party, which favored removal, and the National party, which continued to oppose it. John Ross and the National party viewed their opponents as traitors. They never came to accept removal. Major Ridge, knowing that many of the people he loved considered him an enemy, pleaded with them:

"I am one of the native sons of these wild woods. I have hunted the deer and turkey here more than fifty years. . . . The Georgians have shown a grasping spirit lately; they have extended

**This painting depicts the Cherokee on their forced march to Oklahoma. One soldier noted that he** had seen as many as **22** Cherokee people die in a single night during the journey.

their laws, to which we are unaccustomed, which harass our braves and make the children suffer and cry. . . . I know the Indians have an older title than theirs. We obtained the land from the living God above. . . . Yet they are strong and we are weak. We are few, they are many. We cannot remain here in safety and comfort. I know we love the graves of our fathers. . . . We can never forget these homes, I know, but an unbending, iron necessity tells us we must leave them."

Pressure to complete the Cherokee relocation intensified. The National party, representing about 16,000 Cherokee, adamantly resisted the move. Yet the Jackson administration dealt only with the Treaty party, which had only a small number of members. Its leaders signed a relocation treaty, which was ratified by Congress in 1836.

Still, few of the Cherokee moved voluntarily. Most never understood nor shared the Ridges' viewpoint. In 1838, after the deadline set for removal had passed, soldiers with rifles and bayonets forced more than 18,000 Cherokee from their homes and marched them approximately 1,000 miles to what is now Oklahoma. During the relocation, nearly 4,000 Cherokee died from malnutrition, exposure, cholera, and harsh treatment. Their grueling trek earned the name the "Trail of Tears."

---

## Think About It

1. Jackson spoke well of the Cherokee as hunters who had no right to "tracts of country on which they have neither dwelt nor made improvements, merely because they have seen them from the mountain or passed them in the chase." Why do you think Jackson made this statement? What was he purposely ignoring?

2. Senator Theodore Frelinghuysen, in a speech on the Indian Removal Act, asked: "Do the obligations of justice change with the color of the skin?" Which views presented on page 61 would Frelinghuysen probably agree with?

3. Before the "Trail of Tears," the Ridges had decided that their people had no choice but to go west. What events had changed their minds? Could the *Worcester v. Georgia* case have been one of them? Why?

4. How was Major Ridge in sympathy with the Cherokee who continued to oppose removal? What were some of the values and assumptions he shared with them?

# The Economy Grows

**A**FTER 14 HOURS ON THE JOB, MALENDA ED-WARDS WALKED TO HER BOARDINGHOUSE, WEARILY CLIMBED THE STAIRS, AND SAT AT THE DESK IN HER ROOM. HER EARS STILL ringing from the din of the mill machinery, Malenda found a piece of paper and began a letter to her cousin Sabrina. "You have been informed, I suppose," she wrote, "that I am a factory girl." She continued:

*T*here are many young ladies at work in the factories that have given up millinery dressmaking and school keeping for to work in the mill. But I would not advise anyone to do it, for I was so sick of it at first I wished a factory had never been thought of. But the longer I stay the better I like it.

Malenda Edwards,
*from a letter to Sabrina Bennet*, April 4, 1839

In 1839 Malenda Edwards had left her parents' quiet farm and moved to Nashua, New Hampshire, to work in a textile mill. She traded her days of milking cows, spinning thread, and raking hay for work in a five-story, red-brick factory. Every day but Sunday, she started work at 5:00 A.M. and operated a power loom until 7:00 P.M., with only short breaks for meals. Most of the 250 workers in the factory were women.

Despite the long hours, Malenda was happy to work in the mill. For a 70-hour work week she earned $3.25—more than most women could make as teachers, seamstresses, or servants. In the years between 1839 and 1845, Malenda would work in the factory for part of the year, then return home to enjoy her earnings and take care of her aging parents.

In 1845 Malenda Edwards got married, stopped working in the mills, and moved to a small town. She was just one of thousands of Americans who made the journey from farm to factory in the 1800s.

## From Farms to Factories

**I**n 1800 most Americans worked on farms. Whether raising cotton in the South, planting in the meadow of a western forest, or farming near an eastern town, American farmers led a quiet, rural life. They prided themselves on being self-sufficient. Their farm supplied the family with food, and farm women made day-to-day necessities like soap, candles, and maple sugar.

Most other necessities could be found within a few miles of the farm. Items that could not be made at home were manufactured—by hand, one at a time—by local blacksmiths, shoemakers, and tailors in exchange for corn or wheat. In the more populous areas of the nation, small country stores provided farmers with hard-to-find goods, like gunpowder, coffee, and tea. **Textiles**, or cloth and fabric, from Europe were especially popular in American stores.

### 75 Young Women

From 15 to 35 Years of Age,

**WANTED TO WORK IN THE**

## COTTON MILLS!

IN LOWELL AND CHICOPEE, MASS.

I am authorized by the Agents of said Mills to make the following proposition to persons suitable for their work:—They will be paid $1.00 per week, and board, for the first month. It is presumed they will then be able to go to work at job prices. They will be considered as engaged for one year, cases of sickness excepted. I will pay the expenses of those who have not the means to pay for themselves, and the girls will pay it to the Company by their first labor. All that remain in the employ of the Company eighteen months will have the amount of their expenses to the Mills refunded to them. They will be properly cared for in sickness. It is hoped that none will go except those whose circumstances will admit of their staying at least one year. None but active and healthy girls will be engaged for this work as it would not be advisable for either the girls or the Company.

I shall be at the Howard Hotel, Burlington, on Monday, July 25th ; at Farnham's, St. Albans, Tuesday forenoon, 26th, at Keyse's, Swanton, in the afternoon; at the Massachusetts' House, Rouses Point, on Wednesday, the 27th, to engage girls,—such as would like a place in the Mills would do well to improve the present opportunity, as new hands will not be wanted late in the season. I shall start with my Company, for the Mills, on Friday morning, the 29th inst., from Rouses Point, at 6 o'clock. Such as do not have an opportunity to see me at the above places, can take the cars and go with me the same as though I had engaged them.

I will be responsible for the safety of all baggage that is marked in care of I. M. BOYNTON, and delivered to my charge.

**I. M. BOYNTON,**

Agent for Procuring Help for the Mills.

BAKER LIBRARY, HARVARD UNIVERSITY

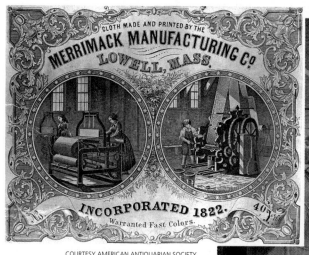

By 1800 all but those farmers living on the most remote fringes of the frontier survived on a mix of homemade goods, products manufactured by local craftsmen, and store-bought items imported from Europe. That way of living began to change in 1807.

**Before the arrival of mills, most women could expect to spend their lives on farms.** *Why do you think women and not men were recruited for the mills?*

## A Changing Economy

U.S. trade had increased steadily with Europe. But in 1803 war broke out between England and France resulting in harassment and capture of U.S. merchant ships. To avoid a war with England or France, President Jefferson signed the Embargo Act in 1807, stopping all trade between Europe and the United States. Trade remained choked until after the War of 1812. The resulting economic slowdown had several effects. First, the British wool, Irish linen, and Indian cotton that had flooded the American market no longer arrived. As a result, the home manufacture of textiles boomed. A second effect of this situation was that merchants who had traded with Europe now looked for other ways to make money.

One of those merchants, a Bostonian named Francis Cabot Lowell, recognized the demand for textiles in the United States. He had seen dozens of tiny spinning mills crop up across New England. Lowell took advantage of the postwar slowdown in trade with Britain and began a bold experiment. He started to organize an entirely new system of textile production that was bigger, more efficient, and more profitable than any in the United States.

## Lowell's Experiment

In 1813 Lowell set about designing a new spinning and weaving machine. With help from employee Paul Moody, the machine was finally perfected. Lowell and his business partners built a three-story brick factory on the banks of the Charles River in Waltham, Massachusetts. The current of the river turned water wheels, which were connected to gears and belts that ran the machinery in the factory.

Unlike the tiny spinning mills of New England, Lowell's plant contained all the stages of textile production under one roof: spinning, weaving, bleaching, dyeing, and printing. The fabric turned out by Lowell's factory was rougher than the fine textiles of Europe, but it suited the needs of Americans who bought his cloth. Lowell's factory—larger and more ambitious than any other in America—launched the nation's **Industrial Revolution**, the change from manufacturing at home to manufacturing in factories.

## New Workers

Where would Lowell find workers to operate his spinning and weaving machines? In the rural areas around Waltham, no farmer wanted to give up his property and independence to earn **wages**, or daily pay, in a textile factory. Lowell discovered

STUDY GUIDE

### Predicting Consequences

Predicting consequences allows you to isolate causes of important events and explore alternative outcomes. The textile industry became successful in the Northeast because Lowell put all his production stages under one roof and found women who would work for low wages. Other factory owners followed Lowell's ideas, mechanizing other industries. What if Lowell had been unable to solve his labor problem? At the very least, the Industrial Revolution in the United States might have had a slower start.

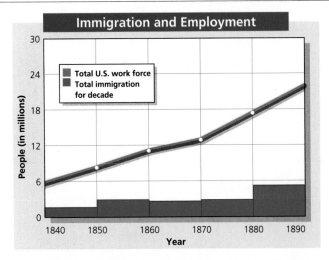

**Immigration and Employment**

People (in millions)

- Total U.S. work force
- Total immigration for decade

**Immigrants helped supply the labor that made the Industrial Revolution possible.** *How did the arrival of immigrants affect the economy of the United States?*

however, that the farmers' daughters were happy for an opportunity to earn money. Many parents were also happy to receive some of these earnings.

Lowell began recruiting young (mostly ages 15–29) farm women to live and work at his factory. He promised parents that their daughters would live under strict moral supervision in company dormitories, be required to attend church services, and be held to a nightly curfew. After persuading many parents to allow their daughters to move to Waltham, Lowell opened his factory in 1814.

Lowell's Waltham mill was an enormous success. In fact, it was so successful that following Lowell's death in 1817, his partners built a new, larger plant on the Merrimack River in 1823. The town that grew up at that spot became known as Lowell, Massachusetts. Other textile mills that were located in Lowell also adopted the factory system. By 1840 textile mills employed 8,000 workers, almost 40 percent of Lowell's population.

Businessmen built textile mills all over New England and the mid-Atlantic states in the 1830s and 1840s. Most of the workers in these factories were women like Malenda Edwards. The rest of the labor force was made up of children from local farms and a growing number of men who sought factory work after failing at farming.

After 1840 another source of labor began arriving in the factories of the Northeast. Political turmoil and failed crops drove thousands of Germans and poor Irish from their European homes. Most of these immigrants arrived on American shores desperate for jobs. Many came to the textile mills of the Northeast and offered to work for lower wages than the farm women.

For factory owners, this new, cheap source of labor came just in time. The success of the factory system had created intense competition between textile companies. Mill owners struggled to find ways to increase production and lower costs. Many cut wages and increased the workload of employees. Some women went out on strike to protest wage cuts. In response, factory owners began to hire more and more immigrants. By 1860 European immigrants had replaced farm women as the largest group of workers in American factories. This influx of labor willing to work for low wages continued to make the factory system profitable in the United States.

**A New Economy** The census of 1850 reported that in the past most "manufacturing was carried on in the shop and the household by the labor of the family." By 1850 it was done by "a system of factory labor, compensated by wages, and assisted by power." Factories producing textiles, shoes, furniture, carriages, and other goods appeared all across the Northeast. Many of these factories were built in growing cities that attracted immigrant workers.

The growth of factories meant that more Americans bought more goods in stores. After 1850 a farmer did not get his shoes handmade from a cobbler two miles from his home. Instead, he bought factory-made shoes from a store that had ordered them from a merchant hundreds of miles away. The transportation revolution that also occurred after 1800 made more goods available to more people in more places than ever before.[1]

## The Transportation Revolution

By 1850 American manufactured goods and farm produce were being transported to most places where people wanted them, whether in Boston or Chicago. However, moving goods and people from one place to another had not always been so simple.

## Roads and Turnpikes

Before 1800 roads and rivers were the most important links between farms, villages, and cities. Yet travel over these roadways and waterways was impossible during some seasons and difficult during the best times. Dry seasons turned many rivers into trickling streams. Hot weather turned roads to dust and rain turned them into muddy troughs. Shipping goods from east to west was expensive: it cost more to haul a ton of goods nine miles inland from the ocean than it did to bring that same ton of goods from Europe.

An early solution to America's transportation problems was the development of **turnpikes**, or roads where travelers had to pay tolls. The first turnpikes were built by private companies which hoped to earn back the cost of the roads by charging tolls. Turnpike companies often built their roads of stone and gravel, making better traveling conditions. By 1832 the United States had nearly 2,400 miles of toll roads linking together most important cities.

Roads to the west were the most common projects during the turnpike era. The federal government funded construction of the most important route west, the National Road. This 80-foot-wide stone road was begun in 1811 and ran westward from Cumberland, Maryland. By 1818 it stretched about 130 miles to Wheeling, in present-day West Virginia. By 1852 it spanned approximately 600 miles, ending in Vandalia, Illinois.

## Rivers and Canals

Transportation by water was much less expensive than by road. During the early 1800s, flatboats floated down the Ohio and Mississippi rivers, carrying crops raised by western farmers to export markets and to pioneers in other areas. Upstream travel remained slow and expensive, but rivers were a popular and cheap way to move people and goods from place to place.

The rise of steam power made the nation's rivers even more crowded. After 1810 steamboats began churning up and down the rivers, bringing trade in their wake. Between 1830 and 1860, riverboats were especially important on the Mississippi, where they helped make western farms profitable.

Of course, rivers had limited usefulness. For one thing, most run from north to south, so travel from east to west was often difficult. "Rivers are ungovernable things," had written Benjamin Franklin. "Canals are quiet and always manageable." Franklin neglected to note that canals were also expensive and hard to build. Nevertheless, the early 1800s witnessed the growth of a network of canals linking the nation's natural waterways.

After the War of 1812, a group of New Yorkers pushed for a canal connecting the Hudson River to Lake Erie. The Erie Canal was to be 363 miles long at a time when the longest existing canal in the nation was less than 28 miles long. Construction began in 1817, and over the next eight years laborers dug by hand a 40-foot-wide and four-foot-deep canal through the wilderness of northern New York.

Completed in 1825, the Erie Canal was a phenomenal success. Thanks to the business generated by the canal, by 1830 New York City replaced Baltimore as the major eastern port leading to the interior of the nation. Freight rates to western New York fell by 90 percent after the canal opened. The benefit of this modification to the nation's geography and transportation system was clear.

The Erie Canal's success spurred the construction of canals throughout the nation between 1830 and

**Improving the transportation network not only helped industry, it also linked the people of different regions.** *How might failure to improve transportation have affected the social development of the nation?*

1850. In the East, canals connected the back country to the ocean. Further inland, canals linked eastern cities with the growing settlements of the Ohio River Valley. In the Midwest, canals connected the Great Lakes with the Mississippi River. By 1840 Americans had constructed over 3,300 miles of canals. In a land of mountains, forests, and plains, however, canals did not solve every transportation problem. Soon, Americans were looking for another way to travel.

**Tracks and Steam Engines**  The success of the Erie Canal took business away from Baltimore merchants who had profited from their location near the National Road. Some of them hatched a plan to restore Baltimore's importance as a seaport by building a railroad from Maryland to Ohio. In 1828 these merchants launched the Baltimore and Ohio, or B & O, Railroad.

Railroads had been invented in Britain. The idea, however, seemed tailor-made for the United States and its huge, varied landscape. Fast transportation that could cover virtually any terrain offered obvious advantages over canals. As a result, people eagerly invested large sums of money in the infant railroad companies. During the 1830s, over 3,300 miles of iron rails were built across the nation. A trip from New York to Cincinnati that had taken two months over roads took only one week by train in 1850.

By 1860 railroads carried goods and passengers at lower cost and in less time than roads, canals, or rivers. They made money for investors, merchants who shipped by rail, and people who settled in the towns and cities that sprouted along the track of the locomotive during the 1840s and 1850s. The need for railroads, like roads and canals before, came from industry and trade. The growth of railroads, in turn, created thousands of jobs and stimulated new industries, such as those for iron, steel, and railroad car manufacturing. **2**

---

## Politics and the Economy

"It is an extraordinary era in which we live," said Daniel Webster, a senator from Massachusetts in 1847. "It is altogether new. The world has seen nothing like it." The new world was made possible by revolutions in industry and transportation in the United States. While private investors had funded many of these developments, government also helped nurture America's economic growth in the 1800s.

One of the strongest supporters of government's role in the economy was Henry Clay. A member of Congress from Kentucky, Clay had gained prominence during the War of 1812 as a western War Hawk. At that time, he opposed a strong national government and programs such as the Bank of the United States, which gave the federal government significant centralized economic power.

As America's economic power grew, however, Clay's views changed. He organized his new ideas into an economic plan called the "American System."

**The American System**  Clay's American System was based on the idea that a stronger national government would benefit each of the different sections of the country. As part of this system Clay supported an 1816 bill to increase **tariffs**, or fees, on imported goods. The tariffs were designed to protect American manufacturers, nearly all of whom were located in the East, from European competition. Clay believed that healthy eastern industries would help the whole nation. This bill passed despite the objections of southerners in Congress. The South, a region with little manufacturing, would gain nothing directly from the tariff. In fact, the tariff would have the effect of higher prices for the South, because southerners imported a great deal of foreign goods.

In 1816 Congress faced the decision of whether to charter a new Bank of the United States (the first Bank had failed in 1811). Clay supported the bank, arguing that it would stabilize the economy and encourage investments. The bank bill passed.

Another part of Clay's American System met with less success than the first two. Clay wanted the government to supply money for improvements such as road and canal building. Other westerners in Congress voted for these plans, which would greatly benefit the frontier regions they represented. Southerners in Congress generally favored Clay's plans because the South also stood to benefit from such improvements. Northerners, however, clashed with Clay over these improvements. For one thing, their roads and canals were already built and dug, so they

**Assessing Outcomes**
The Erie Canal was a phenomenal success, fulfilling all the promises of its promoters. Farmers from upstate New York and the Great Lakes region could transport products to New York's harbor.

Western towns had easy access to eastern manufacturers. Settlers could move west more easily. The result was a national canal boom, as other cities competed for trade with the West.

**2** How did the Erie Canal's success help launch another great transportation era, that of railroads?

would not benefit directly from federal assistance. Also, many northerners feared the growing power of the westerners and did not want to help them grow stronger.

The greatest opposition to Clay's plans, however, came from the president. Between 1817 and 1830, three of Clay's internal improvement bills were passed by Congress and then vetoed by three different presidents. The first was vetoed by President James Madison who argued that the Constitution did not give Congress the power to build roads. In 1822 a proposal to improve the National Road was vetoed by President James Monroe on the same grounds. Finally, in 1830 President Andrew Jackson vetoed the use of federal funds to improve Kentucky's Maysville Road.

Clay was disappointed that these presidents paid so little attention to internal improvements, but the government did encourage the nation's growth in other ways. After 1816 Congress passed a series of tariffs that protected the nation's young industries. Between 1830 and 1860 New York, Pennsylvania, Ohio, and Virginia built many of their canals with state funds. Canal and railroad companies usually obtained land from federal and state governments at bargain prices. The combination of private investments and public policy reshaped American life after 1815.

**A New Nation** Shortly after steamboats began to paddle down the nation's rivers, a newspaper editor exclaimed that steam power would "diminish the size of the globe." It would make Americans "one single people, one nation, one mind." In some ways, the nation did seem more unified after the transportation

THE GRANGER COLLECTION

**This 1831 cartoon uses the theme of a poker game to represent the regional conflicts of the era. Clay is at left, playing the cards "U.S. Bank" and "Tariff."**

and industrial revolutions. After 1850 the farmer's solitary self-sufficiency no longer seemed practical. It was replaced by cooperation between people with different interests and from different regions. New Englanders gave up most of their farming and devoted resources to manufacturing. Farmers from the western side of the Appalachians now produced most of the American grain. Southern planters devoted more land and slave labor to cash crops like cotton.

Regional specialization, however, could lead to conflicts. A law that helped northern manufacturers, such as the tariff, might hurt southern planters. Tensions between different sections of the nation and between different groups of people began to grow. The forces that changed America's economy in the 1800s also changed the politics and beliefs of its people.

## SECTION REVIEW

### Checking Facts

1. Describe Lowell's experiment, and explain its significance.
2. How did political upsets and crop failures in Europe help the owners of American mills?
3. What were the advantages of turnpikes for travelers?
4. Explain the success of the Erie Canal and the railroads.
5. Why were Clay's views on tariffs objectionable to some people?

### Thinking Critically

6. **Assessing Outcomes** Describe the positive and negative outcomes of the 1807 Embargo Act.
7. **Predicting Consequences** Why might factory owners have feared labor shortages in the 1830s when they increased production and cut wages? Who helped solve the owners' labor problems?
8. **Analyzing Behavior** How did events of the early 1800s encour-

age Americans to think of themselves as "one single people, one nation, one mind"?

### Linking Across Time

9. Compare the women in the factories of the 1800s with women starting their first jobs today.

# The Rise of American Cities

Trade and transportation set off a burst of urban growth from 1800 to 1860. All along trade and transportation routes, older cities grew and new ones were born. Topography, too, played a key role in this rise of American cities because terrain usually dictated where trade routes would be established.

A map of the thirteen colonies shows that most American cities grew up along the Atlantic Coast; the ocean linked them with Britain and other countries. Born as ports, coastal cities such as New York, Charleston, and Boston are still important centers of transportation and industry.

Inland cities tended to grow up along rivers that provided easy access to the coast as well as water power to run industries. As American technology overcame geographical obstacles of distance and rugged terrain, the people moved steadily westward.

Steamboats bucked the currents to carry cargo on inland rivers. Mules plodded along towpaths, pulling canal boats laden with everything from beeswax to lumber. Trains spit their sparks and belched their steam while hauling freight at the amazing speed of 15 miles per hour. With these three modes of transportation in full swing west of the Appalachians, the pace of trade picked up in the interior. Soon, river outposts, canal communities, and railroad whistlestops developed into cities, while settlements off the beaten track stagnated, sometimes completely disappearing from the map.

The following three examples indicate how trade, transporta-

THE GRANGER COLLECTION

**The steam locomotive and steamship in this 1864 lithograph would be familiar sights to people in St. Louis, Buffalo, or Chicago in the late 1800s.**

tion, and topography directed the course of urban growth.

**Between 1800 and 1860, major new cities emerged west of the Appalachians. Trade and transportation sparked much of this urban expansion.**

## Riverside City

A bonanza of waterways transformed the fur-trading center of St. Louis into a sizable city. Encircled by farmland, St. Louis is situated on the Mississippi just south of where that mighty river meets two other rivers — the Illinois and the Missouri. By mid-century, steamboats chugged into St. Louis from north and south,

so many that sometimes they lined up for a mile along the docks. From St. Louis, both boats and barges traveled along the Illinois to prairie country, along the Missouri to the western lands that beckoned the pioneers, and to New Orleans, gateway to the Gulf of Mexico. This intense activity helped boost the one-time frontier outpost of the fur trade to a city of 160,773 by 1860.

## Along the Canal

In 1810, Buffalo, New York, was nothing but a small settlement of 1,500 people at the east end of Lake Erie. Then, along came the Erie Canal's gala opening in 1825. Buffalo's population grew to over 2,400, and hundreds of new buildings sprang up. By 1860, Buffalo's population had climbed to 81,000.

The 363-mile canal ran across New York State from Albany to Buffalo. At Albany, the Hudson River linked the canal with the coast, thus tying the Atlantic seaboard to the Great Lakes. Canal boats poked along at speeds between one and five miles an hour, but freight rates were cheap. The canal made it possible to ship goods from New York City to Buffalo for as little as $5.00 a ton. Transporting the same load by wagon cost $100 and took twice as long.

Although railroads soon outran the Erie Canal, it stayed in operation. Today, the canal is part of the 524-mile New York State Barge Canal System, and Buffalo remains a major transportation center.

## The Hub of the Rails

With a roar, railroads changed Chicago from a swampy settlement into a megacity. The community numbered only about 4,500 people in 1840. Eight years later, the first train rumbled into town. Before long, grain, lumber, and livestock rode the rails to Chicago's growing market, helping to push the city's population to 109,260 by 1860.

Chicago was perfectly placed for a rail center. It was located on level land in the heart of the nation with Lake Michigan at its front door. These advantages caused rail tycoons to bypass neighboring landlocked communities and chart their tracks to Chicago. By 1860, Chicago was the nation's top rail city, with 11 lines radiating from its hub.

Transportation and trade served as springboards for numerous cities besides Chicago, Buffalo, and St. Louis. Cities with transportation networks that gave them access to both raw materials and markets soon became booming industrial centers. Gradually, they gained complex political systems, extensive educational facilities, and a rich variety of cultural institutions that gave them identities far beyond those of mere distribution centers.

THINK ABOUT IT:

In 1950 railroads in the United States carried 56 percent of the total intercity freight. By 1988 that figure had dropped to 37 percent. Most railroads now have less impact on the development of cities than they did a century ago. What kinds of transportation might affect urban growth today?

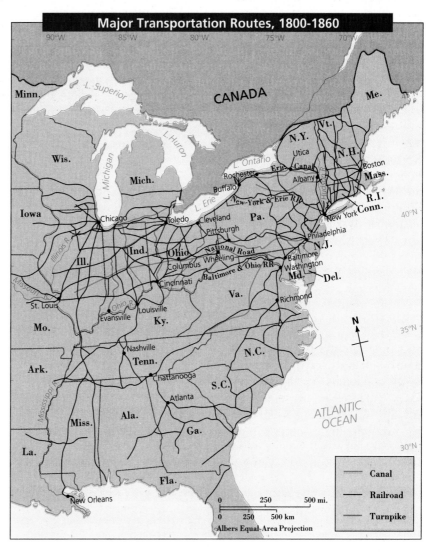

**Major Transportation Routes, 1800-1860**

Canal
Railroad
Turnpike

Albers Equal-Area Projection

**Identify the different kinds of transportation that linked U.S. cities.**
*How did geography help make Chicago a major transportation center?*

# A Changing People

## August 1801: 20,000 Worship at Kentucky Camp Meeting

THE NOISE RISING FROM THE CLEARING IN THE FOREST "WAS LIKE THE THE ROAR OF NIAGARA." THE SOUND OF SINGING, WEEPING, SHOUTING, AND MOANING OF THOUSANDS of people came from the meadow. "The vast sea of human beings," observed young James Finley, "seemed to be agitated as if by a storm." The power that stirred the people at Cane Ridge, Kentucky, on that warm August afternoon was religion.

The Cane Ridge meeting began early one Friday and continued for six full days. More than 20,000 people flocked from the surrounding countryside to attend. For these people, camp meetings were a rare chance for contact with others and for a religious service. At night they slept in a city of canvas tents; by day they heard sermons by traveling preachers.

"I counted seven ministers all preaching at once," reported Finley. Some stood on tree stumps, others in wagons. Using vivid images of Satan and fiery hell, the preachers provoked powerful feelings among the listeners. Their sermons offered straightforward choices: sin or salvation, evil or good, wrong or right. The decision was in each person's hands.

Like many others, James Finley was powerfully affected by what he heard at Cane Ridge. "A peculiar strange sensation came over me," he

COURTESY OF THE NEW-YORK HISTORICAL SOCIETY, NEW YORK CITY

said. "My heart beat tumultuously, my knees trembled, my lips quivered, and I felt as though I must fall to the ground." Finley never forgot this experience; several years later he became a preacher himself.

To many people, religion was the solution to the problems facing the United States in the early 1800s. As the nation expanded, Americans became participants in disturbing conflicts—conflicts between rich and poor, easterner and westerner, northerner and southerner, black and white. Some people tried to escape these tensions by joining religious communities. Others tried to reform American society, while still others turned to politics as a way of bringing change to the nation.

## A New Era in Politics

New ideas about politics were sweeping the United States in the early 1800s. The most important of these ideas involved the question of who should be allowed to vote. Many western states allowed all adult men to vote, regardless of how much land they owned. Many eastern states also eliminated in the 1820s property requirements for voters. During that decade, more white men than ever before gained the vote. Many of these new voters were westerners, men who had left the East to seek wealth and opportunity on the frontier. These new voters wanted a new type of politician. They found one in Andrew Jackson.

**Jackson and the Common Man** Thanks to his exploits in the War of 1812, Andrew Jackson became one of the nation's best known heroes. Though he professed little interest in politics, friends persuaded him to run for president in 1824.

---

### STUDY GUIDE

**As You Read**
Identify major American social, religious, and political movements that took place in the early 1800s.

**Central Concepts**
- understanding how the **Second Great Awakening** helped fuel several major reform movements
- recognizing **abolitionism** as an important social movement

**Thinking Skills**
- recognizing propaganda
- making generalizations
- comparing and contrasting
- drawing conclusions

---

Jackson entered one of the wildest elections Americans had yet seen. After 23 years of solid control over the presidency, the Democratic-Republican party was split by factions battling along sectional lines. John Q. Adams, a northerner and son of the second president, had the support of President James Monroe. Another veteran Democratic-Republican, Henry Clay, hoped to be elected by the westerners he represented. A southern candidate, William Crawford of Georgia, had won the support of many congressmen.

Jackson was the fourth candidate. By far the least experienced politically, he nonetheless impressed people. His image as a no-nonsense frontiersman who had worked his way up the ladder of society, appealed to many voters. His political ideas were as direct as a frontier preacher's sermon: He favored a "Democracy of Numbers" over the "moneyed aristocracy."

Jackson's supporters in the West and South gave him the most electoral and popular votes in the contest, but no candidate had a clear majority. The contest—according to the Constitution's rule—was turned over to the House of Representatives. Henry Clay, who served as Speaker of the House that year, threw his support to Adams. When the House vote was taken in February 1825, Adams won with the votes of 13 states to Jackson's seven. Jackson's supporters claimed that Clay and Adams had made a "corrupt bargain," a charge that seemed justified when Adams named Clay secretary of state.

The election of 1824 split the Democratic-Republican party once and for all. Supporters of Adams and Clay began to call themselves National Republicans. Jackson's supporters, calling themselves Democrats, began to make plans for the 1828 presidential election.

### The Election of 1828

Both Adams and Jackson had observed the changing political climate, and both designed their campaigns with the "common man" in mind. The result was a mean-spirited but lively campaign that avoided most serious issues.

National Republicans called Jackson "a gambler, a cockfighter, a brawler, a drunkard, and a murderer." The Democrats attacked Adams as a "stingy, undemocratic" aristocrat. They asked Americans to choose between "John Quincy Adams, who can write, and Andrew Jackson, who can fight."

But the political tide of democracy favored Jackson in 1828. Almost three times as many people voted as had in 1824, and these new voters helped deliver a resounding victory for Jackson.

Following his inaugural address in March 1829, Jackson rode down Pennsylvania Avenue to the White House, followed by thousands of his celebrating supporters. The crowd swarmed into the White House behind Jackson, grabbing the cakes, ice cream, and punch that had been set out for the inaugural reception. The people broke china, tore curtains, and

LIBRARY OF CONGRESS

**Andrew Jackson was a hero in the spirit of the rugged frontier.** *Do you think Jackson would have been as* *politically successful earlier in the history of the United States?*

knocked over furniture. Jackson had to escape the mob through a window. It was apparent to everyone in Washington that a new era in politics had begun.

"The people expect reform," Jackson said. "They shall not be disappointed." One of his first changes was to fire a number of allegedly "lazy" government workers, many of whom had supported Adams. Jackson replaced them with his own supporters.

This practice of rewarding government supporters with government jobs was known as the **spoils system**. Jackson claimed that replacing workers every so often made the government more democratic. The duties in most government jobs, he argued, were so "plain and simple" that anyone could do them. Dismantling the old bureaucracy, however, was a small matter compared to Jackson's war on the powerful Bank of the United States.

**The Bank Crisis**   The Bank of the United States was an important financial institution that exerted significant influence over Congress and the nation's economy. Twenty percent of the bank's stock was owned by the United States, and the government's money was deposited there. This money, along with private investments, was used to promote commerce and manufacturing. This had the effect of promoting the interests of northeastern industries.

To Jackson, the bank was undemocratic and unconstitutional. It represented the "moneyed aristocracy" that he so hated. He called the bank a "monster" that threatened to "control the Government and change its character."

Henry Clay and Daniel Webster knew how Jackson felt and planned to strengthen the bank and embarrass the president at the same time. Clay and Webster drafted a bill rechartering the bank, even though the bank's original charter still had four years remaining. They reasoned that Jackson would not dare veto a bill—a rare occurrence in that era—in his reelection year. The bill passed Congress and reached the president's desk in July 1832.

Jackson saw this early bank bill as an attack. "The bank . . . is trying to kill me," he told an adviser, "but I will kill the bank." Jackson not only vetoed the bank bill, he also made it the central issue in his campaign that fall. "When the laws," he said, "make the rich richer and the potent more powerful, the humble

members of society—the farmers, mechanics, and laborers—. . . have a right to complain." Many people agreed, and in the 1832 election Jackson defeated his opponent Henry Clay.

During his second term, Jackson was determined to destroy the bank. He closed the government's accounts at the bank and moved federal funds to state banks. In 1836 the bank's charter expired for good.

**The Tariff Controversy**   As Jackson battled the bank, another crisis split his administration and threatened to divide the nation.

Tariffs had been part of the U.S.'s economic policy since 1816. However, tariffs were unpopular in the South. When Congress passed a high tariff on some European imports in 1828, many southerners complained loudly. One of these angry southerners was Jackson's vice president, John Calhoun. Calhoun wrote an essay invoking states' rights and the theory of **nullification**. A state, wrote Calhoun, had the right to nullify, or reject, any law that the state felt violated the Constitution.

Jackson supported states' rights, but as president he could not accept nullification because it threatened the federal government's power and the states' unity. Still, some southerners tried to win Jackson's support on the matter by inviting him to a large ceremonial dinner with Calhoun in 1830. When Jackson stood to make the toast before dinner, he let the nullifiers know exactly where he stood on the matter: "Our Federal Union: It must be preserved." Jackson's toast—which plainly put the power of the federal government above the power of the states—silenced the room. A stunned Calhoun rose with his own toast to defend states' rights: "The Union," he said, "next to our liberty, most dear."

In 1832 the controversy became a crisis when Congress passed yet another high tariff. This act enraged politicians in South Carolina. During the fall of 1832 the state legislature nullified the tariff. They also threatened to **secede**, or leave the Union, if the government tried to collect tariff duties in the state. John Calhoun resigned as vice president and took over one of South Carolina's seats in the Senate.

In December, Jackson directed warships and troops to move toward South Carolina. Then Congress passed a Force Bill permitting the president

**Recognizing Propaganda**
Recognizing propaganda helps you to evaluate the use of communication to shape others' thinking. To gain support for his veto of the bill to recharter the Bank of the United States, Jackson used the language of propaganda. He played on prejudices that many people held against banking and finance. Many people didn't understand finance at all, and they viewed banking as an evil, unproductive activity. Capitalizing on that mistrust, Jackson said the bank was a "monster," a monopoly that advanced the interests of "the few at the expense of the many."

to use military force to collect the state's tariff duties.

As tensions mounted, Henry Clay designed a compromise plan to reduce all tariffs for 10 years. South Carolina accepted this peace offering and withdrew its nullification of the tariff. Clay's compromise bill resolved the crisis, but states' rights would remain a burning issue for the next 30 years as southern and northern politicians battled over slavery.

**The Whig Party**   While Jackson remained a popular figure, he made many political enemies. By 1834 opposition to Jackson had unified as the Whig party. The new party included Republicans like Henry Clay and Federalists like Daniel Webster, plus supporters of the Bank of the United States, manufacturers who favored tariffs, and wealthy businessmen in large cities. The Democrats maintained their support among working people, immigrants, and the small farmers of the South and West.

The Democrats retained the White House in 1836 as Jackson's chosen successor, Martin Van Buren, won the election. In 1840, however, the Whigs retaliated. They portrayed Van Buren as an aristocrat who ate from gold plates. The Whig candidate was a military hero in the Jackson mold, William Henry Harrison. By ignoring the issues and portraying him as a common, cider-drinking man, the Whigs were able to capture the White House.

In the election of 1840, the Whigs made use of the Jacksonian idea that power and success were available to everyone, not just the elite. That idea was echoed in the sermons of preachers on the western frontier. **1**

THE GRANGER COLLECTION

The People's Line--Take care of the Locomotive

*Sold at 104 Nassau, and 18 Division Streets, New-York.*

**Opposition to Jackson inspired the formation of a new political party—the Whig party.** *Why do you think Jackson made so many political enemies?*

## An Awakening Interest in Religion

While voters were expressing displeasure toward the "moneyed aristocracy," many Americans were finding they had little in common with the traditional colonial Christian churches: the Anglican (Episcopal), the Congregationalist, and the Presbyterian. These churches often had an air of wealth and privilege. Services tended to be formal affairs that inspired little enthusiasm. As the nation expanded, Americans began seeking new forms of religion more in keeping with the spirit of a restless, growing young nation.

**Western Revival**   Beginning in the 1790s, a revival in religious interest known as the **Second Great Awakening** swept the western frontier. The style of these growing churches—especially Methodist and Baptist—was less formal than the better established churches of the East. **Circuit riders**, or traveling ministers, rode about the frontier preaching to farmers. Rallies such as the camp meeting at Cane Ridge, Kentucky, attracted people from miles around.

The sermons delivered at these meetings and churches could be frightening—damnation awaited all sinners. But the message behind them remained personal, emotional, practical, and even democratic.

The Expanding Nation    75

**The Second Great Awakening tapped the tremendous energy and spirit of the expanding nation, and applied it** to the nation's spiritual development. Each family member here is shown with a Bible.

The idea that anything—even victory over sin—was possible with hard work and prayer appealed to many Americans.

**Perfecting Society** As the powerful ideas of the Second Great Awakening spread through the country, the nature of its message changed. One preacher who took this message and developed it was Charles Grandison Finney. A tall man with thinning blond hair and blazing eyes, Finney began with the idea that sin was a failure of will. Those who could avoid the temptation of sin could make themselves perfect.

Finney went on to say that not only could Christians make themselves perfect, they could—indeed, must—make the world around them perfect. No Christian could fail to see a thousand evils that needed to be corrected, reformed, and eliminated. The ideas of Finney and other preachers unleashed enormous energy in Americans. The urge to perfect the nation grew stronger during the 1830s and thereafter.[2]

## Reforming American Society

The Second Great Awakening inspired different responses from different groups. Some withdrew to create their own "perfect" communities. For example, the Shakers and the Mormons, two religious groups, attempted to build their own **utopia**, or ideal world, away from mainstream American life. Others set about changing the mainstream itself.

**Comparing and Contrasting**
The frontier churches were presenting a message that was similar in many respects to that of established East Coast churches. However, they differed greatly in style and emphasis. The western churches were far less formal. More importantly, they downplayed the element of privilege that pervaded eastern religion. Western churches appealed to a broader social and economic class.

2 What ideas preached during the Second Great Awakening fit the growing American spirit of democracy?

They saw a host of evils in the rapidly changing society of the 1800s. Churchgoers in the populous areas of the North were among the first to organize reform groups. These groups usually saw social problems in religious terms of "evil" and "sin."

In an era when women had limited opportunities for education or jobs, reform groups offered an outlet for their energy and skills. Women filled the ranks of many reform efforts during the mid-1800s, but others considered it "unfeminine" for women to play an active role in these movements. As a result of these tensions, women's rights became one of the dominant issues during the reform era.

While women's rights concerned some, other evils were more visible and easier to attack. Alcohol, for example, was blamed for crime, insanity, and the breakdown of the family. As a result, the **temperance**, or antidrinking, movement became one of the first organized reform movements in the United States.

### Demon Rum

Starting in the 1830s reformers targeted the evils of "demon rum." They flooded the nation with tracts and articles. One of the bestselling novels of the 1850s, *Ten Nights in a Bar Room and What I Saw There*, warned against the excesses of alcohol. Reformed alcoholics traveled to meetings in city after city, telling their stories. These efforts got results. Hard liquor sales fell by half during the 1830s alone.

Gradually the fight against drunkenness became a war on alcohol itself. More and more Americans chose to avoid all liquor and became "teetotalers." Reformers took their case to state legislatures. In 1838 Tennessee passed the first statewide regulation of liquor. Temperance reformers won another victory when Maine passed a tougher liquor law in 1851. While some citizens protested and bootleg liquor poured into the state from Canada, re-

MASSACHUSETTS HISTORICAL SOCIETY

**This engraving shows the "Great Central Route To Destruction!" and reflects the temperance movement's belief that alcohol drove people to ruination.**

formers counted the Maine law as a victory.

The success of the temperance movement inspired dozens of other reform efforts: the push for better prisons, mental health care, and free public education; and aid for the blind and the deaf. Some reformers, however, perceived an evil much greater than all of these—an evil endorsed by politicians, protected by laws, and defended by an entire section of the nation. That evil was slavery.

### Fighting Slavery

Slavery had troubled some Americans since before the Revolution. In 1787 the Northwest Ordinance forbade slavery in territories north of the Ohio River, and by 1804 every northern state had provided for the end of slavery. Few white Americans, however, took an active stand on slavery after the passage of the Constitution until the 1820s.

At this time dozens of publications appeared spreading the ideas of **abolitionism**, the movement to end slavery. Most of these papers called for a gradual end to slavery, believing that the slow pace would bring **emancipation**—freedom to African Americans —while protecting businesses of southern planters.

Other abolitionists had less patience. David Walker, a former slave living in Boston, called for an immediate end to slavery in 1829. He argued that slaves were entitled to use violence to obtain their freedom from the white masters.

Two years later William Lloyd Garrison began publishing a newspaper called *The Liberator*. In his black suits and steel-rimmed glasses, Garrison looked more like a school master than a radical reformer. His pen, however, spouted fire as he called for the immediate emancipation of all slaves. "I am in earnest," he wrote, "I will not retreat a single inch —AND I WILL BE HEARD!"

Garrison was heard.

BROWN BROTHERS

CHICAGO HISTORICAL SOCIETY

COURTESY OF THE BOSTON PUBLIC LIBRARY, PRINT DEPARTMENT

COURTESY OF THE BOSTON PUBLIC LIBRARY, PRINT DEPARTMENT

**The reform movements spawned the emergence of many important and notable historical figures. From left to right are abolitionists Frederick Douglass and** **Sojourner Truth, both former slaves, and William Lloyd Garrison. At right, is temperance zealot Lucretia C. Mott.**

In 1833 a group of his supporters met in Philadelphia and formed the American Anti-Slavery Society. The goals of the Society were to end slavery in the United States by stirring up public sentiment and flooding the nation with abolitionist literature. The Society grew throughout the 1830s. With success, however, came controversy. Southerners worried about the effect of Garrison's message on their slaves and mounted vicious verbal attacks on him. Northerners blasted his views on the Constitution, which he called a "compromise with tyranny" and "an agreement with hell" because it allowed slavery.

**Tensions Within the Movement**  White leaders of the abolitionist movement discovered that African Americans, especially former slaves, made the most convincing arguments against slavery. Soon, escaped slaves became the star attractions at meetings of the Anti-Slavery Society. One of the best speakers was Frederick Douglass, a brilliant man who had made a dramatic escape from slavery in 1838 at age 21. Douglass was a spellbinding speaker. "I appear before this immense assembly," he addressed one crowd, "as a thief and robber. I stole this head, these limbs, this body from my master, and ran off with them."

Sojourner Truth, a tall, deep-voiced woman, had also become free after serving several masters for 30 years. In the 1840s she attracted large crowds throughout the North and West with her abolitionist speeches.

For all their talent, black abolitionists found that white opponents of slavery were generally unwilling to accept them into their organizations. In addition, blacks and whites often disagreed over how to attack slavery. Some abolitionists advocated the use of violence and urged slave revolts. They felt that the speeches and tracts of the Anti-Slavery Society were useless against a problem like slavery. Others, like Frederick Douglass, believed that change could only come from within the political system.

Women also chafed at their role as second-class citizens within the movement. Recognizing the important contributions of women, Garrison supported women's rights and encouraged their role in the Society. Other male leaders of the Society, however, refused to accept women as equals.

In 1840 all these tensions within the American Anti-Slavery Society splintered it. The split in the Society, however, was not the end of abolitionism. In the 1840s and 1850s abolitionism was one of the issues—along with western expansion and the nation's changing economic identity—that widened the split between northern and southern states.

## SECTION REVIEW

**Checking Facts**

1. Although Jackson supported states' rights, he opposed nullification, which would strengthen states. Explain his opposition.

2. How did Jackson illustrate the saying, "To the victor go the spoils"?

3. How was William Henry Harrison's appeal similar to Jackson's?

4. How did the Second Great Awakening reflect political trends of the time?

5. Describe the antislavery efforts of the 1820s and 1830s.

**Thinking Critically**

6. **Compare and Contrast**  Abolitionists differed among themselves in their strategies for ending slavery. Compare and contrast their opinions.

7. **Making Deductions**  Why might African Americans have expected to share power with whites in the Anti-Slavery Society?

8. **Recognizing Propaganda**  How did both Adams and Jackson use the language of propaganda in the election of 1828?

**Linking Across Time**

9. Is name calling ever used in modern election campaigns? Is it ever effective? Explain your answer.

# Making Telescoping Timelines

William Lloyd Garrison was a vital force in the abolitionist movement. His accomplishments can be highlighted in a telescoping timeline, a detailed timeline covering a relatively short period. A standard timeline places Garrison's achievements in the broader context of historical events.

## Learning the Skill

The upper of the two timelines on this page is a standard timeline beginning in 1615 and ending in 1850. The events on the timeline relate to slavery in America and efforts to abolish it. The first event on the timeline is the arrival of slaves who were brought to work on tobacco plantations at the English settlement at Jamestown. Now read the remaining entries on the standard timeline.

Next, look at the lower timeline, a 14-year telescoping timeline, which focuses on William Lloyd Garrison's contributions to the abolitionist movement. The entries begin with 1828, the year in which Garrison became actively involved in the abolitionist cause as editor of Boston's *National Philanthropist* and of *Journal of the Times*, published in Bennington, Vermont. Read the rest of the entries on the telescoping timeline, which tell of Garrison's activities during the time period of this chapter.

Notice the relationship between events on the two timelines. For example, the entries for 1688 and 1808 on the standard timeline show the origins of the antislavery movement. This movement was then strengthened by Garrison's leadership, as the telescoping timeline entries illustrate.

To decide which timeline an event belongs on, consider the subject it covers and the date of its occurrence. For example, the 1820 Missouri Compromise belongs on the standard timeline because it occurred before 1826 and because it relates to slavery and abolitionism, but not to William Lloyd Garrison.

## Practicing the Skill

1. Visit your school or public library to find biographical information about Frederick Douglass. Make a standard timeline showing events in his entire life. Then make a telescoping timeline that shows what he did in the years 1841 through 1865.
2. How do events in Douglass's early life relate to events described on your telescoping timeline?
3. Try making timelines showing U.S. expansion. Use 1776–1960 for a standard timeline. Show events important to expansion. Your telescoping timeline can focus on major events in the westward movement of the 1800s.

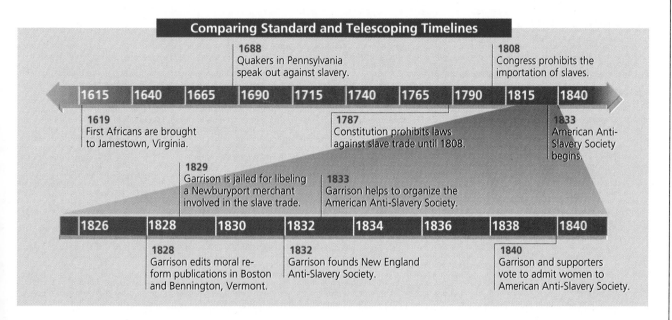

**Comparing Standard and Telescoping Timelines**

**1688**
Quakers in Pennsylvania speak out against slavery.

**1808**
Congress prohibits the importation of slaves.

1615 | 1640 | 1665 | 1690 | 1715 | 1740 | 1765 | 1790 | 1815 | 1840

**1619**
First Africans are brought to Jamestown, Virginia.

**1787**
Constitution prohibits laws against slave trade until 1808.

**1833**
American Anti-Slavery Society begins.

**1829**
Garrison is jailed for libeling a Newburyport merchant involved in the slave trade.

**1833**
Garrison helps to organize the American Anti-Slavery Society.

1826 | 1828 | 1830 | 1832 | 1834 | 1836 | 1838 | 1840

**1828**
Garrison edits moral reform publications in Boston and Bennington, Vermont.

**1832**
Garrison founds New England Anti-Slavery Society.

**1840**
Garrison and supporters vote to admit women to American Anti-Slavery Society.

# Chapter 2 Review

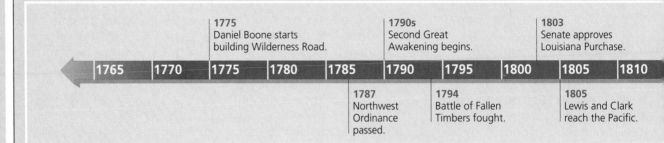

1775
Daniel Boone starts building Wilderness Road.

1790s
Second Great Awakening begins.

1803
Senate approves Louisiana Purchase.

1765　1770　1775　1780　1785　1790　1795　1800　1805　1810

1787
Northwest Ordinance passed.

1794
Battle of Fallen Timbers fought.

1805
Lewis and Clark reach the Pacific.

## Summary

Use the following outline as a tool for reviewing and summarizing the chapter. Copy the outline on your own paper, leaving spaces between headings to jot down notes about key events and concepts.

**I. Territorial Expansion**
A. The Moving Frontier
B. Settling the West
C. Native Americans and the Settlers

**II. The Economy Grows**
A. From Farms to Factories
B. The Transportation Revolution
C. Politics and the Economy

**III. A Changing People**
A. A New Era in Politics
B. An Awakening Interest in Religion
C. Reforming American Society

## Ideas, Events, and People

1. Who was Tenskwatawa? What were his views on relations with white settlers?
2. Identify and explain:
   The Trail of Tears
   Embargo Act
   Sacajawea
   Charles Grandison Finney
   Cumberland Gap
3. Give three purposes of the Lewis and Clark Expedition.
4. Describe the changes in the economic life of the nation between 1800 and 1850. Describe some of the effects on individual Americans.
5. What is the relationship between "Mad" Anthony Wayne, the Battle of Fallen Timbers, the Treaty of Greenville, and the Northwest Territory?
6. Explain the relationship between Tecumseh and Prophet's Town.
7. Identify the *Cherokee Phoenix*.
8. Explain Henry Clay's "American System."
9. What was the "spoils system"?
10. Explain the work of Sojourner Truth.
11. How were women's rights related to the reform movement?

## Social Study Skills

**Making Telescoping Timelines**
Make timelines showing the administrations of the first eight presidents. Use the years 1790 to 1840 for a standard timeline. Show presidential elections as well as important events related to changing economic policy and to the development of national parties. Your telescoping timeline can focus on events occurring during the presidencies of John Quincy Adams and Andrew Jackson.

## Critical Thinking

1. **Making Generalizations**
   The Industrial Revolution and the Great Awakening occurred at about the same time. Are they related in any way?
2. **Cause and Effect**
   After 1850 the system of canals, which had just been completed, was soon abandoned. Why?
3. **Compare and Contrast**
   Compare and contrast the life of a Lowell mill girl with the life of a girl on the farm.
4. **Recognizing Values**
   What was the Lowell experiment? Briefly explain its importance in American industrial development.
5. **Analyzing Behavior**
   Explain the internal improvement bills and the controversy surrounding them.

1815    1820    1825    1830    1835    1840    1845    1850    1855    1860

**1825**
Erie Canal opens.

**1838**
Trail of Tears begins.

**1814**
Lowell's mill opens in Waltham, Mass.

**1830s**
Temperance and antislavery movements attract supporters.

**1850**
Census reports that most goods are factory-made; railroads speed movement of goods.

### 6. Recognizing Propaganda

The picture below shows the cover for a song entitled "Log Cabin March," used in William Henry Harrison's 1840 presidential campaign. How are campaign paraphernalia such as this used to gain voter support?

THE GRANGER COLLECTION

## Extension and Application

### 1. Citizenship

A major movement of the nineteenth century was the crusade against alcohol, or the temperance movement, as it was called. Compare this movement with the present-day campaign against tobacco and drugs. How are they similar? How are they different?

### 2. Global Connection

Investigate the Louisiana Purchase. What international events made it possible? If the slaves had not revolted in Haiti, how might the map of the United States look today? Would your culture, language, and customs be different?

### 3. Linking Across Time

The chapter describes how certain Native American nations were pushed aside in the westward expansion of the United States. Choose one of the Native American nations mentioned in the text and investigate where and how they live today. Use the *Writer's Guide*, Unit 6 (page 829), to help you prepare your report.

### 4. Cooperative Learning

With a small group, construct a timeline for the nineteenth century showing significant events in the history of industrial development. Beneath it, construct another timeline showing the important developments in the history of women's rights. Is there a relationship between the developments in both? Add other timelines for the antislavery moment, the addition of new states, and the growth of railroads. Draw your own conclusions about the period from parallel developments. Do they show that progress always occurs steadily?

## Geography

1. Name the three countries that owned the Louisiana Territory between 1763 and 1803. Why did ownership of the land change during the period?

2. According to the map on page 55, in what era was most of the Mississippi River valley settled? How might some of these settlers have arrived?

3. Why were the early textile mills of New England built along rivers?

4. What were some of the different purposes served by the canals built in the early 1800s? What bodies of water did the canals link?

CHAPTER 3

# Rift and Reunion

## May 1856: Pottawatomie, Kansas

Proslavery and antislavery forces were fighting for control of Kansas by 1855. Proslavery residents of Missouri had poured into Kansas by the hundreds to elect proslavery leaders to office. The legislature that they elected then passed harsh laws to prohibit even the free expression of opinions against slavery. By the fall of 1855, however, more Kansas residents opposed slavery than supported it. These antislavery forces determined to defy the proslavery laws, armed themselves, called for new elections, and then drafted a new state constitution.

In response, in the spring of 1856,

*The conflict in "Bleeding Kansas" foreshadowed the turmoil that later would engulf the nation.*

THE METROPOLITAN MUSEUM OF ART

*This detail from the painting* The Last Moments of John Brown, *by Thomas Hovenden (1884) shows Brown, on the way to his execution, kissing a black child as a statement of his antislavery views.*

a group of proslavery Missourians lugged five cannons to the outskirts of Lawrence, Kansas, the antislavery stronghold. The invaders ransacked and burned homes and businesses and killed several men. Outraged by this action, militant antislavery leader John Brown with his four sons and two other men, kidnapped and brutally executed five proslavery settlers at Pottawatomie, Kansas.

In subsequent raids between the proslavery and antislavery forces, about 200 people were killed before federal troops could stop the violence. The conflict in "Bleeding Kansas" foreshadowed the turmoil that later would engulf the nation.

*Five generations are represented in this African American family. All of them were born on a South Carolina plantation.*

# Slavery and Politics

## March 6, 1857: Washington, D.C.

**D**RED SCOTT AND HIS WIFE HARRIET SCOTT ANXIOUSLY AWAITED THE SUPREME COURT DECISION. THE SCOTTS WERE SLAVES, BUT THEY WERE HOPING THE SUPREME COURT would set them free because they had resided with a former master in Illinois and in the Wisconsin Territory, where slavery was prohibited by the Missouri Compromise. But the year was 1857, and slaves did not have any legal rights in the United States. Furthermore, the Scotts were again living in Missouri, a slave state.

At last, Chief Justice Roger Taney read the majority opinion of the Court and crushed the Scotts' hopes for freedom. Slaves were legal property and no state could deprive citizens of their property without due process of law, Taney said. In addition, the Court ruled the **Missouri Compromise** unconstitutional, declaring that Congress could not prohibit slavery in U.S. territories.

Several weeks later, the Scotts were again sold. Their new owner freed them, and the former slaves quietly slipped into obscurity. But the decision from their lawsuit did not disappear. Northerners were angered by the court's ruling because new U.S. territories could become slave states, upsetting the balance of power between free states and slave states. A heated debate ensued that in 1861 would erupt in a bloody war.

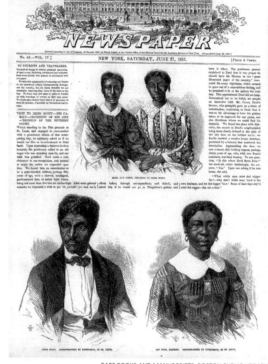

RARE BOOKS AND MANUSCRIPTS, BOSTON PUBLIC LIBRARY

## *The Roots of Conflict*

**I**n the late 1700s, many farmers in the upper South—Maryland, Virginia, and North Carolina—shifted from tobacco to grain crops because these crops required less labor. The result was that a once-booming slave trade declined in this region. However, in 1793 a single event abruptly stopped any possible downward trend in the slave trade. In that year Eli Whitney introduced the cotton gin, a machine that greatly reduced the amount of time and work required to remove the seeds from cotton.

Suddenly, large quantities of cotton could be profitably grown with the aid of slave labor. Almost overnight, vast numbers of landowners throughout the South converted their fields to cotton production and thousands of would-be cotton farmers poured into the South from other regions. These new cotton planters figured they could increase their profit margins if slaves picked and cleaned their cotton. So with the profitability of cotton production ensured by Whitney's invention, slavery quickly gained a new economic foothold. And white southerners were determined to protect it.

By the mid-1800s, the northern economy relied mostly on manufacturing and an ever-increasing immigrant work force. Therefore, the northern econ-

**As You Read**

Identify the economic differences between North and South and the events that led to the war. Also, think about the following concepts and skills.

**Central Concepts**
- identifying the roots of southern **sectionalism**
- recognizing the effects of the **Missouri Compromise**

**Thinking Skills**
- recognizing points of view
- predicting consequences
- assessing outcomes
- analyzing decisions

THE GRANGER COLLECTION

THE GRANGER COLLECTION

**Compare and contrast the two scenes above. In the 1836 lithograph of Lockport, New York, on the left, the Erie Canal dominates the town. The colored** **engraving on the right depicts a scene on a southern cotton plantation.** *How do these images reflect the different economies that developed in the North and the South?*

omy did not rely on a **slave labor force**—a group of people owned by a master and made to do work without pay. In fact, they feared that if slavery were to extend northward, their own jobs would be threatened. In addition, northern abolitionists opposed slavery on moral grounds. Abolitionists such as Frederick Douglass, Sojourner Truth, and William Lloyd Garrison had become adamant that slavery be abolished throughout the nation. As Garrison wrote in his antislavery newspaper *The Liberator,* "I will be as harsh as truth and as uncompromising as justice. On this subject [slavery] I do not wish to think, or speak, or write, with moderation. No! No!"

Thus, by midcentury, North and South had developed two different political agendas based on their very different economies. The Northern agenda called for the extension of free labor into new states. The Southern agenda demanded the maintenance of slavery. The two regions drifted toward **sectionalism,** or an extreme allegiance to their own local interests.

This sectionalism developed because of northern politicians' attempts to pass laws settling the slavery debate for the entire nation. White southerners, angered over increasing federal intervention in their affairs, believed that they should be able to make more decisions—especially about slavery—at the state level of government. Meanwhile, millions of African Americans wondered when their oppression would end.

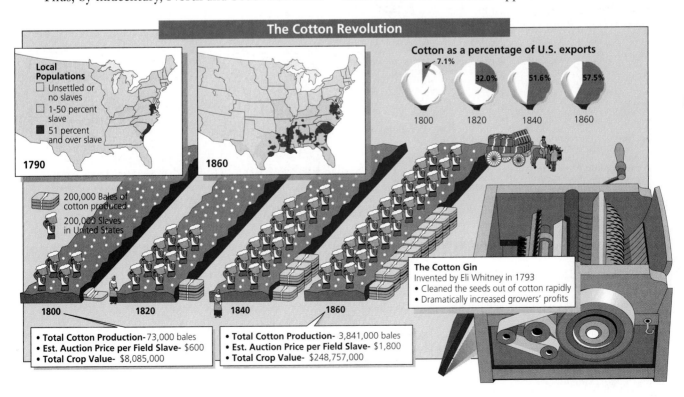

## The Cotton Revolution

**Local Populations**
- ☐ Unsettled or no slaves
- ☐ 1–50 percent slave
- ■ 51 percent and over slave

**1790**

**1860**

**Cotton as a percentage of U.S. exports**

7.1% — 1800
32.0% — 1820
51.6% — 1840
57.5% — 1860

- 200,000 Bales of cotton produced
- 200,000 Slaves in United States

**1800** **1820** **1840** **1860**

**The Cotton Gin**
Invented by Eli Whitney in 1793
- Cleaned the seeds out of cotton rapidly
- Dramatically increased growers' profits

- **Total Cotton Production**- 73,000 bales
- **Est. Auction Price per Field Slave**- $600
- **Total Crop Value**- $8,085,000

- **Total Cotton Production**- 3,841,000 bales
- **Est. Auction Price per Field Slave**- $1,800
- **Total Crop Value**- $248,757,000

## The Slave Community

From about 1800 to the Civil War, about half of all southern African Americans lived on large plantations. On the plantation, most slaves worked in the fields from sunup to sundown, six days a week. Although they were typically given Sundays off, many used that day to cultivate their own garden plots.

Some slaves worked as cooks, maids, and nursemaids in the Big House, where the plantation owner lived. There the slaves might receive better food and clothing, but since they lived in Big House slave quarters (often in the basement), they saw their loved ones less often. On big plantations, slaves also worked as shoemakers, boatmen, seamstresses, and carpenters.

Most slaves were periodically subject to physical abuse. Planters tended to use whips freely and sometimes even branded or maimed slaves to punish them. Many masters also sexually abused female slaves.

The emotional torment imposed on the slaves was as common as the physical abuse. Planters would threaten to "sell a slave down the river," which meant selling the slave to a distant plantation far removed from family and friends. Parents and children were frequently separated on the auction block. One way many slaves coped with these traumatic sep-arations was by substituting "fictive kin" for blood ties. That is, slaves often adopted each other as family.

A great number of slaves also turned to the Christian religion for comfort, adapting African religious beliefs and practices to suit their needs. They took hope from biblical stories of slavery and liberation and transformed Protestant customs into their own African-Christian blend, including African practices such as dancing, drumming, and shouting during worship services. In music, slaves created a gospel tradition. Spirituals are a unique American musical form.

In the Sea Islands of Georgia and South Carolina, slaves known as the "Gullah" people were especially noted for infusing the Christian religion with African cultural practices. One observer described a worship service in 1867, noting, "Song and dance alike are extremely energetic, and often, when the shout lasts into the middle of the night, the monotonous thud, thud, thud of the feet prevents sleep within half a mile of the praisehouse . . ."

## Resistance to Slavery

Religious beliefs offered slaves comfort, and inspired action. By the mid-1800s, hundreds of slaves were fleeing from plantations to freedom in the North and in Mexico each year. Between 1830 and 1860, a network of abolitionists known as the underground railroad helped many of these slaves escape by conducting them to safe houses where they could hide on their way to free territories.

PRIVATE COLLECTION/LAURIE PLATT WINFREY, INC.

**Eyre Crowe's 1852 painting, *Slave Market in Richmond, Virginia*, depicts a romanticized image of a slave sale. In reality, slaves were usually barely clothed and were often in chains.**

## STUDY GUIDE

### Recognizing Points of View
The North favored a strong national government largely because northerners believed that their economy, which was based on industry and business, would flourish under strong federal support. The South, on the other hand, believing that Southern interests were not national interests, preferred that many issues, including slavery, be decided at the state level by legislators who were more aware of the effects federal laws might have on the southern economy.

One of the most famous "conductors" along the underground railroad was Harriet Tubman, a woman who had herself escaped from slavery. Armed with a pistol she wasn't afraid to use, Tubman guided 19 expeditions of slaves out of the South.

Jerry Loguen, another conductor, is said to have helped as many as 1,500 slaves escape. When Loguen's former owner, Sarah Logue, discovered his whereabouts, she wrote demanding that he return or pay her $1,000 to purchase his freedom and the horse he had stolen to escape. This was Loguen's reply:

**Harriet Tubman led over 300 slaves, including her parents, to freedom. Rewards of $40,000 were offered for her capture.**

HISTORICAL PICTURE SERVICE, CHICAGO

M*rs. Sarah Logue . . . You say you have offers to buy me, and that you shall sell me if I do not send you $1000, and in the same breath and almost in the same sentence, you say, "You know we raised you as we did our own children." Woman, did you raise your own children for the market? Did you raise them for the whipping post? Did you raise them to be driven off, bound to a coffle in chains? . . . Shame on you!*

*But you say I am a thief, because I took the old mare along with me. Have you got to learn that I had a better right to the old mare, as you call her, than Manasseth Logue had to me? Is it a greater sin for me to steal his horse, than it was for him to rob my mother's cradle, and steal me? . . . Have you got to learn that human rights are mutual and reciprocal, and if you take my liberty and life, you forfeit your own liberty and life? Before God and high heaven, is there a law for one man which is not a law for every other man?*

J. W. Loguen, from a letter reprinted in The Liberator in the 1850s

Despite the threat of punishment, some slaves made annual forays off the plantations to visit family and friends. Others resisted their masters within the confines of the plantation grounds. They held secret meetings, staged work slowdowns, broke tools, feigned illnesses, and set fires.

Plantation owners feared open defiance from individual slaves but were even more afraid of a collective rebellion. A number of early slave revolts—such as Gabriel Prosser's Revolt in Richmond in 1800 and the Denmark Vesey Conspiracy in Charleston in 1822—aroused concern. This concern turned into panic in 1831 when on August 22, a slave preacher named Nat Turner led 75 armed followers in a rebellion. During the two days before they were subdued, these rebels killed between 55 and 60 whites.

The hysteria that spread throughout the South after the Turner revolt prompted slave owners to take elaborate precautions to protect themselves. They created a complicated system of permits for slave travel and patrols to enforce the system. Believing that literacy would lead to empowerment and revolt, masters tried to prevent slaves from learning to read and write. Additionally, southern legislatures passed laws that made it difficult for masters to free their slaves. They wanted to prevent the free black population from increasing because free blacks could organize revolts much more easily than slaves. While these tactics seemed to halt slave rebellion in the South, northern opposition to the spread of slavery grew.

## Conflict and Compromise

The majority of Northern politicians did not oppose slavery as a labor force or as a way of life. For purely political reasons, they opposed the extension of slavery into the new territories gained by the Louisiana Purchase. If these territories became slave states, the South would have greater representation in the Senate than the North. Greater representation would give Southern politicians a better chance of fulfilling their political agenda.

To protect slavery and their way of life, white southerners insisted that the federal government keep out of all matters which the Constitution had not clearly defined. In addition, southerners wanted tariff laws that encouraged southern development.

As you read in Chapter 2, white southerners were troubled by high tariff laws, which raised prices on many articles from overseas. Because the South bought large quantities of manufactured goods from England, which in turn bought the South's cotton for British cotton mills, the high tariffs threatened the South's prosperity. The Southerners argued that Congress did not have the right to make laws which caused one section of the country to suffer unfairly. They were determined to maintain the political balance.

**The Missouri Compromise**    Until 1818 there had been an equal number of slave and free states, and likewise an equal number of senators representing the interests of the North and South. Then in 1818 when Missouri petitioned to enter the Union as a slave state, this delicate balance of power was threatened. Northern legislators amended Missouri's petition by stipulating that Missouri could become a state only if it outlawed slavery. Southern politicians were outraged.

Lawmakers eventually resolved this conflict with a series of legislative compromises. The northern part of Massachusetts, which had petitioned for statehood soon after Missouri, would be admitted as the separate free state of Maine. Missouri would be admitted to the Union as a slave state. In addition, the region south of 36°30′ latitude in the Louisiana territory would be open to slavery, whereas all the land north of it, except Missouri, would be free. These agreements were collectively known as the Missouri Compromise.

White southerners were unhappy with the compromise because it made more land available for settlement as free territory than as slave territory. Southerners were also concerned because most immigrants pouring into the country were seeking jobs in northern urban centers. This trend meant that the North's population would soon far exceed the South's. The North would then be entitled to far more seats in Congress and would be able to advance the goals of its free-labor agenda. In fact, the North already had more seats, and this had helped them push the Missouri Compromise through.

**War with Mexico**    In 1836 when Texas declared its independence from Mexico, white southerners hoped to acquire Texas as a new slave state. Northerners feared that the admission of Texas to the Union would not only increase the South's power in Congress but would also result in war with Mexico. Nevertheless, by 1845 enough politicians were caught up in the fervor of westward expansion—believing that it was the destiny of the nation to reach from shore to shore—that white Southern politicians were able to prevail in getting Texas admitted to the

**This nineteenth-century engraving shows General Zachary Taylor at Buena Vista, where he defeated Santa Anna in 1847.**

Union. Mexico was outraged at this action. After a border skirmish between U.S. troops and Mexican troops, the United States declared war on Mexico in May 1846.

The principal war aim of the United States was to take possession of the territories that Mexico had refused to give up—New Mexico and California. The early battles of the war were relatively easy victories for the United States. The Mexican troops, though greater in number than the U.S. forces, were poorly trained, poorly led, and inadequately equipped. In July 1846, U.S. naval forces under the command of Commodore John Sloat took possession of the California coast. In the meantime Colonel Stephen Kearney, with 1,700 troops, entered the town of Santa Fe in August and took control of New Mexico. Kearney then proceeded westward, arriving in California just in time to help put down a rebellion of Spanish-speaking Californians who had remained loyal to Mexico.

The bloodiest fighting of the war occurred in the Mexican campaign, which served as a valuable training ground for officers who later would command troops in the Civil War. General Zachary Taylor won a major victory at Monterey in September 1846. The following year in February he soundly defeated Mexican General Santa Anna at Buena Vista.

The final phase of the war began in March 1847 when General Winfield Scott launched a campaign along Mexico's eastern coastline. He captured Veracruz and marched inland toward Mexico City. During the next five months, American troops defeated the Mexicans at Cerro Gordo, Churubusco, and Chapultepec. Mexico City fell on September 14.

The Mexican American War had momentous results. By the terms of the Treaty of Guadalupe Hidalgo, the United States gained nearly half of Mexico, including the areas that today are California, Utah, Nevada, and parts of Arizona, New Mexico, Colorado, and Wyoming. The terms also confirmed the independence of the state of Texas. But the fear that these territories would organize into states intensified sectional conflict. Many northerners opposed the extension of slavery into the newly acquired lands that lay south of the line established by the Missouri Compromise.

**The Compromise of 1850**   In 1850, 15 free states and 15 slave states made up the union. California threatened this delicate balance of power by applying for admission to the Union as a free state. Congress once again faced the need to hammer out a legislative compromise. Kentucky Senator Henry Clay introduced four compromise resolutions that became the basic proposals making up the Compromise of 1850: first, that California be admitted to the Union as a free state; second, that territorial governments in Utah and New Mexico let the people of the territories decide the slavery issue for themselves; third, that the slave trade —but not slavery—be prohibited in the District of Columbia; and fourth, that a new fugitive slave law require federal marshals to assist slaveholders in recovering runaway slaves.

Clay's proposals touched off months of heated debate in Congress. Some of the greatest orators of the time lined up on opposite sides of the issue. John C. Calhoun of South Carolina bitterly opposed Clay's plan. Weak and near death, Calhoun sat silent while his final speech was read to the Senate. In it he warned that the Union could be saved only by giving the South equal rights in the acquired territory and by halting the agitation over slavery. Daniel Webster, who supported Clay's ideas, captivated the Senate with a sentence that has since become famous:

> *I wish to speak today, not as a Massachusetts man, nor as a northern man, but as an American. . . . I speak today for the preservation of the Union. "Hear me for my cause."*
>
> Daniel Webster, March 7, 1850

Webster argued that there was no need to exclude slavery from the territories because it would not prosper there due to the soil and climate.

President Taylor opposed a compromise, but his untimely death in July 1850 brought Millard Fillmore to the presidency. With Fillmore's backing, Clay and his supporters succeeded in pushing the proposals through Congress. The package of four laws that became known as the Compromise of 1850 temporarily settled the question of slavery in the territories. The problems did not go away, however, because they were rooted in the issue of slavery itself.

**The Kansas-Nebraska Act**   Just four years later, in 1854, Illinois Senator Stephen A. Douglas guided a highly controversial bill through Congress. This bill,

**Assessing Outcomes**
Robert E. Lee and Ulysses S. Grant, the opposing commanders in the Civil War, formed impressions of each other during the Mexican War. Grant later wrote that the acquaintance "was of immense service to me in the war of rebellion . . . . A large part of the National Army . . . and most of the press of the country, clothed General Lee with [superhuman] qualities, but I had known him personally, and knew that he was mortal."

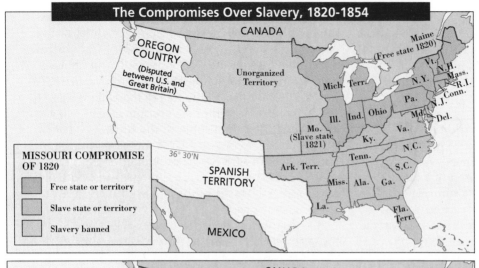

## The Compromises Over Slavery, 1820-1854

**MISSOURI COMPROMISE OF 1820**
- Free state or territory
- Slave state or territory
- Slavery banned

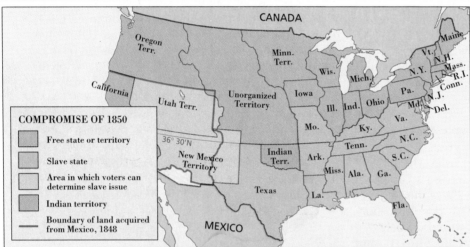

**COMPROMISE OF 1850**
- Free state or territory
- Slave state
- Area in which voters can determine slave issue
- Indian territory
- Boundary of land acquired from Mexico, 1848

**KANSAS - NEBRASKA ACT OF 1854**
- Free state or territory
- Slave state
- Area in which voters can determine slave issue
- Indian territory

which reignited sectional discord, was the Kansas-Nebraska Act.

Douglas was serving as chairman of the Senate Committee on Territories. He wanted to see the unorganized territory west of Missouri and Iowa opened for settlement. Douglas proposed that the people in the territory be allowed to decide for themselves whether or not they wanted slavery.

In 1854 after much negotiation, the Kansas-Nebraska Act was passed. It divided the Nebraska territory into two separate territories, Kansas and Nebraska; and repealed the prohibition of slavery north of the Missouri Compromise line. The citizens of each territory would be able to determine by vote whether their state would be slave or free. In effect, the Act voided the Missouri Compromise, enabling slavery to expand northward.[1]

Many of the antislavery politicians detested Douglas's bill as a violation of the "sacred pledge" of the Missouri Compromise: no slavery north of the 36°30′ line. These politicians broke from traditional party politics to form the

**Three important steps in the slavery dispute are shown in these maps: The Missouri Compromise, the Compromise of 1850, and the Kansas-Nebraska Act. Note the status of the territories in each map.** *How does the territories' slave status change from one map to the next?*

**Analyzing Decisions**

Stephen A. Douglas of Illinois hoped to be elected president someday but needed to generate white southern support. He thought the Kansas-Nebraska Act, which would allow slavery where it was forbidden, would appease southern voters. At the same time, Douglas thought that the settlers in these territories would never vote for slavery and he would not lose northern support.

1 Why would many antislavery politicians oppose the Kansas-Nebraska Act?

SOUTHERN CHIVALRY — ARGUMENT versus CLUB'S.

BOSTON ATHENAEUM

**Violence over slavery spread to the U.S. Congress when a southern Congressman attacked a northern Senator.**

Republican Party in February 1854. The Republicans defended northern sectional interests under the slogan "Free Soil, Free Labor, Free Speech, Free Men."

Kansas meanwhile became the battleground for sectional and party conflicts. By 1856 Kansas had turned into a cauldron of violence between antislavery and proslavery groups.

### Violence Reaches Washington, D.C.

"Bleeding Kansas" became the catchword for the escalating violence over slavery—and the blood spilled all the way to Capitol Hill. In May 1856 Congressman Preston Brooks of South Carolina entered the nearly empty Senate chamber and beat Massachusetts Senator Charles Sumner with a cane. Brooks felt that Sumner's "Crime Against Kansas" speech, which verbally attacked Brooks's kinsman, had warranted this retaliation.

It was in the wake of these events that the Supreme Court handed down its decision in the Dred Scott case in March 1857. Naturally enough, this decision gave rise to fear among northern politicians. The Free Soil Republicans, fearful that the extension of slavery into all the territories was forthcoming, gained more popular support, causing southern forces to defend slavery even more stubbornly.

An unsettled nation approached the 1858 elections, as Abraham Lincoln, a little-known one-term congressman from Springfield, Illinois, opposed Senator Stephen A. Douglas in the race for the Senate and challenged him to a series of debates. The debates gave Lincoln the opportunity to make his political views, including his defense of northern interests, nationally known. Lincoln lost the election, but the debates catapulted him into the national spotlight.

### Hostilities Intensify

Then, in October 1859 a violent clash captured the nation's attention. Abolitionist John Brown, leading an interracial band of 21 men, attacked the federal arsenal at Harpers Ferry, Virginia. Brown said he hoped to spark a slave rebellion that would end slavery and "purge this land with blood."

Although Brown and his men were captured within 36 hours, the revolt prompted intense public reaction. White southerners initially responded hysterically, fearing an outbreak of slave insurrections. The fear calmed as they realized that Brown had not, after all, managed to incite even one slave to join him in the Harpers Ferry revolt. Northern response was initially cool. However, Brown's eloquence during his trial swayed public opinion. Some northerners, including many free blacks, proclaimed Brown a hero.

By the time Brown was sentenced to hang, writer Ralph Waldo Emerson predicted that Brown would "make the gallows as glorious as the cross." The editor of a Kansas newspaper supported this prediction; he wrote, "The death of no man in America has ever produced so profound a sensation. A feeling of deep and sorrowful indignation seems to possess the masses." With northerners gripped by indignation and most white southerners gripped by fear or anger, the nation prepared for the presidential election of 1860.

## SECTION REVIEW

### Checking Facts

1. What were the economic differences between North and South that led to the Civil War?
2. What were some ways slaves coped with the conditions of slavery?
3. How did southern whites react to slave revolts?
4. How did the Kansas-Nebraska act nullify the Missouri Compromise?

### Thinking Critically

5. **Identifying Cause and Effect** High tariff laws protected northern industries. What was the effect of these laws on the South?
6. **Recognizing Assumptions** Northerners strongly opposed the Fugitive Slave Law enacted as part of the Compromise of 1850. Why do you think this was so? What assumptions did the law make about the North?

### Linking Across Time

7. Compare and contrast efforts of African Americans to resist slavery in the mid-1800s with civil rights protests in the 1960s.

# The Civil War

## April 2, 1865: Richmond, Virginia

On Sunday, April 2, 1865, Confederate President Jefferson Davis was praying in a Richmond, Virginia, church when a messenger rushed in. The Union Army had broken through Confederate lines and was advancing on the city. In response, General Lee had ordered his troops to pull out of Richmond. The city would have to be evacuated.

By midafternoon, troops, cavalry, and townspeople were clogging the roads in a frenzied attempt to escape the city. Then, as the sun set, bands of devoted Confederates set fire to their own city of Richmond to destroy any remaining goods and shelter that might be of benefit to the Union soldiers.

On April 4, just 40 hours after Davis had left Richmond, President Lincoln entered the smoldering city. As Lincoln walked the streets of the fallen Confederate capital, freed slaves waved, shouted thanks and praise, and even reached out to touch him. One woman shouted, "I know I am free, for I have seen Father Abraham and felt him."

BOSTON ATHENAEUM

## The Start of the War

In 1860, after a hard-fought campaign, Abraham Lincoln was elected president of the United States. Of the four candidates who had battled for the presidency, Lincoln had obtained an overwhelming majority of electoral votes—but only 40 percent of the popular vote.

Southerners, well aware of Lincoln's pronorthern political views, reacted to his election by calling for **secession**, or formal withdrawal, from the Union. In December 1860 South Carolina became the first state to secede from the Union. By the following year, Mississippi, Florida, Alabama, Georgia, Louisiana, and Texas followed, declaring themselves a new nation, the Confederate States of America.

**The Fall of Fort Sumter** The Confederacy's first military objective was to obtain control of Fort Sumter, a Union military installation in the harbor of Charleston, South Carolina. A prominent Southerner warned against firing on this army stronghold, "You will wantonly strike a hornet's nest. Legions now quiet will swarm out and sting us to death." Nevertheless, on April 12, 1861, the Confederate army began shelling Fort Sumter until its commander surrendered.

Proclaiming an insurrection in the South, Lincoln called for 75,000 volunteers to suppress the rebellion. In response Virginia, Arkansas, North Carolina, and Tennessee left the Union to join the Confederacy. Headed by their newly elected president, Jefferson Davis, the Confederates prepared for a war of independence, likening their status to that of the American revolutionaries in 1776.

**The Union and the Confederacy Compared** The Union could draw its fighting force from a population of 22 million that included foreign-born immigrants, free African Americans, and escaped slaves.

---

### STUDY GUIDE

**As You Read**
Assess the preparedness of the North and South and identify the effects of the Civil War upon the nation. Also, think about the following concepts and skills.

**Central Concepts**
- recognizing the political and military implications of **secession**
- identifying the effects of the **Emancipation Proclamation** on blacks and on the South

**Thinking Skills**
- assessing outcomes
- recognizing bias
- analyzing decisions

With this size population, the North was able to raise a much larger army than the South. The eleven Confederate states had a population of only nine million, nearly three million of whom the Confederacy refused to let fight because they were slaves.

What the South lacked in numbers, it made up for in military skill and experience. The Confederacy could draw from a talented pool of military minds that included many officers from West Point and veterans of the Mexican American War. It was a seasoned West Point general, Robert E. Lee of Virginia, who assumed command of the Confederate army. Also, many white southerners were members of local militia units and were skilled marksmen.

This superior military training might have given the South a clear advantage over the North were it not for the fact that almost all resources for waging war—steel mills and iron mines, important industries, and transportation facilities—were located in the North. Over 70 percent of the nation's railroads ran through the North. Most naval facilities and ships were in the North as well. By comparison, the Confederacy possessed inferior natural resources, industry, and transportation. Furthermore, the South lacked the financial resources to manufacture or acquire these necessities of war.

The South tried to make up for its disadvantages by fighting a defensive war. Southerners fortified their cities and waited for the Union to invade. If the Union forces invaded, Confederate strategists reasoned that southerners would at least be fighting on familiar terrain, amid supporters, and close to supplies.

**African American Soldiers**   Early in the war, northern blacks eagerly tried to enlist in the Union Army in order to join the fight to end slavery, but they were not accepted. Outraged by the army's refusal, Frederick Douglass wrote: "Why does the Government reject the negro? Is he not a man? Can he not wield a sword, fire a gun, march and . . . obey orders like any other?"

In 1863, desperately needing more soldiers, Lincoln announced his decision to use black troops. By the end of the war, about 180,000 African Americans served in the Union Army. Black units took part in more than 500 engagements. During the Mississippi valley

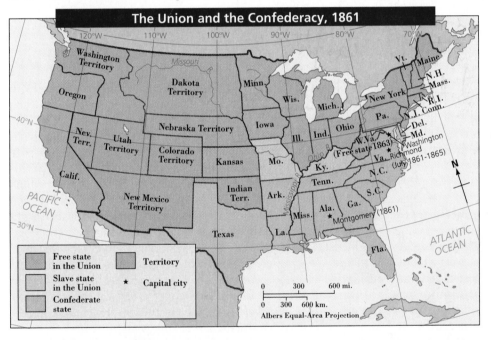

**The Union and the Confederacy, 1861**

**The map on the left shows the opposing sides in the Civil War.** *Which states left the Union and decided to join the Confederacy? Which slave states remained in the Union?*

**In the chart below compare the resources of the North and the South at the start of the Civil War.** *What resources are most valuable during wartime?*

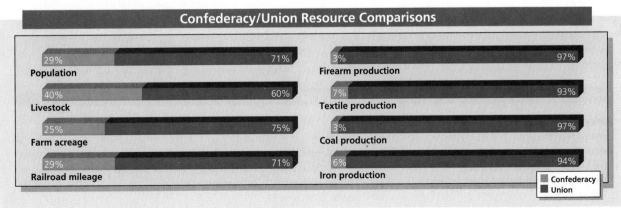

**Confederacy/Union Resource Comparisons**

| | Confederacy | Union |
|---|---|---|
| Population | 29% | 71% |
| Livestock | 40% | 60% |
| Farm acreage | 25% | 75% |
| Railroad mileage | 29% | 71% |
| Firearm production | 3% | 97% |
| Textile production | 7% | 93% |
| Coal production | 3% | 97% |
| Iron production | 6% | 94% |

**Photography captured the gruesome results of war. The photo above, taken by Timothy O'Sullivan in 1863, is titled "Harvest of Death." Photography also enabled a Confederate solder to carry into battle the framed portrait of a loved one, shown on the right.** *How might photos such as the one above have affected Americans' view of the war?*

campaign, one observer wrote: "The self-forgetfulness, the undaunted heroism, and the great endurance of the negro . . . created a new chapter in American history." In spite of the Confederate threat to shoot black soldiers on capture, 23 African Americans won the Medal of Honor.

## Major Military Battles

Neither the Union nor the Confederacy imagined that the war would last as long as it did, or that it would exact such a terrible cost in lives and property throughout the nation. During four years of war, hundreds of thousands of Americans were killed in battle, and property damage was enormous.

**The First Battle of Bull Run** On July 21, 1861, the first battle of the Civil War was fought in Virginia, about twenty miles southwest of Washington, D.C. Northern civilians, believing that they would be able to

witness the easy defeat of the Confederates, came out to picnic and watch the battle. The battle, however, didn't end as the North had expected.

Even though Confederate soldiers were outnumbered more than two to one, they managed to hold their ground until reinforcements arrived. The Confederates then counterattacked, letting out bloodcurdling cries—"rebel yells"—that terrified and confused Union troops. Hastily retreating Union soldiers rushed right into the crowds of spectators. According to one witness:

*Cruel, crazy, mad, hopeless panic possessed them, and communicated to everybody about in front and rear. The heat was awful, although now about six; the men were exhausted—their mouths gaped, their lips cracked and blackened with the powder of the cartridges they had bitten off in the battle, their eyes starting in frenzy; no mortal ever saw such a mass of ghastly wretches.*

Congressman Albert Riddle

## STUDY GUIDE

### Recognizing Bias

During the war about 180,000 African Americans served with heroism in the Union forces. Although they often served at greater risk than their fellow white soldiers, they faced frequent discrimination within the army. For example, African American soldiers received a salary of only $10 a month compared to the white soldier's $13. Black soldiers rarely rose above the rank of captain. Their all-black units were usually led by white officers.

The defeat meant more than losing one battle. It was a psychological setback from which the Union did not quickly recover.

## The Battles of Shiloh and Antietam

On April 6 and 7, 1862, the Union and Confederate armies clashed in the first of several massive battles at Shiloh, Tennessee. After the Battle of Shiloh, Americans realized that this conflict was not going to be a gentlemen's war; rather, it would be the wholesale slaughter of ill-fated men and boys. In just these two days of fighting at Shiloh, over 20,000 Union and Confederate soldiers were killed or wounded—8,000 more than in several previous battles combined.

Another violent clash occurred at Antietam Creek on September 17, 1862, when General Lee marched his Confederate troops northward into Maryland. In the ensuing battle, which eventually stopped Lee's advance north, 30,000 soldiers died. The air, one army surgeon commented, was "vocal with the whistle of bullets and scream of shells." A Confederate officer said a nearby cornfield "looked as if it had been struck down by a storm of bloody hail." The Union's victory was of strategic importance because it made Britain reluctant to respond to the South's request for aid.

## The Battles of Gettysburg and Vicksburg

In 1863 Confederate General Lee tried once again to invade the North. Union troops met his advance, and during the first three days of July the two armies battled outside the town of Gettysburg, Pennsylvania. The Union suffered heavy losses on the first day of battle at Seminary Ridge. A gunner recalled "bullets hissing, humming and whistling everywhere; cannon roaring; all crash on crash and peal on peal."

On the third day, Lee ordered General George Pickett to lead 13,000 men in an assault on Union lines. Nearly half the advancing Confederates were gunned down. By the time the Confederates retreated from Gettysburg, they had sustained 28,000 casualties; the Union had sustained 23,000. As wagons carried the Confederate wounded southward, a Quaker nurse wrote, "There are no words in the English language to express the suffering I witnessed today."

Far west of Gettysburg, meanwhile, Union and Confederate forces battled to control the Mississippi River. Union troops occupied New Orleans, Baton Rouge, Natchez, and Memphis. Finally all that remained in Confederate hands was Vicksburg, located on bluffs high above the

**Major Battles of the Civil War**

Legend:
- Union state
- Confederate state
- Union campaign
- Confederate campaign
- Union victory
- Confederate victory
- Union blockade
- Capital city

0 125 250 mi.
0 125 250 km
Albers Equal-Area Projection

**Using the map, follow the war strategies of the Union and the Confederacy on land and on sea.** *How does the location of most of the battles reflect the Confederates' plan to fight a defensive war? Where did the Union army attack along water routes? Why would the Union forces want to gain control of the Mississippi River?*

river. In mid-May 1863, Union General Ulysses S. Grant ordered a siege of the city. On July 4, the same day Lee began his retreat from Gettysburg, Confederate forces in Vicksburg surrendered. As news of the two strategic victories spread throughout the Union, there were, according to Carl Sandburg, "celebrations with torchlight processions, songs, jubilation, refreshments."

**The War at Sea**   While armies battled their way across the land, another aspect of the war took place in coastal waters and on inland rivers. At the outset of the war, Lincoln had ordered a blockade of all southern ports. The Union Navy's assorted collection of ships patrolled the 3,500 miles of Confederate coastline and eventually cut off southern trade. The daring blockade runners that managed to escape capture could not carry enough goods to supply the South. The greatest blow to Confederate trade came in April 1862 when Commodore David Farragut sailed a fleet into the mouth of the Mississippi River. He steamed past the forts below New Orleans and went on to capture the South's largest city.

The Confederates almost succeeded in breaking the blockade at Chesapeake Bay. Southerners raised the frigate *Merrimack,* scuttled by Union forces when they abandoned the Norfolk navy yard, and converted it into an ironclad warship. In March 1862 the *Merrimack,* renamed the *Virginia,* battled the Union's ironclad *Monitor* for five hours. Neither ship could sink the other, but the battle marked the beginning of a new era in naval warfare.

According to this Union poster, soldiers could avoid the draft by enlisting in the cavalry.

## Social and Economic Battles

The battles of 1863 turned the tide militarily for the Union, but northerners still experienced difficulties on the home front. Social and economic difficulties plagued both sides.

**Emancipation**   Throughout the war, abolitionists pressured President Lincoln to emancipate, or free, enslaved African Americans. Abolitionists argued that Union soldiers were fighting not only to preserve the Union but also to end slavery. They also pointed out that emancipating the slaves would create a new pool of recruits that could be drafted to fight for the North. Further, backers of emancipation reasoned that the Fugitive Slave Law no longer applied to southerners, who after their secession from the Union could no longer claim to be protected by the Union's laws. By this reasoning, the North was finally rid of its obligation to return escaped slaves, and Union troops could confiscate southern property and slaves as spoils of war.

At first, Lincoln evaded the issue of emancipation, fearing it would drive Maryland, Missouri, and Kentucky out of the Union. However, on September 22, 1862, under extreme pressure from Republican senators to declare his position on slavery, Lincoln signed a preliminary version of the **Emancipation Proclamation,** which declared freedom for slaves only in parts of the Confederacy not under the control of the Union army. The proclamation had no effect on enslaved African Americans in the border states that had not joined the Confederacy.

Although this proclamation freed some enslaved African Americans, it did not necessarily express Lincoln's personal views on the subject. Just a few months earlier, Lincoln made his position known in a letter to the abolitionist Horace Greeley.

CHICAGO HISTORICAL SOCIETY

---

### STUDY GUIDE

**Assessing Outcomes**

Throughout the war, a Union naval blockade tried to keep the southerners from receiving supplies from Europe. While the Union Navy stopped only five out of six ships, many ships headed for southern ports lost parts of their cargo as they tried to speed through the blockade. Also, many more ships would have tried to make supply runs if there had been no blockade. On the whole, the Union's blockade effort was more successful than not.

*My paramount object in this struggle is to save the Union, and is not either to save or destroy Slavery. If I could save the Union without freeing any slave, I would do it; and if I could save it by freeing all the slaves, I would do it; and if I could do it by freeing some and leaving others alone, I would also do that. What I do about Slavery and the colored race, I do because it helps to save this Union; and what I forbear, I forbear because I do not believe it would help to save the Union.*

Abraham Lincoln,
from a letter to Horace Greeley, 1862

**Riots** As the bloody battles dragged on, both the North and the South experienced difficulties recruiting soldiers as well as raising money needed to keep up the fight. The Union draft law of March 1863 excused men from military service if they paid the government a $300 fee. Many northerners who thought the law discriminated against the poor angrily took to the streets in protest.

The most violent draft riots erupted in New York City on July 13, in the wake of Union victories at Gettysburg and Vicksburg. There the draft riots had racial overtones as low-paid workers blamed African Americans for the war. Rioters set fire to an orphanage for black children and began lynching African Americans.

Resentment over the draft was also prevalent in the South. But there, homelessness and hunger overshadowed the draft

**Mary Rice Livermore, pictured right, worked throughout the Civil War in support of the Union cause. She organized women's aid societies such as the group pictured on the right. The societies raised money and sent food and clothing to Union soldiers on the battlefield.**

issue. Women, being the majority of those left at home to confront these issues, eventually took matters into their own hands. In 1863 riots broke out in which women looted stores, hijacked trains, and attacked Confederate supply depots to get bread and other food stored there.

**New Roles** As the war dragged on, northern and southern women had to assume many of the roles previously assigned to the men who had gone away to fight. The two armies needed food, clothing, and weapons. Women took responsibility for supplying many of these goods. In addition, many women needed jobs to help support their families. So across the country, women managed their family farms, worked in factories, ran printing presses, shod horses, and also filled government positions. A handful of women even disguised themselves as men and fought in the war.[1]

One of the many significant contributions women made to the war effort was to care for the wounded. Three thousand women served as nurses during the war. Nurses were in great demand to tend the wounded, since twice as many soldiers died of infectious diseases as died of combat. Doctors did not yet understand the importance of sanitation, sterile

CHICAGO HISTORICAL SOCIETY

---

**Analyzing Decisions**

Lincoln's main goal was to preserve the Union, and yet he signed the Emancipation Proclamation, which further alienated the South. Why did he take this step? Lincoln was under intense pressure from Northern legislators and abolitionists to sign. Also, Lincoln realized that North and South could never be united as long as slavery existed.

**1** How did women's everyday responsibilities during the war differ from their everyday responsibilities in peaceful times?

medical equipment, and a balanced diet. As a result, deaths from dysentery, malaria, and typhoid were a byproduct of war.

## The Road to Surrender

Until 1864 Lincoln had been disappointed with the quality of his military commanders. Only General Ulysses S. Grant had performed close to Lincoln's expectations. In March, the president appointed Grant commander of all Union forces.

One of Grant's first official actions was to order Generals William Tecumseh Sherman and Philip Henry Sheridan to pursue a **scorched earth policy** in the South. On Grant's instruction, Sherman's and Sheridan's troops burned farmland, plantation homes, and cities. In so doing, they destroyed the enemy's food, shelter, and supplies and broke the South's will to fight. Sheridan raided the Shenandoah Valley, one of the Confederacy's main sources of food, to starve Lee's hungry troops. Sherman led 60,000 men on a "March to the Sea" from Atlanta to Savannah. On the way they burned homesteads and fields, sacked storehouses, and ripped up and twisted railroad tracks to render them useless. Consequently, Savannah fell to Sherman in December 1864.

Meanwhile, Grant battled Lee in Virginia, hoping eventually to take the Confederate capital of Richmond. Union and Confederate forces clashed in three major battles: in the Virginia wilderness and at Spotsylvania in May, and at Cold Harbor in early June. In three battles, Grant lost almost as many Union soldiers as there were Confederates serving in Lee's army. Yet because of the Union's population advantage, Grant could replace his soldiers, while Lee could not. Grant then settled down to a long siege of Richmond.

BROWN BROTHERS

**General Ulysses S. Grant, commander of all Union forces, exuded the confidence of a capable, aggressive soldier.**

By the fall of 1864, Lincoln called home as many Union troops as he could, hoping to generate support for his reelection. The Union victories in the South helped Lincoln win by an electoral vote of 212 to 21 and a popular majority of more than 400,000 votes.

**The War's End** Increasing desertions among Confederate troops prompted Jefferson Davis in November 1864 to allow enslaved African Americans to enlist. The Confederate Congress did not authorize the act, however, until it was too late to take effect. Still, Davis refused to surrender unless Lincoln acknowledged the South as an independent nation.

Grant and Sheridan finally took Richmond on April 3, 1865, as the city smoldered from the fires set by retreating Confederates. Union troops pursued Lee and his exhausted army. The Confederates made feeble attempts to hold them off, but Lee's army had been reduced to about 30,000 hungry and demoralized men. On the morning of April 9, Lee led his troops into battle for the last time. Union forces had them almost surrounded and badly outnumbered. Facing an almost certain slaughter, Lee decided to surrender. That afternoon he met Grant at Appomattox Court House, Virginia. Grant's terms of surrender ensured that Confederate soldiers would not be prosecuted for treason and that artillery and cavalry soldiers would be permitted to keep their horses. Grant also arranged for three days' rations to be sent to the Confederate soldiers. Lee accepted.

When Union troops heard of the surrender, they began firing their guns to celebrate their victory. Grant put an end to the firing. "The war is over," he said, "the rebels are our countrymen again, and the best sign of rejoicing after the victory will be to abstain from all demonstrations."

Lee echoed these sentiments when he knew the Confederate army was defeated.

*T*he war being at an end, the southern states having laid down their arms, and the question at issue between them and the northern states having been decided, I believe it to be the duty of everyone to unite in the restoration of the country and the reestablishment of peace and harmony.

Robert E. Lee, April 1865

The human costs of the war were staggering. About 360,000 Union soldiers and 260,000 Confederates lay dead. Another 375,000 soldiers were wounded. About one in three Confederate soldiers died in the war. These figures do not include deaths from imprisonment such as at Andersonville, a prison camp operated by Confederates in Georgia, where 13,000 out of 32,000 Union prisoners died.

**Lincoln as Commander in Chief** Lincoln's main goal had been to preserve the Union. In his second inaugural address, he indicated that he would deal compassionately with the South after the war ended:

*W*ith malice toward none; with charity for all; with firmness in the right, as God gives us to see the right, let us strive on to finish the work we are in; to bind up the nation's wounds; to care for him who shall have borne the battle, and for his widow, and his orphan. . . .

Abraham Lincoln,
Second Inaugural Address, March 1865

Unfortunately, Lincoln never got to carry out his plan. On April 14, 1865, five days after the South surrendered, Confederate sympathizer John Wilkes Booth shot President Lincoln at a theater in Washington, D.C. Lincoln died the next morning. The nation, and indeed the world, mourned his death.

Even those who had been sharply critical of Lincoln's policies nevertheless acknowledged his leadership and accomplishments. The New Orleans *Tribune* stated: "Brethren, we are mourning for a benefactor of our race." An outpouring of sympathy came from Britain and others who had supported the Confederate cause. Admirers as well as critics agreed that replacing Lincoln would be difficult.

A funeral train carried Lincoln's body on a 1,700-mile journey from Washington, D.C., to Springfield, Illinois. Millions of people lined the route. At night, bonfires and torches lit the way. By day, bells tolled and cannons fired.

Lincoln's second inaugural address, read at the cemetery, reminded Americans of his plan "to do all which may achieve and cherish a just, and a lasting peace, among ourselves, and with all nations." The future, however, was in the hands of those who favored harsher measures against the former Confederates.

LINCOLN MUSEUM

**The photograph at the top shows President Lincoln before the war. The portrait at the bottom, taken in 1865, shows the toll that the war took on Lincoln's health and appearance.**

CHICAGO HISTORICAL SOCIETY

## SECTION REVIEW

### Checking Facts

1. What advantages did the North have upon entering the war? The South?
2. How did the battles of Shiloh and Antietam change expectations about the war?
3. What were the social and economic battles fought during the Civil War?
4. What was the purpose of Grant's scorched earth policy?

### Thinking Critically

5. **Making Inferences** Why was it important to the Confederate Army that many Southerners personally owned horses and guns?
6. **Assessing Outcomes** Union soldiers at Bull Run had almost completed their three-month term of enlistment. How might this condition have contributed to the Union defeat there?

7. **Analyzing Decisions** From what you've learned about Lincoln, why do you think he initiated a postwar policy of leniency toward the South?

### Linking Across Time

8. Lincoln is remembered today as a hero for his role in liberating the slaves. Did his actions bring genuine freedom to African Americans? Why or why not?

# Combining Information From Maps

Thematic maps aid communication by presenting place-related information in a concise way. Often information can be shown more clearly on a map than in written text. A glance at the map on abolition, for example, gives you an immediate sense of the changes that took place between 1770 and 1865.

## Learning the Skill

Sometimes two or more thematic maps are shown together in order to convey information that cannot be presented easily on a single map.

Showing maps together indicates that there may be a relationship between the information presented on them. Maps may be put together to show different information about an area—for example, the population and economy of the Northeast. Or they may show changes over time, such as the boundaries of the United States in 1789, 1850, and 1960.

The two maps on these pages are about two different subjects—the abolition of slavery, and industry and agriculture in 1860. Combining these maps suggests that whether or not a state chose to abolish slavery may have been related to how people in the state made a living.

Try to visualize possible relationships between the maps on these pages. The first map shows that only three of the original thirteen states abolished slavery before the writing of the Constitution (Maine was then part of Massachusetts). The second map

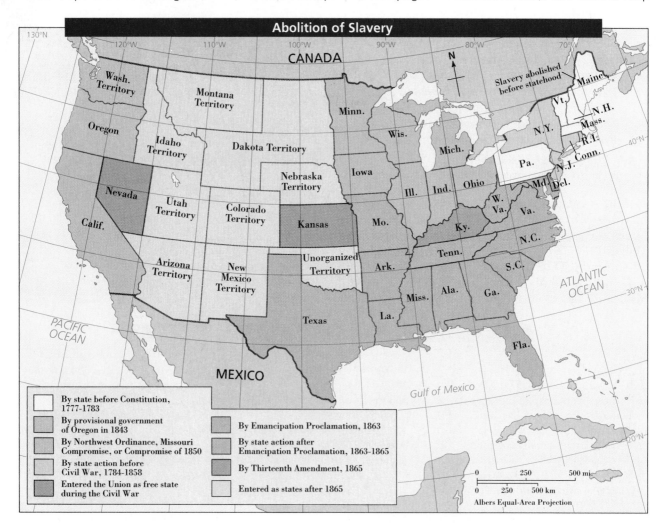

**Abolition of Slavery**

Legend:
- By state before Constitution, 1777-1783
- By provisional government of Oregon in 1843
- By Northwest Ordinance, Missouri Compromise, or Compromise of 1850
- By state action before Civil War, 1784-1858
- Entered the Union as free state during the Civil War
- By Emancipation Proclamation, 1863
- By state action after Emancipation Proclamation, 1863-1865
- By Thirteenth Amendment, 1865
- Entered as states after 1865

Albers Equal-Area Projection

shows that New England farmers mainly raised dairy cattle and grew hay on small family farms.

In this area, America's early textile mills were set up. By 1860 textile mills and shoe manufacturers provided jobs for the children of New England farmers.

Many states in the South had an economy that depended on growing large crops of cotton and tobacco on plantations. What do the maps on these pages tell you about the relationship between plantation crops and the abolition of slavery?

## Practicing the Skill

1. Use the maps on these pages to compare industry in cotton-growing states to industry in other states. What connection can you make between a state's economy and its abolition of slavery?
2. Compare the three maps on page 90. How are they similar? Which symbols do you find in all three? What category that is not on the first map indicates that a major change occurred in the status

of slavery beginning in 1850?
3. How does combining information from the abolition map on page 100 with the Union and Confederacy map on page 93 illustrate why slavery was not abolished in Missouri, Kentucky, Delaware, or Maryland by the Emancipation Proclamation?
4. Compare the maps on pages 93 and 95. Which Civil War battles took place in free states of the Union? In slave states of the Union? In Confederate states?

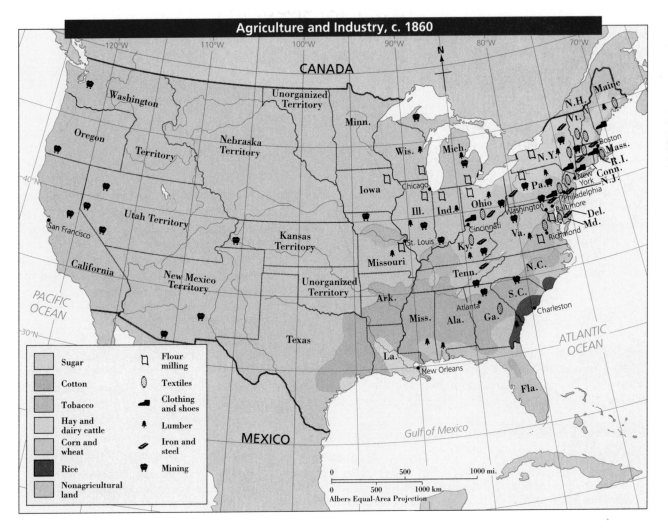

Agriculture and Industry, c. 1860

# Reconstruction

## February 24, 1879: Banks of the Mississippi River

HUNDREDS OF AFRICAN AMERICANS, WITH THEIR BELONGINGS BUNDLED ON THEIR BACKS, WAITED ON THE SHORES OF THE MISSISSIPPI RIVER for the steamer that would carry them across to St. Louis. From there they would head by train to Kansas, where they hoped to begin new lives. These people were called the Exodusters, so named because they left their homes to make better lives in the dusty new land, just as the Israelites had done centuries earlier in their exodus from Egypt to Canaan.

During the exodus of 1879, over 20,000 African Americans migrated to Kansas, their Canaan, or "promised land." A Louisiana preacher explained that they "were not emigrating because of inducements held out to them by parties in Kansas, but because they were terrorized, robbed, and murdered by the bulldozing desperadoes of Louisiana and Mississippi." In fact, the African Americans hoped that their journey to Kansas would take them far from the poverty and terrorism that they experienced in the South despite the many promises of the postwar government.

**Ho for Kansas!**

Brethren, Friends, & Fellow Citizens:
I feel thankful to inform you that the
**REAL ESTATE**
AND
Homestead Association,
Will Leave Here the
**15th of April, 1878,**
In pursuit of Homes in the Southwestern
Lands of America, at Transportation
Rates, cheaper than ever
was known before.
For full information inquire of
Benj. Singleton, better known as old Pap,
NO. 5 NORTH FRONT STREET.
Beware of Speculators and Adventurers, as it is a dangerous thing
to fall in their hands.
Nashville, Tenn., March 18, 1878.

KANSAS STATE HISTORICAL SOCIETY

as legitimate, 10 percent of the men eligible to vote in 1860 had to have sworn allegiance to the Union.

Andrew Johnson, who assumed the presidency after Lincoln's assassination, had expressed harsh sentiments toward Confederate "traitors" during the war. He therefore surprised many northerners when he began to promote policies that seemed to continue Lincoln's intentions of "malice toward none." Congress was not in session when Johnson took office, so he proceeded with his plans for **Reconstruction**—the process of restoring relations with the Confederate states.

In a Reconstruction Proclamation issued in May 1865, Johnson granted **amnesty,** or pardon, to Confederates who would sign an oath of loyalty to the Union. Political and military leaders and landowners whose property was worth more than $20,000 had to apply for special pardons. Johnson granted such pardons regularly. In addition, Johnson appointed provisional governors and set forth minimal requirements for reorganizing southern state governments. By December 1865 all ex-Confederate states except Texas had fulfilled the requirements and had elected representatives to Congress. Johnson announced that the Union had been restored.

When Congress reconvened in December, it refused to seat the newly elected southern representatives. Some members of Congress criticized Johnson's leniency toward the South. They pointed out that Johnson had done nothing

## Presidential Plans

In 1863 before the war had ended, Lincoln made plans to reestablish state governments in the South that would be loyal to the Union after the war. According to Lincoln's plan, for a state to be recognized

---

**STUDY GUIDE**

**As You Read**
Identify Radical Republican goals and analyze the effects of Reconstruction on freed slaves in the South. Also, think about the following concepts and skills.

**Central Concepts**
- analyzing the effects of **Reconstruction** on blacks and on the South
- understanding the effects of **sharecropping**

**Thinking Skills**
- recognizing points of view
- predicting consequences
- identifying cause and effect
- forming hypotheses
- recognizing stereotypes

to prevent new southern state governments from passing **black codes,** laws that severely restricted the rights of newly freed African Americans. In Mississippi, for example, black codes prohibited free blacks from receiving farmland and stipulated that orphaned black children could be assigned to forced labor. Throughout 1866 and 1867, tensions increased as the president and Congress battled over Reconstruction.

**Military Occupation**   In 1867 Congress passed a series of Reconstruction Acts over Johnson's veto. These acts abolished the state governments formed under Johnson's plan. They also divided the South into five military districts, each under the command of a general. Federal troops were stationed in each district to carry out the process of readmitting states to the Union. The functions of the military forces, according to the acts, were "to protect all persons in their rights of person and property, to suppress insurrection, disorder, and violence, and to punish, or cause to be punished, all disturbers of the public peace and criminals."

The provision for military occupation of the southern states changed the tone of Reconstruction. Leadership was in the hands of Congress, and the Army administered Congress's plan. Many northerners felt that the presence of federal troops was necessary to bring about political and social changes in the South. General Sherman, however, was more astute and expressed a different view: "No matter what change we may desire in the feelings and thoughts of people South, we cannot accomplish it by force. Nor can we afford to maintain there an army large enough to hold them in subjugation [control]."

**The Supreme Court's Role**   In the battle between the executive and legislative branches over Reconstruction, the Supreme Court at first seemed to support President Johnson's position. In *ex parte*

*Milligan,* the Court ruled that civilians could not be tried in military courts when civil courts were functioning. Northerners defied this decision, however, and made military tribunals part of legislation. The Court further stated that the administration of military justice in the South was "mere lawless violence." In *ex parte Garland,* a case that involved a law requiring loyalty oaths from ex-Confederate teachers and others who wanted to resume their jobs, the Court handed down a split decision. The majority opinion ruled that such oaths were invalid. The dissenting opinion held that such requirements were valid qualifications for officeholders and voters.

The Court soon upheld Congress's authority to reconstruct the states. In 1867 Georgia and Missouri sought an injunction preventing President Johnson from enforcing Congress's Reconstruction Acts. The Supreme Court refused on the grounds that executive functions were not subject to judicial restraint. Johnson, who had relied on the Court's record of sympathy toward the South, began to feel increasingly isolated.

HISTORICAL PICTURES/STOCK MONTAGE, INC.

**Richmond women are shown snubbing a Union soldier in this photograph. On their way to receive U.S. government rations, these women exhibited the attitude of many southerners to the northern military occupation.**

STUDY GUIDE

**Recognizing Points of View**
President Johnson and Congress had very different points of view about Reconstruction. Johnson favored generous and kind treatment of the people of the Confederacy, whereas Congress wanted to punish the South severely. Johnson believed that the general population of the South had been led into rebellion by wealthy, powerful plantation owners. He also believed that the federal government had no right to pass laws regarding black suffrage when the South was not represented.

# Congressional Plans

The Radical Republican faction of Congress had been formulating plans for Reconstruction since the early 1860s. These Republicans earned the label "radical" because they were strongly antislavery and were not willing to forgive the Confederates. They had been outraged by Lincoln's leniency. They wanted sweeping political change in the South, which they believed would occur only with the strong presence of Union troops. As Thaddeus Stevens, a leading Radical Republican, said, any valid unifying plan "must revolutionize the southern institutions, habits, and manner . . . or all our blood and treasure have been spent in vain."

The Radical Republicans had responded to Lincoln's terms by passing the Wade-Davis bill in 1864. This bill would have required a majority of a state's white male citizenry to swear both past and future loyalty to the Union; only then could the state's government be recognized by the federal government. Considering the bill too harsh, Lincoln vetoed it.

Johnson further outraged the Radical Republicans by promoting Lincoln's lenient policies. In 1866 northerners fought Johnson's policies by electing a Radical Republican majority to Congress. The Radical Republicans quickly enacted legislation designed to punish the former Confederate states, to increase Republican power in the South, and to create conditions that would promote economic development and racial equality in the South.

Much of the legislation passed during Reconstruction increased the rights and freedoms of African Americans. This benefited the Republicans in two ways: it made the Republicans popular with a large new pool of voters, and it diminished white southerners' ability to dominate the South politically and economically. In 1866 Congress passed a Civil Rights Act that granted citizenship to African Americans and prohibited states from diminishing the rights accompanying this citizenship. In addition, ratification of the Fourteenth Amendment in 1868 prevented states from denying rights and privileges to any U.S. citizen. The Fifteenth Amendment of 1870 guaranteed that no citizen could be denied the right to vote based on race, color, or former servitude. The Enforcement Act of 1870 empowered federal authorities to prosecute anyone who violated the Fourteenth or Fifteenth amendments.[1]

**Radical Reconstruction** New state governments were established under the Reconstruction acts. White southerners who protested the acts refused to vote in the elections that set up these governments. Their protest had two results: Republicans, who had little support in the South before the Civil War, won control of every new state government; and African Americans began to exert influence at the polls. One white southerner wrote in his diary:

| Reconstruction Legislation | | |
|---|---|---|
| Year | Law | Provisions |
| 1865 | Thirteenth Amendment | Prohibits slavery in the United States |
| 1866 | Civil Rights Act | Gives citizenship to blacks and guarantees them equal protection of the law |
| 1868 | Fourteenth Amendment | Prevents states from denying rights and privileges to any U.S. citizen |
| 1870 | Fifteenth Amendment | Gives the right to vote to all citizens regardless of their color, race, or condition of former servitude |
| 1870 | Enforcement Act | Empowers federal authorities to prosecute for violations of 14th and 15th amendments |

**Review this chart of the legislation passed during the Reconstruction era.** *Which amendment secured African Americans' right to vote? Why do you think it was necessary to pass the Enforcement Act of 1870?*

> *B*ills have passed both houses of Congress which repudiate and destroy the present civil government of the lately seceded states and substitute in their place a military government. Most of the whites are disenfranchised [deprived of the right to vote] and ineligible for office, whilst the negroes are invested with the right of voting.

Henry William Ravenel
South Carolina, February 24, 1867

---

STUDY GUIDE

**Recognizing Points of View**

Thaddeus Stevens, Radical Republican leader in Congress, expressed this opinion in 1867: ". . . among other reasons, I am for Negro suffrage in every rebel state. If it be just, it should not be denied; if it be necessary, it should be adopted; if it be punishment to traitors, they deserve it."

**1** How did African Americans benefit from the legislation that passed from 1866 through 1870 during Reconstruction?

When African Americans were guaranteed their right to vote, they began to exert influence at the polls in states in which they were a majority of the population: Alabama, Florida, Louisiana, Mississippi, and South Carolina. African American representatives outnumbered white representatives in the South Carolina legislature.

**The Impeachment Effort**   Radical Republicans pushed their legislation through Congress in spite of President Johnson's vetoes. For example, in 1866 Johnson vetoed a bill that would have enabled the Freedmen's Bureau, an organization that assisted former slaves, to continue. He also vetoed the Civil Rights Act of 1866. Congress overrode both vetoes.

At about the same time that Johnson was undermining African Americans' efforts to obtain equality, white supremacist organizations such as the Ku Klux Klan began terrorizing blacks. These organizations used intimidation and violence to prevent African Americans from voting and from holding positions of power. In this environment of violence and hatred, mobs of southern whites periodically lashed out against blacks. For example, in May 1866 in Memphis, Tennessee, a crowd of whites killed 46 blacks and two white sympathizers, and raped five African American women.

Johnson's attempts to undermine congressional legislation coupled with his inability or lack of desire to control the terrorist organizations further angered Radical Republicans. Their anger peaked when the president defied the Tenure of Office Act, which required Senate approval for the removal of cabinet members. Johnson failed to obtain that approval before he fired Secretary of War Edwin Stanton in 1868.

The House responded by voting to impeach the president on eleven charges of misconduct. These included charges that Johnson had violated the Tenure of Office Act. The House appointed seven representatives to present the charges to the Senate. Johnson was defended by a team of lawyers. Chief Justice Salmon P. Chase presided over the trial. Johnson did not attend.

The trial dragged on for eight weeks. Johnson's attackers accused him of everything from alcoholism to plotting Lincoln's murder. But the president's lawyers presented a purely legal defense, arguing that the Tenure of Office Act was unconstitutional and did not

HISTORICAL PICTURES/STOCK MONTAGE, INC.

**Thaddeus Stevens, a Radical Republican leader in Congress, wanted African Americans to receive full rights as citizens.**

apply to Stanton. Conviction required a two-thirds majority of the Senate. The final tally of 35 for conviction and 19 against acquitted Johnson by one vote.

## Limits on Freedom

At the end of the Civil War, most African Americans expected their lives to improve radically. A former slave recalled the excitement she and other freed slaves had felt when they learned of the Union victory and their new freedom:

*When the soldiers marched in to tell us that we were free . . . I remember one woman. She jumped on a barrel and she shouted. She jumped off and she shouted. She jumped back on again and shouted some more. She kept that up for a long time, just jumping on a barrel and back off again.*

Anna Woods, *from a* Federal Writers' Project *interview, 1930s*

THE GRANGER COLLECTION

**This lithograph shows the first African Americans who served in the U.S. Congress. Top row, left to right: Rep. Robert C. De Large of South Carolina, Rep. Jefferson H. Long of Georgia. Bottom row, left to right: Senator H. R. Revels of Mississippi, Rep. Benjamin Turner of Alabama, Rep Josiah T. Walls of Florida, Rep. Joseph H. Rainy and Rep. R. Brown Elliot, both of South Carolina.**

Many white southerners resented African American schools, and teachers often faced intimidation or physical abuse. Progress was slow. Nevertheless, illiteracy among African Americans fell from more than 90 percent in 1860 to about 80 percent in 1870.

**Voting Power** During Reconstruction, African American voters exercised their political power for the first time. W. E. B. DuBois, an important black leader of the early 1900s, wrote that "With northern white leadership, the Negro voters . . . proved apt pupils in politics. They developed their own leadership. They gained clearer and clearer conceptions of how their political powers could be used for their own good."

After the initial happiness passed, however, African Americans realized that they would have to struggle to secure their rights as a freed people. Blacks at an 1865 convention in Alabama demanded "exactly the same rights, privileges, and immunities as are enjoyed by white men—we ask nothing more and will be content with nothing less. . . ."

Blacks were aided in their efforts by the Freedmen's Bureau, an office of the War Department established to provide ex-slaves with food, teachers, legal aid, and other assistance. The Bureau also distributed horses, mules, and land that had been confiscated during the war. With the Bureau's help, about 40,000 African Americans were able to establish their own farms in Georgia and South Carolina.[2]

In the face of much opposition, African Americans obtained an education. At first, the Freedmen's Bureau and charitable organizations paid the cost of African American education. After 1871 the states began to take over the support of both black and white schools.

African Americans were elected to office at the local, state, and national levels. Between 1869 and 1876, two African Americans served in the Senate and fourteen served in the House of Representatives. Most of these men were ex-slaves or born of enslaved parents. Some critics claimed that "they left no mark on the legislation of their time; none of them, in comparison with their white associates, attained the least distinction." Others observed that "The colored men who took seats in both Senate and House did not appear ignorant or helpless. They were as a rule studious, earnest, ambitious men, whose public conduct . . . would be honorable to any race."

**Sharecropping** For many ex-slaves, life changed little in the years after the Civil War. President Johnson returned confiscated estates to the previous Confederate owners. Former slaves who had established farms on that land found themselves back on the plantations. Some worked under contract for meager wages. Others were forced into **sharecropping**, a

---

system in which a wealthy patron would give seeds, supplies, and a small parcel of land to a farmer in exchange for a portion of the person's crop. If the patron required a large portion of the crop, the sharecropper might not be able to survive on what remained. If the crop failed, the sharecropper usually wound up hopelessly in debt to the patron.

"Freedom wasn't no difference I know of," complained one former slave. "I works for Marse John just the same." Many former slaves did stay on the same plantations where they worked under the same overseer. The wage or share of the crop they received hardly made up for the fact that freedom in no way meant equality.

BROWN BROTHERS

COOK COLLECTION, VALENTINE MUSEUM

**Educating African Americans was one of the primary goals of the Freedmen's Bureau. The Bureau was led by O. O. Howard, pictured above, a former Union commander. The children are students at one of many Freedmen's schools in the South.**

## Grant's Presidency

In 1868 the Republican Ulysses S. Grant won the presidency by a margin of 300,000 votes. The more than 500,000 blacks who voted in the election certainly contributed to Grant's victory. Nevertheless, during Grant's two terms in office, from 1869 to 1877, the government began paying less and less attention to the plight of African Americans.

**Government Scandal**  Grant's administration was plagued by scandal and corruption. A Congressional investigation in the mid-1870s found that whiskey distillers and tax officials were stealing excise taxes from the government, and linked a member of Grant's staff to the scandal. In addition, Grant's Secretary of War, William W. Belknap, was accused of accepting bribes. Even Grant wrongly accepted personal gifts.

At the time, successful politicians commonly rewarded their supporters by appointing them to government positions. These appointed individuals often lacked the skills and experience necessary to do their jobs. Quite often they were also greedy and dishonest. This was true of a number of the personal friends, relatives, and fellow army officers Grant appointed.

Such was also the case in the newly created Republican state governments in the South. Although these governments did manage to implement legislation that helped to ease the South's social and economic difficulties, many of the northerners

STUDY GUIDE

**Forming Hypotheses**
Forming hypotheses forces you to state tentative conclusions in a way that can be tested as more evidence is obtained. In the 1870s, the Supreme Court and Congress reversed or reinterpreted much of the legislation that guaranteed the rights of African Americans. What hypothesis does this lead you to make about the durability of legislative reform? You can form the hypothesis that unless such legislation is accompanied by economic and political power, legislation often guarantees very little.

**Shown here is sheet music from a song written in 1869 about the adventures of a carpetbagger.** *How would the songs written about carpetbaggers by southern composers and northern composers differ?*

THE GRANGER COLLECTION

involved in the administrations were inexperienced and even corrupt. White southerners called these northerners **carpetbaggers,** mocking them for having arrived in the South with only the possessions they had been able to stuff inside their luggage. Most white southerners believed the carpetbaggers wanted only to turn a profit or rise to power at the expense of the South. In addition, African Americans newly elected to political positions were often blamed for government wastefulness and dishonesty.

**Democratic Success** As one after another of the carpetbag governments came under attack, Democrats began to regain control of southern legislatures. They also used some underhanded tactics to neutralize the influence blacks had begun to have in the election process. One such technique, called **gerrymandering**, involved redividing voting districts to decrease black representation in a particular area. Another tactic was to institute a poll tax, which the Democrats managed to do in several states. In these states, voting became a privilege that required payment of a fee. Poll taxes excluded poor blacks as well as poor whites from the voting process. By 1875, aided by these strategies, Democrats had gained control of the House of Representatives for the first time since before the Civil War. By 1877 they had completely reestablished control over southern state governments.

**The Panic of 1873** Grant's presidency was plagued with economic as well as political problems. A financial crisis during his second term in office left the country in economic difficulty. The crisis was touched off in 1873 when financier Jay Cooke suddenly closed his Philadelphia bank. The bank closing prompted a panic during which 5,000 businesses closed and thousands of people lost their jobs.

As the panic spread, concern for social reform was quickly replaced by concern for economic reform. In the North, the demands of white workers for economic relief supplanted the demands of blacks for equality. By 1874 one quarter of the population of New York City was out of work. In Chicago 20,000 unemployed people protested in the streets, demanding that government officials solve the problems of the economy.

In the South, the sharecropping system cheated many African American farmers out of landowning. White farmers, who suffered devastating losses during these economic hard times, accused free blacks of causing their economic troubles.

African Americans living in northern states also faced economic and social problems. Although they had gained access to public education and transportation, African Americans were usually trapped in low-paying, unskilled jobs. The black communities in the North lived in poor housing and had little voice in shaping government policies. Unlike the large African American population in the South, northern blacks comprised only 2 percent of the population. In both the North and the South, African Americans had to struggle to claim the political and social rights that Reconstruction promised.

In the midst of the economic and social upheaval of Reconstruction, however, America celebrated its Centennial in 1876. Ten million people paid 50 cents each to visit the Grand Exposition in Philadelphia. Displays of the nation's art, fashion, produce, appliances, and industrial development greeted the visitors. Many Americans were ready to push the problems of the Civil War into the past and forge on optimistically into the nation's second century.

## The End of Reconstruction

In the wake of social and economic crises, government scandals, and outbreaks of violence, the Radical Republicans lost their political power. So, too, the Radical Republican program of Reconstruction came to an end. No longer supported by the majority of voters, Republicans attempted to regain their foothold in the South by backing a moderate candidate for president, Rutherford B. Hayes, who appealed to both the North and South.

Hayes ran against Democratic candidate Samuel Tilden in what was possibly the closest presidential election battle in U.S. history. A dispute arose over the election returns from four states. Three of these states were southern states still under Reconstruction rule. The Democrats insisted that the majority of the people in these states favored Tilden but had been prevented from registering their votes. To settle the dispute, Congress appointed a special Electoral Commission.

To get Hayes elected, Republicans made many concessions to the Democrats, among which was the agreement to withdraw the Union troops that had been stationed in the South since the end of the war. These votes assured, Hayes won the election by one electoral vote. Shortly thereafter, the last Union troops withdrew from the South.

Without the presence of the Union army to combat terrorism, the rights of southern blacks were gravely jeopardized. Even before Hayes's election, blacks received even more bad news. The Supreme Court's 1876 ruling in *U.S. v. Cruikshank* overturned the Enforcement Act of 1870 and ruled that a state could not legally discriminate against African Americans, but nonstate institutions and individuals could. Specifically, the court had overturned the convictions of three whites for their participation in a bloody massacre of African Americans on the grounds that the three individuals did not specify that their actions were racially motivated. In subsequent administrations, the Supreme Court's support of African American rights diminished still further. For example, in 1883, during Chester A. Arthur's presidency, the Supreme Court nullified the Civil Rights Act of 1875.

Although the period of Reconstruction had ended and Republicans and Democrats had temporarily united, African Americans felt as if their needs had been forgotten. Most of the legal decisions that had advanced African American rights during Reconstruction had been overturned. Furthermore, the Radical Republican governments had failed to correct the problem of unequal land distribution in the South, a measure that might have given blacks the economic leverage they needed to protect their rights.

Discontented and afraid for their lives, African Americans left the South by the thousands. Many moved to northern urban centers, such as Chicago and New York. Some moved to Kansas, a state in which there was an abundance of fertile land open to homesteaders and a strong Republican government that promised to treat African Americans fairly. During the 1870s, more than 20,000 southern blacks made the exodus to Kansas. There, many began to enjoy a decent existence.

## SECTION REVIEW

### Checking Facts

1. What legislation passed during Reconstruction aided African Americans?
2. What tactics did white southern Democrats use to increase their influence in southern legislatures and regain political control?
3. What compromise was made to ensure that Hayes won the election of 1876?

### Thinking Critically

4. **Predicting Consequences** The Wade-Davis bill required that a majority of a state's white males swear past and future loyalty to the Union. What consequences might legislators have anticipated from this bill?
5. **Identifying Cause and Effect** Why do you think many northern politicians stopped concentrating their efforts on securing rights for blacks after Grant's election?
6. **Identifying Cause and Effect** What was the overall effect of Reconstruction in the South? On African Americans in the North and South?

### Linking Across Time

7. Did Reconstruction mend the rift between North and South? What differences still exist today between the two regions?

# An Age of Ingenuity

*After the Civil War, Americans yearned to shed their painful memories. Hoping for brighter tomorrows, they channeled their creativity toward peaceful and productive technology, inventing everything from the dentist's drill to the dynamo. They applied their ingenuity to entertainment, too, contriving such stellar attractions as showboat vaudeville, the circus, and exhibitions.*

Thousands thronged to the opening of the **1876 Centennial Exhibition in Philadelphia** to celebrate the nation's 100th birthday. Nearly 200 buildings on 450 landscaped acres showcased the country's growing technology, including the newly invented telephone (top). On this occasion, women shook off their second-class status to present a pavilion all their own—complete with a "lady engineer."

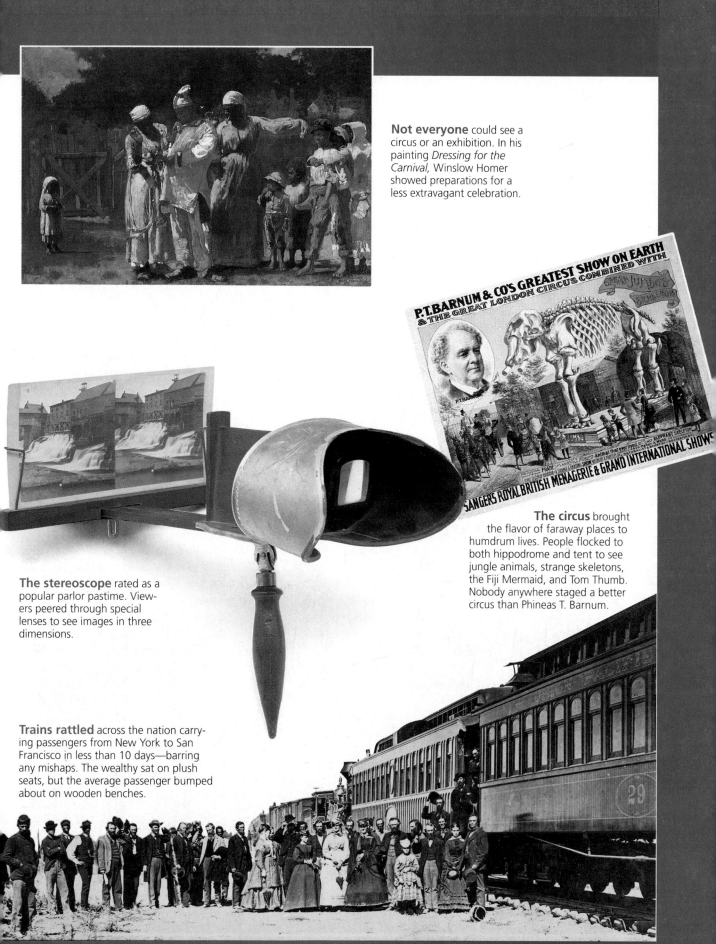

**Not everyone** could see a circus or an exhibition. In his painting *Dressing for the Carnival,* Winslow Homer showed preparations for a less extravagant celebration.

**The circus** brought the flavor of faraway places to humdrum lives. People flocked to both hippodrome and tent to see jungle animals, strange skeletons, the Fiji Mermaid, and Tom Thumb. Nobody anywhere staged a better circus than Phineas T. Barnum.

**The stereoscope** rated as a popular parlor pastime. Viewers peered through special lenses to see images in three dimensions.

**Trains rattled** across the nation carrying passengers from New York to San Francisco in less than 10 days—barring any mishaps. The wealthy sat on plush seats, but the average passenger bumped about on wooden benches.

# Chapter 3 Review

**1793**
Eli Whitney invents the cotton gin; slavery spreads in the South.

**1820**
Missouri Compromise passed.

1787   1792   1797   1802   1807   1812   1817   1822   1827   1832

## Summary

Use the following outline as a tool for reviewing and summarizing the chapter. Copy the outline on your own paper, leaving spaces between headings to jot down notes about key events and concepts.

**I. Slavery and Politics**
  A. The Roots of Conflict
  B. The Slave Community
  C. Resistance to Slavery
  D. Conflict and Suspense

**II. The Civil War**
  A. The Start of the War
  B. Major Military Battles
  C. Social and Economic Battles
  D. The Road to Surrender

**III. Reconstruction**
  A. Presidential Plans
  B. Congressional Plans
  C. Limits on Freedom
  D. Grant's Presidency
  E. The End of Reconstruction

## Ideas, Events, and People

1. Explain how Eli Whitney's improved cotton gin contributed to increasing sectionalism. Include both economic and political factors.
2. Why was the Dred Scott decision significant?
3. How were sectional interests reflected by (a) the Missouri Compromise, (b) the Compromise of 1850, and (c) the Kansas-Nebraska Act.?
4. What led to the secession of eleven southern states?
5. Why were both northerners and southerners at first confident of victory in the Civil War?
6. Explain why Gettysburg and Vicksburg were significant battles.

7. What was the Emancipation Proclamation? Did it achieve the goals of the abolitionists? Explain.
8. What motivated the Radical Republicans to pass civil rights legislation for African Americans?
9. Despite laws passed during Reconstruction, southern African Americans lost many of their civil rights until the 1950s and 1960s. Explain.
10. Did the Civil War and Reconstruction end sectionalism? Why or why not?
11. What is sharecropping? How did it block African American hopes?

## Social Studies Skills

**Combining Information from Maps**
Compare the map of transportation routes on page 71 with the map of Civil War battles on page 95. Why did Union victories in Tennessee and New Orleans cause major hardships for the South?

## Critical Thinking

1. **Making Generalizations**
During the Civil War, women began to assume many jobs once held only by men. What generalizations can you make about the social, economic, and political impact of war?
2. **Analyzing Cause and Effect**
President Lincoln and General Grant expressed that the South not be treated harshly after the Civil War. Was this a wise policy? Explain.
3. **Compare and Contrast**
Make a chart showing the strengths and weaknesses of the Union and the Confederacy at the outbreak of the Civil War. What proved to be the determining factors in the war?
4. **Recognizing Points of View**
White southerners tended to support policies that enlarged the powers of the states, while

| 1837 | 1842 | 1847 | 1852 | 1857 | 1862 | 1867 | 1872 | 1877 | 1882 |

**1850** Compromise of 1850 passed.

**1860** Abraham Lincoln elected president.

**1865** Reconstruction begins.

**1868** Ulysses S. Grant elected president.

**1854** Kansas-Nebraska Act passed.

**1861** Southern states form Confederacy; Civil War begins.

**1865** Civil War ends; Lincoln assassinated; Andrew Johnson assumes presidency.

**1877** Rutherford B. Hayes elected president, effectively ending Reconstruction.

northerners supported limiting the powers of the states in certain important ways. What caused this difference in outlook?

5. **Recognizing Values**

Explain what Jerry Loguen meant when he said "human rights are mutual and reciprocal." How has this idea been applied to other areas, for example, women's rights?

# Extension and Application

1. **Global Connections**

Many countries in the twentieth century have been torn apart by civil war. Choose one country, such as China, Spain, or Mexico, and investigate its civil war period. Identify the causes and effects of its civil war. In what ways was it similar to the American Civil War? How was it different?

2. **Linking Across Time**

Julia Ward Howe's words for "The Battle Hymn of the Republic" stirred Union supporters, while Confederate soldiers marched to the strains of "Dixie." Collect some of the most popular Civil War songs. Compare them with songs popular during World War I. What themes do you find in wartime music? What differences do you find in songs of the two periods?

3. **Cooperative Learning**

The Civil War has inspired numerous books, plays, movies, and TV dramas. For example, Margaret Mitchell's *Gone With the Wind*, Stephen Crane's *The Red Badge of Courage*, and the movie *Glory* take different looks at the war. With a group of your classmates, prepare a review of different works on the Civil War. Include answers to the following questions: How historically accurate are they? What evidence is there of stereotyping? Has stereotyping changed over the years? To help you write your report, consult the *Writer's Guide*, Unit 6 (page 829).

# Geography

1. What product became the basis of the southern economy after 1793? According to the map on page 85, how did this product affect the South's population?

2. On page 90, what do the three maps show about the decisions made at each stage in the conflict over slavery?

3. Look at the map on this page. In what state did most of the eastern Civil War battles take place? Which side won most of these battles?

4. According to the map, where did the last battle take place? Why was it significant?

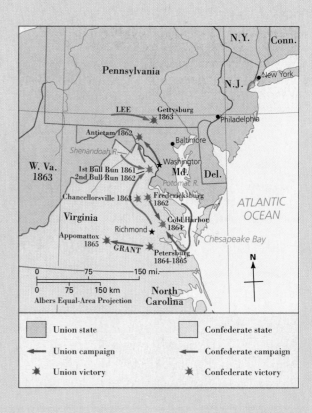

CHAPTER 4

# Farming and Industry

### May 24, 1883: Fanfare Marks Brooklyn Bridge Opening

Church bells rang out all over the city. Guns boomed from forts in New York harbor. After 14 years of construction, marred by worker injuries and deaths, New York City celebrated the opening of the Brooklyn Bridge. President Chester A. Arthur and New York Governor Grover Cleveland joined thousands of New Yorkers in the opening ceremony. The steel bridge stretched over the East River, ready to open the way from the island of Manhattan to Brooklyn.

At the time it was opened, the bridge was the largest suspension bridge in the world. Costing nearly $15 million, the bridge was suspended by four cables. Each cable contained over 5,000 small wires and could hold nearly 3,000 tons. Over 100,000 people would travel over it each day.

The Brooklyn Bridge reflected the industrial progress sweeping the nation in the years following the Civil War. Factories and cities grew, while advancements in technology and communications transformed the way Americans lived. As the nation continued to push its boundaries outward, the United States emerged as one of the great world powers of the twentieth century.

> *The Brooklyn Bridge reflected the industrial progress sweeping the nation in the years following the Civil War.*

UPI/BETTMANN

*The Brooklyn Bridge provides a majestic walkway for these strollers photographed at the turn of the century.*

*This photograph captures the commercial bustle of Chicago's State Street in the late 1890s. American cities such as Chicago boomed after the Civil War.*

# Opening of the West

### April 22, 1889:  Thousands Grab Land in Oklahoma

*THERE WE WERE, THE GIRL ON MY LEFT, THE OLD PLAINSMAN ON MY RIGHT. ELEVEN FORTY-FIVE. ALONG THE BORDER WERE THE SOLDIERS, THEIR guns in one hand, their watches in the other. . . . Twelve o'clock. There went up a roar that drowned the crack of the soldiers' musketry as they fired in the air as the signal of noon and the start of the Run. You could see the puffs of smoke from their guns but you couldn't hear a sound. The thousands surged over the Line. It was like running water going over a broken dam. The rush had started, and it was devil take the hindmost. We swept across the prairie in a cloud of black and red dust that covered our faces and hands in a minute. . . .*

Edna Ferber,
*Cimarron*, 1930

The clock struck noon and gunshots rang out, beginning one of the most remarkable land grabs in American history. Yancey Cravat, the hero in Edna Ferber's novel, *Cimarron*, describes the scene on April 22, 1889, when the U.S. federal government effectively gave away the almost two million acres of land it had purchased from evicted Creek and Seminole.

Over 50,000 men, women, and children participated in the rush. Although the land was free, the settlers would have to **homestead,** or settle on the land, for a number of years before they could own it. Some found their stakes too dry to farm, and disease-causing conditions drove

ARCHIVES AND MANUSCRIPTS DIVISION OF THE OKLAHOMA HISTORICAL SOCIETY

others out; but a year later, the Oklahoma Territory boasted a population of about 259,000 people.

The success of the Oklahoma rush led the government to open more land in the West. The following year, federal authorities authorized settlement on millions of acres of Sioux land in South Dakota. The government could not hold back the tide of eager settlers, and after 1900 thousands descended on the former Native American reservation.

## New Frontiers

After the Civil War, as the nation's population boomed and midwestern agricultural land filled up, farmers looked westward to the Great Plains. When the transcontinental railroad was completed in 1869, railroad companies encouraged eager farmers to buy some of their enormous land holdings. More encouragement came from the Homestead Act of 1862, which awarded 160 acres of public land free to any settler who would farm the land for at least five years. So enticed, many settlers, including thousands of newly arrived immigrants from European countries, poured into the lands west of the Mississippi River.

**The Cattle Frontier**   On the eastern high grass prairie of the Great Plains, enough rain fell to cultivate grain crops. But in the drier western lands, settlers used the land for cattle grazing. Herds of longhorn and other cattle were fattened on the open range lands of Texas, Kansas, Nebraska, the Dakotas, Wyoming, and Montana. They were driven to market and sold to packers and finally were sent east to feed the growing numbers of beef-hungry city dwellers.

The profits from cattle ranching could be enormous. A Texas steer, purchased as a calf for $5–$6, could be set out to graze on public land and later sold for $60–$70. By the late 1880s, however, drought and an oversupply of cattle forced beef prices down. But for two decades after the Civil War, the cowboy and his cattle reigned supreme on the Great Plains.

**Cowhands**  American cowhands, idealized in popular books and movies, had a unique way of life that evolved from the vaqueros, their Mexican counterparts. The cattle industry in the United States developed from the livestock and horses that the Spanish introduced into the Americas. Similarly, cowboy culture—the clothing, equipment, work, and entertainment of American cowhands—had a partly Spanish heritage.

Cowhands' chaps, a word based on the vaqueros' *chaparejos*, protected their legs from thorny brush on the Plains. The words *lariat* and *rodeo* also have Spanish origins. Cowhands' outfits were mostly functional. High-heeled boots kept their feet from slipping out of the stirrups, and broad-brimmed hats kept sun, rain, and dust from their eyes.

A cowhand's work was seasonal. Ranchers hired extra help for the roundup, when cattle

**This photograph, taken around 1910, shows cowhands on a cattle drive. Cowhands, one third of whom were African American or Hispanic American, spent time in cattle boom towns such as Abilene and Dodge City, Kansas. There they sought relief from the dusty, lonely trails.**

were branded. During a trail drive, hired hands kept the herds together and moved them as far as 1,000 miles in three months. The work was exhausting, and the wages were low—$40 or $50 per month. Few cowboys owned a horse, but every cowboy owned a saddle, one of his prized possessions. His worth was measured by his skill at roping and riding. Cattle rancher Joseph G. McCoy said of a cowboy in 1874: "He lives hard, works hard, has but few comforts and fewer necessities. He loves danger but abhors labor of the common kind, and never tires riding."

The profession was more integrated than most walks of American life. African American, Native American, Hispanic, and Anglo cowhands, as well as those of mixed ancestry, all met and worked together. Yet discrimination existed on the frontier as elsewhere. Vaqueros earned less than Anglos and seldom became foremen or trail bosses. Some saloons discriminated against Hispanics, segregated African Americans, and excluded Chinese altogether.

Few women worked as salaried cowhands. Ranchers' wives and daughters did help with many chores, such as tending animals and sewing leather britches. A widow sometimes took over her deceased husband's ranch.

During free time in the bunkhouse, cowboys entertained themselves with card games, tall tales, practical jokes, and songs. In town, after several months

CULVER PICTURES, INC

on the trail, many cowboys let off steam by drinking, gambling, and fighting in local saloons. Cow towns, where cattle were loaded on trains for shipment to market, gained a reputation for lawlessness. Yet the "Wild West" gained its name not so much for gunfights as for the cowhands' rugged life.

**Mountains and Valleys**   West of the Great Plains, people sought their fortune from the vast mineral and forest resources of the Rocky Mountain and Sierra Nevada regions. The timberlands of California and the Northwest yielded much of the wood necessary for thousands of miles of railroad ties, fence posts, and the building of hundreds of towns.

Gold and silver provided much of the capital for an industrializing country. The Comstock Lode, a rich vein of silver in Nevada, yielded more than $292 million between 1859 and 1882. Though western tales celebrate the lone miner toiling with pick and shovel, most mining of valuable metals was done by huge companies. These companies, in pursuit of gold, silver, lead, copper, tin, and zinc, commanded great money and power. They could build railroad lines, bring in heavy machinery, and employ armies of miners.

In California the gold discovered under the ground proved less valuable than the ground itself. As one father told his son: "Plant your lands, these be your best gold fields." Indeed, farmland turned out to be California's most valuable asset. Eager miners, believing the California soil unsuitable for crops, willingly paid high prices for farm produce: "watermelon at from one to five dollars each, apples from Oregon at one and two dollars each, potatoes and onions at fifty cents to one dollar a pound . . . eggs at two dollars a dozen," according to one older resident. More often than not, provisioners in the West made money while miners did not. By 1862 California produced a surplus of some crops.

Like the cattle culture of the Great Plains, the agriculture of California had a partly Spanish heritage. Franciscan missionaries introduced grapes and citrus fruits to California's fertile soils in the late 1700s. With the end of the mission system in the mid-1800s, however, the vineyards and orchards fell into neglect. Enterprising settlers, once in search of gold, displaced Mexican ranchers and turned the rich California valleys into cornucopias of the Far West.

**This Mexican American family lived in California in the mid-1800s, uniting two cultures.**

# Building the Railroad

California's population increased dramatically because of its gold rush and its agricultural successes. Other parts of the West remained sparsely settled, usually because they were far from transportation and markets. In the early 1860s, the federal government proposed that railroad lines should cross the entire United States.

The incredible engineering feat that provided transcontinental transportation began with the Pacific Railroad Act. Passed by Congress in 1862, the act authorized the Union Pacific Railroad to lay track westward from a point near Omaha, Nebraska, while the Central Pacific Railroad laid track eastward from Sacramento. The lines were to meet in Utah. In addition to government loans, the railroads received large land grants, 20 square miles of land for each mile of track laid. The railroad barons made fortunes by selling this land to settlers.

**Recognizing Points of View**
Native Americans lamented how settlers farmed and mined the land in ways never before seen in North America. Chief Seattle gives his perspective in a letter to President Franklin Pierce: "If we sell you our land, love it as we have loved it. Hold in your mind the memory of the land . . . , and with all your might, and with all your strength, and with all your heart—preserve it for your children."

**This 1868 lithograph by Currier and Ives, *Across the Continent: Westward the Course of Empire Takes Its Way*, helps capture the march of Americans to the West. American farmers, settlers, and railroads transform the vast western lands as the Native Americans look on.**

Both railroads faced enormous challenges that required armies of laborers. The Central Pacific had to cross the Sierra Nevada in eastern California, while the Union Pacific had to cross the Rockies. Blasting and tunneling into rock and working through the winters, the crew suffered many injuries and deaths. In January 1865 the Central Pacific advertised for 5,000 more workers.

The quiet efficiency of Chinese laborers impressed the construction boss, and he began recruiting in China. Before the end of the year, about 7,000 Chinese laborers were at work on the line. The Union Pacific relied heavily on Irish immigrant labor, although one worker described the team as "a crowd of ex-Confederates and Federal soldiers, muleskinners, Mexicans, New York Irish, bushwackers, and ex-convicts," with a few African Americans as well.

By 1868 the work of laying track had become a race between the two railroads. The pace quickened as the lines approached each other. When the two sets of tracks met on May 10, 1869, at Promontory, Utah, special trains carrying railroad officials and their guests arrived for the completion ceremony. Leland Stanford, governor of California, drove in a gold spike, symbolically uniting the rail lines. A telegraph message informed the nation, "It is done!" By the end of the 1800s four more transcontinental rail lines crossed the United States. Passengers and freight began to crisscross the nation.

Not everyone benefited from the expansion of the railroads, however. Red Cloud, a Sioux chief, lamented in 1870, "When we first had all this land we were strong; now we are all melting like snow on the hillside, while you are growing like spring grass."

## STUDY GUIDE

### Recognizing Bias

While campaigning for the governorship of California in 1862, Leland Stanford had denounced Chinese immigrants in racial terms. Stanford eventually became governor and a railroad owner. After Chinese workers had proven their value to California's economy later in the decade, Stanford viewed their presence much more favorably.

**This photograph shows federal agents preparing to remove a group of Apaches from Arizona to Oklahoma by train in the late 1800s. Geronimo, of the Chiricahua Apache, sat third from right in front.**

## The Second Great Removal

The rapid settlement of the lands west of the Mississippi River after the Civil War led to a generation of violent conflict. Settlers fought the dozens of Native American nations that had inhabited these lands for generations.

In 1871 the U.S. government decreed that all western Native American nations must agree to relocate to one of two reservation areas. The northern Plains Indians were assigned to the western half of present-day South Dakota; the southern Plains tribes were assigned to what is now Oklahoma. Once placed on the reservations, they would have to accept the U.S. government as their guardian.

Government policy, as well as military conflict with those who resisted, undermined Native American cultures. In 1871 the government ended the practice of treating each Native American nation separately. Under the new policy, Native Americans lost two rights. They could no longer negotiate treaties to protect their lands, and they could no longer vote on laws governing their fate. The Dawes Severalty Act of 1887 continued the attempt to break down Native American loyalty to their own nation. This act decreed that parcels of land be given not to nations but to individuals. Each family head was allowed 160 acres. Reservation land left over was sold to white settlers.

Some reformers compared this act to the Emancipation Proclamation: just as slaves were set free, so Indians would gradually gain citizenship. Few reformers seemed to notice that sending Native Americans to government boarding schools was breaking down Native American culture.

Within 20 years after the Dawes Act, Native Americans retained control of only 20 percent of their original reservation lands. The southern Plains Indians in Oklahoma were severely hurt. By the time of Oklahoma statehood in 1907, most of their original acreage was in the hands of 500,000 white settlers. A newspaper editor in that year summed up the prevailing feeling among the settlers: "Sympathy and sentiment never stand in the way of the onward march of empire."

### SECTION REVIEW

**Checking Facts**

1. How did homesteaders legally acquire the land they settled?
2. What aspects of American cowboy culture reflect its Spanish heritage?
3. Name some of the natural resources that settlers found on the Great Plains and in the Far West.
4. How did the federal government promote the building of a transcontinental railroad?

**Thinking Critically**

5. **Analyzing Decisions**
   Why do you think the government gave two companies instead of just one the contract to build the transcontinental rail line?
6. **Recognizing Points of View**
   How did the Native American view of westward expansion differ from that of settlers?

**Linking Across Time**

7. Some reformers compared the Dawes Severalty Act to the Emancipation Proclamation. Just as slaves were set free, reformers argued, so Indians would gain citizenship. How would you compare the consequences of the Emancipation Proclamation and the Dawes Act? Explain.

# Rise of Industrialism

## Late 1800s: Carnegie Forges a Steel Empire

ANDREW CARNEGIE LEARNED ABOUT THE MEANING OF HARD WORK AS A YOUNG BOY. WHEN HIS FAMILY FELL ON HARD TIMES in Scotland, he helped his mother sew shoes by threading her needles. In 1848 after the Carnegies left Scotland for the United States, 12-year-old Andrew worked with his father in a Pennsylvania cotton factory, earning $1.20 for a 72-hour week.

Little by little, Carnegie made himself a business success. At age 14 Carnegie started work in a telegraph office as a messenger and then quickly rose to the position of telegraph operator. When he got a job at the Pennsylvania Railroad at age 17, his skills and hard work catapulted him in a few years to assistant to the president. Through smart investments in a railroad car company and in oil wells, Carnegie made a small fortune by his early twenties and left the railroad to start his own business, manufacturing iron bridges.

Carnegie was not only a shrewd investor, but also a daring industrial innovator. In 1873 he began building a massive steel plant to produce railroad tracks in Pittsburgh, Pennsylvania. Carnegie introduced the revolutionary Bessemer converter and open-hearth steelmaking method, which converted iron ore into steel with much less labor than was previously required. Carnegie's mill also combined all stages of steel production—smelting, refining, and rolling—into one unified operation. As a result, the price of a ton of steel rails dropped from $107 per ton in 1870 to $32 per ton in 1890.

CULVER PICTURES, INC.

Innovation, ambition, and organizational skill made Carnegie hugely wealthy by the time he was 40 years old. Saying that hard work brought success, he also believed that those who acquired great wealth had a responsibility to return a portion of their profits to society. "The man who dies rich, dies disgraced," the self-made Scottish immigrant avowed.

By the time of his death in 1919, Carnegie had donated over $350 million to worthy causes, including thousands of libraries, and another $30 million was disbursed by his last will and testament. His generosity was legendary throughout the world.

## Industrialism Triumphant

The era in which Andrew Carnegie built his steel empire witnessed a dramatic economic transformation. Between the end of the Civil War in 1865 and the end of the 1800s, the United States became an industrial giant. Manufacturing replaced agriculture as the main source of economic growth; growing **industrialism** turned the United States into a land rich with machines, factories, mines, and railroads.

### STUDY GUIDE

**As You Read**
Trace the developments that led to the shift from agriculture to industry as the basis of the U.S. economy. Also, think about the following skills and concepts.

**Central Concepts**
- recognizing how **industrialism** and the development of **national markets** affected U.S. businesses
- understanding **Social Darwinism** and its relationship to big business

**Thinking Skills**
- predicting consequences
- comparing and contrasting
- identifying cause and effect

**The Rise of Heavy Industry** Before the Civil War, manufacturing in the United States had been tied to the farming economy. Factories processed the products of the farm and forest into consumer goods—turning cotton and wool into cloth; hides into shoes and boots; and trees into ships, barrels, and furniture. After the Civil War, manufacturing branched out and concentrated increased funding and labor in heavy-industry consumer goods such as railroad tracks, steam engines, and farm tractors. Factories could now produce in huge quantities what craftsmen had painstakingly made by hand.

Steelmaking was central to the new heavy industry. Hand in hand with steel production went the intensive development of the nation's mineral resources. Iron ore deposits in Michigan and Minnesota provided the raw substance for the steel making centers that sprang up in Illinois, Ohio, and Pennsylvania. Coal was equally important because it became the fuel that powered a nation of steam-run machines. **1**

**The Technology Boom** In 1876 the most ingenious American inventor since Benjamin Franklin built a long wooden shed in a little town in New Jersey where he promised to produce "a minor invention every ten days and a big thing every six months or so." Thomas Alva Edison, a brash 29-year-old at the time, was nearly as good as his word.

Edison patented over 1,000 inventions in his Menlo Park laboratory before his death in 1931. He lit up the nation through his stunning development of an incandescent light bulb that provided a cheap and efficient replacement for candles and oil lamps. Of equal importance was his invention of the technology for producing and distributing electrical power.

Between 1865 and 1900 thousands of other inventors pushed forward the new age of machines and electrical energy. The U.S. Patent Office, which had issued a total of 36,000 patents in the 70 years before 1860, granted 676,000 between 1860 and 1900. Among the most important was Alexander Graham Bell's telephone. Patented in 1876, the telephone revolutionized communications. By 1884 telephone service from Boston to New York began the boom in rapid long distance communication. By 1900, over 1.3 million telephones were in operation nationwide.

BROWN BROTHERS

**Cotton mills such as this Greensboro, North Carolina, mill, photographed in 1895, provided jobs for many southern people who were forced out of farming by hard times. Whole families worked in the mills.**

Inventions and entrepreneurial skills combined to reshape the face of American manufacturing. New cotton machinery speeded up textile production. By 1886 a worker laboring for 10 hours could turn out three times as much as a worker in 1840 who toiled for 14 hours. Such developments made processed goods and consumer items cheaper and more readily available.

Everywhere in the United States the new technology could be seen in the form of mechanical reapers, blast furnaces, and telegraph offices; in the camera, typewriter, electric motor, and electric light; in the high-speed rotary printing press, iron and steel ships, pressed glass, wire rope, and petroleum. All of these products combined to create a new world of manufacturing, business, and consumerism.

## National Markets

Closely linked to the maturing of the nation's industrial economy was the creation of a transportation network that turned the country into a huge, unified **national market**. Before the Civil War, canal and river boats had carried the bulky farm and forest products from one region to another. After the

### STUDY GUIDE

**Predicting Consequences**
What if Thomas Edison had not invented the light bulb at this time? How would this have affected the growth of U.S. industry at the time? Because other inventors were working on the same

task, someone would probably have soon invented a light bulb or similar device. Manufacturing of bulbs and the vast amount of related equipment, however, would have been slowed.

**1** How did the nation's rich supply of natural resources help industry grow?

Civil War the fledgling railroad system that began in the 1830s surged forward. Soon it became the most popular way of transporting people and goods.

Across these thousands of miles of railroad track, goods could move with such year-round, on-time efficiency that entire industries were revolutionized. One example was the meatpacking industry. Before the Civil War Americans bought meat from their local butchers, who had purchased livestock from nearby farmers. But the railroads allowed for far more efficient cattle raising on the wide open ranges of the Great Plains. This in turn lowered meat prices for the consumer. From the Great Plains cattle were shipped in cattle cars to livestock markets—Chicago was the largest—and then were distributed by the railroads to be slaughtered in eastern and southern cities.

The invention of the refrigerated railroad car further revolutionized the business. Gustavus Swift, a clever Chicago cattle dealer, recognized that if slaughtering and preparing meat for market could be done in one place, money could be saved and meat sold more cheaply. What was needed was the ability to keep meat fresh during its journey to the local butcher shops. The refrigerated railroad car was the answer.

Using the newly invented refrigerated car, Swift created a gigantic national meatpacking network in the 1880s. His wagons carried meat from chilled beef branch houses to local butcher shops. Four other meatpackers copied Swift's innovations, and by the 1890s these five companies completely dominated the nation's meat business.

The refrigerated railroad car also created a national market for fruits and vegetables from the West Coast. In 1888 fresh apricots and cherries were able to survive the train ride from California to New York, and the nation's diet was transformed. Large parts of the country that only ate locally grown fruit and vegetables during the summer months could now have a Florida orange for breakfast, an Oregon apple for lunch, and a California lettuce salad for dinner.

Other businesses quickly followed the move to identify or create a national market. By the 1880s the McCormick Harvesting Machine Company had a national network of dealers who not only sold mechanized farm equipment that arrived by train but also provided credit and repair services. The Singer Sewing Machine dotted the land with retail stores and blanketed the country with door-to-door salespeople.

City dwellers also became connected to huge nationwide chain store systems. F.W. Woolworth's five- and ten-cent stores sprouted in thousands of towns and cities. The Great Atlantic and Pacific Tea Co. replaced "Ma and Pa" grocery stores all over the country because this large grocery chain could undersell the single retailer through mass purchasing. All of their products moved across the nation by rail.

**The Birth of Consumerism**   The creation of a national marketplace changed the way people spent their money. In the cities people no longer purchased solely from pushcarts or small shops, but rushed to the new department stores. John Wanamaker of Philadelphia introduced fixed prices and window displays to entice customers in 1861. He was soon joined by Macy's in New York, Marshall Field in Chicago, and Jordan Marsh in Boston.

These lavish consumer palaces included leaded-glass skylights, polished marble staircases, expensive carpets, and chandeliers. Such stores introduced charge accounts and trained clerks to cater to the customer. They tried to convince buyers that shopping was a great pleasure to be enjoyed. Advertising played

**Trace the development of U.S. railroads in the late 1800s on the graph. When was the refrigerator car introduced in the United States? What inference can you make about how the refrigerator car may have affected the growth of the railroads?**

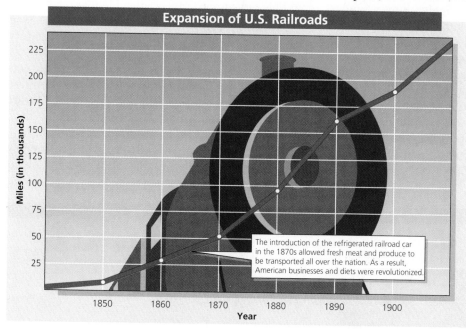

### Expansion of U.S. Railroads

*Miles (in thousands)* vs *Year*

The introduction of the refrigerated railroad car in the 1870s allowed fresh meat and produce to be transported all over the nation. As a result, American businesses and diets were revolutionized.

CATALOGUE AND BUYERS' GUIDE. No. 68 THIS IS OUR ONLY SALESMAN

FALL AND WINTER 1900-1901

MONTGOMERY WARD & CO. MICHIGAN AVE. AND MADISON ST. CHICAGO

CULVER PICTURES, INC.

ELABORATE SILK SHIRT WAIST SUITS

BROWN BROTHERS

Montgomery Ward issued mail order catalogs to rural families across the country. People could buy thousands of items, from barn nails to sunbonnets.

a significant role in this buying craze. Between 1870 and 1900 the amount of money spent on advertising multiplied dramatically, from $50 million to $542 million.[2]

## The Growth of Big Business

The growth of heavy industry and the creation of vast nationwide markets brought about a fundamental change in business organization. Only large businesses, gathering capital from many investors, could afford to set up huge factories, install modern machinery, and employ hundreds of workers.

Railroads led the way in the new era of big business. While the typical railroad line in 1865 was only 100 miles long, by 1885 it had expanded to 1,000 miles of track. Such a large enterprise, with enormous costs of construction, maintenance, and operation, demanded unprecedented amounts of capital and new methods of management.

**The Managerial Revolution** In the early days of railroading, a superintendent could give his personal attention to every detail in running a 50- or 100-mile operation. But how could one person oversee the operations of a business such as the Pennsylvania Railroad? By 1890 the railroad had 50,000 employees, properties spread over great distances, large amounts of capital invested, and hundreds of trains that had to be scheduled and coordinated with precision.

The answer was to separate the various functions of a business and put each "department" under a separate manager. In a railroad, for example, one person would be in charge of people who maintained the tracks; another supervised cargo handling; another oversaw traffic. Managers reported to the central office through well-defined lines of communication.

**The Merger Movement** Led by the railroads, the American industrial economy grew rapidly in the decades after the Civil War. However, businesses were plagued by the cutthroat competition of an uncontrolled marketplace. Business owners feverishly overbuilt their operations in good times and cut back sharply when demand for their products slackened. In such a boom-and-bust marketplace, bankruptcy was common. In the depression of the 1870s, for example, 47,000 firms closed their doors, laying off hundreds of thousands of employees.

Some people felt that the solution to such business instability was a **merger,** or a combining of several competing firms under a single head. By merging companies in a particular industry, a junglelike market could become an orderly, predictable market. "I like a little competition now and then," exclaimed J.P. Morgan, a titan of mergers in the late nineteenth century, "but I like combination a lot better."

The pioneering figure in the late nineteenth-century merger movement was John D. Rockefeller. Rockefeller started out as a clerk in his boyhood town of Cleveland, Ohio. In the 1860s he founded a business that refined kerosene from petroleum and later became Standard Oil. Hundreds of oil refineries, mostly small and badly organized, competed fiercely in the Ohio and Pennsylvania regions.

Both wise and ruthless, Rockefeller purchased as many competing companies as possible, and by the late 1870s his Standard Oil company controlled almost all the oil refineries in Ohio. By 1882 Standard Oil had gobbled up most of the competition throughout the country. His 40 oil companies owned 90 percent of the nation's pipelines and refined 84 percent of the nation's oil. "The day of individual competition [in the oil business] is past and gone," Rockefeller pronounced.

Because he dominated the market, Rockefeller was able to demand rail shipping rates of 10 cents a barrel as compared with his competitors' 35 cents. When Rockefeller turned the business over to his son in 1911, his fortune exceeded one billion dollars.

The merger of competing companies in one area of business such as Rockefeller's oil corporation was known as **horizontal integration**. It was often accompanied by **vertical integration** of industries, in which a firm would strive to control all aspects of production from acquisition of raw materials to final delivery of finished products. In this way a single business might gain total control over a national market, as the chart below shows.[3]

In the merger movement, Swift and Armour dominated meatpacking, and the Duke family controlled tobacco. Andrew Carnegie, however, had the most success with vertical integration. Carnegie bought up coal mines and iron ore deposits for his steel mills, then bought railroads and ships to transport raw materials and send his products to market. By owning every aspect of steel production he could limit risk and guarantee profit.

When J.P. Morgan bought Carnegie's steel company in 1901, he consolidated it with several other firms to form the U.S. Steel Corporation, which controlled 60 percent of American steel production. It was the nation's first billion dollar company.

## The Spirit of the Gilded Age

The wealth generated by industrial capitalism and big business led to the growth of a "nouveau riche" class with its own philosophy. Many of these self-made people proclaimed their importance with showy displays of money, leading humorist Mark Twain to call the late 1800s the "Gilded Age."

Some of these people, known as "robber barons," built lavish mansions in New York City complete with solid gold bathroom fixtures. For the summer months many built castlelike estates in Newport, Rhode Island, which they dubbed their "cottages." Railroad tycoon William Vanderbilt's summer home cost $11

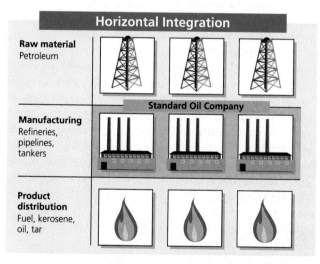

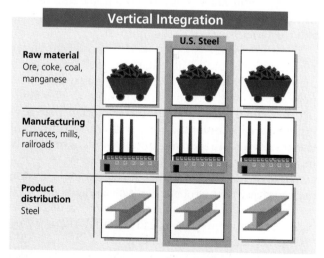

Study the diagrams above which illustrate horizontal and vertical business integration. Note that when a business integrates horizontally, it merges all competing companies in one area of business. In vertical integration, one business controls all aspects of production. Note that U.S. Steel even owned the railroads that transported the materials from one production stage to the next.

### Identifying Cause and Effect

As U.S. businesses merged, the same people often served on the board of directors of many companies. This stifled competition and gave huge corporations an advantage in the marketplace.

By 1913 J.P. Morgan controlled 314 directorships in 112 corporations, with an estimated collective worth of $22 billion.

**3** Did horizontal and vertical integration give corporations an unfair advantage in the marketplace? Explain.

million. Outrageous displays of wealth were popular. At one debutante ball in Philadelphia, a young lady's parents ordered thousands of live butterflies (many of which drowned in champagne glasses) as decorations at the $75,000 party.

**Social Darwinism**   In the heady, expensive atmosphere of the Gilded Age, the struggle for wealth became a way of life for the most ambitious Americans. But how did business leaders, bent on killing off competition in order to increase their control of the marketplace and make as much money as possible, justify their activities to a public raised on the ideology of a fair and open society?

A new theory of human behavior provided an answer. It rested on the scientific theories of Charles Darwin about the origin of species and the evolution of humankind. Darwin argued that the plant and animal world had reached its present state through a long process of "natural selection" in which only the fittest had survived. Herbert Spencer, an English philosopher, loosely adopted these ideas, in a theory known as **Social Darwinism**, to explain the evolution of human society.

Progress, Spencer argued, occurred through competition in which the weak fell and the strong forged ahead. His strongest American supporter, William G. Sumner, put it this way: "If we do not like the survival of the fittest, we have only one possible alternative, and that is the survival of the unfittest."

Leading Americans flocked to honor Spencer when he visited the United States in 1882. Here was a man whose theories justified their aggressive business practices and their attempts to eliminate weaker competitors. They heaped praise on his notion that government should never interfere with the separation of the weak from the strong because this would only hold back progress.

Despite their seeming lack of regard for common people, many of the robber barons who had embraced

CULVER PICTURES, INC.

**Wealthy socialites lounge on the steps of a Newport, Rhode Island summer "cottage" in 1887.**

Social Darwinism also supported the spirit of charity. They believed that the more fortunate should give back to society to benefit the public at large. Carnegie was but one of a host of powerful, rich patrons who supported the arts, education, and culture; funded public works; and established foundations.

These individual efforts had their limitations, however. As Jane Addams, a reformer of this time, commented concerning her native city of Chicago, "Private beneficence [charity] is totally inadequate to deal with vast numbers of the city's disinherited." Americans would have to learn new ways to cope with and solve the enormous problems created by population growth and industrialization in the United States between the Civil War and the end of the nineteenth century.

## SECTION REVIEW

**Checking Facts**

1. How did U.S manufacturing change after the Civil War?
2. Name two technological advances that spurred industrial growth in the late 1800s.
3. How did the growth of railroads help to create national markets ?
4. Why did business mergers decrease competition in the U.S. marketplace?

**Thinking Critically**

5. **Predicting Consequences** There is a saying that "invention and economic progress often go hand in hand." What does this mean? Cite examples from the late 1800s that illustrate this point.
6. **Identifying Cause and Effect** How might workers have reacted to the notion of "survival of the fittest" that Social Darwinists preached?

**Linking Across Time**

7. How do you think technological advances such as computers and robotics in today's work place have influenced the job qualifications that American workers need to have?

# Reading Statistical Tables

Throughout the nineteenth century, patterns of employment in the United States gradually shifted. Statistical tables can help you to spot changes in such patterns or trends.

## Learning the Skill

Tables can present a great deal of detailed statistical information concisely by organizing it into categories that are readily comprehensible. The table on this page is based on figures compiled by the Bureau of the Census. Its title tells you its contents.

All tables use headings, or boxheads, to categorize information. Here the headings "Labor Force" and "Employment" create two broad categories. Two more levels of heads group information into subcategories.

The lefthand column, the stub, lists years. Items in the stub may be organized alphabetically, chronologically, or geographically. Notice that in this table, years are shown from the earliest (at the top of the column) to the most recent (at the bottom).

The vertical columns of figures to the right of the stub are the body of the table. The first column in the body shows the number of people in the labor force, expressed in thousands. In 1960 the total labor force was 74,060,000. What do the next two columns tell? Why are there no figures after 1860? The rest of the columns list percentages of the labor force employed in particular occupations. For example, 14 percent of the labor force worked in trade in 1900.

Use the table below to find out how the percentage of people employed in agriculture has changed. First find the subheading "Agriculture." Figures from the column below it show that smaller and smaller percentages of Americans have worked in agriculture since 1810.

## Practicing the Skill

1. How much did agricultural employment change between 1880 and 1900? For the same time period, what four employment categories showed increases in the percentages of workers employed?
2. Major changes in employment patterns occurred between 1800 and 1960. Which employment category lost the greatest share of workers during this time period? Which two employment categories gained the most workers? Use statistics from the table to support your answer.

### Labor Force and Employment, 1800–1960

| Year | Total Labor Force (in thousands) | Labor Force (percent) | | Employment (percent) | | | | Manufacturing | | | | Transport | | Service | |
|---|---|---|---|---|---|---|---|---|---|---|---|---|---|---|---|
| | | Free | Slave | Agriculture | Fishing | Mining | Construction | Total | Cotton textiles | Primary iron and steel | Trade | Ocean vessels | Railways | Teachers | Domestics |
| 1800 | 1,900 | 72 | 28 | 74 | 0.3 | 1.0 | – | – | 0.1 | 0.1 | – | 2.0 | – | 0.3 | 2 |
| 1810 | 2,330 | 68 | 32 | 84 | 0.3 | 0.5 | – | 3 | 0.4 | 0.2 | – | 3.0 | – | 1.0 | 3 |
| 1820 | 3,135 | 70 | 30 | 79 | 0.4 | 0.4 | – | – | 0.4 | 0.2 | – | 2.0 | – | 1.0 | 4 |
| 1830 | 4,200 | 72 | 28 | 71 | 0.4 | 1.0 | – | – | 1.0 | 0.5 | – | 2.0 | – | 1.0 | 4 |
| 1840 | 5,660 | 74 | 26 | 63 | 0.4 | 1.0 | 5 | 9 | 1.0 | 0.4 | 6 | 2.0 | 0.1 | 1.0 | 4 |
| 1850 | 8,250 | 76 | 24 | 55 | 0.4 | 1.0 | 5 | 15 | 1.0 | 0.4 | 6 | 2.0 | 0.2 | 1.0 | 4 |
| 1860 | 11,110 | 79 | 21 | 53 | 0.3 | 2.0 | 5 | 14 | 1.0 | 0.4 | 8 | 1.0 | 1.0 | 1.0 | 5 |
| 1870 | 12,930 | – | – | 53 | 0.2 | 1.0 | 6 | 19 | 1.0 | 1.0 | 10 | 1.0 | 1.0 | 1.0 | 8 |
| 1880 | 17,390 | – | – | 51 | 0.2 | 2.0 | 5 | 19 | 1.0 | 1.0 | 11 | 1.0 | 2.0 | 1.0 | 6 |
| 1890 | 23,320 | – | – | 43 | 0.3 | 2.0 | 6 | 19 | 1.0 | 1.0 | 13 | 1.0 | 3.0 | 2.0 | 7 |
| 1900 | 29,070 | – | – | 40 | 0.2 | 2.0 | 6 | 20 | 1.0 | 1.0 | 14 | 0.4 | 4.0 | 1.0 | 6 |
| 1910 | 37,480 | – | – | 31 | 0.2 | 3.0 | 5 | 22 | 1.0 | 1.0 | 14 | 0.4 | 5.0 | 2.0 | 6 |
| 1920 | 41,610 | – | – | 26 | 0.1 | 3.0 | 3 | 27 | 1.0 | 1.0 | 14 | 0.5 | 5.0 | 2.0 | 4 |
| 1930 | 48,830 | – | – | 22 | 0.1 | 2.0 | 4 | 20 | 1.0 | 1.0 | 17 | 0.3 | 3.0 | 2.0 | 5 |
| 1940 | 56,290 | – | – | 17 | 0.1 | 2.0 | 3 | 20 | 1.0 | 1.0 | 17 | 0.3 | 2.0 | 2.0 | 4 |
| 1950 | 65,470 | – | – | 12 | 0.1 | 1.0 | 5 | 24 | 1.0 | 1.0 | 19 | 0.2 | 2.0 | 2.0 | 3 |
| 1960 | 74,060 | – | – | 8 | 0.1 | 1.0 | 5 | 23 | 0.4 | 1.0 | 19 | 0.2 | 1.0 | 2.0 | 3 |

# Populism and Protest

## July 2, 1892: People's Party Holds First Convention

**W**E HAVE WITNESSED FOR MORE THAN A QUARTER OF A CENTURY THE STRUGGLES OF THE TWO GREAT POLITICAL *parties for power and plunder, while grievous wrongs have been inflicted upon the suffering people. . . . Assembled on the anniversary of the birthday of the nation . . . we seek to restore the government of the Republic to the hands of "the plain people."*

Omaha Platform,
July 1892

The platform of the People's Party, also called the **Populist Party,** was adopted with great enthusiasm by the convention delegates. The platform not only denounced the existing ills of society but also proposed a third-party remedy. The Populists represented a grand coalition of farmers, laborers, and reformers whose aim was to put government back into the hands of the people.

Populist leaders were as colorful and diverse as the causes they represented. Ignatius Donnelly of Minnesota, who had written the preamble to the party platform, was considered the greatest orator of Populism. Mary E. Lease (pictured here), who forcefully represented farmers' interests, once advised Kansas farmers to "raise less corn and more hell." "Sockless Jerry" Simpson earned his nickname when he told a Kansas audience that he wore no silk socks like his "princely" Republican opponent. Georgia's Thomas E. Watson left the Democratic Party to campaign for Populist ideals.

CULVERS PICTURES INC

The Populists chose their candidates amid calls for restricted immigration and a shorter workday for industrial laborers. Another major aim was to convince the government to allow the free coinage of silver, a measure that would make silver, not just gold, legal tender. Many farmers thought this would be the most effective way to raise prices for farm goods and breathe new life into the faltering economy. The nomination for president in 1892 went to James B. Weaver, a seasoned campaigner from Iowa, who had been the candidate of the Greenback Party in 1880. Second place on the ticket went to James G. Field, an ex-Confederate general from Virginia. As one historian observed, "Whether they knew it or not, the delegates were beginning the last phase of a long and perhaps losing struggle—the struggle to save agricultural America from the devouring jaws of industrial America."

## Farmers Beleaguered

The rapid development of the agricultural West and the reorganization of southern agriculture after the Civil War provided new opportunities for millions of American families. The changes also exposed these families to the financial hardships of rural life. The result was the first mass organization of farmers in American history.

Ironically, the farmers' problem was rooted in their ability to produce so much. Huge tracts of the

---

Great Plains were being tilled for the first time by immigrants as well as American-born farmers. Larger acreage, coupled with improved farming methods, meant bumper crops in most years. By the 1870s farmers produced more than the country—or the world—demanded. Prices dropped, as the graph shows. Adding to the farmers' financial problems were two factors: many farmers borrowed money to put more land under cultivation, and most of them had to pay high transportation costs to get crops to market.

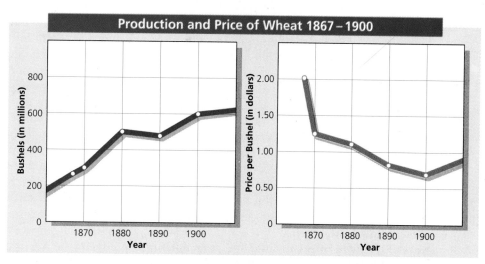

**Production and Price of Wheat 1867–1900**

The graph on the left shows an increase in wheat production during the late 1800s. The graph on the right shows the price of wheat declining during this same period. *What conclusion can you draw from these two graphs?*

Falling farm prices brought widespread rural suffering. On the Great Plains many farmers had to borrow more money to keep afloat financially. In the South many lost their farms and became debt-ridden sharecroppers. When eastern bankers began to foreclose on farm loans, thousands of homesteads were abandoned.[1]

Homesteaders in the late 1800s also faced nature's wrath. In 1874 a plague of grasshoppers devoured crops, clothes, and even plow handles. Droughts parched the earth in 1886, and in January 1888 in the northern Plains the School Children's Storm killed more than 200 youngsters who were stranded at school or starting home. Loneliness could be just as tormenting. One farm mother, who had not seen another woman for a year, walked across the prairie with her small children to see a woman who had come to live several miles away. The two strangers threw their arms around each other and wept.

Some families gave up and headed back East. They left behind bitter slogans: "In God we trusted, in Kansas we busted." The farmers who stayed began to seek political relief. The governor of Kansas received the following letter from a farm woman in 1894:

*I take my pen in hand to let you know we are starving . . . My husband went away to find work and came home last night and told me that he would have to starve. He had been in 10 counties and did not get no work . . . I haven't had nothing to eat today and it is 3 o'clock.*

**Farmers United**  Farmers, like other beleaguered groups in society, realized that there is strength in numbers. As early as 1867, farmers banded together to form the Patrons of Husbandry, also known as the Grange. By 1875 about 1 million Grange members spread from New England to Texas. Mainly they were concentrated in the South and Great Plains. The Grangers wanted the government to regulate railroad freight rates and to fund agricultural colleges. They also formed sales cooperatives, pooling their products and dividing profits.

In the 1880s farmers stepped up their political activism by forming groups known as Farmers' Alliances—one in the South, another on the Plains. The Alliances pooled the credit resources of their members to free themselves from the high interest rates charged by banks. They formed marketing cooperatives to sell directly to large merchants and thus avoided paying extra costs to brokers. Such cooperatives could also buy bulk quantities of the supplies and machinery farmers needed.

## STUDY GUIDE

### Identifying Cause and Effect
Prices go up or down for many reasons. But probably nothing is more important in setting prices than the economic law of supply and demand. When the supply of a product or service is small and the demand is great, the price is high. But when the supply is greater than the demand, the price is low.

**1** What financial problems did many farmers face in the late 1800s?

**The Populist Crusade**  Despite action by Farmers' Alliances and Grangers, the plight of thousands of farmers worsened. By the 1890s they had become politically active as never before. The platform of the Populist Party called for extensive reforms. Reformers believed that farmers and workers should be freed from the exploitative practices of banks, railroads, and merchants. Although James Weaver, the Populist candidate for president, was soundly defeated by Democrat Grover Cleveland in the election of 1892, his party made headway. The Populists gained 14 seats in Congress, won two governorships, and received the largest number of popular votes cast for any third party in the nineteenth century.

Shortly after the election of 1892, the nation plunged into the deepest depression the country had yet known. In 1893 more than 2.5 million Americans, about 20 percent of the labor force, were unemployed. By the following year the ranks of the unemployed had swollen to 4 million.

President Cleveland's seeming indifference to the economic problems caused by the depression created a popular revolt. Jacob S. Coxey, a quiet Ohio businessman, led a march of about 500 people from Ohio to Washington, D.C., to dramatize the plight of those out of jobs. Leaders read their grievances on the steps of Congress and were arrested for trying to enter the Capitol unlawfully.

By the time of the 1896 election, the Populist Party itself had declined, but some of its ideas entered the mainstream. The continuing depression forced the Democratic Party into a more radical position on one key issue—unlimited coinage of silver. This stance led many Populists to support the Democratic candidate, William Jennings Bryan of Nebraska. Bryan waged a campaign in favor of "free silver," and secured endorsement by the Populist Party. He travelled extensively, logging 18,000 miles on the campaign trail.

The Republican nominee, William McKinley, took a more relaxed approach. McKinley had the support of big business. In fact, Standard Oil's $250,000 donation to the Republicans nearly exceeded the total amount in the Democrats' treasury. McKinley merely warned voters of the dangers of Populist-inspired radicalism.

McKinley won by a comfortable 600,000 votes, suggesting that Americans in towns and cities heeded his warning. The discovery of gold in Alaska in 1898 increased the nation's gold reserves and eased more money into circulation, stemming the money crisis for many farmers. Populism began to decline as a political force.

**The Southern Alliance**  One factor limited Populism's strength in the South. By 1890 well over 1 million farmers belonged to the Southern Alliance. In December of that year they met with other farmers' groups at Ocala, Florida, and drew up a list of concerns. These included cheap currency, the abolition of national banks, and the restriction of land ownership to American citizens. Although this list resembled the Populist platform of 1892, the third party failed to gain wide support in the South. The Southern Alliance advised its members to support major party candidates who favored agricultural interests.

The underlying reason for the failure of Populism in the South, however, was the issue of white supremacy. The Southern Alliance feared that support of a third

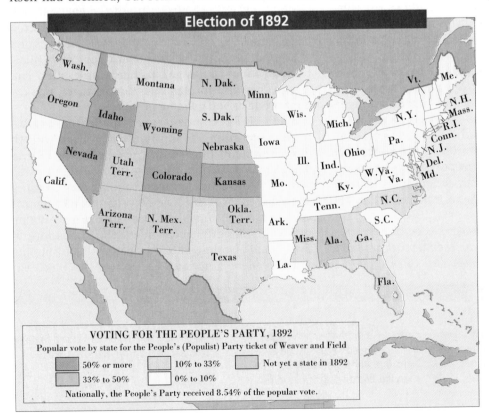

**Election of 1892**

VOTING FOR THE PEOPLE'S PARTY, 1892
Popular vote by state for the People's (Populist) Party ticket of Weaver and Field

- 50% or more
- 33% to 50%
- 10% to 33%
- 0% to 10%
- Not yet a state in 1892

Nationally, the People's Party received 8.54% of the popular vote.

**The Populist candidates for president and vice president in 1892 received very different levels of support from one state to the next.** *In which states or regions did Populists gain the most votes? Whose needs did the Populists hope to serve?*

party might lead to political power for African Americans. Populist leader Thomas Watson tried to form an alliance of poor white and black farmers. He argued that social class was more important than race. He urged blacks and whites to unite against the financial oppression that enslaved them both.

Watson's career mirrored the fate of Populism in the South. He was elected to Congress in 1890 but was defeated two years later as Democratic candidates gained support by promising to exclude African Americans from political power. Watson ran for president on the Populist ticket in 1904 and 1908. Embittered by his defeats, he became racist, anti-Catholic, and anti-Semitic.

## Labor Organizes

As early as the 1810s skilled workers such as carpenters, printers, and tailors had formed city-wide organizations to try to get better pay. Construction workers in many eastern cities succeeded in getting a 10-hour day in 1834. As the workplace changed, however, so did the labor movement. After the Civil War, factory production replaced skilled labor. Employers often cut the cost of wages by hiring women and children. Workers, like farmers, decided to organize to maintain control over their wages and working conditions.

The first nationwide labor organizations developed during the mid-1800s. In 1867 boot and shoemakers, whose wares were being undersold by machine-made products, formed the Knights of St. Crispin to try to block competition from unskilled workers. By 1870 this **union,** an organization for mutual benefit, had nearly 50,000 members. Like most early unions, however, the Knights of St. Crispin could not survive the high unemployment of the 1870s.

In 1877 a national railroad **strike,** or work stoppage, was the first of many violent confrontations between labor and the large corporations in the post–Civil War era. Clashes between railroad workers and state militias or federal troops sent in to break the strike recurred in the 1880s. Then in 1885 successful negotiations with railroad magnate Jay Gould emboldened workers in all fields. It convinced millions of them that they needed stronger labor unions.

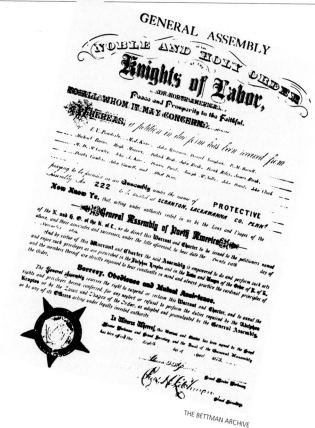

THE BETTMAN ARCHIVE

**Pictured above is the charter of a local Knights of Labor group. The charter instructs members to practice "Secrecy, Obedience, and Mutual Assistance."**

**The Knights of Labor**   The first national labor union to remain active for more than a few years was the Knights of Labor. Tailors in Philadelphia formed it as a secret society in 1869, and it grew to national proportions in the 1880s. The Knights of Labor differed from other labor unions by accepting all gainfully employed persons, including farmers, merchants, and unskilled workers. The union proposed new laws, including one to cut the workday to eight hours. Another proposal was equal pay for men and women doing the same work. Both of these were radical propositions at the time.[2]

Women workers played a role in this growing labor movement. When Irish immigrant Mary Harris Jones lost her husband and children to yellow fever in 1867, she moved to Chicago to work as a seamstress. After losing everything else in a fire, she turned to the Knights of Labor for help. Soon she was one of their strongest campaigners. She traveled on behalf of labor for nearly 50 years—later organizing for the United Mine Workers. Beloved by her followers, she became known as "Mother Jones." The bosses, however, feared her. A West Virginia lawyer working for the mining companies called her "the most dangerous woman in America."

In 1886 the Knights of Labor reached its peak with more than 700,000 members. A less reform-minded group, the American Federation of Labor (AFL), soon replaced it as the leading union. Led by Samuel Gompers, a cigar maker born in England, the AFL concentrated on organizing skilled workers. It advocated using strikes to improve wages and hours.

Gompers was willing to accept the new industrial system as it was, but only if labor got greater rewards. He also advocated **boycotts**—organized agreements not to buy specific products—as one means of peaceful protest. This tactic had only limited success.

**Protests and Violence**   Workers in the late 1800s customarily worked ten hours a day, six days a week. A strike for an eight-hour workday at the huge McCormick Harvester reaper factory in Chicago led to violent confrontation on May 3, 1886. After police

killed four strikers outside the plant during a scuffle, about a thousand workers turned out for a rally at Haymarket Square.

Someone in the crowd threw a bomb during the Haymarket protest, killing 7 police officers and injuring 67 bystanders. The police then fired into the crowd, killing 10 and wounding 50. Uproar over the Haymarket riot continued when 8 radical strike leaders were put on trial for murder. Although no direct evidence could be found that any of them had thrown the bomb, 7 of the 8 were sentenced to death, and 4 eventually were hanged. The public outcry against labor organizers in general helped employers defeat the eight-hour workday reform.

In 1892 another violent dispute took place in Homestead, Pennsylvania. The steelworkers' union called a strike when the Carnegie Steel Company reduced wages. The company hired 300 guards from the Pinkerton Detective Agency to protect its factories. Several people were killed when violence broke out between the strikers and the guards. The Homestead strike failed when most workers quit the union and returned to work.

Labor unrest spread to the West as well. Disputes arose between miners and mine owners over pay and conditions. Disputes also flared between nonunion miners and members of the Western Federation of Miners. Strikes plagued the Coeur d'Alene mining region of Idaho during the 1890s. Twice the strikes were broken when the governor called in federal troops.

**The Pullman Strike**   The depression of 1893 to 1897 brought further setbacks for labor. In 1894 Eugene V. Debs, the dynamic young founder of the new American Railway Union, led a labor action against the Pullman sleeping car works near Chicago.

George Pullman regarded his company town as a model industrial village where workers were paid decently and were carefully disciplined. "We are born in a Pullman house," said one worker, "fed from the Pullman shop, taught in the Pullman school, catechized in the Pullman church, and when we die we shall be buried in the Pullman cemetery and go to the Pullman hell."

As the depression of 1893 worsened, Pullman cut wages by one-third and fired many workers. Prices in the company stores and the rents for the company

DENVER PUBLIC LIBRARY

**A supervisor looks on as miners toil in San Miguel County, Colorado, around 1890. Bad working conditions led miners to try to form labor unions.**

houses, however, stayed the same. Angry Pullman workers joined Debs's railroad union in droves and went out on strike in the spring of 1894.

Debs then led a strike of all American Railway Union workers across the country in sympathy with the Pullman workers. Debs promised to "use no violence" and to "stop no trains." Instead, the railroad workers refused to handle trains pulling Pullman sleeping cars.

Determined to break the growing union movement, 24 railroad owners persuaded President Cleveland to order U.S. Army troops to disperse the strikers. Violence again centered in Chicago where strikers fought bitterly with troops and railroad company guards. Strikers set boxcars on fire and brought rail traffic in the Midwest to a dead halt.

However, labor did not stand together. Samuel Gompers's refusal to swing his powerful AFL behind the railroad workers caused the strike to collapse. The government arrested Debs and other union leaders and sentenced him to six months in prison. In 1895 the Supreme Court upheld the president's right to issue an **injunction,** an order to end a strike. Corporations thereby gained a powerful legal weapon that they used against unions for years.

**Obstacles to Unity**  Government intervention during major strikes repeatedly thwarted the nation's industrial unions. However, the unions also tended to cripple themselves by largely excluding three large groups of people: women, members of minority groups, and unskilled workers. By 1900 only about 1 in every 33 American workers belonged to a union, and fewer than 100,000 of the 5.3 million working women belonged to unions.

In the South the great majority of African American workers could join only a separate, all-black local union. In the North and West white unionists feared the competition of black workers and knew that many bosses would pay blacks less.

CULVER PICTURES, INC

**This print from an 1892 *Harper's Weekly* magazine shows angry strikers taunting security forces sent to break up the Homestead strike in Pennsylvania.**

The hostility of American-born workers toward immigrants was another factor that kept the unions weak. Suspicion often centered on Germans, English, or Russians, some of whom had more radical ideas about society and labor than Americans usually heard.

American-born workers strongly expressed their resentment of immigrants during the anti-Chinese movement in the West during the 1870s and 1880s. Angry mobs rampaged through Chinese areas in San Francisco, Tacoma, Seattle, and Denver in the 1870s. The Chinese Exclusion Act of 1882 reflected hostility against immigrant workers. The law halted immigration of Chinese workers and gained wide support from American labor unions.

By the turn of the century, big business cast its shadow across most of the American economy. In the turbulent labor struggles of the era, government had sided with employers against workers.

## SECTION REVIEW

### Checking Facts

1. What is the economic law of supply and demand? How did this law affect farmers in the late 1800s?
2. What reforms did the Populist Party call for?
3. Why did Populism fail to gain wide support in the South?
4. Why did workers feel it was necessary to create labor unions? What advantages might a labor union have over an individual worker in bargaining with an employer?

### Thinking Critically

5. **Identifying Cause and Effect**  How did attitudes toward women and minorities prevent labor unions from growing larger or gaining more power in the late 1800s?

### Linking Across Time

6. William Jennings Bryan once said, "The great cities rest upon our broad and fertile prairies. Burn down your cities and leave our farms, and your cities will spring up again as if by magic. But destroy our farms, and the grass will grow in the streets of every city in the country." What is Bryan's point? Do you think this argument is valid today? Why or why not?

# Material Culture

## *Looking Back to Former Life Styles*

Everyday items from long ago provide a treasure chest of information for historians. Button-hooks and potbellied stoves, toys and typewriters, curling irons and branding irons—these and countless other objects make up a society's material culture. Such objects help historians piece together a picture of past life styles and assess the technology of the times.

## The Evidence

The examples of material culture pictured on these two pages give historians clues about the life styles of people who lived between 1875 and 1900. The picture below shows a miniature room, a model of the parlor of a midwestern home. Does the model portray a life style of poverty or adequate means? Do the items in the room suggest a simple existence or a taste for comforts? What objects reflect the technology of the late nineteenth century? What do those objects tell you about the technology of the time?

The miniature room reveals a wonderful mixture of styles. In the late 1800s many people wanted their homes to reflect the latest trends. Different furniture designs appeared and disappeared with such dizzying speed that rooms often displayed a mixture of styles. In the model parlor, for example, the pointed arches of the windows are copies of the Gothic style of Medieval Europe. The wooden decoration, or fretwork, at the top of the window enclosure, on the other hand, reflected the latest style; it came into use in the late 1800s.

Notice the ornaments that decorate every surface. During the late 1800s families often used whatnots (open shelves like the ones at the right in the photo) to display cherished souvenirs. A seashell might recall a vacation on the shore, and a glass dish might proclaim "Souvenir of—."

Also treasured were portraits, such as the one over the fireplace. Many homes displayed

**This photograph of a model of a midwestern parlor shows one of a series of miniature rooms furnished** in the style of the late nineteenth century for a sociological study of a typical small city.

formal photographs of dearly loved relatives and respected officials. By the 1870s technological advances made it possible for even amateurs to try their hand at photography. Many a quiet Sunday was spent pouring over albums of family photographs.

## Interpretation

Items like the upholstered platform rocker (left side of parlor) and the telephone on the wall above the platform rocker give evidence that the Industrial Revolution made an impact on home life. A close examination of the platform rocker would reveal that it was machine-made. Because these rockers were mass-produced, they were far more affordable for the average family than handcrafted ones. This rocker also illustrates an innovative design of the time. It was mounted on a small platform so that it rocked back and forth in place, thus saving wear on the colorful, factory-made carpet.

On the wall to the right of the fireplace is a paper rack that was used to hold the daily newspaper. Along with the books in the elaborate secretary to the right, the paper rack is an indication that a family of this economic status valued an education.

The lamp at right is named after Louis Comfort Tiffany, who developed a colored glass called Tiffany Favrile glass. The colors in the glass shade, with its graceful design of fruit or flowers, glowed like jewels when the lamp was lit. The Tiffany lamp reflects a combination of technological advances. Its form took advantage of new machines that allowed designers to use cast iron and wire

in new ways. The lamp was lit by electric light bulbs, first developed by Thomas Edison in 1879.

Examining material culture for historical evidence sometimes presents limitations. For example, an isolated item doesn't tell much. Historians usually depend on additional information from other sources to understand better how an item affected people of the time. Suppose a historian examines the telephone in the parlor. First invented by Alexander Graham Bell in 1876, its placement in the parlor reflects its importance to a family of the late 1800s.

Yet, by itself, the telephone tells almost nothing. When the historian checks newspapers and advertisements of the day, as well as notes and papers in the archives of The American Telephone and Telegraph Company, the research gradually reveals a picture of the telephone in the context of that time. The historian learns that in 1877 installation of a phone line cost more than $100 a mile; therefore, a logical inference is that only affluent individuals or businesses could afford this new invention. Phones also could not be placed more than 20 miles apart, and transmitted words were frequently unclear. Why might a business or bank put up with the inconvenience of an indistinct message?

Another limitation to looking at material culture as evidence relates to identifying who used an object. Historians cannot conclude that a particular item was common to an entire culture at a given time. Only the well-to-do

THE CORNING MUSEUM OF GLASS, CORNING, NY

**This Tiffany lamp was made in the early 1900s. The pieces of colored glass are held together with lead.**

had telephones before 1900. Economic level and ethnic background frequently dictated usage. For example, while children in the middle class received an education, most children in impoverished families worked in factories and did not go to school. To assume that all the children of the period had the same opportunities for an education would give a distorted view of the life styles of the late 1800s.

## Further Exploration

Find a picture of a contemporary living room of a family from any economic level. What items in the room might interest a future historian? What limitations might those items present? What conclusions can be drawn about twentieth-century life style and technology?

# Reaching for Empire

## July 1, 1898: "Rough Riders" Storm San Juan Hill

SHOUTS OF "HURRAH!" WELCOMED TEDDY ROOSEVELT AND HIS BAND OF U.S. SOLDIERS AS THEY BATTLED THEIR WAY UP SAN JUAN Hill near Santiago, Cuba. Nonetheless Roosevelt barked at his troops: "Don't cheer, but fight. Now's the time to fight."

As the weary force struggled one last time to overpower the Spanish forces at the top of the hill, American wagons appeared, heaped with weapons. Grabbing rapid fire rifles, U.S. troops and the Cuban freedom fighters they were allied with finally captured the hill. The

THEODORE ROOSEVELT COLLECTION, HARVARD COLLEGE LIBRARY

U.S. and Cuban fighters won the battle, but the war continued. Finally, sixteen days later, the Spanish garrison at Santiago surrendered.

Roosevelt was but one of over 250,000 Americans who served in the Spanish-American War. When the U.S. government declared war on Spain, Teddy Roosevelt was assistant secretary of the navy. Eager to fight, Roosevelt resigned his government post, ordered a well-tailored uniform, and rushed to volunteer for military service. The secretary of the navy had mixed feelings about Roosevelt, saying, "He means to be thoroughly loyal, but the very devil seemed to possess him. . . . He has gone at things like a bull in a china shop."

Roosevelt proved to be a popular war figure. He organized the First Voluntary Cavalry Regiment,

known as the "Rough Riders." This odd collection of cowboys, college students, ranchers, and rich aristocrats fascinated the press. Roosevelt attracted a large following of wartime newspaper reporters with his colorful style and "bully" spirit. Reporters peppered their articles with Roosevelt's colorful quotes about the war.

The brief war with Spain was the climax of an era marked by the United States's growing involvement with foreign nations. In the late 1800s, the American people were in a mood for expansion as they pushed their boundaries westward, gained new lands, and created new businesses and markets in faraway places for American products.

## The Legacy of the Monroe Doctrine

The United States had a long and complex relationship with its neighbors in the western hemisphere. President James Monroe's address to Congress in 1823 had a significant impact on this relationship. Monroe's message to the European powers was loud and clear: no more European colonies in the western hemisphere.

Any foreign military expeditions sent to the western hemisphere for whatever reason would

---

### STUDY GUIDE

**As You Read**

Recognize how the United States expanded its borders and sought new business opportunities in foreign lands. Also, think about the following skills and concepts.

**Central Concepts**

- understanding U.S. **expansionism** in North America and beyond
- recognizing how the idea of **Manifest Destiny** encouraged Americans to expand

**Thinking Skills**

- recognizing assumptions
- making inferences
- recognizing propaganda

be seen as a threat to the United States, Monroe warned. No European country should interfere in U.S. affairs, at home or abroad, he continued.

Spain's interest in regaining control over former colonies spurred the president into action. Yet Monroe did have some assurance as he made these bold statements. He knew that England was also determined to prevent Spain from gaining any new colonies in the western hemisphere.

The president, relying on this information, decided to seize the moment and chart U.S. foreign policy with his strong words. This was a bold move, to volunteer to be the "police force" protecting emerging nations in the entire hemisphere.

At the time, there was little discussion of Monroe's ground-breaking pronouncement. It was neither widely liked nor sharply contested. More than 20 years passed before President James K. Polk implemented this so-called Monroe Doctrine and laid a cornerstone for American foreign policy.

**From Sea to Shining Sea**  American settlers were flooding into territories throughout the country. Settlers in foreign-owned territories such as Oregon, Texas, and California wanted a government of their own and they wanted to be part of the United States. Taking over these lands, however, would create conflicts with England, which owned part of Oregon, and with Mexico, which held Texas and California and much of today's southwestern United States.

James K. Polk was the settlers' champion. When Polk ran for president in 1844, he warmly supported **expansionism**, the process of increasing U.S. territory. After his election, Polk set out to gain Oregon as well as the Southwest. Polk and many other Americans supported **Manifest Destiny**—the notion that the United States was a superior country and had a right to invade, conquer, and occupy the North American continent and beyond.

In 1845 Polk declared that no European colony could occupy the North American continent. When the British insisted that they would continue to share in the rich Northwest Territory, Polk decided to drive the British out.

In a compromise move in 1846, Britain claimed land above the forty-ninth parallel and the United States retained what have today become the states of Oregon and Washington. War was avoided on the northern border, as the United States prepared for battle with Mexico.

Mexico had broken diplomatic relations with the United States when Congress annexed Texas in 1845. In that same year Polk sent negotiators to Mexico in an attempt to buy other Mexican lands, such as California and the area known as New Mexico. Mexico refused the Americans' $30 million offer. Shortly after, following a border dispute, war erupted. After two years of fighting, a peace was negotiated, and the United States laid claim to nearly half of Mexico for the bargain price of $15 million, with an additional $3.25 million to compensate U.S. citizens with claims against Mexico. You may want to refer to the map of territorial expansion of the United States on page 836.

**Policing the Hemisphere**  The Civil War years, 1861 through 1865, considerably limited American dreams of expansion. The war so consumed American arms and energy that during the long conflict, European nations tried to gain control of weak nations south of the Mexican border.

In 1861, despite warnings by Secretary of State William Seward, Spain seized an opportunity to reclaim its former colony, the Dominican Republic, an island in the Caribbean. At the same time that Spain sailed into the Caribbean, England and France sent troops to Mexico, pretending to collect war debts. The British soon retreated, but in 1864 the French leader, Napoleon III, installed Austrian archduke Ferdinand Maximilian, on the Mexican throne.

After the Union victory in the Civil War, however, American troops massed on the Mexican border, and Secretary of State Seward, citing the Monroe Doctrine, threatened war with France if its troops did not withdraw. By 1867 France complied, and new life was breathed into the Monroe Doctrine.

## Worldwide Ambitions

Many factors contributed to the spread of expansionist fever in the United States after the Civil War. Many Americans were motivated by a patriotic fervor. They felt that the acquisition of new lands would increase American glory and prestige throughout the world. Others saw the United States as a model country and felt a moral obligation to expand. They wanted to spread the American ideals of democracy and Protestant Christian values to people in other lands. Missionaries were sent to foreign lands to convert natives to Christianity. All of these opinions were supported by a new brand of American foreign policy maker who also emerged during this era. These newly established foreign policy professionals wanted to make the United States a world power through trade, diplomacy, and conquest.

Perhaps the greatest motivation for expansion was the need for new economic markets. As settlers filled the western frontier, and farmers and businesses produced more goods than Americans could buy, the country tried to create new markets. Henry Demarest Lloyd, a popular political writer at the time, wrote, "American production has outrun American consumption and we must seek markets for the surplus abroad."[1]

The United States looked especially to Asia. American involvement in Asia actually began long before the Civil War. In 1844 the United States negotiated trade agreements with China and began to export cloth, iron, and fur to the Chinese in exchange for tea, silk, porcelain, and jade. Far Eastern trade became a boon to New England merchants and expanded naval production, especially after Commodore Matthew Perry "opened" Japan in 1854.

Before that year, the Japanese had steadfastly refused contact with western merchants and closed their ports to European and American trade. Yet when Perry sailed into Tokyo's harbor under steam power, he so impressed the authorities that Japan began doing business with the United States.

By the 1880s the United States had made further inroads in the Far East with commercial treaties with Korea. The growth of these

PEABODY MUSEUM OF SALEM

**When trade to the Far East was opened, New England merchants bought and sold Oriental goods such as this Chinese porcelain vase.**

Asian markets stimulated the U.S. economy and became a key factor in the United States's bid for world power.

**Acquiring New Lands**   Under the leadership of Secretary of State William Seward, U.S. foreign policy after the Civil War became more aggressive. Seward dreamed of a U.S. empire that would include Canada, the Caribbean, Mexico, and Central America as well as Hawaii and other Pacific islands.

In 1867 Seward attempted to purchase Danish islands in the Caribbean for $7.5 million—a move rejected by the Senate. Congress also refused to approve Seward's plans for a U.S. naval base in the Dominican Republic.

He succeeded elsewhere. In 1867 the United States seized the Midway Islands in the Pacific Ocean, strategically located in the trade route to China and Japan. In the same year, Seward bought Alaska from Russia for $7.2 million.

Newspapers mocked Seward, and Alaska became known as "Seward's folly" and a worthless "polar bear garden." But Seward was wiser than his critics realized. Alaska paid for itself many times over with the gold that was discovered in the Yukon Valley, its rich copper and oil resources, and its seal and whale trade.

**Moving into the Pacific**   U.S. expansionist ambitions continued in the Pacific in the last three decades of the nineteenth century. In 1878 the United States acquired rights to a naval station in Samoa, astride the trade route to Australia and New Zealand. German and British claims in Samoa led in 1889 to a three-way division of Samoa among the three powers.

The Hawaiian islands became another Pacific prize. American sugar planters and American missionaries had thrived there after 1875, when the Senate allowed Hawaiian sugar to enter the United States duty-free. By 1881 the secretary of state declared the islands "essentially a part of the American

**Making Inferences**

The Hawaiian palace coup was called a "revolution of sugar, by sugar, for sugar." From this saying, we can infer that the American sugar planters held great political power and were extremely influential in shaping the United States's foreign policy in the Pacific islands.

1 Why did the United States feel the need to seek new markets in the era following the Civil War?

**Queen Liliuokalani was determined to keep the United States from seizing control of Hawaii.** *Why were the Hawaiian Islands so valuable to American interests in the Pacific?*

## War with Spain

The expansionist moves from the end of the Civil War through the early 1890s reached a peak in 1898 in the Spanish-American War. The war not only added significant new territory to the growing American overseas empire, but also demonstrated that the United States could turn its industrial muscle into formidable naval power in both of the oceans surrounding North America.

The origins of the Spanish-American War lay in the troubled island of Cuba, only 90 miles off the southern tip of Florida. The Cuban people had struggled since 1868 for independence from Spain.

Many Americans identified that struggle with their own revolution against England. Other Americans, beginning in the 1850s, had regarded Cuba as geographically a natural part of the United States and as an island of great economic potential because of its sugar-growing ability.

In 1895 Cuban rebels led by José Martí renewed their fight for independence, launching their first attacks from U.S. soil. A ferocious war ensued. Spanish troops, commanded by Valeriano Weyler, forced some 300,000 Cubans into concentration camps where tens of thousands died.

While the war wore on, Americans elected William McKinley president in 1896. McKinley's campaign platform included claims to Hawaii and the Virgin Islands and support for Cuban independence. But he had no desire for war with Spain and in 1897 was encouraged by a new Spanish government that promised reforms in Cuba as well as some measure of independence for the Cubans.

**Headline Wars**   Dramatic events early in 1898 ruined McKinley's desire to avoid war. In February, an exploding mine rocked the *Maine*, killing 260 officers and men. Headlines screamed for revenge: "Remember the *Maine*! To Hell With Spain!" Two days later, a New York paper proclaimed: "Whole Country Thrills With the War Fever/Yet President Says 'It Was An Accident'." Most Americans believed the Spanish had blown up the *Maine*, and a naval board of investigation soon concluded that a Spanish mine caused the explosions.

system." In 1887 King Kalakaua was strongly pressured into granting rights for the United States to build a naval base at Pearl Harbor to protect United States interests in the Pacific. Finally, in 1893 American sugar planters in Hawaii staged a rebellion, determined to wrest control from Kalakaua's sister, Queen Liliuokalani. The queen had resisted U.S. control with the slogan "Hawaii for the Hawaiians."

The U.S. Marines surrounded the palace, and the American minister cabled Washington: "The Hawaiian pear is now fully ripe, and this is the golden hour for the United States to pluck it." The palace coup succeeded, leaving U.S. sugar planters and missionaries with political control of the islands. Congress moved toward annexation, but it would take another five years before the islands were officially annexed.

---

**STUDY GUIDE**

### Recognizing Propaganda

Many political writers decried the Americans' seeming love of the war. A great many of these writers attributed it to the press. Critics believed that journalists, with their sensational headlines

and stories pressed politicians into declaring war—especially in the case of the *Maine*. In fact, U.S. Admiral Hyman Rickover conducted a study of the sinking of the *Maine* 78 years later.

Rickover concluded that an accident, probably a faulty boiler, caused the explosion—not a mine.

Against his conscience, President McKinley took action. On April 11, 1898, he sent a message to Congress that called for the use of troops to bring about "a national compromise between the contestants." Congress responded with a more warlike declaration that gave the president authority to use troops to end Spanish control of Cuba and declared the island independent. These acts amounted to a declaration of war against Spain. Spain responded with its own declaration of war on April 24, 1898.

**From Havana to Manila**   Although most U.S. citizens focused on Cuba as the primary target for U.S. military might, others focused on the Philippines, Pacific islands also under Spanish control. One reformer asked: "Why should Cuba with its 1,600,000 people have a right to freedom and self-government and the 8,000,000 people who dwell in the Philippine Islands be denied the same right?" Also, gaining a foothold in the Philippines would help the United States protect Asian business connections.

Shortly after the *Maine* was blown up, Assistant Secretary of the Navy Teddy Roosevelt, anticipating war, instructed Commodore George Dewey to prepare to remove his squadron of six ships from the neutral port of Hong Kong and attack the Spanish fleet in the Philippines.

Dewey confirmed this plan with President McKinley by cable and steamed across the China Sea to enemy waters over 600 miles away. The commodore sailed into Manila Bay on May 1, 1898, and demolished the old Spanish fleet protecting the city. Before noon, every Spanish ship was sunk.

After Dewey's triumph, soldiers training in Florida were eager to launch their attack in Cuba. The battle began on June 22 with great fanfare.

Within days, most of the troops were under fire, wading through waist-deep swamps and dodging shrapnel day and night. U.S. troops finally took San Juan Hill, near the city of Santiago, on July 1, but a strong Spanish naval force remained in the harbor.

On July 3, however, the U.S. Navy chased Spanish cruisers and defeated their fleet in a dramatic battle that left only one U.S. sailor killed and another wounded. By contrast almost 500 Spaniards were killed or wounded and 1,700 taken prisoner.

By July 17 the United States had secured Cuba and only Puerto Rico remained under Spanish control. It fell to the United States in a few days. The fast pace of the war was necessary to bring home the thousands of American soldiers sickened by yellow fever and malaria. Occupation had proved more deadly than battle. By the end of 1898, the death toll exceeded 5,400, of whom fewer than 400 were killed in combat.

**United States Victorious**   On August 12, with two fleets and their colonial armies devastated, Spain signed an armistice, or cease-fire. Diplomats met in Paris in October to negotiate a permanent settlement. It took two months to iron out their differences. Spain granted independence to Cuba and ceded Guam, Puerto Rico, and the Philippines to the United States for $20 million.

Although the United States had seemed to fight to liberate the Philippines, the American government refused to accept the pleas of Filipino nationalists for independence. The leader of the Filipino rebels against Spain, Emilio Aguinaldo, was deported from the islands when he refused to recognize U.S. rule.

President McKinley felt it would be "cowardly and dishonorable" to return the islands to the Spanish and argued that the

THE GRANGER COLLECTION

In the political cartoon below, President McKinley reprimands the press for using sensational headlines such as the one opposite to instigate war against Spain. Publishers were accused of publishing "yellow" journalism that misled the public and stirred Americans to war.

CULVER PICTURES, INC.

Spanish-American War in the Philippines

Spanish-American War in the Caribbean

**Fighting during the Spanish-American War took place in both the Philippines and in the Caribbean. Note**

**Dewey's successful strike against the Spanish fleet in the Philippines and the U.S. blockade of Cuba.**

Filipinos were "unfit for self-government." To keep Europeans from taking over the Philippines, many Americans said that possession of the islands would uplift and Christianize the Philippines, overlooking the fact that the majority of Filipinos were already Catholic. Actually, business interests outweighed all other considerations, as an editor at the *Chicago Times-Herald* wrote: "The commercial and industrial interests of Americans, learning that the islands lie in the gateway of the vast and undeveloped markets of the Orient, say 'Keep the Philippines . . .'"

The war also gave the nation glory and many new heroes. Although Dewey's command to his subordinate, "You may fire when ready," was hardly stirring, the admiral became a cult figure. Eager for a hero, U.S. businesses capitalized on the naval commander's exploits: a song celebrated his bravery, and a chewing

gum was marketed as "Dewey's Chewies."

Teddy Roosevelt reveled in his image as a "Rough Rider" charging up San Juan Hill. He effectively used his military adventures during his political career, first as governor of New York and then as U.S. president. Roosevelt, like many Americans, believed the Spanish-American War had given the United States a new status. In 1898 he wrote "the nation now stands as the peer of any of the Great Powers of the world."

By 1899 America had expanded its dominion to include Puerto Rico, Hawaii, and many Pacific islands, including the newly acquired Philippines. Both the nation and the world recognized the new international role of the United States. The consequences of this economic and political expansion would shape the course of the United States's future well into the next century.

## SECTION REVIEW

**Checking Facts**

1. Define expansionism. Why is Polk remembered as an expansionist president?
2. Why did Europeans try to create new colonies in the western hemisphere during the Civil War years? How did the United States respond?
3. Why did the Japanese finally agree to trade with the United States in 1854 ?

**Thinking Critically**

4. **Comparing** What events led to the Spanish-American War?
5. **Comparing and Contrasting** How are the ideas of Manifest Destiny and Social Darwinism alike?
6. **Drawing Conclusions** Why did the smaller nations in the Pacific play a large role in the United States's plans for expansion?

**Linking Across Time**

7. In recent years, the United States has become involved in conflicts in such Central American countries as Nicaragua and El Salvador. How does this involvement reflect policies set forth by the Monroe Doctrine?

# Chapter 4 Review

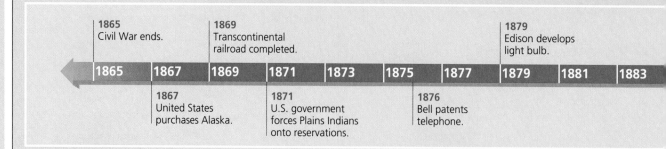

1865
Civil War ends.

1869
Transcontinental railroad completed.

1879
Edison develops light bulb.

| 1865 | 1867 | 1869 | 1871 | 1873 | 1875 | 1877 | 1879 | 1881 | 1883 |

1867
United States purchases Alaska.

1871
U.S. government forces Plains Indians onto reservations.

1876
Bell patents telephone.

## Summary

Use the following outline as a tool for reviewing and summarizing the chapter. Copy the outline on your own paper, leaving spaces between headings to jot down notes about key events and concepts.

I. Opening of the West
  A. New Frontiers
  B. Building the Railroad
  C. The Second Great Removal
II. Rise of Industrialism
  A. Industrialism Triumphant
  B. National Markets
  C. The Growth of Big Business
  D. The Spirit of the Gilded Age
III. Populism and Protest
  A. Farmers Beleaguered
  B. Labor Organizes
IV. Reaching for Empire
  A. The Legacy of the Monroe Doctrine
  B. Worldwide Ambitions
  C. War with Spain

## Ideas, Events, and People

1. Which groups of people benefited from the settlement of the West? Which did not? Why?
2. Identify three major inventions of the era from 1865 to 1900. What effect did these and other inventions have on workers' productivity?
3. John D. Rockefeller once said, "The day of individual competition is past and gone." How does his own life illustrate this belief?
4. Explain the term *robber barons*. Why was it applied to people such as Carnegie and Morgan?
5. What were the main goals of the Populist Party? Whose interests did the party represent?

6. How could labor unions have dramatically increased their size or power? Why didn't they?
7. What was the Monroe Doctrine? Why was it important to the United States after the Civil War?
8. Why did the United States decide to keep control of the Philippines?

## Social Studies Skills

### Reading Statistical Tables

The *Statistical Abstract of the United States* annually publishes tables of statistics from the Bureau of the Census and other governmental agencies. Look at the latest edition in the library for recent information relevant to a topic introduced in this chapter—for example: labor union membership by state, or mergers of corporate enterprises, or income levels of households. Pick one table of interest and photocopy it. What information does the table give in its title and subtitle? According to the headings, in what categories and subcategories does the table group its information? Look at the column on the left side to find out how items in the table are organized. Describe any changes or patterns shown by the statistics in the table.

## Critical Thinking

### 1. Predicting Consequences

In 1907 an Oklahoma newspaper editor wrote that "Sympathy and sentiment never stand in the way of the onward march of empire." Do you think the government could have kept settlers out of Oklahoma? Would telling settlers to respect Native American lands have been effective?

### 2. Recognizing Values

Wanamaker's, Macy's, and other department stores had marble staircases, expensive carpets, and chandeliers. Why do you think the owners spent so

| 1889 | 1898 |
| U.S. government opens Oklahoma for settlement. | United States annexes Hawaii. |

| 1885 | 1887 | 1889 | 1891 | 1893 | 1895 | 1897 | 1899 | 1901 | 1903 |

| 1886 | 1893 | 1894 | 1898 |
| Strikers riot at Haymarket. | Nation plunges into economic depression. | Railroad workers organize Pullman strike. | United States gains Guam, Puerto Rico, and the Philippines in Spanish-American War. |

much money to decorate their stores? What values were they trying to appeal to in customers?

3. **Comparing and Contrasting**

Explain the difference between horizontal and vertical integration of industry. Why did Carnegie and other business leaders try to achieve both?

4. **Making Generalizations**

Reread the material on the Populist Party and on the labor movements. Based on this material, what generalizations can you make about farm and labor movements during the era? What evidence supports your generalizations?

5. **Recognizing Bias**

President McKinley argued that the Filipinos were "unfit for self-government." What bias does this statement reveal? What might account for McKinley's bias?

6. **Analyzing Decisions**

In 1898 Teddy Roosevelt resigned his safe post as assistant secretary of the navy in order to help organize the dangerous "Rough Riders." Why do you think he made this decision? What effect did it have on his career?

## Extension and Application

1. **Citizenship**

Life stories of Carnegie, Rockefeller, and other "robber barons" show the financial success that American citizens can achieve. Do you admire that kind of success? What is its impact on other citizens? How do the "robber barons" compare to today's financially successful people? Discuss your answers with the class.

2. **Global Connections**

Like the United States, many nations held colonies as part of their empires. Using the maps in the back of the book, prepare a world map that shows the colonies held by France and Britain before 1945. How does your map compare to a current world map showing these nations and their possessions? What factors account for the differences?

## Geography

1. How did cattle ranching and the cowhands' work promote settlement on the Great Plains?

2. How did the early railroad lines influence where people settled on the Plains and in the West?

3. Name three factors that made northern and northeastern states the center of industry in the United States after the Civil War.

4. The map on page 130 shows regional differences in the presidential election of 1892. Was regionalism becoming more important or less so in the late 1800s?

5. Name some geographical factors involved in American imperialism in the McKinley and Roosevelt years. Which were economic and which were political factors?

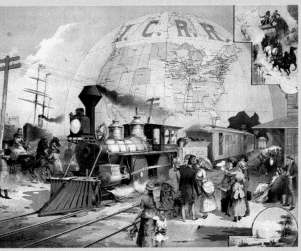

THE GRANGER COLLECTION

# Unit 1 Review

> *I* do believe that we shall continue to grow, to multiply and prosper until we exhibit an assocation powerful, wise, and happy beyond what has yet been seen by men."
>
> Thomas Jefferson,
> *in a letter to John Adams*, 1812

> *A* merica is a land of wonders, in which everything is in constant motion and every change seems an improvement."
>
> Alexis de Tocqueville,
> *Democracy in America*, 1835

## Concepts and Themes

As the nineteenth century ended, the United States emerged as a world power. Only 120 years earlier, the nation was no more than 13 colonies under British rule. After struggling free from Britain, the American people created a democratic government that aimed to please all parts of the country, from the industrialized North to the agricultural South. Regional differences, however, would tear the nation apart in the Civil War. Yet the United States not only survived the war, it flourished after it. U.S. boundaries reached outward, and industries and cities boomed. The nation was ready to establish its influence worldwide.

1. As Thomas Jefferson predicted in the quote above, the United States did grow after the Revolution. Using the territorial acquisition map on page 836, briefly summarize in a paragraph how the United States acquired new territories in North America.
2. Jefferson implies that as the country grew, the people would grow happier. How did the growth of the country in the pre-Civil War years create discontent in the nation?
3. Consider the quote by Tocqueville above, and cite one specfic change that occurred in the United States in this unit. Would all people agree with Tocqueville that this change was an improvement? Why or why not? Use details from the unit to support your answer.

## History Projects

1. **Evidence of the Past**
   Quickly sketch or photograph your living room. What clues do the objects in the room give you about modern values ?
2. **Culture of the Time**
   The Centennial Exposition of 1876 showcased inventions and other developments of the time. Plan an "American Teen in the 1990s" display for a modern exposition. Make a photo collage of the items you would display.
3. **Geography**
   Research how northeastern cities have changed since the 1800s. Locate the U.S. region that has been called the "Rust Belt." List how one city in the region is adapting to today's economy.
4. **One Day in History**
   Using library resource material, research the events following Lincoln's assassination. Create a feature following the format of One Day in History documenting how the American people paid tribute to the fallen president.
5. **Case Study**
   Research the status of a Native American nation today. In writing, explain the issues now confronting those people.

## Writing Activities

1. Research the first transcontinental railroad. Write several paragraphs describing how it was built, the people who built it, and the problems they faced. (See the *Writer's Guide*, page 829, for guidelines on informative writing.)
2. Study the photo of Richmond in ruins on page 117. Imagine you are a Richmonder who has returned home to this devastation. Using the *Writer's Guide* for descriptive writing on page 825, write an essay describing your feelings.

## The Arts

1. *The American Revolutionaries: A History in Their Own Words* by Milton Meltzer; a collection of first-person accounts of life at the time of the American Revolution.
2. "Glory": a film dramatizing free black volunteers facing combat in the Civil War.
3. *My Antonia* by Willa Cather; a novel about a girl living on the Great Plains in the late 1800s.

# UNIT TWO

# The Roots of a Modern Nation

© 1942 Frank Lloyd Wright Foundation

# Visions of the City

*In his novel* Sister Carrie, *Theodore Dreiser captures the allure of rapidly expanding cities like Chicago and New York for ambitious men and women in the late 1800s. Because he pays such careful attention to detail, Dreiser's portrait of city life at the time is as accurate as it is vivid. Poet Amy Lowell paints a different picture of city life in "New York at Night."*

## from *Sister Carrie*

### by Theodore Dreiser

Minnie's flat, as the one-floor resident apartments were then being called, was in a part of West Van Buren Street inhabited by families of labourers and clerks, men who had come, and were still coming, with the rush of population pouring in at the rate of 50,000 a year. It was on the third floor, the front windows looking down into the street, where, at night, the lights of grocery stores were shining and children were playing. To Carrie, the sound of the little bells upon the horse-cars, as they tinkled in and out of hearing, was as pleasing as it was novel. She gazed into the lighted street when Minnie brought her into the front room, and wondered at the sounds, the movement, the murmur of the vast city which stretched for miles and miles in every direction.

Mrs. Hanson, after the first greetings were over, gave Carrie the baby and proceeded to get supper. Her husband asked a few questions and sat down to read the evening paper. He was a silent man, American born, of a Swede father, and now employed as a cleaner of refrigerator cars at the stock-yards. To him the presence or absence of his wife's sister was a matter of indifference. Her personal appearance did not affect him one way or the other. His one observation to the point was concerning the chances of work in Chicago.

"It's a big place," he said. "You can get in somewhere in a few days. Everybody does."

It had been tacitly understood beforehand that she was to get work and pay her board. He was of a clean, saving disposition, and had already paid a number of monthly instalments on two lots far out on the West Side. His ambition was some day to build a house on them.

In the interval which marked the preparation of the meal Carrie found time to study the flat. She had some slight gift of observation and that sense, so rich in every woman—intuition.

She felt the drag of a lean and narrow life. The walls of the rooms were discordantly papered. The floors were covered with matting and the hall laid with a thin rag carpet. One could see that the furniture was of that poor, hurriedly patched together quality sold by the instalment houses.

She sat with Minnie, in the kitchen, holding the baby until it began to cry. Then she walked and sang to it, until Hanson, disturbed in his reading, came and took it. A pleasant side to his nature came out here. He was patient. One could see that he was very much wrapped up in his offspring.

"Now, now," he said, walking. "There, there," and there was a certain Swedish accent noticeable in his voice.

"You'll want to see the city first, won't you?" said Minnie, when they were eating. "Well, we'll go out Sunday and see Lincoln Park."

Carrie noticed that Hanson had said nothing to this. He seemed to be thinking of something else.

"Well," she said, "I think I'll look around to-morrow. I've got Friday and Saturday, and it won't be any trouble. Which way is the business part?"

Minnie began to explain, but her husband took this part of the conversation to himself.

"It's that way," he said, pointing east. "That's east." Then he went off into the longest speech he had yet indulged in, concerning the lay of Chicago. "You'd better look in those big manufacturing houses along Franklin Street and just the other side of the river," he concluded. "Lots of girls work there. You could get home easy, too. It isn't very far."

Carrie nodded and asked her sister about the neighbourhood. The latter talked in a subdued tone, telling the little she knew about it, while Hanson concerned himself with the baby. Finally he jumped up and handed the child to his wife.

"I've got to get up early in the morning, so I'll go to bed," and off he went, disappearing into the dark little bedroom off the hall, for the night.

"He works way down at the stock-yards," explained Minnie, "so he's got to get up at half-past five."

"What time do you get up to get breakfast?" asked Carrie.

"At about twenty minutes of five."

Together they finished the labour of the day, Carrie washing the dishes while Minnie undressed the baby and put it to bed. Minnie's manner was one of trained industry, and Carrie could see that it was a steady round of toil with her.

She began to see that her relations with Drouet would have to be abandoned. He could not come here. She read from the manner of Hanson, in the subdued air of Minnie, and, indeed, the whole atmosphere of the flat, a settled opposition to anything save a conservative round of toil. If Hanson sat every evening in the front room and read his paper, if he went to bed at nine, and Minnie a little later, what would they expect of her? She saw that she would first need to get work and establish herself on a paying basis before she could think of having

company of any sort. Her little flirtation with Drouet seemed now an extraordinary thing.

"No," she said to herself, "he can't come here."

She asked Minnie for ink and paper, which were upon the mantel in the dining-room, and when the latter had gone to bed at ten, got out Drouet's card and wrote him.

"I cannot have you call on me here. You will have to wait until you hear from me again. My sister's place is so small."

She troubled herself over what else to put in the letter. She wanted to make some reference to their relations upon the train, but was too timid. She concluded by thanking him for his kindness in a crude way, then puzzled over the formality of signing her name, and finally decided upon the severe, winding up with a "Very truly," which she subsequently changed to

NATIONAL GALLERY OF ART

**With its abstract geometric shapes, Max Weber's *Rush Hour, New York* (1915) conveys the hustle and bustle of burgeoning, modern cities of the early part of the century.**

"Sincerely." She sealed and addressed the letter, and going in the front room, the alcove of which contained her bed, drew the one small rocking-chair up to the open window, and sat looking out upon the night and streets in silent wonder. Finally, wearied by her own reflections, she began to grow dull in her chair, and feeling the need of sleep, arranged her clothing for the night and went to bed.

When she awoke at eight the next morning, Hanson had gone. Her sister was busy in the dining-room, which was also the sitting-room, sewing. She worked, after dressing, to arrange a little breakfast for herself, and then advised with Minnie as to which way to look. The latter had changed considerably since Carrie had seen her. She was now a thin, though rugged, woman of twenty-seven, with ideas of life coloured by her husband's, and fast hardening into narrower conceptions of pleasure and duty than had ever been hers in a thoroughly circumscribed youth. She had invited Carrie, not because she longed for her presence, but because the latter was dissatisfied at home, and could probably get work and pay her board here. She was pleased to see her in a way but reflected her husband's point of view in the matter of work. Anything was good enough so long as it paid—say, five dollars a week to begin with. A shop girl was the destiny prefigured for the newcomer. She would get in one of the great shops and do well enough until—well, until something happened. Neither of them knew exactly what. They did not figure on promotion. They did not exactly count on marriage. Things would go on, though, in a dim kind of way until the better thing would eventuate, and Carrie would be rewarded for coming and toiling in the city. It was under such auspicious circumstances that she started out this morning to look for work.

Before following her in her round of seeking, let us look at the sphere in which her future was to lie. In 1889 Chicago had the peculiar qualifications of growth which made such adventuresome pilgrimages even on the part of young girls plausible. Its many and growing commercial opportunities gave it widespread fame, which made of it a giant magnet, drawing to itself, from all quarters, the hopeful and the hopeless—those who had their fortune yet to make and those whose fortunes and affairs had reached a disastrous climax elsewhere. It was a city of over 500,000, with the ambition, the daring, the activity of a metropolis of a million. Its streets and houses were already scattered over an area of seventy-five square miles. Its population was not so much thriving upon established commerce as upon the industries which prepared for the arrival of others. The sound of the hammer engaged upon the erection of new structures was everywhere heard. Great industries were moving in. The huge railroad corporations which had long before recognised the prospects of the place had seized upon vast tracts of land for transfer and shipping purposes. Street-car lines had been extended far out into the open country in anticipation of rapid growth. The city had laid miles and miles of streets and sewers through regions where, perhaps, one solitary house stood out alone—a pioneer of the populous ways to be. There were regions open to the sweeping winds and rain, which were yet lighted throughout the night with long, blinking lines of gas-lamps, fluttering in the wind. Narrow board walks extended out, passing here a house, and there a store, at far intervals, eventually ending on the open prairie.

In the central portion was the vast wholesale and shopping district, to which the uninformed seeker for work usually drifted. It was a characteristic of Chicago then, and one not generally shared by other cities, that individual firms of any pretension occupied individual buildings. The presence of ample ground made this possible. It gave an imposing appearance to most of the wholesale houses, whose offices were upon the ground floor and in plain view of the street. The large plates of window glass, now so common, were then rapidly coming into use, and gave to the ground floor offices a distinguished and prosperous look. The casual wanderer could see as he passed a polished array of office fixtures, much frosted glass, clerks hard at work, and genteel business men in "nobby" suits and clean linen lounging about or sitting in groups. Polished brass or nickel signs at the square stone entrances announced the firm and the nature of the business in rather neat and reserved terms. The entire metropolitan center possessed a high and mighty air calculated to overawe and abash the common applicant, and to make the gulf between poverty and success seem both wide and deep.

Into this important commercial region the timid Carrie went. She walked east along Van Buren Street through a region of lessening importance, until it deteriorated into a mass of shanties and coal-yards, and finally verged upon the river. She walked bravely forward, led by an honest desire to find employment and delayed at every step by the interest of the unfolding scene, and a sense of helplessness amid so much evidence of power and force which she did not understand. These vast buildings, what were they? These strange energies and huge interests, for what purposes were they there? She could have understood the meaning of a little stone-cutter's yard at Columbia City, carving little pieces of marble for individual use, but when the yards of some huge stone corporation came into view, filled with spur tracks and flat cars, transpierced by docks from the river and traversed overhead by immense trundling cranes of wood and steel, it lost all significance in her little world.

It was so with the vast railroad yards, with the crowded array of vessels she saw at the river, and the huge factories over the way, lining the water's edge. Through the open windows she could see the figures of men and women in working aprons, moving busily about. The great streets were wall-lined mysteries to her; the vast offices, strange mazes which concerned far-off individuals of importance. She could only think of people connected with them as counting money, dressing magnificently, and riding in carriages. What they dealt in, how they laboured, to what end it all came, she had only the vaguest conception. It was all wonderful, all vast, all far removed, and she sank in spirit inwardly and fluttered feebly at the heart as she thought of entering any one of these mighty concerns and asking for something to do—something that she could do—anything.

# New York at Night

### by Amy Lowell

A near horizon whose sharp jags
    Cut brutally into a sky
Of leaden heaviness, and crags
Of houses lift their masonry
    Ugly and foul, and chimneys lie
And snort, outlined against the gray
    Of lowhung cloud. I hear the sigh
The goaded city gives, not day
Nor night can ease her heart, her
        anguished labours stay.

Below, straight streets, monotonous,
    From north and south, from east and west,
Stretch glittering; and luminous
    Above, one tower tops the rest
    And holds aloft man's constant quest:
Time! Joyless emblem of the greed
    Of millions, robber of the best
Which earth can give, the vulgar creed
Has seared upon the night its flaming
        ruthless screed.

O Night! Whose soothing presence brings
    The quiet shining of the stars.
O Night! Whose cloak of darkness clings
    So intimately close that scars
    Are hid from our own eyes. Beggars
By day, our wealth is having night
    To burn our souls before altars
Dim and tree-shadowed, where the light
Is shed from a young moon, mysteriously
        bright.

Where art thou hiding, where thy peace?
    This is the hour, but thou are not.
Will waking tumult never cease?
    Hast thou thy votary forgot?
    Nature forsakes this man-begot
And festering wilderness, and now
    The long still hours are here, no jot
Of dear communing do I know;
Instead the glaring, man-filled city groans
        below!

## Responding to Literature

1. Review the descriptions of cities in these two selections. Would you have wanted to live in a city at the turn of the century? Why or why not?

2. In *Sister Carrie* the main character believes the city will provide her with new opportunities and a new life. Do cities today represent to you a gateway to opportunity? If not, what does?

*For Further Reading*
Cather, Willa: *O Pioneers!*
Dos Passos, John: *U.S.A.* (a trilogy)
Dreiser, Theodore: *The Financier*
Norris, Frank: *The Octopus*
Steffens, Lincoln: *The Shame of the Cities*

## CHAPTER 5

# Progressive Impulse

### July 7, 1903: Working Children March on the President's Mansion

President Theodore Roosevelt faced a difficult decision. Should he meet with a handful of children who were marching 125 miles from Kensington, Pennsylvania, toward Oyster Bay, New York, to confront him at his home? These marchers represented the thousands of children who worked in factories, mills, and mines. They were seeking the president's support for a law prohibiting child labor.

Though Roosevelt sympathized with the children, he feared supporting any demand voiced by their leader, radical organizer Mother Jones. President Roosevelt advocated reform, not revolution.

*These marchers represented the thousands of children who worked in factories, mills, and mines.*

Finally, on July 27, after 20 days of marching, the children arrived. Through a representative, Roosevelt sent his reply: "No!" His fear outweighed his sympathy. Despite Roosevelt's refusal to meet with Jones and the children, the child labor debate did not go away. However, it was just one issue Americans confronted between 1880 and 1920. Political corruption, labor unrest, and urban decay also plagued the United States during this period of rapid industrial and urban growth. By responding to these issues and yet avoiding radical upheaval, the American people fueled one of the greatest periods of reform in American history, the progressive era.

THE BETTMANN ARCHIVE

*Mary Harris Jones was 73 years old when she led the children's march.*

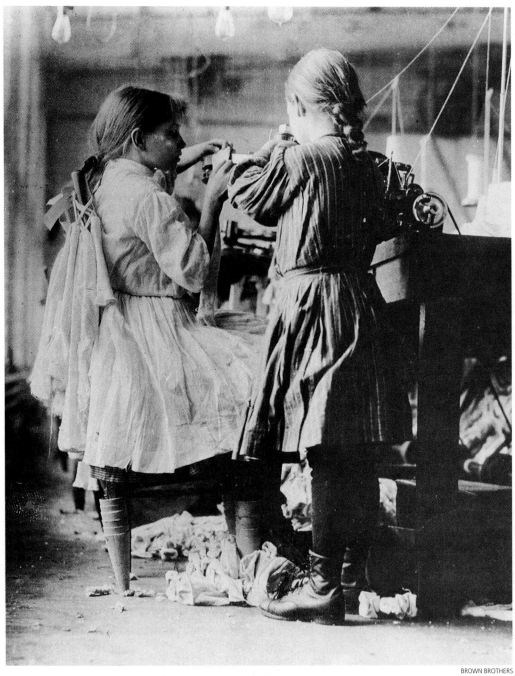

*The two young girls shown here worked in a clothing factory in New York around 1900. Children were paid about one-third or one-half as much as adult workers.*

# Facing a New Order

## 1890: Life and Death in a New York Apartment

PHOTOGRAPHER AND JOURNALIST JACOB RIIS HAD BREATHED ENOUGH STAGNANT AIR, SMELLED ENOUGH ROTTING FOOD, AND SEEN ENOUGH SICKLY CHILDREN TO KNOW how the poor of New York City lived. In one of his writings, he offered to take readers on a guided tour of an overcrowded apartment building:

*Be a little careful, please! The hall is dark and you might stumble over the children pitching pennies back there. Not that it would hurt them; kicks and cuffs are their daily diet. They have little else.*

*Here where the hall turns and dives into utter darkness is a step, and another, another. A flight of stairs. You can feel your way, if you cannot see it. Close? Yes! What would you have? All the fresh air that ever enters these stairs comes from the hall-door that is forever slamming, and from the windows of dark bedrooms. . . .*

*Here is a door. Listen! That short hacking cough, that tiny, helpless wail— what do they mean? They mean that the soiled bow of white you saw on the door downstairs will have another story to tell—oh! a sadly familiar story—before the day is at an end. The child is dying with measles. With half a chance it might have lived; but it had none. The dark bedroom killed it.*

Jacob Riis, *How the Other Half Lives*, 1890

Between 1880 and 1920, people flocked to the cities from the countryside and abroad. While they often found opportunity, many also suffered from low wages, diseases, and wretched housing. How concerned citizens responded to these problems reshaped American government in the progressive era.

## Shame of the Cities

The conditions that Riis described in the New York apartment building, or **tenement,** could be found in many cities around the nation. As these cities grew, so did their problems.

**Urban Growth and Immigration**   Cities in the United States expanded rapidly in the late 1800s. In 1860 only 20 percent of the people in the United States lived in towns or cities with populations greater than 2,500. By 1900 this percentage had doubled.

As American cities grew and became overcrowded, people who could afford to moved to **suburbs.** These communities blossomed at the edges of big cities. New forms of mass transportation developed; these enabled suburban residents to commute more easily to their jobs in the center of the city. In addition, these improvements helped everyone move around the city more efficiently. In 1873 San Francisco began construction of cable-car lines. A large cable powered by a motor at one end of the rail line moved passenger cars along.

THE BETTMANN ARCHIVE

---

### STUDY·GUIDE

**As You Read**
Identify the reasons that people were drawn to the cities and understand how they coped with the challenges they encountered. Also, think about the following concepts and skills.

**Central Concepts**
- analyzing the impact of rapid **urbanization** on American life in the late 1800s
- understanding the experiences of **immigrants** in America

**Thinking Skills**
- identifying cause and effect
- analyzing behavior

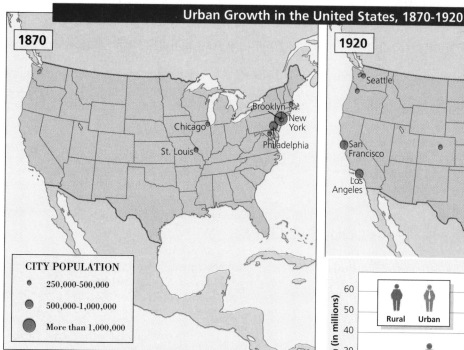

## Urban Growth in the United States, 1870-1920

1870

1920

**CITY POPULATION**
- 250,000-500,000
- 500,000-1,000,000
- More than 1,000,000

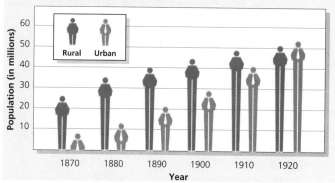

**The map shows rapid urban growth near the Great Lakes, a region with large coal deposits and good transportation.** *According to the chart, how did the rural population change between 1880 and 1920?*

In 1888 Richmond, Virginia, pioneered the use of the trolley car, a motorized train that was powered by electricity supplied through overhead cables. In 1897 Boston opened the nation's first subway, or underground railway.

Changes in transportation were just one advancement in technology that fostered **urbanization,** the growth of cities. Before the mid-1800s water power ran machinery. Therefore, factories had to be near rivers. With the application of steam power in the mid-1800s, though, factories could be established anywhere that fuel, usually coal, was available. Factory owners sought locations where they had dependable access to coal for fueling their steam-driven machinery and to minerals, sand, or other materials they needed to run their factories. They prized sites where rail lines linked with water routes, such as New York, Chicago, and St. Louis.

The opening of a factory in a city was a magnet that pulled in new residents looking for jobs. Many of these people came from rural areas where they could find no work. New machines—reapers, threshers,

binding machines, combines—were rapidly replacing manual labor on farms. One commentator noted in 1898 that "four men with improved agricultural implements now do the work formerly done by fourteen." Those who moved to cities often found work in the expanding factories.[1]

Although jobs were the primary attraction of the cities, people also headed to cities for other reasons. Cities offered pleasures considered luxuries in rural areas—plays, concerts, and stores with fancy clothes. City dwellers got new technology, such as electricity and indoor plumbing, long before rural residents did. Finally, cities offered anonymity. In large urban areas, people could easily disappear from the scrutiny of their friends and families.

The movement to the cities included both whites and blacks. In 1865, at the end of the Civil War, most African Americans lived on farms and in small towns throughout the South. By the late 1800s, though, blacks were beginning to move to cities. Over 40

### STUDY GUIDE

**Identifying Cause and Effect**

As machines replaced hand labor, industrial production levels increased dramatically. Large amounts of coal were needed to power these new machines, and a network of railroads was created

to distribute the goods all over the country. Cities became the hubs of these networks and the centers of industrial production. Industrial growth, then, led to urban growth.

1 How did the development of new farm machines draw people away from rural areas and encourage the growth of cities?

Progressive Impulse    153

percent of the people in Atlanta were African Americans. In most northern cities, the black population was increasing but did not exceed 3 percent in any given city by 1915.

Like rural citizens of the United States, Europeans poured into American cities in the late 1800s and early 1900s. The United States had always been a land of **immigrants.** However, beginning around 1880, the immigrant stream became a flood. Between 1880 and 1920, about 25 million immigrants entered the United States. That was half as many people as lived in the entire country in 1880.

As important as the swelling tide of immigrants was the dramatic shift in their countries of origin, as shown on the chart on this page. Before 1890 most immigrants came from northern and western Europe—Great Britain, Ireland, Germany, and the Scandinavian countries. Many of these people spoke English, and most were Protestants. Between 1890 and 1920, though, about 80 percent of all immigrants came from southern and eastern Europe, from countries such as Italy, Greece, Poland, and Russia. They usually practiced the Roman Catholic, Eastern Orthodox, or Jewish faith. Most were poor, uneducated, and illiterate.

Most immigrants arriving after 1880 settled in cities, because that was where jobs could be found. By 1920 nearly half of all urban dwellers were immigrants or the children of immigrants. The ethnic diversity of American cities impressed Danish

**Immigrants, such as those shown below arriving in New York in the early 1900s, often sailed on dangerously crowded ships.** *When did the number of southern and eastern European immigrants first exceed 400,000, according to the chart?*

immigrant Jacob Riis. Speaking of New York, he said, "A map of the city, colored to designate nationalities, would show more stripes than on the skin of a zebra, and more colors than any rainbow." However, one Polish immigrant found the large number of immigrants frustrating:

> *I am polish man. I want be American citizen. . . . But my friends are polish people—I must live with them—I work in the shoe-shop with polish people—I stay all the time with them—at home—in the shop—anywhere. . . . when I come home—I must speak polish and in the shop also. In this way I can live in your country many years—like my friends—and never speak—write well English—and never be good American citizen.*
>
> Polish immigrant, *Commission on the Problem of Immigration*, 1914

To adjust to the United States, immigrants often relied on help from friends or relatives who had arrived earlier. "When I woke of a morning," one immigrant recalled, "I was never greatly surprised to find in my bed a new family of immigrants."

Not all immigrants stayed in the United States. Some got homesick and returned to the land of their birth. Others came to the United States expecting to leave. They worked for a few years, saved all they could, and returned home. As many as one-third of the immigrants to the United States eventually left. Those who stayed faced a challenging future in American cities.

**Social Problems** Not everyone celebrated the growth of cities. Many Americans agreed with Congregationalist minister Josiah Strong that cities were wicked places and indeed posed threats to the very core of their civilization.

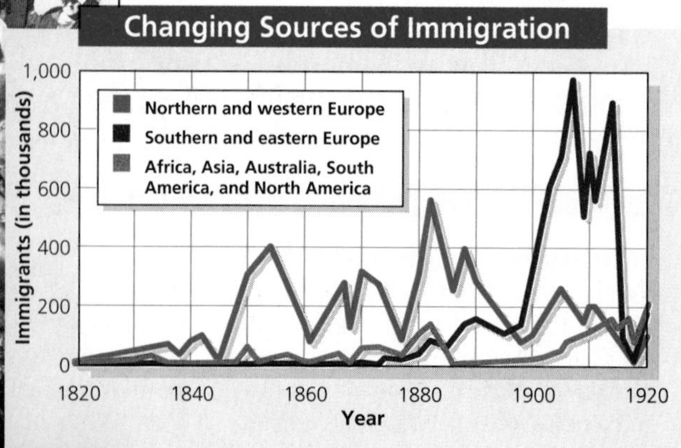

UPI/ BETTMANN NEWSPHOTOS

### Changing Sources of Immigration

- Northern and western Europe
- Southern and eastern Europe
- Africa, Asia, Australia, South America, and North America

Immigrants (in thousands) — Year

*The city has become a serious menace to our civilization. . . . Here [in the city] is heaped the social dynamite; here roughs, gamblers, thieves, robbers, lawless and desperate men of all sorts, congregate; men who are ready on any pretext to raise riots for the purpose of destruction and plunder; here gather foreigners and wage-workers; here skepticism and irreligion abound.*

Josiah Strong,
*Our Country,* 1885

Strong's attack on cities reflected his own dislike of immigrants. However, his views also reflected the existence of real problems in cities. Many jobs paid so poorly that workers had to find other ways, sometimes illegal, to add to their income. Gambling, robbery, and extortion were widespread. In 1906 Chicago had an estimated 10,000 prostitutes, many of whom were under the age of 19. The city also had about 7,000 cocaine addicts. As cities grew, so did violence. The murder rate increased from 1.2 per 100,000 people in 1900 to 6.8 per 100,000 in 1920. Election days were often marred by gang fights between rival political groups.

Cities were not equipped to respond to their growing problems. Without enough police officers, crime was rampant. Without enough firefighters, fires quickly raged out of control. Without adequate sanitation systems, garbage and sewage piled up in the streets and polluted the drinking water. Two of the most severe urban problems were poor housing and political corruption.

Many people pouring into the cities could not afford their own apartments—and not enough places existed even if they could—so people doubled up. Landlords divided small apartments into two or more even smaller units. Property owners converted horse stables, garages, and storage shacks into apartments. They added new buildings in the backyards of existing ones.

As buildings were carved up or constructed ever closer together, many apartments had no source of fresh air. Architects tried to combat this problem by designing dumbbell apartments. These structures were narrower in the middle than on the ends, like the letter *I*. A row of such buildings would have air shafts between each. The air shaft allowed light and air into each apartment.

The air shafts, though, became dangerous. Tenants threw garbage out of their windows into the shafts. The smell on a hot summer day could be so nauseating that tenants had to close their windows. Worse than the putrid smell were the rats, insects, and disease germs that thrived in the garbage.

Tenements were bad for most newcomers to the city, but they were worst for African Americans. As a result of the racial prejudice of most whites, African Americans were restricted to living in only small parts of cities. As their population increased, the black neighborhoods became even more overcrowded than the areas where immigrants lived.

**Political Corruption**   Politicians controlled the valuable contracts for building the new transportation lines, bridges, and firehouses that a growing city needed. However, many showed more concern for filling their own pockets than for solving the problems that Riis and others identified. A mayor could become wealthy overnight by accepting a bribe from a company trying to win a construction contract with the city. Businesses, then, usually added the cost of the bribe onto the contract with the city. The well-connected business prospered, and so did the politician. Taxpayers paid the bill.

In order to keep the wealth flowing to themselves and their allies, politicians had to remain in office. They won the necessary votes by doing favors for people. The poor people of a city, especially immigrants and African Americans, often needed help—a job, a bag of coal, legal advice—that a wealthy politician could provide. All that the politician asked in return was a vote on election day. Some politicians developed and ran sophisticated organizations, known as **machines,** to win votes. In each ward, or political district within a city, a machine representative controlled jobs, contracts, and favors. This person was the ward boss.

The most famous political machine in the country controlled life in New York City and was headquartered in Tammany Hall. George Washington Plunkitt, a member of the New York State Assembly, was a minor boss in the Tammany Hall machine.

## STUDY GUIDE

### Identifying Cause and Effect
The slums and tenements were not just breeding grounds for disease. The conditions in the crowded city neighborhoods also created a cycle of poverty and crime that was difficult to break.

Poor children who worked long hours in the factories could not attend school. Hence, they could not receive the education that could help them escape from poverty.

**2** Without an adequate sanitation system, how did people dispose of their garbage? What effect did this method of disposal have on their lives?

**Jessie Tarbox Beals took this photo, "Room in a Tenement Flat," in New York City in 1910. In poor areas of** New York, where political machines were strong, apartments housed an average of 1.9 people per room.

By observing Plunkitt in action and reading his diaries, a newspaper reporter pieced together a typical workday for Plunkitt. At 6:00 A.M., Plunkitt followed a fire truck to the scene of a fire and provided food, clothes, and temporary shelter for tenants who had just been burned out. "Fires," the reporter noted, "are considered great vote-getters." Later that morning, Plunkitt "paid the rent of a poor family" about to be evicted and "gave them a dollar for food." Then he found jobs for four men who had just been fired.

In the afternoon Plunkitt attended two funerals, one Italian and one Jewish. At each, he sat in the very front so everyone would see him. After dinner Plunkitt went to a church fair, where he bought tickets at every single fund-raising booth, and bought ice cream for all the children, "kissed the little ones, flattered their mothers, and took their fathers out for something down at the corner." At 9:00 P.M., he returned to his office, where he pledged to donate money to help a church buy a new bell. Later that night he attended a wedding reception and gave a "handsome wedding present to the bride." Finally, at midnight, after 18 hours of making friends and winning votes, Plunkitt went to bed.[3]

Plunkitt's long hours paid off handsomely. His Tammany Hall associates rewarded him for his ability to deliver a large number of votes to party candidates each election day. For example, when the park board

## STUDY GUIDE

### Analyzing Behavior

Analyzing behavior helps you understand individuals' motivations for acting as they do. Immigrants used the machines to secure services that they needed but that the government did not provide. Today, when government agencies provide food, jobs, and other benefits directly to individuals in need, people continue to vote for leaders that they think will serve their interests.

**3** How did George Plunkitt and other Tammany Hall machine bosses win the political support of New York voters?

was planning a new park, they slipped word to Plunkitt of the location long before any plans had been made public. Then, from the unsuspecting owners, Plunkitt bought the land where the park would be established. Weeks later, when the board announced its decision to construct a new park, Plunkitt resold the land to the park board at a much higher price than he paid for it. By the time of his death, Plunkitt was a millionaire.

## Industrial Disorder

Plunkitt was not the only person to prosper while others struggled just to survive. In fact, by 1910 the wealthiest 2 percent of Americans accounted for almost 20 percent of the total income of all workers, double what they accounted for in 1896.

One reason for this growing concentration of wealth was the rash of business mergers and buy-outs in the 1890s. Such consolidations usually resulted in the formation of **trusts,** a combination of companies dominating an industry, usually formed for the purpose of reducing competition in that industry. Often a trust was ruled by a a small handful of people, or even a single individual.

The size of these large companies accounted for some benefits to consumers. Large firms could afford to develop and use expensive new machinery that, in turn, lowered the cost of producing goods. Companies were so large that any small cost-cutting measure could save enormous amounts of money. For example, by reducing the cost of each oil storage can by only 15 cents, Standard Oil saved over $5 million a year. Such production efficiency could lead to cheaper retail prices. Items that were once luxuries, such as glass bottles, were now commonly available and inexpensive. "Never in human history was the creation of material wealth so easy and so marvelously abundant," pointed out one U.S. senator.

However, the senator cautioned, "Here are dangers it will behoove us to gravely contemplate." The new, efficient companies exacted a heavy cost in human suffering. Though wages increased slowly between 1890 and 1910, most workers lived just outside the reach of financial ruin. Everyday expenses for rent, food, and clothes absorbed virtually all of the income of typical workers.

In between the wealthy owners and the poorly paid laborers was a growing middle class. This group consisted of managers, clerks, small-business owners, college professors, clergy, lawyers, and other professionals. The middle class, which was able to afford the mass-produced goods, praised the technological triumphs that led to greater production efficiency. However, they felt threatened by both the rich and the poor and blamed the growing problems of society on these groups:

*Nearly all problems which vex society have their sources above or below the middle-class man. From above come the problems of predatory wealth. . . . From below come the problems of poverty and of pigheaded and brutish criminality.*

California Weekly,
December 18, 1908

To many educated, honest, middle-class Americans, the traditional values that they prized were under assault. Trusts, though efficient, threatened to squeeze small businesses out of existence. Workers, plagued with crime and poverty, seemed vulnerable to revolutionary calls for radical change. Middle-class Americans and their allies responded to these threats by calling for a return to traditional values—economic opportunity, religious morality, political honesty, and social stability. This effort to reform the United States and preserve its democratic values became known as the progressive movement.

## SECTION REVIEW

### Checking Facts

1. What combination of factors attracted rural Americans as well as immigrants to cities in the United States?
2. What effect did urban and industrial growth have on life in American cities?
3. Why did many newcomers to the cities have to share apartments?
4. How did consumers benefit from the existence of large trusts?

### Thinking Critically

5. **Identifying Cause and Effect** How do you think the wages of workers were affected by the continuous flow of new workers into the cities?
6. **Analyzing Behavior** Why did many immigrants eventually return to their native land? Explain whether or not such departures should be considered a criticism of American society.

### Linking Across Time

7. In what ways do the conditions described in American cities of the late 1800s and early 1900s resemble those in today's cities? In what ways do they differ?
8. Give examples to show whether or not the reasons immigrants enter the United States today are the same as the reasons they came around 1900.

# Ragtime

*The years called ragtime, named for the sprightly music of black composer Scott Joplin, were an extraordinary time in the nation's history. Industrialization and innovation transformed the way Americans worked and played. The recent discovery of "free time" presented the challenge of what to do with it. The invention of the camera made it possible to record many scenes of people eager to meet this new challenge.*

At the beach, playing in the sand and surf, Americans began enjoying **newfound leisure.** Even when swimming, they remained clothed virtually from head to toe.

**Woolen swimsuit**

BULLY

Scott Joplin entertained audiences with **ragtime piano music**—syncopated, high-stepping dance music born on the Mississippi Delta.

**Amusement parks,** such as Luna Park on New York's Coney Island, provided a "bully" time for everyone. They offered exciting rides for the daring and elaborate slides for the young.

**Celebrations** often combined love of family and love of country. Here Mr. and Mrs. Israel Dow celebrate their fiftieth wedding anniversary at their home near Chicago.

**The Gibson Girl,** drawn by illustrator Charles Dana Gibson, graced numerous ragtime-era magazines. Sophisticated, athletic, and self-reliant, she became the model that young women strove to copy.

**Physical strength** won Fred Winter, Olympic weightlifting hero, popular acclaim.

Frank Merriwell, the **all-American hero,** inspired readers of comics everywhere with his amazing deeds of courage and stamina.

**Tuskegee Institute,** organized by Booker T. Washington in Alabama in 1881, taught African Americans trade skills such as carpentry, printing, and nursing.

# A Generation of Reformers

## Early 1890s: "Saint Jane" Opens Nursery for the Poor

WITHIN A YEAR AFTER MOVING TO CHICAGO IN 1889, YOUNG, IDEALISTIC JANE ADDAMS MET THREE CHILDREN WHOM SHE NEVER FORGOT. "ONE HAD fallen out of a third-story window, another had been burned, and the third had a curved spine due to the fact that for three years he had been tied all day long to the leg of the kitchen table." The children had each been left alone, day after day, while their parents worked. Their parents earned so little money that they could not hire anyone to watch their children.

Addams, a quiet, dignified woman from a well-to-do family in a small Illinois town, had moved to Chicago because she wanted to help the poor. She and a friend had purchased a large, but run-
down, old home known
as Hull House in the
midst of a densely popu-
lated immigrant neigh-
borhood. They repaired
the house and made it
into a community center
where neighborhood res-
idents could learn to
speak English, discuss
political events, and hold
celebrations. In addition,
because of those three
injured children, Addams
opened a day nursery.

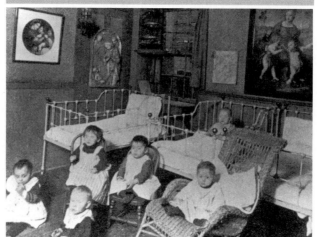

UNIVERSITY OF ILLINOIS AT CHICAGO, THE UNIVERSITY LIBRARY, JANE ADDAMS MEMORIAL COLLECTION

Working parents no longer had to leave their young children unsupervised during the day. For her work, neighbors referred to her as Saint Jane.

Addams realized that the machines that had brought such great prosperity were also the engines of great misery. Jane Addams was just one of many Americans who, at the turn of the century, advocated reforms to confront the problems caused by industrialization and urbanization. The efforts of these reformers, the **progressives,** dominated the political landscape of the early 1900s.

## Progressive Ideals

During Jane Addams's youth, the United States consisted mostly of small towns, small businesses, and small-scale problems. As Addams grew up, though, she watched larger cities, larger businesses, and larger problems develop. Small-town politicians never practiced corruption on the scale of George Washington Plunkitt and his Tammany Hall cronies. Rural poor people did not live in concentrations of garbage and stagnant air as did city tenement dwellers. A village blacksmith could never control a town the way a large steel company could dominate the people of a city.

Like the populists of the 1880s and 1890s, progressives feared the concentration of power in the hands of the wealthy few. While hard-working immigrants could not afford to provide for their hungry and ill children, financiers like J. P. Morgan became

---

**STUDY GUIDE**

**As You Read**
Identify individuals who were progressives and the problems they tried to solve in urban America. Also, think about the following concept and skills.

**Central Concept**
- recognizing that **progressives** worked in different ways to address the problems and upheavals that were associated with urbanization and industrialization

**Thinking Skills**
- comparing and contrasting
- recognizing values
- analyzing behavior

millionaires by manipulating ownership of the companies for which these immigrants toiled. Through campaign contributions and bribes, trusts bought influence with lawmakers. Progressives wanted reforms to protect the public interest.

Unlike the populists, who usually lived in rural areas, the progressives generally lived in cities. By the 1890s cities faced crippling problems: housing shortages, political corruption, and spiraling crime rates. In the chaotic cities, progressives wanted to reestablish order and stability.

Progressives were also unlike populists in their greater faith in experts. While populists emphasized the wisdom of average people, progressives focused on the ability of knowledgeable experts to analyze and solve problems. Just as Thomas Edison had conquered technological problems in developing the light bulb, progressives believed that trained experts could analyze and conquer crime, alcoholism, and political corruption. Many progressives praised business owners for their expertise in solving the problems of producing and distributing goods and in running a store or a factory smoothly. Though fearing the power of big businesses, progressives often respected the efficient methods used by businesses.

## Progressive Profiles: Analysts

Progressives looked to government to solve problems. Virtually all progressives shared the hope that a well-run government could protect the public interest and restore order to society. Beyond this hope, though, progressives differed widely in their beliefs, goals, and actions.

**New Intellectuals**   Many progressives were influenced by changes in higher education. Between 1870 and 1920, college enrollment increased more than tenfold, and many schools established separate social science departments, such as economics, political science, and sociology. These departments attempted to analyze human society with the same objectivity that scientists used to study nature. Their establishment reflected a growing faith in the ability of people to analyze society and solve human problems.[1] Many social science professors and the students they

influenced became progressives. For example, Columbia University historian Charles Beard applied his knowledge of American history to reforming corrupt city governments. Not all intellectuals worked for universities. Mary Ritter Beard, wife of Charles, wrote extensively about how scholars had ignored the contributions of women in history.

One of the influential members of the new social science fraternity was Lester Ward. Much of Ward's childhood was spent "roaming over those boundless prairies" of Illinois and Iowa in the mid-1800s "and admiring nature." After surviving three wounds as a Union Army soldier in the Civil War, he got a job as a minor clerk in the U.S. Treasury Department. For the next 40 years, he held a variety of federal government jobs. For most of this period, he worked for the U.S. Geological Survey, studying rocks, plants, and animals in the lightly settled territories of the West.

In his free time, Ward taught himself Greek, Latin, French, and German, and participated in various book clubs, debating the latest ideas on science, history, and philosophy. In 1869 he began outlining his first book, *Dynamic Sociology*, which he completed in 1883. In this book and five others, Ward analyzed social concerns just as scientifically as he studied natural phenomena. He challenged the widely held belief that it was natural for the strong, such as the owner of a large corporation, to prosper while the weak, the workers, suffered. What was natural, Ward argued, was for people to control and change their social environment—the laws, customs, and relationships among people—for their own benefit. "The day has come for society to take its affairs into its own hands and shape its own destinies."

The shaping of a society's destiny, according to Ward, was the job of the government. For example, if tenements were inadequate, then government should pass laws, spend money, or take other steps to improve housing. Ward believed that a larger role by government would improve the social environment and expand the options of individuals. "The true function of government," Ward proclaimed, "is not to fetter, but to liberate the forces of society, not to diminish but to increase their effectiveness."

In 1906, at age 65, Ward finally took his first full-time academic position. He became professor of sociology at Brown University. Social scientists such

**STUDY GUIDE**

### Comparing and Contrasting

Both progressives and the populists wanted a stronger government, one that would protect the rights of average citizens. Both groups called for a federal income tax and greater regulation of

the railroads. However, the movements responded to different concerns. Populists responded to agricultural problems, and progressives, to urban problems.

**1** How could a college department in economics help the progressives solve some of the problems that plagued American cities?

as Ward claimed that scientific study of human problems would provide better ways to run the cities. However, these new intellectuals often depended upon others to motivate the public and to attack specific problems with specific solutions.

**Angry Writers**  Among those who motivated the public were many writers known as **muckrakers.** That label came from a character in a seventeenth-century book *Pilgrim's Progress* who spent all of his time raking up the dirt and filth, or muck, on the ground. The muckrakers combined careful research, vivid writing, and intense moral outrage. Most of these crusaders wrote long, investigative articles for popular magazines such as *McClure's*, *Collier's*, *Cosmopolitan*, and the *American Magazine*. Writers attacked wealthy corporations that exploited child labor, corrupt police departments that protected prostitution rings, and prestigious churches that owned disease-ridden tenements. Ida Tarbell, a "conventional-minded lady, sweet and gracious," was one of the most famous of the muckrakers. She wrote a series of widely read articles detailing the rise of the Standard Oil Company. Tarbell exposed the ruthless methods used by its owner, John D. Rockefeller, to crush his competition—including Tarbell's father.

Ida Tarbell, a diligent investigator and a skilled writer, spent two years researching her articles on the rise of the Standard Oil Company.

In addition to articles, some muckrakers, such as Upton Sinclair, wrote novels. Sinclair grew up in near-poverty in Baltimore. His father, a salesman, suffered from alcoholism and was never very successful. By 1904 the 26-year-old Sinclair was a gentle, innocent-looking young writer. He had already completed four novels, each featuring a courageous individual who fought against social injustice. In that year a radical newspaper, *Appeal to Reason*, hired Sinclair to write a novel about the exploitation of workers in the United States.

To prepare for the contracted novel, Sinclair lived among the stockyard workers of Chicago for seven weeks. He later recalled how he sat "in their homes at night, and talked with them and then in the daytime they would lay off their work, and take me around, and show me whatever I wished to see. I studied every detail of their lives."

Based on his close observations of how workers lived, Sinclair wrote *The Jungle*, a novel about a Lithuanian immigrant who worked in the meat-packing industry. In focusing on one worker's life, Sinclair intended to arouse public sympathy for the common laborer. However, his graphic descriptions of the unsanitary conditions in the packing plant sparked a reaction to the meat industry itself that completely overshadowed his intended focus. As Sinclair noted somewhat sadly, "I aimed at the public's heart, and by accident I hit it in the stomach." His book made consumers ill—and angry:

> *There would come all the way back from Europe old sausage that had been rejected, and that was moldy and white—it would be dosed with borax and glycerine, and dumped into the hoppers, and made over again for home consumption. There would be meat that had tumbled out on the floor, in the dirt and sawdust, where the workers had tramped and spit uncounted billions of consumption germs. There would be meat stored in great piles in rooms; and the water from leaky roofs would drip over it, and thousands of rats would race about on it.*
>
> Upton Sinclair,
> *The Jungle*, 1906

BROWN BROTHERS

**Complaints about unsafe meat preparation began in 1899, after U.S. soldiers got seriously ill from eating spoiled canned meat.** *How would photos like this one of the Chicago stockyards around 1900 support the charges made by Upton Sinclair?*

Sinclair, like each of the muckrakers, had a vision of a just and orderly society. In Sinclair's society, workers would receive adequate wages and consumers would purchase healthful food. The muckrakers' aim was to awaken people to the growing social, economic, and political evils and inequities in the nation.

**Religious Reformers**  Another group of progressives also appealed to the conscience of Americans. The **social gospel movement** included Christians who emphasized the role of the church in improving life on earth rather than in helping individuals get into heaven.

One leader of the social gospel movement was Walter Rauschenbusch. Described by one journalist as "a tall, spare man, with a twinkle in his eyes," Rauschenbusch followed in the footsteps of six family generations and became a minister. After studying

theology in Rochester, New York, and in Germany, he became pastor of the Second German Baptist Church in New York City.

Rauschenbusch's theological training did not prepare him for what he confronted in New York. His church bordered a region aptly named Hell's Kitchen. Unemployment, alcoholism, and desperation plagued residents of this poverty-stricken neighborhood.

Rauschenbusch, as a devout Christian, turned to the Bible and his faith for a proper response to the new industrial system that made "the margin of life narrow in order to make the margin of profit wide." He concluded that the cause of many social ills was fierce competition. Owners and managers, many of whom were practicing Christians, believed they had to be ruthless or they would go out of business:

> *C*ompetitive commerce . . . makes men who are the gentlest and kindliest friends and neighbors, relentless taskmasters in their shops and stores, who will drain the strength of their men and pay their female employees wages on which no girl can live without supplementing them in some way.
>
> Walter Rauschenbusch,
> *Christianity and the Social Crisis*, 1907

Rauschenbusch and other advocates of the social gospel believed that environmental conditions such as unemployment and poverty, and not an individual's personal depravity, caused the ills in society. Hence,

Progressive Impulse  163

they believed, every Christian should strive to better the economic and political conditions in the world.

## Progressive Profiles: Activists

Most progressives who analyzed problems took action to solve them as well. Sinclair ran for Congress three times and for governor of California once. Rauschenbusch skillfully helped his parish members cope with unemployment, alcoholism, and other social ills. However, Sinclair and Rauschenbusch, like Ward, were more influential as analysts who identified and publicized problems than as activists who solved them.

Other progressives were more influential as activists who successfully won reforms on specific issues rather than as analysts. Progressives usually focused their efforts on the problems they saw firsthand or felt personally. For example, Sinclair wrote about the meat-packing workers he lived with. Rauschenbusch confronted the problems of the urban poor. Similarly, many women who were progressives emphasized the problems faced by women and children. Many black progressives stressed issues affecting blacks.

**Concerned Women**   In most families, whether urban or rural, women had more responsibility for raising the children than did men. Hence, women were particularly outraged about the problems of children laboring in factories.

One of the leaders in the battle against child labor was Florence Kelley. Her father, a member of the U.S. House of Representatives, opposed slavery and supported women's right to vote. He taught Florence to read at a young age and to value education. She graduated from Cornell University in New York and attended graduate school in Switzerland.

In 1891 she went to live and work at Jane Addams's Hull House. During her seven years there, she investigated and reported on the use of child labor. "In the stores on the West Side," Kelley reported in 1895, "large numbers of young girls are employed thirteen hours a day throughout the week, and fifteen hours on Saturday."

Kelley was, in the words of a friend, "explosive, hot-tempered, determined . . . a smoking volcano that at any moment would burst into flames." What she unearthed in her investigations, though, outraged even many mild-mannered people. Kelley charged that "children are found in greatest number where the conditions of labor are most dangerous to life and health." Children working in the tobacco industry suffered from nicotine poisoning. Children in paint factories suffered from breathing in toxic arsenic fumes. Children in clothing factories suffered spinal curvature from hunching over sewing machines 48 hours each week.

Kelley pressed the federal government to outlaw the use of child labor. "Why," she thundered, "are seals, bears, reindeer, fish, wild game in the national parks, buffalo, [and] migratory birds all found suitable for federal protection, but not children?"

BROWN BROTHERS

**This photograph shows one of the many child labor protest marches held in the early 1900s.** *Why would child labor opponents often support unions?*

Kelley continued her battle against child labor after she left Hull House. As general secretary of the National Consumers League (NCL), she helped organize consumer boycotts of goods manufactured by children or by workers toiling in unsanitary or dangerous conditions.

Most members of the NCL were, like Kelley, middle-class or upper-class women concerned about the problems such as exploitation of children in factories. Many NCL members also supported the work of **settlement houses,** institutions that provided educational and social services to poor people. Hull House was the best known of the 400 settlement houses established between 1886 and 1910. In addition to their work in settlement houses, women were very active in clubs that promoted the arts, education, and community health. By the early 1920s, almost one million women joined such clubs. The NCL, the settlement houses, and the women's clubs indicate that women were taking a more active role in confronting political and economic problems than they had in the past.

Some of the reforms advocated by Kelley and other women were not supported by many of the men who were progressives. For example, Walter Rauschenbusch opposed granting women the vote, even though this was a vital issue to Kelley and many female reformers.[2]

**African American Activists**   For the urban black family, racism intensified such problems as high unemployment and inadequate housing. Many white factory owners refused to hire blacks—except as strikebreakers. In most cities African Americans could live only in well-defined areas, which quickly became overcrowded as cities grew. Furthermore, racism remained firmly entrenched in the minds of most whites, including most progressives. Many whites viewed blacks as lazier, less intelligent, and more immoral than whites. In no other period of American history did state governments pass so many laws designed to restrict blacks to a secondary role in society.

African Americans working for reform often felt outside the progressive movement.

The most dangerous problem for blacks was **lynching,** murder by a mob. In 1892 about 230 people were lynched in the United States. Most of these people were African Americans, killed by groups of angry whites. Leading the antilynching movement was Ida B. Wells.

Born to slave parents in Holly Springs, Mississippi, in 1862, Wells remembered how much her parents emphasized education. "Our job," Wells recalled, "was to learn all we could."

When Wells was 14, her parents died in a yellow fever epidemic. Ida, the oldest of the six living children, refused to let her family be broken up. She lied about her age in order to get a job teaching school so that she could support her family.

In 1884 she got a better teaching job in Memphis and began writing for a local newspaper. Soon after arriving in Memphis, Wells became a controversial advocate of equality for African Americans because of an incident on a train. Upon taking a seat, she was told by the conductor that she was in a car reserved for whites and that she would have to move. Wells refused. Though only about four and a half feet tall, Wells put up a fierce struggle:

LIBRARY OF CONGRESS

**The National Women's Trade Union League united workers and middle-class reformers.**
*How do its slogans reflect this?*

> *H*e tried to drag me out of the seat, but the moment he caught hold of my arm I fastened my teeth in the back of his hand. . . . He went forward and got the baggage-man and another man to help him and of course they succeeded in dragging me out. They were encouraged to do this by the attitude of the white ladies and gentlemen in the car. . . . I said I would get off the train rather than go in [to a segregated car]–which I did.
>
> Ida B. Wells, *Crusade for Justice*

In her writing, Wells expressed the same pride and courage that she showed in the train incident.

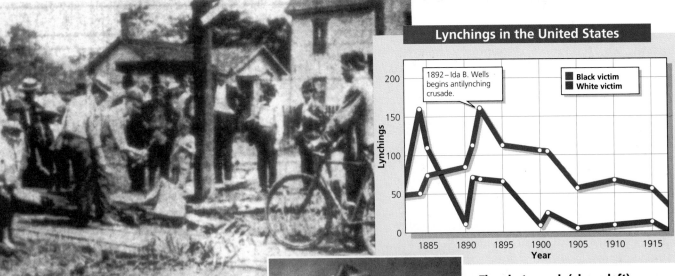

## Lynchings in the United States

1892 – Ida B. Wells begins antilynching crusade.

■ Black victim
■ White victim

Lynchings

Year
1885 1890 1895 1900 1905 1910 1915

© CHICAGO TRIBUNE COMPANY

UNIVERSITY OF CHICAGO

**The photograph (above left) appeared in the *Chicago Tribune* in 1908 with the caption: "Chopping Up Souvenirs, The Tree Upon Which Scott Burton Was Hung." Ida B. Wells (left) led a national battle against lynchings.** *According to the chart (above), when did lynchings of African Americans reach their peak?*

However, after writing articles criticizing the poor education that African Americans received in Memphis schools, she was fired from her teaching position. She became a full-time journalist, writing articles for several black-owned newspapers.

The night of March 9, 1892, changed Ida Wells's life. That night a mob of angry whites lynched three black men in Memphis. Wells wrote a scathing newspaper editorial attacking the lawless treatment of blacks in Memphis. Moving to Chicago in 1894, Wells launched a national campaign to end lynching. From Chicago she wrote articles, gave speeches, and carried out investigations to expose the racism that motivated mob murderers. Within three years the number of lynchings went down by one quarter.

Lynching was an extreme expression of the racism that Wells and other African Americans witnessed.

Wells was not alone in fighting back, though. Racial oppression triggered the founding of the National Association for the Advancement of Colored People (NAACP) in 1909 and the National Urban League in 1910. Both organizations worked to help blacks improve their living conditions. (For more information on the founding of the NAACP, see One Day in History, page 198.)

As Wells and the progressives awakened the public to social ills and organized campaigns to remedy these ills, the number of people pressuring the government to respond increased. Progressives set out their agenda to reform the political structure, to modify the economic system, and to improve the moral climate of communities across the nation.

## SECTION REVIEW

### Checking Facts

1. What role did many of the progressives believe government should play in addressing society's problems?
2. Describe some of the different methods progressives used to combat social, political, and economic injustices.
3. How did the methods of the activists differ from those of the analysts? How were they similar?

### Thinking Critically

4. **Comparing and Contrasting** In your opinion, which of the methods used by the progressives was most effective in combating injustices? Explain your answer using two of the progressives discussed in this section.
5. **Recognizing Values** Identify the values that motivated different individuals to become progressive reformers.

6. **Analyzing Behavior** Why did Jane Addams want to live in a poor, immigrant neighborhood in Chicago?

### Linking Across Time

7. How does the United States today show the impact of progressive reforms?
8. Explain whether or not you think modern-day journalists consider themselves muckrakers.

# Progressive Agendas

## Spring 1901: Wisconsin Challenges the Railroads

THE YOUNG LEGISLATOR LOOKED TERRIFIED AS HE WALKED INTO THE OFFICE OF WISCONSIN GOVERNOR ROBERT LA FOLLETTE. THE GOVERNOR, HOPING TO PROTECT THE legislator's identity, referred to him by a letter. "E., what's the matter?" With that, E. burst into tears.

As a progressive, La Follette was fighting to break the tight grip of the railroad tycoons and political bosses on the state government. He needed E.'s support for his bill requiring the railroads to pay a fair share of taxes.

"Governor, I can't help it. I've got to vote against the railroad taxation bill," E. explained sorrowfully. He went on, "I haven't slept any for two or three nights. I have walked the floor. I have thought of resigning and going home."

"Tell me all about it," La Follette said.

"Well," E. replied, "you know that all I have in the world I have put into that factory of mine. I have told you about how proud I was of the thing. Now," he said, "this railroad lobby [people who try to influence the legislature] tells me that if I vote for that railroad taxation bill they will ruin me. . . . I can't beggar my family. I have a wife and babies." He knew that the railroads could put his factory out of business easily. They simply had to charge his competitors slightly lower rates for transporting their goods than they charged him. His goods would then cost more, and his sales would quickly vanish.

STATE HISTORICAL SOCIETY OF WISCONSIN

La Follette and E. talked for a long time about their duty as elected officials to protect the public interest. Then E. returned to the legislative chamber. Just before casting his vote, E. confessed to the legislator next to him, "It is a question between my honor and my bread and butter, and I propose to vote for my bread and butter." He voted against the bill.

E.'s dilemma over how to vote demonstrated the clout of the railroads in 1901. Their wealth and power undermined the democratic process in Wisconsin, as it did in many other states and cities. However, La Follette did not give up. In 1903 he triumphed. The Wisconsin legislature passed the railroad tax hike. The choice between serving the public interest and giving in to powerful private interests, though, made life difficult for many progressives.

## Political Reform

Hoping to make serving the public interest easier for dedicated officials like La Follette and E., progressives fought to end the stranglehold that the railroads and other powerful special interests had on government. Political machines, declared Kansas newspaper editor William Allen White, had to "be reduced to mere political scrap iron by the rise of the people." Most progressives agreed with White, but

---

### STUDY GUIDE

**As You Read**

Notice that many of the reforms the progressives supported altered the role of government in business, education, and society. Also, think about the following concepts and skills.

**Central Concepts**

- recognizing that progressives worked to eliminate **corruption** within the political system
- analyzing the **reforms** designed to help women, workers, and children

**Thinking Skills**

- recognizing points of view
- identifying cause and effect

few agreed on how to destroy and supplant the machines and the **corruption** that made them powerful. **Reforms** in government were the first steps.

### Galveston: Model of Efficiency

A hurricane helped initiate one alternative to machine politics on the city level. On September 8, 1900, driving rains and a tidal wave devastated Galveston, Texas. The storm killed 6,000 people. Almost the entire city was between 7 and 17 feet underwater.

Galveston's mayor and city council members were effective politicians but poor administrators. The task of rebuilding the city overwhelmed the weak city government. Reformers, including many Galveston business leaders, convinced the state legislature to set up a new local government to replace the large, slow-moving city council with a smaller, more centralized government. In March 1901, the legislature approved a new charter for Galveston that placed the power of the city government into the hands of five commissioners. Of the five, two were elected and three were appointed by the governor. With power centralized in just five people, the city could move quickly to clean up the damage from the storm.

As important as changing the structure of city government was changing the type of people serving as government leaders. Four of the five commissioners were prominent local business leaders rather than Plunkitt-style politicians. They applied their experience in running businesses efficiently to the operation of Galveston's government. Under the guidance of its new government, Galveston soon began to rebuild ruined buildings, to fix its destroyed streets, and to get its finances in order.

Reformers around the nation noted Galveston's quick recovery under its commissioner system. By centralizing power in the hands of a few business-oriented managers, Galveston had developed an efficient city government. Within 20 years, over 500 cities across the United States adopted a commissioner system. Another 158 cities had adopted a city manager system, in which the city council hired a professional to manage all the daily affairs of the city.

Even cities that did not adopt the commissioner system or the city manager system learned from the example of Galveston and reduced the power of machine politicians by streamlining their government.

Cutting government spending reduced the number of padded contracts that politicians could dole out to their friends. Trimming the bloated government payrolls reduced the number of jobs a politician had available to pass out as favors. These reforms made government more efficient.

In addition, many cities changed their election procedures. Electing city council members at large, rather than from each ward, reduced the power of each local ward boss. Holding nonpartisan elections, in which candidates ran as individuals rather than as party representatives, reduced the power of parties. By undercutting the power of ward bosses and parties, reformers hoped that well-qualified candidates would have better chances to win elections.

Some progressives, hoping to make government more efficient, advocated reforms to undercut the machines. Others, though, supported reforms because they feared the power of immigrants and the poor. These progressives wanted to reduce the influence of immigrants and other poor people whom they blamed for causing the crime, prostitution, and disorder in the cities.

### Wisconsin: Laboratory of Democracy

Many progressives believed that the solution to political corruption lay in making government more responsive to citizens. Governor Robert La Follette made Wisconsin the premier example of a state in which citizens directed and controlled their government.

La Follette was born in a two-room log cabin on a Wisconsin farm in 1855. By the time he was a student at the University of Wisconsin, he already displayed the traits that would lead him to political success. One classmate called him "the chairman of the undergraduate greeters" because of his friendly, outgoing manner. However, La Follette opposed with righteous indignation any system by which a minority received special privileges. He felt an "overmastering sense of anger and wrong and injustice" at the gap between poor students like himself and the wealthy fraternity members.

La Follette's anger propelled him into politics. He served six years in Congress before he ran for governor. After losing two races, "Fighting Bob" finally won in 1900. Shortly after La Follette took office, one political boss swaggered into his office to cut a

---

deal and to boast about his power over members of the legislature. "I own them," he told the newly elected governor, "They're mine!" La Follette, fiery and moralistic, refused to compromise with the boss. As he declared in his autobiography, "In legislation, *no bread* is better than *half a loaf*."

As governor, La Follette attacked the power of the bosses through a series of reforms known as the **Wisconsin Idea.** He opposed the conventions at which parties nominated candidates to run for office. Since machine bosses controlled the selection of delegates, the bosses effectively controlled whom the party nominated. Reform candidates had virtually no chance of being selected to run. In 1903 La Follette pressured the legislature to pass a law requiring each party to choose its candidates through a **direct primary,** an election open to all voters within the party. As a result of that law, the power to nominate and select candidates passed from the bosses to the electorate.

In Wisconsin, as in many states, bosses also controlled the introduction and passage of bills in the legislature. Legislators felt more accountable to the bosses than to the citizens who elected them. To work around the power of the bosses, La Follette introduced three reforms, each of which had been developed in other states. The **initiative** allowed citizens to introduce a bill into the legislature and required members to take a vote on it. The **referendum** established a procedure by which voters cast ballots for or against proposed laws. The **recall** gave citizens a chance to remove an elected official from office before the person's term ended. Wisconsin adopted all three of these proposals, thereby giving citizens power to bypass or to punish machine-controlled legislators. Other states under progressive leadership followed the example of Wisconsin and instituted similar reforms.

**Attacking Corruption in the Senate** Another reform favored by La Follette and progressives affected the federal government: the direct election of senators. According to the U.S. Constitution, each state legislature elected the two senators from that state. When a powerful political machine or large trust gained control of a state legislature, it also captured two Senate seats. Then senators repaid the machine or trust with federal contracts and jobs. By the early 1900s, muckraker Charles Edward Russell charged, the Senate had become "only a chamber of butlers for industrialists and financiers."[1]

To counter Senate corruption, progressives called for direct election of senators by the voters of each state. In 1912 Congress proposed a direct-election amendment to the Constitution. In 1913 the states ratified the Seventeenth Amendment.

THE GRANGER COLLECTION

**Locate the two doorways in this 1889 political cartoon by Joseph Keppler.** *How does the difference between them show Keppler's view of the Senate?*

STUDY GUIDE

**Identifying Cause and Effect**

The recall, referendum, and initiative were designed to enable voters to remove corrupt politicians, challenge unfair laws and pass new ones, and, in general, to support reforms. Thus the people would have the power to act on what they had learned. Progressives who favored these reforms had faith in citizens to act wisely once they had adequate information.

1 According to muckraker Charles Russell, whose interests did the Senate serve in the early 1900s? What did he mean by that charge?

### Expanding Voting Rights

Some progressives tried to increase not only the influence but also the number of citizens participating in government. After an 1848 women's rights conference in Seneca Falls, New York, women began organizing to win **suffrage,** the right to vote. By 1890 women had won at least partial suffrage in 19 states. In most of these states, women could vote in local or state elections, but they could not vote in presidential elections. Only Wyoming and Utah gave women full voting rights.

The suffrage movement gathered momentum in the 1890s. The National American Woman Suffrage Association grew from 13,000 members in 1893 to 75,000 members in 1910. By 1912 nine states, all west

SCHLESINGER LIBRARY

of the Mississippi River, allowed women to vote in all elections. Suffrage advocates continued to push for a constitutional amendment to grant women full voting rights in all states. However, they would not achieve that goal until the passage of the Nineteenth Amendment in 1920.

While women fought to win the vote, blacks struggled to regain it. Beginning in Mississippi in 1890, state after state in the South revised its constitution and laws to prevent African Americans from voting. In Louisiana, for example, over 130,000 blacks voted in 1896. In 1900, after changes in the constitution and the laws, the number of African Americans registered to vote there plunged to 5,320. The drive to win voting rights for blacks made little progress before 1915. African American progressives won little support from white progressives for their cause.

## Economic Reform

Progressives hoped that political reform would pave the way for economic reform. Once the political system was rescued from controlling private interests, citizens could use government to protect the public interest.

**Regulating Big Business**   Government regulation proved to be one means of taming powerful special interests. In Wisconsin La Follette established a state railroad commission. This group of experts, many from the University of Wisconsin, oversaw the operation of all railroads in Wisconsin. They held the power to revise, overturn, and thereby regulate rates charged by the railroads. Thus the commission prevented the railroad from unfairly overcharging small farmers whose livelihoods depended on the railroads for shipping their grain to market. Under regulation, factories could no longer bribe the railroads into giving them an unfair rate advantage over other factories in the state. La Follette declared that his goal "was not to 'smash' corporations, but to drive them out of politics, and then to treat them exactly the same as other people are treated."[2]

PHOTOGRAPHIC ARCHIVE, UNIVERSITY OF KENTUCKY LIBRARIES

**In 1916, these activists from Kentucky traveled to St. Louis to urge delegates at the Democratic National Convention to support equal rights for women.**

STUDY GUIDE

### Recognizing Points of View

Supporters of suffrage for women disagreed about why women should vote. One leader, Elizabeth Cady Stanton, emphasized the equality of men and women. Others, though, emphasized the differences between men and women. For example, Jane Addams argued that female voters would be more concerned than men had been about the needs of children, workers, and families.

2   Explain the political and economic reforms Governor Robert La Follette tried to make in the Wisconsin state government.

Other states followed Wisconsin's lead. They established commissions to regulate railroads, electric power companies, and gas companies. Some cities went beyond mere regulation, setting up and running utilities as part of city government.

**Caring for Injured Workers**   Owners and workers clashed repeatedly over issues such as how companies should treat injured workers. Factories, coal mines, and railroads were particularly dangerous places to work. In 1914 about 35,000 people died on the job; another 700,000 were injured. Companies often fired seriously injured workers because they could no longer do their jobs. In a fiercely competitive business climate, no company could afford the expense of caring for its injured workers unless all of its competitors did the same.

Articles by muckrakers and protests by unions slowly roused public anger at the irresponsibility of big business. In 1902 Maryland passed the first state law requiring employers to buy insurance that would compensate workers injured on the job. By 1916 about two-thirds of the states required companies to have some type of workers' compensation program.

**Limiting the Workday**   In 1900 about one-fifth of all people working outside their homes were women. Most progressives believed that women were naturally weaker than men and thus more deserving of protection. Even a Tammany Hall boss, Big Tim Sullivan, worried about the ravages of work on young women: "I had seen me sister go out to work when she was only fourteen and I know we ought to help these gals by giving 'em a law which will prevent 'em from being broken down while they're still young."

In 1903 Oregon passed a law that prohibited employing women in a factory or a laundry for more than 10 hours a day. Portland laundry owner Curt Muller, fined $10 for breaking the law, challenged it. Muller, like other business owners, argued that the government had no right to interfere in a private contract between an owner and a worker. The Oregon Supreme Court disagreed with Muller and upheld the fine. Muller then appealed to the U.S. Supreme Court, which agreed to hear the case.

Progressives, including Florence Kelley and Josephine Goldmark of the National Consumers

THE BETTMANN ARCHIVE

On March 25, 1911, a fire at the Triangle Shirtwaist Factory killed 146 workers. Since the company locked the doors from the outside to prevent workers from taking breaks, many had no chance to escape. Outrage at the deaths caused New York City to pass a strict building code.

League, closely followed the *Muller v. Oregon* case. They had seen both state and federal courts strike down laws like the one passed by Oregon. If the Supreme Court upheld the Oregon law, though, similar laws in other states would also be valid.

Goldmark recruited her brother-in-law, Louis Brandeis, to defend the Oregon law. Brandeis, whose father was a Jewish immigrant from Bohemia, was a prominent Boston lawyer. Tall and wiry, with a shock

STUDY GUIDE

**Identifying Cause and Effect**

During the late 1800s, business leaders in several major industries formed powerful trusts and cut prices to eliminate their competition. Many companies then abused their power by raising prices and limiting production. To regulate these businesses, Congress passed the Sherman Antitrust Act of 1890. In 1911, after Ida Tarbell exposed the abuses committed by the Standard Oil Company, the government used the Sherman Act to break up that company into 33 separate firms. This act helped safeguard competition and protected the public interest.

of unruly hair, Brandeis earned his nickname of the "People's Lawyer" by donating his expertise to defending unions and attacking corrupt politicians.

In January 1908 Brandeis presented his brief, the statement of a client's case, to the Supreme Court. The brief included 95 pages of statistics, quotations, and other evidence collected by Goldmark showing that long hours damaged the health of women and, in effect, threatened the public interest. "The overwork of future mothers," Brandeis wrote, "thus directly attacks the welfare of the nation."

Goldmark's evidence proved persuasive. In a unanimous decision, the Supreme Court upheld the Oregon law. They agreed that a state government, to protect the public interest, had a right to regulate the work of women. After the *Muller* decision, Illinois, Virginia, Michigan, Louisiana, and other states quickly passed similar laws.

Brandeis's use of Goldmark's data revolutionized legal thought. Previously courts evaluated laws only on narrow legal grounds. Beginning with the *Muller* decision, courts considered the law's impact on people's lives. Brandeis and Goldmark won a major victory in the progressives' battle to carve out a new role for government as protector of the public interest.

## Social and Moral Reform

The progressives' desire to protect the public interest included a broad range of social reforms. Many reforms were designed to help children. For example, progressives supported establishing separate courts that would be sensitive to the needs and problems of juveniles. They also backed laws providing financial assistance to children in homes with no father present. One of the key progressive reforms for children was the expansion of public education.

**Educating Children** During the late 1800s, state after state passed laws requiring young people to go to school. The number of schools jumped sharply. Before the Civil War, only a few hundred high schools existed across the nation. By 1900 there were 6,000 high schools; by 1920, there were 14,000. The expansion of public education then led to a sharp

**In the late 1800s, schools developed physical education programs. These Massachusetts students are** doing calisthenics. *What do the images on the wall suggest about the subjects they studied?*

CULVER PICTURES, INC.

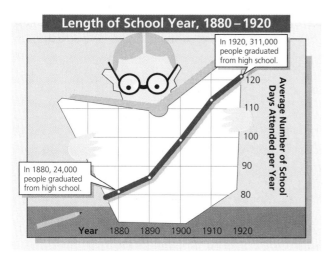

## Length of School Year, 1880–1920

In 1920, 311,000 people graduated from high school.

In 1880, 24,000 people graduated from high school.

Average Number of School Days Attended per Year

Year   1880   1890   1900   1910   1920

**Progressives supported laws requiring attendance at school.** *How many more days did the average student attend school in 1920 than in 1880?*

decline in illiteracy. In 1870 approximately 20 percent of the people in the United States were illiterate. By 1920 only 6 percent could not read.

In addition to growing, public education was changing. Philosopher John Dewey criticized schools for overemphasizing memorization of knowledge. Instead, Dewey argued, schools should relate learning to the interests, problems, and concerns of students. He believed that the "true center" of a child's education was "not science, nor literature, nor history, nor geography, but the child's own social activities." Dewey wanted schools to teach students to be good citizens. "Education," he declared, "is the fundamental method of social progress and reform." Most progressives agreed with him.

**Protecting Women**   Just as some progressives emphasized reforms to protect children, others focused on reforms that primarily affected women. The most controversial of these reforms was the birth control movement. A New York nurse, Margaret

Sanger, had seen many women die from poorly performed abortions. In 1914 she launched a drive to inform women about ways they could prevent pregnancy. Under New York's Comstock Act of 1873, though, information describing methods of birth control was considered obscene. Almost immediately after starting her crusade, Sanger was arrested for violating the Comstock Act. Though the charges against her were dropped in 1916, Sanger faced constant opposition to her work.

Another reform that aimed to protect women was the temperance movement, the drive to restrict or prohibit the use of alcohol. Intoxicated men sometimes beat their wives and children, and the temperance movement aimed to stop such abusive behavior at the source—alcohol. The largest temperance organization was the Women's Christian Temperance Union (WCTU), founded in 1874. By 1900 it had almost 300,000 members. One-fourth of the U.S. population lived in areas with some restrictions on alcohol purchase or consumption.

Frances Willard led the WCTU from 1879 until her death in 1898. She encouraged the organization to attack social ills other than the abuse of alcohol. The WCTU advocated voting rights for women, lobbied for prison reform, promoted world peace, and spoke out on various health issues. Willard's slogan was, "Do everything."

The WCTU under Willard was typical of many progressive organizations. While it focused on one problem that seemed to be rampant in cities, it supported several other reform causes. Although the problem it confronted was nationwide, the organization won its first victories on the city and state level. To achieve a nationwide solution, the temperance movement, like other progressive reforms, would have to convince Congress and the president to take a more active role in social reform. The progressives, then, needed to develop a new role for the federal government in the United States.

## SECTION REVIEW

**Checking Facts**
1. Explain the ruling in the case of *Muller v. Oregon.*
2. How did reforms force employers to act responsibly?
3. Describe the reforms that protected women and children.

**Thinking Critically**
4. **Recognizing Points of View** Why did the progressives feel morally obligated to support

women's and children's rights? Why did they generally believe that the problems women and children faced were related?

5. **Recognizing Points of View** Analyze the view of women that Brandeis expressed in the *Muller* case and explain why you agree or disagree with it.

6. **Identifying Cause and Effect** Why did the progressives believe that political reform was necessary

before economic reform could be achieved?

**Linking Across Time**
7. Do big businesses have more or less influence on government today than they did around 1900? Give examples to support your viewpoint.

# Chapter 5 Review

**September 1889**
Jane Addams starts
Hull House.

**1894**
Ida B. Wells begins a national
antilynching campaign.

**September 1900**
Hurricane devastates
Galveston, Texas.

**April 1901**
Galveston gets a
new city charter.

| 1888 | 1890 | 1892 | 1894 | 1896 | 1898 | 1900 | 1902 | 1904 |
|---|---|---|---|---|---|---|---|---|

**January 1892**
New center for receiving immigrants
opens at Ellis Island, New York.

**November 1900**
La Follette is elected
governor of Wisconsin.

## Summary

Use the following outline as a tool for reviewing and summarizing the chapter. Copy the outline on your own paper, leaving spaces between headings to jot down notes about key events and concepts.

**I. Facing a New Order**
  A. Shame of the Cities
  B. Industrial Disorder
**II. A Generation of Reformers**
  A. Progressive Ideals
  B. Progressive Profiles: Analysts
  C. Progressive Profiles: Activists
**III. Progressive Agendas**
  A. Political Reform
  B. Economic Reform
  C. Social and Moral Reform

## Ideas, Events, and People

1. Identify the major factors that contributed to the growth of the cities in the late 1800s.
2. How did men like John D. Rockefeller and J. P. Morgan amass huge fortunes during this period?
3. Why did the average urban worker live on the edge of poverty?
4. How were the progressives different from the populists?
5. How did intellectuals like Charles Beard, Mary Ritter Beard, and Lester Ward influence the thinking of the reformers?
6. Who were the muckrakers? How did the public react to Upton Sinclair's book *The Jungle?*
7. What were the principal features of the Galveston plan?
8. What was the chief area of concern of each of the following reformers?
    Jane Addams    Ida Tarbell    Ida B. Wells
9. What reforms did Robert La Follette bring about in Wisconsin?
10. How did progressive reforms benefit children?

## Social Studies Skills

**Sequencing Historical Data**
Use an encyclopedia or a biography to identify the major events in the life of one of the reformers mentioned in the chapter. Make a standard timeline showing the major events in the person's life. Then make a telescoping timeline to show an important period in the person's life in greater detail.

## Critical Thinking

1. **Recognizing Points of View**
Do you think progressives believed in democracy? In your answer clarify what you think democracy means. Then indicate whether the progressive view of democracy agrees with your view. Use examples from among the progressive reformers to support your conclusion.

2. **Identifying Cause and Effect**
How did politicians gain power in the cities during this time? Why did this political power often lead to corruption?

3. **Recognizing Values**
What were the chief values that motivated the progressive reformers?

4. **Analyzing Behavior**
Why did Theodore Roosevelt refuse to meet with Mother Jones and the children when they marched to Oyster Bay, New York, in the summer of 1903?

5. **Comparing and Contrasting**
How did the women's struggle to gain the vote parallel the struggle of African Americans? How did it differ?

**1906**
*The Jungle* is published.

**October 1913**
Congress passes the first income tax law.

**September 1916**
Congress passes Workman's Compensation Act.

**August 1920**
The 19th Amendment gives women the vote.

**1908**
The Supreme Court approves Oregon's law limiting women's workdays.

**1913**
The 17th Amendment establishes the direct election of senators.

**January 1919**
The 18th Amendment outlaws manufacture and sale of alcohol.

**6. Making Generalizations**

Make a list of ten progressives described in this chapter. When possible, indicate whether each came from a poor family or a prosperous one. Use this information to write a sentence describing the general background of individuals who became progressives.

**7. Assessing Outcomes**

List and evaluate four changes caused by the growth of cities. In your evaluation explain both the benefits and the costs of the change.

**8. Making Inferences**

The photograph on this page shows a street scene in New York City in 1901 or 1902. What aspects of urban life are shown in this picture?

CULVER PICTURES, INC.

# Extension and Application

**1. Citizenship**

What, in your opinion, is the major problem facing the United States today? Make a list of ways in which you could enlist people to work together to solve the problem.

**2. Community Connection**

The progressives identified a set of problems that needed correction a hundred years ago. What are the major problems facing your community today? Work with your teacher to single one out for discussion. Then prepare to participate in a round-table discussion to explore ways of solving the problem.

**3. Global Connection**

Research the history of Great Britain, Germany, or Australia between 1880 and 1920. Was that country wrestling with the same social and economic problems as the United States? Write a short report discussing your findings and present it to the class.

# Geography

1. Suppose you wanted to build a new steel-producing factory in the 1800s. What natural resources would you need? What factors, besides natural resources, would you need to consider before deciding where to locate the factory?

2. What effect did immigration have on the growth of U.S. cities between 1890 and 1920?

3. How did the characteristics of U.S. immigrants change between 1890 and 1920?

4. What changes were caused by the growth of cities?

5. How did development of new mass transportation change the ways people lived in urban areas?

CHAPTER 6

# Progressivism Takes Hold

## February 25, 1901: Morgan Forges the First Billion Dollar Corporation

For J. P. Morgan, it was a day of triumph. In just four months of feverish activity, Morgan had masterminded the formation of the world's first billion dollar corporation, U.S. Steel. Through buying out leading steel companies, Morgan's steel trust won control of 60 percent of the nation's steel-making capacity.

For many people, though, Morgan's triumph was a frightening one. The 168,000 steel workers, whose 12-hour days spent in dangerous mills made the steel industry so profitable, feared they would have no bargaining power with the giant new corporation. How low would Morgan drive wages? How high would he drive steel prices?

Only one institution seemed big enough to protect average citizens from Morgan: the federal government.

Only one institution seemed big enough to protect average citizens from Morgan: the federal government. Since the founding of the nation, however, the federal government had done far more to nurture corporations than to challenge them. In early 1901, with President McKinley in office, people had no reason to expect much change. Little did Americans realize that the role of the federal government in American life would soon change dramatically as progressives carried out their agenda.

THE GRANGER COLLECTION

*J. P. Morgan, the field marshal of industry*

*Before the days of radio and television, political candidates boarded trains and rode from one small-town station to another to speak to the voters. This train tour became known as a whistle-stop campaign.*

# Theodore Roosevelt and the Modern Presidency

## September 6, 1901: President McKinley Assassinated

PRESIDENT MCKINLEY SHOOK HANDS WITH ADMIRERS AT THE PAN-AMERICAN EXHIBITION IN BUFFALO AS HIS SECRET SERVICE DETECTIVE SAM IRELAND STOOD GUARD. Next in line to greet the president stepped an anarchist, Leon Czolgosz, who caught Ireland's eye:

BROWN BROTHERS

*When Czolgosz came up I noticed that he was a boyish-looking fellow, with an innocent face, perfectly calm, and I also noticed that his right hand was wrapped in what appeared to be a bandage. I watched him closely, but was interrupted by the man in front of him, who held on to the President's hand an unusually long time . . . and it was necessary for me to push him along so that the others could reach the President. Just as he released the President's hand, and as the President was reaching for the hand of the assassin, there were two quick shots. Startled for a moment, I looked and saw the President draw his right hand up under his coat, straighten up, and, pressing his lips together, give Czolgosz the most scornful and contemptuous look possible to imagine.*

Detective Sam Ireland,
in *Our Times*, by Mark Sullivan

At first the doctors who arrived in the emergency room of the hospital where McKinley was taken thought the president might survive Czolgosz's attack. However, despite surgery and other efforts to save McKinley's life, the president died eight days later, on September 14. Czolgosz was later electrocuted, after admitting to a compulsion to kill a "great ruler."

Theodore Roosevelt, the vice president, was away on a hiking trip in the Adirondack Mountains at the time. He succeeded to the presidency shortly before his forty-third birthday. Upon taking the oath of office, Roosevelt became the nation's youngest president. This energetic young man soon changed the American people's idea of what the role of the president should be.

## Early Political Career

Despite ridicule from his educated and respectable friends, Roosevelt entered politics immediately after graduating from Harvard College in 1880. Politics, his friends chided him, was for grasping, disreputable people, like the machine bosses whom they considered corrupt and uncultured. Roosevelt argued that "if this were so, it merely meant that the people I knew did not belong to the governing class, and that

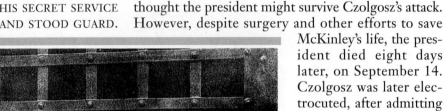

STUDY GUIDE

**As You Read**
Identify actions that show how Roosevelt expanded presidential power. Also, think about the following concepts and skills.

**Central Concepts**
- understanding Roosevelt's policy of **resource management**
- analyzing Roosevelt's actions against **trusts**
- explaining **socialism**

**Thinking Skills**
- analyzing decisions
- recognizing propaganda
- assessing outcomes

the other people did. . . . I intended to be one of the governing class." In 1881, Roosevelt showed the strength of his intention by winning election to the New York State Assembly.

He gained reelection twice before personal tragedy struck. On February 14, 1884, in a tragic coincidence, Roosevelt's young wife died in childbirth just hours after the death of his beloved mother. Emotionally shattered, Roosevelt left politics and fled New York for the Dakota Territory. There he ran a pair of cattle ranches in what he described as "a land of vast silent spaces, of lonely rivers, and of plains where the wild game stared at the passing horseman."

In 1886, after a disastrous winter demolished most of his cattle herd, Roosevelt returned east to politics, his first love. For the next 12 years, he held various government positions, from Civil Service Commissioner to Assistant Secretary of the Navy. When the United States went to war against Spain in 1898, Roosevelt resigned and organized a group of volunteers called the Rough Riders. Their successful assault on San Juan Hill in Cuba made Roosevelt a national hero. He rode his new fame to victory in the 1898 race for governor of New York.

## Roosevelt and McKinley

When President McKinley prepared to run for reelection in 1900, he needed someone to replace Garret Hobart, his first vice president, who had died in 1899. Roosevelt seemed a logical choice. After all, the governor of New York had earned public recognition as a war hero and was equally popular with ranchers in the West and reformers in the cities.

Basically a man of action, Roosevelt considered the vice presidency a do-nothing position leading to political oblivion. However, political oblivion was exactly where New York's Republican party hoped to send the politician whose stubborn independence they found so irksome. The bosses schemed to kick Roosevelt out of New York to serve as McKinley's vice president. After he and McKinley won the election, Roosevelt sadly wrote to a friend, "I do not expect to go any further in politics."

The reserved and serious McKinley, a predictable, solid Republican, provided a sharp contrast to his impulsive vice president. To one senator, the constantly moving Roosevelt resembled "a steam engine in trousers." Wherever Roosevelt went, he became the center of attention. "When Theodore attends a wedding he wants to be the bride," noted a relative, "and when he attends a funeral he wants to be the corpse."

Not all the Republican machine bosses had approved of Roosevelt's nomination as vice president. In fact, when Ohio Senator Mark Hanna heard of the Roosevelt nomination, he shouted at his allies, "Don't any of you realize that there's only one life between that madman and the Presidency?"

Fifteen months later, that "one life" was gone. The "madman" was president. Though Roosevelt pledged to carry out McKinley's moderate policies, the new president's dramatic style transformed the presidency.

Thanks in part to his energetic speeches, Americans perceived Roosevelt as a president who could take charge. For his part, Roosevelt saw the presidency as a "bully pulpit" from which to preach the ideas he advocated. The young president captivated audiences with his toothy grin, vigorous gestures, and somewhat squeaky voice.

Throughout his government career, Roosevelt supported progressive reform in strong language while in practice he pursued a more moderate course of action. In this way, Roosevelt persuaded the public

★ ★ ★ PRESIDENT'S GALLERY ★ ★ ★

"Our relations with the other powers of the world are important; but still more important are our relations among ourselves. Such growth in wealth, in population, and in power as this nation has seen . . . is inevitably accompanied by a like growth in the problems which are ever before every nation that rises to greatness."

Inaugural Address,
March 4, 1905

THEODORE ROOSEVELT COLLECTION, HARVARD COLLEGE LIBRARY

Theodore Roosevelt, 1901–1909

**Background:**
- Born 1858; died 1919
- Republican, New York
- Elected vice president 1900
- Assumed the presidency 1901
- Elected president 1904

**Achievements in Office:**
- Panama Canal begun
- Meat Inspection Act (1906)
- Pure Food and Drug Act (1906)
- U.S. Forest Service established (1905)

he was a reformer at the same time he reassured the business community of his basic conservatism. For example, as governor, Roosevelt had supported progressive labor legislation but repeatedly threatened to bring out armed troops to control strikers. "We Republicans," Roosevelt had written in 1896, "hold the just balance and set our faces as resolutely against the improper corporate influence on the one hand as against demagogy and mob rule on the other."

During the late 1800s, the country had been dominated by strong Congresses and relatively weak presidents. Roosevelt reversed that traditional division of power. The new president employed the considerable powers of his office and his own personal magnetism to bypass congressional opposition. In doing so, Roosevelt became the first modern president.

## Managing Natural Resources

Roosevelt put his stamp on the presidency most clearly in the area of conservation. From his boyhood explorations, Roosevelt had viewed America's minerals, animals, and rugged terrain as priceless national resources. For the good of the nation, thought Roosevelt, these treasures must be protected from greedy private developers, eager to make a quick dollar. As president, Roosevelt eagerly assumed the role of protector. He argued that the government must distinguish "between the man who skins the land and the man who develops the country. I am going to work with, and only with, the man who develops the country."

Roosevelt quickly applied that philosophy in the dry western states, where farmers and city dwellers competed for scarce water. To increase crop yields and to protect themselves from droughts, farmers demanded more water to expand their irrigation systems. Rapidly growing cities such as Los Angeles also thirsted for this precious resource. In 1902 Roosevelt supported passage of the Reclamation Act, which authorized the use of federal funds from the sale of public lands to pay for irrigation and land development projects in the dry farms and cities of the West. Under the new law, Roosevelt supported the construction of 25 irrigation or reclamation projects.

Roosevelt also backed efforts to save the nation's forests by preventing short-sighted lumbering companies from overcutting. He appointed his close friend Gifford Pinchot to head the U.S. Forest Service. Like President Roosevelt, Pinchot was a firm believer in **resource management,** the rational scientific management of natural resources such as forests.

With the president's support, Pinchot's department drew up regulations controlling lumbering on federal lands. This position satisfied neither business nor environmental interests. Business leaders, hoping to profit from unlimited cutting, criticized restrictions instituted by Pinchot as unwarranted government

CULVER PICTURES, INC.

**President Theodore Roosevelt and naturalist John Muir, right, survey Yosemite Valley. As a result of Muir's efforts, Yosemite became one of the nation's national parks.**

**Analyzing Decisions**
Corporate lawyer Richard A. Ballinger and many others who opposed Roosevelt's policy of removing valuable lands from public sale felt the president had overstepped his powers. Roosevelt based his decision on a loose interpretation of the Constitution. In other words, if the Constitution did not specifically prohibit removing land from public sale, the president was free to approve the withdrawal of pastures and other lands rich in timber, coal, and agriculture from the auction block.

interference in the workings of private business. On the other hand, veteran environmental activists like John Muir of California criticized Pinchot for supporting any cutting in the few unspoiled forests remaining. They argued that forests should be kept in a completely unspoiled condition for people to enjoy.

In addition to supporting Pinchot's moderate actions in lumbering, Roosevelt took other steps to provide for the managed use of the nation's resources. He added 150 million acres to the national forests, quadrupling the amount of land they contained. Roosevelt also established five new national parks, created 51 federal bird reservations, and started four national game preserves. These solid conservation accomplishments hardly put an end to private exploitation of the country's natural treasures, but they did initiate government protection of such resources. At the very least, Roosevelt's constant championing of the causes of conservation and resource management served to place the issue on the national agenda.

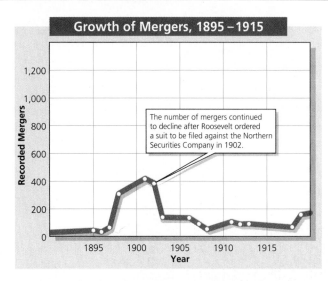

## Growth of Mergers, 1895–1915

The number of mergers continued to decline after Roosevelt ordered a suit to be filed against the Northern Securities Company in 1902.

**The progressive era resembled the 1980s in terms of the large number of recorded mergers that occurred during that time.** *According to the graph above, what effect did the Sherman Antitrust Act have on mergers?*

## Supervising Big Business

Other issues were already on the national agenda when Roosevelt took office. One involved the growth of large **trusts**—giant firms that controlled whole areas of industry by buying up all the companies with which they did business. This concentration of wealth and economic power under control of large trusts had dramatically reshaped the American economy. Buy-outs, takeovers, and mergers reached a feverish pitch between 1897 and 1903. Indeed, by 1899 an elite group of six companies controlled about 95 percent of the railroads in the country.

Most Americans were suspicious of the trusts. Trusts drove smaller companies out of business by lowering prices. They then established monopolies and were able to fix high prices without fear of competition. In 1890 Congress passed the Sherman Antitrust Act, which was designed to prohibit such monopolies, but it had proven hard to enforce. Industrialists simply devised substitute methods of retaining control, for example, the **holding company.** Holding companies bought controlling shares of stock in the member companies instead of purchasing

the companies outright. While the "held" companies remained separate businesses on paper, in reality the holding company controlled them.

In public Roosevelt capitalized on the widespread mistrust of the wealthy industrialists. He called them the "criminal rich," "malefactors of great wealth," and "a miracle of timid and short-sighted selfishness." However, Roosevelt avoided breaking up trusts whenever he could. "I have let up in every case," he said in describing his record of prosecuting trusts, "where I have had any possible excuse for so doing."

Roosevelt's outspoken comments were offset by rather cautious actions. This behavior led one newspaper columnist, Finley Peter Dunne, writing in a thick Irish dialect, to summarize his trust policies as mixed: "On wan hand I wud stamp thim undher fut; on th' other hand not so fast."

**Battling Monopolies** Roosevelt combined dramatic public relations with moderate action in 1902. J. P. Morgan, the head of U.S. Steel, had joined with a handful of the nation's wealthiest men to finance the Northern Securities Company. This holding company combined the stock of the Union Pacific, Northern Pacific, and Burlington railroads to dominate rail service from Chicago to the Pacific Ocean. Roosevelt, deciding

CULVER PICTURES, INC.

**As the coal supply dwindled during the coal strike of 1902, the lines of people fearful of facing a winter without coal grew longer.** *How important a role did coal play as a heating resource?*

**Heating Fuel Sources, 1902**

Oil and gas 8%
Wood 33%
Coal 59%

that the company was a monopoly in violation of the Sherman Antitrust Act, ordered his attorney general to file suit against the company in 1902.

In 1904 the Supreme Court, in a 5–4 vote, sided with Roosevelt, ruling that the Northern Securities Company had indeed violated the Sherman Antitrust Act. Roosevelt declared victory, claiming it as "one of the great achievements of my administration. . . . The most powerful men in the country were held to accountability before the law."

Much of the public hailed Roosevelt as a trustbuster who challenged and defeated the most powerful financiers in the United States. The common, working people felt they had a fearless ally in the White House, one who would defend them from powerful corporations.

Despite the public praise, the Northern Securities case hardly changed the day-to-day operations of the railroad. The railroads west of Chicago continued to operate under the control of a few giant railroad firms, with little competition. None of the organizers of the trust went to jail or suffered significant financial loss for breaking the law. Instead, they remained immensely powerful. Within a few months, in fact, Morgan would help Roosevelt further develop his image as a defender of the public interest.

**Settling Strikes**   In May 1902 the United Mine Workers (UMW) called a strike of the miners who dug the anthracite, or hard, coal that fired most of the furnaces in the United States. The UMW hoped to win a 20 percent pay increase and to reduce their long workday to eight hours, while securing the mine

---

**STUDY·GUIDE**

**Assessing Outcomes**

A single event, such as the coal-strike settlement in 1902, often has many outcomes. For Roosevelt the settlement was a success because of the praise he received. For business owners it was a

moderate success because it stopped a rising tide of public resentment against them. For union members the settlement was a mixed success. While the miners won a shorter workday and a

pay increase, they lost on the major issue of the strike. Although Roosevelt did not send in troops to break the strike, the owners won by not being forced to recognize the union.

owners' recognition of their union. For their part, the mine owners firmly opposed a union that might force them to raise wages and improve mine safety conditions. They simply refused to negotiate with the striking workers.

The strike continued through the summer and into the fall. As the reality of a cold winter approached, the shivering public demanded a settlement. President Roosevelt stepped in and urged the union and the owners to accept **arbitration,** a settlement imposed by an outside party.

Although the UMW agreed, the owners did not. They intended to destroy the union, regardless of the public interest. One of the owners, George Baer, claimed that workers did not need a union, that they should trust the selfless, conscientious owners:

> *The rights and interests of the laboring man will be protected and cared for not by the labor agitators, but by the Christian men to whom God in His infinite wisdom has given the control of the property interests of the country.*
>
> George F. Baer,
> Letter to W. F. Clark, July 17, 1902

The mine owners' stubbornness infuriated Roosevelt, who called Baer's comment "arrogant stupidity." If the owners refused to submit to arbitration, Roosevelt threatened to order federal troops into the mines. Then he sent his Secretary of War, Elihu Root, to meet with J. P. Morgan to work out a settlement proposal. Fearing that Roosevelt would carry through on his threat and responding to the urging of the powerful Morgan, the mine owners finally accepted arbitration. The result was a compromise that gave each side part of what it had sought.

The miners won a nine-hour workday and a 10 percent pay increase, which was passed along to consumers in the form of higher coal prices. However, on the main issue of the strike, the owners won: they did not have to recognize the union.

In 1904, when Roosevelt ran for president in his own right, he coined a phrase that could have been used to describe his approach to the coal strike: "I shall see to it that every man has a square deal, no less and no more." Roosevelt saw himself standing above the battling classes, rendering to each a fair share of the spoils.

Despite the coal price hike, a relieved public felt it had been given a square deal. Americans hailed Roosevelt, whose powerful language shaped the public image of him as a fighter for their protection. Not since Abraham Lincoln had a president seemed to act so boldly on behalf of the public's interest.

**Protecting Consumers**   Roosevelt also defended the public interest on consumer issues. He was president when Upton Sinclair published *The Jungle* in 1906, exposing the unsanitary practices of the meatpacking industry. *The Jungle* provoked a massive crusade. Roosevelt jumped to the head of the crusade and pushed the Meat Inspection Act through Congress.

The Meat Inspection Act of 1906 outlawed misleading labels and dangerous chemical preservatives. It also showed Roosevelt's willingness to compromise with the trusts. For example, Roosevelt agreed that the government, rather than the packers, should pay for the inspection. In addition, he dropped the requirement that meat be dated, which would have informed consumers about the meat's age.

Though *The Jungle* focused specifically on meat, progressives worried about all of the foods and

★ ★ ★ **PRESIDENT'S GALLERY** ★ ★ ★

*"I have had the honor to be one of the advisers of my distinguished predecessor, and, as such, to hold up his hands in the reforms he has initiated. I should be untrue to myself, to my promises, and to the declarations of the party platform upon which I was elected to office, if I did not make the . . . enforcement of those reforms a most important feature of my administration."*

*Inaugural Address,
March 4, 1909*

THE BETTMANN ARCHIVE

William Howard Taft, 1909–1913

**Background:**
- Born 1857; died 1930
- Republican, Ohio
- Federal judge 1892–1900
- Governor of Philippines 1901–1904
- Secretary of War 1904–1908
- Chief Justice of the Supreme Court 1921–1930

**Achievements in Office:**
- Postal Savings System (1910)
- Alaska given territorial government (1912)

medicines that Americans consumed. Quack doctors sold concoctions of alcohol, cocaine, opium, and other drugs that claimed to heal everything from liver ailments to baldness. Many of these patent medicines, or nonprescription drugs, were worthless at best and addictive or dangerous at worst. On the same day that Congress passed the Meat Inspection Act, it also passed the Pure Food and Drug Act. This act prohibited the manufacture, sale, or shipment of impure or falsely labeled food and drugs in interstate commerce. The Food and Drug Administration (FDA) was not established until much later, in 1938. This agency broadly expanded the power of the federal government to protect consumers from fraudulent advertising claims by patent medicine dealers and from unsafe foods.

THE GRANGER COLLECTION

## Going Beyond Roosevelt

No president before had ever served more than two terms. In keeping with that tradition, Roosevelt decided not to run for reelection in 1908. Instead, Roosevelt chose his fellow Republican, William Howard Taft, an experienced diplomat and administrator, to run for president on the Republican ticket. Taft, a large, slow-moving, but extremely intelligent man, ran a mild-mannered campaign. Nevertheless, thanks to Roosevelt's energetic efforts on his behalf, Taft won the election.

In office Taft repeated the pattern he had established on the campaign trail. Instead of dashing about, making fiery speeches and always remaining in the public eye, Taft remained calm, quiet, and often almost unnoticeable.

Although he had none of Roosevelt's flair, Taft carried out—and went beyond—many of his predecessor's policies. In dealing with trusts, he rejected accommodation in favor of prosecution. In only four years as president, Taft prosecuted almost twice as many trusts as did Roosevelt in nearly eight years, including two of the most powerful, Standard Oil and the American Tobacco Company.

In other areas, Taft was at least as strong a progressive as Roosevelt. He expanded the number of acres of national forest. He supported laws requiring mine owners to improve safety. He established the Children's Bureau, a federal agency that protected the rights and interests of children.

Despite all of these achievements, Taft never received the public acclaim Roosevelt did. Taft did not view the presidency as a bully pulpit from which to lead moral crusades. Rather, he considered the presidency an administrative post, a job. He never had the eye for public relations opportunities that Roosevelt had. Nor did he have the ability to mobilize the nation with stirring speeches as Roosevelt had. By 1912 Roosevelt had become completely disillusioned with Taft; he was upset over Taft's failure to exert strong public leadership. With a new presidential election on the horizon, Roosevelt wondered if Taft was enough of a progressive activist to warrant his continued support.

## SECTION REVIEW

### Checking Facts

1. What was the main purpose of the Newlands Act of 1902?
2. List the main provisions of the settlement of the anthracite coal strike imposed by arbitrators.
3. What was the job of the Food and Drug Administration?

### Thinking Critically

4. **Recognizing Propaganda** How do Roosevelt's comments on the Northern Securities case indicate his skill at using emotionally charged language to show his side of an issue?
5. **Analyzing Decisions** Why did Roosevelt lead the fight for the Meat Inspection Act of 1906? How does this show his skill as a politician?
6. **Assessing Outcomes** What effect did Roosevelt have on the attitude of the public toward the use of natural resources?

### Linking Across Time

7. Compare the ideas of Theodore Roosevelt and William Howard Taft regarding the use of government power.
8. Explain how you think Roosevelt would react to or think of the environmental movement today.

# Woodrow Wilson and the New Freedom

## September 1910: Bosses Nominate Wilson for Governor

"LOOK AT THAT MAN'S JAW!" EXCLAIMED A DELEGATE TO THE NEW JERSEY DEMOCRATIC CONVENTION UPON SEEING THE TALL, SHARPLY DRESSED WOODROW WILSON for the first time. Indeed, the long, strong jaw of the just-nominated candidate for governor suggested an unbending moralist, one solidly in the progressive mold. Yet Wilson was not the candidate of New Jersey progressives. Rather, he was the handpicked choice of machine boss James Smith, Jr. The New Jersey machine backed Wilson, the popular president of Princeton University, because he was both electable and, as a political novice, nonthreatening to the entrenched machine. However, when Wilson rose to give his acceptance speech, he expressed views that neither the bosses nor the reformers expected from him:

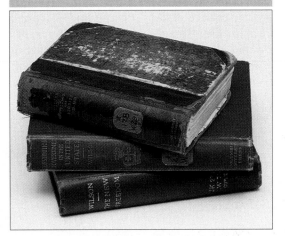

> *I shall enter upon the duties of the office of governor, if elected, with absolutely no pledge of any kind to prevent me from serving the people of the state with singleness of purpose.*
>
> Woodrow Wilson,
> Acceptance Speech, 1910

With these words, Wilson declared his independence from the machine. From a reformer in the delegation came the cry, "Thank God, at last, a leader has come!" "Go on, go on," other delegates shouted. Wilson went on to pledge his support for almost every progressive cause desired by New Jersey reformers, from direct election of senators to the establishment of utility regulatory commissions. At the end of his speech, the reformers, who had greeted him skeptically, applauded wildly. Some reformers ran up to the platform and tried to lift him to their shoulders, but Wilson would have none of this. His sponsors, figuring that the new politician was just playing to the crowd, assumed his backbone was not as strong as his jaw. They were wrong. Soon after election, Wilson began destroying the political machine that brought him to power.

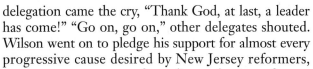

## *Wilson's Rise to Power*

Thomas Woodrow Wilson entered politics with a firm set of moral values that he had learned from his father, a Presbyterian minister, and his mother, the daughter of a Presbyterian minister. Wilson was born in Virginia in 1856 and grew up in Georgia and South Carolina. Although both of his parents were educated and avid readers, "Tommy" did not learn the alphabet until age nine and could not read until age eleven. He may have suffered from a

## STUDY GUIDE

**As You Read**
Explain how Woodrow Wilson extended the role of the president as a national leader in shaping legislation. Also, think about the following concept and skills.

**Central Concept**
- analyze the ideas, goals, and achievements of Wilson's **New Freedom** program

**Thinking Skills**
- recognizing assumptions
- drawing conclusions
- making generalizations
- identifying cause and effect

learning disability. Yet he persevered and became an excellent student. He attended law school, and eventually received a Ph.D. in political science from Johns Hopkins University in 1886. During his 16 years as a professor, he frequently won praise from students for his outstanding skills as a lecturer. In 1902 he was selected president of Princeton University, a post he held until he ran for governor.

When nominated, Wilson possessed no government experience. However, in dozens of articles and several books written during his academic career, he had expressed his political views. Wilson ridiculed Populists as "crude and ignorant" for their unquestioning trust in the wisdom of common citizens. He attacked Theodore Roosevelt and the Republicans for carrying political reforms to "radical lengths." The best model of government, he said, was the British system, which allowed for slow, orderly change under strong leadership from a well-educated elite. Because of his criticisms of most reformers and his praise for the British system, Wilson was generally branded a conservative rather than a progressive Democrat.

Once elected, however, Wilson proved that he was independent of the machine. Smith wanted to return to the seat he had once held in the U.S. Senate. Since the Seventeenth Amendment had not yet been ratified, the New Jersey legislature appointed the state's two senators. Smith, who had recruited Wilson to run for governor, expected Wilson's support in winning the votes of state legislators. In the Democratic primary, Smith had finished behind Thomas E. Martine. Wilson, calling machine bosses "warts upon the body politic," endorsed Martine. Without the governor's backing, an exasperated Smith and his machine lost. As one reporter put it, Wilson had "licked that gang to a frazzle."

From that battle onward, Wilson supported and won one progressive reform after another in New Jersey. He revamped election laws, established utility regulatory boards, and allowed cities to change to the commissioner form of government. To the embarrassment of the New Jersey machine, in less than two years as governor, Wilson transformed the state into a model of progressive reform.

## The Election of 1912

Wilson's success in New Jersey attracted national attention. The Democratic party, which had elected only one president since the Civil War, needed a fresh, new leader. The party met in Baltimore in June 1912 to choose its presidential nominee. The leading contenders were Wilson and Champ Clark, a Missouri representative and long-time reform activist. During a solid week of feverish politicking and 45 rounds of voting, the delegates could not reach agreement on a candidate. Finally, the powerful Illinois machine threw its support to Wilson, and he won the nomination. In the 1912 election, as in 1910, Wilson owed his success to machine politicians.

BROWN BROTHERS

**Eugene Debs, shown wearing a bow tie in a train window, takes time out from his busy whistle-stop campaign to pose with his campaign workers. Debs was one of four candidates battling for the presidency in 1912.**

**The Opponents** The Republicans were even more divided than the Democrats. Taft retained the support of most party officials, but few progressive Republicans stood by him. Widespread Democratic successes in the 1910 congressional elections convinced many Republicans that supporting Taft would cost them the White House in 1912. Progressive Republicans turned to the only person powerful enough to challenge an incumbent president: former president Roosevelt. Fearing that Taft was not progressive enough and that other leaders like Robert La Follette were too radical, Roosevelt entered the race. At the Republican Convention, though, Taft won the nomination.

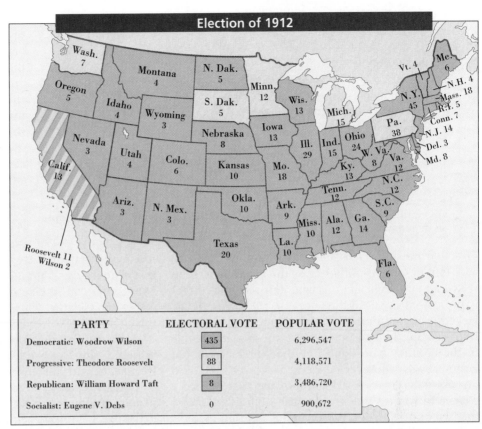

### Election of 1912

| PARTY | ELECTORAL VOTE | POPULAR VOTE |
|---|---|---|
| Democratic: Woodrow Wilson | 435 | 6,296,547 |
| Progressive: Theodore Roosevelt | 88 | 4,118,571 |
| Republican: William Howard Taft | 8 | 3,486,720 |
| Socialist: Eugene V. Debs | 0 | 900,672 |

**In 1908 people had said that the name Taft stood for "Take advice from Teddy." By 1912, however, "Teddy" Roosevelt had formed the Progressive, or Bull Moose, party to run against the incumbent President Taft.** *How might this move on the part of the popular ex-president be applied to words from the old song "By Uniting We Stand, by Dividing We Fall"?*

Instead of quietly accepting defeat, Roosevelt bolted the Republican party. Declaring himself "fit as a bull moose," he created the Progressive party, often called the Bull Moose party. Social reformers, including Jane Addams, eagerly flocked to Roosevelt. "Roosevelt bit me and I went mad," confessed Kansas journalist William Allen White. The Progressive party platform included calls for many longstanding goals of the progressives: a minimum-wage law for women, prohibition of child labor, workers' compensation laws, a federal trade commission to regulate business and industry, women's suffrage, and initiative, referendum, and recall.

In addition to Wilson, Taft, and Roosevelt, Eugene Debs ran for president. Debs, leader of the American Railway Union during the Pullman strike in 1894, had run in 1908, and received about 420,000 votes. Debs believed in **socialism**, an economic theory advocating collective, or social, ownership of factories, mines, and other businesses. As a response to the problems caused by private ownership of big business, socialism gained considerable support in the United States in the early 1900s. Debs rejected the moral and economic basis of **capitalism**, which was that private individuals should profit from the labor of others. If trusts did not serve the public interest, Debs passionately argued, then the government should take them over and run them. His faith in people and his energy won Debs many followers. One supporter commented, "That old man with the burning eyes actually believes that there can be such a thing as the brotherhood of man. And that's not the funniest part of it. As long as he's around I believe it myself."

---

## STUDY GUIDE

### Drawing Conclusions

By examining the effect candidates have on their supporters, you can determine whether or not they are charismatic leaders. Charismatic leaders have such personal magnetism that they attract and inspire devoted supporters. Judging from the emotional reactions of supporters of Theodore Roosevelt and Eugene Debs, it is reasonable to conclude that these men had a powerful hold on their followers and might be considered charismatic leaders.

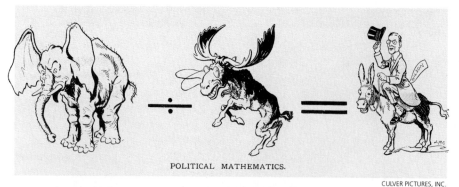

POLITICAL MATHEMATICS.

CULVER PICTURES, INC.

**The cartoon above was printed on September 4, 1912. Using political and mathematical symbols, the cartoonist reduced the election to its lowest common denominator.**

**The Campaign**   Debs, despite his powerful oratory, and Taft, despite his influence as the incumbent, soon realized that they could not win. Taft recognized that many voters opposed him because they thought he lacked leadership on progressive causes. "I might as well give up," he lamented, "there are so many people in the country who don't like me." Debs attracted large crowds wherever he went. However, he could not convince many of his supporters that he had a chance to win, so they threw their support to one of the two front-runners, Wilson and Roosevelt.

Wilson and Roosevelt agreed on many basic issues, such as the need for a stronger federal government to influence the economy. However, to win votes each candidate highlighted their differences, particularly on the great question of the day—the trusts.

Roosevelt believed that trusts must be accepted and regulated. Though known as a trustbuster while president, in 1912 he maintained that breaking up the trusts was "futile madness." Big companies, Roosevelt decided, were as necessary to modern life as big factories, big stores, and big cities. He ridiculed efforts to promote competition in a trust-dominated economy as "preposterous." Instead, government must be big enough and powerful enough to protect the public interest by controlling the excesses of big business. Just as La Follette in Wisconsin tamed the railroads by setting up a commission of experts to oversee their operation, so Roosevelt proposed establishing a federal regulatory commission to oversee trade practices of big businesses. He labeled that regulatory program the New Nationalism.

Wilson criticized Roosevelt's program as one that supported "regulated monopoly." If big businesses were destroying competition, Wilson argued, then government must break up big businesses. He urged that a strong federal government should dismantle—not regulate—the trusts so that small businesses could once again compete freely. Wilson referred to his program of restoring competition as the **New Freedom.** He pledged to make the nation safe for aggressive young entrepreneurs once again: "What this country needs above everything else is a body of laws which will look after the men who are on the make rather than the men who are already made."[1]

Wilson, with a smooth, analytical speaking style honed during years of lecturing as a professor, and Roosevelt, with his energetic personality, captivated audiences wherever they spoke. Crowds of 10,000 people, straining to hear, stood and listened to hour-long speeches from each candidate. In Milwaukee on October 14, less than a month before the election, a would-be assassin shot Roosevelt as he prepared to give a speech. Slowed by his glasses case and the bulky speech still in his coat pocket, the bullet did not stop Roosevelt. "Friends," he began, "I shall have to ask you to be as quiet as possible. I do not know whether you fully understand that I have just been shot, but it takes more than that to kill a Bull Moose." He gave his speech, at times nearly fainting, before going to the hospital for treatment. Wilson, in a show of fair play, suspended his campaign until Roosevelt recovered.

The intensive campaigning and brilliant oratory, though, did not inspire the citizens. On election day, only 59 percent of the voters went to the polls and apparently they followed traditional party loyalties. The only surprise was Debs, who more than doubled his vote total from 1908. Democrats united behind Wilson, while Roosevelt and Taft split the Republican voters. The result: Wilson won a landslide in the electoral college, even though he got only 42 percent of the popular vote.

## STUDY GUIDE

### Making Generalizations
In elections, candidates' positions on issues often reflect the positions of voters. In the election of 1912, three candidates stood for change— Roosevelt, Wilson, and Debs. Adding together the votes of these three suggests that the 1912 election was a mandate for reform.

**1** What were the main campaign issues in the presidential election of 1912?

# The New Freedom in Operation

Once inaugurated, Wilson immediately took charge of the government. "The president is at liberty, both in law and conscience, to be as big a man as he can," Wilson had once written. "His capacity will set the limit." Two weeks into his term, Wilson became the first president to hold regularly scheduled press conferences. Allowing reporters to question him directly, Wilson knew, would make him a more powerful leader in shaping legislation. During his eight years as president, Wilson demonstrated his power as he crafted reforms affecting the tariffs, the banking system, the trusts, and the rights of workers.

**Reducing Tariffs**   Five weeks after taking office, Wilson appeared before Congress—something no president had done since John Adams in 1800—to present his bill to reduce tariffs. High tariffs symbolized the special treatment government accorded big business. Adding taxes to the price of imported goods protected businesses from foreign competition. The consumers paid for this protection of big business in the form of higher prices. Progressives had long attacked high tariffs as an example of how government served the special interests at the expense of the public interest.

Wilson personally lobbied members of Congress to support the tariff reduction bill. Rarely had a president, even Roosevelt, taken such an active role in promoting specific legislation. Representatives for the trusts flooded Washington to defeat the tariff reduction bill. Wilson took the offensive. Charging that the nation's capital was so full of lobbyists for big business that "a brick couldn't be thrown without hitting one of them," he called on Congress to defend "the interests of the public." In 1913, with the attention of the voting public focused on it by Wilson's charges, Congress passed and Wilson signed into the law the Underwood Tariff, which reduced the average tariff on imported goods to about 30 percent of the value of the goods, or about half the tariff rate in the 1890s.[2]

**Reforming Banks**   Wilson's second major legislative initiative attempted to bolster the banking industry. The United States had not had a central bank since the 1830s, when President Andrew Jackson

BROWN BROTHERS

Worried investors gathered outside the closed doors of their banks during the Panic of 1907. In that year 91 banks failed. In 1908 bank failures rose to 155.

**Bank Failures, 1880 – 1915**

Number of Suspended Banks

Economic depression causes bank failures to skyrocket.

Rise in bank failures stimulates debate on banking reform.

Year

---

## STUDY GUIDE

**Identifying Cause and Effect**
One likely effect of the tariff reduction was a decrease in revenue. To make up for this deficit, the Underwood Tariff included a new tax on incomes. People or corporations receiving between $3,000 and $20,000 had to pay 1 percent of their income in tax. Income over $20,000 was taxed at a higher rate.

2  How did President Wilson persuade members of Congress to pass the tariff reduction bill?

destroyed the Second Bank of the United States. During the economic depressions that had hit the United States periodically over the decades that followed, hundreds of small banks collapsed in bankruptcy, wiping out the life savings of many of their depositors. To restore public confidence in the banking system, Wilson proposed establishing a federal reserve system. Banks would have to keep a portion of their deposits in a reserve bank, which would provide a financial cushion against unanticipated losses. If banks prepared better for economic downturns, Wilson reasoned, fewer would go broke when depressions hit. In addition, a reserve system would serve as a central bank for the entire economy, controlling interest rates and the amount of money in circulation.

Advocates of a reserve system disagreed about who should control the reserve banks. Wealthy bank presidents and industrialists argued that the big banks should control the system because they had the expertise. Many progressives favored a government regulatory agency directly controlled by the president and Congress, and thereby responsive to the public. Wilson proposed a compromise system composed of 12 regional banks that would be overseen by a federal reserve board appointed by the president. Congress approved Wilson's proposal at the end of 1913.

**Regulating Trusts**   When he entered the White House, Wilson vowed to break up the trusts. In 1914 Congress passed the Clayton Antitrust Act, which broadened the Sherman Antitrust Act of 1890. For example, the Clayton Act promoted competition by prohibiting interlocking directorates, which allowed companies to work together to reduce competition. The Clayton Act also made corporate officers personally responsible for violations of antitrust laws. Wilson believed that the government must hold individuals responsible for the actions of the corporations they controlled:

*E*very act of business is done at the command . . . of some ascertainable person or group of persons. These should be held individually responsible, and the punishment should fall upon them, not upon the business organization of which they make illegal use.

Woodrow Wilson,
*The Papers of Woodrow Wilson*, Volume 29

Wilson also backed efforts to regulate trusts. In 1914 Congress established the Federal Trade Commission (FTC), which attempted to stop unfair trading and business practices among companies. For example, the FTC could prevent companies from working together in order to keep prices high. Fair trade, Wilson hoped, would give small companies better chances to compete with larger companies.

**Protecting Workers**   As president, Wilson supported a variety of progressive federal labor laws. For example, in 1916, Wilson signed the first federal law regulating the use of children as workers in factories and mines. However, the Supreme Court struck down the law in 1918 claiming that whether or not children could work was a matter for the state courts.

Wilson also supported laws requiring that all companies contracting with the government provide their workers with compensation for injuries on the job. These laws greatly strengthened the role of the federal government in protecting workers.

During his presidency Wilson built upon Roosevelt's foundation. He expanded the role of the federal government and of the president. Like Roosevelt, Wilson saw himself as a crusader, using federal power to protect common citizens. However, for Wilson as for most progressives, the common citizens were white, native born, and capitalists. Other Americans, such as African Americans, immigrants, and socialists, often suffered during the progressive era.

## SECTION REVIEW

### Checking Facts

1. As governor of New Jersey, how did Wilson demonstrate his political independence in the selection of a senator?

2. Why were tariffs such an important issue to progressives?

3. What was the goal of the Clayton Antitrust Act?

4. Explain why the Supreme Court overturned the federal law on child labor.

### Thinking Critically

5. **Making Generalizations** Based on the actions of Roosevelt, Taft, and Wilson, what statement can you make about the value of public relations to politicians?

6. **Recognizing Assumptions** How might Wilson's moral values have caused him to oppose James Smith's bid for the Senate?

7. **Drawing Conclusions** Judging from Wilson's actions as

president, would you consider him a conservative or a progressive democrat? Explain your answer.

8. **Identifying Cause and Effect** Why did Wilson accept the support of political machines?

### Linking Across Time

9. Roosevelt's and Wilson's view of the presidency differed from McKinley's and Taft's. Give examples to show the current president's view.

# Limits to Progressivism

## November 1914: African American Activist Challenges Wilson

"TWO YEARS AGO YOU WERE THOUGHT TO BE A SECOND LINCOLN," WILLIAM MONROE TROTTER ANGRILY REMINDED PRESIDENT WILSON. TROTTER, THE OUTSPOKEN EDITOR of the *Boston Guardian*, and four other African American leaders were meeting with Wilson to protest the segregation of black and white workers in federal offices in Washington, D.C. These offices had been integrated for almost 50 years, since the end of the Civil War, and now the president had tried to change that. Wilson agreed to meet with the black delegation, but he had little sympathy for their complaints. After nearly an hour of tense discussion, an exasperated Trotter challenged President Wilson, "Have you a New Freedom for white Americans and a new slavery for 'your Afro-American fellow citizens'? God forbid!"

Wilson resented anyone challenging his authority, particularly a defiant African American. "You have spoiled the whole cause for which you came!" barked Wilson, as he pointed to the door. The meeting was over, and the five men exited. Though unsuccessful in changing Wilson's policy, Trotter's final question did make his objective clear: he wanted progressives to address the needs of blacks as well as whites.

Few white progressives thought to challenge the racism rampant in American society because they themselves had deeply negative attitudes towards blacks and other peoples. As a result, African Americans found themselves ignored by the mainstream of the progressive movement. Two other groups,

GRANGER COLLECTION

immigrants and radical workers, also found themselves battling progressives on many issues.

## African Americans and Equality

For African Americans, the progressive era was marked by continuing poverty and discrimination. About two-thirds of blacks scratched out livings in the rural South. Most were sharecroppers, farmers who traded a share of their crop in return for land to plant and money to buy seeds and tools. Sharecroppers generally found the tobacco or cotton that they raised barely covered their rent and the money they had borrowed, so they were almost always in debt.

Blacks who could leave their farms joined the flood of whites moving to cities in search of opportunity. Though most African Americans went to southern cities, an increasing number headed north, hoping to escape racism. In northern cities, though, blacks found much of the same discrimination and segregation as they had experienced in the South. In addition, in the North, African Americans competed with immigrants for jobs. This competition created tension and sometimes violence between blacks and immigrants.

In both North and South, segregation was a matter of custom. Beginning in the 1880s, however, southern states and cities started passing laws requiring racial segregation. Taking their name from a black character in an old slave song, the "Jim Crow" laws required, for example, that trains have separate cars

---

### STUDY GUIDE

**As You Read**
Describe the attitudes of progressives toward African Americans, immigrants, and socialists. Also, think about the following concepts and skills.

**Central Concepts**
- describing the policy that urged **accommodation** to racism
- understanding **Americanization**

**Thinking Skills**
- comparing and contrasting
- recognizing bias

BROWN BROTHERS

CULVER PICTURES, INC.

**Booker T. Washington, upper left, was the first African American to be invited to the White House for dinner. As founder and president of Tuskegee Institute, the print shop of which is shown above, Washington was the most admired African American leader at the beginning of the 1900s.**

for black and white passengers. They also mandated segregation in hotels, restaurants, parks, and every facility open to the public. Atlanta even required separate Bibles for whites and blacks to swear upon when called as witnesses in court cases. In 1896, in *Plessy v. Ferguson*, the Supreme Court ruled that separate, segregated facilities were constitutional as long as they were equal. The only dissenter in the "separate but equal" decision was Justice John Harlan, a Southerner and former slave owner. "Our Constitution is color-blind," protested Harlan fruitlessly.

Despite the requirements of the courts that separate facilities must be equal, they rarely if ever were. Black children received a second-class education compared to what white children received. For example, in 1900 in Adams County, Mississippi, the school system spent $22.25 per white student and only $2.00 per black student.

**Accommodating Racism**   Leading one African American response to racism in the progressive era was Booker T. Washington. The son of slave parents, Washington grew up in a log cabin with a dirt floor. He worked as a janitor to pay his way through Hampton Institute, a federally funded school in Virginia established to educate freed slaves. In 1881 the state of Alabama hired the mild-mannered but ambitious 25-year-old Washington to open a vocational school in Tuskegee for African Americans. Over the next 33 years, Washington molded Tuskegee Institute into a nationally prominent school where black students could learn 38 trades and professions, including farming, forestry, plumbing, sewing, and nursing.

Washington believed that African Americans could achieve economic prosperity, independence, and the respect of whites through hard work as farmers, craft-workers, and laborers. By succeeding at such jobs, blacks would become valuable members of their communities without posing a threat to whites. Publicly Washington urged African Americans to bend to white racism by accepting without challenge Jim Crow laws, voting restrictions, and less desirable jobs. This policy, known as **accommodation**, emphasized economic success over racial equality. In 1895 Washington clearly spelled out his views on race relations in a speech in Atlanta:

> *I n all things that are purely social we [blacks and whites] can be separate as the fingers, yet one as the hand in all things essential to mutual progress. . . . The agitation of questions of social equality is the extremest folly.*
>
> Booker T. Washington,
> Speech at the Cotton States Exposition

Many African Americans, particularly poor farmers, agreed with Washington. Struggling to escape

**STUDY GUIDE**

**Comparing and Contrasting**
When comparing two individuals, always compare the same characteristic in each. Did Washington and Du Bois hold similar views about how African Americans should struggle for equality? A comparison of their speeches suggests that they held sharply contrasting views. A comparison of their actions, though, suggests that their views were not far apart. Compare Washington's views above with those of Du Bois on the next page.

poverty, they believed that economic gains were more important than winning the vote, ending segregation, or directly challenging white domination.

**Agitating for Equality**  However, many African Americans opposed Washington's apparently meek acceptance of humiliating discrimination. The leading opponent of accommodation was W. E. B. Du Bois. Born and raised in a free black family in Massachusetts, Du Bois became the first black to receive a Ph.D. from Harvard University. He taught history and social science at Atlanta University before helping found the National Association for the Advancement of Colored People (NAACP) in 1909. He served as that organization's director of publications for 24 years. (For more information on the establishment of the NAACP, see "One Day in History," on pages 198–199.)

A proud and strong-willed man, Du Bois summoned African Americans to demand equality at once. "The way for a people to gain their reasonable rights," he pointed out, "is not by voluntarily throwing them away." Du Bois argued that the key to winning equality was not in developing vocational skills but in voting. With the vote African Americans would gain the political influence to end lynchings, to provide better schools for their children, and, in general, to challenge the white domination of society.

**Reacting to African Americans**  Most whites, including most progressives, ignored or actively opposed the efforts of Du Bois, Washington, and other African Americans to achieve equality. Many agreed with Theodore Roosevelt, who confided to a friend, "Now as to the Negroes! I entirely agree with you that as a race and in the mass [they] are altogether inferior to the whites."

Some progressives—usually women—did support black reformers. Jane Addams, for example, criticized racial discrimination and helped organize the NAACP. The alliance between white female reformers and African Americans reached back to the 1830s. Many white women continued to identify with blacks because they saw that each group was caught in a web of discrimination.

Among sympathetic whites, Washington's ideas were more acceptable than those of Du Bois, because

Washington did not directly challenge white social and political domination. However, these whites might have supported Washington less if they had known that he privately supported many of the same goals as Du Bois. He quietly provided money to pay for court cases challenging Jim Crow laws, to win back voting rights for African Americans, and to support antilynching campaigns.[1]

The activism of Washington, Du Bois, and other African Americans led to some advances in spite of the lack of concern exhibited by progressives. For example, the African American illiteracy rate was cut in half between 1900 and 1910; and the number of African Americans owning land increased by 10 percent.

## Immigrants and the Melting Pot

Like African Americans, immigrants struggled to find their place in American society. After the flood of newcomers from eastern and southern Europe between 1890 and 1914, immigrants and their children constituted about one-third of the American population. The United States became even more of a **melting pot**—a society in which various racial, ethnic, and cultural groups were blended together—than it had been before 1890. Each immigrant went through the assimilation process of absorbing a new culture. For most, the first steps in assimilating the culture of the United States, or **Americanization,** were learning English and understanding the laws and system of government of the United States.

**Americanizing the Newcomers**  Few progressives valued the cultural diversity that immigrants brought to the United States. Most, like Theodore Roosevelt, considered the cultures of all immigrants inferior to that of the United States. Americanization, to Roosevelt, was a process of stripping away an immigrant's old habits and replacing them with new, American ones. With his usual confidence, Roosevelt had no doubt that the American melting pot could assimilate as many European immigrants as wished to come to the United States.

Not everyone shared Roosevelt's optimism about the melting pot. Among those who feared that the

**Recognizing Bias**
Roosevelt clearly stated his prejudice against African Americans. Prejudice stems from bias. The word *bias* comes from a French word meaning "a slope or slant." Roosevelt's views were not objective. They were slanted toward the opinions of the white Anglo-Saxon Protestants, most of whom believed other races and religions to be inferior to theirs.

1 How did Washington and Du Bois differ on the importance of accommodation to the racial views of whites?

**Forgetting they were once immigrants themselves, many Americans demanded immigration restrictions. The number of Roman Catholics in the United States tripled between 1880–1920.** *How did the percentage of Americans who were Catholics change?*

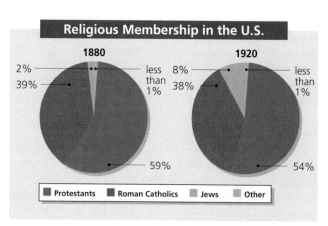

**Religious Membership in the U.S.**

1880

2%
39%
less than 1%
59%

1920

8%
38%
less than 1%
54%

■ Protestants ■ Roman Catholics ■ Jews ■ Other

CULVER PICTURES, INC.

flood of immigrants was destroying American culture were some progressives, as well as advocates of **nativism,** persons who prefer native-born individuals over foreign-born ones.

Many nativists were Protestants who opposed immigration because of the large number of Roman Catholics, Eastern Orthodox Christians, and Jews who arrived between 1890 and 1920. As the chart on this page shows, the Protestant domination of the United States was facing a challenge. Other nativists feared that radical immigrants, though few in number, would undermine the economic system and the government of the United States.

Opposition to immigration existed throughout society. Woodrow Wilson, while a professor at Princeton, complained that countries such as Hungary and Poland were "disburdening themselves of the more sordid and hapless elements of their population." A sign in a restaurant in California read, "John's Restaurant. Pure American. No Rats. No Greeks." Job advertisements often included a footnote, "No Irish Need Apply."

Some opponents of immigration claimed to have scientific evidence proving that some racial or ethnic groups were superior to others. In particular, they asserted that the Anglo-Saxon and Nordic peoples of northern and western Europe were smarter, stronger,

and more moral than the Slavs and Mediterranean peoples of southern and eastern Europe. Jews, African Americans, and Asians, they claimed, were even more inferior. Based on these mistaken beliefs, some people advocated a **eugenics** movement, an effort to improve the human race by controlling breeding. The eugenics movement successfully convinced some state legislatures to allow forced sterilization of criminals and other individuals who were diagnosed as severely mentally retarded.

**Imposing Restrictions**  Nativists had begun calling for sweeping restrictions on immigration in the late 1840s. At that time, about 150,000 Roman Catholics from Ireland entered the United States each year because of a disastrous famine in their homeland.

As immigration swelled after 1880, reaching over a million immigrants a year by 1905, the call for restriction became a loud chorus. The federal government began limiting Chinese immigration in 1882. In 1903 Congress prohibited individuals "dangerous to the public welfare," meaning political radicals, from immigrating. In 1907 Roosevelt worked out a "gentlemen's agreement" with Japan, whereby the Japanese government limited the number of Japanese allowed to leave for the United States. All of these restrictions were targeted at specific groups. However, many Americans wanted much broader restrictions that would dramatically limit immigration from southern and eastern Europe.[2]

In 1907, in response to the concerns of nativists, Congress established a commission to study how well

---

**STUDY GUIDE**

**Comparing and Contrasting**
Compare the beliefs of members of the eugenics movement with progressives' beliefs about the forces shaping human behavior. Jane Addams, Walter

Rauschenbusch, and other progressives emphasized how the environment shaped behavior; eugenicists emphasized the power of heredity.

**2** Describe the major factors that caused nativists to demand immigration restrictions.

immigrants were assimilating into American life. In its report issued in 1911, the Dillingham Commission concluded that the new immigrants from eastern and southern Europe were not assimilating as well as the older immigrants from western and northern Europe and that they never would. Hence, the commission recommended, Congress should restrict immigration, especially from eastern and southern Europe.

Some labor unions also called for immigration restrictions, hoping that a reduction in the number of people looking for work would help push wages upward. Ironically, many labor union members were themselves recent immigrants.

Under these combined pressures, Congress adopted a wide-ranging restriction on immigration in 1917. This law refused entry to immigrants over the age of 16 who could not pass a literacy test. Since schooling was limited in southern and eastern Europe, the literacy requirement affected immigration from these areas most sharply. More severe restrictions would come in the 1920s.

**Responding to Nativism**    In a climate of restrictions and nativism, many immigrants relied upon each other for support. They formed mutual assistance societies, organizations that provided care for the sick and paid for funerals for members who died. Virtually every immigrant group had its own newspapers, its own athletic and social clubs, and its own theater groups. In many immigrant communities, churches and synagogues became centers of social as well as religious activity. There, newly arrived Americans could meet people who spoke the same language and understood their customs.

Though old, ethnic hostilities frequently kept immigrant groups divided, they sometimes joined together for political battles, often in opposition to progressive reforms. For example, many immigrants supported the urban political machines that many progressives attacked. Some poverty-stricken immigrant families who relied on the labor of their children to help them buy food and pay their rent opposed progressives who wanted to ban child labor. Immigrants from cultures in which drinking wine or beer was a traditional social behavior often resented progressives who advocated temperance. These conflicts over economic, social, and political issues increased tensions between immigrants and progressives.

## Workers and Radicals

Progressives also had tense relationships with many labor unions and were deeply opposed to radical labor leaders and ideologies. On one hand, progressives sympathized with workers in factories, mines, and mills who suffered from low wages, dangerous working conditions, and the constant threat of unemployment. Most progressives recognized that workers needed protection. On the other hand, progressives firmly supported capitalism and rejected all other economic systems. Most were horrified by socialists like Eugene Debs, who argued that workers or the government should own the factories and operate them in the public interest.

The IWW organized thousands of textile workers, who went on strike in Lawrence, Massachusetts, in 1912. One of the strikers was killed and many others were sent to prison. The union leader made the following statement: "Bayonets cannot weave cloth." *What did he mean?*

CULVER PICTURES, INC.

IWW FILES

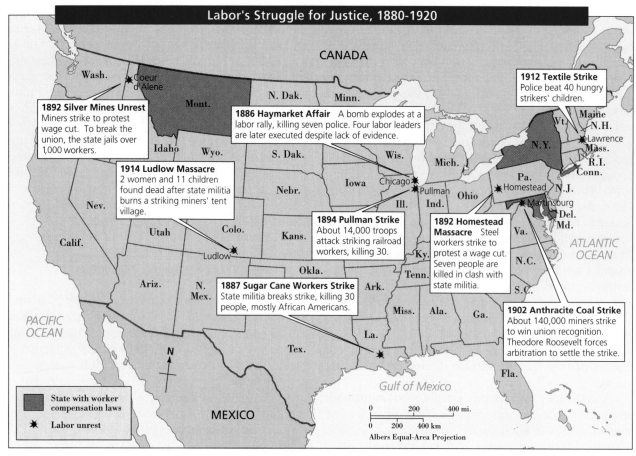

## Labor's Struggle for Justice, 1880–1920

CANADA

**1912 Textile Strike**
Police beat 40 hungry strikers' children.

**1892 Silver Mines Unrest**
Miners strike to protest wage cut. To break the union, the state jails over 1,000 workers.

**1886 Haymarket Affair** A bomb explodes at a labor rally, killing seven police. Four labor leaders are later executed despite lack of evidence.

**1914 Ludlow Massacre**
2 women and 11 children found dead after state militia burns a striking miners' tent village.

**1894 Pullman Strike**
About 14,000 troops attack striking railroad workers, killing 30.

**1892 Homestead Massacre** Steel workers strike to protest a wage cut. Seven people are killed in clash with state militia.

**1887 Sugar Cane Workers Strike**
State militia breaks strike, killing 30 people, mostly African Americans.

**1902 Anthracite Coal Strike**
About 140,000 miners strike to win union recognition. Theodore Roosevelt forces arbitration to settle the strike.

PACIFIC OCEAN

ATLANTIC OCEAN

Gulf of Mexico

MEXICO

☐ State with worker compensation laws

✴ Labor unrest

0    200    400 mi.
0  200  400 km
Albers Equal-Area Projection

**Across the nation, workers and their families walked the picket lines during the progressive era.** *Why was a strike an emotional and often frightening experience for the men, women, and children involved?*

**Supporting Unions** Among progressives, the strongest advocates of unions were those who had most contact with laboring people—the settlement house reformers. Jane Addams and others saw how unions won fairer wages, safer working conditions, and greater job stability for workers.

In addition to backing unions, many progressives supported political reforms advocated by labor unions, such as limits on the length of the workday, a minimum wage for women, and an end to child labor. The largest labor organization was the American Federation of Labor (AFL), a coalition of unions representing about 1.5 million workers by 1904. While the AFL called for these reforms, it trusted government less than did many progressives. The AFL realized that a government that could grant such reforms

could also revoke them. The best protection for a worker, according to the AFL, was a strong union capable of negotiating with the owners.

AFL leaders also distrusted the government because they had frequently seen government side with owners to break strikes and crush unions. State governors or the president often sent in troops to reopen a plant shut down by striking workers. At other times, courts ended strikes by declaring them illegal under the Sherman Antitrust Act, which banned all actions that restrained trade. Although this act was written to break up business monopolies, the courts used it to crack down on unions. Owners who knew that the courts or the troops would end a strike for them had almost no reason to negotiate with unions. Without that ability to strike, unions had little power.

## STUDY GUIDE

### Comparing and Contrasting

Politicians who support contrasting solutions often share similar beliefs. Roosevelt, an ardent capitalist, agreed with most socialists in blaming competition as the source of employees' overwork and inadequate pay. Both believed that a return to a deregulated system would destroy the progress made by large companies in producing consumer goods at low cost. Both realized that, as the economy evolved, so must the government.

**Challenging Capitalism**   Unions often included some socialists as members. While they envisioned radical changes in the long term, socialists often worked for short-term reforms that improved the lives of workers. They generally supported stronger unions that could fight for higher wages, shorter hours, and better working conditions. Socialists also called for public ownership of railroads, trolley lines, and utilities such as water and electricity. Most supported the right of women to vote.

Though progressives shared many of the short-term goals of the socialists, the two groups analyzed problems differently and came up with different solutions. For example, when progressives saw a problem, such as the high number of workers killed on the job, they blamed insensitive owners and supported a factory safety law to solve the problem. Socialists seeing the same problem blamed the capitalist system of competition that forced owners to require workers to risk their lives, so that the company could remain in business. Even if a law improved work-place safety, argued the socialists, the problems of workers would not go away until the competitive system that caused them was eliminated.

Some radical labor organizations not only rejected capitalism, but they also rejected the willingness of socialists to run candidates for political office and to work with progressives. One such group was the Industrial Workers of the World (IWW), formed in Chicago in 1905. Wobblies, as IWW members were known, wanted a single union for all workers. They believed that workers should confront owners directly rather than through political battles. "Shall I tell you what direct action means?" one IWW pamphlet asked. "The worker on the job shall tell the boss when and where he shall work, how long and for what wages and under what conditions." Under the leadership of William D. ("Big Bill") Haywood, the IWW successfully organized unskilled workers that the AFL often ignored, such as miners, lumberjacks, and migrant farm laborers. In the most popular union song sung to the tune of "Battle Hymn of the Republic," an IWW organizer and songwriter expressed the union's belief that workers needed to join together for their own protection:

*When the union's inspiration through
the workers' blood shall run,
There can be no power greater anywhere
beneath the sun.
Yet what force on earth is weaker than the
feeble strength of one?
But the union makes us strong.*

*Solidarity forever!
Solidarity forever!
Solidarity forever!
For the union makes us strong.*

*They have taken untold millions
that they never toiled to earn,
But without our brain and muscle
not a single wheel could turn.
We can break their haughty power,
gain our freedom when we learn
That the union makes us strong.*

Ralph Chaplin,
"Solidarity Forever," 1915

The members of the IWW, in addition to socialists, African Americans, and immigrants, often worked at cross-purposes from most progressives. Ironically, these groups suffered the most from the poverty, corruption, and other social ills that motivated progressives. Despite this irony, the progressives did orchestrate an expansion of government power to meet the problems caused by urbanization and industrialization. That change in the role of government would have a significant and lasting effect on American life.

## SECTION REVIEW

**Checking Facts**
1. What did the Supreme Court rule in the case of *Plessy v. Ferguson*?
2. What led to the immigration law of 1917? How did the 1917 immigration restrictions differ from those passed in 1882 and 1907?
3. How was the Sherman Antitrust Act of 1890 used against unions?

**Thinking Critically**
4. **Recognizing Bias**  Give an example to show that Woodrow Wilson shared the bias against immigrants that existed throughout society in the early 1900s.
5. **Comparing and Contrasting** How were socialists and Wobblies similar? How were they different?

**Linking Across Time**
6. Do you think that the United States is more or less of a melting pot today than it was in the early 1900s? Provide evidence to support your viewpoint.
7. How significant a role does the federal government play in American citizens' lives today? Explain your answer.

## A Call for Equality

*NEW YORK—Signatures of many prominent men and women are attached to a call issued today for a national "Lincoln conference on the negro question." The object of the conference, as outlined in the call, is a "full discussion of present evils, and to awaken a renewed interest and activity in behalf of the colored race, and to secure for it a perfect equality."*
—*Chicago Tribune*, 1909

### Founding of the NAACP

Race riots in Abraham Lincoln's hometown of Springfield, Illinois, in 1908, shamed a few white progressives into meeting with blacks on the hundredth anniversary of Lincoln's birth. After discussing Lincoln's Emancipation Proclamation, W. E. B. Du Bois, Jane Addams, Ida B. Wells, and others took action that eventually led to the formation of the National Association for the Advancement of Colored People (NAACP).

A MAN WAS LYNCHED YESTERDAY

LIBRARY OF CONGRESS; NEW YORK PUBLIC LIBRARY, PRINTS DIVISION

## Elsewhere in the News

### Darwin Centennial

LONDON—Britain celebrated the hundredth anniversary of the birth of scientist Charles Darwin, who explained his controversial theory of evolution in his book *The Origin of Species.*

THE BETTMANN ARCHIVE

## The Crisis

The NAACP's monthly journal brought cases of discrimination to the attention of its readers. Editor W. E. B. Du Bois (below, in the editorial office of *The Crisis*) set out to produce a journal that would be "frank and fearless."

## Lynching Protest

Opponents of lynching (below) appealed to national pride as one reason to end the murder of African Americans.

## Jane Addams

Settlement-house founder Jane Addams suffered frequent attacks for her support of the NAACP.

## Violence in India

CALCUTTA—Opponents of British rule, hoping to send a message to the viceroy governing their country, killed a public prosecutor and bombed a railway.

## South African Constitution

CAPE TOWN—Ex-Prime Minister William Philip Schreiner criticized the new constitution as "narrow, illiberal, and short-sighted" for its discrimination against South Africa's non-European majority.

# Chapter 6 Review

**May 1902**
The United Mine Workers go on strike.

**1904**
AFL membership reaches 1.5 million.

**1906**
*The Jungle* is published.

**June 1906**
The Meat Inspection Act is passed.

1901  1902  1903  1904  1905  1906  1907

**September 1901**
President McKinley is assassinated; Theodore Roosevelt succeeds to the presidency.

**June 1902**
The Newlands Reclamation Act is passed.

**June 1905**
The IWW is formed.

**June 1906**
The Pure Food and Drug Act is passed.

## Summary

Use the following outline as a tool for reviewing and summarizing the chapter. Copy the outline on your own paper, leaving spaces between headings to jot down notes about key events and concepts.

**I. Theodore Roosevelt and the Modern Presidency**
   A. Early Political Career
   B. Roosevelt and McKinley
   C. Managing Natural Resources
   D. Supervising Big Business
   E. Going Beyond Roosevelt

**II. Woodrow Wilson and the New Freedom**
   A. Wilson's Rise to Power
   B. The Election of 1912
   C. The New Freedom in Operation

**III. Limits to Progressivism**
   A. African Americans and Equality
   B. Immigrants and the Melting Pot
   C. Workers and Radicals

## Ideas, Events, and People

1. How did Theodore Roosevelt become president?
2. What event made Theodore Roosevelt a national hero?
3. What experiences in Theodore Roosevelt's early life led him to seek strict conservation measures as a politician?
4. Give two examples of how Theodore Roosevelt expanded the power of the presidency.
5. Why was the Sherman Antitrust Act difficult to enforce?
6. Identify three progressive reforms supported by President Taft.
7. Why did Eugene Debs reject capitalism?
8. How did Woodrow Wilson expand the power of the presidency?

9. How did President Wilson restore public confidence in the banking system?
10. What effect did the Supreme Court decision in *Plessy v. Ferguson* have on the Jim Crow laws?
11. How did the views of Booker T. Washington differ from those of W. E. B. Du Bois?
12. Give two examples of advances made by African Americans during the Progressive era as a result of the activism of black leaders.
13. Briefly explain the concept of socialism. Why did this economic system horrify the progressives?
14. Explain the main difference between the Wobblies' views on workers' rights and those of the progressives.

## Social Studies Skills

**Sequencing Historical Data**

The standard timeline on this page places events in the chapter in historical sequence. Create a telescoping timeline that covers the theme of immigration between 1882 and 1920. Include all laws, agreements, and recommendations regarding immigration during this time period.

## Critical Thinking

**1. Comparing and Contrasting**

Compare and contrast President McKinley's style of leadership with that of his successor, Theodore Roosevelt.

**2. Recognizing Values**

Assume the role of an arbitrator in the United Mine Workers strike of 1902. To settle this strike, you will need to recognize two opposing sets of values. What did the owners of the mines value most? What were the values of those who worked in the mines? How would you mediate this strike?

| 1908 | 1909 | 1910 | 1911 | 1912 | 1913 | 1914 |
|------|------|------|------|------|------|------|

**November 1908**
William H. Taft is elected president.

**1909**
W. E. B. Du Bois helps to found the NAACP.

**1911**
The Dillingham Commission recommends restricting immigration from eastern and southern Europe.

**November 1912**
Woodrow Wilson is elected president.

**October 1913**
The Underwood Tariff reduces duties on imports.

**October 1914**
The Clayton Anti–trust Act is passed.

**3. Comparing and Contrasting**

Compare and contrast the actions of Roosevelt and Taft as presidents.

**4. Identifying Cause and Effect**

Explain how Woodrow Wilson's family background, education, intellectualism, public speaking style, and previous leadership experience affected his actions as a politician.

**5. Identifying Alternatives**

Imagine that you are a registered voter and a member of a trade union. The election of 1912 is one week away. Identify the candidates who are running for election and their platforms. Which candidate will get your vote? Give reasons to support your answer.

**6. Recognizing Bias**

Reread the section entitled Americanizing the Newcomers. What examples of bias do you detect in the attitudes of the progressives toward the immigrants? How do their attitudes differ from those of the nativists?

## Extension and Application

**1. Linking Across Time**

Research environmental issues that are in the news today. Draw up arguments for and against the following statement: The federal government has not gone far enough to protect the nation's natural resources. Then divide into two groups and hold a mock debate. The groups should represent the opposing interests of the environmental activists and of persons owning industries whose interests conflict with protection of resources.

**2. Cooperative Learning**

Divide your class into five groups to research the five tariffs that were passed between 1890 and 1913. Then regroup into teams containing a representative from each of the original five groups. Each group should choose its own means of presenting its findings.

**3. Citizenship**

The year is 1914. You are the resident of a southern state that requires a poll tax to be paid in order to vote in federal elections. Write a letter to President Woodrow Wilson explaining why having to pay this poll tax is a violation of your rights as a U.S. citizen. Why did it take another 50 years before poll taxes were finally abolished? Which amendment to the Constitution prohibits poll taxes?

**4. Community Connection**

Interview a member of your family or a friend who came to the United States as an immigrant. Include the following questions in your interview: Have you ever experienced prejudice from native-born Americans? What are your views on the melting pot theory? Do you think the present immigration laws are fair? Report on your interview to the class.

## Geography

1. How did Teddy Roosevelt contribute to the preservation of natural resources in the United States?

2. Without the passage of the Reclamation Act, how might the development of farming have been different in the dry western states?

3. Based on the 1912 electoral vote shown on page 187, which three states had the largest populations in 1912? Which four states had the smallest populations?

4. According to the map on page 196, in which types of industries were most strikers employed?

5. In which two regions did most of the labor unrest take place?

CHAPTER 7

# Progressivism Abroad

## March 1901: George Washington of Philippines Captured

Senator George F. Hoar once called Emilio Aguinaldo the "George Washington of the Philippines," as Aguinaldo sought to liberate his country from foreign rule. When that rule was Spanish, Hoar and others had encouraged the Philippine liberation struggle. Aguinaldo had responded in kind, shouting *"Viva los Americanos!"*

This enthusiasm did not last long, however. The United States had promised its support of Philippine independence if Aguinaldo joined the United States in their fight against Spain. After the war, that promise was not kept. President McKinley wanted to "civilize" the Filipinos before granting independence. In the meantime, Americans would have access to a port in Manila and to the country's abundant resources.

When the United States refused to accept Aguinaldo's legitimacy to govern, the struggle continued in earnest. U.S. officials no longer praised him as a founding father of his country. Instead they plotted his capture. Aguinaldo marked the United States as an enemy. He led a guerilla war to rid his country of U.S. forces.

Aguinaldo's capture in 1901 did not end the Filipino struggle. The war dragged on for another year.

The story of how the United States became the enemy of Aguinaldo is only part of the larger story of U.S. foreign policy under the progressives—a policy guided by an uneasy mixture of idealism and self-interest.

> *Aguinaldo marked the United States as an enemy.*

THE BETTMANN ARCHIVE

*Emilio Aguinaldo led the Filipino people as they struggled against the threat of foreign rule.*

*World War I began in 1914 with the assassination of Archduke Franz Ferdinand and continued for four gruelling years. Soldiers from around the world made their way to Europe to fight for peace. Armistice finally came in the latter part of 1918.*

# Foreign Policy under Roosevelt and Taft

## January 9, 1900: Beveridge Defends Imperialism

ALBERT J. BEVERIDGE, SENATOR FROM INDIANA, STOOD UP BEFORE THE U.S. SENATE AND SPOKE WITH CANDOR. "MOST FUTURE WARS WILL BE CONFLICTS FOR COMMERCE," he declared. He argued that the United States must secure new markets. As the United States acquired new markets in countries of Asia and Latin America, it should be willing to send troops, if needed, to protect those markets. It should even be willing to **annex,** or put under U.S. dominion, new territories, so that the markets could be controlled only by the United States.

As Beveridge argued his ideas, he recalled that the nation's founding fathers were not afraid to acquire the territories of Louisiana and Florida and other continental territories farther west. "The founders of the nation were not provincial," he noted. "Theirs was the geography of the world. They were soldiers as well as landsmen, and they knew that where our ships should go our flag might follow."

©SAN FRANCISCO CHRONICLE

## America's Special Destiny

Progressives responded to the possibility of gaining foreign commercial markets and annexing new territories in vastly different ways. Some of them wanted to forge ahead; others didn't. They all kept in

mind, however, that the United States was different from the many countries of Europe. The United States for decades had had a special destiny to uphold liberty and freedom. Some progressives agreed with Senator Beveridge that the people of the United States had a duty to spread the American way of life to lands recently acquired during the Spanish-American War of 1898.

To some extent, the idea of exporting American capitalism and democracy to foreign lands overseas gained strength from the progressive movement itself. The progressives had shown that Americans had the ability to organize and mobilize for social, political, economic, and even moral reform within the United States. The progressives reasoned that they could export their knowledge and products to less developed countries overseas.

Deeply engrained racial attitudes added support to the U.S. impulse to become involved in the world affairs of other countries. Some Americans believed that the people of the Philippines, as well as people of most Caribbean islands, were inferior by race and that they should succumb to the leadership of the United States.

**Overseas Markets** Not only progressive ideas, but also the economic realities, helped to spur the debate about the United States engaging in commercial expansion around the world. Senator Beveridge touched upon the economic realities affecting industries and the work force:

*T*oday we are making more than we can use. Today our industrial society is congested; there are more workers than there is work; there is more capital than there is investment. We do not need more money—we need more circulation, more employment. Therefore we must find new markets for our produce, new occupation for our capital, new work for our labor.[1]

Albert J. Beveridge,
Quoted from *The American Spirit*

Beveridge's cry for new markets struck a responsive chord in American farmers, manufacturers, and investors. As shown in the graph below, exports of U.S. products rose dramatically in the early 1900s. Investors, as well as farmers and manufacturers, favored new markets.

Railroads offered a good example of an American industry that was seeking new opportunities for in-

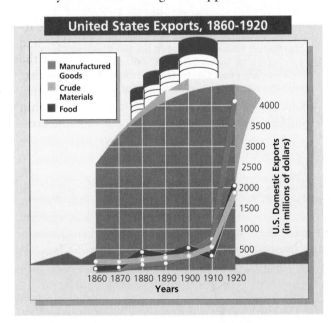

**The rise of U.S. exports led to demands for even more markets.** *What types of products yielded the greatest number of dollars?*

vestment. By the turn of the century, railroads already crisscrossed North America. Entrepreneurs eagerly looked overseas to lands where railroads had yet to be built. One railroad entrepreneur at the World's Fair Railway Conference spoke eloquently on his desire for commercial expansion:

*W*e blow the whistle that's heard round the world, and all peoples stop to heed and welcome it. Its resonance is the diplomacy of peace. The locomotive bell is the true Liberty bell, proclaiming commercial freedom. Its boilers and the reservoirs are the forces of civilization. Its wheels are the wheels of progress, and its headlight is the illumination of dark countries.

*Railway Conference Proceedings*
Quoted from *Spreading the American Dream*

**An Anti-Imperialist Plea**  Not all Americans favored expansion overseas. In 1902 the *Nation* magazine declared, "We made war on Spain four years ago for doing the very things of which we are now guilty ourselves." In this editorial the *Nation* pointed out that many Americans had previously opposed Spanish exploitation of native peoples, but now the United States government engaged in similar exploitation. Some Americans, like the author of the editorial, disapproved of imperialism on humanitarian and moral grounds.

Other anti-imperialists prided themselves as Americans for being different from the Europeans who were caught up in colonialism and militarism. They shared the sentiments of diplomat Carl Schurz, who lamented that extensive trading overseas would mean "wars and rumors of wars, and the time will be forever past when we could look down with condescending pity on the nations of the old world groaning under militarism and its burdens."

## Policies in the Caribbean

In spite of anti-imperialist arguments, the political and economic climate at the turn of the century favored commercial expansion, even if commercial expansion meant sending troops to keep order and defend markets. Such commercial and military endeavors suited the temperament of Theodore Roosevelt who became president in 1901. "I have always been fond of the West African proverb," Roosevelt explained, "Speak softly and carry a big stick; you will go far." Roosevelt preferred not to brag about American power, but rather to be so strong that other countries would bow to the United States. This philosophy came to be known as the **Big Stick**. Roosevelt's Big Stick policies in the Caribbean included the building of a canal in Panama and the extension of the Monroe Doctrine.

**The Big Ditch**   A canal across Central America linking the Pacific and Atlantic oceans had been the dream of people of many different nationalities for years. The map of the Caribbean on page 207 reveals the commercial and military advantages of such a canal. The distance by ship between San Francisco and New York would shrink about 8,500 miles. The average traveling time of early twentieth-century ships would be reduced by 60 days. Such a reduction would save commercial fleets millions of dollars and increase the efficiency of naval fleets. Indeed, the inefficiency of naval fleets during the Spanish-American War had underscored the need for a canal. When the war broke out in 1898, the battleship *Oregon* was sent from Seattle to Cuba. Since a canal did not exist at that time, the ship did not arrive until the war was **nearly over.**

The United States went on to negotiate the Hay-Herrán Treaty with Colombia in 1903, offering $10 million outright and $250,000 annually for a canal zone six miles wide in Panama, which at the time belonged to Colombia. When the Colombian legislature held out for more money, Roosevelt responded angrily and plotted to support a revolution that would make Panama an independent country—one the United States could more easily control.

When Panamanians revolted in November 1903, U.S. warships blocked Colombian troops from landing to fight the rebels in Panama. This helped the Panamanians win their independence from Colombia. The new government had little choice but to accept the terms of the United States in building a canal. The cutting of the canal began in 1904 and was completed 10 years later. Roosevelt took pride in having

THE BETTMANN ARCHIVE

**The Gatun Locks are located on the Panama Canal's western end. Today about 12,000 ships use these locks every year. Concrete chambers enable ships to rise 85 feet above sea level and enter Gatun Lake.**

forcefully secured the canal, forging ahead in spite of reservations from Congress and legal advisers. He noted, "I took the Canal and let Congress debate."[2]

**Expansion of Monroe Doctrine**   Roosevelt had supported the revolution in Panama against Colombia to secure a canal for U.S. interests. In general, though, he did not look kindly upon revolutions or any kind of disorder in the Caribbean. Striving to keep the region stable for U.S. investment, he put down disorders in various Caribbean countries.

In 1904–1905 several European powers threatened the Dominican Republic. They wanted to collect money owed by Dominican customs, but could not do so peacefully because various factions in the Dominican Republic fought for control of customs

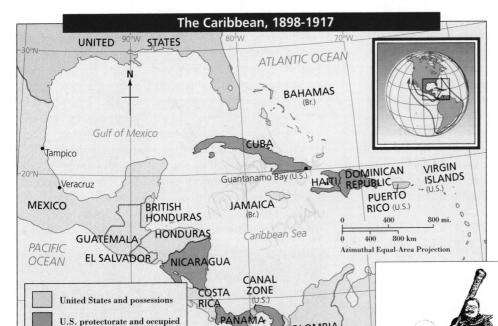

## The Caribbean, 1898-1917

United States and possessions

U.S. protectorate and occupied

The map and timeline on this page show the pattern of United States intervention in the Caribbean from 1898 to 1917. The cartoon below is dated 1904 and is known as "The Big Stick in the Caribbean Sea." *How does this cartoon illustrate Roosevelt's interpretation of the Monroe Doctrine and his Big Stick philosophy?*

revenues. Before Germany could send troops to collect its debts, U.S. troops seized Dominican customhouses and supervised the collection of customs fees and the repayment of debts. Roosevelt justified this action by issuing a **corollary,** or proposition, extending the Monroe Doctrine. His corollary asserted that "chronic wrongdoing" or "impotence" gave the United States the right to exercise "international police powers" in the Western Hemisphere. This changed the original intention of the Monroe Doctrine, which was to ward off European colonization. The United States now committed itself to maintaining stability in the Western Hemisphere. The commitment would cause Roosevelt, Taft, and Wilson to send troops to a number of Caribbean countries—including Cuba, Nicaragua, and Haiti—during their respective terms of office, as illustrated on the timeline below.

CULVER PICTURES, INC.

**Dollar Diplomacy** When William Howard Taft succeeded Roosevelt as president in 1909, he agreed with the spirit of Roosevelt's Big Stick policies, but not his tactics. Taft preferred **Dollar Diplomacy**—a sometimes milder approach to expansion and influencing foreign governments—one that substituted dollars for bullets. Hoping to gain more American influence in the hemisphere, Taft encouraged American bankers to lend money to Central American countries so that they could pay debts owed to Britain. He also

## The United States Intervenes in the Caribbean

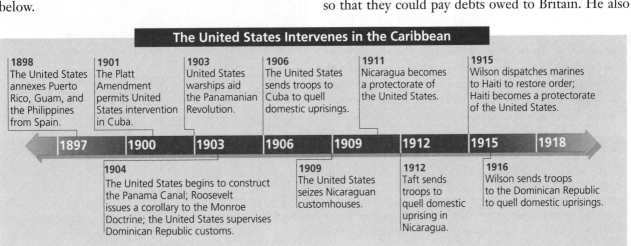

**1898** The United States annexes Puerto Rico, Guam, and the Philippines from Spain.

**1901** The Platt Amendment permits United States intervention in Cuba.

**1903** United States warships aid the Panamanian Revolution.

**1906** The United States sends troops to Cuba to quell domestic uprisings.

**1911** Nicaragua becomes a protectorate of the United States.

**1915** Wilson dispatches marines to Haiti to restore order; Haiti becomes a protectorate of the United States.

1897    1900    1903    1906    1909    1912    1915    1918

**1904** The United States begins to construct the Panama Canal; Roosevelt issues a corollary to the Monroe Doctrine; the United States supervises Dominican Republic customs.

**1909** The United States seizes Nicaraguan customhouses.

**1912** Taft sends troops to quell domestic uprising in Nicaragua.

**1916** Wilson sends troops to the Dominican Republic to quell domestic uprisings.

encouraged entrepreneurial investment. Investment in Central American mines, banana and coffee plantations, and railroads increased by $72 million from 1897 to 1914. Loans and investments had the effect of further impoverishing the fragile economies of Central American countries because most of their resources had to be used to pay back money, rather than to provide goods and services to their citizens. Throughout the twentieth century, the U.S. State Department would use its power and influence in Latin America to protect American investors from loan defaults and unfriendly governments.

## Policies in the Far East

At the same time the United States consolidated its power in Latin America, it also turned to the Far East, or Asia, to look for additional markets and to spread American values. Some Americans regarded Asia as a mysterious and alluring place. Others feared the growing Asian population, especially if it meant large numbers of Asians immigrating to the United States. The stereotypes that emerged in the 1800s lingered into the 1900s and characterized Asians as heathen and exotic—the lawless hordes, the yellow peril. Both prejudice against and fascination with Asia influenced foreign policy during the Progressive Era.

**The Chinese Market**   While Americans at the turn of the century feared and discriminated against Chinese immigrants in the United States, the great numbers of people in China itself attracted them. The lure of souls, more than 400 million of them, to convert to Christianity inspired missionaries. The Student Volunteer Movement for Foreign Missions sprang up on college campuses all over the United States. During the 1890s, the number of U.S. missions in China doubled to over 500.

Missionaries not only attempted to convert Chinese people to Christianity, but also built schools and hospitals and encouraged their converts to buy American products. As missionaries became more and more involved in China, they increasingly looked toward the U.S. government for protection and help, especially when they confronted Chinese resentment and hostility. In 1900 missionaries asked for and received

U.S. military help in putting down the Boxer Rebellion, an attempt by a group of Chinese rebels to expel foreign influence from China.[3]

Four hundred million souls to save inspired missionaries, but 400 million bodies to consume goods inspired American business people. The United States was not alone in its attraction to the Chinese market. China and its promise of wealth attracted Britain, France, Germany, Russia, and Japan as well.

By the latter half of the nineteenth century, these powers competed for influence in a China weakened by a decaying government, the Manchu dynasty. Each power vied for a chance to expand its interests in China. The United States wanted to share in these

BY THE PERMISSION OF THE HOUGHTON LIBRARY, HARVARD UNIVERSITY

**In 1903 U.S. missionary Grace Roberts taught the Bible to Chinese women at a Manchurian outpost.** *In what other ways did the missionaries try to spread American values, traditions, and the American way of life to the Chinese people?*

**Comparing and Contrasting**
Taft's approach to foreign policy was less aggressive than was Roosevelt's. Taft relied more on investment to secure American interests abroad and less on military intervention. Nevertheless, he

did not hesitate to order the Marines into action—in Nicaragua, for example—when he felt that American investments were threatened.

**3** Boxers, so called because they practiced gymnastics and boxing, killed missionaries during the rebellion. Why might the Chinese resent missionary activity?

opportunities as well. Some Americans saw opportunities to build railroads, control ports, and sell manufactured products. However, at least two factors put the United States at a distinct disadvantage: its geographical location, distant from China compared with Russia or Japan; and its navy, inferior to those of Japan, Germany, and Britain.

In 1899 and 1900, Secretary of State John Hay promoted a plan that would strengthen the U.S. position in the scramble to gain control over specific regions of China. He sent notes to Japan and the key European powers asking them to accept the **territorial integrity** of China. In other words, Hay asked them not to control a specific part of China, but to leave the door open to trade for all nations in all parts of China. Since Russia, Japan, Britain, and France were jealous of one another's influence in China, they temporarily agreed with Hay's **Open Door** plan. The Open Door became a key concept in American foreign policy during the first decades of the twentieth century. The hope of getting a share of the Chinese market continued to be the driving force in U.S. policies in Asia and played a role in the U.S. decision to annex the Philippines.

### A War in the Philippines

As the United States celebrated its victory of 1898 against Spain, many wondered if the United States would allow the Philippines its independence. Before the Spanish-American War, the Filipinos had been waging a guerrilla war for independence from their colonial ruler, Spain. Filipino revolutionaries initially welcomed U.S. forces into their country as liberators. The United States had drafted the Teller Amendment promising Cuba complete and unconditional freedom at the end of the war, and the Philippines expected similar treatment.

Expansionists justified annexation of the Philippines using the arguments first put forth by President McKinley who feared "anarchy" and vowed to "educate," "uplift," and "civilize" the population. Not far behind these lofty intentions, other considerations lurked: the Philippines could provide a rich variety of natural resources, as well as a foothold into the Far East—a naval stop on the way to China. McKinley decided to hoist the U.S. flag and take control of the country.

Filipino revolutionaries, led by Emilio Aguinaldo,

did not accept the U.S. decision to annex the Philippines without a fight. They waged guerrilla war at full force in the Philippines until 1902 and at reduced levels until 1906. In total, 120,000 U.S. troops fought in the war, 4,200 of whom died. Filipinos suffered far greater casualties: at least 15,000 rebels and 200,000 civilians died. The novelist Mark Twain depicted the situation's supreme irony:

> *T*here must be two Americas: one that sets the captive free, and one that takes a once-captive's new freedom away from him, and picks a quarrel with him with nothing to found it on; then kills him to get his land. **4**

Mark Twain,
"To the Person Sitting in Darkness," 1901

### Balancing Russia and Japan

A port in Manila would be a stop on the way to the tempting Chinese market and, in part, explained the willingness of the United States to fight for the Philippines. As Albert Beveridge put it: "[J]ust beyond the Philippines are China's illimitable markets." This dream also shaped U.S. policies with Japan. When Theodore Roosevelt assumed the presidency in 1901, Russia posed the greatest danger to an Open Door in China because it controlled the large Chinese province of Manchuria. Like Hay before him, Roosevelt attempted to change the situation through diplomacy.

In 1904 Japan launched an attack against Russia, destroying much of its fleet. Roosevelt opportunistically supported Japan because he regarded Russia as a greater enemy. In 1905 he mediated a peace agreement between the two rivals, which earned him the Nobel Peace Prize. Roosevelt's mediation of the Russo-Japanese War pleased Japan. It gained control over Korea, as well as key ports in China and the railroad in southern Manchuria. Roosevelt, however, made a point of checking Japanese power by negotiating rights for Russia in northern Manchuria and by having Japan agree to noninterference in the Philippines. His main interest was in seeing that no single power reigned supreme in Asia.

### Racial Politics

In addition to shifting the balance of power in China, the settlement of the Russo-Japanese War also had worldwide implications in racial politics. That an Asian people, the Japanese, had humiliated a white people, the Russians, kindled new national and racial pride in both the Chinese and the Japanese.

Japan reacted by protesting the 1906 segregation of Japanese children in San Francisco schools. A respected Japanese journal urged Japan to use its navy, if necessary, to end such humiliation:

> *The whole world knows that the poorly equipped army and navy of the United States are no match for our efficient army and navy. It will be an easy work to awake the United States from her dream of obstinacy when one of our great admirals appears on the other side of the Pacific.*

> *Mainichi Shimbun, 1906*

Roosevelt soothed Japanese humiliation with "A Gentleman's Agreement" in 1907 that ended school segregation in San Francisco—while at the same time controlling Japanese immigration to California. As the controversy raged, Roosevelt began to calculate. Perhaps the delicate balance of power was shifting. Perhaps it was time for the United States to flex its muscles for the Japanese to see. Roosevelt had been building a more modern and stronger U.S. Navy, and now he resolved to send the entire U.S. fleet of 16 battleships around the world in a show of might. The Great White Fleet, shown on this page, made a special stop in Japan in 1908.

**The Great White Fleet began its 14-month world tour in 1907.** *Why do you think Roosevelt sent the U.S. Navy on this 46,000-mile trip?*

## Entanglement with Europe

As the United States experimented in colonial and militaristic adventures overseas, its attitude toward Europe changed. For almost all of the nineteenth century, the United States had shunned entanglement with Europe. The democratic institutions of the United States set it apart from the colonial and militaristic ways of Europe—or so popular opinion believed. However, when Hay shaped his Open Door policy and when Roosevelt mediated the Russo-Japanese War, they both participated in diplomacy that affected politics in Europe. They also showed that the United States could effectively resolve conflicts of interest in other parts of the world.

In the early twentieth century, the United States was frequently called upon to mediate disputes. In 1906, Roosevelt defused a crisis between Germany and France over Morocco. In 1911 Taft arbitrated a dispute between France and Great Britain over Liberia. In part, a desire for trading privileges in Africa motivated the efforts of Roosevelt and Taft in these cases. Far more than keeping an open door for U.S. trade, the presidents hoped to keep peace in Europe. By 1900 the U.S. economy depended on markets all over the world. If tensions in Europe were to explode into war, U.S. trade might suffer disastrously.

## SECTION REVIEW

**Checking Facts**
1. Give examples of how racial ideas figured in U.S. expansion overseas.
2. Give two examples of the arguments against expansion.
3. Why did American farmers, manufacturers, and investors favor expansion overseas?
4. How did Roosevelt justify sending troops to the Dominican Republic?

**Thinking Critically**
5. **Recognizing Bias** When Roosevelt negotiated peace between Russia and Japan he claimed neutrality. What evidence suggests that he actually favored one side? Why would it be to his advantage to pretend he was unbiased?
6. **Comparing and Contrasting** Compare and contrast the interests missionaries and investors had in expanding their work in China.

**Linking Across Time**
7. When Roosevelt felt that Russia might dominate Asia, he favored the Japanese. When Japan became mightier, he decided to demonstrate U.S. strength with the Great White Fleet. How does the United States today show both friendship toward and rivalry with the Japanese?

# Watching Europe's War

## May 7, 1915: Germany Sinks *Lusitania*

*N*OTICE! *TRAVELLERS INTENDING TO EMBARK ON THE ATLANTIC VOYAGE ARE REMINDED THAT A STATE OF WAR EXISTS BETWEEN GERMANY AND HER allies and Great Britain and her allies; . . . and that travellers sailing in the war zone on ships of Great Britain or her allies do so at their own risk.*

New York *World*,
May 1, 1915

The passengers who sailed from New York on the British ship *Lusitania* that day seemingly ignored the warning that appeared in the newspaper. Bound for England, they enjoyed six days of dining and dancing on the luxury liner.

Early in the afternoon of May 7, in calm waters off the coast of Ireland, a German torpedo ripped into the side of the *Lusitania*. The huge ship sank within 18 minutes, taking with it the lives of nearly 1,200 men, women, and children, including 128 Americans.

Germany defended its action on the grounds that the *Lusitania* carried a shipment of arms. It also pointed out that passengers had been warned not to sail in the war zone. Americans, however, were outraged. Some demanded a declaration of war, although most wanted to keep America out of the war. President Wilson chose to apply diplomatic pressure on Germany and try to hold it accountable for its actions. Over the next few months, Wilson sent increasingly severe protests to Germany. He insisted that it

HISTORICAL PICTURES SERVICE, CHICAGO

abandon unrestricted submarine warfare. Americans could no longer merely watch Europe's war.

---

## Wilson's Foreign Policy

President Wilson brought to foreign policy an element of idealism that contrasted with the pragmatism of Roosevelt and Taft. He strongly believed that all peoples of the world had a right to **self-determination,** the right to choose the form of government they live under and to control their internal affairs. Yet President Wilson intervened in the affairs of other countries more than any previous president.

### Revolution in Mexico

President Wilson, like Roosevelt, upheld the principles of the corollary to the Monroe Doctrine. Wilson maintained stability in the Western Hemisphere for U.S. investment by sending American troops to Haiti in 1915, the Dominican Republic in 1916, and Cuba in 1917 to quell domestic uprisings. He also continued Taft's policies of Dollar Diplomacy by encouraging investors to buy out British enterprises in Central America. Dealing with Mexico and Europe, however, proved problematic for Wilson.

For 30 years the powerful Porfirio Díaz ruled Mexico. The stability of his rule encouraged American, British, and German investors, so much so that they controlled 90 percent of Mexico's mines, railroads, and industry. In 1911, however, Díaz fell from power,

---

### STUDY GUIDE

**As You Read**
Identify the policies and decisions that resulted from Wilson's idealism regarding foreign policy. Also, think about the following concepts and skills.

**Central Concepts**
- understanding that Wilson advocated but did not always practice **self-determination**
- recognizing the complexity of U.S. **neutrality** in the Great War

**Thinking Skills**
- analyzing decisions
- analyzing behavior
- identifying cause and effect
- making inferences

MUSEO NACIONAL DE HISTORIA, MEXICO

**This is just a portion of a mural found in Chapultepec Castle near Mexico City, Mexico. It was created by** *David Alfaro Siqueiros. How does this mural depict the period of the Mexican Revolution?*

toppled by angry peasants whose land had been taken and middle-class Mexicans who had been deprived of their civil and voting rights.

Foreign investors feared that Francisco Madero, who replaced Díaz, would confiscate their property. Foreign diplomats—including the U.S. ambassador—and business people plotted with discontented elements of the Mexican army to overthrow Madero. They wanted to replace him with Victoriano Huerta.

By the time President Wilson took office on March 4, 1913, Huerta had seized power, killing Madero in a bloody coup. Wilson thought the violence repulsive. He refused to recognize Huerta's government, but vowed not to interfere directly.

*W*e shall have no right at any time to intervene in Mexico to determine the way in which the Mexicans are to settle their own affairs. . . . [T]hings may happen of which we do not approve and which could not happen in the United States, but I say very solemnly that that is no affair of ours.

Woodrow Wilson,
Letter, 1914

**U.S. Intervention**    A few months after expressing these beliefs, Wilson changed his mind, declaring that he had to teach Mexico to elect good men. A minor incident concerning American honor was one reason for his shift. In April 1914 Mexican officials arrested several sailors from a U.S. naval vessel in the port of Tampico. Local Mexican officials, as well as Huerta, quickly apologized for the incident. The U.S. admiral in charge demanded a 21-gun salute to the American flag. Huerta demanded the same salute to the Mexican flag. This infuriated Wilson, who used the Tampico incident as a pretext for sending marines to the port city of Veracruz.

Another cause for Wilson's change of mind was a rumor that a German ship bound for Veracruz carried guns for Huerta's army. In spite of Mexico's ongoing revolution, most Mexicans were outraged by the occupation of Veracruz. Anti-American riots broke out in Mexico and throughout Latin America. The European press condemned the U.S. military intervention, and so did many Americans. Shocked, Wilson backed off, and agreed to allow the **ABC powers**—Argentina, Brazil, and Chile—to mediate.

In 1915 Venustiano Carranza followed Huerta as president of Mexico. When Wilson backed Carranza,

### STUDY GUIDE

**Analyzing Decisions**

If Wilson believed in self-determination, why did he decide to send troops to Haiti, the Dominican Republic, and Cuba? First, Wilson valued an orderly world that offered opportunities for American economic investment. The chaos in the Caribbean threatened that order—right in the backyard of the United States. Second, Wilson wanted no interference by European nations in the affairs of the Western Hemisphere. If the United States did not restore order in the Caribbean, Britain or Germany may have tried to in order to protect their own interests.

the rebel leader Pancho Villa struck back by killing 18 American mining engineers in Mexico. Villa's band then crossed the border and killed 17 Americans in the town of Columbus, New Mexico.

Wilson sent an expedition of 15,000 troops into Mexico under the command of John J. Pershing to find and capture Villa. Though they never found Villa, both Mexican and American lives were lost in battle.

Despite this military involvement, the United States failed to control events in Mexico. By late January 1917, Wilson decided to withdraw forces from Mexico. Another, much larger war raged in Europe.[1]

## Origins of the Great War

What set off the Great War in Europe? The bullet that killed the heir to the throne of the Austro-Hungarian empire, Archduke Franz Ferdinand, started the Great War—now commonly known as World War I. Austria-Hungary ruled over a large part of the Balkans, a mountainous area of southeastern Europe where many small ethnic groups struggled for their independence. When a Serbian who supported Balkan independence assassinated Franz Ferdinand and his wife, all of Europe held its breath.

**Entangling Alliances**   By June 1914 almost any troublesome event could have sparked a war in Europe. Russia vied with Austria-Hungary and the Ottoman Empire for control over the Balkans. France, Russia, Britain, and Germany wrangled with one another to control ports and colonies overseas. The new naval force of Germany challenged Britain's long-established naval supremacy. Similarly, Germany's disciplined army struck fear into the hearts of neighboring Russia and France.

To gain security, many European countries organized themselves into a number of alliances. Each country that was part of a particular alliance vowed to help the allied countries in case of war. The members of the **Triple Entente**—which came to be called the Allies—were Britain, France, and Russia. Opposing the Allied powers were the **Central Powers,** which consisted of Germany, Austria-Hungary, and the Ottoman Empire.

Because of the alliances, leaders in Europe knew that the assassination of Archduke Franz Ferdinand might mean world war. Russia reacted first by coming to the defense of the Serbian nationalists, in hopes of gaining influence in the Balkans. Russia's move brought the countries of the Triple Entente into the dispute, but Austria-Hungary and Germany needed to protect their interests, too. Soon all of Europe erupted into war.

**Early Years of the War**   Austria-Hungary declared war on Serbia on July 28, 1914, and Germany declared war on Russia and France in the next few days. To avoid the strong defenses on the Franco-German border, German troops stormed through neutral Belgium. As a result, Great Britain, which was committed to the **neutrality,** or impartiality, of Belgium, declared war on Germany on August 4, 1914. A year later, France, Russia, and Great Britain lured Italy into World War I on their side by promising Italy territory from the Austro-Hungarian empire after the war was over. The map of Europe on page 214 shows that battle lines, or fronts, formed in two principal places: the eastern front in Russia and Germany and the western front in Belgium and France.

By November 1914 opposing troops on the western front faced each other in deadlock. French troops stopped a German advance toward Paris, but at heavy cost. For more than three years thereafter, each side held the other in check.

On the eastern front, the Central Powers rapidly pushed back a disorganized and unprepared Russian army. They advanced across hundreds of miles of territory and took hundreds of thousands of prisoners early in the war. Later Russian successes were less decisive. Hardship among the Russian people, coupled with plummeting confidence in the czar's leadership, threatened Russia's ability to fight at all. Talk of mutiny sped through the troops.

**The Fields of Death**   World War I resulted in greater loss of life and property than any previous war. In the Battle of Verdun (February–July 1916), for example, French casualties numbered about 315,000 and German casualties about 280,000. In the Battle of the Somme, Britain suffered 60,000 casualties in one day of fighting. That battle raged from July to November of 1916 and resulted in more than

**Analyzing Behavior**
At first, Wilson vowed not to interfere in Mexican affairs. After Huerta took power, however, he changed his mind. Huerta was acting unfavorably towards U.S. investments in Mexico. Even though Wilson was not able to control events in Mexico before withdrawing American troops, he demonstrated his concern in protecting U.S. interests in foreign countries.

1 How did President Wilson's actions in Mexico conflict with his professed belief in self-determination?

1 million deaths. In the end, the Allies had advanced the front only about 7 miles. A battle at Tannenberg, in East Prussia, was so disastrous that the Russian general shot himself in defeat.

The terrible destruction of World War I resulted from a combination of old-fashioned strategies and new technology. Military commanders continued to order massive infantry offensives. The command "Over the top!" sent soldiers scrambling out of the trenches to dash across a field with fixed bayonets, hurling grenades into enemy trenches. But the attackers were no match for automatic machine guns that could fire hundreds of rounds in rapid succession. Defensive artillery kept each side pinned in the trenches.

Both sides developed new weapons designed to break the deadlock. In April 1915 the Germans first used poison gas in the Second Battle of Ypres. The fumes caused vomiting and suffocation. When the Allies also began using poison gas as a weapon, gas masks became a necessary part of a soldier's equipment. Flamethrowers that shot out streams of burning fuel and tanks that could roll over barbed wire and trenches added to the destruction.

The fields of battle in World War I extended to the seas and to the skies. Germany challenged Britain's sea power with its submarine blockade. The two navies squared off in a major encounter on May 31 and June 1, 1916, in the Battle of Jutland, off the west coast of Denmark. Both sides claimed victory, but Britain retained control of the seas.

Great advances in aviation came about during World War I. At first, planes were used mainly to observe enemy activities. Then Germany developed a machine gun timed to fire between an airplane's propeller blades. This invention led to the use of airplanes for combat. Dogfights, the name given clashes between enemy aircraft, proved deadly for pilots but had little effect on the ground war.

During 1917 France and Britain saw their hopes for victory diminish. A revolution in Russia made the situation seem even more hopeless. Early in 1917, an

**On the map below, find the countries of the Triple Entente alliance and of the Central Powers. Note their positions. Identify and locate the neutral countries during World War I.**

Europe During World War I

NAWROCKI STOCK PHOTO

**Many soldiers and civilians were killed by awesome new weapons never before used—submarines, automatic machine guns, poisonous gases, and tanks.**

NAWROCKI STOCK PHOTO

FIRST DIVISION MUSEUM AT CANTIGNY

uprising in Russia resulted in the overthrow of the czar. In November, Bolshevik party leader Vladimir I. Lenin seized control of the government and began peace talks with Germany. Thus, the Russian Revolution led to the end of fighting on the eastern front, freeing Germany to concentrate all its forces on the western front.[2] The Allies' only hope seemed to be getting help before Germany overwhelmed them.

**In the Trenches**   The soldiers on the western front spent most of their time in muddy trenches. Enemy troops were protected from one another only by dirt, barbed wire, and a stretch of land—called "no man's land"—no more than 30 yards wide in some places.

When not shooting at their enemy, soldiers in trenches fought lice, rats, the dampness and cold, as well as such diseases as dysentery, gangrene, and trench mouth. All understood the suffering they faced daily, if not the politics that created the trenches. By the end of the Great War, roughly 10 million soldiers and about 20 million civilians had died. Exact numbers were impossible to collect.

Many soldiers took the war as a personal challenge. Others became disillusioned. One German novelist portrayed a young German soldier crying out in protest:

> *W* *hile they [government officials] continued to write and talk, we saw the wounded and dying. While they taught that duty to one's country is the greatest thing, we already knew that death-throes are stronger. . . . We loved our country as much as they; we went courageously into every action; but also we distinguished the false from true.*
>
> Erich Maria Remarque,
> *All Quiet on the Western Front*, 1929

## Struggle for Neutrality

Woodrow Wilson longed to keep the United States out of the Great War. In August 1914 he asked for neutrality, urging the American people not to take sides. He said, "We must be impartial in thought as well as in action." Neither side deserved America's support, thought the righteous Wilson. The American people, however, many of whom had recently emigrated from Europe, had their favorite side. Millions had been born in Germany, England, Austria-Hungary, Russia, Ireland, or Italy. Yet for the most part, they, too, preferred to distance themselves from the bloodbath overseas.

**Myth of Neutrality**   While Wilson publicly proclaimed American neutrality, U.S. interests leaned toward the Allies. Although American businesses traded with both sides in the European conflict, ties with the

Allies were much stronger. A representative from the House of Morgan, the mighty New York financial institution explained:

*Those were the days when American citizens were being urged to remain neutral in action, in word, and even in thought. But our firm had never for one moment been neutral: we didn't know how to be. From the very start we did everything that we could to contribute to the cause of the Allies.*

Thomas W. Lamont,
*Manchester Guardian,*
January 27, 1920

American political and business sympathy pleased the Allies. They tried to sway popular support to their side, too. One of the first things Britain did when war broke out was to cut the transatlantic cable to the United States, so all news had to come through Britain. The reports that arrived vilified the Germans. Soon many ordinary Americans favored the Allies in the Great War.

**Bryan and the Submarines**   Although public sentiment was turning toward the Allies, Secretary of State William Jennings Bryan still favored neutrality—even after German submarines attacked ships on which American citizens traveled. Germany had developed a new weapon, the submarine, which it used to surprise enemy merchant ships in the war zone it monitored around the British isles. That strategy was in response to a British blockade of Germany which had effectively begun to starve the German people. Bryan could see that both sides had military reasons for acting as they did. He encouraged Wilson to forbid Americans from traveling in the submarine zones as a way of avoiding trouble with Germany. Wilson argued, however, that free and safe travel was a right of citizens of a neutral country.

The issue reached a crisis on May 7, 1915, when German submarines attacked the *Lusitania*, a British passenger ship. Over 1,000 passengers died, including 128 Americans, as the torpedoed ship quickly sank. Germany knew that the *Lusitania* secretly carried arms and had warned ahead of time that it might be a target for attack. Nevertheless, Americans were outraged. "Damnable! Damnable! Absolutely hellish!" cried Billy Sunday, a fiery evangelist of the time. In spite of the tragedy, Wilson continued to believe that Americans should not be restricted from traveling the seas. In protest, Bryan resigned.

**Reelection**   The American people reelected Woodrow Wilson to the presidency in 1916 in a close race against Charles Evans Hughes. American voters responded to the Democratic campaign slogan, "He kept us out of war!" That slogan, however, made Wilson nervous. In spite of his neutrality efforts, he knew that the nation was edging closer to entering the Great War.

The pressure on Wilson to enter the war came partly from his own moral commitment to the Allies; but it came also from American business leaders and investors. American companies had invested deeply in an Allied victory. By 1917 American loans to the Allies totaled $2.25 billion. If Wilson helped the Allies win, the money would be paid back. Even more important, his commitment to the Allies would ensure a place for American investment in postwar Europe.

In addition to these pragmatic motives, the idealistic Wilson truly wanted to have a say in a peace settlement. He longed to make sure that after the Great War, no other war would ever threaten the world again. He felt that no one would listen seriously to his ideas unless the United States had actually proved itself in battle. Ironically, then, his desire for a peaceful world led him closer to war.

**Closer to War**   Several events led the United States finally to enter the war. In January 1917 a German official named Arthur Zimmermann cabled the German ambassador in Mexico instructing him to make an offer to Mexico. Zimmermann proposed that Mexico ally itself with Germany. In return, Germany would make sure that after the war, Mexico would receive some of the region that it lost to the United States in 1848. A British official intercepted Zimmermann's telegram and spread the news to the United States. This incident occurred shortly after Wilson withdrew from the Pancho Villa chase, so the Zimmermann note made many Americans eager to humiliate both Mexico and Germany.

**Making Inferences**

At the outset of World War I, the official U.S. policy was one of neutrality. However, one can infer that most Americans probably felt anything but neutral. Consider the facts: many U.S. citizens were European immigrants with ties to their former homelands; American businesses had invested heavily in certain European nations; the United States had traditional ties to England, the home of many of the original American colonists; and indiscriminate German submarine warfare had begun to anger many Americans.

PRIVATE COLLECTION

**Early in 1915 several feminist leaders formed the Woman's Peace Party to advocate peace. After the *Lusitania* disaster, they staged a protest parade to** urge the president to search for peace despite German advances. *How can public protests influence government policies?*

Another declaration from Germany led the United States even closer to war. On January 31, 1917, Germany announced an unrestricted submarine campaign. German people were starving, and the country was desperate to end the war. Since the United States was not truly neutral, the Germans felt they had nothing to lose by an onslaught. Germans sank one ship after another, including the U.S. supply ship *Illinois* on March 18, 1917.

By April 1 President Wilson was brooding and pacing the floor. "Once I lead these people into war," he confided to editor Frank Cobb, "they'll forget there was ever such a thing as tolerance. To fight you must be brutal and ruthless, and the spirit of ruthless brutality will enter into the very fabric of our national life." In spite of his doubt and anguish, on April 2, 1917, the president stood before the U.S. Congress and asked its members to declare war on Germany.

*I*t is a fearful thing to lead this great peaceful people into war, into the most terrible and disastrous of all wars, civilization itself seeming to be in the balance. But the right is more precious than peace, and we shall fight for the things which we have always carried nearest our hearts,—for democracy, for the right of those who submit to authority to have a voice in their own Governments, for the rights and liberties of small nations. . . . [W]e dedicate our lives and our fortunes, everything that we are and everything that we have, . . . America is privileged to spend her blood and her might for the principles that gave her birth and happiness and the peace which she has treasured.

Woodrow Wilson,
War Message, April 1917

## SECTION REVIEW

### Checking Facts
1. How did Wilson continue the policies of Roosevelt and Taft?
2. Why did Wilson send marines to Veracruz? How else did he interfere in the Mexican Revolution?
3. What single act set off World War I?
4. What made the United States lean toward the Allied Powers during World War I?

### Thinking Critically
5. **Making Inferences** Wilson wanted Congress to declare war on Mexico because he felt Huerta had offended U.S. honor. What considerations may have been behind Wilson's action?
6. **Analyzing Decisions** Why was the British government so eager to inform the United States of Germany's offer to Mexico? What did it hope to gain?

### Linking Across Time
7. Wilson professed a belief in self-determination; however, he intervened in the affairs of other nations on several occasions. In 1983, the United States sent troops to Grenada to protect U.S. interests. Do you think strong nations should have the right to intervene in the affairs of weaker nations?

# Print Media

## Shaping Public Opinion During World War I

Popular print media—especially newspapers, magazines, and posters—reflect the culture, events, and concerns of their time. News and feature stories, editorials, letters to editors, and advertisements of the past offer today's historians the unique opportunity to experience a past event in much the same way as it was experienced by the people who lived during that time.

### The Evidence

After the United States entered World War I, the print media played a pivotal role in shaping and managing public opinion about the war. Newspapers, magazines, and posters urged Americans to support the war effort.

As the following excerpt from an article in *McClure's* magazine

---

"WELL," said my young friend, "we're in it at last."

"The War?" I queried.

He nodded.

"Your old Uncle Sam is sometimes a bit slow in assimilating an idea, but once he gets it firmly imbedded in his head, he certainly knows what to do with it. And before he's through, the Germans will be sorry they didn't stop pestering him when they had the chance.

"Mr. Dooley said it. Military nations are all right enough in their way. But look out for a country that fights in a plug hat and a long-tailed coat. . . . For, while your Uncle will slough his civilian habiliments, and get right into his working clothes along with the rest of 'em, he still has the plug-hat spirit; which means that he's slow to wrath, but, once wrathful, zowie!

"History piles across the scenery so fast in times like these that things are liable to be over with even while you're talking about them," he went on; "and to write anything at the moment that will be accurate a month from now, one has to be a cross between a clairvoyant and that fellow that tells you what kind of winter we're going to have in 1931 by looking at a goose's wishbone.

"However, we're in the war, and we're raising an army, and we're raising a navy, and when we have finished raising the army and the navy we're going to raise something else that isn't commonly spoken of in mixed gatherings, but in case there remains any uncertainty in your mind, it's what Sherman said war was.

"No nation in the world wanted to go to war except Germany. But Germany did. After going to war, every nation in the war wanted to fight according to the rules except Germany. And Germany didn't. I can't fight you according to Queensbury rules when you're using brass knuckles and a hunk of lead pipe concealed in a stocking; nor when you're polluting me with poison gases can I defend myself successfully by delicately spraying you with an atomizer filled with attar of roses, or Esprit de Joie.

"If it were a man, like yourself, that were attacking you (which in these days is hard to conceive) he would employ only the means of attack that you would employ; hence could you defend yourself by the means that he would employ in defense; which would mean that you would be fighting according to the rules laid down at The Hague; which would probably mean that there wouldn't be any fighting in the first place. But when a mad dog starts to attack you, you've got to kill the dog or get hydrophobia. That's all. And eighty million words of argument can't bring any other answer."

Porter Emerson Browne,
"Please Right Face!"
*McClure's*, July 1917

makes clear, the media ridiculed Germany and its people, prompting a deep mistrust of, and sometimes even outright hatred for, German Americans in the United States.

## The Interpretation

Pride and patriotism are evident in the aggressive tone and language of this article. So, too, are prejudice and ridicule.

Uncle Sam is portrayed as a tough, albeit reluctant, fighter in a plug hat and long-tailed coat who has decided to roll up his sleeves and give Germany the lickin' it deserves. The Germans, in contrast, are painted as street brawlers, mad dogs, and dirty fighters who hide lead pipes in stockings and toss poison gas in your face. Such prose was meant to prompt citizens to cheer on Uncle Sam while heaping scorn and derision on Germany. For the contemporary reader, it also illustrates one of the limitations of using the print media as a venue for historical research.

In any era the media offer a variety of perspectives on current events. Some media are conservative. Some are liberal. Others are extremist. During some eras, such as the period of World War I in the United States, unique pressures may influence what the media report.

For example, historians know that many Americans were strongly opposed to fighting a war in Europe. Yet a survey of popular newspapers and magazines during the war years offers little evidence of this opposition. Why were the media so united in their enthusiasm for the war? Why did so little dissent find its way into print?

The answers to these questions have a significant impact on the way historians interpret what they read in American publications from the war years.

In 1917 President Wilson appointed George Creel to head up a new government agency, the Committee on Public Information (CPI). The CPI acted as both an advertising agency and a public relations firm. It coordinated, disseminated, and censored the information Americans received about the war effort and encouraged the production of posters and other advertisements designed to whip up enthusiasm and support for the U.S. campaign against Germany. In effect the CPI was the U.S. government's propaganda machine.

The CPI did its job so well that the media, with few exceptions, presented a united front in its coverage of the war. Some newspapers even published alleged "news" stories that actually had been composed by CPI writers—without ever revealing the source of the stories. Unwary contemporary historians may imagine they are reading dispatches from the front when in fact the "correspondent" may well have been comfortably billeted in a federal office on the banks of the Potomac!

In addition to understanding the impact of the CPI, historians must be aware of the effect two important pieces of legislation had on the print media. The Espionage Act of 1917 and the 1918 Sedition Amendment to the Espionage Act provided for severe penalties, including lengthy jail terms, for anyone convicted of using "disloyal, profane, scurrilous, or abusive language" about

THE GRANGER COLLECTION

**This poster is just one of many issued by the U.S. goverment during World War I. It is an enlarged depiction of a 1917 War Savings Stamp.** *What message did this poster attempt to send to the American public?*

the U.S. government, the flag, the Constitution, or the military. Such was the political climate during the war, and few dissenters wanted to see their words in print.

## Further Exploration

Search through newspapers and magazines dating from 1917 and 1918. Look for articles, advertisements, stories, and poems relating to the war. Look, also, for contemporary books showing posters from World War I. Try to find a variety of opinions in the media you research. Which point of view is most often represented? Photocopy the most interesting pieces you find. Use them to create a class booklet or display on the print media during World War I.

# The Great War: There and Here

### Fall 1918: Influenza and Bonds Sweep Nation

IN HER NOVELLA *PALE HORSE, PALE RIDER*, KATHERINE ANNE PORTER DESCRIBES LIFE ON THE HOME FRONT THROUGH THE EXPERIENCES OF A WOMAN NAMED MIRANDA. DURING 1918 Miranda's problems, like those of other young working women, were intimately linked to the war. One morning, she awakened with a headache and a queasy feeling in her stomach—symptoms of influenza. This disease had infected the people of Denver, where Miranda worked, as well as people in other cities across the nation. Thousands died. The deadly disease also spread abroad. About 57,000 American soldiers died from influenza during the time America was at war and about 53,500 died in battle.

Miranda tried to ignore her headache and the funeral processions that wound down the city's streets. She needed to concentrate on two other problems. She had just fallen in love with a young man named Adam who had to leave for the front in a few days. She also was being hounded to buy Liberty Bonds—loan certificates the government issued to help pay for the war. As illustrated by the photograph on this page, bonds were sold at rallies throughout the nation. Miranda couldn't afford a bond, but was afraid she'd lose her job if she refused.

That evening Miranda met Adam. The couple strolled to the theater. They could not, however, escape the hawking of the war. When the curtain rose for the third act, the audience beheld, not the actors, but an American flag draped across a backdrop. In front of the flag, a middle-aged man began to sell Liberty Bonds. All of the words Miranda had ever heard about the war ran together in her mind:

BY COURTESY OF ENCYCLOPAEDIA BRITANNICA INC.

*WAR to end WAR, war for Democracy, for humanity, a safe world forever and ever—and to prove our faith in Democracy to each other, and to the world, let everybody get together and buy Liberty Bonds and do without sugar and wool socks.*

Katherine Anne Porter, *Pale Horse, Pale Rider,* 1939

## Mobilization

The pressures Miranda felt to back the war effort were typical for her generation. When President Wilson asked Congress to declare war, he knew that he needed the support of all Americans. War, he said, would involve **mobilization,** or preparation, by citizens and business enterprises. Wilson warned that any

---

disloyalty would be met "with a firm hand." Support in Congress for the war resolution was very strong. To fund the war, Wilson raised income taxes and organized a vigorous Liberty Bond campaign. Secretary of the Treasury William Gibbs McAdoo also pressed the public for financing. "A man who can't lend his government $1.25 per week at the rate of 4% interest," he said, "is not entitled to be an American citizen."

**Drafting an Army**  In addition to raising money, the president initiated **conscription,** or compulsory enrollment in military service. The United States had not enforced a draft since the Civil War, however, and some Americans now spoke out against it. "I feel it is my sacred duty to keep the stalwart young men of today out of a barbarous war 3,500 miles away," said Congressman Issac Sherwood. Jeannette Rankin of Montana, the first woman elected to Congress, also opposed both conscription and the war declaration.

Many progressives, however, supported the war and the draft. They argued that the draft might prove to be a great equalizer. Young men from upper and lower classes and from many ethnic origins would serve side by side, learning to live together as brothers. This equality might then translate into reforms at home.

Secretary of War Newton D. Baker called June 5, 1917, the official day of registration for the draft, "a festival and patriotic occasion." Draft registration proceeded in the midst of local fairs and picnics. Men aged 21 to 30 (later the draft age was extended from 18 to 45) registered by the millions. A lottery decided those to be actually inducted into the military. About 11,000 women also volunteered as nurses, clerical workers, and telephone operators.[1]

**Segregating African Americans**  The military did not prove to be an equalizer for African Americans, who were strictly segregated. The National Association for the Advancement of Colored People (NAACP) demanded that African Americans be allowed to become officers. Its persistence paid off, when over 600 African Americans graduated from an officer-training program at Fort Des Moines. The military, however, did not give high rank to any of these officers. White officers commanded the black 92nd Division. Some black troops were integrated

UPI/BETTMANN NEWSPHOTOS

**The 15th Negro Regiment was made up of New Yorkers and nicknamed "the Buffalos." Here they are seen marching during World War I.**

with French troops once they arrived in Europe. This tolerance added to African Americans' discontent with prejudice back home.

## Fighting Over There

Under the command of General John J. Pershing, the American Expeditionary Force—nicknamed **doughboys** after a cake traditionally baked for sailors—began coming ashore in France in late June 1917. The Allies desperately needed "men, men, men," as one French officer put it. Although most Americans fought separately from the European units, the Allies welcomed the relief the American Expeditionary Force (A.E.F.) offered.

American doughboys arrived in France singing "Pack Up Your Troubles in an Old Kit Bag" and "It's a Grand Old Flag." Aside from their confident air, the doughboys were unprepared for war. Pershing, known for his unbending will and a personality embittered by the death of his wife and children in a fire, described the problem: "a large percentage of them [American troops] were ignorant of practically everything pertaining to the business of the soldier in war." By late 1917, about 200,000 had arrived. Though they lacked training, American soldiers gained a reputation for courage and "pep."

### STUDY GUIDE

**Predicting Consequences**
African American soldiers were surprised to discover that the French treated them with more respect and equality than the Americans did. As frustration and resentment grew after the war, some African Americans—primarily entertainers, writers, artists, and musicians—went to live in France as expatriates.

1 How did the United States mobilize for war?

**The Eastern Front** The A.E.F. filled a breach left by heavy Allied losses in the west and Russia's pullout from the war. Russia had suffered huge losses on the eastern front. Its new revolutionary government wanted no part of what they considered to be the czar's imperialistic—and now unwinnable—war. Russia signed a peace treaty with Germany on March 3, 1918, and gave up large amounts of territory, including Finland, Poland, Ukraine, and the Baltic states.

Yet Germany's strength was waning. American troops and military hardware added punch to the Allied attack in the west, and the military position of all of the Central Powers deteriorated rapidly in the fall of 1918. Bulgaria surrendered on September 29. British forces caused the surrender of the Ottoman Empire on October 30. Italy, with the help of France and Britain, brought about the surrender of Austria-Hungary on November 3.

**The Expeditionary Force's Role** More than 2 million U.S. soldiers went to France during the war, the peak arriving in July 1918. Of these troops, nearly 1.4 million took part in active combat. Most were in the army or marines, but 50,000 U.S. naval forces, under the command of William S. Sims, were indispensable, too. They convoyed troop transports and helped the British fleet chase submarines and keep German ships out of the North Sea.

Beginning in March 1918, the Germans launched a last desperate series of offensives on the western front. In June U.S. troops helped the French block a German advance at Chateau-Thierry. American troops then captured Cantigny. The turning point of the war was at the Second Battle of the Marne in July. About 85,000 American troops helped bring an end to the German offensive. After that, the Allies advanced steadily.

Britain and France attacked the Germans near Amiens, and General Pershing led U.S. troops to a major victory at Saint-Mihiel. The last major offensive of the war took place between the Meuse River and the Argonne Forest, beginning in September 1918. More than 1 million U.S. troops took part in a campaign that convinced the Germans they could no longer overcome the superior strength of the Allies. Germany signed the

armistice on November 11, 1918, and World War I came to an end.

Americans had fought in Europe for just over a year. They felt neither the despair nor the suffering of their European counterparts. Many doughboys, never away from home before, regarded the Great War as a dashing adventure, a romantic scene from movies they had seen in boot camp.

> *Those [Germans] were the Huns. Then there were flags blowing very hard in the wind, and the sound of a band. The Yanks were coming. Everything was lost in a scene from a movie in which khaki-clad regiments marched fast, fast.*
>
> John Dos Passos,
> *Three Soldiers*, 1921

That is how the author John Dos Passos described the musings of one American soldier. Not all soldiers, however, could romanticize the war. They had witnessed sobering scenes such as this one described in the diary of an American draftee:

> *Many dead Germans along the road. One heap on a manure pile. . . . Devastation everywhere. Our barrage has rooted up the*

| World War I Casualties* | | |
|---|---|---|
| **Country** | **Killed** | **Wounded** |
| **Allied Powers** Russia | 1,700,000 | 4,950,000 |
| France | 1,358,000 | 4,266,000 |
| British Empire | 908,400 | 2,090,000 |
| Italy | 650,000 | 947,000 |
| Romania | 335,700 | 120,000 |
| United States | 116,500 | 234,400 |
| **Central Powers** Germany | 1,773,000 | 4,216,000 |
| Austria-Hungary | 1,200,000 | 3,620,000 |
| Turkey | 325,000 | 400,000 |
| Bulgaria | 87,500 | 152,400 |

*Figures are approximate. Not all countries are listed.

**World War I devastated many countries.** *Which five countries suffered most of the casualties?*

**Predicting Consequences**

With so many men leaving the country, the United States had many adjustments to make. To enable the production of food and goods to continue and for the economy to remain stable, someone had to take over the jobs these men left behind. Many women filled these positions. They went to work in factories and operated the nation's farms. In addition, many people from the south moved to the north to find jobs

*entire territory like a ploughed field. Dead horses galore, many of them have a hind quarter cut off—the Huns need food. Dead men here and there.*

Battlefield Diary,
November 3, 1918,
Quoted from *The American Spirit*

## The War Effort at Home

Unity, cooperation, conformity—these key words described the war effort at home. **Propaganda,** or a form of public information to mold public opinion, became the tool by which business, labor, government, and American opinion would be molded to fight and win the Great War. William Gibbs McAdoo, secretary of the treasury, relentlessly pitched patriotism in his Liberty Bond campaigns. Herbert Hoover, food administrator, admonished housewives and urged them to conserve: "Food Will Win the War," "Use All Leftovers," and "Serve Just Enough." George Creel, who headed Wilson's Committee on Public Information, also relied on emotion and peer pressure to mold public opinion. To those who regarded his numerous flyers, movies, conferences, speeches, posters, news bulletins, tracts, pictures, headlines, and exhibits as heavy-handed, he defended his mission without apology. He called his work "the world's greatest adventure in advertising."

**Response from the Heartland**   The patriotism campaigns of McAdoo, Hoover, and Creel reached every city, town, and rural area of the United States. In Geneva, Illinois, for example, women formed the Women's Council of Defense to conserve food for the war effort. Since the Allies desperately needed food, many U.S. crops were shipped overseas and Americans at home were asked to conserve, as shown by the poster to the right.

In addition to conserving food, women along with adolescent girls and boys pitched in to plow fields and plant and harvest corn while young men fought in France. The corn crops of the Midwest fed the whole nation.

Women and teenagers in Geneva also took jobs at the Burgess-Norton Company, a factory booming with war business. In 1916 the government awarded Burgess-Norton a contract for producing ammunition. The factory later received contracts to produce fuses for navy shells, as well as meat cleavers, saws, and brush axes for the army.

**Cooperation of Business**   The Burgess-Norton Company, like thousands of small companies across the United States, willingly cooperated with the government's war mobilization. In doing their part for the war effort, they were also seizing an opportunity to grow and increase profits. For large corporations, the war promised still greater rewards.

In the name of unity and in the expectation of abundant profit, big businesses joined with the government in forming cooperative committees. These

UNIVERSITY OF NORTH CAROLINA LIBRARY

**BLOOD or BREAD**
Others are giving their blood
You will shorten the war—
save life if you eat only what
you need, and waste nothing.
No.16  UNITED STATES FOOD ADMINISTRATION

**This poster by Henry Raleigh could be seen in the United States during 1917 and 1918.** *What message did this poster attempt to send to the American public? What might have been the public's response?*

committees supervised the purchasing of war supplies and the granting of contracts. Progressives who lauded efficiency and cooperation smiled upon this centralized regulation, forgetting, in the heat of the moment, their former distrust of big business. Corporate profits tripled between 1914 and 1919.

**Cooperation of Labor**   Would labor cooperate with government and big business in the effort to win the Great War? In 1917 that question did not have a ready or immediate answer. Antiwar sentiment among **rank and file,** or ordinary, workers had soared since 1914, and labor leadership was sharply divided. The American Federation of Labor and the Women's Trade Union League supported the war, while socialists (members of the American Socialist Party and the Industrial Workers of the World) opposed it as an imperialist ploy to make the world safe only for the profits of big business. Likewise, some women suffragists in the labor movement opposed the war, questioning Wilson's commitment to democracy. After all, most women still could not vote!

Samuel Gompers, who headed the American Federation of Labor, became a key figure in labor's support of the war. He easily shed his earlier pacifist ideals as he calculated the opportunities war might mean for the labor movement. If he cooperated with government by supporting mobilization, Gompers believed he could surely gain concessions from company leaders: higher pay and better working conditions; the right to organize and bargain collectively. Even before the United States entered the war, Gompers had pledged his support to Wilson. In return, the government's Committee of Public Information secretly channeled money to Gomper's American Alliance for Labor and Democracy, a group organized to discredit socialists in the labor movement.

The American Federation of Labor did attract thousands of workers to its ranks during the war years. By 1918, with its membership swelled to nearly three million, labor had won important concessions such as the acceptance of an eight-hour work day in many industries previously opposed to it.

These gains came at a price. For example, during the war, workers labored under no-strike contracts. Also, women of all races and African American and Hispanic men quickly lost their jobs when soldiers returned home to claim them. The labor movement itself lost some of its diversity as Gompers, in cooperation with the government, muzzled socialist opponents. Thus weakened, the labor movement would not be able to effectively face the backlash that would come after the war.[2]

**War and Civil Liberties**   The lack of diversity in the labor movement reflected a similar pattern in society as a whole as the government passed legislation to unify everyone behind the war effort. The Espionage Act of 1917 and the Sedition Amendment of 1918 made any obstruction of the war effort illegal and curbed the **civil liberties,** or democratic rights, of those who spoke against the war. Government agencies broadly interpreted the new laws. Loyalty Leagues, organized by George Creel, encouraged Americans to spy and report on those who might be "disloyal." The Post Office withdrew circulation privileges from socialist and antiwar newspapers such as the *Masses* and the *Milwaukee Leader,* and even hired college professors to translate foreign periodicals to find out if they contained antiwar messages. As officials pressed for efficiency and absolute conformity in order to win the war, Wilson's fears of April 1, 1917, seemed prophetic. Just before he declared war, Wilson had expressed concern that the war would result in widespread intolerance.

During the war, freedom of speech took a severe beating. Socialist Rose Pastor Stokes was punished for a letter she sent to the *Kansas City Star* stating: "No government which is for the profiteers can also be for the people, and I am for the people, while the Government is for the profiteers." For her words, a local court sentenced her to 10 years in prison. That decision was later reversed through a higher court. Socialist leader Eugene Debs served time in prison for telling his followers to "resist militarism, wherever found."

This atmosphere of **legal repression,** or official restriction of dissent, soon led to mindless crowd reaction. One night in Tulsa, Oklahoma, "gowned and masked gunmen" terrorized Wobblies, members of the Industrial Workers of the World. One member remembered the ordeal: "After each one [of us] was whipped another man applied the tar with a large brush, from the head to the seat. Then a brute

**Predicting Consequences**
The Espionage Act of 1917 and its Sedition Amendment of 1918 provided lengthy jail terms for anyone convicted of violating their provisions. Predictably, these two laws had a chilling effect on free speech in the United States. Little published dissent appeared during the war years, although many Americans did oppose the war. Vocal dissent also was limited.

2  How did the government coordinate the war effort at home with business and labor? Why was such coordination necessary during war?

smeared feathers over and rubbed them in."

Americans of German descent, like socialists, suffered wartime harassment. All things German became suspect. Advertisers began to call sauerkraut "liberty cabbage" and hamburgers "liberty sausage" because they wanted to avoid German names. Many schools dropped the German language from their curriculums. In some small towns, anti-German feeling turned into violence. A mob numbering 500 in Collinsville, Illinois, lynched a young German-born man whom they suspected of disloyalty. When a jury found the mob leaders innocent, they shouted, "Nobody can say we aren't loyal now!"

EUGENE V. DEBS FOUNDATION

"The Debs Mural" covers the walls of the entire third floor of the Eugene V. Debs Home, a museum in Terre Haute, Indiana. It was commissioned in the late 1970s to depict the life of Eugene Debs. Even though Debs was convicted under the Espionage Act in 1918, he went on to run for the presidency as a socialist five times.

**Defending Free Speech** Not all Americans were caught up in the wartime frenzy. Some spoke out against the Espionage and Sedition laws and what they considered to be violations of free speech. Senator Robert La Follette and Professor Zechariah Chafee, Jr., of the Harvard Law School openly defended the right of Americans to exercise their freedom of speech with regard to war. Groups were formed to protect the rights of antiwar protestors. The Civil Liberties Union (later the American Civil Liberties Union) assisted pacifists and conscientious objectors who had been subjected to ridicule and abuse. (You can read more about such pacifists in the Case Study on page 226.) Most Americans, however, gave little thought to restrictions of speech and supported the war without questioning the rights they were giving up.

After the war Supreme Court Justice Oliver Wendell Holmes, Jr., ruled that a citizen's freedom of speech should only be curbed when the words uttered constitute a "clear and present danger." He used yelling *Fire!* in a crowded theater as an example of a situation in which freedom of speech would be superseded by the theater-goers' right to safety. The question remained whether critics of the war constituted a "clear and present danger" to the United States.

## SECTION REVIEW

**Checking Facts**
1. Summarize the antiwar argument of Isaac Sherwood.
2. Why did many progressives see a positive side to conscription?
3. Why was the goal of the Women's Council of Defense important to the war effort?
4. Who was Samuel Gompers, and why did he support the war?
5. What was the purpose of the Loyalty Leagues?

**Thinking Critically**
6. **Recognizing Propaganda** Look at the poster on page 223. Explain how language and images can stir up enthusiasm for war.
7. **Predicting Consequences** Think about the conviction of Eugene Debs and Rose Pastor Stokes and the terrorization of I.W.W. members in Oklahoma. In what ways might the abridgement of civil liberties lead to mob rule?

**Linking Across Time**
8. As the United States mobilized for war, government and business joined forces as never before in U.S. history. Today, cooperation between government and business is common. Which industries are most closely connected with government? Why?

# Case Study

# Pacifism in World War I

## *SPRING 1917*

> The No-Conscription League has been formed for the purpose of encouraging conscientious objectors to affirm their liberty of conscience and to make their objection to human slaughter effective by refusing to participate in the killing of their fellow men. The No-Conscription League is to be the voice of protest against the coercion of conscientious objectors to participate in the war. Our platform may be summarized as follows:
>
> We oppose conscription [the military draft] because we are internationalists, anti-militarists, and opposed to all wars waged by capitalistic governments.
>
> We will fight for what we choose to fight for; we will never fight simply because we are ordered to fight.
>
> We believe that the militarization of America is an evil that far outweighs, in anti-social and anti-libertarian effects, any good that may come from America's participation in the war.
>
> We will resist conscription by every means in our power, and we will sustain those who, for similar reasons, refuse to be conscripted.
>
> —No-Conscription League

## The Case

**E**van Thomas, a staff member of the Young Men's Christian Association (YMCA), traveled to Europe in 1916 to spread the word of God to English soldiers fighting in the Great War. Thomas was initially impressed by the patriotic spirit of the soldiers. However, the more he experienced the death and destruction of war at close range, the more disillusioned he became.

Thomas began meeting with others in England who had also started to question the war. As devout Christians, they believed that war was opposed to all the principles for which Jesus stood. However, they were tortured by many doubts. Each asked himself: Am I not responsible to the state and do I not owe it my allegiance? When my beliefs and my duty to the state conflict, which do I choose to follow?

In 1917 the government began drafting young men for the military. Men like Evan Thomas had to make a decision of conscience.

## The Background

**B**efore World War I, religious pacifist organizations had drawn their support largely from Christian sects whose members obeyed religious injunctions against killing. Religious pacifists pursued a policy of nonresistance. They believed that true Christians should not participate in violence or try to resist it, but rather should submit to it.

By 1914, however, the old pacifist organizations had either merged with or been replaced by organizations whose objections to war were based on political or ethical rather than religious principles. Such nonreligious objectors to war were called conscientious objectors. These new pacifists, who included social reformers and feminists active in the progressive movement, viewed war as a social problem that they had a duty to solve. Many of them believed that capitalistic industrialists saw the war as a money-making opportunity, since the manufacture of war weapons would boost production levels for many industries.

When war broke out in Europe, the new pacifist organizations urged that there should be no American intervention. Between 1914 and 1917, leaders of the pacifist organizations encouraged President Woodrow Wilson to mediate between the warring European nations. Despite maintaining a neutral stance, the United States continued to trade with Great Britain during these years. Shortly after Wilson was reelected in 1916, German U-boats began to attack American merchant ships in neutral waters. These acts of aggression led the president to abandon his position of neutrality. In 1917 the United States entered the war, and within six weeks conscription became a reality.

## The Points of View

**R**eligious and conscientious objectors resisted conscription. They could not support an evil, the war, even as a means to an approved end, international peace. The quotes that follow reflect pacifist opinions as well as the opinions of those who supported the United States' involvement in World War I.

*"We are patriots who love our country and desire to serve her and those ideals for which she has stood . . . but we cannot believe that participation in war is the true way of service to America or to humanity. Nor can we persuade ourselves that it is right to do evil that good may come. To us war especially in its modern form is not so much a sacred call to give one's self as it is a stern necessity to do all in one's power to kill others."*

The Fellowship of Reconciliation,
a pacifist organization in 1917

*"We live in society, but we live first of all with ourselves, and we could not live honestly or at peace with ourselves if we had taken human lives in war when all reason cried out against it."*

Ernest Meyer,
conscientious objector

*"The clergyman who does not put the flag above the church had better close his church and keep it closed."*

Theodore Roosevelt

*"The pacifist speaks with the German accent. Even if his words are not against America, the import of all he says is to aid Germany against America and its allies in the war."*

Clarence Darrow

*"I cannot emphasize too strongly that in my view, not only could this war not have been successfully and in a self-respecting way carried on by the United States Government if such an attitude as yours had prevailed, but I think such an attitude would have led inevitably to disorder and finally to the destruction of a [our] Government."*

Judge Julius M. Mayer's remarks in imposing
sentence on a religious objector in 1918

## The Options

**T**he Selective Service Act of 1917 defined two categories of objectors to conscription: religious objectors from recognized religious pacifist sects and conscientious objectors. The first category included members of recognized religious

THE GRANGER COLLECTION                    AP/WIDE WORLD PHOTOS

**Former president Theodore Roosevelt and Judge Julius M. Mayer agreed that conscription was necessary.**

pacifist sects, such as Quakers, Mennonites, and Brethren. Since the Civil War the government had accepted these sects as pacifists and had exempted them from active military service. Military-aged male members of these sects were not required to report to an army base or be in the armed services but were still required to serve the nation in time of war. In World War I, many carried out relief work in devastated areas of France through private groups and through the American Red Cross. For those religious pacifists who felt such work was too closely allied with the war, there were other options, such as working on farms to raise food for people affected by the war.

The second category of objectors to conscription, conscientious objectors, included religious objectors unaffiliated with a pacifist religious denomination and people who objected to conscription for political or ethical reasons. Conscientious objectors were not exempted from military service. These men were drafted and had to report to an army base where they had an opportunity to explain their position to army officers. Only 3,989 men out of the 2.8 million men inducted into the armed services persisted in claiming that they were conscientious objectors once they went through an inquisition from army officers. Most accepted the military's offer of doing noncombatant relief service in the military that was similar to the work that religious pacifists were doing for nonmilitary organizations.

About 1,400 conscientious objectors, however, refused to cooperate with the military in any way. They refused to follow military orders, wear uniforms, or contribute in any way to the war effort.

The military classified these men as "absolutist" war resisters. It was this group that created the most difficulty for the military, for refusing to follow orders set a precedent that the military could not tolerate. Absolutists were court-martialed and then imprisoned in solitary confinement for weeks at a time, forced to live in dark and damp cells with nothing to eat but bread and water. Absolutists were often psychologically tormented and physically tortured by others in the armed services. Seventeen objectors died in jail as a direct result of these conditions; others were driven insane.

## The Significance

After the United States entered the war in 1917, Evan Thomas resigned his position with the YMCA and returned to the United States. Because he did not belong to a religious sect that would allow him exemption from the military, Thomas knew that when he was drafted he would be expected to serve in some capacity. Thomas decided to challenge the authority of the Selective Service System that refused to grant him an exemption just because he was not a member of a recognized pacifist sect. Once drafted, Thomas became an absolutist who refused to perform even noncombatant duties. By carrying out these duties, he reasoned, he would have made it possible for another man to fight. It was important to Thomas to prove to the military that he was a free person, whom they could not force to serve in the military. In order to demonstrate his dissatisfaction with the army, Thomas went on a hunger strike. As a result, Thomas was court-martialed for refusing to follow the order to eat. The military tribunal found him guilty and sentenced him to prison at Fort Leavenworth for 20 years.

Thomas's battle with the military was often lonely and doubt-ridden. He wrote to his brother about his feelings of isolation:

*The comradeship one must give up, the being part of the fun and hardship of all this, yes of fighting and maybe dying along with the rest of your fellows on both sides in this huge tragedy makes my stand seem so terribly aloof, so terribly unhuman.*

However, Thomas hoped that his dedication to the pacifist cause might inspire others. By personally expressing his objection to the war and by supporting other pacifists, Thomas believed he was promoting the greater welfare of society.

After the war ended in November 1918, the War Department released Thomas from prison on a legal technicality. The War Department admitted that the order to eat that Thomas had refused to obey was not a proper military order.

## The Decisions

During the 1920s and 1930s, pacifist organizations continued to work for the ideals they had upheld throughout World War I: peace, justice, and internationalism. International pacifist organizations attracted more peace workers who, like Evan Thomas, did not belong to a religious denomination that granted them exemption from the draft. The Selective Service Act of 1940, which determined who would be eligible for the draft in World War II, allowed exemption to all those who objected to war "by reason of religious training and belief." In other words, membership in a traditionally pacifist denomination was no longer a requirement for exemption. Alternative service outside the army was also an option for these religious conscientious objectors.

The position of non-religious conscientious objectors, however, was much as it had been during the first world war. Pacifists opposed to war on ethical rather than religious grounds had to either submit to the draft or go to prison. This provision continued to be enforced during the Vietnam War in the 1960s.

Yet by the 1960s, the antiwar movement once again included people calling for broad social change. Just as the pacifist movement during World War I had attracted progressive-era reformists, the peace movement during the Vietnam War drew civil rights and women's rights activists. Because these later reformers were more numerous than their World War I counterparts, they had more influence over America's domestic and foreign policies. Peace advocates in the 1960s loudly defended the conscientious objectors, and some people believe that peace demonstrations held during the war hastened its conclusion. In many ways, World War I pacifists had laid the groundwork for later peace workers.

FREEDOM OF CONSCIENCE AT ALL COSTS!

**FRIDAY, MAY 18, 8 P. M.**
**HARLEM RIVER CASINO**
127th Street & Second Avenue

SPEAKERS: Emma Goldman; Harry Weinberger; Leonora O'Reilly; Alexander Berkman; Jacob Panken; Alex Cohen [in Yiddish] Carlo Tresca [in Italian] and others.
Leonard D. Abbott, Chairman

Auspices of No-Conscription League of New York

*Admission Free*

**The pamphlet of the No-Conscription League carried the message, "Resist conscription. Organize meetings. Join our League. Send us money."**

## Think About It

1. List the reasons that religious pacifists thought it was wrong to serve in the military. List the reasons that conscientious objectors thought it was wrong to fight in World War I. Why do you think the United States government treated these two groups differently?

2. Evan Thomas claimed that conscription violated his freedom, and he went to prison for his beliefs. Do you think he had more freedom in prison or out of prison? Explain your answer.

3. Evan Thomas fought a war against conscription. Do you think he won or lost that war? Explain your answer.

# Reshaping the World

## December 1918: Europeans Cheer Wilson

"WE WANT WILSON," THE WAR-WEARY CROWD ROARED. "LONG LIVE DR. WILSON." "HONOR TO WILSON THE JUST." ENGLISH SCHOOL GIRLS WITH American flags smiled, tossing flowers in the president's path. Everywhere in Europe the Wilsons visited—Paris, Rome, Milan—the reception was jubilant. An Italian laborer spoke for millions when he said of Wilson:

> *They say he thinks of us—the poor people; that he wants us all to have a fair chance; that he is going to do something when he gets here that will make it impossible for our government to send us to war again. If he had only come sooner! I have already lost my two sons. Do you believe he is strong enough to stop all wars?*
>
> Overheard conversation, 1918, *My Diplomatic Education*

Europeans had lost about 10 million soldiers in the war and twice as many civilians. Soldiers suffered from wounds in crowded hospitals. French towns had been obliterated from the map. Ordinary Europeans had sacrificed, scrimping on food, often going cold and hungry. No wonder they looked for a saviour—someone to end such brutality forever. They hailed Wilson hopefully because of his plan for lasting peace.

European leaders, however, regarded Wilson with skepticism. French Premier Georges Clemenceau observed, "God has given man Ten Commandments. He broke every one. President Wilson has his Fourteen Points. We shall see."

BROWN BROTHERS

## Points for Peace

Wilson's Fourteen Points for peace had been a brilliant propaganda ploy as well as an earnest effort to steer a middle course between a radical peace settlement and a conservative, opportunistic peace settlement. Wilson presented his Fourteen Points speech to Congress on January 8, 1918, ten months before the end of the Great War. George Creel chose the most lyrical phrases from the speech to print in leaflets—about 60 million of them. He eagerly distributed them around the world, even dropping them from the air above Central Power countries.

Why had Wilson outlined his terms for peace so long before the war was over? The answer lay in the momentous events of the war years. Wilson believed that if he did not act quickly, he might lose the initiative to the Bolsheviks in Russia, who had powerful ideas of their own about reshaping the world.

### Impact of Bolshevism

Russia had dealt a hard blow to the Allied cause when it withdrew from the war in early 1918. On March 3, 1918, V. I. Lenin, the new Bolshevik leader in Russia, signed the Treaty of Brest-Litovsk with Germany, thus formally ending Russian-German conflict. Lenin gave up large areas of land to the Germans because he needed peace to concentrate on domestic reform and on internal opposition by czarist forces, called the Whites. To understand better why **bolshevism,** a radical socialist ideology, posed a threat to President Wilson requires

---

## STUDY GUIDE

**As You Read**
Evaluate Wilson's efforts to reshape the world according to his Fourteen Points. Also, think about the following concepts and skills.

**Central Concepts**
• understanding why Wilson felt threatened by **bolshevism**
• recognizing the importance of the **League of Nations** in the postwar world

**Thinking Skills**
• recognizing points of view
• analyzing behavior
• forming hypotheses

an examination of events in Russia during the war.

When the Great War began, an autocratic czar ruled Russia. Indeed, Wilson's initial hesitation to enter the war stemmed, in part, from his distaste for associating with the cruel czarist rulers. By July 1917 the czar had already surrendered his power and the Russian parliament had set up a provisional government led by a moderate socialist named Aleksandr Kerensky. Because of his liberal policies and commitment to continue fighting in the Great War, Kerensky enjoyed great popularity among the Allies.

At home, however, domestic problems overwhelmed Kerensky. Chief among them was the war's unpopularity and the disintegration of the Russian army. In the midst of chaotic discontent, the Bolsheviks, led by Lenin, seized power from Kerensky in November 1917. All of Europe, indeed all of the world, watched the tumultuous events in Russia. American journalist John Reed described the November Revolution as the "Ten Days That Shook the World."

The Bolshevik Revolution frightened world leaders. They knew that bolshevism could potentially attract millions of discontented, war-weary workers to its ranks. Lenin's beliefs were rooted in the communist ideology of Karl Marx who called for class war between workers and capitalists, rather than world war between capitalist governments. In fact Lenin blamed world war on capitalism and named workers

COURTESY STEPHEN WHITE

**The translated title of this El Lissitsky poster is** *Beat the Whites with the Red Wedge.* **It was created in 1920 to abstractly dramatize the social revolution in Russia.** *How does this piece illustrate the conflict?*

of all nationalities as its hapless victims.

Wilson and other world leaders feared the radical message of the Bolsheviks. They were embarrassed when Lenin published copies of secret pacts made between allied European powers early in the war. These pacts revealed that the Allies were not simply fighting for democracy but, in fact, wanted to divide the world among themselves. The publication of the pacts put Wilson in a difficult position. He did not want to be associated with them, nor did he want to support the Bolsheviks. His answer to this dilemma emerged as

the Fourteen Points. Wilson hoped that his plan for lasting peace would attract the attention of common people, distracting them from bolshevism.

**Wilson's Fourteen Points**    The Fourteen Points promised that all countries signing the peace treaty would enjoy equality of trade and "removal, as far as possible, of all economic barriers" in the postwar world. This provision reassured Germany, who feared harsh reprisals. The points underscored the importance of territorial integrity and self-determination for countries invaded during the war, including Russia, Belgium, France, and Italy. They specifically outlined recommendations for adjusting borders after the war, so that the Austro-Hungarian empire would be divided into several new states based on nationality.

The Fourteen Points also suggested new forms of international conduct: freedom of ocean travel and trade, open agreements instead of secret pacts, and arms reductions. One point stressed "impartial adjustment" of colonial claims, with a voice for both the colonial populations and the colonial governments claiming dominion over them.

Wilson believed the most important point to be the establishment of a **League of Nations,** an international mediating body "affording mutual guarantees of political independence and territorial integrity to great and small states alike." Wilson hoped that such a league would bond all nations of the world together. If the League could provide for the security of each individual state, then the ancient dream of peace among nations might succeed.

**Reaction to the Fourteen Points**    While the European masses greeted the Fourteen Points with great enthusiasm, British and French leaders were more restrained. They did not have time to sit down and leisurely talk with Wilson about his grand ideas. The Great War needed their attention. However, David Lloyd George, the pragmatic prime minister of Britain, knew that he could never agree to freedom of the seas, giving up Britain's naval dominance.

Likewise, Georges Clemenceau knew that France would never concede to ignoring the damage inflicted by Germany. From the onset, the Fourteen Points were no match for the fierce determination of France to punish Germany.

One of the Fourteen Points was ignored seven months after the points were announced—the right of Russia to have "institutions of her own choosing." Yielding to pressure from the Allies, Wilson sent American battalions to the Russian ports of Vladivostok and Murmansk. He did so under the pretense of helping Czech troops stranded there after Russia pulled out of the war. In reality, the intervention gave aid to the White Army, which was waging a civil war against the Bolsheviks.

Wilson also unwittingly endangered his Fourteen Points with a political move at home. As the midterm Congressional elections of 1918 drew near, Wilson issued an appeal urging Americans to vote Democratic. This appeal enraged Republicans, who took it as an affront to their patriotism. When voters later elected Republican majorities to Congress, Wilson lost credibility at the negotiating table with European leaders.

## *A Troubling Treaty*

Woodrow Wilson walked into the Paris peace conference at the Palace of Versailles in January 1919 with the cheers of the European masses still ringing in his ears; but, in fact, he was in a very weak bargaining position. As the conference dragged on for five long months, he would give up more and more of his Fourteen Points as well as his own good spirits and health. By April he appeared thinner, grayer, grimmer, and more nervous. His face twitched as he spoke, and he spoke with greater moral rigidity than ever before. This irritated the European leaders around him. "I never knew anyone to talk more like Jesus Christ," said Clemenceau in exasperation.

**An Atmosphere of Exclusion**    One of the Fourteen Points promised that international negotiations and agreements would be made in the open eliminating secret pacts. From early on, however, this principle was ignored. The press was kept away from the negotiations. The Allied powers also pared down the number of countries actually shaping the final outcome to the Big Four—the United States, Britain, France, and Italy. Germany and Russia—two countries whose futures hinged on the outcome of the

**Recognizing Points of View**
Bolshevism presented a far more radical agenda for reshaping the world than did the Fourteen Points. It advocated the liberation of colonies, recognition of the equality of all races, and diminish-ment of nationalism in favor of internationalism. The working class would rule and capitalism would be abolished. These ideas challenged Wilson's views about lasting peace. He wanted self-de-termination for colonies, free trade, open agreements instead of pacts, arms reductions, and an international mediating body to guarantee independence and territorial integrity.

treaty—were completely shut out of negotiations.

Britain, Italy, and France insisted on the exclusion of a German representative. France even refused Germany the right to have observers at the proceedings. Wilson had argued for peace among equals, but now he deferred to the wishes of his three wartime allies. Before the conference concluded, France obtained concessions to occupy an industrial region of Germany for 15 years, won back its northeastern territories of Lorraine and Alsace, and established a reparations commission to assess money to be paid by Germany for French losses.

The exclusion of Russia at the conference stemmed from confusion and fear. In 1919 Europe seemed on the brink of revolution. The Bolshevik armies had not fallen to the White Russian opposition, in spite of American and Japanese intervention. In Germany radical groups threatened to overthrow the newly established Social Democratic government. Communists gained power in Hungary. For the leaders of the western democracies at Versailles, the question was what to do about the revolutionary movements sweeping Europe.

The Big Four vacillated and disagreed. Should they include Russia to try to soften its impact, or should they use direct military action to subdue the Bolsheviks? Neither of these extremes won the day. Instead, the Big Four simply excluded Russia from the conference; but as one contemporary observer noted, "the black cloud" of Russia remained, "threatening to overwhelm and swallow up the world."[1]

**An Atmosphere of Self-Interest**  The Fourteen Points dwindled down to even fewer as the Big Four debated what to do about German and Turkish colonies in Asia and Africa. According to Wilson's original plan, all colonies would have a say in their own destiny. Colonies of Allied powers hoped this principle would include them. To victorious France and Great Britain, however, the self-determination of their colonies was completely unacceptable. Rather than losing their own colonies, they were eager to enjoy the spoils of war by absorbing the colonies of their defeated enemies.

The final compromise did little to honor Wilson's call for "impartial adjustment of all colonial claims." Allied powers would retain their own colonies and the League of Nations would give them control over Central Power colonies. These controlled or mandated colonies, however, would be ruled in the name of the League.

Italy presented another challenge to the Fourteen points. It, too, wanted some of the spoils of war—parts of the Austro-Hungarian empire including the ports of Fiume and Trieste. Wilson resisted Italy's expansion because his plan had advocated the formation of Balkan states from the land of Austria-Hungary. Much of what Italy wanted would go to the newly created state of Yugoslavia shown on the map on page 234. Soon, Italians would turn to Benito

THE BETTMANN ARCHIVE

**The billions of dollars Germany was required to pay in war reparations helped bankrupt the German economy and cultivated fertile ground for the rise of fascism in the 1930s. Some of Berlin's poorer citizens turned to rummaging through refuse heaps in hopes of finding everyday necessities.**

## STUDY GUIDE

### Analyzing Behavior

Wilson's moralism probably puzzled the Allies. They knew, that despite talk of self-determination, he was capable of intervening in world affairs. During negotiations, his points had little chance for survival. They struck at the economical and political interests of the Allies. European leaders quite predictably opposed Wilson—not for his moral rigidity, but to protect their own interests.

1  Summarize how the principle of open negotiations was ignored at the conference. How did France's attitude about excluding Germany prove to be disastrous for Germany?

## Europe After World War I

**BOUNDARIES OF FORMER EMPIRES**

━━ Austria-Hungary     ★ Capital city

━━ Germany             ── National boundary

━━ Russia

**After the war the European empires were divided into smaller countries. Compare this map of Europe to the map of Europe during World War I** *on page 214. What new countries were formed? Which new countries make up what were once Austria-Hungary and the German and Russian empires?*

Mussolini who vowed to avenge their humiliation.

Japan, the mighty force of the Pacific, also came to Versailles to make its demands as the world shifted and realigned. Japan wanted full recognition of its rights in the Shandong Province of China, which Germany had influenced before the war. During the heat of the war, world powers had little time to protect their stake in China, leaving Japan to consolidate its interests there. Japan's demand to control the province directly opposed the self-determination provisions of the Fourteen Points.

Nonetheless, Japan devised a scheme to secure its control of Shandong. Japanese delegates asked that an article formally declaring the equality of all races be attached to the peace agreement. This request exposed the limitations of Wilson's progressive approach. Much of progressive foreign policy, especially in the Caribbean, had been based on the assumption that white people knew best. While the Fourteen Points provided for a degree of self-determination, Wilson was not ready to change the power structure of the world radically. The Japanese proposal directly challenged not only Wilson, but all of the colonial powers present at the conference who held dominion

## STUDY GUIDE

### Forming Hypotheses

The treaty that ended World War I may have sowed the seeds of World War II. Think about these facts as you consider that hypothesis: the humiliation of Germany and Italy; the division of Austria-Hungary into many nationalistic states; the exclusion of Russia and Germany from the treaty process; Allied rule over the Central Powers' colonies; and the revolutionary movements sweeping Europe. Some say that the Treaty of Versailles ensured another war as much as it resolved the problems that caused World War I.

over people of color in Asia and Africa. Rather than deal with the troubling concept of racial equality, the conference let Japan expand its influence in China, provided that it drop its racial equality proposal. Thus, by cleverly manipulating the issue of race, Japan gained power in China. The Japanese victory, however, enraged student radicals in China who rioted in protest through the streets of Beijing.

By June 28, 1919, when the Treaty of Versailles was signed, a beleaguered and ill Woodrow Wilson had only one consolation left: the provision for the League of Nations had not been rejected, even though most of his original Fourteen Points had vanished. He returned to the United States as a man driven by the idea that the League of Nations must not fail. Only an international league could deal with the injustices that had shaped the Treaty of Versailles.[2]

## Rejection at Home

Woodrow Wilson's long stay in Europe took its toll on his health. Moreover, his rivals in Congress had consolidated against him. Approval for a League of Nations now hinged on ratification of the Treaty of Versailles by the U.S. Senate.

**Opposition in Congress**   Opposition to the League had consolidated around two camps in the Congress. One camp, the **irreconcilables,** were mostly progressive Republicans, many of whose service dated back to the turn of the century. They included Robert La Follette, William Borah, Hiram Johnson, and a handful of others. They called themselves irreconcilables because under no circumstances would they be reconciled to voting for the League of Nations.

Irreconcilables clung to the old argument that the United States was better off steering clear of the corrupting influence of Europe. For the most part, they were anti-imperialists. They feared that if the United States joined the League of Nations, it would be put in the immoral position of defending the colonial activities of European powers. They preferred to focus attention on reform at home, rather than on politics abroad. Nevertheless, they did not completely favor isolationism—a policy that supported indifference in affairs outside the United States.

The **reservationists,** on the other hand, approved of the idea of the League of Nations but wished to modify Wilson's particular proposal. The aspect of his plan that they found controversial was the article specifying that the League preserve "the territorial integrity and existing political independence of all Members of the League." Vague wording described how such an obligation would be fulfilled.

Both reservationists and irreconcilables feared that this article—Article Ten—could involve the United States in armed conflict. The article also seemed to suggest that the League itself would have the authority to decide if and when the United States, or any of the League members, would enter a conflict in defense of a member nation's independence. If this were so, the power of the League superseded the power of Congress to declare war.

By late summer 1919, anti-League of Nations sentiment spread from Washington throughout the country. An advertisement in the *Boston Herald* on July 8, 1919, for an anti-League meeting warned: "AMERICANS, AWAKE! Shall We Bind Ourselves to the War Breeding Covenant? It Impairs American Sovereignty! Surrenders the Monroe Doctrine! . . . Entangles us in European and Asiatic Intrigues!"

In addition to the concern the reservationists expressed in regard to Article Ten, they also objected to the League for other reasons. Led by Senator Henry Cabot Lodge, they hoped to embarrass the president. Lodge, like Wilson, had formerly been a scholar. Though Lodge himself often acted in an aristocratic manner, he resented the same behavior in Wilson. He seethed with anger at the idea that Wilson would get full credit for the League, when he himself had often put forth the idea of an international peacekeeping body. Motivated by anger as well as genuine misgivings, Lodge fought to attach his amendments to the original proposal for the League. Wilson, however, refused to consider a compromise.

**Speaking to the People**   Growing impatient with senators and critics, Wilson decided to take his case to the people of the United States. If he had their overwhelming support, the Senate would not dare defy him. In September 1919 President Wilson organized a gruelling, 9,000-mile cross-country

### Recognizing Points of View

The League created two camps in Congress. The irreconcilables opposed the League to avoid European involvement. The reservationists, on the other hand, approved of the League but wanted to modify the proposal. Even though these groups disagreed, they both feared that part of the proposal could lead to armed conflict and take away the power of Congress to declare war.

**2** Describe the negotiations that went on during the peace conference before the final peace treaty was signed.

ME IDEA IS TO HIT TH' LAD WITHOUT TOUCHIN' THE APPLE

LIBRARY OF CONGRESS

**This cartoon characterizes the partisan opposition to the Treaty of Versailles.** *How can personal opinions about an individual color one's decisions to support or not support that individual's policies?*

speaking tour by train: 26 different stops in 27 days.

As in Europe, cheering crowds greeted Woodrow Wilson during his tour. In spite of his failing health, he often spoke eloquently:

> *For the first time in the history of a civilized society, a great international convention, made up of the leading statesmen of the world, has proposed a settlement which is for the benefit of the weak and not the benefit of the strong.*

> Woodrow Wilson,
> Speech in Los Angeles,
> September 1919

The crowds gathered and cheered. The president waved and rallied. His dream, though, was not to be. On September 25, 1919, as he spoke in Pueblo, Colorado, he fell violently ill and was rushed back to Washington. A few days later, he suffered a paralytic stroke. For weeks Wilson could not function as president. When finally he was able to make decisions, he refused to modify any of his ideas. As both Lodge and Wilson remained entrenched in their positions, the U.S. Senate voted to reject the Versailles Peace Treaty with its League of Nations.

Wilson refused to give up. He looked forward to the presidential election of 1920. The Democratic party did not seriously consider renominating President Wilson because of his illness. Wilson, however, pinned his hopes to the party's nominee, Governor James M. Cox from Ohio. Woodrow Wilson saw the election of 1920 as a "solemn referendum" on the League of Nations.

Most of the United States, however, was not listening. Other concerns captured their attention. The Red Scare—a fear of bolshevism—spread throughout the United States. Wilson himself had helped to bring on this hysteria during the war by supporting the Espionage Act of 1917 and its Sedition Amendment of 1918 that had led to the arrest of several socialist labor leaders. Even on his last speaking tour, Wilson had warned "there are apostles of Lenin in our midst."

By the election of 1920, the country responded to this fear by isolating itself, turning away from Europe and a world of troubling revolutions. Repudiating the League of Nations and the idea of internationalism, the American people opted for a promise of "normalcy" by electing the Republican Warren Gamaliel Harding to the presidency. Woodrow Wilson lived for three years after leaving office, but he never regained his health. He died on February 3, 1924, shortly after telling some of his friends that he was "tired of swimming upstream."

## SECTION REVIEW

### Checking Facts

1. How did George Creel help spread Wilson's ideas about peace?
2. Why did Russia withdraw from the Great War and make a separate peace with Germany?
3. Why was the League of Nations so important to Wilson?
4. Who were the irreconcilables and what did they stand for? Who were the reservationists and what did they stand for?

### Thinking Critically

5. **Analyzing Behavior**
   During negotiations, Japan demanded recognition of its rights to China's Shandong Province. This opposed the self-determination provisions of the Fourteen Points. To secure its control of Shandong, Japan asked that an article declaring the equality of races be attached to the peace treaty. Rather than dealing with the concept of racial equality, the conference let Japan expand its influence in China. Why did Wilson and other leaders accept Japan's proposal?

### Linking Across Time

6. Think about the international organizations that exist today, such as the United Nations. What can such organizations accomplish? What are the limitations of such organizations?

Suppose you want to prepare a research paper on a topic related to World War I. As you research this topic, you will need to use information from a variety of reference materials. Becoming familiar with such materials will sharpen your research skills and help you determine which source is most likely to contain the information you are seeking.

## Learning the Skill

Visit a library and familiarize yourself with its reference department. Try to locate the following types of reference sources:

### Encyclopedias

Encyclopedia articles provide an overview of information related to a given topic. Most encyclopedia articles also offer suggestions for further research. This information usually appears at the conclusion of an article and may include a bibliography of sources used in preparing the article, a list of related articles elsewhere in the encyclopedia, or a list of additional sources of information.

### Indexes of Periodicals

Periodicals from the past reflect the culture, events, and concerns of their time; current periodicals provide the most recent research on a given topic. Several indexes can help you find information in periodicals. One frequently used index is the *Readers' Guide to Periodical Literature,* a set of reference books that lists magazine articles by topic.

### Historical Atlases

All historical atlases contain maps that give information about people and events of the past; many also include informative articles and timelines. One source of information on U.S. history is National Geographic's *Historical Atlas of the United States.*

### Statistical Sources

If you need statistical information about the United States, the *Statistical Abstract of the United States* is a good place to start. It was compiled by the Bureau of the Census and contains data on over 30 topics. The statistical information dates back to 1790, the year the first census was taken in the United States.

### Biographical Dictionaries

To learn more about the life or achievements of a noteworthy person, you may want to consult a biographical dictionary. Good sources of information on historical figures include *Webster's American Biographies,* the *Dictionary of American Biography,* and *Notable American Women.*

## Practicing the Skill

1. Read the chart below. For each of the five sources listed, make up your own research questions that relate to material from the chapter. Answer the questions by consulting the appropriate reference materials.
2. Write a short report about one of the key figures in this chapter. Tell what sources you used during your research.

### Tools of Reference

| Sources of Information | Uses | Sample Research Questions |
|---|---|---|
| Encyclopedias | Provide topic overviews; offer suggestions for further research | What were the main provisions of the Treaty of Versailles? |
| Periodicals | Reflect the past; supply current research on a topic | How did U.S. journalists react to the November Revolution? |
| Historical Atlases | Provide geographic context for historical information | Locate the eastern and western fronts during World War I. |
| Statistical Sources | Convey statistical information | What was the estimated total cost of the war to the United States? |
| Biographical Dictionaries | Describe the backgrounds and achievements of historical figures | Who were Emilio Aguinaldo, V. I. Lenin, and Georges Clemenceau? |

# Chapter 7 Review

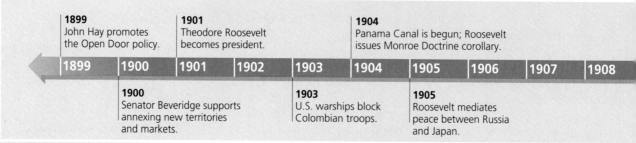

**1899**
John Hay promotes the Open Door policy.

**1901**
Theodore Roosevelt becomes president.

**1904**
Panama Canal is begun; Roosevelt issues Monroe Doctrine corollary.

| 1899 | 1900 | 1901 | 1902 | 1903 | 1904 | 1905 | 1906 | 1907 | 1908 |

**1900**
Senator Beveridge supports annexing new territories and markets.

**1903**
U.S. warships block Colombian troops.

**1905**
Roosevelt mediates peace between Russia and Japan.

## Summary

Use the following outline as a tool for reviewing and summarizing the chapter. Copy the outline on your own paper, leaving spaces between headings to jot down notes about key events and concepts.

**I. Foreign Policy under Roosevelt and Taft**
  A. America's Special Destiny
  B. Policies in the Caribbean
  C. Policies in the Far East
  D. Entanglement with Europe

**II. Watching Europe's War**
  A. Wilson's Foreign Policy
  B. Origins of the Great War
  C. Struggle for Neutrality

**III. The Great War: There and Here**
  A. Mobilization
  B. Fighting Over There
  C. The War Effort at Home

**IV. Reshaping the World**
  A. Points for Peace
  B. A Troubling Treaty
  C. Rejection at Home

## Ideas, Events, and People

1. Why did overseas markets appeal to many Americans? Why did others oppose commercial expansion overseas?
2. What policies did Roosevelt and Taft implement in the Caribbean?
3. What is self-determination? What actions did Wilson take that were not consistent with his belief in self-determination?
4. Describe U.S. involvement in Mexico during the first two decades of the 1900s.
5. Why did Wilson claim neutrality prior to World War I?
6. Give examples of print media that historians might use to study public opinion during World War I.
7. Describe the racial bias that existed in the U.S. military during World War I.
8. What actions were taken to support the war on the home front during World War I?
9. What happened to pacifists during World War I?
10. Why did bolshevism frighten President Wilson and other world leaders?

## Social Studies Skills

**Using Reference Materials**

Imagine that you are a reporter and that you have been assigned a feature story commemorating Theodore Roosevelt. Think about the various reference materials that could enable you to gather information about his family, accomplishments, and career. Refer to the Tools of Reference chart on page 237 as you consider the various reference materials you could use. Make a list of the reference materials you could use and the type of information each source would provide.

## Critical Thinking

1. **Predicting Consequences**
In the early 1900s, imperialists wanted the United States to seek commercial markets overseas and to annex new territories. These demands led to U.S. intervention in the internal affairs of other nations. What do you think would have happened if the United States had not intervened in foreign affairs during the early 1900s?

2. **Identifying Cause and Effect**
President Woodrow Wilson did not want to involve the United States in World War I. Instead, he wished to remain neutral, supporting neither

**1909**
William Howard Taft becomes president.

**1913**
Woodrow Wilson becomes president.

**1916**
Woodrow Wilson is reelected.

**1918**
Wilson presents his Fourteen Points to Congress.

| 1909 | 1910 | 1911 | 1912 | 1913 | 1914 | 1915 | 1916 | 1917 | 1918 | 1919 |

**1910**
Mexican Revolution begins.

**1914**
Wilson urges Congress to send troops to Mexico; World War I begins.

**1917**
Wilson asks Congress to declare war on Germany.

**1919**
Versailles Treaty is signed but later rejected by Congress.

Germany nor Russia. The president wanted the people of the United States to be "impartial in thought as well as in action." However, on April 2, 1917, the president asked the members of Congress to declare war on the country of Germany. What factors or international incidents involving the United States caused President Wilson to reverse his position?

## Extension and Application

### 1. Global Connections
Select a country in Europe that was involved in the Great War. Research what life was like for the citizens of the country during the war. Combine your findings with those of students who researched other countries. Prepare an oral report about "life during the Great War."

### 2. Linking Across Time
In 1978 the U.S. Senate agreed to transfer the control of the Panama Canal and the canal zone to Panama in December 1999. The transfer of the canal and its zone will probably have major effects on the Panamanian economy. For example, many jobs related to the operation and the maintenance of the canal are presently held by U.S. citizens. These positions will gradually have to be taken over by Panamanians. Research the present U.S. relationship with Panama and discuss other possible ramifications.

### 3. Cooperative Learning
With a small group, stage the debate over the selective exclusion that occurred during the 1919 peace conference in Paris. Use information from Section 4, as well as additional research, to represent the Big Four countries. Try to identify the reasons the Big Four finally excluded the countries of Germany and Russia from the peace negotiations.

## Geography

1. In which two areas did most of the fighting take place during World War I?
2. Why were German submarines most active in the waters surrounding Great Britain and Ireland? How did Allied navies try to block this tactic?
3. Which capital city of western Europe was most threatened by nearby warfare? Did this affect how the war was fought?
4. Look at the map on page 207. How might U.S. intervention in the Caribbean and Mexico have protected the Panama Canal? Explain.
5. Compare the map on page 234 with the one below. Do you think the many new countries formed after World War I made Europe's political situation more stable or less so? Why?

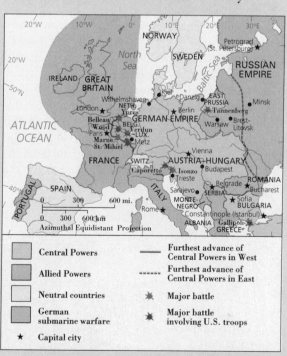

# Unit 2 Review

NO MOLLY-CODDLING HERE

THE GRANGER COLLECTION

## Concepts and Themes

In the 1890s fearing the potential chaos of radical change, the progressives called for a more moral, stable, and orderly society. At home they fought to clean up slums, evict machine bosses, help women and workers, and free children from factories. Their reform umbrella, however, rarely protected African Americans and immigrants. In foreign policy some progressives felt duty-bound to "educate and civilize" people they viewed as inferior. This paternalistic attitude proved a handy companion to the nation's growing imperialism. During the early 1900s, Theodore Roosevelt and Woodrow Wilson forged a stronger role for the president. They also advanced the federal government's role within U.S. society and the role of the United States within the world.

1. In the cartoon above, Roosevelt swings his stick at trusts and "everything in general." What actions of Roosevelt might come under the "everything" label?
2. Who used the bigger stick in trust-busting, Roosevelt or Taft? Defend your choice.
3. Ill and tired, Wilson was unable to wield sufficient big-stick force to fight for his League of Nations. Summarize the opposition he encountered.

## History Project

1. **Evidence of the Past**
   Research one incident in the Philippine annexation. Write three brief accounts of it, each with a different viewpoint. Make the first reflect an anti-United States point of view; the second, pro-United States. The third should present an objective account.
2. **Culture of the Time**
   Research a personality from the ragtime era. Examples are Edgar Rice Burroughs, Frank Baum, John Sloan, Jim Thorpe, D.W. Griffith, Alfred Stieglitz, Irving Berlin, John Muir, Helen Keller. Give an oral report.
3. **One Day in History**
   List with examples the discriminatory practices used against blacks at the time of the NAACP founding. Research such books as Milton Meltzer's *In Their Own Words* and Herbert Aptheker's *A Documentary History of the Negro People in the United States.*
4. **Case Study**
   President Woodrow Wilson's League of Nations met strong criticism. Use newspaper microfiches and library sources to find and write down quotes expressing pro and con opinions. Conclude with a paragraph telling if you think the quotes are applicable to today's United Nations.

## Writing Activities

1. Select the Dominican Republic, Haiti, or Cuba. Research and write an informative article comparing "Then" (early 1900s) and "Now." Emphasize political and social conditions. (See the Writer's Guide, pages 825 to 827.)
2. Imagine you are touring a textile mill or tenement. Write an eyewitness account.

## The Arts

- "Maple Leaf Rag" and other ragtime compositions by pianist Scott Joplin.
- The action-packed western paintings and sculpture by Frederic Remington.
- *My Ántonia* by Willa Cather; a novel about Bohemian immigrants and frontier farming.
- *The Birth of a Nation;* D.W. Griffith's classic film of 1915 about the Civil War and the rise of the Ku Klux Klan.

# UNIT THREE

# The New Era of the Twenties

Courtesy, The Blue Lantern Studio

# Voices of the Twenties

*In F. Scott Fitzgerald's* The Great Gatsby, *the narrator describes a party at his neighbor's mansion on Long Island. Music, dancing, and parties occupied the lives of many in the Jazz Age of the 1920s. However, Harlem Renaissance writer Langston Hughes reveals another side of life during this period in his poem "The Weary Blues."*

## from *The Great Gatsby*

### by F. Scott Fitzgerald

There was music from my neighbor's house through the summer nights. In his blue gardens men and girls came and went like moths among the whisperings and the champagne and the stars. At high tide in the afternoon I watched his guests diving from the tower of his raft, or taking the sun on the hot sand of his beach while his two motor-boats slit the waters of the Sound, drawing aqua planes over cataracts of foam. On week-ends his Rolls-Royce became an omnibus, bearing parties to and from the city between nine in the morning and long past midnight, while his station wagon scampered like a brisk yellow bug to meet all trains. And on Mondays eight servants, including an extra gardener, toiled all day with mops and scrubbing-brushes and hammers and garden-shears, repairing the ravages of the night before.

Every Friday five crates of oranges and lemons arrived from a fruiterer in New York—every Monday these same oranges and lemons left his back door in a pyramid of pulpless halves. There was a machine in the kitchen which could extract the juice of two hundred oranges in half an hour if a little button was pressed two hundred times by a butler's thumb.

At least once a fortnight a crop of caterers came down with several hundred feet of canvas and enough colored lights to make a Christmas tree of Gatsby's enormous garden. On buffet tables, garnished with glistening hors-d'oeuvre, spiced baked hams crowded against salads of harlequin designs and pastry pigs and turkeys bewitched to a dark gold. In the main hall a bar with a real brass rail was set up, and stocked with gins and liquors and with cordials so long forgotten that most of his female guests were too young to know one from another.

By seven o'clock the orchestra has arrived, no thin five-piece affair, but a whole pitful of oboes and trombones and saxophones and viols and cornets and piccolos, and low and high drums. The last swimmers have come in from the beach now and are dressing upstairs; the cars from New York are parked five deep in the drive, and already the halls and salons and verandas are gaudy with primary colors, and hair shorn in strange new ways, and shawls beyond the dreams of Castile. The bar is in full swing, and floating rounds of cocktails permeate the garden outside, until the air is alive with chatter and laughter, and casual innuendo and introductions forgotten on the spot, and enthusiastic meetings between women who never knew each other's names.

The lights grow brighter as the earth lurches away from the sun, and now the orchestra is playing yellow cocktail music, and the opera of voices pitches a key higher. Laughter is easier minute by minute, spilled with prodigality, tipped out at a cheerful word. The groups change more swiftly, swell with new arrivals, dissolve and form in the same breath; already there are wanderers, confident girls who weave here and there among the stouter and more stable, become for a sharp, joyous moment the center of a group, and then, excited with triumph, glide on through the sea-change of faces and voices and color under the constantly changing light.

Suddenly one of these gypsies, in trembling opal, seizes a cocktail out of the air, dumps it down for courage and, moving her hands like Frisco, dances out alone on the canvas platform. A momentary hush; the orchestra leader varies his rhythm obligingly for her, and there is a burst of chatter as the erroneous news goes around that she is Gilda Gray's understudy from the *Follies*. The party has begun.

I believe that on the first night I went to Gatsby's house I was one of the few guests who had actually been invited. People were not invited—they went there. They got into automobiles which bore them out to Long Island, and somehow they ended up at Gatsby's door. Once there they were introduced by somebody who knew Gatsby, and after that they conducted themselves according to the rules of behavior associated with an amusement park. Sometimes they came and went without having met Gatsby at all, came for the party with a simplicity of heart that was its own ticket of admission.

I had been actually invited. A chauffeur in a uniform of robin's-egg blue crossed my lawn early that Saturday morning with a surprisingly formal note from his employer: the honor would be entirely Gatsby's, it said, if I would attend his "little party" that night. He had seen me several times, and had intended to call on me long before, but a peculiar combination of circumstances had prevented it—signed Jay Gatsby, in a majestic hand.

Dressed up in white flannels I went over to his lawn a little after seven, and wandered around rather ill at ease among swirls and eddies of people I didn't know—though here and there was a face I had noticed on the commuting train. I was immediately struck by the number of young Englishmen dotted about; all well dressed, all looking a little hungry, and all talking in low, earnest voices to solid and prosperous Americans. I was sure that they were selling something: bonds or insurance or automobiles. They were at least agonizingly aware of the easy money in the vicinity and convinced that it was theirs for a few words in the right key.

As soon as I arrived I made an attempt to find my host, but the two or three people of whom I asked his whereabouts stared at me in such an amazed way, and denied so vehemently any knowledge of his movements, that I slunk off in the direction of the cocktail table—the only place in the garden where a single man could linger without looking purposeless and alone.

I was on my way to get roaring drunk from sheer embarrassment when Jordan Baker came out of the house and stood at the head of the marble steps, leaning a little backward and looking with contemptuous interest down into the garden.

Welcome or not, I found it necessary to attach myself

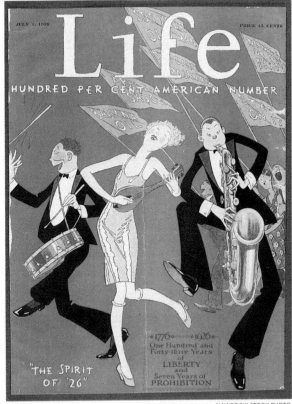

NAWROCKI STOCK PHOTO

**The illustrator of this *Life* magazine cover, dating from July 1, 1926, captured the verve that jazzed up the twenties.**

to some one before I should begin to address cordial remarks to the passers-by.

"Hello!" I roared, advancing toward her. My voice seemed unnaturally loud across the garden.

"I thought you might be here," she responded absently, as I came up. "I remembered you lived next door to——"

She held my hand impersonally, as a promise that she'd take care of me in a minute, and gave ear to two girls in twin yellow dresses who stopped at the foot of the steps.

"Hello!" they cried together. "Sorry you didn't win."

That was for the golf tournament. She had lost in the finals the week before.

"You don't know who we are," said one of the girls in yellow, "but we met you here about a month ago."

"You've dyed your hair since then," remarked Jordan, and I started, but the girls had moved casually on and her remark was addressed to the premature moon, produced like the supper, no doubt, out of a caterer's basket. With Jordan's slender golden arm resting in mine, we descended the steps and sauntered about the garden. A tray of cocktails floated at us through the twilight, and we sat down at a table with the two girls in yellow and three men, each one introduced to us as Mr. Mumble.

"Do you come to these parties often?" inquired Jordan of the girl beside her.

"The last one was the one I met you at," answered the girl, in an alert confident voice. She turned to her companion: "Wasn't it for you, Lucille?"

It was for Lucille, too.

"I like to come," Lucille said. "I never care what I do, so I always have a good time. When I was here last I tore my gown on a chair, and he asked me my name and address—inside of a week I got a package from Croirier's with a new evening gown in it."

"Did you keep it?" asked Jordan.

"Sure I did. I was going to wear it tonight, but it was too big in the bust and had to be altered. It was gas blue with lavender beads. Two hundred and sixty-five dollars."

"There's something funny about a fellow that'll do a thing like that," said the other girl eagerly. "He doesn't want any trouble with *any*body."

"Who doesn't?" I inquired.

"Gatsby. Somebody told me——"

The two girls and Jordan leaned together confidentially.

"Somebody told me they thought he killed a man once."

A thrill passed over all of us. The three Mr. Mumbles bent forward and listened eagerly.

"I don't think it's so much *that*," argued Lucille sceptically; "it's more that he was a German spy during the war."

One of the men nodded in confirmation.

"I heard that from a man who knew all about him, grew up with him in Germany," he assured us positively.

"Oh, no," said the first girl, "it couldn't be that, because he was in the American army during the war." As our credulity switched back to her she leaned forward with enthusiasm. "You look at him sometimes when he thinks nobody's looking at him. I'll bet he killed a man."

She narrowed her eyes and shivered. Lucille shivered. We all turned and looked around for Gatsby. It was testimony to the romantic speculation he inspired that there were whispers about him from those who had found little that it was necessary to whisper about in this world.

The first supper—there would be another one after midnight—was now being served, and Jordan invited me to join her own party, who were spread around a table on the other side of the garden. There were three married couples and Jordan's escort, a persistent undergraduate given to violent innuendo, and obviously under the impression that sooner or later Jordan was going to yield him up her person to a greater or lesser degree. Instead of rambling, this party had preserved a dignified homogeneity, and assumed to itself the function of representing the staid nobility of the countryside—East Egg condescending to West Egg, and carefully on guard against its spectroscopic gayety.

"Let's get out," whispered Jordan, after a somehow wasteful and inappropriate half-hour. "This is much too polite for me."

We got up, and she explained that we were going to find the host: I had never met him, she said, and it was making me uneasy. The undergraduate nodded in a cynical, melancholy way.

The bar, where we glanced first, was crowded, but Gatsby was not there. She couldn't find him from the top of the steps, and he wasn't on the veranda. On a chance we tried an important-looking door, and walked into a high Gothic library, panelled with carved English oak, and probably transported complete from some ruin overseas.

A stout, middle-aged man, with enormous owl-eyed spectacles, was sitting somewhat drunk on the edge of a great table, staring with unsteady concentration at the shelves of books. As we entered he wheeled excitedly around and examined Jordan from head to foot.

"What do you think?" he demanded impetuously.

"About what?"

He waved his hand toward the book-shelves.

"About that. As a matter of fact you needn't bother to ascertain. I ascertained. They're real."

"The books?"

He nodded.

"Absolutely real—have pages and everything. I thought they'd be a nice durable cardboard. Matter of fact, they're absolutely real. Pages and—Here! Lemme show you."

Taking our scepticism for granted, he rushed to the bookcases and returned with Volume One of the "Stoddard Lectures."

"See!" he cried triumphantly. "It's a bona-fide piece of printed matter. It fooled me. This fella's a regular Belasco. It's a triumph. What thoroughness! What realism! Knew when to stop, too—didn't cut the pages. But what do you want? What do you expect?"

He snatched the book from me and replaced it hastily on its shelf, muttering that if one brick was removed the whole library was liable to collapse.

"Who brought you?" he demanded. "Or did you just come? I was brought. Most people were brought."

Jordan looked at him alertly, cheerfully, without answering.

"I was brought by a woman named Roosevelt," he continued. "Mrs. Claude Roosevelt. Do you know her? I met her somewhere last night. I've been drunk for about a week now, and I thought it might sober me up to sit in a library."

"Has it?"

"A little bit, I think. I can't tell yet. I've only been here an hour. Did I tell you about the books? They're real. They're——"

"You told us."

We shook hands with him gravely and went back outdoors.

There was dancing now on the canvas in the garden; old men pushing young girls backward in eternal graceless circles, superior couples holding each other tortuously, fashionably, and keeping in the corners—and a great number of single girls dancing individualistically or relieving the orchestra for a moment of the burden of the banjo or the taps. By midnight the hilarity had increased. A celebrated tenor had sung in Italian, and a notorious contralto had sung in jazz, and between the numbers people were doing "stunts" all over the garden, while happy, vacuous bursts of laughter rose toward the summer sky. A pair of stage twins, who turned out to be the girls in yellow, did a baby act in costume, and champagne was served in glasses bigger than finger-bowls. The moon had risen higher, and floating in the Sound was a triangle of silver scales, trembling a little to the stiff, tinny drip of the banjoes on the lawn.

# The Weary Blues

### by Langston Hughes

Droning a drowsy syncopated tune,
Rocking back and forth to a mellow croon,
    I heard a Negro play.
Down on Lenox Avenue the other night
By the pale dull pallor of an old gas light
    He did a lazy sway. . . .
    He did a lazy sway. . . .
To the tune o' those Weary Blues.
With his ebony hands on each ivory key
He made that poor piano moan with melody.
    O Blues!
Swaying to and fro on his rickety stool
He played that sad raggy tune like a musical fool.
    Sweet Blues!
Coming from a black man's soul.
    O Blues!
In a deep song voice with a melancholy tone
I heard that Negro sing, that old piano moan—

"Ain't got nobody in all this world,
Ain't got nobody but ma self.
I's gwine to quit ma frownin'
And put ma troubles on the shelf."
Thump, thump, thump went his foot on the floor.
He played a few chords then he sang some more—
    "I got the Weary Blues
    And I can't be satisfied.
    Got the Weary Blues
    And can't be satisfied—
    I ain't happy no mo'
    And I wish that I had died."
And far into the night he crooned that tune.
The stars went out and so did the moon.
The singer stopped playing and went to bed
While the Weary Blues echoed through his head.
He slept like a rock or a man that's dead.

## Responding to Literature

1. *The Great Gatsby* was published in 1925; "The Weary Blues" came out one year later. How do the two selections reflect the diversity of experience in the 1920s?

2. What do you think the narrator's attitude is toward the life style and values of the wealthy? Explain.

**For Further Reading**
Fitzgerald, F. Scott: *The Stories of F. Scott Fitzgerald*
Hemingway, Ernest: *The Short Stories of Ernest Hemingway*
Honey, Maureen, ed.: *Shadowed Dreams: Women's Poetry of the Harlem Renaissance*

CHAPTER 8

# Getting On with Business

### October 28, 1925: Missing Episode of "Annie" Published

From the moment the orphan with the frizzy curls appeared in American homes on August 5, 1924, she found her way into the hearts of all.

On October 27, 1925, the *Chicago Tribune* accidentally left Annie out of their papers. Reader response was so strong that an apology along with two Annie strips were seen in the next day's paper.

How could a cartoon strip capture so much attention? In part, Annie's innocent strength seemed to resemble the United States as it came to see itself

in the era that followed World War I. Annie's creator, Harold Gray, had left her without relatives or entanglements. This gave Annie the freedom to do what she wanted and go where she pleased.

*Annie's innocent strength seemed to resemble the United States as it came to see itself.*

THE CHICAGO TRIBUNE

*Because many existing cartoon characters were boys, Harold Gray changed "Andy" to "Annie."*

Annie's foster father, Daddy Warbucks, was a weapons tycoon who showered Annie with kindness, gifts, and love. His character stood as resounding proof that businesspeople could be honest and decent. In the big business era of the 1920s, millions of people in the United States seemed to agree.

*The Chrysler Building in New York City stands as testimony to the growth of business during the 1920s. The brainchild of architect William Van Alen, it towers 77 stories above midtown Manhattan as one of the nation's first skyscrapers.*

# Postwar Turmoil

## August 23, 1927: Sacco and Vanzetti Executed; Riots Worldwide

IN 1921 NICOLA SACCO AND BARTOLOMEO VANZETTI HAD BEEN CONVICTED OF MURDERING A PAYMASTER AND SHOE FACTORY GUARD DURING A ROBBERY IN SOUTH BRAINTREE, Massachusetts. Many people believed that the men had been found guilty only because they were immigrants and radicals. By 1927 Sacco and Vanzetti had exhausted every legal appeal. Now they were about to be executed.

In his final defiant words to Judge Thayer, Vanzetti declared that he was innocent of the murders but unshakable in his unpopular beliefs:

> *I am suffering because I am a radical and indeed I am a radical; I have suffered because I was an Italian, and indeed I am an Italian; I have suffered more for my family and for my beloved than for myself; but I am so convinced to be right that if you could execute me two times, and if I could be reborn two other times, I would live again to do what I have done already.*

Bartolomeo Vanzetti,
speech to Judge Thayer, 1927

The years of the trial of Sacco and Vanzetti showed the United States desperately struggling to defend itself against the dangers following World War I. Many Americans feared immigrants whose ways appeared different and threatening. For a time, many Americans also believed that the radical politics of the 1917 Russian Revolution might overtake this country. Sacco and Vanzetti seemed to represent all the fears of the United States during the turbulent postwar years.

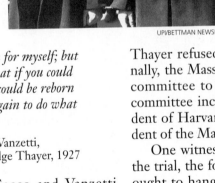

UPI/BETTMAN NEWSPHOTOS

## Sacco and Vanzetti

Some criminal evidence linked Sacco, a shoemaker, and Vanzetti, a fish peddler, to the murders. Neither man had ever been accused of a crime before his arrest, and none of the money from the robbery was ever traced to the men.

Their trial, too, was marked by serious breaches of fairness. The judge, Webster Thayer, had repeatedly denounced Sacco and Vanzetti for their immigrant backgrounds and for their belief in a radical political theory called **anarchism.** Anarchists believe that the restraint of one person by another is evil, and they do not recognize the authority of any government.

During the six years the men stayed in jail, Judge Thayer refused repeated motions for a new trial. Finally, the Massachusetts governor appointed a special committee to review the case one more time. The committee included Abbott Lawrence Lowell, president of Harvard, and Dr. Samuel W. Stratton, president of the Massachusetts Institute of Technology.

One witness told the committee that, even before the trial, the foreman of the jury had declared, "They ought to hang anyway." The committee agreed that the judge had not behaved properly when he had referred to Sacco and Vanzetti as "dagos" and worse. However, the committee still backed Judge Thayer's decision to execute the prisoners.

Prominent Americans, including future Supreme Court Justice Felix Frankfurter, protested the scheduled executions. Sacco and Vanzetti, Frankfurter argued, were being punished for their "alien blood and abhorrent philosophy," rather than for murder.

## STUDY GUIDE

**As You Read**
Identify the roots of America's postwar turmoil in threats stemming from the Russian Revolution and the Great Migration. Also, think about the following concept and skills.

**Central Concept**
- understanding how America's fear of **anarchism** and bolshevism led to a turning away from the progressive agenda of an earlier era

**Thinking Skills**
- recognizing bias
- recognizing points of view
- identifying cause and effect

## Major Events in the Case of Sacco and Vanzetti

**September 11, 1920**
Sacco and Vanzetti indicted for South Braintree murders.

**October 21, 1921**
Hand grenade injures twenty people in Paris protesting guilty verdict.

**May 16, 1926**
Sympathizers explode bomb at U.S. Embassy in Buenos Aires.

**April 9, 1927**
Judge Thayer sentences Sacco and Vanzetti to die in electric chair.

**June 1, 1927**
Governor Fuller appoints advisory committee to reconsider verdict.

| 1920 | 1921 | 1922 | 1923 | 1924 | 1925 | 1926 | 1927 |

**July 14, 1921**
Jury finds Sacco and Vanzetti guilty of murder.

**October 1, 1924**
Judge Thayer dismisses five motions to set aside guilty verdict.

**January 10, 1926**
Convicted murderer says he saw Morelli gang commit the murders.

**August 19, 1927**
Supreme Court rejects pleas filed by Sacco and Vanzetti defense.

**August 23, 1927**
Sacco and Vanzetti electrocuted at Charlestown Prison.

**This photograph shows people gathered in New York to protest the verdict of the Sacco and Vanzetti trial. People in foreign countries also staged demonstrations upon hearing the news.** *How were other nations affected by the Sacco and Vanzetti case? Why do you think people of other nations protested the verdict?*

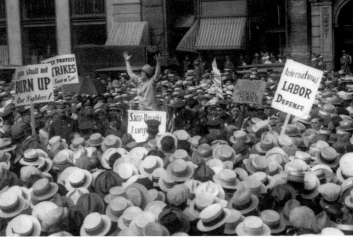

UPI/BETTMANN NEWSPHOTOS

Americans weren't the only protesters. During the six years of appeals, the Sacco and Vanzetti case had become world famous. When Sacco and Vanzetti were executed, riots broke out from Japan to Warsaw, from Paris to Buenos Aires. Crowds menaced the United States Embassy in Rome, and workers went on strike in France, Italy, and the United States.

Sacco's last words were "Long live anarchy!" Before he died, Vanzetti gave an interview to a reporter. In broken but eloquent English, he said:

*I f it had not been for these thing, I might have live out my life, talking at street corners to scorning men. I might have die, unmarked, unknown, a failure. Now we are not a failure. This is our career and our triumph. Never in our full life can we hope to do such work for tolerance, for joostice [justice], for man's onderstanding [understanding] of man, as now we do by an accident.*

Bartolomeo Vanzetti,
*New York World,* May 13, 1927

Fifty years to the day of their execution, August 23, 1977, Massachusetts Governor Michael Dukakis cleared the names of Sacco and Vanzetti. Their trial, Dukakis said, had been "permeated with prejudice."[1]

## The Red Scare

Judge Felix Frankfurter described the atmosphere in Boston during Sacco and Vanzetti's trial. He said that outside the courtroom "the Red hysteria was rampant; it was allowed to dominate within."

Indeed, Boston had become one of the centers for the Red Scare, a violent wave of anti-communist panic that swept through the United States in 1919 and 1920. In November 1917 the Bolshevik Revolution had installed a communist government in Russia. Communist uprisings in Hungary and Bavaria made it seem as though communism were spreading rapidly.

Two small communist parties had formed in the United States in 1919. Their total membership never exceeded 70,000, just one-tenth of one percent of the adult population. Even so, many people began to fear

---

## STUDY GUIDE

**Recognizing Bias**

The U.S. criminal justice system depends on the presumption of innocence. The judge and the foreman of the jury that convicted Sacco and Vanzetti presumed that the defendants were guilty before the evidence was heard. Their bias against Sacco and Vanzetti rendered the trial unfair and spurred the worldwide protest against the verdict.

**1** How did Sacco and Vanzetti's trial and execution help to spread their beliefs in a way that never would have happened if they had not been brought to trial?

that a communist revolution like the one in Russia was brewing in this country.

During World War I, George Creel's Committee on Public Information had whipped up public hatred of Germans. After the war many Americans transferred this hatred to anyone who had been born in another country. Foreigners were especially vulnerable to attack when, like Sacco and Vanzetti, they favored radical politics.

Public officials, business leaders, and the press all contributed to the Red Scare. More than any other person, President Wilson's attorney general, A. Mitchell Palmer, directed the Red Scare.

**The Palmer Raids**  A progressive lawyer and politician from Pennsylvania, Palmer had no doubt that communists were about to take over his country's government. For one thing, Palmer had spent the war serving as an alien property custodian. In this job, he had collected and been shocked by reams of anti-American propaganda. As a pacifist Quaker, Palmer despised the Bolshevik theory that promoted violent revolution.

To Palmer, the Bolshevik plan to take over the world seemed to become a reality on June 2, 1919, when bombs exploded in eight cities throughout the United States. One of the bombs shattered the front of Palmer's Washington, D.C., home. Although the bomb-thrower was killed in the blast, evidence suggested he was an Italian immigrant and anarchist.

After the bombings, Palmer asked for and got an appropriation of $500,000 from Congress to launch a campaign to "tear out the radical seeds that have entangled American ideas in their poisonous theories." Within the Justice Department's Bureau of Investigation, Palmer established the General Intelligence or anti-radical division. Under the direction of J. Edgar Hoover, this division began to gather information about domestic radical activities.

In November Palmer's men staged raids on the Union of Russian Workers in 12 cities. In December, 249 aliens were deported to Russia on a ship the popular press nicknamed "The Soviet Ark." Most of the deportees had never participated in any terrorist or criminal activity but merely favored nonviolent radical causes. However, many Americans believed they were ridding their country of a terrible danger. The

*New York Evening Mail* declared with certainty, "Just as the sailing of the Ark that Noah built was a pledge for the preservation of the human race, so the sailing of the Ark of the Soviet is a pledge for the preservation of America."

The following month Palmer's men arrested more than 4,000 people, many of them U.S. citizens, in 33 major cities during a single night of raids. Seized without warrants, many of these prisoners were denied attorneys and deprived of food, water, heat, and even bathroom facilities. In Boston one detainee leaped five stories to his death, two prisoners died of pneumonia, and another went insane. In New York guards beat many prisoners.

Some critics challenged Palmer's methods. William Allen White, newspaper editor, called Palmer's raids "un-American." He went on to argue:

*A*nd if a man desires to preach any doctrine under the shining sun, and to advocate the realization of his vision by lawful, orderly, constitutional means—let him alone. If he is Socialist, anarchist, or Mormon, and merely preaches his creed and does not preach violence, he can do no harm. For the folly of his doctrine will be its answer. The deportation business is going to make martyrs of a lot of idiots whose cause is not worth it.

William Allen White,
*Emporia* (Kansas) *Gazette*, January 8, 1920

However, the public generally applauded Palmer's January raids. Even though most of the prisoners eventually were released because they had nothing to do with radical politics, the *Washington Post* proclaimed that this was "no time to waste on hairsplitting over infringement of liberty." Six hundred radicals were expelled from the country before the Department of Labor, in charge of aliens, halted the deportations.

By midsummer 1920 the height of the Red Scare seemed to be over. American radicals had been demoralized by the raids and deportations. Businesses had broken a rash of strikes. Bolshevism had failed to spread beyond Russia.

In September 1920 a bomb exploded at the corner of Broad and Wall Streets, the center of New York

**Recognizing Points of View**
During the Red Scare, many Americans believed that immigrants and others who promoted radical causes posed an immediate threat to the U.S. government and should be treated without consideration for their rights. Others, such as journalist William Allen White, argued that the arrests and deportations of alleged communists gave radical causes more publicity than they deserved. Preserving freedom of speech would allow Americans to consider the merits of various theories of government without being swayed by pity or fear.

City's financial district, killing more than thirty people and injuring hundreds more. If the bombing had occurred the year before, Americans might have interpreted it as part of a plot to overthrow the government. Now the United States seemed to be determined not to give way to panic. One newspaper reported:

> *T*he public is merely shocked, not terrorized, much less converted to the merits of anarchism. Business and life as usual. Society, government, industry functioning precisely as if nothing had happened.
>
> Cleveland Plain Dealer,
> September 18, 1920

HISTORICAL PICTURES SERVICE - CHICAGO

**During the Red Scare, strikes were often regarded as direct threats to the stability of our government.**
*Why was this so?*

**Labor Unrest**  In the middle of the Red Scare, an outbreak of strikes brought the threat of revolution uncomfortably close to home. The cost of living had more than doubled from prewar levels. When their wages lagged far behind, angry workers went on strike.

Of the 3,600 strikes during 1919, the Seattle General Strike, the Police Strike in Boston, the Steel Strike, and the Coal Strike proved the most disruptive. (The Seattle Strike is presented as a Case Study on page 256.)

Each major strike further inflamed an already fearful public. During the Boston Police Strike, all the Boston newspapers called the policemen's decision to strike "Bolshevistic." When labor leader Samuel Gompers asked Massachusetts Governor Calvin Coolidge to help settle the strike, Coolidge wired back the refusal that launched his national political career: "There is no right to strike against the public safety by anybody, anywhere, anytime."

The 350,000 steel workers who went on strike in September 1919 worked a 12-hour day, seven days a week. Each time they changed between the day and the night shift, they had to work 24 hours straight, risking injury and death. Their simple demand—one day's rest out of the week—was denied by Elbert Gary, the head of U.S. Steel. At first, the public sympathized with the strikers. However, supported by the press, the steel companies portrayed the strike as a radical outbreak and dangerous uprising. As public opinion began to turn against them, the strikers had little chance.

The steel owners provoked riots, broke up union meetings, and employed police and soldiers to end the strike. African Americans recruited from the impoverished South to replace the striking workers also helped break the strikes. In the end, 18 strikers were killed, and the steel workers' union won none of their demands.

The Coal Strike lasted for a month in the late fall of 1919 and threatened to paralyze a country that depended on coal to heat its homes and run its factories. When the 394,000 striking miners finally obeyed a presidential order to go back to work, they went back to the same working conditions.

All the major strikes of 1919 were portrayed in the press as anti-American actions that threatened the United States government. The issues of long hours and poor working conditions got lost in the shuffle.[2]

## The Great Migration

**B**etween 1916 and 1920, half a million African Americans left the South for new jobs in the North. Many of these migrants were World War I veterans. Black soldiers bitterly resented the discrimination they had experienced in the war. No longer satisfied to struggle on southern farms, African Americans began to seek better opportunities in the North.

Many African Americans corresponded with a newspaper, the *Chicago Defender*, a key source of information about jobs and conditions in the North. One man wrote to the *Defender* to explain why so many African Americans were migrating north. In the South, he wrote, the wages of a grown man were fifty

**STUDY GUIDE**

**Identifying Cause and Effect**
During the Red Scare, labor strikes affected more than just the business leaders and their companies. Each major strike caused the public to be less tolerant of strikers and blame was laid more heavily on communist influences. Even though the strikers only wanted safer working conditions, public fear of violence and revolution overrode the real strike issues.

**2** What were the results of the major strikes during the Red Scare? How did the press influence the outcomes of the strikes?

to seventy-five cents a day for all labor. "He is compelled to go where there is better wages and sociable conditions, . . . many places here in this state the only thing that the black man gets is a peck of meal and from three to four lbs. of bacon per week, and he is treated as a slave."

### African Americans Find Better Pay

In the North, African Americans took jobs as meat packers, metal workers, and auto workers, all for more pay than they could have made in the South. A migrant to Chicago who had found employment in the sausage department of a meat-packing plant wrote: "We get $1.50 a day and we pack so many sausages we don't have much time to play but it is a matter of a dollar with me. . . ."

Only 50 African Americans worked for the Ford Motor Company in 1916. By 1920 Ford had 2,500 black employees. Six years later their numbers had quadrupled to 10,000.

Between 1910 and 1930, the Great Black Migration swelled Chicago's African American population from 44,000 to almost 234,000. Cleveland, the home of 8,500 blacks in 1910, sheltered 68,000 by the end of the 1920s.

Northern whites, however, were no more eager than southern whites had been to share power and opportunity with blacks. Many northern whites reacted violently to this northern migration.

*According to the chart on the right, which city had the greatest increase in black population during the 1920s?* **Service workers like the fire fighter recruits shown below were part of growing black communities in the North.**

### Racial Unrest

In 1917 race riots erupted in 26 northern cities. Racial conflicts escalated even further after the war. Riots broke out in many cities, including the nation's capital, during the hot summer of 1919.

Southern blacks who had migrated to Washington, D.C., during the war had been competing for jobs in an atmosphere of mounting racial tension. Newspaper reports of rumored black violence against whites contributed to the tension.

Following one such newspaper story, 200 sailors and marines marched into the city, beating black men and women. A group of whites also tried to break through military barriers to attack blacks in their homes. Determined to fight back, a group of blacks boarded a streetcar and attacked the motorman and conductors. Blacks also exchanged gunfire with whites who drove or walked through their neighborhoods.

President Wilson had to call in federal troops to control the crowds, who finally dispersed in a driving rain. When the Washington riot ended, four days after it began, four men had been killed, eleven had

| Urban Black Population, 1920–1930 | | | |
|---|---|---|---|
| City | 1920 | 1930 | Increase |
| New York | 152,467 | 327,706 | 114.9% |
| Chicago | 109,458 | 233,903 | 113.7% |
| Philadelphia | 134,229 | 219,599 | 63.6% |
| Detroit | 40,838 | 120,066 | 194.0% |
| Los Angeles | 15,579 | 38,894 | 149.7% |

INDIANA STATE LIBRARY

Fire Station #1. 1926.

suffered serious wounds, and dozens more had been injured. Three hundred people were arrested for rioting or for carrying weapons.

Few cities escaped racial violence during the early 1920s. Knoxville, Omaha, and Tulsa all experienced deadly struggles between blacks and whites. Several radical African American groups sprang out of this ferment. Marcus Garvey's "Back to Africa" movement became the most famous.

**The Garvey Movement**  A black man from Jamaica, Marcus Garvey had grown up at the very bottom of Jamaican society. Black Jamaicans had no economic or political voice in this white-controlled British colony.

Educated as a journalist and filled with ambition, Garvey arrived in New York City at the age of 28. There he found an enthusiastic audience for his particular version of Booker T. Washington's black self-help doctrine.

Where Washington advocated separate development in the United States, Garvey encouraged African Americans to return to Africa "to establish a country and a government absolutely on their own." To this end, Garvey founded the Universal Negro Improvement Association, which peaked at a membership of 250,000. With its program of black pride and power, Garvey's "Back to Africa" movement foreshadowed the Black Muslim movement of the 1960s.

Garvey's message encouraged poor African Americans who were his most fervent supporters. A member of the NAACP's Board of Directors said:

*T*he sweeper in the subway, the elevator boy eternally carrying fat office men and perky girls up and down a shaft, knew that when night came he might march with the African army and bear a wonderful banner to be raised some day in a distant, beautiful land.

Mary White Ovington,
*Portraits in Color,* 1927

A master showman, Garvey dressed in a hat with a white plume and a fancy uniform of purple, black, and green. He declared himself the president of the African Empire and gave his close followers positions of authority within his empire.

BROWN BROTHERS

**Marcus Garvey, fourth from the left, rewarded the lieutenants of his movement with titles such as Duke of Uganda and Knight Commander of the Nile.**

Thousands invested in Garvey's Black Star Line of ships that would bring African Americans back to their "home" in Africa. However, the Black Star Line collapsed, partly because unscrupulous white business dealers sold Garvey leaky ships and faulty equipment. Arrested and charged with mail fraud, Garvey was deported as an undesirable alien.

Whites called Garvey the "Moses of the Negroes," but other black leaders, particularly W.E.B. Du Bois, criticized his unconventional methods and personal flamboyance. However, Marcus Garvey gave blacks pride and hope for the future.

## The Progressive Spirit in the 1920s

Even during this period of labor unrest and social tension, the reform impulse endured. For example, Senator George Norris of Tennessee successfully resisted efforts to turn over the government power plant at Muscle Shoals to business interests. The Women's Joint Congressional Committee lobbied for social reforms throughout the 1920s. On the state level, reformers also succeeded in instituting such programs as old-age pensions, workers' compensation, and city planning.

Indeed, the postwar decade began with two important reforms whose roots were firmly planted in the Progressive Era. The Eighteenth Amendment established national Prohibition in 1919, and the Nineteenth Amendment gave women the right to vote in 1920.

**Prohibition** Between 1906 and 1919, twenty-six states had passed laws limiting the sale of liquor. Progressives who supported national Prohibition, a law that would forbid the manufacturing, transporting, and selling of liquor, argued that an outright ban on drinking would be a great boon to society. In the House of Representatives debate on the Prohibition amendment, Congressman Richard Austin from Tennessee predicted that "a [prohibition] law which has emptied the jails in Tennessee and virtually wiped out the criminal side of the dockets of the courts will do the same in every State."

During the war, anti-saloon advocates successfully linked Prohibition with patriotism. Conserving the grain that would have gone into liquor became part of the war effort. The anti-saloon league also stirred up the country's anti-German hysteria, blaming German brewers for making American soldiers unfit.

By 1918, three quarters of the population lived in "dry" states or counties. However, the cities with their large immigrant populations remained "wet" until the national amendment was passed. When the Volstead Act took effect in January, 1920, many Americans had high hopes that the new law would reduce poverty and wipe out prostitution and crime. John Kramer, the first Prohibition

Commissioner of the United States, enthusiastically proclaimed: "We shall see that it [liquor] is not manufactured. Nor sold, nor given away, nor hauled in anything on the surface of the earth or under the earth or in the air."

**Suffrage** Like the fight for Prohibition, women's struggle for voting rights got its final push from the war experience. Women had begun pursuing the right to vote in 1848, but the fight died down in the decades before the Progressive Era.

Progressives supported suffrage because they believed women's votes could help pass a variety of reforms, especially those that protected women and children. A new period of activism beginning around 1910 won rewards when several states—mostly in the west—approved suffrage.

Agnes Geelan, who later became mayor of her town and state senator from North Dakota, remembered: "We were allowed to vote in state elections . . . but there were restrictions. Women could only vote for women candidates. Men could vote for either men or women, and I didn't like that discrimination."

The campaign for national suffrage gathered steam in 1916, thanks to Carrie Chapman Catt's

**Women had voting rights in four western states before 1900.** *Why might this have happened?*

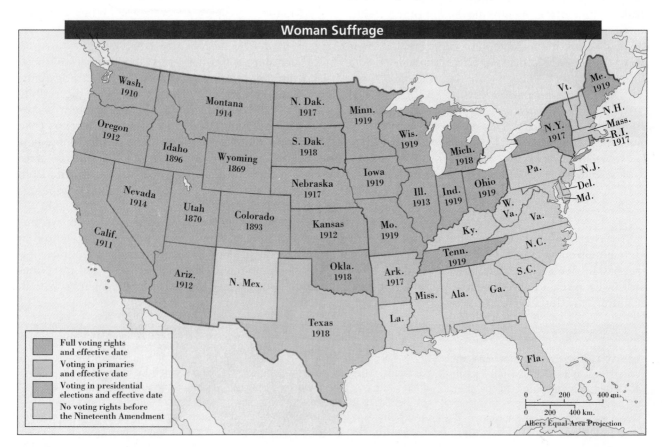

**Suffrage champion Carrie Chapman Catt (left) also founded the League of Women Voters.** *Why did progressives support suffrage?*

National American Woman Suffrage Association (NAWSA) and Alice Paul's Congressional Union, later the National Woman's Party. The two groups argued intensely over tactics. The Woman's Party favored radical actions, such as picketing the White House and going on hunger strikes when arrested. In a somewhat less radical way, NAWSA publicized women's contributions to the war effort, an argument President Wilson used in urging Congress to approve suffrage. Ratification of the national Suffrage Amendment finally came on August 26, 1920.

The right to vote did not grant women full equality. In many states, a woman still could not serve on juries, hold office, enter business, or sign contracts without her husband's permission. Despite the years of hard work that went into gaining the right to vote, two out of three women who had the vote failed to use it in the 1920 election.

After winning the vote, women united to support one important piece of legislation, the Sheppard-Towner Maternity Act of 1921. Stimulated by high rates of maternal and infant mortality, the act provided funds for states to employ public health nurses, hold child care conferences, and educate new mothers. The Sheppard-Towner Act was the first allocation of federal funds for welfare purposes. It had faced opposition from the American Medical Association. Other opponents argued that the bill was "inspired by foreign experiments in communism." Even so, Congress passed the Sheppard-Towner Act almost unanimously. It stayed in effect until 1929 when Congress failed to renew it.

**Turning Away from Progressivism**   Despite the passage of Sheppard-Towner, the 1920s hardly provided a friendly environment for reform. Progressive legislation that survived Congress or the state legislatures frequently perished as a victim of a hostile Supreme Court.

For example, in 1916 the Congress had passed a Child Labor Act, controlling the employment of children. Two years later, the Court declared the act unconstitutional on the grounds that Congress could not use its commerce power to regulate labor conditions. To make it uneconomical for businesses to hire children, Congress passed a new law establishing a prohibitive tax on child-manufactured products. The Court found the new law unconstitutional as well.

Progressive legislation to benefit working women fared little better. In 1923 the Court struck down a Washington, D.C., law enacting a minimum wage for women.

Progressivism declined for other reasons besides a hostile Supreme Court. After the brutality of the war, many reformers had lost faith in finding political solutions to social problems. The turmoil of the postwar years also helped to weaken the progressive movement. Many progressives were middle-class property owners. Shocked by the violence of the strikes and fearful of radical political ideas, many former progressives found their sympathies more firmly on the side of big business.

## SECTION REVIEW

### Checking Facts

1. How did Sacco and Vanzetti symbolize the fears of many Americans in the postwar era?

2. How did the Palmer raids deprive radicals of their civil rights?

3. How did the press contribute to America's feeling that labor unrest might lead to a Bolshevist takeover?

4. Who were Marcus Garvey's biggest supporters?

5. List three factors that contributed to the decline of the progressive movement during the 1920s.

### Thinking Critically

6. **Identifying Cause and Effect** Why did Americans not react more strongly to the Wall Street bombing in September 1920?

7. **Recognizing Bias** What measures were used to sway public opinion in favor of Prohibition?

### Linking Across Time

8. In many big cities of the United States, infant mortality rates are as high as they are in countries without excellent medical resources. Should the United States enact another bill like the Sheppard-Towner Act? Why or why not?

# The Seattle General Strike

## FEBRUARY 6-11, 1919

## The Case

*S*treet car gongs ceased their clamor; newsboys cast their unsold papers into the streets; from the doors of mill and factory, store and workshop, streamed 65,000 working men. School children with fear in their hearts hurried homeward. The lifestream of a great city stopped.

—Ole Hanson, Mayor of Seattle

When the 10 A.M. whistle blew on Thursday, February 6, 1919, Seattle workers belonging to the American Federation of Labor (AFL) and other unions walked off their jobs. This strike was different from other recent labor disputes because workers in every kind of business and industry, from carpen-

ters to garbage collectors, were striking together.

This general strike had been called by the Seattle Central Labor Council, led by its secretary James A. Duncan. The Council was composed of delegates from every union and trade organization in the Seattle area. Its purpose in calling the strike was to demonstrate union workers' solidarity with 35,000 workers in the Seattle shipyards.

The shipyard workers had been on strike since January 21, demanding higher wages and shorter hours. Charles Piez, the director of the shipyards, refused to discuss with the striking workers any issues relating to their jobs and flatly ordered them back to work. Piez denied that his workers had a right to strike. In effect, he said the workers should accept the present salary and hours or give up their jobs, play by his rules or quit. Duncan and other union leaders feared that

UNIVERSITY OF WASHINGTON LIBRARIES                    UPI/BETTMANN

**Anna Louise Strong and Ole Hanson were on opposing sides in the Seattle General Strike.**

Piez was trying to undermine the authority of the whole labor movement in Seattle.

In the days before the general strike, Seattle citizens stocked up on groceries and fuel. Many also bought guns and rifles. Some wealthier families left the city seeking shelter in Portland hotels. Most people feared the disruption the strike would bring. But some also feared that the strike was the beginning of a revolution to try to overthrow the government of the United States.

The mayor of Seattle, Ole Hanson, was one who believed that the strike was the beginning of a revolution. He asked that federal troops from Camp Lewis be sent to Seattle, and personally led the soldiers into the city in his flag-draped car.

## The Background

Ole Hanson's view that the Seattle strike was the beginning of a revolution was founded on recent international events. Just two years before, in November 1917, a political faction known as the Bolsheviks, led by V. I. Lenin and Leon Trotsky, had seized power in Russia.

The Bolsheviks, who later formed the Communist party, called on the workers of the world to overthrow capitalist governments, which they defined as those serving the interests of business. The Bolsheviks also called for the peoples' ownership of businesses and other private property, a prospect that terrified American business owners.

Moreover, after seizing power in Russia, the Bolshevik government deserted the American side in World War I and signed the treaty of Brest Litovsk with Germany. Because of this action,

many Americans assumed that the Bolsheviks were agents of Germany and thus traitors to the United States.

However, not every American hated and feared the Bolsheviks. Embittered by their struggle for better working conditions and higher wages, the leaders and members of some American labor unions found new hope in the Bolshevik victory. One such union was the International Workers of the World (IWW), also known as the Wobblies. It called for American workers to join together in "one big union" to overthrow their bosses.

Other labor unions spoke out against the Bolsheviks. The American Federation of Labor, for example, denounced bolshevism and its goal of a workers' revolution as incompatible with the American economic system. Samuel Gompers and other AFL leaders insisted that strikes were not revolutionary. Rather, they were a legitimate way for workers to fight for higher wages, shorter hours, and the right of unions to organize workers and to bargain collectively for their demands. To protect the labor movement against charges that it was anti-American, Gompers asked local trade unions to expel members sympathetic to the Bolsheviks. However, Gompers worked on the East Coast and had little influence in Seattle, where both the AFL local and the Labor Council continued to include Bolshevik sympathizers.

Many newspapers ignored the distinction between these opposing labor positions. In 1919, editorials routinely suggested that any strike was for bolshevism. Like Seattle mayor Ole Hanson, many government officials, business owners, and ordinary citizens began to distrust all workers and their demands. They came to regard all strikers, even those with legitimate grievances, as radicals, Bolsheviks, and troublemakers.

## The Opinions

The opinions about the general strike in Seattle ranged from a call to workers' revolution, a goal that was not widely shared among the striking workers, to a warning that the city government was prepared to use violent means to end the strike. Between these extremes are opinions expressing concern for the effects of the strike on the ordinary citizens of Seattle.

"The Russians have shown you the way out. What are you going to do about it? You are doomed to die of wage slavery unless you wake up, realize that you and the boss have not one thing in common, that the employing class must be overthrown, and that you, the workers, must take over control of your jobs, and through them, control over your lives instead of offering yourself up to the masters as sacrifice six days a week, so that they may coin profits out of your sweat and toil."

Harvey O'Connor,
in a leaflet passed out along Seattle's
waterfront and downtown streets

"We are undertaking the most tremendous move ever made by LABOR in this country, a move that will lead—NO ONE KNOWS WHERE! We do not need hysteria. We need the iron march of labor. LABOR WILL FEED THE PEOPLE. Twelve great kitchens have been offered, and from them food will be distributed by the provision trades at low cost to all. LABOR WILL CARE FOR THE BABIES AND THE SICK. The milk-wagons and the laundry truck drivers are arranging plans for supplying milk to babies, invalids, and hospitals, and taking care of the cleaning of linen for hospitals.... THE POWER OF THE STRIKERS TO MANAGE WILL WIN THIS STRIKE."

Anna Louise Strong,
Editorial in the Seattle Union Record,
February 4, 1919

"This is plain talk to the common-sense union men of Seattle. You are being rushed pell-mell into a general strike. You are being urged to use a dangerous weapon—the general strike, which you have never used before—which in fact, has never been used anywhere in the United States. It isn't too late to avert the tragic results that are sure to come from its use....The issue at stake is merely a better wage to the average unskilled worker in the shipyards. To a large extent public opinion is with these unskilled workers now, but public opinion will turn against them if their wage issue brings chaos and disaster upon the whole community unnecessarily. Seattle today is awake to the fact that she is on the brink of disaster, and Seattle is getting fighting mad...."

Editorial in the Seattle Star, Feb. 4, 1919

"By virtue of the authority vested in me as mayor, I hereby guarantee to all the people of Seattle absolute and complete protection....We have fifteen hundred policemen, fifteen hundred regular soldiers from Camp Lewis, and can and will secure, if necessary, every soldier in the Northwest to protect life, business, and property....The anarchists in this community shall not rule its affairs. All persons violating the laws will be dealt with summarily."

Ole Hanson, Mayor of Seattle

## The Outcome

One hour after the general strike began, a car backfired in downtown Seattle. A huge crowd gathered, eager to witness the opening battle of what most assumed was a revolution. However, there was no revolution. Though rumors to the contrary swept the city, there was also no violence. During the five days of the strike, no striker was arrested on any charge related to the strike. In fact, the number of people arrested by Seattle police for any offense fell from the usual number of 100 a day to about 30, probably because most people stayed home.

Seattle's essential services continued to operate during the strike. The city light plant produced electricity at full capacity. Hospital workers, exempted from the strike by union leaders, stayed on the job. Milk truck drivers delivered fresh milk from local farms to 36 milk stations in residential neighborhoods, where citizens could bring their own quart bottles to be filled. Strikers and other citizens could buy hot meals of stew or spaghetti at one of 21 feeding stations set up by the committee of union leaders in charge of the strike.

Despite efforts by strikers to meet citizens' needs, public opinion grew increasingly hostile as the strike continued. Furthermore, the grievances of the shipyard workers were lost in the hysterical debate over whether the strike was a revolution. Thus it seemed unlikely that the strike could force a victory for the shipyard workers. Even more damaging to the strikers' cause, the national leaders of the American Federation of Labor condemned general strikes as a labor tactic. Fearing that public opinion against the Seattle strike would damage the labor movement across the U.S., national AFL officials pressured the Seattle AFL to end its participation in the strike.

In the face of attacks from without and within, union leaders issued orders on February 10 for the general strike to cease. On the morning of February 11, a jubilant Mayor Hanson proclaimed, "The rebellion is quelled." Newspapers and magazines were equally enthusiastic. They heaped praise on Hanson as a new American hero, calling him "the man of the hour," "a red-blooded patriot," and a man "with a backbone that would serve as a girder of a railroad bridge."

After other union workers in Seattle returned to their jobs, the shipyard workers continued their strike alone until March 17. However, as a direct result of the strike, government contracts for the construction of 25 ships in Seattle were canceled. By the summer of 1919, thousands of shipyard workers had been laid off and several giant shipyards were closed.

Hanson used the shower of favorable publicity to launch a new career. Within a few months of the strike, he resigned his $7,500-a-year job as mayor and began touring the country giving speeches on the dangers of bolshevism. His speaking tour earned him $38,000 in seven months, though it did not win him the 1920 Republican nomination for president, as he had hoped.

COURTESY PAUL DORPAT

**The general strike was called to show solidarity with the Seattle shipyard workers who were on strike.**

The Red Scare that swept the United States in 1919 and 1920 was based on the fear that a revolution like the one in Russia could happen in this country. The Seattle strike suggested to some that this fear was justified. Praise in the press for the strong stand taken by Seattle Mayor Ole Hanson also led some Americans to believe that extreme, or even violent, actions were necessary to protect the nation against aliens, radicals, and anarchists.

## The Significance

Historians have examined the significance of the Seattle strike to the labor movement specifically and to Americans in general.

The Seattle general strike created ill will toward the American labor movement. In spite of the fact that no one acted violently and that no one seized private property, the American public became even more suspicious about bolshevism in the labor movement. Furthermore, since the strike did not succeed in improving workers' conditions, it damaged the self-esteem of the workers within the movement. On the other hand, workers gained a feeling of solidarity and proved to themselves that they could conduct a general strike without violence or damage to property.

## Think About It

1. Make a two column chart. On one side of the chart indicate the values of the strikers and on the other side show the values of the shipyard owners. Decide which side has values that are more like your own.
2. Discuss why each side in this dispute ultimately made the decision to strike or to stop the strike.
3. Study the four statements in The Opinion section. Which of these four opinions comes closest to your own feelings. Why?
4. When other newspapers reprinted Anna Louise Strong's editorial from the Union Record, public opinion turned against the strikers. Why do you think her editorial frightened people?
5. Describe how you think government officials should respond to a general strike.

# The Republican Influence

## November 2, 1920: Harding Defeats Cox

RICHARD STROUT BEGAN REPORTING FOR THE *CHRISTIAN SCIENCE MONITOR* IN 1922 AND CONTINUED FOR 62 YEARS. THE FIRST THREE PRESIDENTS HE COVERED— Warren Harding, Calvin Coolidge, and Herbert Hoover—could not have been more different.

Richard Strout said that Warren Gamaliel Harding, a fun-loving man who was elected in a landslide in 1920, didn't have the answers. "He was furthermore aware of his inadequacies, and he was pathetic. . . . He said, 'Gentlemen, gentlemen, go easy on me. I just want to go out on the golf course today and shoot a round.' "

Calvin Coolidge, Harding's stern vice president, succeeded to the presidency when Harding died. Coolidge then handily won the 1924 election. In an interview concerning the thirtieth U.S. president, Strout said:

*Calvin Coolidge only answered written questions from the press, and so, one time, we all got together and wrote down the same question. We wanted to know if he was going to run for re-election in 1928. So Coolidge looked at the first question and put it aside. Then he looked at the second and did the same thing. He went through all the slips of papers, I think there were a total of twelve, and on the last one he paused, read it to himself, and went on dryly: "I have a question about the condition of the children in Poland." We all smiled. He may have smiled too. And that concluded the press conference.*

As told to Tom Tiede,
*American Tapestry,* 1988

Herbert Hoover, the engineer who had performed brilliantly as secretary of commerce under Harding and Coolidge, easily won the presidency in 1928 after Coolidge declined to run. In the same interview, Strout said:

*Herbert Hoover was the first great man in my life. I thought he was going to be the greatest president we ever had. . . . He had each of us ask our questions, and then he would remember all of the questions and answer them one by one. It was remarkable. "As for your question, Mr. Strout, blah, blah, blah." He did it perfectly. I always thought he had a great mind, and he did.*

Although their personalities were strikingly different, the three Republican presidents pursued similar policies in the 1920s. Rejecting the social reforms of the Progressive Era, the Republican presidents—Harding, Coolidge, and Hoover—put their faith in big business, both at home and abroad. If government allowed business to prosper, all Americans would reap the rewards.

## Harding and the Teapot Dome

In 1920 Warren G. Harding trounced Democrat James M. Cox in the general election. Many observers saw this as a rejection of Wilson's brand of internationalism. As a senator, Harding had fought against joining Wilson's League of Nations. Now he promised, "We do not mean to be entangled."

## STUDY GUIDE

**As You Read**

Analyze how the presidents of this era pursued policies that promoted big business interests at home and abroad. Also, think about the following concept and skills.

**Central Concept**

- understanding how the United States, disillusioned with war and eager for business opportunities in foreign lands, initiated the first modern **disarmament** conference

**Thinking Skills**

- assessing outcomes
- recognizing assumptions
- analyzing decisions

Harding owed his success to Americans' exhaustion with the war years, with progressivism, and with the turbulence of 1919. Tired of reformers' attacks and Wilson's demands for self-sacrifice, the country longed for a rest.

Harding reassured Americans. In a campaign speech in 1920 he said, "America's present need is not heroics, but healing; not nostrums, but normalcy; not revolution, but restoration; not agitation, but adjustment; not surgery, but serenity."

People weren't always sure exactly what the word "normalcy" meant—it wasn't even in the dictionary. But Harding sounded presidential, and he most certainly looked presidential—tall, handsome, and stately.

Harding's first two years in office began well. He called a presidential conference to consider the problems of unemployment. Well aware of his own limitations, Harding named some bright and able officers to his cabinet: Secretary of State Charles Evans Hughes, Secretary of the Treasury Andrew Mellon, and Secretary of Commerce Herbert Hoover.

Harding also surrounded himself with his old friends from Ohio. People called these friends "The Poker Cabinet" or "The Ohio Gang." Alice Roosevelt Longworth described the White House atmosphere

THE BETTMAN ARCHIVE

**Harding enjoys an outing in 1922 with businessmen Henry Ford and Thomas Edison.**
*What kinds of people did Harding surround himself with?*

under Harding: "the air heavy with tobacco smoke, . . . cards and poker chips at hand—a general atmosphere of waistcoat unbuttoned, feet on desk, and spittoons alongside."

Some of Harding's poker buddies used their positions to line their pockets with money. The head of the Veteran's Bureau was fined and sent to jail for selling off veteran's hospital supplies for a personal profit. Eventually, another advisor resigned in disgrace and yet another narrowly avoided going to prison. Two of Harding's other advisors committed suicide rather than face public humiliation.

Of the many scandalous situations that occurred during Harding's administration, the **Teapot Dome Affair** became the most famous. Harding's secretary

---

of the interior, Albert Fall, leased government oil fields—one at Teapot Dome, Wyoming—to wealthy friends in exchange for hundreds of thousands of dollars in bribes. Eventually, Fall made history by being the first cabinet officer to go to prison, but the wealthy business people who bribed him were never punished. A popular joke at the time quipped, "In America, everyone is assumed guilty until proved rich."

**This political cartoon of the 1920s depicts the fall of public officials as scandals were brought to light.**

Upon hearing the news of a Senate investigation of oil leases, Harding grew depressed and distraught over his friends' betrayal. He became ill in Seattle, contracted pneumonia, and died in San Francisco on August 2, 1923, before the press began to reveal news of his administration's corruption. Americans mourned Harding, whom they had loved. Indeed the public seemed less angry at the corrupt government officials than they did at the exposers of the scandals. Senators Thomas J. Walsh and Burton K. Wheeler, who attempted to bring the crimes to light, were labeled "the Montana scandalmongers" by the *New York Tribune* and "assassins of character" by the *New York Times*. After decades of exposure, the American public had tired of muckraking and truly wanted a return to "normalcy." They got it when Harding's vice president, Calvin Coolidge, succeeded to the presidency.[1]

## Silent Cal and Big Business

Coolidge had a dry personality that symbolized the old-fashioned virtues of the New England where he had been raised. The journalist William Allen White once remarked that Coolidge had the expression of one "looking down his nose to locate that evil smell which seemed forever to affront him." Alice Roosevelt Longworth said he looked as if he had been "weaned on a pickle."

Born on a Vermont farm that had been worked by his family for five generations, Coolidge attended a one-room school house. After Harding's death, Coolidge's father, a justice of the peace, administered the presidential oath to his son by the light of a kerosene lamp. With his upright Yankee background and unquestioned reputation for complete honesty, Coolidge soon erased any damage the Harding scandals had caused the Republican administration.

Although he lacked Harding's personal warmth, Coolidge carried out Harding's programs. Both administrations rejected government programs to help ordinary citizens. When the victims of a Mississippi River flood appealed to the government for help, for example, President Coolidge replied, "The government is not an insurer of its citizens against the hazards of the elements."

Big business was another matter. The *Wall Street Journal* could justly brag that "Never before, here or anywhere else, has a government been so completely fused with business." The Harding and Coolidge administrations gave big business a boost in three ways. They appointed business people to commissions that were supposed to regulate business. They selected Supreme Court justices who ruled against progressive legislation. Finally, they named conservatives to powerful cabinet positions.

Harding and Coolidge appointed to regulatory commissions people who opposed regulation. The Interstate Commerce Commission, the Federal Trade Commission, and the Bureau of Corporations soon began to overlook business's violations of antitrust laws.

### Assessing Outcomes

Warren Harding appointed several men to government positions who had no qualifications except their relationship with the president. The head of the Veteran's Bureau, for example, was a one- time deserter from the army whom Harding had befriended on a vacation. Harding's loyalty to such "friends" provided the atmosphere in which government corruption flourished.

**1** Describe the most famous scandal in Harding's administration. Why didn't people blame Harding when scandals conducted during his administration were revealed?

**Coolidge often allowed himself to be photographed wearing outfits that attracted publicity.** *How might this have affected the public's image of him?*

Harding and Coolidge made five conservative appointments to the Supreme Court. From its origin in 1789 until 1925, the Supreme Court had struck down only 53 acts of Congress. During the 1920s the Supreme Court found 12 progressive laws unconstitutional, including the child labor law and the Washington, D.C., minimum wage law for women.

Cabinet positions in the Republican administrations went to wealthy business leaders who used their positions to protect big business interests. Andrew Mellon—secretary of the treasury under Harding, Coolidge, and Hoover—showed where the heart of 1920s politics lay. The third wealthiest person in the United States, Mellon immediately set out to cut government spending and reduce taxes on corporations and on people with high incomes.

Mellon feared that if high taxes relieved a businessman of too much of his earnings, "he will no longer exert himself and the country will be deprived of the energy on which its continued greatness depends." The multimillionaire with the straggly bow tie almost completely overturned the progressive tax policies of the Wilson years. Thanks to Mellon's efforts, a person making a million dollars a year in 1926 paid less than one third of the taxes a millionaire had paid in 1921.

Coolidge agreed with Mellon; government should interfere with big business as little as possible. "Four-fifths of all our troubles in this life would disappear if we would only sit down and keep still," said Silent Cal. When Coolidge chose not to run in 1928, America's beloved humorist, Will Rogers, commented that Coolidge retired a hero "not only because he hadent [*sic*] done anything, but because he had done it better than anyone."

## Herbert Hoover, The Wonder Boy

As secretary of commerce under both Harding and Coolidge, Herbert Hoover was a key architect of the Republican era. An intelligent and dedicated president, Hoover inherited the blame when the Republican prosperity later came crashing down.

Hoover, a successful mining engineer, had brilliantly managed the U.S. Food Administration during World War I. As director of the Belgian Relief Committee that provided food to starving Europeans, Hoover's name was a household word in the United States years before he became president.

Coolidge, who prided himself on restraint, sneered at Hoover's optimistic energy and called his secretary of commerce the "Wonder Boy." Indeed,

---

★ ★ ★ **PRESIDENT'S GALLERY** ★ ★ ★

*"I favor the policy of economy, not because I wish to save money, but because I wish to save people. The men and women of this country who toil are the ones who bear the cost of the Government. Every dollar that we carelessly waste means that their life will be so much the more meager. Every dollar that we prudently save means that their life will be so much the more abundant."*

Inaugural Address,
March 4, 1925

AP / WIDE WORLD PHOTOS

Calvin Coolidge 1923–1929

**Background:**
- Born 1872; died 1933
- Republican, Massachusetts
- Elected governor of Massachusetts 1918
- Elected vice president in 1920
- Assumed presidency 1923
- Elected president 1924

**Achievements in Office:**
- Kellogg-Briand Pact (1928)
- Improvement of relations with Mexico
- Support of American business

during the 1920s, it seemed there was nothing the "Wonder Boy" couldn't do.

Hoover expanded his Commerce department to control and regulate airlines, radio, and other new industries. He helped organize trade associations—groups of firms in the same line of business—to minimize price competition, which Hoover thought inefficient. Hoover also pushed the Bureau of Standards to standardize everything manufactured in the nation—from nuts and bolts to tires, mattresses, and electrical fixtures.

Hoover supported zoning codes, eight-hour days in major industries, better nutrition for children, and conservation of natural resources. He even pushed through the Pollution Act of 1924, the first effort to control coastline oil pollution.

Hoover believed above all in volunteer effort and free enterprise. As secretary of commerce, Hoover had argued that American business was entering a new era. With the growth of trade associations, Hoover hoped businesses would show a new spirit of public service.

In 1928 many Americans agreed with Will Rogers, who said, "I always did want to see [Hoover] elected. I wanted to see how far a competent man could go in politics. It has never been tried before." Hoover's campaign slogans proudly proclaimed, "Help Hoover Help Business" and "Let's Keep What We've Got: Prosperity Didn't Just Happen."[2]

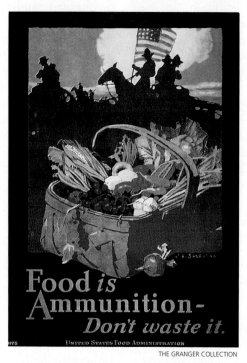

THE GRANGER COLLECTION

**Posters like this promoted Hoover's "meatless meals" and "wheatless days" when he was the food administrator during World War I. To *Hooverize* meant to *economize*.**

## Republican Foreign Policy

After World War I, the United States shied away from political involvement in Europe. Nevertheless, all three Republican administrations increased U.S. economic ties to Europe and the rest of the

world. During the 1920s military assistance gave way to economic expansion and control. Herbert Feis, an influential historian of United States policy, wrote, "The soldiers and sailors had done their part, [and now] the dollar was counted on to carry on their work. It was regarded as a kind of universal balm."

In the twenties the government encouraged U.S. firms to dramatically expand their international business. During this decade, American businesses came to dominate world markets in cars, tractors, electrical equipment, and farm machinery. "World peace through world trade," was how business leaders like Thomas J. Watson of International Business Machines (IBM) put it.

**The Dawes Plan** Although the United States government did not direct this worldwide economic expansion, its policies fostered the international expansion of big business. The Dawes Plan showed how the United States influenced European economics without direct government intervention.

After World War I, the Allies owed $10 billion in war debts to the United States. Americans insisted on repayment, but the Allies could not pay unless they got the $33 billion Germany owed them.

When Germany defaulted on its war payments in December 1922 and January 1923, French soldiers marched into Germany's Ruhr valley. To avert another war, the United States stepped in. However, the United States sent a business leader instead of an army. Charles G. Dawes, a wealthy Chicago banker, negotiated loans from private U.S. banks to Germany and set up a new payment schedule. Now Germany could pay its reparations to the Allies and the Allies could repay the United States.

**Recognizing Assumptions**

Herbert Hoover believed that government should help make business more efficient. As secretary of commerce, Hoover had promoted trade associations. He thought competition between

businesses was inefficient. However, he failed to foresee that some corporate executives would use such associations for price fixing.

2  How was Hoover's view of big business slightly different from that of Harding and Coolidge? What were some of Hoover's accomplishments that benefited ordinary citizens?

The Dawes Plan was a way for Germany to meet its financial obligations and avert war. U.S. banks loaned Germany $2.5 billion so that Germany could make war reparations to the Allies. In turn, the Allies repaid this money to the U.S. government. Even though this money represented only a fraction of what the Allies and the United States were actually owed, the Dawes Plan restored payments that otherwise would not have been made. As a result the potential for war was averted.[3]

**The Disarmament Movement** The most powerful nation in the world during the 1920s, the United States proved to be a reluctant giant. To stay clear of Europe's power struggles, the United States embarked on a two-fold policy. The United States attempted to destroy the weapons of war through the Washington Conference. The United States also signed the Kellogg-Briand Pact to outlaw armed struggle.

In November 1921 Charles E. Hughes addressed the nine nations meeting at the Washington Naval Conference to discuss **disarmament,** the limiting of arms. The delegates knew they were to discuss specifically limitation of naval arms. But the U.S. secretary of state shocked his fellow world leaders when he asked them to destroy their battleships. Eventually, three major treaties emerged from the first successful disarmament conference in modern history.

After much controversy, the United States, England, Japan, France, and Italy pledged to limit the number of their largest ships and to stop constructing new ships. Great Britain and the United States got to keep 500,000 tons of ships each; Japan, 300,000 tons; and France and Italy, 167,000 tons each. The Japanese ambassador complained that the ratio of 5:5:3 sounded like "Rolls-Royce, Rolls-Royce, Ford." Japan agreed only after winning concessions that prohibited new U.S., British, and Japanese naval bases on the Western Pacific islands.

**During World War I, the United States provided the Allies with loans and supplies. The Dawes Plan was set up to help recover the debt.** *Which countries were paying war debts to the United States? How much money did Germany borrow?*

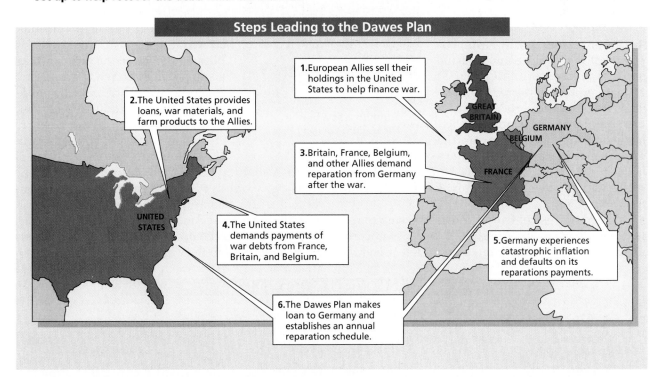

**Steps Leading to the Dawes Plan**

1. European Allies sell their holdings in the United States to help finance war.

2. The United States provides loans, war materials, and farm products to the Allies.

3. Britain, France, Belgium, and other Allies demand reparation from Germany after the war.

4. The United States demands payments of war debts from France, Britain, and Belgium.

5. Germany experiences catastrophic inflation and defaults on its reparations payments.

6. The Dawes Plan makes loan to Germany and establishes an annual reparation schedule.

GREAT BRITAIN
GERMANY
BELGIUM
FRANCE
UNITED STATES

## STUDY GUIDE

**Analyzing Decisions**
The Washington Naval Conference, initially called by President Harding, was based on a necessity of understanding. The United States, as well as other nations, feared there could be a Japanese-American war over the islands in the Pacific. The nations who were principal powers in World War I were invited to negotiate a pact to eliminate this threat of war.

**3** How did the Dawes Plan illustrate U.S. influence in European economics?

For its part, Japan promised to respect China's sovereignty and independence. Despite this pledge, which kept the China market open to U.S. business, the United States was concerned about Japanese power and ambitions in the Pacific.

The United States' second attempt to free itself from involvement in Europe, the Kellogg-Briand Pact, began as a two-nation pact initiated by France's foreign minister, Aristide Briand, to outlaw war and ensure France's security. However, Secretary of State Frank Kellogg wanted a world treaty to outlaw war.

Fourteen nations initially signed the Kellogg-Briand Pact of 1928. Although the treaty declared war illegal, it failed to include punishments for future attackers. Many people scorned it as a "parchment peace." But the pact demonstrated high U.S. hopes for an end to military entanglements with Europe.

### Relations with Latin America

Although the U.S. wanted to avoid political involvement in Europe, it chose to protect its interests in Latin America. During the twenties U.S. business firms continued their long-standing expansion to the south, searching for markets and raw materials. In fact, by 1924 the United States controlled the financial policies of 14 out of 20 Latin American countries.

United States control of Latin America represented more than an extension of business-government cooperation. The United States felt it had the right and duty to extend its civilization south of the border. Little had changed since the turn of the century. Teddy Roosevelt's "Big Stick" lived on.

Though the U.S. government had begun to reduce its military presence in Latin America after World War I, the United States still did not hesitate to protect its business interests with soldiers. Coolidge had withdrawn U.S. troops from Nicaragua briefly in 1925, but he sent Marines back in 1926 when a U.S. backed conservative government experienced revolt.

The revolt was a home-grown movement under rebel César Augusto Sandino. When Congress criticized his action, Coolidge argued that the United States was "not making war on Nicaragua any more than a policeman on the street is making war on passersby."

Bowing to vocal Latin American objections and U.S. domestic criticism, the United States temporarily withdrew its troops from Nicaragua in 1925. Congressional resistance to Coolidge's use of troops in Nicaragua showed the beginnings of a shift in U.S. policy toward Latin America. By 1929 U.S. policy makers had finally begun to recognize that U.S. troops in Latin America created resentment abroad and criticism at home.

Both domestically and internationally the Harding, Coolidge, and Hoover administrations showed a firm commitment to promoting U.S. business interests. Most Americans shared the firm belief that U.S. business could spread peace and prosperity to the nation and to the world at large.

LIBRARY OF CONGRESS

**Sandino was a hero in Nicaragua.** *Why did he want U.S. troops out of his country?*

---

## SECTION REVIEW

### Checking Facts

1. What do you think Harding meant by "normalcy"?
2. Why were Americans reassured when Calvin Coolidge took over Harding's presidency?
3. Why did Mellon believe millionaires should not pay high taxes?
4. List three of Hoover's accomplishments as secretary of commerce.
5. How did the Dawes Plan show the Republicans' belief that the interests of big business and government were the same?
6. Why was Japan initially unhappy with the disarmament treaty it signed with the United States, England, France, and Italy?

### Thinking Critically

7. **Comparing and Contrasting** Briefly characterize Harding, Coolidge, and Hoover to show their differences and similarities.

8. **Recognizing Assumptions** What did Coolidge mean when he compared the U.S. Marines enforcing order in Nicaragua to "a policeman on the street"?

### Linking Across Time

9. Do you think a treaty such as the Kellogg-Briand Pact could have helped prevent World War I? Why or why not?

# Prosperity and American Business

## 1925: *The Man Nobody Knows* Is Best-Seller

**B**RUCE BARTON'S SUBJECT—BIG BUSI-NESS—AND HIS HERO—JESUS—SEEMED AN UNLIKELY COMBINATION FOR A BOOK. HOWEVER, BARTON'S *The Man Nobody Knows* became America's best-seller during 1925 and 1926. A one-time journalist and the founder of a large advertising agency, Barton told Americans that Jesus had been the first modern businessman. After all, he wrote, Jesus "picked up twelve men from the bottom ranks of business and forged them into an organization that conquered the world."

Barton explained that when Jesus said he must be about his father's business, he had meant much more than simply religion. Barton wrote:

*A*sk any ten people what Jesus meant by his "Father's business," and nine of them will answer "preaching." To interpret the words in this narrow sense is to lose the real significance of his life. It was not to preach that he came into the world; nor to teach; nor to heal. These are all departments of his Father's business, but the business itself is far larger, more inclusive. For if human life has any significance it is this—that God has set going here an experiment to which all His resources are committed. He seeks to develop perfect human beings, superior to circumstance, victorious over Fate. No single kind of human

THE BETTMANN ARCHIVE

talent or effort can be spared if the experiment is to succeed. The race must be fed and clothed and housed and transported, as well as preached to, and taught and healed. Thus all business is his Father's business. All work is worship; all useful service prayer.

Bruce Barton,
*The Man Nobody Knows*, 1925

## The Glorification of Business

**T**he America that made Bruce Barton's book a best-seller changed business almost into a religion and elevated the successful businessperson to the status of a religious hero. In 1921, after touring and examining 12 of the country's biggest businesses, writer Edward Earl Purinton published an article idolizing big business. Purinton praised the business manager of Gary, Indiana, the world's largest one-industry city, saying that successful business leaders were naturally suited to be powerful religious leaders:

*H*e is called upon by the pastors and priests of churches of a dozen different faiths and nationalities, whose members are employees of the U.S. Steel Corporation, to address the congregations in some helpful, appropriate way. Because he is a fine business

### STUDY GUIDE

**As You Read**
Trace the increase in productivity that fueled America's economic growth, revolutionized corporate structure, and glorified big business. Also, think about the following concepts and skills.

**Central Concepts**
• tracing the reorganization of U.S. business into a system of **oligopoly**
• understanding how the system of **welfare capitalism** reduced the appeal of independent unions

**Thinking Skills**
• recognizing values
• identifying cause and effect
• assessing outcomes

*man, with power, skill and money back of him, the men of the city want to hear what he has to say. And because he is a gentleman, kind, thoughtful, and sympathetic, the women of the church listen gladly to his lay sermons.*

> Edward Earl Purinton,
> "Big Ideas from Big Business,"
> *The Independent*, April 16, 1921

Not only wealthy Americans revered business. After all, President Coolidge had said, "The man who builds a factory builds a temple—the man who works there worships there." As profits, salaries, dividends, and industrial wages rose during this decade, the gospel of big business became a national creed. Popular magazines printed articles praising corporate leaders, such as Walter Chrysler, *Time* magazine's Man of the Year in 1929.

A list of 59 people who "ruled" the United States appeared in newspapers in the 1920s. The list omitted all elected officials but included John D. Rockefeller, J.P. Morgan, a number of Du Ponts, and Treasury Secretary Andrew Mellon. The person who had compiled the list explained, "These men rule by virtue of their ability." Too busy to hold public office themselves, "they determine who shall hold such office."

Even universities, traditionally hostile to business matters, joined in the universal admiration for business leaders. In 1925, the Princeton University newspaper asked:

> *What class of men is it that keeps governments, businesses, families, solidly on their feet? What class of men is it that endows universities, hospitals, Foundations? . . . What class of men are the fathers of most of us— fathers who provide decently for their families, who educate their children, who believe in order and justice, who pay taxes to support jails, insane asylums and poor houses, which neither they nor theirs are likely to occupy?*

> *Daily Princetonian*,
> January 7, 1925

Predictably, the one answer to all the questions was *business*men.[1]

## A Booming Economy

Americans thanked big business for the prosperity the country enjoyed during the twenties. Indeed, the United States had emerged from World War I in a splendid economic position. At the beginning of the war, the United States had owed other countries money. Now the United States was a creditor nation, collecting debts from war-torn Europe.

In contrast to other major powers whose farms and factories had been devastated by the war, America's productive capacity had expanded. Following a short period of social and economic unrest immediately after the war, the United States bounded into several years of record-breaking prosperity.

Between 1922 and 1928, **industrial productivity**— the amount of goods produced by each hour of labor—rose by 70 percent. Corporate investors reaped the largest rewards, but many ordinary Americans also benefited. Workers earned higher wages than at any previous time in the history of the United States.

CULVER PICTURES, INC.

**The use of electric generators improved industrial productivity.** *How did new technology contribute to the expanding economy?*

America's productivity soared as new technology and techniques introduced greater efficiency into manufacturing. Electrical motors powered 70 percent of machines in 1929, compared with only 30 percent in 1914. The assembly line that revolutionized the auto industry in 1914 soon moved into other industries as well.

When American business boomed, companies needed bigger and better offices. A growing urban population required new apartment buildings, and a spreading suburban population demanded new roads and houses. As a result, building and road construction took off during the decade.

**New Industry**   New industries also sprang up, all helping to continue the rapid growth of the decade. The manufacturing of light metals, such as aluminum; a brand-new synthetics industry; motion pictures; and radio manufacturing—all provided new jobs and new products for the American public.

Automobile manufacturing ranked as the most important of all the new industries. Henry Ford was one of several automobile makers, but it was his name that became a synonym for the booming new industry. In 1923 a public opinion poll declared Henry Ford would be a more popular candidate for president than President Harding. In another contest college students voted Ford the third greatest figure of all time. Only Napoleon and Jesus got more votes.

In 1907 Ford had declared:

> *I will build a motor car for the great multitude. It will be large enough for the family but small enough for the individual to run and care for. It will be constructed of the best materials, by the best men to be hired, after the simplest designs that modern engineering can devise. But it will be so low in price that no man making a good salary will be unable to own one—and enjoy with his family the blessing of hours of pleasure in God's great open spaces.*

> Henry Ford, quoted in
> *American Civilization in the First Machine Age: 1890–1940*, 1970

In 1913–1914 Ford introduced the moving production line, an innovation that made it possible to assemble his car in 93 minutes instead of the 14 hours it had taken a year before. By 1925 a completed auto rolled off the Ford assembly lines every 10 seconds. The auto industry's dramatic expansion in the 1920s gave birth to a host of related industries: steel, rubber, petroleum, machine tools, and road building.[2]

**The New Commercial Downtowns**   As roads and automobiles remade the horizontal landscape of the United States, skyscrapers began to revolutionize the country's vertical landscape. During the war, construction had been abruptly halted. Now it seemed Americans were reaching for the sky as they made up for lost time.

In 1910 European travelers to New York City had been surprised by 20-story skyscrapers. By 1930 they found themselves in the shadows of 60-story

ALFRED STIEGLITZ COLLECTION, FISK UNIVERSITY, NASHVILLE

**The Radiator Building, shown here in a painting by Georgia O'Keeffe, was an architectural display of the glorification of business.**

STUDY GUIDE

**Identifying Cause and Effect**
Because the United States was no longer a debtor nation after World War I, business had enough capital to introduce the new technologies of mass production and electricity. These innovations increased productivity. Some new industries, especially automobile manufacturing, spurred the growth of related industries, which led to even greater productivity.

**2** How did the moving production line affect the automobile industry? What effects did the moving production line have on industry as a whole?

buildings. On May 1, 1931, the new Empire State Building dwarfed even the Bank of Manhattan's 71 stories and the Chrysler Building's 77 stories. At 102 stories, topped by a slender mast, the Empire State Building had become the tallest building in the world.

If New York had its skyscrapers, the rest of the United States would have theirs, too. Houston had its Petroleum Building, Chicago its Tribune Tower, and Cleveland its Terminal Tower. Even prairie towns raised the giant buildings. Tulsa and Oklahoma City had not even existed when the first skyscraper was completed in 1885. By the end of the 1920s, these cities, too, celebrated their own new skylines.

## The Corporate Revolution

During the 1920s American industry produced new products and constructed soaring new monuments. In this decade the United States also witnessed the culmination of the corporate revolution that had begun in the late nineteenth century. Many family-run firms could no longer raise enough **capital**—an accumulation of money—to invest in research and development. Unable to purchase the new technology or to afford national advertising, small companies could not compete. American business became big business, as thousands of small firms went out of business or were absorbed into larger companies or **corporations**—businesses legally separate from their stockholders.

**The Urge to Merge**     Between 1920 and 1928, more than 5,000 mergers took place, resulting in the loss of hundreds of firms. The Federal Trade Commission (FTC) had protected small businesses against such takeovers. But the person President Coolidge appointed to the chairmanship of the FTC scorned the commission as a "publicity bureau to spread socialistic propaganda" and "an instrument of oppression and disturbance and injury instead of help to business." Under William E. Humphrey, the FTC soon began to encourage instead of to prosecute trade associations and business mergers.

Some of the most obvious examples of business mergers were seen among utility companies. Many local electric companies were absorbed into huge regional systems and utility empires. During the period from 1919 to 1927, 3,700 local power companies turned their lights off for good. By 1930 ten holding companies supplied 72 percent of the nation's power.

Four meat packers, three major baked goods companies, and four tobacco producers dominated their industries during the 1920s. Such a situation, in which a few major producers control an entire industry, is called an **oligopoly**. Oligopoly prevailed in banking, too, as large banks swallowed smaller ones. By 1929, 1 percent of the banks controlled more than 46 percent of the country's banking resources.

A smaller and smaller number of American businesses began to wield unmatched economic power. By 1929, in fact, half of America's corporate wealth belonged to its 200 largest corporations.

**The National Dollar Stores, Inc., was founded by Chinese American Joe Shoong as one small store in 1903. It had grown into a chain of stores by the**

*1920s. How might management of a group of chain stores differ from that of a single store?*

THE NATONAL DOLLAR STORES, LTD.

CULVER PICTURES, INC.

The National Negro Business League, founded by Booker T. Washington (seated, second from left), encouraged black enterprises in the 1920s. This photo dates from the early 1900s.

As small firms went out of business, chain stores and other large companies thrived. The Great Atlantic and Pacific Tea Company (A & P) expanded from 400 stores in 1912 to 15,500 stores by 1932. Big businesses like the A & P could no longer be run by one strong leader. The new companies demanded a new type of leadership.

**The Managerial Revolution**   Everyone knew who Henry Ford was, but during the 1920s, the average American could no longer identify the chairperson of the board of directors of any other large corporation. Big firms were now being directed by anonymous, replaceable managers rather than by the strong personalities of the past.

Colleges stepped in to train the new leaders for the large corporations. Indeed, during the 1920s, almost every leading university established its own business school. In 1924 the Harvard Graduate School of Business Administration dedicated 23 elegant new buildings on a site across the Charles River from the university. The president of the First National Bank of New York had given $6 million toward the building of Harvard's business school.

During the 1927–28 school year, Northwestern University offered more than 30 courses on business, from "Bank Practice and Policy" to "Psychology of Business Relations." New York University students could even take a course in "Restaurant, Tea Room, and Cafeteria Organization."

Smaller businesses that had grown more complicated also required a more specialized kind of managerial know-how. New college-trained business managers soon began to replace the company-trained general manager of an earlier generation.

By 1924 in Muncie, Indiana, for example, the old job of general manager of the glass factory had been divided into five new jobs: production manager, sales manager, advertising manager, personnel manager, and office manager. Companies grew by adding laborers. But to supervise larger work forces, they now seemed to need more layers of management.

Another plant in the same city had employed 200 workers in 1890 and supervised them with a small staff: a president, a vice president who was also general manager, a secretary and treasurer, and two foremen. By 1924 the same plant had six times as many workers, but now required fifteen times as many foremen, as well as the addition of two superintendents, an auditor, and assistants to the secretary and treasurer.

## Industry's Labor Policies

Big corporations with specialized managerial staffs had almost complete control over the work force during the 1920s. Immediately after the war, the Red Scare had struck a crushing blow to labor by associating unions with communists. For the rest of the decade, corporations kept labor submissive with an effective combination of punishment and reward. The

Getting On with Business    271

American Plan was the punishment, and welfare capitalism was the reward.

### The American Plan

The American Plan was a variety of activities companies used after the war to demoralize and destroy unions. Corporations called it the *American Plan* to give it the ring of patriotism. One of the plan measures, open-shop associations, allowed employers to stick together in blacklisting union members. Companies also employed spies who joined unions and then informed employers about labor discontent and identified labor organizers.

As part of the American Plan, many companies offered their workers only "yellow-dog" contracts. With a yellow-dog contract as a condition of employment, an employee agreed not to become a member of a union or to organize fellow employees.

Big business, of course, tried to make it sound as though the American Plan was in the worker's best interest. Elbert H. Gary, head of U.S. Steel, wrote:

> *The principle of the "open shop" is vital to the greatest industrial progress and prosperity. It is of equal benefit to employer and employee. It means that every man may engage in any line of employment that he selects and under such terms as he and the employer may agree upon; that he may arrange for the kind and character of work which he believes will bring to him the largest compensation and the most satisfactory conditions, depending upon his own merit and disposition.*
>
> Elbert H. Gary,
> *New York Times*, September 18, 1919

The Supreme Court favored management over labor with several key rulings. In 1915 the Court had upheld the yellow-dog contract. In 1921 it declared a union boycott illegal and drastically limited workers' rights to picket. In the 1922 Coronado Case, the same Court that so carefully guarded the rights of big businesses ruled that unions could be sued for damages under antitrust rules.

Between 1921 and 1929, union membership dropped from about 5 million to about 3.5 million people. Phil Bart, a lifelong union organizer, recalled how difficult it was to organize strikes in the auto industry in 1928:

> *There were no laws to protect strikers then, and there wasn't much public sympathy either. We had to struggle against the place and time. The authorities were intolerant, and when we set up a line the police might come right in and knock hell out of us. The strikers could try to protect themselves by putting up a fight or something, but you could not go to the courts, you could not go to the government; they didn't care. . . . We never forced management to bargain, but working conditions did get better.[3]*
>
> Phil Bart, quoted in
> *American Tapestry*, 1988

### Welfare Capitalism

Working conditions got better partly because employers sought to reduce the appeal of independent unions. The combination of programs employers adopted in order to convince workers they did not need unions became known as **welfare capitalism.**

During the 1920s most employers improved plant conditions, hired company doctors and nurses, and provided a variety of activities from glee clubs to sports teams. For example, the Hammermill Paper Company sold its workers cheap gasoline, while Bausch and Lomb established dental and eye care clinics for its employees.

In 1922 the president of General Electric, Gerard Swope, had told a group of foremen in Schenectady, New York, "You are constantly being hounded to increase your output. One of the ways of getting it is to have your men cooperate with you." U.S. business leaders heeded this message and began practicing welfare capitalism in their own companies.

During the 1920s most U.S. companies offered safety programs and group insurance. A few of the largest corporations instituted stock purchase opportunities and pension plans. In the 1920s U.S. Steel alone paid out more than $10 million a year in worker benefits. Even Elbert Gary, the head of U.S. Steel, had come to believe that such generosity to workers actually profited his company. In 1923 he told his stockholders, "it pays to treat men in that way."

---

#### STUDY GUIDE

**Recognizing Values**

During the Red Scare, many employers seemed more concerned with making profits and fighting unionization than with employee welfare. Later, they found that satisfied workers were more productive and less likely to unionize. As a result, conditions improved. However, company values had not really changed. Making money and avoiding unions were still company goals.

**3** What policies did corporations institute as part of the American Plan? How did the Supreme Court show support for big business?

**A company sponsored basketball team was one of the benefits given these employees under welfare capitalism.**
*What were other benefits of welfare capitalism and why were they offered?*

Many companies also began programs in which workers could elect representatives to speak to management. Employers called this "industrial democracy" and boasted that it would erase the differences between workers and bosses. Edward Purinton wrote that by providing employee representation on the board of directors, "owners of a business now give the manual workers a chance to think and feel in unison with [the bosses.] All enmity is between strangers. Those who really know each other cannot fight."

Employers may have believed that the interests of the worker and employer were identical and that company unions were a form of democracy. However, the workers knew that the company unions had no real power and called them "Kiss Me Clubs." In the absence of worker-led unions, welfare capitalism maintained the power inequalities that gave management full authority over labor. Indeed, Charles M. Schwab, the head of Bethlehem Steel, made the owners' position very clear: "I will not permit myself to be in a position of having labor dictate to management."

Welfare capitalism may not have done away with the vast inequities between employer and employed, but by the 1920s, worker-led unions were in a serious decline. By 1929, only about one in twelve workers belonged to a union.

While the United States was prosperous, welfare capitalism seemed to keep the work force content. In January 1929 the head of the Chicago and Alton Railroad boasted, "In our shops since the strike of 1922, the shop employees have been very quiet. The employee is much happier. . . . He is a peaceful worker and a peaceful citizen."

Since employee well-being increased efficiency and profits, welfare capitalism paid off for big business. Corporations also used welfare capitalism to restore their public image after the muckraking scandals of the Progressive Era.

During the twenties, professional public relations experts promoted the idea of humane businesses that not only looked out for the welfare of their employees but also acted in the service of society. The Western Electric Company for example, offered to send literature teaching household management to women.

> *T*he science of managing a home indicates the use of electrical appliances, but the company wants to teach the science whether it sells the goods or not. This is "good business" because [it is] genuine service.
>
> Edward Earl Purinton,
> "Big Ideas from Big Business," *The Independent*,
> April 16, 1921

Indeed, the idea of public service became an ideal for big business during the 1920s. Business leaders joined service groups such as the Rotary Club, whose motto became "He profits most who serves best." According to the Rotarians, "the businessman was no longer a profit-maker or even a bread-winner, he was a public servant."

## SECTION REVIEW

**Checking Facts**

1. Give three examples of America's new admiration for big business during the 1920s.
2. List five new industries that helped propel the U.S. economy during the 1920s.
3. Before Henry Ford's time, only the rich could afford to buy automobiles. Why was Ford's statement of 1907 so revolutionary?
4. Why did many small firms have so much trouble competing during the 1920s?
5. What two methods did corporations use to manage labor in the 1920s?

**Thinking Critically**

6. **Recognizing Values** Why did big business begin to promote service activities during the 1920s?
7. **Identifying Cause and Effect** Why would Coolidge appoint someone opposed to the activities of the FTC to be its chairperson?

**Linking Across Time**

8. The names "American Plan" and "open shop" cast opponents in a negative light because no one should want to support an "un-American Plan" or a "closed shop." What groups today have names that suggest nonmembers oppose something highly valued?

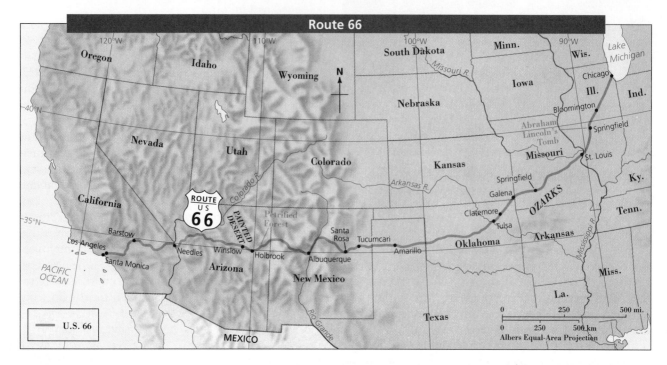

**Route 66**

- — U.S. 66

The path of Route 66 was the subject of intense negotiating as many small towns petitioned to have the road run through their community.

Pulitzer prize-winning author James Agee described the American story as having five main characters: the continent, the people, the automobile, the road, and the roadside. According to Agee, these five characters met because of the restless nature of Americans:

*The twenties made him [the American] rich and more restive still and he found the automobile not merely good but better and better. It was good because continually it satisfied and at the same time greatly sharpened his hunger for movement.*

James Agee,
*Fortune*, September 1934

Cars alone could not satisfy the American hunger for movement. Only the construction of a vast network of highways would finally enable Americans to travel freely. This increased movement of people and goods had dramatic

> ## Only the construction of a vast network of highways would finally enable Americans to travel freely. This increased movement of people and goods had dramatic effects on the nation's culture and economy.

effects on the nation's culture and economy.

One famous highway, U.S. Highway 66, allowed Americans to fulfill their desire to take to the road. How did the U.S. highway system, including roads such as Route 66, come about?

## Building the Roadway

Americans enjoyed driving their cars and soon wanted better roads on which to drive. People were interested in what Americans in other parts of the country were doing: what they ate, wore, lived in, and looked like.

Car owners and manufacturers were not the only ones demanding new roads. Since the early 1900s farmers in the Midwest and the Southwest had cried out for roads on which to transport their products to market. Farmers had been dependent on trains to freight their produce at whatever rate the railroad monopoly set.

Local political action groups

pressed Congress to legislate highway building and to break the railroad's stranglehold over transportation. In 1916 the Federal Aid Road Act responded to the pleas of these groups. The Road Act provided federal aid for half of the construction costs of any rural highway intended to carry mail. The new state highway departments were to plan the routes of the new roads. A second federal provision in 1921 granted money to states that would connect their roads to the roads of other states, forming a main thoroughfare. These acts set the foundation for a national highway system.

When U.S. Highway 66 officially opened on November 11, 1926, it became one of the main arteries of the national highway system. This "great diagonal highway" between Chicago and Los Angeles cut through the Middle West, straddled the Great Plains, crossed the deserts of the Southwest and reached to the very edge of the Pacific Ocean. In its 2,400-mile course, Route 66 spanned eight states and ran through 200 towns. In the late 1920s, Route 66 was an autotourist's vacation land.

During the Depression of the 1930s, Route 66 became famous as the road followed by migrants on their way to California in search of jobs. John Steinbeck once wrote "66 is the mother road, the road of flight."

## Building the Roadside

The car and the highways provided Americans with a new form of recreation and business in the 1920s: autocamping. Millions of Americans packed tents and headed for the open countryside. Car dealers even advertised autotourism as a way to strengthen the family. They pictured the prosperous middle-class family traveling together down Route 66 exploring the United States.

Much of the land Route 66 crossed had not experienced the same prosperity as the rest of the nation in the 1920s. The same technology that brought cars and highways also revolutionized farming with new machinery. However, when the overproduction of grains glutted the market during the 1920s, prices fell. Many farmers went bust, losing their farms as well as their jobs.

The unemployed farmers and other people who lived in rural areas were not quite sure what the new highways were, nor what businesses the highways could bring. But when Route 66 opened, they found out. Many unemployed farmers enthusiastically joined the retail petroleum business selling gasoline, oil, and other services to passing tourists. After these new entrepreneurs opened gas stations, they went on to build tourist courts and cafes where tourists could rest and try local foods. Billboards began advertising such roadside attractions as man-eating pythons. In those days any promise became fair in the battle to get the tourist to stop and spend money.

**THINK ABOUT IT:** Today franchised service stations and restaurants line the interstates of the United States from coast to coast. How has this standarization contributed to the reduction of regional differences?

**Americans enjoyed the fresh air and fellowship they found at roadside auto-camps.** *What kinds of goods and services would these autotourists require?*

CULVER PICTURES, INC.

# The Changing Nature of Work

## 1924: Assembly Line Boosts Sales and Earnings

IN 1924 THE TYPICAL FACTORY WORKER WORKED ON AN ASSEMBLY LINE, REPEATING ONE SMALL TASK. SOCIOLOGISTS ROBERT AND HELEN LYND WROTE OF ONE SUCH WORKER: "The worker is drilling metal joint rings for the front of a well-known automobile. He stands all day in front of his multiple drill-press, undrilled rings being brought constantly to his elbow and his product carted away."

The man described above drilled a pair of joint rings three times each minute, over and over again. In a nine-hour day, he performed his job 1,620 times.

Although a worker's contribution to making an automobile usually involved tedious work, many factory laborers could still hop into their own cars and drive home at the end of the work day. In that sense, Henry Ford's dream of 1907 had come true. The assembly line sped up car manufacturing and reduced the cost of producing automobiles. Ford passed that savings on to his customers by slashing the prices of his cars.

## *Henry Ford and the Assembly Line*

Henry Ford was one of the first industrialists to act on the realization that each worker is also a consumer. If workers had more money, Ford reasoned, they could purchase more of his cars. So in 1914 Ford took the revolutionary action of doubling the wages of the workers at his plant in Highland Park, Michigan.

**Working for Henry Ford**   In an era when $2 a day was considered a generous wage, Ford offered $5

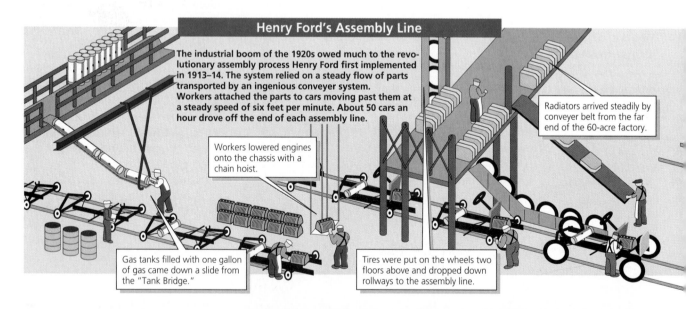

**Henry Ford's Assembly Line**

The industrial boom of the 1920s owed much to the revolutionary assembly process Henry Ford first implemented in 1913–14. The system relied on a steady flow of parts transported by an ingenious conveyer system. Workers attached the parts to cars moving past them at a steady speed of six feet per minute. About 50 cars an hour drove off the end of each assembly line.

Workers lowered engines onto the chassis with a chain hoist.

Radiators arrived steadily by conveyer belt from the far end of the 60-acre factory.

Gas tanks filled with one gallon of gas came down a slide from the "Tank Bridge."

Tires were put on the wheels two floors above and dropped down rollways to the assembly line.

## STUDY GUIDE

**As You Read**
Analyze the changes in the workplace for factory and white collar workers, and examine the trend for women to enter offices in new jobs. Also, think about the following concept and skills.

**Central Concept**
- understanding how **scientific management** changed the lives of factory and office workers and revolutionized American production during the 1920s

**Thinking Skills**
- recognizing assumptions
- comparing and contrasting
- identifying cause and effect

a day to workers of "thrifty habits." Workers who refused to learn English, rejected the company detective's advice, gambled, drank, or pursued "any malicious practice derogatory to . . . moral behavior" did not get the raise. In two years, three-quarters of Ford's workers made $5 a day.[1]

Other industrialists called Ford a "traitor to his class" because his actions defied the conventional wisdom of keeping wages low and prices high. However, Ford reasoned that well-paid workers would be less likely to seek other jobs and more likely to do their boring jobs willingly. In 1926 Ford again delighted the workers and shocked the business world by reducing the work week at his plant from a 48-hour, six-day week to a 40-hour, five-day week.

Ford could easily afford to cut back his worker's hours and increase their pay beyond the standards of the time. The assembly line methods that permitted mass production made tremendous profits for Ford, whose company earned an estimated $264,000 per day in 1922.

In addition to their increased wages, Ford's workers gained some other benefits from the new assembly line work. Because the jobs required no skills and little training, laborers could master their work quickly. In fact, almost anyone who wanted to work could do the new jobs.

Henry Ford employed ex-convicts, as well the physically and mentally handicapped. He believed a worker to be "equally acceptable whether he has been in Sing Sing or at Harvard and we do not even inquire from which place he has graduated. All that he needs is the desire to work." Indeed, Henry Ford prided himself on hiring thousands of immigrants and members of minority groups who might not otherwise have had good job opportunities.

**Man or Machine?**   The Czech immigrants who worked for Henry Ford and in other factories brought a new word to the United States with them during the 1920s. The word *robot* came to mean a machine that acts like a person or a person who acts like a machine. In the new factories, it began to be difficult to tell where the worker ended and the machine began.

Typically, a mechanized assembly line delivered the material to workers at waist level, so they did not have to waste valuable time in walking, stooping, reaching, or bending. Each worker, doing a tiny part of the total job, worked at a pace set by the machine.

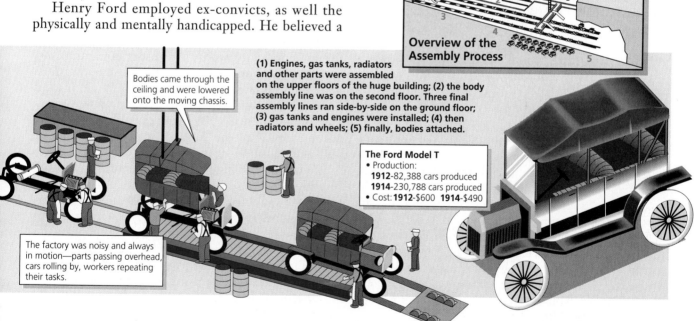

**Overview of the Assembly Process**

Bodies came through the ceiling and were lowered onto the moving chassis.

(1) Engines, gas tanks, radiators and other parts were assembled on the upper floors of the huge building; (2) the body assembly line was on the second floor. Three final assembly lines ran side-by-side on the ground floor; (3) gas tanks and engines were installed; (4) then radiators and wheels; (5) finally, bodies attached.

**The Ford Model T**
• Production:
  **1912**-82,388 cars produced
  **1914**-230,788 cars produced
• Cost: **1912**-$600  **1914**-$490

The factory was noisy and always in motion—parts passing overhead, cars rolling by, workers repeating their tasks.

STUDY GUIDE

**Recognizing Assumptions**
Many people praised Henry Ford's generosity in raising his workers' wages, citing his idealism and his "faith in human nature." But Ford knew that mass production could yield high profits only if plenty of workers could afford to buy the goods they produced. "Profits," Ford said, "belong primarily to the business and the workers are only part of the business."

1  How could workers in Ford's Highland Park plant qualify for the $5 daily wage?

*T*here were presses that punched sheet steel. *All that the worker had to do was to insert the steel before the press descended and withdraw his hands quickly. But some men became fatigued, or surrendered to the numbness or monotony, or were simply careless. The machines cut off their hands.*

Geoffrey Perrett,
*America in the Twenties*, 1982

The steel company prevented these accidents by chaining the workers' hands to their machines. All day, the men's hands jerked back and forth, even when they were out of material. As one visitor to a model steel plant wrote, "There they work, chained to their machines, as galley slaves were chained to their oars."

Indeed, mass production meant skilled jobs got broken down into their most basic operations, to be repeated without pause almost all day long. Many workers, not just those who worked in Ford plants, held these repetitive jobs on assembly lines. Skills that had taken a lifetime to master soon became unnecessary. In 1924 a steel worker lamented:

*Y*ou had to know how to use the old carbon *steel to keep it from gettin' hot and spoilin' the edge. But this "high speed steel" and this new "stelite" don't absorb the heat and are harder than carbon steel. You can take a boy fresh from the farm and in three days he can manage a machine as well as I can, and I've been at it twenty-seven years.*

Robert S. Lynd and Helen Merrell Lynd,
*Middletown*, 1929

The new simple factory jobs did not require much training or thought. But to do the job quickly and efficiently demanded discipline. Foremen at the Ford plant prohibited the workers from leaning on their machines, sitting, squatting, singing, talking, whistling, smoking, or smiling on the job. Laborers had to talk like ventriloquists, not moving their lips, in what they called the "Ford whisper." They set their faces in frozen grimaces that became known as "Fordization of the face." Describing the atmosphere in his auto plant, Ford explained, "There is not much personal contact. The men do their work and go home."

Breaking down skilled work into tiny jobs increased production and profits, raised the wages of laborers, and provided jobs for thousands of people in need of work. However, it also threatened to turn the workers into machines. Although Henry Ford was the first to use the assembly line for large-scale mass production, the blessings and curses of the new mass production both stemmed from the theories of Frederick Taylor.[2]

## Scientific Management

*B*orn into an upper-class family in Pennsylvania, Frederick Taylor joined the Midvale Steel Works in Philadelphia as a laborer in 1878 at the age of 22. Within six years, the young man had become chief engineer and a careful observer of his co-workers.

For himself, Taylor appreciated the virtue of hard work, calling it "the real monotonous grind which trains character." But the wealthy young man concluded that most of his fellow factory workers were lazy and sloppy in performing their jobs. Taylor argued that developing more efficient working methods would heighten the workers' productivity, raise their wages, and profit the company.

Taylor's theory, which came to be known as **scientific management,** suggested that efficiency, or time-study, experts analyze each work operation and find ways to minimize the time necessary to do a job. Breaking each job into its simplest operations, time-study experts would train workers to carry out their simplified tasks and then time them to see if they could meet the new standards. Taylor advised management to offer cash incentives to workers who produced more than the standard quantities that had been established for their jobs.

Taylor successfully tested scientific management at Midvale Steel. At first both management and labor criticized Taylor's ideas. The bosses at Midvale opposed scientific management because it disrupted their long-established routines. For their part, the workers remained unimpressed by the money incentives. They suspected scientific management of being simply the "scientific sweating of labor."

One new industry, however, had no traditional routines to be upset by Taylor's revolutionary new

**Comparing and Contrasting**
Before mass production, many factory workers took pride in their skills and in the goods their work produced. Furthermore, workers set the speed and rhythm of their own work.

Mass production meant endless repetition of a few easily learned movements at a speed set by the machine. After a day on the assembly line, workers could claim no one thing they had made.

2 The assembly line made mass production possible. What were some of the advantages and disadvantages of mass production?

methods. The auto industry adapted Taylor's ideas from the very beginning.

In 1911 Taylor published his major work, *The Principles of Scientific Management*. That year, the Taylor Society was founded to spread Taylor's ideas. Four years later, Taylor's book had been translated into eight European languages and Japanese.

By the 1920s many established industries had gotten the message that saving time meant greater profits. Scientific management truly came into its own during the anti-union era that followed the post-World War I strikes. In the 1920s the Taylor Society boasted new members from some of the country's biggest corporations: General Electric, DuPont, and American Telephone and Telegraph (A. T. & T.)

Taylor's ideas about the organization of the workplace influenced not just factories, but offices as well. During the 1920s even the physical layout of offices began to resemble factories with their assembly lines. Papers passed from worker to worker along a moving belt. A writer described one such firm in 1929:

*Orders are passed along by means of a belt and lights from a chief clerk to a series of checkers and typists, each of whom does one operation. The girl at the head of the line interprets the order, puts down the number and indicates the trade discount; the second girl prices the order, takes off the discount, adds carriage charges and totals; the third girl gives the order and number and makes a daily record; the fourth girl puts this information on an alphabetical index; the fifth girl time-stamps it: it next goes along the belt to one of several typists, who makes a copy in sextuplicate and puts on address labels; the seventh girl checks it and sends it to the storeroom.*[3]

C. Wright Mills,
*White Collar*, 1951

## *The New White Collar Workers*

During the 1920s more new workers than ever before were going to work each day dressed in business clothes. Although women were among their ranks, these workers became known as "white collar workers" because of the white shirts and ties uniformly worn by the men.

As corporations grew larger and more complex, the industrial transformation of the early twentieth century gave rise to a host of new occupations—from typist, clerk, and stenographer to junior manager. Thriving insurance and banking industries added to the growing need for still more white collar jobs.

Indeed, between 1920 and 1930, the ranks of white collar workers—professionals, wholesale and retail salespeople, and clerks—swelled by 36 percent, from 10.5 to 14.3 million people. During the same decade, the number of manual workers increased only 13 percent, from 16.9 to 19.2 million.

White collar work got another boost from thriving U.S. factories. By 1929, led by the supercharged automobile industry, nine of the 20 biggest U.S. corporations were turning out consumer goods. Exploding with new products, businesses now needed to persuade consumers to buy these new goods. Two growing white collar professions—sales and advertising—proved indispensable to big business.

**The Lure of Sales**   Popular magazines in the 1920s advertised, "Don't envy successful salesmen—be one!" Descriptions of salespeople making $5,000 to $30,000 a year at a time when even autoworkers were earning less than $2,000 a year, lured thousands of young people into the profession.

If they showed brashness and drive, salespeople could make a lot of money. But the pressure to succeed could be devastating. Many companies used the quota system in which, to keep the job, each salesperson had to sell 20 or 25 percent more every year.

To make a quota, a salesperson needed to learn and apply sales psychology taught in a variety of books. According to a 1925 essay by famed lawyer Clarence Darrow, a leading sales textbook of the time even compared selling to hunting for prey: "The expert fisherman tries out the fish—if one kind of bait doesn't get the strike, he changes. . . . He carefully lays his snares, places his bait and then the unsuspecting Prospect falls into the trap."

Sometimes a salesperson couldn't simply wait for a prospect to fall into the trap. A more aggressive approach was in order. *Selling News*, a magazine for salespeople, awarded a cash prize for this winning

**Identifying Cause and Effect**

Like factories, offices eagerly adopted the new assembly line methods to save time and money. Because the new office machines cost so much, managers hesitated to leave them idle. Type-writers, adding machines, dicta-phones—all were centralized into pools. Like factory workers, white collar employees worked on only one machine and performed the same job all day long.

3  Describe how Frederick Taylor's scientific management heightened workers' productivity, raised wages, and increased a company's profits.

entry to a "sales ideas" contest. An electric cleaner salesperson who had seen a woman shaking a rug out of a second-story window told the following story. Since the door to her upstairs rooms was open, the salesman walked right in, pretending that he had an appointment to clean the woman's house. In the words of the salesman, the woman was "very much surprised, assuring me that I had the wrong number. But during my very courteous apologies I had managed to get my cleaner connected and in action. The result was that I walked out minus the cleaner, plus her contract and check."

The salespeople who could succeed, using whatever methods, won the biggest rewards. One company gave a yearly banquet at which the best salesperson feasted on oysters, roast turkey, and an ice cream dessert. The runner-up was served the same feast, but without the oysters. So it went, down to the one with the worst sales record. This poor person's humiliation was served up before the group on a small plate of boiled beans and crackers.[4]

**The Advertising Worker** If the salesperson sold Americans what they needed and wanted, it was the advertising worker who persuaded Americans to need and want what was being offered for sale. Indeed, by 1925, U.S. corporations spent over a billion dollars a year on advertising. In the 1920s advertiser and author Bruce Barton argued, "Advertising is the spark plug on the cylinder of mass production . . . and sustains a system that has made us leaders of the free world." The advertising company Barton began started with a $10,000 loan in 1919 and eventually became a multi-million-dollar business.

Who worked for a typical large advertising company? Most advertising workers were young, white college graduates or former newspaper writers. Advertising companies hired women for the special knowledge only they could provide about the types of products women used and wanted. However, in the largest ad agencies, male employees outnumbered females by ten to one. As in many other businesses, men in advertising occupied almost all the positions that carried executive authority. Even the best paid women copywriters earned far less than men who performed the same jobs.

Advertising workers got used to producing at a hectic pace. One ad copy writer later recalled, "If you have never wrapped a cold towel around your head at three o'clock in the morning in an effort to get a piece of copy ready for delivery before nine,

As electricity became available to all, salespeople like these found a ready market for their wares.

UNIVERSITY OF LOUISVILLE PHOTOGRAPHIC ARCHIVES

**Comparing and Contrasting**
Before the 1920s salespersons sold Americans what they wanted to buy and advertisers described products in a factual way. Neither profession paid well. When business expanded during the 1920s, salespersons and advertisers used psychology to persuade Americans to buy things that they hadn't known they wanted. Both professions became better paying.

4 Give examples of the kinds of pressure that made selling so hectic during the 1920s. Why do you think people chose this kind of work despite the pressure?

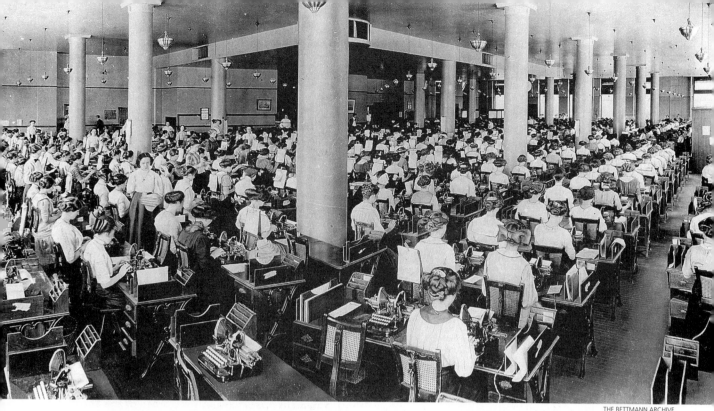

THE BETTMANN ARCHIVE

**In the 1920s many young women spent their working hours in large typing "pools" like this one.**

*What may have motivated women to choose this kind of work?*

you have never given it your all." The job turnover was high: More than one out of three advertising workers switched employers each year. But if an advertising worker could stand the exhausting pace, he or she could make an annual salary exceeding $5,000, more than three times what an automobile worker earned.

Advertisers prided themselves on knowing what Americans wanted. Indeed, they liked to consider themselves not advertising workers but "consumption engineers." Great business leaders, a 1920s advertising magazine boasted, might someday "learn almost as much about what the people of the United States really know about and are interested in as does the junior copy writer of a fourth rate advertising agency."

## Women in the Work Force

At the turn of the century, less than one in five women workers held clerical, managerial, sales, and professional positions. But when women began to flood the work force during the 1920s, many left their

houses dressed in black skirts and starched white blouses. These women workers were heading for offices and stores, not factories. By 1930, 44 percent of employed women worked at white collar jobs.

**Typecasting Women**  It all started with the typewriter. E. Remington and Sons sold the first typewriting machines in 1874. Almost all the new typists were middle class, high school educated, and female. Why? To do the job, a worker needed to be a good speller and possess a knowledge of grammar, capitalization, and punctuation. Most lower-class men and women lacked these skills; a middle-class man with a high school diploma could find a much better-paying job.

For female high school graduates, however, the story was different. Before the typewriter, an educated working woman had few choices: she could become a teacher or a nurse or take a factory job for which she was overqualified. Even if typing paid no better than operating a machine in a factory, the new office work allowed an educated young woman to work in a clean, attractive environment.[5]

## STUDY GUIDE

**Recognizing Assumptions**
As young women began to work in new white collar professions such as typist, stenographer, and cashier, these professions became known as "woman's work." Employers assumed

that women worked only for luxuries or would work only until they got married. Therefore, these jobs paid far less than jobs requiring similar responsibility performed by men.

5 Why did women with high school educations flock to the new office and department store jobs even though the jobs paid no more than jobs in factories?

Previously, the clerical work in a typical office had been done by one man or a small group of male clerks, who could expect eventual promotion to managerial positions. All the new office technology—typewriters, dictaphones, telephones— could be operated by women who did not command high wages or look forward to advancement.

Since any of the new jobs could be performed as easily at one firm as another, the stenographer or typist found herself in a large "pool" of similarly skilled workers. In a book called *The Job*, Sinclair Lewis described such a pool, in which an "unrecognized horde of girls . . . merely copied or took the bright young men's dictation." He added, "They were expected to keep clean and be quick-moving; beyond that they were as unimportant to the larger phases of office politics as frogs to a summer hotel."

**Shop Clerks and Telephone Operators**   In the same way that secretarial work provided an alternative to nursing or teaching for female high school graduates, telephone companies and the new department stores offered women without a high school diploma a pleasant alternative to factory work or domestic service. By 1930, 736,000 women had gone to work as shop clerks, cash girls, wrappers, stock clerks, cashiers, or switchboard operators.

Women proved to be polite and eager employees. After all, shop work was easier than factory work and the environment was cleaner. The pay equalled or exceeded what they could earn performing unskilled labor. The job was important, too. It was up to the sales clerk to see that people's new needs and wants were satisfied.

**Men and Women in the Office**   By the 1920s offices and stores had two distinct cultures, neatly divided by sex. Women dominated in the clerical, unskilled occupations. There, neatness, orderliness, and courtesy played a big role, but job responsibility in-

CULVER PICTURES, INC.

**Ever-growing communications systems provided employment opportunities for women of the 1920s.**

volved simple, repetitive routines. Women's jobs provided little chance for advancement except to the positions of cashier or executive secretary, or, perhaps, to marriage. In fact, because secretarial work taught a woman endurance, modesty, and obedience, many people considered it perfect preparation for marriage.

Men, on the other hand, found jobs as managers, senior cashiers, chief clerks, head bookkeepers, floorwalkers, salespeople, or advertising workers. In these jobs, energy, initiative, and creativity paid off and could lead to a better position in the company.

Though the new work environment of the 1920s clearly defined the separate jobs of each sex, it also provided for the first time an opportunity for educated men and women to meet and share the workplace. These new co-workers would soon become consumers of a host of new products produced by thriving U.S. factories.

**SECTION REVIEW**

**Checking Facts**

1. Give three reasons why Henry Ford doubled his workers' wages in 1914.
2. Describe some of the difficulties of being an automotive worker during the 1920s.
3. Why did management and labor at Midvale Steel oppose scientific management at first? Why did the auto industry adopt the new methods from the beginning?

4. Contrast the growth of white collar workers with that of manual workers during the 1920s.
5. List three white collar jobs held by men in the 1920s. Compare these to white collar jobs held by women in terms of qualifications, salary, and opportunity for advancement.

**Thinking Critically**

6. **Recognizing Assumptions** What assumptions lay behind Henry Ford's hiring practices?
7. **Identifying Cause and Effect** Why were there suddenly so many new white collar workers during the 1920s?

**Linking Across Time**

8. Are any jobs today thought to be primarily for men or for women?

# Identifying Text Patterns

A clear organizational pattern helps a writer communicate an intended message. Recognizing organizational patterns and identifying the intent of each can improve reading comprehension and writing effectiveness.

## Learning the Skill

Historical writing is often organized chronologically, relating events in the order that they occur. Look for other organizational patterns as you read:

### Cause-and-Effect Pattern

The cause-and-effect pattern expresses causal relationships: it clarifies which events caused other events to happen. Often, key words make the relationship explicit, as in the sentence: "Between 1920 and 1928, about 2,000 mergers took place, *resulting in* the loss of hundreds of firms."

Turn to page 278 and read the paragraph on scientific management. In this example, the causal relationship is implicit. Note that the cause is stated first: time-study experts analyze each work operation. The causal link to the four effects that follow is implied rather than stated.

In both these examples, the cause precedes the effects. Sometimes an effect will be stated first, followed by its cause or causes.

### Compare-and-Contrast Pattern

The compare-and-contrast pattern highlights similarities or differences. In historical writing, this pattern is often used to show how ideas or methods change over time. Read the two paragraphs on page 282 that describe differences in office positions held by men and women in the 1920s. Women held clerical positions that stressed obedience and endurance, while men filled managerial positions that rewarded assertiveness and creativity. Words such as *distinct* and phrases such as *on the other hand* are text clues that point to a compare-and-contrast pattern.

### Spatial Pattern

A spatial pattern explains how places, people, objects, or events relate to one another in terms of location. Examine the description of the diagonal path of Route 66 on page 275. Find the key words that show place relationships, such as *straddled and between.*

### Other Patterns

The chart on this page summarizes the patterns discussed above, as well as several others.

## Practicing the Skill

1. Refer back to the chapter to find examples of at least four organizational patterns shown below.
2. Find magazine articles that discuss the relationship between business and government today. Identify any organizational patterns.

### Organizational Patterns

| Organization | Description | Text Clues |
|---|---|---|
| Cause-and-effect | Clarifies causal relationships | because, consequently, led to, resulted in, therefore |
| Compare-and-contrast | Highlights similarities or differences | although, by comparison, however, in contrast, similarly, unlike |
| Chronological | Describes events in the order in which they occurred | in 1917, at 10 a.m., after, as, before, finally, first, second, last, next, when |
| Pro-and-con | Juxtaposes arguments in favor of and against an idea, proposal, or action | in favor of, in support of, on the plus side, the case against, the downside is, the disadvantages are |
| Problem-and-solution | States problems and discusses actual or possible solutions | the problem is, the challenge we face, the difficulty is, the trouble was, answered, resolved, solved, the answer is, the solution was |
| Spatial | Explains locational relationships | above, beneath, beyond, next to, north, south, east, west Place names: Chicago, Oklahoma |
| Question-and-answer | Links questions and answers | how, why. when, where, what, who clearly, undoubtedly, obviously, the answer is, the correct response is |

# The Jazz Age

*During the 1920s, the golden age of jazz, Americans danced to its joyous music at a frantic and ever-accelerating pace. Inspired by jazz, Americans began to improvise leisure-time activities that had no purpose other than having fun. People roared through the decade intent on enjoying every exciting moment of it, as though the entire group shared an unspoken premonition that it could not last.*

Louis Armstrong played the trumpet, and his wife, Lil Hardin, played the piano in **King Oliver's Dixieland Jazz Band,** also called King Oliver's Creole Jazz Band.

**Jazz** was born in the streets of the South, migrated north, and spread into urban neighborhoods, where amateur street musicians enjoyed re-creating the sounds.

Poised and chic **flappers,** like this one, set a sophisticated style of dress for women in the jazz age.

# 23 SKIDOO

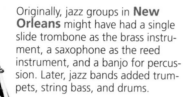

Originally, jazz groups in **New Orleans** might have had a single slide trombone as the brass instrument, a saxophone as the reed instrument, and a banjo for percussion. Later, jazz bands added trumpets, string bass, and drums.

In the 1920s **women's amateur golf** was dominated by the British, but in the United States the sport was catching on fast, and more women took to the fairways.

By 1920 one million African Americans had migrated north. As entertainment, this crowded **street fair in Harlem** had two advantages: it was free, and it was right in the neighborhood.

# Chapter 8 Review

**1916**
Many African Americans
migrate north for jobs.

**November 1918**
World War I ends.

**August 1920**
Suffrage Amendment gives
women the right to vote.

| 1915 | 1916 | 1917 | 1918 | 1919 | 1920 | 1921 | 1922 |

**November 1917**
Bolshevik Revolution
installs a communist
government in Russia.

**January 1920**
Palmer raids jail
thousands during
Red Scare.

## Summary

Use the following outline as a tool for reviewing and summarizing the chapter. Copy the outline on your own paper, leaving spaces between headings to jot down notes about key events and concepts.

I. **Postwar Turmoil**
   A. Sacco and Vanzetti
   B. The Red Scare
   C. The Great Migration
   D. The Progressive Spirit in the 1920s

II. **The Republican Influence**
   A. Harding and the Teapot Dome
   B. Silent Cal and Big Business
   C. Herbert Hoover, the Wonder Boy
   D. Republican Foreign Policy

III. **Prosperity and American Business**
   A. The Glorification of Business
   B. A Booming Economy
   C. The Corporate Revolution
   D. Industry's Labor Policies

IV. **Changing Nature of Work**
   A. Henry Ford and the Assembly Line
   B. Scientific Management
   C. The New White Collar Workers
   D. Women in the Work Force

## Ideas, Events, and People

1. What were some of the causes of the Red Scare? Name at least three contributing factors.
2. Why did so many blacks migrate from the South to the North between 1916 and 1920?
3. What was the basis for Ole Hanson's view that the general strike in Seattle was the beginning of a revolution?
4. How did the Republican administrations of Harding and Coolidge aid big business?

5. In what two ways did the United States attempt to free itself from involvement in Europe during the 1920s?
6. Name two factors that contributed to the development of oligopolies in the 1920s.
7. List three types of welfare capitalism programs.
8. Why did Americans clamor for a national highway system?
9. How did Henry Ford implement the theory of scientific management?
10. List five white collar professions that grew during the 1920s.

## Social Studies Skills

**Identifying Text Patterns**

Name the organizational pattern of each of the following: the last three paragraphs in the first column on page 250, the last paragraph in the first column on page 268, and the second paragraph in the second column on page 268. Choose from these text patterns: cause-and-effect, compare-and-contrast, chronological, pro-and-con, problem-and-solution, spatial, and question-and-answer.

## Critical Thinking

1. **Recognizing Points of View**
   Identify the points of view held by whites and African Americans regarding the Great Black Migration. How did newspaper reports influence the formation of these viewpoints, especially in the Washington, D.C., area?

2. **Assessing Outcomes**
   The Republican presidents of the 1920s supported big business and rejected programs for the public welfare. How did the government's support of big business affect ordinary citizens both positively and negatively?

**August 1923**
President Harding dies.
Calvin Coolidge succeeds.

**March 1929**
Herbert Hoover
becomes president.

| 1923 | 1924 | 1925 | 1926 | 1927 | 1928 | 1929 | |

**August 1927**
Sacco and Vanzetti
are executed.

**August 1928**
Kellogg-Briand
Pact is signed.

**3. Identifying Cause and Effect**

The idolizing of businessmen created a national climate that benefited big business. What do you think might have been some negative effects of the glorification of business?

**4. Comparing and Contrasting**

Compare and contrast the careers of women and men in white collar professions in the 1920s.

## Extension and Application

**1. Linking Across Time**

The photo below shows Dr. Anna Shaw and Mrs. Carrie Chapman Catt in 1918 leading 20,000 women down New York's Fifth Avenue in a march for suffrage. How have women's roles in politics changed or remained the same since the 1920s? Interview adult women about how they perceive their role in politics. Present the results of your interviews in an essay.

CULVER PICTURES

**2. Citizenship**

Research the requirements for setting up a small business in your community. Investigate areas such as government regulations, financing, and the costs of leasing space and buying equipment. The local chamber of commerce might direct you in your research. Write a report on your findings.

**3. Global Connections**

The United States emerged from World War I in a strong economic position. In contrast, the countries of war-torn Europe were burdened with debts and their farms and factories had been devastated. Choose one European nation that was involved in World War I and investigate its economy during the 1920s. Make charts, graphs, or other aids to compare the economy of the European nation with that of the United States.

**4. Cooperative Learning**

Work in small groups to research one aspect of the Sacco and Vanzetti trial. Then choose a medium for presenting your findings, such as a newspaper article, skit, or collage.

## Geography

1. Describe how cities such as New York, Chicago, Cleveland, and Washington, D.C., changed in the years after World War I. Why did they change?
2. On the map on page 254, which region had the most states denying women the right to vote before the Nineteenth Amendment passed? What factors made this region oppose woman suffrage?
3. Why was Chicago a likely location for the eastern end of Route 66?
4. The moving assembly line, scientific management, salespeople, and typing pools were part of the 1920s revolution in the workplace. Which change would be most likely to affect rural America? Why?

## CHAPTER 9

# A Prospering Society

### October 6, 1926: The Babe Sets World Series Record!

Sportsman's Park in St. Louis, Missouri, was the setting for 40,000 fans to witness the fourth game of baseball's World Series. Millions more were listening to popular radio announcer Graham McNamee as Babe Ruth came to bat. McNamee reported, "The Babe is waving that wand of his over the plate. Bell is loosening up his arm. The Babe hits it clear into the center-field bleachers for a home run! For a home run! Did you hear what I said? Oh, what a shot! . . . Oh, boy! Wow! That is a World Series record, three home runs in one series game, and what a home run!"

No one better symbolized the period of the 1920s than home run hit-

> *No one better symbolized the period of the 1920s than home run hitter Babe Ruth.*

THE BETTMANN ARCHIVE

*The birth of mass communications in the 1920s made sports stars like Babe Ruth famous all over the world. Babe's name was known worldwide.*

ter Babe Ruth. He was a contradictory man with an amazing athletic talent, a gigantic appetite for pleasure, and a casual disregard for rules.

Like its baseball hero, the United States also exhibited some basic contradictions during the 1920s. At the same time most of the country was plunging breathlessly into the new era, many Americans sought to return to a simpler past. Deep conflicts in the United States over religion and immigration added turmoil to the excitement of this decade, rapidly becoming full of radios, newspapers, movies, and advertising.

Babe Ruth was a perfect hero for a country undergoing vast change in a bold, hungry, and lawless era.

*Part of the exciting cinema scene in this prospering era, Mexican actress Dolores Del Rio starred in the United States in the 1920s.*

# Growth of the Middle Class

## 1922: Sinclair Lewis Publishes *Babbitt*

WRITER SINCLAIR LEWIS INVENTED THE BOOMING TOWN OF ZENITH IN 1922 FOR HIS NOVEL *BABBITT*. IT COULD HAVE BEEN ANY ONE OF MANY AMERICAN cities in the 1920s. George Babbitt declared that:

*Zenith manufactures more condensed milk and evaporated cream, more paper boxes, and more lighting-fixtures, than any other city in the United States, if not in the world. But it is not so universally known that we also stand second in the manufacture of package-butter, sixth in the giant realm of motors and automobiles, and somewhere about third in cheese, leather bindings, tar roofing, breakfast food, and overalls!*

*. . . When I add that we have an unparalleled number of miles of paved streets, bathrooms, vacuum cleaners, and all the other signs of civilization; that our library and art museum are well supported and housed in convenient and roomy buildings; that our park-system is more than up to par, with its handsome driveways adorned with grass, shrubs, and statuary, then I give but a hint of the all-round unlimited greatness of Zenith!*

Sinclair Lewis,
*Babbitt*, 1922

HOWARD GISKE PHOTOGRAPHS

## Americans as Consumers

The industrialization of the late nineteenth century was finally beginning to offer real rewards to residents of towns like Zenith. Between 1923 and 1929, American workers saw their real income rise 11 percent. With more than enough money simply to live on, many American workers could buy more of the goods they produced. They began to feel that they were part of a growing middle class.

In the 1920s many middle-class American consumers improved their **standard of living.** This means the necessities and luxuries an individual or group enjoys. Compared to people overseas, Americans like George Babbitt could afford to buy more goods and, compared to people overseas, Americans like George Babbitt had a higher standard of living.

### New Consumer Products
Thanks to refrigeration, Americans ate fresh fruits and vegetables, now available in stores year round. Thanks to improved packaging, they bought a wider variety of packaged food, including that great invention, sliced bread. They now purchased ready-made clothes, which replaced home-sewn or tailored garments, especially for men.

---

## STUDY GUIDE

### As You Read
Identify the changes industrialization, the automobile, advertising, and the new youth culture brought to American life. Also, think about the following concepts and skills.

### Central Concepts
• understanding how the **standard of living** rose for many, though not all, Americans during the 1920s
• recognizing how the new **mass media** changed buying habits

### Thinking Skills
• making generalizations
• identifying cause and effect

Some regional differences between Americans began to blur as clothing and other mass-produced goods became cheaper and more popular. In most parts of the country, workers were buying identical electric irons, vacuum cleaners, washing machines, toasters, fans, and refrigerators.

These marvelous machines reduced the time it took to do housework. In their new leisure time, Americans could now listen to radios and phonographs, or talk to each other on the telephone.

Without electricity, all these machines would have stayed on their inventors' drawing boards. During the 1920s the electrical current to run the machines became more widely available, not just in the houses of the wealthy but also in the homes of many average Americans.

Not all American homes had electricity. Many parts of rural America, especially in the South, were not electrified for many years. But even without electricity, some working-class homes still showed an improvement in their standard of living during this decade. In the 1920s many poor people traded wood fuel for coal, walked on linoleum floors instead of wooden ones, and retired their water buckets when fresh water began to gush out of indoor faucets.

**Poverty in the Midst of Plenty** However, not all Americans were able to improve their standard of living during this period. Low wages and unemployment combined to drive many American families into poverty. Farmers and other workers suffered when the goods they produced dropped in price.

For example, thousands of farmers had replaced their workhorses with Henry Ford's Fordson tractor. This efficient machine allowed farmers to produce more wheat and corn than America could consume. In a market economy, when supply exceeds demand, prices tend to drop. During the 1920s a glut of produce sent farm prices into a steep decline. In 1919 a bushel of corn could buy five gallons of gasoline. By 1921 it only fetched a half gallon.

The period brought hardships for coal miners and textile workers, too. During the 1920s industries began to use electricity rather than coal to power their machinery. This drop in demand for coal drove the price down and put many miners out of work.

Due to changes in fashion—rising hemlines and a new demand for silk stockings—Americans now were buying less cotton. As cotton prices plunged, many textile factories in the Northeast and South were forced to shut down. In fact, for the first time in a century, America's overall factory employment decreased.

By some estimates, a third of American families lived below minimum levels for a decent life. Their inability to buy what the United States produced would contribute to the unraveling of the booming economy by the end of the decade.

Despite the plight of farmers and workers in depressed industries, however, most Americans in the 1920s shared George Babbitt's satisfaction. The automobile was beginning to give even ordinary Americans a share in the United States' plenty.

**Average Annual Employee Income**

Mining
Manufacturing
Public Education
Agriculture

**Not all workers' wages increased during the 1920s.**
*In which areas did income decrease?*

## Americans Take to the Road

More than any single consumer item, the automobile defined the America of the 1920s. In 1927 Americans owned four out of five of the world's cars, averaging one motor vehicle for every 5.3 persons. The Model T car Henry Ford introduced in 1908 transformed the automobile from a high-priced item to one many moderate-income families could afford. On May 27, 1927, when the last of 15 million Model T's rolled off the line, the average

STUDY GUIDE

**Making Generalizations**
During the 1920s new tractors allowed farmers to produce their crops more efficiently, but prices for farm products fell because the supply far outstripped demand. Coal miners and textile workers, too, found their standard of living falling in the 1920s when their products were no longer needed in great quantities. Thus we can generalize that American workers who suffered economically during the 1920s tended to work in fields where production grew faster than demand (agriculture), or where demand had suddenly dropped (mining and textiles).

American family made $2,000 a year and could buy a new car for under $300.

Sharing so visibly in the wealth of society, more and more Americans came to feel that the booming Coolidge economy was working for them. They enthusiastically entered a new era, the age of the automobile. In turn, the age of the automobile would revolutionize American life for decades to come.

**Shifting the Economy**  Automobile manufacturing became America's biggest industry during the 1920s, and it soon boosted the entire economy. Cars required vast quantities of steel, lead, nickel, and gasoline. Workers in all these industries thrived. An-

other five million Americans labored to produce the glass and rubber that automobile making demanded.

Businesses flourished to serve the needs of a newly mobile nation. Garages, filling stations, hot dog stands, restaurants, tearooms, tourists' roadside camps—all sprang into existence only after the automobile drove onto the American scene.

Besides boosting industry, the automobile radically changed the face of the country. Villages along the new automobile routes thrived, while villages along the railroad lines began to disappear.

At the end of World War I, the United States had just 7,000 miles of concrete roads. By 1927 a network of 50,000 miles was growing at the rate of 10,000 miles each year. Even-numbered highways like Route 66 ran east to west, and odd-numbered highways ran north and south. States paid for these roads by taxing gasoline, which few Americans minded.

**The Romance of the Automobile**  The automobile was more than just a convenient way to get from one place to another. It soon became part of the American dream. Henry Ford boasted that customers could have a Model T in any color "so long as it is black." But by the middle 1920s, Americans wanted

The 1920s road map to the left shows the growing network of roads drivers used. Automobiles crowd Nantasket Beach, Massachusetts, on the Fourth of July in the early 1920s in the photo below.

their cars to make a fashion statement. With the invention of lacquer finishes, automobiles of 1925 and 1926 delighted buyers with bold new shades from Arabian Sand to Versailles Violet.

Even Henry Ford had to give in. In May 1927 Ford shut down his plant and scrapped the plain black Model T that had been America's first real car. Ford's announcement of the brand-new Model A was a key event of 1927. Beginning at 3:00 A.M. on December 2, almost one million people lined up in front of Ford's New York headquarters, eagerly trying to catch the first glimpse of Ford's colorful new cars.

**Driving the Culture**    The car changed American culture in countless ways. The dating habits of young people, the Sunday outings of families, the places people lived and vacationed, and the ways people shopped—all were affected by the automobile.

By 1927, four out of five cars had closed tops, compared with only one in ten in 1919. The new, closed car was a room on wheels. Now protected from the weather, teenagers especially enjoyed the privacy of closed cars.

On Sundays, many families hopped into their cars for short day-trips. With their new mobility, many city workers moved to houses in the new suburbs. Families with cars traveled to once-distant places.

One such traveler described his stay at a roadside camp in North Carolina. The tourists had come from as far away as Washington state:

> *There were fourteen cars in the camp, ranging all the way from dusty Fords to big and glittering limousines with balloon tires and tremendous horse-power. . . . And for the first time in history, the common, ordinary "fo'kes" of the North and South are meeting one another on a really large scale, mostly by means of the National chariot—the Ford car.*
>
> C. P. Russell,
> "The Pneumatic Hegira,"
> *The Outlook*, December 9, 1925

In addition to bringing far-flung Americans together for the first time, the automobile also saddled many people with their first debt. Eager to own a car, a person could now put a deposit down, drive a new

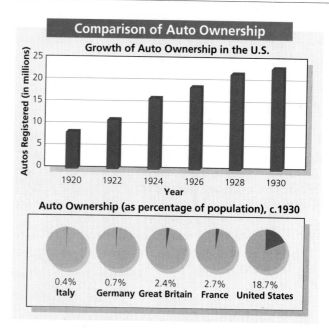

### Comparison of Auto Ownership
**Growth of Auto Ownership in the U.S.**

**Auto Ownership (as percentage of population), c.1930**

0.4% Italy    0.7% Germany    2.4% Great Britain    2.7% France    18.7% United States

**The automobile industry boomed in the United States during the 1920s.** *According to the graphs, about how many more automobiles were registered in the United States in 1930 than 1920? How did automobile ownership in the United States in 1930 compare with automobile ownership in Italy, Germany, Great Britain, and France?*

car away, and pay off the balance, plus interest, in installments. By 1927, two out of three cars were purchased on the installment, or time-payment, plan.

A banker who loaned money to prospective car buyers bemoaned the change in American habits of thrift, including his own, in an essay, written in 1925:

> *The ease with which a car can be purchased on the time-payment plan is all too easy a road to ruin. The habit of thrift can never be acquired through so wasteful a medium as an automobile. Instead, the habit of spending must be acquired, for with the constant demand for fuel, oil, and repairs, together with the heavy depreciation, the automobile stands unique as the most extravagant piece of machinery ever devised for the pleasure of man. But—I still drive one myself. I must keep up with the procession.*[1]
>
> William Ashdown,
> "Confessions of an Automobilist,"
> *Atlantic Monthly*, June 1925

## STUDY GUIDE

### Identifying Cause and Effect
The automobile industry had a great impact on the United States. The new industry put Americans to work, producing both the automobile itself and the goods that automobile making required. Businesses came into existence specifically to serve car owners. The auto fostered the growth of suburbs, and changed the dating, recreational, and buying patterns of Americans.

1 What effects did the automobile have on American culture?

## Selling America

Even thrifty Americans like William Ashdown felt pressured to buy cars on the installment plan. One reason was the brash salesmanship practiced by the dealers.

A Ford dealer speaking with Jesse Rainsford Sprague said he had been instructed by his boss to sell 20 cars a month in a depressed rural area. In speaking of one customer, the dealer said:

> *The man was a poor devil of a renter seven or eight miles out of town who never had enough cash ahead to buy a wheelbarrow, but Burke insisted that one of my salesmen go out there with him to try and land a sale. When they got there a couple of the children were down with whooping cough and a hailstorm had laid out his bean crop, but Burke came back and told me he would expect me to put over a Ford on the fellow before he came on his next trip.*

"Confessions of a Ford Dealer," *Harper's Monthly Magazine*, June 1927

**Buying on Time** Automobiles weren't the only product Americans were buying on **credit**, by putting money down and paying the balance in installments. In 1928, 85 percent of furniture, 80 percent of phonographs, 75 percent of washing machines and radios, and 70 percent of refrigerators were also bought on credit.

Buying on time could add as much as 40 percent to the price consumers eventually paid. But for the first time, buyers could have an item without having

saved enough money to pay for it. That $43.50 phonograph became irresistible when the price read, "$5 down and $5 a month."

Most Americans no longer looked at debt as shameful. Instead, they began to regard installment buying as an easy way to raise their standard of living.

**Chain Stores** If Americans were buying more and buying on the installment plan, they were also shopping in a different type of store. In the twenties, Americans flocked to the new chain stores that began to spring up all over the country—grocery stores like A&P, Safeway, and Piggly Wiggly, and department stores like J.C. Penney and Sears, Roebuck. In 1918 there were 29,000 such stores. By 1929 there were 160,000.

Now that customers could hop into their cars and drive to a chain store, the owners of the traditional corner stores lost their main advantage—convenience. In addition to being convenient, the chainstores also offered lower prices, greater reliability, better service, and wider choice. At Woolworth, for example, a shopper could for ten cents or less buy anything from Hebrew New Year cards to Venetian Night Incense, from a Mammoth Tulip sundae to a packet of gumdrops or foreign stamps.[2]

**Advertising** Americans' buying habits changed most of all because of the sudden growth of advertising. Advertising itself wasn't new, of course. Since colonial times, American retailers had used newspapers to inform the public about products and prices. What revolutionized advertising in the 1920s was the idea of using it to create consumer demand.

Even President Calvin Coolidge, that tight-lipped and thrifty man, acknowledged the power of advertis-

*Holeproof Hosiery*

HOLEPROOF is the hosiery of lustrous beauty and fine texture that wears so well. It is not surprising, therefore, that it is selected by many people who can afford to pay far more for their hose, but who prefer the Holeproof combination of style and serviceability at such reasonable prices.

Obtainable in Pure Silk, Silk Faced, and Lusterized Lisle styles for men, women and children in the season's popular colors. If your dealer cannot supply you, write for price list and illustrated booklets.

HOLEPROOF HOSIERY COMPANY, Milwaukee, Wisconsin
Holeproof Hosiery Company of Canada, Limited, London, Ontario

CULVER PICTURES

**Advertisements like this induced the American public to buy many goods.**

**Making Generalizations**
Generalizations based on statistical data are more reliable than those based on opinion. The generalization that advertising became big business in the 1920s is based on statistics such as these: In

1929 corporations spent $1.8 billion on ads; advertising agencies in the 1920s employed 600,000 people; in 1927 Henry Ford spent $1.3 million on newspaper ads for his new Model A Ford.

**2** List two ways American buying habits changed during the 1920s.

Movies, as well as advertising, emphasized youth and beauty in the 1920s. Actress Helene Costello is shown above dancing in *Lights of New York* (1928).

**Every well-dressed flapper carried a fancy purse similar to the beaded bag shown at the right.**

ing to make "new thoughts, new desires and new actions" seem attractive to an impressionable public. He added, "It is the most potent influence in adopting, and changing the habits and modes of life, affecting what we eat, what we wear, and the work and play of the whole nation."

Advertising suddenly sprang into prominence because Americans' purchases could barely keep pace with the factories' explosion of new goods. Advertisers helped sell their clients' products.

The new **mass media** allowed advertisers to reach large numbers of people at the same time. Newspapers, radio stations, billboards, and national magazines all bombarded consumers with the message: Buy, buy, buy!

Advertising was big business in the 1920s. In fact, critics complained that for every dollar spent to educate consumers in what to buy, a mere 70 cents went to pay for schools.

## Youth Sets the Scene

During this decade advertisers took advantage of the nation's growing fascination with youth to sell their products. Indeed, never before had American culture idolized the young as it did in the twenties. The destruction of so many young men in World War I seemed to place a special premium on youth.

Now, instead of young people modeling themselves on their elders, adults tried to act like children.

**Fashions and Fads** As youth came to mean stylishness, young people became the models for fashion, dress, music, and language. Styles that began on college campuses spread quickly to the public, thanks to cheap mass production and advertising in the national mass media. Women all over the country wore yellow rain slickers and multi-colored bandannas at the waist. Men sported raccoon coats and golf stockings.

Other fads spread equally quickly. In fact, the 1920s could be called the age of the **fad**—a sudden explosion of interest in some product or activity. In Baltimore, for example, 15-year-old Avon Foreman sat on a flagpole for 10 days, 10 hours, 10 minutes, and 10 seconds in 1929. For months, Americans everywhere tried to do the same. Then they turned their attention elsewhere. Like the automobile, mass-produced items, and national advertising, the fads of the 1920s helped establish a common culture.[3]

**New Ideals of Beauty** The Gibson Girl, an ideal of feminine beauty before World War I, had long, flowing hair. Her dress emphasized her womanly figure, highlighted her tiny waist, and covered her legs.

### STUDY GUIDE

**Identifying Cause and Effect**
During the 1920s advertisers increasingly turned their attention to youthful buyers. Because young people were eager consumers who changed their styles often, they promoted a rapid turnover of clothing and accessories. This led to business growth and the expansion of certain industries, promoting the general prosperity of the 1920s.

3  How did fashions spread during the 1920s? How do fashions spread today?

The 1920s girl—at least the one promoted in advertising and the movies—turned this modest image upside down and inside out, and emerged as a flapper. Named for the open galoshes she flapped around in, the flapper bound her chest to flatten it, loosened her blouse and dropped its waist, lifted her hemline, and rolled down her stockings. She bobbed her hair short and crowned the shorn locks with a close-fitting hat.

In 1928 the *Journal of Commerce* estimated that, in the previous 15 years, the average woman had stripped away 12¼ yards of material from her outfit, leaving only a scant 7 yards of cloth in addition to her rolled-down stockings. These were now silk or the new rayon, no longer the practical cotton or wool ones of the past.

The flapper may have looked like a little girl or even a little boy, but she applied makeup with a bold hand. So did her mother.

**Women's New Freedoms** Before World War I, women had been arrested for smoking or using profanity in public. Appearing at the beach without stockings or going without a corset was considered indecent exposure, even in cities as large and sophisticated as Chicago. Ten years later, the flapper smoked, drank, left her corset in the cloakroom at the dance, and went for joyrides in automobiles. Mainstream society, far from curbing women's new openness, seemed to encourage it.

For one thing, the women's movement and new laws gave women a greater measure of economic and intellectual independence than they had had before the war. In addition, the automobile gave the young a new and exciting independence from their families.

**School Days** If American teenagers were taking to the road in the evening, they were spending more time at school during the day. Most Americans could afford to keep their children in school longer now because many were finally prosperous enough not to need the children's wages. By 1930, 51 percent of all high school age youth were in school, compared with less than 6 percent in 1890.

The schools Americans built to accommodate their teenagers looked nothing like the little red schoolhouse of earlier years. In the 1920s the new high school building with its huge gym and gleaming laboratory was the pride of the neighborhood.

Only one out of eight young people went to college in 1930, but that was three times the number who had attended college at the turn of the century. Both high school and college students were eager consumers who helped set national trends for fashion and amusement. The mass media helped to make youth the bestselling image of the 1920s.

UNIVERSITY OF LOUISVILLE, PHOTOGRAPHIC ARCHIVES

**Classrooms in the United States were fuller in the 1920s than they had been in previous decades. The students in this class are conscious of health chores.** *Why do you think this class is having a fingernail inspection?*

## SECTION REVIEW

### Checking facts

1. Explain what we mean by the term **standard of living**. List three ways that it improved for most Americans during the 1920s.
2. How did the automobile change dating patterns of the young and the vacation habits of families?
3. Explain why the plain black Model T Ford no longer satisfied Americans in the late 1920s.
4. How did the increasing school attendance of young people show that most Americans were more prosperous during the 1920s?
5. Compare a fad of the 1920s with a fad of today.

### Thinking Critically

6. **Making Generalizations** Give evidence to support this generalization: The1920s would not have been as prosperous without the automobile industry.

7. **Identifying Cause and Effect** How did changes in women's fashion affect the cotton industry?

### Linking Across Time

8. The practice of buying products on time still exists today with the use of charge cards or payment plans. List at least two benefits and two drawbacks of this practice.

# Synthesizing

The writers of this book gathered information from many sources in order to present a story of how Americans have lived in the twentieth century. To integrate all the information into a cohesive story, the writers used a process called synthesis.

Being able to synthesize can be a useful skill for you as a student. Suppose you were called upon to write a research paper on the status of women in the 1920s. You would need to synthesize what you learn in your research to communicate it to others.

## Learning the Skill

To synthesize is to combine information obtained from separate sources or at different times. The skill involves analyzing information in order to make logical connections. The following three steps are basic to the process of synthesizing:

1. Select relevant information.
2. Analyze information and build connections.
3. Reinforce or modify connections as you acquire new information.

### Organizing Existing Ideas

Begin by detailing the ideas you already have about the status of women in the 1920s. You might use a graphic organizer to categorize facts. The graphic organizer on this page categorizes facts about women's status in four areas.

### Adding New Information

Now read the following article about women in the 1920s. Note how the relevant information, highlighted in blue, could be added to categories in the graphic organizer. Finally, incorporate the new information with your existing knowledge to verify some ideas and modify others.

*In 1923 the National Woman's Party first proposed an Equal Rights Amendment (ERA) to the Constitution. This amendment stated that "men and women shall have equal rights throughout the United States and every place subject to its jurisdiction." The National Woman's Party pointed out that legislation discriminating against women existed in every state. For example, in some states, the law gave husbands control over the earnings of their wives and prevented women from sitting on juries. Women could not attend some of the best schools, and they were delegated to the lower levels of professions.*

*However, some progressive women reformers opposed the goals of the National Woman's Party. These progressives favored protective legislation, which had brought shorter hours and better working conditions for many women. The progressives succeeded in their efforts to defeat the ERA.*

## Practicing the Skill

1. On a sheet of paper, revise the graphic organizer to incorporate the information highlighted in the article.
2. Using only your existing knowledge, write a paragraph about how the automobile affected Americans in the 1920s. Next go back through section 1 of this chapter. Then rewrite your paragraph, integrating ideas from the text and illustrations.
3. Discuss with a partner ideals of the twenties, synthesizing information from Chapter 8 and section 1 of Chapter 9.

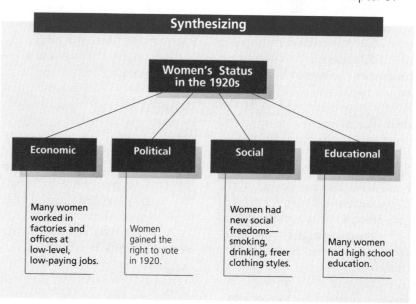

**Synthesizing**

**Women's Status in the 1920s**

**Economic** — Many women worked in factories and offices at low-level, low-paying jobs.

**Political** — Women gained the right to vote in 1920.

**Social** — Women had new social freedoms—smoking, drinking, freer clothing styles.

**Educational** — Many women had high school education.

# Advertising

## The Wills Sainte Claire: Illustrating Fashion

*A*dvertisements are important to historians because they reflect the values and aspirations and even the prejudices and fears of the people they were designed to reach. Ads also help shape culture by introducing new ideas and by influencing people's tastes and purchasing habits. During the 1920s automobile manufacturers bought millions of dollars of advertising in newspapers and magazines. Money spent by car makers for colorful ads in magazines alone climbed from $3.5 million in 1921, to $6.2 million in 1923, to $9.2 million in 1927. To the historian, these ads offer valuable evidence of what was important to Americans of the 1920s.

### The Evidence

The advertisement on the opposite page appeared in a magazine in the 1920s. It is typical of the glossy ads car makers placed in popular magazines during this period. As you study the ad, ask yourself questions such as these: What kind of people was this ad designed to reach? What do you think the values of the ad's target audience were? How can you tell?

### The Interpretation

To the historian, this ad illustrates that American consumers of the 1920s wanted manufactured products to be elegant rather than simply useful and well-made. Car buyers valued cars that reflected their idea of up-to-date style and good taste. No longer satisfied with some car of older design, such as the plain black Model T Ford, wealthier car buyers of the 1920s demanded such features as gray mohair velvet upholstery and real walnut steering wheels. Automobile companies contributed to this change of taste by using ads like this one to stimulate consumer desire for new colors, styles, accessories, and technical improvements.

Of course the ad's main thrust is to persuade people that they will gain social prestige by owning the latest style. The slender, fashionable young woman in the foreground of the ad wearing the latest flapper dress suggests that the owner of a Wills Sainte Claire will also live a life of fashion.

One problem with using ads as evidence is that a historian cannot be sure whether a particular ad reflects what is already true about people's values or whether it represents an advertiser's attempt to introduce new ideas and values. For example, does the ad for the Wills Sainte Claire reflect consumer boredom with plain black cars? Or does it demonstrate that car makers tried to increase sales by using psychological appeals to create demand for something new? Both interpretations may be valid. To be effective, an ad must reflect the current values of its audience and stimulate this audience to aspire to something better.

Another limitation of using advertisements as historical evidence is that ads are often designed to reflect the tastes and aspirations of a specific audience. A historian studying an ad for clues about consumer values must consider whether an ad reflects the tastes and aspirations of the American public in general or of only a specific group of consumers.

### Further Evidence

As was true in the 1920s, car ads that appear in current magazines reflect what is important to consumers today. Examine the car ads in several popular magazines. Choose an ad that you think is especially revealing of contemporary values and aspirations. As you study the illustration and read the words of the ad, try to decide what a historian of the future who sees this ad might conclude about Americans of the 1990s. What kind of consumers do you think this ad was designed to reach? What does the ad reveal about the values, aspirations, or life style of this target audience? Does the ad imply that these consumers buy cars because of how they look, how they drive, how much they cost, or for other reasons? In what ways does the ad present a valid picture of Americans, and in what ways does it try to influence our tastes and purchasing habits?

# WILLS SAINTE CLAIRE

WHEN quality car owners ultimately discover Wills Sainte Claire, their restless seeking after something different abruptly ends. Aware, after driving the car, that there is nothing finer anywhere to be found, they cease to seek.

That is why it has become an adage throughout the Wills Sainte Claire organization, that the best prospect for a Wills Sainte Claire is the Wills Sainte Claire owner himself.

WILLS SAINTE CLAIRE, INC.
*Marysville, Michigan*

© W.S.C. Inc.

# The Jazz Age

## October 6, 1927: First Talking Motion Picture Released

TEENAGERS ENTERED THE HUSHED THEATER AS THOUGH IT WERE THE PALACE IT LOOKED LIKE. FURNITURE, STATUES, AND RUGS FROM ALL OVER THE WORLD FILLED the lobby. A couple stopped in surprise as they caught sight of themselves in the huge mirrors that covered every wall. For just a moment, they thought they had become their favorite movie stars. Like guests at a grand ball, the girl and her date got ready to descend the marble staircase. Inside the huge auditorium with its painted ceiling, the couple rested back in their plush seats. Fans blowing over ice cooled the summer air. The movie started!

More than any other entertainment, movies defined and helped create American culture in the twenties. Glamorous settings like the movie house described above showed that many Americans in the twenties had new-found leisure as well as the wealth to enjoy it. By the millions, Americans were now discovering the pleasures of movies, sports, live music, dancing, radio, and an abundance of newspapers, magazines, and books.

THEATRE HISTORICAL SOCIETY

### At the Movies

In the 1920s Americans went to the movies about once a week. Sociologists Robert S. Lynd and Helen Merrell Lynd profiled an average American city—Muncie, Indiana—in their 1929 book *Middletown*. In the 1920s Muncie boasted nine motion picture theaters for a town of 35,000. The movies at these theaters operated from 1:00 to 11:00 P.M. every day of the year.

**Escaping Together** At the movies, Americans escaped to a different world, both on and off the screen. The movies, silent until *The Jazz Singer* in 1927, spoke powerfully to their audiences. A *Saturday Evening Post* ad encouraged Americans to "Go to a movie . . . and let yourself go." Each week, Americans of all ages, but especially high school and college students, paid as little as ten cents for a few hours of fantasy.

Since every seat in the movie palace cost exactly the same admission price, going to the movies helped level the differences among Americans. A team of white-gloved ushers treated modest workers with the same courtesy they showed to rich business people.

Even more important, because many of the major movie studios had chains of outlets, people in Muncie were now watching exactly the same stories people watched in California. The movies quickly became more popular than regional forms of entertainment.

Some people worried that the movies promoted immoral behavior. Indeed, the ads for a movie called *Flaming Youth* promised "neckers, petters, white kisses, red kisses, pleasure-mad daughters, sensation-craving mothers, . . . the truth—bold, naked, sensational." In 1922 the Motion Picture Producers and Distributors Association tacked a moral message onto the end of each movie. But the movies themselves stayed as suggestive as ever.

### STUDY GUIDE

**As You Read**
Describe the ways people used their leisure time during the Jazz Age, and explain the decade's explosion of musical and literary creativity. Also, think about the following concept and skills.

**Central Concept**
- understanding how American prosperity led to an atmosphere of **materialism** that provoked an intense critical response from the Lost Generation

**Thinking Skills**
- recognizing values
- drawing conclusions
- comparing and contrasting

COURTESY OF THE ACADEMY OF MOTION PICTURE ARTS AND SCIENCES

**Rudolph Valentino, a famous silent film actor, and Agnes Ayres are pictured above in *The Sheik* (1921).**

**Wishing on Stars**    Seated in the dark, audiences could easily imagine themselves on the screen. Americans also relished reading about the stars' private lives in gossip columns by Louella Parsons and Hedda Hopper. The major movie studios hired publicity departments to make up and publicize stories that kept fans attached to "their" stars' loves, marriages, and divorces. When the romantic leading man, Rudolph Valentino died at age 31 in 1926, nearly 30,000 tearful women thronged his funeral.

Through the fans' identification with stars, movies transformed Americans' tastes and behaviors. When stars like Mary Pickford or Gloria Swanson appeared in a new dress style or hair style, millions of women suddenly began to demand the same look.

## Bat, Ball, Glove, and Club

Now that so many Americans had the time, energy, and money to play, they took to sports almost as avidly as they had embraced the movies. Before this decade, 300 private clubs and a handful of public courts easily served the few people who played tennis. By the late twenties, America boasted nearly a thousand tennis clubs and enough municipal courts to accommodate more than a million players, who swatted at 300,000 new tennis balls each month.

Golf, too, became widely popular during the twenties. Before the war, golf had been a rich man's game. By 1927, two million players were putting away on 5,000 courses, many of them open to working class people. Cities also constructed swimming pools, baseball diamonds, summer camps, playgrounds, and recreation centers.[1]

**Sports Stars**    Hard-playing Americans also provided huge audiences for professional sports. The era's popular sports heroes—baseball's Babe Ruth and Oscar Charleston, boxing's Jack Dempsey, tennis's Helen Wills, football's Red Grange, golf's Bobby Jones—became as newsworthy off the field as movie stars. Explaining America's fascination with sports heroes, the historian George Mowry wrote:

> *On the battlefield, in the factory production line, at home in a city apartment, and increasingly even in the business world the individual was becoming lost in a welter of the hive. The sporting field was one of the few remaining areas of pure individual expression where success or failure depended precisely upon individual physical and intellectual prowess. And if the masses themselves could not or would not participate directly they could at least, by a process of identification, salute the old virtues.*
>
> George E. Mowry,
> *The Twenties: Fords, Flappers,*
> *& Fanatics,* 1963

Americans learned about their heroes by watching them perform. They also devoured newspaper and magazine articles about them. In 1926 Jack Dempsey, the "Manassa Mauler," lost his heavyweight boxing title to Gene Tunney. Sports fans all over the country chuckled at the aging fighter's answer when his wife asked him what had happened. "Honey," Dempsey answered, "I forgot to duck."

**Heavyweight boxing champion Jack Dempsey was a hero to millions of Americans.** *Why did Americans idolize sports figures in the 1920s?*

AP/WIDE WORLD PHOTOS

In 1926 a 19-year-old girl named Gertrude Ederle, popularly known as "Our Trudy," became the first woman to swim the English Channel, beating the fastest man's record by a full two hours. Before her swim, W. O. McGeehan wrote in the *New York Herald Tribune*, "If there is one woman who can make the swim, it is this girl, with the shoulders and back of Jack Dempsey and the frankest and bravest pair of eyes that ever looked into a face." After swimming the English Channel, Gertrude Ederle said simply, "I just knew if it could be done it had to be done, and I did it." A huge ticker tape parade greeted her return to New York.

UPI/BETTMANN NEWSPHOTOS

**Covered with grease to help keep her warm, Gertrude Ederle prepares to swim the English Channel in 1926. Involved in professional baseball from 1915 to 1941, Oscar Charleston was inducted into the National Baseball Hall of Fame in 1976.**

NATIONAL BASEBALL LIBRARY, COOPERSTOWN, N.Y.

One of the greats in baseball's Negro League, Oscar Charleston led the league in home runs six times between 1921 and 1933. Regarded as one of the greatest players of all time, Charleston was never allowed to play in the major leagues because of the color of his skin.

**Lucky Lindy**   No American hero of the twenties equalled Charles Lindbergh, whose solo flight across the Atlantic in 1927 excited more enthusiasm than any single event before or since. The modest young man in his flying machine served to join America's pioneer past with an optimistic view of the country's technological future.

Lindbergh's flight and the public response to it could never have taken place without modern machinery and the combined efforts of thousands of people. Many Americans, however, still preferred to regard their hero as a traditional pioneer, "the lone eagle." To them, Lindbergh's accomplishment seemed to demonstrate the triumph of individual American heroism in a bewildering new age of machines.

## New Rhythms in the Air

During the 1920s Americans entertained themselves at movies and sports events. They also began to listen to two exciting new types of African American music: soulful blues and the frantic jazz that would give its name to the entire era.

The blues grew out of the work songs and field chants of African American slaves. In the 1920s black singers, such as Bessie Smith and Gertrude "Ma" Rainey, sang their sad songs to huge audiences in clubs on Chicago's South Side and recorded them on black-oriented labels for major record companies.

Jazz began in black New Orleans and moved north when African Americans migrated during the Great War. Not a single note was written down, but the musicians all seemed to know what to play.[2]

Singing of joy in the face of oppression, jazz contains strands of music from many European countries. However, jazz is above all African American, and it could have developed only in a U.S. city. In 1925 J. A. Rogers wrote, "With its cowbells, auto horns, calliopes, rattles, dinner gongs, kitchen utensils, cymbals, screams, crashes, clankings and monotonous rhythm [jazz] bears all the marks of a nerve-strung, strident, mechanized civilization."

Joseph "King" Oliver's Creole Jazz Band found a ready audience of urban blacks when they moved to Chicago in 1920. In 1922 King Oliver invited his talented former cornet student to join the band. When the student, Louis Armstrong, later switched to the trumpet, he became perhaps the most famous jazz musician of all time.

**The first to write lengthy jazz compositions, pianist and director Duke Ellington made great contributions to jazz. He and the Duke Ellington Band became** **famous during the twenties playing at Harlem's Cotton Club. Here they are pictured in Chicago at the Oriental Theatre.** *How did jazz make its way to northern cities?*

Imitating the black jazz bands, white bands, such as those of Paul Whiteman and Bix Beiderbecke, performed widely at dances for young people. Supper clubs and country clubs provided settings for the slow dancing and the Charleston that young people so enjoyed and that older people declared immoral, shocking, and scandalous.

The Charleston was by no means the only dance of the 1920s, an era that has been called "The Dance Age" as well as "The Jazz Age." However, with its flying beads, knocking knees, and crossing hands, the Charleston will forever represent the 1920s. The Charleston first appeared in a black revue called "Runnin' Wild" in 1924. Although initially considered too difficult for amateurs to master, within a year this whirlwind had swept the country.

While live music defined the twenties, recorded music became part of the mainstream only after electricity made the phonograph and radio possible. Commercial radio had a modest start when stations in Detroit and Pittsburgh broadcast the 1920 presidential election returns. By the middle of the decade, few people found themselves out of earshot of a radio speaker. In the late 1920s, the roof of practically every tenement house on the Lower East Side of New York City looked like a forest of radio antennae. Radio brought entertainment and advertising to a mass market and helped spur the explosive growth of the mass market economy.

## Time to Read

With time on their hands and with more education than any previous generation, more Americans in the 1920s read. During the 1920s scores of new magazines came into existence. At least 20 boasted circulations of a million readers. *Reader's Digest* debuted in 1922, *Time* in 1923, and *The New Yorker* in 1925.

## STUDY GUIDE

### Comparing and Contrasting

In the 1920s radio played the role television plays in today's culture. People from every income group listened to the same programs and advertisements. The voices of popular radio announcers reached the entire country. Some people even put ads in the newspaper to tell their friends not to call them while their favorite programs were on! The first television transmission took place during the height of this age of radio. In April 1927 a hand-sized screen showed a grainy image of Herbert Hoover, transmitted from Washington to New York.

More people were reading newspapers as well, although the number of newspapers dropped as papers gathered into **syndicates**—chains of newspapers under centralized direction. The contents of the newspapers began to look more similar as the syndicates provided editorials, sports, gossip, and Sunday features for a national audience.

With their small pages and large type, tabloid newspapers made ideal reading for crowded, rocking subway cars. Tabloids swept the country in the 1920s. New York alone had three, with a combined circulation of 1.6 million readers. The tabloids battled each other, attempting to sell papers by publicizing scandals, or fads, such as dance marathons in which young people danced until they dropped.

Most of the fads reported in the tabloids grew old very quickly. But one fad thrived long enough to launch a publishing empire. Two young men, Richard Simon and Lincoln Schuster, began their publishing company by bringing out a crossword puzzle book that eventually sold two million copies.

Americans were hungry for books and the twenties saw the birth of several major publishing houses, including Simon and Schuster, Morrow, Viking, and Harcourt, Brace. The Book-of-the-Month Club and the Literary Guild began mass distribution of books within months of each other in 1926.

## The Lost Generation

While ordinary Americans happily pursued new leisure activities—movies, radio, music, dance, and reading—some writers began to attack America's **materialism.** They questioned a society that placed more importance on money and material goods than it did on intellectual, spiritual, and artistic concerns.

**Leaving America Behind**   During the 1920s some prominent American writers and artists moved to Europe, partly because they felt the United States was "the enemy of the artist, of the man who cannot produce something tangible when the five o'clock whistle blows." The expatriates also felt that it was cheaper to live in Europe than it was to stay at home.[3]

The dollar was especially strong in Paris where writers Gertrude Stein, Ernest Hemingway, and F. Scott Fitzgerald took up residence in the 1920s. Gertrude Stein made bold experiments with language in her plays, operas, and books. She also gave the literary era its name when she told her friend Hemingway, "You are all a lost generation."

THE METROPOLITAN MUSEUM OF ART, BEQUEST OF GERTRUDE STEIN, 1946

**The Spanish artist Pablo Picasso painted *Gertrude Stein* in 1906. Stein encouraged such experimental painters as Picasso and Henri Matisse.** *Why did Gertrude Stein encourage artistic experimentation?*

Ernest Hemingway set most of his novels in Europe and portrayed the ruined innocence of his postwar generation. His masterpiece *The Sun Also Rises*, published in 1926, quoted Gertrude Stein's comment on its title page. The book tells of Jake, an expatriate American who bears physical and psychological wounds from the war. It ends on a note of quiet despair.

F. Scott Fitzgerald's earliest novels and stories were set in the United States where he wrote about daring college students. *The Great Gatsby*, published

**Recognizing Values**

To a striking degree, F. Scott Fitzgerald and Ernest Hemingway lived the life styles of their characters. Fitzgerald and his wife, Zelda, threw lavish jazz parties. Hemingway hunted and fished.

While Hemingway promoted these traditional masculine values in his writing, Fitzgerald's writing evoked nostalgia for the solid midwestern values his Jazz Age characters scorned.

3  Why did the expatriate writers forsake the United States for Europe after World War I?

in 1925 and considered Fitzgerald's greatest work, explored the empty lives of Americans with too much money. Daisy, the main female character, feels purposeless and lost.

**Criticizing America from Within**  Many of the most significant writers of the 1920s never left the United States or left for only brief periods. But like the expatriates, American writers who stayed home took up their pens to expose what they considered the shallow and money-centered culture of their nation.

In his trilogy, *U.S.A.*, John Dos Passos suggested America had become two nations, one rich and one poor. Experimenting with free-form writing and leaving punctuation behind, Dos Passos wrote, " 'on the streets you see only the downcast faces of the beaten the streets belong to the beaten nation . .

" 'we stand defeated America.' "

Sinclair Lewis attacked the materialism of small town America in satiric novels such as *Main Street*, which was a best seller in 1920, and *Babbitt*, which was equally popular two years later. The term "Babbitt" is still used to refer to the ordinary 1920s American—a narrow-minded, obsessed businessman whose deepest desires are determined by advertising.

Ironically, just as intellectuals were complaining that art could not possibly flourish in the United States, American writers were publishing some of the country's best literature ever.

The wittiest critic of America during this period was H. L. Mencken, a newspaperman and magazine editor. His targets often richly deserved his nasty insults. However, when Mencken labeled the South the "Sahara of the Bozart," or wasteland of the fine arts, he could not have been more mistaken. From his home in Oxford, Mississippi, William Faulkner was crafting the brilliant and difficult works that would eventually win him a Nobel Prize in literature.

DENVER CENTER THEATRE COMPANY

**The plays of Eugene O'Neill brought serious themes to Broadway in the 1920s. Such O' Neill plays as *Emperor Jones* (1920), pictured above, still influence audiences today.**

## The Harlem Renaissance

At the same time the Lost Generation of white writers was questioning materialistic American culture, African American writers who had migrated to the nation's northern cities began to express their own identity and a rising anger at northern racism. Bustling with nightclubs and cafes and alive with blues and jazz, a section of New York City called Harlem lured black and white intellectuals. The African American literary and artistic movement that resulted became known as the Harlem Renaissance.[4]

Alain Locke was a Professor of Literature at Howard University, a graduate of Harvard, and the first African American Rhodes scholar. Locke urged his fellow blacks to create a new literature. In *The New Negro*, Locke wrote that the younger generation of African Americans is "vibrant with a new psychology . . . the new spirit is awake in the masses."

Inspired by Locke, writers like Langston Hughes and Claude McKay spoke out in the strongest voices of the Harlem Renaissance. Hughes, a gifted poet, was one of the first

**Comparing and Contrasting**
The themes of writers during the 1920s reflected their different experiences in the United States. White writers attacked the materialism of their culture. Black writers expressed anger at racism and the inequalities between blacks and whites. Blacks had not yet experienced affluence on a large enough scale to be critical of it.

4 What prompted the movement known as the Harlem Renaissance?

**(left to right) Langston Hughes, Charles S. Johnson, E. Franklin Frazier, Rudolph Fisher, and Hubert Delaney helped shape the Harlem Renaissance.**

African American writers to use jazz and blues themes and rhythms in his poetry. In a 1926 essay called "The Negro Artist and the Racial Mountain," Hughes argued that what was truly worth expressing would be found in the culture of the poorest black people: "If white people are pleased we are glad. If they are not, it doesn't matter. We know we are beautiful. And ugly too. The tom tom cries and the tom tom laughs."

Claude McKay migrated from his native Jamaica to Harlem. There he wrote poems such as "If We Must Die" and "The White City" that challenged African Americans to fight for their rights. McKay's autobiographical novel, *Home to Harlem*, published in 1928, expressed his fascination with all the shades of people who could be called black: "Brown girls rouged and painted like dark pansies. Brown flesh draped in soft colorful clothes. . . . The cabaret singer, a shiny coffee-colored girl in a green frock . . . chocolate, chestnut, coffee, ebony, cream, yellow . . . "

In addition to Langston Hughes and Claude McKay, many other talented African American men and women launched their writing careers during this exciting period. For example, Arna Bontemps, a poet and friend of Langston Hughes, wrote the following poem in which the images of planting grain pointed out the inequalities between blacks and whites:

*I have sown beside all waters in my day.*
*I planted deep, within my heart the fear*
*That wind or fowl would take the grain away.*
*I planted safe against this stark, lean year.*

*I scattered seed enough to plant the land*
*In rows from Canada to Mexico*
*But for my reaping only what the hand*
*Can hold at once is all that I can show.*

*Yet what I sowed and what the orchard yields*
*My brother's sons are gathering stalk and root,*
*Small wonder then my children glean in fields*
*They have not sown, and feed on bitter fruit.*

Arna Bontemps,
"A Black Man Talks of Reaping," 1927

Of the many gifted black women involved in the movement, a young anthropologist named Zora Neale Hurston eventually became the best known. Hurston's plays, short stories, and articles began to appear in the 1920s, and featured the African American folklore she had listened to as a child. Her 1937 masterpiece, *Their Eyes Were Watching God*, portrayed the first heroic black woman in American literature.

In the 1920s African Americans began to find their own unique voice in a new and exciting literature. The writers of the Harlem Renaissance proclaimed that blacks would no longer accept second-class citizenship in any area of American life.

## SECTION REVIEW

**Checking Facts**

1. How did movies and radio increase the similarities between Americans in different parts of the country?

2. How did Charles Lindbergh's accomplishment link the values of the nation's past and future?

3. Why did tabloid newspapers become popular during the 1920s?

4. Why did so many American writers criticize American values during the postwar period?

5. What do you think Bontemps meant by "bitter fruit" in "A Black Man Talks of Reaping"?

**Thinking Critically**

6. **Recognizing Values** Why do you think the Motion Picture Producers and Distributors Association tacked a moral message onto the end of movies in the 1920s?

7. **Drawing Conclusions** Give at least two examples to support the conclusion that African American writers developed a powerful new voice during the Harlem Renaissance.

**Linking Across Time**

8. Give an example of a sports or movie hero from the 1920s and a modern hero. Explain how each hero helped to shape American fashions and/or values.

# Cultural Conflicts

## July 10, 1925: Scopes Trial Begins, Dayton, Tennessee

**D**URING A SIZZLING HOT JULY IN 1925, A SIMPLE TRIAL IN THE SMALL TOWN OF DAYTON, TENNESSEE, TURNED INTO A SHOWDOWN BETWEEN RELIGION AND science. A local science teacher, John Scopes, was on trial for teaching evolution. Scopes and all the other teachers who used the state-approved textbook had broken the Butler Act, a new state law against teaching "any theory that denies the story of the Divine Creation of man as taught in the Bible."

When the Butler Act was passed in 1925, Tennessee's governor had signed it reluctantly, commenting, "Nobody believes that it is going to be an active statute." He was wrong. When a small item about the law appeared in the *New York Times*, the American Civil Liberties Union (ACLU) raised money to test the law in court. All they needed was a Tennessee teacher who would volunteer to be arrested for breaking the Butler Act.

In 1925 John Scopes agreed to go on trial to test the legality of the Butler Act. Clarence Darrow, an urban liberal, volunteered as Scopes's defense lawyer. William Jennings Bryan, three times a candidate for president and a hero to rural America, joined the prosecution.

Broadcast over the radio and reported in hundreds of newspapers, the Scopes trial symbolized many of the bitter conflicts that rocked the United States during the 1920s. In this decade, struggles between Americans erupted over religion, over drinking, and even over who was to be considered an American.

AP/WIDE WORLD PHOTOS

## The Familiarity of Religion

The turning point of the Scopes trial came on the last day, when Darrow put Bryan on the stand and questioned him at length about the Bible's account of creation, which Bryan claimed to believe literally. Darrow, who saw the case as an important constitutional issue, asked Bryan if he thought the earth had been made in six days, and Bryan had to admit, "Not six days of twenty-four hours." The judge finally halted the questioning when the two adversaries ended up shaking their fists at one another.

When the trial was over, both sides claimed victory: the jury had taken less than ten minutes to find John Scopes guilty and fine him $100, but the Supreme Court later freed him on a technicality. The Butler Act remained the law in Tennessee, even if biology teachers continued to teach evolution. To many, it seemed that **fundamentalism**—a movement that affirmed the literal truth of the Bible—had won.

However, Darrow's piercing questions disturbed Bryan, who had been forced to admit that a "day" in the Bible might be a million years or more. Since Bryan had based his position on the idea that the Bible must be read literally and not interpreted, he was aware of contradicting himself. The elderly statesman died less than a week later and was mourned by millions.

AP/WIDE WORLD PHOTOS

**Some evangelists of the 1920s mixed religion and show business. In this picture, evangelist Aimee Semple McPherson dramatically pleads with her Los Angeles congregation for contributions.**

## The Failure of Prohibition

Like the battle over whether fundamentalism belonged in schools, the struggle to enforce Prohibition, enacted by an amendment in 1919, pitted small town residents and farmers against a newer, more urban America. Most fundamentalists stood firmly in favor of Prohibition, claiming that people's behavior could and should be controlled by strict law. Opponents of Prohibition, on the other hand, preferred more tolerance.

Prohibition succeeded in eradicating the saloon. The demise of the saloon decreased alcohol consumption among lower class people who could not afford to go to the new speakeasies, where liquor was sold in violation of the law. However, most middle-class people simply refused to obey the Volstead Act that was enacted to enforce Prohibition. This widespread refusal gave the 1920s its well-deserved reputation as a lawless decade.

Prohibition was hard to enforce for many reasons. For one thing, the United States offered over 10,000 miles of coastlines and land borders to smugglers, who were all too happy to sneak in the alcohol thirsty

The Scopes case may have dealt fundamentalism a blow, but it continued to thrive in the United States. Rural people, especially in the South and Midwest, remained faithful to their churches. When large numbers of farmers migrated to cities during the 1920s, they brought fundamentalism with them. The familiar religion helped them make sense of their new lives.

In the 1920s, though, even the traditional religions began to take on some modern aspects. In Southern California, several fundamentalist preachers used radio to reach many people.

Aimee Semple McPherson used show business techniques to attract a radio following to her "Four Square Gospel." McPherson barnstormed the country in 1921 and 1922, raising $1.5 million for the construction of her Angelus Temple. After the temple was completed in 1923, McPherson kept it filled every night.[1]

THE NEW YORK HISTORICAL SOCIETY

**Before Prohibition, groups opposed to the use of alcohol encouraged people to sign pledge cards like the one shown here.**

Americans refused to give up. People who made, sold, or transported illegal liquor were called bootleggers. A former bootlegger from Barre, Vermont, later recalled, "We ran mostly ale. We got it in Canada for five bucks a case and sold it here for fifteen or twenty. You could load a lot of ale into those big crates we had. We kept five or six cars on the road at the time."

In 1924 the Department of Commerce estimated the value of liquor smuggled into the country at $40 million. In addition, hundreds of ships anchored in international waters dispensed legal liquor to anyone who came out by boat.

Thousands of druggists sold alcohol quite legally on doctors' prescriptions. During the 1920s some doctors began to prescribe alcohol for a variety of real and imagined complaints. Women who had not been

STUDY GUIDE

**Analyzing Behavior**
When Aimee Semple McPherson built her huge temple in Los Angeles, she particularly appealed to uprooted farmers who were thronging to the growing city at the rate of almost 3,000 a day.

McPherson staged extravagant musical productions that dramatized Bible stories or enacted the ongoing battle between good and evil. Her approach made exciting and appealing theater.

1 Explain the outcome of the Scopes trial. What effect did the case have on fundamentalism?

able to drink in saloons went to the new speakeasies, where both men and women eagerly gulped down Prohibition's new drink, the cocktail.

Illegal distilling could and did take place anywhere. An industrious bootlegger could make his own home brew with a portable still that sold for six or seven dollars. Between 1919 and 1929, the production of corn sugar increased six-fold, and most of it ended up in illegal liquor.

When you are Blue and Dry,
Don't Sit there and Sigh,

**SERVICE**

JUST CALL
DIgby 4-7298 - 7347

AL GOLDMAN

47 BROADWAY
NEW YORK

THE NEW YORK HISTORICAL SOCIETY

**To better guard against raids during Prohibition, speakeasy owners required customers to have membership cards like the ones shown on this page.**

Prohibition had other ill effects. Americans came to have a casual attitude about disobeying the law. A tiny force of Prohibition agents received very little pay for the thankless job of enforcing a law many Americans hated. In 1923 one Prohibition agent toured several American cities to see how difficult it would be to purchase an illegal drink. It took him only three minutes in Detroit; in New Orleans, a drink could be had in a mere 35 seconds.

Many people simply refused to take the law seriously. In fact, a San Francisco jury trying a Prohibition case drank up the liquor that had been used in court as evidence!

As federal courts choked on too many liquor cases, many government officials took part in the bribery and corruption that accompanied the unenforceable law. Fiorello La Guardia, a Congressman from New York who would later become a reform-minded mayor of New York City, estimated it would take a police force of 250,000 to enforce Prohibition in New York, and another 200,000 agents to police the police.

Perhaps the worst effect of Prohibition was its contribution to the explosive growth of big-city crime. Gangsters had been around before Prohibition, but when they took over bootlegging, crime soared to new heights.

The gangs bought out hundreds of breweries and transported illegal beer in armored trucks. They stationed "soldiers" to hijack other gangs' shipments, and they killed their rivals in a series of gruesome slayings. Al Capone, the head of a gang of Chicago bootleggers, became a multi-millionaire, driving through the streets in an armor-plated car with bullet-proof windows.

The **Hunt Club**
125A WEST 45TH STREET
NEW YORK

GUY E. MAYER

REGULAR MEMBER 1933

Henry E. Stores
SECRETARY

THE NEW YORK HISTORICAL SOCIETY

**Prohibition became a joke to many Americans. In this picture, speakeasy owner Texas Guinan smiles after being arrested at her club in 1927. Guinan simply moved from one club to another after raids.**

UPI/BETTMANN NEWSPHOTOS

**Chicago gangster Al Capone (second from left) leaves a Chicago courthouse after being convicted of income tax evasion.** *How did prohibition contribute to a soaring crime rate in the 1920s?*

AP/WIDE WORLD PHOTOS

## Crosses in the Night

The forces favoring Prohibition centered in rural areas and small towns where fundamentalist preachers warned their congregations against the sinful ways of the big city. The Ku Klux Klan, which suddenly blazed back onto the American scene in the 1920s, also flourished in small towns, and it fought some of its fiercest battles with the liquor interests. The rebirth of the Klan pointed up many of the conflicts dividing American society during this period.

Like the hooded secret order of Reconstruction days, the new Klan began in the South under a burning cross and fanned some southern whites' hatred for blacks. When the Klan spread from Georgia in the twenties, however, it added new enemies to its list. In Texas the Klan attacked Mexicans; in California, it fought Japanese immigrants; in New York, the Klan's targets were Jews and European immigrants; and in New England, it stirred up hatred of French Canadians.

All over the country, Klan members participated in violent activities—tarring and feathering, flogging, and lynching. The Southwest saw some of the worst terror. In a single year, Oklahoma's Klan was responsible for no less than 2,500 floggings.

With its secret initiation rites, hooded robes, and burning crosses, the Klan provided a fellowship of prejudice for ill-educated men whose lives offered few other satisfactions. It soon became strong in northern cities such as Detroit, Pittsburgh, and Indianapolis, where many African Americans had recently migrated.

In fact, the Ku Klux Klan claimed its greatest strength in Indiana where almost half a million men had joined. David Stephenson, state head of the Klan

THE BETTMANN ARCHIVE

**Ku Klux Klansmen accompany the hearse of one of their members in Freeport, Long Island.** *Why did Klan membership and activity increase during the 1920s?*

in Indiana, bragged with some truth, "I am the law in Indiana." On Kokomo's parade nights, the police disappeared and white-sheeted figures directed traffic.

The new Klan even gained a foothold in the industrial Northeast, and in California. In 1923, 10,000 New Jersey Klansmen burned a cross in New Brunswick, New Jersey, almost in sight of Manhattan. Similar scenes took place in Anaheim, California.

Klan members believed that as "pure" Americans, they should be the guardians of society's behavior and morals. In America's cities, Klan members enjoyed a kind of superiority in their common hatred for whichever group they thought was beneath them.

Under Hiram Wesley Evans, a Texas dentist and the Klan's Imperial Wizard and Emperor, the secret society's rolls swelled to almost 5 million members. Evans believed the Klan represented "the great mass of Americans of the old pioneer stock." By this, he meant "a blend of various peoples of the so-called Nordic race, the race which, with all its faults, has given the world almost the whole of modern civilization."[2]

Evans and his followers felt modern America had forced them to become strangers in their own land:

> *O*ne by one all our traditional moral standards went by the boards, or were so disregarded that they ceased to be binding. The sacredness of our Sabbath, of our homes, of chastity, and finally even of our right to teach our own children in our own schools fundamental facts and truths were torn away from us.
>
> Hiram Wesley Evans,
> "The Klan's Fight for Americanism,"
> *The North American Review,*
> March-May, 1926

## STUDY GUIDE

### Recognizing Bias

Most Ku Klux Klan members shared a particular hatred for Catholics. Klansmen assumed Catholics' allegiance to the pope meant they could not be loyal U.S. citizens. A Catholic teenager who grew up in Indiana recalled that word spread that "the Pope was finally pulling into town on the south-bound from Chicago to take over. A mob formed and stoned the train."

**2** Give two facts to show that the new Klan targeted newcomers to the United States.

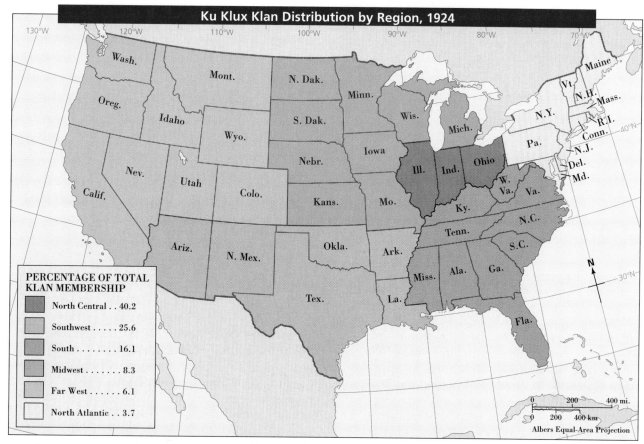

## Ku Klux Klan Distribution by Region, 1924

**PERCENTAGE OF TOTAL KLAN MEMBERSHIP**

North Central . . 40.2
Southwest . . . . . 25.6
South . . . . . . . . 16.1
Midwest . . . . . . . 8.3
Far West . . . . . . 6.1
North Atlantic . . 3.7

Albers Equal-Area Projection

**While the Ku Klux Klan thrived during the 1920s, it was not equally popular throughout all areas of the** **United States.** *Which three regions of the country accounted for over 80 percent of Klan membership?*

Evans expected to win "a return of power into the hands of the everyday, not highly cultured, not overly intellectualized, but entirely unspoiled and not de-Americanized, average citizen of the old stock."

The Klan prided itself on its pure-blooded Americanism, but it shared many similarities with German and Italian movements of this period. Like the European groups, the Klan stressed nationalism and racial purity, attacked alien minority groups, disapproved of the urban culture, and called for a return to the past.

The Ku Klux Klan began to sink back into obscurity in 1925 when David Stephenson, who had insisted he was the law in Indiana, went to jail for the second-degree murder of a woman he had kidnapped and brutally abused. Klan members who had believed in its stated ideals of chastity and morality deserted the organization in large numbers.

In 1928 the Klan could not prevent the nomination of Al Smith, a Catholic, for President of the United States. Although Smith could see crosses burning in the fields as his campaign train crossed Oklahoma, the Klan itself was almost burned out.[3]

## Closing the Doors

The Ku Klux Klan's drive for "pure Americanism," if not their methods, found a sympathetic echo in mainstream America. Many Americans associated immigrants with radicalism and disloyalty. These fears had fueled the Red Scare, the Palmer raids, and the case against Sacco and Vanzetti. Rural Americans in particular believed that immigrants had somehow caused erosion of old-fashioned American values.

---

### STUDY GUIDE

**Analyzing Behavior**

In the 1920s Ku Klux Klan prejudice erupted in violence against the Klan's traditional enemy, African Americans. However, the new Klan was as likely to attack Catholics, bootleggers, political opponents, or people Klan members believed to be immoral. For example, in Alabama in 1927 the Klan beat a white woman who had been divorced.

**3** Why did the Ku Klux Klan suddenly lose so many members during the late 1920s?

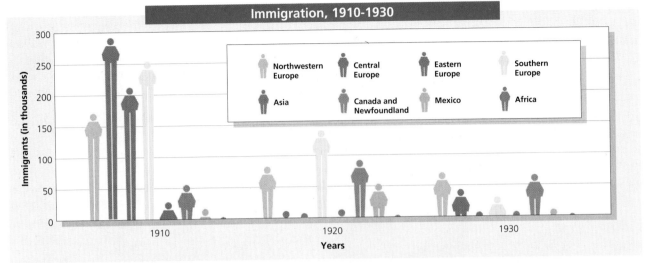

## Immigration, 1910-1930

**Immigrants (in thousands)** vs **Years**

Legend:
- Northwestern Europe
- Central Europe
- Eastern Europe
- Southern Europe
- Asia
- Canada and Newfoundland
- Mexico
- Africa

**During the 1920s Congress passed several laws that limited immigration and applied a quota system.**

*According to the graph, from which four areas of the world did the fewest immigrants come in the 1920s?*

An immigration act in 1921 attached the force of law to bigotry when it reversed the century-long tradition of open immigration from Europe. The law limited the number of immigrants by applying a quota system. The number of immigrants from any country in a year could not exceed 3 percent of the number of people in the United States from that country according to the 1910 census. That favored immigrants from northern and western Europe since most of the immigrants from these areas had arrived by this time.

In 1924 the National Origins Act reduced the number of immigrants and excluded Asians altogether. It also decreased the quota percentage from three to two. Congress also changed the census year used as the basis for the quotas from 1910 to 1890. By using the 1890 census instead of the 1910 census, the law slashed the number of immigrants allowed in from eastern and southern Europe, since the large immigrations after 1890 came from these areas.

In the debate on the bill, congressmen vented their hatred of immigrants, especially immigrants who lived in New York. One representative from Kansas contrasted the "beer, bolshevism, unassimilating settlements and perhaps many flags" to his idealized view of America: "constitutional government; one flag, stars and stripes."

The law attempted to maintain America's ethnic mixture as it existed in 1890 in order to ensure that America would stay "American." The authors of the law assumed that Asians, Italians, and Poles were less American than were the Irish and Germans who had come in large numbers in the nineteenth century and therefore had a larger quota in the law.

The National Origins Act made it exceptionally difficult for groups with low quotas to immigrate to the United States. In the 1930s immigration to the United States dwindled to a trickle.[4]

## The Challenge of Change

During this decade Americans found themselves suddenly thrust, sometimes unwillingly, into a modern, urban world. In 1910 more than half of all Americans had lived in villages of less than 2,500 people. During the 1920s six million people left the farm for the city, and by 1930 only 44 percent of Americans still lived in rural areas.

The battles fought in the twenties over religion, over drinking, and over who could be considered an American, shared a common thread of fear and hostility to everything an urban society seemed to represent. But the laws passed to try and stop change at best merely postponed it.

For example, Tennessee's law to prevent the teaching of evolution received world attention in the Scopes trial. The Eighteenth Amendment to curb Americans' thirst for liquor was often ignored before its repeal in 1933. After the late 1920s the Ku Klux Klan and the values it represented had all but disappeared, except in the South. While the National Origins Act stemmed the tide of eastern European immigration, it did not stop immigrants from the Western Hemisphere. After the 1920s Mexicans, French Canadians, and Puerto Ricans became the new American immigrants.

Tensions between the city and the country erupted into national election politics for the first time in 1928 when New York Governor Al Smith made his bid for national power. Probably no Democrat could have defeated Herbert Hoover in the middle of this prosperous Republican decade. However, Smith seemed to stand for everything small-town Americans feared most: the big city with sinful and foreign ways.

For example, the Governor had been born in a tenement house near the East River in New York City. Fearful voters saw Smith as a spokesman for immigrants. He openly opposed Prohibition, which small-town America supported.

Rural voters and city voters who held traditional values gaped at Smith's brown derby hat, his expensive tailor-made suits, and his ever-present cigar. Even the accent with which Smith pronounced "radio" as "raddio" or said "foist" for "first" made the candidate seem un-American. Most important of all, many Americans wondered whether the devout Catholic governor could remain independent of the pope if he were to be elected president.

Hoover, on the other hand, presented himself as a typical Iowa farmboy, who recalled diving in the swimming hole under the willow branches and trapping rabbits in the woods. Of course, he had since become a millionaire mining engineer. Hoover had also spearheaded relief efforts after World War I and had successfully served under two Republican presidents as secretary of commerce. But when he accepted the Republican nomination for president, Hoover spoke of himself as "a boy from a country village, without inheritance or influential friends."

The popular vote of 1928 reflected America's intense interest in the election. Only half the eligible voters had cast ballots in the 1924 contest. In 1928 more than two-thirds of the eligible voters turned out. Many of the new voters in 1928 were Catholic women, casting ballots for the first time.

To no one's surprise, Hoover won in a landslide. However, lost in the excitement of Hoover's victory was the fact that for the first time in a decade of Republican prosperity, a president had failed to win the 12 largest U.S. cities. In 1924 the Republicans had carried these big cities by 1.3 million votes. Political change was already clearly in the wind.

The 1920s, a time of rapid social change in America, was an exciting and troubling decade. The promise of an easier, more bountiful and modern life existed side by side with old suspicions, fears, and hatreds. The change that thrilled some people threatened others who tried unsuccessfully to cling to older ways. The people in power—white, Protestant, and male—still gave lip service to the small-town virtues of the past. But in the 1920s, the United States was changing rapidly into a modern, urban society. It would change even more with the great crash in 1929.

## SECTION REVIEW

### Checking Facts

1. Why did both sides claim victory in the Scopes trial?
2. Name one good effect of Prohibition. How did Prohibition fail?
3. Why were so many people attracted to the Ku Klux Klan during the 1920s? Why did the Klan's popularity die out so suddenly?
4. Why did many Americans seek to restrict immigration during the 1920s? How did the National Origins Act of 1924 affect Asian immigration to the United States?
5. Why was the presidential election of 1928 seen as a contest between rural and urban values?
6. In what ways did Al Smith's showing in the presidential election of 1928 indicate change?

### Thinking Critically

7. **Analyzing Behavior** Why do you think so many Americans disobeyed the Prohibition Amendment?
8. **Recognizing Bias** Why did small-town Americans fear the presidential candidacy of Al Smith in 1928?

### Linking Across Time

9. Does racial and ethnic bias still exist in the United States today? Give evidence to support your claim.

## Lindbergh Crosses the Atlantic

*PARIS—Lindbergh did it. Twenty minutes after 10 o'clock tonight suddenly and softly there slipped out of the darkness a gray-white airplane as 25,000 pairs of eyes strained toward it. At 10:24 the* Spirit of St. Louis *landed and lines of soldiers, ranks of policemen and stout steel fences went down before a mad rush as irresistible as the tides in the ocean.*
— *New York Times, 1927*

### "Lone Eagle" Lands – World Sighs in Relief

Just 33 hours and 29 minutes after he took off from New York, Lindbergh landed at Le Bourget airfield in Paris. The 25-year-old "Lone Eagle" became the first person to survive a nonstop flight across the Atlantic. "No man before me had commanded such freedom of movement over earth," said Lindbergh. "For me the *Spirit of St. Louis* was a lens focused on the future, a forerunner of mechanisms that would conquer time and space."

UPI/BETTMANN NEWSPHOTOS

## Elsewhere in the News

### Hoover Views Flooding

NEW ORLEANS – Secretary Herbert Hoover, shocked at the disaster caused by the Mississippi River flood that left half a million homeless, said, "There never has been a calamity such as this flood."

### Border Battle over Rum

WASHINGTON, D.C. – The Canadian government abandoned its prohibition policy, making the problem of American prohibition enforcement across the shared border even more difficult.

## "Lucky Lindy"

"Lucky Lindy" insisted that his "luck" consisted chiefly of three years' flying experience on the St. Louis-to-Chicago airmail route and an innovative plane that he helped design.

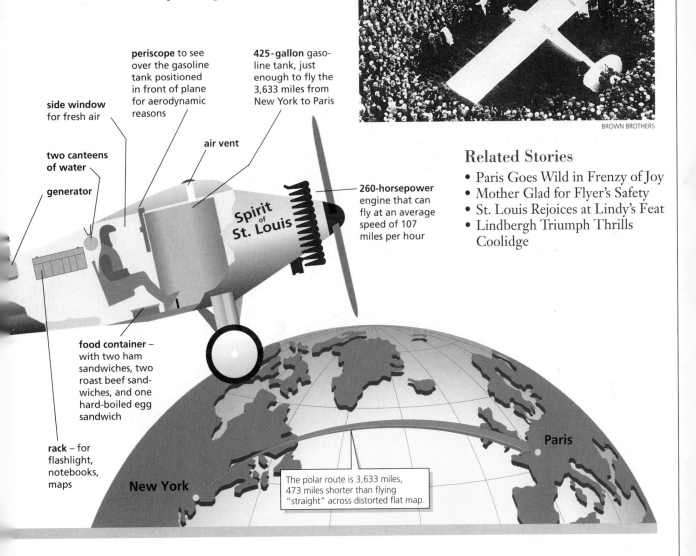

BROWN BROTHERS

**periscope** to see over the gasoline tank positioned in front of plane for aerodynamic reasons

**425-gallon** gasoline tank, just enough to fly the 3,633 miles from New York to Paris

**side window** for fresh air

**air vent**

**two canteens of water**

**generator**

**260-horsepower** engine that can fly at an average speed of 107 miles per hour

Spirit of St. Louis

**food container** – with two ham sandwiches, two roast beef sandwiches, and one hard-boiled egg sandwich

**rack** – for flashlight, notebooks, maps

### Related Stories

- Paris Goes Wild in Frenzy of Joy
- Mother Glad for Flyer's Safety
- St. Louis Rejoices at Lindy's Feat
- Lindbergh Triumph Thrills Coolidge

Paris

New York

The polar route is 3,633 miles, 473 miles shorter than flying "straight" across distorted flat map.

---

## Taxicabs Pose Menace

NEW YORK – Chief Magistrate McAdoo complained that the city's 17,000 taxicabs continue to increase. "After a while we'll have to leave New York and turn it over to the taxicabs."

KOBAL COLLECTION

## Bow Takes Bow

HOLLYWOOD – Clara Bow (she's got It) starred in *Rough House Rosie* as a newly successful society songstress who missed her boxer-boyfriend. Punning subtitles added to the film's fun.

# Chapter 9 Review

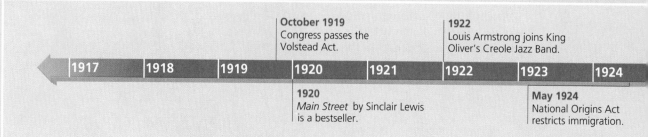

October 1919
Congress passes the Volstead Act.

1922
Louis Armstrong joins King Oliver's Creole Jazz Band.

1917 | 1918 | 1919 | 1920 | 1921 | 1922 | 1923 | 1924

1920
*Main Street* by Sinclair Lewis is a bestseller.

May 1924
National Origins Act restricts immigration.

## Summary

Use the following outline as a tool for reviewing and summarizing the chapter. Copy the outline on your own paper, leaving spaces between headings to jot down notes about key events and concepts.

**I. Growth of the Middle Class**
  A. Americans as Consumers
  B. Americans Take to the Road
  C. Selling America
  D. Youth Sets the Scene
**II. The Jazz Age**
  A. At the Movies
  B. Bat, Ball, Glove, and Club
  C. New Rhythms in the Air
  D. Time to Read
  E. The Lost Generation
  F. The Harlem Renaissance
**III. Cultural Conflicts**
  A. The Familiarity of Religion
  B. The Failure of Prohibition
  C. Crosses in the Night
  D. Closing the Doors
  E. The Challenge of Change

## Ideas, Events, and People

1. How much did the real income of American workers increase between 1923 and 1929? How did this increase affect their standard of living?
2. Give examples of some occupations that were adversely affected by the prosperity of the twenties.
3. How did advertising reflect the materialism of the 1920s?
4. Identify three sports heroes of the twenties. What ideals of the age did these people represent?
5. Who inspired the Harlem Renaissance? Identify three writers of this literary movement and a work of each.
6. How did the Scopes trial test fundamentalism?
7. Why was Prohibition hard to enforce?
8. How was David Stephenson responsible in part for the decline of the Ku Klux Klan?

## Social Studies Skills

### Synthesizing Information

Imagine that you are living in the 1920s. Decide whether you are a city or a farm dweller. Select material from each section of Chapter 9, and synthesize the material into an account of a day in your life.

## Critical Thinking

1. **Making Generalizations**
   This chapter discusses the work of writers like Sinclair Lewis, Alain Locke, Langston Hughes, Gertrude Stein, and Zora Neale Hurston. Consider the works for which they are remembered. What generalization can you make about the topics these writers selected?
2. **Identifying Cause and Effect**
   What were some effects of mass-media advertising and high-pressure salesmanship in the 1920s?
3. **Drawing Conclusions**
   In many ways the 1920s were delightful yet troubled. What events support that conclusion?
4. **Recognizing Values**
   Support for and opposition to the Volstead Act marked opposing sets of values in different segments of the population. Identify the values represented by each group. What are some present-day issues that are vigorously debated by people with opposing sets of values?
5. **Analyzing Behavior**
   Besides sitting on flagpoles and dancing the

| July 1925<br>John Scopes goes on trial<br>for teaching evolution. | 1927<br>*The Jazz Singer*, the first talking<br>motion picture, is shown. | June 1928<br>Al Smith wins Democratic<br>nomination for president. |
|---|---|---|

| 1925 | 1926 | 1927 | 1928 | 1929 | 1930 | 1931 |

| February 1925<br>*New Yorker*<br>magazine<br>is introduced. | August 1926<br>Rudolph<br>Valentino<br>dies. | May 1927<br>Lindbergh completes<br>nonstop flight across<br>the Atlantic. | December 1927<br>Henry Ford introduces<br>the Model A car. |
|---|---|---|---|

Charleston, dance marathons were another fad of the twenties. What political, social, and economic factors led to the widespread interest in and imitation of such behavior?

## Extension and Application

### 1. Citizenship

Organizations like the Ku Klux Klan that use violent means to obtain their ends often violate the civil rights of other citizens. To what extent are such organizations protected by the Constitution? What laws protect citizens from the threats and intimidation practiced by such groups?

### 2. Community Connection

Research the lives of people who were teenagers during the twenties. Your local history museum or back issues of newspapers may be helpful. Try to learn about some of the following topics: the effects of the automobile on their lives, their education, styles of clothing, forms of recreation, and music. You may wish to explore family albums. Look for pictures that record styles of clothing, hairdos, and social events of that period. Report your findings orally to the class.

### 3. Linking Across Time

Consult a periodical index for reports on installment buying in the nineties. Read articles on credit card usage, another form of installment buying. What evidence exists that easy credit encourages people to live beyond their means? What are the effects of installment buying? Are they any different now than they were in the twenties?

### 4. Cooperative Learning

Plan a cooperative learning project on automobile advertising in the 1920s and now. Work in groups of five. As a group analyze the advertisement on page 299. Then find current advertisements that compare or contrast with it. Present the results of your research to the class as a whole.

## Geography

1. How did the use of tractors instead of workhorses produce mixed results for farmers?
2. How did the Model T and chain stores such as Woolworth and J.C. Penney diminish the differences between city life and country life? What other innovations of the twenties had a similar influence?
3. Compare the map below with the 1920 city population map on page 153. Between 1920 and 1930, which region of the country experienced the greatest urban growth?
4. On the map, which cities clearly show the shift from rural to city life during the 1920s? Explain.

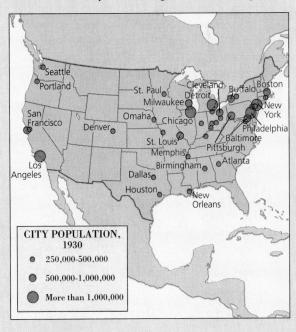

**CITY POPULATION, 1930**
- 250,000–500,000
- 500,000–1,000,000
- More than 1,000,000

# Unit 3 Review

> mericans . . . have put a high value upon the . . . qualities of curiosity and daring, and so they have acquired that character of restlessness, that impatience of forms, . . . which now broadly marks them. . . . A new fallacy in politics spreads faster in the United States than anywhere else on earth, and so does a new fashion in hats, or a new revelation of God, or a new means of killing time, or a new shibboleth, or metaphor, or piece of slang.
>
> H. L. Mencken,
> *The American Language*, 1919

## Concepts and Themes

Writing in 1919, Mencken saw that the United States was changing rapidly from a nation with strong rural roots into a modern, urban society. Mencken witnessed the promise of prosperity, along with fears, old suspicions, and hatreds. Both industry and individual life styles were affected by these changes.

1. Mencken wrote about the American quality of daring. Cite examples of how prosperity and affluence developed in the United States during the 1920s because of this trait.
2. Cite examples of the turmoil created in the United States during the 1920s by some of the "American" characteristics Mencken mentioned.

## History Projects

### 1. Case Study
Pick an industry that is heavily unionized and research a recent strike of its workers. What were the major causes of the strike? Try to find out some effects of the strike on the families of the workers. Share your findings in a short oral presentation.

### 2. Geography
Route 66 helped change the economy of the United States. Research the construction of the Alaska Highway, which was completed in 1942 and opened to the public in 1947. In a brief oral report, explain the main effects of the Alaska Highway.

### 3. Culture of the Time
What is mah-jongg? Briefly describe mah-jongg and give directions for how to play it.

### 4. Evidence of the Past
Collect advertisements aimed at teenagers. Analyze each ad with a partner. Decide which values the advertiser assumes that you hold. Make a list. Do you think the advertiser's assumptions are correct? Present a panel discussion or debate on the validity of the assumptions.

### 5. One Day in History
What was the Lindy? Why was it so named? Report about or demonstrate the dance for your class.

## Writing Activities

1. Research the beginnings of organized crime in the United States. Present your findings in a three- to five-page report. Use at least three sources in your research. (See the Writer's Guide, page 829, for guidelines on writing a research report.)
2. Choose one group that existed in the United States during the twenties, such as affluent urban workers or struggling farmers. Write a journal entry for Sunday, May 21, 1927, as if you were a member of that group. Include your reactions to news of the day, such as Charles Lindbergh's accomplishment, and a description of your typical week. (See the Writer's Guide, pages 825–827, for guidelines on writing for different purposes.)

## The Arts

- *Cane* by Jean Toomer; collection of poems, short fiction, and poetic prose about frustrated African Americans in the North and South
- *Women's Suffrage in Politics: The Inner Story of the Suffrage Movement* by Carrie Catt; a personal account of the struggle for the right to vote
- *You Know Me, Al* by Ring Lardner; collection of humorous stories and letters by a baseball-playing character

# UNIT FOUR

# Economic Crisis and the New Deal

VANITY FAIR

FEBRUARY 1934
PRICE 35 CENTS
©THE CONDÉ NAST
PUBLICATIONS, INC.

# "To Mark the Dust"

*At the height of the Depression, drought turned the Great Plains into a huge, arid dust bowl. Unable to make their land produce, thousands of farmers fell hopelessly into debt. In* The Grapes of Wrath, *novelist John Steinbeck traces the journey of one family that moves from Oklahoma to California in search of work. In this selection, Steinbeck depicts the Oklahoma farmers' frustration as they confront an unseen, unknown foe.*

## from *The Grapes of Wrath*

### by John Steinbeck

The owners of the land came onto the land, or more often a spokesman for the owners came. They came in closed cars, and they felt the dry earth with their fingers, and sometimes they drove big earth augers into the ground for soil tests. The tenants, from their sun-beaten dooryards, watched uneasily when the closed cars drove along the fields. And at last the owner men drove into the dooryards and sat in their cars to talk out of the windows. The tenant men stood beside the cars for a while, and then squatted on their hams and found sticks with which to mark the dust.

In the open doors the women stood looking out, and behind them the children—corn-headed children, with wide eyes, one bare foot on top of the other bare foot, and the toes working. The women and the children watched their men talking to the owner men. They were silent.

Some of the owner men were kind because they hated what they had to do, and some of them were angry because they hated to be cruel, and some of them were cold because they had long ago found that one could not be an owner unless one were cold. And all of them were caught in something larger than themselves. Some of them hated the mathematics that drove them, and some were afraid, and some worshiped the mathematics because it provided a refuge from thought and from feeling. If a bank or a finance company owned the land, the owner man said, The Bank—or the Company—needs—wants—insists—must have—as though the Bank or the Company were a monster, with thought and feeling, which had ensnared them. These last would take no responsibility for the banks or the companies because they were men and slaves, while the banks were machines and masters all at the same time. Some of the owner men were a little proud to be slaves to such cold and powerful masters. The owner men sat in the cars and explained. You know the land is poor. You've scrabbled at it long enough, God knows.

The squatting tenant men nodded and wondered and drew figures in the dust, and yes, they knew, God knows. If the dust only wouldn't fly. If the top would only stay on the soil, it might not be so bad.

The owner men went on leading to their point: You know the land's getting poorer. You know what cotton does to the land; robs it, sucks all the blood out of it.

The squatters nodded—they knew, God knew. If they could only rotate the crops they might pump blood back into the land.

Well, it's too late. And the owner men explained the workings and the thinkings of the monster that was stronger than they were. A man can hold land if he can just eat and pay taxes; he can do that.

Yes, he can do that until his crops fail one day and he has to borrow money from the bank.

But—you see, a bank or a company can't do that, because those creatures don't breathe air, don't eat sidemeat. They breathe profits; they eat the interest on money. If they don't get it, they die the way you die without air, without side-meat. It is a sad thing, but it is so. It is just so.

The squatting men raised their eyes to understand. Can't we just hang on? Maybe the next year will be a good year. God knows how much cotton next year. And with all the wars—God knows what price cotton will bring. Don't they make explosives out of cotton? And uniforms? Get enough wars and cotton'll hit the ceiling. Next year, maybe. They looked up questioningly.

We can't depend on it. The bank—the monster has to have profits all the time. It can't wait. It'll die. No, taxes go on. When the monster stops growing, it dies. It can't stay one size. . . .

The squatting men looked down again. What do you want us to do? We can't take less share of the crop—we're half starved now. The kids are hungry all the time. We got no clothes, torn an' ragged. If all the neighbors weren't the same, we'd be ashamed to go to meeting.

And at last the owner men came to the point. The tenant system won't work any more. One man on a tractor can take the place of twelve or fourteen families. Pay him a wage and take all the crop. We have to do it. We don't like to do it. But the monster's sick. Something's happened to the monster.

But you'll kill the land with cotton.

We know. We've got to take cotton quick before the land dies. Then we'll sell the land. Lots of families in the East would like to own a piece of land.

The tenant men looked up alarmed. But what'll happen to us? How'll we eat?

You'll have to get off the land. The plows'll go through the dooryard.

And now the squatting men stood up angrily. Grampa took up the land, and he had to kill the Indians and drive them away. And Pa was born here, and he killed weeds and snakes. Then a bad year came and he had to borrow a little money. An' we was born here. There in the door—our children born here. And Pa had to borrow money. The bank owned the land then, but we stayed and we got a little bit of what we raised.

We know that—all that. It's not us, it's the bank. A bank isn't like a man. Or an owner with fifty thousand acres, he isn't like a man either. That's the monster.

Sure, cried the tenant men, but it's our land. We measured it and broke it up. We were born on it, and we got killed on it, died on it. Even if it's no good, it's still ours. That's what makes it ours—being born on it, working it, dying on it. That makes ownership, not a paper with numbers on it.

We're sorry. It's not us. It's the monster. The bank isn't like a man.

Yes, but the bank is only made of men.

No, you're wrong there—quite wrong there. The bank is something else than men. It happens that every man in a bank hates what the bank does, and yet the bank does it. The bank is something more than men, I tell you. It's the monster. Men made it, but they can't control it.

The tenants cried, Grampa killed Indians, Pa killed snakes for the land. Maybe we can kill banks—they're worse than Indians and snakes. Maybe we got to fight to keep our land, like Pa and Grampa did.

And now the owner men grew angry. You'll have to go.

But it's ours, the tenant men cried. We—

No. The bank, the monster owns it. You'll have to go.

We'll get our guns, like Grampa when the Indians came. What then?

Well—first the sheriff, and then the troops. You'll be stealing if you try to stay, you'll be murderers if you kill to stay. The monster isn't men, but it can make men do what it wants.

But if we go, where'll we go? How'll we go? We got no money.

We're sorry, said the owner men. The bank, the fifty-thousand-acre owner can't be responsible. You're on land that isn't yours. Once over the line maybe you can pick cotton in the fall. Maybe you can go on relief. Why don't you go on west to California? There's work there, and it never gets cold. Why, you can reach out anywhere and pick an orange. Why, there's always some kind of crop to work in. Why don't you go there? And the owner men started their cars and rolled away.

The tenant men squatted down on their hams again to mark the dust with a stick, to figure, to wonder. Their sunburned faces were dark, and their sun-whipped eyes were light. The women moved cautiously out of the doorways toward their men, and the children crept behind the women, cautiously, ready to run. The bigger boys squatted beside their fathers, because that made them men. After a time the women asked, What did he want?

And the men looked up for a second, and the smolder of pain was in their eyes. We got to get off. A tractor and a superintendent. Like factories.

Where'll we go? the women asked.

We don't know. We don't know.

And the women went quickly, quietly back into the houses and herded the children ahead of them. They knew that a man so hurt and so perplexed may turn in anger, even on people he loves. They left the men alone to figure and to wonder in the dust.

THE GRANGER COLLECTION

**Dorothea Lange's portrait of a family evicted from the land is one of many stories that photographers of the Depression recorded.**

gulches, water courses, fences, houses.

The man sitting in the iron seat did not look like a man; gloved, goggled, rubber dust mask over nose and mouth, he was a part of the monster, a robot in the seat. . . .

At noon the tractor driver stopped sometimes near a tenant house and opened his lunch: sandwiches wrapped in waxed paper, white bread, pickle, cheese, Spam, a piece of pie branded like an engine part. He ate without relish. And tenants not yet moved away came out to see him, looked curiously while the goggles were taken off, and the rubber dust mask, leaving white circles around the eyes and a large white circle around nose and mouth. The exhaust of the tractor puttered on, for fuel is so cheap it is more efficient to leave the engine running than to heat the Diesel nose for a new start. Curious children crowded close, ragged children who ate their fried dough as they watched. They watched hungrily the unwrapping of the sandwiches, and their hunger-sharpened noses smelled the pickle, cheese, and Spam. They didn't speak to the driver. They watched his hand as it carried food to his mouth. They did not watch him chewing; their eyes followed the hand that held the sandwich. After a while the tenant who could not leave the place came out and squatted in the shade beside the tractor.

"Why, you're Joe Davis's boy!"

"Sure," the driver said.

"Well, what you doing this kind of work for—against your own people?"

"Three dollars a day. I got damn sick of creeping for my dinner—and not getting it. I got a wife and kids. We got to eat. Three dollars a day, and it comes every day."

"That's right," the tenant said. "But for your three dollars a day fifteen or twenty families can't eat at all. Nearly a hundred people have to go out and wander on the roads for your three dollars a day. Is that right?"

And the driver said, "Can't think of that. Got to think of my own kids. Three dollars a day, and it comes every day. Times are changing, mister, don't you know? Can't make a living on the land unless you've got two, five, ten thousand acres and a tractor. Crop land isn't for little guys like us any more. You don't kick up a howl because you can't make Fords, or because you're not the

After a time perhaps the tenant man looked about—at the pump put in ten years ago, with a goose-neck handle and iron flowers on the spout, at the chopping block where a thousand chickens had been killed, at the hand plow lying in the shed, and the patent crib hanging in the rafters over it.

The children crowded about the women in the houses. What we going to do, Ma? Where we going to go?

The women said, We don't know, yet. Go out and play. But don't go near your father. He might whale you if you go near him. And the women went on with the work, but all the time they watched the men squatting in the dust—perplexed and figuring.

The tractors came over the roads and into the fields, great crawlers moving like insects, having the incredible strength of insects. They crawled over the ground, laying the track and rolling on it and picking it up. Diesel tractors, puttering while they stood idle; they thundered when they moved, and then settled down to a droning roar. Snub-nosed monsters, raising the dust and sticking their snouts into it, straight down the country, across the country, through fences, through dooryards, in and out of gullies in straight lines. They did not run on the ground, but on their own roadbeds. They ignored hills and

telephone company. Well, crops are like that now. Nothing to do about it. You try to get three dollars a day someplace. That's the only way."

The tenant pondered. "Funny thing how it is. If a man owns a little property, that property is him, it's part of him, and it's like him. If he owns property only so he can walk on it and handle it and be sad when it isn't doing well, and feel fine when the rain falls on it, that property is him, and some way he's bigger because he owns it. Even if he isn't successful he's big with his property. That is so."

And the tenant pondered more. "But let a man get property he doesn't see, or can't take time to get his fingers in, or can't be there to walk on it—why, then the property is the man. He can't do what he wants, he can't think what he wants. The property is the man, stronger than he is. And he is small, not big. Only his possessions are big—and he's the servant of his property. That is so, too."

The driver munched the branded pie and threw the crust away. "Times are changed, don't you know? Thinking about stuff like that don't feed the kids. Get your three dollars a day, feed your kids. You got no call to worry about anybody's kids but your own. You get a reputation for talking like that, and you'll never get three dollars a day. Big shots won't give you three dollars a day if you worry about anything but your three dollars a day."

"Nearly a hundred people on the road for your three dollars. Where will we go?"

"And that reminds me," the driver said, "you better get out soon. I'm going through the dooryard after dinner."

"You filled in the well this morning."

"I know. Had to keep the line straight. But I'm going through the dooryard after dinner. Got to keep the lines straight. And—well, you know Joe Davis, my old man, so I'll tell you this. I got orders wherever there's a family not moved out—if I have an accident—you know, get too close and cave the house in a little—well, I might get a couple of dollars. And my youngest kid never had no shoes yet."

"I built it with my hands. Straightened old nails to put the sheathing on. Rafters are wired to the stringers with baling wire. It's mine. I built it. You bump it down—I'll be in the window with a rifle. You even come too close and I'll pot you like a rabbit."

"It's not me. There's nothing I can do. I'll lose my job if I don't do it. And look—suppose you kill me? They'll just hang you, but long before you're hung there'll be another guy on the tractor, and he'll bump the house down. You're not killing the right guy."

"That's so," the tenant said. "Who gave you orders? I'll go after him. He's the one to kill."

"You're wrong. He got his orders from the bank. The bank told him, 'Clear those people out or it's your job.' "

"Well, there's a president of the bank. There's a board of directors. I'll fill up the magazine of the rifle and go into the bank."

The driver said, "Fellow was telling me the bank gets orders from the East. The orders were, 'Make the land show profit or we'll close you up.' "

"But where does it stop? Who can we shoot? I don't aim to starve to death before I kill the man that's starving me."

"I don't know. Maybe there's nobody to shoot. Maybe the thing isn't men at all. Maybe, like you said, the property's doing it. Anyway I told you my orders."

"I got to figure," the tenant said. "We all got to figure. There's some way to stop this. It's not like lightning or earthquakes. We've got a bad thing made by men, and by God that's something we can change." . . . Across the dooryard the tractor cut, and the hard, foot-beaten ground was seeded field, and the tractor cut through again; the uncut space was ten feet wide. And back he came. The iron guard bit into the house-corner, crumbled the wall, and wrenched the little house from its foundation so that it fell sideways, crushed like a bug. And the driver was goggled and a rubber mask covered his nose and mouth. The tractor cut a straight line on, and the air and the ground vibrated with its thunder. The tenant man stared after it, his rifle in his hand. His wife was beside him, and the quiet children behind. And all of them stared after the tractor.

## Responding to Literature

1. The tenant says about the land, "That's what makes it ours—being born on it, working it, dying on it." Do you agree or disagree? Explain.

2. Who do you think Steinbeck believes is ultimately responsible for the destruction of the tenant's house? What events support your conclusion?

*For Further Reading*
Agee, James: *Let Us Now Praise Famous Men*
Hurston, Zora Neale: *Their Eyes Were Watching God*
McCullers, Carson: *The Heart Is a Lonely Hunter*
Saroyan, William: *The Daring Young Man on the Flying Trapeze*

CHAPTER 10

# The Great Depression

## December 1932: New York Responds to Its Neediest Cases

Daily stories printed in the *New York Times* in 1932 described the city's neediest families and asked readers to contribute to a fund to help these people. In one of these stories the paper described an unemployed plasterer, Mr. C., who had not been eating so that his two-year-old daughter could have enough food. One morning he "fell to the floor and could not rise. A doctor said he had injured himself so seriously by voluntarily starving himself that an operation was imperative. Help is asked to keep the family in food and shelter until Mr. C. is able to work."

Mr. C. was only one of millions of

*The 1930s witnessed one of the longest, the deepest, and the most devastating economic depressions ever experienced by the people of the United States.*

UPI/BETTMANN NEWSPHOTOS

*On the brink of destitution, people who had been wiped out by the stock market crash became desperate for money.*

people who had enjoyed prosperity during the 1920s but whose fortunes fell in the early 1930s. Between 1929 and 1932 millions of hard-working men and women lost their jobs. Most of these people were proud and used to providing for their own families. They felt ashamed to take charity.

The 1930s witnessed one of the longest, the deepest, and the most devastating economic depressions ever experienced by the people of the United States. After a decade of high living, the abrupt financial breakdown came as a severe shock. The affluence enjoyed during the Roaring Twenties suddenly began to evaporate in the autumn of 1929.

*This classic photograph by Dorothea Lange shows a mother and children on the road in Tulelake, California. Lange was a photographer for the Farm Security Administration from 1935 to 1939.*

# The Economy Hits Bottom

## October 24, 1929: New York Stock Exchange Crashes

THURSDAY MORNING AT 10:00, WALL STREET WAS JAMMED. A CROWD OF THOUSANDS GATHERED OUTSIDE THE NEW York Stock Exchange, waiting for news. The rumble of loud voices hinted to spectators of the bedlam inside. Traders shouted out their orders to sell, sell, sell. Few were willing to buy the stocks, so prices plunged steeply in the stampede.

At noon five of the nation's leading bankers met in the building across the street from the Exchange. In an effort to stabilize the plummeting market, these men pledged to pump undisclosed millions into the stock market. By buying stocks, they hoped to make prices rise. Rumors of the meeting had a calming effect on the stock market. Selling slowed and the panic began to subside. When the bankers' representative, Richard Whitney, strode across the floor later that afternoon to deliver his orders for large blocks of stock above asking prices, the stock market had already begun to rally. At closing time stock prices started to rebound from the morning's slump.

The stock market's recovery was short-lived. The following Monday the Exchange opened with a rush of sales that wiped out all the gains of the preceding week. The bankers met again and decided they could do nothing to check the decline. On Tuesday, October 29, the flood of sales continued. Historians have called this "the most devastating day in the history of markets." A gloomy quiet pervaded the trading floor. The week before, traders ran across the floor in

© VARIETY

panic, trying to submit their orders before prices dropped further. That day, however, the stock exchange was as dour as a funeral parlor. A reporter from the *New York Times* described the somber scene: "Orderly crowds lined up before each [selling] post, talking in subdued tones, without any pushing." In that last week in October 1929, the stock market began a momentous decline that came to be known as the great crash. During that time $30 billion in stock value—about the same amount of money the United States spent in World War I—evaporated completely along with people's dreams of achieving permanent prosperity.

## Why Did the Crash Occur?

According to economists and politicians of the late 1920s, the United States had entered a new era in which everyone could be rich. Many people agreed with a leading politician who stated:

> *If a man saves $15 a week, and invests in good common stocks, and allows the dividends and rights to accumulate, at the end of twenty years he will have at least $80,000 and an income from investments of around $400 a month. He will be rich.*

> John J. Raskob, Democratic
> National Committee chairman, 1929

---

### STUDY GUIDE

**As You Read**

Analyze why the nation's economy hit bottom and why it stayed there. Also, think about the following concepts and skills.

**Central Concepts**

- recognizing how **speculation** led to the stock market crash
- understanding the diverse causes and effects of the economic **depression**

**Thinking Skills**

- identifying cause and effect
- making generalizations

**Stock Market Speculation** Such advice inspired thousands of people to pour their savings into stocks. However, many investors wanted to make their fortunes immediately. Hoping that heavy financial risks would pay off quickly, people in the late 1920s speculated in the stock market. **Speculation** was a way of gambling with short-term investments. Speculators would buy stocks they thought would rise in price quickly. After the price of their stocks went up, they would sell the stocks for a profit.

The table below shows the large gains stocks made between 1927 and 1929. A speculator who bought stock in Hershey Chocolate in August 1928, for example, and sold it in September 1929, made over 100 percent profit on the investment. Banks at the time commonly paid an annual rate of under 7 percent on savings accounts. The dramatic difference between the return on a savings account and the return on stock speculation made the stock market an attractive gamble for thousands of Americans.

Speculation was further fueled by the common practice of buying on margin. In such a transaction, an investor put down as little as 5 percent of the stock price and borrowed the rest of the money from a stockbroker. The stock itself was collateral for the loan. In other words, if the investor could not repay the loan, the broker gained ownership of the stock.

**On the March 1929 cover of *Life* magazine, a young woman rapidly reads the stock market ticker tape, with its ever-rising prices.** *If you had bought 10 shares of AT&T on August 31, 1927, and sold them on September 3, 1929, how much profit would you have made?*

Investors buying on margin could buy more stock with their money than investors who did not borrow from brokers. For example, an investor with $500 could buy 5 shares of a stock costing $100 per share. Buying on margin, however, the investor could use the $500 to buy 100 shares, in effect buying $10,000 worth of stock. As long as the price of the stock continued to rise, the buyer could sell later, pay back what had been borrowed, and realize a tidy profit.[1]

In the boom years of the late 1920s, savvy margin buyers made fortunes. Buying stocks at low prices, they watched gleefully as stock values soared. When they thought a stock had reached its peak price, they sold it, paying off the stockbroker with the money they made from the sale.

As long as stock prices kept going up, brokers were happy to lend money to speculators. After all, they received up to 20 percent interest on their loans. However, as soon as prices began to slide, brokers had to protect their loans. Since the stocks were their only collateral, when stock prices began to decline, brokers called in their margins. In other words, they asked

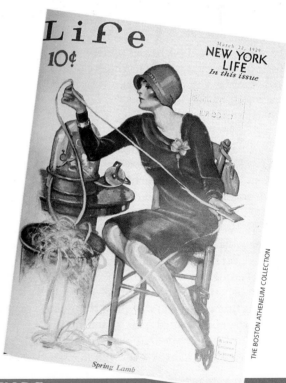

THE BOSTON ATHENEUM COLLECTION

### Selected Stock Prices, 1927–1929

| Stock | Aug. 31, 1927 | Aug. 31, 1928 | Sept. 3, 1929 |
|---|---|---|---|
| American and Foreign Power | $ 23.86 | $ 38.00 | $167.75 |
| American Telephone and Telegraph (AT&T) | $169.00 | $182.00 | $304.00 |
| Detroit Edison Co. | $151.00 | $205.00 | $350.00 |
| General Electric Co. | $142.00 | $168.13 | $396.25 |
| Hershey Chocolate | not listed | $ 53.25 | $128.00 |
| International Business Machines (IBM) | $ 93.00 | $130.86 | $241.75 |
| People's Gas Chicago | $147.13 | $182.86 | $374.75 |

*Spring Lamb*

**Identifying Cause and Effect**
Speculators invested in stocks because stocks returned greater profits than savings accounts did. Stockbrokers allowed investors to buy on 5 percent margin, and that encouraged even more investment in stocks. When stock prices fell and investors could not pay their debts, investors lost their money and brokers held worthless stocks as collateral.

1 Compare the responsibility of both investors and brokers in starting the frenzy of speculation that occurred in the stock market.

NATIONAL MUSEUM OF AMERICAN ART, SMITHSONIAN INSTITUTION, MUSEUM PURCHASE

## Selected Stock Prices, 1929

| Stock | Sept. 3, 1929 | Oct. 29, 1929 | Nov. 15, 1929 |
|---|---|---|---|
| American and Foreign Power | $167.75 | $ 73.00 | $ 67.86 |
| American Telephone and Telegraph (AT&T) | $304.00 | $230.00 | $222.00 |
| Detroit Edison Co. | $350.00 | not listed | $195.00 |
| General Electric Co. | $396.25 | $210.00 | $201.00 |
| Hershey Chocolate | $128.00 | $108.00 | $ 68.00 |
| International Business Machines (IBM) | $241.75 | not listed | $129.86 |
| People's Gas Chicago | $374.75 | not listed | $230.00 |

**The Latin words *Dies Irae* literally mean "Day of Wrath," but colloquially the expression means "Judgment Day."** *When the stock market crash came, which of the stocks listed in the table had the greatest decline in value? How much would you have lost on 10 shares of that stock if you had bought them on September 3, 1929, and sold them on November 15, 1929?*

investors who had borrowed money from them to put down more cash. If the customer could not pay, the broker sold the stock, keeping the proceeds as repayment for the loan.

**The Beginning of the End**  By the summer of 1929, brokers had lent out more than $6 billion in margin loans to their customers. Realizing that the huge number of people investing in the stock market meant the market was saturated, a few investors began to sell, and stock prices slowly declined in the autumn of 1929. Brokers began calling in their margins. Many investors did not have cash to pay for their stocks, so brokers were forced to sell. Enforced selling pushed prices down further. Noticing the downturn, other investors began selling their stock in panic. Amid the flood of unmet margin calls and the deluge of panic selling, the crash gained speed and force.

By the last week in October, the bottom fell out of the stock market. Stocks tumbled even further in

November. As shown in the table above, in a few months the prices of major stocks fell 75 percent. People who had been millionaires suddenly were deep in debt.

However, stock market investors were not the only people brought down by the crash. Since savings deposits were not federally insured, people who had prudently tucked their money in banks found their savings had vanished. Many banks had lent their cash reserves to stockbrokers. The brokers lost the money when their customers could not respond to the margin calls and failed to repay their loans. Thus, the stock market crash caught millions of innocent bystanders in the financial crunch.

**The Onset of the Depression**  In the first few months after the crash, business leaders and economists spoke confidently, predicting a quick recovery. In December 1929 Secretary of the Treasury Andrew Mellon announced, "I see nothing in the present situation that is either menacing or warrants pessimism." However, as the new decade dawned, the United States fell into a deep business depression.

A period of severely reduced economic activity, known as a **depression,** is characterized by a sharp rise in unemployment. The depression that began in

## STUDY GUIDE

### Identifying Cause and Effect

Before the Depression, people who invested in stocks knew they took a risk, but people who put their savings in a bank for a lower rate of interest thought their money would be safe. In one of the catastrophes of the Depression, people with bank savings accounts also lost their money, because the bankers had lent the money out to stockbrokers who could not pay it back.

Today the Federal Deposit Insurance Corporation, a government agency, protects savings accounts up to $100,000.

October 1929 was the most devastating economic downturn in U.S. history. Raging through most of the 1930s, this sickening decline became known as the Great Depression.

## The Causes of the Great Depression

After that disastrous week in October 1929, the economy began unraveling. Economists then saw flaws few had noticed during the get-rich-quick era of the mid-1920s.

**Depressed Farms and Industries**  The shiny glow of prosperity had not rubbed off on all Americans in the 1920s. Farmers' incomes fell throughout the decade. The textile, lumber, mining, and railroad industries also declined. In the months preceding the crash, the automobile and construction industries suffered from a decrease in orders. As a result, wages dropped and employers laid off workers. With their incomes cut, many farmers and workers could not afford the manufactured goods that the United States' industries had been churning out at impressive rates in the 1920s. This underconsumption became a major weakness in the economy.

**Wealth Distribution**  Another factor contributing to the underconsumption that fueled the Depression was the growing gap in wealth between rich people and Americans of more ordinary means. Although business profits in many industries rose throughout the 1920s, not all workers received a proportionate share of these profits. This meant that there was not enough consumer buying power to keep up with all the goods being produced. By the late 1920s, radios, telephones, refrigerators, washing machines, and other goods were stacking up in warehouses across the country.

**Monetary Policy**  Errors in monetary policy also contributed to the crash. After the crash, the Federal Reserve system, charged with regulating the amount of money in circulation, followed a restrictive policy that dried up credit. This policy left the country with a supply of money in circulation that was not large enough to allow the economy to bounce back after the stock market bubble burst.

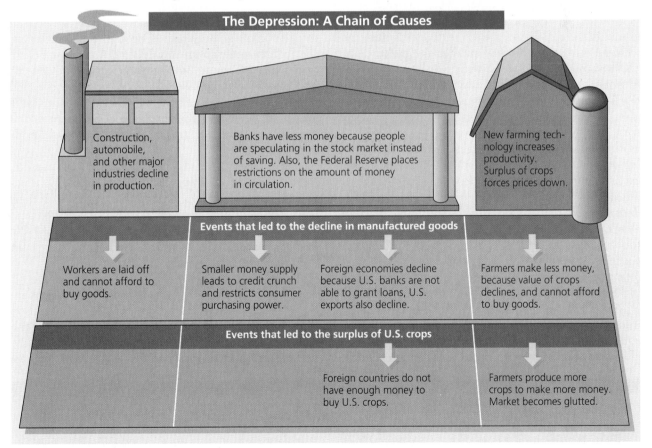

**The Depression: A Chain of Causes**

Construction, automobile, and other major industries decline in production.

Banks have less money because people are speculating in the stock market instead of saving. Also, the Federal Reserve places restrictions on the amount of money in circulation.

New farming technology increases productivity. Surplus of crops forces prices down.

**Events that led to the decline in manufactured goods**

Workers are laid off and cannot afford to buy goods.

Smaller money supply leads to credit crunch and restricts consumer purchasing power.

Foreign economies decline because U.S. banks are not able to grant loans, U.S. exports also decline.

Farmers make less money, because value of crops declines, and cannot afford to buy goods.

**Events that led to the surplus of U.S. crops**

Foreign countries do not have enough money to buy U.S. crops.

Farmers produce more crops to make more money. Market becomes glutted.

**The symbols at the top of the chart represent industry, banking (domestic and international), and agriculture.** *How might the decline in industrial production have affected the agricultural surplus? How might the decline in the amount of money available domestically have affected the agricultural surplus?*

**Decline in Foreign Trade** Weaknesses in the American economy also sapped the strength of foreign economies, some of which were already unstable. Throughout the 1920s the United States served as a bank for other nations, lending money to aid foreign industries and speed recovery from the Great War. During the late 1920s, however, as Americans began pouring borrowed money into the stock market, bank funds for loans to other nations dried up. International trade slowed down because, without American loans, other nations had less money to spend on our nation's goods. High tariffs—taxes on imported products—further blocked international trade. This decline fed into the cycle of underconsumption, further weakening the American economy.

After the stock market crash, all these problems with the economy began to take their toll. The economic slowdown frightened everyone, from East Coast executives to midwestern store owners, from Utah miners to the president of the United States.

---

## Hoover's Response

Occupying the White House when the Depression began was Herbert C. Hoover. Nicknamed the Great Engineer, Hoover was elected president by a wide margin in 1928. Orphaned at age eight, he left his Iowa home to move in with relatives in Oregon. Although his early childhood was sad, in young adulthood Hoover buried unhappiness with driving ambition. He graduated from Stanford University in 1895 with an engineering degree. For the next 18 years he worked on engineering projects all over the world, building an unshakable reputation for solving technical problems and amassing a personal fortune.

Hoover's Quaker upbringing gave him a strong desire to serve humanity. After the outbreak of World War I, he coordinated war relief efforts in Europe and food production in the United States. Efficient and successful, Hoover inspired confidence. He quickly rose as an important political figure. President Harding appointed him Secretary of Commerce in 1921.

From this influential post, Hoover tried to put into practice his vision for the United States. He encouraged voluntary associations of business leaders to eliminate inefficiency in industry. He suggested that federal, state, and local governments coordinate efforts to dampen harmful swings in the business cycle. With these and other measures, Hoover was sure that the United States in 1928 was "nearer to the final triumph over poverty than ever before in the history of any land." His optimism and confidence matched the mood of the country and won him the presidency.

**Initial Reaction to the Depression** Only months after Hoover made that prediction, the stock market crashed. Realizing that people's plummeting faith in the economy hindered chances of recovery, Hoover tried to bolster confidence. "We have now passed the worst," he told Americans in May 1930, "and . . . shall rapidly recover."

Even with his optimistic pronouncements, the president took immediate action to try to arrest the economic downturn. Following his own faith in voluntary action, he called a meeting of business leaders and asked them to pledge not to cut wages or production of goods. He suggested that city and state governments stimulate their local economies by funding building projects to provide new jobs.

Hoover also funneled aid to farmers through the Agricultural Marketing Act, which Congress had passed even before the economy began to weaken in the aftermath of the crash. Through this legislation, the federal government established the Farm Board, which lent money to farmers to help them set up cooperative marketing associations. Farmers who joined these associations agreed to sell their crops as a group. If they could not get the prices they wanted at the time of the harvest, they would store their crops until prices rose.

Voluntary marketing associations might, in time, have raised crop prices. However, many farmers needed immediate help paying the mortgages on their land. But the Farm Board was not authorized to lend money to individual farmers, so thousands of farm families went bankrupt in the early 1930s, losing both their jobs and their homes.

**The Depression Deepens** Despite Hoover's efforts to help farmers and others, business conditions in the United States worsened in the two years after the crash. Twenty-three thousand businesses failed in 1929. In 1932, 32,000 businesses went under. The average

**Making Generalizations**
As Secretary of Commerce for eight years under Presidents Harding and Coolidge, Hoover realized the importance of being optimistic about the economy. He built confidence in the economy by boasting, "The slogan of progress is changing from the full dinner pail to the full garage." After the crash he continued his attempts to stimulate optimism about the American economy. He asked businesses to maintain production levels and full staffs. In summary, Hoover believed that an optimistic attitude was extremely important in combating the Depression.

**WORLD'S HIGHEST STANDARD OF LIVING**

*There's no way like the American Way*

MARGARET BOURKE-WHITE, *LIFE* MAGAZINE © TIME WARNER INC.

**Margaret Bourke-White was one of the four original staff photographers for *Life*. This photograph,** **probably the most famous of her career, was taken at a relief station in Louisville, Kentucky, in 1937.[2]**

family's annual income dropped from $2,300 in 1929 to $1,600 in 1935. Unemployment rose from about 5 percent in 1929 to almost 25 percent in 1932.

The early 1930s saw mounting poverty and destitution. In major cities bread lines stretched for blocks, as people waited for one scant meal a day. (You can read more about the bread lines in Evidence of the Past on pages 334–335.) With the number of unemployed growing every month, charity funds soon proved completely inadequate. Toledo, Ohio, could afford to spend only two cents per relief meal per day. New York City gave only $2.39 to each family on relief per week. Thousands of people were turned away.

With poverty pressing down on them, some people wrote President Hoover in anger and frustration:

*Why should we hafto . . . have foodless days . . . and our children have Schoolless days and Shoeless days and the land full of plenty and Banks bursting with money? Why does Every Thing have Exceptional Value Except the Human being? Why are we reduced to poverty and starving and anxiety and Sorrow So quickly under your administration?*

Robert S. McElvaine,
*Down & Out in the Great Depression*

---

## STUDY GUIDE

**Identifying Cause and Effect**
A cause and effect chain of events set the economy on a downward spiral from 5 percent unemployment to 25 percent. As more people were unemployed, there were fewer people with money to buy products. Stores began to lay off salespeople. This in turn led to more unemployment and fewer customers. Soon the factories stopped producing goods and laid off their workers.

**2** Identify examples of irony in Margaret Bourke-White's photograph of the bread line.

## Too Little Too Late

Facing such harsh criticism, Hoover reluctantly introduced new government programs to deal with the economic crisis. He still insisted that voluntary action and local programs were the best ways to relieve the Depression. However, by early 1932 he had to admit that these measures had failed.

Trying to respond to the deepening economic crisis, Hoover obtained congressional approval for a federal relief agency called the Reconstruction Finance Corporation (RFC) in February 1932. The RFC was the largest federal program of economic aid that any president had ever proposed. The agency was authorized to dispense $2 billion in loans to faltering banks, insurance companies, and railroads. Hoover hoped that the RFC would inspire confidence in business. The theory was that funding such institutions would stimulate industry and eventually create more jobs.

The trickle-down measure, however, could not relieve the immediate suffering of the unemployed. The Emergency Relief Act, passed in July 1932, enabled the RFC to distribute an additional $300 million in loans to state governments for unemployment relief. However, these governments did not qualify for RFC loans unless they were on the verge of bankruptcy. By the end of the year, the RFC had distributed only half of its available money.

**Mounting Protests**   With wages dropping, unemployment growing, and so little money trickling into relief measures, resentment grew among people beaten down by the Depression. One group, veterans from the Great War, organized a massive lobbying effort to get aid for themselves and their families. The government had promised these veterans a bonus for serving in the war, payable in 1945. Organizing themselves into disciplined companies, a group of jobless veterans from Portland, Oregon, traveled to Washington, D.C., in May 1932, to try to convince Congress to grant them their bonus 13 years early. The bonus army, as this group was called, enforced strict rules to keep their movement united and respectable. Among these rules were "no panhandling, no drinking, and no radicalism."

The group from Portland started with 1,000 veterans. By the time Congress was to vote on the bonus in June, the ranks of the bonus army had swelled to 17,000. Setting up camp in abandoned buildings in Washington, D.C., and on the marshy flats along the shores of the Anacostia River, the veterans remained orderly. Many veterans had brought their families with them. Wives set up housekeeping while the children made new friends from all over the country.

On June 17, the day the Senate was slated to vote on the bonus bill, the veterans marched to the Capitol steps to await the outcome. Late in the afternoon, Oklahoma Senator Elmer Thomas appeared on the Capitol steps and told the leader of the group, Walter W. Waters, that the bill had been defeated. As the men began to hiss and boo, Waters took charge: "Let us show them that we can take it on the chin. Let us show them that we are patriotic Americans. I call on you to sing 'America.'" Thousands of the men joined in singing and then formed ranks and marched back to their camps.

With the bonus bill dead, several thousand veterans left Washington. However, about 2,000 remained throughout the month, hoping that the bill would be revived before the congressional session ended in July. After Congress again refused to approve the bonus bill, the veterans slowly began to disperse. However, they did not leave quickly enough for Hoover, who

---

### ★ ★ ★  PRESIDENT'S GALLERY  ★ ★ ★

*"Ours is a land rich in resources; stimulating in its glorious beauty; filled with millions of happy homes; blessed with comfort and opportunity. . . . No country is more loved by its people. I have an abiding faith in their capacity, integrity, and high purpose. I have no fears for the future of our country. It is bright with hope."*

*Inaugural Address,
March 4, 1929*

AP, HERBERT HOOVER PRESIDENTIAL LIBRARY-MUSEUM

Herbert Hoover, 1929–1933

**Background:**
- Born 1874; died 1964
- Republican, Iowa
- Headed the Commission for Relief in Belgium 1914–1917
- Secretary of Commerce 1921–1928

**Achievements in Office:**
- Federal Farm Board (1929)
- Smoot-Hawley Tariff Act (1930)
- Reconstruction Finance Corporation (1932)

AP/WIDE WORLD PHOTOS

**Bonus-seeking veterans were attacked by soldiers near the veterans' makeshift shacks in the Anacostia Flats, approximately three miles from the White House.** *Why did Hoover feel threatened by the veterans?*

AP/WIDE WORLD PHOTOS

saw the bonus army as a hostile force. On July 28 Hoover dispatched Army Chief of Staff Douglas MacArthur and his aide Dwight D. Eisenhower to clear the veterans from the federal buildings. Cavalry units, tanks, infantry with fixed bayonets, and a machine-gun detachment marched on the unarmed veterans. Fleeing in terror, the veterans crossed the Anacostia River to the bonus army encampments. MacArthur pursued the veterans and torched the camp. More than 100 people were injured and a baby died, asphyxiated by tear gas. The press, appalled at the brutal attack, commented: "What a pitiful spectacle is that of the great American Government, mightiest in the world, chasing unarmed men, women, and children with Army tanks."

**The Election of 1932**   The routing of the bonus army was the last nail in Hoover's political coffin. The public, which already considered the president cold

and unfeeling because he refused to pay for unemployment relief, now saw him also as a vicious bully. On hearing about the attack on the veterans at Anacostia by MacArthur's troops, Democratic presidential candidate Franklin D. Roosevelt turned to his friend Felix Frankfurter and said, "Well, Felix, this will elect me."

Roosevelt's prediction proved correct. Hoover stayed in Washington through most of the campaign. When he did make public appearances, he was often booed into retreat. On election day, on his way to vote, people hurling stink bombs attacked his car. Roosevelt won the presidency by a landslide. Herbert Hoover, for all of his early optimism and organizational skills, was defeated by the Depression and its crushing economic problems.

## SECTION REVIEW

**Checking Facts**

1. What does buying on margin mean and how did it partially cause the stock market crash?
2. What three major flaws appeared in the economy after the stock market crash?
3. Describe Hoover's first efforts to deal with the Depression.
4. How did the treatment of the bonus army affect feelings toward Hoover?

**Thinking Critically**

5. **Identifying Cause and Effect** Discuss the major causes of the Depression.
6. **Making Generalizations** Discuss which people the Depression hurt the most.
7. **Identifying Cause and Effect** Comment on the relationship between the consumption and the production of goods. Which is cause and which is effect?

**Linking Across Time**

8. Today investors can buy on 50 percent margin if their broker has a guarantee that they have collateral or property equal in value to the remaining 50 percent. How might this practice have prevented some of the problems that led to the crash?

# Oral History

## E. Y. Harburg: A Testimony About the Depression

*O**ne important way in which historians gather evidence about the recent past is by interviewing people who lived through those times and recording their own stories as told by them. Historians refer to such personal remembrances as oral history. By interviewing people from many different social backgrounds, a historian can put together a rich and complex picture of a particular historical period.*

### The Evidence

In 1970 Studs Terkel published an oral history of the Depression called *Hard Times*. In preparation Terkel transcribed over 150 taped interviews. This excerpt is from an interview with E. Y. (Yip) Harburg, song lyricist. Among Harburg's works are "Somewhere Over the Rainbow" and the most famous song of the Depression era,

"Brother, Can You Spare a Dime?" All the bands played this song in 1930 and 1931. During the 1932 presidential campaign, the Republicans tried to discourage the radio networks from playing the song, but it had already impressed voters. As you read Harburg's account, think about the effects of the great crash, the explosion of the American dream. How did it affect people? How did it affect Harburg?

### The Interpretation

Testimonies like Harburg's reveal how the Depression affected people's lives. Harburg hated his business, so when the Depression came, he rejoiced at losing his job and finding his creativity. However, Harburg himself says, "Other people didn't see it that way." Because oral histories are so subjective, the oral historian

---

*I* never liked the idea of living on scallions in a left bank garret. I like writing in comfort. So I went into business, a classmate and I. I thought I'd retire in a year or two. And a thing called Collapse, bango! socked everything out. 1929. All I had left was a pencil.

Luckily, I had a friend named Ira Gershwin, and he said to me, "You've got your pencil. Get your rhyming dictionary and go to work." I did. There was nothing else to do. I was doing light verse at the time, writing a poem here and there for ten bucks a crack. It was an era when kids at college were interested in light verse and ballads and sonnets. This is the early Thirties.

I was relieved when the Crash came. I was released. Being in business was something I detested. When I found that I could sell a song or a poem, I became me, I became alive. Other people didn't see it that way. They were throwing themselves out of windows.

Someone who lost money found that his life was gone. When I lost my possessions, I found my creativity. I felt I was being born for the first

time. So for me the world became beautiful.

With the Crash, I realized that the greatest fantasy of all was business. The only realistic way of making a living was versifying. Living off your imagination.

We thought American business was the Rock of Gibraltar. We were the prosperous nation, and nothing could stop us now. A brownstone house was forever. You gave it to your kids and they put marble fronts on it. There was a feeling of continuity. If you made it, it was there forever. Suddenly the big dream exploded. The impact was unbelievable.

I was walking along the street at that time, and you'd see the bread lines. The biggest one in New York City was owned by William Randolph Hearst. He had a big truck with several people on it, and big cauldrons of hot soup, bread. Fellows with burlap on their shoes were lined up all around Columbus Circle, and went for blocks and blocks around the park, waiting.

E. Y. Harburg, in *Hard Times*, by Studs Terkel

---

needs many in order to discover the total picture. A historian would want to interview people who achieved success in the Great Depression but would also want the thoughts of those people who stood in bread lines. Harburg only imagines these thoughts in his famous lyrics:

*They used to tell me I was building a dream,*
*And so I followed the mob—*
*When there was earth to plow or guns to bear*
*I was always there— right on the job.*

*They used to tell me I was building a dream*
*With peace and glory ahead—*
*Why should I be standing on line*
*Just waiting for bread?*

*Once I built a railroad, made it run,*
*Made it run against time.*
*Once I built a railroad,*
*Now it's done—*
*Brother, can you spare a dime?*

*Once I built a tower, to the sun.*
*Brick and rivet and lime,*
*Once I built a tower,*
*Now it's done—*
*Brother, can you spare a dime?*

*Once in khaki suits,*
*Gee we looked swell,*

COURTESY OF THE DOROTHEA LANGE COLLECTION, THE OAKLAND MUSEUM

**Dorothea Lange described "White Angel Bread Line" as her most famous photograph and added that life for people in 1932 had begun to crumble on the edges.**

*Full of that Yankee Doodle-de-dum*
*Half a million boots went sloggin' through Hell,*
*I was the kid with the drum.*

*Say don't you remember, they called me Al—*
*It was Al all of the time.*
*Say don't you remember I'm your pal—*
*Buddy, can you spare a dime?*

"Brother, Can You Spare a Dime?"
E. Y. Harburg, 1932

Studs Terkel interviewed Harburg almost 40 years after the events he described. For a memory to persist that long, it must

have made a powerful impact on the person. However, a historian cannot be sure whether Harburg's memories of the Depression are the emotions he originally experienced. Because Harburg began his successful career as a lyricist during the Depression, he may now have positive memories of that time. Over his lengthy career, he probably has been interviewed about his early memories many times. In recalling these memories, Harburg may have created an idealized image of the past. When he thinks of the past, what he is remembering may be the often repeated story of his past rather than the original events themselves. A historian should question the accuracy of memories.

## Further Exploration

Ask neighbors and members of your family to tell you about their experiences during the 1960s and 1970s, another period of economic, political, and social upheaval in our nation's history. Record your interviews on video cassette, audio tape, or in writing. Once you have interviewed several people, ask yourself some questions about the evidence. What is the overall impression each person had of the sixties and seventies? What conclusions can you draw about the period based on your evidence? Do you think time has affected the memories of the people you interviewed?

The Great Depression        335

# The Dream Foreclosed

### April 14, 1935: Dust Storm Socks Meade County, Kansas

ONE PERSON THOUGHT THAT LIFE ITSELF WAS COMING TO AN END. ANOTHER WAS SURE THAT JUDGMENT DAY WAS UPON THEM. A THIRD SIMPLY BROUGHT HER ROCKING CHAIR to the center of her living room and waited out the storm. She was content because the tape over her window frames was blocking out almost every particle of dust. She boasted that under such conditions "almost any housewife could have died happily."

On Sunday, April 14, 1935, one of the biggest dust storms of this century swept over the Great Plains of the United States. Huge black clouds of dust, more than 1,000 feet high, formed a wall miles wide. Birds flew frantically trying to escape suffocation in the roiling storm. Motorists were stranded for hours along the highway, totally blinded by the impenetrable cloud. The rain sent mud balls splattering to the ground. Dust from the "black blizzard" piled up on railroad lines, and it took snow plows several days to clear off the tracks.

Dust storms like these plagued the Great Plains during the drought years from 1932 to 1939. Especially hard hit were the Dakotas, Nebraska, Kansas, Oklahoma, eastern Colorado and New Mexico, and the Texas Panhandle. Burying crops and killing livestock, the natural disasters of dust storms and drought worked in tandem with the economic disaster of the Depression to bring thousands of farmers to financial ruin. Although Dust Bowl farmers were among the hardest hit, farmers throughout the country suffered severe hardship during the Depression.

UPI/BETTMANN NEWSPHOTOS

## On the Farms

Heading into their second decade of economic depression, farmers received severely low prices for their crops. Falling incomes made it impossible for many to pay their mortgages. A bank that held an unpaid farm loan would have a **foreclosure,** or take back ownership of the property without letting the farmer pay off the rest of the mortgage. In the early years of the Depression, thousands of farmers lost their land. As the Depression deepened, however, some of the farmers thought of their own inventive ways to get around their financial problems. One Iowan recalled how farmers connived to resist the foreclosures by the banks, saying, "[The] mortgaging of farms was getting home to us. . . . [The bankers would] put up a farmer's property and have a sale." He continued:

*All the neighbors'd come in, and they got the idea of spending twenty-five cents for a horse. They was paying ten cents for a plow. And when it was all over, they'd all give it [the property] back to him [the farmer being foreclosed upon]. It was legal and anybody that bid against that thing, that was trying to get that man's land, they would be dealt with seriously, as it were.*

Harry Terrell,
in *Hard Times*

---

## STUDY GUIDE

**As You Read**
Consider the effects of the Depression on all Americans. Also, think about the following concepts and skills.

**Central Concepts**
- understanding **foreclosure**
- realizing why Mexican Americans sought **repatriation**
- understanding the extent of **unemployment**

**Thinking Skills**
- predicting consequences
- analyzing behavior

Penny auctions, as they were called, helped some farmers stay on their land. Borrowing money from relatives saved the farms of others. However, on the drought-ridden plains, where for seven successive years crops were pulverized, thousands of farmers had no choice but to abandon their fields. The Okies, as these Great Plains farmers were called, headed westward in search of a better life for themselves and their families.

**Migration of the Okies**   The plight of the Okies dramatized that of the desperately unemployed throughout the United States. They exhausted any savings they had. They sacrificed everything they owned except what they could carry with them. Uprooted, the Okies drifted anywhere they thought they might have a chance to find work. California, with its huge farms, lured many. Leaflets advertising jobs for seasonal work drew them onward, across the highways of the United States. As described by a writer late in the thirties:

*They came along U.S. Highway 30 through the Idaho hills, along Highway 66 across New Mexico and Arizona, along the Old Spanish Trail through El Paso, along all the other westward trails. They came in decrepit, square-shouldered 1925 Dodges and 1927 La Salles; in battered 1923 Model-T Fords that looked like relics of some antique culture; in trucks piled high with mattresses and cooking utensils and children, with suitcases, jugs, and sacks strapped to the running boards.*

Frederick Lewis Allen,
*Since Yesterday*

When they reached California, the Okies were in for even more hard times. Although a few jobs were available, competition for those jobs was fierce. With Okies entering the state by the hundreds daily, the number of unemployed in the labor market quickly skyrocketed. Yet, bouncing down rutted roads, driven by hope and false rumor, the Okies still kept coming. For the California farm owners, the migration of the Okies was a boon. The owners could lower wages nearly to starvation levels and still find takers for the most wretched of jobs. Huddled on the outskirts of farm towns, luckless Okies without employment set up temporary camps. People living within the towns often saw these unemployed as dirty, ignorant outsiders and sent the police to dislodge them. Bitter and dispirited, the Okies continued their migration, wandering up and down the West Coast, searching for a lucky break.

**Tenant Farmers, Black and White**   The farm crisis of the 1930s also hit tenant farmers, most of whom lived in the South. Tenant farmers did not own the land that they farmed. Therefore they were extremely vulnerable to changes in the farm economy during the thirties.

**This map shows the route the Okies took to get to California. Look at the precipitation map on page 343 to see why the Okies were heading to California.**
*How did California differ from the Dust Bowl?*

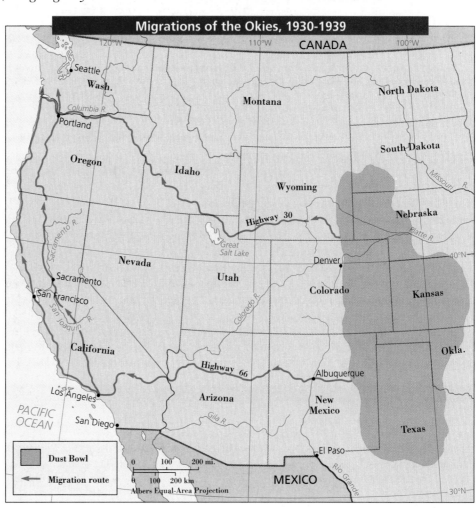

Migrations of the Okies, 1930-1939

UPI/BETTMANN NEWSPHOTOS

**Tenant farmers rented fields from the landowner, but the sharecropper and his family exchanged their** **labor for a share of the crop they raised.** *What are these sharecroppers in Caruthersville, Missouri, doing beside the road?*

As the Depression dragged on, the government began to pay landowners to let some of their land lie fallow, or go unplanted. This reduced surplus crops, causing prices for those remaining crops to rise. Most landowners decided to take out of production the land their tenant farmers used rather than the land they used. Tenant farmers lost their jobs and were also thrown off the land where some had worked and lived for many years. Also, as landowners used their government checks to buy farm equipment such as tractors and cultivators, they no longer needed year-round farmhands. Instead, they would hire a few day laborers on a temporary basis for the essential seasonal work.

The following letter, from a Georgia farmer to a government relief official, highlights the tenant farmers' situation.

*I have Bin farming all my life But the man I live with Has Turned me loose taking my mule [and] all my feed. . . . I have 7 in my family. I ploud up cotton last yeare. I can rent 9 acres and plant. . . . But I haven't got a mule [or] no feed. . . .*

From a letter to Harry Hopkins

Evicted from the farms, with little hope of finding work with other landowners, tenant farmers and their families took to the roads to look for work, often leaving behind many possessions of a lifetime. Since most of the African Americans living in the South had been tenant farmers, they suffered disproportionately from the upheaval in agriculture. However, white tenant farmers suffered severe hardship as well.

### Predicting Consequences
During the 1920s new technology stimulated overproduction on farms, and consequently, prices fell. Farmers unable to meet mortgage payments lost their farms. The dust storms of the 1930s blew away the fertile topsoil of the Great Plains states, leaving even more farmers without work. As a result, many farmers chose to move to the cities to look for work. This stream of new workers into an urban environment would create a whole new set of problems because of their lack of industrial skills and urban experience.

**Mexican American Workers**   The tenant farmers were not the only group who faced discrimination during the Depression. Mexican Americans, many whose families had been in this country for several generations, found themselves branded illegal aliens, foreigners who had no right to live and work in the United States.

Although farm owners in California welcomed a surplus of Mexican and Mexican American migrant workers to help keep wages low during the harvest season, city officials wanted to send all people of Mexican descent back to Mexico. For example, between 1931 and 1934, Los Angeles officials rounded up more than 12,000 people of Mexican descent and forced them to return to Mexico. A number were United States citizens. Nevertheless, they were denied their legal rights and threatened with deportation if they refused to leave on their own. With no choice in the matter, many Mexican Americans gathered their belongings and boarded the government-sponsored trains that dumped them across the border.

Mexicans and Mexican Americans living in the Southwest and Texas also faced increased discrimination and threats of deportation during the Depression years. Many were agricultural workers caught in the crunch of the depressed farm economy of the United States. Out of work, they fled to the cities to apply for relief. Here, they were easy prey for immigration officials, who denied them fair hearings and summarily deported them. Seeing the hopelessness of the situation, many Mexican Americans decided to return to their former homeland, and they applied to the Mexican consulate for **repatriation.** In Austin, Texas, for example, 60 percent of all people of Mexican descent had returned to Mexico by January 1931.

## In the City

The prospect for people without jobs was just as bleak in the cities as on the farms. By 1933 one of every four people was out of work. However, in some cities, the jobless rate soared above the national level. **Unemployment** ran 30 percent in Buffalo, New York, 50 percent in Chicago and Cleveland, and 80 percent in Toledo, Ohio.

Evidence of the economic crisis was clearly visible in most cities. "For Rent" notices festooned closed-down shop windows. Apple sellers hawked their wares on street corners. These unemployed men and women had bought surplus apples on credit from Pacific Coast apple growers and hoped to sell the fruit to passersby at a small profit. Those with less of an entrepreneurial spirit turned to panhandling. Beggars roved the sidewalks in most cities, accosting better-off citizens for spare change.

However, the most telling sign of the Depression was the absence of activity. In the most depressed areas, factory smokestacks spewed no smoke. Loading docks received no deliveries. Construction sites were eerily silent, the skeletons of half-finished buildings rusting in the rain. Pedestrians slowed their pace. Time seemed to dawdle during the Depression years. This was especially true for the unemployed, who had little but time on their hands.

**Unemployed Workers**   Despite promises to President Hoover to keep factories running full tilt, many factory owners began to lay off workers after a year or two of economic decline. The layoffs followed a pattern. African Americans and members of other minorities were usually the first to lose their jobs. Next, full-time employees were asked to share their jobs with others. Then, even these scaled-down jobs were cut. With wage reductions many working people were no better off than people who qualified for relief. In many cities the jobless and those with jobs became economic equals.

To reduce living expenses, people moved in with relatives. As many as 15 people would crowd into an apartment built for a couple or a family of three. Evictions of

AP/WIDE WORLD PHOTOS

**Fred Bell, known as "Champagne Fred" in San Francisco, had inherited a fortune in the 1920s but was reduced to selling apples in 1931.**

renters who could not make their monthly payments were so common in some neighborhoods that children invented a new game based on their own experience:

*They would pile all the doll furniture up first in one corner and then in another. "We ain't got no money for the rent, so we's moved into a new house," a tot explained to the teacher. "Then we got the constable on us, so we's moving again."*

Caroline Bird,
*The Invisible Scar*

Just as these children adapted to their transient situation by making a game out of it, people from all levels of society had to adapt to immense changes and learn how to do without. People lost their jobs, their homes, most of their possessions, but still they survived. Among the saddest and most touching testaments to human adaptability and survival were the makeshift cities that sprang up on the fringes of metropolitan areas. People sarcastically nicknamed these communities Hoovervilles.

**Hoovervilles and the Homeless** During the early years of the Depression, the number of homeless people in the United States skyrocketed. Although no one ever took an official census, it was estimated that by 1932 about two million people were on the road, job seekers and their families looking for work and a place to settle. At least that many had constructed temporary or not-so-temporary shelters in Hoovervilles. One woman described her amazement when she first saw the sprawling Hooverville in Oklahoma City:

THE BETTMANN ARCHIVE

**People called shantytown slums Hoovervilles, newspapers became Hoover blankets, and empty pockets turned inside out were Hoover flags.**

*Here were all these people living in old, rusted-out car bodies. I mean that was their home. There were people living in shacks made of orange crates. One family with a whole lot of kids were living in a piano box. This wasn't just a little section, this was maybe ten-miles wide and ten-miles long. People living in what ever they could junk together.*

Peggy Terry,
in *Hard Times*

For some, life on the Hooverville streets was squalid beyond belief. Garbage scraps were all these poor people could scrounge for food. For other people, life was simple and pleasant. They kept their homes, however humble, sparkling clean and shared food with neighbors.[1]

Helping others became a way of life, even among people who had not previously known each other. Those who did know each other often developed a trust that transcended the hard times. A young girl, orphaned during the Depression, remembered her friendship with the owners of a local grocery store.

*L ouise was a Bohemian girl. Her mother had a grocery store that they lived behind. Louise used to do the books, and there was always owing. You never said to the people: "Do you have the money to pay me?" They would say, "Write it in the book." And you wrote it in the book, because this was their family food, and they had to have it. It wasn't that you were giving it away. Eventually, you'd be paid.*

Dorothe Bernstein,
in *Hard Times*

**The Better-Off** Even relatively well-to-do people sometimes had to depend on the aid and charity of their neighbors during the Depression. For example, people who owned rental property did not qualify for food supplements in most city relief programs. Unable to collect rents, some landlords let their unemployed tenants stay on for free, and the tenants shared their food with the landlord.

Nevertheless, people who were wealthy before the Depression had much greater chances of weathering the economic storm and coming out with minimal financial damage. Such people might have had to sell a summer home or give up a vacation trip. They might postpone buying a new car or forego the latest fashions. However, most were able to make ends meet and live a comfortable, if less luxurious, life.

A handful of people took advantage of the rock-bottom prices brought on by the Depression to increase their wealth. For example, J. Paul Getty eventually became one of the richest men in the world by buying up oil companies at bargain prices during the 1930s. Such people were the exception.

For most Americans the loss of money and material possessions was not nearly as damaging as the sense of lost hope and pride brought on by years of unemployment or underemployment. These losses, along with changing roles and expectations, were most apparent within families.

## In the Family

In many families the father—the traditional provider—lost status and self-esteem during the Depression. With loss of income, many men were no longer able to support their families or maintain their former life styles. Some hid out at home, discouraged, listless, and cranky. Others hit the pavement every day, hoping against hope to land a new job. Still others set themselves daily tasks to keep busy. One person remembered:

*M y father spent two years painting his father's house. He painted it twice. It gave him something to do. It prevented him from losing all his—well, I wouldn't say self-respect, because there were many, many people who were also out of work. He wasn't alone.*

Bob Leary,
in *Hard Times*

**The Woman's World** Women, traditionally taking the role of homemakers, suffered less upheaval throughout the depression years. In fact, their families came to depend on them even more during those lean years, because their efforts at economizing kept many families from starvation. Many women revived traditional home crafts, such as canning vegetables, drying food, and sewing clothes. They started home industries, such as taking in laundry, selling baked goods, or renting out rooms to boarders. In many families not only did women run the household, but they also held a job outside the home.

During the Depression, women faced increasing discrimination in professional fields. However, jobs that traditionally went to women, such as clerical work and retail sales, did not decline as extensively as professional and manufacturing jobs that traditionally went to men. Therefore, many employment opportunities were open to women during the 1930s. Throughout the Depression the number of working women grew in the United States.[2]

**Growing Up in the Thirties** Domestic upheaval, with many fathers unemployed and many mothers working long hours for low wages, took its toll

## STUDY GUIDE

**Predicting Consequences**
Jobs help form a person's self-image. When people lost their jobs during the Depression, a predictable consequence was that their self-image suffered. Men particularly suffered a loss of self-esteem

during the Depression. Men, no longer the breadwinners, had never been the homemakers. They now had no defined role in the family. Psychological depression often follows a loss of role.

**2** Explain why women's traditional jobs in homemaking and in service fields survived while men's traditional jobs on the farms and in the factories evaporated.

PHOTO BY W.P.A. IN KENTUCKY

CULVER PICTURES, INC.

**More employment opportunities were available for women than for men during the Depression.** *Was the Depression harder on women or men?*

*On weekends and holidays, I'd go traipsin' up to grandma's and we'd all be together, the whole family; and everybody played an instrument and we sang. We just got closer as a family during that time.*

Hope Moat,
in *Making Do:
How Women
Survived the '30s,*
by Jeane Westin

on families. In fact, the Depression tore some families apart. Many of the hoboes who hitchhiked across the country on freight trains were unemployed men who had set out at first in search of work in other parts of the country. Unsuccessful and ashamed to return home, they deserted their families and lived together in hobo camps along the side of the railroad tracks.

With other families hard times actually brought family members closer. Hope Moat's family, from Cincinnati, Ohio, lost everything during the Depression, and they had to split up. Hope's mother and brother went to live with her grandparents on their farm. Her father traveled in search of work, and Hope herself worked in town in exchange for board.

Although some people came away from the Depression with an increased sense of inner strength or with stronger bonds to their family, for most the Depression was aptly named. It was a time of psychological and spiritual as well as economic depression. People stayed home and avoided socializing, ashamed of their worn clothes or their decline in fortune. Young people put off getting married, and married couples avoided having children. Undernourishment in children was common throughout the country. Milk consumption dropped in state after state. Economic factors shaped these choices, but so did a deep lack of hope and faith in the future. Everywhere, health officials reported that at the city and state levels child welfare and public nursing were usually the first services to be cut. During the 1930s deep despair entered the grain of American life. Some have called the Depression an invisible scar, one that, though unseen, would take many years to heal.

## SECTION REVIEW

### Checking Facts

1. What did penny auctions show about the community's reaction to bank foreclosures?

2. What conditions led to the establishment of Hoovervilles?

3. Discuss three ways the Depression affected women's role in the family.

4. Why did Mexican Americans go back to Mexico?

### Thinking Critically

5. **Predicting Consequences** Discuss both the economic and psychological effects of the Depression on a typical American family.

6. **Analyzing Behavior** Explain why for some people the Depression was the worst time in their life and why for others surviving this challenge was exhilarating.

### Linking Across Time

7. Although there is not a depression today, there are still people who are unemployed. Suggest reasons for unemployment in the United States today. In your opinion what, if anything, should the government be doing about current unemployment?

# Drawing Inferences from Maps

A logical conclusion derived from facts is called an inference. As you know, maps present facts in a visual format. For example, a temperature and precipitation map of the United States in the 1930s provides a great deal of factual information. From this information you can make inferences about the causes of the devastating dust storms that occurred throughout the decade.

## Learning the Skill

The map on this page is both thematic and historical. Its title tells you that it shows precipitation and temperature for the years 1932 through 1939, years when dust storms swept across the Great Plains. The map was created using data recorded at 27 weather stations throughout the United States. The key explains what the colored numerals on the map mean. Plus and minus symbols tell whether the deviation was an increase or a decrease from normal.

Study the map carefully to see whether any patterns emerge. Note the location of the Dust Bowl, shown in tan on the map. You can see that every weather station in the Dust Bowl and most stations in the immediately surrounding area recorded *both* decreased precipitation and increased temperature. From this data you might infer that drastically decreased precipitation and increased temperature were factors that contributed to the dust storms.

This inference is, in fact, correct. The combination of greatly decreased precipitation and increased temperature, along with high winds and poor farming practices, led to the dust storms.

## Practicing the Skill

1. Which was a more important cause of the dust storms—decreased precipitation or increased temperature? Use facts from the map to support your answer.
2. Based on the map, would you expect to find crop damage was worse in North Dakota or in Oklahoma?

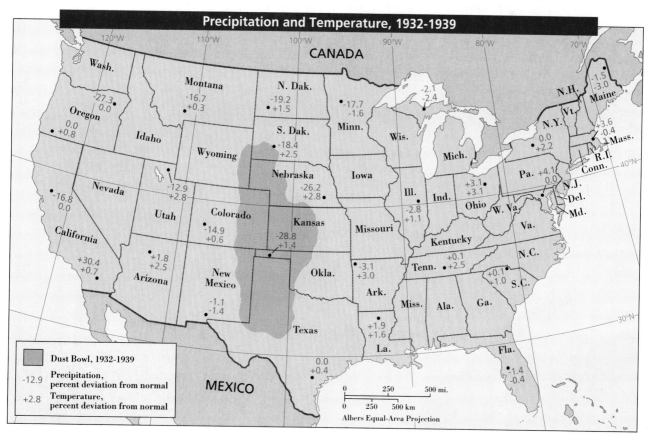

**Precipitation and Temperature, 1932-1939**

Key:
- Dust Bowl, 1932-1939
- -12.9 Precipitation, percent deviation from normal
- +2.8 Temperature, percent deviation from normal

Albers Equal-Area Projection

# Hard Times

*The reality of the Great Depression was something that most Americans lived with every day. The most they could hope for in their leisure time was that for a few hours a week they could escape from that reality into a fantasy world in which life was beautiful and problems could be easily solved. Movies, radio, and comics provided that escape.*

**Lavish production numbers** of Busby Berkeley showed Americans an extravagant life-style that many had never known, least of all in a time of economic depression. This scene is typical of Berkeley, the master of 1930s musicals.

*Love Finds Andy Hardy* starred Mickey Rooney in the title role being "found" by Judy Garland, Ann Rutherford, and Lana Turner. The **Andy Hardy series** of the 1930s kept filmgoers returning to neighborhood theaters to see their favorite film family.

The colorful world somewhere over the rainbow was a fun place to visit in **The Wizard of Oz**, but the important message at the movie's end was that "there's no place like home."

At a time when big-time gangsters were running wild and getting off scot free, cartoonist Chester Gould created a crime-fighting hero **Dick Tracy**. Such strips entertained and reassured Americans.

IN THE GROOVE

Americans of all ages gathered around the radio to listen to such weekly music and comedy shows as **"Edgar Bergen and Charlie McCarthy."** Even on radio it was amazing how the ventriloquist Bergen could create a sophisticated personality for his dummy Charlie, who was definitely in the groove.

Going to the movies and being scared by the giant gorilla, **King Kong,** was exciting. When airplanes finally shot Kong from the top of the Empire State Building, the audience felt reassured that a problem this big could be solved by American technology.

Even though the price of movies, radio, and comics was low, the cost was more than some people could afford. For the poorest people during the Depression, simple pleasures like a **guitar** could provide hours of entertainment for free.

# Culture During the Depression

## June 30, 1936: *Gone with the Wind* Smashes Sales Records

PENNED BY AN UNKNOWN JOURNALIST WHO HAD NEVER WRITTEN A BOOK BEFORE, MARGARET MITCHELL'S THOUSAND-PAGE novel, *Gone with the Wind*, became an instant success during the Depression. Through its pages readers stepped back in time to the world of Scarlett O'Hara and Rhett Butler in plantation Georgia, during and after the Civil War. Vivid with description, the book told of plantation life in a land only recently tamed:

*It was a savagely red land, blood-colored after rains, brick dust in droughts, the best cotton land in the world. It was a pleasant land of white houses, peaceful plowed fields and sluggish yellow rivers, but a land of contrasts, of brightest sun glare and densest shade. The plantation clearings and miles of cotton fields smiled up to a warm sun, placid, complacent. At their edges rose the virgin forests, dark and cool even in the hottest noons, mysterious, a little sinister, the soughing pines seeming to wait with an age-old patience, to threaten with soft sighs: "Be careful! Be careful! We had you once. We can take you back again."*

Margaret Mitchell,
*Gone with the Wind*, 1936

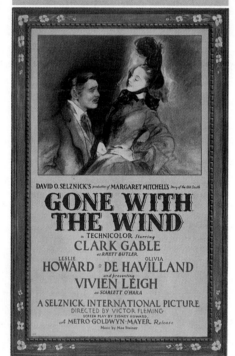

COURTESY OF THE ACADEMY OF MOTION PICTURE ARTS AND SCIENCES

The outbreak of the Civil War brought upheaval to this peaceful world. Readers were caught in the flames of Atlanta burning and dragged through the decimated fields of the O'Hara family's plantation, Tara. Lost in this broken world of postwar Reconstruction, millions of readers momentarily escaped from their own troubled time. They put aside their worries as they experienced the epic drama, defeat, and triumphs of Margaret Mitchell's memorable cast of characters.

*Gone with the Wind* won the 1937 Pulitzer prize for fiction and in 1939 was made into one of the most popular movies of all time. During the Depression fans had the fun of reading the book and anticipating the casting of the movie before finally seeing the characters come to life on the big screen. Other works of historical fiction also enjoyed immense popularity transporting readers to another era and allowing them to forget the ordeals of the Depression.

## *The Car Craze Continues*

Just as reading books provided an emotional escape from the dire circumstances of the Depression, owning an automobile gave people the sense that they could physically escape their problems. America's

---

### STUDY GUIDE

**As You Read**
Consider how people lived, coped, and even escaped during the Depression era. Also, think about the following concepts and skills.

**Central Concepts**
- understanding the importance of a **status symbol** during the Depression
- realizing the effect that the **mass media** had on people during the Depression

**Thinking Skills**
- comparing and contrasting
- drawing conclusions

romance with cars, which began in the prosperous years of the 1920s, continued through the poverty-ridden 1930s. Auto shows drew tens of thousands. Then, as now, a new car was a sign of wealth, a **status symbol** of great prestige.

**Cars for Show**   The Depression highlighted the status value of the automobile. Even people who could not afford the fuel to drive, considered their cars among their most prized possessions. One person recalled his grandfather's car:

> *My grandfather owned a car [during the Depression] but it never left the garage. He had it jacked up for two years. Gasoline was just too expensive. He told how he polished the car once a week. How he took good care of it, but he never drove it. Couldn't afford it.*
>
> Ben,
> in *Hard Times*

Whether they could afford their cars or not, many Americans kept the autos and continued to drive them despite the expense. A restless spirit lured thousands to the highways during the Depression.

**On the Move**   By the mid-1930s a maze of two-lane roads crisscrossed the United States. Heading down these bumpy byways, people took off for parts unknown. Some were searching for work. Others were seeking adventure. Many were pioneering what

would soon become an American institution: the driving trip as a family vacation.

During the 1930s tourism grew to be the third largest industry in the United States. Thirty-five million vacationers took to the roads in 1935 alone. One woman recalled a yearlong journey she took with her husband and son in the middle of the decade:

> *The roads in those days were not the way they are now, and there weren't many motels, although in the East they had what they called auto courts; sometimes these were little better than primitive log cabins. We camped beside the road when we couldn't find a tourist home or a hotel. . . .*
>
> *This country was so different for families traveling in the thirties. You stayed with local people and ate the food the region was famous for. For instance, in the South there were antebellum houses that were turned into tourist homes, and I think it only cost about $1.50 a night—for the three of us—with an absolutely gigantic dinner and breakfast thrown in.*
>
> Marion Conrad,
> in *Making Do: How Women Survived the '30s*

Trailers—mobile homes that could be hitched to the back of a car—became popular in the 1930s. Ideal for vacations in isolated areas or for rent-free accommodations in a city, trailers tapped into the American dream, promoting freedom and opportunity. The

**The year 1935 was a banner year for the American automobile. Auto show attendance zoomed, car sales** dramatically increased, two-lane highways crisscrossed the country, and vacationers took to the roads.

trailer fad peaked in the summer of 1937, when a Florida observer reported that an average of 25 trailers entered his state each hour. (You can read more about auto camping in Geography: Impact on History on pages 274–275.)

The automobile industry itself just kept growing. The number of registered automobiles in the United States jumped from 24 million in 1933 to 32 million in 1940. Even in the early 1930s, more than half of the families in the United States owned a car.

## Escape from Household Drudgery

The car was the ultimate escape machine for the Depression decade. However, it was not the only machine prized for its powers. The appliance revolution that began in the twenties continued into the thirties. As more and more houses were wired with electricity, the market for remarkable new household appliances grew. In the late 1930s, government programs helped bring electricity to many isolated regions of the country, such as the mountains of Arkansas.[1]

The refrigerator was, by far, the most sought after of the new appliances. Even during the worst years of the Depression, refrigerator sales continued to climb. Replacing the clunky old icebox, the refrigerator promised a cleaner, safer way to store food. Gone was the incessant drip-drop of melting ice and the creeping puddle of water that always seemed to spill over the edge of the icebox's collecting pan. With the hum of the refrigerator's whirring motor, families could rest assured that their food would stay fresh.

The spread of electrification also eased burdensome household chores such as washing and ironing clothes. Doing laundry had traditionally involved a whole day of bending over tubs full of scalding water and another full day of heating and reheating a heavy iron for pressing. Simple washing machines and the electric iron transformed this work from a weekly ritual of torture. With modern appliances, doing laundry became a set of relatively painless tasks to be squeezed in between other household chores.

For some people, electrical power seemed no less than a miracle. An Arkansas congressman remembered the day it miraculously appeared.

*I wanted to be at my parents' house when electricity came. It was in 1940. We'd all go around flipping the switch to make sure it hadn't come on yet. We didn't want to miss it. When they finally came on, the lights just barely glowed. I remember my mother smiling. When they came on full, tears started to run down her cheeks.*

Clyde T. Ellis,
in *Hard Times*

People in these regions welcomed the escape from drudgery that new appliances afforded them. (For more information about electrification in rural areas, read One Day in History on pages 384–385.)

To Gladden Hearts and *Lighten* Labor

DOWMETAL···THE WORLD'S LIGHTEST STRUCTURAL ALLOY

THE DOW CHEMICAL COMPANY, MIDLAND, MICHIGAN

DOW
CHEMICALS INDISPENSABLE
TO INDUSTRY

**This advertisement stressing the wonders of light alloy metals makes the point that electrical equipment manufactured in the 1930s was making household work lighter and easier.** *Would this advertisement still be effective in selling electrical appliances today? Would a vacuum cleaner be appreciated as a gift today?*

# Escape Through Entertainment

In the 1930s a dime would buy round-trip fare on a streetcar or city bus, two apples from a corner vendor, a double thick malt at the drugstore fountain, or an afternoon's escape to the movies. Faced with these choices, many people walked instead of rode the bus and did without afternoon snacks in order to claim a seat in the local theater for a Saturday double-feature matinee.

**The Silver Screen**   Movies changed dramatically as "talkies"—movies with sound—became more common in the early 1930s. At first, all sound was taped live in the studio at the same time the movie was being filmed. Any editing of the movie threw the sound track out of sync with the picture. As a result, the actors looked as if they were mouthing their lines, but the words did not match up. Immobile microphones also stunted acting and directing styles. When speaking, the actors and actresses had to stand in place in front of the microphones. They could not change positions or even turn their heads for fear of spoiling the sound. For these reasons, early talkies had a stiffness to them that contrasted with the smooth pace of the old silent movies.

Continued improvement of sound technology ushered in the era of musicals. Watching such gems as *Flying Down to Rio* and *42nd Street*, audiences swooned at the sensuous steps of Fred Astaire and Ginger Rogers. They thrilled at the spectacle of rows of high-stepping dancers. So far removed from the dreariness of the Depression, these sumptuous pageants transported people to a world of glitz and glamour.

Color-film technology added another appealing dimension to 1930s movies. Over the decade more and more movie theaters bought the equipment to

ACADEMY OF MOTION PICTURE ARTS AND SCIENCES

**Fred Astaire and Ginger Rogers became film's most successful dance team, making nine hits in all. They began dancing together in *Flying Down to Rio* in 1933.**

project the full-color films the studios began making. The release of the movie version of *Gone with the Wind* in 1939 converted any diehards who preferred black and white. The searing scenes of Atlanta under Union General William Sherman's torch had some viewers shielding their eyes from the imagined heat of dancing flames.

*Gone with the Wind* was the epitome of a Depression-era film. It drew viewers into a romantic, faraway world. It engaged them with a twisting, dramatic plot. It tugged at all the emotions—love, anger, fear, pity, and hope. Best of all, it lasted for nearly four hours, not including an intermission for a meal. A more satisfying afternoon of entertainment could not be had for the price of just one thin dime.

During an average week in the mid-1930s between 60 and 90 million people flocked to the movies. For their daily entertainment, however, most people turned on the radio.

**The Golden Age of Radio**   Unlike today's compact radios that people carry in the palm of the hand, the radio of the thirties was a substantial piece of furniture. Granted an honored place in the living room, the radio, with its rich wood cabinet, often served as a visual focus, the mantel for family photographs and mementos. It also served as a social focus, the gathering place for hours of spirit-lifting amusement.

More than ten million households owned radios in 1929. A decade later that number had almost tripled. Like television today, radio served many purposes. It was the family's communication link to the outside world. It was the housewife's companion as she did her daily chores. It gave the unemployed the comfort of company. It occupied young children when they returned home from school. Radio enlivened long winter evenings with engrossing family entertainment.

## STUDY GUIDE

### Drawing Conclusions

Attendance at movies and radio ownership both increased during the Depression. One might conclude that people must have been willing to spend some of their limited money to escape the unhappiness of their own circumstances. In order to get people to spend money on movies, films featured spectacles. In addition, theaters also tried such gimmicks as dish nights, when people got free glassware for attending, and presented continuing serials that would encourage viewers to return.

LIBRARY OF CONGRESS

The radio was not only a source of entertainment but also a piece of furniture that became the entertainment center and focal point of the living room in some homes.

Radio programming in the thirties set a pattern that would be followed by television in later years. Daytime radio included soap operas, panel discussions, and quiz shows designed to appeal to women working at home. During the late afternoon, children's programs came on. Adventure stories, such as "The Lone Ranger" and "Superman," originated in the 1930s and captured young audiences well into the 1950s. The evening was reserved for news programs, variety shows, comedy hours, dramatic presentations of plays, and live musical performances.

Sponsored by big-name corporations, radio programs tended to avoid controversial issues. Most audiences considered movies, radio, and other forms of **mass media** means of escape. Few used it as a forum to discuss difficult questions or unpopular views.

## Voices That Would Not Be Stilled

Despite many Americans' obsession with escape, quite a few people took an interest in defining the nation's problems and exploring solutions. Angry at injustices, they spoke out candidly. Many were artists—writers, painters, photographers, playwrights—whose works still inspire social awareness and empathy today.

**The Mirror of Literature**   During the thirties many serious writers shifted their focus from the anxiety of the individual to the mass struggles of people caught in a system that robbed them of their vitality. John Steinbeck and John Dos Passos, two writers acclaimed during this turbulent decade, stressed the struggles of individuals in society. In addition, both writers evaluated the effectiveness of society in upholding the rights of people of different classes. They intended that their writing serve as a mirror in which society could see itself. These writers wanted their readers to take a long, hard look at the evils and injustices of society. They wanted to inspire their readers to fight for social change.[2]

*The Grapes of Wrath* by Steinbeck was one of the most famous and influential novels of the 1930s. This American classic focused on an Okie family driven from their land:

Pa borrowed money from the bank, and now the bank wants the land—wants tractors, not families on the land. Is a tractor bad? Is the power that turns the long furrows wrong? If this tractor were ours it would be good— not mine, but ours. If our tractor turned the long furrows of our land, it would be good. Not my land, but ours. We could love that tractor then as we have loved this land when it was ours. But this tractor does two things—it turns the land and turns us off the land. There is little difference between this tractor and a tank. The people are driven, intimidated, hurt by both. We must think about this.

John Steinbeck,
*The Grapes of Wrath*, 1939

**Thomas Hart Benton was the most famous painter of the American scene. His murals, such as *Rural Family Life and Law* above, measuring 14 feet by 23 feet,** **were based on layouts of picture pages from the Sunday newspapers.** *What statement is Benton making in this mural?*

**Statements in the Arts**   No less insistent than the 1930s writers were the artists of the time who clamored for social change. They sought to show the United States in all its Depression-era bleakness. Thomas Hart Benton, Edward Hopper, and Grant Wood each focused on a particular region of the country and tried to convey the flavor of life there as they saw it. Through these works of art, viewers perceived the trials of poor farmers, unemployed workers, and others struggling to hold on to their ideals during years of hardship.

Playwrights and theater directors also used their works to make statements about society. Emphasizing the struggle of labor against exploitative factory owners, the play *Waiting for Lefty* by Clifford Odets glorified the Depression-era worker. This and other plays promoted the visions of playwrights for a just world.

In contrast, documentary photography showed the United States of the Depression era stripped of hopes and dreams. Staring into the faces of destitute migrant workers from Alabama, the evicted wheat farmers from the Dust Bowl, and the hungry children in Hoovervilles, few viewers could avoid sensing these people's anger, shame, and misery. The photographs immediately convey the scope of the Depression, which shattered the lives of so many Americans.

## SECTION REVIEW

**Checking Facts**

1. Explain the importance of the car as a status symbol of the 1930s.
2. What three new electrical appliances of the 1930s do you think made the most difference in people's lives? Explain your choices.
3. Discuss how the addition of sound and color changed movies. Examine ways that movies might have been better without color or sound.

4. Explain why escapist films and realistic fiction were both popular during the thirties.

**Thinking Critically**

5. **Drawing Conclusions** Unemployment remained high during the 1930s, but sales of cars and radios and movie attendance rose. Decide if the 1930s constituted a depressing time to be a teenager and explain why or why not.

6. **Comparing and Contrasting** Compare the culture of the Depression decade with today's culture.

**Linking Across Time**

7. Explain why so much of the art, music, literature, and film of the 1930s is still popular today.

# Art and Politics at Rockefeller Center

## SPRING 1933

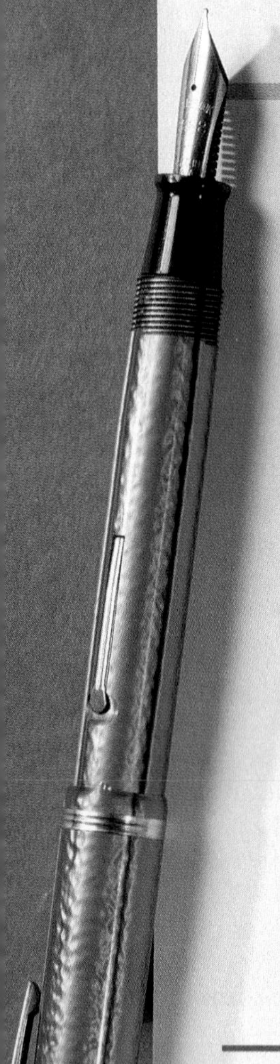

May 4, 1933

Dear Mr. Rivera,

While I was in the No. 1 building at Rockefeller Center yesterday viewing the progress of your thrilling mural, I noticed that in the most recent portion of the painting you had included a portrait of Lenin. This piece is beautifully painted but it seems to me that his portrait, appearing in this mural, might very easily seriously offend a great many people. If it were in a private house it would be one thing but this mural is in a public building and the situation is therefore quite different. As much as I dislike to do so I am afraid we must ask you to substitute the face of some unknown man where Lenin's face now appears.

You know how enthusiastic I am about the work which you have been doing and that to date we have in no way restricted you in either subject or treatment. I am sure you will understand our feeling in this situation and we will greatly appreciate your making the suggested substitution.

With best wishes, I remain sincerely,
Nelson A. Rockefeller

## The Case

Nelson Rockefeller commissioned Diego Rivera, the Mexican muralist, to paint a fresco mural into the fresh, moist plaster in the grand hall of the 77-story RCA Building in Rockefeller Center. The mural's middle panel was nearly 41 feet by 19 feet.

The mural's proposed title was *Man at the Crossroads Looking with Hope and High Vision to the Choosing of a New and Better Future.* The Rockefeller family approved a preliminary sketch by Rivera that showed man at a crossroads between the bad times of the past and the good times of the future. A faceless leader united the people and brought order out of chaos.

Rivera began painting the mural in March 1933, according to his original plan. However, on May Day (May 1), an international day in honor of workers, Rivera painted a portrait of the late Russian communist ruler, V. I. Lenin, in place of the faceless leader. Rivera described his mural:

*On the left . . . I showed a night club scene of the debauched rich, a battlefield with men in the holocaust of war, and unemployed workers in a demonstration being clubbed by the police. On the right, I painted corresponding scenes of life in a socialist country: a May Day demonstration of marching, singing workers; an athletic stadium filled with girls exercising their bodies; and a figure of Lenin, symbolically clasping the hands of a black American and a white Russian soldier and worker, as allies of the future.*

When Rockefeller suggested Rivera alter the design, Rivera responded:

*I am sure that that class of person who is capable of being offended by the portrait of a deceased great man, would feel offended, given such a mentality, by the entire conception of my painting. Therefore, rather than mutilate the conception, I should prefer the physical destruction of the conception in its entirety, but conserving, at least, its integrity. . . . I could change the sector which shows society people playing bridge and dancing, and put in its place, in perfect balance with the Lenin portion, a figure of some great American historical leader, such as Lincoln, who symbolizes the unification of the country and the abolition of slavery.*

The next move was up to Rockefeller. If he insisted that Rivera change the portrait of Lenin to an unknown man, would that constitute censorship of Rivera? Did the painting belong to Rivera or Rockefeller? Who owns a work of art—the artist who creates it, the person who buys it, or the public?

## The Background

The Rockefeller family developed Rockefeller Center between 1929 and 1939. Its 14 buildings cost more than $100 million. In 1932, when 64 percent of the workers in the building trades were unemployed, 75,000 men were employed in constructing Rockefeller Center. John D. Rockefeller, Jr., was the epitome of the successful American capitalist. While all around him workers were

losing faith in an economy that could not employ them, Rockefeller provided meaningful, profitable work for thousands of people.

Mrs. John D. Rockefeller, Jr., was a founder of the Museum of Modern Art in New York City. In 1931 she brought Rivera to the United States, where he gave a show the next year. Some of the images in that show had realistically depicted starving workers and idle mills that existed in the

UPI/BETTMANN NEWSPHOTOS

**Diego Rivera painted the controversial mural in Rockefeller Center, New York.**

United States. She was also aware that in his Mexico City murals Rivera had painted a mocking caricature of John D. Rockefeller, Sr., the founder of the family's fortune. When the Rockefeller family commissioned Rivera to paint the mural, there was no discussion as to how his feelings about capitalism might influence the work.

As a believer in communist philosophy, Rivera regarded Lenin as the father of a unified and successful working class. Lenin provided the rallying point for what Rivera thought was an impending world revolution. Rivera explained the use of Lenin in the mural in this way:

*If the United States wished to preserve its democratic forms, it would ally itself with Russia against [Nazi] fascism. Since Lenin was the pre-eminent founder of the Soviet Union and also the first and most altruistic theorist of modern communism, I used him as the center of the inevitable alliance between the Russian and the American [against fascism].*

**When Diego Rivera could not paint his mural for Rockefeller Center, he asked the Mexican** **government for a duplicate space and was given a wall on the third floor of the Palacio de Bellas Artes.**

## The Points of View

To Rivera this dispute was between individual ownership as championed by capitalism and collective ownership as advocated by communism. He stated:

> There are only two real points of view from which to choose: the point of view of capitalist economy and morality . . . the right of individual property. . ., and the point of view of socialist economy and morality . . . the rights of the human collectivity.

Bertram Wolfe,
*Diego Rivera: His Life and Times*, 1939

Many other artists saw the issue of censorship at the heart of this dispute. They claimed that the Rockefellers were attempting to censor Rivera's free speech as expressed through his art.

To refute this view, a newspaper editorial expressed the opinion that it was not censorship that was at issue but rather logic. It was illogical to have a communistic mural in a capitalist building:

*The issue between Rivera and Rockefeller Center would thus have nothing to do with the right of the artist to represent the world as he sees it. The mural painter is not concerned with visions and intuitions but with telling a story and inculcating a lesson. His message must therefore make sense. There is no sense in making a monumental wall-painting cry "Liar" to the wall on which it is spread.*

New York Times, May 11, 1933

## The Options

After Rockefeller wrote his letter of May 4 to Rivera, the muralist declined to change the portrait, but he offered to balance the painting by putting an American figure of historical importance on the capitalist side of the mural. That left the decision up to Rockefeller, who could resolve the conflict in any of the following ways:

**1.** Display the painting as Rivera had originally created it.

2. Accept the changes that Rivera offered to make on the capitalist side of the mural.
3. Use a chisel to remove the mural from the wall's plaster into which it was painted.

## The Decision

On May 9 Rockefeller ordered Rivera to stop work on the mural, and the carpenters covered it with large frames of stretched canvas. After the guards drove Rivera from his scaffold, the building manager paid off the artist's $21,000 contract and gave him a letter of dismissal.

Nearly 100 admirers of Rivera's art paraded in front of the RCA Building, carrying signs that read "Save Rivera's Art" and "We Want Rivera." There was a great uproar; committees of artists agitated for and against the mural.

Rockefeller was eager to avoid controversy and said in a letter to his father, "We are hoping that the disagreeable public criticism which has been leveled at us this past week will be turned to sympathetic understanding of our position." On May 12, 1933, the *World-Telegram* reported Rockefeller's assurance that the "uncompleted fresco of Diego Rivera will not be destroyed or in any way mutilated, but . . . will be covered, to remain hidden for an indefinite time."

The Rockefellers allowed the mural to remain covered until February 9, 1934. At midnight, just as the weekend was beginning, workmen rolled wheelbarrows into the building and crumbled the fresco into powder, which was wheeled away.

## The Significance

When Rivera learned that his painting had been smashed, he made his goal clear: "My object was attained when the painting was destroyed. I thank the Rockefellers for its destruction because the act will advance the cause of the labor revolution."

In Mexico City, Rivera applied to the Mexican government for a wall at the Palace of Fine Arts where he could let people see what kind of painting it was that these "patrons of the arts" had chosen to destroy. He introduced into the new mural's nightclub scene a portrait of John D. Rockefeller, Jr., drinking champagne. Rockefeller actually did not drink alcohol.

To Rivera the significance of the dispute lay in the distinction between the individual's rights (as represented by capitalism) and the rights of the group (as represented by communism):

*Let us take, as an example, an American millionaire who buys the Sistine Chapel, which contains the work of Michelangelo. . . . Would that millionaire have the right to destroy the Sistine Chapel?. . . In human creation there is something which belongs to humanity at large, and . . . no individual owner has the right to destroy it or keep it solely for his own enjoyment.*

Diego Rivera

But the lawyers of Rockefeller Center completely deflated the protests that were planned by the artistic community. They made public the year-old letter in which Rivera told the Rockefellers that he would prefer to see the whole mural destroyed rather than change Lenin's portrait.

## Think About It

1. Make two columns on a sheet of paper. On one side list the arguments made by Rivera and on the other side list the arguments made by Nelson Rockefeller on behalf of his family. Explain which side appears to have the stronger position.
2. Identify a point in this study where one side or the other could have avoided the controversy by making its position clear to the other side. Decide what could have been done at that particular point.
3. Discuss whether a person who owns a work but does not let it be seen is guilty of censorship. For example, could a newspaper publisher/owner who stopped an objectionable story from being printed be considered guilty of censorship?
4. Which, if any, of Rockefeller's responses constituted censorship: his request that Lenin's portrait be changed, his covering the mural with canvas for nine months, or his chiseling it off the wall? Defend your answer.
5. Discuss whether a painting is owned by the painter who created it, the person who bought it, or the general public.

# Chapter 10 Review

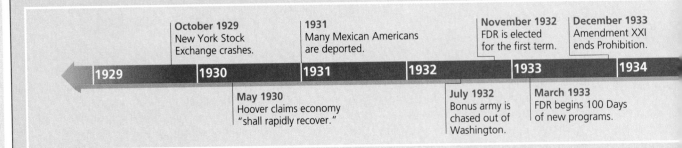

| | October 1929<br>New York Stock<br>Exchange crashes. | 1931<br>Many Mexican Americans<br>are deported. | | November 1932<br>FDR is elected<br>for the first term. | December 1933<br>Amendment XXI<br>ends Prohibition. |
|---|---|---|---|---|---|
| **1929** | **1930** | **1931** | **1932** | **1933** | **1934** |
| | May 1930<br>Hoover claims economy<br>"shall rapidly recover." | | July 1932<br>Bonus army is<br>chased out of<br>Washington. | March 1933<br>FDR begins 100 Days<br>of new programs. | |

## Summary

Use the following outline as a tool for reviewing and summarizing the chapter. Copy the outline on your own paper, leaving spaces between headings to jot down notes about key events and concepts.

**I. The Economy Hits Bottom**
  A. Why Did the Crash Occur?
  B. The Causes of the Great Depression
  C. Hoover's Response
  D. Too Little Too Late

**II. The Dream Foreclosed**
  A. On the Farms
  B. In the City
  C. In the Family

**III. Culture During the Depression**
  A. The Car Craze Continues
  B. Escape from Household Drudgery
  C. Escape Through Entertainment
  D. Voices That Would Not Be Stilled

## Ideas, Events, and People

1. Why did the stock market crash of 1929 occur?
2. Name several causes of the Depression.
3. State two steps President Hoover took to end the Depression.
4. Why were President Hoover's economic policies unsuccessful?
5. Why did the Republican party discourage radio stations from playing "Brother, Can You Spare a Dime"?
6. State three reasons why many farmers were out of work during the Depression.
7. Explain what Hoovervilles were.
8. What effects did the Depression have on the American family?
9. During the Depression why was so much of the entertainment extravagant and unrealistic?
10. Explain why automobiles were so popular during the Depression.
11. How did electric appliances change the lives of homemakers in the 1930s?
12. Identify an approach in literature and photography that highlighted social problems during the Depression.
13. Why was the Rockefeller family so concerned about Diego Rivera's painting of Lenin during this time of economic depression?

## Social Studies Skills

**Drawing Inferences from Maps**

Look at the map on page 337 showing the migration of the Okies between 1930 and 1939. Highways 30 and 66 extend from the edge of the Dust Bowl to the West Coast. What can you infer about why the Okies were going to the West?

## Critical Thinking

1. **Comparing and Contrasting**
Compare and contrast the ways people in the cities and rural areas helped one another during the Depression.
2. **Analyzing Behavior**
Why were many people speculating in the stock market and even going into debt borrowing money to invest in stocks?
3. **Drawing Conclusions**
Mexican Americans and African Americans were among the first to lose their jobs during the Depression. Why did this occur?
4. **Predicting Consequences**
What would the consequences be for a factory that produced goods of high quality and value

| 1935 Dust storms sweep the Great Plains. | | January 1937 FDR begins his second term. | | 1939 John Steinbeck's *The Grapes of Wrath* is published. | |
|---|---|---|---|---|---|
| **1935** | **1936** | **1937** | **1938** | **1939** | **1940** |
| 1935 Automobile sales increase. | | November 1936 FDR is elected for second term. | | 1939 *Gone with the Wind* and *The Wizard of Oz* appear on screen. | |

that were too expensive for workers to buy? How could this problem be alleviated?

**5. Identifying Cause and Effect**

In the 1930s electronic devices, such as refrigerators and radios, were new products for Americans to manufacture and purchase. Did people's need for these devices stimulate new industries, or was the desire for these products created in people's minds by businesses that needed customers? Explain your answer.

## Extension and Application

**1. Global Connections**

The Depression era was a worldwide event. Investigate and report on how Germany handled unemployment and the economic hard times of the Depression.

**2. Evidence of the Past**

This photograph showing Herbert Hoover and Franklin Roosevelt riding together in an open limousine was taken on a special occasion. Using your knowledge of American history and the evidence in the photograph, such as the contrasting expressions on their faces, tell the day, the approximate time, and the event that this photograph records.

**3. Linking Across Time**

Consult a bank and a savings and loan institution in your community and determine how much money from a single depositor they insure. Also check with a stockbroker to determine what collateral you must produce when buying stocks on margin. How do these current provisions in banking and investing differ from those of the 1920s? How will these new provisions help prevent future depressions?

**4. Cooperative Learning**

Form a film-review group and divide up the responsibility for analyzing videotapes of some of the film classics of the 1930s. Present a panel discussion on these films, evaluating them and comparing them with some of the popular films of the 1990s.

**5. Community Connection**

Use the library to research and write a report on how the Depression affected unemployment and the economy in your community.

## Geography

1. After leaving the Dust Bowl, how far did Okie families travel to Los Angeles and Portland? What difficulties did they encounter during the journey?
2. Why was California an attractive destination to Dust Bowl farmers?
3. Identify the factors that influenced the lives of southern farmers during the Depression. How did these factors change their lives?
4. How was the Depression visible in urban areas? In rural areas?
5. What opportunities did cross-country highways provide for people during the Depression?

UPI/BETTMANN NEWSPHOTOS

## CHAPTER 11

# The New Deal

### May 27, 1938: Eleanor Roosevelt Visits Arthurdale, West Virginia

First Lady Eleanor Roosevelt and her square dance partner promenaded down the aisle of clapping onlookers in the Arthurdale High School Auditorium. Five years had passed since Mrs. Roosevelt helped to establish the resettlement community of Arthurdale, West Virginia, and she wanted to be on hand to celebrate the graduation of its first high school senior class.

In 1933, in the midst of the Depression, the federal government convinced a number of families to move from Morgantown, where most farm families could barely eke out a living, to Arthurdale. Residents there would ideally be able to remain employed and self-sufficient during the year by combining subsistence farming with small industry. To encourage individuals to move to Arthurdale, the federal government promised each family a house with plumbing and electricity, a plot of land, and a job in a nearby factory.

Arthurdale was the first of the government-sponsored communities established by the Resettlement Administration, one of President Roosevelt's New Deal programs. These communities gave hope to people mired in the Depression. Under the president's leadership, the United States government assumed a new responsibility for the welfare of the American people and for the future of the nation's economy.

> *These new communities gave hope to people mired in the Depression.*

MARGARET BOURKE-WHITE, LIFE MAGAZINE © TIME WARNER INC.

*This western town took its name from Roosevelt's promise to give Americans a new deal.*

*People employed by the WPA worked on intricate wiring, such as that shown in the 1938 photograph above, to transmit electricity for the first time to communities in the nation's rural areas.*

# FDR and the First New Deal

## March 4, 1933: Franklin D. Roosevelt Takes Presidential Oath

DULL, GRAY SKIES HUNG OVER WASHING-TON. AN ICY WIND GUSTED DOWN THE CITY'S BROAD BOULEVARDS, chilling the crowd that packed the walk in front of the Capitol steps. Suddenly, the high, clear notes of a bugle sounded out a fanfare. Franklin Delano Roosevelt, partially paralyzed from polio, leaning on the arm of his son, mounted the inaugural platform. As he walked up the steps to the podium, the band began playing "Hail to the Chief."

After Roosevelt took the oath of the office of the president, he turned to face the crowd. He had planned his first words as president carefully, because he knew that the nation would be listening closely to find out just what kind of president he would be.

Three-and-a-half years of economic depression had left millions unemployed, hungry, and homeless. Thousands of banks had closed. Assembly lines had ground to a halt while bread lines stretched for blocks down city streets. Farmland lay fallow, abandoned by angry farmers unable to recover even the costs of planting. Americans had lost faith in their country. Roosevelt considered his first major task to restore that faith.

FRANKLIN D. ROOSEVELT LIBRARY

FPG INTERNATIONAL

His voice echoing over the public address system, Roosevelt declared the following:

*This great Nation will endure as it has endured, will revive and will prosper. So, first of all, let me assert my firm belief that the only thing we have to fear is fear itself—nameless, unreasoning, unjustified terror which paralyzes needed efforts to convert retreat into advance.*

Inaugural Address, March 4, 1933

Cheers and roaring applause burst from the crowd at the end of the president's address. For the first time that day, Roosevelt grinned. Then he descended the steps, determined to lead this country out of its prolonged economic depression.

## FDR Takes the Helm

Franklin Delano Roosevelt was born on January 30, 1882, into a wealthy, well-connected family. As a child, Roosevelt was popular with his classmates and received good grades in school. Nevertheless, the future president showed no signs of distinction.

## STUDY GUIDE

**As You Read**
Identify Roosevelt's policies during the Hundred Days and the methods by which he gained the public's confidence. Also, think about the following concept and skills.

**Central Concept**
- identifying the legislation of the **New Deal**

**Thinking Skills**
- identifying cause and effect
- predicting consequences
- recognizing bias
- making inferences

In this picture, young Franklin, in the midst of his cousins, leans on his grandfather's wheelchair. At right, newlyweds Franklin and Eleanor pose for the photographer.

A classmate described Roosevelt as "nice but colorless." Several decades later, when Roosevelt was running for office, a political analyst would confirm the classmate's opinion:

> *Franklin Roosevelt is no crusader. He is no tribune of the people. He is no enemy of entrenched privilege. He is a pleasant man who, without any important qualifications for the office, would very much like to be President.*

Walter Lippmann, 1932

**Marriage to Eleanor Roosevelt**   Franklin's distant cousin Eleanor introduced him to a world he had not seen in his sheltered youth. At the age of 20, Eleanor had volunteered at a settlement house in the slums of New York City. Franklin, accompanying Eleanor to the home of one of her students, exclaimed, "I didn't know people lived like that!"

On March 17, 1905, Franklin and Eleanor were joined in marriage. Republican President Theodore Roosevelt, Franklin's distant cousin and Eleanor's uncle, led Eleanor down the aisle. A few years later, Franklin followed in Theodore Roosevelt's footsteps, launching a political career.

**An Emerging Politician**   In 1910 FDR, as Franklin Roosevelt came to be known, was elected as a Democrat to the New York state legislature. In 1913 President Wilson appointed him Assistant Secretary of the Navy. He served in this post for seven years until 1920, when, at the age of 38, he gained the Democratic nomination for vice president. However, Roosevelt did not become vice president because the Democratic presidential candidate lost the election.

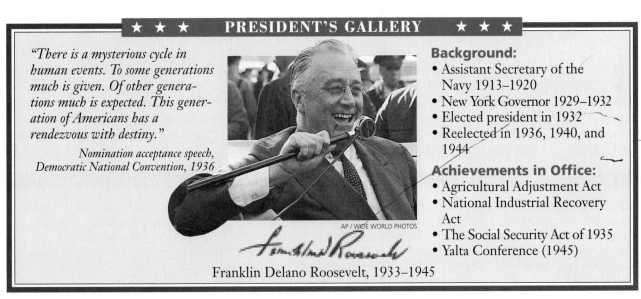

★ ★ ★   **PRESIDENT'S GALLERY**   ★ ★ ★

*"There is a mysterious cycle in human events. To some generations much is given. Of other generations much is expected. This generation of Americans has a rendezvous with destiny."*

*Nomination acceptance speech, Democratic National Convention, 1936*

AP / WIDE WORLD PHOTOS

**Background:**
- Assistant Secretary of the Navy 1913–1920
- New York Governor 1929–1932
- Elected president in 1932
- Reelected in 1936, 1940, and 1944

**Achievements in Office:**
- Agricultural Adjustment Act
- National Industrial Recovery Act
- The Social Security Act of 1935
- Yalta Conference (1945)

Franklin Delano Roosevelt, 1933–1945

In 1921 while vacationing at his family's summer home, FDR suffered an attack of poliomyelitis that left his legs completely paralyzed. But Roosevelt was determined to return to active political life.

Years of treatment never did restore the use of his legs, but the experience increased his ability to empathize with others and strengthened his spirit. As he remarked, "If you have spent two years in bed trying to wiggle your big toe, everything else seems easy."

At the Democratic Convention in 1924, Roosevelt made his first public political appearance since having been stricken with polio. From that appearance on, Roosevelt's political career skyrocketed. Twice he won the governorship of New York—in 1928 by a slim margin and in 1930 by a landslide. His innovative relief measures, including a statewide relief program, won him national praise. Then in 1932 he accepted the Democratic nomination for president.

**The Roosevelt Victory**   Both Roosevelt and Hoover promoted conservative measures to end the Depression. However, President Hoover was reluctant to institute direct relief measures, and he projected a grim attitude. Both of these things made him widely unpopular. Roosevelt, on the other hand, possessed a buoyant spirit and warm smile and promised direct action. These were enough to sweep him into office and to get a wide Democratic majority elected to both houses of Congress.

An experimenter at heart, Roosevelt was open to all ideas. He employed Republicans as well as Democrats, conservatives as well as liberals, university intellectuals as well as experienced politicians.

The day Roosevelt took office a flurry of activity began that did not let up for over three months. This time of intensive legislation and policy setting came to be called the Hundred Days.

---

## The Hundred Days

**M**onths before Roosevelt's inauguration, thousands of panicky Michigan residents had begun flocking to their local banks to withdraw cash from savings accounts. This activity depleted bank funds to such an extent that many banks actually closed. In mid-February, the governor of Michigan declared a banking **moratorium,** a temporary shutdown of operations, in effect closing all state banks. He hoped that this would give the banks enough time to replenish their supplies of ready cash and, thus, restore depositors' confidence. However, the moratorium actually had the opposite effect: It caused the panic to spread and intensify. Overnight, people throughout the nation began to panic. By inauguration day, 38 states had closed their banks, and the remaining 10 states had sharply restricted banking operations. The majority of Americans, having lost faith in their financial institutions, were hoarding money, hiding cash under mattresses, and storing gold in pillow cases.

**Stemming the Bank Crisis**   Even before the inauguration, Roosevelt had directed his future Secretary of the Treasury William Woodin to develop a plan for dealing with the bank crisis. Woodin proposed that Roosevelt call a special session of Congress and declare a partial bank holiday for all financial institutions until after Congress met on March 9. The president announced the plan on the afternoon of March 5, directing the banks to accept all deposits and make emergency loans for food and animal feed over the course of the next four days but to refrain from conducting any other business.

From March 5 to noon on March 9, Secretary Woodin and his advisers worked around the clock to hammer out legislation that would end the banking crisis. When Congress met on the afternoon of March 9, the president's representative read the bill aloud. It stated that banks in sound financial shape would be reopened immediately. Those lacking assets would remain closed until the government could develop a way to open them safely. Congress promptly passed the bill, and Roosevelt signed it that evening.

FDR reassured people that their money would be safer in the newly reopened banks than hidden in their homes. Within a few days, deposits exceeded withdrawals. The banking crisis was over.[1]

**A New Deal**   When Roosevelt accepted the Democratic nomination for president, he had pledged "a new deal for the American people." Now that he had taken office, it was time to fulfill that promise and put the rest of his legislative program, the **New Deal,** into effect.

---

**Identifying Cause and Effect**
Roosevelt's open-minded approach to new ideas had the effect of making him seem interested and approachable. Because he often responded so positively to people's ideas, they felt mistakenly encouraged to believe that he would implement them. When he didn't, people felt Roosevelt had misled them, and they labeled him a hypocrite.

**1** What steps did Roosevelt take to end the banking crisis?

The overwhelming approval that the Democrat-controlled Congress gave his banking bill persuaded Roosevelt to extend the special session to work on other New Deal legislation. The bills Roosevelt introduced—some of which actually had been first proposed by the Hoover administration—addressed the three R's: relief for the unemployed, recovery measures to stimulate the economy, and reform laws to help lessen the threat of another economic disaster.

**Relief** By 1933 many of the millions of people who had been unemployed for more than three years had no choice left to them but to apply for public aid. However, local relief agencies could not meet the growing demand for aid. In response, FDR asked Congress to appropriate $500 million to be distributed by a new agency, the Federal Emergency Relief Administration (FERA), to state and local relief agencies. The bill passed on May 12.

Eight days later the FERA swung into action. Headed by experienced administrator and social worker Harry Hopkins, the agency distributed $5 million in its first two hours of operation. One government official, worried about this fast pace of spending, suggested that a slower, more conservative distribution of funds might work out better in the long run. Hopkins responded, "People don't eat in the long run—they [have to] eat every day."

Although Hopkins disbursed the millions allotted to FERA quite freely, he disliked the **dole,** which is what government charity was called. He, along with Roosevelt, felt that giving money to people broke down their self-respect and their will to work. To combat this weakening of morale, Roosevelt proposed relief programs that would put people back to work.

One of these programs was the Civilian Conservation Corps (CCC). The CCC put hundreds of thousands of unemployed men to work each season on environmental projects. Many of the facilities in the state and national parks today were constructed by the CCC.

Members of the CCC lived in barracks, ate together in mess halls, and followed a strict schedule. This room and board and a salary of $30 a month were provided to each man in exchange for his labor. The workers sent most of their salaries back to their families. (Turn to the Geography feature on pages 376 and 377 to learn more about the CCC.)

Among the first recruits to the CCC were several thousand members of the bonus army. This army had

U.S. DEPARTMENT OF THE INTERIOR

**William Gropper painted the mural "Construction of the Dam" in 1939. In it Gropper depicts the energy and productivity engendered by New Deal programs.**

**He also conveys a sense of harmony among the construction workers.** *How does he achieve this?*

returned to Washington, D.C., in the spring of 1933 to lobby again for early payment on the bonus certificates they had received as veterans of World War I. Roosevelt, like Hoover, was reluctant to grant them the money. However, instead of sending in troops to run the veterans out of Washington as Hoover had done, Roosevelt had coffee served to the veterans and then arranged for them to meet with his aides. These aides first gave the veterans the idea of seeking employment in the CCC.

The Public Works Administration (PWA) was another New Deal program that helped provide jobs for the unemployed. With a grant of $3.3 billion dollars to carry out public projects, the PWA put people back to work building schools and dams, refurbishing government buildings, planning sewage systems, improving highways, and generally modernizing the nation.

The PWA also revitalized the economy in communities throughout the United States. For example, in 1934 the PWA granted New York Mills, a small town in Minnesota, money to build a village water system. All the unemployed men of New York Mills were put back to work on this construction project. In addition, local businesses, including engineering firms, building contractors, plumbers, and materials suppliers, participated in the project. The PWA's massive spending on wages, materials, and supplies for projects nationwide was intended to stimulate industry and spur economic recovery.

**Recovery Measures**   Another of Roosevelt's goals was to increase the productivity of industry. Between 1929 and 1933, America's factories had decreased their production levels by about 40 percent. To help factories recover, Roosevelt sponsored the National Industrial Recovery Act (NIRA). After its passage on June 16, 1933, the NIRA established the National Recovery Administration (NRA), to carry out the new law.

The NIRA relaxed the antitrust laws of the early 1900s and called for business leaders to confer and establish codes to set quality standards, production levels, prices, maximum work hours, and minimum wages. The NIRA also declared that workers should be allowed to organize labor unions and to bargain collectively. Shortening individual workers' hours forced businesses to hire more people, which, in turn, created two million additional jobs.

Business leaders who decided not to adhere to the industry-set standards could not effectively be penalized by the NRA. So to encourage business leaders to comply voluntarily with the codes, the NRA launched a huge publicity campaign. It adopted as its symbol the blue eagle and asked businesses that followed the codes to prominently display a blue-eagle poster. Then the NRA asked people to buy their goods only from businesses displaying the blue eagle.

The public rallied in support of businesses displaying the eagle. However, despite the public's enthusiasm, the NRA's policies had controversial results. Owners of large companies established codes that put small businesses at such a disadvantage that many small-business owners felt that they were being forced into bankruptcy, and for this they blamed the NRA.

The Agricultural Adjustment Administration (AAA) was equally controversial. This agency was established to help farmers who had been hard hit by the Depression. The AAA paid farmers a **subsidy,** or financial assistance, to reduce the production of crops and the number of animals they raised. Such cutbacks would help bring the supply of agricultural products more in line with the demand for them, causing prices to rise.

Although the plan was sound in theory, problems developed as it was put into practice. For example, by the time the AAA was established in the spring of 1933, farmers had already planted their fields and farm animals had already produced many young. Therefore, in order to meet the AAA's guidelines, farmers had to plow under portions of their crops and kill the newborn animals. At a time when thousands of people were suffering from malnutrition, this action struck many as immoral and wasteful.

In response, Roosevelt authorized the FERA to buy some of the crops and livestock before they were destroyed to distribute them to the needy. Yet not all the farm products could be redistributed. For example, most of the animals slaughtered were too young to be used as food. To explain the apparent waste, Secretary of Agriculture Henry A. Wallace stated, "Agriculture cannot survive in a capitalistic society as a philanthropic enterprise." His explanation did little to appease the people distressed by the AAA's policies.

Another New Deal recovery program was the Tennessee Valley Authority (TVA). The TVA built

STUDY GUIDE

**Predicting Consequences**
If Roosevelt had used only the dole without taking any other measures to help needy citizens, there would have been unwelcome consequences. The nation's economy would have suffered because people on the dole would not have been contributing to the economy. Furthermore, government funds would have eventually become depleted by the dole.

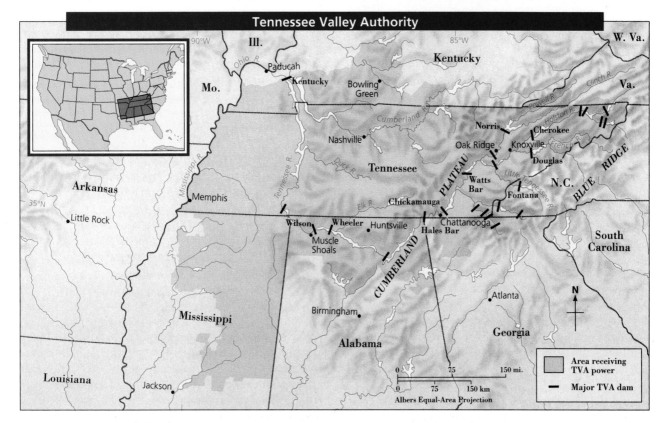

## Tennessee Valley Authority

**Plotted on this map are the sites in which major TVA dams are located. Also shown is the area receiving TVA power.** *Locate these sites and identify the area that receives TVA power. In what other states besides Tennessee were there TVA dams? Besides Tennessee, what other states benefit from TVA power?*

dams in the Tennessee River to turn the river's water power into electricity. A reporter outlined the TVA's plan as follows:

> *First, says the TVA, you fill up your gullies, terrace your land, strip-plow your slopes, and let the water flow down as slowly as possible. You collect the water behind dams and produce power. You use part of this power to make phosphate fertilizer, and with the fertilizer you grow legumes which enrich and hold your soil. You use some of the rest of the power on the farm itself.*

> "A Dream Takes Form in TVA's Domain,"
> *New York Times Magazine*, April 19, 1936

The TVA aimed to do much more than just generate electricity. It was also intended to enrich the land, create fish-filled lakes that would, in turn, increase tourism, and to provide jobs for the residents of the Tennessee Valley. However, although the TVA achieved some of these goals, it was not well received by everyone. Farmers whose lands were permanently flooded by backwaters created by the dams were certainly not pleased by the project. Also, some business leaders considered the government-sponsored agency an unfair competitor, resenting the rock-bottom rates the TVA charged. They lobbied to prevent similar programs from being approved for other regions of the country.

**Reform Laws** In addition to providing relief and stimulating recovery, the New Deal legislation enacted reform measures. Among the most important reform measures were the Truth-in-Securities Act and the Glass-Steagall Banking Act.

## STUDY GUIDE

### Recognizing Bias

Socialism is an economic system in which big businesses are not privately owned, but, rather, all members of a society own and profit from them.

Private owners of big businesses were thus threatened by anything even faintly resembling socialism—such as the TVA, which was government

owned and operated. Their bias against socialism was so strong, in fact, that although the TVA helped many people, big-business owners opposed it.

The Truth-in-Securities Act was designed to eliminate fraud in the stock market. Under this law, a company that deliberately deceived investors about its financial status could be sued. The Glass-Steagall Banking Act prohibited banks from investing savings deposits in the stock market, which was too unpredictable to assure the safety of these funds. It also established the Federal Deposit Insurance Corporation (FDIC) to insure bank deposits in all member banks. With this insurance, people regained confidence that their money would be safe in FDIC banks.

During the Hundred Days between March 9 and June 16, President Roosevelt proposed 15 bills. These came to be known collectively as the *First* New Deal. Congress, with only minor changes, passed all 15 of his proposals. For a president to be able to collaborate so successfully with a Congress was a major victory for a new president. However, FDR was a Democrat at a time when Congress was controlled by Democrats, a fact that greatly facilitated the passage of FDR's legislative programs.

## The President and the People

President Roosevelt's positive, vigorous style was reflected not only in his legislative programs but also in life at the White House, where glumness had reigned during the last few months of the Hoover administration. On inauguration day, the head of the secret service, Colonel Edmund Starling, drove the brooding ex-president and his wife to the train station. When Starling returned, he reported that the White House was "transformed during my absence into a gay place, full of people who oozed confidence." The friendly informality of the White House made many Americans feel personally connected to the president.

**Fireside Chats** FDR promoted this feeling by informally addressing the American public in frequent radio broadcasts known as fireside chats. In these chats, Roosevelt explained the legislation of the New Deal in simple, straightforward terms. Humorist Will Rogers quipped that in Roosevelt's first fireside chat on March 12, 1933, the president explained the complex subject of banking in terms that even bankers could understand. His steady, relaxed voice reassured people across the nation that their problems would be solved, and, more importantly, that they could participate in solving them.[2] In his broadcast about the NRA, Roosevelt said the following:

> *The essence of the plan is a universal limitation of hours of work per week for any individual by common consent, and a universal payment of wages above a minimum, also by common consent. I cannot guarantee the success of this nation-wide plan, but the people of this country can guarantee its success. . . . [I] do have faith, and retain faith, in the strength of common purpose, and in the strength of unified action taken by the American people.*

> Franklin D. Roosevelt,
> *Fireside Chat*, July 24, 1933

FDR's masterful management of radio publicity was matched by his skillful handling of the press. Hoover had met infrequently with reporters and only answered questions that had been written out beforehand. Roosevelt, on the other hand, held weekly press conferences in which he was willing to answer all questions. This made him very popular with reporters—a relationship that often worked to his advantage.

**Eleanor's Influence** Eleanor Roosevelt first became involved in politics during her husband's battle with polio. Hoping to keep FDR's name before the public, Eleanor became active in the Democratic party. She soon took up other causes, joining the Women's Trade Union League and the League of Women Voters. When FDR returned to politics, Eleanor did not give up her own political activities. Instead, she lobbied for laws to end child labor, worked for better conditions in state hospitals, discussed with her husband the appalling plight of people stranded by the Depression, and used her influence to help relieve their suffering.

Eleanor gave people throughout the nation the sense that they had access to the president. Hundreds of thousands of people wrote to her each year, seeking help and offering solutions to the nation's problems.

**Making Inferences**
FDR prohibited banks from investing savings account funds in the stock market because he believed that people had withdrawn their money from banks to keep them from losing it in the unstable stock market. Indeed, he appears to have inferred correctly. After Roosevelt implemented this measure, bank deposits once again began to exceed withdrawals.

**2** For what purpose did Roosevelt hold the fireside chats?

*This letter comes to you from the . . . lead and zinc field of southeastern Kansas. Thirty-eight percent of the entire world supply of lead and zinc ore is produced in this district. We have here health hazards known as "lead poisoning" in the smelters and silicosis, the most dreaded industrial disease known to medical science. . . . These health hazards can be eliminated if the mining trusts will install air cleaning devices. This, of course, costs money and the greedy, grasping employers apparently haven't any extra. . . . Why [doesn't] the labor department make a health and hygiene survey of this district? Will you add your voice to ours in requesting this be done[?]*

Letter from the Cherokee
County Central Labor Body,
Columbus, Kansas, 1938

AP/WIDE WORLD PHOTOS

**While touring Puerto Rico in 1934, Mrs. Roosevelt enjoys listening to a young girl read from her school book. In addition to speaking English, the First Lady spoke Spanish, French, and German.**

Eleanor saw to it that all the letters that she received were answered. Those letters that were of special concern to her, like the one reprinted above, she showed to the president, often persuading him to take action. She held her own press conferences regularly and traveled across the country, giving lectures on a variety of topics that were of great concern to her and the American people. According to her friend Adlai Stevenson, "What rendered this unforgettable woman so extraordinary was not merely her response to suffering; it was her comprehension of the complexity of the human condition." Showing concern for everyone she met, the First Lady symbolized the energy, empathy, and responsiveness of the Roosevelt administration.

The Roosevelts' warm public image aligned the majority of Americans behind President Roosevelt and his New Deal. However, throughout 1934, the country remained mired deep in economic depression. Critics quickly arose to attack Roosevelt and the New Deal.

## SECTION REVIEW

### Checking Facts

1. What are some of the reasons Roosevelt won the election of 1932?
2. What were the Three R's Roosevelt's legislation addressed?
3. How did the CCC and the PWA differ?
4. What was Eleanor Roosevelt's role in her husband's administration?

### Thinking Critically

5. **Making Inferences** Why do you think Franklin Delano Roosevelt was so popular with the American people?
6. **Predicting Consequences** What might have happened if Roosevelt's legislation had failed to address any one of the Three R's?
7. **Identifying Cause and Effect** Why did the Roosevelts' decision to speak frequently with reporters, answer all correspondence, and broadcast fireside chats work to FDR's advantage?

### Linking Across Time

8. Compare and contrast the leadership styles of President Coolidge and of President Roosevelt.

Many painters and photographers documented their impressions of American life during the Depression. You can learn about the period from their works. But these works are chronicles of painters' and photographers' impressions and not objective records of the subjects they portray. To interpret an image, therefore, you must understand how it reflects the views of the person who created it.

## Learning the Skill

Both painter and photographer make choices about what to include and how to show it. These choices can affect the impressions their works give.

### Interpreting a Painting

From a painting you can get an idea of how people dressed, what technology they used, and where they lived and worked. But don't assume that this information is unbiased. The painter might have idealized the subject. If painting from memory, the artist might not have portrayed the subject exactly as it was. Further, the painter might have chosen to represent only a narrow segment of society or to symbolize the subject rather than to document it precisely.

Look below at the section of Thomas Hart Benton's mural *America Today*. What impression of steelworkers and the steel industry does this painting give you? Notice that Benton has chosen to portray the workers as being very industrious. How else has he idealized the workers and the industry?

### Interpreting a Photograph

You can learn many of the same historical details from a photograph as from a painting, usually with less chance of distortion since a camera captures in an instant everything the lens "sees." However, photographers can control what the lens "sees" just as painters can control what appears on a canvas. Photographers can exclude elements that do not support the impression they want to convey and they can stage pictures, posing people as they want them to appear. A photographer's opinion, or point of view, is usually reflected in his or her work.

Study the 1913 photograph of the construction of the Woolworth Building. What can you learn from it? What ideas and feelings does it convey about the steelworkers' relationship to the steel girders and to the city? How has the photographer communicated these ideas and feelings?

### Practicing the Skill

1. Examine the mural on page 363. What can you learn about the New Deal from this image? How did the painter create this impression?
2. Review the two photographs of Eleanor Roosevelt in the chapter. How does each photograph give a different impression of her?

© THE EQUITABLE LIFE ASSURANCE SOCIETY OF THE UNITED STATES

CULVER PICTURES, INC.

# Criticism and Reformulation

## September, 1933: Doctor Launches Crusade to Aid the Elderly

ONE DAY IN 1933, DR. FRANCIS E. TOWNSEND, A 66-YEAR-OLD RETIRED PHYSICIAN, WITNESSED something that changed his life. While standing at his bathroom window shaving, he saw "three very haggard old women, stooped with great age, bending over the [trash] barrels, clawing into the contents." That these elderly people should be reduced to such poverty and degradation infuriated him.

Townsend channeled his fury into formulating a plan to aid America's aged and, at the same time, to stimulate the economy. According to his plan, every person over age 60 would be asked to retire, freeing up jobs for younger people. Each retired person would receive a pension of $200 per month on the condition that the person spend the entire sum in 30 days. Townsend claimed that the pension would rescue the elderly from poverty, and the enforced spending would act as a transfusion of cash into the economy. Furthermore, it would create a demand for products, which, in turn, would result in a demand for more workers to produce them. Townsend believed that his social security program would bring about an immediate end to the Depression.

UPI/BETTMANN NEWSPHOTOS

In the southern California community where Townsend lived, the idea gained widespread appeal. To publicize the plan, Townsend began circulating petitions, speaking at meetings, and organizing clubs. Within a few years, Townsend clubs had sprung up throughout the nation.

The overnight success of Dr. Townsend's movement indicated the level of discontent felt by many elderly people during Roosevelt's first term. Older people, however, were not the only ones to find fault with Roosevelt. By the end of 1934, people from all walks of life were attacking Roosevelt's policies.

## New Deal: Big Deal!

Under Roosevelt's New Deal, the economy had begun to recover. Between 1933 and 1934, the national income rose 25 percent. By 1934, hundreds of factories that had closed in the early 1930s were again producing goods. Many farmers had refinanced their mortgages with government assistance. Millions of people who had been unemployed were receiving relief or held federally funded jobs.

---

### STUDY GUIDE

**As You Read**

Learn the criticisms of the New Deal to understand the formulation of the Second New Deal. Also, think about the following concepts and skills.

**Central Concepts**
- recognizing the causes and effects of **unionization**
- understanding the policies of the **Second New Deal**

**Thinking Skills**
- recognizing points of view
- drawing conclusions
- making inferences
- identifying cause and effect
- recognizing propaganda

Nevertheless, the recovery was incomplete. Although by 1934 incomes had risen substantially, they were still far below pre-crash levels. On average, workers in the cities made 13 percent less than they had made in 1929. Farm prices lagged 28 percent behind 1929 prices. More than 20 percent of the working population was still unemployed. For many farmers, factory workers, and unemployed citizens, the New Deal had taken too long to accomplish too little.

**Protests of Tenant Farmers**   The New Deal's agricultural program, the AAA, actually did some farmers more harm than good. To reduce the amount of crops that would be produced, the AAA paid landowners to let some of their land lie unused. Technically, the landowners were supposed to divide their AAA checks with their tenant farmers. In reality, however, few landowners complied with this requirement. Instead, they tended to reduce the number of acres planted by evicting their tenant farmers and didn't even share with them the AAA subsidy. Poverty-stricken before the New Deal, tenant farmers were then also homeless and jobless.

A group of southern tenant farmers who were outraged by this situation organized the interracial Southern Tenant Farmers' Union (STFU). They went on strike to obtain raises for working tenant farmers and day laborers. They petitioned the Department of Agriculture to give them a guarantee that tenant farmers would get their fair share of AAA payments. They also promoted nonviolent protest and showed that blacks and whites could work together effectively.

The STFU met with strong opposition. Landowners worked with law enforcement agents to harass STFU leaders, threaten union members, and break up STFU meetings. Desperate for help, the STFU appealed to Roosevelt for aid. Roosevelt responded with promises but no action. Bitterly disappointed, one STFU leader wrote, "Too often he [Roosevelt] has talked like a cropper [tenant farmer] and acted like a planter [landowner]."

**Voices of Labor**   The National Industrial Recovery Act (NIRA) of 1933 had permitted all workers to join unions of their choice, bargain collectively for wage increases and other work benefits, and go on strike to try to force employers to meet their demands. The NIRA thus renewed most workers' hopes for change. In just the first two years following its passage, unions added about 1 million new workers to their ranks.

Although unions organized workers' efforts and provided them with

AP/WIDE WORLD PHOTOS

**Although blacks and whites were segregated in most work and social situations, in the STFU, black and white tenant farmers joined forces to fight the landowners who had unjustly evicted them.**

## STUDY GUIDE

### Recognizing Points of View

Landowners felt justified in evicting their tenant farmers and in pocketing the AAA reimbursement for letting their lands lie unused. They felt that, since the land was theirs, they should be entitled to the entire subsidy paid for not using it. Tenants, on the other hand, felt that, since they were the ones who had been evicted to comply with the AAA, they should be the ones to receive the reimbursement.

## Labor Union Membership

Legend:
- Independent unions
- CIO
- AFL

Membership (in millions) vs Year (1929, 1931, 1933, 1935, 1937, 1939, 1941)

**Membership in unions rallied after the NIRA passed. Some union leaders formed a Committee for Industrial Organization (CIO). In 1938 the CIO became the Congress of Industrial Organizations.**
*Judging from the graph, about when did the NIRA pass?*

LIBRARY OF CONGRESS

UPI/BETTMANN NEWSPHOTOS

**Minneapolis police attack unarmed teamsters during the strike of 1934, shown in the photo above. The worker at left proudly displays his union membership book.**

leaders who could negotiate with owners and managers, some workers believed that unions were not as effective as worker-organized strikes and protests. Unions tended to dissipate revolutionary energy by focusing on contracts and negotiations rather than on rebellion.

However, **unionization,** or the formation of unions, did not generally ease the conflict between workers and management. In fact, the number and intensity of such conflicts increased after passage of the NIRA. An especially heated conflict occurred in 1934 when Minneapolis truck drivers tried to get local business representatives to negotiate with their union. Business leaders responded by banding together to break the strike. Then, on July 16, the police opened fire on unarmed picketers, shooting 67 people and killing two. One hundred thousand Minneapolis citizens marched in the funeral procession for the slain workers. Confronted by such strong union sympathy, business leaders agreed to negotiate with unions.

During 1934, similarly bitter strikes took place throughout the nation. Textile workers from Georgia to Massachusetts staged a massive strike, while San Francisco workers from various unions struck together. That year, over 1.5 million workers staged 1,800 strikes.

Because unionization tended to increase the number of strikes and protests, business leaders and factory owners generally tried to prevent workers from unionizing. Although it was illegal, many employers fired or intimidated workers who tried to start unions. Even Roosevelt, who had supported the NIRA, was more worried about labor's power to halt economic recovery with strikes than he was about protecting the rights supposedly ensured by the bill.[1]

**Reactionary and Radical Voices** Frustrated with the slowness and limited scope of Roosevelt's New Deal, many Americans turned to leaders who

---

STUDY GUIDE

### Drawing Conclusions

A sit-down strike—a strike in which workers stopped work but remained at their posts—was a very effective means of protest. It kept strikers' morale up since they were close enough to give each other support. It kept out strikebreakers since the strikers occupied the plant. Also, it kept the police from interfering, since a police invasion might damage the plant's equipment.

**1** Why were most business leaders opposed to unionization?

AP/WIDE WORLD PHOTOS (left)

AP/WIDE WORLD PHOTOS (right)

**Father Charles Coughlin, at left, claimed approximately nine million supporters' votes before the church ordered him to step out of the public spotlight. Huey P. Long, at right, also possessed an enormous following.** *If Senator Long had not been assassinated, do you think he would have become the first dictator of the United States? Why or why not?*

promised simple and sometimes radical solutions to the nation's pressing problems. These leaders gained huge followings during the mid-1930s.

Dr. Townsend, who organized more than five million supporters for his pension plan, was one such leader. Townsend focused on getting Congress to approve his plan. However, in 1935 Townsend's plan was soundly defeated in Congress.

Another popular leader was Father Charles E. Coughlin, a Roman Catholic priest with his own weekly radio show. Coughlin was a **demagogue,** a leader who gains power by appealing to people's prejudices and fears rather than to reason.

In 1933 and 1934, Coughlin supported Roosevelt because he thought the president agreed with his ideas such as nationalizing the banks and running them as a federal business like the post office. However, by 1935 Coughlin realized that Roosevelt had no intention of changing the nation's financial system. At that point he began calling the president a "great betrayer and a liar."

FDR was not the only person Coughlin attacked. He also spoke out against powerful bankers and later extended his hatred of particular bankers who happened to be Jewish to all Jews. Although the Jewish people were clearly not responsible for the plight of the nation, Coughlin's anti-Semitism gave his followers a group of people to blame for their troubles. Coughlin also preached that the wealth of the few should be redistributed among the many, an idea that appealed to the working class.

Coughlin's impassioned speeches increased his following. In the mid-1930s, he commanded a radio audience of 30 million. However, superiors in the church, embarrassed by Coughlin's behavior, finally imposed silence upon the priest in 1942.

A contemporary of Coughlin, Senator Huey P. Long of Louisiana was equally popular and just as opposed to FDR's programs. Long had achieved almost instant popularity when, as governor of Louisiana, he had pushed through a bill to levy new taxes to raise funds for schools and hospitals that would serve the poor. Long had seen to it that roads were improved and bridges built in previously neglected areas of the state.

While retaining power in Louisiana state government, Long was elected to the U.S. Senate in 1930. However, just before he left the office of governor to take his seat in the Senate, he replaced the lieutenant governor with two successors who would follow his commands while he was in Washington, D.C. Then, as senator, he abolished local Louisiana governments, putting himself in control of all appointments to government offices such as those of the police and fire departments.

As senator, he also launched his Share Our Wealth campaign with the slogan, "Every man a king, but no one wears a crown." According to Long's proposal, all incomes over $5 million dollars would be confiscated and redistributed, providing each family with a $5,000 income. Long's plan, like Coughlin's, appealed to the working class, helping him to gain widespread support.

Having taken complete control of the Louisiana government, Long then set his sights on controlling the U.S. government. However, in September 1935 Long was assassinated, putting an end to his plans.

## STUDY GUIDE

**Making Inferences**

What did Coughlin's and Long's popularity reveal about the American public at the time? Americans were eager to find a leader with an actual plan that promised to solve their financial problems and rectify the imbalance in the distribution of wealth throughout the nation. They were also eager to find a group of people to blame for their troubles—Coughlin blamed the Jews and Long blamed the rich.

## New Deal: No Deal!

Roosevelt not only faced opposition from people who demanded that the government do more for the needy but also from people who demanded it do less. Among his greatest enemies were the bankers and politicians with whom he had worked so successfully when he first took office.

**Attack from the Conservatives**   Many business leaders charged that Roosevelt was interfering too much with private businesses and spending an excessive amount of money on relief. They attacked the president's top advisers for lacking the political and business experience necessary to address adequately the needs of businesses. Most claimed that Roosevelt had created an unmanageable bureaucracy and was leading the nation toward socialism.

In 1934 a number of unhappy politicians and businessmen formed the American Liberty League, an organization dedicated to "upholding the Constitution." This goal masked the League's real purpose: to destroy the New Deal. By waging a propaganda war, League members hoped to force Roosevelt supporters out of office. However, the Liberty League, described by one reporter as "the largest collection of millionaires ever assembled under the same roof," never gained much support.

**Attack from the Courts**   The courts were more successful in attacking the New Deal than were the millionaires. In the mid-1930s the Supreme Court overturned two key pieces of New Deal legislation, the NIRA and the AAA, on the grounds that they were both unconstitutional. It objected to the multitude of NIRA codes the executive branch had helped design and found that the NIRA's regulation of all industries—from dog food to shoulder pads—gave the executive branch too much power over small, local businesses. In addition, the Court faulted NIRA codes that regulated intrastate as well as interstate business, arguing that the Constitution gave the federal government power only to regulate commerce between states—not within states. The Court also objected to the means by which the AAA funded its agricultural subsidies: by levying a processing tax on businesses that bought the agricultural products. The Court deemed taxation was an improper method of regulating agricultural production.

Faced with attacks by radicals, liberals, and conservatives, and hampered by the Supreme Court, Roosevelt revamped his recovery and reform policies. In 1935 he launched his new program—the **Second New Deal**.

## The Second New Deal

Like the First New Deal, the Second New Deal included sweeping legislation in many different areas. The new laws expanded relief programs, aided farmers and workers, and provided economic reforms.

**Expanding Relief**   Despite the success of the First New Deal, 10 million people remained unemployed in 1934. To put more people back to work, Roosevelt therefore proposed a $4.8 billion relief program, the Works Progress Administration (WPA), in his Second New Deal.

Congress approved the proposed WPA in April 1935. Headed by Harry Hopkins, the administrator who had so forcefully taken charge of the FERA, the WPA then began processing the applications it received for a huge variety of projects nationwide. Building projects, including hospitals, schools, airports, and playgrounds, were the mainstay of the program. The WPA also put unemployed teachers, artists, writers, and actors back to work. Teachers taught people to read. Painters designed murals for public buildings. Writers wrote guidebooks describing America's historical and cultural heritage. Actors traveled the country, bringing live theater to people who had never seen a play before.[2]

A single WPA project might benefit a community in a variety of ways. For example, in San Antonio, Texas, in 1939, the WPA sponsored a $300,000 project that included building a scenic walkway along the San Antonio River, deepening the river channel to permit small-craft navigation, landscaping the riverfront, and building an outdoor theater. This project stimulated the local economy and beautified the city.

Both directly and indirectly the WPA improved the quality of life in communities across the nation. In

---

**Identifying Cause and Effect**
The WPA had some positive effects on the nation. The program created millions of jobs and improved communities. However, the WPA also had a negative effect. It needed a huge bureaucracy to function. In fact, people coined a word to refer to the WPA's projects: *boondoggling,* which means "to waste time or money."

**2** Whom did the WPA employ? In what types of projects were they involved?

FRANKLIN D. ROOSEVELT LIBRARY

**During a flood WPA workers sandbag a street.** *Why might the poster at left have succeeded in getting people to join the WPA?*

LIBRARY OF CONGRESS

When the Supreme Court declared the NIRA unconstitutional in May 1935, workers lost their right to join unions of their choice and to bargain collectively. The July 1935 Wagner Act, however, restored those rights. It also set up a federal agency, the National Labor Relations Board (NLRB), to ensure that employers followed the new law.

After the Supreme Court struck down the AAA, Roosevelt proposed the Soil Conservation Act of 1936, which required farmers to reduce the acreage of the same crops the AAA had previously paid them not to plant. Under this act, the money for farm subsidies would not come from a processing tax—as it had under the AAA—but from the treasury.

The Rural Electrification Act (REA) of 1935 lent money to groups of farmers who organized to build power plants. For years utility companies had refused to extend service to isolated rural areas, arguing that it was not profitable. As a result, before the REA, fewer than one in ten American farms had electricity. By the late 1940s, however, electricity had been extended to 90 percent of all farms.

all, during its five years of operation, the WPA gave jobs to over eight million people.

In August 1935 another relief program, the Social Security Act, was passed. With its passage, the government was accepting direct responsibility for meeting the basic needs of its citizens. This program instituted pension and survivors' benefits for the elderly and the orphaned and aid to individuals injured in industrial accidents. Monthly social security payments ranged from $12 to $85. However, millions of people did not even qualify for the program. Many of those who did not qualify were members of minority groups.

**Aiding Recovery** Roosevelt further aided recovery by restoring the rights and privileges of workers and farmers that the Supreme Court had revoked.

**Pushing for New Reforms** The REA indirectly attacked utility companies by enabling people to obtain electricity without them. Roosevelt also attacked these huge conglomerates directly with the Public Utility Holding Company Act, passed in June 1935. This act, which pared down the holding companies, helped eliminate corruption and inefficiency in the utilities industries and reduce consumers' costs.

The legislation regulating the utility companies enraged many business leaders who believed that the

## STUDY GUIDE

### Recognizing Propaganda

Propaganda is the governmental promotion of a particular message or idea or the material being used to promote the message. The WPA poster above is a good example of the type of propaganda the Roosevelt administration used to popularize its programs. Notice that the worker in the poster is portrayed as a strong man and that the message links work to confidence. This implies that working for the WPA will make you strong and confident. At a time when most Americans felt weak and insecure, such promises must have generated much support for the WPA.

government was assuming too much power over businesses. These people became even angrier when the president proposed increased taxes on the incomes of wealthy corporations and individuals. This revenue bill passed Congress in 1935.

The Revenue Act of 1935 as well as other Second New Deal legislation convinced millions of Americans that the president was on their side. Roosevelt's popularity soared as the 1936 election season began.

## Reelection and Redirection

Roosevelt geared his campaign toward the lower and middle classes, who had been hardest hit by the Depression, promising legislation that was not only charitable but that helped people to help themselves. The Republican candidate, Kansas Governor Alfred Landon, supported most of Roosevelt's New Deal programs but said that he would run them more efficiently. Nevertheless, Landon gave people little reason to switch to him. In the most lopsided election since 1820, FDR won the majority of votes in every state but Maine and Vermont. Backed by 60 percent of the voters, Roosevelt believed the American people had endorsed his New Deal.

Forging ahead, in February 1937 Roosevelt introduced a bill to increase the number of justices on the Supreme Court. Having been distressed by the Court's rulings against New Deal legislation, FDR wanted to appoint additional judges sympathetic to his programs. However, publicly Roosevelt insisted that he was merely trying to ease the workload of the aging justices. People reacted negatively to his tampering with the delicately balanced judicial system. Republican critics accused Roosevelt of wanting to become a dictator.

Although even some Democrats eventually criticized him, Roosevelt stuck to his proposal. Then, in the middle of the fight, the Supreme Court upheld several key New Deal programs. At this point, FDR backed down. To save face, he eventually signed a watered-down bill enacting measures to speed up judicial processes.

Opposition to Roosevelt's proposed judicial system changes and an economic recession that began in 1937 slowed down his political momentum. In 1937 and 1938, Roosevelt proposed numerous other programs. However, he only secured passage of one New Deal law in 1938, the Fair Labor Standards Act, which regulated wages and working hours. Then, as tensions in Europe and Asia grew, the president began to concentrate on international issues and the New Deal slowly ground to a halt.

BROWN BROTHERS

**When FDR proposed that up to six more seats be added to the Supreme Court, most people believed that he was trying to "pack the court" with justices who would favor his legislation. In this way, FDR could ensure that other New Deal legislation would not be overturned by future Supreme Court rulings. However, FDR denied that this was his objective.**

## SECTION REVIEW

### Checking Facts
1. List the failures of the New Deal.
2. Why did some people, particularly, bankers and conservative politicians, oppose the New Deal?
3. What people did the WPA and the Social Security Act not help?
4. What decision hurt Roosevelt politically during his second term? Why?

### Thinking Critically
5. **Identifying Cause and Effect** How did unionization actually help business and factory owners?
6. **Recognizing Points of View** Why might business owners not want the government to interfere with their operation?
7. **Making Inferences** Why do you think the government was interested in helping farmers receive electricity?

8. **Drawing Conclusions** How might FDR's attempt to increase the number of Supreme Court justices have worked partly to his advantage?

### Linking Across Time
9. Compare criticisms of FDR with criticisms of the president today. Are any of the criticisms the same?

In the 1930s one form of recreation still within the reach of a family on a budget was a camping trip. The national parks were most vacationers' favorite campgrounds. Although the National Park Service was supposed to maintain these areas, the parks deteriorated during the Depression.

## Roosevelt's Corps

In 1933, within the first three weeks of his administration, President Roosevelt proposed the Civilian Conservation Corps (CCC) to improve the national parks and employ young people. Roosevelt hoped the CCC would create "a mass exodus of unemployed to the forests." Instead of going on relief, unmarried men between the ages of 18 and 25 would work here to preserve the environment. According to Roosevelt's plan, the Labor Department would recruit the workers, the War Department would run the camps, and the Interior Department would supervise the work projects.

The CCC became a showpiece for the Roosevelt administration. Reporter Ernie Pyle visited Shenandoah Park in Virginia and reported that "the boys build stone guard-rails, trim ledges, fix overlooks so you can park and see. The camps are neat and clean, their green barracks and little gravel streets as trim as any Army camp you ever saw. The boys at work wave as you drive by."

All told, by 1942 when the CCC was disbanded, 2,650 camps had been built and a total of 2.5 million men had served in them.

The CCC excluded women and limited the numbers of African Americans, Hispanic Americans, and Native Americans it accepted

> **People are shaped by their environment but also have the capacity to shape their environment. Environmental modifications have made our national parks accessible to millions.**

into its ranks. Furthermore, the minorities who were permitted to join the corps were segregated from the white workers. So, although the CCC helped many people, it still discriminated against minorities and women—some of the people hardest hit by the Depression.

## The Tree Army

The CCC primarily worked to preserve and enhance the environment and improve outdoor facilities. Workers built reservoirs and fish ponds, then stocked them with fish. In fact, the CCC put almost one billion fish into ponds. Crews built dams to stop erosion, dug ditches, created bridges, and built truck trails as well as roads throughout the parks. They also restored historic battlefields, cleared

beaches and camping grounds, and created more than 30,000 shelters for wildlife.

Although the CCC's tasks were varied, CCC workers became best known for their efforts to protect and preserve the trees of the forests. In fact, people referred to the CCC as the tree army.

After the dust storms of 1935, Roosevelt pushed for the construction of a "shelterbelt" of trees in a 100-mile-wide region in the Great Plains. He believed that the root structure of the trees would hold tightly to the topsoil

**Graphic artist Albert Bender produced this energetic design to promote the CCC.**

A YOUNG MAN'S OPPORTUNITY

CCC

FOR WORK PLAY STUDY & HEALTH

APPLICATIONS TAKEN BY
ILLINOIS EMERGENCY RELIEF COMMISSION
ILLINOIS SELECTING AGENCY

LIBRARY OF CONGRESS

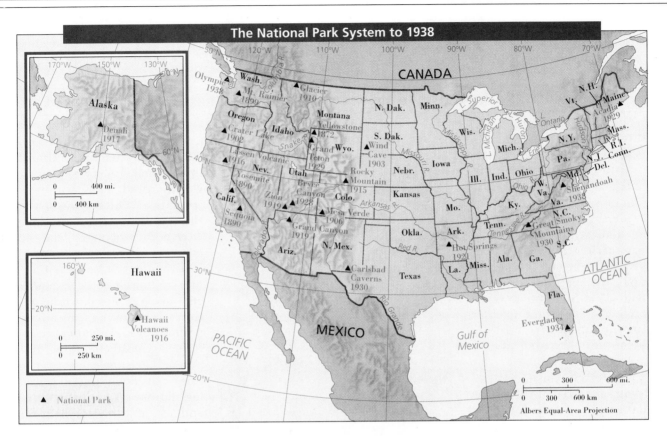

## The National Park System to 1938

Alaska
Denali 1917

Hawaii
Hawaii Volcanoes 1916

CANADA

Olympic 1938
Wash.
Mt. Rainier 1899
Glacier 1910
Oregon
Crater Lake 1902
Idaho
Montana
Yellowstone 1872
N. Dak.
Minn.
Lassen Volcanic 1916
Nev.
Utah
Grand Teton 1929
Wyo.
Wind Cave 1903
S. Dak.
Wis.
Mich.
N.Y.
Vt.
N.H.
Maine
Acadia 1929
Mass.
R.I.
Conn.
Yosemite 1890
Calif.
Zion 1919
Bryce Canyon 1928
Colo.
Rocky Mountain 1915
Nebr.
Iowa
Ill.
Ind.
Ohio
Pa.
N.J.
Del.
Md.
W. Va.
Va.
Shenandoah 1938
Sequoia 1890
Grand Canyon 1919
Mesa Verde 1906
Kansas
Mo.
Ky.
Tenn.
N.C.
Great Smoky Mountains 1930
S.C.
Ariz.
N. Mex.
Okla.
Ark.
Hot Springs 1921
Ala.
Ga.
Carlsbad Caverns 1930
Texas
La.
Miss.
ATLANTIC OCEAN
MEXICO
Gulf of Mexico
Fla.
Everglades 1934

PACIFIC OCEAN

▲ National Park

Albers Equal-Area Projection

**At right, CCC workers help reforest Oregon in 1939. On the map, find the national parks created by 1938.** *When was the first national park established?*

## Parks and Men

while the foliage would break the force of the wind, preventing it from blowing away the good soil. Although critics predicted that trees wouldn't grow on the Great Plains, the CCC took on this project, planting over 200 million trees to break the wind's force.

During the nine years the tree army existed, it planted a total of two billion trees and constructed a network of forest-fire lookout towers. The corps also lost 47 workers to forest fires.

One young CCC worker from Cleveland who had gone west for his assignment said, "I almost feel as if I owned that land. Some day when those trees I planted grow large I want to go back and look at them."

While working at these daily jobs, the men learned new work skills. According to one supervisor, "Here they teach them how to pour concrete and lay stones and drive trucks, and if a boy wants to go and get a job after he's been in the C's, he'll know how to work."

In the words of historian Arthur M. Schlesinger, Jr., "The CCC left its monuments in the preservation and purification of the land, the water, the forests, and the young men of America." Today our national parks, which were preserved and maintained by the CCC, are popular tourist attractions visited by nearly 270 million people each year.

UPI/BETTMANN NEWSPHOTOS

**THINK ABOUT IT**: Discuss why national parks are such popular vacation sites. Also discuss the ways in which the national parks are affected by the millions of tourists who visit them each year. In what ways is this heavy tourist traffic beneficial and harmful to the parks?

The New Deal    377

# The Impact of the New Deal

## Easter Sunday, 1939: Marian Anderson Dazzles Crowd at Lincoln Memorial Concert

THE WHITE MARBLE OF THE LINCOLN MEMORIAL GLEAMED IN THE SUNSHINE. A CROWD OF 75,000 PEOPLE GATHERED IN front of it on the grassy hill and beside the reflecting pool. At the dedication ceremony 10 years earlier, blacks had been assigned seats in a separate, roped-off section across the road. This Sunday, however, blacks and whites sat together, awaiting the appearance of the famous opera singer, Marian Anderson.

The crowd hushed as Anderson appeared at the foot of the monument and turned to face the crowd. She began singing, "My country 'tis of thee, sweet land of liberty." She sang slowly as if singing a solemn hymn.

It was an inspiring moment, since plans for the concert had almost had to be abandoned. There was no concert hall in the capital large enough to seat the enormous crowd expected to attend her performance other than Constitution Hall. However, the Daughters of the American Revolution (DAR), which owned the hall, had refused Anderson the right to sing there simply because she was an African American. Dismayed, Anderson had turned to the Roosevelts for help.

When Eleanor Roosevelt heard about the DAR's refusal to host the famous singer, she not only resigned from the organization but also encouraged

UPI/BETTMANN NEWSPHOTOS

Anderson to apply for permission to give a free concert on the steps of the Lincoln Memorial. Almost immediately Anderson's request was approved. Thus, with help from the White House, the thousands of Anderson's fans were not disappointed, and the concert was a majestic success.

Although the Roosevelt administration's record on gender and race was mixed, to the nation's women and minority groups it was the most accessible and sympathetic administration in the nation's history. The Roosevelt administration passed legislation, created programs, and made other significant changes that benefited African Americans, Native Americans, and women. Such changes were among the most important legacies of FDR's New Deal.

## *Women Gain Political Recognition*

On March 6, 1933, two days after President Roosevelt's inauguration, approximately 35 reporters gathered in the Red Room of the White House to wait for the First Lady. The scene looked like any other press conference—reporters quietly talking and reviewing their lists of questions—except that all of the reporters were women. This was the first of what Eleanor Roosevelt promised would be weekly press conferences.

---

## STUDY GUIDE

**As You Read**
Identify the long-term effects of the New Deal on women, African Americans, and Native Americans. Also, think about the following concepts and skills.

**Central Concepts**
- examining **discrimination** during FDR's administration
- understanding the role of **federal regulation** during the New Deal

**Thinking Skills**
- recognizing bias
- making inferences
- drawing conclusions

HISTORICAL PICTURES SERVICE, CHICAGO

**The candid and informal way the Roosevelts addressed reporters won the press over completely. Here Eleanor is holding one of her regular press conferences to which only women were admitted.**

In addition to what the First Lady had to say to the press, the mere fact that she had decided to hold weekly press conferences made news in Washington. Mrs. Hoover had met with reporters just once in her four-year tenure as First Lady—and then only reluctantly. Eleanor Roosevelt had been politically active even before she came to the White House, and, as First Lady, she increased her political activities. One of her causes was helping women gain economic and political power. She restricted her press conferences to women reporters so as to help them keep their jobs. During the Depression many newspapers cut back their staffs, and women were often the first to be let go. Eleanor felt that if she would only meet with women reporters, at least these women would be retained by their employers.

Partly because of Eleanor's influence, women gained political recognition. Women, she felt, were in the best position to promote child welfare, education, fair labor standards, and even world peace. To this end, in addition to publicizing these causes, the First Lady worked to get women appointed to political posts. Women's roles in government expanded substantially during the Roosevelt years.

**Women in Power** In his first term as president, Roosevelt appointed the first female in American history to a cabinet post: Frances Perkins, a former social worker, who had served as Industrial Commissioner for New York state. As secretary of labor, Perkins pushed hard to obtain a social security program and a minimum-wage law that would boost the pay of thousands of poorly paid women in the work force.

Roosevelt also appointed the first woman to the federal appeals court, the first women ambassadors, and a woman as director of the mint. Women were asked to serve as advisers in many New Deal agencies. In all, more than 100 women held senior positions in the federal government during FDR's administration. However, this was still only a fraction of the number of such positions held by men.

**Facing Discrimination** Even though a greater number of women entered public life during Roosevelt's administration, in general they still faced **discrimination,** or prejudicial treatment. For example, although Roosevelt was a strong supporter of women's rights, he tended to appoint women to government posts that would be least likely to lead to conflicts with men. Thus, the women in his administration had more limited influence than it might seem.

Therefore, despite the fact that there were women in government, they could not prevent women in the work force from experiencing unfair treatment. NRA codes often granted women lower pay than men, even for the same jobs. Many businesses refused to hire married women during the Depression, and married women whose husbands worked were often forced to resign from their jobs.

The reasons for these severe practices were twofold. First, most people believed that unless a woman's wages were essential for family survival, the woman should not work but stay at home. Second, the majority of Americans thought that because jobs were so scarce, working wives should give up their jobs so that men could take their places. People believed in these arguments even in the face of logical contradictions. For example, many men would not have taken the jobs vacated by women anyway because they were jobs thought to be inappropriate for men, such as secretarial work, nursing, and teaching.

## African Americans Gain a Voice

The year 1934 was a dramatic one in American political history. In the congressional elections, most African Americans switched their allegiance from the Republican party to the Democratic party. Although they had voted overwhelmingly for Republicans since Reconstruction, blacks changed allegiance mainly to support Roosevelt and the New Deal.

At the urging of Eleanor Roosevelt and other key political advisers, FDR kept himself informed about issues important to African Americans. Much of his information came from a group of about 50 African American appointees who served in various branches of his administration. This group came to be known as the black cabinet.

**The Black Cabinet**   Although most African Americans in the Roosevelt administration were appointed to secondary posts, they nevertheless exerted influence collectively as the black cabinet. Mary McLeod Bethune, head of the Negro Affairs Division of the National Youth Administration, was the most influential member of the black cabinet. A personal friend of Eleanor Roosevelt, Bethune often shared the black cabinet's ideas with the First Lady. Eleanor then discussed them with FDR.

CULVER PICTURES, INC.

**Mary McLeod Bethune held meetings of the black cabinet in her home. There members outlined the concerns they wanted Roosevelt to address.**

Harold Ickes, Secretary of the Interior, also worked closely with African Americans to improve race relations and to pass along their concerns to FDR. He integrated his department, appointing several prominent blacks to key positions. Under Ickes, the PWA allocated funds for the construction of black hospitals, universities, and housing projects. PWA building contracts also contained a clause requiring that the number of blacks hired be at least equal in proportion to the number of blacks in the local population. This practice would become a basis for civil rights legislation in the 1960s and 1970s.

Other New Deal agencies also greatly aided African Americans during the Depression. The WPA gave jobs to hundreds of thousands of blacks. The FERA and other relief agencies granted aid to 30 percent of all African American families.[1]

**Failure to Stand for Justice**   The Roosevelt administration exceeded all previous administrations in the number of African Americans that it appointed to government positions and in the amount of federal aid that it provided African Americans. The president, however, failed to take a strong stand on civil rights issues.

Roosevelt did little to eliminate unfair hiring practices and discriminatory job conditions. Some government agencies, such as the TVA, often refused to hire black workers. Most of the government agencies that did hire African Americans, including the CCC and the armed forces, segregated blacks and whites. In addition, black workers often received lower wages and were prevented from obtaining many jobs by stiff restrictions on the hiring of blacks.

Roosevelt also failed to push for a federal antilynching law. Acts of mob violence, such as lynching, increased during the early years of the Depression. Unlike Hoover, Roosevelt publicly condemned what he called "that vile form of collective murder." However, Roosevelt hesitated to support antilynching legislation because he was afraid that he would alienate the southern white leaders who strongly opposed such laws.

Roosevelt's desire to maintain the support of southern whites also kept him from abolishing the poll tax. This tax was levied by election officials to prevent poor blacks and whites from voting in elections.[2]

Roosevelt expressed the views of many liberal Americans at the time about race relations. He advocated only slow, cautious change, a stand that exasperated racial and ethnic minorities. Nevertheless, the president recognized the vital importance of working toward social equality. During a meeting with black cabinet member Mary McLeod Bethune, FDR said the following:

*People like you and me are fighting and must continue to fight for the day when a man will be regarded as a man regardless of his race or faith or country. That day will come, but we must pass through perilous times before we realize it.*

Franklin D. Roosevelt

## Native Americans Gain an Ally

Native Americans, like African Americans, had long been subject to discrimination, deprivation, and degrading policies. Earning an average annual income of $48, Native American families were the poorest in the nation. New Deal agencies and policies provided many Native Americans with jobs and aid.

The most significant New Deal program to aid Native Americans was the Indian Reorganization Act of 1934, authored by John Collier, the Commissioner of Indian Affairs. Collier had been involved in Native American politics since 1923, when he had founded

UPI/BETTMANN NEWSPHOTOS

**John Collier speaks with Blackfoot Nation member at the Rapid City, South Dakota, Federal Indian Conclave sometime in 1934.**

### STUDY GUIDE

**Drawing Conclusions**

Given the barriers black people faced—racial segregation, lower wages, lynchings, and poll taxes—you could conclude that the majority of white Americans were still prejudiced against

blacks. You could also conclude that, at the time, African Americans experienced greater hardships than white Americans.

2 What is one reason that Roosevelt did not work harder to end racial discrimination?

the American Indian Defense Association. In this and the Reorganization Act of 1934, Collier built upon the ideas and initiatives of Winnebago teacher Henry Roe Cloud and Sioux writer Gertrude Bonnin. The goals of both the association and the reorganization act were to promote Native American culture and preserve tribal ownership of reservation lands.

Collier's Indian Reorganization Act furthered these goals by preventing the government from seizing unclaimed reservation land and selling it off to people who were not Native American. Government seizure of reservation territory, which had been going on since the late 1800s, had deprived Native Americans of their most valuable land and reduced the reservations to one-third of their original size. With the Indian Reorganization Act, Native Americans gained control of the reservations and could decide how their lands would be used and managed.

The Indian Reorganization Act also encouraged Native Americans to establish their own governments on the reservations. Once these governments had been established, the Indian Bureau was authorized to provide the reservations with the funds needed to build schools and hospitals, to establish businesses, and to start arts and crafts cooperatives.

## An Expanded Government Role

By including the excluded—women, African Americans, Native Americans, farmers, common laborers, the poor—the New Deal brought government closer to all the people. During the Roosevelt administration, 14 percent of all families obtained aid or relief from the federal government. Millions were able to stay off relief because of government jobs with the CCC, the PWA, and the WPA. Other New Deal agencies helped people hold on to their farms, keep their homes, stay in business, and bargain with employers for better pay.

**Federal regulation,** or the expansion of the federal government into almost all aspects of people's

**Joe Jones painted *Harvest* in about 1935. In this and similar works, Jones wanted "the working people, the people producing useful things with their hands," to enjoy seeing themselves portrayed with understanding. In all of his works, Jones depicted farmers as craftspeople.**

## New Deal Legislation and Agencies

| Date | Name and Purpose | Date | Name and Purpose |
|------|------------------|------|------------------|
| 1933 | **Emergency Banking Act:** Reopened banks under government supervision | 1935 | **Resettlement Administration (RA):** Helped resettle destitute farmers on better land and unemployed workers in planned communities |
| | **Civilian Conservation Corps (CCC):** Employed young men in environmental projects | | **Works Progress Administration (WPA):** Employed people for construction, maintenance, education, and creative projects |
| | **Federal Emergency Relief:** Provided funds for local and state relief organizations | | **Social Security Act:** Instituted pension and survivors' benefits for the elderly and the orphaned and provided aid to people injured in industrial accidents |
| | **Agricultural Adjustment Act (AAA):** Subsidized farmers to reduce crop and livestock production | | **National Labor Relations Board (NLRB):** Guaranteed workers the right to join labor unions of their choice, bargain collectively, and call strikes |
| | **Emergency Farm Mortgage Act:** Provided funds for the refinancing of farm mortgages | | **Rural Electrification Act (REA):** Lent money to rural cooperatives for the building of power plants |
| | **Tennessee Valley Authority (TVA):** Provided funds for the development and electrification of the Tennessee River Valley | | **Public Utility Holding Company Act:** Allowed a maximum of only two holding companies to control any one utility company |
| | **Truth-in-Securities Act:** Required full disclosure of information about stocks and bonds | 1936 | **Soil Conservation Act:** Subsidized farmers to reduce soil-depleting crops and to employ soil conservation measures |
| | **Home Owner's Loan Act:** Provided funds for the refinancing of home mortgages | 1937 | **National Housing Act:** Authorized low-rent public housing projects |
| | **National Industry Recovery Act (NIRA):** Created work codes and industry standards | | **Farm Security Administration (FSA):** Lent money to sharecroppers and tenant farmers to help them buy their own farms; established camps for migrant workers |
| | **Public Works Administration (PWA):** Funded projects to revive industry and fight unemployment | | |
| | **Glass-Steagall Banking Act:** Guaranteed bank deposits with the Federal Deposit Insurance Corporation (FDIC) | | |
| 1934 | **Federal Housing Administration (FHA):** Insured bank loans for the construction and rehabilitation of homes | 1938 | **Fair Labor Standards Act:** Established minimum wages and maximum hours for all employees of businesses engaged in interstate commerce |
| | **Indian Reorganization Act:** Restored tribal ownership of reservation land to Native Americans | | |

**Examine the legislation of Roosevelt's New Deal shown on the chart above. On a piece of paper, write the following categories: housing, agriculture, labor, civil rights, relief, unemployment, banking, industry, and utilities. Then list the name of each piece of legislation under the appropriate category head.** *Judging from the chart, what issues concerned FDR the most? What issues concerned him the least?*

lives, was a direct legacy of the New Deal. Under President Roosevelt, for the first time, the federal government assumed responsibility for the economic welfare of individuals as well as for the health of the nation's economy at large. In taking on such obligations, FDR's New Deal proved to be a turning point in American history.

The New Deal increased many people's confidence in the nation's political and economic systems. However, the government programs of the New Deal neither eliminated individual poverty nor ended the Depression. In fact, the U.S. economy did not completely recover from the Depression until the Second World War was well under way.

## SECTION REVIEW

### Checking Facts

1. What causes did Eleanor Roosevelt believe women were in the best position to promote?

2. How did the WPA, PWA, and FERA work to end discrimination against African Americans?

3. What were the goals of the Indian Reorganization Act?

4. What new responsibilities did the government acknowledge during FDR's administration?

### Thinking Critically

5. **Making Inferences** Why would Eleanor Roosevelt have suggested that women were in the best position to promote certain political programs?

6. **Recognizing Bias** FDR advocated taking only cautious steps to end racial discrimination. Was his attitude biased? Why or why not?

7. **Drawing Conclusions** Some New Deal legislation seemed to benefit minority groups and the poor. Did the New Deal provide long-term solutions to those groups' problems? Explain.

8. **Drawing Conclusions** Could FDR have achieved his economic goals without extensive government regulation? Explain.

### Linking Across Time

9. What evidence of the New Deal do you still see today?

## Electricity Comes to the Farms

*FLORENCE, ALABAMA—*
*Within the next 30 days cheap*
*electrical power from the Ten-*
*nessee Valley Authority and*
*Wilson Dam will begin flowing*
*to a host of rural consumers in*
*Colbert County, bringing the*
*blessings of the TVA and all its*
*attendant benefits to the farm-*
*ers of this section.*
*—The Florence Times, 1936*

### Democrats Electrify Farmers

In many farm communities of the Tennessee Valley, townspeople reacted to the news that, thanks to the REA and TVA, their towns would soon be receiving electrical power. By the time the news broke, the REA had already extended 20 loans to farmers' cooperatives to finance the cost of connecting farm communities to existing power sources such as the TVA.

TENNESSEE VALLEY AUTHORITY

## Elsewhere in the News

### Lindbergh in Germany

BERLIN—Charles Lindbergh inspected the German Air Force while visiting from England. Lindbergh warned that airplanes had become "more dangerous than battleships and guns."

### A Royal Romance

LONDON—King Edward VIII waited to hear whether he would be asked to choose between keeping his throne of six months and marrying the American divorcee, Mrs. Wallis Simpson.

LIBRARY OF CONGRESS

## REA Energizing Celebrations

Farm communities across the nation celebrated the coming of electricity with electrical displays and fireworks. Many towns also chose a "Polly Power" to bury a kerosene lamp, symbolizing the end of the pre-electrical age.

### Related Stories

- Electric Fence Stops Bull Roaming
- Business Leaders Call TVA Unfair
- Farmers Fear TVA Dam Will Cause Flooding

UPI/BETTMANN NEWSPHOTOS

## Seeing the Light

After linemen finished hooking up power lines in one area of rural Alabama, a farm woman noticed spider webs on her newly lit ceiling. As she swept them away, her child yelled, "Don't sweep the spider down—he just wants to see the light."

## Olympic Games

BERLIN—Berliners prepared to host next month's Olympics. Meanwhile, Americans wondered if Jesse Owens would break as many track records in Berlin as he had at home in 1935.

AP/WIDE WORLD PHOTOS

# Chapter 11 Review

**November 1932**
Roosevelt is
elected president.

**May 1933**
Congress passes Federal
Emergency Relief Act.

**Summer 1934**
Strikes rock
the nation.

**August 1935**
Congress passes
Social Security Act.

1932    1933    1934    1935

**March 1933**
Roosevelt's inauguration
begins Hundred Days.

**April 1935**
WPA expands relief aid.
Roosevelt begins implementing
Second New Deal.

## Summary

Use the following outline as a tool for reviewing and summarizing the chapter. Copy the outline on your own paper, leaving spaces between headings to jot down notes about key events and concepts.

**I. FDR and the First New Deal**
  A. FDR Takes the Helm
  B. The Hundred Days
  C. The President and the People

**II. Criticism and Reformulation**
  A. New Deal: Big Deal!
  B. New Deal: No Deal!
  C. The Second New Deal
  D. Reelection and Redirection

**III. The Impact of the New Deal**
  A. Women Gain Political Recognition
  B. African Americans Gain a Voice
  C. Native Americans Gain an Ally
  D. An Expanded Government Role

## Ideas, Events, and People

1. What major problems did President Roosevelt face as he entered the White House in 1933?
2. What were the Hundred Days?
3. Describe the life and work of a member of the Civilian Conservation Corps.
4. Why was the National Recovery Administration (NRA) controversial?
5. How did Eleanor Roosevelt help women gain recognition in politics?
6. What New Deal legislation created problems for farmers? What were those problems?
7. What opposition did Roosevelt meet from business leaders? From the Supreme Court?
8. What did the Roosevelt administration do for African and Native Americans?
9. What New Deal projects brought electricity to rural Alabama?
10. What legislation benefited organized labor during the 1930s?
11. What is a demagogue? Were Dr. Townsend, Father Coughlin, and Senator Long demagogues? Why or why not?

## Social Studies Skills

**Interpreting Images**

Turn to page 325. Examine the photograph and read the caption. "Mother and Children, on the Road" is the work of Dorothea Lange, one of several photographers who observed and documented the Depression era for the government Farm Service Administration (FSA), a New Deal program. The purpose of FSA photography was to show people's needs to gain support for federal aid. How does this photo serve that purpose? What impression of these people do you get from the photograph? Why?

## Critical Thinking

1. **Comparing and Contrasting**
In what ways did Hoover's and Roosevelt's solutions to Depression problems differ?
2. **Analyzing Behavior**
How was Roosevelt's personal style reflected in White House life? In the fireside chats?
3. **Identifying Cause and Effect**
How might the circumstances of FDR's early life have made him the kind of president he became?
4. **Recognizing Points of View**
Toward whom did Roosevelt direct his 1936 campaign? Why?
5. **Analyzing Behavior**
What made some Americans turn to demagogues like Coughlin and Long?

July 1936
TVA brings electricity
to Alabama farms.

February 1937
Roosevelt introduces a bill to add
up to six justices to the Supreme Court.

April 1939
Marian Anderson sings
in Washington, D.C.

1936       1937       1938       1939

November 1936
Roosevelt
is reelected.

6. **Analyzing Decisions**

What discriminatory practices did Roosevelt fail to address? Why?

7. **Assessing Outcomes**

Why did Roosevelt try to add Supreme Court justices? What were the results?

## Extension and Application

1. **Linking Across Time**

Compare and contrast the goals of the modern environmentalist movement with those of the Civilian Conservation Corps. Refer to your text and do research if necessary. Summarize your findings in a chart.

2. **Citizenship**

Social security still exists today. Interview a friend or relative who is a senior citizen. Ask for the person's opinions about the social security program. Report your findings in a letter to an imaginary newspaper editor. In your letter, urge people to support legislation that will leave social security as it is, modify it, or abolish it. Include reasons.

3. **Cooperative Learning**

Divide your class into small groups, and have each group research the life of one person prominent during the Roosevelt years. For example, you could look up Frances Perkins, the first woman to serve on a president's cabinet. Each group member might find out about a different aspect of the person's life such as his or her childhood, education, or early career. Then, as a group, prepare a presentation of your material for the rest of the class.

## Geography

1. According to page 365, what characteristics of the Tennessee River valley made it a likely location for a program such as the TVA?

2. According to page 374, how did programs like the TVA and the REA affect people living in urban areas?

3. According to pages 376–377, what benefits did the Great Plains receive from the shelterbelt of trees? How did other regions also benefit from the trees?

4. Use the map on this page to explain why CCC workers lived in barracks while working in the national parks.

5. What regions of the country benefited from CCC National Park projects? How do Americans today benefit from these projects?

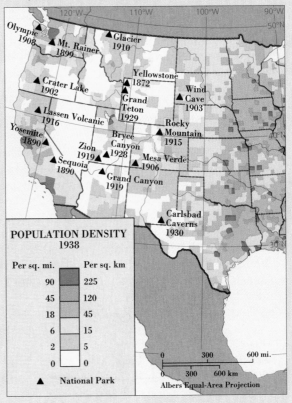

POPULATION DENSITY
1938

| Per sq. mi. | Per sq. km |
| --- | --- |
| 90 | 225 |
| 45 | 120 |
| 18 | 45 |
| 6 | 15 |
| 2 | 5 |
| 0 | 0 |

▲ National Park

Albers Equal-Area Projection

# Unit 4 Review

> *T*hese unhappy times call for the building of plans . . . that build from the bottom up and not from the top down, that put their faith once more in the forgotten man at the bottom of the economic pyramid.
>
> Franklin D. Roosevelt,
> Radio Address, April 7, 1932

> *I*n the Presidents inaugural address . . . he made mention of The Forgotten Man, and I with thousands of others am wondering if the folk who was born here in America some 60 and 70 years ago are this Forgotten Man . . . if we are this Forgotten Man then we are still Forgotten.
>
> Mr. R. A., age 69, Letter to
> Eleanor Roosevelt, Nebraska, May 1934

## Concepts and Themes

As the twenties roared to a close, more and more people had less cash to spend on products pouring off assembly lines. This combination of underconsumption and overproduction led to the devastating Depression of the 1930s. Millions milled about without jobs, food, homes, or hope. Then came Franklin D. Roosevelt's New Deal. Although it did not wipe away poverty, the New Deal did much to cure the nation's economic woes by means of work programs, relief, reform measures, and a promise for tomorrow. Never before had the United States government marched so boldly into individuals' lives.

1. Herbert Hoover advocated voluntary action and trickle-down measures to help the "forgotten man." Contrast his approach with Roosevelt's method of demanding legislation for direct help to the unemployed.
2. What were some of the effects of the CCC, WPA, and Wagner Act on "the forgotten man"?
3. Analyze why Mr. R. A., quoted above, might have been forgotten. What New Deal legislation eventually aided such people?

## History Projects

1. **Evidence of the Past**
   Conduct an interview with a family member or friend who was an adult during the 1930s. Be prepared with written questions but also allow the interview to evolve spontaneously. Write a theme from the notes.
2. **Culture of the Time**
   Create a collage contrasting today's pop culture with that of the 1930s.
3. **Geography**
   Research the geography of the Tennessee Valley before the TVA project, right after it, and today. Make a chart explaining the geographical and technological changes.
4. **One Day in History**
   Examine library microfiches of newspapers for Black Thursday, October 24, 1929. Create a feature following the format of One Day in History on page 384.
5. **Case Study**
   Franklin D. Roosevelt's attempt in 1937 to increase the number of Supreme Court justices encountered opposition. Research Roosevelt's proposal and present the background. Check library sources to find quotations representing opposite views. In a written conclusion, tell the outcome.

## Writing Activities

1. Research the rich and poor of the 1930s. Write several paragraphs contrasting their shelter, clothing, food, and entertainment. (See the Writer's Guide, pages 825–827.)
2. Study Dorothea Lange's photo on page 338. Write a short imaginary narrative from the mother's viewpoint.

## The Arts

- *You Can't Take It with You* by George Kaufman and Moss Hart; a zany Broadway comedy.
- *Native Son* by Richard Wright; a novel depicting the frustrations of a black youth in Chicago during the Depression.
- *Number One* by John Dos Passos; a novel based on the life of Huey Long.
- *My Life and Hard Times* by James Thurber; humorous vignettes about the author's life.

# UNIT FIVE

# The United States Transformed

George C. Marshall Foundation

**7th WAR LOAN   NOW··ALL TOGETHER**

OFFICIAL U. S. TREASURY POSTER

Chapter 12: The World in Crisis     Chapter 13: The Home Front

# Personalizing the War

*Popular World War II correspondent Ernie Pyle brought the war home by writing about the experiences, thoughts, and feelings of Army soldiers at the front lines of combat. The following excerpt from one of Pyle's columns recounts the 9th Infantry Division's fight to recapture a French town from the Germans. Muriel Rukeyser's poem "To Be a Jew in the Twentieth Century" also reveals the impact of the war on the individual.*

## Dispatches from the Front
### by Ernie Pyle

IN NORMANDY, *July 14, 1944*—Gradually we moved on, a few feet at a time. The soldiers hugged the walls on both sides of the street, crouching all the time. The city around us was still full of sound and fury. You couldn't tell where anything was coming from or going to.

The houses had not been blown down along this street. But now and then a wall would have a round hole through it, and the windows had all been knocked out by concussion and shattered glass littered the pavements. Gnarled telephone wire was lying everywhere.

It was a poor district. Most of the people had left the city. Shots, incidentally, always sound louder and distorted in the vacuumlike emptiness of a nearly deserted city. Lonely doors and shutters banged noisily back and forth.

All of a sudden a bunch of dogs came yowling down the street, chasing each other. Apparently their owners had left without them, and they were running wild. They made such a noise that we shooed them on in the erroneous fear that they would attract the Germans' attention.

The street was a winding one and we couldn't see as far ahead as our forward platoon. But soon we could hear rifle shots not far ahead, and the rat-tat-tat of our machine guns, and the quick blirp-blirp of German machine pistols.

For a long time we didn't move at all. While we were waiting the lieutenant decided to go into the house we were in front of. A middle-aged Frenchman and his wife were in the kitchen. They were poor people.

The woman was holding a terrier dog in her arms, belly up, the way you cuddle a baby, and soothing it by rubbing her cheek against its head. The dog was trembling with fear from the noise.

Pretty soon the word was passed back down the line that the street had been cleared as far as a German hospital about a quarter of a mile ahead. There were lots of our wounded in that hospital and they were now being liberated.

So Lt. Shockley and (Charles) Wertenbaker and (Robert) Capa and myself got up and went up the street, still keeping close to the walls. I lost the others before I had gone far. For as I would pass doorways soldiers would call out to me and I would duck in and talk for a moment and put down a name or two.

By now the boys along the line were feeling cheerier, for no word of casualties had been passed back. And up here the city was built up enough so that the waiting riflemen had the protection of doorways. It took me half an hour to work my way up to the hospital—and then the excitement began.

IN NORMANDY, *July 15, 1944* — The hospital was in our hands, but just barely. On up the street a block, there seemed to be fighting. I say *seemed* to be, because actually you can't always tell. Street fighting is just as confusing as field fighting.

One side will bang away for a while, then the other side. Between these sallies there are long lulls, with only stray and isolated shots. Just an occasional soldier is sneaking about, and you don't see anything of the enemy at all. You can't tell half the time just what the situation is, and neither can the soldiers.

About a block beyond the hospital entrance two American tanks were sitting in the middle of the street, one about fifty yards ahead of the other. I walked toward them. Our infantrymen were in doorways along the street.

I got within about fifty feet of our front tank when it let go its seventy-five-mm gun. The blast was terrific there in the narrow street. Glass came tinkling down from nearby windows, smoke puffed around the tank, and the empty street was shaking and trembling with the concussion.

As the tank continued to shoot I ducked into a doorway, because I figured the Germans would shoot back. Inside the doorway there was a sort of street-level cellar, dirt-floored. Apparently there was a wine shop above, for the cellar was stacked with wire crates for holding wine bottles on their sides. There were lots of bottles, but they were all empty.

I went back to the doorway and stood peeking out at the tank. It started backing up. Then suddenly a yellow flame pierced the bottom of the tank and there was a crash of such intensity that I automatically blinked my eyes. The tank, hardly fifty feet from where I was standing, had been hit by an enemy shell.

A second shot ripped the pavement at the side of the tank. There was smoke all around, but the tank didn't catch fire. In a moment the crew came boiling out of the turret.

Grim as it was, I almost had to laugh as they ran toward us. I have never seen men run so violently. They ran all over, with arms and heads going up and down and with marathon-race grimaces. They plunged into my doorway.

I spent the next excited hour with them. We changed

During their induction into the Army and Navy, men sing the National Anthem. Americans who went to war during the forties sacrificed their civilian clothes, their day-to-day freedoms, and sometimes their lives in the service of the cause.

to another doorway and sat on boxes in the empty hallway. The floor and steps were thick with blood where a soldier had been treated within the hour.

What had happened to the tank was this:

They had been firing away at a pillbox ahead when theirs backfired, filling the tank with smoke and blinding them.

They decided to back up in order to get their bearings, but after backing a few yards the driver was so blinded that he stopped. Unfortunately he stopped exactly at the foot of a side street. More unfortunately there was another German pillbox up the side street. All the Germans had to do was take easy aim and let go at the sitting duck.

The first shot hit a tread, so the tank couldn't move. That was when the boys got out. I don't know why the Germans didn't fire at them as they poured out.

The escaped tankers naturally were excited, but they were as jubilant as June bugs and ready for more. They had never been in combat before the invasion of Normandy, yet in three weeks their tank had been shot up three times. Each time it was repaired and put back in action. And it can be repaired again this time. The name of their tank, appropriately, is *Be Back Soon*.

The main worry of these boys was the fact that they had left the engine running. We could hear it chugging away. It's bad for a tank motor to idle very long. But now they were afraid to go back and turn the motor off, for the tank was still right in line with the hidden German gun.

Also, they had come out wearing their leather crash helmets. Their steel helmets were still inside the tank, and so were their rifles.

"We'll be a lot of good without helmets or rifles!" one of them said.

The crew consisted of Corp. Martin Kennelly of Chicago, the tank commander; Sgt. L. Wortham of Leeds, Alabama, driver; Pvt. Ralph Ogren of Minneapolis, assistant driver; Corp. Albin Stoops of Marshalltown, Delaware, gunner; and Pvt. Charles Rains of Kansas City, the loader.

Private Rains was the oldest of the bunch, and the only married one. He used to work as a guard at the Sears, Roebuck plant in Kansas City.

"I was M.P. to fifteen hundred women," he said with a grin, "and how I'd like to be back doing that!"

The other tankers all expressed loud approval of this sentiment.

IN NORMANDY, *July 17, 1944* — Tank Commander Martin Kennelly wanted to show me just where his tank had been hit. As a matter of fact he hadn't seen it for himself yet, for he came running up the street the moment he jumped out of the tank.

So when the firing died down a little we sneaked up the street until we were almost even with the disabled tank. But we were careful not to get our heads around the corner of the side street, for that was where the Germans had fired from.

The first shell had hit the heavy steel brace that the tread runs on, and then plunged on through the side of the tank, very low.

"Say!" Kennelly said in amazement. "It went right through our lower ammunition storage box! I don't know what kept the ammunition from going off. We'd have been a mess if it had. Boy, it sure would have got hot in there in a hurry!"

The street was still empty. Beyond the tank about two blocks was a German truck, sitting all alone in the middle of the street. It had been blown up, and its tires had burned off. This truck was the only thing you could see. There wasn't a human being in sight anywhere.

Then an American soldier came running up the street shouting for somebody to send up a medic. He said a man was badly wounded just ahead. He was extremely excited, yelling, and getting madder because there was no medic in sight.

Word was passed down the line, and pretty soon a medic came out of a doorway and started up the street. The excited soldier yelled at him and began cussing, and the medic broke into a run. They ran past the tanks together, and up the street a way they ducked into a doorway.

On the corner just across the street from where we were standing was a smashed pillbox. It was in a cutaway corner like the entrances to some of our corner drugstores at home, except that instead of there being a door there was a pillbox of reinforced concrete, with gun slits.

The tank boys had shot it to extinction and then moved their tank up even with it to get the range of the next pillbox. That one was about a block ahead, set in a niche in the wall of a building. That's what the boys had been shooting at when their tank was hit. They knocked it out, however, before being knocked out themselves.

For an hour there was a lull in the fighting. Nobody did anything about a third pillbox, around the corner. Our second tank pulled back a little and just waited. Infantrymen worked their way up to second-story windows and fired their rifles up the side street without actually seeing anything to shoot at.

Now and then blasts from a 20-mm gun would splatter the buildings around us. Then our second tank would blast back in that general direction, over the low roofs, with its machine gun. There was a lot of dangerous-sounding noise, but I don't think anybody on either side got hit.

Then we saw coming up the street, past the wrecked German truck I spoke of, a group of German soldiers. An officer walked in front, carrying a Red Cross flag on a stick. Bob Capa, the photographer, braved the dangerous funnel at the end of the side street where the damaged tank stood, leapfrogging past it and on down the street to meet the Germans.

First he snapped some pictures of them. Then, since he speaks German, he led them on back to our side of the invisible fence of battle. Eight of them were carrying two litters bearing two wounded German soldiers. The others walked behind with their hands up. They went on past us to the hospital. We assumed they were from the second knocked-out pillbox.

I didn't stay to see how the remaining pillbox was knocked out. But I suppose our second tank eventually pulled up to the corner, turned, and let the pillbox have it. After that the area would be clear of everything but snipers.

The infantry, who up till then had been forced to keep in doorways, would now continue up the street and poke into the side streets into the houses until everything was clear.

That's how a strong point in a city is taken. At least that's how ours was taken. You don't always have tanks to help, and you don't always do it with so little shedding of blood.

But the city was already crumbling when we started in on this strong point, which was one of the last, and they didn't hold on too bitterly. But we didn't know that when we started.

I hope this has given you a faint idea of what street fighting is like. If you got out of it much more than a headful of confusion, then you've got out of it exactly the same thing as the soldiers who do it.

# To Be a Jew in the Twentieth Century

### from "Letter to the Front"
### by Muriel Rukeyser

To be a Jew in the twentieth century
Is to be offered a gift.   If you refuse,
Wishing to be invisible, you choose
Death of the spirit, the stone insanity.
Accepting, take full life, full agonies:
Your evening deep in labyrinthine blood
Of those who resist, fail and resist; and God

Reduced to a hostage among hostages.
The gift is torment.   Not alone the still
Torture, isolation; or torture of the flesh.
That may come also.   But the accepting wish,
The whole and fertile spirit as guarantee
For every human freedom, suffering to be free,
Daring to live for the impossible.

## Responding to Literature

1. If you had been a teenager during World War II, do you think you would have been a regular reader of Ernie Pyle's dispatches from the front? Why or why not? How might they have influenced you?

2. After reading Muriel Rukeyser's poem, do you think denying one's heritage might lead to a "death of the spirit"? Why or why not?

**For Further Reading**
Heller, Joseph: *Catch-22*
Hersey, John: *Hiroshima*
Houston, Jeanne Wakatsuki: *Farewell to Manzanar*
Jones, James: *The Thin Red Line*
Vonnegut, Kurt: *Slaughterhouse Five*

# The World in Crisis

## September 1, 1939: Germany Invades Poland

President Franklin Roosevelt was wakened by a telephone call at 2:30 A.M. on September 1, 1939. Bill Bullitt, United States Ambassador to France, reported a call from Tony Biddle in Warsaw. "Several German divisions are deep in Polish territory, and fighting is heavy. Tony said there were reports of bombers over the city. Then he was cut off."

"Well, Bill," Roosevelt said, "it's come at last. God help us all."

"It" was war in Europe. Only 21 years after the end of World War I, war had begun again. In response to Germany's invasion of Poland, Great Britain began moving troops. Two days later Great Britain and France declared war on Germany.

*Only 21 years after the end of World War I, war had begun again.*

AP/ WIDE WORLD PHOTOS

*WACs show incoming candidates the uniform they would wear while serving in World War II.*

Bringing the country out of the Great Depression was Roosevelt's most pressing concern, but political unrest in Europe and Asia also demanded his attention. The invasion of Poland was only the latest international crisis of the 1930s.

Looking back, Roosevelt could see the roots of the crisis in Europe in the rise to power of Benito Mussolini and of Adolf Hitler. He had also watched as Japan flexed its military might. It was clear to Roosevelt that these events could hurl the United States into global conflict. He could not know that the war to come would be the most devastating in history, or that it would make the United States the richest and most powerful nation in the world.

*During the fighting on Guadalcanal, lookouts like the one pictured above kept a constant watch from their foxholes on the hills overlooking Japanese lines. Down below, the U.S. Army was launching its offensives to retake the Pacific.*

# The Road to War

## July 13, 1934: Hitler Addresses the Reichstag

ADOLF HITLER RECOGNIZED AND MADE USE OF THE POWER OF THE SPOKEN WORD. "Every great movement on this globe owes its rise to the great speakers," he had said. As he stood before the Reichstag, the German house of representatives, on July 13, 1934, Hitler sensed that the moment for a powerful speech was at hand. Two weeks before, he had ruthlessly eliminated those members of his own political party who stood in the way of his rise to absolute power. In a night of blood and terror, Hitler's storm troopers had shot or stabbed hundreds of Hitler's political enemies.

Though he began speaking in a hoarse whisper, Hitler's voice soon rose to a screech. Stabbing the air with his hands, he spit out words like *traitor, poison,* and *blood.* As Reichstag members sat in stunned silence, Hitler took full responsibility for the murders of his countrymen. He had killed, he declared, from the highest of motives—his love for the German people and the German state:

*I gave the order to shoot those who were the ringleaders in this treason, and I further gave the order to burn out down to the raw flesh the ulcers of this poisoning of the wells in our domestic life and of the poisoning of the outside world. And I further ordered that if any of the mutineers should attempt to resist arrest, they were immediately to be struck down with armed force. . . . I am ready to undertake the responsibility at the bar of*

THE BETTMANN ARCHIVE

*history for the twenty-four hours in which the bitterest decisions of my life were made . . . to hold fast to the dearest thing that has been given us in this world—the German people and the German Reich!*

Adolf Hitler, 1934

Hitler's bold justification of the murders swept millions of Germans off their feet and united them behind his government. It also frightened into silence those Germans who still opposed his rule. Hitler's speech warned the rest of the world that this new German Reich was a force not to be ignored.

## The Rise of Totalitarianism

Before 1934, Americans had been too preoccupied with their own problems to take Hitler's emotional speeches seriously. The suffering caused by the Great Depression convinced most people in the United States that their first priority lay at home, not overseas. The enormous cost in money and lives of victory in World War I also convinced many that the nation should stay out of Europe's troubles.

Keeping with public sentiment, Roosevelt's foreign policy concentrated at first on making the United States a "good neighbor" to the countries in this hemisphere. At his inauguration in 1933, he announced the **Good Neighbor policy.** This policy supported the idea of nonintervention among nations. Roosevelt pledged that the United States would not interfere in the internal affairs of its

Latin American neighbors. However, events in Italy and Germany would soon make it impossible for the United States to avoid intervention in Europe.

**Mussolini's Rise in Italy**   The events that brought Italy to the center of the world stage began after World War I. Though Italy had fought on the victorious Allied side, the war had left the country in economic chaos. Thousands of soldiers returning to civilian life could not find jobs.

A wounded veteran himself, Benito Mussolini burst onto the Italian political scene with a threat and a promise of change. Painting himself as a modernizer and as a champion of order and efficiency, *Il Duce* (the leader), as he called himself, challenged Italians to join with him in rebuilding their shattered economy and in restoring Italy's power in the Mediterranean region. Mussolini gained a following of political demonstrators who became known as **fascists,** a political party that preached that the nation and the race were more important than the individual. Fascists won elections by frightening people into supporting them. Black-shirted gangs roamed the streets smashing the offices of opposing political parties and breaking up their meetings. As leader of the Fascist Party, Mussolini became a **totalitarian** dictator, completely controlling all aspects of Italian life.

In spite of these ruthless tactics, many Italians, and even some Americans, saw Mussolini as a model of strength and determination. Once in power, he succeeded in bringing energy and discipline to Italian society with a flood of new government economic and social programs. Under Mussolini, for example, Italian trains ran on time, and engineers built 400 new bridges and 4,000 miles of roads.

Mussolini also kept his promise to restore Italy's power in the Mediterranean. In October 1935 his armies invaded the African nation of Ethiopia. Ethiopian soldiers on horseback, armed with outdated guns and spears, were no match for the bombers and machine guns of the modern Italian army. By May 1936, Mussolini controlled Ethiopia.

**Hitler Founds the Nazi Party**   In the same way as Mussolini, Adolf Hitler rose to power in Germany during the troubled times after World War I. Wounded and gassed during the war, Hitler nursed his personal bitterness by taking a tiny workers party and building it into the mighty National Socialist German Workers Party, which soon became known as the **Nazis.** In a series of speeches during the 1920s, Hitler spelled out the Nazi program. The German people, he said, had been divided into warring social classes for too long. By eliminating the differences between rich and poor, the Nazis would make the German people strong and united. Moreover, Hitler said, Germany had been betrayed in World War I by Jews and others who were not blond, blue-eyed members of what he called the "Aryan" or Germanic race. The Jews, Hitler said, were to blame for Germany's economic problems.[1]

**Building the Third Reich**   When the Depression struck Germany in 1929, the German government was unable to find jobs for 6 million unemployed workers. Hitler took advantage of the discontent to appeal to the German people to rebuild their economy and to revive their honor by bringing him to power. He denounced the Treaty of Versailles, which dismantled the German military and required Germany to pay huge sums of money to the Allies. In an election held in July 1932, the Nazi Party became the most powerful in Germany though it failed to win a clear majority. Nevertheless, Hitler held out for full powers as Chancellor, which he got in January, 1933.

Once in power, Hitler moved to eliminate opposition. In February 1933, he persuaded German president Paul von Hindenberg to suspend most German civil rights. A month later, by false promises and threats of violence, Hitler convinced the Reichstag to give him the power to make laws without its consent. In June 1934 Hitler demanded that members of the military swear personal allegiance to him. After Hindenberg's death in August 1934, Hitler abolished the office of president and declared himself Fuehrer, or supreme leader of the Third Reich, the German Empire. Thus, Hitler also became a totalitarian dictator.

With all power concentrated in his hands, Hitler defied the Treaty of Versailles by rebuilding the German military. In 1936, he took his defiance a step further and sent troops into Germany's Rhineland. This put German soldiers on the eastern border of France. When Great Britain and France did not resist the action, Hitler's plans grew even more ambitious.

**Recognizing Points of View**
The early support Mussolini and Hitler received shows how points of view can affect judgment. Many Italians, disturbed by the disorder they saw, admired Mussolini for the energy and discipline he brought to Italian society. Many Germans admired the way Hitler worked to make Germany strong and united. Point of view can hide the truth about people, at least for a time.

1  How did the disorder resulting from World War I and the Depression help Fascists and Nazis to gain power?

## The Axis Tests Its Strength

**H**itler and Mussolini were two powerful leaders who had dreams of expanding their borders, and both were building armies mighty enough to seize new lands at will. When these two dictators formed an alliance in 1936, dubbed the **Axis powers,** fear struck the hearts of many Europeans, including the Soviets whose communism clashed with fascism.

**Fighting the Spanish Civil War** The situation in Europe was complicated by the outbreak of a bitter and bloody civil war in Spain. In 1931, the Spanish monarchy had been replaced by a parliamentary government under a democratic constitution. Led by Spanish army general Francisco Franco, conservative and pro-monarchy rebel troops attempted to overthrow the Spanish government in 1936. The war quickly grew into an international struggle. Since Franco, like Mussolini, strongly opposed communism,

Mussolini felt compelled to aid Franco's cause. He sent airplanes and thousands of soldiers from the Italian army. Hitler also sent Franco bombers and troops.

On the other side, the Soviet Union supported the Republicans who fought for the elected government. Though the governments of Great Britain, France, and the United States were officially neutral, the Republicans were backed by many citizens in these countries. Some 3,000 Americans who opposed Franco's political stance formed the Abraham Lincoln Brigade and fought in Spain for the Republican cause. Many were far-left supporters of Stalin. Some of the Americans who volunteered felt that if Germany and Italy could come to the aid of Franco and overturn a democracy in Spain, nothing would stop them from moving on to France. "And after France?" many asked. In the end, Franco's fascist forces prevailed.

**Appeasing Hitler in Munich**  Intervening in the Spanish Civil War did not satisfy Hitler's drive to increase German power. In March 1938, he proclaimed

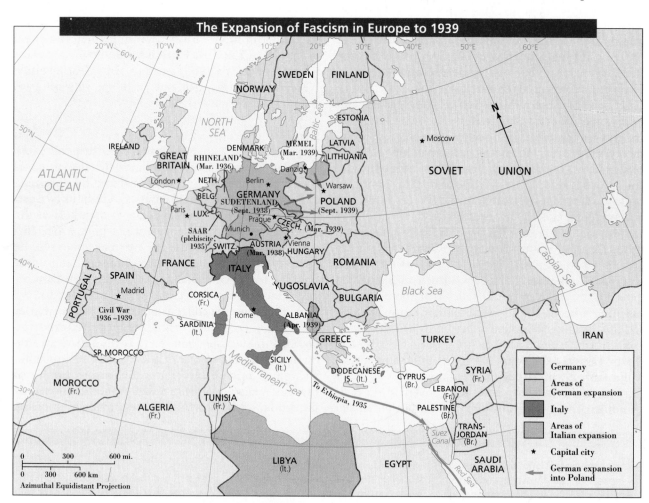

### The Expansion of Fascism in Europe to 1939

**Once in power, the totalitarian regimes of Mussolini and Hitler moved across Europe and parts of Africa, conquering every small and weak country in their** paths. *Both geographically and politically, why was the defeat and ultimate control of France and Great Britain so important to Hitler?*

THE PRADO

**Pablo Picasso's famous painting *Guernica* is a masterpiece of protest against the bombing of the town of Guernica during the Spanish Civil War.** *How does his un-conventional portrayal of this event contribute to its overall effect as a protest statement against war?*

that Austria was part of Germany, and German tanks rolled into Vienna, Austria's capital, to seal a shotgun marriage between the two countries. Six months later, Hitler's armies occupied the Sudetenland region of Czechoslovakia, an area with a large ethnic German population. To justify his aggression, Hitler explained that he had taken the Sudetenland to satisfy the wish of Germans living there to become part of Germany. His only goal, he said, was to defend the German-speaking people of Czechoslovakia against political oppression by the Czechs.

Eager to avoid another war, the leaders of England and France adopted a policy of **appeasement** toward Hitler, in which they gave in to his demands in an attempt to keep the peace. At a conference in Munich in September 1938, British Prime Minister Neville Chamberlain and French Premier Edouard Daladier agreed not to oppose Hitler's move against the Sudetenland. Describing this crisis as a family affair, Hitler promised that he would respect the rest of Czechoslovakia and make no new territorial demands in Europe. A joyful Chamberlain, supported by President Roosevelt, told a jittery world that war had been averted and that the Munich Pact meant "peace for our time." However, not all British politicians agreed. Winston Churchill, who would soon replace Chamberlain as Prime Minister, remarked, "Britain and France had to choose between war and dishonor. They chose dishonor. They will have war."

**Invading Poland Leads to War**   When Hitler seized the rest of Czechoslovakia just five and a half months later, Churchill's words proved prophetic. Any remaining hope that Hitler could be stopped short of waging all-out war was shattered on August 23, 1939, when Germany signed a nonaggression pact with the Soviet Union. The agreement pledged that neither country would attack the other. By securing his eastern border against Soviet attack, Hitler freed himself to direct his forces against the rest of Europe.

The suspense over where Hitler would strike next was short-lived. Poland, a country historically beset by its stronger neighbors, was once again the fuse igniting the powder keg. In a secret section of their non-aggression treaty, Germany and the Soviet Union had already agreed to divide Poland between them. With Soviet approval, Hitler's tanks rumbled across the border into Poland at dawn on September 1, 1939,

The World in Crisis   399

while his *Luftwaffe* (air force) bombarded Polish cities. This swift, all-out style of attack, known as *Blitzkrieg* (lightning war), was devastatingly effective. Two days later, Great Britain and France, who had pledged to defend Poland against outside aggression, declared war on Germany. World War II had begun.

## Japan Flexes Its Muscles

Japan was as aggressive a nation in Asia as Hitler's Germany was in Europe. During the 1930s, ambitious Japanese military leaders began a policy of territorial expansion. Confined to a chain of small islands and Korea, Japan's growing population strained its resources. Though rich in industrial know-how, Japan was poor in land for agriculture and in raw materials for its industries. It depended on imports from the United States and other countries for such essential commodities as wheat, petroleum, rubber, coal, iron, and timber. Japanese military leaders resented this dependence on foreign suppliers, which made them vulnerable to economic and military pressure from abroad. To make Japan secure and self-sufficient, these leaders pushed to expand Japan's borders beyond its home islands onto the Asian mainland.

Military leaders occupied a special place in Japanese society. The chiefs of the imperial army and navy were independent of the civilian government and answered only to the Emperor in matters of national defense. These leaders regarded foreign conquest as a badge of personal honor. They had already savored the sweetness of victory when Japan won the large and potentially productive island of Taiwan in a war with China in 1895. Ten years later, they tasted conquest again when Japan won footholds in Manchuria and Korea on the Asian mainland by defeating Russia in the Russo-Japanese War in 1904 and 1905. Now they looked to the rest of Manchuria and East Asia for new lands to add to their empire.[2]

**Japan Invades Manchuria** The most tempting target for Japanese expansion was Manchuria, in northern China. This vast region was poorly defended, and it had abundant resources. Japanese military leaders hoped that Manchuria would provide living space for Japan's surplus population and enough raw materials, food, and manufactured goods to make Japan self-sufficient. In September 1931 Japan launched an attack on Manchuria. Within a few months, the Japanese army had overpowered the province. In September 1932 Japan installed a Japanese-controlled puppet government and renamed the region "Manchukuo."

The League of Nations, of which Japan was a key member, condemned Japan for its aggression. In contempt, Japan merely withdrew from the League. Meanwhile, Japan argued that its military actions in Manchuria were essential to its long-term security. The world remained unconvinced.

**Shutting the Open Door** The United States protested Japan's expansion into China but did little more. Roosevelt refused to recognize Japan's puppet government in Manchuria. Later, when Japan used its base in Manchuria to launch a full-scale assault on China, Roosevelt authorized small loans to the government of China to help them buy military supplies. He also urged Americans to boycott Japanese silk.

Perhaps the strongest critics of Japanese aggression against China were the American people. Many Americans felt a special sympathy and kinship with the Chinese. Fiction such as *The Good Earth* by Pearl Buck painted a picture of Chinese peasants as noble and long-suffering. Jiang Jieshi (Chiang Kai-shek), the leader of China, and Soong Meiling, his American-educated wife, were popular figures in the United States, even appearing on the cover of *Time* magazine. American missionaries had long been active in China, and many Americans saw themselves as China's protectors. Some Americans even believed that, in time, China would come to resemble the United States.

However, the most important reason for Americans' alarm at the Japanese invasion of China was economic. The American business community saw China as a boundless market for U.S. goods. To protect this market, the United States had long asserted its Open Door policy, assuring all countries equal access to China's commercial markets. If Japan succeeded in conquering China and in closing that open door, the United States stood to lose close to $100 million in annual cotton sales. As Japan grew stronger and gained control of more natural resources, its industries would be better able to compete with American

**Recognizing Values**

Most Japanese held certain values that made their nation's aggressive actions seem acceptable to them. They could not get along without certain resources unavailable on their small island nation. However, they valued security and self-sufficiency, and they viewed conquest as the means to those ends. They also admired their military leaders, for whom foreign conquest was a badge of honor.

2  What motivations helped shape Japan's foreign policy from 1895 on?

THE NATIONAL ARCHIVES

**Propaganda posters such as the one above depicted Japan as a powerful and ruthless aggressor.**

businesses for world sales. For these reasons, many feared the possibility of a confrontation with Japan.

**The China Incident**   By 1937 Japanese forces moved south from Manchuria against Shanghai and Nanking, major Chinese cities. Japanese soldiers killed tens of thousands of Chinese civilians. Leaders in Tokyo tried to play down the military actions in China, referring to them as the "China Incident." In reality, the "China Incident" was a full-scale war.

The Japanese attacks on Shanghai and Nanking alarmed already anxious Americans. Even such a strong opponent of American involvement in foreign conflicts as Senator George Norris condemned the Japanese actions as "disgraceful" and "barbarous." However, the United States leveled nothing stronger than words at the Japanese.

## America's Unneutral Neutrality

With hostilities spreading in Europe and Asia, Congress took action to try to keep the United States from becoming involved. After Italy's invasion of Ethiopia in 1935, and again after the outbreak of the Spanish Civil War in 1936, Congress passed a series of laws called the Neutrality Acts. These laws prohibited the sale of American weapons to nations at war and tried to keep U.S. citizens from traveling on ships belonging to warring countries. The laws also required that countries at war pay cash for non-military trade goods like cotton or wheat.

Roosevelt signed the Neutrality Acts reluctantly. In doing so, he bowed to strong public sentiment against American involvement in another war. A 1937 Gallup Poll found that nearly two-thirds of Americans thought that U.S. participation in World War I had been a mistake. Although Roosevelt regarded both Germany and Japan as serious threats to U.S. security, he faced an uphill battle in preparing the United States for the possibility of another war.

Roosevelt knew that to fight a war, the United States would need tanks, planes, guns, and other supplies. To this end, he asked Congress in 1938 for $300 million in additional spending. By 1939 Roosevelt was asking Congress for a $1.3 billion military budget. He had decided that Hitler and Mussolini were "two madmen," who "respect force and force alone." History would prove Roosevelt correct.

## Nazi Terrorism Erupts

*BERLIN—Systematic destruction of Jewish property, looting, arson, and wholesale arrests of Jews without official charges swept Germany today. It is estimated that 20,000 Jews were arrested in Germany and what was Austria.*
*—Chicago Tribune, 1938*

### Synagogues Torched

Three days earlier in Paris, a young Polish Jew had shot a German embassy official. The official died, and the Nazis turned the event into an excuse for violent anti-Jewish demonstrations in many cities.

Storm troopers and Nazi party members, aided by mobs of private citizens, burned, wrecked, and looted about 200 synagogues and 8,000 shops. At least three dozen Jews were killed. Police didn't try to stop the violence. Firefighters stood idly by, acting only to save the nearby property of non-Jews.

THE WIENER LIBRARY, LONDON

## Elsewhere in the News

### Celebrations Planned

SAN FRANCISCO—Americans were busy preparing for a variety of Armistice Day ceremonies. November 11 would mark the 20th anniversary of the armistice that ended the Great War in 1918.

### Girl Scout Cookies for Sale

NEW YORK—Girl Scouts began ringing doorbells, selling cookies at 25 cents a box. First Lady Eleanor Roosevelt was on hand for the sale's kickoff.

## Jews Forced to Wear the Star

The night of terror was later called *Kristallnacht*, or "night of crystal glass," for the shattered glass of the synagogue and shop windows. The Nazis had forced the Jews to wear a yellow Star of David. On Kristallnacht, the stars helped the Nazis to identify the Jews.

### Related Stories

- Goebbels Claims Demonstrations "Spontaneous"
- Riots Sweep Germany

## Propaganda Spreads

Signs warned: "Germans! Defend yourselves! Do not buy from Jews." According to the Nazis, "good" Germans did not shop in Jewish stores. The signs were part of a Nazi propaganda campaign that was designed to turn the Germans against the Jews.

## Nobel Prize Awarded

STOCKHOLM—The Swedish Academy awarded the Nobel prize for literature to American Pearl Buck. Her well-known novel, *The Good Earth*, portrays peasant life in China.

# The Gathering Storm

## June 14, 1940: German Troops Occupy Paris

PARIS WAS SILENT AND OMINOUSLY DESERTED AS DAWN BROKE ON FRIDAY, JUNE 14, 1940. THE SHUTTERS OVER HOUSE AND SHOP WINDOWS WERE CLOSED AND barred. The Metro was not running. No cars, trucks, or bicycles moved down the magnificent boulevards or along the narrow, twisting streets. Three million of the nearly five million people who lived in Paris and its surrounding neighborhoods had already fled. The rest stayed indoors and waited.

The night before, under a flag of truce, French officers had met with German officials near Paris. The French knew Paris would fall under a German assault. Rather than see their beautiful city destroyed, they handed it over to the Germans.

By 5 A.M. on Friday morning, columns of German infantry were marching three abreast toward railroad stations and other key points in Paris. Roger Langeron, chief of the Paris police, watched as German soldiers entered the city. Writing in his diary for that fateful Friday, Langeron described the "terrible thing" that had befallen France. He mourned the "interminable defile of motorized troops" that made its way through Paris from Saint-Denis toward Montrouge. He recorded the dark parade of leather-clad motorcyclists and armored tanks that moved down empty streets before "shuttered" houses.

In the midafternoon, Langeron was summoned to meet the new German military governor at the Crillon Hotel. By then swastika flags were already flying over the public buildings of Paris.

LIBRARY OF CONGRESS

## Hitler Crushes Europe

The unopposed German occupation of Paris was a triumph for Hitler's forces, which in two months had conquered most of Western Europe. On April 9, 1940, nearly eight months after his invasion of Poland, Hitler unleashed an air and sea assault against Denmark and Norway. A few weeks later, German tanks and bombers drove the Netherlands, Belgium, and Luxembourg to their knees. "The small countries are smashed up, one by one, like matchwood," England's new prime minister, Winston Churchill, complained.

**France Surrenders** Despite Germany's victories, the French had prepared to make a stand. About a million French soldiers held positions along the Maginot line, a system of heavily armed steel and concrete bunkers built after World War I stretching hundreds of kilometers along the German border, from Belgium to Switzerland. In addition, England had sent troops and supplies to aid in the defense of France.

In early May 1940, German tanks stormed across the French border from Belgium, swept around the north end of the Maginot line, and attacked French positions from the rear. Fixed firmly in concrete and pointing toward Germany, the heavy artillery pieces of the Maginot line were never fired.

France had placed its faith in the strength of the Maginot line, and its failure demoralized the French. Within a few short weeks France's fate was sealed.

**As You Read**
Trace the growing U.S. involvement in the war after the fall of France. Also, think about the following concepts and skills.

**Central Concepts**
- understanding how the fall of France and the blitz increased support for **interventionism**
- understanding how American **isolationism** delayed entry into the war

**Thinking Skills**
- making inferences
- analyzing behavior
- identifying cause and effect

**In the photo above, British destroyers loaded with troops stranded at Dunkirk arrive safely at a British port. The photo at the right shows civilians huddled in a cramped subway tunnel during the London *blitz*.**

The pulverizing attacks of the German tank corps, supported by massive air power, sent the French and British armies reeling backward. By the end of May, French soldiers were throwing down their weapons in the face of the German advance, and the British forces had retreated to the seacoast town of Dunkirk, across the English Channel from Great Britain. A fleet of private ships saved the British army from destruction by evacuating 338,000 French and British troops from Dunkirk between May 28 and June 4, 1940. French forces were left to face the German invaders alone. **1**

French resistance lasted about a month more. On June 3, German bombers had attacked Paris airports. A week later Italy declared war on France, and Mussolini's forces attacked from the south. On June 14, German troops marched into Paris. Finally, in a railway car on June 22, a jubilant Hitler personally accepted the French surrender.

**The Battle of Britain** With France secure, Hitler began an all-out attack on Great Britain in the summer of 1940. However, Great Britain was not as easily conquered. Although badly outnumbered, Britain's Royal Air Force had better planes and more highly skilled pilots than Hitler's *Luftwaffe*. So many German planes were shot down by British fighter pilots that Germany had to abandon daylight attacks. A proud Prime Minister Churchill declared that "never in the field of human conflict was so much owed by so many to so few."

Hoping to avoid further defeat, Hitler sought the cover of darkness. From September 1940 to May 1941, German aircraft dropped tons of bombs on London almost every night. The **blitz,** as the British called the bombing raids, killed more than 20,000 Londoners alone. The entire city of Coventry and large parts of London were reduced to smoking rubble. In the face of this assault, Churchill pleaded for more American aid. However, the future course of the United States at this point was far from clear.

STUDY GUIDE

**Making Inferences**

In March 1940, 43 percent of Americans believed that a German victory would threaten American security. After France fell on June 22, 1940, that number had risen to 69 percent. We can infer that fears increased because Germany seemed to be winning the war and also because countries friendly to the United States were falling.

**1** What was France's Maginot line, and why wasn't it successful?

## The Americans Respond

The rapid fall of France stunned people in the United States. However, Americans still disagreed about what should be done. Some who supported **interventionism** believed the United States should give all possible support to Britain short of declaring war on Germany. Others who supported **isolationism** thought the United States should stay out of the war.

One influential interventionist was William Allen White, a Kansas City journalist. He formed the Committee to Defend America by Aiding the Allies. With more than 600 local branches, the group promoted vigorous American support of Britain, short of active participation in the war.

Isolationists banded together to form the Committee to Defend America First. Its members thought the United States should keep its nose out of Europe's business. America First drew support from a broad range of Americans, including pacifists and socialists, Democrats and Republicans. Former president Herbert Hoover, historian Charles Beard, union activist John L. Lewis, and architect Frank Lloyd Wright belonged, as did representatives from German and Italian ethnic groups. The governing committee was headed by Robert E. Wood, the chairman of Sears, Roebuck and Co. The most famous speaker for the group was aviator Charles Lindbergh. He argued that the United States was strong enough to stand alone, despite Hitler's victories. Within a few months of its founding, America First had about 60,000 members.

**Selective Service** Aware of the split in public opinion and mindful of the upcoming presidential election, Roosevelt continued on a cautious course of aid to the Allies. In September 1940, Roosevelt arranged the transfer of 50 overage American destroy-

1940 HERBLOCK COPYRIGHT CARTOON FOR NEA SERVICE

**Many Americans were indecisive about involvement in World War II.**
*Does the cartoon above support interventionism or isolationism?*

ers to Britain. In return, the United States was given the right to establish naval and air bases on British territory in Newfoundland, Bermuda, and British Guiana (now Guyana). The same month, the president signed the Selective Training and Service Act, which established the first peacetime draft in American history. The law applied to all men between 21 and 35. Over one million men were to serve in the military for one year, but they were authorized to serve only in the Western Hemisphere. The Selective Service Act laid the groundwork for an American military capable of fighting a global war.

On the surface these moves brought the United States closer to involvement. Yet Roosevelt explained them as strengthening U.S. defenses and keeping the nation out of the war. Roosevelt took a similar stance during the 1940 election campaign: "Your president says this country is not going to war!" Approving voters returned him to the presidency for a third term.[2]

**Lend-Lease** With the election won, Roosevelt moved to support the Allies openly. In January 1941 he proposed the Lend-Lease bill. This bill gave the president the right to sell, lend, or lease military supplies to any nation deemed "vital to the defense of the United States." Roosevelt defended this plan by explaining that Britain did not have the money to purchase arms. If a neighbor's house were on fire, Roosevelt argued, you would loan that person your garden hose without worrying about the price. The United States, the president declared, must become the "great arsenal of democracy."

Polls indicated that most Americans agreed with Roosevelt. Nearly 80 percent of those questioned in one poll favored the Lend-Lease plan. Given these results, Congress approved the **Lend-Lease Act** in March 1941, providing an initial budget of $7 billion. Before Lend-Lease ended, over $50 billion in weapons, ammunition, vehicles, and other supplies

---

### STUDY GUIDE

**Analyzing Behavior**

Like all presidents who intend to seek reelection, Roosevelt had his finger on the pulse of public opinion. Even after the fall of France, he remained cautious about aiding the Allies, partly because of the upcoming election in November. He assured Americans that the country was not going to war. Only with the election safely over did he support the Allies more openly.

**2** How did the Selective Service Act bring the United States closer to war?

would go to support the Allied war effort. Shipments to Britain began at once. Economically, at least, the United States was at war with Germany.

Lend-Lease heated up America's involvement in the war in another way. During the spring and summer of 1941, German submarines patrolling in "wolf packs" sent tens of thousands of tons of British and American supply ships to the bottom of the Atlantic every week. To make sure that Lend-Lease supplies arrived safely in Britain, in April Roosevelt ordered the Navy to help the British track German U-boats. By summer, the Navy had orders to guard British ships as they traveled across the Atlantic and to destroy enemy submarines that threatened their passage.

The undeclared naval war between German and American ships worsened throughout the fall of 1941. In September, a German submarine opened fire on the *Greer*, an American destroyer. Calling the Germans "the rattlesnakes of the Atlantic," Roosevelt ordered the Navy to shoot Axis vessels on sight. In October, German U-boats torpedoed the destroyer *Kearny* and sank the destroyer *Reuben James*, killing about 100 American sailors. Congress revised the Neutrality Acts to allow armed U.S. merchant ships to carry munitions directly to England.

Though Lend-Lease seemed to be pulling the United States into the war, most U.S. citizens supported it in principle. However, when Germany suddenly attacked the Soviet Union in June 1941, the United States extended Lend-Lease aid to the USSR. Some people in the United States were outraged at the idea of sending Lend-Lease aid to a communist country. Isolationist Charles Lindbergh said he would prefer an alliance with Nazi Germany, with all its faults, to an alliance with "the godlessness and barbarism that exist in the Soviet Union."

However, Churchill, who had criticized the communists for years, cheered U.S. aid to the Soviets. "I have only one purpose," Churchill remarked, "the destruction of Hitler. . . . If Hitler invaded Hell I would at least make a favorable reference to the Devil in the House of Commons." Churchill was aware that Germany's opening of an eastern front would take some of the pressure off Britain. Battles against the Soviets in the east tied up 200 German divisions that might otherwise have been used in an invasion of Britain.

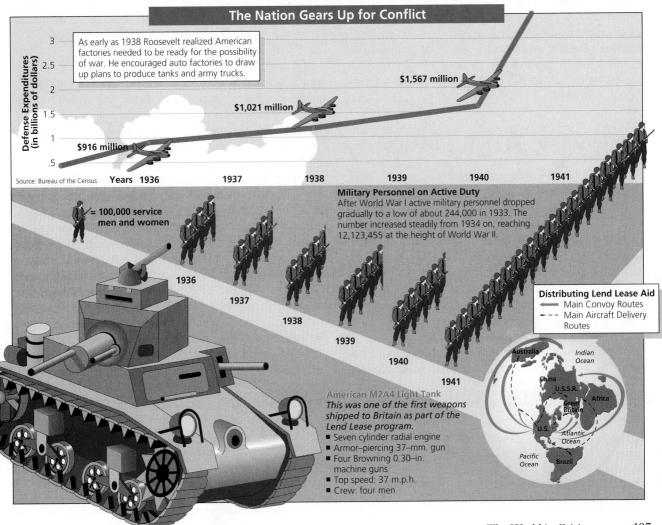

**The Nation Gears Up for Conflict**

As early as 1938 Roosevelt realized American factories needed to be ready for the possibility of war. He encouraged auto factories to draw up plans to produce tanks and army trucks.

**Defense Expenditures (in billions of dollars)**

$916 million
$1,021 million
$1,567 million

Source: Bureau of the Census    Years    1936    1937    1938    1939    1940    1941

= 100,000 service men and women

1936
1937
1938
1939
1940
1941

**Military Personnel on Active Duty**
After World War I active military personnel dropped gradually to a low of about 244,000 in 1933. The number increased steadily from 1934 on, reaching 12,123,455 at the height of World War II.

**Distributing Lend Lease Aid**
— Main Convoy Routes
- - - Main Aircraft Delivery Routes

Australia    Indian Ocean
China
U.S.S.R.
Great Britain    Africa
U.S.
Atlantic Ocean
Pacific Ocean    Brazil

**American M2A4 Light Tank**
*This was one of the first weapons shipped to Britain as part of the Lend Lease program.*
- Seven cylinder radial engine
- Armor–piercing 37–mm. gun
- Four Browning 0.30–in. machine guns
- Top speed: 37 m.p.h.
- Crew: four men

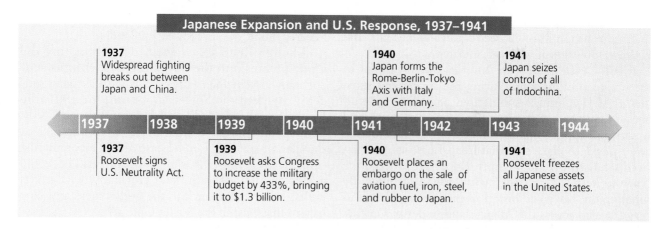

**Japanese Expansion and U.S. Response, 1937–1941**

**1937** Widespread fighting breaks out between Japan and China.

**1940** Japan forms the Rome-Berlin-Tokyo Axis with Italy and Germany.

**1941** Japan seizes control of all of Indochina.

1937 | 1938 | 1939 | 1940 | 1941 | 1942 | 1943 | 1944

**1937** Roosevelt signs U.S. Neutrality Act.

**1939** Roosevelt asks Congress to increase the military budget by 433%, bringing it to $1.3 billion.

**1940** Roosevelt places an embargo on the sale of aviation fuel, iron, steel, and rubber to Japan.

**1941** Roosevelt freezes all Japanese assets in the United States.

**The Atlantic Charter**  Stopping Hitler was not the only goal Roosevelt and Churchill shared. In August 1941, the two met for four days on a warship off the coast of Newfoundland. In addition to discussing military strategy, Roosevelt and Churchill agreed on a set of common principles establishing their goals for a postwar world. Their joint public statement was known as the Atlantic Charter. Recalling Wilson's Fourteen Points, the Charter affirmed each nation's right to choose its own government, free from fear of aggression. To protect this right, the United States, Britain, and the 15 others who had signed the charter by September 24, resolved to create an international organization to protect the security of all countries. Later, this dream took shape in the founding of the United Nations (UN).

## The Japanese Threat Increases

In the Pacific, Japan's continued aggression clearly violated the principles that Roosevelt and Churchill supported in the Atlantic Charter. In July 1940, Japan announced a plan for the future of Asia called the Greater East Asia Co-Prosperity Sphere. The sphere was in reality a Japanese empire, to include much of China, Southeast Asia, and the western Pacific. On September 27, Japan concluded an alliance with Germany and Italy, the Rome-Berlin-Tokyo Axis, which promised that each would defend the other if attacked by the United States.

The United States responded to Japan's aggressive stance by applying economic pressure. Roosevelt's goal was to limit Japanese expansion by cutting off the supplies Japan needed, without provoking Japan to war. He placed an embargo on the sale of scrap metal to Japan. In September 1940, when Japan occupied French colonial possessions in northern Indochina, Roosevelt extended the embargo to include aviation fuel, all metals, chemicals, machine parts, and other products with military uses to Japan. This game of check and counter-check continued into 1941. When in July of that year, Japan seized control of the rest of Indochina, Roosevelt retaliated by freezing all Japanese assets in the United States and ending all trade with Japan.

Despite mounting tensions, the United States continued to negotiate with the Japanese. In part, the negotiations were an attempt to buy time for the nation to fortify the Philippines and to build the "two-ocean navy" authorized by Congress in 1940. However, Roosevelt's Secretary of State Cordell Hull did not budge from his principles. He refused to meet with General Hideki Tojo in October 1941 and insisted that Japan honor the Open Door policy with China and that it stop its expansionism. The United States would resume trade with Japan, Hull said, only if Japan withdrew from China and Indochina.

By November 1941, the U.S. government knew that war with Japan could not be averted. With negotiations deadlocked and its oil supplies dwindling, the Japanese high command decided to take the offensive. Some Americans suspected an attack on British Malaya or the American Philippines. However, the Japanese high command had accepted the plan of Admiral Isoroku Yamamoto, who advised Japan to

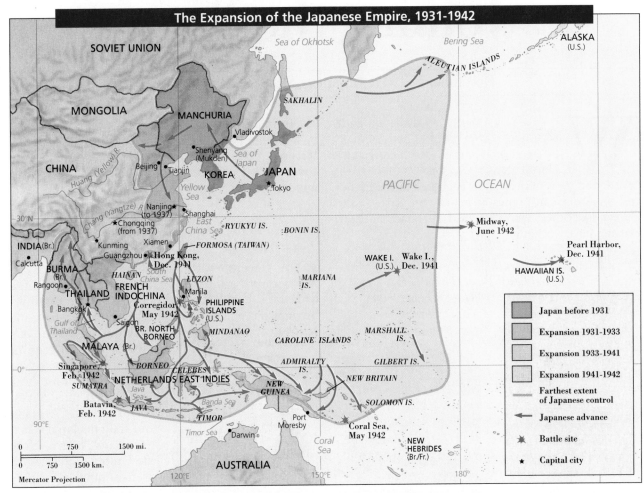

## The Expansion of the Japanese Empire, 1931-1942

**Legend:**
- Japan before 1931
- Expansion 1931-1933
- Expansion 1933-1941
- Expansion 1941-1942
- Farthest extent of Japanese control
- Japanese advance
- Battle site
- Capital city

**From 1931 to 1941 Japan's expansionism led to its control of most of East Asia. When Japan decided to attack the United States, Pearl Harbor was the chosen target.** *Geographically, what might have influenced this decision?*

strike the United States closer to home. An attack on the American naval base at Pearl Harbor offered Japan the possibility of delivering a knockout blow against the American fleet in the Pacific. However, Yamamoto himself was far from optimistic about Japan's long-range prospects in a war with the United States. "In the first six months to a year of war with the United States and England I will run wild," Yamamoto told his government prophetically. "I will show you an uninterrupted succession of victories, but if the war is prolonged for two or three years I have no confidence in the ultimate victory."

# Joining the War

## December 7, 1941: Japanese Attack Pearl Harbor

WITHOUT WARNING, JAPANESE DIVE BOMBERS AND TORPEDO PLANES SWOOPED OUT OF THE CLEAR, BLUE HAWAIIAN SKY AND RAINED DEATH AND devastation on American ships anchored in the harbor and on American planes at nearby air bases. John Garcia, like others who witnessed the attack on Pearl Harbor, never forgot it:

*I was sixteen years old, employed as a pipe fitter apprentice at Pearl Harbor Navy Yard. On December 7, 1941, oh, around 8:00 A.M., my grandmother woke me. She informed me that the Japanese were bombing Pearl Harbor. I said, "They're just practicing." She said, no, it was real and the announcer is requesting that all Pearl Harbor workers report to work. I went out on the porch and I could see the anti-aircraft fire up in the sky. . . . I was asked . . . to go into the water and get sailors out that had been blown off the ships. Some were unconscious, some were dead. So I spent the rest of the day swimming inside the harbor, along with some other Hawaiians. . . . We worked all day at that.*

As told to Studs Terkel, "The Good War," 1984

In less than three hours, the Japanese destroyed 19 ships, including five battleships, and 188 planes. Over 2,400 Americans were killed. It was the worst defeat by a foreign power in U.S. military history. Yet Pearl Harbor aroused and united Americans as nothing else could have done. It hurled the nation into war bent on revenge and committed to victory.

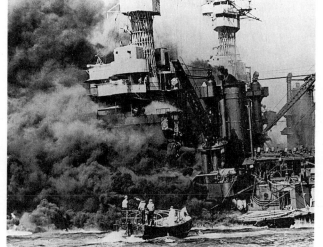

UPI/ BETTMANN NEWSPHOTOS

## Mobilizing at Home

On December 8, President Roosevelt asked Congress to declare war on Japan to avenge what he called a "date which will live in infamy." Because the United States had not attacked first, the pact between the Axis Powers did not require Hitler and Mussolini to follow Japan into war against the United States. Nevertheless, Germany and Italy declared war a few days later. Now the United States had to prepare quickly for global war on two fronts.

The Selective Service Act had been in force for over a year, but American armed forces had only 1.8 million men when war was declared. Increased draft calls soon began to fill the ranks, as thousands of men and women enlisted.

Their reasons for signing up varied from one person to the next. Patriotism, anger toward the Axis, a desire for adventure, and joblessness all played parts in decisions to join the military. By 1942, nearly 3.9 million Americans were in uniform. The number more than doubled by 1943, and in 1945 it peaked at more than 12 million. By the end of the war, more than 15 million men and nearly 216,000 women had served.

## STUDY GUIDE

### As You Read
Identify the major events that brought the United States from the bombing of Pearl Harbor to the end of World War II. Also, think about these concepts and skills.

### Central Concepts
- recognizing in the **holocaust** the consequences of Hitler's fanaticism
- recognizing the complexity of Allied strategic decisions.

### Thinking Skills
- recognizing cause and effect
- analyzing decisions
- recognizing assumptions
- comparing and contrasting

The armed forces included about one million African Americans. Their experiences differed in several significant ways from those of white personnel. Like much of the rest of American society, the military was officially segregated. When African Americans enlisted, they were assigned to all-black units, usually commanded by white officers. African Americans were often given jobs as cooks or laborers. Many white commanders would not send black units into combat.

Those African American units that did fight, however, performed with distinction. In late 1944 General Dwight D. Eisenhower called for black service troops to volunteer for combat in integrated units. Many did so, and Eisenhower and other generals became convinced that racially integrated combat units were more successful than segregated units. One Marine Corps leader commented, "Negro Marines are no longer on trial. They are Marines, period."

Other minority groups also enlisted. Nearly 350,000 Hispanic Americans served, and suffered many of the same kinds of discrimination as African Americans. Hispanics were the most decorated American ethnic group, while the Japanese American 442nd Regiment was the most decorated unit. Japanese American soldiers fought loyally in spite of the severe discrimination suffered by their families back home during the war. Special units decoded captured Japanese documents and helped the United States anticipate enemy moves. Many Native Americans also joined the war effort. One group of Navajo became part of the Marine Signal Corps. They outwitted the Japanese by sending messages in a code based on the Navajo language.

THE BETTMAN ARCHIVE

**Black troops in France during 1944 proved their skill in field artillery units.** *By serving in combat, how did black soldiers alter the U.S. military's attitude toward minorities?*

## The European Front

As the military geared up for combat, Allied political leaders met to determine overall strategy for the war. Shortly after Pearl Harbor, Roosevelt and Churchill decided that defeating Germany would be their first priority. Later, in 1943 at the Casablanca Conference in Morocco, where Stalin was not present, the Allied leaders agreed to wage war until the Axis Powers surrendered unconditionally. The United States would fight a defensive war against Japan in the Pacific while the Allies concentrated their joint offensive efforts on defeating Nazi Germany.

**Invasion of the Soviet Union** Although the Soviets and the Nazis had signed a nonaggression pact in 1939, Soviet leader Josef Stalin distrusted Hitler. The German invasion of the Soviet Union on June 22, 1941, however, took the Soviets by surprise. Using blitzkrieg tactics on a vast scale now, German troops surged north toward Leningrad and south toward the Crimean peninsula. By November, they had begun to encircle Moscow. An unusually severe winter and the determination of Soviet troops and civilians drove back the attackers. In the north, German troops surrounded Leningrad for almost 900 days, starving more than half a million residents to death.

In spring 1942 the Germans launched a new attack on the Soviet oil fields in southwestern Russia. By September, 300,000 Nazi troops had begun a major assault on the city of Stalingrad. The battle continued for five months amid the ruins and rubble of the city, until the Germans surrendered in February 1943. As many as 250,000 German troops, and many more

STUDY GUIDE

**Recognizing Cause and Effect**
World War II did not do away with racial discrimination, but it caused changes that would help launch the civil rights movement. Black workers successfully protested discrimination in defense plants. Black farmers took jobs in wartime industries. Military leaders discovered that segregation had been wasteful and unnecessary.

1 What was the war like for various American ethnic groups? Why?

Russians, were killed or froze to death. The Battle of Stalingrad halted Germany's eastward advance, but Stalin never forgave the Allies for failing to support Russia's defense. His country had suffered more casualties at Stalingrad than the United States did during the entire war. After the war, U.S. General George C. Marshall called the British and Russian people's refusal to accept defeat "the great factor in the salvage of our civilization."

SOVFOTO

**The Soviets paid dearly for a victory at Stalingrad, but their efforts gave the Allies an advantage in Europe.**

**Allied Offensives**   Rather than face a winter deep within Russia, the Allies decided on a less-risky assault. In November 1942 American and British troops landed in North Africa, advancing into Morocco and Algeria against a German tank division led by General Erwin Rommel, dubbed "the desert fox." The British gained an important victory in Egypt at El Alamein. This battle, like Stalingrad, marked a turning point in the war. Although 5,000 Americans died in a German counterattack in Tunisia, the Allies were victorious in North Africa by May 1943.

The Allies then used bases in North Africa to launch an invasion of southern Europe, landing in Sicily in July 1943. They battled German troops for more than a month before finally driving them out of Sicily. In the meantime, Mussolini's Fascist government fell from power. British forces invaded Italy from Sicily. On September 8, Italy announced its unconditional surrender to the Allies.

Germany, however, was determined to fight the Allies for control of Italy. Some of the most bitter fighting of the war occurred at Anzio beach and at Cassino Pass in central Italy. It was this kind of fighting—months of bombing, destruction, and death—that led cartoonist Bill Mauldin to write one of his darker captions: "Look at an infantryman's eyes and you can tell how much war he has seen." The Allies finally broke through German defenses in May, and Rome was liberated on June 4, 1944.

**D-Day**   The spotlight on the victory in Italy quickly shifted west. On June 6, 1944, General Eisenhower directed the largest combined land-sea-air invasion in history. The code name for the offensive was Operation Overlord, but most Americans remember the assault as D-Day. The D-Day invasion was, according to Churchill, "the most difficult and complicated that has ever taken place." Some 175,000 Allied soldiers began to come ashore before dawn along a 60-mile stretch of the Normandy coast of France. Once they had established a beachhead, at a cost of 2,245 killed and 1,670 wounded, the Allied forces had a base from which they would try to sweep the Germans out of France.

The success of D-Day also hinged on American industry. For months before the invasion, American and British planes dropped thousands of tons of bombs on German railroad lines, factories, and cities. Moreover, the huge Allied invasion force was carried by American transports of all kinds. Without the industrial workers who made this equipment, the Allied forces could not have landed in or retaken France.

**The Beginning of the End**   As the war progressed, the Allies gradually proved their dominance in the skies. Both experienced and new pilots flew fighters, bombers, and spy planes. That done, ground troops could advance cautiously eastward toward Germany. On August 25, 1944, American and Free French forces liberated Paris to great rejoicing by most inhabitants. In the meantime, Allied forces had launched an invasion of France's Rhône Valley from the south. By summer's end, France, Belgium, and Luxembourg were in Allied hands. Soviet troops advanced on Germany from the east.

**Analyzing Decisions**

At the time and later, controversy arose over the decision to launch the first British and American offensive in Africa instead of Europe. Some said Britain wanted to protect its own colonial interests in Africa. Others said that, by not taking action to divert German forces from the eastern front, Britain and the United States were deliberately refusing to help the Soviets. Others said the Allies were too cautious. The real reason was probably that Roosevelt believed the Allies still lacked the necessary military strength and hardware to invade Europe successfully.

**Legend:**
- Axis Powers
- Axis-controlled, 1942
- Allied Powers
- Neutral countries
- → Allied advance
- ✳ Battle site
- ★ Capital city

Azimuthal Equidistant Projection

**The European phase of World War II lasted five years, eight months, and seven days. Civilians suffered heavy losses in both life and property from bomb-** **ings, forced evacuations, and starvation.** *According to the battle sites marked on the map above, which European cities experienced the greatest loss of civilian life and property?*

Sea power was also crucial to Allied planning. Before the United States had entered the war, German U-boats preyed on North Atlantic shipping, even briefly threatening U.S. east-coast cities. While at sea, sailors faced the triple peril of attack from above, surface, and below—from planes, battleships, and U-boats. By late 1943 advances in sonar technology had given the Allies an edge in locating and sinking U-boats. More and more Allied naval convoys were safely crossing the Atlantic, keeping the Allies' enormous armies well provisioned. This lifeline made possible an offensive, not just defensive, strategy.

While the Allies prepared for an invasion of Germany itself, Hitler launched a last desperate strike. In December, Germany mounted a counteroffensive in the Ardennes Forest of Belgium. Hitler's tanks drove a bulge of troops and artillery 80 miles long and 50 miles deep into the Allied lines. After weeks of heavy fighting, during which 76,000 Allied soldiers were killed or wounded, the Germans were pushed back. The so-called Battle of the Bulge was the final German offensive of the war. The road into Germany, blocked for six weeks, was now open. As the Allied armies advanced, however, they had to confront the horrors committed by Hitler's government.

## STUDY GUIDE

### Recognizing Assumptions

The D-Day invasion took years of planning. Allied forces spent months before the actual invasion bombing strategic sites in Germany in order to weaken German defenses. The Allies assumed that with these added blows the German army would not be able to withstand an attack by Allied soldiers moving inland from the beach at Normandy. This assumption proved correct.

The D-Day invasion led to the liberation of Paris and ultimately to the defeat of Germany.

**The Holocaust** When Allied soldiers entered Germany in 1945, they found the terrible consequences of Hitler's fanatical hatred of Jews and other peoples. In early 1942 Hitler had put into action what he called "the final solution" to his "Jewish problem." Nazi soldiers rounded up Jews from all over Europe and shipped them to concentration camps. In these camps, Jews were used for slave labor, subjected to medical experiments and other atrocities, starved, beaten, shot, and put to death in gas chambers. Their bodies were buried in mass graves or incinerated in fiendishly efficient crematoriums.

Reports about these horrors were circulating as early as 1942. Only when the Allies liberated the death camps in 1945, however, did the world learn for certain the ghastly extent of Hitler's plan to wipe out the Jews of Europe. Walter Rosenblum, an American soldier, helped liberate Dachau, a concentration camp in southern Germany. He recalled:

> *T*he first thing I saw as I went down this road to Dachau were about forty boxcars on a railroad siding. . . . I looked into these boxcars and they were full of emaciated bodies, loaded all the way to the top. Forty boxcars full of dead people.
>
> As told to Studs Terkel, *"The Good War,"* 1984

Hitler's henchmen, along with thousands of Nazi collaborators, massacred about 6 million Jewish men, women, and children. More than two-thirds of the total Jewish population in Europe was destroyed. They also killed some 6 million Slavs, gypsies, communists, homosexuals, and others, most of them civilians. This mass extermination lives in infamy as the **holocaust,** which has come to mean the "great destruction."

Some critics have charged that Roosevelt could have lessened the extent of this tragedy. They point out that only 21,000 Jewish refugees were admitted to the United States in the early 1940s. This was a small fraction of the number permitted under existing immigration quotas. Moreover, some people thought Roosevelt was indifferent to the mass suffering of European Jews. In 1944 the U.S. War Department resisted proposals to bomb the gas chambers at the Auschwitz concentration camp. Roosevelt countered that his policy was to defeat Germany quickly and thus save all of Hitler's victims from further persecution.

**Victory in Europe** After turning back the Nazi onslaught on their homeland, Soviet troops moved west. They ousted Nazi governments or aided anti-German forces throughout eastern and central Europe in 1944 and 1945. They encircled Vienna and Prague, prize capitals of central Europe, and warned off the western Allies from challenging their control. Residents of the formerly Nazi-occupied countries, fearing new foreign armies, were not always sure which army to surrender to. Already it was clear to the world that the Soviet Union and the United States were replacing Germany as superpowers in Europe.

Allied forces began their final assault on Germany early in 1945. Soviet troops crossed Poland, as British and American troops swept into northern Germany from the Netherlands. Crossing rivers was among the gravest dangers, as retreating Nazis often tried to mine the bridges. By the end of March, U.S. forces had crossed the Rhine River and were advancing steadily toward Berlin, Germany's capital.

In the midst of Allied successes in Europe, however, a tragedy occurred in the United States. On April 12, Franklin Roosevelt died, after twelve years

**Nazis rounded up and transported Jews, Slavs, gypsies, and others to concentration camps. Millions of them were tortured, starved and murdered.**

in office. Vice President Harry S Truman took the oath of office and assumed leadership of the country. Roosevelt's death did not halt the Allied advance. By late April, Soviet troops had surrounded the city of Berlin. On April 30, Hitler committed suicide.

Berlin fell on May 2, and Germany surrendered unconditionally on May 7. War-weary Allied soldiers could look forward to being sent home. Sergeant Harold Murphy of Decatur, Illinois, expressed the feelings of thousands of other fathers in a postcard mailed to his baby daughter that day: "The War ended today, honey, and I hope to see you soon." The Allies declared May 8, 1945, V-E Day, or Victory in Europe Day.

## The Pacific Front

The war in Europe was over, but the United States continued to fight a very different kind of war in the Pacific. After their devastating attack on Pearl Harbor, the Japanese army swept to victory after victory. In early 1942, they captured the Dutch East Indies, which were rich in oil and other natural resources. Then they took Burma, Wake Island, and Guam and forced the surrender of 12,000 American soldiers in the Philippines.

By May 1942, American forces in the Pacific began to reverse the tide that had been flowing against them. In the battle of the Coral Sea, American carrier-based planes bombarded the Japanese fleet, stopping the Japanese advance toward Australia. A month later at the Battle of Midway, American planes sank four Japanese aircraft carriers and destroyed over 300 planes. This was the first major Japanese defeat, and it greatly reduced the threat to Hawaii.

Despite these setbacks, Japan still held many heavily fortified Pacific islands. To counter this advantage, American military planners adopted an "island hopping" strategy. American Marines captured key islands, building bases from which to attack the Philippines and eventually Japan itself. With this tactic, they hoped to surround Japanese strongholds and cut them off from supplies.

**Guadalcanal**    A typical American offensive in the Pacific was the attack on Guadalcanal, in the Solomon Islands. During the summer of 1942, the Japanese began building an airfield on the island, preparing for an invasion of Australia. To keep the Japanese from finishing the airfield, 10,000 marines waded ashore to seize the island on August 7, 1942.

Once on land, the marines battled both the enemy and the steaming jungle environment. Scorching heat, relentless humidity, rotting gear, poisonous insects, and tropical fevers such as malaria and dysentery were the everyday conditions of jungle warfare.

The battle for Guadalcanal continued over six grueling months, as Japanese soldiers were ordered to fight to the death to hold the island. Even after the U.S. Navy destroyed Japanese ships in the area, isolating the enemy remaining on the island, it took three months to drive the Japanese off.

Guadalcanal was the first territory Japan lost in the war. In their unsuccessful attempt to hold the island, the Japanese lost 25,000 men. Americans learned that every Pacific battle would be bloody and hard fought and that the Japanese could be beaten.

Battles for islands like Guadalcanal cost thousands of American lives from 1942 to 1945. In a six-week battle for Iwo Jima in early 1945, for example, the Marines suffered about 20,000 casualties to secure this tiny island 700 miles from Japan. About the same time, the United States achieved another objective when General Douglas MacArthur directed the American recapture of the Philippines. The strategy of inching island by island toward an eventual invasion of Japan was working. However, the United States and its allies agreed it might take years and up to a million deaths to conquer the Japanese home islands.

To step up the pressure on Japan, American long-range B-29 bombers began sustained strikes on the Japanese mainland in June 1944. By November they were bombing Tokyo itself. In one raid on Tokyo in March 1945, napalm bombs caused a fire storm in the city, incinerating 83,000 Japanese citizens. Despite casualties like these and the near total destruction of Japanese sea and air power, Japanese military leaders refused to accept an unconditional surrender that the United States demanded.[2]

**The Atomic Bomb**    With little hope of forcing a Japanese surrender, President Truman scheduled an invasion of Japan for late 1945 and early 1946. Then on July 16, 1945, American scientists, led by physicist

**Comparing and Contrasting**

In Europe, Allied forces waged a tough battle against German troops, eventually emerging the victor. Though this stage of the war had been a terrific struggle, the climate of Europe was not completely foreign to American soldiers. In the Pacific, however, U.S. forces had to survive not only enemy attacks but also the sometimes fatal effects of the jungle environment.

2  Explain the "island hopping" strategy used in the Pacific. Why was it eventually abandoned?

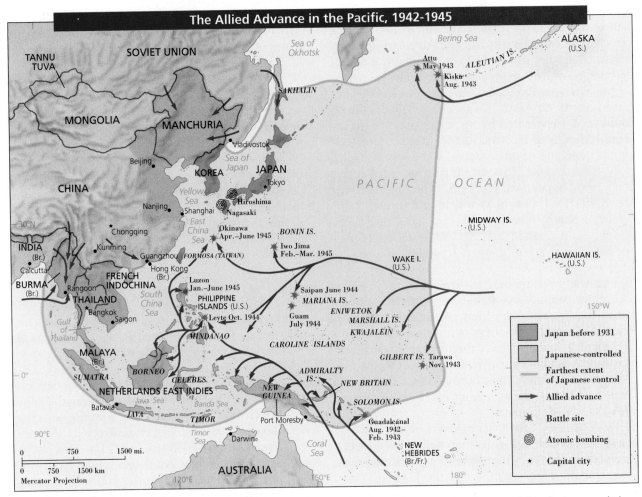

## The Allied Advance in the Pacific, 1942-1945

| | |
|---|---|
| ■ | Japan before 1931 |
| ▨ | Japanese-controlled |
| ── | Farthest extent of Japanese control |
| → | Allied advance |
| ✳ | Battle site |
| ◎ | Atomic bombing |
| ★ | Capital city |

**The map above shows the advance of Allied forces to retake areas in the Pacific captured by the Japanese** **Army during 1942-1945.** *What areas fell to the Japanese during these years? What major battles occurred during their recapture?*

J. Robert Oppenheimer, gave Truman another choice when they successfully detonated the first atomic bomb in the desert near Alamogordo, New Mexico. Truman chose to use the bomb on Japan in the hopes of ending the war without an invasion. (See page 418.) On August 6, 1945, the *Enola Gay*, an American B-29, dropped a single atomic bomb code-named "Little Boy" on the Japanese city of Hiroshima. A Japanese journalist described the bomb's effects:

*S*uddenly a glaring whitish pinkish light appeared in the sky accompanied by an unnatural tremor. . . . Within a few seconds

*the thousands of people in the streets . . . and in the gardens in the center of town were scorched by a wave of searing heat.*

. . . . . . . . . . . . . . . . . . . . . . . . . . . .

*By the evening the fire began to burn down and then it went out. There was nothing left to burn. Hiroshima had ceased to exist.*

Barrington Boardman,
*From Harding to Hiroshima*, 1987

The atomic blast killed 100,000 people instantly, and another 100,000 men, women, and children died later from burns, radiation, or other wounds caused

## STUDY GUIDE

### Recognizing Cause and Effect

After the communist revolution in 1917, the mistrust that already existed between Americans and Russians increased. During World War II, the two great powers had laid their differences aside. However, some wartime decisions increased Soviet animosity, such as delaying the invasion of Europe and leaving the Russians to fight alone on the Continent for two years. Though both governments praised each other's courage in battle, old and new differences would loom even larger during the postwar period, resulting in the Cold War.

by the blast. The bomb destroyed 4 square miles of the city. On August 8, the Soviet Union entered the war against Japan as it had promised. When the Japanese still did not surrender, the United States dropped a second atomic bomb on the city of Nagasaki on August 9. The bomb killed 40,000 more Japanese citizens. Five days later, on August 14, the Japanese government surrendered. After six years of fighting, World War II was over.

## The Impact of War

For the Axis Powers as well as for the Allies, World War II was the most devastating war in history and the first to bring mass civilian deaths. Grigori Baklanov, who served in the Soviet military, expresses in stark terms the tragedy these numbers represent: "Of my generation, out of one hundred who went to fight, three came back. Three percent." Baklanov notes with despair, "I was the only one from our class of all the boys who went to the front who remained alive after the war. What else is there to say?"

Beyond the tragic loss of life, the war also devastated thousands of cities and villages throughout Europe and Asia. Capitals like Berlin, Tokyo, London, and Manila suffered heavy damage. Everywhere, transportation systems were mangled, factories were destroyed, and economies were left in shambles.

As the chart above indicates, the United States suffered fewer deaths than many nations, and it had less destruction of property. Fewer than 1 percent of U.S. citizens were killed or wounded in the war. By contrast, the Soviet Union lost more than 8 percent of its population. Also, the demand for war supplies pulled the American economy out of the Great Depression and made it more productive and prosperous.

The war changed the lives of the men and women who served in it. Many left their homes for the first time to travel across the country and around the

| World War II Dead* | | |
|---|---|---|
| Country | Military Dead | Civilian Dead |
| United States | 405,000 | 2,000 |
| Great Britain | 271,300 | 60,600 |
| Germany | 2,850,000 | 2,300,000 |
| France | 210,700 | 173,300 |
| USSR | 14,500,000 | 7,000,000 |
| Poland | 850,000 | 5,778,000 |
| Italy | 279,800 | 93,000 |
| China | 1,324,000 | 10,000,000 |
| Japan | 1,506,000 | 300,000 |
| Spain | 12,000 | 10,000 |

*Approximate

**The United States suffered approximately 2,000 civilian deaths during World War II.** *What factors account for this comparatively low estimate?*

world. They were exposed to new ideas and opinions. Anne Bosanko Green described life in the WACs.

> We suddenly left our humdrum lives, our jobs, and schools and were moved all around the vast United States or across the Atlantic and Pacific oceans to lands we had never thought we would see. We did not have to worry about our families and homelands being destroyed while we were off seeing the world. We were learning new skills, [and] meeting new people. . . .
>
> Anne Bosanko Green,
> *One Woman's War*, 1989

In addition to its effects on returning servicemen and women, the war transformed the lives of millions of Americans on the home front. In all areas of American society—business, agriculture, labor, and government—the war brought varied and lasting changes.

## SECTION REVIEW

### Checking Facts
1. How did the United States go about mobilizing for the war once it had been declared?
2. What was the importance of the Soviet victory at Stalingrad?
3. What was the role of American industry in the success of D-Day?
4. Why was Hitler's last strike called the Battle of the Bulge? How did the battle end?
5. What people did the Nazis send to

concentration camps in Germany and Poland? Why?

### Thinking Critically
6. **Recognizing Assumptions** What are some assumptions behind this comment of a Marine Corps leader: "Negro marines are no longer on trial. They are Marines, period."
7. **Analyzing Decisions** Why did America decide to drop an

A-bomb on Hiroshima, and a second one on Nagasaki?

8. **Recognizing Cause and Effect** How did advanced technology make World War II the most devastating war in history?

### Linking Across Time
9. How have conditions changed for women and ethnic minorities since World War II? How might the war have influenced these changes?

# Dropping the Bomb

> Dear Mr. President,
> I think it is very important that I should have a talk
> with you as soon as possible on a highly secret matter.
> I mentioned it to you shortly after you took office, but
> have not urged it since on account of the pressure you
> have been under. It, however, has such a bearing on our
> present foreign relations and has such an important
> effect upon all my thinking in this field that I think
> you ought to know about it without much further
> delay.
>
> —Secretary of War Henry L. Stimson to
> President Harry S Truman, April 24, 1945

## The Case

When Truman received Stimson's note, he had been president for only 12 days. Roosevelt's sudden death had thrust Truman into the presidency at a critical point in the war. This great responsibility reportedly prompted Eleanor Roosevelt to say to Truman, "Is there anything we can do for you? For you are the one in trouble now."

What Stimson wanted to talk with Truman about was the atomic bomb. Within two weeks the war in Europe would be over, and the President was already turning his attention to ending the war with Japan and to the negotiations that would shape the postwar world. Truman met with Stimson the very next day, and the information Stimson shared would significantly influence Truman's strategy both for ending the war and negotiating the peace.

Truman faced a critical question: Now that the atomic bomb was nearing completion, would the United States use this fearsome new weapon against Japan? Truman later insisted that he "regarded the bomb as a military weapon and never had any doubt that it should be used." Some others did have doubts, but the evidence available to us today indicates that Truman and other leading policy makers did not really question the assumption that the atomic bomb should be used to end the war. However, the decisions they made about when and how to use the weapon had major military, political, and ethical consequences for the postwar world.

## The Background

Truman's meeting with Stimson gave him his first knowledge of the atomic bomb. Many months earlier while still a senator, Truman had become aware of the existence of the Manhattan Project, but he did not learn of its purpose. In fact, when Truman tried to investigate the project, Secretary Stimson himself persuaded Truman to abandon his investigation. Truman recalled their discussion this way in his memoirs:

*"Senator," the Secretary told me as he sat beside my desk, "I can't tell you what it is, but it is the greatest project in the history of the world. It is most top secret. Many of the people who actually engaged in the work have no idea what it is, and we who do would appreciate your not going into those plants."*

*I had long known Henry L. Stimson to be a great American patriot and statesman. "I'll take you at your word," I told him. "I'll order the investigations into those plants called off."*

When Secretary Stimson met with President Truman on April 25, he briefed the president on the full history of the Manhattan Project and informed him that the atomic bomb would probably be available within four months. Although Stimson supported using the bomb to end the war, he also pointed out some serious problems that the bomb would pose for the world after the war. Chief among these were a possible atomic arms race and the danger of an atomic war. To address these challenges, Stimson proposed that Truman appoint a committee to advise him on policy regarding atomic weapons. The president took Stimson's advice, and the Interim Committee, as it was called, met in Washington on May 31.

The goal of Truman and the Interim Committee appears to have been to find the most effective way to use the bomb to shock Japan into surrendering. Even though the Russians had promised to enter the war against Japan by August 8, many American military leaders assumed that an amphibious landing on the Japanese mainland would be necessary to end the war. The cost in American lives would be high, and many believed that using the bomb could end the war without an invasion.

## The Opinions

The quotes on this page represent the range of opinions about using the atomic bomb that were expressed during the summer of 1945. Stimson's statement expresses the majority opinion, that the bomb had to be used to end the war quickly and to save American lives. Secretary of State James Byrnes and the Interim Committee strongly supported this position. The other statements question the use of this new weapon.

*"In the light of the alternatives which, on a fair estimate, were open to us I believe that no man, in our position and subject to our responsibilities, holding in his hands a weapon of such possibilities for accomplishing this purpose and saving those lives, could have failed to use it and afterwards looked his countrymen in the face."*

Henry L. Stimson, Secretary of War

*"I told him [Stimson] I was against it on two counts. First, the Japanese were ready to surrender and it wasn't necessary to hit them with that awful thing. Second, I hated to see our country be the first to use such a weapon."*

General Dwight D. Eisenhower
Supreme Allied Commander

*"I have had a feeling that before the bomb is actually used against Japan that Japan should have some preliminary warning of say two or three days in advance. . . . The position of the United States as a great humanitarian nation and the fair play attitude of our people generally is responsible in the main for this feeling."*

Ralph A. Bard, Undersecretary of the Navy

*"If the United States were to be the first to release this new means of indiscriminate destruction upon mankind, she would sacrifice public support throughout the world, precipitate the race for armaments, and prejudice the possibility of reaching an international agreement on the future control of such weapons."*

James Franck, University of Chicago

## The Options

The opinions you have read indicate that Truman had these options to consider:

1. Drop the bomb on Japanese cities to force an immediate end to the war.
2. Carry out a demonstration of the weapon to persuade Japan to surrender.
3. Launch an invasion of Japan.
4. Rely on Japan's deteriorating military situation and the entry of the Soviet Union into the war to force Japanese surrender.
5. Negotiate surrender terms acceptable to Japan and the United States.

## The Decision

The Interim Committee made its decision and gave it to Truman on June 1:

*The present view of the Committee was that the bomb should be used against Japan as soon as possible; that it be used on a war plant surrounded by workers' homes; and that it be used without prior warning.*
—Recording Secretary R. Gordon Arneson, from minutes taken on May 31

Secretary of State Byrnes informed the president of the Interim Committee's decision. Later, he said that "with reluctance [Truman] had to agree that he could think of no alternative and found himself in accord with what I told him the Committee was going to recommend."

Truman seems to have made his decision the day he received the report, though he did not give the order to drop the bomb until later. Why did he agree with the Interim Committee? Why did he choose option 1?

Apparently, Truman rejected option 2, a demonstration, for reasons offered by the Interim Committee and its Scientific Panel. A demonstration would not help to end the war. The committee did not offer evidence to support this judgment. They knew, however, that a successful test would not necessarily cause the Japanese to surrender unconditionally. An unsuccessful test, they believed, would be worse than none.

Truman placed the highest value on ending the war with the loss of as few American lives as possible. Both options 3 and 4 would cost countless American lives and bring an indefinite extension of the war with no certain outcome. The Japanese might never surrender. They seemed prepared to fight to the end, whatever that would mean, even the loss of many Japanese lives. Option 4 had an added disadvantage. If the Soviets entered the fighting, they would gain an advantage in postwar negotiations about new governments in Eastern Europe. Truman and other U.S. leaders preferred not to be indebted to the Soviets for any help in ending the war with Japan.

Truman probably never viewed option 5 as a real possibility. The only surrender acceptable to American leaders would be unconditional. The only surrender acceptable to the Japanese would include at least one condition: that they be allowed to keep their emperor. Truman saw the bomb as just another weapon—legitimate in wartime, when the goal was to win. He saw it as more destructive, perhaps, but not ethically different from the fire bombing of Dresden or Tokyo.

## The Outcome

The bomb was successfully tested on July 16, 1945, at a remote desert site near Alamogordo, New Mexico. Scientists saw for the first time the blinding flash and the enormous multicolored cloud of an atomic explosion. J. Robert Oppenheimer, the physicist who directed the production of the bomb, said, "We waited until the blast had passed, walked out of the shelter and then it was extremely solemn. We knew the world would not be the same."

On August 6, 1945, an atomic bomb, carrying more power than 20,000 tons of TNT, was dropped on Hiroshima, Japan, an important military center. The next day President Truman gave a statement that included the following: "Let there be no mistake: we shall completely destroy Japan's power to make war. Only a Japanese surrender will stop us."

Most Americans and their allies breathed a sigh of relief, knowing that the war would soon end. But they also recognized that, as the London Daily Express put it, "The world has changed overnight."

## The Interpretations

Almost half a century has passed since that summer in 1945. The years have brought knowledge and perspectives unavailable to Truman and other decision makers of that time. During these years, three main interpretations have emerged.

One is that Truman and Stimson were correct in their idea that the bombings were necessary to end the war and save lives. According to this view, these were the only significant motives of those who ordered the bombing of Hiroshima and, three days later, Nagasaki.

Another interpretation is that dropping the bomb was unnecessary, even immoral. People holding this view argued that while Truman and the others were honest, they were also naive; they failed to take into account the long-term effects of dropping the bomb, such as the arms race and the Cold War.

A third group also saw the bombings as unnecessary and unwise. In addition, they said that Truman and the other policy makers had ulterior motives, that they engaged in "atomic diplomacy." That is they used the bombings to try to intimidate the Soviets. As a result, said this group, they failed to seriously consider alternatives to dropping the bomb.

Today, controversy over the decision to drop the atomic bomb continues. As time passes, new evidence becomes available. For example, the first viewpoint found support in later evidence from Japan which seemed to show that without the bombings, the war might have continued for many months. Such findings support the often repeated but much challenged idea that the bombings saved as many as 1,000,000 American lives.

Another source of new evidence has been medical reports about those who survived the bombings at Hiroshima and Nagasaki. Many sickened and died soon afterward. Over the years, more evidence has emerged about long-term effects of atomic radiation. Today, for example, survivors of the bombings have a higher than average incidence of leukemia and thyroid cancer. Thus, medical reports about survivors add to the evidence used by those who raise ethical questions about the bomb.

AP/WIDE WORLD PHOTOS

**A tall column of smoke billows 20,000 feet above Hiroshima, Japan, after the first atomic bomb strike by American forces on August 6.**

## Think About It

1. Look again at the opinions of Henry L. Stimson and James Franck, and contrast their predictions of the consequences of using the bomb. Why do you think they differed so much?
2. Which consequences of using the bomb did Truman predict correctly? Which consequences were different from those that he might have expected?
3. Some scientists were more likely than political leaders to oppose the use of the atomic bomb. What could account for these differences?
4. What conflicts in values did you discover as you read the quotations on page 419? Have our values as Americans changed over time, giving new meanings to the events of the 1940s?
5. Think of some current issues, and describe opposing points of view. One example is global warming. Some say we lack evidence that global warming is a genuine threat. Others say we need to take action now, no matter what it costs. Otherwise, it may be too late.

# Chapter 12 Review

**September 1931**
Japan attacks
Manchuria.

**October 1935**
Italy invades
Ethiopia.

**1936**
Axis Powers Alliance
is formed.

1931  1932  1933  1934  1935  1936  1937  1938

**1933**
Roosevelt introduces
"Good Neighbor Policy."

**July 1936**
The Spanish Civil
War begins.

## Summary

Use the following outline as a tool for reviewing and summarizing the chapter. Copy the outline on your own paper, leaving spaces between headings to jot down notes about key events and concepts.

**I. The Road to War**
  A. The Rise of Totalitarianism
  B. The Axis Tests Its Strength
  C. Japan Flexes Its Muscles
  D. America's Unneutral Neutrality
**II. The Gathering Storm**
  A. Hitler Crushes Europe
  B. The Americans Respond
  C. The Japanese Threat Increases
**III. Joining the War**
  A. Mobilizing at Home
  B. The European Front
  C. The Pacific Front
  D. The Impact of War

## Ideas, Events, and People

1. In his speech before the Reichstag, how did Hitler justify his orders to murder those who stood in his way to political power? What effect did his words have on the German people?
2. Describe the Good Neighbor policy. Why did Roosevelt employ it?
3. Germany and Italy formed an alliance in 1936 known as the Axis Powers. How did this alliance affect the outcome of the Spanish Civil War?
4. Why did Japan wish to expand its territory during the 1930s and 1940s?
5. What was the function of the Neutrality Acts?
6. Why was the Battle of Britain an initial failure for Germany? What strategy did Hitler try in his "blitz" of London to ward off further failure?

7. Why did the Battle of Stalingrad cause Stalin to resent Britain and the United States?
8. What famous battle led to the liberation of France? How was it accomplished?
9. Why is the name *holocaust* used to describe Hitler's atrocities against Jews in Europe during World War II?

## Social Studies Skills

**Drawing Inferences from Maps**
Analyze the map on page 413. Locate battle sites, and trace the path of Allied offensive attacks that led to the defeat of Germany. Make a chronological list.

## Critical Thinking

1. **Recognizing Assumptions**
Many people in the United States supported the Republican cause in Spain. Some even volunteered to fight in the Spanish Civil War. What assumptions might they have made about the expansion of totalitarian governments in Europe that led them to become involved in what could have been seen as strictly Spain's problem?
2. **Identifying Cause and Effect**
Admiral Isoroku Yamamoto promised Japan a series of victories for the first year of a war with the United States and Britain if Japan took his advice to strike the United States close to home. He also said, however, that unless Japan won the war quickly victory would be impossible. Considering what you now know about Japan during this time period, identify the cause and effect relationship that caused Yamamoto to hold this view.
3. **Analyzing Decisions**
Once Japan attacked Pearl Harbor and the United States entered the war, many men and women volunteered for duty. What reasons did

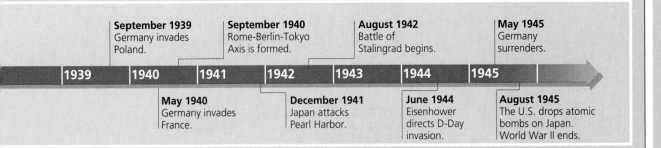

September 1939
Germany invades
Poland.

September 1940
Rome-Berlin-Tokyo
Axis is formed.

August 1942
Battle of
Stalingrad begins.

May 1945
Germany
surrenders.

1939 | 1940 | 1941 | 1942 | 1943 | 1944 | 1945

May 1940
Germany invades
France.

December 1941
Japan attacks
Pearl Harbor.

June 1944
Eisenhower
directs D-Day
invasion.

August 1945
The U.S. drops atomic
bombs on Japan.
World War II ends.

they give for enlisting? Why do you think these reasons were important to them?

# Extension and Application

### 1. Citizenship
Isolationists and interventionists held different opinions about United States involvement in World War II and the responsibilities of its citizens. What were the basic views, priorities, and values of both sides?

### 2. Global Connection
During World War II, most countries in Europe either supported the Allies or the Axis Powers. Some countries, however, remained neutral, including Portugal, Spain, Ireland, Sweden, Turkey, and Switzerland. Choose one of these neutral countries and research the reasons for its neutrality. Write a report on what you discover. Share your information in a class discussion.

### 3. Linking Across Time
During World War II, people in the United States felt "a special sympathy and kinship" for the Chinese. Conversely, they felt loathing for the Japanese, a feeling that grew stronger as the war continued. With a partner, research the present U.S. relationships with China and Japan. Newspapers and news magazines are good sources of current information. Pay particular attention to the topics of trade, technology, and human rights. Give an oral report to the class.

### 4. Cooperative Learning
Working in small groups, analyze the propaganda used during World War II by the Axis Powers and by the Allies. Assign group members specific tasks of gathering information, writing descriptions and summaries of what you find, analyzing the propaganda, and then making a presentation to the class.

# Geography

1. Use the map on page 398 to name the countries or parts of countries taken over by Italy and by Germany between 1935 and 1939.

2. Use the map on page 409 to trace Japanese expansion after 1931. Which countries did Japan invade, and which countries' possessions did it invade?

3. According to page 415, why were Guadalcanal and islands near it difficult for American forces to attack?

4. The map below shows the Allied invasion routes to Normandy beginning June 6, 1944. Why do you think the invasion was launched from five sites rather than one?

5. The Nazis were fooled into thinking the D-Day invasion would come near Calais. Why do you think the Allies chose to land on a peninsula?

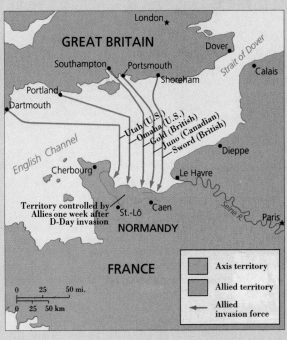

## CHAPTER 13

# The Home Front

## 1942: Americans Pull Together

The Second World War jolted the American people—still suffering from a long depression—with an electric sense of purpose. After a decade of severe job shortages, American men and women willingly served in the armed forces and worked on farms and in factories to produce the food and weapons to win the war.

During the war years, the United States became a country on the move. Many of the new recruits had never before left their hometowns.

The war disrupted the homes, families, and lives of all Americans. Many women followed their husbands to military bases. Both men and women went in search of high-paying jobs in the defense industry. African Americans traveled north and west hoping to escape poverty and discrimination.

This mingling of people from different economic, social, and cultural backgrounds altered the way Americans looked at themselves. The people of the United States began to recognize some of the political, social, and economic consequences of living in such a diverse society. The prosperity that Americans experienced from a full-employment economy during the war years enabled them to live better after the war.

*The war disrupted the homes, families, and lives of all Americans.*

CULVER PICTURES

*Entertainers and movie stars made special trips to raise the morale of U.S. troops abroad.*

*During World War II, the American work force took on a whole new look. Many women started working in the nation's factories—doing jobs they never would have done before. These women worked as welders in a factory in Connecticut.*

# Mobilizing the Home Front

## December 7, 1941: Japanese Bomb Pearl Harbor

AT THE BEGINNING OF DECEMBER 1941, THE UNITED STATES WAS AT PEACE, AND MOST AMERICANS WERE PREPARING FOR THE HOLIDAYS. THE JAPANESE ATTACK on Pearl Harbor on December 7 stunned Americans and permanently changed their lives. Everyone had a story to tell about how he or she first heard the startling news. Maxine Andrews, one of the famous Andrews Sisters singing trio, remembers that day.

*B**ut oh, I remember the day war was de-*
*clared. We were in Cincinnati. It looked*
*like we were gonna break the house record in*
*the theater. It didn't matter how cold it was*
*or how high the snow,*
*people were lined up*
*for blocks. . . . This*
*Sunday morning,*
*I walked over and*
*there were no lines. I*
*thought, "Now, this*
*is funny." I walked*
*onto the stage, which*
*was very dark. The*
*doorman and the*
*stagehands were*
*sitting around the*
*radio. They had just one light on. They were*
*talking about Pearl Harbor being bombed. I*
*asked the doorman, "Where is Pearl Harbor?"*

As told to Studs Terkel,
*"The Good War,"* 1984

The Andrews Sisters, like other stars and celebrities, bolstered the morale of Americans both at home

and abroad. In small towns and big cities, on Army posts and Navy ships, entertainers lifted spirits and helped unify the country.

## Building National Morale

Japan's surprise attack on Pearl Harbor ended the bitter argument between isolationists and those who favored intervention in the war. Shocked and angered by the attack, Americans rallied to support their government. Most believed they were fighting for what President Roosevelt called the Four Freedoms: freedom of speech and expression, freedom of worship, freedom from want, and freedom from fear.

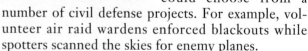
AP/ WIDE WORLD PHOTOS

**Calling All Volunteers**
To raise and maintain the country's morale, the government created the Office of Civilian Defense (OCD). Each citizen was asked to contribute "an hour a day for the U.S.A." They could choose from a number of civil defense projects. For example, volunteer air raid wardens enforced blackouts while spotters scanned the skies for enemy planes.

Other Americans helped the war effort by growing their own vegetables. In 1941 the Secretary of Agriculture suggested that because farmers were busy feeding the Army, people who wanted fresh vegetables should plant "victory gardens." A few months

**As You Read**
Identify the methods the government employed to maintain morale and to mobilize the economy for war. Also, think about the following concepts and skills.

**Central Concepts**
- understanding the causes of **inflation** in the wartime economy
- recognizing the role **rationing** played in keeping prices down

**Thinking Skills**
- recognizing propaganda
- identifying cause and effect
- recognizing points of view

later, backyards, vacant lots, and such unlikely places as zoos, racetracks, and jails sprouted a colorful array of vegetables planted by conscientious citizens. Victory gardens eventually produced 40 percent of all the vegetables grown in the country during the war.

Volunteers also collected materials for the war effort. Newspapers, rubber, scrap metal, aluminum pots, tin cans, box springs—anything that could be turned into armaments—were deposited on designated street corners. Students brought these materials to collection centers. By June 1942 the Boy Scouts had salvaged so much waste paper that paper collection was temporarily called off. Eventually these efforts supplied much of the steel, half of the tin, and half the paper that was needed to fight the war.

**The Media Goes to War** To keep Americans informed about the war, the government established the Office of War Information. Its function was to coordinate war news from various federal agencies. The agency also encouraged newspapers, radio stations, and the movie industry to help Americans understand the progress of the war and the government's policies.

The entertainment industry, however, needed no encouragement from the government. Hollywood rushed to copyright titles such as *Bombing of Honolulu, Yellow Peril, My Four Years in Japan,* and *V for Victory.* A month after Pearl Harbor, filmmakers were hard at work on their versions of the war. The heroes were gallant Americans played by actors such as John Wayne. The villains—all stereotypes—were sadistic Germans, bumbling Italians, and sneaky Japanese.

Comic strip characters also went to war. "Terry and the Pirates" fought the Japanese instead of pirates. "Little Orphan Annie" called on readers to collect scrap metal, and her father, Daddy Warbucks, served as a general. Superman promoted the Red Cross and war bonds. New comic strips with titles such as *G.I. Joe, War,* and *Don Winslow of the Navy* appeared.

Songwriters, too, joined in. A popular song told how the war changed one musician's life:

*He was a famous trumpet man from out Chicago way,*

AP/ WIDE WORLD PHOTOS

**In answer to Roosevelt's appeal, a recycling parade in Stevens Point, Wisconsin, boasts 106 trucks carrying more than 80 tons of scrap rubber. At left, a c1943 comic book cover shows Captain Freedom and his friends fighting the Axis.** *How did both of these things help raise morale?*

THE GRANGER COLLECTION

*He had a boogie sound that no one else could play,*
*He was top man at his craft.*
*But then his number came up and he was called in the draft.*
*He's in the army now ablowin' reveille.*
*He's the boogie woogie bugle boy of Company B.*

Hughie Price and Don Raye, "The Boogie Woogie Bugle Boy of Company B," 1941

Patriotic songs such as "This Is the Army Mister Jones," and "American Patrol" were popular at the beginning of the war. After 1942, though, patriotism gave way to more sentimental songs such as "I Left My Heart At the Stage Door Canteen" and "You'd Be So Nice To Come Home To."[1]

National unity was also stimulated by advertisements in magazines and newspapers and on billboards and radio shows. Advertisers reversed their usual emphasis on selling goods and instead urged Americans to use less rather than buy more. The popular slogan was "Use it up, wear it out, make it do or do with-

**Recognizing Propaganda**

How did the government use propaganda to help mobilize Americans to support the war effort?

The Office of War Information worked with the media to publicize slo-

gans, promote the sale of bonds, and provide Americans with information about the war.

1 Describe how Americans at home supported the war effort. How did the media respond to the war?

out." The materials and energy that ordinarily went into producing consumer goods would now be needed to make the instruments of war.

## *Staging a Production Miracle*

Although the Roosevelt administration had taken steps to prepare the country for war before Pearl Harbor, much remained to be done. In 1941 only 15 percent of industrial production was going to military needs. To help U.S. industry convert to war production, President Roosevelt created the War Production Board (WPB) in January 1942. The WPB's job was to "exercise general responsibility" over the nation's economy.

First came the task of getting industrialists to convert their factories from civilian to military production. To accomplish this, the WPB issued orders limiting the production of materials not essential to the war effort. Manufacturers switched from making consumer goods such as shirts, toys, and cars to making uniforms, bombs, tanks, and aircraft.

Next came the job of convincing businesses to build new plants to increase production. The government often paid for the new plants and equipment, and also agreed to grant relief from antitrust laws to war-related industries. To eliminate the risk for businesses, military contractors were reimbursed for their costs and guaranteed a fixed and generous profit. "If you . . . go to war . . . in a capitalist country, you have to let business make money out of the process or business won't work," said Secretary of War Henry Stimson.

The WPB's plan succeeded, and industrial production nearly doubled. This was accomplished with the help of people like Henry Kaiser, the genius of ship construction. His Richmond, California, shipyard cut the time needed to build merchant ships from

105 days to 46, then to 29, then to 14 days from start to finish! By 1944 the United States had created such a surplus of armaments that the government ordered some defense plants to stop hiring and to cut back on items like anti-tank guns and trainer planes.

At a meeting between Roosevelt, Churchill, and Stalin in Teheran, late in 1943, the Soviet leader offered a toast: "To American production, without which this war would have been lost."

## *Directing a Wartime Economy*

The United States economy grew at a staggering rate during the war. The **gross national product** (GNP), the dollar value of all goods and services produced annually, increased in the U.S. from $90.5 billion in 1939 to $211.9 billion in 1945.

The war created 17 million new jobs, and many workers put in long hours of overtime. Farmers shared in the prosperity as crop prices doubled between 1940 and 1945. As people made more money, they sought more of the consumer goods that were in short supply. This increased demand pushed prices up. By spring of 1942, the cost of living had risen 15 percent above 1939 levels.

Roosevelt worried about the effects of this **inflation,** or general rise in wages and prices. The first step he took to control inflation was to freeze wages. Trade unions, however, opposed a wage freeze. Since they were enthusiastic political supporters of FDR, the administration moved slowly and cautiously.

**Controlling Wages and Prices** The administration set up the National War Labor Board (NWLB) to control wages and monitor inflation. In July 1942 the NWLB adopted a wage formula that allowed

AP/ WIDE WORLD PHOTOS

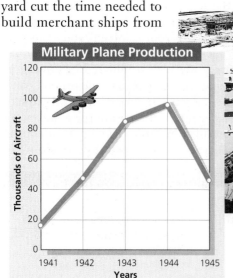

**Military Plane Production**

*Thousands of Aircraft* (y-axis: 0, 20, 40, 60, 80, 100, 120)

*Years* (x-axis: 1941, 1942, 1943, 1944, 1945)

**Workers in Burbank, California, finish the final assembly of Lightning P-38 fighter planes in July 1943. Mechanized assembly lines doubled the daily output and reduced production hours. As the graph on the left shows, production had not yet reached peak capacity by 1943.**

wage increases up to 15 percent over January 1, 1941, levels, the amount the NWLB had estimated living costs had risen.

In April 1943, faced with continued inflation, the government issued a "hold the line" order. Restrictions, however, applied to hourly wages, not to weekly earnings. By working overtime, workers could still earn a good deal more money. Consequently, while wage rates rose by a relatively modest 24 percent during the war, weekly earnings rose by a tremendous 70 percent.

If wages were to be limited, workers wanted prices controlled as well. Early in 1942 Congress let the Office of Price Administration (OPA) fix maximum prices. The OPA soon set a ceiling on all prices.

Overall, however, a reasonable balance existed between wages and prices throughout the war. The **consumer price index** (CPI), a statistic showing the change in the prices of selected goods and services, rose about the same percentage as wages between 1939 and 1945.[2]

**Reducing Demand through Rationing**   One method the OPA used in hopes of keeping prices down was **rationing,** a way of distributing limited goods fairly. Rationing reduced demand because ration coupons were needed to purchase many goods, such as meat and butter. The OPA set up local rationing boards that set quotas for each family's coupons. Families received ration coupons based on the number of people in a household and their needs. They presented coupons when buying rationed items. Merchants, in turn, gave these coupons to suppliers in order to restock their shelves. In this way the government controlled demand and kept prices from rising.

Rationing was one of the most controversial elements of the war effort. Although Americans were earning more, government restrictions

**Every World War II family was familiar with ration coupons like these.** *Do you agree with the principle of rationing? Why or why not?*

limited their spending. They could afford automobiles and gasoline, but Detroit was producing tanks, not cars, and gasoline was limited. Because they found gasoline rationing so irritating, some Americans learned to bend the rules.

*I was a certified ski instructor and was with the National Ski Patrol, so the army hired me to certify skiers and mountaineers for the mountain troops that were trained in Leadville, Colorado. They gave me a 'C' card for an unlimited amount of gasoline to go skiing on the weekends. . . .*

*But you'd better believe I had a long waiting list of people to ride up to the mountains with me every weekend. One of the guys who went with me owned a small butcher shop and had a contract to supply a hotel, and he seemed to be able to get unlimited quantities of meat. So every month I turned my meat stamps over to him and was able to get meat anytime I wanted it. You had to work the angles—good old American ingenuity I guess—and it didn't hurt anything.*

As quoted by Archie Satterfield, *The Home Front,* 1981

**Paying for a Costly War**   World War II cost the United States ten times more than World War I. From 1941 to 1945, the government's operating budget was $321 billion, nearly twice as much as its total spending in the preceding 150 years. About 40 percent of the war costs were met by taxes; the government borrowed the rest.

Before the war began, many Americans did not pay any federal income tax. Only about 26 million tax returns were filed in 1941. In 1942 Congress passed a Revenue Act that FDR called "the greatest tax bill in American history." This legislation increased corporate taxes and required nearly all Americans to pay income taxes.

In 1943 Congress approved a system for withholding taxes through monthly payroll deductions. Now the modern tax structure, which had been laid in 1913 when Congress instituted a direct tax on income, was completed.

While taxes provided for 40 percent of the cost of

**Identifying Cause and Effect**
How did rationing help hold down inflation? Americans could buy only as much of a product as their share of ration coupons allowed. The amount they could buy was less than they would have purchased without rationing. As a result demand was held down. In theory, then, shortages would not develop, and so manufacturers and merchants would not raise prices.

**2** Why weren't wage restrictions more successful in bringing down inflation?

MYRON DAVIS, LIFE MAGAZINE

**Movie star Carole Lombard "sells" the war by selling over two million war bonds in one day at a rally in Indianapolis.** *How did such rallies boost the country's morale?*

later. Adult Americans bought bonds to help family members in the armed services, to invest their money safely, to preserve "the American way of life," to combat inflation, and to save for postwar purchases. When the war ended, Americans had saved $129 billion that they could spend on homes, appliances, and goods that they were unable to buy during the war.[3]

## Upholding a No-Strike Pledge

While the wages of many Americans increased dramatically during the war, not everyone shared in this prosperity. However, the major labor unions had issued a pledge that, as long as the war continued, their workers would not strike for higher salaries and better working conditions.

In return, the National War Labor Board enforced settlements between companies and their workers on hours, wages, and working conditions. It also had authority to seize plants whose owners refused to cooperate. The no-strike pledge, however, was not legally binding, and more than three million workers went on strike in 1943.

The most serious strikes occurred in the coal fields. Wages had been frozen in 1942, but prices and profits had continued to rise, and miners thought they were entitled to a raise. They were led by United Mine Workers president John L. Lewis. A miner himself, Lewis led nearly 450,000 coal miners out on strike in 1943 when the NWLB denied them a raise. At congressional hearings, when Lewis was reminded that the government was trying to hold down wages to control inflation, he replied, "Do you mind first inflating the stomachs of my members?"

After his pleas to miners to return to work failed, President Roosevelt took over the mines. When FDR was urged to put striking miners in jail, though, one adviser cautioned: "There are not enough jails in the country to hold these men, and, if there were, I must point out that a jailed miner produces no more coal than a striking miner." Eventually Lewis, the mine operators, and the administration agreed on a raise.

Workers in the coal, steel, and railroad industries went out on strike during the war. Despite these strikes, labor largely lived up to the no-strike pledge.

the war, the remaining 60 percent was paid for by borrowing, mostly from Americans. To borrow money, the government sold war bonds, certificates that promised the government would pay the holder the amount borrowed plus interest. The bonds also controlled inflation by reducing the money consumers had to spend and helped sell the war to the American public.

The Treasury Department recruited both Madison Avenue advertisers and Hollywood stars to help sell bonds. Creative public relations stunts boosted sales. The publishers of *Batman* comic books devoted a cover to a picture of their hero urging the purchase of war bonds. Hollywood stars traveled across the country to perform at bond rallies and auctioned their personal possessions. In the first big war bond sale in 1942, 337 actors and actresses participated, working eighteen hours a day.

Even children helped pay for the war. At the post office, they bought war stamps that they pasted into albums. When their stamps totaled $18.75, they received a war bond redeemable for $25 ten years

---

**STUDY GUIDE**

**Recognizing Points of View**
Compare the government's view on inflation and wage increases with that of the miners. The government focused on the broad economic picture in its efforts to control inflation and influence the

country's economy. Miners focused on their need to keep up with rising prices and improve their way of life. They also wanted a share of the increased profits the war brought to mine owners.

**3** How did the government finance the high cost of war?

MARGARET BOURKE-WHITE, LIFE MAGAZINE

**Entitled "Women in Steel," this photo shows women using acetylene torches to shape edges on armor plate for tanks at a plant in Gary, Indiana.**

## Recruiting New Workers

Over 15 million Americans left work to serve in the armed forces during the war. Many of the remaining adults, as well as adolescents, assumed those positions. As new war-related plants were built, the need for civilian workers increased dramatically.

At first, jobs were easily filled by the unemployed. Wartime labor demands wiped out the unemployment of the depression years and created other opportunities. Between 1940 and 1945, about 6 million women joined the civilian labor force. The proportion of women who worked rose from 27 to 37 percent as women replaced the men who were at war.

The labor shortage opened up doors for women in many occupations. The most startling increase in numbers of working women occurred in defense industries, such as airplane plants and shipyards, where female employment jumped by 460 percent. There women worked on assembly lines as welders, riveters, and mechanics. Although "Rosie the Riveter" transformed the nature of the labor force, women generally had a hard time gaining acceptance by male workers. Helen Studer, a riveter at Douglas Aircraft in Los Angeles during the war, told her story.

*The men really resented the women very much, and in the beginning it was a little bit rough. . . . The men that you worked with, after a while, they realized that it was essential that the women worked there, 'cause there wasn't enough men and the women were doing a pretty good job. So the resentment eased. However, I always felt that they thought it wasn't your place to be there.*

As reported by Sherna B. Gluck,
*Rosie the Riveter Revisited,* 1987

Three of every four new women workers were married. All women, however, suffered two disadvantages. They received 60 percent less pay than men, and they had little job security. The NWLB called for equal pay for equal work, but women were often placed in lower job classifications, so the gap between male and female earnings increased.

For the most part, women found that wartime opportunities were only temporary. As the war ended, so did their jobs. Between 1944 and 1946, about 4 million women either lost their jobs or left them.

Faced with mobilizing for the greatest international conflict in their history, American workers performed production miracles. They were rewarded with full employment and a higher standard of living. Yet fighting the war on the home front created new problems. Women entered the work force only to be pushed out at the end of the war. The war also strained the American family and society in new ways.

## SECTION REVIEW

**Checking Facts**

1. Define Gross National Product (GNP). How much did it grow during the war?
2. What is the consumer price index (CPI)?
3. What were some contributions volunteers made during the war?

**Thinking Critically**

4. **Recognizing Propaganda** Find an example of propaganda in one of the visuals used in this section. Explain its purpose. Is it effective? Why or why not?
5. **Identifying Cause and Effect** What effect did buying war bonds have on inflation?
6. **Recognizing Points of View** What problems did women face as they replaced men in the workplace?

**Linking Across Time**

7. How does selling bonds affect inflation? In what ways does the government attempt to influence the economy today?
8. In 1981 President Reagan fired air traffic controllers who would not return to work from an illegal strike. Was this an option for Roosevelt when the miners went out on strike? Why or why not?

# The War and Social Change

## 1941–1945: Americans Migrate

BETWEEN 1941 AND 1945 ONE IN EVERY FIVE AMERICANS MOVED FROM ONE AREA OF THE COUNTRY TO ANOTHER. AMONG THEM WERE OVER 700,000 AFRICAN Americans who left the South to escape grueling working hours, poverty, and demeaning segregation. Sybil Lewis was one of these Americans. This is what she said about leaving Oklahoma and heading west.

AP/ WIDE WORLD PHOTOS

*I had always been told that California was a liberal state and there was no segregation there. "Go west," that was the theme. "Everything is great in California, all doors are open, no prejudice, good jobs, plenty of money." . . . When I arrived, though, I found it wasn't quite the way I had imagined.*
*. . . In many ways California was no different from Oklahoma or the South, because people brought their feelings with them.*

As told to Mark Jonathan Harris, Franklin D. Mitchell, and Steven J. Schechter, *The Homefront*, 1984

### Americans on the Move

After the United States declared war, more than 15 million Americans joined the military. Blacks and whites who remained at home sought jobs that opened up in shipyards, aircraft plants, munitions factories, and military bases. This reshuffling made up the greatest short-term **migration,** or movement, of people in American history.

In general, Americans migrated from rural to urban areas, from the East to the West, and from the North to the South. The largest gains were in the Far West, which included California, Washington, and Oregon. Much of the wartime shipbuilding and airplane manufacturing took place there. More than 1.4 million Americans migrated to California alone. Next in population gain were Texas and the three South Atlantic states of Maryland, Florida, and Virginia.

Other areas of the country also grew. Big war contracts went to the auto manufacturers of Detroit and the arms manufacturers of New England. New arsenals, steel and other metal plants, and new military bases sprang up in both rural and urban areas.

The movement of Americans from farms to cities reflected both the wartime demand for workers and changes in American agriculture. Between 1940 and 1945, the number of farm workers fell by 11 percent while farm output increased more than 15 percent. By using more fertilizer and more machinery and by consolidating small farms into larger ones, fewer farmers were able to grow more crops.

It seemed that almost everyone in the United States was moving. Migrants drove until their cars' tires were worn smooth. Others stood on crowded trains and buses. Young wives with babies joined their husbands at defense jobs or in army camps. Old men and young boys went west and south for jobs.

---

### STUDY GUIDE

**As You Read**
Note the population shifts caused by military and civilian wartime needs and identify the problems that resulted. Also, think about the following concepts and skills.

**Central Concepts**
- understandinging the complex causes and effects of **migration**
- recognizing the role of **deficit spending** to counteract economic downturns

**Thinking Skills**
- recognizing stereotypes
- identifying cause and effect
- assessing outcomes

African Americans made up a large part of this migrating stream. In areas where most wartime production took place, the black population almost doubled. In contrast to other groups who stayed only temporarily, blacks tended to remain in their new homes.

One of the most congested areas was Mobile, Alabama. From 1940 to 1943, Mobile's population climbed by 61 percent. The novelist John Dos Passos described the impact of this sudden massive population growth on Mobile.

*S idewalks are crowded. Gutters are stacked with litter that drifts back and forth in the brisk spring wind. . . . Cues[lines] wait outside of movies and lunchrooms. The trailer army has filled all the open lots with its regular ranks. In cluttered backyards people camp out in tents and chickenhouses and shelters tacked together out of packingcases.*

John Dos Passos,
*State of the Nation,* 1944

## Boom Towns Emerge

Many migrants headed for large industrial cities. Others went to the small towns that grew into boom towns in the shadows of smoking defense plants and shipyards. The rapid growth of such communities overburdened services that Americans often took for granted. New arrivals looking for work in these places found housing scarce, medical facilities inadequate, sanitary conditions terrible, schools overcrowded, and day-care centers almost nonexistent.

Housing was a problem for almost all migrant war workers. The National Housing Agency figured that it had to house 9,000,000 migrating workers and their families during the war years. Thus, lodging for new workers was often temporary—barracks, trailers, and even tents.

Schools lacked money, teachers, and equipment. One high school in Mobile accommodated twice the number of students for which it was designed. Teachers there earned only $1,150 per year while a typist could make $1,440 and a laborer in the shipyards $2,600.

Perhaps the best known example of these boom town problems was Willow Run, a community located 27 miles west of Detroit. The Ford Motor Company built a huge factory to produce bomber planes there, and the factory attracted more than 32,000 people. They crowded into small trailers, drank impure water, and lived in dread of a fire or epidemic. Eventually, the government built about 10,000 units of temporary housing, which only partially solved the overcrowding.

Other boom towns experienced similar problems, though on a smaller scale. Pascagoula, Mississippi, a small town with a fine shipyard, nearly quadrupled its

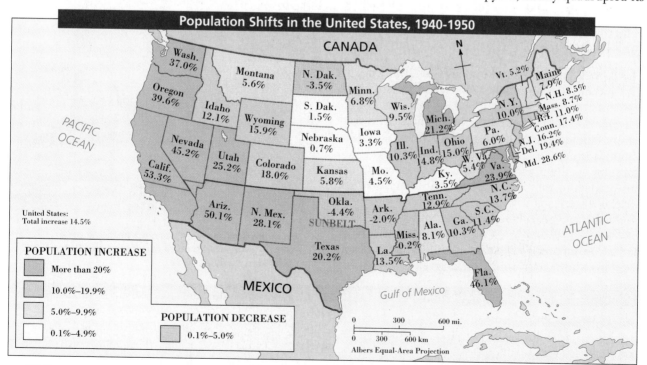

Population Shifts in the United States, 1940-1950

While some states experienced similar percentage increases in population, the actual number of people gained was quite different. For example, Nevada and Florida had similar percentage gains, but Nevada actually gained 50,000 people while Florida gained 874,000 people. *Which states experienced actual population loss?*

The Home Front     433

population during the war. Older residents often refused to accept the new arrivals. Recent arrivals complained that they were made to feel inferior because they lived in trailers instead of houses. Lacking an adequate sewage system, the town allowed waste to be discharged into a river, causing considerable ecological damage.

San Diego was once a quiet waterfront town, but an aircraft factory there grew from a work force of six in the 1930s to over 50,000 in the 1940s. In addition, San Diego was the home of the largest naval base on the West Coast as well as a thriving shipbuilding center. One longtime resident remembers the changes brought about by this population increase.

*W*e used to go to bed by ten, or anyway, by eleven. Now some theaters and cafes never close! I remember it was like that in the Klondike. Now when boatloads of sailors hurry ashore, and all those soldiers from Fort Rosecrans and Camp Callan swarm in on payday, this town goes crazy. In one day they eat 50,000 hot dogs! Even shoe shine boys get the jitters. Sherman's Cafe has ten bars, and a dance floor so big that 5,000 can dance at once.[1]

Quoted in *National Geographic*,
January, 1942

## Social Stresses Multiply

The rapid movement of migrants into new regions and cities created severe social stresses. Native residents of cities such as Los Angeles, San Diego, and Detroit often resented the newcomers. Midwesterners labeled the migrants from Arkansas, Oklahoma, Tennessee, and Kentucky "hillbillies" and stereotyped them as poor and lazy. Workers in the shipyards and factories discriminated against the African Americans who came in search of jobs. The situation was especially tense in Detroit.

**Racial Tensions Explode**  By 1943 Detroit was home to about half a million migrants, including many southern whites and 60,000 African Americans. As a result, housing, transportation, and recreational facilities were overcrowded. Most African Americans, both the newly arrived and native Detroiters, were wedged into an area called Paradise Valley. There, according to the Detroit Housing Commission, more than half the dwellings were substandard.

Bottled-up racial tensions finally erupted in violence on a hot summer night in June 1943. Picnickers, most of them African Americans, were returning home from a Sunday outing when a fight broke out. Nobody remembered why. Apparently some black teenagers had bumped a white sailor and his girlfriend. Sailors from the Navy Arsenal nearby joined the fray. As rumors spread of sexual assaults and murders, rioters smashed windows and stoned cars. Black crowds attacked white workers returning from the night shift. The overworked police force, short-handed because many experienced officers had joined the military, could not control the violence.

THE BETTMANN ARCHIVE

**An explosion showers burning gasoline on a passenger-packed trolley car during the Detroit race riots, June 21, 1943.**

The next day, Bloody Monday, large crowds of whites roamed up and down Detroit's main street in search of African Americans to beat or kill. Whites dragged blacks off trolley cars and beat them; police shot looters and battled it out with rooftop snipers. After a day of violence, the governor of Michigan requested federal assistance. Six thousand soldiers moved into Detroit to control the crowds and restore order. In the 36 hours of rioting, 25 blacks and nine whites lost their lives, and nearly 700 people were injured. Also, $2 million worth of property was destroyed.

Discrimination also led to other race riots in 1943. Black soldiers, who resented unfair treatment, inferior housing, and the brutality of military police, were involved in riots at nine army training camps, mostly in the South. In August 1943 Harlem exploded when rumors circulated that a white New York City policeman had killed a black soldier. Unlike the Detroit riot, the Harlem riot did not see pitched battles; however, five African Americans were killed and 410 people were injured before the police restored order.

UPI/BETTMANN

**Zoot-suiters wore long key chains that almost touched the ground. They also often sported knives and wide-brimmed hats.**

**The Zoot Suit Riots** African Americans were not the only minority group involved in violent clashes in the summer of 1943. Opportunities for farm workers in the Southwest brought thousands of Mexicans illegally to the United States. At the same time, many **Chicanos,** Americans of Mexican descent, shifted from agricultural work to industrial and manufacturing jobs. They worked at factories in and around Los Angeles. There, as elsewhere, they suffered discrimination and prejudice. They were segregated from other Americans, insulted by the police, and given only the lowest paying jobs.

In Los Angeles this prejudice turned to hatred of Hispanic American teenagers, many of whom wore zoot suits. A zoot suit included a long jacket that reached to the finger tips and had heavily padded shoulders and pleated trousers tightly tapered at the cuffs.

Mexican Americans did not have a monopoly on zoot suits, however. On the whole, zoot-suiters were young people seeking escape from the burdens of life in the slums. The zoot suit set them apart from the rest of society and served as a badge of independence. In Los Angeles, many of the zoot-suiters were underemployed teenagers, many of whom were caught between two cultures.

For several months, zoot-suiters and white sailors had clashed in Los Angeles. Sailors stationed at the nearby Chavez Ravine Naval Base blamed zoot-suiters for stabbing and robbing military personnel. In June they cruised the Mexican American sections of Los Angeles in cars, beating up people they found wearing zoot suits. Even though the sailors had started the trouble, the police arrested only the zoot-suiters. To end the violence, the city had to be declared off limits to naval personnel. When the city council outlawed zoot suits, the situation cooled.[2]

The violence in Los Angeles and other cities prompted Philip Murray, president of the Congress of Industrial Organizations (CIO), to write President Roosevelt. He urged the administration to prepare an educational campaign "to eradicate the misconceptions and prejudices" that had contributed to the riots. The president replied in a short note that read in part, "I join you and all true Americans in condemning mob violence, whatever form it takes and whoever its victims."

One idealistic black student had expected that Roosevelt would stand behind the demands of minorities for fair treatment. After Roosevelt's reply to Murray, she expressed her feelings of hopelessness in this poem entitled "Mr. Roosevelt Regrets."

*What'd you get, black boy,*
*  When they knocked you down in*
*    the gutter,*
*And they kicked your teeth out,*
*And they broke your skull with clubs,*
*And they bashed your stomach in?*

**Identifying Cause and Effect**
The spread of mob violence in the Detroit and zoot suit riots had many contributing factors. Police forces were understaffed, tension had been increasing for months, and mob psychology took over. Mob psychology allows individuals to abdicate responsibility for their actions. This enables large groups to act in violent ways that individuals would never attempt on their own.

2  Explain how living conditions and changing populations contributed to the riots in Detroit and Los Angeles.

*What'd you get when the police shot you in the back,*
*And they chained you to the beds*
*While they wiped the blood off?*
*What'd you get when you cried out to the Top Man?*
*When you called the man next to God, as you thought,*
*And you asked him to speak out to save you?*
*What'd the Top Man say, black boy?*
*Mr. Roosevelt regrets. . . .*

Pauli Murray,
as printed in *The Crisis*, August 1943

## *Wartime Family Stresses*

Other stresses caused by the war itself fell indiscriminately on both whites and blacks. As families migrated, children and adolescents moved from familiar neighborhoods to strange surroundings. Men and women worked long hours of overtime at their defense jobs, sometimes leaving children unattended. Single parent families became common as men went into the armed forces leaving their wives and children behind.

As more mothers of young children took jobs, newspapers and magazines complained about "latchkey children" and "eight-hour orphans." Agnes Meyer, the wife of the publisher of the *Washington Post*, traveled around the country investigating social conditions in boom towns. She wrote:

*In the San Fernando Valley, in the city limits of Los Angeles, where several war plants are located, a social worker counted 45 infants locked in cars of a single parking space [lot]. In Vallejo, the children sit in the movies, seeing the same film over and over again until mother comes off the swing shift and picks them up. Some children of working parents are locked in their homes, others locked out.*

Agnes E. Meyer,
*Journey Through Chaos*, 1943

Teenagers were also often left to care for themselves. Unlike younger children, though, teenagers could find jobs of their own. From 1940 to 1944, the number of teenage workers nearly tripled to 2.9 million. More than a million teenagers dropped out of school. Although child labor laws governed the kind of work they did and the number of hours they worked, these laws were often ignored. Because of the widespread disregard for these laws, nineteen states extended the number of hours teenagers could work.

With teenagers left to fend for themselves in a society, it was not surprising that juvenile delinquency increased. During the war years, a widely viewed documentary film, *Youth in Crisis*, aroused public concern. The film described how adolescents, abandoned by their parents and subjected to wartime stress, picked up a "spirit of recklessness and violence." To help curb rising juvenile delinquency, some communities enforced curfews.

Even though the war caused new problems for American children, many later remembered this period as the most exciting time of their lives. Memories include collecting scrap, watching war movies in which the "good guys" always won, and being intensely interested in news of the war.[3]

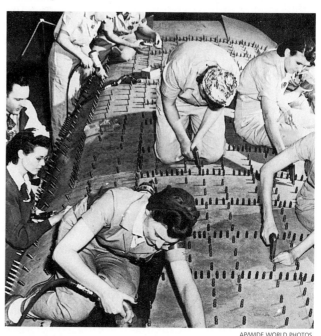

AP/WIDE WORLD PHOTOS

**These students are turning out the covering for the belly of a military transport.** *How did women working affect family life in the United States?*

STUDY·GUIDE

**Assessing Outcomes**
Juvenile delinquency and "latchkey" children were much publicized during the war. Did this "neglect" of the young cause a rise in crime later in the United States or affect the stability of

American society? The country suffered no later ill effects, and, in fact, memories of the home front during the war were positive.

3 Describe some of the conditions that teenagers dealt with during the war.

# The New Deal Comes to an End

In December 1943 President Roosevelt announced that "Dr. New Deal" had outlived his usefulness and would have to make way for "Dr. Win-the-War." This was simply a way of saying that military objectives needed to take priority over social reform. However, many of the New Deal programs, such as Social Security, unemployment compensation, old-age benefits, and the Tennessee Valley Authority (TVA) had become, and would remain, a permanent part of American life. Even the generally conservative Republican party, by 1944, incorporated most New Deal programs into its platform.

Both liberals and conservatives, however, agreed with the president to shelve any reforms that could interfere with war production. For example, bringing electricity to rural areas had to be postponed since copper wire was needed for military purposes. The work week was lengthened from 40 to 48 hours in order to boost industrial output. Many antitrust prosecutions were suspended so as not to interfere with efficiently run businesses. Child labor laws were changed to permit teenagers to join the labor force. "Progressives should understand that programs which do not forward the war must be given up or drastically curtailed," wrote David Lilienthal, head of the TVA.

The war made it possible to phase out a number of New Deal agencies. These included the Civilian Conservation Corps, the Works Progress Administration, and the National Youth Administration. Congress had created these agencies to ease unemployment. With full employment during the war, they were no longer needed.

However, World War II extended the New Deal in some respects by continuing the role of government in economic planning. Wartime economic growth convinced many people that government spending could ensure full employment and prosperity. In the future the government would resort to **deficit spending,** using borrowed money, to counteract economic downturns.

AP/WIDE WORLD

**After World War II, people indulged in the latest fads. Here, members of New York's Madison Square Boys Club wear special glasses to read their "3-D comics."**

The war also made possible the election of Franklin D. Roosevelt to an unprecedented fourth term as president in 1944. However, his margin of victory over Republican Thomas E. Dewey was the narrowest in all of his four campaigns.

Americans on the home front suffered from housing shortages, overcrowding, a breakdown of law and order, and juvenile delinquency during the war years. At the same time, most people reaped the financial rewards of a wartime, full-employment economy. Although minority groups had not yet reaped many benefits, the war did provide new opportunities in employment and enabled them to make some headway in their struggle for civil rights. Some of the New Deal reform measures had to be set aside during the war but were not forgotten. They would be taken up again when the war ended.

## SECTION REVIEW

### Checking Facts

1. What areas of the country experienced a permanent increase in population as a result of wartime migration?

2. What characteristics did boom towns share?

3. What characteristics made up the zoot suit culture?

4. Define deficit spending as it relates to the government.

### Thinking Critically

5. **Recognizing Stereotypes** Why might stereotyping lead to discrimination?

6. **Identifying Cause and Effect** What effect did the war have on New Deal agencies and reforms?

7. **Assessing Outcomes** How did the migration of Americans during the war affect industrial cities in the short and long run?

### Linking Across Time

8. How do the destinations of wartime migrants compare to migration within the United States today?

9. Compare the problems of working mothers during the war with those of today's working mothers.

# The Big Band Era

*Newspaper headlines screamed of battles and bombings. In thousands of windows hung blue stars, telling that loved ones had gone to war. Factories rumbled with assembly lines manned by both women and men. Paychecks hit an all-time high, but there was little to buy—everything from silk to steel fueled the war. No wonder people turned to entertainment for escape.*

**Big-name bands like Count Basie's** helped wipe away people's wartime woes. The Count could tickle the 88 without missing a beat, all the while sending musical cues to his band.

**Slicked-back hair**

**Jitterbuggers** went wild in the war years with routines that demanded rhythm and stamina. Couples jived to both big-name bands and juke box platters.

# KILROY WAS HERE

This whimsical character named **Kilroy** became the GI's graffiti. Scribbled on walls, bunkers, and latrines, Kilroy let everyone know GI Joe had been there.

Comedian **Bob Hope** quipped his way to stardom in the forties. He teamed with crooner Bing Crosby and sarong-queen Dorothy Lamour in "Road to Bali," one in a series of "road" films that began during WWII. Hope also hit the road to entertain troops at home and overseas.

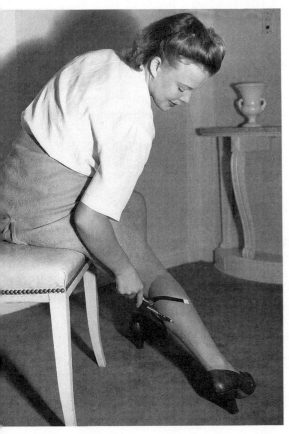

When silk and nylon went to war to make parachutes, women painted their legs with makeup, simulating **stockings**. They even drew seams—with difficulty, of course.

When **blue stars in windows** turned to gold, a passerby knew someone within had died in battle. Alleta Sullivan of Waterloo, Iowa, lost all five sons at once when their ship was sunk off Guadalcanal.

# The War and Civil Rights

## 1941: Racist Hiring Practices Meet with Resistance

ALTHOUGH AFRICAN AMERICANS FOUGHT AND DIED FOR THE UNITED STATES IN BOTH WORLD WARS, THEY FACED DISCRIMINATION AS THEY SEARCHED FOR JOBS AT home. The hiring policy of North American Aviation, one of the nation's largest aircraft manufacturers, was typical of the discrimination practiced by many companies. The president of North American Aviation publicly stated its policy in 1941.

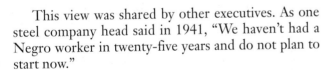
AP/ WIDE WORLD PHOTOS

*While we are in complete sympathy with the Negro, it is against company policy to employ them as aircraft workers or mechanics . . . regardless of their training, but there will be some jobs as janitors for Negroes.*

As quoted by Daniel S. Davis,
*Mr. Black Labor,* 1972

This view was shared by other executives. As one steel company head said in 1941, "We haven't had a Negro worker in twenty-five years and do not plan to start now."

## Civil Rights Movement Grows

DURING World War II, the demands of African Americans for equal treatment grew louder. Many whites as well as blacks came to recognize the uncomfortable similarity between racial tensions in the United States and Hitler's belief in a superior race. A leading black newspaper, the *Amsterdam News,* deplored the "race discrimination and segregation, mob brutality—the entire Nazi pattern of U.S. racial conditions."

**Racism** is the belief that race determines human capacities and that some races are superior to others. Racism was the basis for the system of segregation and discrimination that existed in law and in fact throughout most of the United States. For many years anthropologists had been challenging the once popular idea that certain races were superior. By the 1940s scholars considered doctrines of racial supremacy to be unscientific and false. The differences that mattered, they said, were not between races but between individuals. Racial traits or characteristics were really a product of environmental influences, they concluded.

White Americans who continued to justify segregation felt increasingly uncomfortable with comparisons of American discrimination and Hitler's theories of racial superiority. One southern politician conceded in 1944 that the Nazis "have wrecked the theories of the master race with which we were so contented so long."

African Americans responded to this heightened awareness of racism with a new militancy. As they moved from the South, where they could not vote, to the North and West, African Americans began to flex their political muscles. They became more vocal, insisting on opportunities that they had long been denied. Some picketed factories with signs such as: HITLER MUST OWN THIS PLANT, NEGROES

---

**STUDY·GUIDE**

**As You Read**
Recognize the effects of the war in Europe on civil rights and civil liberties in the United States. Also, think about the following concepts and skills.

**Central Concepts**
- understanding how **racism** affected the lives of African Americans in the United States
- recognizing the role of **civil disobedience** in gaining civil rights

**Thinking Skills**
- recognizing assumptions
- predicting consequences
- assessing outcomes
- recognizing bias
- analyzing decisions

CAN'T WORK HERE. IF WE MUST FIGHT, WHY CAN'T WE WORK?

The black press pushed a "Double V" campaign—victory at home as well as abroad. They insisted that fighting the war should not diminish the struggle for equality; on the contrary, progress toward equality should help win the war.

## A March on Washington

In the South, blacks were legally segregated from whites in all public facilities. In much of the rest of the country, trains, buses, restaurants, and movie theaters were segregated, too. Throughout the nation, poverty kept most African Americans confined to slums and ghettos, and those who could afford better housing faced exclusion by homeowners and real estate salespeople in middle-class neighborhoods.

The war led civil rights groups to develop new forms of protest against these injustices. In the summer of 1941, A. Philip Randolph led the movement for black equality. The son of a minister, he had grown up in the South where the Ku Klux Klan terrorized African Americans to keep them in line. After arriving in New York in 1906 at the age of 17, Randolph attended college at night and worked at various jobs during the day.

Quiet but determined, Randolph became a respected leader of African Americans. By following his goal of "creating unrest among the Negroes," Randolph eventually became known as the Father of the Civil Rights Movement.

Randolph's leadership qualities first surfaced in 1925 when he led a movement to organize the porters who worked on the sleeping cars of the nation's trains. The Brotherhood of Sleeping Car Porters that Randolph organized worked to obtain higher wages and better working conditions for its members. New Deal reforms prior to the war, such as the Wagner Act,

helped the organization win its fight to bargain as a union.

By May 1941 Randolph had turned his energies to battles in the national political arena. He was appalled by discrimination in the armed forces, in which African Americans had already fought for their country during World War I. The exclusion of African Americans from well-paying jobs in war industries to which billions of federal dollars were flowing also angered him. To help right these wrongs, Randolph organized a March on Washington Movement (MOWM). Supporters rallied behind the slogan, "We Loyal American Citizens Demand the Right to Work and Fight for Our Country."[1]

Randolph's approach differed from the mainstream civil rights organization of the time, the National Association for the Advancement of Colored People (NAACP). The NAACP, the largest organization fighting for equal treatment for blacks, urged African Americans to "persuade, embarrass, compel and shame our government and our nation" to end discrimination. In contrast to the NAACP, Randolph

AP/WIDE WORLD PHOTOS

**Asa Philip Randolph, seated on the right, is shown above before the Senate Armed Services Committee testifying that millions of African Americans would refuse to register for or be drafted into the military unless racial segregation and discrimination ended. The photograph on the left shows African American members of an engineer battalion in Algeria during World War II lining up for noon mess.**

THE BETTMANN ARCHIVE

called for direct action, a "thundering march" on Washington rather than the use of cumbersome political and legal processes. In addition, Randolph demanded changes that would benefit northern urban blacks as well as those living in the South. Finally, he excluded white people from the MOWM because he maintained that the victims of discrimination must assume responsibility for abolishing it. "No one will fight as hard to remove and relieve pain as he who suffers from it," Randolph counseled.

**Roosevelt and Randolph Compromise**  As preparations for the March on Washington moved ahead, government officials began to worry. Roosevelt wanted to prevent the march, which would embarrass the government. He was also afraid that a march that brought 50,000 to 100,000 people to Washington might end in violence. The president sent his wife, Eleanor, as well as government officials, to persuade Randolph to call off the march. To show his sympathy, Roosevelt even publicly condemned job discrimination and ordered his defense chiefs to do something about it.

When Randolph refused to call off the march, Roosevelt finally met with him. Randolph demanded three key changes in government policy, all of which could be brought about by an executive order of the president. First, he wanted defense contracts denied to employers who practiced discrimination. Next, he asked that job segregation in federal agencies be abolished. Finally, he asked for the desegregation of the armed forces.

Randolph did not get all he demanded, but his threat of a mass demonstration in the nation's capital marked a real

breakthrough in equal treatment and opportunities for African Americans. Roosevelt's Executive Order 8802, issued on June 25, 1941, stipulated that government agencies, job training programs, and defense contractors put an end to discrimination. It also created the Fair Employment Practices Committee (FEPC) to investigate violations of the order. The president, however, did not agree to integrate the armed forces.

As Randolph canceled the march, black leaders hailed the Executive Order as a major step forward. However, the MOWM did not disband. Randolph continued to urge mass marches and protest rallies to focus attention on discrimination. He also encouraged boycotts of segregated facilities and acts of **civil disobedience** to show nonviolent opposition to government laws or policies. Black protesters willingly accepted punishment for such illegal actions.[2]

**Other Victories**  Encouraged by Randolph's success in protesting discrimination, other black civil rights leaders organized the Congress of Racial Equality (CORE) in 1942. CORE continued the

| Occupation | Percentage of Work Force | |
|---|---|---|
| | 1940 | 1944 |
| Agriculture | 32.1% | 21% |
| Business, repair, and recreation | 1.5% | 1.2% |
| Construction | 2.5% | 1.9% |
| Domestic services | 36.5% | 29.3% |
| Government | 1.2% | 3.5% |
| Manufacturing | 9.5% | 18.3% |
| Mining | 0.9% | 2.1% |
| Professional services | 4.3% | 5.3% |
| Trade and finance | 8.1% | 11.9% |
| Transportation and utilities | 3.4% | 5.5% |

**African American Job Distribution Before and During War**

**This graph shows some of the gains made by African Americans in nonagricultural jobs during World War II.** *Despite these gains, which job remained number one?*

**STUDY GUIDE**

**Predicting Consequences**
What consequences did government officials fear would result from the March on Washington? The march would embarrass the government in the eyes of its allies. Also, Roosevelt

feared the large number of marchers might lead to rioting and violence. This would endanger human life and personal property.

2  Summarize and evaluate the Roosevelt–Randolph compromise. What did each side have to concede? What did each side gain?

## The FEPC Fights Discrimination

Through the efforts of the NAACP, CORE, and MOWM, but mainly due to the critical labor shortage during the war, the share of jobs held by African Americans in war industries grew. The Fair Employment Practices Committee (FEPC) helped open up some jobs in the federal government for African Americans and Hispanic Americans.

But the FEPC faced major obstacles in battling racial discrimination. The committee could act only on formal complaints about hiring practices or discrimination on the job, but many people were afraid to file complaints. Moreover, the committee's authority was severely limited. The FEPC was given no power to enforce its orders but had to rely on support from other federal agencies. For example, the only action the FEPC could take against defense contractors who discriminated against minorities was to recommend that their government contract be canceled. However, since canceling defense contracts would jeopardize military production, the cancellation was unlikely to occur.

The FEPC was equally ineffective when the railroad unions ignored its order to end discrimination. Other government agencies reasoned that the United States could not afford a nationwide transportation walkout in wartime.

The committee also fought public opinion which was prejudiced against it. Members of Congress, especially southern Democrats, claimed the agency fostered racial discord and saw it as a first step toward communism. The FEPC withstood a congressional investigation, but it had to fight with Congress for every scarce dollar that it received.

Far from being a radical organization, the FEPC was led by moderates who moved slowly and cautiously. Significantly, the FEPC did not consider segregation, as opposed to discrimination, a cause for action. In several instances, the FEPC approved the creation of separate facilities for black and white workers.

In all, the FEPC received 8,000 complaints, only one-third of which were resolved successfully. More often than not, employers defied its directives. In the summer of 1945, just before the war ended, Congress

UPI/BETTMAN

**This photograph shows a skilled worker fitting the sidings of U.S. warships during World War II.**

strategy of mobilizing mass resistance to discrimination and employed acts of nonviolent civil disobedience such as sit-ins at movie theaters and restaurants. Through the use of such tactics, shunned by more conservative organizations, CORE helped end segregation in public accommodations in several northern cities.

Meanwhile, the membership of the NAACP grew. By 1946 its membership had risen to 450,000, almost ten times the membership in 1940. The NAACP continued to rely on traditional, noncontroversial means of protesting such as education, political pressure, and legal action. The organization won an important victory in 1944 when the Supreme Court ruled that it was unconstitutional to bar African Americans from voting in Democratic primaries in eight southern states. In *Smith v. Allwright*, the Court held that political parties were agents of the state and they could not nullify the right to vote by practicing racial discrimination. **3**

The Home Front     443

slashed the FEPC's budget in half and shortly there-after dissolved the agency. **4**

## *Internment of Japanese Americans*

Generally, World War II brought about few re-strictions on **civil liberties**, or rights guaranteed to all citizens. Almost no one vocally opposed the war after Pearl Harbor, and little danger existed of an attack on the United States. As a result, there was not a repetition of the hysteria and pressure to conform that occurred during World War I. Most Americans showed tolerance toward persons of foreign ancestry, including citizens of German and Italian descent. The treatment of Japanese Americans, however, became the exception.

Spring 1942 brought events that are burned into the memories of Japanese Americans. Despite the fact that they showed no evidence of disloyalty, over 100,000 Japanese Americans were moved from their homes to relocation camps. One evacuee, Helen Murao, explained why. "We looked like them [the enemy]. That was our sin."

Of the 110,000 Japanese Americans who lived on the West Coast and in Hawaii, about one-third were **Issei**—foreign-born Japanese who had entered the United States before the National Origins Act of 1924 dramatically cut the number of immigrants allowed into the country. Two-thirds were **Nisei**—mainly children of Issei who were citizens because they had been born in the United States. In February 1942, the government decided that all Japanese Americans, citizens as well as aliens, would be relocated from their homes and confined in internment camps located in Arkansas and the western states.

Japanese Americans were vulnerable because they could easily be singled out and they lacked political power. In addition, they had little economic influence.

Popular sentiment against Japanese Americans on the West Coast grew intense after the bombing of Pearl Harbor. The *San Francisco Chronicle* pushed to have the Japanese interned. Others, including California's Attorney General Earl Warren (later Chief Justice of the Supreme Court) and several members

MUSEUM OF HISTORY AND INDUSTRY, SEATTLE, WASHINGTON

**On March 30, 1942, Japanese American evacuees are led from their homes on Bainbridge Island, Washington. According to regulations, they are taking only what they can carry with them.** *What does the armed escort suggest about the nature of their relocation?*

## STUDY GUIDE

### Recognizing Bias

Many Americans used the war with Japan as a pretext to express racial bias that was already present. People feared that Japanese Americans would betray the United States, despite the fact that no evidence of such activities existed. On the contrary, the Japanese American community had shown itself to be comprised of hardworking, constructive, and loyal citizens.

**4** Recount some difficulties encountered by the FEPC. What kind of resistance do you think it would have met if it *had* considered segregation as a sign of discrimination?

AP/ WIDE WORLD PHOTOS

**Shigeo Nagaishi and his Nisei family find broken windows in their home and garage when they return to Seattle, Washington, from the relocation center in Hunt, Idaho, on May 10, 1945.**

of Congress, supported relocating Japanese Americans. Finally, on February 19, 1942, President Roosevelt signed Executive Order 9066 authorizing the removal of Japanese Americans from the West Coast.

The Executive Order subjected Japanese Americans to extreme economic hardship. Since they were permitted to take only a few belongings with them to the camps, they were forced to sell most of their possessions. Bargain hunters descended on their farms and businesses to take advantage of the evacuees. Signs began to appear reading: EVACUATION SALE—FURNITURE MUST ALL BE SOLD. In the end most Japanese families received about five cents for every dollar's worth of their possessions. Property not immediately sold was either stored or left with friends. Much of this was stolen, vandalized, or sold through legal loopholes. Even more devastating was the loss of real property—farms, houses, and places of business. Estimates of this loss hover around $500 million.

Over the course of several months, the Japanese Americans were ordered to report to relocation centers. The military justified this action on the basis that Japanese Americans would commit sabotage to aid Japan in an attack on the West Coast. General John DeWitt, head of the Western Defense Command argued: "The very fact that no sabotage to aid Japan has taken place to date is a disturbing and confirming indication that such action will be taken."

But other motives were equally important. Farmers and business associations thought they would gain from eliminating Japanese American competitors. Politicians believed they would increase their popular support by favoring relocation. General DeWitt expressed the commonly held view, "the Japanese race is an enemy race."[5]

From the relocation centers, Japanese Americans were moved to one of ten armed and guarded internment camps located in sparsely settled areas. For example, Topaz, a camp in Utah, was 4,600 feet above sea level. Here inmates endured temperatures ranging from 106° F in summer to minus 30° F in winter. They also lived in a constant whirlwind of dust.

The other camps were similarly barren. Japanese Americans taken to Heart Mountain, Wyoming, suffered from winter temperatures as low as 30° F below zero. For those from the mild California valleys, the camps were tolerable at best. One camp resident wrote a poem in the camp newspaper, the *Sentinel.*

*S now upon the rooftop*
*Snow upon the coal;*
*Winter in Wyoming—*
*Winter in my soul.*

## STUDY GUIDE

**Analyzing Decisions**

The evacuation decision was based on many factors: the economic gain of special interest groups, the prejudice against Asian Americans, and the ease of identifying Japanese Americans.

The fact that an absence of sabotage was cited as proof that it was likely to happen casts doubt on whether national security was the main consideration in making the decision.

5  What factors, in addition to prejudice, led to the internment of Japanese Americans?

One evacuee, Peter Ota, recalled that the camp was in a

*Desolate, flat, barren area. The barracks was all there was. There were no trees, no kind of landscaping. It was like a prison camp. Coming from our environment, it was just devastating.*

As quoted by Studs Terkel,
*"The Good War,"* 1984

This was no exaggeration. Entire families lived in a single room in the barracks, sparsely furnished with cots, makeshift dressers, and bare light bulbs.

Despite the stark surroundings, the evacuees created a number of alternative communities to serve their cultural needs. The Japanese Americans published newspapers, started schools, churches, bands, Boy Scout groups, softball leagues, built tennis courts, landscaped flower and vegetable gardens, and gave trumpet and tap dancing lessons. They were determined to replenish their lives with the dignity and resources that they and their children would need when the war was over.

Some of the evacuees were released to work at jobs in the interior of the United States before the end of the war. They were allowed to resettle in the East or Midwest. Most, however, remained in the camps for the duration of the war.

The Supreme Court upheld the wartime policies that deprived Japanese Americans of their civil rights. In 1943, in *Hirabayashi v. United States*, the Court unanimously decided that a curfew order affecting only Japanese Americans did not violate their constitutional rights. Chief Justice Harlan Fiske Stone wrote that "In time of war residents having ethnic affiliations with an invading enemy may be a greater source of danger than those of a different ancestry."

In December 1944, in *Korematsu v. United States*, the Court upheld the order providing for the relocation of Japanese Americans. It based its decision largely on the grounds that the judiciary could not second-guess military decisions. One of the dissenting justices, however, termed the decision a "legalization of racism." Nevertheless the Court also ruled that citizens could not be held in relocation centers once their loyalty had been established. By then, however, the camps were being closed down.

The United States recorded both gains and losses in the areas of civil rights and civil liberties during the war years. While African Americans fought hard to win the smallest of victories, Japanese Americans found themselves regarded as enemies of the United States and suffered humiliation and a loss of their liberties. However, as the war ended all Americans looked ahead and hoped for prosperity and justice in a peaceful postwar world.

NATIONAL ARCHIVES

**President Ronald Reagan signs Public Law 100-383 on August 10, 1988. Among other things, this law makes apologies and restitution of $1.25 billion to individuals of Japanese ancestry who were interned during World War II. This amounts to $20,000 in tax-free payments per eligible person over a ten-year period.** *What does this law indicate about government attitudes regarding the Japanese internment?*

## SECTION REVIEW

**Checking Facts**

1. What is racism?
2. How did Randolph's approach to protest differ from that of the National Association for the Advancement of Colored People?
3. What steps did Roosevelt take to stop the March on Washington Movement?
4. Explain ways in which the Japanese Americans adjusted to life inside the internment camps.

**Thinking Critically**

5. **Analyzing Decisions** What factors kept Roosevelt from making Executive Order 8802 stronger?
6. **Recognizing Bias** Why were people afraid to file complaints to the Fair Employment Practices Committee?

**Linking Across Time**

7. Explain one reason protesters continue to use civil disobedience.

8. Do you think Public Law 100-383 signed by President Reagan provided adequate compensation for victims of internment? Why?
9. What methods does the government employ today to help alleviate racial discrimination?

# Reading Economic Graphs

During the 1920s and 1930s, dramatic economic changes affected many Americans. For example, the factory production of automobiles experienced a wave pattern of rising production, peak, declining production, and bottom. Patterns of this kind—in prices, interest rates, or wages—form what is called a business cycle. Business cycle graphs can help you visualize the direction and extent of economic change.

## Learning the Skill

Line graphs illustrate change over time. A business cycle graph, such as the one below, is a particular kind of line graph that shows changes in economic activity, as measured by the value of goods and services produced. The line in the center of the graph represents a long-term trend, an average based on the level of economic activity over a period of years. The long-term trend on the graph below is recorded as zero and is meant to show variances from the long-term trend.

The horizontal axis indicates the years the graph covers. The vertical axis gives the percentages above and below the long-term trend. The data line compares the value of goods and services produced at any time to the trend.

To interpret a business cycle graph, first compare the data line to the trend line. For example, find the lowest level of economic activity in 1925. The value of goods and services produced at that time was about 4 percent more than the long-term trend.

### Rising and Falling Production

A downward slope of the data line, such as the one from 1929 to 1931, indicates falling production. An upward slope, such as the one during 1933, shows rising production.

In a business cycle, economic activity may rise higher or fall lower than the trend. Alternatively, a complete cycle may occur either above or below the trend line and may last for any length of time. During 1933 Americans experienced a complete cycle without once reaching the level of the long-term trend.

### Supply and Demand

Now trace the business cycle that began in the early 1940s. At that time government spending on such war materials as weapons, ships, and aircraft boosted production. To meet rising production, manufacturers hired more workers. More people with more money to spend further increased demand and production.

In 1942 thousands of American men left their jobs to serve in the armed forces. Production dropped. Soon other Americans filled the open positions, stopping the decline in production.

## Practicing the Skill

1. On the graph below find the business cycle that began with rising production during 1942. When did this cycle end?
2. Describe the economic effect of the war's end in 1945.
3. During which Depression years might Americans have felt most hopeful? Explain.

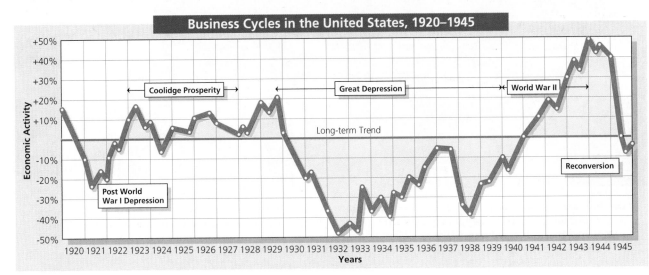

**Business Cycles in the United States, 1920–1945**

## The Internment Camps: A Story in Pictures

*P*hotographs provide rich visual evidence about past events. Historians search long and hard for photos—everywhere from the National Archives in Washington, D.C., to your great-grandmother's album. Photographs provide information unavailable anywhere else. They describe the settings of events more precisely than words, and they reveal people's emotions by letting us read their facial expressions. Photographs are especially good at answering questions like "What was it like to live in that time? In that place?"

### The Evidence

Photographs tell the story of the more than 100,000 Japanese Americans who spent much of World War II confined in internment camps.

Study the photos on these pages. What do they show about the locations of the camps? What do they suggest about the people and how they spent their time; how they felt about being interned; their qualities of mind and spirit? Which photos suggest contradictions between what the United States stood for and what the United States actually did?

### The Interpretation

The photographs on these pages present facts and feelings. They describe the inhospitable

LIBRARY OF CONGRESS

On their way to the internment camps, the Japanese Americans were placed in temporary detention camps like this one at Salinas, California. Families were allowed to take along only as many possessions as they could carry, and many carried their household goods in large bundles tied together with rope.

**Mrs. Shigeko Kitamoto and her three children await transportation to a Japanese American internment camp. Notice the tags, which identify the children by number.**

environments where most of the camps were built—desolate places that no one had ever lived in before or since. The photographs suggest the confusion and sadness that people felt at being uprooted. They also show the energy, ingenuity, and creativity of people who, in adverse situations, worked hard to make their own lives and their children's lives rich and productive.

When a photographer aims a camera, the viewfinder frames only a small part of the scene. The photographer chooses what to include and what to omit. Thus, like words, photos often reflect personal opinion, or bias —the photographer's own point of view. What examples on these pages express a photographer's viewpoint? What did each photographer focus on, and why? What might have been left out? What values do the photographs reflect? Does bias in a photograph help or hinder the historian who

wishes to use it as evidence? Might it do both? How?

The possible bias of the photographer is one limitation in the historian's use of photographs as evidence. Another is that you often need more information to grasp a photo's message fully. You would miss the irony, or contradiction, in one of the photos below if you didn't know more than it shows—that the garden is a Victory Garden, and that the gardeners are loyal Americans held under military guard.

Finally, photos can serve in ways that go well beyond their original purpose. In recent years internment photos, along with other evidence, were used to document the breach of civil rights suffered by Japanese Americans in the 1940s. Such documentation built support for making redress

to those who were interned. In 1988 Congress voted to make payments totaling $20,000 to each Japanese American interned during World War II. In this case, photos did more than record history; they helped to make it.

## Further Exploration

Ask older relatives to show you photos taken when they were young. If possible, bring some of those photos to class and discuss what they reveal about life in the forties, fifties, sixties, and so forth.

If you cannot get old family photos, bring in three or four recent ones taken by you or someone else. Show your pictures to classmates. Choose a classmate's photo, one you never saw before, and tell what it shows about American life today.

**The Japanese Americans shown above are cultivating a large community Victory Garden in the camp at Manzanar, California. The barracks in the background were typical, with four families sharing one barracks.**

# Chapter 13 Review

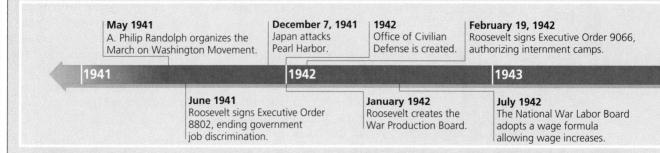

**May 1941**
A. Philip Randolph organizes the March on Washington Movement.

**December 7, 1941**
Japan attacks Pearl Harbor.

**1942**
Office of Civilian Defense is created.

**February 19, 1942**
Roosevelt signs Executive Order 9066, authorizing internment camps.

1941     1942     1943

**June 1941**
Roosevelt signs Executive Order 8802, ending government job discrimination.

**January 1942**
Roosevelt creates the War Production Board.

**July 1942**
The National War Labor Board adopts a wage formula allowing wage increases.

## Summary

Use the following outline as a tool for reviewing and summarizing the chapter. Copy the outline on your own paper, leaving spaces between headings to jot down notes about key events and concepts.

**I. Mobilizing the Home Front**
 A. Building National Morale
 B. Staging a Production Miracle
 C. Directing a Wartime Economy
 D. Upholding a No-Strike Pledge
 E. Recruiting New Workers

**II. The War and Social Change**
 A. Americans on the Move
 B. Boom Towns Emerge
 C. Social Stresses Multiply
 D. Wartime Family Stresses
 E. The New Deal Comes to an End

**III. The War and Civil Rights**
 A. Civil Rights Movement Grows
 B. A March on Washington
 C. The FEPC Fights Discrimination
 D. Internment of Japanese Americans

## Ideas, Events, and People

1. The U.S. government spent $321 billion between 1941 and 1945, nearly twice as much as it had spent in the preceding 150 years. How did the government raise the money to finance World War II?
2. How did rationing help the war effort?
3. What is civil disobedience? Who used civil disobedience between 1941 and 1945 and what did they accomplish?
4. Explain why inflation occurred during the war and how the government tried to fight it.
5. Who was John L. Lewis?

6. What are some of the advantages and disadvantages that society experienced as a result of having women enter the work force during World War II?
7. Describe migration patterns in the United States during World War II.
8. How did Executive Order 9066 come about?
9. What aspects of the New Deal became a permanent part of U.S. political policy?
10. Give examples of how the war furthered the cause of racial equality.

## Social Studies Skills

**Reading Economic Graphs**
Business cycle graphs are line graphs that show changes in economic activity relative to some long-term trend. Such information indicates shorter-term phases, or cycles, which exceed or fall short of the long-term trends. Look at the graph on page 447.
1. During which decade was the business cycle entirely below the long-term trend?
2. Compare the business cycle during 1924 to the cycle during 1941. How do these cycles differ?

## Critical Thinking

1. **Recognizing Bias**
Even though navy personnel roamed the streets of Los Angeles in 1943 beating zoot-suiters, only the zoot-suiters were arrested. What can you infer about the attitudes of the arresting police officers?

2. **Recognizing Assumptions**
How did the military justify the relocation of Japanese Americans? On what assumptions was the justification based?

3. **Comparing and Contrasting**
A. Philip Randolph and members of the NAACP

**June 1943**
Race riots occur
in Detroit.

**November 1944**
Roosevelt is elected
to a fourth term.

1944

1945

**December 1944**
The U.S. Supreme Court up-
holds the order to relocate
Japanese Americans.

had differing philosophies about how to bring about social change. Compare and contrast the methods of civil disobedience and the less controversial tactics of the NAACP. Which do you think is more effective?

# Extension and Application

## 1. Citizenship

Write an essay that discusses ways in which an individual can cope with and ease racial tensions today. You might relate incidents, jokes, or casual comments that you or someone you know may have witnessed or participated in. Conclude by making recommendations that you can apply to everyday social situations. (An example might be speaking out among peers when racial comments or jokes are made.)

## 2. Community Connection

Interview family members or older neighbors who lived at home during World War II. Find out about their memories of the social changes and about how important entertainment was to them. You might bring to class examples of some of the music they listened and danced to.

## 3. Linking Across Time

Use the *Readers' Guide to Periodical Literature* and other sources to find information about the actual gains of African Americans, Chicanos, or Japanese Americans since World War II. Has the earning power of this minority gone up or down in comparison to white Americans? Has the percentage of this minority group that lives below the poverty line gone up or down compared to that of white Americans? Make a chart to present to your class.

## 4. Evidence of the Past: Photography

Look at the photograph and analyze it. Describe the subject, what is included and what is left out, what the photographer's biases might have been, and the purpose and audience for which the photograph may have been intended. Then present your analysis to the class.

# Geography

1. Which natural resources were saved in large quantities during World War II because of reuse of old materials?
2. What were the major population shifts during World War II? Which shift continued a trend caused by improvements in technology and modernization of techniques?
3. What were some reasons African Americans left the South and moved to the North between 1941 and 1945?
4. What hardships did Japanese Americans endure because of their relocation and internment during the war?

LIBRARY OF CONGRESS

# Unit 5 Review

W e have learned that we cannot
live alone, at peace; that our
own well-being is dependent
on the well-being of other nations, far away.
We have learned that we must live as men,
and not as ostriches, nor as dogs in the
manger. We have learned to be citizens
of the world, members of the human
community.

Franklin Delano Roosevelt,
*Fourth Inaugural Address,*
January 20, 1945

## Concepts and Themes

In 1933 the United States strongly opposed
becoming involved in the European war. Notice
how Roosevelt's position has changed by 1945.

1. Why did the United States adopt and then
   abandon its isolationist policy?
2. How did the people of the United States learn
   to be "citizens of the world, members of the
   human community" during this period of history? How were their everyday lives affected?

## History Projects

1. **One Day In History**
   Check with a synagogue near you to see if and
   how that congregation commemorates Kristallnacht. Share your findings in a brief oral report.
2. **Case Study**
   Examine the editorial pages of one U.S. newspaper for August 7, 1945, and the following few
   days. Note the opinions regarding the use of
   the atomic bomb. Did you find more editorials
   that supported the decision to use the bomb or
   that disapproved of its use? Present your findings in a two- to three-minute oral report.
3. **Culture of the Time**
   Record a sample of one band's music recorded
   during the 1940s and play it for your class.
4. **Evidence of the Past**
   *Life* magazine, begun in 1936, and *Look* magazine, begun in 1937, are famous for in-depth
   photojournalism. This method of reporting the
   news involves heavy use of pictures, usually
   photographs. Sometimes text is also used. Examine some of these magazines from the 1940s.
   What do the images tell you about the United
   States and its culture during the 1940s? Write a
   description of one event that impresses you.

## Writing Activities

1. Research United States military strategies during World War II. Write an essay comparing
   two different strategies for fighting on land.
   (See the Writer's Guide, pages 825-827, for
   guidelines on writing for different purposes.)
2. Imagine that you are living in the early 1940s.
   Write a letter to President Roosevelt stating your
   opinions about the U.S. policy of refusing to
   allow more Jewish immigrants to enter our country. Include reasons that support your opinions.
   (See the Writer's Guide, pages 825-827, for
   guidelines on writing for different purposes.)

## The Arts

- *For Whom the Bell Tolls* by Ernest Hemingway;
  a novel about an idealistic American fighting
  fascist forces during the Spanish Civil War.
- *Hiroshima* by John Hersey; nonfiction account of
  the destruction of the Japanese city when the
  United States dropped the first atomic bomb.
- *All My Sons* by Arthur Miller; a play exposing
  the moral conflicts of a manufacturer who sold
  defective airplane parts to the government
  during World War II.
- *This Is My Story* by Eleanor Roosevelt; an
  autobiography.
- *Native Son* by Richard Wright; a novel about
  one man's discouragement due to racial discrimination.

# UNIT SIX

# The Postwar World

"The Homecoming G.I.", *Saturday Evening Post*, May 26, 1945, courtesy of the estate of Norman Rockwell

# The Quiet and the Storm

*While some Americans find contentment in the postwar quiet and solitude, others, such as Annie Dillard in the following passage from* An American Childhood, *find the silence hypnotic and deadening. Still others were caught in a rapidly spreading web of fear, frightened by the postwar threat of communism. E. L. Doctorow captures the spirit of paranoia in* The Book of Daniel, *as young Daniel's home is visited by the FBI, which suspects his parents of involvement in communist espionage.*

## from *An American Childhood*
### by Annie Dillard

The story starts back in 1950, when I was five. Oh, the great humming silence of the empty neighborhoods in those days, the neighborhoods abandoned everywhere across continental America—the city residential areas, the new "suburbs," the towns and villages on the peopled highways, the cities, towns, and villages on the rivers, the shores, in the Rocky and Appalachian mountains, the piedmont, the dells, the bayous, the hills, the Great Basin, the Great Valley, the Great Plains—oh, the silence!

For every morning the neighborhoods emptied, and all vital activity, it seemed, set forth for parts unknown.

The men left in a rush: they flung on coats, they slid kisses at everybody's cheeks, they slammed house doors, they slammed car doors; they ground their cars' starters till the motors caught with a jump.

And the Catholic schoolchildren left in a rush; I saw them from our dining-room windows. They burst into the street buttoning their jackets; they threw dry catalpa pods at the stop sign and at each other. They hugged their brown-and-tan workbooks to them, clumped and parted, and proceeded toward St. Bede's church school almost by accident.

The men in their oval, empty cars drove slowly among the schoolchildren. The boys banged the cars' fenders with their hands, with their jackets' elbows, or their books. The men in cars inched among the children; they edged around corners and vanished from sight. The waving knots of children zigzagged and hollered up the street and vanished from sight. And inside all the forgotten houses in all the abandoned neighborhoods, the day of silence and waiting had begun.

The war was over. People wanted to settle down, apparently, and calmly blow their way out of years of rationing. They wanted to bake sugary cakes, burn gas, go to church together, get rich, and make babies.

I had been born at the end of April 1945, on the day Hitler died; Roosevelt had died eighteen days before. My father had been 4-F in the war, because of a collapsing lung—despite his repeated and chagrined efforts to enlist. Now—five years after V-J Day—he still went out one night a week as a volunteer to the Civil Air Patrol; he searched the Pittsburgh skies for new enemy bombers. By day he worked downtown for American Standard.

Every woman stayed alone in her house in those days, like a coin in a safe. Amy and I lived alone with our mother most of the day. Amy was three years younger than I. Mother and Amy and I went our separate ways in peace.

The men had driven away and the schoolchildren had paraded out of sight. Now a self-conscious and stricken silence overtook the neighborhood, overtook our white corner house and myself inside. "Am I living?" In the kitchen I watched the unselfconscious trees through the screen door, until the trees' autumn branches like fins waved away the silence. I forgot myself, and sank into dim and watery oblivion.

A car passed. Its rush and whine jolted me from my blankness. The sound faded again and I faded again down into my hushed brain until the icebox motor kicked on and prodded me awake. "You are living," the icebox motor said. "It is morning, morning, here in the kitchen, and you are in it," the icebox motor said, or the dripping faucet said, or any of the hundred other noisy things that only children can't stop hearing. Cars started, leaves rubbed, trucks' brakes whistled, sparrows peeped. Whenever it rained, the rain spattered, dripped, and ran, for the entire length of the shower, for the entire length of days-long rains, until we children were almost insane from hearing it rain because we couldn't stop hearing it rain. "Rinso white!" cried the man on the radio. "Rinso blue." The silence, like all silences, was made poignant and distinct by its sounds. . . .

In the living room the mail slot clicked open and envelopes clattered down. In the back room, where our maid, Margaret Butler, was ironing, the steam iron thumped the muffled ironing board and hissed. The walls squeaked, the pipes knocked, the screen door trembled, the furnace banged, and the radiators clanged. This was the fall the loud trucks went by. I sat mindless and eternal on the kitchen floor, stony of head and solemn, playing with my fingers. Time streamed in full flood beside me on the kitchen floor; time roared raging beside me down its swollen banks; and when I woke I was so startled I fell in. . . .

Six xylophone notes chimed evenly from the radio in the back room where Margaret was ironing, and then seven xylophone notes chimed. With carefully controlled emotion, a radio woman sang:

What will the weather be?
Tell us, Mister Weather Man.

Mother picked up Amy, who was afraid of the trucks. She called the painters on the phone; it was time to paint the outside trim again. She ordered groceries on the phone. Larry, from Lloyd's Market, delivered. He joked with us in the kitchen while Mother unpacked the groceries' cardboard box.

I wandered outside. It was afternoon. No cars

ROBERT MILLER GALLERY, NEW YORK

**After reading both literature selections, consider how *Blue and Black* (1951–1953) by Lee Krasner reflects the period.** *What effects do the boldness of color, interlocking shapes, and repetition in the painting have?*

passed on the empty streets; no people passed on the empty sidewalks. The brick houses, the frame and stucco houses, white and red behind their high hedges, were still. A small woman appeared at the far, high end of the street, in silhouette against the sky; she pushed a black baby carriage tall and chromed as a hearse. The leaves in the Lombardy poplars were turning brown.

"Lie on your back," my mother said. She was kind, imaginative. She had joined me in one of the side yards. "Look at the clouds and figure out what they look like. A hat? I see a camel."

Must I? Could this be anybody's idea of something worth doing?

I was hoping the war would break out again, here. I was hoping the streets would fill and I could shoot my cap gun at people instead of at mere sparrows. My project was to ride my swing all around, over the top. I bounced a ball against the house; I fired gravel bits from an illegal slingshot Mother gave me. Sometimes I looked at the back of my hand and tried to memorize it. Sometimes I dreamed of a coal furnace, a blue lake, a redheaded woodpecker who turned into a screeching hag. Sometimes I sang uselessly in the yard, "Blithar, blithar, blithar, blithar."

It rained and it cleared and I sent Popsicle sticks and twigs down the gritty rivulet below the curb. Soon the separated neighborhood trees lost their leaves, one by one. On Saturday afternoons I watched the men rake leaves into low heaps at the curb. They tried to ignite the heaps with matches. At length my father went into the house and returned with a yellow can of lighter fluid. The daylight ended early, before all the men had burned all their leaves.

It snowed and it cleared and I kicked and pounded the snow. I roamed the darkening snowy neighborhood, oblivious. I bit and crumbled on my tongue the sweet, metallic worms of ice that had formed in rows on my mittens. I took a mitten off to fetch some wool strands from my mouth. Deeper the blue shadows grew on the sidewalk snow, and longer; the blue shadows joined and spread upward from the streets like rising water. I walked wordless and unseeing, dumb and sunk in my skull, until—what was that?

The streetlights had come on—yellow, bing—and the new light woke me like noise. I surfaced once again and saw: it was winter now, winter again. The air had grown blue dark; the skies were shrinking; the streetlights had come on; and I was here outside in the dimming day's snow, alive.

---

## from *The Book of Daniel*
### *by E. L. Doctorow*

Early the next morning, as I was leaving for school, the doorbell rang and I opened the door and two men were standing on the porch. They were dressed neatly, and did not appear to be of the neighborhood. They had thin, neat faces and small noses, and crew-cut hair. They held their hats in their hands and wore nice overcoats. I thought maybe they were from one of those Christian religions that sent people from door to door to sell their religious magazines.

"Sonny," said one, "is your mother or father home?"

"Yes," I said. "They're both home."

My mother did not allow me to delay going to school just because the FBI had come to the door. I don't know what happened on that first visit. The men went inside and, going down the splintery front steps, I turned and caught a glimpse of Paul coming out of the kitchen to meet them just as the door closed. My mother was holding the door and my father was coming forward in his ribbed undershirt, looking much skinnier than the two men who rang the bell.

When the FBI knocks on your door and wants only to ask a few questions, you do not have to consent to be asked questions. You are not required to talk to them just because they would like to talk to you. You don't have to go with them to their office. You don't have to do anything if you are not subpoenaed or arrested. But you only learn the law as you go along.

"They don't know what they want," Paul says to Rochelle. "It's routine. If you don't talk to them, they have nothing to pin their lies on. They are clumsy, obvious people."

"I'm frightened," my mother says. "*Polizei* don't have to be smart."

"Don't worry," Paul says. "Mindish won't suffer from anything we said." He is walking back and forth in the kitchen and he is pounding his fist into his palm. "We have done nothing wrong. There is nothing to be afraid of."

It develops that all of Mindish's friends are being questioned. Nobody knows what he is being held for. There has been no announcement on the radio, there has been no story in the newspaper. Sadie Mindish is in a state of hysterical collapse. Her apartment has been searched. Her daughter has stayed home from school. Nobody knows if they even have a lawyer.

The next day the same two FBI men come back again, this time in the early evening. They sit on the stuffed, sprung couch in the living room parlor with their knees together and their hats in their hands. They are very soft-spoken and friendly. Their strange names are Tom Davis and John Bradley. They smile at me while my mother goes to the phone to call my father.

"What grade are you in, young fellow?"

I don't answer. I have never seen a real FBI man this close before. I peer at them, looking for superhuman powers, but there is no evidence that they have any. They look neither as handsome as in the movies nor as ugly as my parents' revulsion makes them. I search their faces for a clue to their real nature. But their faces do not give clues.

When Paul comes home, he is very nervous.

"My lawyer has advised me that I don't have to talk to you if I don't want to," my father said. "That particular fact you neglected yesterday to mention."

"Well, yes sir, Mr. Isaacson, but we were hoping you would be cooperative. We're only looking for information. It's nothing mysterious. We thought you were a friend of Doctor Mindish. As his friend, you may be in a position to help him."

"I will be glad to answer any questions in a court of law."

"Do you deny now that you know him?"

"I will answer any questions in a court of law."

The two men leave after a few minutes, and then they sit in their car, double-parked in front of the house, for ten or fifteen minutes more. They appear to be writing on clipboards or on pads, I can't tell exactly. It is dark and they have turned on the interior car light. I am reminded of a patrol man writing a parking ticket. But the sense is of serious and irrevocable paperwork, and I find it frightening. There is some small, grey light in the dark sky over the schoolyard. The wind is making whistling noises at the edges of the window.

"Danny!" Rochelle says sharply. "Get away from there."

My father takes my place at the curtains. "That is outrageous," he says. "Don't you see, it is part of the treatment. They are trying to shake us up. But we're too smart for them. We're onto them. They can sit out there all night for all I care."

The next day is worse. At lunch my father tells my mother he is sure someone has searched the shop. When he unlocked the door this morning, he felt that things were slightly out of place. It wasn't anything he could pinpoint exactly. Maybe the tubes in the trash barrel. Maybe the customer tickets. It was more like a sense of things having been disturbed.

Our lunch is muenster cheese sandwiches on pumpernickel and canned tomato soup. My father doesn't eat. He sits with his elbow on the table and his hand to his head. He nods, as if he agrees with something he has decided.

"That's it. That's why they came here and asked you to call me home. They could just as easily have come to the store, couldn't they? But they didn't. They wanted to make sure I was home when they wanted to search my store."

My mother discounts this. She says they could have waited until late at night and achieved the same thing. I understand that she is deliberately minimizing the situation. She suggests that perhaps my father is imagining the whole thing about the store being searched. As the pressure increases, she seems to be calming down. Her own hysteria has passed. She is worried about Paul. She is into the mental process which in the next three years will harden into a fortitude many people will find repugnant.

"Did you have your test, Danny?"

"This afternoon."

"Do you know all the words?"

"Yes."

But there are dark circles under her eyes. When I come home from school, the FBI men are sitting outside again in their car. My mother is lying down on the couch with a washcloth across her head. Her left forearm is bandaged. While ironing she gave herself a terrible burn. The edges of our existence seem to be crumbling. The house is cold and Williams has come up from the cellar to say in his deepest voice of menace that the furnace is not working properly and has to be cleaned. He will get to it when he can. I understand this means he will get to it when he does not feel abused by the situation. All my senses are in a state of magnification. I hang around the house feeling the different lights of the day. I drink the air. I taste the food I eat. Every moment of my waking life is intensified and I know exactly what is happening. A giant eye machine, like the mysterious black apparatus at the Hayden Planetarium with the two diving helmet heads and the black rivets and its insect legs, is turning its planetary beam slowly in our direction. And that is what is bringing on the dark skies and the cold weather. And when it reaches us, like the prison searchlight in the Nazi concentration camp, it will stop. And we will be pinned, like the lady jammed through the schoolyard fence with her blood mixed with the milk and broken bottles. And our blood will hurt as if it had glass in it. And it will be hot in that beam and our house will smell and smoke and turn brown at the edges and flare up in a great, sucking floop of flame.

And that is exactly what happens.

## Responding to Literature

1. The two passages present different views of the postwar United States, but in what ways are the two views similar?

2. Daniel likens the FBI investigation to a searchlight in a Nazi concentration camp. Why is this ironic in the 1950s?

*For Further Reading*
Cheever, John: *The Stories of John Cheever*
Ellison, Ralph: *Invisible Man*
Hellman, Lillian: *Scoundrel Time*
Wilson, Sloan: *The Man in the Grey Flannel Suit*

## CHAPTER 14

# The Uneasy Peace

### October 22, 1962: The White House

President John F. Kennedy walked into the Oval Office at 6:59 P.M., stepping over TV cables on the way to his desk. He was about to deliver some frightening news to the American people—news of a mounting Soviet threat in Cuba.

In a controlled, almost dull tone, Kennedy explained what the U.S. government would do in response. It would ask for a United Nations meeting. It would blockade Cuban shipping lanes with American destroyers in order to keep more weapons from reaching the island, and it would put the U.S. military forces on full alert. If even one missile were fired from Cuba on any country in the Western Hemisphere, the United States would launch a nuclear attack on the Soviet Union. Suddenly, the world teetered on the brink of disaster.

What had happened? Just 17 years before, the United States and the Soviet Union had embraced and toasted their stunning World War II victory. Roosevelt's warmth and diplomacy in dealing with the Soviets toward the end of the war had raised hopes of continued cooperation between the two powers. Now, however, the wartime alliance had soured into a bitter and dangerous rivalry, a cold war, affecting the entire world.

> *Suddenly, the world teetered on the brink of disaster.*

AP/WIDE WORLD PHOTOS

*Aerial photographs provided concrete evidence that Russian freighters bound for Cuba were carrying missiles.*

*Chief Petty Officer Graham Jackson weeps as President Roosevelt's funeral procession passes. The death of Roosevelt and the succession of Truman to the presidency ushered in the tense period known as the cold war.*

# The Cold War Begins

## April 25, 1945: GIs Meet Soviet Troops

LILACS BLOOMED AND THE SUN SHONE ON APRIL 25, 1945, AS AMERICAN SOLDIERS BATTLING THE GERMANS FROM THE WEST APPROACHED THEIR SOVIET ALLIES fighting from the east. Victory was in the air, and as the armies neared the Elbe River south of Berlin, small patrols of Americans drove out in jeeps to meet their Soviet comrades in arms. Throughout the day Soviet and American soldiers embraced for the first time. Andy Rooney, staff writer for the armed forces newspaper, *Stars & Stripes*, caught the moment:

*There was a mad scene of jubilation on the east and west banks of the Elbe at Torgau as infantrymen of Lieutenant General Courtney H. Hodges . . . swapped K rations for a vodka with soldiers of Marshal Kornian's Ukrainian Army, congratulating each other . . . on the linkup.*

*Men of the 69th Division sat on the banks of the Elbe in warm sunshine today with no enemy in front of them or behind them and . . . watched their new Russian friends and listened to them as they played accordions and sang Russian songs.*

*The Russian soldiers are the most carefree bunch . . . that ever came together in an army. They would best be described as exactly like Americans, only twice as much. . . . You get the feeling of exuberance, a great new world opening up.*

Andy Rooney, "Good Soldiers Meet," *Stars & Stripes*, April 28, 1945

AP/WIDE WORLD PHOTOS

## An Iron Curtain Starts to Fall

The possibility of the opening of that "great new world" evaporated quickly. The war had left the United States and the Soviet Union as the world's dominant powers. Cautious allies during the struggle, the two nations emerged from the war with misgivings about one another. Each viewed the other with deep mistrust. Each had special interests to protect. And each carried the weight of its own history to the moment.

**An Uneasy Alliance** During the war Britain, the Soviet Union, the United States, and 23 other nations had joined forces as the Allied powers. Having pooled their military might, the 26 set out to crush the Axis powers in Europe and Asia.

The organization was a strong, but uneasy, alliance. Among its members were nations with old hatreds and misunderstandings of one another, bound together by a common enemy. At the heart of the alliance stood the United States and the Soviet Union.

While the Soviets praised the courage of American fighting men and the leadership of President Roosevelt, old hostilities simmered beneath the surface. The Soviets resented the fact that American troops, along with British and French forces, tried to undo their revolution of 1917. When that attempt failed, the United States still refused to recognize the Soviet government until 1933. Furthermore, Soviet propaganda stirred up popular fears of American capitalism with its divisions between rich and poor and its swings between prosperity and depression.

---

### STUDY GUIDE

**As You Read**
Identify the events that led to Soviet dominance in eastern Europe, the Truman Doctrine, and the cold war. Also, think about the following concepts and skills.

**Central Concepts**
- understanding how differing ideologies shaped postwar Europe and fueled the **cold war**
- understanding the main elements of the **Truman Doctrine**

**Thinking Skills**
- comparing and contrasting
- recognizing points of view
- analyzing behavior

CULVER PICTURES, INC.

SOVPHOTO

**After World War II, victory celebrations took place in both American and Soviet cities.** *What effects of the war are evident in the picture on the right?*

The Allies' delay in launching a second front also made Stalin suspicious. He had counted on an invasion of France in 1942 to divert German forces from his country. The United States and Britain's two-year delay made him think that the Americans secretly wanted a weakened Soviet Union.

Americans also harbored fears of the Soviet Union. Communism, with its emphasis on world revolution, had always frightened Americans. Furthermore, past Soviet agreements with Germany rankled Americans. In 1918 the Soviets struck a separate peace with Germany, forcing the West to fight Germany without Soviet help. In 1939 Stalin signed a short-lived nonaggression pact with Hitler. Adding to American fears were memories of Stalin's bloody attacks on his internal enemies in the 1930s.

During the war Roosevelt struggled to keep the Allies focused on military issues—the common problem—and off the areas of disagreement. As the war came to an end, the United States and the Soviet Union faced their greatest challenge.

**Two Views of the World**   At the end of the war, the western Soviet Union was a scene of awful destruction. More than 20 million Soviets had died in the struggle. Ground fighting and air bombing had destroyed more than 4.7 million homes, nearly 2,000 towns, and 70,000 villages. Through the ruins wandered the hungry and homeless—25 million of them—seeking a place to settle.

Nothing was more important to Soviet leaders than protecting themselves from a rearmed Germany and rebuilding their shattered economy. One key to their security, they believed, was a permanently weakened Germany. Another was a ring of pro-Soviet nations protecting their western border. From Napoleon's attack on Moscow in 1812 through the German invasions of World Wars I and II, enemy armies had always swept in from the west.

Unlike the Soviets, the Americans emerged from the war more powerful than when they entered it. American deaths of 405,000 were tragic, but small, compared with the millions of Soviet dead. A booming American economy controlled nearly 50 percent of the world's wealth, and most Americans felt proud of their successful fight for democracy.[1]

American leaders envisioned a future of international peace and prosperity. They imagined a world patterned after the United States—democratic, open to business expansion and free trade. In this world free nations would solve their differences by talking, not by fighting. Like the Puritans and believers in Manifest Destiny before them, many Americans felt

**STUDY GUIDE**

**Comparing and Contrasting**
The Soviets feared capitalism because it is essentially a free-market economic system in which individuals own and operate privately financed businesses. In a socialist economy, the system the communists favored, the state (the government) owns and operates businesses for the benefit of society at large. Strict socialism does not allow for private ownership.

**1** How did America's position at the end of the war compare with the Soviet Union's?

they had a mission: to build a free world with the United States leading the way.

## Turning Point at Yalta

In February 1945, near the end of the war, the Big Three—Roosevelt, Churchill, and Stalin—met in the Soviet city of Yalta to work out control of the postwar world. The three men and their advisers arrived at a moment when victorious Soviet armies were sweeping across eastern Europe.

Each leader brought his own concerns to the table. Churchill hoped to save the British Empire; Stalin intended to protect his borders and rebuild his country. Unlike Churchill and Stalin, who believed in great powers controlling spheres of influence, Roosevelt sought the worldwide spread of democracy and free trade. However, the American president also needed Soviet aid in the war against Japan. All agreed, however, that working out these interests together was the only path to peace.

**At Yalta Churchill, Roosevelt, and Stalin reached a number of historic agreements.** *Which of these agreements affected the future of Germany?*

FRANKLIN D. ROOSEVELT LIBRARY

Every day for a week, the Big Three met in the ballroom of the former czar's palace along the Black Sea. They talked, debated, and compromised.

The meeting at Yalta marked a high point of cooperation among the Big Three. However, it also became a turning point in the relationship between the major powers, and in many ways it determined the form the postwar world would take.

**Big Three Agreements** Many key agreements came out of the Yalta talks. Much to Roosevelt's relief, Stalin agreed to join the fight against Japan "two or three" months after Germany surrendered. In return, Stalin would receive territories in Asia. Stalin also pledged Soviet support for the United Nations (UN), an international body that would be formed to help keep world peace.

Agreement broke down over Germany and eastern Europe. Even though all three leaders feared a re-armed Germany, they disagreed on how to keep Germany under control. Stalin wanted to punish Germany by demanding $20 billion in war payments. Half of the money would go to the Soviet Union to help rebuild its shattered economy. Roosevelt and Churchill knew that Germany could not afford the payments without their help; they feared having to support Germany so it could pay Stalin.

Rather than debate the issue, the three agreed that each nation would control the part of Germany its troops held at the end of the war. Later a commission would solve the problem of war payments.

**Control in Eastern Europe** Eastern Europe and Poland were even touchier issues. Stalin demanded recognition of Soviet power in Poland, Romania, Bulgaria, Austria, Hungary, and Czechoslovakia to protect his western border. Soviet forces already occupied much of eastern Europe, and Stalin had installed a government in Poland. Roosevelt and Churchill protested strongly. Britain went to war "so that Poland should be free," Churchill exclaimed.

In the end, however, Roosevelt and Churchill had little choice but to give in. With the Pacific war still raging, they had no means of forcing Stalin to back down. Reluctantly they agreed to Soviet influence in eastern Europe but insisted that Stalin hold "free and unfettered elections" at an "early date."

## STUDY GUIDE

### Recognizing Points of View
At Yalta major differences of opinion arose over the political future of postwar Europe. Roosevelt's vision was influenced by economic considerations. A free, democratic Europe would represent fertile new markets for American business and trade. Churchill and Stalin, on the other hand, were driven by security considerations. Each of their nations had suffered through two world wars during the previous three decades, and both leaders wanted a postwar Europe over which they could exert influence and control.

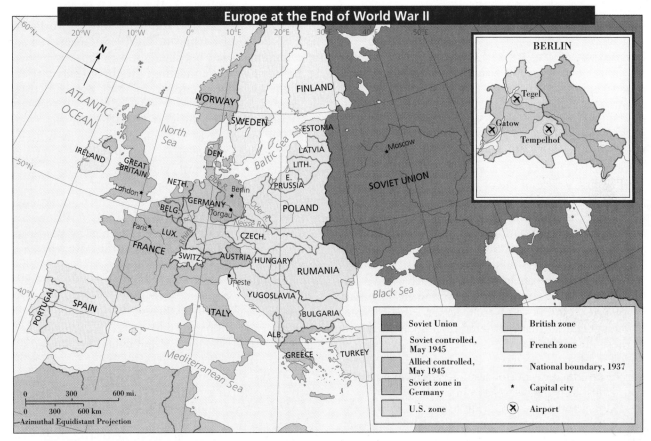

## Europe at the End of World War II

BERLIN

**Legend:**
- Soviet Union
- Soviet controlled, May 1945
- Allied controlled, May 1945
- Soviet zone in Germany
- U.S. zone
- British zone
- French zone
- National boundary, 1937
- ★ Capital city
- ⊗ Airport

**At the close of World War II, the political map of Europe underwent massive changes.** *Which parts of Europe were controlled by the Soviet Union in May 1945? Compare this area with the land held by Soviet troops at the end of the war.*

In the weeks after the conference at Yalta, Roosevelt worried as the Soviets installed communist governments in country after country. Still, he had faith in his ability to win Stalin's trust of the West. Newly elected to a fourth term, Roosevelt believed he could persuade Stalin that the Soviets had nothing to fear and could relax their iron grip on eastern Europe. However, any such hopes were dashed when Roosevelt died suddenly on April 12, 1945.

## Truman Comes to Power

I don't know whether you fellows ever had a load of hay or a bull fall on you, but last night the moon, stars, and all the planets fell on me." Harry S Truman could well feel overwhelmed on his first day as president—April 13, 1945. Nations were still battling, and the world had reached a turning point in its history: The old system of power was crumbling and a new, unknown system remained to be built.

Truman stepped into the presidency unprepared. Raised in a small Missouri town with little chance for an education, the gritty, intelligent Truman worked his way up from the farm to business and finally to the U.S. Senate. Nominated as Roosevelt's running mate in 1944, he spent only 12 weeks as vice president before Roosevelt's death.

During those 83 days, Truman got little information from Roosevelt. The president shared no details of key military or foreign policies with him, and Truman received only two short foreign relations briefings. According to Roosevelt's key adviser, Harry Hopkins, Truman himself knew "absolutely nothing

### Analyzing Behavior

Stalin promised to hold free elections throughout eastern Europe, but were his promises sincere? Stalin had demanded control of the eastern European nations in order to protect the western border of the Soviet Union from invasion. If he granted these nations their freedom, how could he prevent any one of them from invading Soviet territory or from making it possible for another nation to do so? Despite all of Stalin's promises, the fate of eastern Europe's "captive nations" was firmly sealed at Yalta.

of world affairs." Yet only 10 days after Truman assumed the presidency, international events took center stage.

**Formation of the United Nations** At Yalta, the Big Three had agreed in principle to an international peacekeeping organization. On April 25, 1945, fifty countries met in San Francisco to draft the charter for the United Nations. United States support was voiced in Truman's address to the conference: "We must build a new world, a far better world—one in which the eternal dignity of man is respected."

The first article of the charter stated that the purpose of the United Nations was to maintain international peace and security. By October 1945 a majority of the participating nations had ratified the charter, and the United Nations officially came into existence.

The United States hoped that the United Nations would help to bring about a world in which every country would be free to run its own government. However, the Soviet Union—and to a lesser extent Great Britain—believed that self-determination applied only to those countries that did not have strategic value to Soviet, or British, interests. In particular, the Soviets were determined to control eastern Europe as a protection against future aggression from the West.

Truman's advisers urged him to get tough with the Soviets, and Truman exhibited his hard-line approach during the visit of Soviet ambassador V. M. Molotov. Truman sharply criticized Molotov for failing to support the Yalta agreements. Specifically, Truman demanded to know why the Soviets had not held free elections in Poland.

Accustomed to Roosevelt's friendly, patient style, Molotov was shaken. "I have never been talked to like that in my life," he reportedly said to Truman.

"Carry out your agreements and you won't get talked to like that," Truman snapped.

**Meetings at Potsdam** In this mood of growing hostility, Truman, Stalin, and Churchill met in Potsdam, a suburb of Berlin, in July 1945. Germany had surrendered in May, but the fight with Japan wore on. At this final wartime meeting, the three leaders tried to tie up some loose ends from Yalta, especially the future of Germany.

Truman and Stalin were meeting for the first time, and Truman was determined to be hard-nosed. A few days into the sessions, the already determined Truman learned that American scientists had successfully exploded the atomic bomb. He kept the news to himself, but it was soon clear that something had happened. Churchill recalled, "When he [Truman] got to the meeting after having read the report he was a changed man. He told the Russians just where they got off and generally bossed the whole meeting."

In spite of Truman's attitude, the three leaders reached agreement on Germany. The country would be completely disarmed and its war industries dismantled. Each occupying nation would be allowed to take war payments from its zone.

With this decision the three leaders began moving down the path to a divided Germany. The western half of Germany would remain under British, French, and U.S. control. The eastern half would stay in Soviet hands. The capital city of Berlin, 110 miles deep in the Soviet zone, would also be carved up among the four nations.

All too quickly the world was dividing into two camps, dominated by the United States and the Soviet Union.

**The Idea of Containment** Over the next seven months, Truman's and Stalin's mistrust of one another grew. Stalin continued to oppress most of eastern

---

★ ★ ★ **PRESIDENT'S GALLERY** ★ ★ ★

*"The American people desire, and are determined to work for, a world in which all nations and all peoples are free to govern themselves as they see fit. . . . Democracy alone can supply the vitalizing force to stir the peoples of the world into triumphant action, not only against their human oppressors, but also against their ancient enemies—hunger, misery, and despair."*

*Inaugural Address*
*January 20, 1949*

THE HARRY S. TRUMAN LIBRARY

*Harry S Truman*

Harry S Truman 1945–1953

**Background:**
- Born 1884; died 1972
- Democrat, Missouri
- Served in U.S. Senate 1935–1944
- Elected vice president 1944
- Assumed presidency 1945
- Elected president 1948

**Achievements in Office:**
- United Nations founded (1945)
- Marshall Plan (1947)
- North Atlantic Treaty Organization (1949)

Europe, forcing loyalty to the Soviet Union through phony trials and executions. In the Middle East, Stalin kept his troops in Iran long after U.S. and British troops had pulled out. Iran complained before the United Nations, and Truman protested as well. In early 1946 the United States gave Britain a $3.5 billion loan but ignored a Soviet request for help.

On February 9, 1946, Stalin added to the growing tension with an important speech in which he declared that capitalism was a danger to world peace. Capitalism and communism, he said, would eventually clash. Because of that danger, he would protect Soviet security by stopping trade with the West and developing modern weaponry no matter how high the cost. In America Supreme Court Justice William Douglas said the speech sounded like "a declaration of World War III."

Truman then received a momentous 16-page telegram from George Kennan, a brilliant young diplomat at the American embassy in Moscow. An expert in Soviet history and culture, Kennan advised Truman that the United States needed to pursue "long-term, patient, but firm and vigilant containment of Russian expansive tendencies." **Containment**—the restriction of communism to its current borders—was the only way to secure the peace.

A few weeks later, in March 1946, Winston Churchill supported this view in a famous speech at Westminster College in Fulton, Missouri. Somberly he warned that "from Stettin in the Baltic to Trieste in the Adriatic, an iron curtain has descended across the continent." Furthermore, Churchill warned, English-speaking people should join forces against the Soviet threat. "There is nothing the Communists admire so much as strength and nothing for which they have less respect than for military weakness."

## Cold War Is Declared

Churchill's speech gave the world a clear picture of the future: The West, led by the United States, would resist any Soviet attempts to expand its influence in the world. The **cold war** had begun—a U.S.–Soviet conflict in which the two powers would avoid fighting each other directly but would block each other's goals around the world.

**The Truman Doctrine**   In February 1947 the British gave the United States a chance to put containment to work. Nearly bankrupt at the end of the war, the British asked the U.S. government to take over support of the Greek and Turkish governments. The Soviet Union was trying to force the Turks to share control of a key shipping channel between the Black Sea and the Mediterranean. In Greece, the government was fighting communist rebels, although the Soviet Union was not directly involved.

Truman talked to his advisers, who convinced him that America had to act. Otherwise, they believed, the communists might succeed, and that would "open three continents to Soviet penetration."

Truman agreed but knew he had to convince a Congress that wanted to reduce taxes—not raise them. He would have to "scare the American people" and Congress into supporting the plan.

On March 12, 1947, Truman called a joint session of Congress. In his speech he grimly pictured a threatening world:

*At the present moment, nearly every nation must choose between alternative ways of life. The choice is too often not a free one.*

*One way of life is based upon the will of the majority and is distinguished by free institutions, representative government, free elections, guarantees of individual liberty, freedom of speech and religion, and freedom from political oppression.*

*The second way of life is based upon the will of a minority forcibly imposed upon the majority. It relies upon terror and oppression, a controlled press and radio, fixed elections, and the suppression of personal freedoms.*

Harry S Truman,
Speech to Joint Session of Congress,
March 12, 1947

Truman went on to state that America must help all free people who were "resisting attempted subjugation by armed minorities or outside pressures." Then he asked for $400 million in military and economic aid to support the Greek and Turkish governments.[2] Although many observers felt that Truman painted too harsh a picture, his dramatic appeal

## STUDY GUIDE

### Analyzing Behavior
Truman's speech was meant to instill fear in the American people and generate support for anticommunist activity, and it worked. Over the next three decades, virtually every use of American military power was justified as necessary to thwart the imminent spread of communism somewhere around the world.

**2** What motivated Truman to take on the task of supporting the Greek and Turkish governments?

worked. Congress approved the request about one month later.

This view, which came to be known as the **Truman Doctrine,** defined American foreign policy for the next 20 years. From this moment on, most Americans would view communism as a worldwide threat to democracy that they had a duty to resist. The cold war would become not just a struggle for territory but a fight between two opposing views of the world.

**The Marshall Plan** While military aid could help contain communism, Truman and his advisers knew it was only part of the answer. In June 1947 Secretary of State George Marshall suggested another way to bolster freedom—a plan for helping Europe rebuild.

The war had been over for two years, but Europeans were still struggling to survive. Cities and towns had been bombed into ruin. Roads and canals were destroyed. Worst of all, millions of people were sick, homeless, and hungry. In May 1947 Churchill lamented that Europe was "a rubble heap . . . a breeding ground of pestilence [disease] and hate."

Conditions like these were not only heartbreaking but also dangerous. Such terrible suffering provided ideal conditions for communism to grow, and already Communist parties were gathering strength in France and Italy. However, a ruined, starving Europe would drain the American economy—and American businesses desperately depended on European markets.

Marshall's plan involved spending billions of dollars to help put Europe, including the USSR, back on its feet. To qualify for the aid, nations had to agree to spend the dollars on goods from the United States. At first many conservatives in Congress disagreed with the plan, but events in eastern Europe soon changed their minds. The Soviets refused to take part in the plan, criticizing it as America's way of taking over Europe. In February 1948 the Communist party seized control of Czechoslovakia, completing the Soviet domination of eastern Europe.

GEORGE C. MARSHALL FOUNDATION

**The slogan on this poster—"For the lifting up of self and a better life"—tells the benefits of the European Recovery Program, also called the Marshall Plan.**

Two months later Truman approved Congress's bill for $17 billion in aid to Europe over five years. Sixteen nations participated in the plan, and by 1952 they were more successful than anyone had dreamed. The Communist party in western Europe was severely weakened. Western European industries had increased their output by 64 percent, and American prosperity was ensured. At the same time, however, tensions with the Soviet Union continued to grow.

## SECTION REVIEW

**Checking Facts**

1. Tension existed within the Grand Alliance. Why were the Soviets hostile toward the Americans? Why did the Americans fear the Soviets?

2. What was the toll taken in Russian life and property during World War II?

3. Over which six eastern European nations did Stalin demand control at Yalta?

4. How was Germany divided at the Potsdam conference?

5. Describe the U.S. commitment to rebuild Europe as part of the Marshall Plan.

**Thinking Critically**

6. **Analyzing Behavior** Why might the United States have waited 16 years after the Russian Revolution to officially recognize the Soviet government?

7. **Comparing and Contrasting** Why did the Soviets prefer Roosevelt's style of diplomacy to Truman's?

**Linking Across Time**

8. What was the political status of eastern Europe at the start of the cold war? How has that status changed today?

# The Cold War Deepens

## June 1948: U.S. Air Force Heads for Berlin

O N A LAZY SATURDAY MORNING IN 1948, LT. COLONEL GUY B. DUNN, JR., HEADED FOR A GOLF GAME NEAR BROOKLEY AIR FORCE BASE IN ALABAMA. BEFORE HE COULD GET to the course, though, Colonel George S. Cassidy stopped him and told him they had to get to work—fast. They had to organize 12 aircraft, three crews per aircraft, and 62 maintenance people to start a squadron of 12 planes. Their destination—Berlin.

Dunn and his group got under way quickly. Once airborne and droning over the Atlantic, Dunn's colleague Lt. Colonel Jim Haun got on the radio. From the air he organized the rest of the squadron, calling on crews from Fairfield-Suisan Air Force Base in California and Great Falls Air Force Base in Montana.

The 12 planes heading to Berlin were cargo planes on a mission of mercy—not bombers. Just two weeks later, though, the Security Council ordered 60 B-29 bombers—the "atomic bombers"—to bases in Great Britain. There they would be within easy striking range of Moscow.

UPI/BETTMANN NEWSPHOTOS

Since the end of the war, Soviet and American plans for Germany had put the two nations on a collision course. The United States wanted a strong Germany to promote western European recovery and to help contain communism. The Soviets demanded a powerless Germany that could never attack the Soviet Union again.

Unable to find a common solution, the two powers pursued their own aims in the zones of Germany and Berlin they controlled. The United States, Britain, and France hammered out plans to rebuild the three western zones, tie their economies to the rest of Europe, and lay the groundwork for a free West German state. The Soviets viewed these plans with growing anger and alarm.

On June 18, 1948, tensions reached a breaking point when the United States, Britain, and France announced a new currency for the three western zones and West Berlin. Outraged, the Soviet governor angrily reminded the Western powers that at Potsdam they had agreed to treat Germany as one country. The Soviets warned them to scrap their currency plan or to accept a Soviet currency system for the eastern zone and *all* of Berlin.

Over the next three days, tempers flared. Western leaders reminded the Soviets they had no authority in West Berlin. The Soviets insisted on seeing Berlin as a part of their territory. At meetings on June 22, the powers searched for a compromise but gave up at 10:00 P.M. with no solution.

## Crisis in Berlin

N ot since the **cold war** began had the United States and the Soviet Union inched so close to war. Threatening speeches and hostile policies had deepened the two countries' fear of each other. Now they had a powder keg on their hands—Berlin.

## STUDY GUIDE

**As You Read**
Identify the events that led to the Berlin blockade and airlift, the civil war in China, and the Korean War. Also, think about the following concept and skills.

**Central Concept**
- understanding how the **cold war** led to the establishment of two Germanies, the victory of communism in China, and a bitter and divisive war in Korea

**Thinking Skills**
- identifying cause and effect
- drawing conclusions

**Showdown in Berlin**  In a surprise announcement the next morning, Soviet leaders declared that their currency would start circulating the following day. It would be the official currency in the Soviet zone and all four zones of Berlin. At the same time, Soviet troops blockaded the highways and railroads crossing the eastern zone to West Berlin. Finally, the Soviets shut off West Berlin's electric power.

Suddenly two million West Berliners became hostages. Sealed off from the outside world, they had no way to import the 4,000 tons of food, fuel, and clothes they needed every day. By isolating West Berlin, Stalin hoped to force the Allies into giving up their plans for West Germany or surrendering Berlin—a key Allied listening point—to the communists.

At this point Truman seemingly faced two terrible choices. He could order American troops to force open the roads and railroads and risk provoking World War III, or he could hand Berlin over to Stalin. Truman's advisers had another idea, though, and after he heard them out, he declared, "We are going to stay—period."

Taking advantage of a 1945 agreement to keep three air corridors open to Berlin, Truman launched an airlift to the trapped city. More than 50 C-54 and 80 C-47 cargo planes, all war weary and badly in need of repair, were pressed into service. A lifeline to the West, they would fly everything from milk and potatoes, blankets and coal, to clothing and vitamin pills into West Berlin's Templehof and Gatow airports.

**Airlift Saves Berlin**  For 11 months American and British pilots worked themselves to exhaustion, flying through summer thunderstorms and the dangerous fog and rain of Berlin's winter. At first they landed every three minutes, carrying in 2,400 pounds of supplies a day. At the peak of the airlift, the planes set down on makeshift runways every 45 seconds, day and night. Feverishly, crews unloaded some 13,000 tons of supplies a day and sent the planes on their way.

The massive effort—some 277,000 flights delivering two million tons of supplies—melted the hatred between former American and German enemies. Before long West Berliners by the hundreds were traveling out to Templehof to thank the pilots. They brought whatever gifts they had—flowers, hand-knitted sweaters, treasured family heirlooms. "An old man, so thin you could see through him showed up with a watch that would have fed him for months on the black market," recalled the American public affairs officer. "He insisted on giving it to an American. He called it 'a little token from an old and grateful heart.'"

The blockade was a complete disaster for Stalin. World opinion turned against the Soviet Union and its tactic of starving innocent people to achieve its

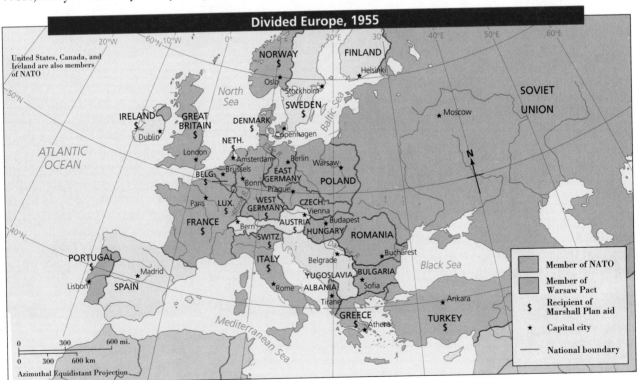

Divided Europe, 1955

**In 1955 NATO and the Warsaw Pact divided Europe into two sections as shown on the map.** *Which European countries belonged to NATO? What correlation existed between NATO members and participants in the Marshall Plan?*

ends. The United States, however, emerged a resourceful hero, and Berlin quickly became a symbol of America's fight against communism.

In May 1949 Stalin lifted the blockade, but the strong West Germany he had tried to prevent now became a reality. Late in May the United States, Britain, and France agreed to form the Federal Republic of Germany, sealing tight the once-loose border between the eastern and western zones. In October 1949 Stalin countered by declaring the German Democratic Republic of Eastern Germany. With those decisions Europe lay divided in half, and the Allied powers saw that a new alliance was needed.[1]

**Allies Form NATO**   The Berlin blockade convinced the Allies that western Europe needed military as well as economic support to remain free. In April 1949, a month before Stalin lifted the blockade, the United States, Canada, and 10 European nations formed the North Atlantic Treaty Organization (NATO). Not since the Revolutionary War had the United States joined a military alliance with Europe.

In Truman's mind, NATO would work like a "tripwire." If the Soviet Union dared to invade western Europe, they would "trip the wire" and set off an American military response. Said Truman, "An armed attack against one or more [nations] in Europe or North America shall be considered an attack against them all." NATO knit western Europe together as a force and discouraged individual countries from staying uncommitted to the rest.

Truman also persuaded Congress to spend $1.5 billion for military aid to NATO countries, beginning a military buildup in the United States. A few years later, in 1955, the Soviet Union matched NATO with the Warsaw Pact, a Soviet–eastern Europe alliance planted squarely across the Iron Curtain.

## The Cold War Moves to Asia

While the cold war unfolded in Europe, massive changes rocked the Far East. Throughout Asia, colonies ruled by the British, French, and Dutch began demanding their freedom. Stretched thin by the job of rebuilding at home, the European powers had little choice but to give in. In 1947 Britain

UPI/BETTMANN NEWSPHOTOS          THE BETTMANN ARCHIVE

**Mao Zedong (left) led the Communist forces and Jiang Jieshi (right) headed the Nationalists in the struggle for control of China.** *Which leader gained the support of Chinese peasants and why?*

granted freedom to India and modern-day Pakistan and Bangladesh, and in 1949 the Dutch gave up control of Indonesia.

**Civil War in China**   At the end of World War II, revolution was also raging in China, one of the key allies of the United States. There, Jiang Jieshi (Chiang Kai-shek), leader of the Nationalist government, was fighting a civil war with Mao Zedong (Mao Tse-tung), leader of Communist forces.

To most Americans, Jiang's success seemed essential to world peace. They believed a strong anti-communist government in China, the most populous country in the world, would block Soviet expansion and give the United States an important trading partner. Mao's success, many feared, could open the doors of Asia to Soviet control.

Yet this view of China was too simple. For one thing, Americans did not understand the Soviets' mistrust of Mao. A brilliant leader, Mao described himself as part tiger and part monkey—part ruthless and part clever. Stalin did not trust Mao or his brand of communism, saying once that "the Chinese communists are not really communists. They are 'margarine' communists." A weak China, like a weak Germany, would have pleased Stalin more. Likewise, Americans failed to understand the causes of the Chinese civil war—the oppression by a landlord class of millions of peasant farmers.

### STUDY GUIDE

**Identifying Cause and Effect**
The Berlin crisis might never have escalated to such dangerous proportions had the Soviets not sealed off the city and shut off electricity to West Berlin.

However, once those steps were taken, Truman believed he had little choice but to intervene.

**1** What alliances were formed after the Berlin crisis?

In the early 1920s, the Nationalist party swept into power, promising to rid China of foreign powers and redistribute property to the land-hungry peasants. Once in power, however, the Nationalists ignored the needs of the peasants and put up with corruption at all levels of government. Furthermore, Jiang forced the Communists who helped put him in power out of the government. By the late 1920s, the Communists and Nationalists were locked in battle.

When the Japanese invaded China in 1937, the Nationalists and Communists joined forces to defeat the Japanese. As the fighting wore on, however, the fortunes of the Nationalists and Communists changed dramatically.

Within a year Japanese forces crushed the Nationalist armies and conquered China's coast and river valleys—the industrial and farming heart of the country. With this defeat, the Nationalists lost much of their military strength and their power base.

By contrast, the Communists took advantage of the war to expand their control in the countryside. Stepping in where the Japanese had destroyed normal life, the Communists set up governments and small police forces. They gave peasants their own plots of land. In time, more and more people felt protected and taken care of by Mao's Communists.

By the end of World War II, Communist forces had grown from about 100,000 in 1937 to more than 900,000. As their shoestring army attracted more followers, they began to fight Jiang. Soon they were welcoming deserters from Jiang's poorly fed, sickly army into their own ranks.

**Truman Steps In**   Late in 1945 Truman sent George Marshall to meet with Jiang and Mao and find a way for both groups to share control. But the idea, however good, was doomed. Mao believed he should control China, and Jiang believed he should.

At this point, Truman had to choose sides, and he chose Jiang's. To fuel the Nationalist cause, the United States poured more than $3 billion in aid into China. In return, Truman also told Jiang to solve China's problems—answer the cry for land reforms, stop his friends from helping themselves to the treasury, take care of his tattered army.

Jiang continued to ignore these problems, while Mao's forces began winning battles. By January 1949

Jiang's forces abandoned Beijing. In May, Mao seized Shanghai; in October, he took Guangzhou and declared the People's Republic of China. Jiang fled to the offshore island of Taiwan in December, and in the American view, 500 million Chinese were "lost" to communism.

**The American Response**   To many Americans Mao's victory represented a frightening failure of containment. The most populous nation on earth had fallen into the enemy camp. "Who lost China?" many demanded to know.

Republican congressmen and leaders blamed Truman and the State Department. They believed more military support would have stopped Mao.

Truman responded that China was not America's to lose. Jiang, Truman said, lost because he refused to solve his nation's problems. The United States already had expensive programs to pay for in Europe. A full-scale war in China would have been too costly.

Still, the failure of containment was disturbing. To anchor freedom in Asia, the National Security Council urged the president to support the remaining friendly nations in Asia. Jiang's government was one. Another was Bao Dai's regime in Vietnam.

**The Arms Race Begins**   As hard as the Truman administration tried to keep people calm, events in Berlin and China unnerved everybody—including Truman himself. In January 1950 he ordered a high-level study of America's defenses. The outcome of that study—the top secret National Security Council Report NSC-68—suggested a change in direction.

According to NSC-68, the Soviet Union should be considered an enemy with a "design for world domination." As the leader of the "free world," only the United States could be expected to lead the fight against Soviet expansion. However, that job would require a huge standing army and navy and the best weapons that money could buy. To pay for such a massive defense system would require more than tripling the $13 billion defense budget.

Truman and his advisers agreed with the report. However, they worried about persuading Congress and the public to support a huge increase in taxes. "We were sweating over it," said a State Department aide, "and then, thank God, Korea came along."

### Identifying Cause and Effect

The civil war between the Chinese Nationalists and the Chinese Communists might have been avoided had the Nationalists kept their promises to the people. However, by denying peasants the land they were promised, by forcing friendly Communists out of the government, and by ignoring corruption, the Nationalists practically guaranteed their unpopularity and a bitter struggle for power with the Communists.

## Hot War Flares in Korea

Around 4:00 A.M. on a rainy June 25, 1950, about 75,000 North Korean troops following Soviet-made tanks poured across the 38th parallel into South Korea. They "struck like a cobra," recalled General Douglas MacArthur. While the attack took everyone by surprise, it followed years of squabbling.

At the end of World War II, Korea suffered a fate much like Germany's. The victors divided Korea along the 38th parallel, leaving a communist government and a powerful army in the north and a pro-Western government in the south. Both governments wanted to reunify Korea on their own terms. Now the North Koreans had made the first move.

**Truman Responds**  Truman decided to fight back, viewing the assault as a test of containment. Without seeking approval from Congress, Truman ordered air and naval forces to Korea on June 27. The same day, he sought the help of the United Nations.

In a strange twist of fate, the Soviet delegate to the UN Security Council was not present to block Truman's request. He had walked out of the United Nations to protest the council's unwillingness to seat a representative from Mao's China. With little debate, the Security Council condemned the Korean invasion and voted to provide money to help South Korean, American, and supporting UN forces repel the attack.[2]

Through the summer the North Korean army swept southward, cornering UN forces in the southeast around Pusan. On September 15, however, MacArthur launched a brilliant naval invasion behind enemy lines at Inchon, a port city near Seoul. With 18,000 marines and tanks, he rolled east and freed Seoul. From there the UN forces drove the North Koreans back to the 38th parallel.

MacArthur smelled victory, and he persuaded Truman to let him fight on to free all of Korea. Through the autumn MacArthur's troops pushed the North Korean army deeper into their own territory. By November MacArthur had them backed against the Chinese border at the Yalu River.

As MacArthur's troops approached the Yalu River and aircraft began bombing bridges crossing into China, Mao warned MacArthur to back off. Stubborn and overconfident, MacArthur paid no attention to Mao. Instead, he launched another attack to the north. In late November, however, huge numbers of Chinese troops surged across the Yalu and attacked the UN forces, taking MacArthur by surprise. Through the bitterly cold Korean winter, Chinese forces drove the UN troops back across the 38th parallel. There the war ground into a brutal stalemate, with both Chinese and UN troops fighting and dying over small, snow-covered hills.

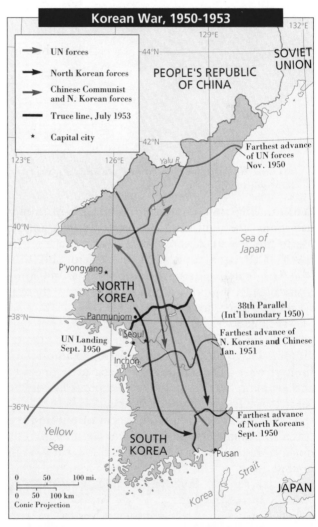

**The Korean War raged up and down the Korean peninsula between 1950 and 1953.** *Using the dates and arrows on the map, trace the movement of the opposing forces.*

---

## STUDY GUIDE

**Drawing Conclusions**
Taken together, the crisis in Berlin, the civil war in China, and the Korean conflict led many people to these conclusions: the Soviets were intent on exporting communism throughout the world, and the Americans had to be equally determined to resist communism wherever it appeared.

**2** What led to the involvement of UN forces in Korea? How successful were they?

THE BETTMANN ARCHIVE

**An American soldier tries to find warmth during the hard winter fighting in Korea.**

**Truman Fires MacArthur** After Chinese troops had joined the fight, Truman decided to give up the idea of freeing all of Korea and to seek a peace settlement. Outraged and anxious to win the war, MacArthur demanded permission to attack China, using nuclear weapons if necessary. "In war there is no substitute for victory," he insisted.

"We are trying to prevent a world war—not start one," Truman shot back. But MacArthur was bent on victory. He publicly criticized Truman's policy of **limited war**—keeping the fight confined to one area and avoiding the use of nuclear weapons. Finally, in April 1951, Truman fired MacArthur.

Truman's action ignited a storm of public fury. After all, Americans had just won a world war. Why not let MacArthur, a warrior and hero, rid Asia of communism? Truman's popularity took a nosedive; only 29 percent of the public agreed with the action he had taken.

Many government officials supported Truman, however. They knew that the United States could not afford to provoke the Soviets into open warfare. Nor could the United States expend all of its resources in Asia, leaving Europe unprotected.

In July 1951, shortly after MacArthur's firing, UN representatives and North Koreans met to begin peace talks. But the fighting and the talks dragged on for two more years, only to be settled by the next president, Dwight D. Eisenhower.

## The Impact of the Korean War

The Korean War settled little in Asia. When it ended in 1953, the official border was set at the cease-fire line, not far from where the fighting began. Korea continued to be divided in half with a communist regime in the north and a pro-Western government in the south. Still, the conflict had far-reaching effects.

First, the Korean War convinced Americans that a huge military buildup was a good idea. Moving faster than NSC-68 suggested, Congress increased defense spending from $22.3 billion in 1951 to $50.4 billion in 1953. America emerged from the Korean War with an army of 3.5 million men as well as overseas military bases and powerful new weapons like the long-range B-52 bomber. Moreover, the country now had a stockpile of 750 nuclear warheads, an increase of 600 in two years.

The public also supported Truman's decisive actions in Korea, overlooking the fact that he never sought or received a declaration of war from Congress. Truman's independent action enhanced the power of the presidency and laid the foundation for later undeclared wars.

## SECTION REVIEW

**Checking Facts**

1. What does the acronym NATO stand for? What is the name of its Soviet counterpart?
2. To where did Jiang Jieshi retreat after the defeat of his Nationalist forces by the Communists?
3. What was NSC-68, and what did it suggest?
4. Why did President Truman relieve General Douglas MacArthur of his command in Korea?

**Thinking Critically**

5. **Identifying Cause and Effect** What might have caused the Allies to band together to form NATO? Use evidence from the section to support your answer.
6. **Drawing Conclusions** How might a Nationalist victory in the Chinese civil war have affected the outcome of the Korean conflict?

**Linking Across Time**

7. The reunification of East and West Germany took place in 1990. At that time newly independent Poland expressed strong reservations about a reunified Germany and even asked that Soviet troops stationed in Poland remain to buttress Poland's defenses. How did Poland's concerns in 1990 mirror Soviet concerns about Germany immediately after World War II?

# Cold War in the Atomic Age

## August 1949: Russia Joins the Nuclear Club

THUNDER BOOMED OMINOUSLY, AND HAIL CLATTERED DOWN ON THE WHITE HOUSE ROOF THE MORNING OF SEPTEMBER 23, 1949. JUST AFTER 10:30 A.M., WHITE House reporters finished a routine meeting with Charles Ross, President Truman's press secretary. On their way out, however, Ross's secretary, Myrtle Bergheim, told the reporters to stick around. She called them out of the nearby press room and back into Ross's office just seconds before 11:00 A.M. None of them knew what was coming, and none of them realized how perfectly the storm outside would fit the news.

As the last reporter filed in, Ross said, "Close the door. Nobody is leaving until everybody has this statement."

Ross handed each reporter a single sheet of paper carrying a short statement by Truman. The first reporter to scan the copy gasped; in seconds the whole group tore out of Ross's office and down the hall for the press room phones. In the mad rush, somebody crashed into a stuffed deer head and broke off its nose.

When the presidential statement hit the papers, it stunned the nation. "We have evidence," Truman announced, "that within recent weeks an atomic explosion occurred in the USSR."

## *Living with Fear*

With this chilling announcement, America's sense of security went up in a cloud of smoke—a dark, fearsome mushroom cloud. The world now had two nuclear powers, and what happened to Hiroshima and Nagasaki could just as easily happen to New York or Chicago or Los Angeles.

**Public Worry**   When the atomic age burst into history at Hiroshima in 1945, Americans were shocked, confused, and terrified. Like children whistling in the dark, they also joked about the bomb. Stores had atomic sales, bars sold atomic cocktails, musicians wrote ballads and polkas about the bomb, but under the surface laughter ran a deep current of fear. Months passed before Americans got used to the idea of life with the bomb.

With Truman's announcement America's fears surged back to the surface. The media jumped on the story, both soothing the panic with helpful advice and intensifying fears with hair-raising descriptions. One radio show broadcast the following account of a make-believe nuclear attack on Chicago:

> *Most of those in the center of the city were violently killed by the blast or by the following vacuum, which explosively burst their stomachs. . . . Those few who escaped the blast, but not the gamma rays, died slowly after they had left the ruined city. No attempt at identification of the bodies or burial ever took place. Chicago was simply closed.*
>
> — NBC Radio Program, August 1949

To calm the public's jangled nerves, Truman organized the Federal Civil Defense Administration (FCDA). Within months the agency flooded the

---

## STUDY GUIDE

**As You Read**
Watch for the political influences, military plans, scientific breakthroughs, and public fears that accompanied the arms race. Also, think about the following concepts and skills.

**Central Concepts**
- understanding the strategy of **massive retaliation**
- recognizing how the **arms race** affected the cold war and American public opinion

**Thinking Skills**
- recognizing assumptions
- identifying cause and effect
- predicting consequences

country with posters and booklets telling people they *could* survive a nuclear war—if they were prepared.

How should Americans prepare? Best of all, they could build some kind of underground bomb shelter. A simple one could be a trench covered with dirt. They could also take shelter in the family car or a well-stocked basement protected with piles of dirt around the outside walls.

If a shelter wasn't handy when an attack came, people learned to "jump in any . . . ditch or gutter" and "bury their faces in their arms." Grade schools instructed children in these procedures. To keep from panic during an attack, people were encouraged to use "little tricks to help steady their nerves—reciting jingles or the multiplication tables."

Once again, all of America seemed preoccupied with nuclear war. Real estate agents offered houses in "safe locations." Doctors and ministers took courses on coping with radiation injuries and panic. Entrepreneurs tried to sell every product they could dream up—burn medicine, ready-made bomb shelters, dog tags, even radiation-proof clothing for dad, mom, kids, and the dog.[1]

**The Game Gets Deadlier** Scary as nuclear bombs were, most Americans thought the best way to prevent nuclear war was to have more and better bombs than the Soviets. Truman agreed. In January 1950, after a heated debate with his advisers, the president ordered scientists to develop a deadly hydrogen bomb, a superbomb. By late 1952, the scientists were ready to test the first H-bomb—nicknamed *Mike*—on a coral island in the South Pacific.

No one who saw the explosion after the bomb was dropped ever forgot it. Out of a blast of white heat, five times hotter than the center of the sun, billowed a monstrous mushroom cloud. Purple, gray, and yellow and nearly 100 miles wide, it climbed 25 miles into the sky. The blast carved a mile-long crater in the bottom of the ocean and spilled radioactive dust over thousands of square miles. Nuclear scientists had let a terrible genie out of the bottle, and now there was no way to put it back.

**Public fear of nuclear attack resulted in the building of backyard bomb shelters, weekly safety drills in schools, and numerous publications from the FCDA.**

UPI/BETTMANN NEWSPHOTOS

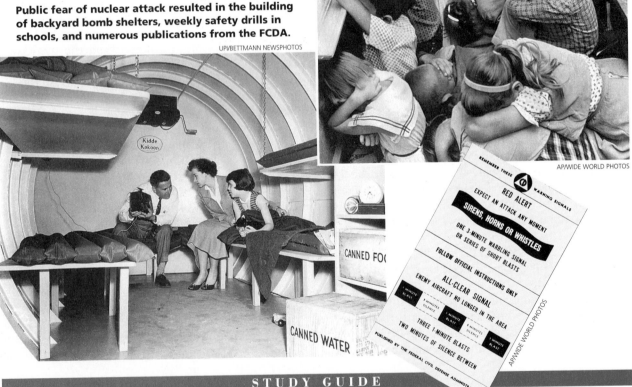

AP/WIDE WORLD PHOTOS

AP/WIDE WORLD PHOTOS

STUDY GUIDE

**Recognizing Assumptions**

The use of nuclear weapons made all previous concepts of warfare obsolete. Nevertheless, Americans supported the building of a huge arsenal of nuclear weapons. They assumed that peaceful negotiations with the Soviets were an impossibility.

**1** How did Americans respond to the possibility of nuclear war?

# Eisenhower Comes to Power

**T**hree days after *Mike* blew a coral island to smithereens, Republican Dwight D. Eisenhower won the 1952 presidential election. The World War II hero stepped into the White House at the height of the cold war. China had fallen. American troops were bogged down in Korea. Growing stockpiles of atomic bombs had Americans on edge. In the midst of mounting danger, Ike seemed like the perfect leader.

Raised on the Kansas frontier and honed into a tough army officer by West Point and World War II, Eisenhower was both a seasoned soldier and a grandfather figure. He had an instinct for people, and his homespun charm won hearts instantly. Said one of Eisenhower's World War II compatriots: "He has the power of drawing the hearts of men towards him as a magnet attracts bits of metal. He merely has to smile at you, and you trust him at once." People, as the campaign buttons said, liked Ike.

AP?WIDE WORLD

**Mamie and Ike's eight years in the White House was the longest time they had lived in one place.**

**Eisenhower in Korea**   Americans found Eisenhower's upbeat outlook and his practicality comforting in dangerous times. But they also liked his determination to settle the Korean War.

Before the election in 1952, Eisenhower had accused the Democrats of "mishandling the war," and vowed that his first job as president would be "to bring the Korean war to an early and honorable end. If that job requires a personal trip to Korea," Eisenhower had declared, "I shall make that trip."

True to his word, three weeks after the election, Eisenhower toured the Korean front and confirmed his hunch that peace talks offered the only way out. "Small attacks on small hills would not end this war."

Still, Eisenhower took time to review other ways of ending the war, including full-scale war against China and nuclear attacks on Korea. Finally, though, he decided to demand peace talks backed up by a veiled threat to use nuclear weapons.

Eisenhower's search for peace was aided by the death of Josef Stalin in March 1953. Communist leaders in China and North Korea could no longer be sure of Soviet help; nor could they be sure whether Eisenhower was bluffing or telling the truth about a nuclear attack. With little choice but to settle the fight, UN and communist delegates finally signed an agreement in July 1953 dividing North and South Korea at the truce line.

## Eisenhower and Dulles

With the Korean War behind him, Eisenhower could focus on the cold war and the mounting arms race. Like Truman, Eisenhower was a passionate anticommunist. Unlike Truman, however, Eisenhower stepped into office with a solid grasp of world affairs. He had lived in Latin America, Europe, and Asia. As a World War II general and, later, the commander of NATO, he had mingled with heads of state. Even so, Eisenhower wanted a strong secretary of state who would hold the line on communism and advise him on areas like the Middle East and Asia.[2]

John Foster Dulles fit the bill. A polished international attorney, Dulles had spent more than 40 years in foreign relations. The son of a Presbyterian minister, white-haired Dulles was also deeply religious and fiercely anticommunist. Many Americans found Dulles humorless and argumentative. Churchill once said that Dulles was the only "bull he knew who carried his own china shop with him." However, Soviet Premier Nikita Khrushchev would later say of Dulles that he "knew how far he could push us and he never pushed us too far."

## A New Cold War Strategy

Together, Eisenhower and Dulles took a fresh look at the cold war game board. Problems and unknowns were everywhere. Who would replace Stalin in the Soviet Union? How long could the United States afford to build bigger armies and navies and bombs? Was containment the best defense against communism? How did nuclear weapons figure into all of this?

In May 1953 Eisenhower assigned three top-level groups to study the situation, while he worked with defense officials to cut military costs. Out of these studies emerged a new containment policy.

**Massive Retaliation**   Instead of depending on costly armies and navies to fight limited wars as Truman did, Eisenhower decided to rely on cheaper air power and nuclear weapons. This program, called the New Look, would retire 500,000 soldiers and 100,000 sailors but increase the air force by 30,000 men. The new defense plan would save about $4 billion a year, thereby providing "a bigger bang for the buck."

Smaller armies and navies required a different way to fight communism, so Eisenhower and Dulles proposed a new policy. If the Soviet Union attacked any nation, the United States would launch **massive retaliation**—an instant nuclear attack "by means and at places of our own choosing." Such a vague threat, Eisenhower believed, would force the communists to think twice before attacking because they couldn't be sure where the United States might strike.

Critics called this tough stance **brinksmanship**—the art of never backing down from a crisis, even if it meant pushing the nation to the brink of war. By keeping the communists from testing every weak spot along their borders, the United States could stay out of small, limited wars that cost huge amounts of money.

To back up this tough stance, Eisenhower and Dulles also circled the Soviet Union and China with more American military bases and allies. By the end of the decade, Dulles had worked out mutual defense treaties with 43 countries around the globe.

**Policy Dangers**   The policy of massive retaliation had two dangerous results. First, it gave the United States only two extreme ways of responding to a communist attack: either fight a nuclear battle or do nothing. The middle ground, using armies to fight small wars, virtually disappeared. The United States had to gamble on threats and Soviet insecurity to keep the peace.

Second, the Soviets did not sit idly by and let the United States sprint ahead in the arms race. Heavy U.S. spending for nuclear weapons spurred the Soviets to step up their own research, and in July 1953 they exploded an H-bomb in Siberia. "The U.S. and Soviet Union are like two scorpions in a bottle, each capable of killing the other but only at the risk of his own life," observed J. Robert Oppenheimer, father of the atomic bomb. The world had reached, in Churchill's words, a new "balance of terror."

## Eisenhower Wages Peace

Eisenhower was a realist. He knew he had to be tough with the Soviets, so he kept the war machine in good running order. But like Oppenheimer, he also understood that nuclear war was pointless. From the early days of his presidency, Eisenhower searched for ways to disarm atomic weapons.

★ ★ ★  **PRESIDENT'S GALLERY**  ★ ★ ★

"*We must be ready to dare all for our country. For history does not long entrust the care of freedom to the weak or the timid. We must acquire proficiency in defense and display stamina in purpose. We must be willing, individually and as a Nation, to accept whatever sacrifices may be required of us. A people that values its privileges above its principles soon loses both.*"

*Inaugural Address, January 20, 1953*

UPI/BETTMANN NEWSPHOTO

Dwight David Eisenhower 1953–1961

**Background:**
- Born 1890; died 1969
- Republican, Kansas
- Graduated West Point 1915
- Commanding general of American forces in Europe 1942
- Supreme commander of the Allied Expeditionary Force in Europe 1943

**Achievements in Office:**
- Southeast Asia Treaty Organization formed (1954)
- NASA formed (1958)

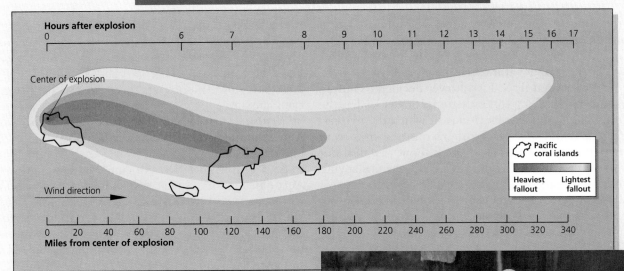

## Nuclear Fallout from *Bravo* H-Bomb Test

**Hours after explosion**
0   6   7   8   9   10   11   12   13   14   15   16   17

Center of explosion

Wind direction

Pacific coral islands

Heaviest fallout    Lightest fallout

**Miles from center of explosion**
0   20   40   60   80   100   120   140   160   180   200   220   240   260   280   300   320   340

**Aabbno Masuda was one of the Japanese fishermen injured by fallout from *Bravo*. In addition, 239 natives of the Marshall Islands and 28 American service personnel were affected.** *How did the publicity surrounding the Bravo accident affect public reaction to the tests?*

UPI/BETTMANN NEWSPHOTOS

A few weeks after Stalin's death, Eisenhower made his famous "Chance for Peace" speech before a group of newspaper editors. "An era ended with the death of Josef Stalin," Eisenhower said, inviting friendlier relations with the Soviet Union. He went on to spell out the high costs of cold war. "Every gun that is made, every warship launched, every rocket fired signifies . . . a theft from those who hunger and are not fed, those who are cold and not clothed." Eisenhower closed with an appeal for nuclear disarmament.

In December 1953 Eisenhower carried his appeal to the United Nations. There he proposed an "atoms for peace" plan in which Soviets and Americans would contribute radioactive materials to a stockpile for peaceful uses.[3]

**Fallout Fears** As Eisenhower worked for peace, arms research continued. On March 1, 1954, the United States set off the biggest H-bomb it has ever tested—the equivalent of 15 million tons of TNT, nicknamed *Bravo*.

The massive explosion in the South Pacific created a radioactive cloud that rained deadly silver ash on 7,000 square miles of ocean waters and islands. Worst of all, radioactive ash fell on 23 Japanese

fishermen aboard the *Lucky Dragon*, some 80 miles from the blast. By the time the fishermen got back to Japan, all 23 were sick with radiation poisoning. A few months later, Aikichi Kuboyama, the radioman, died.

Suddenly people had something new to worry about—radioactive fallout. It was possible to live hundreds of miles from a nuclear blast and still be killed. Around the world, concern grew about nuclear tests and the effects of their deadly, radioactive clouds.

**Talks in Geneva** By the autumn of 1954, international voices were clamoring for a halt to the arms race. Late that year Communist and Western leaders finally agreed to meet the following summer—their first face-to-face talk since 1945.

Eisenhower flew to the meeting in Geneva, Switzerland, with high hopes of improving U.S. and Soviet relations. But the first few days of meetings went poorly. The Soviet leaders—Nikolai Bulganin and Nikita Khrushchev, the real power—"drank little and smiled much," Eisenhower commented. Their actions seemed unnatural, rehearsed.

After several days, Eisenhower decided to loosen things up. Speaking earnestly to the Soviet leaders, he proposed the "open skies" idea in which the two nations would inspect each other's military sites from the air. Bulganin agreed to think about the idea, but Khrushchev dismissed the plan as an obvious spying ploy. Ten years of bitter mistrust stood in the way of the idea, and in the end the Soviets let it die. Even so, the Geneva conference did end on an upbeat note—the powers had begun to talk again.

## Back into the Deep Freeze

Through the rest of 1955 and into 1956, the cold war seemed to be thawing. The talks in Geneva had broken the ice, and back home Khrushchev made some astounding statements. In a momentous speech before the Party Congress in February 1956, he openly condemned Stalin's crimes against the Soviet people. Moreover, he stated that communists and capitalists might be able to live together peacefully and even declared that the Soviets might tolerate different kinds of communism.

Throughout eastern Europe Khrushchev's words inspired people to seek more freedom. In Hungary a new government announced that the country would leave the Warsaw Pact and remain neutral. The Soviets responded with force. On November 4, 1956, Khrushchev sent 200,000 troops and 2,500 tanks into Budapest to put down an uprising of poorly armed students and workers. Khrushchev, the "bare-knuckle slugger" who was taking control, had revealed another side. Clearly, the cold war was far from over.

**Sputnik Fires the Arms Race**   If any hopes remained of slowing the **arms race,** they fizzled completely in the fall of 1957. On August 1 the Soviets tested their first successful intercontinental missile, a long-range missile carrying a nuclear warhead. On October 4 the Soviets jolted Americans when they launched *Sputnik,* a 184-pound satellite, into orbit around the earth.

People read the news with awe and fear: America was running second in the survival race. Critics accused Eisenhower of "permitting a technological Pearl Harbor." A missile gap had developed, they cried, and now America was threatened by bomb-carrying missiles!

*Sputnik* shifted the arms race into high gear. Almost immediately Eisenhower increased the funding for missile development from $4.3 billion in 1958 to $5.3 billion in 1959. He launched the National Aeronautics and Space Administration (NASA), which worked feverishly to close the missile gap. With large, new congressional appropriations, the Defense Department expanded the B-52 bomber fleet, built submarines outfitted with nuclear missiles, and installed a ring of short-range missiles in Europe.

To be sure the United States wouldn't be caught short again, the government poured huge sums of money into education to train scientists and engineers. Billions of dollars also went to universities; nearly one-third of all university scientists and engineers directed their energies to full-time weapons research. A powerful military-educational-industrial combination was taking shape.

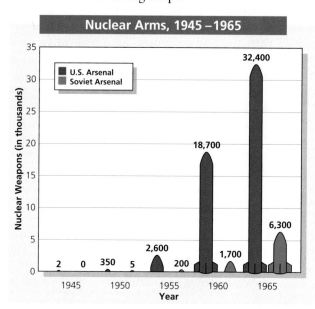

*How does the number of Soviet warheads in 1960 compare with the number of American warheads in that year? What accounts for this difference?*

### Predicting Consequences

*Sputnik* and the missile gap led to great increases in military spending on both sides throughout the next three decades. What were the consequences of such enormous military spending? By the time arms-reduction treaties finally were being signed in the late 1980s and early 1990s, the Soviet economy was faltering. Although the United States fared somewhat better, neverthe-less, vital social programs had either been cancelled, underfunded, or abandoned before they were begun.

**Protests Slow Testing**   In spite of the Soviets' military achievements and America's headlong race to keep up, strong pressure was still building for arms control. The nuclear-fallout scare of 1954 continued into 1955 when radioactive rain fell in Chicago. Scientists and doctors began to warn of fallout dangers like bone cancer and leukemia.

In 1957, the same year that *Sputnik* roared into orbit, a group of business, scientific, and publishing leaders established SANE, the Committee for a Sane Nuclear Policy. Within a year their membership grew to 25,000, and the group began pressuring for change with powerful newspaper ads: "We must stop the contamination of the air, the milk children drink, the food we eat."

In 1957, Nevil Shute's novel *On the Beach* hit the best-seller list, adding its strength to the growing antinuclear movement. Terrifyingly real, the book told the story of massive nuclear war that destroyed the Northern Hemisphere and sent clouds of radioactive dust swirling into the Southern Hemisphere. There, millions of people talked, planned, worried, cried—and waited for the end. In the book, Moira Davidson, a young Australian woman, rages at her friend, submarine commander Dwight Towers:

> *I*t's not fair. No one in the Southern Hemisphere ever dropped a bomb. . . . We had nothing to do with it. Why should we have to die because other countries nine or ten thousand miles away from us wanted to have a war?"
>
> *There was a pause, and then she said angrily. "It's not that I'm afraid of dying, Dwight. We've all got to do that sometime. It's all the things I'm going to have to miss. . . . All my life I've wanted to see the Rue de Rivoli. I suppose it's the romantic name. It's silly because it's just a street like any other street. But that's what I've wanted, and I'm*

*never going to see it. Because there isn't any Paris now, or London or New York."*

Nevil Shute, *On the Beach*, 1957

Forty newspapers serialized *On the Beach*, and eventually the book was made into a movie. The book contributed its weight to shifting public opinion. In 1957 a Gallup Poll found that 63 percent of Americans wanted the government to halt H-bomb tests.

In response to a growing worldwide outcry, the United States and the Soviet Union agreed to stop nuclear testing in the atmosphere. That agreement held until the Soviets set off another bomb in 1961. In 1963 the nuclear powers finally signed a test ban treaty that outlawed nuclear tests in the atmosphere but permitted them underground and in outer space. Ultimately 100 nations signed the agreement.

**The Military-Industrial Threat**   Changes in nuclear testing solved the immediate problem. Yet the United States and the Soviet Union continued to invent new doomsday weapons and build huge stockpiles. In the process, a new threat was growing in the United States—the vast, interwoven military establishment and arms industry. At the end of his presidency, Eisenhower alerted the nation to the danger of this **military-industrial complex** that could threaten freedom in America:

> *I*n the councils of government we must guard against the acquisition of unwarranted influence . . . by the military-industrial complex. The potential for the disastrous rise of misplaced power exists and will persist.
>
> *We must never let the weight of this combination endanger our liberties or democratic processes.*

President Dwight Eisenhower, Farewell Speech, 1961

## SECTION REVIEW

### Checking Facts

1. When and where was the first H-bomb tested?
2. Why did Eisenhower appoint Dulles as his secretary of state?
3. Explain the policy of massive retaliation. What is the other name for this policy?
4. Explain Eisenhower's "open skies" proposal.
5. What was *Sputnik*?

### Thinking Critically

6. **Predicting Consequences**
Just before he left office, President Eisenhower predicted the rise of a military-industrial complex in the United States. What are some possible consequences of an alliance between industry and the military?

7. **Recognizing Assumptions**
During the late 1980s, the United States and the Soviet Union agreed to allow mutual inspections

of each country's military installations. What assumptions underlie such an agreement?

### Linking Across Time

8. During the Geneva convention in 1955, President Eisenhower proposed an "open skies" policy. Although neither nation agreed to it, it is practiced today. How?

## Soviet "Moon" Circles the Earth

*MOSCOW, OCT. 5—Russia announced this morning it had launched yesterday the first man-made "moon" and that it was spinning around the earth at a speed of five miles a second.*

*The artificial moon is about 23 inches in diameter. It was launched by a carrier rocket which was believed to have given it the necessary spin to fly round the world in 1 hour and 35 minutes.*
*—Chicago Tribune, 1957*

### United States Left on Launching Pad

The 184-pound *Sputnik* was put into orbit by one of Russia's intercontinental ballistic missiles, capable of delivering satellites into space and bombs across the ocean. Since June the U.S. Project Vanguard has hoped to send a 21.5-pound satellite into space. However, America's own satellite has not successfully gotten off the launching pad.

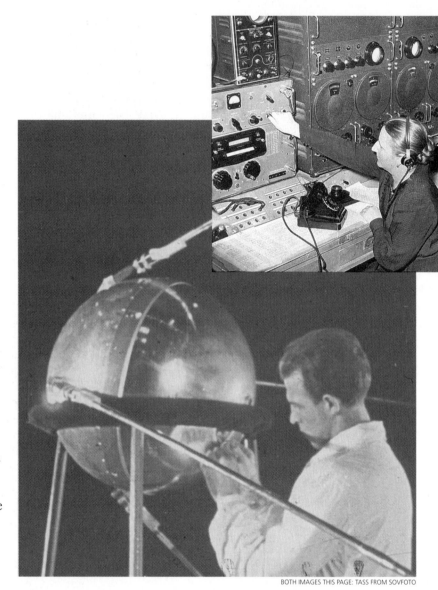

BOTH IMAGES THIS PAGE: TASS FROM SOVFOTO

## Elsewhere in the News

### Leave It to Beaver

NEW YORK—The Cleaver family, with Beaver and older brother, Wally, made its TV debut. In the first episode, one of the boys tried to avoid being "spelled from school."

### Presley Rocks

LOS ANGELES—Elvis Presley's newest recording, "Jailhouse Rock," climbed the charts. However, the Everly Brothers' "Wake Up Little Suzie" topped the national hit parade this week.

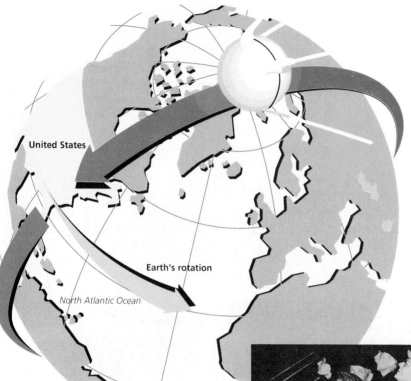

United States

Earth's rotation

North Atlantic Ocean

Equator

AP/WIDE WORLD

## Ike Not Worried

At his press conference, President Eisenhower denied the United States had ever been in a space race. Insisting that the satellite was for science and not defense, he added it "does not raise my apprehensions. Not one iota."

## Related Stories

- **Satellite Visible with Binoculars**
- **Navy Picks Up Radio Signals**
- **U.S. Delay Draws Scientists' Fire**
- **Politicians Push Panic Button**

AP/WIDE WORLD PHOTOS

FPG

## New Champion Honored

NEW YORK—Featured on this month's cover of *Ebony* was Althea Gibson, world-famous tennis champion. A ticker-tape parade welcomed her home from her victory at Wimbledon.

# Analyzing Secondary Sources

The book *War and Peace in the Nuclear Age,* by John Newhouse, is a secondary source that analyzes events described in this chapter. The value and accuracy of a secondary source depends on its use of primary sources.

## Learning the Skill

A source created at or near the time of the events it reports is called a primary source. Primary sources may be written or oral accounts by participants or witnesses. Materials produced from primary sources are called secondary sources.

### Spotting Primary Sources

Clues in a secondary source often tell you what primary sources have been used. Acknowledgments or "A Note on Sources" at the front of a book or the bibliography at the back of the book list primary sources.

Watch for references to primary sources, as in this excerpt from Newhouse's book:

*Eisenhower was very taken with the Open Skies idea. He even thought the idea might be negotiable. . . . Eisenhower described in his memoirs the . . . [reaction] of Soviet Prime Minister Bulganin, who said it had real merit and would be studied sympathetically. "The tone of his talk seemed as encouraging as his words," wrote Eisenhower. A few minutes later, walking toward the bar with Khrushchev, he was disabused but enlightened. " 'I don't*
*agree with the Chairman,' Khrushchev said, smiling—but there was no smile in his voice. I saw clearly then, for the first time, the identity of the real boss of the Soviet delegation." From then on, said Eisenhower, "I wasted no more time probing Mr. Bulganin; I devoted myself exclusively to an attempt to persuade Mr. Khrushchev of the merits of the Open Skies plan, but to no avail. He said the idea was nothing more than a bald espionage plot against the U.S.S.R."*

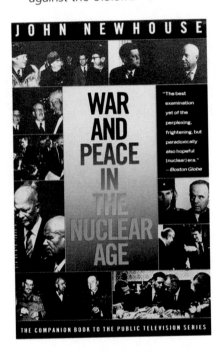

Newhouse alerts the reader to the primary source in three ways. First, he mentions the primary source, Eisenhower's memoirs. Then he puts primary source material in quotation marks. Third, he provides a footnote, which identifies the primary source as Eisenhower's memoirs, *The White House Years: Mandate for Change, 1953–1956.*

## Evaluating Effectiveness

To determine whether the historian has used primary sources effectively, ask these questions about the secondary source:

1. Are the primary sources relevant? The historian may use a primary source not only to support a particular historical fact but also to create a sense of immediacy. Newhouse's use of Eisenhower's words provides a vivid impression of how Eisenhower felt.

2. Is a wide enough range of primary sources considered? Careful historians consider many different kinds of primary sources. For the Eisenhower years, primary sources could include bumper stickers about the bomb, government documents, or the text of a speech. Look for balance. Ask whether the account presents enough varied testimony.

3. Is the interpretation sound? Check the context of the primary source to see whether the sense of the excerpt is accurate. Then consider whether the historian's interpretation seems correct.

4. Is information synthesized effectively? Good secondary sources interweave information from primary sources to support a thesis or tell a story.

## Practicing the Skill

1. Read magazine articles that analyze nuclear arms control today. Evaluate how well primary sources were used.

2. Find a secondary source that discusses a major topic in this chapter. Analyze how effectively it uses primary sources.

# A New Battleground

## Midnight, August 2, 1953: CIA Plots the Takeover of Iran

LATE IN THE SUMMER OF 1953, TROUBLE WAS BREWING IN IRAN, AND EISENHOWER WAS WORRIED. THIS MIDDLE EASTERN COUNTRY WAS IMPORTANT TO THE UNITED STATES for two reasons: Iran bordered the Soviet Union and it had some of the richest pools of oil in the world.

Eisenhower worried about Iran's troubled economy and its increasing reliance on the Soviet Union. If the communists seized Iran's government, yet another country—and one with a huge supply of valuable oil—would join the Soviet bloc. Something had to be done quickly. That something began this way:

*A large, ornate garden in Teheran [Iran's capital]. A medium-sized, medium-height, rather nondescript American wearing a dark turtleneck shirt, Oxford gray slacks, and Persian sandals, opens the gate to the garden, slips out, glances up and down the street, and silently climbs into the back seat of an ordinary looking black sedan. Without a backward glance, the driver pulls away slowly, smoothly and heads toward the royal palace. In the back seat, the American huddles down on the floor and pulls a blanket over him.*

*At the palace gate, the sentry flashes a light in the driver's face, grunts, and waves the car through. Halfway between the gate and the palace steps, the driver parks, gets out, and walks away. A slim, nervous man walks down the drive, glancing left and right as he*

*approaches. The American pulls the blanket out of the way and sits up as the man enters the car. . . .*

*They look at each other. Then His Imperial Majesty, Mohammed Reza Shah Pahlavi, Shahanshah of Iran, Light of the Aryans, allows himself to relax and even smile.*

Kermit Roosevelt,
*Countercoup: The Struggle for Control of Iran,* 1979

UPI/BETTMANN NEWSPHOTOS

The American hiding under the blanket in the back seat that night was Kermit (Kim) Roosevelt, the grandson of President Theodore Roosevelt and a cousin of Franklin Delano Roosevelt. A top American spy, Roosevelt had entered Iran under a phony name to meet secretly with Iran's 34-year-old Shah, or ruler.

Why were Roosevelt and the Shah sneaking around in the middle of the night? What was going on?

## New Worlds to Conquer

Iran, like many emerging nations, found itself in turmoil after World War II. These **third world** lands—the mostly nonwhite, developing countries in Asia, Latin America, Africa, and the Middle East—were shaking off colonial rule and taking charge of their futures. So widespread and powerful were these movements for national independence that between 1946 and 1960 alone 37 new countries emerged. Loyal to neither of the two worlds—the

### STUDY GUIDE

**As You Read**
Notice how the cold war affected events in third world countries and influenced the development and activities of the CIA. Also, think about the following concept and skills.

**Central Concept**
- recognizing the influence of the cold war on the politics of the **third world**

**Thinking Skills**
- analyzing decisions
- predicting consequences
- identifying cause and effect

United States and its democratic allies or the Soviet Union and the communist bloc—these third world nations became a new cold war battleground.

**U.S. Interests**   Winning the loyalty of emerging nations was crucial to Eisenhower. The United States depended on rich stores of rubber, oil, and other natural resources in third world countries and on their vast markets for American products. Just as important, third world nations that were allied with the United States could help defend against communist expansion.

Eisenhower and Dulles believed they needed to act decisively. They assumed that third world struggles for self-determination were really revolutions directed by the Soviet Union. Left unopposed, these revolutions could result in neutral states or, worse, communist ones throughout the Southern Hemisphere. If the Soviets managed to increase their influence in the third world, said Dulles, the scales would tip decisively against the Western democracies.

**Third World Views**   Drawing third world countries into the American camp was difficult, however. Many newly independent nations, like India and Egypt, wanted no part of outside control—American *or* Soviet. Having just gotten rid of one foreign ruler, they had no desire for another.

Even establishing friendships with emerging nations proved difficult. For the millions of third world poor, life was a grim daily struggle to stay alive. They resented America's wealth, which they glimpsed in the luxurious life styles of American tourists and diplomats. Likewise, Soviet propagandists pointed to America's troubled race relations and asked nonwhite people of the third world: If America does not treat its fellow citizens equally, how will it treat you? Finally, in third world struggles, the United States often sided with the wealthy, not the common, people. Even though America itself was born of revolution, the United States now worried about protecting its overseas investments and military bases. To people struggling for freedom, America seemed like just another threat.

Facing so much resistance in the third world, the United States used many methods to win friends and wage cold war. Massive amounts of foreign aid—the primary method—helped improve farming, schools, and medical care in third world countries. When Eisenhower became president, he relied increasingly on the Central Intelligence Agency, the **CIA,** to promote the allegiance of newly independent nations. The CIA spied and conducted **covert operations,** or undercover missions, of all kinds.

## The CIA Joins the Fight

The CIA wasn't Eisenhower's idea but rather a government agency created by President Truman. After World War II, Truman decided that peacetime America no longer needed a network of spies. By 1946, however, Truman changed his mind as U.S.–Soviet relations soured and intelligence gathering began to seem necessary again.

**CIA Powers**   In 1947 Congress passed the historic National Security Act, which streamlined the defense system and created the CIA and the National Security Council (NSC). The newly created NSC and the CIA reported directly to the president.

The act also gave the CIA sweeping powers with this loose definition of its job: The CIA shall perform "functions and duties related to intelligence affecting national security as the National Security Council will direct." This language left the CIA free to spy and to carry on covert operations. Used with care, the CIA enabled the president to take quick, controversial action in foreign trouble spots without waiting for congressional or public approval. This resource gave the White House virtual control of foreign policy.

In its early years, the CIA carried out few covert operations. Its main job was to spy on the Soviet military and prop up European democracies by secretly funding democratic political parties, labor unions, and other pro-Western groups.

The CIA was so successful that in 1949 Congress gave that agency the right to spend unlimited amounts of money without telling anyone except the director where the money went and for what. This authority gave the president and the CIA a free hand. In time they would bribe overseas politicians, hire secret armies, and even plot the assassination of troublesome leaders.[1]

**STUDY GUIDE**

**Analyzing Decisions**
Both the United States and the Soviet Union were eager to secure the loyalty of third world countries. Using economic aid as an inducement, these powers could obtain permission from third world countries to establish military bases within their borders.

1   What enabled the CIA to become such a powerful force in foreign affairs?

**The CIA Grows Powerful**   With its increase in power and funding, the CIA mushroomed. In 1949 the agency had about 300 employees and spent $4.7 million. Just three years later, the CIA had grown to 20 times its original size. It employed nearly 6,000 people located all over the world and spent nearly $82 million.

As the CIA grew, more Americans saw it as "the good way to fight communism." Exciting, glamorous, and challenging, the agency attracted talented young graduates from Harvard, Yale, and other top universities. Eventually the CIA would have an important role, instead of just a hand, in shaping events all over the world. As the map below shows, CIA agents worked behind the scenes worldwide to overthrow neutral or pro-Soviet governments and to prop up pro-Western ones.

## The CIA and the Shah

The CIA's first attempt to overthrow a government took place in Iran. At the end of World War II, oil-rich Iran was ruled by a monarch and a two-house parliament. The Shah (king), Mohammed Reza Pahlavi, was a dark, handsome man who looked dashing and powerful but was actually young and insecure.

After the war the Shah faced a tough problem—Iranian hatred of the British-owned Anglo-Persian Oil Company. Through Anglo-Persian Oil, the British controlled most of Iran's oil industry and drained the country of great wealth. Angry Iranians wanted to take control of their oil, but they needed a leader.

The man who stepped forward to lead the Iranians was not the Shah, but wealthy 70-year-old Dr. Mohammed Mossadegh. On the surface Mossadegh seemed harmless. He was small, thin, and often emotional. He appeared to be no threat to the Shah. Beneath the surface, however, the rich landowner was a masterful politician.

In 1951 the popular Mossadegh had become prime minister and pushed through a bill authorizing **nationalization** of the oil fields, or declaring them the property of Iran. Outraged, the British refused to accept the payment Mossadegh offered. Instead, the British shut down their refineries, stopped buying Iranian oil, and convinced other countries to do the same. As Iran's oil market dried up, its economy slipped toward bankruptcy.

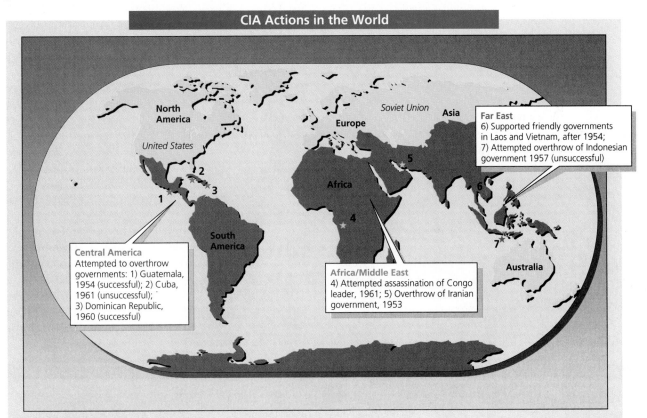

**CIA Actions in the World**

**Far East**
6) Supported friendly governments in Laos and Vietnam, after 1954;
7) Attempted overthrow of Indonesian government 1957 (unsuccessful)

**Central America**
Attempted to overthrow governments: 1) Guatemala, 1954 (successful); 2) Cuba, 1961 (unsuccessful); 3) Dominican Republic, 1960 (successful)

**Africa/Middle East**
4) Attempted assassination of Congo leader, 1961; 5) Overthrow of Iranian government, 1953

**The shaded areas of the map colored green represent the third world. In these countries the CIA exerted its extensive covert powers.** *How did the United States justify the interference of the CIA in foreign governments? How successful were CIA attempts to control political situations?*

**Eisenhower Steps In**  By the time Eisenhower took office, Iran was in serious trouble. In Eisenhower's mind, the situation in Iran was a perfect breeding ground for communism. The best way to protect Iran's oil supply for the West, Eisenhower thought, was to keep the Shah and get rid of Mossadegh.

Eisenhower ordered CIA agent Kim Roosevelt to engineer Mossadegh's overthrow from a "safe house" in Teheran. In a plan nicknamed AJAX, Roosevelt would organize military and public support for the Shah. Then the Shah would sign a royal decree deposing Mossadegh.

**The CIA Operation**  AJAX got off to a bad start in August 1953 when the Shah grew nervous about the plot and fled Teheran without signing the decree. It took Roosevelt four days to find the Shah, get the signed document, and deliver it to Mossadegh. By that time, though, the prime minister had discovered the plot. Mossadegh announced the attempted takeover on the radio and demanded the arrest of the Shah's supporters. In response, mobs of Iranians, including Communist supporters, ran wild in the streets, rioting, looting, and searching for enemies. Mossadegh called a stop to the violence only after the U.S. ambassador threatened to order all Americans out of Iran. Mossadegh knew that his government would look like a failure if the Americans pulled out.

With the mobs under control, Roosevelt sent his Iranian agents into action. On August 19, 200 Zirkaneh giants—huge, frightening-looking weightlifters—marched through Teheran's bazaars chanting, "Long live the Shah!" Other agents ran alongside, passing out Iranian money and gathering a crowd of artisans, students, police, and professionals. As the crowd headed for Mossadegh's house, Roosevelt rounded up the Shah's military supporters, who set off with tanks and guns.

The CIA agents and the Shah's men met and clashed with Mossadegh's supporters near Mossadegh's house. The battle lasted several hours and left 400 dead and injured. When Mossadegh's forces ran out of ammunition, the resistance ran out of steam. On the following day Mossadegh surrendered, and the Shah's supporters begged the Shah to come home.

Soon afterward the Shah returned victorious, and soon after, Mossadegh was jailed. With the Shah in power, a group of Western oil companies was able to sign an agreement to buy and sell Iranian oil and share the profits with the Shah. AJAX had ensured the CIA's future. It had also planted the seeds of later Iranian hatred of the United States.

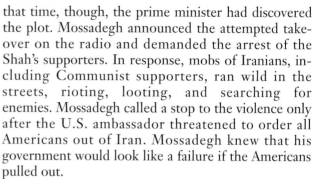

AP/WIDE WORLD PHOTOS

**The Shah's supporters rioted outside Mossadegh's home in Teheran. Mossadegh, top left, surrendered and the Shah, bottom left, celebrated his return to power.**

UPI/BETTMAN NEWSPHOTOS

AP/NEW YORK TIMES PICTURE SERVICE

**Predicting Consequences**

The outcome of operation AJAX was an indication of things to come. What might the consequences of this CIA success be? Presumably, the agency would make other attempts. Some historians believe that the CIA orchestrated the overthrow of other foreign governments, notably those of South Vietnam's repressive dictator Diem in 1963 and Chile's socialist leader Allende in 1973.

## War in Egypt

Three years later another hot spot ignited in the Middle East. This time the CIA was not involved, but the event showed Eisenhower that the third world would present difficult and dangerous problems.

In 1953 Egypt declared itself an independent republic, and in 1954 the passionate Arab nationalist General Gamal Abdel Nasser demanded that Britain give up control of the Suez Canal, which cut through his country. More than 75 percent of western Europe's oil imports were shipped through the Suez Canal, a key link between the Persian Gulf and the Mediterranean Sea. Nasser wanted to collect the $25 million annual profit from tolls. As part of his plan for modernizing Egypt, Nasser also wanted to build a dam on the Nile River to provide electric power and irrigation water for farms.

To help draw Egypt into the American camp, Dulles had offered to help Nasser build his dam. Soon afterward, though, the independent Nasser made an arms deal with the Soviets, and Dulles angrily cancelled the loan. In July 1956 Nasser fought back by seizing the Suez Canal. With the millions in tolls from the canal, he would finance the Nile River dam.

In October 1956, before Eisenhower could work out a solution to the crisis, Israel, Britain, and France invaded Egypt to seize the canal. Eisenhower and Dulles were appalled, fearing the action would drive the Middle East into the Soviet camp and threaten vital oil resources. Eisenhower called for a UN resolution condemning the actions of the three American allies. Without U.S. support, they pulled out, and the canal was returned to Egypt—full of sunken ships.

While Eisenhower managed to head off a full-scale war, the incident had serious consequences. It opened the Middle East to the Soviets, who appeared to side with Egyptian nationalists and eventually built Nasser's dam. The conflict also revealed weaknesses in the Western camp and pulled the United States deeper into Middle Eastern affairs. Afraid of growing Soviet influence in the oil-rich Middle East, Eisenhower promised U.S. aid, both economic and military, to pro-Western governments in the region. Soon this policy, known as the Eisenhower Doctrine, would involve fighting communism *and* Arab governments that did not join the Western camp.[2]

## The Cold War in Latin America

The spirit of nationalism fired up people in Central and South America during this period, too. For decades the United States had invested in their economies, and by the mid-1950s, U.S. companies controlled more than $7 billion of oil, mineral, and agricultural resources in Latin America. U.S. firms enjoyed rich profits from these investments, but little wealth trickled down to the masses of people who lived in poverty. Nationalistic leaders knew they had to loosen the grip of the U.S. firms on their economies. Revolution was simmering.

**Revolution in Cuba**  By the early 1950s, U.S. corporations virtually controlled the island nation of Cuba. Nearly 90 percent of its mines, ranches, and oil, half of its sugar crop, and three million acres of its land belonged to Americans. Only a few high-level Cubans lived well. Most suffered in grinding poverty.

In 1952 Fulgencio Batista, an army officer, overthrew the government and installed himself as dictator, friendly to the United States. He did little to improve life for the Cuban people, however, and in 1958 a young lawyer named Fidel Castro led a group of peasants and middle-class Cubans in a successful revolt against Batista.

Once in power, Castro moved quickly to solve Cuba's problems by demanding control of American properties. When the U.S. government refused to discuss the matter, Castro turned to the Soviets for economic help. Soon after, Eisenhower ordered the CIA to train a secret force of anti-Castro Cubans called La Brigada, which could be used to overthrow Castro. Before Eisenhower left office in 1961, Castro had seized all American businesses and signed a trade agreement with Moscow. The United States and Cuba had broken diplomatic relations.

**Kennedy and Cuba**  In 1961 John F. Kennedy became president and faced, in his words, the problem of a "communist satellite on our very doorstep." With

---

**Identifying Cause and Effect**
Economic warfare became an important cold war tactic among the three "worlds." When Iran seized Anglo-Persian Oil, Great Britain organized a multinational boycott of Iranian oil.

When Egypt's Nasser signed an arms deal with the Soviets, the United States cancelled an important loan to Egypt. When Great Britain refused to give up the Suez Canal, Nasser seized it.

2  What was the outcome of the 1956 struggle over the Suez Canal? What effect did the struggle have on American foreign relations?

AP/WIDE WORLD PHOTOS

**At a public rally, Fidel Castro outlines his plans for improving the lot of the Cuban people.** *What led to Castro's ascent to power?*

Castro's success in Cuba and growing crises in Africa and Southeast Asia, Kennedy feared a Soviet upper hand in the cold war. Before leaving office Eisenhower had urged Kennedy to step up the training of La Brigada. Now in office Kennedy took the advice of CIA operatives and ordered La Brigada to land secretly in Cuba, inspire a popular uprising, and sweep Castro out of power.

The invasion on April 17, 1961, failed miserably. When the 1,500 commandos tried to land at the Bay of Pigs on Cuba's southern coast, they met disaster at every turn. Their boats ran aground on coral reefs; Kennedy cancelled their air support to keep U.S. involvement secret; and the promised uprising of the Cuban people never happened. Within two days Castro's forces killed several hundred members of La Brigada and captured nearly all the rest.

The Bay of Pigs was a dark moment for Kennedy. The action exposed an American plot to overthrow a neighbor's government, and the clumsy affair made the United States look weak, like a paper tiger.

**To the Brink of War** To assert America's strength, Kennedy searched for other ways to unseat Castro. Using the CIA in a plan called Operation Mongoose,

he interrupted Cuban trade, ordered more raids by exiles, even plotted Castro's assassination.

For Castro and Khrushchev, these activities were outrageous. Khrushchev did not want to lose his foothold in the Western Hemisphere, and Castro did not want to lose his freedom from U.S. influence. "We had to think of some way of confronting America with more than words," Khrushchev recalled. Their solution was to install Soviet nuclear missiles and bombers near Havana, Cuba's capital, as a warning to the United States.

On October 14, 1962, a U.S. spy plane flying over Cuba got clear photos of crews installing Soviet missiles. Afraid that the Soviets were taking advantage of American weakness, Kennedy called a meeting of his closest advisers to decide what to do.

For a solid, nerve-racking week, the group thrashed out every possible response. Negotiations were ruled out at once; the group feared that drawn-out talks would give the Soviets time to install the missiles. Bombing the missile sites and invading Cuba were both proposed, but Kennedy feared that either could ignite a nuclear war. Finally Kennedy agreed to block Cuban shipping lanes to halt further deliveries of nuclear weapons, then quietly push Khrushchev to remove the missiles.

On the evening of October 22, Kennedy announced this decision on national TV. Within two days 180 warships were sailing to Cuba, B-52 bombers were in the air, loaded with nuclear weapons, and military forces worldwide were on full alert—more than 200,000 in Florida alone. For the next two days, Soviet ships steamed toward Cuba, and the world waited to see what would happen. It was a time when "the smell of burning hung in the air," Khrushchev remembered later. The United States and the Soviet Union had edged to the brink of nuclear war.

On October 26 Khrushchev agreed to remove the missiles if the United States vowed never to attack Cuba. But the next day he demanded the removal of U.S. missiles from Turkey. After hours of frantic meetings, Kennedy agreed to the first demand but ignored the second. He also ordered Khrushchev to get the missiles out of Cuba—or the United States would take them out. Finally, on October 28, Khrushchev backed down and the crisis ended.[3]

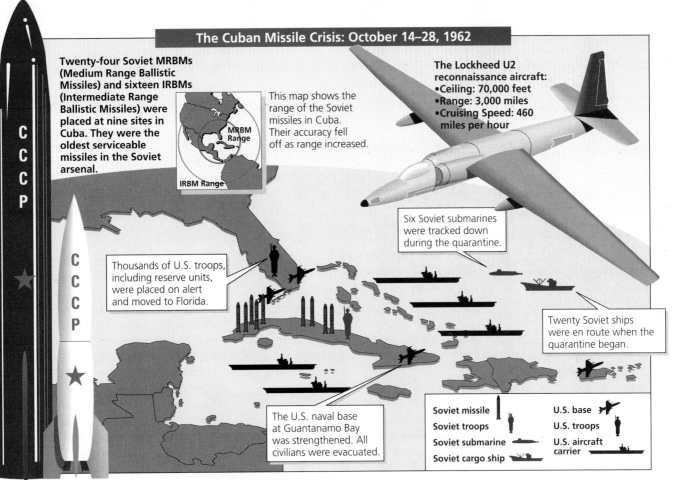

## The Cuban Missile Crisis: October 14–28, 1962

Twenty-four Soviet MRBMs (Medium Range Ballistic Missiles) and sixteen IRBMs (Intermediate Range Ballistic Missiles) were placed at nine sites in Cuba. They were the oldest serviceable missiles in the Soviet arsenal.

This map shows the range of the Soviet missiles in Cuba. Their accuracy fell off as range increased.

MRBM Range

IRBM Range

The Lockheed U2 reconnaissance aircraft:
- Ceiling: 70,000 feet
- Range: 3,000 miles
- Cruising Speed: 460 miles per hour

Six Soviet submarines were tracked down during the quarantine.

Thousands of U.S. troops, including reserve units, were placed on alert and moved to Florida.

Twenty Soviet ships were en route when the quarantine began.

The U.S. naval base at Guantanamo Bay was strengthened. All civilians were evacuated.

| | |
|---|---|
| Soviet missile | U.S. base |
| Soviet troops | U.S. troops |
| Soviet submarine | U.S. aircraft carrier |
| Soviet cargo ship | |

**Enemy nuclear warheads positioned close to the United States posed an immediate danger to the** country and raised the specter of all-out nuclear war between the United States and the Soviet Union.

**After the Crisis**   As the missiles left Cuba, the world stepped back from the brink and breathed a huge sigh of relief. War had been averted.

The standoff also changed the character of the cold war. At last the United States and the Soviet Union accepted each other's power and admitted the importance of negotiation. In this spirit, American and Soviet leaders installed a hot line, a teletype link for communication when future crises arose.

The brush with nuclear war did nothing to slow the arms race, however. For the Soviet Union, the missile crisis had ended in public humiliation. The Soviets vowed, in the words of one official, "Never [to] be caught like this again." Back home they launched a huge military buildup.

America's victory in the missile crisis renewed the nation's pride and its belief in containment. Through the rest of Kennedy's administration, the United States continued to stockpile nuclear weapons and serve as the world's policeman. Before long, though, America's beliefs would be put to the test in the small Asian country of Vietnam.

## SECTION REVIEW

**Checking Facts**

1. Why was winning the loyalty of emerging third world nations of great importance to the United States?

2. Who created the CIA, and why?

3. What sparked the controversy between Iran and Great Britain in 1951?

4. What was the major political effect of Operation AJAX? What was its major economic effect?

5. Why was Castro's revolution politically worrisome to the United States? Why was it economically worrisome?

**Thinking Critically**

6. **Analyzing Decisions**  Why was the United States so interested in seeing Castro's revolution fail?

7. **Predicting Consequences**  What might life have been like for the majority of Cuban people if

the invasion at the Bay of Pigs had succeeded?

**Linking Across Time**

8. In 1979 the Iranian people overthrew the Shah, an event that inaugurated a decade of extreme anti-Americanism. What might account for the Iranian hatred of the United States?

The Uneasy Peace   489

## John F. Kennedy: An Urgent Letter to Khrushchev

Presidential papers, which include the speeches, diaries, memos, and correspondence of U.S. presidents, are a rich source of information about the conduct of domestic and foreign policy and about the style and philosophy of the chief executives themselves. A president's papers, ordinarily published after he has left office, offer historians an inside look at the workings of the U.S. government.

### The Evidence

For 13 days in October 1962, the United States and the Soviet Union held each other and all the nations of the world hostage to a potential nuclear holocaust. U.S. spy planes had recorded photographic evidence that the Soviets were constructing launch facilities for nuclear missiles on the island of Cuba, just 90 miles from the coast of Florida. The United States initiated a naval quarantine of Cuba, and both superpowers readied their arsenals for the ultimate military conflict: nuclear warfare.

During the tense standoff, Soviet Chairman Nikita Khrushchev and U.S. President John Kennedy exchanged a series of letters about the crisis. As you read the letter on the opposite page, sent by President Kennedy to Chairman Khrushchev on October 27, look for language that suggests the seriousness of the crisis.

### The Interpretation

When historians study presidential papers relating to a specific subject, it is important that they bring to their research strong background knowledge of the subject. Such knowledge can add to their ability to interpret what they read.

For example, background knowledge enables historians studying presidential papers to read between the lines. That is, they can search for meaning beyond the words themselves.

President Kennedy's letter to Chairman Khrushchev offers an example of how reading between the lines can provide historians with information about the Cuban crisis not stated explicitly in the letter itself. Historians know that the crisis was grave. On the day this letter was written, Soviet cargo ships, apparently loaded with nuclear armaments, were steaming toward Cuba, headed for a confrontation with U.S. naval ships enforcing the quarantine of the island. Both nations had placed their nuclear forces on the highest alert status. Just how close was the world, however, to atomic destruction?

Clues can be found in the language of Kennedy's letter. All but two paragraphs contain the words *prompt*, *promptly*, and *quickly*. Clearly, the President wanted Khrushchev to believe that any delay in settling the crisis could result in a military conflict with the United States involving the use of nuclear weapons.

In addition, Kennedy warns Khrushchev in the final paragraph of the letter that linking the solution of the missile crisis with other issues involving European and world security would only delay settlement and intensify the crisis. Again Kennedy's message is clear—the missile crisis must be solved immediately to avoid war. Reading between the lines suggests that on this date in history the world was indeed edging toward nuclear destruction.

### Further Exploration

Choose an important event from the 1960s that involved the president of the United States. Possible choices include the invasion of Cuba at the Bay of Pigs (Kennedy), the Gulf of Tonkin incident that accelerated the country's involvement in Vietnam (Johnson), and the first landing of Americans on the moon (Nixon).

First, do some background reading about the event you have chosen. Then search for presidential papers relating to the event. The librarian at your school or a nearby college may be able to assist you in finding these materials. After reading these papers, prepare a report that includes the following information: the event you researched, the types of papers you found, what the papers told you about the event, and any other insights you gained from reading between the lines of the papers.

Dear Mr. Chairman:

I have read your letter of October 26th with great care and welcomed the statement of your desire to seek a prompt solution to the problem. The first thing that needs to be done, however, is for work to cease on offensive missile bases in Cuba and for all weapons systems in Cuba capable of offensive use to be rendered inoperable, under effective United Nations arrangements.

Assuming this is done promptly, I have given my representatives in New York instructions that will permit them to work out this weekend—in cooperation with the Acting Secretary General and your representative—an arrangement for a permanent solution to the Cuban problem along the lines suggested in your letter of October 26th. As I read your letter, the key elements of your proposals—which seem generally acceptable as I understand them—are as follows:

1. You would agree to remove these weapons systems from Cuba under appropriate United Nations observation and supervision; and undertake, with suitable safeguards, to halt the further introduction of such weapons systems into Cuba.

2. We, on our part, would agree—upon the establishment of adequate arrangements through the United Nations to ensure the carrying out and continuation of these commitments—(a) to remove promptly the quarantine measures now in effect, and (b) to give assurances against an invasion of Cuba. I am confident that other nations of the Western Hemisphere would be prepared to do likewise.

If you will give your representative similar instructions, there is no reason why we should not be able to complete these arrangements and announce them to the world within a couple of days. The effect of such a settlement on easing world tensions would enable us to work toward a more general arrangement regarding "other armaments," as proposed in your second letter, which you made public. I would like to say again that the United States is very much interested in reducing tensions and halting the arms race; and if your letter signifies that you are prepared to discuss a détente affecting NATO and the Warsaw Pact, we are quite prepared to consider with our allies any useful proposals.

But the first ingredient, let me emphasize, is the cessation of work on missile sites in Cuba and measures to render such weapons inoperable, under effective international guarantees. The continuation of this threat, or a prolonging of this discussion concerning Cuba by linking these problems to the broader questions of European and world security, would surely lead to an intensification of the Cuban crisis and a grave risk to the peace of the world. For this reason, I hope we can quickly agree along the lines outlined in this letter and in your letter of October 26th.

John F. Kennedy

# Chapter 14 Review

| March 1946<br>"Iron curtain" descends.<br>Cold war deepens. | June 1948<br>Soviets<br>blockade Berlin. | April 1949<br>NATO<br>is formed. | June 1950<br>Korean War<br>begins. | November 1952<br>Eisenhower is<br>elected president. | July 1953<br>Korean<br>War ends. |
|---|---|---|---|---|---|

**1945** **1946** **1947** **1948** **1949** **1950** **1951** **1952** **1953** **1954**

| April 1945<br>Roosevelt dies suddenly.<br>Truman becomes president. | April 1948<br>Marshall Plan begins<br>aid to Europe. | October 1949<br>Mao declares<br>People's Republic<br>of China. | November 1952<br>United States tests<br>hydrogen bomb. |
|---|---|---|---|

## Summary

Use the following outline as a tool for reviewing and summarizing the chapter. Copy the outline on your own paper, leaving spaces between headings to jot down notes about key events and concepts.

**I. The Cold War Begins**
A. An Iron Curtain Starts to Fall
B. Turning Point at Yalta
C. Truman Comes to Power
D. Cold War Is Declared

**II. The Cold War Deepens**
A. Crisis in Berlin
B. The Cold War Moves to Asia
C. Hot War Flares in Korea
D. The Impact of the Korean War

**III. Cold War in the Atomic Age**
A. Living with Fear
B. Eisenhower Comes to Power
C. A New Cold War Strategy
D. Eisenhower Wages Peace
E. Back into the Deep Freeze

**IV. A New Battleground**
A. New Worlds to Conquer
B. The CIA Joins the Fight
C. The CIA and the Shah
D. War in Eygpt
E. The Cold War in Latin America

## Ideas, Events, and People

1. What were some outcomes of the talks at Yalta and Potsdam for Germany and eastern Europe?
2. How did the Marshall Plan benefit western European countries?
3. How did the Berlin blockade and the subsequent airlift affect world opinion about the Americans and Soviets?
4. Why did most Americans hope for a Nationalist victory in the Chinese civil war?
5. Why did Truman view the invasion of South Korea as an important test of containment?
6. What were some advantages and some dangers of Eisenhower's policy of massive retaliation?
7. Why didn't Khrushchev agree to Eisenhower's proposal to inspect each other's military sites?
8. What methods did the United States use to gain the friendship of third world countries? How was the CIA involved in that effort?
9. What conditions in Cuba helped to prepare the way for Castro's takeover?

## Social Studies Skills

**Analyzing Secondary Sources**

The photograph below, taken on September 20, 1960, is a primary source document that catches Castro and Khrushchev in a jovial moment. Write a paragraph that might appear in a secondary source about the 1960s. Explain how the friendship between the two men created a crisis for the world.

AP/WIDE WORLD PHOTOS

**July 1956**
Nasser seizes
Suez Canal.

**October 1957**
Soviets launch *Sputnik*

**November 1960**
Kennedy is
elected president.

**November 1956**
Soviets crush
uprising in Budapest.

**January 1959**
Castro becomes
dictator of Cuba.

**April 1961**
Bay of Pigs
invasion fails.

**October 1962**
Soviets remove
missiles from Cuba.

# Critical Thinking

**1. Comparing and Contrasting**

Compare and contrast the concerns that Roosevelt, Churchill, and Stalin brought to the conference at Yalta.

**2. Recognizing Cause and Effect**

What were some causes of the mistrust that grew up between Truman and Stalin?

**3. Analyzing Decisions**

How did the NSC-68 report and the Korean War cause Congress to vote massive increases in defense spending?

**4. Recognizing Assumptions**

In 1956 Khrushchev condemned Stalin's crimes and spoke of tolerating different kinds of communism. What did eastern European nations assume from such statements? How were such assumptions proven false in Hungary?

**5. Recognizing Points of View**

How might a nation's views on nuclear testing depend on whether it was a large or small power? On whether it was or was not a member of the "nuclear club"?

# Extension and Application

**1. Evidence of the Past**

In a library find information about the Yalta and Potsdam conferences. Write a short report explaining Roosevelt's and Truman's ideas about the postwar world.

**2. Community Connection**

Interview friends or family members who took part in World War II, the Korean War, or the war in Vietnam. Ask whether their opinions about the war have changed over the years and, if so, how. Discuss your findings with the class.

**3. Global Connection**

Research everyday life in China following the civil war and communist takeover. Focus on one aspect of the topic, such as how the commune system affected peasant life or how urban life changed under Mao Zedong.

**4. Linking Across Time**

George Washington said, "Liberty, when it begins to take root, is a plant of rapid growth." The 1990s might remind us of the era that followed World War II. Then, as now, a number of nations were in the midst of nationalist movements. Research a recent nationalist movement and write a news article or editorial about it.

**5. Cooperative Learning**

The Soviet launching of *Sputnik* resulted in intense efforts to improve America's educational system. Find out what the media are reporting about America's educational system today. Divide your class into groups of four. Have each group investigate one part of the topic, such as curriculum, teacher training, or textbooks. Have each group present the findings by a different means.

# Geography

**1.** How did the location of fighting in World War II influence the Soviet economy? The U.S. economy?

**2.** Identify the strategy used in waging the cold war. How was it different from strategy used in previous struggles? Where were the battlefields?

**3.** How did Berlin's location deep in East Germany work to the advantage of the United States?

**4.** During the height of the cold war what pressures might countries such as Spain, Yugoslavia, Austria, and Finland experience?

**5.** How does the spread of nuclear arms affect a country's ability to be neutral in a conflict?

## CHAPTER 15

# The Postwar Era

### 1955: Middle-Class Suburbanites Blind to Urban Poverty

The sun glinted off the tail fins and chrome bumpers of the new Chevrolet in the driveway as the Wilsons piled into the car for their weekly ritual—the Sunday afternoon drive. After a brief struggle over who would get the window seats, Sally, Tom, and Susan settled themselves in the back seat.

The car turned onto one of Chicago's newly completed expressways, and shortly the Wilsons were driving north on Michigan Avenue with its exclusive shops and fine restaurants. They parked to window shop a bit, and when the children clamored for ice cream, the family stopped at an ice cream parlor. Then they headed home to the tree-lined streets of their comfortable suburb of Morton Grove.

The Wilsons were a lucky family. Exactly 10 years ago, John Wilson was one of thousands of exhausted GIs marching on the road to Berlin. Now John and Julie had three great kids with a fourth on the way and a beautiful home in the suburbs. John had a college degree (something his parents had never achieved) and a promising future with a large company.

On their drive the Wilsons never saw the other not-so-lucky Americans who lived on the West Side: women talking on the steps of decaying buildings; men slumped in doorways; children playing ball on a sidewalk strewn with broken glass.

> *On their drive the Wilsons never saw the other not-so-lucky Americans.*

MAGNUM

*In the midst of postwar prosperity, millions still lived in desperate poverty.*

*During the 1950s almost two million people a year moved to the suburbs. The typical suburb was filled mainly with young families (few non-white or elderly). The suburban value system stressed togetherness, family, and the "good life."*

# Postwar Economy Booms

## Fall 1947: Vets Enroll in College on GI Bill

WORLD WAR II VETERAN KENNETH BAKER, HIS WIFE LAURA, AND THEIR BABY DAUGHTER ARRIVED ON THE CAMPUS OF THE UNIVERSITY OF MINNESOTA on a cool September morning in 1947. Ken was one of 6,000 married "vets" on campus ready to begin the fall semester. His family was assigned to one of the 674 housing units in Veterans' Village, a university community for ex-GIs where rents were based on each vet's ability to pay. Veterans who had the most seniority were assigned to the best units—converted steel barracks with gas heat and indoor bathrooms. As newcomers, Kenneth and Laura would be living in a trailer with no plumbing. That meant that they would have to use the public bathhouse and the public laundry.

Nevertheless, the Bakers considered themselves lucky. As Ken observed, "Even a hovel in Veterans' Village is heaven compared to the way I lived in the service." Living in Veterans' Village meant that Ken and Laura could get by on their $90 monthly government allowance.

Life in Veterans' Village fostered a spirit of cooperation. With over 900 babies among the village population, every adult became a guardian to every child. The Bakers shopped in the village grocery store, which was owned and operated by the veterans' campus community. Ken and several of his buddies joined the veterans' bowling league. Laura took special classes in sewing, cooking, and child care. On Friday nights, Laura and Ken joined other residents of Veterans' Village in the

UNIVERSITY OF MINNESOTA

recreation center to dance to the recorded music of popular big bands of the day.

Similar veterans' communities could be found on most large college campuses in postwar United States, thanks to the **GI Bill of Rights**. The GI Bill was designed to ease the transition from military to civilian life by providing veterans with financial aid for education and housing and to begin small businesses. Nearly eight million veterans took advantage of educational assistance. Armed with college degrees or technical training, the vets contributed their energy and talent to what would become the nation's longest unbroken period of prosperity.

## The Shift from War to Peace

More than 16 million Americans had served in the armed forces during World War II. **Demobilization,** the dismantling of the huge U.S. war machine, was a daunting task, somewhat like trying to reverse the direction of a river's flow. After peace was achieved in 1945, war-weary soldiers stationed around the world waited eagerly to come home. After thousands of citizens appealed to their congressional representatives to speed up the process, the number of soldiers on active duty dropped from 12 million in 1945 to 1.6 million by mid-1947. This rapid demobilization provided much-needed workers for U.S. industry, which was in the process of converting from wartime to peacetime production.

---

### STUDY GUIDE

**As You Read**

Identify postwar developments in government, business, agriculture, and technology that brought many Americans an affluent life style. Also, think about the following concepts and skills.

**Central Concepts**
- understanding the effects of **demobilization** on the U.S. economy
- recognizing the role of the **GI Bill of Rights** in helping veterans make the transition to civilian life

**Thinking Skills**
- assessing outcomes
- predicting consequences
- recognizing assumptions

**Economic Growth**    After years of "going without" during the Great Depression and the war, Americans hungered for new cars, electronics, appliances, and gadgets. Industry set out to fill the growing demand for consumer goods. The automobile industry produced two million cars in 1946 and nearly four times that many by 1955. Americans bought 975,000 television sets in 1948, and two years later they bought 7.5 million sets. By 1960 about 75 percent of all American families owned at least one automobile, and 87 percent owned at least one TV set. Consumers also purchased more refrigerators, washing machines, vacuum cleaners, and cameras than ever before. Electric can openers, electric garage door openers, and electric pencil sharpeners appeared on the market and quickly became part of the new American way of life.

The GNP, or gross national product (the total value of a country's goods and services), rose rapidly—from just over $100 billion in 1940 to about $300 billion in 1950 and then to $500 billion by 1960. The economic growth, the increase in GNP, that characterized the postwar period gave Americans the highest standard of living the world had ever known. People lived more comfortably than ever before. The United States, home to just 6 percent of the world's population, produced and consumed nearly half the world's goods.

**Wage and Price Issues**
The reconversion to a peacetime economy brought problems, too. During the war, civilian paychecks included plenty of overtime pay. In addition, government policies had kept a lid on prices. When postwar wages failed to keep up with now rising prices, blue-collar workers launched a wave of strikes and work stoppages, refusing to work until their demands were met.

Despite rising prices, most American workers continued to prosper. Average annual earnings for factory workers rose from $3,302 in 1950 to $5,352 in 1960. Real income, the amount of income earned taking into account an increase in prices, increased more than 20 percent during the same period. Working-class Americans began to accumulate discretionary income—money to buy what they wanted as well as what they needed. This increased purchasing power further fueled the rapid economic growth.

THE GRANGER COLLECTION

THE GRANGER COLLECTION

**During the 1950s, the consumption of electricity more than doubled in this country, due in large part to the purchases of so many electrical appliances.** *How did television contribute to this increased consumption of electricity?*

**Persuading the Consumer**   Advertising became the fastest-growing industry in the postwar United States. Manufacturers employed new marketing techniques. These techniques were carefully planned to whet the consumer's appetite. It was also the purpose of these advertisers to influence choices among brands of goods that were essentially the same. In his 1957 best seller, *The Hidden Persuaders*, Vance Packard described the role of advertisers:

> *T*hese motivational analysts . . . are adding depth to the selling of ideas and products. They are learning, for example, to offer us considerably more than the actual item involved. A Milwaukee advertising executive commented to colleagues in print on the fact that women will pay two dollars and a half for skin cream but no more than twenty-five cents for a cake of soap. Why? Soap, he explained, only promises to make them clean. The cream promises to make them beautiful.
>
> Vance Packard,
> *The Hidden Persuaders*, 1957

According to these hidden messages, a freezer became a promise of plenty, a second car became a symbol of status, and mouthwash became the key to immediate social success.

The increased popularity of television played a major role in the development of the advertising industry and the gospel of consumerism. Television networks depended on advertising revenues to pay for the programs they produced. At the same time, advertisers found television a perfect medium for reaching consumers. Television, after all, was still a novelty for most people in the United States during the early 1950s, and they watched the television commercials just as avidly as the television programs.

Television ads became something of an art form in themselves. They not only sold products, they also entertained the viewers with showy dramatizations and catchy jingles. As the decade progressed, the presence and influence of television advertising became pervasive, and acquiring material goods like those shown on TV became a goal of the growing, status-conscious middle class.

## Impact of the G.I. Bill

*M*ore than any other factor, the GI Bill of Rights passed by Congress in 1944 shaped American society in the postwar period. As one veteran said:

> *T*he GI Bill of Rights, of course, had more to do with thrusting us into a new era than anything else. Millions of people whose parents or grandparents had never dreamed of going to college saw that they could go. . . . Essentially I think it made us a far more democratic people.
>
> Nelson Poynter, former GI,
> quoted in *Americans Remember the Home Front*

As a result of the GI Bill, the greatest wave of college building in American history took place during the postwar years. Many states vastly increased their support of higher education. For example, during the postwar period California State University opened campuses at Sacramento, Los Angeles, Long Beach, Fullerton, Hayward, Northridge, and San Bernardino.

In addition to educational benefits, the GI Bill offered low-interest mortgages to veterans who wanted to purchase homes. This spurred a huge demand for housing after the war, creating a construction boom and fostering a trend toward mass production. Using mass production methods, the housing industry built 13 million new homes during the 1950s. Home ownership had always been a part of the American dream. The rate of home ownership increased between 1940 and 1960 from 44 to 62 percent of American households. The GI Bill allowed millions of Americans to achieve a standard of living that was generally better than that enjoyed by their parents.

## The New World of Business

*D*uring the postwar years, the motto of major corporations became "bigger is better." Business mergers, the combining of several companies, created conglomerates—firms that had holdings

---

**STUDY·GUIDE**

### Predicting Consequences

After the war, some people feared that demobilization and the return to a peacetime economy might bring back the unemployment of the Great Depression. Dire predictions of a new depression did not come true. The increased demand for consumer goods more than made up for the loss of war production. Many people had saved money when goods were scarce, and now they were ready to spend it. The GI Bill increased spending even further.

in a variety of unrelated industries. Many of the nation's biggest corporations grew even bigger during the postwar years. The net sales of IBM jumped from $119.4 million in 1946 to $1.7 *billion* in 1961. General Motors doubled their net assets during the 1950s from $1.5 billion in 1951 to $2.8 billion in 1960.

IBM

**Large corporations encouraged conformity and offered training programs—some critics considered them schools of indoctrination—that helped develop the "corporate image." At some large companies holding the proper beliefs was just as important as wearing the proper necktie.**

**Up the Corporate Ladder** Rapid corporate growth during the 1950s gave rise to new employment opportunities and a new life style for the nation's white-collar workers (clerical and professional workers) who viewed the corporate life as a secure career. Major corporations provided their employees with everything from company neckties to memberships in exclusive country clubs. Training programs encouraged employees to adopt the company point of view. Companies such as IBM sent their managers to schools to teach not only management techniques, but company beliefs as well.

Critics charged corporations with destroying individuality by expecting employees to conform to company standards of thinking, dressing, and behaving. As sociologist C. Wright Mills commented, "When white-collar people get jobs, they sell not only their time and energy but their personalities as well."

Major corporations greatly influenced American life and values in the 1950s. To those climbing the corporate ladder, that is, being promoted to higher and higher levels of responsibility, wages were but one concern. Equally important were benefits such as a pension plan, medical insurance, performance bonus, expense account, paid vacation, and company car. For employees who dedicated themselves to the corporate life style and successfully met the expectations of their superiors, the rewards of corporate life were further proof that the United States was a land of opportunity—at least for some Americans.[1]

During the 1950s positions of power and authority within the corporate world belonged predominantly to white males. Minority representation was very rare. Women were expected to fill different roles in the postwar American work force. As the widely read *Life* magazine explained:

> *Household skills take her into the garment trades; neat and personable, she becomes office worker and sales lady; patient and dextrous, she does well on competitive, detailed factory work; compassionate, she becomes teacher and nurse.*
>
> *Life,* 1956

**Opportunities in the Service Sector** The nation's public and private service industries enjoyed tremendous expansion during the postwar years. Government jobs at the national, state, city, and county level included social workers, teachers, and civil servants. In private business, there was a big growth in the number of secretarial and clerical workers, bank tellers, telephone operators, as well as service workers in the insurance, transportation, and retail sales areas. Hospitality and recreation industries needed more service workers with the increased number of bowling alleys, skating rinks, movie theaters, hotels, and restaurants. The unprecedented number of cars, appliances, radios, and television sets purchased by consumers created a need for skilled mechanics and repair people. For the first time in U.S. history, workers who performed services began to outnumber those who manufactured products.

**STUDY GUIDE**

**Recognizing Assumptions**

During the war, women filled jobs in manufacturing that had once been closed to them. Afterward, they were told to "go back home." Most males assumed that women did not need to work and ought to be caring for a family. Many women agreed. Assumptions that both men and women have about women's roles have changed in recent decades.

**1** In what ways did the growth of large corporations affect the lives and values of their employees?

## From Agriculture to Agribusiness

The postwar years also saw a transformation in agriculture from family business to corporate enterprise. Two studies conducted of Plainville, pseudonym for a small rural community in southeast Missouri, told a large story. The first study, conducted in 1939, revealed a community of small farmers growing a variety of small crops, raising a few chickens, and breeding a few cows. Fifteen years later, Plainville had been transformed. Farming had become big business. As incomes doubled, or even tripled, residents joined the consumer society. Nearly every home had a television set. The way of life in rural Plainville was almost indistinguishable from that in suburban areas.

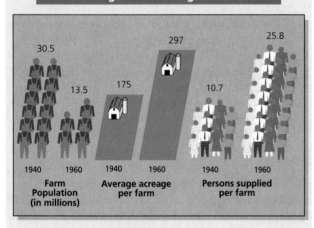

**Farming Becomes Big Business**

| Farm Population (in millions) | | Average acreage per farm | | Persons supplied per farm | |
|---|---|---|---|---|---|
| 30.5 | 13.5 | 175 | 297 | 10.7 | 25.8 |
| 1940 | 1960 | 1940 | 1960 | 1940 | 1960 |

**As farm size grew, farm population dropped.** *What happened to farm production?*

Plainville was typical of the changing nature of farming throughout postwar United States. The size of farms increased. Farmers learned that large-scale farming lowered the cost of production. For example, in 1960 the average cost of corn production was $61 per acre when grown on 160 acres; on 640 acres, the cost dropped to $54 per acre. As the size of farms grew, the value of fertile farmland rose rapidly.

While a few farmers benefited from these changes, others suffered. Since small farms could not compete with large farms, many small farm families sold their land and migrated to urban areas. So, as farm size doubled, the total number of farms dropped from more than six million in 1940 to fewer than four million in 1960 and the farm population fell from about 30 million to about 13 million. By 1960 only 8 percent of the nation's population lived on farms.[2]

## An Automobile Culture

The migration of farm families to the city was characteristic of the population as a whole. Americans were on the move, and the automobile became indispensable to their way of life. Auto dealers sold a record 58 million cars during the decade of the 1950s. Car manufacturers kept the public buying by changing body styles and adding more options, which made the previous year's models obsolete, at least in style. Turning out large, high-powered, steel-and-chrome fantasies in every color of the rainbow, the automakers provided sparkling steel chariots for every taste and income level.

**Curb Service and Drive-ins**   Americans practically lived in their automobiles. "Come as you are, eat in your car" became a popular slogan of fast-food drive-ins that provided curb service. Waitresses, and waiters, called "car hops," and sometimes traveling on roller skates, took orders and delivered food directly to the customer's car window. Drive-in theaters showed movies on large outdoor screens that the audience watched from the privacy of their own cars.

**Ribbons of Highway**   The development of an extensive interstate highway system encouraged automobile travel. The Highway Act of 1956 authorized $32 billion for the construction of over 40,000 miles of federal highways across the United States. President Eisenhower proudly described his administration's commitment to the interstate highway system:

*The amount of concrete poured to form these roadways would build . . . six sidewalks to the moon. . . . More than any single action by the government since the end of the war, this one would change the face of America.*

President Dwight D. Eisenhower

**From the end of World War II until 1960, the number of cars in the United States increased enormously. Aside from the practical uses such as commuting to** work from the suburbs, the automobile popularized drive-in movies, drive-in restaurants, and even drive-in churches.

**Migration to the Suburbs**   The moving van became the symbol of American mobility in the postwar period. During each year of the 1950s, nearly one-fifth of the population changed residences. Attracted by warm climates and plentiful jobs, Americans began to head to the West and the Southwest. Houston, Dallas, Phoenix, and Albuquerque were among cities whose populations soared from this migration. The greatest growth phenomenon, however, took place in California, which accounted for one-fifth of the nation's population growth in the 1950s. By 1963 Cali-

fornia had surpassed New York as the nation's most populous state.

The most significant population shift was the migration of white Americans from cities to suburbs. Greater availability of automobiles, expansion of the highway system, and the affordability of mass-produced suburban housing spurred the movement. By the end of the 1950s, more than one-fifth of all Americans lived in the suburbs. Suburbanization changed the landscape of the nation and the life style of middle-class Americans.

## SECTION REVIEW

**Checking Facts**

1. What caused the heavy demand for consumer goods after the war?
2. What made television so attractive to the advertising industry?
3. What kinds of benefits did the GI Bill of Rights offer to veterans?
4. What were some advantages and disadvantages of corporate life?
5. In what ways did Americans demonstrate their attachment to automobiles after World War II?

**Thinking Critically**

6. **Predicting Consequences**  What are some possible consequences of the failure to understand the techniques advertisers use to sell their products?
7. **Assessing Outcomes**  How did the return of the GIs change the job market for women? Were any of the changes positive? How?
8. **Recognizing Assumptions**  What assumptions resulted in mas-

sive migration to warm climates, especially to California?

**Linking Across Time**

9. What trend in business today is an extension of the "bigger is better" trend of the postwar years?

# The New American Landscape

By the time Japanese military officers signed the terms of unconditional surrender that ended World War II, a severe housing shortage had developed in the United States. During the war, new housing starts had slowed to a standstill. Now hundreds of thousands of GIs were coming home, getting married, and needing homes to raise families. The United States needed 5 million new housing units—and the sooner, the better.

The construction industry in the United States was ready to meet the challenge. Since the cities were too crowded for much new construction to take place, and relocating millions of people to homes in remote, sparsely populated areas of the country would be both expensive and impractical, the builders' solution was to create a new addition to the country's landscape—carefully planned communities on the outskirts of cities. This decision would transform not only the landscape of the country but the life styles of the many white, middle-class Americans who began migrating from the crowded cities to the open, quieter environment of the suburbs.

## Levittown, U.S.A.

The first and most famous postwar planned community was begun in 1946 on Long Island, about 30 miles from midtown Manhattan. The community, called Levittown, was named for the family-owned company that built it, Levitt & Sons, and was constructed on 1,200 acres of potato farmland.

LIFE MAGAZINE

**All the streets in Levittown curved at exactly the same angle, and trees were planted along them, one every 28 feet. Despite such rigid conformity, people loved the openness and country feel of this new suburb.**

**Following World War II, planned communities were constructed just outside many of the nation's big cities. This resulted in a migration of people from the cities to these new "suburban areas."**

Levittown was designed as a planned community that included single-family homes, parks, playgrounds, shopping centers, swimming pools, baseball diamonds, handball courts, and clubhouses for fraternal and veterans' organizations. Each home was exactly the same and sold for the same price: $7,990.

The homes at Levittown were mass-produced. Specialized construction crews hurried from one homesite to the next, digging foundations, pouring concrete, erecting walls and roofs, and installing plumbing and electrical fixtures. During the height of the construction at Levittown, workers completed a brand new home every 15 minutes.

Levittown was an immediate success. Just three years after the start of construction, 10,600 houses had been built and the suburb's population had swelled to over 40,000. The residents loved their new community. Said one ex-GI who had moved to Levittown with his wife and another relative from a one-bedroom apartment in Brooklyn, "That was so awful I'd rather not talk about it. Getting into this house was like being emancipated."

## A New Landscape

The construction of planned communities such as Levittown accounted for several important changes in the landscape. First, these types of planned communities, or subdivisions, had never existed before. They combined elements of city life with features of rural living, blurring the sharp distinctions that had once existed between these two ways of life.

Second, the new communities were an attractive alternative to the increasingly crowded, polluted cities where most Americans lived. So people who could afford to move did so, resulting in a migration of the white middle-class Americans out of the cities and into surrounding suburbs.

Finally, the suburbs created a new way of life for many Americans. Long, daily commutes to and from jobs in the cities became more commonplace. New local governments had to be created to administer the affairs of these fledgling communities, and new school systems were needed to educate the children of the suburbs. In short, out of the postwar housing shortage had come a transformation in the way this country looked and the ways Americans lived.

**THINK ABOUT IT:** After a decade of middle-class migration to the suburbs, the quality of life in the big cities began to decline. What were some possible reasons for this decline?

LIFE MAGAZINE

Homes in Levittown had a living room with a fireplace, two bedrooms, and a large attic that could be converted to two additional bedrooms. They had the latest conveniences—radiant heat, an electric kitchen, an automatic washing machine, and a built-in television in the living room.

# Suburban Life Styles

## 1950s: Americans Migrate to Suburbs

JILL JOHNSON PARKED THE GREEN AND WHITE STATION WAGON NEXT TO A NUMBER OF OTHER SIMILAR VEHICLES AT THE TRAIN STATION. AS BOB JOHNSON JOINED THE CROWD waiting for the 8:22 A.M. commuter into the city, the Johnson children waved and blew kisses to their dad. Jill Johnson's next stop was Eisenhower Elementary School where Bill, a fourth grader, and Susan, a second grader, spent their day. Mary Ann, age four, and baby Jimmy then accompanied their mom to the shopping center.

The Village Market Mall provided ample parking for its 30 or more stores and offices. Shoppers had access to a large department store, a bank, a beauty salon and a barber shop, a drug store, a dry cleaner, and a supermarket. Physicians, dentists, and attorneys occupied offices on the second floor of the two-story buildings in the shopping center.

Jill dropped off Bob's suits at the dry cleaners then stopped at the supermarket to pick up cookies for the Cub Scout meeting and steaks to barbecue on Sunday. She also picked out frozen TV dinners so that the family could eat while they watched "The Adventures of Ozzie and Harriet" on Friday night.

With the morning errands completed, Jill Johnson and her children headed for home, a neat one-story frame house with a picture window and attached garage, located on a street with many similar houses. The neighborhood's well-kept lawns and newly planted flowers and trees reflected pride of ownership. The Johnsons, along with 60 million other white Americans, were enjoying the comfortable life style of the suburbs.

## Growth of Surburbia

During the 1950s, 85 percent of new home construction took place in **suburbia**. The number of suburban dwellers doubled, while the population of central cities rose only 10 percent. Reasons for the

THE BETTMANN ARCHIVE

rapid growth of suburbia varied. Some whites wanted to escape the crime and congestion of city neighborhoods. Others fled because of prejudice against African Americans and Hispanic Americans who were moving to cities in growing numbers. Generally, middle-class white Americans considered migration to the suburbs a move upward to a better life for themselves and their children.

In contrast to city life, suburbia offered a retreat to the picturesque countryside. As developers in earlier periods had done, the developers of the 1950s attracted home buyers with promises of fresh air, green lawns, and trees. Many suburbs had "park," "forest," "woods," "grove," or "hill" as part of their names.

The new suburbs were usually located on the fringes of major cities. Farmland or vacant wooded areas became sites for new subdivisions. In southern California, development of the San Fernando Valley, formerly sprinkled with orange groves, helped make Los Angeles the fastest-growing area in the postwar period.

Suburbs had low population densities compared to cities. Single-family homes on large plots of land, wide streets, and open spaces gave suburbs the "country" feeling that new middle-class homeowners craved. This openness was possible because residents

---

### STUDY·GUIDE

**As You Read**
Identify characteristics of the suburban life style that reflect both success and failure in achieving the American dream. Also, think about the following concepts and skills.

**Central Concepts**
- understanding some positive and negative features of life in **suburbia**
- recognizing the effects of the **baby boom** on life styles and on the economy

**Thinking Skills**
- identifying cause and effect
- analyzing behavior
- recognizing values
- comparing and contrasting

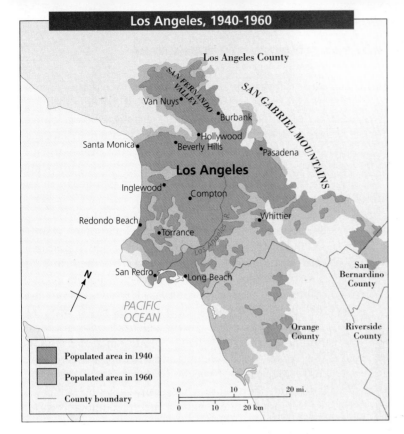

**Los Angeles, 1940-1960**

Los Angeles County

Van Nuys •
SAN FERNANDO VALLEY
• Burbank
SAN GABRIEL MOUNTAINS

• Hollywood
Santa Monica •
Beverly Hills
• Pasadena

**Los Angeles**

Inglewood •
• Compton

Redondo Beach •
• Whittier

• Torrance

San Pedro •
• Long Beach

San Bernardino County

PACIFIC OCEAN

Orange County     Riverside County

Populated area in 1940

Populated area in 1960

County boundary

0      10      20 mi.

0      10      20 km

Millions of people migrated to "sunny California" between 1940 and 1960. The Los Angeles area was one of the most rapidly growing parts of the state. *According to the map, which counties experienced the most growth between 1940 and 1960?*

**Minorities were excluded from white middle-class suburbia. However, in Richmond, California, a group of African American community leaders worked to develop a planned community, named Parchester Village, for middle-class African Americans. The first families moved into their new suburban homes in the spring of 1950.**

owned automobiles, which allowed them to travel to jobs, schools, and shopping facilities.

Affordability became a key factor in attracting home buyers to the suburbs. Because the GI Bill offered low-interest loans, new housing was more affordable during the postwar period than at any other time in American history. Equally attractive was the government's offer of income tax deductions for home mortgage interest payments and property taxes.

Though affordable, the suburbs did not offer opportunities for home ownership to everyone. Many American cities had small but growing populations of middle-class minorities, particularly African Americans and Hispanic Americans, who also longed to escape the noise, dirt, and crime of the cities. By and large, however, the developers of the nation's postwar suburbs refused to sell homes to minorities. By 1960, for example, Levittown, Long Island, had a population of over 65,000, but not a single African American resident. Despite having achieved a measure of finan-

cial success, America's middle-class minorities were still denied full access to the American dream.[1]

## Living the American Dream

Low-income and minority groups were largely excluded from suburban society. Millions of white, middle-class Americans, however, shared a life style that represented to them the American dream. They owned their homes, sent their children to good schools, lived in safe communities, and were economically secure. Such were the dreams of the immigrants who had sailed into New York harbor half a century before, and now those dreams finally had been realized by many of their children.

Nevertheless, some Americans found fault with the "dream." Social critics of the 1950s deplored the conformity of suburban life. They mocked what they regarded as the sameness of the "cookie-cutter"

## STUDY GUIDE

**Identifying Cause and Effect**

The construction of roads was both a cause and an effect of the growth of suburbs. As highways extended outward from the cities, suburbs grew up alongside them. This residential growth led to a further need for new highways. Also, the lack of public transportation between homes in the suburbs and jobs in the cities made the highways necessary for commuting.

**1** Why was suburban life denied to many Americans in the 1950s?

houses, the lack of privacy, and the decline of individuality. Folk singer Malvina Reynolds satirized the middle-class suburbanites in a popular song titled "Little Boxes":

*A nd they all play on the golf course*
*And drink their martinis dry,*
*And they all have pretty children*
*And the children go to school,*
*And the children go to summer camp*
*And then to the university,*
*Where they are put in boxes*
*And they come out all the same.*

Malvina Reynolds,
"Little Boxes"[2]

H. ARMSTRONG ROBERTS

**Togetherness and social participation were important values during the 1950s. These values were exemplified by such diverse things as the backyard family barbecue and increased church attendance.** *How do these things exemplify togetherness?*

KEEP THE LIGHT OF EVANGELISM BURNING!

© WAYNE MILLER, MAGNUM PHOTOS, INC.

Such criticism would not have rung true with most suburbanites. Emerging from an era of depression and world war, the residents of suburbia during the 1950s saw themselves creating thousands of new communities built on a common desire for a decent existence. Moreover, they prized the informality and togetherness of suburban life. New families were greeted by the "Welcome Wagon," a community organization that provided information and offered gifts

and coupons from local stores. Most newcomers moved easily into the social life of the neighborhood by joining a bowling league, bridge club, or church group. One suburban resident observed: "Before we came here, we used to live pretty much to ourselves. . . . Now we stop around and visit with people or they visit with us. I really think [suburban living] has broadened us."

Cooperation and group participation helped forge community spirit in the suburbs. This spirit extended to church membership, which increased from 48 percent of the population in 1940 to 63 percent in 1960. The resurgence of religion became evident in all areas of life, from movies to politics. Hollywood's hit films included such religious extravaganzas as *The Robe*, *The Ten Commandments*, and *Ben Hur*. Congress added "under God" to the Pledge of Allegiance and "In God We Trust" to all U.S. currency. President Eisenhower told Americans, "Everybody should have a religious faith, and I don't care what it is."

Religious leaders helped spread religious commitment with the aid of modern communications. They had their own radio and television programs, best selling books, and newspaper columns. Billy Graham, a popular Protestant minister and preacher, attracted thousands of people throughout the United States and in other parts of the world with his large-scale evangelical campaigns. Fulton J. Sheen, a Roman Catholic bishop, became a television personality through his weekly program optimistically titled "Life Is Worth Living." Protestant minister Norman Vincent Peale attracted many thousands of followers with his message of "positive thinking."

Critics claimed that churches downplayed faith and emphasized comfort and security. Instead of searching for God, the critics said, most Americans turned to religion for peace of mind and a sense of belonging. For whatever reasons, American families flocked to their churches and synagogues throughout the 1950s. Billboards and television commercials proclaimed: "Bring the whole family to church" and

"The family that prays together stays together." Messages like these clearly indicated that postwar society was focused on the family.

## Baby Boom

Like the economy, the family enjoyed unprecedented growth in the postwar years. The nation's population increased by 19 million in the 1940s and by almost 30 million in the 1950s. The fertility rate—the number of births per thousand women—peaked at 123 in 1957, up about 20 percent from the depression years of the 1930s. That meant that a baby was born in the United States every seven seconds! This phenomenal population growth known as the **baby boom** continued until the mid-1960s.

Like the resurgence of religion in the 1950s, the emphasis on family reflected a desire for close social and emotional ties. A *McCall's* magazine article in 1954 coined the term "togetherness" to describe young married couples whose lives centered on raising large families. Americans in the 1950s married at an earlier age and had more babies than their parents. Between the years 1940 and 1960, the birthrate for third and fourth children in a family more than doubled.[3]

The baby boom further fueled the economy and helped sustain prosperity. Growing families needed larger houses, so the construction industry prospered. As the baby boomers progressed from diapers to school classrooms to college diplomas, industries and institutions grew to satisfy their needs. During the 1950s school enrollments increased by 13 million. School districts struggled to erect new buildings and temporary classrooms to accommodate the nation's children. In California, a new school was completed every seven days throughout the 1950s, and still the state faced a shortage of classrooms.

**Catering to the Kids** Many of the baby boom kids enjoyed a life style of unprecedented privilege. Schools became not only institutions of learning but also centers of social activity. After-school programs included an endless variety of lessons and sports events. These activities were enthusiastically supported by parents who wanted to give their children

all the advantages their new prosperity would allow. Music lessons in the schools drove up the sale of musical instruments from $86 million in 1950 to $149 million in 1960. The number of Girl Scouts and Brownies doubled, and the number of Little Leagues grew from around 800 to nearly 6,000 during the 1950s.

Baby boomers were the nation's first generation raised on television from their earliest years. Programming for children included everything from puppet shows to tales of the Old West. Young viewers gathered around the TV to watch Buffalo Bob and his freckle-faced marionette, and when the youngsters heard the familiar opening line, "Say kids, what time is it?" they responded in unison, "It's Howdy Doody time!" At its height, the popular "Kukla, Fran, and Ollie" puppet show attracted an audience of 10 million viewers. Kukla (a clown), Ollie (a snaggle-toothed dragon), and several other Kuklapolitan puppets visited with Fran Allison in an unrehearsed weekly program that charmed the adults as well as the children.

TV heroes included the Lone Ranger, Hopalong Cassidy, and Captain Video (Guardian of the Universe). Also popular were shows featuring heroic dogs and horses—"Lassie," "Rin-Tin-Tin," and "My Friend Flicka." On "Ding Dong School," kindly Miss Frances led her television audience in constructive preschool activities and songs. Millions of viewers joined Annette, Cubby, Karen, and the other

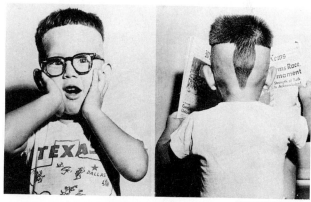

AP/WIDE WORLD PHOTOS

**Enthusiasm for the television characterization of Davy Crockett led some children to get their hair cut in the shape of a coonskin cap.** *What does this tell you about the impact of television on "baby boomers"?*

Mouseketeers on "The Mickey Mouse Club." Captain Kangaroo, Mr. Green Jeans, and a collection of puppet friends entertained more than one generation of youngsters.

Advertisers and toymakers jumped on the television bandwagon. Products aimed at the growing market of five- to fourteen-year-olds rang up big sales. In 1954 the popular Walt Disney television program introduced folk hero Davy Crockett, portrayed by Fess Parker. The resulting Davy Crockett "cult" created a $100 million market for coonskin caps and dozens of other items with Davy's picture on them. The theme song, "The Ballad of Davy Crockett," sold four million records.

Critics argued that television produced passive children. Children's programming, they claimed, was boring, mindless, and often violent. Still, some programs carried positive messages. Good triumphed over evil. Gentleness, kindness, and truthfulness prevailed. The joy and wonder of childhood were encouraged and celebrated.

**Healthier, Happier Children**   By the 1950s medical science had made great strides toward combatting childhood diseases. Antibiotics and vaccines helped control diseases such as diphtheria, influenza, and typhoid fever. Polio, however, continued to baffle the

medical profession. In 1952 a record number of 58,000 cases of polio were reported in the United States. Those who survived were often permanently paralyzed. The most severe cases were confined to iron lungs—large metal tanks with pumps that helped patients breathe. Polio became the most feared disease of the postwar period.

Dr. Jonas Salk finally developed an effective vaccine against polio and in doing so became the medical hero of the 1950s. Salk first tested the vaccine on himself, his wife, and their three sons. In 1954, two million schoolchildren took part in a mass testing program. The test, which was the largest effort of its kind in history, utilized the services of thousands of physicians and millions of volunteers. On April 12, 1955, the Salk vaccine was declared a safe and effective weapon against polio. Through the work of Dr. Salk, who became a hero to people throughout the world, and Dr. Albert Sabin, who developed an oral version of the vaccine, the threat of polio was virtually eliminated.

Dr. Salk's fame was paralleled by that of another medical person, Dr. Benjamin Spock. During the 1950s only the Bible sold more copies than Spock's

*CHICAGO DAILY TRIBUNE*

**When the Salk vaccine was approved for use on April 12, 1955, the day became almost a holiday. People rang bells and honked horns, and some schools were closed. A massive nationwide vaccination program began.** *Why do you think people were so jubilant about the approval of the Salk vaccine?*

MARCH OF DIMES BIRTH DEFECTS FOUNDATION

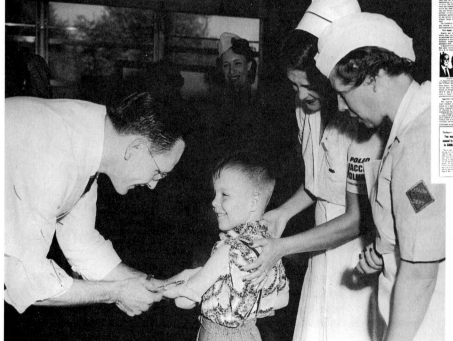

book *Baby and Child Care*. Spock popularized the theory that early childhood experiences influence an individual's entire life. He urged mothers to spare the rod and to devote themselves to creating an atmosphere of warmth and trust for their children so that they would grow into happy, well-adjusted adults. "You can think of it this way: useful, well-adjusted citizens are the most valuable possessions a country has, and good mother care during early childhood is the surest way to produce them." Dr. Spock suggested that the government should pay mothers so that they would not have to seek outside employment. This idea failed to gain popular support, and opponents even suggested that it smacked of socialism.

## A Woman's Place

Spock's theories helped reinforce the concept of motherhood as a profession in itself and strengthened the old idea that a woman's place was in the home. "No job is more exacting, more necessary, or more rewarding than that of housewife and mother," stated an article in the *Atlantic* in 1950. Statistics indicated that American women agreed. The median age of marriage for women fell from 21.5 in 1940 to 20.1 in 1956. By 1950 nearly 60 percent of all women between the ages of eighteen and twenty-four were married.

UPI/BETTMANN NEWSPHOTOS

**Women of the 1950s were encouraged to stay home and care for their young children. Mothers were counseled to reject strict regimentation in favor of freedom for children.** *How might this attitude have contributed to the "permissive generation" of the 1960s?*

**Mother and Homemaker** In the 1950s women were discouraged from attending college. A high school textbook on family living counseled young women that "Men are not interested in college degrees, but in the warmth and humanness of the girls they marry." Many women who did graduate from college concentrated their studies in such fields as home economics or child development. A survey found that most college women believed "it is natural for a woman to be satisfied with her husband's success and not crave personal achievement."

The suburban life style strengthened the distinctions between male and female roles. Fathers often left home early in the morning to commute to jobs in the city. When they returned home in the evening, the children had been fed, bathed, and dressed for bed. Most mothers assumed responsibility for the daily routine of child rearing in addition to cooking, cleaning, shopping, washing clothes, and participating in school and community activities. John Cheever, who set many of his novels and short stories in the suburbs of New York, described one such woman.

*She gets up at seven and turns the radio on. After she is dressed, she rouses the children and cooks the breakfast. Our son has to be walked to the school bus at eight o'clock. When Ethel returns from this trip, Carol's hair has to be braided. I leave the house at eight-thirty, but I know that every move that Ethel makes for the rest of the day will be determined by the housework, the cooking, the shopping, and the demands of the children. I know that on Tuesdays and Thursdays she will be at the A & P between eleven and noon, that on every clear afternoon she will be on a certain bench in a playground from three until five, that she cleans the house on Mondays, Wednesdays, and Fridays, and polishes the silver when it rains. When I return at six, she is usually cleaning the vegetables or making some other preparation for dinner. Then when the children have been fed and bathed, when the dinner is ready, when the table in the living room is set with food and china, she stands in the middle of the room as if she has lost or forgotten something, and this moment of reflection is so deep that she*

**Recognizing Values**

Dr. Benjamin Spock's famous baby book reinforced a traditional idea, one that the feminist movement would later take issue with: a woman's place is in the home. However, Dr. Spock's book is still popular, and some of the ideas he emphasized are still widely accepted. One such idea is that early childhood experiences influence a person's entire life. This idea is reflected in many aspects of modern life from television programming to government-funded Head Start programs for disadvantaged children.

*will not hear me if I speak to her, or the children if they call. Then it is over. She lights the four white candles in their silver sticks, and we sit down to a supper of corned-beef hash or some other modest fare.*

John Cheever,
"The Season of Divorce" from
*The Stories of John Cheever*

Popular culture reinforced the image of women as cute and perky rather than intelligent or career-minded. Actresses such as Doris Day, Debbie Reynolds, and Sandra Dee became role models for white women of the 1950s. Each portrayed the sweet, funny, innocent, wholesome, blond girl-next-door in popular box-office hits of the decade. Television situation comedies (sitcoms) emphasized the role of woman as wife and mother. In such shows as "Father Knows Best" and "Leave It to Beaver," Dad dispensed wisdom and advice while apron-clad Mom tended to domestic matters. In programs such as "Our Miss Brooks" and "Private Secretary," the main character was a single career woman whose goal in life was simply to find a husband.

The educational system often encouraged school girls of the 1950s to follow in their mothers' footsteps. While boys studied woodworking, auto mechanics, or courses preparing them for college, girls learned typing, cooking, and etiquette. Ironically, a Gallup Poll in 1962 showed that 90 percent of the mothers surveyed hoped that their daughters would not lead the same lives as they had.

**Women Question Their Role**   Despite the apparent happiness of the middle-class American woman, something was amiss. Many of these women did not feel the complete fulfillment that devotion to their homes and families was supposed to provide. Yet women who were dissatisfied with this role were considered by many to be either mentally disordered, unfeminine, or both. Truly feminine women, psychiatrist Helene Deutsch declared, related to the outside world only through identification with their husbands and children.

In 1957 Smith College graduates of the class of 1942 answered an alumnae questionnaire prepared by Betty Friedan that raised the issue of a woman's role

in society. Years of such research and interviews with women led to Friedan's landmark book, *The Feminine Mystique*, published in 1963.  As Friedan saw the situation:

*The problem lay buried, unspoken, for many years in the minds of American women. It was a strange stirring, a sense of dissatisfaction, a yearning that women suffered in the middle of the twentieth century in the United States. Each suburban wife struggled with it alone. As she made the beds, shopped for groceries, matched slipcover material, ate peanut butter sandwiches with her children, chauffeured Cub Scouts and Brownies . . . she was afraid to ask even of herself the silent question—"Is this all?"*

Betty Friedan,
*The Feminine Mystique*, 1963

The "problem that had no name" had finally been identified by Friedan. While many American women were happy with their roles as housewives and mothers, many others felt they had been relegated by social pressures to roles as life-long domestics.

**Women in the Work Force**   At the end of World War II, the government and industries urged women to "go back home" and "give your job to a vet." Women, who were largely excluded from important jobs in the corporate world, were also squeezed out of the manufacturing jobs they had held during the war.

So, whether by pressure or by choice, many women who had taken on nontraditional jobs during the war returned to the familiar roles of full-time homemakers and mothers.  However, for women in the lower economic ranks, staying at home was not an option.  Millions of such women continued to enter the job market while still maintaining their roles as housewives and mothers. During the 1950s the rate of female employment increased four times faster than that of males. The number of working wives doubled from 15 percent in 1940 to 30 percent in 1960. The number of working mothers leaped from 1.5 million to 6.6 million. By 1960, nearly 40 percent of women with children between the ages of six and seventeen had jobs outside the home.

**Comparing and Contrasting**
Women who grew up in the 1950s usually had a narrow view of the possibilities open to them in the world of work. Many expected that if they ever worked outside their homes, they would be waitresses, store clerks, or factory workers. Those who planned careers usually prepared to become secretaries, nurses, or teachers. Because of the feminist movement of the 1960s and 1970s, young women now feel encouraged to pursue any career that interests them and for which they have some aptitude. Nearly all careers are open to both women and men.

UPI/BETTMANN

**During World War II women had held traditionally male jobs such as shipbuilding, welding, and carpentry, which were often more interesting and always higher paying than the employment they had been used to. During the postwar years, women were forced back into traditional patterns of employment in low-paying jobs such as clerks, secretaries, waitresses, and textile workers.** *What accounted for this shift in women's job patterns?*

Married women over thirty-five represented the greatest increase in female employment in the 1950s. Many of these women had worked outside the home before having a family. They then had stayed home to raise their children, who were now either married or off to school. These women filled the millions of clerical and secretarial positions created in the postwar pe-

riod that could not be filled by the relatively small number of young single women who were entering the job market.

When surveyed about why they worked, married women no longer talked about professional advancement or job satisfaction. They claimed their motives for working were to make money for the children's education or the mortgage or a second car or a vacation—in other words, to get a piece of the "American Dream." In households where the husband earned between $7,000 and $10,000 a year, the rate of women's employment increased from 7 percent in 1950 to 25 percent in 1960. The 1960 census indicated that the number of households earning $15,000 or more would be cut in half if women's earnings were excluded. Women thus faced a dilemma. Economic pressures to maintain a comfortable life style forced them into the work place, while social pressures led them to believe their proper place was at home.

However, most women's jobs were low-paying and were either temporary, part-time, or held no opportunity for advancement. In areas such as insurance and banking, for example, women made up 50 percent or more of the work force, but they held 20 percent or less of higher-level managerial positions.

Stereotyped images of women's proper roles erected barriers to women's equal treatment. After World War II, the salary gap between full-time male and female wage earners widened. In 1955 women earned 64 percent of average male wages; in 1963 they earned only 60 percent as much as men. A 1959 study concluded that women could not expect a professional career. Men simply would not take women's professional aspirations seriously.

Women were not alone in their plight. Despite the prosperity of postwar society, many Americans—victims of racial prejudice and discrimination, neglect, and cultural differences—were denied full participation in the American dream.

## SECTION REVIEW

### Checking Facts

1. What happened after World War II to make a home in the suburbs affordable for many Americans?
2. Who did not share in the life style of postwar suburbia, and why?
3. How and why did the baby boom kids enjoy privileges not available to their parents?
4. Why was there a resurgence of religion during the postwar period?

### Thinking Critically

5. **Identifying Cause and Effect** How did television promote and maintain postwar consumerism?
6. **Comparing and Contrasting** How are employment opportunities different for women today than they were during the postwar years?
7. **Recognizing Values** What values are reflected by the fact that women wage earners in 1955

earned only 64 percent of the average wages for men?

### Linking Across Time

8. Compare the children's television programs today with those of the 1950s. How are they similar? How are they different? What can you conclude about the values of both periods?

# Happy Days

*After the upheaval of World War II, Americans sought security in an uncertain world.  Many women left wartime jobs to become full-time housewives. Veterans returned to a pumped-up economy full of opportunity. Parents who had experienced the Depression lavished their new affluence on children.*

Dick Clark

**"American Bandstand"** featured hit singers and teen fans exhibiting the latest dances in front of the TV camera. "Bandstand" helped spread the urban rock scene from its studio in Philadelphia throughout the country and tapped into a growing market for records.

**Poodle skirts,** fluffed up with layers of starched crinolines, were popular. Blue jeans, with cuffs rolled up, were the uniform for informal occasions. With allowance money to spend on clothing, teens exerted a new-found influence on style.

The **boomerang** shape was part of the design of everything from lamps to motel signs.

Gathered around their new TV set, many families watched such programs as **"Father Knows Best."** The show's strong but wise father, stay-at-home mother, and respectful children represented an ideal of fifties' life.

## HANG LOOSE

Rebelling against middle-class American culture, the **Beats** adopted an unconventional life style. They haunted smoke-filled coffeehouses where jazz musicians played and poets read their avant-garde works. The men often wore beards; and the women, long straight hair and black leotards.

Teenagers could **hang loose** as they spun their **crazy** hula hoops. Chubby Checker's new dance, **the twist,** used the same hip action that made the hula hoop spin.

# Poverty amid Plenty

## 1955: Families Struggle in El Barrio

PEDRO AND MARIA LOPEZ AND THEIR FIVE CHILDREN LIVED IN AN UNFURNISHED APARTMENT IN EAST HARLEM. EL BARRIO, AS THIS SECTION OF NEW YORK CITY WAS called, had become one of the most densely populated places in the world, with nearly 300,000 people per square mile.

The Lopez family paid $40 a week rent for their fourth-floor walkup, which consisted of a living room, bathroom, kitchen, and one bedroom. Despite Maria's scrupulous housekeeping, the apartment was infested with rats and roaches.

Six days a week, Pedro got up at 4:30 A.M. to commute to his job as a die cutter, for which he earned $75 weekly. Maria earned another $60 weekly by working part-time and weekends in a supermarket, which was a 45-minute trip from home.

© BRUCE DAVIDSON, MAGNUM PHOTOS, INC.

When Pedro had to miss work because of a stomach ulcer, Maria applied for temporary aid from the Department of Social Services. The application was denied because her son Anthony had been suspended from school for truancy.

Because of additional medical expenses, Pedro and Maria came up five dollars short that month when the rent was due. Their landlord promptly issued an eviction notice. In desperation, Pedro ignored his doctor's orders and returned to his job and even took a second job evenings and Sundays. Ten-year-old Manuel dropped out of school and found a job to help pay his family's bills.

Like many American families in the 1950s, the Lopezes were dedicated to the values of thrift, hard work, and a good education for their children. The American dream, however, seemed always beyond their grasp. Pedro, Maria, and their children belonged to a class of Americans whose dreams rarely came true and whose problems went largely unnoticed by the rest of society. The Lopezes were unfortunate members of the nation's **culture of poverty**.

## The Invisible Poor

Picture postcards of New York City in the 1950s reflected the glory of postwar United States. Skyscrapers soared heavenward; the waters swarmed with commercial traffic; sleek passenger jets cruised a cloudless sky; and in the harbor, Madame Liberty beckoned with promises of freedom, equality, and opportunity.

Hidden behind the tall buildings, away from the bustling harbor was a very different United States—a nation of crumbling streets and tenements, of hungry and sometimes homeless people; a nation not of freedom and equality but of prejudice and discrimination; a nation not of plenty but of desperate need.

The "invisible poor" were so well hidden that many Americans believed that poverty in the United States had been nearly eliminated. In 1956 historian Arthur Schlesinger stated that "the central problems of our times are no longer problems of want and privation." Four years later *Fortune* magazine declared that there were fewer than one million poor people

---

### STUDY GUIDE

**As You Read**

Identify the social and political factors that combined to create an invisible poor in the postwar United States. Also, think about the following concept and skills.

**Central Concept**
- understanding and analyzing the reasons that the **culture of poverty** is not limited by age, geography, race, or ethnic group

**Thinking Skills**
- drawing conclusions
- recognizing assumptions
- identifying cause and effect
- assessing outcomes

left in the United States and predicted that by 1970 there would be none at all. *Time* magazine agreed, stating that "nothing less than the elimination of poverty as a fact of life is in sight."

Social and political factors combined to make the poor invisible. Many prosperous Americans, for example, simply closed their eyes to the poverty around them because the postwar popular culture glorified the "good life" and the accomplishments of economic productivity and technological innovation.

Also, as the middle class moved to the suburbs after World War II, they left the poor behind. The inner cities became isolated islands of poverty—out of sight and out of mind. The population of midtown Manhattan dropped from 1.5 million during the day to 2,000 at night. Writer John Brooks noted that midtown Manhattan was "tidally swamped with bustling humanity every weekday morning . . . and abandoned again at nightfall when the wave sucked back." Working in midtown Manhattan, the suburbanites rarely saw the hundreds of thousands of poor families who lived in the Bronx, Brooklyn, and Queens.

The lack of any effective political voice also kept the poor invisible. In the past the urban poor had included large numbers of European immigrants who were aided by big-city political bosses, most of whom had European backgrounds themselves. With such aid the immigrants and their children often struggled out of poverty and fled the noisy, dirty cities for the calm and quiet of the suburbs. However, progressive urban reforms of the 1900s and the increase in federal programs in the 1930s helped undermine the political boss system's monopoly on social services. The urban poor of the 1950s included displaced white people from Appalachia, African Americans, Hispanic Americans, and Native Americans who flooded into the cities during and after World War II. Largely unrepresented, they would only slowly acquire a political voice in the 1960s and thereafter.[1]

AP/WIDE WORLD PHOTOS

**When Michael Harrington, pictured above, published *The Other America* in 1962, many people denied his findings. They did not want to believe that poverty was a significant problem in the United States.** *Why do you think Harrington titled his book* The Other America?

In 1962 author Michael Harrington shocked prosperous Americans by revealing the extent of poverty in their midst. In his book, *The Other America*, Harrington wrote that 50 million Americans lived in poverty. He explained that poverty was defined not only by a lack of money but also by the absence of hope:

> *The poor live in a culture of poverty . . . [and] for reasons beyond their control, cannot help themselves. . . . The poor get sick more than anyone else in the society. . . . When they become sick, they are sick longer than any other group in the society. Because they are sick more often and longer than anyone else, they lose wages and work, and find it difficult to hold a steady job. And because of this, they cannot pay for good housing, for a nutritious diet, for doctors . . . [and] their prospect is to move to an even lower level . . . toward even more suffering.*
>
> Michael Harrington,
> *The Other America*, 1962

---

## STUDY GUIDE

**Drawing Conclusions**

During his research for *The Other America*, Michael Harrington lived among the poor he was studying. He noted that the poverty was being passed on from one generation to the next, resulting in an unbroken cycle of misery. Harrington concluded that poverty had actually become part of the culture of the people he had come to care so much about.

**1** Why were the urban poor of the 1950s "invisible"?

# The Culture of Poverty

Harrington and others pointed out that the poverty of the 1950s was a "new" poverty. The poverty of the Depression era was a general condition that affected large parts of society. Nationally organized, large-scale social welfare programs and labor organizations had responded with work programs and relief payments. When the economy began to recover, so too did the people. In contrast, the poor in the postwar era had no such massive social welfare programs to enable them to break out of poverty.

Additional studies supported Harrington's findings. One study concluded that 40 percent of the American people were ill-housed, ill-clothed, and ill-fed. Another study found that 34.5 million Americans lived on less than $2.10 a day. Americans could no longer deny that poverty was a major social problem.

The reasons for poverty in the United States were varied. Some of the poor, particularly African and Hispanic Americans, faced longstanding racial and ethnic prejudice and discrimination. The poor also included jobless Appalachian whites, who moved to the cities because of the lack of opportunity in the hills, and Native Americans, who lived both in the cities and on reservations. Finally, there were the growing numbers of elderly Americans who were not covered by social security and had never received pensions from their employers. Whatever the reasons for the existence of poverty, the problem was not limited by age, race, or ethnic heritage.[2]

**The Young and the Old**　Almost half the poor were children under the age of eighteen. By the early 1960s, many of the nation's poor children were the third generation in their families to have been raised on welfare. A depressing cycle of poverty was born—generation after generation totally dependent on government aid for their sustenance, knowing no other way of life.

While many children were born into poverty, many elderly Americans simply grew into it. Approximately eight million Americans over the age of sixty-five had incomes of less than $1,000 a year. The following testimony details the problems afflicting the elderly during the 1950s and 1960s:

THE CINCINNATI HISTORICAL SOCIETY

In *The Other America,* published in 1962, Michael Harrington estimated that there were over 8,000,000 elderly poor in the United States. Many of these poor had earned decent wages during their working years but had drifted into poverty during their old age.

*Louise W_____, age 73, lives by herself in a single furnished room on the third floor of a rooming house located in a substandard section of the city. In this one room, she cooks, eats, and sleeps. . . . . Widowed at 64, she has few friends remaining from her younger years. Those who do remain do not live near her, and it is difficult for her to see them. . . . And so she stays confined to her one room and the bathroom shared by nine other people. When the weather is warm enough, she ventures down the long flight of stairs about once a week for a walk to the corner and back.*

Testimony before 1960 Senate hearing on the aged

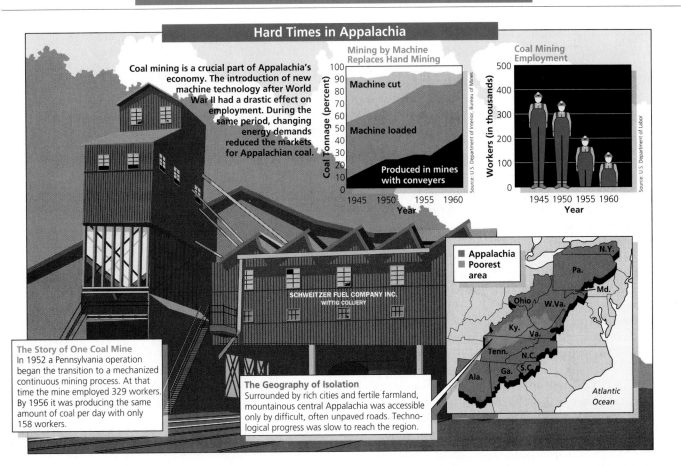

## Hard Times in Appalachia

Coal mining is a crucial part of Appalachia's economy. The introduction of new machine technology after World War II had a drastic effect on employment. During the same period, changing energy demands reduced the markets for Appalachian coal.

**Mining by Machine Replaces Hand Mining**

Coal Tonnage (percent)

Machine cut
Machine loaded
Produced in mines with conveyers

1945 1950 1955 1960
Year

Source: U.S. Department of Interior, Bureau of Mines

**Coal Mining Employment**

Workers (in thousands)

500 400 300 200 100 0

1945 1950 1955 1960
Year

Source: U.S. Department of Labor

SCHWEITZER FUEL COMPANY INC.
WITTIG COLLIERY

**The Story of One Coal Mine**
In 1952 a Pennsylvania operation began the transition to a mechanized continuous mining process. At that time the mine employed 329 workers. By 1956 it was producing the same amount of coal per day with only 158 workers.

**The Geography of Isolation**
Surrounded by rich cities and fertile farmland, mountainous central Appalachia was accessible only by difficult, often unpaved roads. Technological progress was slow to reach the region.

■ Appalachia
■ Poorest area

N.Y.
Pa.
Md.
Ohio
W.Va.
Ky.
Va.
Tenn.
N.C.
S.C.
Ala.
Ga.
Atlantic Ocean

The plight of the nation's elderly citizens was, ironically, partly the result of scientific and technological progress. Modern medicine prolonged their lives, while modern technology often left them unemployed. Mechanization wiped out the farm chores and factory jobs formerly available to older workers. Thus, many elderly Americans spent their final years without work and without dignity. **3**

**Rural and Urban Poverty**   At least a third of the poor worked on farms or lived in depressed rural areas. Changes in modern farming created deep pockets of rural poverty. As corporate farms and big farm owners came to dominate production, many small independent farmers found it difficult to compete and slipped into poverty. Across the southern United States, thousands of small farm families, both black and white, lacked adequate diets in the midst of the world's most productive agricultural system.

Residents of Appalachia, a region covering 80,000 square miles and parts of nine states, suffered severely. In 1960 about three-fourths of Appalachia's eight million people had a median family income of about $2,000 a year. A drop in the demand for coal coupled with the increased use of machinery put almost 70 percent of the region's coal miners out of work.

Rural poverty drove thousands of people to the cities, straining already inadequate housing, school systems, and transportation facilities. Governmental efforts to provide low-cost housing often did more harm than good. Slum clearance merely shoved the poor from one part of the city to another. The projects—low-rent public housing complexes—imposed harsh restrictions on tenants. Large families with low incomes had priority. A family could be evicted if the marriage broke up or the family income exceeded the limits set by the housing authority. Housing projects often actually contributed to the cycle of poverty.

## STUDY GUIDE

### Identifying Cause and Effect
In rural areas, changing farming methods displaced already impoverished small farmers. In Appalachia, modernization of mines and a drop in demand for coal left thousands without a way to earn a living. In both farming and mining, economic or technological change displaced groups from their traditional role in society. This displacement was the first step in the cycle of poverty.

**3** What are some of the conditions that cause the elderly to become impoverished?

## The African American Experience

The poverty of African Americans had a unique quality that was not shared by other groups. African Americans, unlike many of the other poor, had to contend with deep-seated racial prejudice. While southern black farmers suffered the same poverty as their white counterparts, the rural South harbored that force of racial terrorism, the Ku Klux Klan. The Klan used physical violence, including many instances of torture and lynchings, to intimidate blacks and keep them "in their place."[4]

African Americans carried this fear of white terrorism with them when they migrated to northern cities. By the mid-1950s, nearly half the African American population lived in cities. Atlanta, Los Angeles, Detroit, Chicago, New York—each had its ghetto. African American novelist, essayist, and activist, James Baldwin, described Harlem in the postwar period.

*Harlem, physically at least, has changed very little in my parents' lifetime or in mine. Now as then the buildings are old and in desperate need of repair, the streets are crowded and dirty, there are too many human beings per square block. Rents are 10 to 58 per cent higher than anywhere else in the city; food, expensive everywhere, is more expensive here and of an inferior quality; and now that the war is over and money is dwindling, clothes are carefully shopped for and seldom bought. Negroes, traditionally the last to be hired and the first to be fired, are finding jobs harder to get, and, while prices are rising implacably, wages are going down. All over Harlem now there is felt the same bitter expectancy with which, in my childhood, we awaited winter: it is coming and it will be hard; there is nothing anyone can do about it.*

James Baldwin
*Notes of a Native Son*, 1955

In New York City in 1955, 50 percent of black families had incomes under $4,000 a year (compared with 20 percent of the white families), and 40 percent of all New York's welfare recipients were black. Unemployment among black workers was double that of white workers, and average wages were about half of what white workers earned.

Racial prejudice formed a barrier to economic as well as social advancement. Many black workers, because of their color, were denied access to all but the lowest-paying jobs. Many black students lacked opportunities in a segregated school system. Black doctors and lawyers often found it difficult to practice anywhere but in the ghetto, where they would never earn as much as their white colleagues.

**The photo below shows members of a poor black family in an urban ghetto. The "culture of poverty" was particularly devastating to minorities.**

© BRUCE DAVIDSON, MAGNUM PHOTOS, INC.

## Hispanic Hardships

Spanish-speaking Americans made up the nation's second-largest minority group. Puerto Ricans, like Pedro and Maria Lopez who were described earlier, flocked to the United States in the 1950s, drawn by stories of abundance and a desire to escape the poverty of their island homeland. During the decade, the Puerto Rican population of the United States grew from 300,000 to nearly one million. Many of the immigrants crowded into the slum neighborhoods of New York City.

**Assessing Outcomes**

James Baldwin's look at Harlem at the end of World War II is a remarkable description of what Martin Luther King, Jr., would call life "on a lonely island of poverty in the midst of a vast ocean of material prosperity." The themes noted by Baldwin—isolation, powerlessness, lack of opportunity—would be sounded by blacks all over the country during the civil rights movement of the 1960s.

**4** How was the poverty of African Americans during the 1950s different from the poverty of other groups?

Puerto Rican immigrants faced other difficulties in addition to their poverty. The language barrier retarded their assimilation into U.S. society. Native culture and strong family traditions were slowly lost as young Puerto Ricans adopted American ways. Women found jobs more easily than men did, which strained the traditional husband-wife relationship.

Mexican Americans suffered from the same discriminations that Puerto Ricans faced, with an added burden—they rarely felt politically secure. Because Puerto Rico is a Commonwealth of the United States, Puerto Ricans are U.S. citizens, free to travel, work, and live within the United States. Mexico, however, is a sovereign foreign state, and Mexican immigrants are legally defined as aliens. Immigration and Naturalization officers were charged with tracking down immigrants who were in this country illegally. In the process, they could stop any Mexican American on the street and demand proof of citizenship.

Many Mexican American families had been citizens of the United States for generations. Many lived in urban centers, especially in California, Texas, and the Midwest. However, they were less noticed than the migrant farm workers. While Mexican Americans made up the largest group of migrant farm workers, blacks, Puerto Ricans, and poor whites lived and worked under the same oppressive conditions. Migrant workers followed the crops from state to state for seven or eight months a year, from harvesting spring vegetables in Texas to picking fall apples in Washington. They slept in shacks or in labor camps and worked 10 or 12 hours a day in the fields. Some migrant workers worked for piece rates; others received an hourly wage of 50 cents. Migrant workers toiled outside the protection of labor laws. Children worked the fields with their parents, often on ladders or using hazardous machinery. Injured farm workers received no worker's compensation.

Some Mexicans illegally entered the United States to work in the fields. Others entered this country legally, under the bracero program—an agreement forged with the Mexican government during World War II to permit seasonal immigration of farm workers. State employment officials recruited Mexican *braceros*, or temporary workers, to harvest crops. Braceros were expected to return to Mexico after the harvest, but many stayed on illegally.

In 1953 the government launched a deportation

**Migrant farm workers were the focus of a 1960 TV documentary titled "Harvest of Shame." Viewers were surprised that U.S. agriculture still depended so heavily on "stoop" labor and were shocked to learn about the living conditions of the nation's two million migrant farm workers.**

program that became known as Operation Wetback. Illegal Mexican aliens were called "wetbacks"—still considered a derogatory term—because thousands of them entered the United States by swimming across the Rio Grande. During a three-year period, Operation Wetback rounded up and deported more than three million people.

## Displaced Native Americans

O ne of America's smallest minorities—Native Americans—continued to be its poorest, most ignored group. By 1960 almost two-thirds of the nation's 600,000 Native Americans lived on reservations. Unemployment rates were staggering—more than 70 percent among the Blackfeet of Montana and the Hopi of New Mexico; 86 percent among the Choctaw of Mississippi. Many Native Americans migrated to the cities where they encountered much of the same discrimination and poverty African and Hispanic Americans endured.

In 1953 the federal government adopted a new Native American policy called "termination." The Indian Reorganization Act of 1934 had attempted to restore lands to tribal ownership; however, the purpose of this new policy was to end the reservation system and terminate all federal services to tribes. The result of the termination policy was the loss of hundreds of thousands of acres of Native American lands to agricultural, lumber, and mining interests.

As an incentive to leave the reservations, the government helped Native Americans relocate to cities through the Voluntary Relocation program. Relocation offices provided moving expenses, help in finding housing and jobs, and temporary living expenses. However, relocating to the cities proved to be disorienting and culturally wrenching for thousands of Native Americans who left their tribal group. A Seminole petition to President Eisenhower sounded

© PAUL FUSCO, MAGNUM PHOTOS, INC.

**Under the relocation program, more than 60,000 Native Americans had left their reservations and moved to cities by 1960. Some ended up in the poorest sections of the cities, while some became middle-class. However, nearly a third decided to return to their tribes.**

the cry of all Native American groups who struggled for identity in the 1950s:

> *W e do not say that we are superior or inferior to the White Man and we do not say that the White Man is superior or inferior to us. We do say that we are not White Men . . . do not wish to become White Men but wish to . . . have an outlook on all things different from the outlook of the White Man.*
>
> Seminole Petition to
> President Eisenhower

The termination policy of the 1950s, like nearly every Native American policy before it, ended up victimizing Native Americans. Individual tribes and organizations of Native Americans officially protested termination. Lacking political representation, their protests went unanswered, and Native Americans remained the most "invisible" of all minority groups.

## SECTION REVIEW

**Checking Facts**

1. What is the culture of poverty?
2. How was the poverty of the 1950s different from the poverty of the Great Depression?
3. Why did Mexican Americans rarely feel politically secure in the United States?
4. Describe the policy of "termination." How did this policy affect Native Americans?

**Thinking Critically**

5. **Drawing Conclusions** What conclusions can you reach about the causes of poverty in postwar United States?
6. **Recognizing Assumptions** Keeping in mind that during the 1950s the poor were "invisible," what do you think many middle-class Americans of the 1950s assumed about the poor?

7. **Assessing Outcomes** What impact did technological, scientific, and medical advances have on coal miners, farmers, and the elderly during the 1950s?

**Linking Across Time**

8. What are the characteristics of poverty today? Is poverty still hidden? Have different groups become impoverished?

# Recognizing Biases

The role Lucille Ball played in "I Love Lucy" took the show to the top of the ratings from 1951 to 1957. The show's main purpose was humor and entertainment. However, Lucy's wacky behavior and her dependence on husband Ricky shows the bias in this era regarding the appropriate role of women.

## Learning the Skill

A bias is a personal outlook that inhibits impartial judgment. Everyone has some biases—for example, thinking cats make better pets without ever having had any experience with dogs.

Television programs reflect the biases of a society or certain groups within the society. Through the selections they make, the people who control the content of a program—writers, producers, and advertising sponsors—reveal their own biases or the biases they expect will appeal to their audiences.

The way a character is depicted can convey a positive or negative attitude toward particular groups and issues. Being aware of this can help prevent you from accepting a biased point of view as the truth. In fact, accepting a biased view as the truth may indicate that you have similar biases.

When checking for biases, look for clues in costume, setting, and dialogue that make you think that the character's life style is desirable or undesirable. What image is the character projecting, and how closely does it represent real life? What do your reactions indicate about your biases?

NEAL PETERS

**TV Women of the 1950s**

Notice how the clothing and setting in Lucy's picture on this page emphasize her main role in the kitchen and contribute to the bias that being a housewife is the key to happiness.

Lucy was always made to look particularly silly (and lovable) when she was ineptly trying her hand at a new job or role. Everything got back to "normal" when Lucy obeyed her husband and went home.

GLOBE PHOTOS

**Modern TV Women**

By contrast, the role of Murphy Brown, portrayed by Candice Bergen, glorifies the life of an independent career woman. As a news anchor, she has a high level of education and responsibility. Murphy is single and lives alone. By making no effort to search for a husband, she makes it clear that marriage is not the most important thing in her life; she values personal achievement as well.

Taking pride in one's career is seen as a key to happiness. It contributes to a bias that women are happiest when they exercise power in their work. What aspects of Murphy Brown's character could make a person want to be more like her?

## Practicing the Skill

1. Review paragraph five on this page. Then look at the pictures on this page and decide what message each character seems to be conveying about women. List the clues you see in each picture.

2. Imagine what Lucy and Murphy would have been like as high school students. How would their classmates and teachers have reacted to them? Work with one or more classmates to role-play a scene from life at school with Lucy or with Murphy. Then discuss with the class how the biases of you and your classmates affect how you each acted a role and how you reacted to the roles of others.

3. Think of a television program you have seen with a strong male or female character. Identify the bias you think is shown in the way the character is depicted. List the clues that help you identify the bias.

# Chapter 15 Review

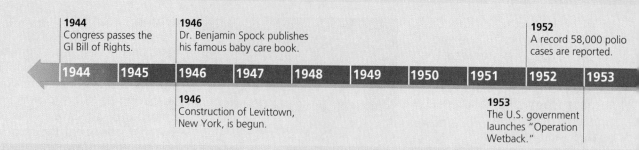

**1944**
Congress passes the GI Bill of Rights.

**1946**
Dr. Benjamin Spock publishes his famous baby care book.

**1952**
A record 58,000 polio cases are reported.

| 1944 | 1945 | 1946 | 1947 | 1948 | 1949 | 1950 | 1951 | 1952 | 1953 |

**1946**
Construction of Levittown, New York, is begun.

**1953**
The U.S. government launches "Operation Wetback."

## Summary

Use the following outline as a tool for reviewing and summarizing the chapter. Copy the outline on your own paper, leaving spaces between headings to jot down notes about key events and concepts.

**I. Postwar Economy Booms**
  A. The Shift from War to Peace
  B. Impact of the GI Bill
  C. The New World of Business
  D. From Agriculture to Agribusiness
  E. An Automobile Culture

**II. Suburban Life Styles**
  A. Growth of Suburbia
  B. Living the American Dream
  C. Baby Boom
  D. A Woman's Place

**III. Poverty amid Plenty**
  A. The Invisible Poor
  B. The Culture of Poverty
  C. The African American Experience
  D. Hispanic Hardships
  E. Displaced Native Americans

## Ideas, Events, and People

1. Describe a "Veterans' Village." How many veterans took advantage of the educational assistance offered by the GI Bill?
2. What happened to the economy as working-class Americans accumulated discretionary income?
3. How did advertising affect the demand for consumer goods?
4. Where were most new homes of the 1950s built?
5. What kinds of people lived in "suburbia"? Describe their life style.
6. Many teenagers shared in the affluence of the 1950s. As their parents' discretionary income increased, teenagers had more money to spend as well. How did teen affluence affect the culture of the 1950s?
7. What was the problem identified by Betty Friedan in *The Feminine Mystique?*
8. How was the poverty of the 1950s different from the poverty of the Depression era?
9. Describe some of the hardships in the life of a migrant farm worker.

## Social Studies Skills

**Recognizing Biases**
Choose some group of society, such as the elderly, the handicapped, motorcycle riders, athletes, or another group. Collect information about how the group is portrayed in our society. Examine television programs and commercials, movies, newspaper articles, magazine advertisements, or other sources. Then decide what biases society has toward the group. Explain how you reach your conclusion. Do you think society's biases about the group have any basis in fact? Why or why not?

## Critical Thinking

**1. Cause and Effect**
What were some of the causes of the baby boom, and how did the baby boom affect the economy?

**2. Assessing Outcomes**
The postwar period saw a dramatic increase in the production of automobiles. In what ways did the life style of Americans in the 1950s revolve around the automobile?

**3. Compare and Contrast**
The growth of suburbia in the 1950s affected the quality of life in urban areas. Compare and contrast suburban life of the 1950s with city life of the same period.

| 1954 | 1955 | 1956 | 1957 | 1958 | 1959 | 1960 | 1961 | 1962 | 1963 |
|------|------|------|------|------|------|------|------|------|------|

**1954**
"Davy Crockett" premieres on TV.

**1956**
Congress authorizes $32 billion for highway construction.

**1960**
U.S. GNP reaches $500 billion.

**1962**
Michael Harrington publishes *The Other America.*

**1955**
Salk vaccine is declared safe and effective weapon against polio.

**1963**
Betty Friedan publishes *The Feminine Mystique.*

**4. Making Inferences**

In 1960 *Fortune* magazine claimed that there were fewer than one million poor in the United States and that poverty would be completely eliminated by 1970. Why do you think society was unaware of the problem of poverty at that time?

## Extension and Application

**1. Citizenship**

The "white flight" from the cities to the suburbs, begun in the postwar period, has continued in most large cities. What might reverse this trend? What social and economic conditions would persuade people to move back to the cities?

**2. Global Connections**

During the 1950s the United States enjoyed an unprecedented period of prosperity. Select a country in Europe. Research the standard of living in that country during the 1950s. Describe the lives of citizens in that country compared to the lives of middle-class Americans during the 1950s.

**3. Linking Across Time**

The baby boom reached a peak in 1957. By 1975 the population growth rate had dropped dramatically, with only 3,144,000 births during the year compared to 4,308,000 in 1957. The generations following the baby boom have fewer members. As the disproportionately large numbers of baby boomers reach retirement age, how do you think that will affect society?

## Geography

**1.** The map pictured here shows a section of the interstate highway system. How might a city such as Lubbock, Texas, benefit from the highway?

**2.** How might a city such as Amarillo benefit from the interstate? How are these benefits related to Lubbock, Texas?

**3.** Find several highway intersections shown on the map on this page. Describe the location of these intersections.

**4.** According to pages 504–505, how did the area around cities change during the 1950s?

**5.** Compare and contrast the uses of the family automobile in the 1920s with the uses of the family automobile in the 1950s, as explained on pages 500–501. What conclusions can you draw from the comparison?

**6.** Based on page 517, what characteristics of Appalachia in the 1950s contributed to its being one of the nation's poorest regions?

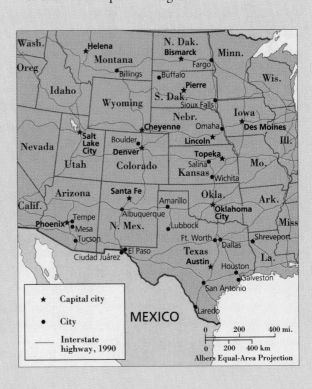

Capital city
City
Interstate highway, 1990

MEXICO

0    200    400 mi.
0    200    400 km
Albers Equal-Area Projection

## CHAPTER 16

# Cold War Politics

## June 9, 1954: McCarthy versus the Army

Joseph Welch was one of a long line of people caught up in the controversy surrounding congressional hearings on the subject of communism. Dozens of people, under questioning, had helplessly watched their careers and their reputations slip away. They left the hearings marked with labels such as "communist," "spy," or "subversive."

The questioner Welch faced was Senator Joseph McCarthy, the nation's self-appointed communist hunter of the early 1950s. He was a dreaded man who was determined to prove that communists were lurking in every office and department of the U.S. government.

McCarthy rarely offered any evidence against people he accused. But in the cold war atmosphere of the 1950s, proof didn't matter. Fear, rather than reason, ruled.

The McCarthy hearings were an extreme example of a wave of conservatism that dominated political life of this time. His campaign of intimidation went unchecked for nearly four years. Few people were willing, or able, to confront McCarthy effectively.

Welch, a Boston attorney, appeared before McCarthy to defend the U.S. Army against charges that it was harboring communists. Under the glare of hot lights and with the nation attentively watching on TV, Welch, weary of McCarthy's slander, replied calmly and firmly. His famous rebuttal challenged the senator. "I think I never really gauged your cruelty or your recklessness," Welch said. "Have you no sense of decency, sir, at long last? Have you left no sense of decency?"

> *"Have you no sense of decency, sir, at long last? Have you left no sense of decency?"*

UPI/BETTMANN

*Senator McCarthy uses a map of Communist party strongholds to attack army attorney Joseph Welch.*

*Alger Hiss and his wife leave the federal court during the 1949 perjury trial
that ended in his conviction.*

# Retreat from the New Deal

## 1946: Veterans Return to a Changing Country After World War II

THE NEWSREELS SHOWED THOUSANDS OF CHEERING SAILORS, SOLDIERS, AND AIRMEN CROWDING INTO TIMES SQUARE OR POURING OFF TROOP SHIPS. THEIR FAMILIES AND girlfriends and wives leaped into their arms, shedding tears of joy. Caps were flung into the air. The ground was kissed. But when the homecomings were over, World War II veterans faced the task of rebuilding their lives and careers in a very uncertain time.

Many men were able to pick up their jobs more or less where they had left off before the war. Others, however, had put education and career decisions on hold to serve in the military. There was, at first, a great deal of turmoil in the job market, as the economy adjusted to peacetime production and to the flood of returning workers.

The 1946 movie *The Best Years of Our Lives* dramatized the difficulties of veterans during the first weeks of their return. In the following scene, a drugstore manager, Mr. Thorpe, is talking to Fred Derry, a much-decorated bombardier:

PHOTOFEST

*Thorpe: I can see that you had a splendid war record, Derry.*

*Derry: Just average, Mr. Thorpe.*

*Thorpe: But you'll understand that since this business changed hands we're under no legal obligation to give you your old job back.*

*Derry: I wasn't thinking of getting my old job back, Mr. Thorpe. I'm looking for a better one.*

*Thorpe: What are your qualifications, your experience?*

*Derry: Two years behind a soda fountain, and three years behind a Norden bomb sight. . . . I was only responsible for getting the bombs on the target. I didn't command anybody.*

*Thorpe: I see; I'm sure that work required great skill. But unfortunately, we've no opportunities for that with Midway Drugs.*

RKO Pictures, *The Best Years of Our Lives*, 1946

Not everybody faced what Fred Derry did, going back to the drugstore where he once worked. One of Derry's compatriots resumes his prestigious work as a bank manager. The character in the picture at left, injured in the war, struggles to find new direction. The nation as a whole was also looking in a new direction. People wanted to put wartime sacrifices behind them, put veterans back to work, and enjoy the prosperity and freedom for which they had fought.

## A Conservative Turn

Richard M. Nixon carried a law degree and a modest war record with him when he came home. Like thousands of other veterans, he was looking for a job. Within two years he would begin to work the levers of power in Washington.

Nixon's quick political climb began when a group of California businessmen backed him as a candidate for Congress in 1946. Nixon was part of the conservative **backlash**, or opposition, to the New Deal. He

---

was also an outspoken anticommunist who would soon become a prominent figure in the cold war politics of the 1950s.

The Twelfth Congressional District in southern California in many ways mirrored the political makeup of the nation. There were slightly more Democrats than Republicans registered in the voting rolls, but that advantage was vanishing because of a growing resentment among voters over postwar shortages in jobs, goods, and housing. Business leaders, farmers, and bankers were generally hopeful but nervous about the nation's economic outlook.

Often in times of uncertainty, voters look with suspicion at the policies of the party in power. In 1946 many voters turned against the Democrats and the New Deal.

There were "two definite opinions on the American system," Nixon told a group of prominent people in his congressional district. "One advocated by the New Deal is government control regulating our lives. The other calls for individual freedom and all that initiative can produce." He was talking to a handful of California Republicans, but he might as well have been addressing disaffected voters in many states who would soon sweep Republicans into Congress.

In congressional districts throughout the country, growing fears about communism resulted in particularly nasty campaign battles. Candidates whipped up anticommunist rhetoric, publicly and subtly accusing their opponents of being "red," the slang term for communists and communist sympathizers. The accusations, even if unfounded, were often hard to erase from the minds of voters.

When the Eightieth Congress convened in January 1947 many incumbents had been replaced. The conservative shift brought a new group of Republicans to Washington and gave the Republican Party control of Congress.

They came ready to correct what they saw as a threat to the nation's peacetime economy: the New Deal. That meant taking on the man who now embodied the spirit of the New Deal—President Harry Truman.[1]

## Fears About the Economy

While Nixon and the other 1946 congressional hopefuls were campaigning, the nation's economy had been following a precarious path. Business leaders and conservatives were pressuring Truman to lift the government's wartime limits on prices. Finally, he gave in, and prices for basic goods immediately shot up.

The president called on businesses to keep prices down voluntarily, as a patriotic measure to help stabilize the economy. Nevertheless, the inflation rate climbed to about 25 percent in mid-1946. The price hikes did little to dampen the spending desires of more prosperous Americans, who eagerly snatched up items such as refrigerators that were now beginning to return to stores after wartime shortages. But many workers watched the purchasing power of their wages shrink. They began to protest. Labor union membership had been growing during the war, but the unions generally had neither asked for nor received wage increases. After the war, unions grew restless and began to make more demands on employers.

Americans started their days with a full breakfast of news about strikes in their morning papers. Unions were stopping production in industries across the nation. There were more strikes, measured in lost work hours, than at any other time in American history.

In 1946 and 1947 many people were getting fed up with

UPI/BETTMANN

**Richard Nixon, a new congressman from California, tapes his name to the door of his Washington office.** *Why did Nixon advocate "individual freedom" in his 1946 campaign speeches?*

rising prices and with lingering shortages in basics such as beef and gasoline. Many targeted their frustrations at the unions. They felt that the unions had become greedy in their demands, forcing up the cost of goods. Critics accused the Truman administration of not having the courage, or the alertness, to confront the economic problems.

**Backlash Against the New Deal** The Republicans in the Eightieth Congress had been elected, by and large, on the promise to "clean up the mess in Washington." Senator Robert Taft of Ohio observed that their task was "the restoration of freedom and the elimination or reduction of constantly increasing interference with family life and with business" by the government. His comment was reflected in two of the Republicans' goals: cut back New Deal spending and rein in labor. The controversy over labor quickly became focused on a single issue: the Taft-Hartley bill.

The 1935 National Labor Relations Act, a major New Deal protection for workers, had recognized the unions' right to bargain collectively. Companies complained that the act had given unions too much power. Companies cited crippling strikes and broken agreements by unions, and complained that they had lost the ability to manage their employees. Conservative members of Congress thought the time had come to strengthen the management position.

The Taft-Hartley bill sought to ban the "closed shop," a workplace where only union members could be hired. The bill also allowed states to pass "right to work" laws to outlaw union shops, in which new workers were required to join the union.

The bill tipped the balance of power in other ways as well. It allowed employers to sue if the unions did not live up to their contracts. It provided for "cooling off" periods during which labor and management would resume bargaining. The bill also enabled the president to intervene in strikes that endangered national health and safety, by ordering workers back to their jobs for 80 days.

Truman and the Congress went to war over Taft-Hartley, which the president called "a slave labor bill." The president shared the public concern about union power. He had on some occasions locked horns with union leaders and forced them to back down in their demands. But he felt that the new bill threatened important worker protections. Congress passed the bill, Truman vetoed it, and Congress voted to override the veto.

The act proved to be less of a threat to labor than was feared. But it had an important side effect. Truman's strong opposition to the measure gave him a new political ally: labor. After months of souring relations with the unions, Truman had in a single stroke become a friend of the worker. "I don't give a hang what the unions say about me, or do to me politically: that isn't my job," Tru-

| Rising Food Prices, 1946 | | | |
|---|---|---|---|
| Month | A loaf of bread | A pound of butter | A dozen eggs |
| March | $ 0.09 | $ 0.55 | $ 0.48 |
| June | $ 0.11 | $ 0.61 | $ 0.51 |
| September | $ 0.12 | $ 0.83 | $ 0.67 |
| December | $ 0.12 | $ 0.92 | $ 0.70 |

AP/WIDE WORLD PHOTOS

**Tedaldo Guido above stands in front of his grocery store in North Tonawanda, N.Y., in 1947. Merchants like Guido cut their prices in response to President Truman's pleas to help keep inflation under control. The efforts of some retailers, however, weren't** enough to prevent prices from soaring when wartime controls were lifted. The chart, above right, shows how quickly the price of basic goods rose before and after the price controls. *Find the prices of these items today to see how inflation has affected costs since the late 1940s.*

man had growled to his aides after tangling with striking mine and railroad workers. "But when they run a balance sheet on Harry Truman, they'll realize they got a fine fair shake."

Truman's balance sheet got plenty of credit from his veto of Taft-Hartley. It gave Truman labor support, a formidable weapon he would carry into the 1948 presidential election—a race in which he would need all the help he could get.

## The Uphill Race in '48

Harry Truman had never wanted to be president. Over and over again, he wished out loud that someone else would take the dubious honor of toiling away in the big drafty house he and his family referred to as the "Great White Jail."

Yet a strange paradox resided in this outwardly simple man. He knew he lacked the understanding of foreign policy and the passion for domestic reform of his predecessor. But he had one quality in himself that he trusted supremely: the determination to do the right thing.

In the end, Harry Truman trusted his ability to do the right thing more than he trusted anybody else he saw looming on the presidential horizon. The man who as senator had called himself "just a country jake who works at the job" liked being Just Plain Harry and thought a "country jake" could run the country just fine.

**Daunting Prospects**  Political experts and members of Truman's own Democratic party thought he should let someone else run for president in 1948. Only 36 percent of the voters approved of his administration. His public image floundered. Many saw him as soft on labor and on communism.

He was blamed for prices that had doubled since 1939. In many opinion columns, news stories, and cartoons, he was portrayed as weak and incompetent. A popular quip of the time was: "To err is Truman." One of his campaign jingles, "We're just wild about Harry," was mockingly rendered as "We're just mild about Harry."

Before confronting the Republicans, Truman first had to face attacks from his own party that promised

Workers march through New York City in a 1946 labor parade. Truman's sour relations with labor turned sweeter after his veto of the Taft-Hartley bill.
THE BETTMANN ARCHIVE

to rob him of votes from conservative and liberal Democrats. Henry Wallace, a former member of Truman's cabinet, split from the party to form the Progressive Party and took many liberals with him. Wallace advocated stronger civil rights legislation, more federal spending for social programs, and a less confrontational stance toward the Soviet Union. The latter position gained him the support of the Communist party, which he did not reject. Wallace's refusal to take a strong anticommunist stand proved disastrous to his candidacy. However, for a time, the Progressive party appeared a serious political contender that could spoil Truman's chances for reelection.

The other threat to Truman's campaign came over the issue of civil rights. The president was a longtime supporter of equal rights for African Americans. He had begun the desegregation of the armed forces and had urged the Justice Department to prosecute cases in which blacks were deprived of their civil rights. Prior to the 1948 Democratic convention he had

**Identifying Cause and Effect**
Truman's decision to remove wartime price controls was one cause that led to rapidly rising prices. But several other economic factors helped drive prices upward. Following the war, workers in factories began demanding long-postponed wage increases. In order to pay these higher wages, manufacturers had to raise prices. Also, postwar consumers were eager to buy all kinds of goods. Manufacturers raised their prices in order to take advantage of the great demand.

unveiled a civil rights plan that included an antilynching bill and a ban on poll taxes, which had previously blocked poor people from voting.

Civil rights issues shattered the Democratic national convention. Liberals managed to insert in the Democratic platform a mildly worded plank affirming the party's commitment to eliminate "racial, religious, and economic discrimination." It also commended Truman's "courageous stand" on civil rights.

A group of conservative southern Democrats, the so-called Dixiecrats, broke from the party to form a States' Rights Democratic Party. It nominated South Carolina Governor Strom Thurmond as its candidate. The party attracted some conservatives who wanted a repeal of New Deal measures. But the Dixiecrats' main issue was their own support of racial segregation and their opposition to federal government action on civil rights—action they insisted violated the authority of states. Asked why southern congressmen revolted against Truman's civil rights proposals when Roosevelt had advocated virtually the same measures, Dixiecrat Strom Thurmond replied, "Yeah, but he means it." **2**

UPI/BETTMANN

**Truman received the Robert S. Abbot award for making the most significant contribution to democracy in 1948. Truman's civil rights plans earned him the respect of many African Americans.** *How would a Dixiecrat have reacted to this photo taken in 1948?*

During the campaign, Truman was warned by friends to soften his stand in order not to offend southern conservative Democrats. To one such friend Truman wrote:

*I am not asking for social equality, because no such thing exists, but I am asking for equality of opportunity for all human beings and, as long as I stay here, I am going to continue that fight. When the mob gangs can take four people out and shoot them in the back, and everybody in the country is acquainted with who did the shooting and nothing is done about it, that country is in a pretty bad fix from a law enforcement standpoint. . . . I am going to try to remedy it and if that ends up in my failure to be reelected, that failure will be in a good cause.*

Harry S Truman, *letter*, August 18, 1948

Truman indeed faced failure. With the Democrats in disarray and their candidate weakened, the Republicans believed that anyone they nominated could crush Truman in November.

The Republican nomination went to the man FDR had trounced in 1944, New York Governor Thomas E. Dewey. He presented a sharp contrast to Truman's feisty, free-wheeling style: Dewey was reserved and meticulous. He was known as an intelligent and efficient administrator.

Although dapper and confident, Dewey wasn't going to sweep the nation off its feet with charisma. However, the Republicans weren't worried. In his speeches, Dewey never even referred to Truman; he campaigned like a man who had already won the election. Indeed, it seemed that the race was Dewey's to win.

**Running on the Rails** While Truman's campaign staff was pessimistic about his chances, the president remained confident. In a particularly shrewd move, Truman waited until the end of the Republican national convention, then called a special session of Congress and challenged Republicans to make good on their platform promises. He had handed Congress a string of his own proposals, including his civil rights legislation. When Congress failed to pass a single bill,

UPI/BETTMANN

UPI/BETTMANN NEWSPHOTOS

**Truman won the support of Americans as he crossed the country on his whistle-stopping campaign tour, above. At right, one of the most famous photos in U.S. history.** *Why would such an error be unlikely in newspapers today?*

Truman was able to claim that the Republicans were not serious about solving the nation's problems.

Truman could now point to a whole menu of New Deal-style measures that the Eightieth Congress rejected: aid to farmers; a minimum-wage hike from 40 to 75 cents; a housing bill; increased social security coverage; and new price controls. This gave him the ammunition he needed against the Republicans in an unprecedented national campaign tour.

Many past presidents had stayed put in the White House during their campaigns—to do otherwise was thought undignified. But Truman wanted to take his case to the people; so he took the White House on the road. From Labor Day to Election Day, Truman conducted his famous "whistle-stop" tour of the country in the Ferdinand Magellan, an ornately appointed suite of railroad cars that once belonged to FDR. More than 20 staff members and dozens of reporters accompanied the president on his 32,000-mile trip.

Stopping in town after town, he spoke to enthusiastic crowds from the rear platform of the train. To people who had only seen pictures of the president

and heard him speak on the radio, the impression was strong. Truman told his listeners about the troubles in Washington. He ticked off the failures of "that do-nothing Eightieth Congress." After that, he asked the crowd if they wanted to meet his family. They did, of course. Bess and daughter Margaret joined him on the platform. And the crowds ate it up.

Still, few people believed Truman could win. In the last weeks before the election, polls showed him trailing by up to 10 percentage points. *Newsweek* polled 50 experts from across the country; not one gave Truman a chance. When one of his aides handed the magazine to Truman, he looked at it, grinned, and said, "Forget it, they're always wrong."

Truman went home to Independence, Missouri,

**STUDY GUIDE**

## Analyzing Behavior

Analyzing a person's behavior may give you insight into the events of a certain time and into the personalities of important people. Harry Truman's campaign strategy reveals much about

Truman himself and about the American people. His aggressive, tireless effort to reach out to thousands of voters successfully conveyed his straightforward style. Meanwhile, Dewey's cool,

reserved manner failed to reach voters. By failing to inspire people, Dewey helped seal his own fate.

Cold War Politics    531

on election day, where he voted, took a Turkish bath, and confidently awaited the results. He went to bed early and was awakened at midnight and 4:00 A.M. by aides telling him he was winning. Radio commentators kept predicting that Dewey would come on strong as new precincts reported in. The *Chicago Tribune* went to press with the historic and later embarrassing banner headline: "Dewey Defeats Truman."

Nothing of the sort happened. Truman won big.

## The New Deal Revisited

The romantic view of the 1948 election is that of the underdog overcoming the odds through grit and determination. But in recent times, historians have noted that Truman's victory was really due to the resilience of FDR's Democratic Party, which was sufficient to overcome Truman's unpopularity. In effect, the vote for Truman was a vote for Roosevelt's fifth term. The strength of the party was also indicated by the fact that the Democrats regained the majority in both houses of Congress in the 1948 election.

For nearly four years, Congress had thwarted the president's hopes of continuing and expanding the New Deal. Now, fresh from his victory, he marched into the Democrat-controlled Congress with a State of the Union message that unveiled the Fair Deal, Truman's new lease on life for the New Deal. It called for legislation on such items as national medical insurance, extension of social security, new public

"Who does Truman think he is — the PRESIDENT?"

REPRINTED WITH PERMISSION, CHICAGO SUN-TIMES/1990. COURTESY OF THE TRUMAN LIBRARY, INDEPENDENCE, MO

power projects, public housing, and repeal of the Taft-Hartley Act. It was bold, ambitious, and liberal.

The Fair Deal registered its successes. The social security system was broadened to cover 10 million more people. The minimum wage rose from 40 to 75 cents an hour. The Housing Act of 1949 authorized the construction of about 800,000 low-income units.

But the Fair Deal was in many ways doomed. Republicans and conservative Dixiecrats often voted as a bloc to defeat many of Truman's legislative proposals, especially in the area of civil rights. Events in the country, and in the world, also helped to undermine the Fair Deal. The fresh wave of support Truman gained in the election gradually faded as charges of corruption riddled his administration. Truman was blamed for not taking stronger action to prevent the communist takeover of China. The United States became bogged down in a costly and stalemated war in Korea. As military spending again soared, Congress had little interest in funding social programs.

Truman's presidency fell victim to these changes. By the end of his term, when he decided not to run for reelection, his popularity had sunk to a new low. Events inside and outside of Washington contributed to Truman's fall. However, another factor was Truman himself, and the nation's growing fear of communism that he helped create.

**Truman's dismissal of General MacArthur was the first event that led to a rapid decline in the president's popularity. Throughout his second term Truman was broadly criticized by the press and by people within his party.**

## SECTION REVIEW

### Checking Facts

1. What issue did Richard Nixon and other Republican candidates try to use to their advantage in the election of 1946?
2. Why did inflation become a problem following the war?
3. Why did Truman's chances seem so slim heading into the 1948 election?
4. How successful was Truman's Fair Deal after the 1948 election?

### Thinking Critically

5. **Recognizing Values** In what way did Truman's values help and hurt him during his presidency?
6. **Recognizing Propaganda** Find an example from the text in which Truman engaged in actions that might be called "propaganda."
7. **Identifying Cause and Effect** What effect did the confrontational actions of the Eightieth Congress have on Truman?

8. **Analyzing Behavior** Why do you think Truman chose not to run for reelection in 1952?

### Linking Across Time

9. How do you think Roosevelt's actions at Yalta influenced the mood of the nation, the rise of conservative power in Congress, and Truman's presidency?

# The Cold War at Home

## May 1, 1950: Wisconsin Town Falls to the "Communists"

MOSINEE, WISCONSIN, WAS A TYPICAL QUIET AMERICAN TOWN—UNTIL THE DAY THE "COMMUNISTS" TOOK OVER. ON MAY 1, 1950, ARMED SOLDIERS stormed into Mosinee, seizing Mayor Ralph Kronenwetter. The mayor and Police Chief Carl Gewiss were arrested and taken to city hall, where the Soviet hammer-and-sickle flag was raised high. When Gewiss refused to cooperate with the invaders, he was "liquidated."

The communist forces circled the town and set up roadblocks to prevent escape. Red guards took over the Mosinee power plant; they arrested the local newspaper editor and began converting his printing presses to publish the new propaganda paper, the *Red Star*.

Soldiers then raided the public library and private homes to "purge" them of anticommunist literature. Clergymen and business leaders were rounded up and put in concentration camps.

Meanwhile, at the high school, Communist party workers organized a parade to celebrate the new regime. They marched down Main Street and gathered for a rally in the center of town—newly dubbed "Red Square."

Then, at 7:00 P.M. the soldiers put down their weapons, the prisoners were freed, and Mosinee residents held a good old-fashioned picnic to celebrate the joys of freedom and democracy. They raised the American flag as the high school band played the "Star Spangled Banner." An American Legion commander addressed the crowd about the virtues of the American way of life.

The takeover was a hoax, of course. The armed subversives were actually patriotic U.S. servicemen;

COURTESY MOSINEE TIMES

the leader of the "coup" was an excommunist. Project organizers, including the American Legion, chose May Day as their date because it was a major holiday in the Soviet Union, celebrating communism. The Mosinee event received nationwide news coverage.

Although the takeover seems rather humorous now, it reflected a pervasive fear. Mayor Kronenwetter died the next day of a heart attack; a clergyman died days later. Town historians said the deaths were associated with the stress of the event. The Mosinee story is an extreme example of a wave of anticommunism that swept the country during the late 1940s and early 1950s. Watching the spread of communism around the world, and listening to the rhetoric of politicians and commentators, millions of Americans feared that seemingly friendly citizens—the local PTA president, a bank secretary, the railroad worker next door—were working feverishly for the communist takeover of the United States government.

The menace of communist traitors poisoning the life of small-town America was very real to many people. Some of them felt that their fellow citizens were not taking the threat seriously enough.

## *The Rise of Anticommunism*

The fear of communism did not start with the cold war. But it grew, explosively, in the climate produced by the development of the Soviet atomic bomb, the spread of communism in the world, and the efforts of some unscrupulous Americans to use fear as a way to defeat their enemies and to propel themselves to positions of political power.

Long after the Red Scare of 1919, and well before the heyday of anticommunism in the 1950s, conservatives in Congress had looked for a way to discredit President Roosevelt and his New Deal administration. The House Un-American Activities Committee, or HUAC, held hearings that explored the issue of communist influence in the New Deal. Little came of the hearings, largely because World War II intervened and the country rallied behind its president. Concern about communism was put aside as Stalin's Soviet government became a temporary ally.

Almost immediately after the war, the mood began to change. Stalin turned more openly belligerent toward the United States. Winston Churchill delivered his famous "iron curtain" speech. The cold war was launched. After the war the HUAC hearings resumed. For months the committee loudly declared the existence of communists in the Truman administration but failed to find any. In 1947, however, the committee got a new cast of characters, most notably a young congressman with a keen mind and an ability to skewer a reluctant witness during cross-examination. The postwar history of HUAC quickly became the story of Richard Nixon and Alger Hiss. It was a case that made one man and broke another.

**The Mysterious Case of Alger Hiss** Surrounded by men who were, at times, emotional, vindictive, and racist, Congressman Nixon became the voice of reason on HUAC. Some committee members resorted to demagoguery—stirring people up by appealing to their emotions—and to character assassinations. Nixon, by contrast, spoke quietly, usually from a brief of carefully gathered facts.

To be sure, there were communists and communist sympathizers to be found. But there were far more *former* communists. The American Communist party was in its heyday during the Depression, when much of the nation was suffering and out of work. Marxist and Leninist writings and the speeches of Stalin—touting the rights of the working class and criticizing the failures of capitalism—appealed to many liberals in the United States. The party drew workers, intellectuals, artists, and college students to its ranks. Interest in communism became a chic intellectual trend. In a time of extensive poverty, racial injustice, and the abuse of workers by powerful corporations, communism seemed to promise relief. The ideology had not yet acquired an association with evil and repression.

This association came in the late 1930s, when Stalin stepped up his campaign of terror against his enemies and tightened internal security in the Soviet Union. His strong-arm tactics caused many sympathizers in the United States to become disillusioned with communism. By World War II, public interest in communism in the United States had virtually died.

The rise of the cold war, however, caused changes that brought HUAC's activities into the spotlight once again. The cold war resulted in increased espionage activity by Stalin against the United States. That legitimized fears that the Soviet Union was trying to undermine the U.S. government.[1]

Politicians and voters wanted to see a strong case brought against the spies they thought had infiltrated the government. That case came along in 1948, when Nixon met Whittaker Chambers, a senior editor at *Time* magazine. Like many intellectuals, Chambers had been attracted to the Communist party in the 1930s. But unlike most intellectuals, he had become deeply involved in communist espionage activities. He later joined the ranks of those disillusioned with the party. He then became as staunch an anticommunist as he had been a fervent communist.

UPI/BETTMANN

Chambers told Nixon and HUAC that during his communist days he had become closely involved with a man named Alger Hiss. Hiss was the spy suspect a redhunter dreamed of catching. He had served in influential positions in government and society. If it could be proved that Hiss was a communist,

---

**Identifying Cause and Effect**
Anticommunist fear found a fertile environment in the postwar United States. One cause of the growing fear was the Soviet Union's successful testing of an atomic weapon in August 1949. This was followed within weeks by the stunning "loss" of China, the world's most populous nation, to communism. To many Americans, the order of the world was unraveling.

**1** What made the postwar United States so ripe for anticommunist fears?

that would support the allegations that HUAC had been making for years.

Alger Hiss was a graduate of Harvard Law School who gained a coveted spot as clerk for Supreme Court Justice Oliver Wendell Holmes. He had served as a New Dealer under Roosevelt and had even gone to Yalta as a member of FDR's staff.

Many conservative Republicans believed that Roosevelt had sold out to the Soviet Union at Yalta, and the Hiss connection made that argument even more plausible. At the time of his arrest, Hiss was president of the Carnegie Endowment for International Peace. Peace organizations in general were highly suspect as instruments for "softening" the United States, so the Soviets could take the nation over by surprise. Hiss was the perfect target for HUAC.

Chambers had been seeking an audience for his accusations against Hiss for almost a decade by the time he was introduced to Nixon. The FBI had investigated the case and had been unable to make much of the charges by Chambers. FDR heard about the allegations and dismissed them. A New York grand jury failed to bring an indictment against Alger Hiss.

Now Chambers told Nixon that Hiss had been, and probably still was, a high ranking Communist party operative. In highly publicized hearings, Nixon staked his personal career on the guilt of Hiss and the integrity of Chambers. Showing talents honed as a high school and college debater and an experienced lawyer, Nixon bore down on Hiss and discredited him with a style of questioning that observers called both brilliant and ruthless. At first Hiss denied ever knowing Chambers. Then, confronted with Chambers in person, Hiss lost his composure and admitted having known Chambers under another name.

Although the FBI continued its investigation of Hiss, the attorney general's office did not yet have sufficient evidence from Chambers to press its case against Hiss in the hearings. The story seemed to end there, with Hiss's reputation smeared but with nothing proven.

**Proof in a Pumpkin Patch?** It was at this point that the case took its most bizarre turn. Late in 1948 two investigators visited Chambers's farm in Maryland, and Chambers, who had not previously accused Hiss of engaging in espionage, suddenly said: "I think I have what you're looking for." Taking the investigators out to a pumpkin patch, he rummaged through the pumpkins, finally finding the one for which he was looking. As his guests watched in amazement, Chambers dramatically pulled off the top, reached into the pumpkin, and pulled out a roll of microfilm.

The microfilm showed copies of secret State Department documents that

TRANSCRIPT OF RECORD, SECOND TRIAL, USA V. ALGER HISS

AP/WIDE WORLD PHOTOS

**Top: One of the sensitive government documents presented as evidence at the Alger Hiss trial. Middle: A HUAC investigator points at Whittaker Chambers as Hiss looks on. Right: The pumpkin patch where Chambers revealed a roll of microfilm that eventually led to Alger Hiss's conviction.**

### Recognizing Stereotypes

Alger Hiss was a perfect villain for communist-hunting politicians. His intellectual credentials, especially his East Coast background and Harvard educa-tion, fit neatly into the public's stereotype of the kind of person who would be sympathetic to communism. The ease with which Hiss fit this stereotype made it less difficult for politicians to persuade people of Hiss's guilt.

became known in national headlines as the Pumpkin Papers. Some documents had been copied on a typewriter that was eventually traced to Alger Hiss.

This was the bombshell Nixon and HUAC had been looking for. The committee hearings led the courts to take up the case against Alger Hiss again. He could no longer be tried for espionage, since the alleged spying had taken place so long before. But Hiss was convicted in 1950 on two counts of perjury and sentenced to five years in prison.

Many books have been written debating Hiss's guilt or innocence. In many he is portrayed as a man who destroyed himself, partly with statements like: "Until the day I die, I shall wonder how Whittaker Chambers got into my house to use my typewriter." When he made the statement in court, laughter erupted in the room. Alger Hiss was a ruined man.

Richard Nixon emerged the real victor in the case. The press, which initially supported Hiss, wound up running dramatic pictures of Nixon scrutinizing the microfilm and making tough public statements about the case. He became identified as a relentless pursuer of communist subversion. In his memoirs Nixon explains that when he later decided to run for the Senate, "I recognized the worth of the nationwide publicity that the Hiss case had given me—publicity on a scale that most congressmen only dream of achieving."

**Truman Joins the Red Hunt**  Compared with FDR, Harry Truman had a far greater suspicion and dislike of communists. His own rhetoric about "the enemy within" contributed to the fears of subversion. But he was forced into taking an even stronger, highly public stand on the subject to defend himself against the accusations of headline-hunting congressmen.

Responding to the label of being "soft," in 1947 Truman instituted the Federal Employee Loyalty Program, designed to evaluate the loyalty of government employees. Although the program had checks meant to protect individuals' rights, it was often abused by ambitious officials.

Under the program, even the slightest suspicion of disloyalty or the slimmest connection to a Communist party member was enough to put a government worker out of a job. Employees were suspect for openly criticizing American foreign policy, advocating equal rights for women, owning books on socialism, and attending foreign films. Others lost jobs because of associations or former associations with radicals, or because they belonged to a group classified as dangerous. From 1947 to 1951 a "loyalty board" investigated more than three million government employees; nearly 3,000 were forced to resign, and 212 were fired. Yet the probes uncovered no positive proof of subversion or espionage.

To many in Congress, Truman's anticommunist measures were not enough. So in 1950 Congress passed its own tough law, the McCarran Act. This act did not directly outlaw the Communist party but made it illegal for Americans to engage in activities that would create a communist government. It required communist organizations to register with the federal government. Communists were not allowed to work in defense plants or to obtain U.S. passports.

Truman vetoed the McCarran Act, declaring, "In a free country, we punish men for crimes they commit, but never for the opinions they hold." Congress easily overrode the veto.

**Seeking U.S. Secrets**  On the heels of the Hiss conviction, a new case broke into the headlines and served to heighten people's fears of communist espi-

THE BETTMANN ARCHIVE

**Women demonstrate against the conviction of Ethel and Julius Rosenberg.**
*What message do these demonstrators want to send? Whom do they want to influence?*

Notice that the Hiss trial and the Rosenbergs' arrest occurred during the same year.

## Postwar Anticommunism

| | November 1946 80th Congress elected. | August 1948 HUAC takes on the Hiss case. | January 1950 Hiss convicted of perjury. | September 1950 McCarran Act passed. | | May–June 1954 Army/McCarthy hearings. |
|---|---|---|---|---|---|---|
| 1946 | 1947 | 1948 | 1949 | 1950 | 1951 | 1952 | 1953 | 1954 | 1955 |
| | March 1947 Federal Employee Loyalty Program | | June 1950 War breaks out in Korea. | August 1950 Rosenbergs arrested on espionage charge. | | June 1953 Rosenbergs executed. | December 1954 McCarthy censured. |

onage. In 1950 a young British scientist, Klaus Fuchs, admitted he had handed over to the Soviets American government specifications for the manufacture of the atomic bomb. A bizarre series of circumstances led investigators to Ethel and Julius Rosenberg, a New York City couple who had likely been members of the Communist party.

The government charged the Rosenbergs with conspiracy in a plot that prosecutors said was intended to transmit top secret bomb specifications to the Soviets. They were accused by Ethel's brother, a soldier stationed at the Manhattan Project in New Mexico, who said the Rosenbergs had recruited him to collect the information. The couple was convicted and sentenced to death.

On June 19, 1953, at 8:06 P.M., Julius Rosenberg walked calmly into the electric chair chamber at Sing Sing prison in New York state. Moments later, his wife, Ethel, followed him. A reporter who witnessed the executions said of Ethel afterward that she had "gone to meet her maker, and would have a lot of explaining to do."

Ethel and Julius Rosenberg died protesting their innocence. Appeals and worldwide protests failed to save them. Ethel's brother served 10 years of a 15-year sentence.

The Rosenbergs had frequently been offered a deal: Testify against others and avoid the death penalty. "Since we are guilty of no crime, we will not be party to the nefarious plot to bear false witness against other innocent progressives to heighten hysteria in our land," Julius wrote.

Ever since, in books, movies, and magazine and newspaper articles, people have been trying to uncover the truth about the Rosenbergs. Arguments abound on both sides as to whether they were guilty or simply victims of a "hysteria in our land."

ECLIPSE: PORTRAIT OF ETHEL AND JULIUS ROSENBERG, LEE JAFFE, 1983, SAATCHI COLLECTION, LONDON, COURTESY ROSENBERG ERA ART PROJECT

**Decades after their execution, the Rosenbergs are still the subject of investigation by historians and comment by artists.**

## The McCarthy Era

Even before Ethel and Julius Rosenberg had been arrested and charged with spying for the Soviet Union in July 1950, Senator Joseph McCarthy took up the anticommunist cause. McCarthy had impressed few people in his first three years in Congress, which began in 1947. The congressional press corps sized him up as a small-time politician. He drank too much, and could get offensive and even violent at those times. He was not well-liked; but he learned how to be feared.

On February 9, 1950, McCarthy stood up at a Republican women's club in Wheeling, West Virginia, waved some papers in the air, and announced he had a list of 205 communists working in the State Department. In follow-up investigations of McCarthy's claim, he wavered on the exact number—from 205 to 81 to 57 to "a lot." However, his basic theme remained the same: Communists thrived in the administration of President Truman. They had to be rooted out. And Joe McCarthy was the man to do it.

McCarthy never produced a shred of credible evidence; but, in hearings and public statements, he attacked and ruined official after official of the U.S. government. Almost nobody was safe from his accusations. The accused either resigned under a cloud of suspicion or were fired as security risks.

These accusatory, anticommunist times were named after him. They became known as "the McCarthy era." He gave a new word, **McCarthyism,** to the language. It referred to the use of intimidation and often unfounded accusations in the name of fighting communism.

Despite his tactics, McCarthy won considerable public support, at least at first. Millions of Americans believed that he was fighting a lonely battle—that he was a patriot challenging traitors and subversives. He was making the country safe for democracy.

The Senate subcommittee on investigations, of which McCarthy became chairman in 1953, provided him with an official forum from which to launch public attacks on government employees. His wasn't the only show in town. Numerous other congressmen conducted their own hearings and investigations, and HUAC's activities continued as well.

For Republicans, McCarthy was a loose cannon, and his conservative colleagues often distanced themselves from him, except when it suited their own purposes. Although few people liked him, some took advantage of his talent for keeping himself and his issue in the spotlight.[2]

In his highly public role, the senator accumulated enormous power. At the height of his power, he could make politicians, bank presidents, network executives, and average citizens quake. For a long time, few people dared challenge him. Harry Truman, in his retirement, acknowledged the extent of McCarthy's hold on the nation's affairs:

*M cCarthyism . . . the meaning of the word is the corruption of truth, the abandonment of our historical devotion to fair*

AP/WIDE WORLD PHOTOS

**Senator Joseph McCarthy publicized his concern about communist infiltration into the U.S. government by making accusations in public speeches.** *Why do you think the nation at first supported McCarthy's actions?*

*play. It is the abandonment of 'due process' of law. It is the use of the big lie and the unfounded accusation against any citizen in the name of Americanism and security. . . .*

*This horrible cancer is eating at the vitals of America and it can destroy the great edifice of freedom.*

Harry S Truman, *radio and TV address,* November 17, 1953

McCarthy's rise to power was swift and heady. The senator eventually grew reckless with it, throwing accusations around fearlessly—but also, many noted, with a growing sense that if he ever ran out of names to smear, his bubble would burst.

That's just what happened. McCarthy went too far. When President Eisenhower took office in 1953, he decided to ignore the senator as much as possible, hoping McCarthy would eventually do himself in. In addition, Eisenhower didn't want to offend conservatives in his own party by engaging in a risky battle with one of their own.

Hunting for ever more sensational targets, Mc-

## STUDY GUIDE

**Assessing Outcomes**

The McCarthy era officially ended with McCarthy's death in 1957. In the end, few if any spies were purged from the United States government. Yet for many people the impact of McCarthy-ism continued to be felt for a lifetime. During the 1950s, thousands of workers in hundreds of different industries lost their jobs because of false accusations of communist sympathies.

**2** Why do you think McCarthy's fellow conservatives kept their distance from him?

Carthy hurled his next accusations against the United States Army in 1954; and the Army was ready. Meeting the senator's unsupported allegations with a quiet presentation of the facts, Army attorney Joseph Welch calmly shredded McCarthy's charges of a communist conspiracy in the U.S. Army. To a nation watching the subcommittee hearings on TV, Welch presented an intelligent contrast to McCarthy's sensational theatrics. McCarthy sealed his own fate.

A political cartoon of the time showed McCarthy trapped in a spider's web, crying, "I can't do this to me!" But he did, along with the efforts of a growing number of opponents that finally broke their silence to take a public stand against him. In 1954 the Senate voted to condemn McCarthy.

When the senator died in 1957, sickened from alcohol and exhaustion, few people mourned. Many hoped an era had died with him—but it had not.

## Citizens Under Suspicion

Just as red-hunting did not begin with McCarthy, it did not end with him, either. The business of spying on neighbors, friends, teachers, even clergy had spread throughout the society. Government films and brochures urged citizens to expose anyone they suspected of having communist leanings.

The McCarthy era spawned hundreds of vigilante-style watchdog groups run by private citizens. Their motives and methods could be vicious and often illegal. John Henry Faulk found this out the hard way in 1957, the year of McCarthy's death.

A Texan with a quick mind and an affection for radical ideas, Faulk had a radio program in New York City in which he dispensed his own brand of whimsy and humor. In the mid-1950s Faulk was elected vice president of a local chapter of the American Federation of Television and Radio Actors. He won partly because of his stand against **blacklisting**, the effort by conservative groups to brand people as communists and prevent them from holding jobs. One such group, called AWARE, had ruined the careers of many performers, and Faulk and others sought to stem the group's influence. AWARE responded with a nasty campaign to associate Faulk with communism. It then pressured the advertisers on Faulk's radio show to cancel their ads. Faced with negative publicity and the loss of advertising dollars, CBS fired Faulk.

Faulk countered with a lawsuit against AWARE, which took six years to settle. In 1963 a jury awarded him $3.5 million in damages, although the award was reduced to $550,000 on appeal. In the meantime, Faulk could find no work for years. His career had been effectively ruined. Ironically, years later CBS made a highly successful TV movie sympathetically dramatizing the Faulk story.

The legacy of the red-hunters had by then faded—but not completely. There remained the living memory of the thousands of people who had been smeared, blacklisted, and ostracized. In 1963, when Faulk's name was finally cleared, the memory of such things was still very fresh.

As late as 1960, for instance, city and state employees all over the country were forced to swear to and sign an oath of loyalty. In Massachusetts, teachers had to make the following promise:

*I do solemnly swear or affirm that I will uphold and defend the Constitution of the United States of America and the Commonwealth of Massachusetts and that I will oppose the overthrow of the government of the United States of America or of the Commonwealth by force or violence or any illegal or unconstitutional method: I am not a member of the Communist party.*

*Subscribed by me under penalty of perjury, this day of      , 1960.*

**Checking Facts**

1. Give two examples of the government's response to growing fears of communism.
2. What was the significance of the Alger Hiss case?
3. Why was the Rosenberg case so shocking to the country?
4. What evidence did McCarthy have to support his accusations?
5. In what ways did communist hunting continue after McCarthy?

**Thinking Critically**

6. **Identifying Cause and Effect** Politicians struggled to prove to voters that they were not "soft" on communism. What were some of the effects of this struggle?
7. **Recognizing Stereotypes** Why do you think that at the time of the Hiss trial many peace activists were stereotyped as being anti-American?
8. **Evaluating Sources** Considering the behavior of Chambers and the facts of the Hiss case, do you think the Pumpkin Papers were believable?
9. **Assessing Outcomes** Do you think John Henry Faulk received justice? Explain your answer.

**Linking Across Time**

10. How did Nixon's career benefit from the fear of communism before the Hiss case?

# The Hollywood Ten

## OCTOBER 1947

Robert Stripling [Chief Investigator]:Mr. Lawson, are you now or have you ever been a member of the Communist Party of the United States?

John Howard Lawson [Screen Writer #1]: The question of Communism is in no way related to this inquiry, which is an attempt to get control of the screen and to invade the basic rights of American citizens in all fields.

Ring Lardner, Jr. [Screen Writer #2]: I could answer that question, but I'd hate myself in the morning.
    ....
J. Parnell Thomas [Committee Chairman]: Any real American would be proud to answer that question.

### The Case

Congress formed the House Un-American Activities Committee (HUAC) in the late 1930s to combat extremist movements. Following World War II, the committee became concerned about Communist activity in Hollywood. In 1947 the committee obtained the membership files of the Communist party in Hollywood and subpoenaed a group of prominent writers and directors on the list to ask them what the committee already knew —whether they had ever been members of the Communist party. During the committee hearings the following witnesses became known in the press as the "Hollywood Ten":

Alvah Bessie, screen writer
Herbert Biberman, screen writer
   and director
Lester Cole, screen writer
Edward Dmytryk, director
Ring Lardner, Jr., screen writer

John Howard Lawson, screen writer
Albert Maltz, screen writer
Samuel Ornitz, screen writer
Adrian Scott, screen writer and producer
Dalton Trumbo, screen writer

The committee had no legal power to prosecute, and it was not illegal to belong to the Communist party. It was the announced goal of the committee, in the words of chairman J. Parnell Thomas, to "uncover the truth and let Hollywood and the American public do the rest."

### The Background

From the mid-1930s to the mid-1950s, about 300 film directors, actors, writers, and designers, along with many people in other walks of life, joined the Communist party. Interest in communist philosophy grew among people who had doubts about capitalism and felt that it led to the exploitation of workers. Communism seemed to offer the promise of improved conditions for

**HUAC suspected Dalton Trumbo (left) and Herbert Biberman (right) of Communist loyalties.**

workers and equity for people of all races. Joining the party was popular in the 1930s, when being a Communist often meant being concerned about workers' rights and about racism in the United States. By the late 1930s many of the craft unions in the film industry were forming, and the Communist party was involved in this struggle for workers' benefits. During World War II the Communists in the Soviet Union were allies of the United States in the fight against Nazi Germany. Before and during U.S. involvement in World War II, the federal government encouraged Hollywood movie moguls to make upbeat movies about the Soviet Union so that Americans would support their fight against the Nazis.

With the defeat of Germany and the end of World War II, however, attitudes toward the Soviet Union quickly began to shift. Americans became increasingly fearful of Soviet leader Josef Stalin and his interest in the spread of communism worldwide. As the cold war heightened, tolerance of communism—and of those involved in it—dissolved. Stalin's repressive tactics against his own people caused many party members to quit. Although membership in the Communist party was never made illegal, the party lost popularity.

People became worried that Communists were trying to influence many aspects of American society. They suspected that Communists in Hollywood were not just working to secure the rights of film workers, but to control the content of films. The federal government now encouraged movies showing Communists in a bad light and depicting the Soviet Union as an enemy. In this atmosphere the House Un-American Activities

Committee decided to turn a spotlight on Hollywood and investigate Communists in the movie business. The probe was a way to influence the movie industry and gain publicity for HUAC.

## The Points of View

The Hollywood community was divided on whether to cooperate with HUAC. Some Hollywood witnesses who appeared before the committee were people who, like HUAC, saw evidence of Communist activity around them. The committee responded favorably to these "friendly witnesses." Those less willing to cooperate with the committee received less cordial treatment. These people were termed "unfriendly witnesses."

*"There has been a small group within the Screen Actors Guild which has consistently opposed the policy of the Guild board and officers of the Guild, as evidenced by the vote on various issues. That small clique . . . has been suspected of more or less following the tactics that we associate with the Communist Party."*

> Ronald Reagan, president of
> the Screen Actors Guild

*"I am convinced that these Hollywood Commies are agents of a foreign country. If I have any doubt that they are [Communists], then I haven't any mind."*

> Sam Wood,
> producer and director

*"You [Sam Wood] really laid it on the line. You've got guts. If every other man had the same courage you have, we wouldn't have to worry about Communism."*

> J. Parnell Thomas,
> committee chairman

*"You [the committee] are using the old technique, . . . in order to create a scare here, . . . in order that you can smear the motion picture industry. . . .The Bill of Rights was established . . . to prevent the operation of any committee which could invade the basic rights of Americans."*

> John Howard Lawson,
> screen writer

The nation's press reported the antics of witnesses and committee members alike, such as the time HUAC Chairman Thomas smashed a gavel to splinters while calling for order. On the editorial page of the *New York Times*, the hearings themselves were deplored:

*"Finally, an investigation of this kind, once begun, has no ready stopping-place. One of the Government's witnesses has already declared that Broadway is worse than Hollywood in the matter of Communist penetration, and that the reading departments of the publishing houses are 'very, very heavily infiltrated with Communists.' Are we now to go on from Hollywood to Broadway, and then from Broadway to the publishing houses, searching for suspects all along the line, and after that carry the hunt into the radio and then into the American press?"*

—*The New York Times*

## The Options

Witnesses who appeared before the House Un-American Activities Committee were asked the question, "Are you now or have you ever been a member of the Communist party?" When considering their responses, they had several options. The witnesses could:

1. Refuse to answer on the grounds that congressional committees have no authority to investigate behavior protected by the First Amendment, the right to freedom of speech and political thought. The witnesses' lawyers warned that this might bring a charge of contempt of Congress since the Supreme Court had established Congress's right to inquire during the process of creating legislation. The Hollywood Ten maintained that Congress could not legislate away the First Amendment of the Bill of Rights and, therefore, had no right to investigate where they could not legislate.
2. Refuse to answer, pleading the Fifth Amendment, which confers upon a person the right to not testify against oneself. However, use of this tactic was assumed by many to be an implicit admission of Communist party membership.
3. Answer yes and place themselves at the mercy of the committee. This tactic would make them

subject to many more questions, such as requests for the names of other individuals in the Communist party.
4. Answer no and risk being charged with perjury if the committee proved they were not telling the truth. Perjury carried a greater penalty than contempt of Congress.

## The Decision

On October 1947, the Hollywood Ten agreed among themselves to plead the First Amendment and remain silent as a protest against questions they believed HUAC had no right even to ask.

The Ten were held in contempt of Congress for refusing to testify. In December 1947 they were indicted by a grand jury and in a trial were found guilty of contempt. The appeals process ran on until 1950, when the Supreme Court refused to hear the case and thus let the verdict stand. The Ten then served jail terms of about one year.

In one of the ironies of history, some of the Hollywood Ten and Chairman Thomas would meet again. While Thomas was becoming a public figure as a result of the HUAC hearings, a newspaper columnist discovered that Thomas had raised the salaries of his staff members in return for payments, or kickbacks, from the grateful employees. Thomas was indicted for fraud and pleaded no contest. He was fined $10,000 and served a nine-month sentence in the same prison in which some of the Hollywood Ten were confined.

In December 1947, one week after the Hollywood Ten had been cited for contempt, the film industry decided to fire them. The industry, facing a serious economic crisis, desperately needed favorable publicity. Industry officials hoped that firing the Ten would boost Hollywood's image.

Fifty top film executives met at the Waldorf-Astoria Hotel in New York City. After two days of conferences, they fired the Hollywood Ten and released a statement saying, "We will not knowingly employ a Communist."

In addition to the jail sentences and firings, the Hollywood Ten were blacklisted. Many were unable to find any work in the film industry for the next 10 years. Others, like Ring Lardner, Jr., could work only under pseudonyms. The Hollywood Ten

HISTORICAL PICTURES SERVICE, CHICAGO

HISTORICAL PICTURES SERVICE, CHICAGO

**Screen writer John Howard Lawson (left) and film director Edward Dmytryk (right), members of the** **Hollywood Ten, were questioned by the House Un-American Activities Committee.**

were not the only ones to be penalized, however. The Ten had support from some of their colleagues in Hollywood. Famous actors such as Gene Kelly, Judy Garland, and Humphrey Bogart had participated in benefits and speeches on behalf of the Ten. Many who supported the Hollywood Ten had their reputations tainted. MGM Studios received so many letters critical of Katharine Hepburn that officials told the famous actress they could not use her in films again until public opinion of her improved.

## The Significance

The HUAC hearings on Communism in Hollywood ended a few days after the Ten refused to testify. Four years later, in 1951, the HUAC again investigated Communism in the Hollywood film industry. This time witnesses pleaded the Fifth Amendment to avoid contempt charges. The committee sent no one to jail, but the industry again responded by denying work to some 250 actors, writers, and directors.

Following the HUAC hearings there was a noticeable increase in the number of movies with an anticommunist point of view. By some estimates, between 1947 and 1954 more than 50 films were released preaching the view that Communists were the enemies of the United States.

The Hollywood Ten decided to go to prison rather than to submit to questioning from HUAC. They believed that the United States Constitution protected them from having to answer to the committee. Screen writer Dalton Trumbo expressed his feelings about the experience in this poem, which he wrote to his family from prison:

> *Say then but this of me:*
> *Preferring not to crawl on his knees*
> *In freedom to a bowl of buttered slops*
> *Set out for him by some contemptuous clown,*
> *He walked to jail on his feet.*

## Think About It

1. List the reasons the committee felt it needed to investigate Communism in the Hollywood film industry. List the arguments of the Hollywood Ten for not answering the committee's questions. Explain which side appears to have the stronger position.
2. How might the Hollywood Ten have responded to the committee's questions without showing contempt but at the same time remaining true to their own beliefs in the freedom of thought guaranteed in the Bill of Rights?
3. What might have happened if the Hollywood Ten had not refused to testify at the HUAC hearing?

# The Eisenhower Years

## April 5, 1954: President Eisenhower Addresses the Nation

H IS WAS A VOICE OF REASON IN AN UNREA-SONABLE AGE. HE HAD THE INNER ASSUR-ANCE AND FIVE-STAR STRENGTH OF A MAN WHO HAD MET THE ENEMY AND WON. When he spoke, you felt that things might come out all right, if we'd all pull together, as we did on the European battlefields of World War II.

Dwight David Eisenhower won the confidence of the nation. Maybe it had something do to with the innocent grin he wore when he held up a big fish he'd just caught; or his commanding eyes; or his baldish dome, which made him appear taller than he was. Maybe it was his halting speech, which seemed to hold six decades of experience and caution in each pause.

Eisenhower was not a fist-pounding speechmaker. He hadn't the flair of Generals MacArthur or Patton for dropping verbal bombs. He counseled calmly, like the family doctor. Ike spoke to a generation watching communism advance on the world's continents—that built bomb shelters and bought lead-lined suits in the naive hope of surviving a nuclear holocaust. Imagine the effect of words like these, in his soothing tones:

WE LIKE IKE

UPI/BETTMANN NEWSPHOTOS

> *N o one can say to you that there are no dangers. Of course there are risks, if we are not vigilant. But we do not have to be hysterical. . . . We can stand up and hold up our heads and say, "America is the greatest force that God has ever allowed to exist on his footstool." As such it is up to us to lead this world to a peaceful and secure existence.*
>
> President Eisenhower, *radio and TV address*, April 5, 1954

## Warrior in the White House

T he U.S.'s favorite patriot, the Supreme Allied Commander in Europe, had never in his life voted when the Republicans began urging him to run for the presidency in 1952. Living in Paris, General Eisenhower began reading United States history books and studying economics. But he was not quick to commit himself to a run for the White House. In fact, he even refused an offer of $40,000 from *McCall's* magazine just to say whether he was a Republican. Ike was not a man of haste. In 1952, however, he answered the call of duty to his country.

### A New Kind of Campaign

Given Eisenhower's popularity and lack of involvement in political controversy, the outcome of the election was never much in doubt. The Democratic candidate, Governor Adlai E. Stevenson of Illinois, conducted a respectable, even admirable, race. The governor was a witty, eloquent speaker who appealed to liberal intellectuals. But the country as a whole was not in a liberal frame of mind in 1952.

For every voter who found Stevenson sophisticated, there were two who dubbed him and his followers "eggheads." He was articulate, sophisticated; not a man who could win the average voter with a folksy style. But Stevenson's greatest obstacle was that he belonged to the same party as Harry Truman.

Although new to politics, Eisenhower did not lack political instincts, as was shown in his choice of Senator Richard Nixon as his running mate. By adding an experienced politician and champion of anticommunism to his ticket, Ike clinched the conservative vote and eased the fears of those who wondered about his grasp of domestic issues.

At first, however, the choice of Nixon threatened to blow up in Ike's face. Early in the campaign, a newspaper revealed the existence of a "secret fund" of contributions from citizens, which it said was used to support Nixon in an extravagant life style. Some party members called for Nixon to quit the ticket.

Nixon, the prosecutor, went on the offensive. At Ike's suggestion, he took his case to the voters in a live TV broadcast on September 23, 1952. In quiet tones, Nixon gave a lengthy and thorough accounting of all his financial holdings, which were quite modest. The fund, he said, was used for travel from his Washington home to California, and it was neither illegal nor immoral.

In this politically shrewd talk, he clearly implied that those who attacked him were those who opposed his efforts to fight communism. Nixon did admit to one contribution for his personal use. An admirer had sent his family a dog. His young daughters loved that dog, which they named Checkers, and he wasn't going to give it back.

The emotional appeal from Nixon won him a wave of support from viewers. The broadcast became known as the "Checkers" speech. As in the Hiss case, Nixon came out on top. Calling him "my boy," Ike embraced Nixon, and the campaign rolled on.

Ike's election campaign resembled his military campaigns: It was organized, efficient, and determined. His speeches offered little in the way of specifics—he promised to "clean up the mess in Washington." Adlai Stevenson warned that the Republican platform was "as slippery as a bunch of eels—you can't stand on it." But it didn't matter. The Republicans hammered away at the themes of Truman-era weakness and incompetence—with Nixon slamming the "scandal-a-day administration," and Ike promising to go to Korea personally to put an end to

AP/WIDE WORLD PHOTOS

**In his "Checkers" speech, Nixon introduced his wife, Pat, to the viewers and emphasized his family values.** *Do you think this tactic would work in a similar situation today?*

the war. This was what voters wanted to hear. "We like Ike" echoed in the auditoriums of the country, and the Republicans marched on to victory. The 1952 election was not so much a win for the Republican Party as a measure of the personal popularity of the smiling hero of World War II.

**A New Command**   The seasoned soldier knows that in battle lives depend not only on good generals but also on the cooperative efforts of every fighting man. So it is no surprise that President Eisenhower used **consensus decision-making**, a management style based on group efforts, to solve problems. "No one has a monopoly on the truth," he declared.

Eisenhower had a firm vision of what he thought was right, and he was comfortable in an administrative role. He focused on major issues only, delegating other matters to his advisers. Everything moved through proper channels in the new administration.

The president had great respect for successful businessmen, and he was convinced that the country would best function on proven business principles. In fact, he named corporate executives to most key posts in his administration. To the government's regulatory agencies he appointed businessmen friendly to the industries they were supposed to regulate.

One of Eisenhower's major initiatives during his first term was to encourage private development of hydroelectric and nuclear power. He unsuccessfully urged Congress to turn over to private companies the operation of one New Deal program, the Tennessee Valley Authority. He did, however, approve the Atomic Energy Act of 1954, which allowed private companies to operate nuclear power plants. The first nuclear-powered generator to produce electricity for public use began operation in Arco, Idaho, in 1955.

Ike unwaveringly followed "middle of the road" policies. His emphasis on consensus decision-making was increasingly criticized by political observers as cumbersome and ineffective. But as a columnist noted in 1959: "The public loves Ike. The less he does, the more they love him. That, probably, is the secret. Here is a man who doesn't rock the boat."[1]

## A Second Term

This "secret" was the strategy that successfully carried him through a second presidential race in 1956. The race was practically a rerun of 1952. Once again Eisenhower squared off against Adlai Stevenson, and once again Ike won by a wide margin.

Although the outcomes of the two campaigns were the same, the tone was somewhat different. Eisenhower had suffered a heart attack in 1955 and was running a less energetic campaign on his record of "peace, progress, and prosperity." The nation still liked Ike but was lukewarm to his party. Democrats retained control of Congress in the 1956 elections.

Eisenhower's second term was notable both for decisions made and for decisions postponed. As in his first term, domestic problems often took a back seat to foreign policy matters. Trouble threatened close to home when Fidel Castro came to power in Cuba. Although the president had ended the Korean War as promised, the cold war grew even icier. In 1957 the Soviets shocked the United States by sending up *Sputnik I*, the first satellite in space.

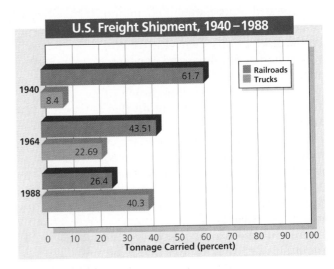

### U.S. Freight Shipment, 1940–1988

Railroads
Trucks

1940 — Railroads 61.7, Trucks 8.4
1964 — Railroads 43.51, Trucks 22.69
1988 — Railroads 26.4, Trucks 40.3

Tonnage Carried (percent)

**Compare the amount of freight carried by train in 1940 and 1988. Determine reasons why railroads are still an important form of freight transport.** *What effect would the building of an interstate highway have on small towns that were bypassed by the highway?*

The United States hurried to catch up in the space race, although Eisenhower was not eager to spend lots of money to do it. *Explorer I*, the country's answer to *Sputnik I*, went up less than four months later, on January 31, 1958. Later that year, Congress created the National Aeronautics and Space Administration, or NASA.

**Paving America**  Ike was much less concerned with blazing a path into space than he was in paving new roads across the country. The second Eisenhower term witnessed the most ambitious and most expensive public works program in U.S. history: the construction of the federal interstate highway system.

Eisenhower's pet program, launched in 1956, was a departure from his generally conservative approach to spending. The president believed the country needed a network of highways to increase road safety, promote commerce, and preserve the nation's unity.

Besides Ike's personal support, the program had the backing of a powerful coalition that included oil companies, automobile and rubber manufacturers, letter carriers, bakers, truckers, and other groups. All stood to benefit from the road building.

## STUDY GUIDE

### Analyzing Decisions
The Federal Interstate and Defense Highways System literally transformed the nation. In a single stroke, it committed the nation to a transportation system based primarily on motor vehicles.

The new highway system proved a boon for many industries. Yet it also led to increases in oil consumption and pollution, effects that have grown more severe in recent years.

1 What were the advantages and disadvantages of Eisenhower's consensus decision-making?

Congress appropriated $32 billion to build 41,000 miles of highways. Ten years later, cars and trucks crisscrossed the nation along the world's finest highway system. (See the map below.) The final cost was more than $80 billion.

**Ike's Legacy**   Ike described himself as "conservative when it comes to money and liberal when it comes to human beings." During his tenure, Congress voted to extend the social security system to cover another seven million people and unemployment compensation to cover an additional four million. The minimum wage increased from 75 cents per hour to one dollar, and federally financed housing for low income families increased. The president also approved the building of the St. Lawrence Seaway, connecting the Great Lakes to the Atlantic Ocean through Canada.

By 1960 the Eisenhower administration was stalled. Lack of progress in easing the cold war was personally crushing to Ike. The president's physical health, mirroring the prestige of the nation, sank lower. It was an opportunity tailor-made for a young political hopeful from Massachusetts, Senator John F. Kennedy.

**The construction of the present Interstate Highway System began under the Eisenhower administration in the 1950s.** *Why do you think oil companies supported Eisenhower's highway construction programs?*

## In with the New

The 1960 presidential contest between Richard Nixon, son of a California shopkeeper, and John F. Kennedy, son of a Massachusetts millionaire, pitted against each other two men and two political philosophies that seemed to offer the country a real choice.

On the surface, Kennedy versus Nixon meant Catholic versus Protestant; a Harvard elite facing a self-styled middle American. It was Kennedy the spender against Nixon the fiscal conservative; the Kennedy style and wit versus the proven Nixon experience.

But in reality many of these much-celebrated differences mattered little. The two men had similar opinions on foreign and domestic issues. When Nixon ran for the Senate in 1950 against Helen Gahagan Douglas, Kennedy showed up at his office with a $1,000 campaign contribution from his father for Nixon's campaign. The Kennedys thought Douglas just as dangerously left-leaning as Nixon did.

When Kennedy advocated an armed invasion of Cuba during the campaign, he was taking just the position Nixon had privately urged under Eisenhower. Ironically, Nixon had to disagree publicly with Kennedy because he had to support his administration's view. In 1960 Kennedy was not a vigorous advocate of civil rights, and Nixon had long been a moderate on the issue.

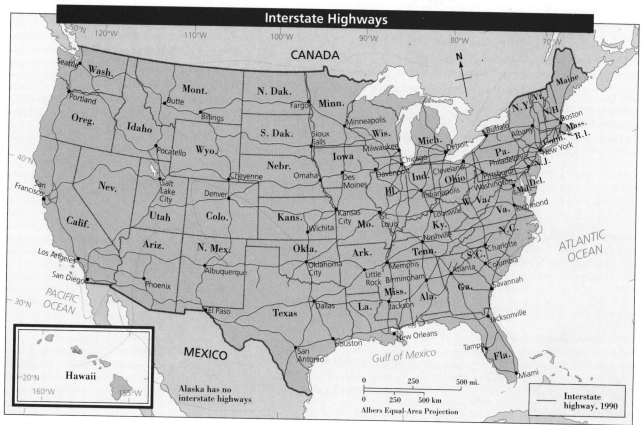

**Interstate Highways**

CANADA

Alaska has no interstate highways

Interstate highway, 1990

Albers Equal-Area Projection

Actually, the 1960 campaign provided something much more interesting than the stereotypes of the two men. It was a political battle waged over issues of national and international importance. Cuba, just off the tip of Florida, was fast becoming a perceived communist threat. The United States had been left behind again when the Soviets sent a dog—the papers nicknamed it "mutnik"— into space. Violent communist movements in Asia had not ended with the Korean War but were only shifting to southeast Asia in a little country called Vietnam.

The 1960 campaign for the presidency was fought over such issues to a virtual standoff—a result that indicates how closely the two young candidates resembled each other. Of the two, Kennedy was younger by several years; but that didn't seem to cost him many votes. He was a Roman Catholic, and surveys indicated that that cost him 1.5 million votes. Nixon had far more experience in foreign affairs. He had confronted violent anti-American crowds in Venezuela, met Khrushchev in a debate in Moscow, and talked with leaders around the world.

However, it was the choice that Nixon made to adopt the whistle-stopping campaign strategy of Harry Truman that helped to defeat him. Truman's recipe for victory turned out to be Richard Nixon's recipe for defeat. The **electronic media**—TV and radio—for the first time were becoming a big factor in a presidential campaign, something that Kennedy exploited with his boyish good looks and infectious humor. The televised debate between Nixon and Kennedy in 1960 became a contest between a weary campaigner who was being squeezed dry by his grueling campaign schedule and a candidate whose aides knew how to help him work smarter, not harder.

The candidates met in a tide-turning televised debate on September 26, 1960. Viewers saw in Nixon a man stretched to his limits. Early in the whistle-stop campaign, Nixon had injured his knee, and for weeks it continued to jolt him with pain. But he had carried on, racking up mile after mile in a desperate push to keep his promise to campaign in every state. He lost weight and became haggard and drawn.

UPI/BETTMANN NEWSPHOTOS

During the 1960 televised debates between Nixon and Kennedy, the public was influenced by Kennedy's wit and youthful appearance.

Kennedy, meanwhile, arrived for the debate tan and fit from a rest in Florida. It didn't matter that radio listeners scored the debate for Nixon on the strength of his arguments. TV conveyed Kennedy's warmth and ease to 70 million viewers.

The election returns were the closest in history. Kennedy took 49.7 percent of the popular vote to 49.5 percent for Nixon, although the difference in electoral votes (303 to 219, respectively) proved more substantial. Many Republicans and some independent observers cried foul, claiming election fraud in Texas and Illinois, where a single county might have wiped out Kennedy's victory of just over 100,000 votes out of the 69 million that were cast.

A New York *Herald Tribune* writer, Earl Mazo, who had long been friendly to Nixon, started a journalistic investigation of vote fraud. However, Nixon called him off, telling him that such an investigation was pointless. "Earl," he said, "no one steals the presidency of the United States."

## SECTION REVIEW

**Checking Facts**

1. List three characteristics that made Eisenhower an attractive candidate to voters.

2. Why did Eisenhower choose Nixon as his running mate?

3. True or false: Eisenhower's policies brought about widespread change in the government. Explain your reasoning.

4. How did television influence the election of 1960?

**Thinking Critically**

5. **Recognizing Values** What does Eisenhower's emphasis on consensus decision-making tell you about his values?

6. **Recognizing Assumptions** What evidence can you find in the text to support historians' assumption that Ike's victory in 1952 was more a measure of his personal popularity rather than of broad support for Republican policies?

**Linking Across Time**

7. Find an example from an earlier chapter of the importance of electronic media in national affairs.

# Recognizing Fact and Opinion

When people talk about any issue, from choosing a place to eat lunch to discussing a political matter, their conversations are full of facts and opinions. A fact is a statement that can be proved or observed. An opinion is a statement of personal belief or preference. It expresses a person's feelings or conclusions. An opinion cannot be proved or disproved, but it *can* be supported by facts. Separating fact and opinion can be difficult. People's opinions are often based on facts, even when they don't state the facts directly. What is important is how facts are used. Do they support the statements being made? Are the facts used to appeal to emotions rather than reason? Are they used to obscure what the writer or speaker is really saying?

## Learning the Skill

You want to be able to recognize any contradictions, inconsistencies, or exaggerations in what you read or hear. The following steps will help you to sift facts from opinions and to judge the reliability of what you read or hear.

1. Pick out statements you think are facts. Ask yourself: Can these statements be proved? Where might I find information to verify them?
2. Check the sources. Reliable sources include almanacs, encyclopedias, the *Congressional Record*, and similar references. Often statistics may sound impressive but come from an unreliable source such as an interest group that is trying to gain support for its programs.
3. Identify the statements of opinion. Sometimes they contain phrases such as *in my view, I believe, it is my conviction, I think.* Such phrases are cues that the assertion may be an opinion. Be careful, however, not to rely solely on cue phrases; sometimes they are used in statements of fact: "I think the meeting will be at 10:00 A.M."
4. Identify the author's purpose. What does he or she want you to believe or do?

In 1960, during their campaigns for the presidency, Senator John F. Kennedy and Vice President Richard M. Nixon met in a series of four television debates. The following quotation is part of Senator Kennedy's opening remarks for the first debate, on September 26.

> This is a great country, but I think it could be a greater country; and this is a powerful country, but I think it could be a more powerful country. I'm not satisfied to have 50 percent of our steel mill capacity unused. I'm not satisfied when the United States had last year the lowest rate of economic growth of any major industrialized society in the world, because economic growth means strength and vitality; it means we're able to sustain our defenses; it means we're able to meet our commitments abroad.

Notice Kennedy's use of the cue words *I think*. Do these words signal an opinion? How can you tell? How does Kennedy support his assertions? Do you think his information is reliable? Why or why not?

## Practicing the Skill

1. Read the following comments that Vice President Nixon made during the debate. What facts does he provide? Which of his statements are opinions? How can you tell?

> I counted out the cost of the Democratic program. It runs . . . a maximum of $18 billion a year more than we're presently spending.
>
> Now the Republican platform will cost . . . a maximum of $4.9 billion a year more than we're presently spending.
>
> Now, does this mean that their program is better than ours? Not at all. Because it isn't a question of how much the federal government spends. . . . It's a question of which administration does the right thing.
>
> And in our case, I do believe that our programs will stimulate the creative energies of 180 million free Americans.

2. Record or take notes on a television interview. List three facts and three opinions that were stated. Tell how facts were used to support opinions. Do the facts seem reliable? Why or why not? Were unsupported opinions stated? What was the speaker trying to get the listener to believe? Was he or she successful?

# Chapter 16 Review

## Summary

Use the following outline as a tool for reviewing and summarizing the chapter. Copy the outline on your own paper, leaving spaces between headings to jot down notes about key events and concepts.

**I. Truman's Fair Deal**
  A. A Conservative Turn
  B. Fears About the Economy
  C. The Uphill Race in '48
  D. The New Deal Revisited
**II. The Cold War at Home**
  A. The Rise of Anticommunism
  B. The McCarthy Era
  C. Citizens Under Suspicion
**III. The Eisenhower Years**
  A. Warrior in the White House
  B. A Second Term
  C. In with the New

## Ideas, Events, and People

1. What was the significance of Truman's whistle-stop tactic in the 1948 presidential election?
2. Who were the Dixiecrats, and how did they influence the politics of the postwar United States?
3. Briefly describe the Federal Loyalty Program.
4. The photograph to the right shows police and strikers at the General Electric plant in Philadelphia in February 1946. This strike was but one of the many that took place in the postwar period. Why did so many strikes and other labor disputes occur following World War II?
5. Why were consumers eager to purchase new cars and appliances following the war?
6. How did television affect the outcome of the Army-McCarthy hearings?

7. Write a paragraph describing the anticommunism of the 1950s. Include major figures and their significance. Use the *Writer's Guide*, Unit 1 (page 822), for help in preparing a well-developed paragraph.
8. Briefly explain the impact of *Sputnik* on the mood of the United States.
9. Adlai Stevenson's critics referred to him as an egghead. Why? What does the use of this term

AP/WIDE WORLD PHOTOS

| 1953 | 1954 | 1955 | 1956 | 1957 | 1958 | 1959 | 1960 |
|------|------|------|------|------|------|------|------|

**1956**
Ike wins second term;
Interstate highways begun.

**1960**
Kennedy-Nixon debates;
JFK wins election.

**1954**
Army-McCarthy hearings;
senator censured.

**1958**
NASA created; United States
enters space race with Soviets.

suggest about American ideals of political leadership in the 1950s?

10. The chapter text often describes the appearance and personality of various political figures of the era. From the following list choose two and describe how the public perception of them affected their careers: Alger Hiss, Dwight D. Eisenhower, Adlai Stevenson, Richard Nixon, Thomas Dewey, Joseph McCarthy.

## Social Studies Skills

**Recognizing Fact and Opinion**

Read the excerpt on page 538 from President Truman's 1953 speech on McCarthyism. Which of his statements are opinions and which are facts? How can you tell? Are there facts in the lesson text on pages 537–538 that support or dispute the opinions in the speech?

## Critical Thinking

1. **Recognizing Values**

   The chapter deals largely with perceptions—how an idea, event, or person is perceived by the public—rather than with an understanding of the basic issues involved. Give one example from the chapter that supports this statement.

2. **Making Generalizations**

   What trend can you identify with regard to the role of government during the cold war period?

3. **Identifying Cause and Effect**

   Name three international events that contributed to cold war fears at home in the 1940s, and three events from the 1950s.

4. **Recognizing Values**

   Identify ways in which the methods of Joseph McCarthy ran counter to American political ideals and constitutional protections.

## Extension and Application

1. **Evidence of the past**

   Portions of the Army-McCarthy hearings are available on recording (Caedmon Records). Obtain this recording from a library and play it in class.

2. **Citizenship**

   Identify a current labor dispute, local or national, and summarize the points at issue between labor and management. Imagine that you are judge or arbitrator. How would you decide this particular case? Does the Taft-Hartley Act apply?

3. **Global Connection**

   Perhaps the most vivid symbol of the cold war was the Berlin Wall and the division of Germany. Today the Berlin Wall has been torn down, and Germany reunited. How do you think this will affect American domestic and foreign politics?

## Geography

1. What part did radio and television play in the spread of suspicion and fear concerning communism? What part did television play in McCarthy's ultimate fate?

2. Use the maps in the Sourcebook to determine what states, in addition to Idaho, have the natural resources necessary for nuclear power. How will the economies of these states be affected as additional nuclear power plants are built?

3. In recent years, railroad cars have begun to carry trucks from one place to another. Why do you think this is so?

4. Use the maps in the Sourcebook to find the distance between Cuba and Miami, Florida. Compare this distance with the distance between cities such as Boston and New York and Los Angeles and San Francisco. How might this distance influence cold war politics?

# Unit 6 Review

*I*t is clear that the main element of any United States policy toward the Soviet Union must be that of a long term, patient but firm and vigilant containment of Russian expansive tendencies. . . .

Soviet society may well contain deficiencies which will eventually weaken its own total potential. This would of itself warrant the United States entering with reasonable confidence upon a policy of firm containment, designed to confront the Russians with unalterable counter-force at every point where they show signs of encroaching upon the interests of a peaceful and stable world.

Diplomat George F. Kennan,
July 1947

## Concepts and Themes

After World War II, Americans were fearful and suspicious of their former allies, the Soviets. Three presidents—Truman, Eisenhower, and Kennedy—enjoyed a broad consensus based on two ideas—the greatness of the United States as a democracy and the global threat posed by the Soviets and communism. All three presidents worked hard to contain communism, or keep it within its present boundaries. This policy, called "containment" by Kennan, would do much to shape events worldwide for three decades.

1. How did the Yalta conference prove to be a major setback for containment?
2. How did the Truman Doctrine, the Marshall Plan, and the Korean conflict support the containment policy in different ways?
3. How did the containment policy and Russia's launching of *Sputnik* lead to an arms race?
4. Why did many in the United States view the rise of Mao Zedong as a failure of containment?
5. What recent events might Kennan interpret as victories for containment? Would you agree?
6. Who were the Americans that remained poor in the midst of postwar affluence? Why were they invisible to much of the population?

## History Projects

1. **Evidence of the Past**
   Locate a book of presidential speeches and read Eisenhower's commencement address of June 14, 1953, at Dartmouth College. Find the part that encouraged opponents of Joseph McCarthy.
2. **Geography**
   Decide where you would rather live—the city, the suburbs, or the country. Write an imaginary real estate ad for an apartment, house, or home-site stressing the advantages of the location.
3. **Culture of the Time**
   Among the word usages of the 1950s were *hot rod, cool* (first rate), *whirlybird, junk mail, shook up, flipped,* and *carry-out.* Research usages of the 1950s. Make a Fifties Glossary.
4. **One Day in History**
   *Sputnik* led to some important "days in history." Research the story of space flight, and make a chart of the important dates, events, and people.
5. **Case Study**
   Truman's 1951 decision to fire General MacArthur was extremely controversial at the time. Research the event in books and periodicals. Find quotations expressing opposing views. Conclude by explaining the outcome.

## Writing Activities

1. Watch a rerun or video of a 1950s television series depicting daily life, such as "I Love Lucy" or "Father Knows Best." Write an essay comparing it with a popular series about family life today. (See the Writer's Guide, page 826, for information on comparative writing.)
2. The 1950s have been criticized as an era of conformity, when people lived in "little boxes" in the suburbs, and their lives and thoughts were all alike. Write an editorial assessing the values of your own era. (See the Writer's Guide, page 827, for information on persuasive writing.)

## The Arts

- *The Spy Who Came in from the Cold* by John LeCarre; a novel of cold war espionage.
- *Death of a Salesman* by Arthur Miller; a play about a man whose shallow values destroy him.
- "Rock Around the Clock" by Bill Haley and His Comets; a record, the first rock hit.

# UNIT SEVEN

# Toward Equality and Social Reform

Family Dog Productions, DBA Chester Helms, 771 Bush Street, San Francisco, California 94108, (415) 391-2423

# Voices of Change

*During the 1960s and 1970s, women and people of color began
to challenge predominant ethnic, racial, and gender stereotypes and worked
to overturn laws that restricted their rights and freedoms. The authors of the
following poems assert their identities by linking personal experiences to a
broader understanding of culture, gender, tradition, and family. They represent the diversity of American culture during this period.*

## To Be of Use
### by Marge Piercy

The people I love the best
jump into work head first
without dallying in the shallows
and swim off with sure strokes almost out
  of sight.
They seem to become natives of that element.
the black sleek heads of seals
bouncing like half-submerged balls.

I love people who harness themselves, an ox to a
  heavy cart.
who pull like the water buffalo, with massive
  patience,
who strain in the mud and the muck to move
  things forward,
who do what has to be done, again and again.

I want to be with people who submerge
in the task, who go into the fields to harvest
and work in a row and pass the bags along,
who stand in the line and haul in their places,
who are not parlor generals and field deserters
but move in common rhythm
when the food must come in or the fire be put out.

## A Good Assassination Should Be Quiet
### by Mari Evans

he had
A Dream
e x p loded
down
  his
    th r o a t.

whereon
a million hard white eyes
swung impiously heavenward
  to mourn
the gross indelicate demise

Such public death
transgresses
all known rules

A good assassination
should be quiet

and occupy the heart
four hundred
years

*Royal Tide II* (1961–1963), by Louise Nevelson, uses objects found in the environment to create a unified three-dimensional assemblage.

## For deLawd
### by Lucille Clifton

people say they have a hard time
understanding how I
go on about my business
playing my Ray Charles
hollering at the kids—
seem like my Afro
cut off in some old image
would show I got a long memory
and I come from a line
of black and going on women
who got used to making it through murdered sons
and who grief kept on pushing
who fried chicken
ironed
swept off the back steps
who grief kept
for their still alive sons
for their sons coming
for their sons gone
just pushing

## The Immigrant Experience
### by Richard Olivas

I'm sitting in my history class,
The instructor commences rapping,
I'm in my U.S. History class,
And I'm on the verge of napping.

The Mayflower landed on Plymouth Rock.
Tell me more! Tell me more!
Thirteen colonies were settled.
I've heard it all before.

What did he say?
Dare I ask him to reiterate?
Oh, why bother,
It sounded like he said,
George Washington's my father.

I'm reluctant to believe it,
I suddenly raise my *mano*.
If George Washington's my father,
Why wasn't he Chicano?

## To Other Women Who Were Ugly Once
*by Inés Hernandez Tovar*

Do you remember how we used to panic
when Cosmo, Vogue and Mademoiselle
    ladies
        would Glamour-us
        out of existence
            so ultra bright
            would be their smile
            so lovely their
            complexion
    their confianza[1] based on
    someone else's fashion
    and their mascara'd mascaras[2]
        hiding the cascaras[3]
        that hide their ser?[4]

I would always become cold inside
                mata*onda*[5] to compete
      to need
      to dress right
      speak right
      laugh in just the
      right places
      dance in just
      the right way

My resistance to this type of
      existence
      grows stronger every day
Y al cabo ahora se
      que se vale
      preferir natural luz[6]

          to neon.

---

1 Confidence.
2 Masks.
3 Shells.
4 Being.
5 Something that is disheartening, roughly translated.
6 And now anyway I know that it is worthy to prefer natural light.

## Offspring
*by Naomi Long Madgett*

I tried to tell her:
    This way the twig is bent.
    Born of my trunk and strengthened by my roots,
    you must stretch newgrown branches
    closer to the sun
    than I can reach.
I wanted to say:
    Extend my self to that far atmosphere
    only my dreams allow.

But the twig broke,
and yesterday I saw her
walking down an unfamiliar street,
    feet confident,
    face slanted upward toward a threatening sky,
and
    she was smiling
    and she was
    her very free
    her very individual
    unpliable
own.

## Eating Together
*by Li-Young Lee*

In the steamer is the trout
seasoned with slivers of ginger,
two sprigs of green onion, and sesame oil.
We shall eat it with rice for lunch,
brothers, sister, my mother who will
taste the sweetest meat of the head,
holding it between her fingers
deftly, the way my father did
weeks ago. Then he lay down
to sleep like a snow-covered road
winding through pines older than him,
without any travelers, and lonely for no one.

## Freeway 280

### by Lorna Dee Cervantes

Las casitas[1] near the gray cannery,
nestled amid wild abrazos[2] of climbing roses
and man-high red geraniums
are gone now. The freeway conceals it
all beneath a raised scar.

But under the fake windsounds of the open lanes,
in the abandoned lots below, new grasses sprout,
wild mustard remembers, old gardens
come back stronger than they were,
trees have been left standing in their yards.
Albaricoqueros, cerezos, nogales . . .[3]
Viejitas[4] come here with paper bags to gather greens.
Espinaca, verdolagas, yerbabuena . . .[5]

I scramble over the wire fence
that would have kept me out.
Once, I wanted out, wanted the rigid lanes
to take me to a place without sun,
without the smell of tomatoes burning
on swing shift in the greasy summer air.

Maybe it's here
en los campos extraños de esta ciudad[6]
where I'll find it, that part of me
mown under
like a corpse
or a loose seed.

---

1 Little houses. [Author's note]
2 Bear hugs.
3 Apricot trees, cherry trees, walnut trees. [Author's note]
4 Old women.
5 Spinach, purslane, mint. [Author's note]
6 In the strange fields of this city. [Author's note]

## Women

### by Alice Walker

They were women then
My mama's generation
Husky of voice—Stout of
Step
With fists as well as
Hands
How they battered down
Doors
And ironed
Starched white
Shirts
How they led
Armies
Headragged Generals
Across mined
Fields
Booby-trapped
Ditches
To discover books
Desks
A place for us
How they knew what we
*Must* know
Without knowing a page
Of it
Themselves.

## Responding to Literature

1. What does each poet say about his or her identity?

2. Walker and Tovar write about the plight of women in different ways. How do they agree?

3. What do you think Madgett and Lee would say are the greatest gifts parents could give their children?

*For Further Reading*
Kesey, Ken: *Sometimes a Great Notion*
Kingston, Maxine Hong: *The Woman Warrior*
Morrison, Toni: *Song of Solomon*
Walker, Alice: *Meridian*

CHAPTER 17

# The Civil Rights Struggle

## September 4, 1957: School Opens at Little Rock Central High

Elizabeth Ann Eckford and her mother made a crisp black and white dress for Elizabeth to wear her first day in the new school. The other eight black students arranged to go together, but Elizabeth never got the message. She went instead by bus and once at Little Rock Central High School headed for the front door. To her surprise, she found the way blocked by an angry crowd of white townspeople and hundreds of armed soldiers.

Elizabeth tried to follow a white student through the door but was stopped by a soldier. "When I tried to squeeze past him," she recalled later, "he raised his bayonet, and then the other guards moved in and raised their bayonets. . . .

Somebody started yelling, 'Lynch her! Lynch her!'"

Elizabeth and the other eight students never made it into Central High that day. It took three more weeks, intervention by the president, 1,000 paratroopers, and 10,000 members of the Arkansas National Guard to integrate the school.

It was a pattern repeated many times in the years to come. Legislation and court orders were not enough. Grass roots efforts by the local black community and nonviolent demonstrations were not enough. It took the efforts of all these people together. Only then could the nation bring the Constitution's promise of guaranteed equality for all a little closer to reality.

> *"Somebody started yelling, 'Lynch her! Lynch her!'"*

FRANCIS MILLER, LIFE MAGAZINE © 1957, TIME, INC.

*Elizabeth Ann Eckford was not prepared for the angry reception she received as she approached Little Rock Central High School.*

*On September 10, soldiers stood outside the all-white Little Rock Central High School in order to prevent black students from entering.*

# The American Dilemma

---

## Early 1950s: The United States

---

DESPITE MAKING SOME GAINS DURING WORLD WAR II, AFRICAN AMERICANS DID NOT SHARE EQUALLY WITH MOST WHITE PEOPLE IN THE PROMISE AND PROSPERITY that came with the 1950s. Worse, many white Americans simply seemed unaware of the social injustices suffered by African Americans. Novelist Ralph Ellison described the plight of the ordinary African American this way:

*I am an invisible man. . . . I am invisible, understand, simply because people refuse to see me. . . . When they approach me they see only my surroundings, themselves, or figments of their imagination—indeed everything and anything except me.*

Ralph Ellison,
Invisible Man, *1952*

In the South, this invisibility was enforced by laws that ensured **segregation.** Indeed, separation of black and white formed a fundamental part of southern culture. All across the region, African Americans had to enter public buses by the back door, sit in separate waiting rooms at train stations, eat in separate restaurants, and attend school in separate classrooms. The power to vote was regularly withheld.

In the North, the pattern of urban life often resulted in *de facto* segregation—segregation in fact though not by law. As African Americans migrated to northern cities, white people moved out to the suburbs. Other, more subtle means of separating whites

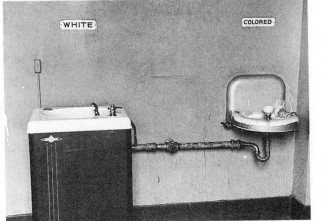

©ELLIOTT ERWITT, MAGNUM

and African Americans emerged. For example, school districts were carefully drawn so that they included only black neighborhoods or only white ones.

Indeed, all across the country there were two Americas, one white and one black. But the invisible world of the African Americans was about to make its presence known.

---

## The Segregation System

While the American people struggled to adjust to post-World War II life, they faced a number of troubling social issues. Among these issues was the question of what place African Americans would occupy in the country they had bravely helped to defend. In the North, African Americans began achieving modest gains in fair housing and fair employment protections. But in much of the South, there was widespread resistance to changing the rights of African Americans.

The issue that most inflamed both segregationists and integrationists was public education. The reason was that public schools placed children from the age of six on in daily social situations of playing and learning. Attitudes learned in the classroom could be expected to influence the students the rest of their lives.

In the early 1950s, 17 states and the District of Columbia prohibited black and white children from attending school together. Only 16 states required their public schools to be integrated, and even these

---

**As You Read**

Analyze the reasons why the Supreme Court declared segregation in public schools unconstitutional in *Brown v. Board of Education*. Also, think about the following concepts and skills.

**Central Concepts**
- understanding the role of segregation, especially in the South
- recognizing the importance of the *Brown* decision in the civil rights struggle

**Thinking Skills**
- comparing and contrasting
- making inferences

requirements were often violated by individual school districts.

Then in 1950 three Supreme Court decisions handed down on a single day gave a new direction to those who were fighting for **civil rights.** First, the Court ruled that railroad dining cars operating in the South must provide equal service to all travelers, regardless of race. Second, the court ruled that African American students could not be segregated within a school also attended by whites. Third, the Court recognized that "intangible factors," not just buildings or books, had to be considered when comparing the education provided African Americans and whites.

## The Challenge of the Courts

For over 50 years *Plessy v. Ferguson* had stood as the legal precedent for the "separate but equal" doctrine. This 1896 Supreme Court opinion held that if separate accommodations provided in railroad cars were equal for both black and white passengers, then the resulting segregation was constitutional. Soon the "separate but equal" principle was being used to justify segregation in housing, restaurants, public swimming pools, and a variety of other public facilities.

**NAACP Strategy**   After World War II the National Association for the Advancement of Colored People (NAACP) initiated a series of court cases that chipped away at the *Plessy* ruling. And in case after case, the Supreme Court held that the separate facilities provided African Americans were not, in fact, equal to those provided white people.

The NAACP had worked out a careful strategy that concentrated first on desegregating graduate and specialized schools. They reasoned that if they could prove that the facilities for nonwhites were not in fact equal, instead of building expensive new school buildings for use by only a handful of African American students, states would be forced to integrate. After succeeding on this level, the NAACP planned to attack segregation in elementary and high schools.

Then in 1950 the NAACP weighed the recent actions of the Supreme Court and made a bold decision. Rather than trying to prove case by case that the "separate but equal" doctrine was unworkable, they agreed to fight segregation head on. They would challenge the courts that segregation itself was illegal.

Leading this effort for the NAACP was Thurgood Marshall, who later became the first African American justice on the Supreme Court. Marshall was extremely popular among southern blacks. As one

**School segregation was law in schools throughout the South, and well-established practice elsewhere.**

*In what ways do you think legal segregation might be easier to combat than de facto segregation?*

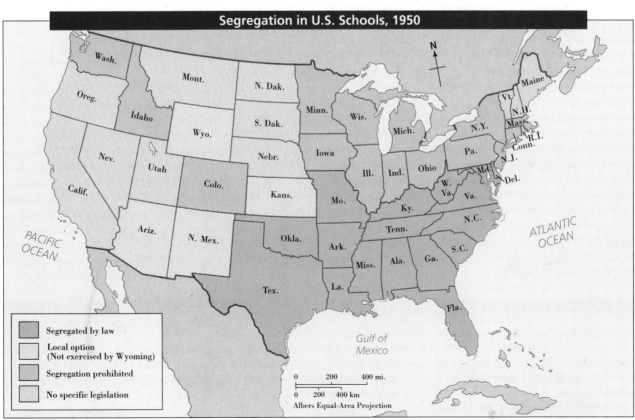

Segregation in U.S. Schools, 1950

Segregated by law

Local option (Not exercised by Wyoming)

Segregation prohibited

No specific legislation

0        200        400 mi.

0     200     400 km

Albers Equal-Area Projection

AP/WIDE WORLD PHOTOS

**Thurgood Marshall had argued 15 cases before the Supreme Court and won 13 before the _Brown_ case.**

called _Brown v. the Board of Education of Topeka, Kansas._ By selecting a case from outside the South, the Court hoped to emphasize that the question of school segregation was a national one.

In fact, the "separate but equal" school facilities in Topeka were of comparable quality. But seven-year-old Linda Brown had to cross through a railroad switching yard to catch the bus to her all-black elementary school, which was miles away. Why, her father insisted, couldn't she attend the all-white school just a few blocks from her home instead of riding a bus to a school located miles away?

Oral arguments before the Supreme Court were set for December 9, 1952. As usual, the NAACP lawyers rehearsed their presentation before the mostly nonwhite faculty and students of Howard Law School in Washington, D.C. After the hearing came months of waiting. The Court then asked for more information, but before arguments were heard again, Chief Justice Fred M. Vinson died suddenly. President Eisenhower appointed in his place the former governor of California, Earl Warren.

Warren felt that such a sensitive decision required a unanimous decision. Such a decision would send a clear message to all parts of the country. Again, weeks of negotiations went on before the Court announced its decision. That historic moment came on May 17, 1954. Chief Justice Warren, in delivering the opinion, said:

> _D_oes segregation of children in public schools solely on the basis of race, even though the physical facilities and other tangible factors may be equal, deprive children of the minority group of equal educational opportunities? We believe it does. . . . To separate them from others of similar age and qualifications solely because of their race generates a feeling of inferiority as to their status in the community that may affect their hearts and minds in a way very unlikely ever to be undone.
>
> We conclude that in the field of public education the doctrine of 'separate but equal' has no place. Separate educational facilities are inherently unequal.
>
> _Brown v. Board of Education,_ 1954[1]

supporter explained, Marshall was "of the people. He knew how to get through to them. Out in Texas or Oklahoma or down the street here in Washington at the Baptist Church, he would make these rousing speeches that would have them all jumping out of their seats."

Then the NAACP began to decide which among the nation's segregated school districts to bring before the Supreme Court. A suitable case required parents courageous enough to sign a court petition despite pressure from local officials. It also required patience. The NAACP expected to lose when the suits were first tried. This would provide the opportunity to appeal to the Supreme Court.

**Brown v. Board of Education** The Supreme Court case that helped overturn school segregation did not originate in the South at all. The case was

**Comparing and Contrasting**
_Plessy v. Ferguson_ and _Brown v. Board of Education_ dealt with the same issue but reached different conclusions. _Plessy_ declared that segregation of railroads was constitutional if the accom- modations were comparable. _Brown_ rejected this reasoning when applied to schools, stating that the harm inflicted on minority children deprived them of equal protection under the law.

1 What might have happened if the Supreme Court had been unable to reach a unanimous decision?

## Resistance to the Brown Decision

When the Supreme Court declared in 1954 that school segregation was illegal, they said nothing about how integration was to be carried out. That announcement came a year later. The rather vague ruling of the court, pronounced in May 1955, was that integration should take place "with all deliberate speed" and "at the earliest possible date." The reluctance to give definite guidelines for ending segregation may have been the price that Chief Justice Warren had to pay for his justices' unanimous decision. After all, the integration decision was not a popular one among many groups. Polls showed that 80 percent of southern whites opposed the Brown decision.

As the nation's school districts took steps to comply with the ruling, other districts, particularly in the South, devised plans to resist the decision.

BROWN FAMILY COLLECTION

**Linda Brown (center) is shown here with two white friends. She became the focus of a national debate.**

**Massive Resistance** In southern districts where resistance was strong, white students, encouraged by parents, refused to attend integrated schools. The Ku Klux Klan reemerged, while other white southerners joined the less militant White Citizens' Councils.

Resistance often received encouragement from those in high offices. Virginia's Governor Thomas Stanley declared, "I shall use every legal means at my command to continue segregated schools in Virginia." Southern state legislatures passed more than 450 laws and resolutions aimed at preventing enforcement of the Brown decision. In 1956 the Virginia state legislature passed a massive resistance measure that cut off state aid to all desegregated schools.

In the same year 100 southern congressmen signed what came to be called the Southern Manifesto praising "the motives of those states which have declared their intention to resist forced integration by any lawful means." One of the three southern congressmen who refused to sign was Lyndon B. Johnson of Texas, future president of the United States.

**Eisenhower and Brown** When elected president in 1952, Dwight Eisenhower carried four of the eleven states of the old Confederacy, only the second time the Republicans had made inroads in the solidly Democratic South since Reconstruction. Out of personal conviction, and out of loyalty to his southern constituents, Eisenhower attempted to be neutral toward desegregation. He neither endorsed nor refuted the Supreme Court decision, saying instead "I don't believe you can change the hearts of men with laws or decisions." Privately, he called his appointment of Earl Warren his biggest mistake.

In 1956 Autherine Lucy was suspended and then expelled from the University of Alabama after whites rioted to prevent her from remaining. Eisenhower said, "I would certainly hope that we could avoid any interference with anybody as long as that state, from its governor down, will do its best to straighten it out." The university continued to exclude African Americans for the next seven years.[2]

## Crisis at Little Rock

Little Rock, Arkansas, seemed an unlikely place for a showdown on school segregation. Just five days after the Brown decision, the Little Rock school board announced its willingness to obey the new law. The school district superintendent worked out a careful plan that consisted in its first stage of placing nine African American students in Central High School, a

**Making Inferences**

The Supreme Court was vague in setting a timetable for the integration of public schools; government officials all over the South declared that they would never yield; and President Eisenhower refused to take a leadership role. Given these facts, we can understand why the road to full integration of public schools was going to be long and hard, full of frustration and struggle.

2 Summarize the initial reaction of the North and the South to the Supreme Court's decision in Brown v. Board of Education.

The Civil Rights Struggle    563

**Opposition by most white citizens of Arkansas was so strong that African American students had to be pro-** **tected by armed soldiers.** *Why do you think the nine African American students themselves became targets of abuse?*

school with approximately 2,000 white students.

Then on September 2, 1957—the night before the first day of school—Arkansas's governor, Orval Faubus, appeared on statewide television. He announced that he had ordered state National Guard soldiers to surround the school the next morning. This move was necessary, he claimed, because of "evidence of disorder and threats of disorder."

The nine new students stayed away from school the next day, as school plans to delay and federal court orders to desegregate followed one another in quick succession. Many saw the issue as a fight between federal and state authority, but President Eisenhower was reluctant to intervene. Finally Governor Faubus met with Eisenhower. Faubus asked for but was denied a one-year delay in implementing desegregation. The meeting ended with the president thinking he had persuaded Faubus to allow integration of the school.

Then, in a surprising show of defiance, Faubus removed the National Guard and left Little Rock. The result was chaos, as an angry crowd of nearly 1,000 white people gathered at the school the next day,

September 4. The "Little Rock Nine," as the students had been dubbed, were forced to leave school at midday under police protection.

President Eisenhower was forced to intervene. Reluctantly he ordered federal troops into Little Rock and nationalized the Arkansas National Guard, this time to protect the students. For the first time since Reconstruction a president had sent federal troops into the South to enforce the Constitution.

On September 25, the day after the president's action, hundreds of paratroopers lined the route to the school. The nine students arrived in a military convoy and were escorted by armed federal soldiers .

The paratroopers were withdrawn at the end of the month, but the federalized National Guard remained for the rest of the school year. The next year, Little Rock public schools closed entirely. White students attended private schools, schools outside the city, or none at all. Most black students had no school to attend. Finally, in August 1959, following another Supreme Court ruling, the Little Rock school board gave in to integration and reopened its public schools.

## SECTION REVIEW

**Checking Facts**

1. Describe some of the social and political conditions in the segregated South and North following World War II.

2. What was the special significance of the Supreme Court's decision in *Plessy v. Ferguson*?

3. What was the special significance of the Supreme Court's decision in the case of *Brown v. Board of Education*?

4. What was President Eisenhower's initial reaction to the *Brown* decision? How was he drawn into the school integration dispute in Little Rock?

**Thinking Critically**

5. **Comparing and Contrasting** How was segregation in the North similar to segregation in the South during the 1950s? How was it different?

6. **Making Inferences** Why does it often take years of struggle before a minority group is able to achieve their civil rights?

**Linking Across Time**

7. What events over the course of the first half of the 1900s may have led the Supreme Court to reconsider the decision in *Plessy v. Ferguson*?

# Presenting Statistical Data

Statistics can help clarify facts and strengthen both spoken and written messages. For example, NAACP lawyers presented statistical evidence in each of the cases they brought against segregated school systems. Very often, however, statistics must be converted from one kind of presentation to another in order to make the intended point most effectively.

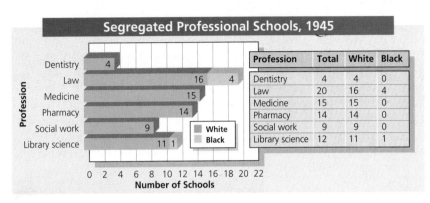

**Segregated Professional Schools, 1945**

| Profession | Total | White | Black |
| --- | --- | --- | --- |
| Dentistry | 4 | 4 | 0 |
| Law | 20 | 16 | 4 |
| Medicine | 15 | 15 | 0 |
| Pharmacy | 14 | 14 | 0 |
| Social work | 9 | 9 | 0 |
| Library science | 12 | 11 | 1 |

## Learning the Skill

Suppose you are comparing schools available to black students seeking to learn a profession with similar opportunities available to white students in the 1940s.

### Presenting the Data

The first step is to locate the necessary statistics. How you present these statistics will depend on the nature of the data, and which aspects of those data you choose to emphasize. The most common ways to present statistics are tables and graphs. Each of these ways serves a different purpose. Tables, such as the one on this page, generally present a lot of statistical information in a concise, easy-to-interpret form.

Bar graphs compare quantities of related categories. The bar graph on this page uses two colors. The different colors on the bars permit easy comparison of the educational opportunities for blacks and whites in each of the professions that were open to both.

Circle graphs also provide comparisons among related categories. The emphasis, however, is not on the individual comparisons, but on each category as a part of the whole.

Line graphs show change over time. While they allow comparisons of quantities at different times, line graphs emphasize direction and extent of change, rather than individual differences.

### Choosing a Focus

Notice the difference in emphasis of Focus statements A and B below.

A. In states requiring segregation, whites could choose from among 4 to 16 schools in each of these professions: medicine, dentistry, pharmacy, law, social work, and library science. African American students had access to only five professional schools—a school of library science and four law schools.

B. In the 17 states that required segregated schools, only 7 percent of all professional schools accepted African Americans.

Statement A contrasts the availability of schools for blacks and whites in certain fields of professional study. Statement B calls attention to the total number of professional schools for African Americans as a proportion of all professional schools in states with segregated schools.

Deciding to focus your message on the effects of segregation in individual professions, you select a bar graph as the most effective way of using statistics to illustrate Statement A. What would be the most effective way to present Statement B?

## Practicing the Skill

1. Use statistics from the table above to create a circle graph illustrating Statement B.
2. Write a statement giving the message of the line graph below.
3. Study the bar graph on page 588. What information does it give you? How does this graph support the Kerner Report's findings?

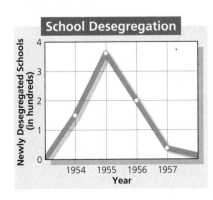

**School Desegregation**

# Freedom Now

## December 1, 1955: Montgomery, Alabama—Bus Boycott Begins

ROSA PARKS WAS TIRED. IT WAS THE CHRISTMAS SHOPPING SEASON, AND THE 43-YEAR-OLD BESPECTACLED WOMAN WORKED HARD AS A TAILOR'S ASSISTANT IN a Montgomery, Alabama, store.

When Parks boarded the Cleveland Avenue bus, she was pleased to find a seat in the middle section. In Montgomery, African American riders could occupy the middle section seats unless the front seats reserved for whites were fully occupied. Then, in order to provide more seats for white riders, African American passengers had to move to seats farther back in the bus or stand.

By the third stop, the seats reserved for whites had filled up, and one white man was left standing. The other black passengers in Parks's row of seats got up and stood in the back of the bus. But she didn't move.

The bus driver, James Blake, called out, "If you don't stand up, I'm going to have to call the police and have you arrested."

"You may do that," Rosa Parks replied.

AP/WIDE WORLD PHOTOS

## The Montgomery Bus Boycott

Rosa Parks's simple decision not to give up her seat set in motion a series of events with far-reaching consequences for all America. Later, many people came to regard her action as the true begin-

ning of the civil rights movement of the 1950s and 1960s. Out of Montgomery emerged the courage, leadership, and strategies for an entire movement.

The news of Parks's arrest soon spread through Montgomery's black community. Protests like Parks's were not new. But hers was the kind of case community leaders had been waiting for. Parks was dignified, soft spoken, well liked. She was a former secretary of the local NAACP chapter and was active in her church. The previous summer she had attended an interracial workshop at the Highlander Folk School, in Tennessee. Now, local civil rights leaders asked if she would be willing to fight her case for as long as it took to win. Despite her mother's and husband's fears, she said yes.

Immediately the call went out for a **boycott** of the Montgomery bus system. By refusing to have anything to do with the bus company, African Americans hoped to exert economic pressure on the company. Jo Ann Robinson, an English professor at Alabama State College, worked through the night writing and mimeographing 35,000 leaflets that instructed, "Don't ride the buses to work, to town, to school, or anywhere on Monday."

Meanwhile, ministers and community leaders met and pledged their support of the one-day boycott. They agreed to a second meeting at Holt Street Baptist Church on Monday evening to decide whether to continue the boycott for more than one day.

Dr. Martin Luther King, Jr., the new minister of

the Dexter Avenue Baptist Church, announced the boycott during his Sunday morning services, asking for the congregation's support. So did other ministers, including the white minister of the Trinity Lutheran Church.

On Monday, nearly empty buses rolled through Montgomery. Although Rosa Parks was found guilty and fined $10 plus $4 in court charges, the boycott was a success. Of the 52,000 passengers who normally rode the bus every day, 40,000 were African American, and they had stayed away in droves. That afternoon the ministers and community leaders met again to organize. They named themselves the Montgomery Improvement Association and selected a president—King.

That evening some 5,000 people packed into the Holt Street Baptist Church. Loudspeakers were hastily set up for the thousands more who gathered outside. King told the crowd:

DAN WEINER, COURTESY SANDRA WEINER

**The ability to communicate was one of Dr. Martin Luther King, Jr.'s greatest strengths.** *Was King's speaking ability important to the acceptance of his philosophies?*

> *T*here comes a time when people get tired. We are here this evening to say to those who have mistreated us so long that we are tired—tired of being segregated and humiliated, tired of being kicked about by the brutal feet of oppression . . .
> If you will protest courageously and yet with dignity and Christian love, in the history books that are written in future generations, historians will have to pause and say 'there lived a great people—a black people—who injected a new meaning and dignity into the veins of civilization.' This is our challenge and our overwhelming responsibility.
>
> Dr. Martin Luther King, Jr., *1955*

The Montgomery bus boycott lasted nearly 400 days. At first the city's 18 African American–owned cab companies filled in, by agreeing to accept black passengers for the bus fare of 10 cents. Then the city threatened to fine the taxi companies for not charging the full 45-cent taxi fare.

Next, boycott leaders worked out an elaborate plan of car pooling. Station wagons picked up riders at 42 separate locations. Funds to buy and operate the station wagons—called "rolling churches" because they were painted with the names of churches—came from white and black supporters of the boycott in Montgomery and throughout the nation. When city officials countered by preventing the "rolling churches" from getting the necessary insurance, King arranged coverage with Lloyd's of London, an insurer known for covering almost any risk.

City officials had not expected such strong resistance from the African American community. As the bus company continued to lose money day after day, the segregationists in power became increasingly frustrated. The mayor, city commissioners, police commissioner, and city council all publicly joined the

**Recognizing Values**

What were the values of the people who started the Montgomery boycott? One way to find out is to examine their speeches and writings. Consider the values that King reveals in his first speech as president of the Montgomery Improvement Association. He admires courage—he himself showed unflinching courage in the face of bombings and arrests. However, for King, courage must always be tempered with charity: "If you will protest courageously and yet with dignity and Christian love . . . historians will . . . say 'there lived a great people.'"

The Civil Rights Struggle     567

DAN WEINER, COURTESY SANDRA WEINER

**Though African Americans enjoyed few rights in the South, their numbers gave them economic power. The Montgomery bus boycott was successful because** of the almost total participation of the African American community. *What sacrifices do you think African Americans had to endure to make the bus boycott a success?*

White Citizens' Council. King's house was bombed. King and 88 other African American leaders were arrested and fined for conspiring to boycott.

The end of the boycott finally came when the U.S. Supreme Court ruled that segregation on Montgomery buses was unconstitutional. This ruling was challenged by the city officials, on the grounds that it violated states' rights. But when the Court's written order was received on December 20, 1956, the segregationists gave up. All riders sat where they pleased on buses that rolled through Montgomery.

> *A* in't gonna ride them buses no more,
>  *Ain't gonna ride no more.*
> *Why don't all the white folk know*
> *That I ain't gonna ride no more.*
>
> —Sung by Montgomery boycotters, *1955–1956*[1]

## *Martin Luther King, Jr.*

After the Montgomery boycott, Dr. Martin Luther King, Jr., had emerged as the unchallenged leader of the African American protest movement. Short in stature and gentle in manner, King was at that time only 27 years old. What had propelled him into this demanding role in history?

The son of a Baptist minister, King and his father were named after Martin Luther, the founder of the Protestant branch of Christianity. The younger King grew up in a comfortable, middle-class home in Atlanta. He attended Morehouse College there, and when he was 18 years old, decided on a career in the ministry. He already showed a gift for the eloquent, emotion-arousing art of popular speaking in southern churches. After a trial sermon in his father's Ebenezer Baptist Church, he was ordained a Baptist minister.

King then went north for more schooling, to Crozer Theological Seminary in Pennsylvania, and then to Boston University for a Ph.D. in religion. By the time he first arrived in Montgomery in September 1954 as pastor of the Dexter Avenue Baptist Church, he had also met and married Coretta Scott.

**Southern Christian Leadership Conference (SCLC)** Following the success of the Montgomery bus boycott, King faced the question of how to extend the lessons learned there to other cities and other civil rights arenas. In January 1957 King called a meeting in Atlanta of 60 southern ministers to discuss nonviolent integration.

The beginning of the conference was marred by the news that the home and church of King's friend and fellow minister Ralph Abernathy had been

STUDY ·GUIDE

**Asssessing Outcomes**

The Montgomery boycott ended in victory for African Americans, but one must take care in assessing the outcome. They won because the Supreme Court declared segregation of public transportation unconstitutional. Many southerners were ready to obey the Court, but they didn't like it. In the future, segregationists would do everything they could to delay changes.

**1** What do you think the African American community of Montgomery—and the nation—discovered about themselves during the course of the bus boycott?

bombed. After a hurried trip back to Montgomery to survey the damage, King returned to Atlanta to assume the presidency of the new organization, the Southern Christian Leadership Conference (SCLC).

**Nonviolence**    From the beginning of the Montgomery boycott, King encouraged his followers to use **nonviolent resistance**. This meant that those who carried out the demonstrations should not fight with authorities, even if provoked to do so.

The SCLC and the Fellowship of Reconciliation (FOR), the latter an interracial organization founded in 1914, conducted workshops in nonviolent methods for civil rights activists. Those attending learned how to sit quietly while others jeered at them, called them names, even spat on them. Workshop participants also learned how to guard themselves against blows and how to protect each other by forming a circle of bodies around someone who was under attack.

King's use of nonviolent tactics has often been compared to those used by Mohandas Gandhi in India's struggle for independence from Great Britain. In both cases, the final victory depended on using moral arguments to change the minds of the oppressors. King linked nonviolence to the Christian theme of "love one's enemy." However, he was certainly familiar with Gandhi's teachings, and in 1959 traveled to India to talk with some of Gandhi's followers.

The Gandhian strategy of nonviolence involved four steps: investigation, negotiation, publicity, and demonstration. Applied to civil rights actions, this meant that the activist ought first to look into a situation and gather the facts. Next, the activist should attempt to negotiate with the person responsible for the segregation. Failing that, others should be made aware of the situation and what the activists intended to do. Only then should the action, such as a march or a demonstration, be carried out.

Soon after the victory in Montgomery, nonviolent methods began to be applied in a startlingly fresh way. Students in universities and colleges all over the country were tired of waiting for change. They vowed to integrate the nation's segregated lunch counters, hotels, and entertainment facilities by a simple new strategy of nonviolent resistence—sitting.[2]

## A Season of Sit-ins

The first sit-in was not elaborately planned. The group of four freshmen from North Carolina Agricultural and Technical College had never attended a workshop on nonviolence. But late one night they began to talk about what they could do to fight segregation. Earlier in the day Joseph McNeil, one of the four, had tried to get something to eat at the local bus station, but had been turned down. He was hurt and resentful.

"We should just sit at the counter and refuse to go until they serve us," one suggested.

"You really mean it?" his friend said.

"Sure I mean it," the first replied.

The next day, February 1, 1960, the four walked into a local store. Nervous, they first tested the waters to see if their business was welcome. One bought a tube of toothpaste, another some school supplies. Then the four sat down at the whites-only lunch counter and asked for coffee and doughnuts.

"I'm sorry but we don't serve colored here," the waitress said.

"I beg your pardon," Franklin McCain said. "You just served me at a counter two feet away. Why is it that you serve me at one counter and [not] at another?"

The four continued to sit at the counter until it closed, about half an hour later. The next day they came back, accompanied by 27 other students. The third day, 63 students sat down at the lunch counter. They were not served, so they just sat. On the fourth day the students were joined by three white students from the Women's College of the University of North Carolina. By Friday, the fifth day, the demonstrators had grown to about 300. They sat in shifts. If some students had to leave to attend class, their place at the lunch counter was taken by other students who stood waiting behind them.

On Saturday evening 1,600 students attended a victory rally, exhilarated by the announcement that the company was ready to negotiate. They soon discovered that the celebration was premature, for the company was willing to make only token changes in its segregation policy.

Two months later students resumed their lunch-counter sit-ins. Adopting a new hard line, the city arrested 45 students and charged them with trespassing. This in turn so enraged the students and their supporters that they launched a massive boycott of stores with segregated lunch counters. As sales dropped by a third, the merchants reluctantly gave in. Six months after the four freshmen first sat down and asked for coffee, they were finally served.

### The Sit-ins Spread

Meanwhile, the spontaneous grass roots movement in Greensboro started a reaction that spread like a brush fire throughout the border states and the upper South. By April 1960, college and high school students in 78 communities had staged sit-ins, and 2,000 protestors had been arrested. A year later, those numbers had nearly doubled. By September 1961, 70,000 black students and white students were sitting-in for social change.

The targets of many sit-ins were southern stores of national chains. However, in some northern cities students picketed stores of the same chains, carrying signs that read "We walk so they may sit."

As more lunch counters integrated under the pressure of sit-ins, variations of the technique emerged. Students held "kneel-ins" to integrate churches, "read-ins" in libraries, "wade-ins" at beaches, and "sleep-ins" in motel lobbies.

### A Student Movement

The driving center of the civil rights movement had spread from the legal committees of the NAACP and African American churches to college campuses. The students were impatient. As schoolchildren in 1954 when the Supreme Court ruled on the *Brown* decision, they had expected immediate results. But progress had been slow. In 1957 African Americans had shared in the excitement of Ghana's independence from Great Britain. During 1960 alone, 11 African countries threw off the shackles of colonialism. "All of Africa will be free before we can get a lousy cup of coffee," writer James Baldwin complained.

The nonviolence of the students provoked increasingly hostile reactions from those who opposed them. In Nashville, after four students had successfully desegregated a bus terminal, they were badly beaten. In other cities, white teenagers poked students in the ribs, ground cigarettes out on their backs, or threw ketchup on them as they ate.

### The Creation of SNCC

Ella J. Baker, executive secretary of King's SCLC, was impressed with the students' commitment and courage, but she was concerned about their lack of coordination and leadership. She invited 100 student leaders of the sit-ins to a conference at Shaw University in Raleigh, North Carolina, over Easter weekend in April 1960. To her surprise, some 300 students showed up, mostly from southern African American communities, but a few also from northern colleges. Out of that meeting came a new civil rights organization, the Student Nonviolent Coordinating Committee (SNCC, pronounced *snick*).

King addressed the students that weekend. He stressed the moral power of nonviolence, saying,

**Nonviolent tactics meant enduring abuse not just from authorities, but also from people who disagreed with the protesters.** *How do you think these people felt when their provocations brought no response from the students at the counter?*

"The tactics of nonviolence without the spirit of nonviolence may become a new kind of violence."

One of the slogans students most warmly applauded at the conference was: "Jail not bail." The decision to refuse bail and to remain in jail came about for practical as well as philosophical reasons. Supporters of the sit-ins throughout the country had been contributing bail money so that students who were arrested could be quickly released on bail. As the number of arrests grew, the bail money became a heavy drain on the treasuries of civil rights organizations. Philosophically, opting for jail placed the burden of supporting the arrested protesters onto the police and local officials. Also, through press coverage, jail service kept the eyes of the nation focused on the protesters and their conflict with the authorities.

In adopting "jail not bail" as a tool, SNCC followed a tradition of **civil disobedience** in U.S. history. Henry David Thoreau, for example, spent a night in jail in 1846 for refusing to pay his poll tax as a protest against slavery and the Mexican War. Thoreau wrote in his essay, "Civil Disobedience":

> *How does it become a man to behave toward this American government today? I answer, that he cannot without disgrace be associated with it. I cannot for an instant recognize that political organization as my government which is the slave's government also.*
>
> Henry David Thoreau,
> *Civil Disobedience*, 1849

Within a year SNCC evolved from an activity that students engaged in between classes to a full-time commitment. The most active students postponed their studies and dropped out of college to work for the movement. In the fall of 1961, SNCC sent 16 "field secretaries" to areas most resistant to integra-tion. By early 1964 that number had grown to 150.

A field secretary could count on only about $10 a week from SNCC, so most roomed and boarded with local African American residents. This arrangement sometimes meant considerable hardship to many southern African Americans who lived constantly on the edge of poverty. SNCC workers and their hosts were also subject to physical harassment, even danger.

More than federal court decisions and more than civil disobedience would be required before the segregation system of 100 years finally broke down. The active committment of the nation's president would be needed as well. The year that the sit-ins erupted and SNCC was formed, John F. Kennedy became the presidential nominee of the Democratic party.

come let us build a new world together
STUDENT NONVIOLENT COORDINATING COMMITTEE 8½ RAYMOND STREET, N.W. ATLANTA 14, GEORGIA

**SNCC was powered by the energy and activism of students and helped bring the goals of the civil rights movement out of the courtroom and into the segregated communities of the South.**

## SECTION REVIEW

### Checking Facts

1. Why is the Montgomery bus boycott of special significance in the struggle for civil rights?
2. What personal qualities helped make King an effective civil rights leader?
3. How did college students first become involved in the sit-ins?
4. What special message did King stress when he addressed SNCC during its first meeting?

### Thinking Critically

5. **Recognizing Values** How did the students who engaged in sit-ins display their own deep commitment to nonviolence?
6. **Assessing Outcomes** How successful were the student sit-ins? Did they have any success in integrating public facilities in the South? Do you think they have had much lasting effect on attitudes in the South?

### Linking Across Time

7. What were the goals of the abolitionists of the 1850s? How were the goals of people such as Dr. Martin Luther King, Jr., and Ralph Abernathy similar to those of the abolitionists? How were they different?

# Government Response

## May 21, 1961: Freedom Riders Mobbed in Montgomery, Alabama

THE PASSENGERS WERE EXPECTING TROUBLE. ON THE WAY TO BIRMINGHAM, ALABAMA, FROM ATLANTA, GEORGIA, ONE OF THEIR BUSES HAD BEEN FIREBOMBED, BURNED TO an iron skeleton. An angry, violent mob had met the second bus as it limped into the Birmingham terminal. After that, the bus drivers, all white, refused to go on. For two days the "Freedom Riders," as bus passengers were called, waited for the bus company to find another driver. Others of their group recuperated in hospital beds. Finally, frustrated, they left the city by plane.

Some thought the Freedom Rides were over then. But a group of students fresh from sit-ins in Nashville, Tennessee, flew to Birmingham intent on continuing the integrated journey. U.S. Attorney General Robert Kennedy asked for, and thought he had received, a pledge from the governor of Alabama to protect the bus and its passengers.

The ride was calm during the first leg of the journey to Montgomery, Alabama. Alabama state patrol cars were seen at intervals. But when the bus pulled into the Montgomery terminal, the bus was quickly surrounded by an angry mob of about 1,000 white people. No police were present.

John Doar, a justice department lawyer on the scene, placed a call to the attorney general's office as the bus rolled into the station. "Now the passengers are coming off," Doar reported. "They're standing on a corner of the platform. Oh, there are fists, punching. A bunch of men led by a guy with a bleeding face

AP/ WIDE WORLD PHOTOS

are beating them," Doar continued. "There are no cops. It's terrible. It's terrible. There's not a cop in sight. People are yelling, 'Get 'em, get 'em.' It's awful."

The mob violence and the city's indifference became front-page news throughout the world. Deeply disturbed and faced with international embarrassment, President Kennedy and his brother Robert sent federal marshals to keep order in Alabama. The segregationists never forgave them for this move.

The next night Robert Kennedy called Governor John Patterson and pleaded with him to reinforce the marshals protecting Dr. Martin Luther King, Jr., and a group of his followers who were trapped inside a church by a crowd of several thousand whites. At the last minute, Patterson did send in Alabama National Guard troops to assist the marshals, but not until after the following exchange:

"You are destroying us politically," Patterson told Kennedy.

Kennedy replied, "It's more important that the people in the church survive physically than for us to survive politically."

## JFK and Civil Rights

John F. Kennedy had not demonstrated a strong commitment to civil rights when he became a candidate for the presidency in 1960. Like many other

### STUDY GUIDE

**As You Read**
Trace the growing involvement of the Kennedy and Johnson administrations in the civil rights struggle between 1961 and 1965. Also, think about the following concepts and skills.

**Central Concepts**
- recognizing the role that **militants** played in the civil rights struggle
- understanding the difficulties involved in the effort to **enfranchise** African Americans

**Thinking Skills**
- analyzing decisions
- predicting consequences
- assessing outcomes
- recognizing points of view

politicians on the state and national scene, his views on civil rights reflected mainly its political importance to him. The question to him was how his stand on the issue would help him defeat his Republican opponent, Richard Nixon.

**On the Campaign Trail**   The dilemma Kennedy faced was this: To win, he needed both segregationists in the South and the black vote in the North. Kennedy relied upon his vice presidential running mate, Texas Senator Lyndon Johnson, to bring the white southern vote. Eisenhower had attracted significant black support in the 1956 election, and Kennedy expected that Nixon would make a bid for that support by endorsing civil rights.

Kennedy decided to make an all-out effort for the African American vote. He endorsed the sit-ins, and promised to sponsor a civil rights bill during the next Congressional session. He also pledged—"with a stroke of the presidential pen," he said—to end racial discrimination in federally supported public housing.

In the closing days of the campaign, King's arrest during a sit-in at an Atlanta department store put both presidential candidates to the test. The other protesters were quickly released, but not King. The judge had ruled that King's sit-in arrest was a violation of his probation, which King had received as a result of an earlier conviction for driving without a valid driver's license. As a result, King was sentenced to four months' hard labor on a Georgia road gang. He was led off in handcuffs and shackles to a rural state prison.

Coretta King and other King supporters feared that King might not come out of that prison alive. There followed a flurry of phone calls to whomever the civil rights leaders thought might be able to help.

Nixon did nothing. John Kennedy, however, telephoned Coretta King and expressed to her his concern, and Robert Kennedy phoned the judge on King's behalf. When King was released a day later, the Kennedys were given much of the credit. "It's time for all of us to take off our Nixon button," Martin Luther King, Sr., exclaimed gratefully.

John Kennedy won the election by the narrowest margin of popular votes in any presidential election in the twentieth century. His ability to carry seven of the eleven states of the old Confederacy and 70 percent

UPI/BETTMANN NEWSPHOTOS

**The Kennedys were politicians who understood the political significance of the civil rights issue.** *Do you believe that political considerations influenced their decisions in a positive or negative way?*

of the black vote were major factors in his political success at that time.

**Kennedy's Civil Rights Strategy**   Despite his campaign promises, Kennedy made no mention of civil rights in his inaugural address. Instead, in his first two years in office he tried to avoid losing either white southern or black support. He failed to back the promised civil rights bill, which would have required southern school districts to submit desegregation plans by 1963. When he finally did issue an executive order on housing discrimination in late 1962, it was so weak that it had little effect.

Rather than by attacking segregation, Kennedy sought to keep black support by promising African Americans jobs and votes. To find more jobs, Kennedy created a presidential committee, headed by Vice President Johnson. The committee was charged with ending job discrimination in federal government departments and businesses that contracted with the federal government. Johnson relied on voluntary efforts rather than strict measures such as canceling

STUDY GUIDE

**Analyzing Decisions**

Both Kennedy and Nixon had a difficult choice to make when King was jailed in Atlanta late in the campaign. Kennedy made the decision to telephone Coretta Scott King and express his concern for the well-being of her husband and appeared to assist in securing King's release. Meanwhile, Nixon did nothing. Exactly how Kennedy's decision to call Mrs. King affected the outcome of the election is impossible to say. What we do know is that Kennedy's aides believed that the decision would help his candidacy.

The Civil Rights Struggle   573

contracts. The result was that during Kennedy's term the committee accomplished little.

Kennedy was not any more successful in helping African Americans obtain voting rights. In 100 counties of the Deep South, only five percent of voting-age African Americans were registered to vote. The civil rights acts passed in 1957 and in 1960 gave the Attorney General power to sue in federal courts on behalf of blacks denied the right to vote because of their race. Accordingly, Robert Kennedy sent a group of lawyers south, to sue when necessary. In three years the Justice Department filed 50 voting-rights cases.

However, the results of this effort at **enfranchisement**, or obtaining the rights of citizenship, for African Americans through the courts was largely unsuccessful. This was so in part because President Kennedy himself had appointed a number of federal judges who were unsympathetic to civil rights.

Although President Kennedy could produce neither the jobs nor the votes he promised, he did appoint a number of African Americans to his administration. He invited prominent African Americans to social events at the White House and made other symbolic gestures that the black community appreciated. At the same time, many politicians appreciated his reluctance to address segregation issues head-on. His efforts to appeal to both sides of the civil rights issue might have continued if **militants**—activists who would not tolerate any compromise—on both sides had not forced his hand.[1]

## Kennedy and the Militants

Civil rights demonstrators demanded "Freedom Now!" and white segregationists countered with the cry "Segregation Forever." If violent whites attacked nonviolent demonstrators, Kennedy would have to make a choice. Either he would have to stay aloof, losing the support of the civil rights movement, or he would have to intervene, alienating segregationists. This presented Kennedy with a difficult political dilemma.

**The Freedom Riders** The first crisis occurred with the arrival on the scene of the Freedom Riders. James Farmer, executive director of the Congress of Racial Equality (CORE), organized these carefully selected groups of interracial bus passengers. In December 1960 the Supreme Court had ruled that all bus stations and terminals serving interstate travelers should be integrated. The purpose of the Freedom Rides was to test that court decision.

On May 4, 1961, the first busload of 13 CORE volunteers rolled out of the Washington, D.C., bus terminal bound for New Orleans. On the bus, whites sat in the back of the bus and African American volunteers in the front. At each stop, black volunteers got off the bus and entered the whites-only waiting rooms to test if facilities were integrated.

The first leg of the journey went well. Violence, however, soon caught up with the Freedom Riders at Anniston, Alabama, where one of the buses was fire-bombed. When Robert Kennedy finally intervened in Montgomery (see page 572), he appealed for the Freedom Riders to wait for the situation to calm down before continuing. But they insisted on moving on to Jackson, Mississippi, and potentially more danger. Each of the 26 blacks and two whites aboard the bus wrote out the names and addresses of persons to be notified in case they were killed. "Everyone on the bus was prepared to die," one Freedom Rider recalled.

Kennedy made a deal with Mississippi senator James O. Eastland. Kennedy would not interfere by sending in federal marshals if Eastland would guarantee there would be no mob violence.

There were no mobs waiting for the Freedom Riders in Jackson. Police, state troopers, and Mississippi National Guard soldiers, however, were everywhere. As the Riders stepped off the bus and tried to enter the whites-only waiting room, each was quickly arrested and taken to jail.

Despite the violence and the jail sentences, more Freedom Riders kept coming all summer. Over 300 were jailed in Jackson alone. Finally, the attorney general petitioned the Interstate Commerce Commission to issue a ruling against segregation of interstate facilities. The ICC made such an announcement on September 22; CORE's victory was secured.

**The Voter Education Project** In an effort to steer the civil rights organizations away from violent confrontations with southern segregationists, Robert

**Predicting Consequences**

Early in his presidency, Kennedy avoided controversial decisions involving civil rights. Black militants were determined to force the issue, however, and it is easy to predict the consequences. Black pressure would meet white resistance, and violence would follow. The situation demanded presidential leadership, and there would be no civil peace until Kennedy took control.

**1** What evidence can you find to support the statement that Kennedy was interested in civil rights primarily in proportion to its political significance?

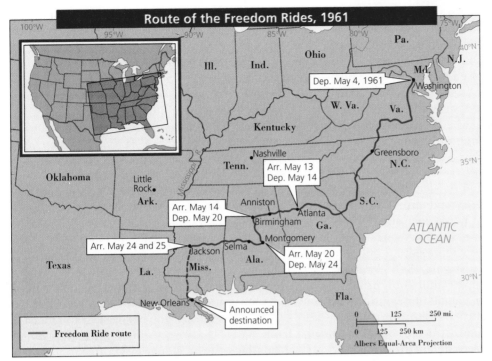

## Route of the Freedom Rides, 1961

Dep. May 4, 1961

Arr. May 13
Dep. May 14

Arr. May 14
Dep. May 20

Arr. May 24 and 25

Arr. May 20
Dep. May 24

Announced destination

Freedom Ride route

**The Freedom Rides helped open the nation's eyes to the violent extremism of parts of the white South.** *What do you think would have happened had the Freedom Rides stopped in the face of the violence they met?*

Kennedy began to stress the importance of black voter registration. He reasoned that if more African Americans voted in elections, they would be able to wield some power on important issues, such as housing and education.

Of course, the idea of encouraging registration of African Americans was not a new idea. Groups such as SNCC had been working to increase black registration for some time. To encourage collaboration on voter registration Kennedy called for a meeting in June 1961 of representatives of SCLC, SNCC, CORE, and NAACP. The result was the Voter Education Project, staffed mainly by SNCC workers. (In Mississippi, voter registration was carried out by an umbrella group called the Council of Federated Organizations, or COFO.)

To increase the number of blacks on voting rolls, SNCC workers held workshops. They explained the sometimes lengthy application forms and they accompanied eligible voters to the registration offices.

Few of the eligible voters were able to get their names on the rolls. They were turned away because the registration dates were changed, or they made spelling mistakes, or they failed outrageously difficult tests on the state constitutions. "Sometimes out of 20 or 25 Negroes who went to register, only one or two would pass the test," SNCC worker Anne Moody recalled. "Some of them were flunked because they used a title (Mr. or Mrs.) on the application blank; others because they didn't."[2]

The presence of so many SNCC workers and their effectiveness in organizing local black communities brought terrorist responses from some white segregationists. In Georgia four black churches that had been used to register African American voters were bombed. Workers were beaten, assaulted, and shot. African Americans who dared to vote were evicted from their land, fired from their jobs, and cut off from their credit.

At the organizational meeting, Robert Kennedy's representatives seemed to have pledged money and protection for the workers. Although some private foundation funds were made available, the Justice Department in fact failed to protect the civil rights volunteers it had encouraged to work in the South. It reasoned that maintaining law and order was the responsibility of local governments. The result was that the militants in the civil rights movement became as alienated from the Kennedy administration as were the white segregationists. On September 30, 1962, President Kennedy had to send the U.S. Army to enforce a court order to enroll James Meredith in the University of Mississippi. It was clear Kennedy was losing control of the segregation issue.

## STUDY GUIDE

### Assessing Outcomes

As an early attempt to enfranchise African Americans, the Voter Education Project was a failure. Volunteers faced intimidation, beatings, and bombings, and few new voters went on the rolls.

Nevertheless, Robert Kennedy had learned an important lesson. He had refused to provide protection for the voting rights workers. He was not going to make the same mistake again.

**2** In one case, the police arrested a group of blacks who arrived at the courthouse steps in a yellow bus, not for trying to register, but because the bus was too yellow!

**Decision at Birmingham** In the spring of 1963, President Kennedy finally chose sides in the segregation struggle. It happened during King's campaign of massive civil disobedience in Birmingham, Alabama.

In 1962 Birmingham closed parks, playgrounds, swimming pools, and golf courses to avoid desegregating them. "We believed that while a campaign in Birmingham would surely be the toughest fight of our civil rights careers," King wrote later, "it could, if successful, break the back of segregation all over the nation."

Civil rights leaders planned the demonstrations to gradually increase in frequency and size. The effect was to keep the attention of newspaper and TV reporters focused on the streets of Birmingham.

The conflict was dramatic. Representing one side was the police commissioner Eugene "Bull" Connor. Thickset and heavily jowled, Connor took pride in the toughness with which he handled integrationists. People around the world watched in horror as he set snarling police dogs on demonstrators, or washed small children across the street under the impact of fire hoses.

Representing the opposition was King, who timed the demonstrations to include his arrest on Good Friday, the Christian holy day marking the death of Jesus. During King's two weeks in jail he wrote the eloquent "Letter from Birmingham Jail." King began the letter on the margins of a full-page newspaper ad that had been taken out by a group of white ministers. The ad called for an end to the demonstrations. King's letter from jail attempts to explain his use of civil disobedience:

*We know through painful experience that freedom is never voluntarily given by the oppressor; it must be demanded by the oppressed. Frankly, I have yet to engage in a direct-action campaign that was "well- timed" in the view of those who have not suffered unduly from the disease of segregation. For years now I have heard the word "Wait!" It rings in the ear of every Negro with piercing familiarity. This "Wait" has almost always meant "Never." We must come to see, with one of our distinguished jurists, that "justice too long delayed is justice denied."*

Dr. Martin Luther King, Jr.,
*Letter from Birmingham Jail*, 1963

After his release from jail, King began a new phase in the demonstrations, using black schoolchildren. To those who protested that the children, who ranged in age from six to 18, were too young, King replied, "Children face the stinging darts of segregation as well as adults."

The first day about 1,000 singing children marched out from the church headquarters and in small groups headed toward the city's downtown. They were quickly arrested. The next day the police cast aside all restraint, and set upon the child marchers with dogs, clubs, and fire hoses. At one point more than 2,000 children and adults were in jail.

The police tactics swung public opinion squarely around in favor of the protesters. Adult demonstrators came out into the streets in record numbers.

**The decision to expose young people to violence and hatred was criticized by many. However, the scenes of powerful jets of water from fire hoses knocking down defenseless people turned the tide of public opinion in the civil rights movement.**

King described the scene on May 27, 1963, when white businessmen were meeting privately to work out a settlement:

> *On that day several thousand Negroes had marched on the town, the jails were so full that police could only arrest a handful. There were Negroes on the sidewalks, in the streets, standing, sitting in the aisles of downtown stores. There were square blocks of Negroes, a veritable sea of black faces. They were committing no violence; they were just present and singing. Downtown Birmingham echoed to the strains of freedom songs.*
>
> Martin Luther King, Jr.,
> *Why We Can't Wait*, 1964

Local business leaders gave in and agreed to desegregate the big department stores; King called off the demonstrations. But shortly after, on May 11, 1963, bombs exploded at King's motel and at his brother's home, and rioting erupted. Alarmed that the black protest might turn violent, President Kennedy decided to cast his lot with Martin Luther King, Jr.[3]

June 11, 1963, was a historic day for the civil rights movement. In the afternoon, President Kennedy federalized the Alabama National Guard to enforce a court order requiring the admission of two African American students to the University of Alabama. That evening, Kennedy appeared on national TV. "We are confronted primarily with a moral issue," he said. "It is as old as the scriptures and is as clear as the American Constitution." He then announced that he would send Congress a civil rights bill, which, it turned out, would deliver crushing blows to segregation.

Later that night in Jackson, Mississippi, a white sniper killed Medgar Evers, head of the state NAACP. By the time President Kennedy himself was assassinated in November 1963, his civil rights bill was moving toward passage in the House.

**The March on Washington**   The massive protest march on the nation's capital on August 28, 1963, began as a cry for jobs. But as planning went on, the goals of the march grew to embrace the entire civil rights movement. A key demand was support for passage of Kennedy's civil rights bill. The march's organizers were a coalition of labor leaders, clergy, white liberals, and grass roots workers.

Trains and buses brought in thousands of demonstrators from all over the country. It was the largest crowd ever to attend a civil rights demonstration up to that time.

There were two highlights, most people agreed, in a day of memorable songs, speeches, and appearances. They were Mahalia Jackson's singing of the spiritual "I Been 'Buked and I Been Scorned," and an emotional speech delivered by King. For further details about the march on Washington see "One Day in History" on pages 580–581.

LEONARD FREED, MAGNUM

**The march on Washington was a high point of the movement up to that time.** *Why do you think organizers chose to go to Washington for the march?*

## The Triumph of Civil Rights

Following President Kennedy's assassination on November 22, 1963, presidential leadership of civil rights efforts fell on Lyndon B. Johnson. Born and raised in the South, Johnson had removed himself from the segregationist ranks in 1956 when he refused to sign the Southern Manifesto. In addition, Johnson had overseen the passage of a limited civil rights act in 1957.

**LBJ Carries On**   Johnson was determined to overcome liberal doubts about his presidency by achieving passage of Kennedy's civil rights bill without compromising any of its most important elements. The bill passed the House in February 1964 but faced an uncertain future in the Senate.

The southerners in the Senate intended to prevent a vote by launching a **filibuster**, that is, they would debate the bill nonstop to keep it from coming to a

UPI/BETTMANN NEWSPHOTOS

**Edmund Pettus Bridge was another place where civil rights activists met violence—and won sympathy for their cause.** *Why do you think the white segregationists failed to recognize how their own violence hurt their cause?*

vote. According to Senate rules, a motion to end debate could carry only if it had the support of two-thirds of those present and voting. With southern Democrats solidly behind the filibuster, 26 of the 33 Republicans in the Senate would have to vote with northern Democrats in order to end it.

The one man who could deliver these votes was the Senate minority leader, Everett McKinley Dirksen. A conservative Republican from Illinois, he was not known as a friend of civil rights. Dirksen ended months of suspense by lining up the Republican votes to end debate and to pass the bill. Dirksen explained his decision with a quote from Victor Hugo: "No army can withstand the strength of an idea whose time has come."

On July 2, 1964, President Johnson signed into law the most comprehensive civil rights legislation enacted up to that time. It met the demands of the civil rights activists in several key ways. For example, the civil rights movement had protested the forced exclusion or separation of black and white in public places. Title II of the 1964 Act forbid segregation in hotels, motels, restaurants, lunch counters, theaters, and sporting arenas that did business in interstate commerce. As a result, most businesses in the South's cities and larger towns desegregated immediately after passage of the Civil Rights Act. The act also relieved individuals of the responsibility for bringing discrimination complaints to court themselves. The act made bringing discrimination cases the job of the federal government.

**Selma** The passage of the Civil Rights Act did not mean that the work of the civil rights movement was over. Legislation still did not exist to enforce the Fifteenth Amendment, which forbids any state from depriving citizens of the right to vote because of race. King decided to force this issue by mounting another campaign of nonviolent resistance, this time in Selma, Alabama. At the start of King's campaign there, only 383 African American citizens were registered out of a possible 15,000.

Selma was an excellent choice for another reason as well. After Birmingham, King had begun to rely increasingly on the power of television and newspapers to reach the conscience of America. Selma had in the person of its sheriff, Jim Clark, a civil rights antagonist that rivaled Birmingham's Bull Connor for ruthlessness.

After two months of beatings, arrests, and one murder, civil rights leaders in Selma announced a climactic protest march from Selma to the state capital in Montgomery, 54 miles away. When Governor George Wallace banned the march, Hosea Williams, who was King's chief aide in Selma, and John Lewis, a SNCC leader, decided to defy Wallace and march anyway.

On March 7, 1965, Williams and Lewis led 600 demonstrators onto the Edmund Pettus Bridge outside Selma on the way to Mongomery. Sheriff Clark's deputies lined both sides of the bridge and 100 state troopers blocked the opposite end.

The leader of the troopers gave the marchers two

---

## STUDY GUIDE

### Recognizing Points of View

The Civil Rights Act of 1964 provided for the complete integration of public facilities. The civil rights movement had won a major victory, but the battle was not over. One last bastion of southern control over African Americans remained—the voting booth. SNCC became the spearhead in the drive for enfranchisement of African Americans. Civil rights activists had won the battle over segregation, and they were confident they could win this one, too. The segregationists were determined to prove them wrong.

minutes to disperse, then set upon them with tear gas and clubs, driving them back to Selma and into the reach of Sheriff Clark's men. (For a description of what it was like to be under attack, see the Evidence of the Past feature on pages 582–583.)

King, who had been out of town for the Sunday march, returned to lead a second one on March 9. When he reached the middle of the bridge, he halted, led the marchers in prayer, and sang "We Shall Overcome." Then, to the astonishment of his followers, he wheeled around and led the marchers back to Selma.

No one knew that King had reluctantly agreed, at the request of the Johnson administration, not to complete the march. King needed the support of the president. In addition, he felt that the first bloody march had accomplished its purpose.

Once again public opinion in the North rallied to King's cause, and once again a president moved to join him. On March 15, 1965, in an emotional televised speech to Congress, Johnson promised to send a bill to Congress that would extend to African Americans in the Deep South the most basic right of citizenship—the right to vote. Finally on March 21, the march from Selma to Montgomery already twice turned back, proceeded peacefully under the protection of the federalized Alabama National Guard.

© EVE ARNOLD, MAGNUM

**Women played a prominent role in SNCC's campaign to register voters in the South.**

**Black Voting Power**

**Black Elected Officials in Mississippi, 1970–1976**

| Year | Number |
| --- | --- |
| 1970 | 81 |
| 1972 | 129 |
| 1974 | 191 |
| 1976 | 210 |

**With expanded black voting rights came success at the polls.** *Predict the consequences of this growing political power.*

**The Voting Rights Act of 1965** At Selma the civil rights movement protested laws designed to prevent African Americans from voting. Of special concern were literacy tests, which were used to deny blacks the right to vote in Alabama, Mississippi, Louisiana, South Carolina, Georgia, Virginia, and 39 counties of North Carolina.

The 1965 Voting Rights Act provided that if literacy or other similar tests were used, and if less than 50 percent of all its voting-age citizens were registered, then racial discrimination could be presumed. In such cases literacy tests were automatically suspended and eligible black citizens could be enrolled whether or not they could read. The act further provided that if local registrars would not enroll African Americans, the president could send federal examiners who would.

As a result of the act, 740,000 African American voters registered to vote in three years. They used their new political power to help win elections for hundreds of African American officials. Blacks also used their power to help defeat Sheriff Jim Clark, who lost his reelection campaign to a racial moderate.

## SECTION REVIEW

**Checking Facts**

1. How did politics help shape President Kennedy's cautious civil rights strategy in the election of 1960?

2. How did militants wreck Kennedy's strategy of appealing to both sides of the civil rights issue?

3. How did President Johnson exert leadership in the civil rights struggle after the death of Kennedy? What were the chief issues addressed by the Civil Rights Act of 1964? Why was the Voting Rights Act of 1965 crucial?

**Thinking Critically**

4. **Analyzing Decisions** Why did King select Selma as the battleground in the struggle for voting rights?

5. **Predicting Consequences** How did the civil rights acts affect the lives of African Americans? How did the Voting Rights Act of 1965 change politics at the state and local level?

**Linking Across Time**

6. With the passage of the 1964 and 1965 civil rights acts, President Johnson felt that African Americans had all the tools they needed to achieve the rights of full citizenship. Was he right?

# Wednesday, August 28, 1963

## *March on Washington*

*WASHINGTON—More than 200,000 Americans, most of them black but many of them white, demonstrated here today for a full and speedy program of civil rights and equal job opportunities. It was the greatest assembly for a redress of grievance that this capital has ever seen.*
—New York Times, 1963

### The Dream Lives On

Civil rights marchers gathered at the Lincoln Memorial to remind Americans that blacks were still looking for freedom a hundred years after the signing of the Emancipation Proclamation. Dr. Martin Luther King, Jr., summed up their hopes for the future in a moving speech: "I have a dream," he cried. "I have a dream that one day this nation will rise up and live out the true meaning of its creed: 'We hold these truths to be self-evident, that all men are created equal.' "

ROBERT KELLY, LIFE MAGAZINE © TIME

the time is NOW
for ALL Americans to join the . . .

**MARCH ON WASHINGTON**
★ FOR JOBS and FREEDOM ★
**WEDNESDAY, AUGUST 28th, 1963**

America faces a crisis . . .
Millions of Negroes are denied freedom . . . .
Millions of citizens, black and white, are unemployed . . . .
The twin evils of discrimination and economic deprivation plague the Nation and rob all people, Negro and White, of dignity and self-respect. As long as black workers are voteless, exploited, ill-housed, denied education and underpaid the fight of the white workers for decent wages and working conditions will fail.

**We Are Marching . . .**
for freedom

• To demand the passage of effective civil rights legislation in the present session which will guarantee to all;
  decent housing
  access to all accommodations
  immediate desegregation of the Nation's schools
  the right to vote
• An end to police brutality directed against citizens using constitutional right of peaceful demonstration.
• To prevent compromise or filibuster against such legislation

**for jobs**
• To demand a Federal massive works and training program that puts all unemployed workers, black and white, back to work
• To demand an FEP Act which bars discrimination by Federal, state and municipal governments, by private employers, by contractors, employment agencies and trade unions
• To demand a national minimum wage of not less than $2.00 per hour which covers all workers

Ride the Chicago **FREEDOM TRAIN**
Special rate $27.00 per passenger — round trip
Leaves Chicago late afternoon Tuesday, August 27th / Arrives back in Chicago
afternoon Thursday, August 29th

For Further Information:
CHICAGO COMMITTEE
**MARCH ON WASHINGTON**
FOR JOBS AND FREEDOM      Phone 624-1810
• Chicago 15, Illinois
4859 South Wabash Avenue      (see other side for reservation form)

ISTORICAL SOCIETY

## *Elsewhere in the News*

### Rocket Engines Pass Test

WHITE SANDS NEW MEXICO— The Apollo rocket engines performed flawlessly as they lifted a Little Joe rocket to an altitude of 24,000 feet. NASA hopes to land a man on the moon before 1970.

## Related Stories

- Marchers Sing and Voice Hope
- Three Rights Buses Are Stoned
- Demonstrator Falls into Reflecting Pool

## Rights Workshop Proposed

A group of New Yorkers suggested turning Ellis Island into "a living workshop to promote the ideas of civil rights and racial equality."

## Industry Backs Trim

PORTLAND, OREGON—The lumber industry proposed trimming the dimensions of the standard 2 by 4 to 3 1/2 by 1 1/2. This would shave about $60 from the cost of the average frame home.

## Yankees Beat Red Sox

NEW YORK—The New York Yankees defeated the Boston Red Sox by a score of 4 to 1. Whitey Ford allowed only five hits as he won his 19th game of the season.

# Memoirs

## Confrontation in Selma

Thousands of people became deeply involved in the civil rights movement, and many of them wrote detailed accounts of the people they met and the events in which they participated. Such accounts are called **memoirs**. Memoirs provide a rich source of information for the historian attempting to reconstruct events of the past.

### The Evidence

On this page and the next are two memoirs that describe the march at Selma, Alabama, on March 7, 1965. (Reread pages 578–579 to refresh your memory of the march.) The first account, published in 1976, is by Governor George Wallace. He describes the confrontation from the point of view of a besieged public official doing everything in his power to prevent a tragedy.

The second account, published in 1980, is by two people who were active participants in the confrontation, Sheyann Webb and Rachel West Nelson. Webb was eight years old in 1965, and Nelson was nine. Webb and Nelson provide a first-hand account of the events from the perspective of the marchers. They were at Edmund Pettus Bridge that day, and they heard the screams, felt the blows, and experienced the terror. As you read these memoirs, think about the different points of view presented in each selection. How do they affect the content of the memoirs?

### The Interpretation

Like any historical source, memoirs must be used carefully. Different people with different concerns remember events differently, and they do not always agree on the significance of the events in which they participated. Historians have to be careful as they thread their way through conflicting evidence. They also have to guard against generalizing too much from just two memoirs. A conscientious historian may consult hundreds of sources in the

---

I would like to tell Alabama's side of the story [of the confrontation at Selma].

We agreed that troopers would be stationed across the highway east of Edmund Pettus Bridge and would halt the march at that point. Under no circumstances were the troops to advance against the marchers. . . . If necessary, the troopers were to fall back and use tear gas to disperse the crowd. I wanted no tragedies, either intentional or accidental, and I gave firm orders to use minimal force.

Tension was high as the demonstrators started toward Pettus Bridge, led by Hosea Williams, from Atlanta, Georgia. The marchers came closer and closer to the troopers, finally stopping perhaps a hundred feet from them.

Major Cloud shouted over his bullhorn, "Turn around and go back to your church. You will not be allowed to march any farther."

The marchers started to move ahead. Cloud told them they were an unlawful assembly. "If you disperse, you will be allowed to return freely to town. You have two minutes."

At the end of the two-minute period, the troopers moved into the waiting demonstrators with their clubs swinging and kept driving into the crowd after the tear gas was fired. As Major Cloud tells the story, he gave no orders to attack, and because of the noise of the melee it was almost impossible to hear commands. When it was over, there were mercifully no serious injuries— and no deaths. But this was not at all the way I had wanted things to turn out. I was saddened and angry.

From *Stand Up for America*, by George C. Wallace

search to discover what really happened in the past.

As you study the memoirs, try to read as a historian would. How are the accounts similar? How are they different? What main concerns did Wallace have on the day of the march? How did he feel about what happened at Edmund Pettus Bridge? What were the main concerns of Webb and Nelson? How did they feel about the events of the day? How do their views on the significance of Selma differ from Wallace's? Think of other sources you could consult in order to learn all the facts about the confrontation. Which sources might provide more reliable information? How might a writer's opinions affect his or her account?

© 1979 VERNON MERRITT, BLACK STAR

**A joyous Sheyann Webb (left) and Rachel West greet Dr. Martin Luther King, Jr., in Selma two weeks after the confrontation at Pettus Bridge.**

## Further Exploration

Find a memoir that recounts the story of another event in the civil rights movement—for example, Rosa Parks telling about the day when she refused to get up to move to the back of the bus, or Dr. Martin Luther King, Jr., writing about the Birmingham demonstrations of 1963. Or find a memoir about a major event in another historical period that interests you.

Read the memoir carefully. What insights does the memoir add to your knowledge of the event? How does the writer's point of view influence the memoir? What other sources could you consult to get another point of view?

---

**S**heyann  I saw those horsemen coming toward me and they had those awful masks on; they rode right through the cloud of tear gas. Some of them had clubs, others had ropes or whips, which they swung about them like they were driving cattle. . . .

I began running and not seeing where I was going. I remember being scared that I might fall over the railing and into the water. . . . I heard more horses and I turned back and saw two of them and the riders were leaning over to one side. It was like a nightmare seeing it through the tears. I just knew then that I was going to die . . .

**Rachel**  Later that evening we went back to the church. What I saw there I will always remember—the faces of the people. They . . . all just sat there staring to the front. I had never seen such looks before. They were hurt, they were angry, they were outraged. . . .

And everything was so quiet. The only sound was the sobbing. We had really been hurt. The movement, I mean. There had never been a time like this. Nobody was praying, nobody was singing. They just sat and stared and cried.

**Sheyann**  But then later in the night, maybe nine-thirty or ten, I don't know for sure, all of a sudden somebody there started humming. I think they were moaning and it just went into the humming of a freedom song. It was real low, but some of us children began humming along, soft and slow.

. . . [P]eople began to pick it up. It started to swell, the humming. Then we began singing the words. We sang, "Ain't gonna let George Wallace turn me 'round. . . . "   And everybody's singing now, and some of them are clapping their hands, and they're still crying, but it's a different kind of crying. It's the kind of crying that's got spirit. . . .

We was singing and telling the world that we hadn't been whipped, that we had won.

*Just all of a sudden something happened that night and we knew in that church that—Lord Almighty— we had really won, after all. We had won!*

From *Selma, Lord, Selma* by Sheyann Webb and Rachel West Nelson, as told to Frank Sikora

# Disappointed Hopes

## June 1966: King and SNCC March Together One Last Time

W HAT BEGAN IN JUNE 1966 AS A SOLO MARCH THROUGH MISSISSIPPI IN DEMONSTRATION OF BLACKS' RIGHT TO VOTE TURNED INTO ONE LAST MARCH in unity. After that the civil rights movement disintegrated into separate factions with radically different goals, ideals, and strategies.

James Meredith, the first African American to attend the University of Mississippi in 1962, undertook the 220-mile walk to demonstrate blacks' right to vote and their right to move without fear through the state. When he fell wounded on the roadside, his back full of buckshot, civil rights workers rushed to Mississippi to complete his march.

During the day they trudged down U.S. Highway 51 arm in arm: Martin Luther King, Jr., of SCLC; Floyd McKissick, of CORE; and Stokely Carmichael, of SNCC. As they stopped to speak in courthouse squares, King and Carmichael preached two separate gospels.

King, despite the increasing numbers of killings and assaults, continued to call on his followers to answer violence with nonviolence. But the SNCC and CORE marchers had given up on nonviolence, and sang a new tune. When King and his supporters began their theme song, "We Shall Overcome," they were often drowned out by the militants' new version, "We Shall Overrun."

The climactic moment came in Greenwood. Carmichael, just released from a few hours in jail for erecting a tent against a state trooper's orders, leaped onto a flatbed truck and raised his hand in a clenched fist salute. "This is the twenty-seventh time I have

UPI/BETTMANN NEWSPHOTOS

been arrested—and I ain't going to jail no more," he shouted. "We been saying freedom for six years and we ain't got nothin'. What we gonna start saying now is Black Power!" King tried to calm the crowd, but his call of "Freedom *Now!*" was drowned out by the new cry of "Black Power." By the time the march reached Jackson, Mississippi, the new call had replaced the old one.

## New Directions in Civil Rights

T he change in direction in SNCC had been in the making for a long time. In the early 1960s the students shared in the ideal of a new, better American society. But after the 1964 and 1965 civil rights acts, when the new laws were not immediately enforced, SNCC volunteers became disillusioned. Indeed, the progress that did occur seemed to come at enormous cost. One **martyr**, or person who dies in the name of an important cause, followed another: the four young girls killed when their church was bombed in Birmingham in 1963; the three civil rights workers shot in Mississippi in 1964; and on and on. As time went on, SNCC leaders began to discuss three key issues: the role that white volunteers should play within the organization; a growing move among some blacks toward black separatism; and the continued use of nonviolence as a strategy for change.

SNCC's efforts to work within the political system also left them disillusioned. In 1964 the Mississippi Freedom Democratic Party (MFDP), a grass roots group supported by SNCC, asked to be recog-

---

### STUDY GUIDE

**As You Read**

Identify the conflicts within the civil rights movement that led to turmoil and disillusionment during the long hot summers of 1965–1967. Also, think about the following concepts and skills.

**Central Concepts**

- understanding the significance of **black pride** and **black power** in the civil rights struggle
- recognizing the divisive effects of black power and **separatism**

**Thinking Skills**

- analyzing behavior
- comparing and contrasting
- identifying cause and effect

nized at the national Democratic party convention as the legitimate Democratic party in the state. They challenged the regular Democratic party principally on the grounds that fewer than five percent of the black population in the state were allowed to vote.

President Johnson, however, was not sympathetic to the MFDP. He did not want the convention distracted from its main job of enthusiastically supporting his policies. Also, he did not want to risk sending white southern Democrats in flight to the Republican party. Johnson assigned Minnesota Senator Hubert Humphrey the job of sidetracking the MFDP challenge, and suggested that the vice presidential nomination Humphrey was hoping for might be at stake.

The compromise Humphrey pushed through gave the MFDP only two of the 40 Mississippi seats. SNCC and MFDP members, who had risked their lives by openly challenging the local regular Democrats, felt they had been let down by the white liberals at the convention. Fannie Lou Hamer of the MFDP summed it up by exclaiming, "We didn't come all this way for no two votes."

**Black Pride** The success of the civil rights movements in the early 1960s gave rise to growing pride in being African American. Ralph Bunche, who gained fame for his skills as a diplomat, wrote in 1961, "I am confident that I reflect accurately the views of virtually all Negro Americans when I say that I am proud of my ancestry, just as I am proud of my nationality." Other black leaders recognized the importance of **black pride,** as well as the harm done by the feelings of inferiority that had long afflicted African Americans. Malcolm X bitterly recalled his youthful efforts at straightening his hair in order to look more like a white person:

> *This was my first big step toward self-degradation: when I endured all of that pain, literally burning my flesh to have it look like a white man's hair. I had joined that multitude of Negro men and women in America who are brainwashed into believing that the black people are "inferior"—and white people "superior."*
>
> Malcolm X
> *Autobiography of Malcolm X, 1965*

AP/WIDE WORLD PHOTOS

**Fannie Lou Hamer, a cotton sharecropper, helped lead the fight for recognition of the MFDP.**

As the 1960s progressed, younger and more race-conscious blacks adopted natural "Afro" haircuts and put on African-inspired *dashikis* in place of shirts and ties. The new pride was reflected also in language, music, life style, and many other aspects of African American culture. Even the words African Americans used to describe themselves changed. The term "Negro," used for years by many prominent leaders, was abandoned because of its evocation of the slave trade. The word "colored" was rejected as not being sufficiently precise. The new preferred term was the simple adjective turned into a noun—black.[1]

Sometimes the powerful desire of African Americans to proclaim their own self-worth was expressed in antiwhite feelings. This was part of the background when some SNCC workers raised in their planning group the troublesome question of the role of white volunteers.

Some within SNCC argued that white college-trained workers thoughtlessly took over the jobs African Americans with little schooling were just learning to do. Moreover, some accused white volunteers of being insensitive to the local conditions under which blacks lived. "Let the whites go fight racism in their own communities," they said. Others pointed out the sacrifices and efforts made by white SNCC

**Analyzing Behavior**
African Americans changed in many fundamental ways during the 1960s—in simple ways like getting Afro haircuts and in more substantive ways like demanding more leadership roles in the civil rights movement. These changes were signs of a reawakening pride in African heritage and a determination to take charge after so many centuries of oppression.

[1] In 1989 Jesse Jackson proposed the term "African American" to replace the term *black.*

workers. Some activists protested that by excluding whites, SNCC itself could be accused of racism. Ultimately, the new view won, and the white workers were asked to give up leadership positions in SNCC.

### Malcolm X and Black Separatism

Emerging African American pride was one factor in the move toward black separatism, which called for a separation of the races in America. According to its promoters, this could best be achieved by African Americans returning to Africa, or by occupying an exclusive area within the United States, on land supplied them by the federal government.

Black **separatism** was the antithesis of the civil rights movement's goal of racial integration. It was a view promoted by, among others, the Nation of Islam, a subgroup of the Islamic religion commonly known as the Black Muslims.

The most vocal Black Muslim was Malcolm X. A brilliant and bold orator, Malcolm X preached a message that included religious justification for black separatism. He was ousted from the Nation of Islam in a fight over leadership, and went on a pilgrimage to the Islamic holy city of Mecca. There he was exposed to more traditional Islamic religious teachings, which do not include racial separatism. On his return to the United States, he softened his views on the separation of blacks and whites. On February 21, 1965, three members of the Nation of Islam assassinated Malcolm X as he spoke in Harlem.

Though Malcolm X's views on separatism gradually softened toward the end of his life, he never supported King's nonviolent methods. Instead, he advocated the use of weapons for self defense, believing that black nonviolence simply emboldened violent white racists. Shortly before his death, Malcolm X pointed out in a speech at Selma, "The white people should thank Dr. King for holding black people in check."

### SNCC's New Leadership

The rhetoric of Malcolm X lived on long after his death, and influenced SNCC and other young militants. The final turnaround in SNCC's orientation came in 1966 with the election of Stokely Carmichael as chairman.

Carmichael was arrested many times during freedom rides, sit-ins, and marches. Jailers were happy to see him go, because he was never reluctant to argue with them over the condition of mattresses and other jail comforts. Once, when six other riders were put in solitary confinement, he banged on his cell door asking for equal treatment, which he finally received.

One of Carmichael's projects during his leadership of SNCC was the formation of a black political party in Lowndes County in Alabama. The party failed to put any of its candidates into office in the 1966 election. However, it was a bold attempt to seize political power, or **black power** as it was called. The symbol used for the Lowndes County Freedom Organization was a black panther about to spring.

## The Long, Hot Summers

Although civil rights activists fought their major campaigns in the South, the pattern of segregation was not confined to states that belonged to the former Confederacy. In fact, it was a growing frustration among African Americans over conditions in the North that led to some of the most dramatic and tragic confrontations of the 1960s.

The migration to northern cities that began in the

**The growing movement for black separatism and militancy, led by people such as Malcolm X (speaking at left), unsettled many white people.** *Why do you think the message of black separatism was troubling to many white people?*

CHICAGO HISTORICAL SOCIETY

WIDE WORLD PHOTOS, INC.

early 1900s had by 1965 resulted in the relocation of some three million southern blacks. More than two-thirds of the total African American population were now urban dwellers. Of these, more than half were concentrated in just 12 cities.

Perhaps more than in the South, life in northern cities bred frustration among many African Americans. Problems of poverty, unemployment, and racial discrimination followed the migrants as they fled the South. The empty promise of racial equality in the North ignited a smoldering fire of rage in many African American communities. Langston Hughes's 1951 poem captures the emotions of many city-dwelling African Americans of the mid-1960s:

*What happens to a*
*dream deferred?*

*Does it dry up*
*like a raisin in the sun?*
*Or fester like a sore—*
*And then run?*
*Does it stink like rotten*
*meat?*
*Or crust and sugar over—*
*like a syrupy sweet?*

*Maybe it just sags*
*like a heavy load.*

*Or does it explode?*

Langston Hughes,
"Harlem," 1951

© DECLAN HAUN, BLACK STAR

**The riots in the Watts section of Los Angeles in 1965 were the first of many riots to erupt in other U.S. cities.**

**Watts, First of a Series**   The arrest for a traffic violation of the young African American in the Los Angeles ghetto should have been routine. Perhaps it was the warm, humid August weather that drew people onto the streets. Or perhaps it was the time, 7:00 P.M., still early enough in the evening to attract a restless crowd.

For whatever reason, that simple arrest in Watts on August 11, 1965, exploded into a major riot that lasted six days. Before it was over, 34 people were dead, 1,072 were injured, and 4,000 arrested. Close to 1,000 buildings were damaged or destroyed, with a property loss that totaled nearly $40 million.

The Watts riot was the first, but not the most destructive, of a series of racial disorders that hit cities throughout the United States in the summers of 1965, 1966, and 1967. Like some kind of seasonal plague, a fever of rage, looting, and arson seemed to erupt in one crowded city after another.

Many of the riots began in similar ways, with an arrest or a police raid that was followed by rumors of resistance and police brutality. The numbers of men, women, and children involved were immense: there were 30,000 rioters in Watts, while another 60,000 milled about in the streets; in the 1967 Detroit, Michigan, riot, 7,000 people were arrested.

Typically, looters headed for white-owned businesses, stripping them clean of merchandise, then setting fire to the buildings. Some stores escaped destruction by putting up signs that read "Negro owned" or "Blood" (meaning African American). Nevertheless, black-owned businesses were often destroyed. As the fires burned, snipers prevented firefighters from doing their work. As a result, whole blocks were left to burn. In Watts in 1965, and again in Detroit in 1967, National Guard troops were sent in to help local police.

While the riots were raging, a new African American political group appeared. In 1966 the Black Panther Party was formed in Oakland, California. Its goals included protecting African American communities from police harassment, and assuming neighborhood control of police, schools, and other services. The Black Panthers differed significantly from other African American groups in that they supported the use of weapons for self defense and retaliation.

**Reasons Why**   During the first nine months of 1967, more than 150 U.S. cities reported incidents of racial disorders. In Newark, New Jersey, and in Detroit, Michigan, the incidents erupted into full-scale riots.

**Comparing and Contrasting**
Stokely Carmichael was typical of the fiery young civil rights veterans who began challenging the leadership of Dr. Martin Luther King, Jr., in the mid-1960s. Throughout his successes and his setbacks, King remained patient and hopeful that the strategy of nonviolent resistance would succeed. Carmichael, in contrast, was less patient. He became convinced that the only way African Americans would attain full civil rights was through violent confrontation. After King's death, leaders like Carmichael failed to inspire large numbers of followers as King had.

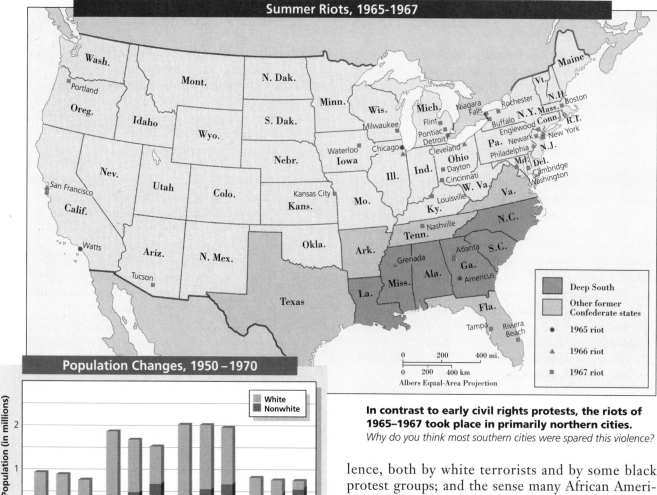

## Summer Riots, 1965-1967

Legend:
- Deep South
- Other former Confederate states
- ● 1965 riot
- ▲ 1966 riot
- ■ 1967 riot

0  200  400 mi.
0  200  400 km
Albers Equal-Area Projection

## Population Changes, 1950–1970

Population (in millions)

Legend: White / Nonwhite

Cleveland 1950 1960 1970
Detroit 1950 1960 1970
Philadelphia 1950 1960 1970
Washington 1950 1960 1970

**In contrast to early civil rights protests, the riots of 1965–1967 took place in primarily northern cities.**
*Why do you think most southern cities were spared this violence?*

To answer the questions of why, and what to do about the riots, President Johnson appointed a National Advisory Commission on Civil Disorders, headed by Governor Otto Kerner of Illinois.

The Kerner Report, as the Commission's findings came to be known, was released in March 1968. As a basic cause of the rioting, the Kerner report pointed to the "racial attitude and behavior of white Americans toward black Americans." This could be visible, the report said, in patterns of racial discrimination and prejudice, in black migration to the cities followed by white flight to the suburbs, and in the existence of black ghettos. The report cited three triggers for the racial violence: frustrated hopes of African Americans; the approval and encouragement of violence, both by white terrorists and by some black protest groups; and the sense many African Americans had of being powerless in a society dominated by whites.

The Kerner Report concluded that "The nation is rapidly moving toward two increasingly separate Americas." To divert that move, the report recommended the elimination of all racial barriers in jobs, education, and housing; greater public response to problems of racial minorities; and increased communication across racial lines.[2]

---

## One More Assassination

The Kerner Report did not end U.S. race riots. One more outburst of rage swept through nearly 130 ghettos following the April 4, 1968, death of Dr. Martin Luther King, Jr., at the hands of a white assassin. The 39-year-old minister was shot while standing on a balcony with friends in Memphis, Tennessee.

### STUDY GUIDE

**Identifying Cause and Effect**

The "long, hot summers" from 1965 to 1967 saw an explosion of violent demonstrations and rioting, with African Americans of all backgrounds joining the protest. The Kerner Commission identified white racism as the chief cause of the unrest. African Americans were frustrated by the slow rate of progress, and saw little hope that the situation would improve.

**2** Name two ways in which the rioting of 1965–1967 differed from the civil rights protests of the late 1950s and early 1960s.

The acceptance of violence as a means of social protest continued to concern King up until his death. Protesters against the war in Vietnam had long been pressing him to come out with an antiwar statement. The issue was not only the war itself but also its financial cost, which was at the expense, many thought, of the war against poverty at home.

King was reluctant to oppose the Johnson government, a stand he knew would be unpopular among many of his supporters. However, the logic of his commitment to nonviolence demanded it. Finally, in 1967 he began to make speeches denouncing the war. He declared that "The promises of the Great Society," the name given Johnson's social program, "have been shot down on the battlefield of Vietnam."

King did lose many supporters because of his antiwar statements. Partly in an effort to rebuild his political strength, he turned toward organizing an interracial coalition of the poor. His final trip to Memphis was to rally support for the mostly black garbage collectors who were attempting to unionize.

The night before his death King spoke at a church rally. He might have had a premonition when he said, "We've got some difficult days ahead. But it doesn't matter with me now. Because I've been to the mountaintop." King went on to say, "I may not get there with you, but I want you to know tonight . . . that we as a people will get to the promised land!"

UPI/BETTMANN NEWSPHOTOS

**As Coretta Scott King mourned the death of her husband, she also mourned the death of a leader that the civil rights movement has not fully replaced.**

## The Movement Appraised

The civil rights movement floundered without strong leadership in the years following King's death. Middle-class Americans, both black and white, tired of the violence and struggle. The war in Vietnam and crime in the streets at home became the new issues at the forefront of the nation's consciousness.

In retrospect, the 14 years between the Supreme Court's momentous *Brown* decision and King's death were years of great progress in civil rights. Not since the passage of the thirteenth, fourteenth, and fifteenth amendments during Reconstruction had so many gains been made. It is for this reason that the years are sometimes called the Second Reconstruction. However, the fear among some civil rights leaders today is that, as in the original Reconstruction, the ensuing years will be marked by a gradual slipping away of hard-won victories. To guard against this, civil rights groups remain vigilant in their quest for progress.

Through the combined efforts of state and federal legislatures, the courts, and the people themselves, some measure of political power was given to African Americans. The next gains to be made would have to come through the political process. Meanwhile, other minorities who also thought of themselves as disenfranchised looked to the civil rights movement of the 1950s and 1960s as a model for their own efforts.

# Chapter 17 Review

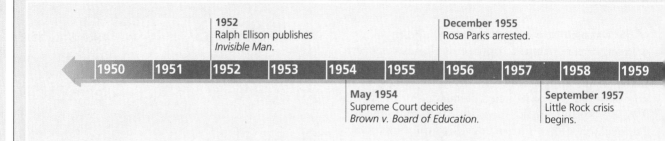

**1952**
Ralph Ellison publishes
*Invisible Man.*

**December 1955**
Rosa Parks arrested.

1950 | 1951 | 1952 | 1953 | 1954 | 1955 | 1956 | 1957 | 1958 | 1959

**May 1954**
Supreme Court decides
*Brown v. Board of Education.*

**September 1957**
Little Rock crisis
begins.

## Summary

Use the following outline as a tool for reviewing and summarizing the chapter. Copy the outline on your own paper, leaving spaces between headings to jot down notes about key events and concepts.

**I. The American Dilemma**
A. The Segregation System
B. Challenges in the Courts
C. Resistance to the Brown Decision
D. Crisis at Little Rock

**II. Freedom Now**
A. The Montgomery Bus Boycott
B. Martin Luther King, Jr.
C. A Season of Sit-ins

**III. Government Response**
A. JFK and Civil Rights
B. Kennedy and the Militants
C. The Triumph of Civil Rights

**IV. Disappointed Hopes**
A. New Directions in Civil Rights
B. The Long, Hot Summers
C. One More Assassination
D. The Movement Appraised

## Ideas, Events, and People

1. What was the most important civil rights issue in the early days of the movement?
2. What were some of the practices used to enforce segregation prior to 1964?
3. What do the acronyms NAACP, SNCC, CORE, and SCLC stand for?
4. What legal doctrine was embodied in the Supreme Court case *Plessy v. Ferguson*? In the case of *Brown v. Board of Education*?
5. Why did the Court argue that separate facilities for whites and blacks were unconstitutional even

when the facilities were physically equal?
6. For what kinds of errors did so-called literacy tests fail blacks at the polls? How were literacy tests used to keep African Americans from power?
7. Briefly explain the significance of each of the following places in the civil rights movement: Little Rock, Montgomery, Selma, Watts, Birmingham, and Washington, D.C.
8. What did Kennedy say about civil rights during his campaign for the presidency? What did he say at his inauguration? Why do you think he changed his mind?
9. Following WW II, the United States enjoyed great prosperity. How did this economic well-being contribute to the civil rights movement?
10. What was the Kerner Report? What did it identify as the causes of urban violence? What recommendations did it make?
11. What does the concept of black pride include? How did black separatism grow out of it?

## Critical Thinking

1. **Making Generalizations**
By 1960, most Americans watched the evening news on television. Why was this custom significant to the modern civil rights movement?

2. **Identifying Cause and Effect**
In the early and mid twentieth century, the cotton industry in the Deep South declined. How did this decline affect the status of African Americans?

3. **Compare and Contrast**
Compare and contrast the methods used by Martin Luther King, Jr., Thurgood Marshall, Stokely Carmichael, and Malcolm X. What were the reasons behind each approach? Which proved most successful?

**February 1960**
Sit-ins begin in North Carolina.

**August 1965**
Rioting begins in Watts.

**April 1968**
Dr. Martin Luther King, Jr., assassinated.

| 1960 | 1961 | 1962 | 1963 | 1964 | 1965 | 1966 | 1967 | 1968 | 1969 |

**May 1961**
Freedom Rides begin.

**July 1964**
Civil Rights Act passed.

**1966**
Black Panthers formed.

## Social Studies Skills

### Presenting Statistical Data

Study the bar graph, Black Voting Power, on page 579. What information does it give you? Use the graph to write a brief statement about the trend in the number of black elected officials.

## Extension and Application

### 1. Community Connection

Interview people in your community who were involved in the civil rights movement. Include law enforcement officials and news people as well as activists. Put together a tape of their reminiscences to play for the class.

### 2. Linking Across Time

The chapter quotes works of Ralph Ellison and Langston Hughes. List some speeches, documents, poems, and novels related to civil rights struggles. Include works from 1800 to the present.

Deep South

Other former Confederate states

● 1965 riot

▲ 1966 riot

■ 1967 riot

Choose a work that you feel is noteworthy and write a brief paragraph describing its significance.

### 3. Linking Across Time

Choose a subject for time comparison, such as the number of African American and Hispanic American officials elected to local, state, and federal offices in 1960 and in 1990. Make a bar graph reflecting these figures.

### 4. Cooperative Learning

In *Brown v. Board of Education*, the Supreme Court handed down a unanimous decision. But in recent civil rights cases the court has been divided five to four. Working with a small group, consult newspapers and periodicals to identify some of these cases. List the arguments on both sides and organize a debate on one of these issues.

### 5. Global Connections

The American civil rights movement added momentum to human rights movements around the world. (a) Trace the movement for human rights in Argentina, China, or South Africa since 1960. (b) Report on the history, founders, goals, and achievements of an international civil rights group.

## Geography

1. According to pages 560–561, how were patterns of racial segregation different in the North and South?

2. In what two regions shown on the map (left) did most of the riots take place between 1966 and 1967? What might have been the reasons for this?

3. Which cities on the map had more than one riot? What might these cities have had in common?

4. Look at the chart on page 588. Which city experienced the greatest change in the proportion of white and nonwhite population between 1950 and 1970? Why did a similar change occur in all of the cities on the chart?

CHAPTER 18

# High Tide of Reform

## November 23, 1963:  A Peruvian Village Mourns Kennedy's Death

Saturday morning was a time for sleeping late in the sleepy little mountain village in Peru where Peace Corps volunteer Nancy Norton worked. But the knock at her door about 7:30 one morning would not stop. Norton came to the door. As she recalled later, in a letter to her parents:

"It was Vilma, a Peruvian friend. 'Tu Presidente esta muerto!' she said. I rubbed my eyes, trying to understand. 'Whose President?' I asked. 'Señor Kennedy,' she answered. . . .

"The paper said the whole world is in mourning. I don't know about the whole world, only about Huarocondo. Huarocondo is mourning. Every-

> *"Were I not here, I would never have believed that the world really cared."*

one knows the president of the United States. They would be stricken if we weren't here. But they know we are here because of John Kennedy. They know we are sad because he is dead. They love us, so they are sad, too. Were I not here, I would never have believed that the world really cared."

Kennedy established the Peace Corps in his first few months in office to help newly developing areas in the third world. The Peace Corps, with its focus on helping others, symbolized the best in John F. Kennedy's "New Frontier." It also represented a new era of social responsibility that was not to be stopped by an assassin's bullet.

COURTESY HOWARD ELLEGANT

*A Peace Corps volunteer speaks to local people about the construction of a new community school.*

*Seated outside of his old school, President Lyndon Johnson hands the pen to Mrs. Chester Loney, his first grade school teacher, after signing an education bill in 1965.*

# New Frontier and Great Society

## January 20, 1961: John F. Kennedy Sworn in as President

THEY STOOD TOGETHER ON THE INAUGURAL PLATFORM: THE 43-YEAR-OLD JOHN F. KENNEDY, TANNED, VIGOROUS, AND COATLESS DESPITE THE subfreezing weather; and 70-year-old Dwight D. Eisenhower, wearing a muffler, looking like a tired general. The appearances of the two men—the youngest and the oldest elected president—symbolized the change of leadership. Kennedy, many voters believed, would get America moving again.

Behind him on the platform were the other members of his glamorous family: his beautiful wife, Jackie; his younger brother, Robert, soon to be attorney general of the United States; and his parents, Rose and Joseph P. Kennedy, founders of a political dynasty. As Kennedy began his inaugural address, his hands chopped at the air in the style familiar to those who had seen his campaign appearances on TV. His speech promised so much:

*L*et *the word go forth . . . that the torch has been passed to a new generation of Americans—born in this century, tempered by war, disciplined by a hard and bitter peace. . . .*
*Let every nation know, whether it wishes us well or ill, that we shall pay any price, bear*

PAUL SCHUTZER, LIFE MAGAZINE © TIME WARNER, INC.

*any burden, meet any hardship, support any friend, oppose any foe to assure the survival and the success of liberty. . . . All this will not be finished in the first 100 days. Nor will it be finished in the first 1,000 days. . . . But let us begin. . . . And so, my fellow Americans—ask not what your country can do for you—ask what you can do for your country.*

John F. Kennedy,
*Inaugural Address,* 1961

The promise John Fitzgerald Kennedy gave the United States was never realized. JFK had scarcely more than 1,000 days himself—1,036 to be exact—before he was cut down by an assassin's bullet.

But looking back at his brief presidency, from the buoyant wintry inaugural in January 1961 to the funeral procession through the grief-soaked streets of Washington, D.C., in 1963, what survives is a strong impression of the Kennedy spirit. It was a force that propelled the nation into a new political era.

## The Kennedy Years

In the eyes of most historians, the scattered accomplishments of Kennedy's abruptly ended term hardly amounted to a finished political record.

**As You Read**
Identify the major social reforms of the Kennedy and Johnson administrations. Also, think about the following concepts and skills.

**Central Concepts**
- recognizing the significance of electoral **mandates** to Presidents Kennedy and Johnson
- understanding the importance of political **coalitions** to Johnson

**Thinking Skills**
- comparing and contrasting
- drawing conclusions
- recognizing values
- analyzing decisions

Compared to the hard-driving presidencies of FDR and Lyndon Johnson, whose first years were packed with new initiatives, Kennedy's young administration moved slowly. He came into office with the narrowest margin of victory of any modern president, not enough to claim a **mandate,** or clear endorsement of his ideas, from the American public. In Congress, Kennedy faced a powerful conservative coalition. So he pursued his course with more caution than boldness.

He grew into the job. His days were long, hard, and fast-paced. As his term progressed, his initiatives became bolder, and his handling of Congress became more aggressive and assured.

**The New Frontier**  Kennedy may not be remembered as a president who accomplished a great deal in terms of domestic legislation. He may stand, however, as one who effected a great change of thinking among the American people. His idealism rang out in this speech:

> *We stand today on the edge of a new frontier—the frontier of the 1960s, a frontier of unknown opportunities and paths, a frontier of unfulfilled hopes and threats. . . . The new frontier of which I speak is not a set of promises—it is a set of challenges.*
>
> John F. Kennedy,
> Presidential nomination acceptance speech, 1960

"The New Frontier" became the label for Kennedy's vision of progress at home. It was not an organized set of legislative initiatives for economic change, like Roosevelt's New Deal or Johnson's "Great Society" that was to come. In fact, Kennedy was often in a position of reacting to events—such as civil rights disturbances and the Cuban missile crisis—instead of blazing new trails. The New Frontier, then, was more a personal vision of Kennedy's, a progressive ideology but by no means a radical one.

As Kennedy began the campaign that ushered him into office, many liberals had become complacent. Although in 1960 the economy was sluggish, the country still enjoyed the prosperity that followed on the heels of World War II. Issues that had consumed the liberals of the New Deal era—the overhaul of large corporations, and economic inequalities—no longer seemed so critical. As economist John Kenneth Galbraith, in a 1958 study of the United States, summarized, "[Capitalism] works, and in the years since World War II, quite brilliantly."

Liberals in the 1960s reasoned that if the country maintained its current progress, those at the bottom of the economic heap would in time better themselves. According to this view, two major issues still to be resolved in the 1960s were civil rights and civil liberties. Other problems, such as slums, inadequate education, and poverty, could be solved by fine tuning.

**The Kennedy Aura**  Jack Kennedy cultivated a stylish, charismatic image that moved people to very strong views of him, both positive and negative. "Since the thirty-fifth president and his wife are about the most physically attractive people to have lived in the White House, the urge of the publicists, magazines, networks, and photographers to fuse two American dreams and reveal the White House as the ultimate movie set is irresistible," Alistair Cooke wrote in 1963. "To put it mildly, the president has yielded to this urge and has manipulated it."

Many considered JFK a hero. Others distrusted him. Their reasons ranged from dislike of his wealthy father and the threat of a family dynasty to anti-Catholic and anti-eastern biases. "All that Mozart string music and ballet dancing down there, and all

★ ★ ★  **PRESIDENT'S GALLERY**  ★ ★ ★

*"Now the trumpet summons us again—not as a call to bear arms, though arms we need—not as a call to battle, though embattled we are—but a call to bear the burden of a long twilight struggle . . . against the common enemies of man: tyranny, poverty, disease, and war itself."*

*Inaugural Address, January 20, 1961*

UPI / BETTMAN NEWSPHOTOS

John Fitzgerald Kennedy 1961–1963

**Background:**
- Born 1917; died 1963
- Democrat, Massachusetts
- Served in the navy 1941–1945
- Elected to the House of Representatives 1946
- Elected to the Senate 1952
- Assassinated in Dallas, Texas, November 1963

**Achievements in Office:**
- U.S. Peace Corps (1961)
- Trade Expansion Act (1962)
- Nuclear Test Ban Treaty (1963)

that fox hunting and London clothes," one congressman said. "He's too elegant for me."

**Kennedy's Working Style**   The team that Kennedy gathered around him in his administration were, as one journalist noted, "the best and the brightest" of the president's generation. Most were educated at top eastern schools, and many were recruited from the executive rooms of big business.

Kennedy and his team were content, on the domestic front, to nudge along economic growth and to strengthen public programs. This is what he meant by "getting the country moving again" and restoring U.S. prestige abroad. The president's interests were centered on foreign policy—the cold war and containing communism.

In August 1961 Communists built a wall between East Berlin and West Berlin to prevent East Germans from fleeing to the West. Kennedy reaffirmed his support for West Berliners in a speech delivered near the Berlin Wall in 1963. He said, "All free men, wherever they may live, are citizens of Berlin, and, therefore, as a free man, I take pride in the words, 'Ich bin ein Berliner.'"

Kennedy considered himself more a **pragmatist,** someone interested in practical solutions to problems, than a liberal. Most of America's problems "are *technical* problems, are administrative problems," he explained. "They [involve] sophisticated judgments which do not lend themselves to the great sort of 'passionate movements' which have stirred this country so often in the past."

**The Space Race**   During the early 1960s, a nation's accomplishments in space became a test of leadership in technology and defense. The Soviet Union gained an edge in the so-called space race when cosmonaut Yuri Gagarin orbited the earth in April 1961. The following month, in a message to Congress, President Kennedy asked for a commitment to the goal of "landing a man on the moon and returning him safely to earth" before the end of the decade.

The challenge caught the imagination of the public and ensured the dedication of American astronauts. The space agency, NASA, developed a three-stage program to put Americans in space. The first stage, Project Mercury, consisted of a series of test flights between 1961 and 1963. John H. Glenn, Jr., became the first American to orbit the earth during a Mercury flight in February 1962. During 1965 and 1966 Project Gemini launched a second series of flights in which two-man teams practiced maneuvering and docking spacecraft while orbiting the earth. The Apollo program, which would accomplish the moon-landing goal established by Kennedy, began in 1968.

**Programs at Home and Abroad**   Kennedy's efforts to perk up the economy were among his successes. Increased spending for defense and for the space program poured billions of dollars into government contracts that would increase employment. The Area Redevelopment Act channeled federal funds into needy regions. Congress raised the minimum wage from $1 to $1.25 an hour. These measures contributed to a general economic upswing that lasted until the early 1970s.

During his administration Kennedy initiated several programs for international development. The Alliance for Progress was a series of aid projects undertaken cooperatively with Latin American countries that agreed to democratic reform. The Peace Corps sent volunteers to developing countries, where they lived among the local people and assisted in education and rural development projects. Among the

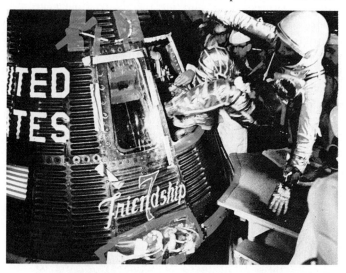

NASA

**In the *Friendship* spacecraft, John Glenn became the first American to orbit the earth.**

**The film frame at left shows First Lady Jacqueline Kennedy with her wounded husband. Later that day Lyndon Johnson took the oath of office aboard Air Force One. At right, Kennedy's funeral procession passes mourners in Washington.**

most popular of the Kennedy programs, the Peace Corps continues today. In its first 20 years, the Peace Corps sent more than 80,000 Americans to 88 countries.

Kennedy's efforts to pass an education aid bill showed the obstacles he faced. The coalition of Republicans and southern Democrats feared that increased federal support for education might mean less state control. The issue of aid to parochial schools was a further complication. Kennedy felt that supporting such aid would open him to the accusation that as a Catholic he favored parochial schools. As negotiations wore on, both Protestants and Catholics became displeased with him. Kennedy was unable to push the education bill through Congress, something that Lyndon Johnson, a Protestant, later managed to do. **1**

## *Hopes Cut Off*

Many people expected more than they were getting from Kennedy on issues such as civil rights. "I was furious with the administration's civil rights posture," recalled Roger Wilkins, a lawyer with the Agency for International Development. "I thought it was slow, lethargic, and unresponsive."

But Arthur Schlesinger, Jr., who served as special assistant to Kennedy, notes that the president "was soon educated by events. . . ." Later in his term, Kennedy seemed to be seizing control of events. He called for a thawing of the cold war with the Soviet Union. Two months later the two nations signed a treaty limiting nuclear testing. As one of his last efforts, Kennedy requested his economic advisers to prepare a plan directed at poverty in the United States. He also promised action on civil rights.

Kennedy's hope was to achieve a greater mandate for his programs in the 1964 elections. With this in mind, in late November 1963 he took a trip to Dallas, Texas, to smooth over party differences and gather electoral support.

**Tragedy in Dallas** CBS television anchorman Walter Cronkite cried as he gave the nation the news: President Kennedy had been fatally shot in Dallas while riding in a motorcade. For four days Americans throughout the nation sat hunched in front of their television sets, as images of violence and of mourning were etched forever into their minds. They pored over newspaper accounts of the grisly shooting, trying to understand why or how the tragedy could have happened.

They saw the pictures of Kennedy waving to cheering crowds as his open limousine wove through the streets of Dallas shortly before noon on November 22. As the motorcade approached an expressway,

**Comparing and Contrasting**
Kennedy and the liberals shared many of the same values and worked for many of the same economic goals, but Kennedy preferred to think of himself as a pragmatist, not a liberal. What was the distinction? Liberals believe in government spending for new programs as an economic stimulant. Pragmatists believe in making spending decisions on a case-by-case basis.

**1** How did the lack of an election mandate affect Kennedy's ability to govern?

shots rang out and Kennedy slumped forward in his seat. Jackie Kennedy cradled her dying husband's head in her lap as the limousine raced to nearby Parkland Hospital. Kennedy was pronounced dead at 1:00 P.M. Vice President Lyndon Johnson was sworn in almost immediately as president.

Police determined that the shots had been fired from a warehouse that overlooked the route of the motorcade. They arrested Lee Harvey Oswald, a 24-year-old warehouse worker, and charged him with the murder. Two days later Oswald was transferred from the city jail to the county jail. TV cameras covered the event live. As viewers across the country watched in disbelief, a Dallas nightclub owner, Jack Ruby, pushed through a circle of police officers and journalists and shot and killed Oswald at point-blank range.

Investigations of the murder were hampered by the death of Oswald. But the Warren Commission, headed by Chief Justice Earl Warren, concluded in 1964 that Oswald had acted alone and not in a conspiracy of any kind. Critics of the Warren Commission maintain that the investigations were hastily concluded and that Oswald most likely was aided by some group whose identity is as yet unknown.

**The Nation Mourns**   The answer to the question, "Where were you when Kennedy was shot?" became frozen in people's memories. "I was in social studies class at Woodlands High School," said Bonnie Steinboch of White Plains, New York. "In the corridor, I saw Mr. Courtney, the art teacher, sobbing against the wall, and I was astonished that a grown-up, a teacher, would be so openly upset. Kennedy was the most important person in my life to die. . . . Months after he died, I realized one night in bed that I would never hear his voice again, and I sobbed for a long time."

Americans cried as they saw three-year-old John F. Kennedy, Jr., salute his father's funeral procession, and they stared at the riderless horse in the procession, symbolizing the fallen hero. The nation grieved as much for the president that John F. Kennedy might have become had he lived, as for the leader he had been. Commentator Richard Neustadt wrote, "He left a broken promise, that 'the torch has been passed to a new generation,' and the youngsters who identified with him felt cheated as the promise, like the glamour, disappeared."

His widow compared the Kennedy years in the White House to Camelot, the site of King Arthur's legendary court, about which a popular musical was written in the 1960s. The romantic hero and heroine, the battle between good and evil, a time of great happiness forever lost—all these images were more commonly applied to ballads and to myths than to political figures.[2]

## Johnson's Great Society

Johnson's administration began in the tragedy of Kennedy's assassination and ended in the tragedy of the disastrous war in Vietnam. In between he carried forward Kennedy's dream of a New Frontier, then went beyond Kennedy's own domestic programs to launch his own vision of the "Great Society."

In the days following Kennedy's assassination, Johnson took several steps to reassure the world that he would carry on in the same tradition as Kennedy. In his first speech following his succession to office, he said, "All I have, I would have given gladly not to be standing here today," and asked for the nation's prayers and support. Looking back on those days, Johnson told his biographer, Doris Kearns:

> We were all spinning around and around, trying to come to grips with what had happened, but the more we tried to understand it, the more confused we got. We were like a bunch of cattle caught in the swamp, unable to move in either direction, simply circling 'round and 'round. I understood that; I knew what had to be done. There is but one way to get the cattle out of the swamp. And that is for the man on the horse to take the lead, to assume command, to provide direction. In the period of confusion after the assassination, I was that man.
>
> Doris Kearns, *Lyndon Johnson and the American Dream*, 1976

The differences between the two men, Kennedy and Johnson, were striking. Whereas Kennedy was handsome, sophisticated, and well-educated, Johnson could be crude and intimidating; politeness and polish

**Drawing Conclusions**
The unfulfilled Kennedy agenda included a civil rights bill banning discrimination against blacks and a plan to attack poverty in the United States. Major legislation on these issues did not come until Johnson took over. To deny Kennedy a share of the credit, however, would be the same as not attributing the 13th Amendment to Lincoln because it was ratified after his death.

**2** What role did the news media play in binding the nation together after the tragedy in Dallas?

were not among his attributes. But he was, as he said, the man for the job. He had been an apt student of politics. A congressman in 1937 at age 29, he advanced to the Senate in 1949 and rose quickly to the powerful position of Senate majority leader in 1955.

Johnson was a genius at building **coalitions**, that is, at bringing people of different opinions together for temporary action. "Let us reason together," he would say, with a touch of understatement. He then used what those who received it called "the Treatment."

Johnson's method was to find out everything he could about the person he was talking to—family, friends, strengths, weaknesses, special interests. Then Johnson would proceed to flatter, cajole, promise, threaten, all the while suggesting that the other person's decision was going to make the difference between success or failure. "Lyndon got me by the lapels and put his face on top of mine and he talked and talked," a colleague said. "I figured [the choice] was getting drowned or joining."

**Fashioning a Legacy** As president, Lyndon Johnson had boundless confidence in himself, and he knew what he wanted to do. He promised to realize the Kennedy vision, and he did—perhaps better than Kennedy ever could have.

In 1963 Kennedy's program for social change was only an emerging vision. His liberalism was cautious and uncertain. Johnson had no such uncertainties. He was a man determined to do great things, and now he had the power to change the country. But what needed changing?

The answer depended on where you looked. In the suburban shopping malls that were springing up around the country, the United States looked robust. Measured in auto sales and economic indicators, the

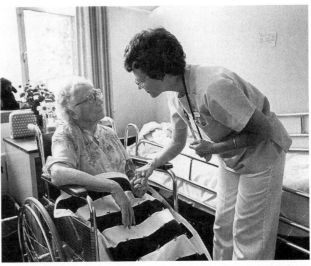

© CATHY CHENEY, STOCK BOSTON

**One of the key accomplishments of Johnson's Great Society program was the creation of Medicare, which, for the first time in U.S. history, guaranteed medical care for the nation's elderly.** *Why do you think there was opposition to such a program that helped so many people?*

country hummed with prosperity. This was the nation TV viewers watched on "I Love Lucy" and other situation comedies, where everyday problems were solvable within a 22-minute show.

There was, of course, another America, as Michael Harrington revealed in his book, *The Other America*. (See Chapter 15.) He described a country within a country, where people were hungry when they went to bed, if in fact they had a bed. Chronic joblessness, unbudged by the New Deal or the postwar economic boom, set like cement in rural towns and big-city slums.

During the 1960s a vision of this other America slowly revealed itself to public consciousness.

---

★ ★ ★ **PRESIDENT'S GALLERY** ★ ★ ★

*"Let us now join reason to faith and action to experience, to transform our unity of interest into a unity of purpose. For the hour and the day and the time are here to achieve progress without strife, to achieve change without hatred— not without difference of opinion, but without the deep and abiding divisions which scar the union for generations."*

*Inaugural Address, January 20, 1965*

THE LYNDON BAINES JOHNSON LIBRARY, AUSTIN

Lyndon Baines Johnson 1963–1969

**Background:**
- Born 1908; died 1973
- Democrat, Texas
- Served in the House of Representatives 1937–1948
- Served in the Senate 1949–1960
- Assumed the presidency 1963; elected to full term 1964

**Achievements in Office:**
- Civil Rights Act (1964)
- Voting Rights Act (1965)
- Medicare (1965)

Strangely enough, it was Lyndon Johnson, the wheeling-dealing politician and friend of the rich, who understood the problem.

Johnson's homespun tales of his rag-poor past may have stretched the truth a bit; but he certainly knew hard times as a child growing up in central Texas. Later, as a teacher of the rural poor in his home state, he felt a great empathy for people living in grinding, persistent poverty.

LBJ cared about the poor, and he cared about his place in history. He felt he could become the first president to create a just society that all but eliminated chronic poverty and hardship in the United States.

Johnson told Congress on March 16, 1964, that "in the past we have often been called upon to wage war against foreign enemies which threaten our freedom today. Now, we are asked to declare a war on a domestic enemy which threatens the strength of our nation and the welfare of our people."[3]

That enemy, of course, was poverty. LBJ's ambitious war on poverty would be the cornerstone of his "Great Society."

**The Great Society**   Johnson moved quickly to push Kennedy initiatives, including the Civil Rights Act, through Congress. He launched his war on poverty with the Economic Opportunity Act, the most ambitious attempt to aid the poor in the nation's history. It established Volunteers in Service for America (VISTA), a kind of domestic peace corps of citizens working in poor neighborhoods. The act also funded Head Start to give preschoolers from disadvantaged families a leg up on elementary education.

The mood of the country, still affected by the shock of Kennedy's assassination, worked in Johnson's favor during the 1964 presidential election. Johnson overwhelmingly defeated Arizona Senator Barry Goldwater and seized the mandate to introduce his own program of reform called the Great Society.

## Major Great Society Programs, 1964–1966

| 1964 | 1965 | 1966 |
| --- | --- | --- |
| **Civil Rights Act** Banned discrimination in public accommodations, in federally assisted programs, and in employment; gave federal government new power to enforce desegregation and prosecute voting rights violations | **Elementary and Secondary Education Act** First major federal aid package for education in U.S. history | **Traffic and Motor Vehicle Safety Act** Set standards for auto and tire manufacturing |
| **Economic Opportunity Act** Launched the 'war on poverty,' creating nationwide federal programs such as Head Start, the Job Corps, and VISTA, within the Office of Economic Opportunity | **Medical Care Act** Federally funded health care for the elderly (Medicare) and for welfare recipients (Medicaid) | **Minimum wage law** Raised the rate from $1.25 to $1.40 an hour |
| **Wilderness Preservation Act** Protected 9.1 million acres of national forest land from commercial development | **Voting Rights Act** Ended literacy tests for voting; allowed federal agents to monitor registration | **Truth in Packaging Act** Established standards for accurate labeling of foods, drugs, cosmetics, and household items |
| | **Omnibus Housing Act** Provided funds to build and subsidize low-income housing | **Model Cities Act** Funded the clearing of slums and building of new housing projects, recreational facilities and mass transit |
| | **National endowments for the arts and for the humanities** Provided aid to individual artists and arts organizations | |
| | **Water Quality Act** Required states to clean up interstate waters within their boundaries | |
| | **Immigration Act** Ended discriminatory ethnic quotas | |
| | **Higher Education Act** Provided student scholarships and loans | |

## STUDY GUIDE

**Recognizing Values**

A president reveals his values in the kinds of programs he tries to push through Congress. Think about the major legislative initiatives of the Johnson years—better education for the young, housing for the poor, medical care for the elderly, voting rights for all. Johnson believed government had an obligation to ensure that all citizens had a chance to live free from poverty.

**3** How did the reality of the nation's economic health in the 1960s differ from earlier common perceptions about it?

*T*he Great Society rests on abundance and liberty for all. It demands an end to poverty and racial injustice . . . [It] is a place where every child can find knowledge to enrich his mind . . . where the city of man serves not only the needs of the body and the demands for commerce, but the desire for beauty and the hunger for community.

Lyndon B. Johnson, *University of Michigan commencement address,* 1964

The president knew that what he called the "honeymoon" of his election would not last for long. "You've got to give it all you can that first year," he said. The result was the most comprehensive reform package to pass through Congress since the New Deal reforms of 1935.

Among the most significant pieces of legislation were Medicare, federally funded health care for the elderly, and Medicaid, its companion program for the needy too young to qualify for Medicare. These programs were the first to make health care available to those who could not afford it. The Voting Rights Act of 1965 put teeth into the Fifteenth Amendment by providing for federal supervision of voter registration. Cities benefited from the Model Cities Act, which encouraged slum rehabilitation. A new department of Housing and Urban Development was created; its secretary, Robert Weaver, became the first African American to serve in a presidential Cabinet.

The immigration act did away with a quota system that had existed for more than 50 years. (For a look at how that affected the nation's ethnic makeup, see pages 608–609.) The chart on the facing page describes other Great Society programs.

**Successes and Limitations** Johnson's Great Society program of social and political reform is often compared to FDR's New Deal. The goals of the two were somewhat different. The New Deal sought

COURTESY BENNY ANDREWS

**In 1965 the government set up a funding program for artists and arts organizations. This 1969 painting uses strong images to comment on African Americans' fight for civil rights in the United States.** *What do you think the symbols represent?*

social reforms in some areas—the creation of the social security system is an example. Its main goals, however, were to provide relief for the unemployed and the poor and to stimulate economic recovery.

The Great Society program achieved greater success in creating legislative programs than in implementing them. It was underfunded, partly because the financing of the Vietnam War claimed a greater and greater proportion of the tax dollar. Still, the percentage of impoverished Americans, as measured by government standards, dropped from 22 percent in 1959 to 12 percent in 1969. The civil rights acts of 1964 and 1965 were landmark achievements of the Johnson presidency. Perhaps the greatest weakness in the Great Society program was that it promised so much that despite its successes, critics could point to problems yet unresolved.

## SECTION REVIEW

### Checking Facts

1. How was Kennedy's pragmatism reflected in his approach to legislative reforms?
2. How did the Peace Corps symbolize the best in Kennedy's New Frontier program?
3. What reforms was Kennedy beginning to take action on when he was assassinated?
4. What were Johnson's major legislative reforms?

### Thinking Critically

5. **Drawing Conclusions** What was the connection between the civil rights movement of the 1950s and the push for reform during the 1960s?
6. **Comparing and Contrasting** How were Kennedy and Johnson alike in their legislative goals? How did they differ in the way they worked with Congress?
7. **Drawing Conclusions** How did

problems associated with the Vietnam War limit the success of some of the programs of the Great Society?

### Linking Across Time

8. How do the legislative achievements of the Great Society compare with the achievements of the New Deal? Which, do you think, will have a more lasting impact on American society?

# Recognizing Stereotypes

**B**oth knowledge and cultural tolerance are needed in order to recognize and overcome stereotypes—as Peace Corps volunteers to the Philippines discovered. A stereotype is an oversimplified idea about a group of people or a culture. Often, stereotyping occurs when people from one culture make generalizations based on an incomplete understanding of another culture.

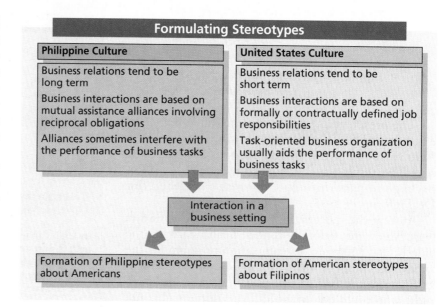

**Formulating Stereotypes**

| Philippine Culture | United States Culture |
| --- | --- |
| Business relations tend to be long term | Business relations tend to be short term |
| Business interactions are based on mutual assistance alliances involving reciprocal obligations | Business interactions are based on formally or contractually defined job responsibilities |
| Alliances sometimes interfere with the performance of business tasks | Task-oriented business organization usually aids the performance of business tasks |

Interaction in a business setting

Formation of Philippine stereotypes about Americans

Formation of American stereotypes about Filipinos

## Learning the Skill

The first Peace Corps volunteers arrived in the Philippines in the fall of 1961. Most were frustrated when they confronted the differences between their culture and the culture of the Philippines. Different value systems led to many misunderstandings.

David L. Szanton, a former Peace Corps volunteer, explains these misunderstandings in the book *Cultural Frontiers of the Peace Corps*. He tells of many cases in which Peace Corps volunteers discussed with local officials the need for additional classrooms, health clinics, or reading rooms. Invariably, the volunteers went away feeling that a commitment had been made and that their recommendations would be acted upon. Usually, nothing happened. When the volunteers raised the issues again, the Filipinos often blamed their lack of progress on unforeseen circumstances. The volunteers concluded that the Filipinos had broken their promises and were dishonest and unreliable.

The volunteers were stereotyping the Filipinos because the volunteers did not understand Filipino culture. In fact, the Filipinos did not favor the volunteers' recommendations. The Filipinos were trying to maintain harmony by avoiding a face-to-face disagreement.

Filipinos and Americans handle conflict differently because of a difference in value systems. Szanton says Philippine culture values "smooth interpersonal relations." Filipinos usually handle disagreements by "ignoring them, by pretending they do not exist, or by designating intermediaries to conduct negotiations between the parties involved." Coming from a culture that values open discussion, the American volunteers tended to handle conflict directly.

Thus, in the Philippines, many situations arose in which Filipinos stereotyped Americans as rude, and Americans stereotyped Filipinos as dishonest. Yet as the volunteers and the Filipinos gained more insight into each other's cultures, they were able to overcome stereotypes and recognize the validity of a culture different from their own.

## Practicing the Skill

1. The chart on this page shows cultural differences in how Filipinos and Americans tend to act and interact in a business setting. Assume that Filipinos and Americans wanted to work together on a business venture. Based on the differences the chart describes, what stereotypes might Filipinos have about Americans? What stereotypes might Americans have about Filipinos? How might these stereotypes be overcome?

2. Think back on what you have learned about American history. What stereotypes have some Americans had about people of other races or nationalities? Choose two or three important examples and write a paragraph about each one. Be sure to tell why these attitudes are stereotypes.

# The Supreme Court and Civil Liberties

## January 8, 1962:  Gideon Petitions the Supreme Court

CLARENCE EARL GIDEON WAS A MAN BEATEN DOWN BY LIFE'S CIRCUMSTANCES AND BY HIS OWN FOOLISH MISTAKES. IN 1962 HE WAS AN INMATE OF THE FLORIDA STATE Prison, serving time for breaking into a poolroom and stealing money. He was a frail man, 51 years old, though he looked 10 years older. His face was gray and wrinkled and his lower lip continually trembled.

Prison life wasn't new to Gideon. He had served four previous jail terms. Poverty was also no stranger, since he had been a runaway at age 14. But now he wanted out. He worried about his family; his wife had started drinking and his children were in foster homes. He insisted he was convicted in an unfair trial for a crime he did not commit.

So Gideon wrote the Supreme Court a letter. In pencil, on lined prison paper, he petitioned the court to release him on the grounds that the state had denied him his rights. At the time of his trial, with no money for a lawyer, he had asked the lower court to provide him with one, but the court had refused. Gideon had conducted his own defense.

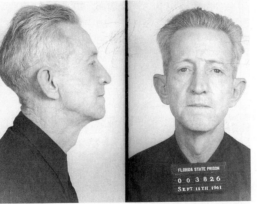

DEPARTMENT OF CORRECTIONS OF THE STATE OF FLORIDA

Fourteen months after Gideon mailed off his plea to the Supreme Court, his conviction was overturned. The *Gideon v. Wainwright* ruling reversed an earlier decision and declared that, according to the Sixth Amendment, if a defendant cannot afford a lawyer, the court must supply one. The appeal to the Supreme Court by Gideon, a poor man with few resources, made legal history.

## The Court's Authority

The Supreme Court, the branch of government that Alexander Hamilton called "the weakest of the three departments of power," has become mighty throughout its history. In its earliest days, the high court simply ruled on whether laws had been broken. In 1803 the court expanded its powers by taking on the role of judging the validity, or constitutionality, of laws. That step sent shock waves through the young government. Presidents from Jefferson to Lincoln bridled at the expansion of judicial power that followed. But there was much more to come.

A further question remained, and it was one that would touch the lives of politicians, families, minorities, and children in modern times: Should the court have a hand in making the country a better, safer, fairer place? That is, when legislatures are failing to bring about reform in social, economic, and political systems, should the court step in? At issue was whether court rulings should merely take into account precedents and laws, or consider the needs of the country.

Dwight Eisenhower didn't realize it, but when he appointed Earl Warren as chief justice of the Supreme Court, he was answering these questions for some time to come. No court in U.S. history went further in making reform its business than the Warren Court of the 1950s and 1960s.

---

## STUDY GUIDE

**As You Read**

Analyze the major decisions of the Warren Court dealing with voting, school prayer, and the exercise of criminal justice. Also, think about the following concepts and skills.

**Central Concepts**
- understanding the role of **due process** in protecting civil liberties
- recognizing the relationship between political power and **reapportionment**

**Thinking Skills**
- identifying cause and effect
- comparing and contrasting

# The Warren Court

When Earl Warren came to Washington, D.C., in 1953, most Americans saw their country as a place of prosperity, liberty, and justice. The Warren Court, however, saw a place where equal justice under the law was elusive if you happened to be black, poor, an accused criminal, an immigrant, or a city dweller. When Warren finished his historic 16-year term as chief justice in 1969, the court had taken direct, far-reaching action to correct what it saw as the nation's social ills. In doing so, the reform-minded court wielded more power and made a bigger impact on the country than had many presidents.

President Eisenhower appointed Warren to head the nation's highest court, following Warren's years as a crime-fighting district attorney and then as governor of California. Despite his conservative image, Warren's beliefs grew more liberal over the years. The chief justice's written opinions were sometimes a reversal of positions he had taken as governor.

The Warren Court era of liberal activism was launched with the 1954 *Brown v. Board of Education* decision on school desegregation. Critics from Joseph McCarthy to more moderate thinkers said the court was stepping far beyond its limits—infringing on the rights of state and local governments, intruding on family life, and threatening the moral fabric of the United States.

Calls for the chief justice's impeachment were heard periodically throughout his tenure. "Impeach Earl Warren" billboards and pamphlets appeared throughout the South, and even at Earl Warren High School in Downey, California. The movement, to which Warren gave little heed, heated up when the court entered its most active period of reform, in the early 1960s.

In 1962 changes in the makeup of the Supreme Court gave Warren a clear majority of judges who were likely to side with him on most issues. In the 1960s the court handed down a series of historic decisions affecting the nation's political process, the civil liberties of individuals, and the operation of the criminal justice system. The chart below highlights some of those decisions.

**One Person, One Vote** Warren called *Baker v. Carr* "the most important case of my tenure on the Court." He was referring to one of a series of cases from 1962 to 1964 that redistributed political power in the United States.

The old methods by which states carved up voting districts were devised when this was a nation of country dwellers. But when twentieth-century industrialization drew more and more people to cities, the size and shape of districts did not change to reflect the shifts in population.

For example, the six million people living in Los Angeles County in 1960 were represented by one state legislator, whose vote carried the same weight as the legislator from a rural district of 14,000 people.

## Warren Court Decisions on Key Issues of the 1960s

### Reapportionment

**Gomillion v. Lightfoot, 1960**
Outlawed racial gerrymandering in case involving the city limits of Tuskegee, Alabama

**Baker v. Carr, 1962**
Established federal authority to oversee that state voting districts ensure equal representation for all citizens; the ruling opened the door to Supreme Court involvement in what previously had been seen as a 'political' issue outside the court's jurisdiction

**Wesberry v. Sanders, 1964**
Required that states redraw their voting districts for the U.S. Congress according to population; each district had to have roughly the same number of people, so every citizen's vote carried the same weight, according to the 'one person, one vote' principle

**Reynolds v. Sims, 1964**
Applied the 'one person, one vote' standard to their state legislatures, requiring state elective districts to be reapportioned; the ruling also demanded the apportionment by population of both houses of a bicameral state legislature

### School Prayer

**Engel v. Vitale, 1962**
Ruled unconstitutional a nondenominational prayer drafted by the State of New York and read voluntarily in school classrooms; the decision banned prayer in public schools

**Abington v. Schempp, 1963**
Banned Bible reading and other religious exercises in public schools, saying this constituted the government establishment of religion

### Rights of the Accused

**Gideon v. Wainwright, 1963**
Established that people accused of a crime have the right to a lawyer, even if they cannot afford one

**Escobedo v. Illinois, 1964**
Ruled that one has the right to a lawyer from the time of arrest or when one becomes the subject of a criminal investigation

**Miranda v. Arizona, 1966**
Required that accused people be informed of their right to a lawyer and their right not to testify against themselves

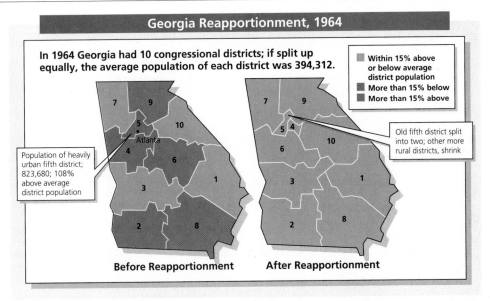

## Georgia Reapportionment, 1964

In 1964 Georgia had 10 congressional districts; if split up equally, the average population of each district was 394,312.

Within 15% above or below average district population
More than 15% below
More than 15% above

Population of heavily urban fifth district; 823,680; 108% above average district population

Old fifth district split into two; other more rural districts, shrink

**Before Reapportionment**

**After Reapportionment**

**Before reapportionment, Atlanta's fifth district, which included the large city of Atlanta, had the same number of state legislators as some rural districts with far fewer people.** *Why was this unfair? According to this chart, what was done to solve the problem?*

This, in effect, made the vote of each citizen in Los Angeles County worth less. A **reapportionment** proposal—that is, a plan changing the number of legislative seats assigned to each district—was opposed by farm groups and others who wished to preserve their voting power. The plan was defeated with the help of California's then-governor, Earl Warren.

But in 1962 Chief Justice Earl Warren had a new constituency—the nation. In many places, legislative districts were drawn in ways that favored a particular political party, a practice known as **gerrymandering**. Throughout the nation, there was a need for a redrawing of political districts according to a "one person, one vote" principle of equal representation.[1]

In Florida, for example, one-fifth of the population lived in Dade County, where Miami is located. But Dade County residents elected only four of Florida's 133 state legislators. Traditionally, the Supreme Court had left such political matters as apportionment up to the state legislatures. But some citizens, frustrated when the legislatures did not take action, brought suits against state officials. In time, these suits came before the Supreme Court on appeal.

In the *Baker v. Carr* suit, the residents of Memphis, Tennessee, complained that their votes were worth less than the vote of a rural resident. The

Supreme Court ruled that the federal courts, which had originally declined to hear the case, should decide it. The court's 1962 decision opened the door for the courts to involve themselves with the question of reapportionment. "Never in American history has a single judicial decision opened the gates for such a massive change in the nation's political structure," wrote the Washington Post.

Subsequent cases went further in forcing states to reorganize their voting systems. In 1964 the court demanded that states redraw their voting districts—for representation to state legislatures as well as to Congress—to make them roughly equal in population. The Court also directed that in state legislatures with two houses, both should be apportioned according to population. In a majority opinion, Warren wrote:

> *Legislators represent people, not trees or acres. Legislators are elected by voters, not farms or cities or economic interests. As long as ours is a representative form of government, and our legislatures are those instruments of government elected directly by and directly representative of the people, the right to elect legislators in a free and unimpaired fashion is a bedrock of our political system.*
>
> *Reynolds v. Sims, 1964*

The 1964 reapportionment rulings and the cases grouped with them affected one-third of the nation's states. In time all 50 states reshaped their legislatures.

**Prayer in Schools** People knew Earl Warren to be a deeply religious man who read the Bible regularly. Justice Hugo Black had been a Sunday School teacher for 20 years. Yet in 1962 these two justices led the

### Identifying Cause and Effect

During the first half of the century, legislatures in state after state blocked election reforms designed to bring voting patterns in line with population distribution. The result was widespread political inequality. With no other recourse, voters appealed to the Supreme Court, and the Court responded with the "one person, one vote" decision.

**1** What does the phrase "one person, one vote" mean?

Court in banning prayer in public schools, a decision that was shocking to many Americans.

At issue in *Engel v. Vitale* was a 22-word nondenominational prayer drafted by the State of New York and recommended to be recited daily by public school children. The prayer read: "Almighty God, we acknowledge our dependence upon Thee, and we beg Thy blessings upon us, our parents, our teachers, and our country."

Parents of 10 students in Hyde Park, New York, objected to the voluntary readings. The court agreed with them, saying that even voluntary prayer subjected religious minorities or nonbelievers to "indirect coercive pressure." Citing the First Amendment provision that "Congress shall make no law respecting an establishment of religion," Justice Black wrote in the majority opinion that this "must at least mean that in this country it is no part of the business of government to compose official prayers for any group of the American people to recite as a part of a religious program carried on by government."

In later decisions, the court also prohibited Bible reading and other religious exercises in the classroom. Some parents and clergy were disturbed by the rulings. Others, including some teachers, atheists, and religious people, were relieved. Legislators tried, and failed, to pass a constitutional amendment permitting school prayer.

**The Rights of the Accused** When police arrested Ernesto Miranda at his home on a charge of kidnaping and rape, he had no idea that his name would become a shorthand term for the rights of accused criminals, and that his case would be a required course of study for every police recruit and law student. But in *Miranda* and other key cases, the Warren Court handed down decisions that revolutionized

UPI/BETTMANN

Before *Engel v. Vitale*, **many public school students, like these in South Carolina, started their day by praying.** *Why do you think the ruling was so controversial?*

how criminal justice is exercised in this country.

Warren, a former prosecutor, personally showed a great deal of concern for the rights of accused criminals and the conduct of police during arrests and interrogation of suspects. The court's rulings reinforced the right of accused citizens to **due process**, or the established legal rules and procedures.

The last major criminal justice ruling had come in 1936, when police were barred from torturing suspects in order to obtain confessions from them. The new wave of reform rulings began in 1963 when Clarence Earl Gideon won his appeal to the Supreme Court. The ruling upheld the right of an accused to have an attorney, even when the accused could not afford one. The decision resulted in a new trial for Gideon, in which he was represented by a local attorney and was acquitted.

In the 1964 case of *Escobedo v. Illinois*, the court ruled that the right to legal counsel begins at the moment of arrest or as soon as someone becomes the subject of police suspicion. But Warren felt that the court needed to take stronger action to protect accused criminals. This led to one of most controversial rulings in the Supreme Court's history.

The case was *Miranda v. Arizona*,[2] which came

STUDY GUIDE

**Comparing and Contrasting**
*Gideon*, *Escobedo*, and *Miranda* all involve the right to legal counsel, but there are subtle differences. *Gideon* asserts that everyone has a right to counsel during a trial, even the poor.

*Escobedo* states that the right to counsel begins when a person first comes under suspicion. *Miranda* requires police to tell suspects about their right to counsel from the moment of arrest.

**2** Why was *Miranda v. Arizona* the most controversial of the three Supreme Court decisions dealing with criminal justice?

before the court in 1966. Police had arrested Ernesto Miranda for kidnaping and rape. After the police interrogated him for two hours, Miranda signed a confession. In a divided 5–4 ruling, the Court set aside his conviction.

Chief Justice Warren gave specific instructions that would sound familiar to anyone who has watched police shows on television: "Prior to any questioning, the person must be warned that he has a right to remain silent, that any statement he does make may be used as evidence against him, and that he has a right to the presence of an attorney, either retained or appointed."

The "Miranda card," used by police departments today, lists instructions to read to suspects at the time of their arrest. Arresting officers must prove that a defendant has waived the right to legal counsel.

Police departments were disturbed by the Miranda ruling, saying it restricted them in performing their duties. Richard Nixon used the ruling to boost the "crime in the streets" issue during the 1968 presidential race. On the other hand, a supporter of the ruling quoted Winston Churchill: "The quality of a nation's civilization can be largely measured by the methods it uses in the enforcement of its criminal law."

**Chicago Patrolmen's Association**

RA-6-4045

**REQUIRED WARNINGS**
1. "YOU HAVE A RIGHT TO REMAIN SILENT."
2. "IF YOU CHOOSE NOT TO REMAIN SILENT ANYTHING YOU SAY OR WRITE CAN AND WILL BE USED AS EVIDENCE AGAINST YOU IN COURT."
3. "YOU HAVE A RIGHT TO CONSULT A LAWYER BEFORE ANY QUESTIONING AND YOU HAVE A RIGHT TO HAVE THE LAWYER PRESENT WITH YOU DURING ANY QUESTIONING."
4. "YOU NOT ONLY HAVE A RIGHT TO CONSULT WITH A LAWYER BEFORE ANY QUESTIONING BUT, IF YOU LACK THE FINANCIAL ABILITY TO RETAIN A LAWYER, A LAWYER WILL BE APPOINTED TO REPRESENT YOU BEFORE ANY QUESTIONING, AND YOU MAY HAVE THE APPOINTED LAWYER PRESENT WITH YOU DURING ANY QUESTIONING."

An Association Made of Policemen . . .
By Policemen . . . For Policemen

AMERICAN POLICE CENTER AND MUSEUM

**The police officer at right uses the so-called Miranda card, above, to read a suspect's rights to him at the time of arrest.**

© BOB DAEMMRICH, STOCK BOSTON

## The Reform Achievements

The Supreme Court, Congress, and the president did not always speak with one voice on the subject of social reform. Controversies marked the reform period from 1954 to 1969. Decisions made during this time are still being argued about and fought in the courts. Congress today faces tough decisions about how to pay for aid programs launched with such promise 30 years ago.

Nevertheless, the efforts of the three branches of government combined to bring about the greatest package of reform measures since FDR's New Deal. One measure of the change is to recall how, in 1948, civil rights proposals by President Truman splintered the Democratic party. Some 20 years later a Democratic president, Lyndon Johnson, worked with Congress in providing for minorities, the poor, and the elderly. The Supreme Court upheld much of this legislation, and extended individual liberties.

But some groups still remained in the shadows of reform. One group was women, who were not a minority in terms of their numbers, but who frequently played a secondary role to men. Women watched with interest the changes of the Kennedy-Johnson era and planned their own strategies for reform, which would extend into the next decade.

---

### SECTION REVIEW

**Checking Facts**

1. Why did the Supreme Court order states to reapportion their voting districts on the basis of the "one person, one vote" principle?

2. Why did the Supreme Court rule that prayer in the public schools was unconstitutional?

3. What were the main Supreme Court decisions protecting the rights of the accused?

**Thinking Critically**

4. **Comparing and Contrasting** What are two historical views of the responsibilities of the Supreme Court toward social, economic, and political reform?

5. **Identifying Cause and Effect** Why did Chief Justice Warren consider the reapportionment decisions the most significant actions taken by his court?

6. **Making Inferences** In what ways have the Warren Court's decisions on school prayer and the rights of the accused remained controversial to this day?

**Linking Across Time**

7. The 1950s and 1960s saw advances in the rights of blacks and criminal suspects, and equal political representation. Which minority groups are pressing for full civil rights today?

# Effects of Immigration

From its beginnings the United States has been a microcosm of the world's cultures, a country that shares in the cultures of many lands yet remains uniquely itself. In U.S. streets today one can see people from every geographical region in the world—from the forests of Scandinavia to the deltas of Southeast Asia, from the deserts of the Middle East to the valleys of China, from the plains of central Europe to the mountains of South America. This diversity is a result of the immigrants who have made the United States their home.

© OWEN FRANKEN, STOCK BOSTON

## Early Immigration

The first great wave of immigrants to arrive in the United States after the American Revolution included 4 million Irish, 6 million Germans, and 2 million Scandinavians—all from western Europe—and 400,000 Chinese from Asia. A second group of immigrants arrived between 1880 and 1920; they included 5 million Italians and Greeks from southern Europe and 8 million Poles, Hungarians, and Russians from eastern Europe.

During the 1920s the pace of immigration slowed considerably. At that time, Americans of northern European descent controlled the political and economic power centers in Congress and throughout the nation. Many feared that immigrants, by accepting lower pay for jobs, would take work away from U.S. citizens. Some

also feared that unregulated immigration of people with different cultural backgrounds would change the fundamental character of American society. Accordingly, Congress passed a series of laws establishing quotas that sharply limited immigration from southern and eastern Europe. This effectively shut the door to mass immigration for 50 years.

> The Immigration Act of 1965 helped produce a dramatic movement of Asian and Hispanic immigrants into the United States. The culture these immigrants have brought with them will change the face of America.

## Changes in 1965

Governments play a major role in the movement of people around the world. Some governments create political refugees

through war and conquest or through social and economic oppression at home. Others try to regulate the movement of people from country to country by passing immigration laws.

The United States has always been a haven for immigrants seeking political freedom and economic opportunity. The quota system sharply restricted entry into the United States. Determined to remedy this injustice, President Johnson helped steer the Immigration Act of 1965 through Congress. The Act encouraged the admission of immigrants from countries all over the world on a first-come, first-served basis. The only exception was that immigrants with relatives already living in the United States had precedence over other immigrants. Artists, scientists, and political refugees were given preference under the 1965 law.

The act more than doubled the number of immigrants admitted to the United States each year. The majority of the most recent immigrants come from the many countries of Asia and Latin America.

## Time of Transition

The United States in the next century will be very different as a result of the Immigration Act of 1965. The new wave of immigrants that is now entering the country is introducing new customs and beliefs, new languages, and new ideas to the rich mosaic that already exists in the United

States.

To the tradition of European and African folk tales that enchant each generation the new immigrants have added tales from China, Southeast Asia, Haiti, and the many countries of Latin America. Immigrants from China and Japan are contributing new talent to the great symphony orchestras of the United States, which earlier immigrants tied to the European musical tradition. Reggae from the Caribbean islands and the Latin American beat now mix with jazz and rock.

To the great variety of ethnic foods that already delight U.S. diners have been added foods such as Korean kim chee, Jamaican pasties, Brazilian rice and black beans, Vietnamese lemon chicken, pad thai from Thailand, and Colombian empanadas. The presence of Filipinos, Vietnamese, Haitians, and Hispanics from all over Latin America is evident in news stories on television and radio and in the many new foreign language newspapers.

From the earliest days of the republic, immigrants have provided new energy and talent. The most recent group of immigrants, like their predecessors, is also contributing to the vitality of American life.

---

### THINK ABOUT IT

1. Many Hispanic American immigrants move directly into Spanish-speaking communities in cities such as Miami, San Antonio, and Los Angeles. They have the richness of bilingualism, knowing two languages —Spanish for home and community life and English for their jobs. What are the advantages of this situation for the immigrants? What are the drawbacks?

2. Look in your local newspaper or listen to local newscasts for evidence of the latest immigrants in your town, city, or state. What contributions have these immigrants made? What problems have they faced? Are these problems similar to those faced by earlier immigrants? Why or why not?

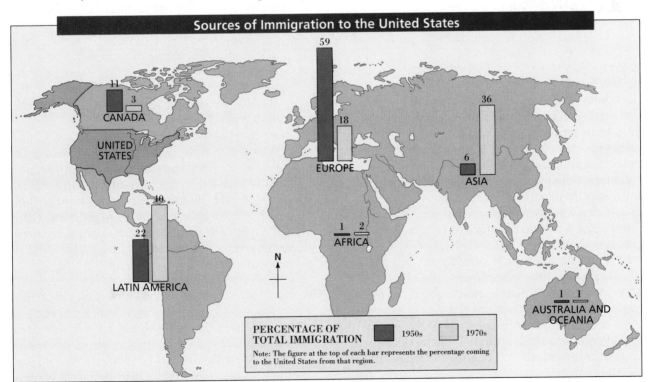

**Note the impact of the Immigration Act of 1965 on the map above.** *Where did the great majority of immigrants to the United States come from before passage of the Immigration Act of 1965? Where did they come from after it?*

# Chapter 18 Review

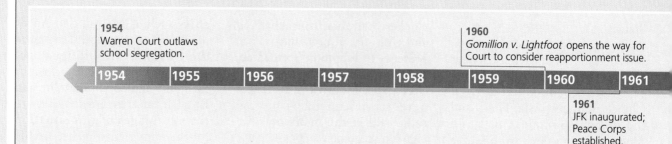

1954
Warren Court outlaws school segregation.

1960
*Gomillion v. Lightfoot* opens the way for Court to consider reapportionment issue.

| 1954 | 1955 | 1956 | 1957 | 1958 | 1959 | 1960 | 1961 |

1961
JFK inaugurated; Peace Corps established.

## Summary

Use the following outline as a tool for reviewing and summarizing the chapter. Copy the outline on your own paper, leaving spaces between headings to jot down notes about key events and concepts.

**I. New Frontier and Great Society**
  A. The Kennedy Years
  B. Hopes Cut Off
  C. Johnson's Great Society
**II. The Supreme Court and Civil Liberties**
  A. The Court's Authority
  B. The Warren Court
  C. The Reform Achievements

## Ideas, Events, and People

1. Why did Kennedy call himself a pragmatist rather than a liberal? Cite an example of his pragmatism.
2. What is a mandate? How were Kennedy's and Johnson's abilities to carry out their programs affected by their respective electoral mandates?
3. Explain how the New Frontier differed from the Great Society. Which was more effective? Why?
4. What weakened Kennedy's efforts to pass a bill for aid to education?
5. What ideals of the Kennedy years does the establishment of the Peace Corps reflect?
6. Describe how gerrymandering affected the rights of voters. What actions did the Supreme Court take to eliminate this obstacle to political rights?
7. What was the Supreme Court's reasoning for banning prayer and religious exercises in public schools?
8. Cite one example for each of the years 1964, 1965, and 1966 of reforms enacted during the Johnson administration.
9. Although many of Johnson's programs were accepted, some of them were not as successful as hoped. Why?
10. Describe how the rights of an accused person were expanded during the 1960s.

## Social Studies Skills

### Recognizing Stereotypes
Review Chapter 17. What stereotypes did the civil rights movement of the 1960s seek to overcome? Why is the elimination of stereotypes important socially, politically, and economically?

## Critical Thinking

### 1. Making Generalizations
Review the various laws and court decisions described in this chapter and try to identify a theme common to all or most of them.

### 2. Identifying Cause and Effect
Concern with rising health costs that made it difficult for the poor and elderly to obtain adequate medical care led to the introduction of Medicaid and Medicare. Did these programs achieve their goals? Why or why not? What might proponents and opponents of these programs argue today regarding their continued funding by the Federal government?

### 3. Compare and Contrast
Kennedy has been called "the first television president." Compare and contrast the public images of Kennedy and Johnson and tell how those images affected their political careers.

### 4. Recognizing Values
Some have argued that expanding the rights of the accused has made it more difficult to prosecute criminals. They say the protection the law gives to the accused is responsible for increases in

**1963**
JFK assassinated;
LBJ sworn in.

**1965**
Voting Rights Act
passed.

**1969**
Earl Warren
retires.

**1962**
Warren Court launches series
of reapportionment decisions,
bans prayer in public schools.

**1964**
Great Society launched;
Civil Rights Act passed.

**1966**
*Miranda* decision affirms
rights of accused.

crime. Use Unit 5 of the *Writer's Guide* (page 828) to prepare an essay giving your opinion.

**5. Analyzing Behavior**

When Johnson became president, he at first kept all of Kennedy's cabinet appointees, even though he recognized the great personal and political differences between himself and Kennedy, and knew that Kennedy's appointees resented him. Why do you think Johnson retained these officials?

**6. Making Inferences**

The cold war was based on fear, mistrust, and the attempts of the Soviets and Americans to curtail each other's influence in the world. How was the cold war rivalry between the United States and the Soviet Union fueled by the space race?

## Extension and Application

**1. Citizenship**

In recent years the Supreme Court has modified the *Miranda* ruling, granting broader powers to the police. Look up the new rulings, then research recent periodicals for discussions about them. Summarize the arguments for and against the original *Miranda* ruling.

**2. Community Connections**

In *Baker v. Carr* and subsequent rulings, the Supreme Court made decisions that led to the reapportionment of electoral districts. Find out how reapportionment affected your state. Has any further reapportionment taken place in your state since the 1960s?

**3. Global Connection**

The widespread unrest and the spirit of change that characterized the United States during the 1960s also was apparent in other parts of the world. Like the programs initiated by Kennedy and Johnson, the following events have had lasting effects. Investigate one of the following

events and find out how it contributed to the world situation today.

Green revolution boosts food production (1960s)

Panamanians riot over U.S. control of the Panama Canal (1964)

Six Day War occurs in Middle East (1967)

Dubček introduces "Prague spring" in Czechoslovakia (1968)

**4. Linking Across Time**

Calling Kennedy's presidency the New Frontier was a reference to the presidency of FDR, who took office in 1933, and called his presidency "The New Deal." Compare and contrast the two administrations and their goals.

**5. Cooperative Learning**

The 1960s was an important period in the history of popular music. With a small group, find the top 10 popular songs for each of the years 1961 through 1968. Discuss how these songs reflect the events of the time. Report your conclusions to the class.

## Geography

1. Study the map on page 605. Before reapportionment in 1964, how many congressional districts in Georgia were more than 15 percent below average in population? How far above average was the fifth district? What was the significance of this?

2. What was the result of reapportionment in Georgia after 1964?

3. Why do you think the Supreme Court took such an active role in reapportionment during the 1960s?

4. What single most important event in Southeast Asia do you think was responsible for the huge increase in Asian immigration in 1970? Based on the Immigration Act of 1965, what impact might this have on future admissions from this country?

## CHAPTER 19

# Voices of Protest

### 1966: Grape Growers and Workers Meet

Picking grapes in the California fields is difficult, hot, sweaty work. As the workers kneel in the dirt, smoke from nearby tractors fills their lungs. If they want water, they must go for it themselves, a trip that costs them valuable picking time. So the new union, the United Farm Workers, sent its best negotiator to work out contract terms with the ranch owner.

A small, quiet woman, Dolores Huerta was a tough negotiator. She demanded protective clothing for the workers, and a smoke pollution device for the tractors. She insisted that each crew receive a can of drinking water. She demanded better wages for the grape pickers.

"Sister, it sounds to me like you're asking for the moon for these people," said one of the rancher's lawyers.

*"All we want is just a little ray of sunshine for them."*

J.R. EYERMAN, TIME MAGAZINE

*Dolores Huerta was inspired by the spirit of protest and change sweeping the nation.*

"Brother, I'm not asking for the moon for the farm workers. All we want is just a little ray of sunshine for them," Huerta replied.

Huerta and her fellow Mexican Americans, like members of other minorities, followed the civil rights movement with great interest. They hoped the time was right for them to achieve progress in their own struggle for equality.

Meanwhile, the nation itself faced social turbulence that turned into a social revolution. White, middle-class women looked about their comfortable suburban homes and began questioning their traditional roles. Many young people began to reject the values of their parents. Some of them attempted to establish their own culture, a counterculture to the one they had known before.

*Feminist leaders of the 1960s inspired women across the nation to fight for equal rights for women.*

# The Revival of Feminism

## November 1964: Women Speak Out Against Oppression

DURING THE SUMMER OF 1964, CASEY HAYDEN AND MARY KING SHARED WITH OTHER STUDENT NONVIOLENT COORDINATING COMMITTEE MEMBERS THE DANGERS OF working for civil rights in the South. The tear gas, the water from the fire hoses, the snarling dogs, and the policemen's clubs did not distinguish between women or men, but hit both with equal force. Hayden and King, both white women, learned about bravery by seeing their African American "sisters" beaten so badly they could only whisper the word "freedom." They learned about commitment from Fannie Lou Hamer, who was evicted from her home when she tried to register to vote, but who never gave up.

Hayden and King gained another insight from working for SNCC that summer. They concluded that as white, middle-class women they, too, were second-class citizens.

In the early 1960s nearly half the students sitting-in at the lunch counters and riding the freedom buses were women. Yet few women played leadership roles within SNCC itself. Ironically, "women's work" was to type memos, make sandwiches, take minutes at meetings, and perform other menial tasks, but not to make decisions. Finally, Hayden and King wrote an unsigned memo protesting the men's attitude:

*Assumptions of male superiority [among SNCC men] are as widespread and deep-rooted and every much as crippling to the woman as the assumptions of white supremacy*

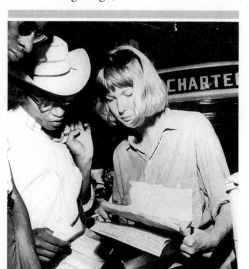

AP/WIDE WORLD PHOTOS

*are to the Negro. . . . [We need to] stop the discrimination and start the slow process of changing values and ideas so that all of us gradually come to understand that this is no more a man's world than it is a white world.*

SNCC Position Paper, 1964

The response to the memo was laughter and scorn. The next fall the two women tried again, this time in a signed memo addressed to other SNCC women. "Perhaps we can start to talk with each other more openly than in the past," they wrote, "and create a community of support for each other." But the time was not right for such an appeal. A few months later, whites of both sexes would be pushed out of SNCC by the pressures of black separatism.

Hayden and King concluded that the fight for **women's liberation**—freedom from the limits of traditionally female roles—was a separate fight. The women's experience in the civil rights movement provided them with some strategies. But equality for women would require its own organization and its own movement.

## Origins of the Women's Movement

The women's movement that sprang up in the 1960s had multiple origins, which perhaps accounted for how quickly it swept the country. One wing of the women's movement, founded on the ex-

---

periences of women like Hayden and King, grew out of the civil rights struggle. Another got its start with Betty Friedan, who first identified the "problem that had no name." In addition, President Kennedy in 1961 appointed a Presidential Commission on the Status of Women, chaired at first by Eleanor Roosevelt and later by Esther Peterson.

Although the movement began primarily among white, middle-class women, by the 1970s it had spread across all racial, social, and economic lines. The movement did not achieve all its legislative goals. Nevertheless, it accomplished major changes in the status of women at home, in school, at work, and in their professional and personal relationships.

**The Early History** In the 1800s the struggle for women's rights was a parallel movement to the antislavery crusade and involved many of the same people. Susan B. Anthony and Elizabeth Cady Stanton, for example, were reformers who were active in both struggles. For a time achieving both objectives seemed possible. An 1838 issue of the abolitionist newspaper *The Liberator* stated, "As our object is universal emancipation, to redeem women as well as men from a servile to an equal condition—we shall go for the rights of women to their utmost extent." The women, however, eventually split with the abolitionist men, who worried that the issue of women's equality might weaken support for the fight against slavery.

Women gained the right to vote only after a long struggle. As late as 1910 only Wyoming, Colorado, Utah, and Idaho had given women full voting rights. Then in 1919 Congress finally passed the Nineteenth Amendment, guaranteeing these rights to all women. The amendment was ratified the following year.

After the voting rights victory, little happened in the women's movement. Although more and more women joined the labor force, most of them were steered into low-paying categories of so-called women's work, such as clerical, teaching, and factory jobs.

Such was the situation when Betty Friedan published her landmark book *The Feminine Mystique* in 1963. The book ridiculed the notions that women were only suited for low-paying jobs and that achievement for women was measured only by their success as wives and mothers. Her ideas struck a chord with many women across the country, and they began to consider alternatives to marriage, childbearing, and homemaking. Yet at the same time, the book inspired strong opposition among many women who rejected Friedan's ideas as an attack on traditional roles.

**The Woman's Dilemma** Minority women faced a special problem in that they encountered sexual and racial discrimination at the same time. They experienced sexual discrimination by men, both white and black; and they faced racial discrimination by whites, men, and other women. In describing that period, the author Toni Morrison explained how black women "look at white women and see the enemy, for they know that racism is not confined to white men and that there are more white women than men in this country."

Many African American, Hispanic American, Native American, and Asian American women chose to delay their fight for equality in one sphere while they struggled for recognition in the other. Because priorities needed to be established, many women chose to seek full civil liberties for their ethnic group as their first objective. Equality between men and women would have to come later.[1]

## Women's Issues in the 1960s

When the President's Commission on the Status of Women issued its report in October 1963 relatively few people noticed. The civil rights struggle at home and the Vietnam war abroad claimed much more public attention. As a follow-up to the commission, however, a permanent Citizens' Advisory Council on the Status of Women was formed, and 32 states set up their own commissions. These actions produced a strong network for the future of **feminists**, or activists for women's equal rights.

The commission's report identified many of the issues that would occupy feminists over the next decades. It presented statistics on how women fared in employment, in education, and in government.

**Economic Rights** In 1960 women made up one-third of the nation's work force. However, most of these jobs offered less pay and prestige than those

**Identifying Cause and Effect**
Three events in the early 1960s helped revive the dormant women's rights movement—the civil rights struggle, publication of *The Feminine Mystique*, and the report of the Presidential Commission on the Status of Women. All drew the same conclusion: women were second-class citizens. The result was a groundswell of protest from women demanding change.

1 Why were women who took part in the social reforms of the 1800s and early 1900s unhappy with the way they had been treated?

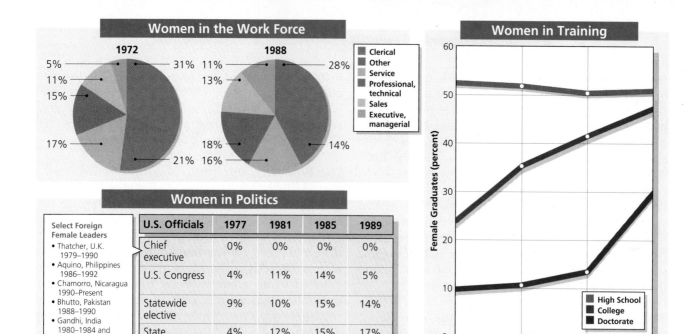

## Women in the Work Force

**1972**

| | |
|---|---|
| 5% | 31% |
| 11% | |
| 15% | |
| 17% | |
| 21% | |

**1988**

| | |
|---|---|
| 11% | 28% |
| 13% | |
| 18% | 14% |
| 16% | |

Legend:
- Clerical
- Other
- Service
- Professional, technical
- Sales
- Executive, managerial

## Women in Politics

| U.S. Officials | 1977 | 1981 | 1985 | 1989 |
|---|---|---|---|---|
| Chief executive | 0% | 0% | 0% | 0% |
| U.S. Congress | 4% | 11% | 14% | 5% |
| Statewide elective | 9% | 10% | 15% | 14% |
| State legislatures | 4% | 12% | 15% | 17% |

**Select Foreign Female Leaders**
- Thatcher, U.K. 1979–1990
- Aquino, Philippines 1986–1992
- Chamorro, Nicaragua 1990–Present
- Bhutto, Pakistan 1988–1990
- Gandhi, India 1980–1984 and 1966–1977

## Women in Training

(Line graph: Female Graduates (percent) vs. Year 1950–1980; lines for High School, College, Doctorate)

**In spite of many legal freedoms and opportunities in this nation, statistics reveal that many real obstacles to equal opportunity exist.** *What kinds of barriers do you think exist that prevent women from taking advantage of opportunities that equal rights laws attempt to provide?*

positions held by men. For example, women made up only 5 percent of the nation's managers and administrators and 12 percent of all professional and technical workers.

For every dollar on average that a man earned on a job in the 1960s, a woman with the same job earned only 59 cents. The Equal Pay Act of 1963 required employers to pay women the same as men for the same work. This act provided a remedy for thousands of women. However, it did not address the discrimination women faced in actually getting jobs.

More important gains came through the inclusion of women in Title VII of the Civil Rights Act of 1964, which prohibited discrimination in employment on the basis of sex as well as of race. (For a case study of how Title VII affected women in one industry, see pages 622–625.)

Still, laws alone would never be able to ensure equal job opportunities for women until they also received equal education and training. In 1960 women made up only 37 percent of the nation's undergraduate students and received just 10 percent of the doctoral degrees conferred.

**Political Rights** By the early 1960s women had been voting for 40 years, but they had achieved little success in obtaining political office, either elected or appointed. In 1963, for example, 351 women served in state legislatures, only 5 percent of the total legislative seats. Thirteen women held seats in Congress, down from a record number of 19 in 1961. The chart above compares the number of women holding high office in the United States and in other nations.

**Reproductive Rights** At the same time that women were growing more aware of the limits on their economic and political freedoms, many also began demanding more personal freedoms. The right to control their own sexuality and reproductivity became a rallying cry of many feminists.

In 1960 the Food and Drug Administration approved the sale of the birth control pill, ushering in a period of new sexual freedom. Married and unmarried women became more knowledgeable about their own health and their bodies. Many women felt that the pill gave them the freedom to be sexually active without the risk of pregnancy. The pill gave these

## STUDY GUIDE

### Identifying Cause and Effect

The Presidential Commission on the Status of Women identified many of the key issues facing women in their struggle for equality and presented hard statistics to support women's claims of inequality. The commission was also instrumental in the formation of Citizens' Advisory Councils on the Status of Women all across the country. As a result of the findings of these organizations, legislation was passed that required equal pay for women for equal work, and that prohibited discrimination in employment on the basis of sex.

women more opportunity to make their own decisions about their bodies.

Meanwhile, many women had been making these decisions another way—through abortion. Because abortions were illegal, finding a qualified physician who was willing to illegally perform the procedure was difficult and costly. Many who could not afford to have a safe abortion resorted to procedures performed by unqualified people. Many women suffered injury, sterility, or death because of unsafe abortions.

Some women took this risk because they did not want to be mothers; others chose abortion because they felt they were too poor or otherwise unfit to care for a baby. Still others were terrified of being pregnant and unmarried, a condition that carried a heavy social stigma at the time.

The push for reform of existing abortion laws came first from some doctors and lawyers, who were acutely aware of the dangers of illegal abortions. They were soon joined by many feminists. However, many people believed that abortions should not be allowed, so that by the time of the 1972 Democratic party convention, abortion had become an explosive political issue. Although feminists were not successful in including a plank on abortion in the 1972 Democratic platform, the issue has refused to fade and is still bitterly contested today.

**Social and Gender Relationships**   As women reexamined their roles in society, old ways of relating to family members, husbands, friends, bosses, and fellow workers all came under question. Women postponed marriages as they prepared themselves for careers, and the divorce rate climbed as more and more women chose to exercise their options rather than remain in unsatisfactory marriages.

Many men willingly examined and adjusted their attitudes in response to the evolving consciousness of women. For other men, reaching an understanding of their changing roles was a frustrating struggle in which they could not get beyond the most trivial issues. "It's getting so you don't know what to do when you come to a door," one man complained. "Open it and a women's libber comes through, you get a dirty look. Don't open it and you feel like an unmannered slob who just kicked his grandmother in the shins."[2]

## *Women's Responses to the Issues*

Two distinct types of women's organizations had sprung up in the United States by the mid-1960s, and both were made up primarily of white, middle-class, college-educated women. The organizations differed in the age groups they represented and in their organizational structures. However, both groups frequently worked together on legislative and political issues, exchanging ideas and strategies.

**The Founding of NOW**   It started as a statement scribbled on Betty Friedan's luncheon napkin. It became a large and powerful national organization that has helped elect politicians; that has helped correct inequality in women's employment; and that wields considerable lobbying power today in the halls of government in Washington, D.C.

The National Organization for Women (NOW) began in 1966 at a conference on the status of women. The women were concerned that complaints of sex discrimination before the Equal Employment Opportunity Commission (EEOC) were not being given serious consideration. This is because the complaints were filed by individual women rather than organizations or government agencies, as in cases of racial discrimination. So they decided to form a civil rights organization for women.

During lunch the following day, 28 women and men each contributed $5 for expenses, and Friedan scribbled out the name of the new organization and its purpose on a paper napkin. The statement of purpose was accepted virtually unchanged four months later at

**NOW quickly became a leader in the fight for women's rights.** *What is the meaning of the 59¢ button?*

### Comparing and Contrasting

Women and men reacted to the ferment of the women's movement in different ways. Most women knew that they had to reorder their priorities in order to achieve full economic, political, and social equality. Some men, on the other hand, were slow to grasp the full implications of the movement. They had full rights themselves, and many saw no need to alter the existing order.

**2** What were the main political issues facing women in the 1960s?

the first formal meeting of the organization, which named Friedan president. The statement of purpose read:

> *To take action to bring women into full participation in the mainstream of American society now, assuming all the privileges and responsibilities thereof in truly equal partnership with men.*
>
> NOW, *Statement of Purpose*, 1966

Eight years later NOW membership had soared to 40,000 people in 1,000 chapters. By 1990 its membership had reached 270,000, and the organization had an annual budget of $11 million. At its first national conference NOW outlined its goals: passage of a constitutional amendment guaranteeing equal rights for all, enforcement of Title VII of the Civil Rights Act, maternity leave benefits, better child care, equal and unsegregated education, equal job training opportunities, and abortion rights.

NOW's success has helped inspire the creation of several other women's organizations. The National Women's Political Caucus, founded in 1971, worked to put women in public office and also supported political candidates of both sexes who were sympathetic to feminist issues. In 1974 the Women's Campaign Fund began to raise money for female candidates. Two women achieved important political breakthroughs that year. Ella Grasso was elected governor of Connecticut, the first woman to head a state in her own right, not as a successor to her husband. Voters in San Jose, California, elected Janet Gray Hayes as mayor, the first woman to head a large city.

Minority women also formed separate organizations. These included the North American Indian Women's Association, in 1970; a conference of Mexican American Women, in 1971; the Conference of Puerto Rican Women, in 1972; and the National Black Feminist Organization, in 1972.

The growing momentum of the women's movement was evident by July 1972, when *Ms.*, a feminist magazine, published its first issue. A preview edition of 300,000 copies completely sold out in eight days. The magazine took up issues that up until then had never found their way into the pages of more traditional women's magazines such as *Good Housekeeping* and *Cosmopolitan*. *Ms.* also helped popularize the title "Ms." as an alternative to "Miss" or "Mrs." used when the marital status was unknown or irrelevant. Women's studies courses appeared at universities, and several men's colleges began opening their doors to women. By 1980 women made up 51 percent of all college undergraduates and received 30 percent of all doctorates.

© ADAM SCULL, GLOBE PHOTOS

**The Women's Liberation movement brought new leaders forward in several fields. Bella Abzug, left, represented New York in Congress and helped found the National Women's Political Caucus. Gloria Steinem (right) not only helped Abzug found the caucus, but also founded *Ms.* magazine.**

**Radical Feminism**

Since to many women in the United States equality of the sexes was a revolutionary idea, NOW was by definition a radical organization. To some women, however, it was not radical enough. The more radical women were mostly white and well-educated, but generally younger than their counterparts in NOW. Many of them had learned about social reform through their civil rights and student protest activities.

The younger feminists lacked the national network of NOW but excelled in grass roots organization. The women practiced participatory democracy—every woman had a voice in the discussion and a chance to develop her own skills and talents.

STUDY GUIDE

**Analyzing Decisions**

By 1966 Betty Friedan and other women activists, troubled by the slow pace of progress, decided that the only way women were going to achieve full equality was to take up the struggle themselves. Accordingly, they formed their own civil rights organization, the National Organization for Women. From the very beginning, they decided to focus on a wide range of issues affecting women, from discrimination in education and employment to encouraging more women to run for political office.

Small, informal discussion groups met regularly at participants' homes for "consciousness-raising" sessions. Women talked openly about their experiences in childhood, school, their families, marriages, and careers. They analyzed issues of common concern to all women and tried to identify those that were most open to political change.

The radical feminists tended to favor more dramatic protests than their NOW sisters. They ridiculed the 1968 Miss America contest by crowning a sheep as the winner. In one widely reported episode, they threw girdles, bras, hair curlers, false eyelashes, and other symbols of what they called feminine enslavement into a "freedom trash can." Such events resulted in a great deal of media attention and, often, negative reaction from the public.

UPI/BETTMANN NEWSPHOTOS

**These NOW members march down New York City's 5th Avenue in a women's liberation parade. Betty Friedan (at right) was one of NOW's founders.**

AP/WIDE WORLD PHOTOS

**The Opposition** Not all women embraced the new ideas of women's liberation with equal enthusiasm. A great many women accepted certain feminist ideas but rejected others. Some disagreed with the radical feminists' methods. Some were adamantly opposed to the movement's general support of a woman's right to abortion. Still other women saw the basis of feminism as an attack on traditional values, which included the subordination of women to men and the importance of a full-time commitment to family.

Among the most prominent of the antifeminists was author and attorney Phyllis Schlafly. Schlafly had long been active in Illinois and national politics where she was a strong voice for conservative causes. As the feminist movement gained strength, Schlafly

directed her energies against it. In her 1977 book *The Power of the Positive Woman*, she argued that a woman's most important and satisfying role was in the home, and that the primary duty of women was to uphold the traditional values of the church, family, and country. Schlafly asserted that feminist organizations did not represent the views of all women. Her leadership offered a powerful choice for many women.[3]

## Response of Congress and the Courts

Despite the opposition of the antifeminists, the accumulated effect of the women's movement began to be visible in the responses of Congress and the courts. In 1970 the Labor Department issued an order calling for all federal contracts to require the

STUDY GUIDE

**Recognizing Points of View**
Many feminists appeared to hold the traditional "home and family" role of women in low regard because it reflected the limited opportunities available to women. However, women such as Phyllis Schlafly were offended by some feminists' denigration of various traditional values. These antifeminists regarded family and motherhood as life's most important jobs.

3 Summarize the national debate over feminist issues in the 1960s and 1970s.

employment of a certain percentage of women. In 1972 the Education Amendments Act outlawed sex discrimination in education. On the local level, that required school boards to rewrite policies that limited cooking classes to girls and shop classes to boys. It also obliged schools to increase their support of girls' athletics. The U.S. armed forces relaxed some restrictions against women in 1973 and in 1976 opened up the military academies of Annapolis and West Point to women.

In the 1970s, however, two legislative and court issues divided American society into opposing camps. These were the proposed Equal Rights Amendment and the Supreme Court's decision on abortion. These two issues galvanized the opposition, which until that time had been somewhat dispersed, and gave it a new focus and sense of purpose.

**The Fight for ERA** The idea of a constitutional amendment specifically addressing the issue of women's equality was not a new one. The National Woman's Party had first proposed an Equal Rights Amendment (ERA) in 1923 and reintroduced it in every subsequent session of Congress.

As late as 1962, the President's Commission on the Status of Women did not favor the passage of the amendment. This view was shared by many women's groups, including the League of Women Voters, who were concerned that passage of the ERA would cancel legal protections women already enjoyed. But in the late 1960s the courts began to strike down these protective laws because they were in conflict with Title VII of the Civil Rights Act of 1964. As a result, the League withdrew its objection to the amendment.

The proposed amendment was a simple one. It read: "Equality of rights under the law shall not be denied or abridged by the United States or by any State on account of sex." Two other brief clauses provided Congress with enforcement power and established that the amendment would go into effect two years after ratification.

The proponents of the amendment felt that in 1970 the time was right for its passage. That year the amendment flew through the House of Representatives on a voice vote of 350 to 15. Two years later, it carried the Senate by a vote of 84 to 8. To become law, the amendment needed to be ratified, or approved, by three-fourths of the state legislatures within the next seven years.

Thirty states quickly approved the amendment by 1973; then the drive for ratification stalled. NOW, which took over leadership of the drive for ratification after a short power struggle among women's groups, was taken by surprise.

AP/WIDE WORLD PHOTOS

AP/WIDE WORLD PHOTOS

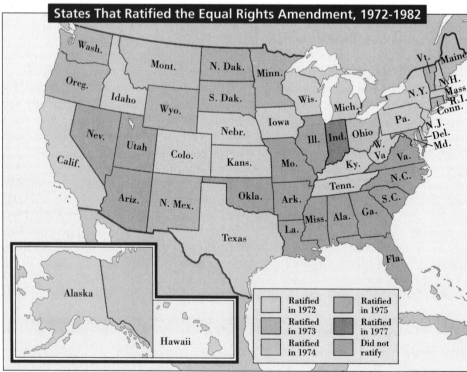

**States That Ratified the Equal Rights Amendment, 1972–1982**

| | | |
|---|---|---|
| Ratified in 1972 | | Ratified in 1975 |
| Ratified in 1973 | | Ratified in 1977 |
| Ratified in 1974 | | Did not ratify |

**Women have always been active in the debate over their political rights.** *What conclusion can you draw from the distribution of states that did not approve the ERA?*

The feminists had underestimated the opposition to the amendment and the ability of conservative women's groups to mobilize opinion against women's liberation. Although opinion polls showed that the majority of Americans favored the concept of equality between men and women, the same polls also indicated that an even larger percentage of the population did not wish to change men's and women's social and family roles. For these concerned people, the ERA represented too radical a change.

**The Defeat of ERA** Schlafly and her supporters charged that passage of the ERA would lead directly to women in combat in wartime, the breakdown of the family, government funding of abortion, and elimination of separate public bathrooms for men and women. The "STOP ERA" forces dramatized their concerns in California by presenting state senators with live mice and asking, "Do you want to be a man or a mouse?" In Illinois they handed out apple pies in the state legislature as symbols of traditional homemaking values, and brought in baby girls bearing signs that read "Don't draft me."

As the original ratification period ran out, supporters of ERA managed to obtain a three-year extension from Congress. They failed, however, to add a single state during that period, and by the 1982 deadline they were still three short of the 38 state approvals required.

**Roe v. Wade** In 1973 the Supreme Court announced its decision in *Roe v. Wade*, which established a woman's right to have an abortion. Even before the

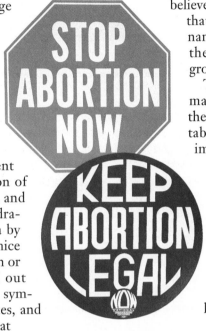

**Much of today's women's rights debate focuses on the issue of abortion.** *What do you think are some of the reasons people might have for opposing abortion?*

court's historic pronouncement, several states had modified their laws to permit abortion under specific conditions. Many feminists, however, wanted all abortion limits repealed on the grounds that women should have absolute control over their own bodies. However, many people, including some feminists, were against abortion. These people believed that life begins at conception, and that abortion at any time during pregnancy constituted murder. Therefore, they opposed abortion on moral grounds.

The Court's decision set forth the manner in which states could limit the right to abortion. The decision established that no limitations could be imposed by the states during the first trimester, or first three months, of pregnancy. State law could restrict abortions during the second trimester to cases that were potentially dangerous to a woman's health. The state could choose to restrict abortion during the third trimester to protect the life of the unborn child capable of sustaining life outside the womb.

In the process of moving through the Supreme Court, the abortion issue shifted in focus from the rights of the mother to the rights of the unborn child. Rather than settling the issue of abortion, however, the Supreme Court decision intensified controversy. The political and moral battle between the "prochoice" supporters (for the individual's right to choose on abortion) and the "prolife" forces (against abortion) dominated many political contests. Indeed, the debate has continued no less passionately into the 1990s.

## SECTION REVIEW

**Checking Facts**

1. Why did some women decide to leave the civil rights struggle of the early 1960s to form their own movement?

2. What were the major economic issues facing women in the 1960s? What were the major political issues? How did women make progress on each front?

3. Why did the Equal Rights Amendment arouse such controversy?

4. What are the major provisions of *Roe v. Wade*?

**Thinking Critically**

5. **Recognizing Points of View** Why did African Americans and other minorities have conflicts about joining the women's movement?

6. **Comparing and Contrasting** What is the difference between moderate feminists and radical feminists? How are the moderates and radicals alike in goals? How are they different?

**Linking Across Time**

7. What were the major changes that the women's movement caused in this country? How is life for a young woman growing up in the United States today different from life in the 1950s?

# Case Study

# Equal Opportunity

*JANUARY 1973*

> It shall be an unlawful employment practice for any employer, labor organization, or joint labor-management committee controlling apprenticeship or other training or retraining, including on-the-job training programs, to discriminate against any individual because of his race, color, religion, sex, or national origin in admission to, or employment in, any program established to provide apprenticeship or other training.
>
> Title VII, Section 703
> Civil Rights Act of 1964

## The Case

On November 19, 1970, the American Telephone and Telegraph Company (AT&T) asked the Federal Communications Commission (FCC) to approve a rate increase for long distance telephone calls. On December 10, the Equal Employment Opportunity Commission, in an unusual move, filed a petition asking the FCC to hold up the rate hike until AT&T reformed its discriminatory practices against women and minorities. The EEOC accused AT&T of steering new female employees into low-paying clerical and telephone operator jobs, where the opportunity for substantial promotion and salary increase was slight.

AT&T employed more than 400,000 women at the time, and, according to the EEOC, the economic repercussions of their policies on women were enormous. The EEOC estimated that restricting women to low paying, dead-end jobs cost them nearly $1 billion a year in lost pay and benefits. The EEOC declared that AT&T was "without doubt the largest oppressor of women workers in the United States."

## The Background

The Civil Rights Act of 1964 gave women and minorities a legal basis for challenging discriminatory employment practices. Litigation was expensive, however, and few individuals could afford the luxury of filing a lawsuit. To help remedy this situation, Congress set up the EEOC to enforce the equal employment provisions of Title VII of the act. Women and minorities could go to the commission to get help in fighting discrimination.

During the first five years, the EEOC concentrated on fighting employment discrimination battles for minorities. It did not take a serious look at employment opportunities open to women until 1970. The EEOC decided to start with AT&T, also called the Bell System, because it was the largest employer of women in the country. The EEOC reasoned that if the government could get AT&T to change its employment practices, other businesses would follow suit.

The EEOC devised a novel approach for dealing with AT&T. It would go before the Federal Communications Commission and challenge a rate increase on the grounds that AT&T was not following the law and thus did not merit a rate increase. The strategy was clear. AT&T would comply with the law and change its policies, or it would have to wait for a rate hike.

Back in the 1870s, all telephone company employees, including switchboard operators, were male. Some of the men were rude to customers, so as an experiment, the company decided to hire a woman. Emma Nutt began working as an operator in September 1879, and she was an immediate success. Soon, virtually all operators in the company were female. Ironically, that was the crux of the EEOC complaint. The EEOC accused AT&T of failing to provide employment opportunities for women other than low paying jobs. To prove its case, the EEOC presented the following information.

- The EEOC cited two facts to support its contention that most jobs at AT&T were segregated by sex. 99.9 percent of all switchboard operators were women. In contrast, 99.9 percent of all telephone installers were men.
- The EEOC claimed it could prove the relation between job segregation and the company's pay scale. The most significant figure contrasted average starting salaries for women and men. Women averaged about $5,500 during their first year of employment. Men earned about $7,500.
- The EEOC cited the following statistics to argue that AT&T's promotion policies were discriminatory. Women held only 6 percent of all middle management jobs in the company, and just 1.2 percent of all top management positions.

## Initial Reactions

AT&T executives reacted to the EEOC charges with indignation and outrage. H. I. Romner, the company chairman, seemed genuinely puzzled by the EEOC action. To his way of thinking, AT&T had always been a leader in the field of fair employment practices. Robert D. Lilley, the executive

vice president, echoed Romner's view. He insisted that AT&T had always tried to follow the law in the employment of women and minorities. John W. Kingsbury, vice president for personnel, took a more aggressive stance. The company was not running a social welfare program, he said. It was in business to provide a service and make a profit. It was not responsible for the hiring practices of the United States.

AP/WIDE WORLD PHOTOS

"The EEOC's intervention in proceedings before the FCC on grounds of discriminatory practices by the Bell System is outrageous. . . . In the field of equal employment, we have been leaders, not followers."

H. I. Romner
Chairman, AT&T

AP/WIDE WORLD PHOTOS

"Many of the specific kinds of allegations made against us are ancient history. . . . We are now . . . actively supporting the national policy of equal employment opportunity."

Robert D. Lilley
Executive Vice President, AT&T

COURTESY AT&T ARCHIVES

"In its zeal in trying this case against the Bell System, the EEOC had failed to recognize that the primary reason the Bell System exists is to provide communications services to the American public, not merely to provide employment to all comers."

John W. Kingsbury
Assistant Vice President, AT&T

## The Options

**D**espite their initial reactions to the EEOC complaint, AT&T executives had a serious problem on their hands. They had to respond to the EEOC complaint, and they had to provide convincing evidence that the company was in compliance with the provisions of Title VII. Otherwise, the FCC would not approve the rate increase. In their view, they had three major options:

1. They could maintain that the company did not discriminate against women at all, argue their case, and let the FCC make a determination.
2. If the FCC ruled against the company, they could litigate in the courts.
3. They could accept the EEOC evidence, admitting discrimination in the past and setting up an affirmative action program to change company policies.

For a time, it looked as though AT&T had opted to fight. The company's reputation for fairness had been questioned, and the top executives were ready for battle. On August 1, 1972, they filed a 2,000-page report with the FCC, responding to each charge. John W. Kingsbury reviewed the long history of employment relations at AT&T, and he insisted the company was doing everything possible to comply with Title VII of the Civil Rights Act of 1964. "To brand actions in 1965 or 1966 as discriminatory because they are not consonant with [today's] views is unfair and improper."

## The Agreements

**E**veryone involved in the dispute expected a long, drawn-out battle. AT&T had a history of litigating disputes in the courts, and nobody expected the company to change that policy now. If the company followed this course, however, they would effectively delay the implementation of the nation's employment goals for years. The EEOC didn't want such a delay to happen, and neither did the company executives. In January 1973 AT&T signed an agreement committing the company to a new employment policy free of discriminatory practices. The agreement included four important provisions.

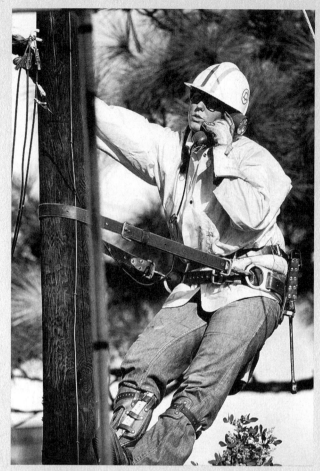

The suit against AT&T resulted in many new job opportunities and equal pay for women and men at AT&T.

- AT&T agreed to open up jobs to all qualified applicants without regard to sex.
- It published a new salary scale, ensuring that everyone doing the same job would be paid at the same rate.
- It instituted a new promotion policy, opening up more management positions to women, as well as to minority men.
- It agreed to pay $15 million to 15,000 workers to make up for lost income due to discriminatory employment practices of the past.

Reactions to the settlement were generally positive. Leon A. Higginbotham, Jr., the judge who oversaw the settlement, called the agreement "the largest and most impressive civil rights settlement in the history of the nation."

Robert D. Lilley took a more practical view of the outcome of the settlement. He summed up AT&T's position in these words: "Yes, I think it's a good agreement. All the litigation and questions are cleared up. It relieves the uncertainty and releases our energies to get the job done. That's what counts."

Wilma Scott Heide, president of NOW, thought the settlement fair because it "vastly expanded job opportunities for females and minority males." However, she called the $15 million in back pay "chickenfeed"; she said that AT&T owed women employees more than $4 billion.

## The Significance

The AT&T case is generally seen as a landmark in the struggle for equal employment opportunities for women. David Copus, an EEOC lawyer, predicted that corporations around the United States would start revamping their employment practices immediately. "Employers won't have any trouble reading between the lines of this settlement," Copus said. "They are threatened if they discriminate."

That is exactly what happened. During the next few months, company after company responded to the pressure and followed AT&T's lead. General Motors, for example, revised its hiring practices to open up more assembly-line jobs to women. The Consolidated Coal Company agreed to reserve 20 percent of its miner trainee jobs for women. The New York Times announced a plan to ensure that women filled at least 25 percent of the editorial jobs in the company. The Prudential Insurance Company promised to institute new hiring policies that would substantially increase the number of women in their sales force. Merrill Lynch set up an aggressive affirmative action program to attract women to careers in the financial industry. Bethlehem Steel and eight other steel companies agreed to pay $30 million in back pay to make up for discriminatory employment practices in the past. Rutgers University in New Jersey admitted that they had been guilty of discrimination against women faculty members and agreed to pay $375,000 in compensation.

## Summing Up

On January 14, 1980, almost 10 years after the initial EEOC complaint, AT&T chairman Charles L. Brown delivered a major address to the National Organization of Women. Looking back at the long, difficult struggle to eliminate sex discrimination at AT&T, Brown admitted that the company had been slow to understand the significance of Title VII of the Civil Rights Act of 1964 and slower still to grasp the implications of the sex discrimination provision.

"We have come to agree with the very fundamental observation that many of the leaders of the women's movement have been making for some time—that feminism and humanism are one and the same and only by insuring that women are treated as equal in the work place, equal in the community, and equal in the home can it be assumed that ours is a fully civilized society."

## Think About It

1. Why did the EEOC decide to use AT&T as a test case in the struggle to gain equal opportunities for women? Why were the AT&T executives outraged when the EEOC singled them out for scrutiny?

2. All the top AT&T executives featured in the photos on page 623 are men. In a sense, they were living proof of the EEOC contention that the company discriminated against women in its failure to promote them to top management positions. Do you think the executives were aware of the irony of the situation? Why or why not?

3. Many people back in 1973 saw the AT&T case as a landmark in the struggle for equal employment rights for women. Today we can look back and judge the case from the perspective of two decades. Do you think the original analysis was correct? Why or why not?

4. Following the settlement of the AT&T case, many corporations set targets of 20 or 25 percent for female employment. Why do you think this was a satisfactory target in the 1970s? Would it be satisfactory today?

The founder and first president of the National Organization for Women (NOW), Betty Friedan (pictured below) became a key leader in the struggle for women's rights. Her activism continues today. In 1970 Friedan made the following assessment of the barriers facing women.

> *We are beginning to know that no woman can achieve a real breakthrough alone, as long as sex discrimination exists in employment, under the law, in education, in mores, and in denigration of the image of women.*
>
> *Even those of us who have managed to achieve a precarious success in a given field still walk as freaks in a "man's world" since every profession—politics, the church, teaching—is still structured as a man's world.*
>
> Betty Friedan, *Voices of the New Feminism, 1970*

Suppose that you had the opportunity to interview Betty Friedan. What questions would you like to ask her? Such an interview could reveal Friedan's personal insights into feminists' accomplishments and the challenges that remain.

## Learning the Skill

Interviews allow people to give their unique perspectives in their own words. Following these steps can help make your interview successful:

1. **Make an appointment.**
   Contact the person you wish to interview. Explain why you want to interview him or her, what kinds of things you hope to learn, and how you will use information from the interview. For example, you might use information from an interview with Betty Friedan to help you prepare a report or organize a class project on feminism. Discuss where the interview will be conducted

UPI/BETTMAN NEWSPHOTOS

and whether you may use a tape recorder.

2. **Gather background information.**
   Find out about the early life, education, and career or other accomplishments of the person you will interview. Familiarize yourself with books or articles he or she has published. Before interviewing Friedan, for example, you might read portions of her book, *The Feminine Mystique*. Then do research on the topics you will discuss.

3. **Prepare questions.**
   Group questions into subject categories, beginning each category with general questions and working toward more specific questions. Formulate your questions carefully, phrasing them in a way that encourages well-developed answers. For instance, consider how Friedan might answer each question. If she could simply say *yes* or *no,* revise your question.

4. **Conduct the interview.**
   Introduce yourself and restate the purpose of the interview. Ask questions and record responses accurately, preferably by using a tape recorder. Be sure to indicate your interest in what the interviewee is saying. Ask follow-up questions to fill in gaps in information.

5. **Transcribe the interview.**
   Convert your written notes or tape recording into a transcript, a written record of the interview presented in a question-and-answer format.

## Practicing the Skill

1. Gather biographical information that would help you prepare for an interview with Betty Friedan. Use this information and material from the chapter to help you develop a list of at least 10 questions to ask.

2. The women's movement also includes women you know—your mother, aunts, grandmothers, neighbors. All these women have had to find their own answers in a society in which gender makes a difference. Interview women of three different generations about their experiences as women in the United States, and about their attitudes toward feminist issues. Did you find any common themes or surprising differences?

# Hispanic Americans and Native Americans

## 1966: Support Grows Nationwide for UFW Grape Boycott

DURING THE LATE 1960S IT WAS A SCENE RE-PEATED IN MANY SUPERMARKETS AND NEIGHBORHOOD GROCERY STORES THROUGH-OUT AMERICA. GRAPES WERE ON SALE. Green and purple, luscious, full of juice, they were appealing to the sight and to the taste. If you were doing the family shopping, you might be tempted to reach for a bunch—until you remembered what you had seen on TV or read in the newspapers about the California grape industry. For those who had not heard the news, some grocers even posted this sign above the fruit as a reminder:

*Notice: California Grape Boycott United Farm Workers led by César Chávez are calling for a boycott of California table grapes. . . . It is this grocer's current policy to inform consumers of the boycott request so that each consumer can make his or her own purchase decision. It's your decision—to boycott or not.*

Table grape boycott notice, *1966*

Shoppers did decide, and many put the grapes back into the bin. By appealing to the nation's consumers, César Chávez, founder of the United Farm Workers of America, gained the support he needed to win recognition of his union among California farm owners. The union used the new strategy of a nation-wide boycott alongside the more familiar tactics of strikes, pickets, and demonstrations. Chávez would use it successfully again, when bargaining with the owners of vineyards and lettuce fields.

## Recent Hispanic American History

Look at a map of the United States. Read out the names of places in the Southwest and Southeast: San Francisco, Los Angeles, Santa Fe, San Antonio, Rio Grande, Ponce de Leon Bay. These names all suggest the long history of Hispanic culture in North America. From the first explorers in the 1500s to the most recent immigrants, Hispanic Americans have added a distinctive element to the language and culture of the United States.

The term *Hispanic American* refers to those Americans who have come, or are descended from others who came, from Spanish-speaking lands such as Mexico, Puerto Rico, and Cuba. They are the fastest-growing minority in the country. From three million in 1960, the Hispanic population rose to nine million in 1970, and nearly 20 million by 1990. Just as many feminists began to demand their rights in the 1960s and 1970s, many Hispanic Americans did as well. The two groups were both characterized by diversity: their members came from many different places and had varying interests.

**Similarities and Differences** Regardless of their country of origin, Hispanic Americans shared the Spanish language and culture and a strong loyalty to family and community. The majority were Roman

---

## STUDY GUIDE

**As You Read**
Identify the special problems Hispanic Americans and Native Americans have had in dealing with the culture of the United States. Also, think about the following concepts and skills.

**Central Concepts**
- understanding why **assimilation** is a major issue for Hispanic Americans
- understanding the importance of **self-determination** to Native Americans

**Thinking Skills**
- comparing and contrasting
- recognizing values
- identifying cause and effect

Catholic. They maintained close ties with their **extended families**, which include grandparents, aunts, uncles, and cousins as well as parents, brothers, and sisters. Economic and social pressures forced many urban Hispanic Americans to live in mostly Hispanic neighborhoods, or **barrios.**

In other ways Hispanic Americans were and are a diverse group. The successful Cuban American banker in Miami, the Puerto Rican teenager in New York City's South Bronx, and the Mexican American fieldworker in California's San Joaquin Valley all faced different political and economic issues.

**Five Major Groups**   Hispanic Americans may be divided into five major subgroups: Mexican Americans, Puerto Ricans, Cuban Americans, and those from Central America and South America. Each group had its own history and settlement pattern.

Many Mexican Americans were grandchildren or great-grandchildren of the one million people who fled Mexico in the 20 years following Mexico's 1910 revolution. Others traced their origins to families who lived in Mexican territories that were incorporated into the United States after the Mexican War. Others first came to this country as *braceros*, farm

workers who were issued temporary work permits by the U.S. government during World War II and after. Still others were **undocumented immigrants**—people who lacked legal papers for residing in the United States. Many Mexican Americans maintained ties with relatives and friends in Mexico through frequent visits or moves back and forth.

Because Puerto Rico is a possession of the United States, Puerto Ricans may enter this country as citizens. After World War II one out of every six Puerto Ricans came to this country seeking economic opportunities not available in Puerto Rico. In the 1960s, of the one million Puerto Ricans in the United States, 600,000 lived in New York City. Most were unskilled, poorly educated, and forced into low-paying jobs.

Cubans began arriving in this country in large numbers after Fidel Castro's revolutionary movement overthrew the dictator Fulgencio Batista in 1959. One great migration began following the Cuban missile crisis of 1962, when 3,000 people a week arrived for several months. A second migration took place between 1965 and 1970, when 368,000 Cubans immigrated to the United States. In 1980, 130,000 Cubans left their homes for this country in what is known as the Mariel Boatlift. A great number of this nation's

**By 1970 the Hispanic American population had grown significantly in cities all across the nation.** *What* conclusions might you draw from studying the map about where Hispanic Americans prefer to live, and why?

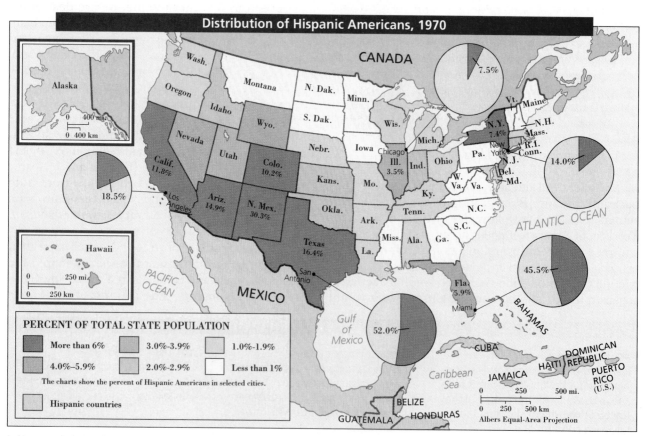

**Distribution of Hispanic Americans, 1970**

PERCENT OF TOTAL STATE POPULATION

- More than 6%
- 4.0%–5.9%
- 3.0%–3.9%
- 2.0%–2.9%
- 1.0%–1.9%
- Less than 1%

The charts show the percent of Hispanic Americans in selected cities.

Hispanic countries

Cuban Americans have settled in and around Miami; large Cuban communities also grew up in New York City and in New Jersey. Many of these immigrants left Cuba for political and not economic reasons and had little difficulty establishing themselves in the United States.

Two other groups of Hispanic Americans have roots in Central America and South America. Civil war has caused tens of thousands of Salvadorans, Guatemalans, and Nicaraguans to seek asylum here. Economic changes and chronic poverty have led many thousands of South Americans to enter this country. The largest number of these are from Colombia. More than 100,000 Colombians immigrated between 1966 and 1979. Most settled in New York, Miami, and Los Angeles.[1]

## Hispanic Americans Respond

While the numbers of Hispanic Americans increased dramatically during the 1960s and 1970s, their development as a political force occurred more slowly. Because of the Hispanic Americans' diversity, it was difficult for any one leader to unite all the segments into a single force.

**Political Issues**   For Hispanic Americans, as for other minorities, a major political issue was **representation**, electing to public office people who would represent their views. In some border towns such as El Paso, Texas, Hispanic American voters outnumbered other voters two to one, but few Hispanic American candidates were nominated or elected to office. Gerrymandering in other cities, such as Los Angeles, helped to keep Hispanic Americans from massing their votes. Gradually, with changes such as reapportionment, a few Hispanic American candidates were elected. For example, in 1961 voters in San Antonio, Texas, elected Democrat Henry B. González to the House of Representatives. In 1964 Texans elected E. "Kika" de la Garza to represent the Lower Rio Grande Valley in the House.

Gradually, Hispanic Americans began to organize politically. La Raza Unida, which translates roughly as "the people united," resulted from an effort to organize a national political party to unite the sometimes divided Hispanic American elements. José Angel Gutiérrez, a 25-year-old Texan, formed the party early in 1970 to give Mexican Americans political control over some 20 southern Texas counties in which they were in the majority. In September of that year, Rodolfo "Corky" González, an activist and poet from Colorado, formed the Colorado La Raza Unida. Two years later a national convention drew 3,000 Chicanos, the ethnic label adopted by many Mexican Americans.

Another pressing political issue concerned the bracero program. In periods of labor shortage such as occurred during World War II, American growers pressed the U.S. government to allow farm laborers to enter on temporary, restricted permits. Although Mexico disliked the program, fearing that the workers would face ethnic discrimination, it reluctantly consented to accept it. The program was scrapped in 1965 when Mexican Americans complained about the poor working conditions suffered by the workers.

The plight of the undocumented immigrant and the related problem of controlling the United States-Mexico border were other troublesome issues. Poverty in Mexico was the source of much illegal immigration. No one really could be sure how many people had crossed over the 2,000-mile-long border without proper documents.

The journey to the United States was a difficult and dangerous one for these undocumented immigrants. They were vulnerable to exploitation—first by "coyotes," often-unscrupulous guides who demanded large sums of money for transporting the immigrants across the border. Coyotes frequently robbed the immigrants, sometimes abandoning them in the wilderness. Immigrants who successfully reached the United States often faced exploitation by employers. Because the workers were in the country illegally, they had no place to turn to for protection, and were often forced to work under poor conditions for little pay.

Undocumented immigrants were not the only ones who suffered. Many Hispanic Americans who were in this country legally faced discrimination from employers as the federal government's Immigration and Naturalization Service (INS) pressured businesses not to hire undocumented immigrants. Many employers, in order to avoid drawing the attention of the INS, simply stopped hiring people of color

**Comparing and Contrasting**
Both the braceros who entered the U.S. legally and undocumented immigrants from Mexico have experienced discrimination and harsh working conditions. However, participants in the bracero program enjoyed some protection not available to undocumented immigrants. This is one reason why braceros were often paid more than workers who were not in the program.

**1** What were some of the reasons Hispanic Americans immigrated to the United States?

PAUL FUSCO, MAGNUM PHOTOS

**By leading the UFW boycotts on grapes and other produce, César Chávez became perhaps the best known** **Hispanic American in the United States.** *Why was public support so important to his movement's success?*

or those with Hispanic-sounding names, regardless of their legal status.

Other challenges awaited undocumented immigrants once they reached this country. Communities generally provided education and emergency health care to anyone who needed it. But undocumented immigrants were often denied other social services, such as unemployment insurance and food stamps, even though most of them paid taxes. In addition, families in need often would not apply for aid for fear of being deported—that is, sent back to their native land.[2]

**Economic Issues** Among minorities, economic questions such as wages and working conditions were not easily distinguished from broader political and social issues. César Chávez believed that they must be treated as a single issue.

Partly as a result of Chávez's leadership, farm workers became unionized for the first time. Chávez, a soft-spoken, patient man, has been called a "quiet explosion." Much of his work has centered on the grape-growing area around Delano, in California's San Joaquin Valley. There he faced bitter opposition from the growers as well as from the Teamsters Union, which had received permission from the growers to represent the workers, even though the workers had not been consulted.

In his union work, Chávez followed the nonviolent philosophy of India's Mohandas K. Gandhi and our own country's Martin Luther King, Jr. Chávez explains:

> *If someone commits violence against us, it is much better—if we can—not to react against the violence, but to react in such a way as to get closer to our goal. People don't like to see a nonviolent movement subjected to violence. . . . That's the key point we have going for us. . . . By some strange chemistry, every time the opposition commits an unjust act against our hopes and aspirations, we get tenfold paid back in benefits.*
>
> César Chávez,
> *Labor Leaders in America,* 1987

Realizing the limits of his resources in Delano, Chávez hit upon the idea of organizing national and international boycotts of farm products. He first used the boycott tactic when negotiating with the growers of table grapes. He then later called successfully for boycotts of wine grapes and of lettuce.

---

## STUDY GUIDE

**Recognizing Values**
César Chávez extended the traditional Hispanic American values of loyalty to family and community to the labor movement. In addition, Chávez helped instill in workers everywhere a commit-ment to nonviolence as a means of achieving their goal. Chávez believed that nonviolent struggle was "the truest act of courage."

**2** What were the most pressing political issues for Hispanic Americans in the 1960s and 1970s?

**Social and Cultural Issues** Some social and cultural problems were shared by all Hispanic Americans. As people of color, all have been subject to some degree to the pervasive racial and ethnic prejudices in U.S. society.

Social reforms brought about through the civil rights movement did not immediately benefit Hispanic Americans. Public facilities such as schools and swimming pools remained segregated in some southwestern cities long after the *Brown* decision. Hispanic Americans were regarded as white, and therefore did not receive many of the legal protections granted other minorities. Not until 1970 did a federal district court rule that Mexican Americans constituted an "identifiable ethnic minority with a pattern of discrimination."

In the 1970s **bilingualism**, the use of two languages, became a storm center of controversy. The proponents of bilingualism claimed that educating children in their native tongue as well as in English was the only way to ensure that minority students would receive an education equal to that of English-speaking classmates. Those who objected to the plan felt this delayed the successful **assimilation**, or incorporation, of minorities into the mainstream of society. A small group of opponents expressed fears that the United States would become a bilingual country. The legal issues were decided in favor of bilingual education in 1974, when the Supreme Court ruled that schools had to meet the needs of those children who had a limited knowledge of English. Nevertheless, the issues of bilingualism and assimilation remain contentious ones in communities across the nation.[3]

## Recent History of Native Americans

Assimilation was also a major issue among Native Americans and a factor in government decisions for several decades. Unlike all other minorities, the Native Americans had never been immigrants, since they were already here when the country was first colonized by Europeans. Nevertheless, starting in the late 1880s, Native Americans became virtual wards of the state—powerless, with little voice in their own affairs. During FDR's administration, a limited amount of control was returned to Native Americans living on reservations. However, policies initiated during Eisenhower's administration reversed Roosevelt's New Deal policy on Native Americans.

In spite of the political developments between the 1930s and the 1950s, the cultural identity of the Native American was still threatened as the 1960s began. From 1960 to 1970, their population soared from 551,500 to 792,730, a rate of increase four times the national average. About two-thirds of all Native Americans lived off the reservations, most in large cities such as Los Angeles and Chicago. The 285 reservations, mostly west of the Mississippi River, were managed by the federal government's Bureau of Indian Affairs with no input from the Native Americans themselves.

Both on and off the reservations, Native Americans were the most disadvantaged of this nation's racial and ethnic minorities. Over 38 percent lived below the poverty line, as compared to 33 percent of African Americans, and only 12 percent of the United States as a whole. Unemployment was widespread, frequently as high as 50 percent, and with a school dropout rate of 50 percent, many Native Americans were unprepared to compete. Life expectancy was only 46 years, as compared to a national average of 69. The rates of tuberculosis and alcoholism were the highest in the nation, while the suicide rate among Native Americans was double that of the rest of the country.[4]

## Native American Responses

During the 1960s and 1970s Native Americans began to organize in order to combat these problems. They met on and off their reservations, on college campuses, in tribal powwows, and in conferences. They negotiated with museums and universities to regain sacred objects that had been removed from Native American lands. They sued to reclaim land, water, and other rights lost when treaties were broken. Some of the younger activists formed militant groups, such as the American Indian Movement (AIM), and tried to achieve social reform by force.

Many Native Americans did not want to assimilate their traditional cultures into the American mainstream. They wanted **self-determination**, the oppor-

---

**STUDY GUIDE**

### Identifying Cause and Effect
One by one, the policies of the U.S. government for resolving problems with Native Americans failed to achieve lasting or satisfying solutions. By the 1960s a new generation of Native Americans were reacting to the continued failure of the U.S. government. These leaders resolved to seize the initiative and work for the right of self-determination.

**3** How is bilingualism related to the assimilation of Hispanic Americans?

**4** How have U.S. government policies over the past 100 years affected Native Americans?

UPI/BETTMAN

**Native Americans have made several dramatic, sometimes violent protests in recent years.** *How are such protests different from sit-ins or UFW boycotts?*

When the siege was lifted, two Native Americans had been killed and one marshal wounded. The issues cited—alleged corruption in the white-sponsored government on the reservation, broken treaties, and lack of self-determination—were not resolved.

What the demonstration did achieve was to focus the nation's attention on the deplorable living conditions of Native Americans. Like earlier dramatic occupations of U.S. property— at Alcatraz Island in 1969 and the Bureau of Indian Affairs building in Washington, D.C., in 1972—the occupation of Wounded Knee brought into the open a problem that had been ignored for almost a century.

tunity to participate in the political and economic decisions that affected their lives.

**Radical Movements** Frustrated by what they saw as their failure to achieve justice through legal channels, a group of Oglala Sioux decided to take matters into their own hands.

On the evening of February 27, 1973, a caravan of 54 cars rolled into a small, quiet town just after dusk. Many of the cars' occupants were armed. First they shot out streetlights; then they seized ammunition and rifles from a trading post. All the town's white people were herded into one house. Roadblocks were set up on all the roads leading into the town, which the Sioux then declared liberated.

The liberated town was Wounded Knee, little more than a fork in the road on the Pine Ridge reservation in southwestern South Dakota. Its significance to its liberators was that Wounded Knee was the site of a massacre more than 80 years earlier by U.S. troops of almost 300 Sioux men, women, and children. Responding to this Sioux militancy, U.S. marshals began a 71-day siege of the town to starve out the Sioux. The Sioux were soon joined by members of the AIM and other sympathetic Native Americans from across the nation.

**Challenges Through the Courts** In spite of their frustrations, Native Americans did have some success in the courts. The Indian Claims Commission (ICC) was created by President Truman in 1946 to hear and settle all outstanding land claims brought by Native Americans against the government. When the commission was dissolved in 1978, its work was taken up by the U.S. Court of Claims. During its lifetime the ICC heard 670 cases and awarded about $775 million to the claimants. Most of the claims stemmed from broken treaties and seizures of Native American land without agreement or compensation.

Many Native Americans were not satisfied with the results. They would have preferred to have their lands restored to them rather than payment in cash. However, the act setting up the ICC provided that compensation could be made only in money.

The claims of Native American peoples in Alaska, who include Aleut and Inuit, had not been dealt with since the purchase of Alaska from Russia in 1867. The Alaska Native Land Claims Settlement Act of 1971 gave over 40 million acres to native peoples and paid out $962.5 million in cash. The act established 12 regional corporations to manage these resources. This action helped fulfill the Alaskan natives' desire for

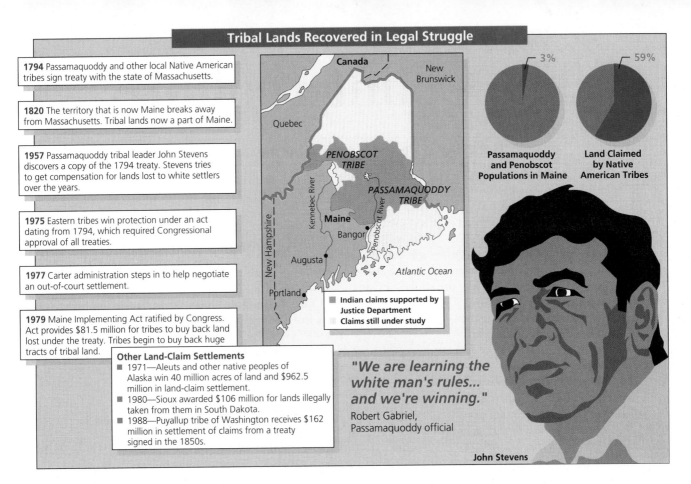

## Tribal Lands Recovered in Legal Struggle

**1794** Passamaquoddy and other local Native American tribes sign treaty with the state of Massachusetts.

**1820** The territory that is now Maine breaks away from Massachusetts. Tribal lands now a part of Maine.

**1957** Passamaquoddy tribal leader John Stevens discovers a copy of the 1794 treaty. Stevens tries to get compensation for lands lost to white settlers over the years.

**1975** Eastern tribes win protection under an act dating from 1794, which required Congressional approval of all treaties.

**1977** Carter administration steps in to help negotiate an out-of-court settlement.

**1979** Maine Implementing Act ratified by Congress. Act provides $81.5 million for tribes to buy back land lost under the treaty. Tribes begin to buy back huge tracts of tribal land.

**Other Land-Claim Settlements**
- 1971—Aleuts and other native peoples of Alaska win 40 million acres of land and $962.5 million in land-claim settlement.
- 1980—Sioux awarded $106 million for lands illegally taken from them in South Dakota.
- 1988—Puyallup tribe of Washington receives $162 million in settlement of claims from a treaty signed in the 1850s.

Canada
New Brunswick
Quebec
PENOBSCOT TRIBE
Kennebec River
PASSAMAQUODDY TRIBE
Maine
New Hampshire
Bangor
Penobscot River
Augusta
Atlantic Ocean
Portland

**Indian claims supported by Justice Department**
**Claims still under study**

Passamaquoddy and Penobscot Populations in Maine — 3%

Land Claimed by Native American Tribes — 59%

*"We are learning the white man's rules... and we're winning."*

Robert Gabriel, Passamaquoddy official

**John Stevens**

---

self-determination but created many difficulties. Few Alaskan natives were experienced in managing large corporations, and the regional division tended to weaken the traditional pattern of organization in Native American societies.

The issue of sacred lands was also addressed by Congress. For example, the Taos of New Mexico struggled for decades before they regained possession of their sacred Blue Lake. After the ICC acknowledged Taos title to the land, Congress passed an act in 1970 approving a return of a portion of the national forest and the lake area to the Taos people. In exchange, the Taos gave up their claims to the Taos township.

The courts of the United States have also helped resolve long-standing disputes within Native American nations. For example, disagreements between the Hopi and the Navajo stemmed from the government's establishment of reservation borders in 1882. The Hopi claimed that these borders favored the Navajo. The court's 1962 ruling restored some of the disputed land to the Hopi and provided joint use of a larger area. However, the ruling required the relocation of some 13,000 Navajo. Also at issue were water and timber rights, oil and mineral rights, and hunting and fishing rights. Many of these cases were not completely resolved by the ICC and are still being fought in the courts.

## SECTION REVIEW

### Checking Facts
1. What were the major issues that Hispanic Americans faced during the 1960s and 1970s?
2. Why are boycotts, such as the one led by Chavéz, often able to achieve dramatic economic results?
3. What were the major problems facing Native Americans during the 1960s and 1970s?
4. Why have many Native Americans resisted assimilation and insisted on retaining their traditional identities?

### Thinking Critically
5. **Recognizing Values** Native Americans have expressed a preference for obtaining control of their traditional homelands rather than cash settlements. What does this tell you about the values of these Native Americans?

6. **Identifying Cause and Effect** Why are Native Americans one of the most disadvantaged of the nation's racial and ethnic minorities?

### Linking Across Time
7. How has Native American resistance to domination by the United States changed since the early 1800s? Are the new Native American strategies more, or less, successful than the old ones?

# The Counterculture

## 1965: Rock Music Provides a Voice for the Counterculture

THE YOUNG PEOPLE WHO STRUGGLED FOR SOCIAL REFORM IN THE 1960S HAILED BOB DYLAN AS THEIR GUERILLA MINSTREL. HE FOUGHT FOR SOCIAL JUSTICE WITH A guitar and a song. More than any other musician of the time, Dylan gave popular music a social consciousness. Many agreed that he was the spokesperson for his generation. In a 1962 song Dylan asked one question after another about racism, war, pollution, apathy—the major issues of the day:

*How many roads must a man walk down*
*Before you call him a man? yes, 'n'*
*How many seas must a white dove sail*
*Before she sleeps in the sand? yes 'n'*
*How many times must the cannon balls fly*
*Before they're forever banned?*
*The answer, my friend, is blowin' in the wind,*
*The answer is blowin' in the wind.*
　　　　　Bob Dylan, "Blowin' in the Wind," 1962

Then in 1965 Dylan changed his tune. In albums such as *Bringing It All Back Home* and in an appearance at the Newport Folk Festival he signaled that change by playing half his music on an acoustic guitar and half on an electric guitar backed up by a rock group. The reaction was electrifying. Where had the old Dylan gone? Who was this new hard-driving musician with tousled hair who sounded so sarcastic, so sneering, so accusing:

*How does it feel,*
*To be without a home,*
*Like a complete unknown,*
*Like a rolling stone?*
　　　　　Bob Dylan, "Like a Rolling Stone," 1965

Once again Bob Dylan had caught the heartbeat of American youth, even before they felt the beat themselves. His unbridled energy, explosive anger, and rejection of what had gone before were all signs that the days of the counterculture had arrived.

## Profile of a Generation

The 1950s had been a turbulent time politically. The majority of American youth, however, did not seriously challenge the social order of the time. Of course, that age had its social critics, writers such as Jack Kerouac and Allen Ginsberg, who turned their backs on the social and cultural values of their time. But these critics were few in number and did not gain many followers.

In the 1960s the first of the baby boomers became teenagers. Having grown up during the cold war, many of these young people felt they were living on the edge of disaster. The threat of nuclear war was ever present as was the possibility of fighting in a faraway jungle war. Many blamed their elders, who

AP/WIDE WORLD PHOTOS

---

## STUDY GUIDE

**As You Read**
Identify the major beliefs and values of the counterculture of the 1960s, and evaluate its influence on American society as a whole. Also, think about the following concepts and skills.

**Central Concepts**
- understanding how the **generation gap** influenced the counterculture
- recognizing aspects of the counterculture that spread to the mainstream through **cultural diffusion**

**Thinking Skills**
- recognizing points of view
- recognizing values
- comparing and contrasting

included not only their parents but everyone over the age of 30, for creating the world in which they lived. The **generation gap**, the differences in attitudes between people of different age groups, became a divisive force in society.

Music was perhaps the main instrument of communication within the young generation. Listening to and discussing the new music—rock and roll—was the way these young people identified one another as members of the same group. The affluence that carried over from the 1950s and the availability of small, cheap, portable radios and of record players meant that teenagers could listen to their own music while parents were tuned in to something completely different.

**Beliefs and Values** Not all the young people of the 1960s hopped on the counterculture bandwagon. For that matter, a few of those who did could no longer be considered young. In fact, there was no such thing as a typical member of the movement, and different counterculture groups had different goals. What the members of the counterculture did have in common was a rejection of the prevailing middle-class values, the attitudes and beliefs of what they called the "Establishment"—people and institutions that represented power, authority, and the status quo.

In the counterculture's way of thinking, the older generation was inhibited, so the young placed a premium on "doing your own thing." The Establishment was materialistic, so the youth culture attempted to break from habits of regular employment and consumerism. Better, so the thinking went, to make what you need, share what you have with others, and not want what you do not have. Science, technology, and the emphasis on reason were blamed for bringing the world to the brink of nuclear disaster, so the counterculture stressed intuition and inner feelings over intellect.

© CHARLES GATEWOOD, STOCK BOSTON

**The generation gap was not unique to the 1960s. Conflict between young and old is a common theme in history.** *Why do you think different generations so often have difficulty understanding each other?*

**New Views** "Hippies," as members of the counterculture came to be called, searched for peak moments, or emotional highs, in sex and drugs. Their rejection of more conservative morals against premarital sex, plus the availability of the birth control pill, opened the door to a new era of sexual freedom. These new views attempted to separate sex from love. Some of the flaunting of the new sexuality, such as explicit song lyrics or public nudity, were self-indulgences meant to shock the older generation; however, there was a price to be paid. For example, venereal disease climbed at an alarming rate among young people during the 1960s.

The self-appointed **guru**, or spiritual leader, of many drug users was Timothy Leary, an academic dropout who experimented with the mind-altering drug lysergic acid diethylamide (LSD). He was fired by Harvard University for violating a pledge not to involve undergraduates in his experiments. Leary then became an advocate of drug use and coined the slogan: "Turn on, tune in, drop out."

The use of LSD declined when word got around about unpleasant side effects, "bad trips," and possible genetic effects. Meanwhile, the smoking of marijuana, also known as grass, or pot, increased. In the absence of today's scientific evidence of marijuana's dangers, its proponents favorably compared the use of the drug to the older generation's use of alcohol and tobacco. Later, some marijuana users moved on to more powerful and more harmful drugs. **1**

**New Religious Movements** In their rejection of materialism many members of the counterculture embraced spiritualism. This included a broad range of beliefs, from astrology and magic to Eastern religions and new forms of Christianity. Many of the religious groups centered around **charismatic** leaders, individuals who possessed remarkable personal appeal. Some

## STUDY GUIDE

**Recognizing Points of View**
During the 1960s, many older people saw the United States as a land of opportunity. In contrast, many young people saw a need for improvement in many elements of American society.

The result was the so-called generation gap, with the older generation unable to understand the deepest ideals and concerns of the young.

**1** What are some of the dangerous health consequences that can result from promiscuity and drug use?

of the religious groups had strict rules against drug use and premarital sex. Their centers, therefore, were frequently refuges to young people who had lost control of their lives through using drugs.

Although not all religious groups were authoritarian in structure, some were. In these groups, the leader dominated others and controlled their lives, sometimes to the point of arranging marriages between members. Religion became the central experience in the believer's life. The authoritarian figure was a sort of parent figure, and believers formed an extended family that took the place of the family into which a member was born. Some followers seemed to reject many aspects of their previous lives when they entered these groups. This could lead to painful conflicts. Parents accused religious sects of using mind-control methods; some attempted to recapture and deprogram their children. Also at issue was the right to choose one's own religion, even when that religion was at odds with widely held beliefs about individual free will.

Two examples of authoritarian, mind-controlling religious groups that attracted considerable attention beginning in the 1960s were the Unification Church and the Hare Krishna movement. Both were the offspring of established religions, and both were imports from abroad. Members of the Unification Church were popularly known as "Moonies," after their Korean-born founder, the Reverend Sun Myung Moon. He claimed to have had a vision in which Jesus told him that he, Moon, was the next messiah and was charged with restoring the Kingdom of God on earth. The Hare Krishnas traced their spiritual lineage through Swami Bhaktivedanta, founder of the American sect, to a Hindu sect that began in fifteenth-century India and that worshiped the god Krishna. In dress, diet, worship, and general style of living they tried to emulate Hindu practitioners of another time and place.

## Living Arrangements

Looking at American society in 1967, author Joan Didion wrote:

*Adolescents drifted from city to torn city sloughing off both the past and the future as snakes shed their skins, children who were never taught and would never now learn the games that had held the society together.*

Joan Didion,
*Slouching Towards Bethlehem*, 1967

In San Francisco, such adolescents gravitated to Haight-Ashbury, a district near Golden Gate Park. In New York City, they concentrated in the East Village.

**City Hangouts**  A common practice was for individuals to organize into groups that shared living quarters, without regard to sex or marital status. Many coffeehouses had a "pad"—a room with a few

The counterculture went beyond the boundaries of behavior that had predominated in previous generations. The use of drugs and casual sexual behavior were two of the most troubling developments to older people. *How do your styles of dress and music differ from the earlier generations?*

© PETER MENZEL, STOCK BOSTON

© 1967 BILL GRAHAM #75, ARTIST: BONNIE MACLEAN

mattresses on the floor or horizontal space sufficient at least to roll out a sleeping bag—where anyone who wished could "crash" for a night. The Diggers, a loosely formed group in San Francisco, operated a "free store" of used clothing. Something was always happening in the street—a performance by a free theater, or an unplanned concert. Drugs were easily available.

Thousands of young people converged on the cities during the summer, some of them disturbed runaways. City hangouts became crowded. In the fall of 1967 some particularly violent murders shook up everyone. Small groups began retreating to the country, where they formed **communes**, communities that shared property in common.

© GREGG MANCUSO, STOCK BOSTON

**Drama, color, and public display were important elements of the counterculture.**
*How do you think the Establishment reacted to this flamboyant behavior?*

**Rural Communes** The practice of people with similar religious, political, or cultural ideals retreating into the countryside to create their own utopian community has a long tradition in American society. Two highly successful examples were the Shakers, a religious order founded in the 1700s, and the Harmony Society, which lasted from 1804 to 1906.

At the height of the modern commune movement, in 1970, the *New York Times* estimated the number of rural communes at over 2,000, though few of them had more than 30 members. Some held meetings, wrote out bylaws, and discussed the ideal community. Communes such as Twin Oaks near Louisa, Virginia, for example, responded to the new women's liberation movement by eliminating distinctions between women's work and men's work. Any member was as likely to work in the kitchen as in the fields.

Other communes, as one observer noted, searched for "Eden rather than Utopia." They sought out secluded spots of natural beauty where commune members could act as they wished without disturbing their neighbors. They also praised spontaneity and resisted making decisions, imposing order, or doing anything else that resembled planning or organization.

Community relationships were prized. One member of a Vermont commune described her experience:

> *The things that make up community are terribly subtle; it's the little things . . . someone getting his hair cut on the porch, the children around sweeping up the hair, each taking a turn snipping . . . making dinner with a crew once a week, remembering who's a vegetarian and needs a special meal. Expanded consciousness of others. . . nothing big and spectacular. The scenes that move me are the little things about our life together.*
>
> Rosabeth Moss Kanter,
> *Commitment and Community, 1971*

## STUDY GUIDE

### Recognizing Values

Many of the people who went to live in communes during the 1960s were pursuing a life based on values that they believed were incompatible with those of the rest of society. They rejected the technological and materialistic ethic they felt had a stranglehold on mainstream society. They wanted to live cooperatively, without the jarring competition that they believed spoiled human relations. By forming large communities, these people hoped to be able to provide for their material needs, while being free to pursue their ideals.

The problems that arose on the Edenlike communes often stemmed from lack of organization. Without rules regarding visitors and new members, the communes were often overrun by the curious or the "weekend hipster." Privacy was in short supply. So was money, and without an economic base such as a home industry, some residents were forced to work outside the commune to raise cash. Despite the counterculture rhetoric of equality, women were often assigned traditional cooking and child-rearing roles. Nearly all of the communes were short-lived, or changed members frequently.[2]

## Counterculture and the Mainstream

Those who were influenced by the counterculture responded in various ways. The radicals rejected mainstream American culture and dropped out for a few years or permanently. The moderates enjoyed aspects of the counterculture such as the music yet managed to hold down demanding jobs. In cities across the nation some young professionals in the 1960s lived together in familylike urban communes. During the day they practiced law, or accounting, and in the evening returned to the house or apartment they shared with like-minded professionals who sought an alternative life style.

While many if not most of the counterculture generation eventually returned to more conventional life styles, some aspects of the counterculture were adopted by the U.S. mainstream, a process called **cultural diffusion**. Examples of cultural diffusion can be seen in aspects of the mainstream's diet, fashion, music, and art.

**Diet** The rapid growth of health food stores and of vegetarian restaurants across the nation, along with the availability of many new food products, can be credited partly to the counterculture's interest in diet and food production. The back-to-the-land movement made consumers aware of the advantages of stone ground cereals and organically grown produce. New items in the American diet, such as yogurt and ranch-fed chicken became available in supermarkets. Environmental concerns prompted people to analyze the economics of feeding a nation on beef as opposed to fish, poultry, or vegetables. Some adopted an exclusively vegetarian diet.

**Fashion** The counterculture generation, as one observer of the 1960s noted, dressed in costumes rather than in occupational or class uniforms. The colorful, beaded, braided, patched, and fringed garments worn by both men and women turned the fashion industry upside down. The international world of high fashion took its cues from young men and women on the street. Men's clothing became more colorful and women's clothing more comfortable.

RALPH J. BRUNKE

Protest often expressed itself in clothing. The counterculture adopted military surplus attire not only because it was inexpensive, but also because it expressed rejection of materialist values and blurred the lines of social class. For the same reasons, clothing of another age was recycled, and worn-out clothing repaired with patches. A mark of high distinction was to wear a patch that had been patched.

Ethnic clothing was popular for similar reasons. Beads and fringes imitated Native American costumes; tie-dyed shirts borrowed techniques from India and Africa. Ideally, each person created his or her own costume, but specialists became entrepreneurs—small-business owners—and sold their products at street fairs and rock concerts.

Perhaps the most potent symbol of the era was hair; a popular 1967 musical about the period was titled, fittingly, *Hair*. Long hair on a young man was the ultimate symbol of defiance. Slogans appeared, such as "Make America beautiful—give a hippie a haircut." School officials debated the acceptable length of a student's hair—could it curl over the collar or not? Once the initial shock wore off, longer hair on men and more individual clothes for both men and women became generally accepted. What was once anti-Establishment clothing was soon mainstream.

**Music and Dance** The counterculture hoped that their music—rock and roll—would be the means of toppling the Establishment and reforming society. It did not succeed because rock stars and their music were absorbed into the mainstream where the music brought material success worth billions of dollars to performers, promoters, and record companies.

Rock and roll was an international phenomenon that combined African American music with elements of popular white music. In the early 1950s only black musicians played rhythm and blues (R&B), a high energy music that emphasized the beat over the lyrics. When a few black singers such as Chuck Berry and Little Richard began to add lyrics that spoke to the trials and tribulations of adolescents, they created a whole new audience. Sam Phillips, a Memphis recording engineer, said in 1951, "If I could find a white man who had the Negro sound and the Negro feel, I could make a billion dollars." A few years later he found that man in Elvis Presley. Not only did Presley have the sound and the feel, he also put on an electrifying show, dancing wildly while singing and playing his guitar. Presley was soon joined in stardom by other white performers such as Buddy Holly.

Meanwhile, in England, four young men from Liverpool with working-class backgrounds began learning popular music by listening to the recordings of African American musicians. Calling themselves the Beatles, they took England by storm in 1963, and a year later made their American debut on the Ed Sullivan TV show. "Beatlemania" soon swept the country, inspiring many rock and roll imitators.

The final ingredient in the rock and roll mix was the addition of lyrics that spoke to the fears and hopes

**The Woodstock Festival, August 15–18, 1969**

For one hot weekend the youth of the nation gathered on Max Yasgur's 600-acre dairy farm in Bethel, New York, for the "Woodstock Music and Art Fair, An Aquarian Exposition." The event made headlines around the country, shocking adults and raising young people's hopes for a peaceful, alternative culture.

The gigantic plywood stage was built at the bottom of a sloping field. Steel towers supported one of the largest sound systems ever assembled.

**The Music**
Nearly all of the most important musicians of the time were scheduled to play: Jefferson Airplane, the Grateful Dead, The Who, Sly and the Family Stone, Janis Joplin, and more. New groups and singers, like Santana, thrilled the crowd and launched their careers. Friday night's music ended just after 2:00 in the morning. On Saturday and Sunday the music ran all night. Jimi Hendrix was the last to perform, at 8:30 Monday morning.

400,000 Arrived

120,000 Anticipated

**The Crowd: "The Woodstock Nation"**
The promotors vastly underestimated the audience their festival would attract.

"There's lots and lots of us, more than anybody ever thought before. We used to think of ourselves as little clumps of weirdos. But now we're a whole new minority group."

*Janis Joplin*

• Most were between 16 and 30 years old.
• Most were white and from the middle and upper classes.

"We are now the third largest city in New York..."
*Newsletter distributed 8:00 Saturday evening*

Mass.

N.Y.

Roads became so jammed that people abandoned their cars and walked as much as 10 miles to the site.

Liberty

**Bethel**
Monticello

The musicians stayed in a motel and were flown to and from the concert in helicopters. Medical supplies were also flown in.

Conn.

Citizens of this nearby town pitched in and made 30,000 sandwiches for the hungry festival-goers.

Pa.

New York City

N.J.

Despite rain and crowded conditions, the mood was one of fun and friendship.

Officials marveled that no fights or thefts were reported. "This is the nicest bunch of kids I've ever dealt with," a sheriff said.

0    25    50

of the new generation and to the widening rift between the young and their parents. Bob Dylan provided these lyrics, as did the Beatles and many other musicians.

The use of electrically amplified instruments also drastically changed the sound and feel of the new music. One master of this new guitar sound was Jimi Hendrix, a musician from Seattle who lived overseas and achieved stardom only after returning to the United States with the influx of musicians from Great Britain.

At rock festivals such as Woodstock, in August 1969, and Altamont in December of that same year, hundreds of thousands of people got together to celebrate the new music. And the fast-paced, energetic beat of rock and roll was made for dancing, but the style of dancing changed dramatically. Each individual danced without a partner, surrounded by others who also danced alone—a perfect metaphor for the counterculture, which stressed individuality within the group.

AP/WIDE WORLD PHOTOS

**Electric guitars revolutionized music—and Jimi Hendrix revolutionized the electric guitar.**

**Art**   During the 1960s, one art critic observed, the distinctions between high art and popular, or pop, art dissolved. The primary purpose of pop art seemed to be to entertain. However, the entertainment had a bite to it, a bite that for many gave the art enormous significance. In poking fun at the established culture, pop artists selected many of the same targets as the counterculture—for example, a consumer society's love of material possessions.

Pop art took as its subject matter the popular culture of the times, such as photographs, comics, advertisements, and brand-name products. Artist Andy Warhol, for example, used images of famous people, such as Marilyn Monroe and Elizabeth Taylor, and repeated them over and over. Warhol also reproduced items such as boxes of household cleaning products, making the paintings as realistic as possible. Roy Lichtenstein used as his inspiration frames from comic strips. He employed the same bold primary colors of red, yellow, and black, and in comic book fashion put words like "blam" and "pow" into his paintings.

Robert Rauschenberg incorporated actual objects into his art to break down the distinction between art and reality. A 1955 composition titled "Bed" included a real quilt and pillow. Claes Oldenburg reproduced common, everyday objects such as a three-way electric plug or a toilet bowl in giant scale.

Pop artists expected these symbols of popular culture to carry, as art, some of the same meaning as they did in their original form. The artists sometimes referred to themselves as only the "agents" of the art, and said it was up to the observer to give meaning to the work and thus become part of it.

An outgrowth of this philosophy was a new kind of theater, called a Happening, which was staged by some pop artists in the 1960s. The artist set the scene, which differed at each performance, and expected each observer to respond differently to the experience. This response became a part of the performance, and each performance was unique.[3]

## The Counterculture Appraised

When the music faded away and the crowds at the corner of Haight and Ashbury packed up and returned home, what remained? The young people of the 1960s had forced the rest of the country to look inside themselves for a brief moment and to question some fundamental values about the individual and society. Musical sounds were never the same again, colors were forever brighter.

On the other hand, the use of drugs took its toll. Many plans for social change were never achieved. People learned the hard way that ideals—love, not war, sharing versus possessing—are not effective un-

**Comparing and Contrasting**
Rock music and pop art had a lot in common. Both were popular with young people, and both carried a heavy load of social commentary. Rock frequently dealt with themes like racism, war, and poverty. Pop artists directed their fire at materialism. However, both popular music and art placed a heavy emphasis on entertainment—and on shocking the Establishment.

**3** How has cultural diffusion helped fuse the counterculture and the mainstream?

COLLECTION OF JOHN JENKINS III

**Andy Warhol's reproductions of famous images, such as this one of Elizabeth Taylor, made icons out of the familiar.**

less there is a plan to put them into action. Planning required organization and careful thought—actions many rejected as the Establishment's way of operating.

The complications and contradictions in the movement were also apparent in the diversity of its members. Although there were those who were sincerely dedicated to specific goals of social justice for African Americans, women, Native Americans, and Hispanic Americans, even within these groups there were differences in thought and strategy that often undermined their efforts at social change.

In the last analysis, was the counterculture a real movement? Not in the sense of the other modern efforts at social reform. These other efforts generally worked within the established social system and advocated organized political, legislative, and economic measures to accomplish concrete goals. Although there were many in the counterculture who chose to effect change by working within the existing social system, there were also those who completely rejected this strategy. Commune members, for example, hoped that their success in establishing new ways for people to live together could encourage others to do the same. Some people were primarily interested in economic reforms, such as better wages and improved working conditions for the poor. Still others were dissatisfied with their lives and found in the symbols of the counterculture—long hair, peace signs, unconventional dress—the security and status of belonging to a group. All in all, many members of the counterculture were more concerned about their own inner adventures rather than social reform.

There was one issue, however, that had the power to draw together different elements from the counterculture and beyond. This issue was the war in Vietnam. The war itself, in turn, became the dominant issue on the social and political landscape of the United States, an issue that would reshape the nation's self-image in the decades to come.

## SECTION REVIEW

**Checking Facts**

1. Why did so many young people drop out of the mainstream during the 1960s to explore the world of the counterculture?

2. Why did rock music hold a central place in the counterculture?

3. Who were the major musicians in the history of rock music? Who were the major artists in the pop art movement? What did each contribute?

4. What aspects of the counterculture spread to the mainstream through cultural diffusion?

**Thinking Critically**

5. **Recognizing Values** What were the major values of the counterculture? Which new life styles and fashions grew out of these values? Which ones became part of the mainstream?

6. **Identifying Cause and Effect** Why was there a renewed interest in religion during the 1960s, and why do you think this interest often included a rejection of established American religions and churches?

**Linking Across Time**

7. How did the counterculture help change the way Americans today think about food and diet?

# The Beat of the Sixties

*During the mid-1960s four British rock singers with a fresh new musical sound took our country by storm. Cheerfully optimistic, flamboyant, often irreverent, the Beatles captivated the hearts of millions of young Americans who came to listen to their music and stayed to imitate their life style. In the process, the Beatles helped influence the culture of a whole generation. America would never be the same again.*

Young people around the country copied Beatle fashions and Beatle hairstyles, half in rebellion against the conformity of the older generation, half as a put-on. The country was in the grip of **Beatlemania.**

American singers like **Paul Butterfield** and **Tina Turner** made their own special contribution to the music of the time. Butterfield helped integrate traditional American blues themes into the new beat, and Tina Turner did the same with soul music. With just three musicians and a wall of amplifiers, **Cream** rose to the top as the ultimate **heavy** guitar band.

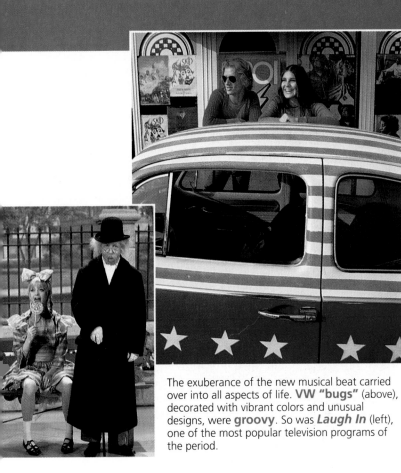

The exuberance of the new musical beat carried over into all aspects of life. **VW "bugs"** (above), decorated with vibrant colors and unusual designs, were **groovy**. So was *Laugh In* (left), one of the most popular television programs of the period.

The aerodynamic **Frisbee** (above) and the psychedelic **lava lamp** (below) became national fads for a time. Wham-O, the company that manufactured the Frisbee, sponsored a national Frisbee tournament in the Hollywood Bowl.

# Heavy

The cultural ferment of the sixties did not affect every facet of society. Beatlemania had no effect on the **Miss America** competition, for example. The sponsors of that pageant would not begin to react to the winds of change until the women's movement challenged their basic premises in the next decade.

# Chapter 19 Review

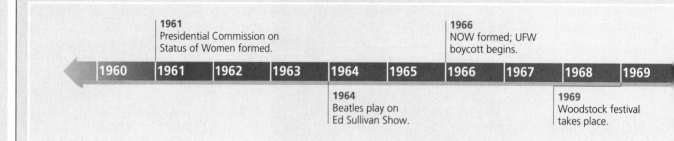

**1961**
Presidential Commission on Status of Women formed.

**1966**
NOW formed; UFW boycott begins.

1960 1961 1962 1963 1964 1965 1966 1967 1968 1969

**1964**
Beatles play on Ed Sullivan Show.

**1969**
Woodstock festival takes place.

## Summary

Use the following outline as a tool for reviewing and summarizing the chapter. Copy the outline on your own paper, leaving spaces between headings to jot down notes about key events and concepts.

**I. The Revival of Feminism**
  A. Origins of the Women's Movement
  B. Women's Issues in the 1960s
  C. Women's Responses to the Issues
  D. Response of Congress and the Courts
**II. Hispanic Americans and Native Americans**
  A. Recent Hispanic American History
  B. Hispanics Respond to the Issues
  C. Recent History of Native Americans
  D. Native Americans Respond
**III. The Counterculture**
  A. Profile of a Generation
  B. Living Arrangements
  C. Cultural Aspects of the Counterculture
  D. The Counterculture Appraised

## Ideas, Events, and People

1. Explain the provisions of the Equal Pay Act of 1963.
2. Describe briefly the major goals in the feminist movement. What is the relation of each of the following to many feminists' goals: Phyllis Schlafly, *The Feminine Mystique*, reproductive rights, ERA?
3. Hispanic Americans are not a single group. They include Mexicans, Puerto Ricans, Cubans, Dominicans, Spaniards, South Americans from many countries, and others. How has this diversity affected their campaign for civil rights?
4. How did the civil rights situation and goals of Hispanic Americans differ from those of other groups seeking their civil rights?
5. Although the Equal Rights Amendment passed both houses of Congress, it did not become law. Why not?
6. What was the principal goal of the National Women's Political Caucus?
7. Explain the concept of *consciousness raising*.
8. Explain *Roe v. Wade*. Give some current examples from the newspapers on how that decision is still being debated and contested today.
9. Define and explain *assimilation* as it applies to the various groups discussed in the chapter.

## Social Studies Skills

### Conducting Interviews

Gather biographical information that would help you prepare for an interview with Phyllis Schlafly. Use this information and material from the chapter to develop a list of 10 questions to ask. If you were to conduct two interviews, one with Phyllis Schlafly and one with Betty Friedan, how could you use the answers in a report on women's issues in the 1970s and 1980s?

## Critical Thinking

1. **Making generalizations**
Summarize, in a single phrase, a goal that is common to all the groups described in the chapter.
2. **Identifying Cause and Effect**
What event caused the first major increase in Cuban immigration to the United States in the late 1950s? Name the approximate dates of two other large Cuban migrations.
3. **Identifying Cause and Effect**
Explain the causes for the increases in the U. S. population of each of the largest Hispanic American groups.

**July 1972**
*Ms.* magazine first published.

**1977**
*Power of the Positive Woman* published.

| 1970 | 1971 | 1972 | 1973 | 1974 | 1975 | 1976 | 1977 | 1978 | 1979 |

**1970**
*New York Times* article claims 2,000 communes exist.

**February 1973**
Wounded Knee occupied by group of Oglala Sioux.

**4. Recognizing Values**

How did pop artists such as Andy Warhol, whose work appears below, challenge people's conception of art?

## Extension and Application

**1. Evidence of the past**

Explain how the problems of Native Americans today are related to decisions made 100 years ago or more. Use Unit 4 of the *Writer's Guide* (pages 825–827) to develop an expository paper.

**2. Citizenship**

Choose three of the reforms described in this chapter and relate them to your future career plans. Describe the effect each of them will have on how you will live and work.

ART RESOURCE

**3. Community Connection**

In the public library, review old newspapers to see how the various movements were carried out in your community. Is your community different today because of them?

**4. Global Connection**

Based on this chapter's account of Hispanic immigration to the United States, what three factors usually account for mass migrations of people?

**5. Linking Across Time**

In the twentieth century, Native Americans faced continuing resistance to their land claims. For example, FDR's administration returned to Native Americans living on reservations a limited amount of control which Eisenhower's administration reversed. Truman set up the ICC to hear and settle all outstanding land claims. How have Native Americans used the ICC in their current struggle for justice?

## Geography

**1.** Compare the maps on pages 254 and 620. Why do you think that many of the same states that did not give voting rights to women before the Nineteenth Amendment also did not ratify the Equal Rights Amendment by 1982? Name those states.

**2.** What ethnic group makes up the fastest-growing minority in the United States? From what different countries or regions have the members of this group come to the United States?

**3.** According to the map on page 628, where in the United States were the most states with large Hispanic American populations in 1970?

**4.** The Aleuts and other native peoples of Alaska were awarded large areas of land in the 1970s that once belonged to them. What positive impact did this have on the Alaskan natives? What were the negative results?

# Unit 7 Review

Women helped fight for American independence.
Women helped fight for abolition.
Women helped fight for child labor laws.
Women helped fight for unions.
Women helped fight for the 40-hour week.
Women helped fight for consumers rights.
Women helped fight for civil rights.
Women helped fight for peace.

**Won't you help women fight for equal rights?**

For more information, write NOW Legal Defense & Education Fund (E)
132 W. 43rd Street, N.Y., N.Y. 10036

## Concepts and Themes

World War II created new opportunities for African Americans, women, and other minorities. The postwar period saw a push for greater participation for minority groups in civilian life, and for an end to segregation and discrimination. These efforts led to a series of court decisions and legislative action outlawing discrimination. The success of the black civil rights movement encouraged similar efforts among Hispanic Americans, Native Americans, and women. These movements merged with growing opposition to the war in Vietnam to produce the counterculture, a youth movement that challenged, sometimes violently, many widely held assumptions about American society.

1. Why did many women feel that the accomplishments listed in the poster above justified their call for equal rights? What reasons did their opponents give for fighting equal rights?
2. How did Native Americans' demands in the 1960s differ from those of women and blacks?
3. Compare and contrast the methods used by various African American civil rights leaders to achieve social reform.

## History Projects

1. **Evidence of the Past**
   Review some popular magazines of the 1950s, such as *Life*, *Saturday Evening Post*, or *Colliers*. Photocopy pictures and advertisements that feature women. In a paragraph, explain how women would be shown differently today.
2. **Culture of the Time**
   The 1960s are often presented as a kind of "Golden Age" in which feelings of peace and love predominated. Create a collage that presents a more balanced view of the counterculture, including images of conflict.
3. **Geography**
   Make a list of the states that did not ratify the Equal Rights Amendment. What conclusions can you draw about the relationship between geography and political orientation?
4. **One Day in History**
   Write an essay explaining how events on one of these days influenced the history of the period: (a) the day John F. Kennedy or Martin Luther King, Jr., was assassinated, (b) the Woodstock festival, (c) the march on Washington.
5. **Case Study**
   Research and write a brief report about the recent activities of NOW. Include a discussion of NOW's opponents and their beliefs.

## Writing Activities

1. Research the history of the Black Panther party. Write several paragraphs summarizing their role in the civil rights movement and the counterculture. (See *Writer's Guide*, page 829, for guidelines on informative writing.)
2. Research the communes of the 1960s counterculture and those of the 1830s–1840s. Compare and contrast the two movements in an essay.

## The Arts

1. "Yellow Submarine," animated film featuring music of the Beatles and many 1960s themes.
2. *The Fire Next Time* by James Baldwin; 1963 book about racial tension in the United States.
3. *The Second Sex* by Simone de Beauvoir; 1949 book exploring the modern role of women.
4. *Bury My Heart at Wounded Knee*, by Dee Brown; history from a Native American point of view.

# UNIT EIGHT

# The Troubled Years

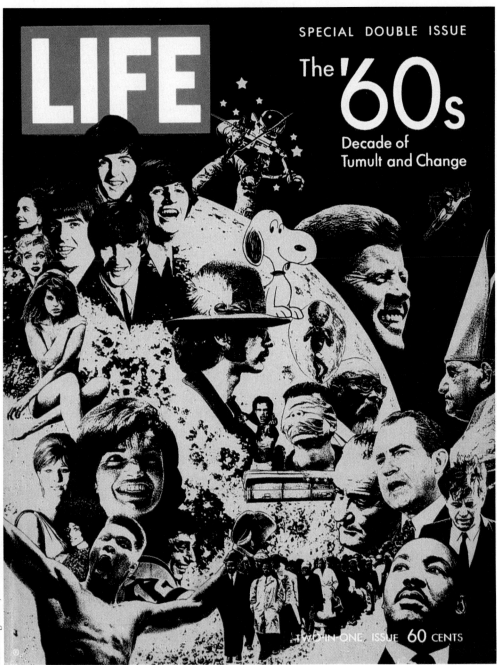

Life Magazine, © Time Warner Inc.

# War Memorial

*Americans responded to U.S. involvement in the Vietnam War in a variety of ways. Some sought to end the war by protesting at home. Others supported the war by enlisting to fight in Vietnam. Vietnam veterans Ron Kovic and Ray A. Young Bear share their perspective on the war after returning to the United States. High school student Sue Halpern tells how she too is a veteran, having experienced the war in her own home.*

## from *Born on the Fourth of July*

### *by Ron Kovic*

I was in Vietnam when I first heard about the thousands of people protesting the war in the streets of America. I didn't want to believe it at first—people protesting against *us* when we were putting our lives on the line for our country. The men in my outfit used to talk about it a lot. How could they do this to us? Many of us would not be coming back and many others would be wounded or maimed. We swore they would pay, the hippies and draftcard burners. They would pay if we ever ran into them.

But the hospital had changed all that. It was the end of whatever belief I'd still had in what I'd done in Vietnam. Now I wanted to know what I had lost my legs for, why I and the others had gone at all. But it was still very hard for me to think of speaking out against the war, to think of joining those I'd once called traitors.

I settled into my apartment again and went back to classes at the university. It was the spring of 1970. I still wore a tie and sweater every day to school and had a short haircut. I was very sensitive to people looking at me in the wheelchair. I buried myself in my books, cutting myself off from the other students. It was as if they threatened me—particularly the activists, the radicals.

I was sitting alone in my apartment listening to the radio when I first heard the news about Kent State. Four students had just been shot in a demonstration against the invasion of Cambodia. For a moment there was a shock through my body. I felt like crying. The last time I had felt that way was the day Kennedy was killed. I remember saying to myself, The whole thing is coming down now. I wheeled out to my car. I didn't know where I was going but I had to find other people who felt the way I did. I drove down the street to the university. Students were congregating in small groups all over the place. The campus looked as if it were going to explode. Banners were going up and monitors with red armbands were walking up and down handing out leaflets. There was going to be a march and demonstration. I thought carefully for a moment or two, then decided to participate, driving my car past the hundreds of students marching down to the big parking lot where the rally was to be held. I honked my horn in support but I was still feeling a little hesitant. I stayed in my car all during the rally, listening intently to each speaker and cheering and shouting with the crowd. I was still acting like an observer. The last speaker was a woman who said there would be a huge rally in Washington that Saturday and that it was hoped that everyone would make it down. I decided I would go.

That night I called my cousin Ginny's husband Skip. He used to come and visit me at the hospital when I first came back and after I got out we became

**In its use of the American flag as icon, Jasper John's *Three Flags* (1958) heralds the transition to** **Pop Art, in which familiar items are treated as aesthetic objects.**

good friends. Sometimes we'd stay up all night at his house playing cards and talking about Vietnam and what had happened to me. Skip's views were very different from mine back then. He was against the war. And each time I left his house to go home, he'd give me books to read—books about the black people and poor people of the country. I laughed at him at first and didn't take the books too seriously, but it was lonely in my room and soon I began to read. And before long, every time I went to his house I asked for more books. Skip seemed surprised when I asked him to go to the rally with me but he said yes, and early Saturday morning we left for Washington.

The New Jersey Turnpike was packed with cars painted with flags and signs, and everywhere there were people hitching, holding up big cardboard peace symbols. You didn't have to ask where anyone was going. We were all going to the same place. Washington was a madhouse with buses and trucks and cars coming in from all directions.

We got a parking space and I gave up my tie and sweater for no shirt and a big red bandana around my head. Skip pushed the wheelchair for what seemed a

mile or so. We could feel the tremendous tension. People were handing out leaflets reminding everyone that this was a nonviolent demonstration, and that no purpose would be served in violent confrontation. I remember feeling a little scared, the way I did before a firefight. After reading the leaflet I felt content that no one was going to get hurt.

Skip and I moved as close to the speakers' platform as we could and Skip lifted me out of my chair and laid me on my cushion. People were streaming into the Ellipse from all around us—an army of everyday people. There was a guy with a stereo tape deck blasting out music, and dogs running after Frisbees on the lawn. The Hari Krishna people started to dance and the whole thing seemed like a weird carnival. But there was a warmth to it, a feeling that we were all together in a very important place. A young girl sat down next to me and handed me a canteen of cool water. "Here," she said, "have a drink." I drank it down and passed it to Skip who passed it to someone else. That was the feeling that day. We all seemed to be sharing everything.

We listened as the speakers one after another

denounced the invasion of Cambodia and the slaying of the students at Kent State. The sun was getting very hot and Skip and I decided to move around. We wanted to get to the White House where Nixon was holed up, probably watching television. We were in a great sea of people, thousands and thousands all around us. We finally made it to Lafayette Park. On the other side of the avenue the government had lined up thirty or forty buses, making a huge wall between the people and the White House. I remember wondering back then why they had to put all those buses in front of the president. Was the government so afraid of its own people that it needed such a gigantic barricade? I'll always remember those buses lined up that day and not being able to see the White House from my wheelchair.

We went back to the rally for a while, then went on down to the Reflecting Pool. Hundreds of people had taken off their clothes. They were jumping up and down to the beat of bongo drums and metal cans. A man in his fifties had stripped completely naked. Wearing only a crazy-looking hat and a pair of enormous black glasses, he was dancing on a platform in the middle of hundreds of naked people. The crowd was clapping wildly. Skip hesitated for a moment, then stripped all his clothes off, jumping into the pool and joining the rest of the people. I didn't know what all of this had to do with the invasion of Cambodia or the students slain at Kent State, but it was total freedom. As I sat there in my wheelchair at the edge of the Reflecting Pool with everyone running naked all around me and the clapping and the drums resounding in my ears, I wanted to join them. I wanted to take off my clothes like Skip and the rest of them and wade into the pool and rub my body with all those others. Everything seemed to be hitting me all at once. One part of me was upset that people were swimming naked in the national monument and the other part of me completely understood that now it was their pool, and what good is a pool if you can't swim in it.

I remember how the police came later that day, very suddenly, when we were watching the sun go down—a blue legion of police in cars and on motorcycles and others with angry faces on big horses. A tall cop walked into the crowd near the Reflecting Pool and read something into a bullhorn no one could make out. The drums stopped and a few of the naked people began to put their clothes back on. It was almost evening and with most of the invading army's forces heading back along the Jersey Turnpike, the blue legion had decided to attack. And they did—

© PETER MARLOW, MAGNUM PHOTOS, INC.

wading their horses into the pool, flailing their clubs, smashing skulls. People were running everywhere as gas canisters began to pop. I couldn't understand why this was happening, why the police would attack the people, running them into the grass with their horses and beating them with their clubs. Two or three horses charged into the crowd at full gallop, driving the invading army into retreat toward the Lincoln Memorial. A girl was crying and screaming, trying to help her bleeding friend. She was yelling something about the pigs and kept stepping backward away from the horses and the flying clubs. For the first time that day I felt anger surge up inside me. I was no longer an observer, sitting in my car at the edge of a demonstration. I was right in the middle of it and it was ugly. Skip started pushing the chair as fast as he could up the path toward the Lincoln Memorial. I kept turning, looking back. I wanted to shout back at the charging police, tell them I was a veteran.

When we got to the memorial, I remember looking at Lincoln's face and reading the words carved on the walls in back of him. I felt certain that if he were alive he would be there with us.

I told Skip that I was never going to be the same. The demonstration had stirred something in my mind that would be there from now on. It was so very different from boot camp and fighting in the war. There was a togetherness, just as there had been in Vietnam, but it was a togetherness of a different kind of people and for a much different reason. In the war we were killing and maiming people. In Washington on that Saturday afternoon in May we were trying to heal them and set them free.

## Wadasa Nakamoon, Vietnam Memorial

### by Ray A. Young Bear

Last night when the yellow moon
of November broke through the last line
of turbulent Midwestern clouds,
a lone frog, the same one
who probably announced
the premature spring floods,
attempted to sing.
Veterans' Day, and it was
sore-throat weather.
In reality the invisible musician
reminded me of my own doubt.
The knowledge that my grandfathers
were singers as well as composers—
one of whom felt the simple utterance
of a vowel made for the start
of a melody—did not produce
the necessary memory or feeling
to make a Wadasa Nakamoon,
Veterans' Song.
All I could think of
was the absence of my name
on a distant black rock.
Without this monument
I felt I would not be here.
For a moment, I questioned
why I had to immerse myself
in country, controversy and guilt,
but I wanted to honor them.
Surely, the song they presently
listened to along with my grandfathers
was the ethereal kind which did not stop.

## I Am a Veteran of Vietnam

### by Sue Halpern

I
am a veteran
of Vietnam.
I've been from
Hamburger Hill to the DMZ
and back again
with a mere flick
of my wrist.
Through my own eyes
I've seen people
Tortured.
Bombed.
Burned.
Destroyed.
Beyond hope of recovery
While I
sit contently
watching . . .
and let it
go on

## Responding to Literature

1. Describe each author's attitude toward the Vietnam War. What is Ron Kovic's attitude toward those who protested against it?

2. If you had been a teenager during the Vietnam War, what do you think your attitudes toward the war and war protestors might have been? Why?

**For Further Reading**
Atkinson, Rick: *The Long Gray Line*
Caputo, Philip: *A Rumor of War*
Curry, Richard: *Fatal Light*
O'Brien, Tim: *Going After Cacciato*

CHAPTER 20

# The Vietnam War

### January 30, 1968: Communist Guerillas Attack U.S. Embassy

The time was nearly 3:00 A.M. on the first night of Tet, the Vietnamese New Year. A small truck and a taxicab filled with Vietcong guerillas rolled through the quiet city streets. As they turned onto Thong Nhut Boulevard, a broad tree-lined avenue that ran past the American embassy, the guerillas opened fire. Two U.S. soldiers inside the embassy grounds returned the fire. A soldier, 23-year-old Charles Daniel, shouted: "They're coming in! They're coming in! Help me! Help me!" Moments later Daniel and his companion, 20-year-old William Sebast, lay dead.

Thus began a bloody six-hour assault on the U.S. embassy in the heart of Saigon, capital of South Vietnam. When the fighting was over, 19 guerillas and 5 American soldiers had lost their lives. According to one reporter, the embassy grounds looked like "a butcher shop in Eden."

By 1968 U.S. troops had already been fighting for three years. Cold war policymakers saw Vietnam as a battle to prevent the spread of communism in Southeast Asia. In pursuing this policy of containment, the United States became entangled in a tragic war 9,000 miles from home.

This would be the nation's longest war, claiming the lives of more than 58,000 U.S. soldiers and more than two million Vietnamese. The war would leave Southeast Asia in ruins and would divide American society as had no other issue since the Civil War.

> *"They're coming in! They're coming in! Help me! Help me!"*

AP/WIDE WORLD PHOTOS

*Two army nurses await transportation to a field hospital in South Vietnam.*

© P.J. Griffiths, Magnum Photos, Inc.

*Americans went to Vietnam believing that their main mission was to protect the freedom of the South Vietnamese.*

# War in Southeast Asia

## September 2, 1945: Vietnam Declares Its Independence

HALF A MILLION VIETNAMESE SWARMED INTO BA DINH SQUARE IN CENTRAL HANOI ON SUNDAY, SEPTEMBER 2, 1945. PEASANTS IN STRAW HATS, MANY OF whom had come on foot from distant villages, mingled with Hanoi residents on the grassy square. At noon a frail figure with piercing black eyes and a wispy black beard climbed onto a wooden platform set up at one end of the square. He was Ho Chi Minh, the 55-year-old leader of the Vietnamese nationalist force known as the Vietminh. The crowd began chanting, "Doc-Lap, Doc-Lap"—"independence, independence." For several minutes Ho stood there smiling, buoyed by the crowd's enthusiasm. Finally he raised his hands, and the crowd grew still.

"We hold these truths to be self-evident, that all men are created equal, that they are endowed by their creator with certain inalienable rights, among them life, liberty, and the pursuit of happiness." With those words borrowed from the American Declaration of Independence, Ho proclaimed the independence of Vietnam from French colonial rule. The crowd roared its approval.

TASS FROM SOVFOTO

Later in the day, U.S. army officers joined Vietnamese leaders to celebrate Vietnam's liberation. During the war Japan had occupied Vietnam. The Americans and the Vietminh had fought side by side to drive out the Japanese. When the Japanese surrendered in August 1945, the Vietminh took over the capital of Hanoi and declared Vietnam independent.

Yet the warm friendship of that September day soon chilled, as Vietnam became a battleground in the cold war that followed World War II. In just 20 years, Vietnamese nationalists and the United States would become bitter enemies, embroiled in war.

## The French War in Indochina

Although the Vietnamese had declared their independence, the French were unwilling to give up the empire they had ruled for more than 60 years. The colonies in Indochina—the modern nations of Cambodia, Laos, and Vietnam—were among the richest of France's overseas colonies, supplying such valuable resources as rice, rubber, tin, and oil.

The French, however, faced a powerful foe in Ho Chi Minh. Ho was a staunch, and at times ruthless, revolutionary committed to the struggle for Vietnamese independence. Ho founded the Vietminh in 1941 to drive the French from Vietnam. Like Ho, most Vietminh leaders were committed communists. Their primary goals were extensive land reform and the creation of an independent unified Vietnam. They were waging a war of **national liberation** to free their country from foreign control.

By 1945 the Vietminh army numbered 5,000 and had a firm base of support in northern Vietnam. The French, meanwhile, tried to regain control of southern

Vietnam as the Japanese withdrew. Tensions mounted, and fighting broke out between the French and the Vietminh. In November 1946 a French ship shelled the port city of Haiphong, setting off a full-scale war.

The French entered the war confident of victory. Ho, however, predicted a different outcome. "If ever the tiger [the Vietminh] pauses," he said, "the elephant [France] will impale him on his mighty tusks. But the tiger will not pause, and the elephant will die of exhaustion and loss of blood."

The French soon controlled the major cities and towns, while the Vietminh retreated into the countryside. There they waged a relentless war—avoiding major battles, ambushing French troops, and staging hit-and-run raids on French outposts—all the while building support among the peasants.

**U.S. Support for the French**  In 1950 the French, unable to crush the Vietminh, appealed to Washington for aid. President Truman was not eager to support France's colonial ambitions. Yet the cold war had increased tensions in Europe. Truman was afraid to lose France as an ally against the Soviets, who in August 1949 had exploded their first atomic bomb.

Also, Indochina had assumed a new importance. The communist victory in China in 1949 fed American fears of communist takeovers elsewhere in Asia. If the United States failed to stop communism in Indochina, Truman believed, it would sweep across the rest of Asia like a red tide. The U.S. policy of **containment,** opposing communism wherever it appeared in an effort to "contain" its spread, would pull the United States closer to war in Southeast Asia.

In 1950, just before the outbreak of the Korean War, Truman agreed to send $20 million in direct military aid to the French. Over the next four years, the United States paid for most of the French war effort, pumping more than $2.6 billion into the French effort to "save" Vietnam from communism.

**The End of French Rule**  Despite U.S. aid, France was losing the war. When in May 1954 the Vietminh overran Dien Bien Phu, a French outpost in northwestern Vietnam, it signaled the end of French control of Vietnam.

The day after the French surrendered at Dien Bien Phu, representatives of the United States, Great Britain, France, the Soviet Union, China, Laos, Cambodia, and the Vietminh met in Geneva to hammer out a peace agreement. According to its terms, Vietnam would be temporarily divided along the 17th parallel. The Vietminh would withdraw to the north of that line, and the French would withdraw to the south. Vietnam would be reunified in 1956 after national elections. The Vietminh agreed, confident that they would win the promised elections.

## The United States Enters the War

Fearful of just such a communist victory, the United States refused to sign the agreement. President Eisenhower believed that the loss of South Vietnam would deny the United States access to the

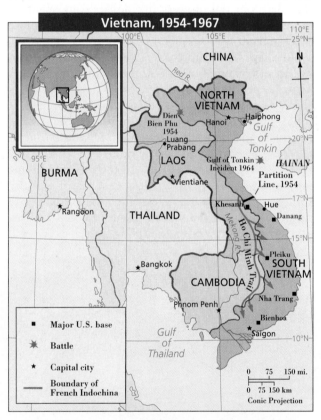

**Ho Chi Minh agreed to the partition of Vietnam in 1954 because he expected to gain control of the whole country in national elections two years later.** *How did the United States upset his plans?*

STUDY GUIDE

**Recognizing Assumptions**
American policymakers in the 1950s assumed that all communists were alike, so it was natural to see China and Vietnam as allies. In fact, the reverse was true. China had been invading Vietnam on and off since 100 B.C. Each invasion was met by a Vietnamese nationalist movement determined to win back the country. Many historians now think that the United States could have used the historical animosity between the two countries as a way to avoid involvement in Vietnam.

resources and markets of all Southeast Asia. In 1954 Eisenhower explained the "domino theory" to a group of reporters. "You have a row of dominoes set up," he said. "You knock over the first one, and what will happen to the last one is a certainty that it will go over very quickly." If South Vietnam fell to communism, the other nations of Southeast Asia would fall in turn, just like dominoes.

### The Diem Regime

Years of war and colonial rule had left South Vietnam in disarray. A tiny ruling class controlled the wealth, while millions of landless peasants toiled in poverty. Political and economic reforms were desperately needed. The United States pinned its hopes on Ngo Dinh Diem, a nationalist and fierce anticommunist. From 1954 to 1961, the United States pumped more than $1 billion into South Vietnam, but four out of every five dollars were spent on the military, leaving only a fraction for economic development.

An aloof man who always dressed in white, Diem was an aristocratic Catholic who had little in common with the people he ruled, most of whom were Buddhist peasants. He ran the country as if it were a personal empire. Half his cabinet members were relatives, and he imprisoned anyone who dared to speak out against his autocratic rule.

U.S. advisers urged Diem to try to win peasant support by breaking up the huge estates of wealthy landowners and handing out farming plots to the landless peasants. However, Diem rejected any reforms that would weaken the ruling class.

### Civil War

In 1957, with American support, Diem cancelled the elections promised by the Geneva Accords. As even Eisenhower admitted, if the elections had been held, Ho Chi Minh would have won.

Instead of elections Diem held a "referendum" to prove he had the support of the people in South Vietnam. American advisers assured Diem that they would be satisfied if he had 60 percent approval, but he rigged the vote so that he won by a whopping 98 percent. In Saigon, for example, he claimed 605,000 votes even though the city had only 405,000 registered voters.

Diem's brutal policies and his refusal to hold elections angered many Vietnamese. Their discontent proved fertile ground for the Vietminh. As one Vietminh guerilla later said, the peasants were "like a mound of straw ready to be ignited."

In late 1960 the Vietminh and other groups opposed to Diem united in South Vietnam to form the National Liberation Front (NLF). Like the Vietminh, most of the NLF leaders were communists. They promised economic reform, reunification with the North, and genuine independence. They also waged a campaign of terror, assassinating 2,000 government officials in 1960. The NLF, also known as the Vietcong, had close ties to the government of Ho Chi Minh. Over the years the NLF would get increasing support from North Vietnam and, indirectly, from China and the Soviet Union as well. The new president of the United States, John Kennedy, faced a difficult choice: abandon Diem or deepen American involvement in Vietnam.

**Vietnam is an agricultural country with towering mountain ranges, dense jungles, and lush coastal plains. Rice is the main crop. Before the Vietnam War, the Mekong River delta was the rice bowl for all of Southeast Asia.**

© PINCHES, SYGMA

© ROGER GAIN, GAMMA-LIAISON

**The Kennedy Years**  Like Truman and Eisenhower, President Kennedy saw Vietnam as part of the global struggle in the fight against communism. "Vietnam represents the cornerstone of the Free World in Southeast Asia," he declared. Despite some misgivings, Kennedy greatly expanded the U.S. role in Vietnam. Kennedy's plan was twofold. The first was to strengthen the South Vietnamese army with U.S. technology and military advisers to help them win the war against the Vietcong. The second was to pressure Diem to make political and economic reforms to eliminate the conditions that had allowed communism to take root in the first place. By 1963 Kennedy had tripled the amount of aid and increased the number of U.S. military advisers to 16,000.

Once again, however, Diem refused to go along. Instead of paying for new schools, health clinics, or land reform, American funds often ended up in the pockets of corrupt Saigon officials. Despite U.S. aid, the ineffective South Vietnamese army failed to score major victories against the Vietcong.

**The Overthrow of Diem**  The crisis in Vietnam deepened in the spring of 1963. As a crowd of Buddhists gathered in the city of Hue on May 8 to protest a government ruling forbidding the display of Buddhist flags, government troops fired on them. The attack stirred new and powerful protests.

A month after the attack at Hue, a Buddhist monk set himself on fire as a protest against the Diem regime. Other monks soon followed his example. A horrifying photograph of a monk engulfed in flames appeared in newspapers and on television screens around the world. Almost overnight, world opinion turned against Diem.

By early August the Diem regime teetered on the brink of collapse; yet Kennedy feared he had no alternative to Diem. In late August, however, a group of South Vietnamese army generals met secretly with U.S. officials to propose the overthrow of Diem. With U.S. support, the plan went forward.

On the night of November 1, 1963, army officers seized control of the government. In the confusion surrounding the takeover, Diem was killed. Just three weeks later, Kennedy himself was assassinated, and the war in Vietnam now troubled his successor, President Lyndon Johnson.

## Johnson's War

Like his predecessors, President Johnson believed that Vietnam was a battle in the cold war. He rejected any settlement of the war that did not guarantee a noncommunist government in South Vietnam.

Like Truman, Johnson was haunted by the loss of China. "I am not going to be the president who saw Southeast Asia go the way China went," he vowed. Johnson also believed he had to take a strong anticommunist stand to fend off the 1964 election challenge by conservative Republican Barry Goldwater.

Like Truman, Johnson took over the presidency with little experience in international affairs. He surrounded himself with the same team that had guided Kennedy's foreign policies—Secretary of State Dean Rusk, Secretary of Defense Robert McNamara, and National Security Adviser McGeorge Bundy—the architects of the U.S. war in Vietnam. Johnson, like Kennedy, hoped to keep the Vietcong from overrunning South Vietnam.[1] By 1964, however, Diem's successors had proved just as unsuccessful in waging the war and just as unpopular with the South Vietnamese. Only massive U.S. economic and military aid would keep the regime from toppling.

Johnson did not want to lose Vietnam, but he did not want to be seen as recklessly plunging the nation deeper into war. He needed the support of Congress and the American public to expand U.S. involvement. He got it in August 1964.

**The Gulf of Tonkin Resolution**  In early August Johnson announced that North Vietnamese torpedo boats had attacked two U.S. destroyers patrolling in the Gulf of Tonkin off the coast of North Vietnam. Johnson angrily declared that Americans had been the victims of "unprovoked" attacks. He urged Congress to pass a resolution giving him authority to "take all necessary measures to repel any armed attack against the forces of the United States and to prevent further aggression." An alarmed Congress almost unanimously passed the so-called Gulf of Tonkin Resolution. The resolution was not a declaration of war, but it authorized Johnson to widen the war. The resolution, he said, "was like grandma's nightshirt—it covered everything."

---

### STUDY GUIDE

**Recognizing Bias**

The bias of U.S. policymakers against anything communist had a pragmatic as well as a political basis. The attacks on communists in this country by Senator Joseph McCarthy made many policymakers fear anything that might seem to be an endorsement of communism. Indeed, after China fell to communists in 1949, key U.S. diplomats were blamed for the fall.

**1** Why did Johnson feel he had to continue Kennedy's policy of supporting South Vietnam in the struggle against communism?

Few Americans questioned the president's account of the incident. Years later, however, it was revealed that Johnson had withheld the truth from the public and Congress. The American warships had been helping South Vietnamese commandos raid two North Vietnamese islands the night of the attacks.

**Operation Rolling Thunder**   Six months later a second incident provided another excuse for deeper involvement. In February 1965 Vietcong forces attacked a U.S. military base at Pleiku, South Vietnam, and killed eight Americans. Johnson retaliated by ordering the first U.S. bombing of North Vietnam. Code-named Operation Rolling Thunder, the bombing would continue almost nonstop for three years.

In addition to bases, roads, and railways in North Vietnam, the air attacks targeted the so-called Ho Chi Minh Trail, a tangled network of dirt roads and muddy trails along which soldiers and supplies flowed from North Vietnam through Laos and Cambodia into South Vietnam. Yet the raids failed to cut off North Vietnamese aid to the NLF. The South Vietnamese army continued to suffer heavy losses at the hands of the Vietcong.

Meanwhile, a new regime had taken power in South Vietnam in 1967 under General Nguyen Van Thieu. Like Diem, Thieu lacked popular support. As a result, the NLF continued to grow, soon controlling the majority of villages in the countryside. Johnson believed that the Saigon government would fall without direct U.S. support. In March 1965 he made a fateful decision.

**U.S. Troops in Vietnam**   One month after the attack on Pleiku, two battalions of U.S. Marines waded ashore at Da Nang, South Vietnam. General William Westmoreland, the commander of U.S. forces in Vietnam, had asked Johnson to send the troops to guard the U.S. air base at Da Nang. Johnson agreed, assuring Americans that peace was on the horizon.

The trickle of U.S. troops soon swelled to a torrent. By the end of 1965, more than 180,000 U.S. troops were fighting in South Vietnam. By the end of 1966 that number had doubled, and by the end of 1967, nearly 500,000 soldiers had been sent to Vietnam—more than all the U.S. troops in Korea at the height of that conflict.

## Fighting the War

The first U.S. troops to land in Vietnam shared the optimism of policymakers at home. As Marine Lieutenant Philip Caputo wrote, "When we marched into the rice paddies on that damp March afternoon, we carried, along with our packs and rifles, the . . . conviction that the Vietcong would be quickly beaten." Within just two years, however, that optimism had turned to bitter frustration.[2]

Through relentless bombing and combat, the United States hoped to destroy the Vietcong's will to fight and force them to the bargaining table. The measure of U.S. success in the war was not territory gained but body counts, the number of enemy killed. In fact, optimistic reports of body counts from the field led many at home to believe the United States was winning the war.

U.S. officials, however, underestimated the Vietcong and their North Vietnamese allies. As Ho Chi Minh had warned the French, "You can kill ten of my men for every one I kill of yours, but even at those odds, you will lose and I will win." Indeed, although U.S. forces claimed to have killed 220,000 communists by the end of 1967, the war raged on.

LARRY BURROWS, LIFE MAGAZINE © TIME WARNER INC.

**Larry Burrows captured the sheer horror of the fighting in Vietnam in this 1966 photograph. A medical evacuation team leads Jeremiah Purdie to a waiting helicopter following a firefight.**

**Recognizing Bias**
The emphasis the United States placed on a military solution to the war in Vietnam had its roots in the domino theory. As early as 1953, for example, the National Security Council decided

that "under present conditions any negotiated settlement would mean the eventual loss to communism not only of Indochina but of the whole of Southeast Asia."

**2** Why were U.S. policymakers in 1965 still optimistic about defeating the Vietcong and preserving the independence of South Vietnam?

**The Air War** Because bombing cost fewer American lives than ground combat, the United States relied more and more on air power. Once Johnson unleashed Operation Rolling Thunder, the air war over Vietnam escalated dramatically—from 25,000 bombing raids in 1965 to more than 108,000 in 1967.

At first the attacks were limited to military targets and supply routes in North Vietnam, but soon the B-52s hammered roads, railways, factories, and homes in South Vietnam and neighboring Laos and Cambodia. By 1967 the United States had dropped more bombs on Vietnam than the Allies dropped during all of World War II. The air raids leveled dozens of cities, killed thousands of civilians, and turned the once lush rice fields and forests into a moonscape pitted with craters.

Yet the immense firepower of the U.S. Air Force failed to rout the Vietcong. To evade the bombers, they burrowed underground, digging more than 30,000 miles of tunnels through which soldiers and supplies continued to flow south from North Vietnam.

AP/WIDE WORLD PHOTOS

AP/WIDE WORLD PHOTOS

**Twin-engine C-123s sprayed over 12 million gallons of a chemical defoliant called Agent Orange in an effort to eliminate Vietcong staging areas in the thick underbrush. These photographs reveal the results. The top photo shows a mangrove forest before spraying in 1965; the lower photo shows the same forest five years later.**

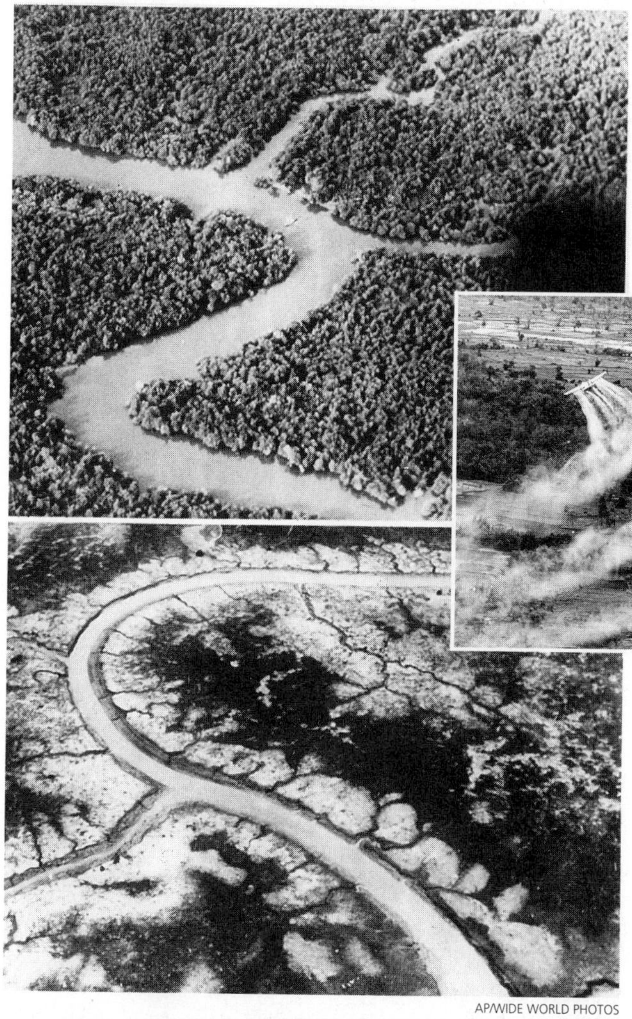

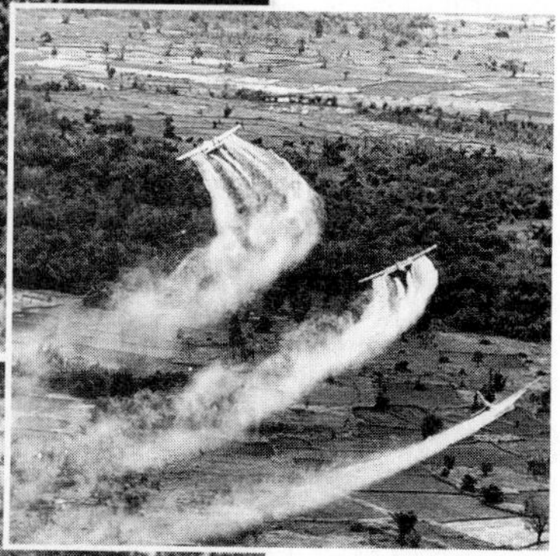

**The Ground War** While U.S. bombers rained terror on Vietnam from above, U.S. forces attempted to wipe out the Vietcong on the ground through "search-and-destroy" missions. To the inexperienced U.S. troops, the first challenge was simply finding the enemy in these unfamiliar jungles. Flying into Vietnam for the first time, Philip Caputo described the terrain:

> *An unbroken mass of green stretched westward, one ridgeline and mountain range after another, some more than a mile high and covered with forests that looked solid enough to walk on. It had no end. It just went on to the horizon. I could see neither villages, nor fields, roads, or anything but endless rain forests the color of old moss. . . . "Out there" they called that humid wilderness where the Bengal tiger stalked and the cobra coiled beneath its rock and the Viet Cong lurked in ambush.*
>
> Philip Caputo,
> *A Rumor of War,* 1977

Once on the ground, the troops slogged through the countryside on endless patrols—plagued by suffocating heat, clouds of mosquitoes, razor-sharp jungle grasses, and hungry leeches. Soaked in sweat and weighed down by 50 to 70 pounds of equipment, U.S. soldiers waded knee-deep along muddy trails and through flooded rice fields. Cautiously they inched

STUDY GUIDE

**Recognizing Assumptions**

U.S. policymakers and military leaders assumed that high casualties would drive the North Vietnamese to the bargaining table. This assumption did not take into consideration that the Vietnamese viewed the war as a continuation of 2,000 years of fighting against the Chinese and later the French. Casualties were accepted as necessary for victory. Ho Chi Minh's famous statement to the effect that the Vietcong could lose 10 men to every one of the enemy and still win expresses this philosophy.

along. Each rock, each clump of weeds, might hide a mine that would cripple or kill in an instant. One especially lethal booby trap was called a "Bouncing Betty" by U.S. troops. It leaped out of the ground just before it exploded.

All South Vietnam became a war zone, as U.S. troops searched the fields, forests, and villages for Vietcong. Yet how could they be sure whether a peasant was friend or enemy? They were all Vietnamese. As one soldier explained, "The Vietcong would be the farmer you waved to from your jeep in the day who would be the guy with the gun out looking for you at night." The enemy was everywhere and nowhere.

The Vietcong employed **guerilla warfare** tactics, using small bands of fighters to harass U.S. troops. Unlike conventional forces, guerilla fighters avoid open battles. Instead they try to wear down the enemy—with ambushes, hit-and-run raids, and sabotage—and force them to withdraw. As one observer noted, "The guerilla wins if he does not lose; the conventional army loses if it does not win." By that definition, the United States was losing the war.

The Vietcong guerillas had two advantages over the U.S. forces. First, they knew the terrain and could move unseen through the mountains and jungles. Second, through a combination of terrorism and the genuine appeal of their nationalist struggle, they had the support of many South Vietnamese peasants who supplied food and shelter and kept them informed of U.S. troop movements.

To deprive the Vietcong of their peasant support, U.S. troops undertook a "pacification" program, uprooting entire villages and forcing the people to move to cities or refugee camps surrounded by barbed wire. Then the army burned the fields and empty villages.

The program, however, failed to stop the Vietcong, who simply moved elsewhere. Instead, the pacification program created new enemies for the Americans—the peasants who were forced to leave the beloved land of their ancestors. "I have to stay behind to look after this piece of garden," one grandfather pleaded with Americans evacuating his village. "Of all the property handed down to me by my ancestors, only this garden now remains. . . . If I leave, the graves of my ancestors, too, will become forests. How can I have the heart to leave?"

Despite these policies, the United States also tried to win friends among the Vietnamese peasants

© 1968 MARC RIBOUD, MAGNUM PHOTOS, INC.

**North Vietnam kept the Vietcong resupplied throughout the war by sending equipment and ammunition down the Ho Chi Minh Trail by bicycle. The trail was narrow and dangerous, scarcely more than two feet wide in places. The Vietnamese modified the bicycles so they could carry up to two tons of equipment each trip.** *Why was the U.S. Air Force unsuccessful in its attempts to shut down the trail?*

through development projects. Teams of volunteers visited villages, offering medical care and farming advice. These efforts to win Vietnamese "hearts and minds," however, were undermined by U.S. bombs and bullets.

Meanwhile, American losses in Vietnam continued to mount. By 1967, over 14,000 U.S. soldiers had been killed. Yet U.S. military power still failed to crush the Vietcong. As one reporter observed, every

STUDY GUIDE

**Recognizing Assumptions**
In guerilla wars the mobility of a single soldier is as important as the mobility of an army. The United States mistakenly assumed that it could fight the Vietcong with conventional troops trained to fight on the battlefields of western Europe, not in the rice fields and jungles of Vietnam. One veteran said the U.S. effort to defeat the guerillas was "like a bull charging the toreador's cape rather than the toreador."

powerful blow from the American war machine "was like a sledgehammer on a floating cork. . . . Somehow the cork refused to stay down."

**The Endless War** For Americans fighting a seemingly unwinnable war, Vietnam was a frustrating and terrifying nightmare. Nurses working in mobile army surgical hospital (MASH) units near the front and on hospital ships off the coast probably had a better feeling for the Vietnam tragedy than anyone. They saw the wounded every day, day after day. Ruth Sidisin of the air force nurse corps said: "Vietnam was not John Wayne. In Vietnam, every day was disaster day."

Most of the U.S. troops were young and inexperienced; the average soldier was just 19 years old, seven years younger than the average soldier in World War II. These young people found themselves miles from home in a steamy jungle filled with daily horrors—mud, heat, booby traps, and an invisible enemy. They fought bravely, but the war seemed endless. Some turned to drugs to escape. Some snapped under pressure, no longer able to tell friend from foe. Others asked, What are we fighting for? Who is the enemy? David Ross, a 19-year-old army medic, had volunteered to fight in Vietnam, but his faith in his country's goals had been shaken by two years of war:

*I volunteered, you know. Ever since the American Revolution my family had people in all the different wars, and that was always the thing—when your country needs you, you go. You don't ask a lot of questions, because the country's always right. This time it didn't turn out that way.*

David Ross,
in *Everything We Had*, 1981

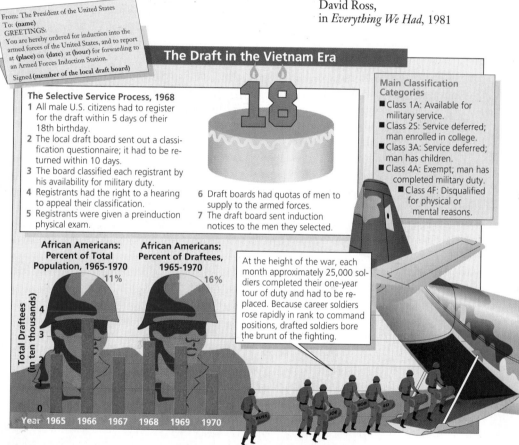

**The Draft in the Vietnam Era**

From: The President of the United States
To: (name)
GREETINGS:
You are hereby ordered for induction into the armed forces of the United States, and to report at (place) on (date) at (hour) for forwarding to an Armed Forces Induction Station.
Signed (member of the local draft board)

**The Selective Service Process, 1968**
1 All male U.S. citizens had to register for the draft within 5 days of their 18th birthday.
2 The local draft board sent out a classification questionnaire; it had to be returned within 10 days.
3 The board classified each registrant by his availability for military duty.
4 Registrants had the right to a hearing to appeal their classification.
5 Registrants were given a preinduction physical exam.
6 Draft boards had quotas of men to supply to the armed forces.
7 The draft board sent induction notices to the men they selected.

**Main Classification Categories**
- Class 1A: Available for military service.
- Class 2S: Service deferred; man enrolled in college.
- Class 3A: Service deferred; man has children.
- Class 4A: Exempt; man has completed military duty.
  - Class 4F: Disqualified for physical or mental reasons.

**African Americans: Percent of Total Population, 1965-1970** 11%

**African Americans: Percent of Draftees, 1965-1970** 16%

Total Draftees (in ten thousands)

Year 1965 1966 1967 1968 1969 1970

At the height of the war, each month approximately 25,000 soldiers completed their one-year tour of duty and had to be replaced. Because career soldiers rose rapidly in rank to command positions, drafted soldiers bore the brunt of the fighting.

## SECTION REVIEW

**Checking Facts**
1. Why did the United States support the French war effort in Vietnam?
2. Describe the domino theory of containment as it applied to Vietnam.
3. Why did the war in Vietnam escalate under President Johnson?
4. Describe how the Vietcong fought the war. What advantages did the Vietcong have over U.S. troops?

5. Why was all of South Vietnam a war zone? How did this affect American troops?

**Thinking Critically**
6. **Recognizing Assumptions** What assumptions did U.S. policymakers make about Vietnam based on events that had taken place in China?

7. **Recognizing Bias** In what ways did U.S. military planners fail to understand the Vietnamese culture? How did this affect pacification programs in South Vietnam?

**Linking Across Time**
8. The domino theory is still used by some politicians to explain global politics. Do you agree with the theory? Explain why or why not.

# An Era of Consciousness

*By the early 1970s, millions and millions of Americans—especially those on college campuses—were protesting against the ills of society. The war, poverty, racial and sexual discrimination, technology, and pollution were all targets. Many traditional values, too, seemed under siege.*

The rainbow, symbol of optimism

**Cloth patches** carried the symbols of the day. Peace, equality, and a better world were in. War and pollution were out.

The **ecology flag** designed in 1970 for the first Earth Day

A popular slogan protesting the war in Vietnam and all wars, past and future

The **keep on truckin'** character, by cartoonist R. Crumb, became a symbol of independence, a carefree attitude, and perseverance in the face of adversity.

**The raised fist** became a symbol of black power, and *Soul on Ice*, by Eldridge Cleaver, became required reading.

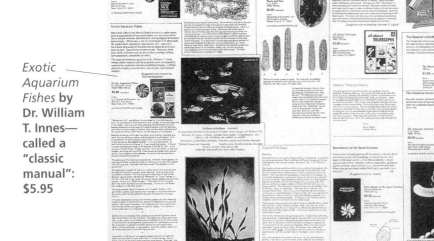

*Exotic Aquarium Fishes* **by Dr. William T. Innes— called a "classic manual": $5.95**

**Catalog of astronomical photos**

**"Divine Right's Trip," an original folktale, appeared regularly throughout the catalog on right-hand pages.**

The *Whole Earth Catalog* was a massive compilation of everything you might need to "do your own thing." Entries in the 448-page book included everything from how to buy army surplus vehicles to how to build alternative housing in the wilderness.

Joan Chandos Baez was one of a **new generation of folk singers** who used their lyrics for social and political ends. Baez was active in the civil rights movement and the antiwar movement, and many of her songs reflected those concerns.

The upheavals of the 1960s caused a **conservative backlash** among some groups, like these Young Republicans at a Nixon for President convention.

# 1968: A Year of Crises

## November 21, 1967: General Westmoreland Reports End Is Near

FACED WITH GROWING OPPOSITION TO THE WAR AT HOME, PRESIDENT JOHNSON BROUGHT GENERAL WILLIAM WESTMORELAND BACK FROM SAIGON TO REASSURE the American public about the war. On November 21, 1967, in an address to the National Press Club in Washington, D.C., Westmoreland delivered an upbeat report: "I am absolutely certain that whereas in 1965 the enemy was winning, today he is certainly losing," he said. "There are indications that the Vietcong and even Hanoi know this. . . . We have reached an important point when the end begins to come into view."

Just 10 weeks later, however, General Westmoreland's words rang hollow. On January 30, 1968, the first day of the Vietnamese New Year, or Tet, communist forces launched a massive attack, striking without warning at civilian and military targets throughout South Vietnam. Within 24 hours, about 84,000 communist soldiers had stormed more than 100 South Vietnamese cities and towns, a dozen U.S. military bases, and even the U.S. embassy in Saigon.

NATIONAL PRESS CLUB

AP/WIDE WORLD PHOTOS

forces hammered its streets with bombs and artillery fire. The fighting left the beautiful city of old temples and palaces a "shattered, stinking hulk, its streets choked with rubble and rotting bodies."

U.S. forces routed the Vietcong, killing an estimated 33,000 enemy troops in the first two weeks of the month-long Tet offensive. The cost was high, however. More than 1,100 American soldiers, 2,300 South Vietnamese troops, and 12,500 Vietnamese civilians were killed. More than one million Vietnamese became refugees. Dozens of towns and villages lay in ruins. As one American army officer said of the battle for the village of Ben Tre, "We had to destroy the town to save it."

Westmoreland quickly claimed Tet as a victory for the United States and boasted that "the enemy is on the ropes." Even the communists admitted that Tet had not achieved their major goal, "to spur uprisings throughout the south." However, Tet also marked a turning point in the war. It showed that no place in South Vietnam—not even the American embassy— was safe from attack. It shattered American confidence and raised grave doubts about Johnson's policies in Vietnam.

**Critics of U.S. Policy** "What the hell is going on?" asked Walter Cronkite, the respected CBS news anchorman. "I thought we were winning the war!" After returning from a trip to Saigon after the Tet offensive, Cronkite reported that "it seems now more

## Tet: A Turning Point

Though most of the targets were retaken by U.S. and South Vietnamese forces within hours or days, a bitter battle over the ancient city of Hue raged for nearly three weeks. To recapture the city, U.S.

---

certain than ever that the bloody experience in Vietnam is to end in a stalemate . . . [and] that the only rational way out . . . will be to negotiate."

"If I've lost Walter," lamented President Johnson, "then it's over. I've lost Mr. Average Citizen." Editorials in *Newsweek*, *Time*, and the *Wall Street Journal* also called for a negotiated settlement of the war and a prompt withdrawal of American troops.

Televised reports challenged official statements and brought home the brutality and hopelessness of the war. American viewers were stunned by the scenes of fighting in South Vietnam—the desperate struggle to regain the U.S. embassy, the destruction of Hue. Millions were shocked by the brutality of America's ally as they watched a South Vietnamese police chief draw his revolver, place it against the head of a young Vietcong prisoner, and pull the trigger. Such images prompted many Americans to question U.S. policy: Was the United States really defending democracy in Vietnam? If so, at what cost?

**The United States began bombing North Vietnam in 1965 to relieve military pressure on the South.** *Why did the United States stage so many bombing raids in Laos and Cambodia, just west of Vietnam?*

The horrifying images of Tet contradicted the rosy picture of the war painted by Westmoreland the previous fall. Public opinion polls showed that in the six weeks after the Tet offensive, the percentage of Americans who approved of Johnson's handling of the war plunged from 40 to 26; Johnson's overall approval ratings dropped from 48 to 36 percent. The massive antiwar protests of the previous year grew even larger. Crowds of angry demonstrators chanted, "Hey, hey, LBJ. How many kids did you kill today?"

**Democratic Challengers** As President Johnson's popularity took a nose dive, he faced another crisis. The liberal Minnesota senator, Eugene McCarthy,

---

## STUDY GUIDE

**Comparing and Contrasting**
The war in Vietnam was not new to television at the time of Tet. What was new was the imagery flashed into American homes. Prior to Tet, the war took place in the jungle. Viewers were used to seeing troops scrambling out of helicopters into high grass or patrolling single file down a muddy path. Violence was brief and faceless: a shot from a hidden guerilla, an exploding grenade. Tet brought the war closer to home. The fighting was intense and personal, involving both civilians and soldiers. Destruction and agony were the rule, not the exception.

© DONALD MCMULLIN, MAGNUM PHOTOS, INC.

© RENE BURRI, MAGNUM PHOTOS, INC.

**The Tet offensive brought widespread destruction in its wake, touching the lives of soldiers and civilians alike. Three Marines in flak jackets drag a sniper victim out of the line of fire during the battle of Hue in February 1968, left. A Vietnamese peasant mourns the death of a loved one, right.** *What effect did Tet have on the American people?*

had entered the New Hampshire Democratic primary. Running on an antiwar platform, McCarthy challenged Johnson for the presidential nomination.

Since the summer of 1967, antiwar Democrats had been searching for a candidate to replace President Johnson. They first tried to recruit New York Senator Robert Kennedy, a vocal critic of the war and the brother of slain President John Kennedy. Reluctant to challenge the president and split the party, Kennedy at first refused. The antiwar Democrats then turned to McCarthy.

At the beginning of January, with support from just 17 percent of the Democratic party, McCarthy had seemed to pose little threat to Johnson's reelection bid. Then came Tet.

McCarthy's antiwar stand attracted thousands of college students. With the motto, "Be clean for Gene," the students trimmed their hair, dressed in suits and ties, and swarmed across New Hampshire, knocking on doors and urging residents to vote for McCarthy. On March 12 McCarthy surprised everyone by winning nearly half the popular vote as well as 20 out of 24 state delegates to the national nominating convention.

Not all of those who voted for McCarthy favored United States withdrawal from Vietnam; many favored stepping up the U.S. effort to win the war. Whatever their politics, New Hampshire voters agreed that Johnson's policies had failed.

On March 16 another antiwar candidate entered the race—Robert Kennedy. His challenge, however, embittered many of McCarthy's supporters, who feared that McCarthy and Kennedy would split the antiwar vote. With a promise to carry on the goals of his brother's New Frontier, Kennedy attracted widespread support from minorities, the poor, and the working class, as well as better-off mainstream Democrats. As the Vietnam War drained more and more money from social reform at home, Kennedy's ranks of supporters swelled.[1]

---

## STUDY GUIDE

### Analyzing Decisions

McCarthy's decision to challenge Johnson for the presidential nomination was based on principle. He announced his candidacy long before anyone thought he had a chance of success. Kennedy

also had grave doubts about the war, but he had another consideration. No Democrat had ever challenged a sitting president for the nomination. Kennedy did not want to break the tradition.

**1** Why were McCarthy's supporters upset and angry when Robert Kennedy announced his candidacy?

**Johnson's Decision**  Shaken by Tet, McCarthy's success in New Hampshire, and Kennedy's entry in the presidential race, President Johnson faced a further dilemma. Following the Tet offensive, General Westmoreland and the Joint Chiefs of Staff had requested an additional 206,000 American troops—a 40 percent increase. Westmoreland claimed that Tet losses had weakened the Vietcong. With additional troops, he argued, the United States could take advantage of their weakness and score a military victory. Uneasy about the request for additional troops, Johnson asked his new secretary of defense, Clark Clifford, to make a recommendation.

After questioning the Joint Chiefs of Staff, Clifford became convinced that "the military course we were pursuing was not only endless but hopeless." The top military commanders could give him no reason to believe the communists could be beaten by "an additional 200,000 American troops, or double or triple that quantity." As a result, Clifford recommended that the president reject Westmoreland's request and, instead, encourage the South Vietnamese to do more of the fighting. Bitterly, Johnson accepted Clifford's recommendation. He would send only a few thousand additional troops to Vietnam, and, for the first time in three years of war, Johnson refused to support Westmoreland. (You can learn more about the decision to stop the escalation of the war in the Case Study on pages 672-675.)

On March 31, three years after the first American troops landed in Vietnam, Johnson made a televised speech. He announced that the United States would limit the bombing of North Vietnam, and he appealed to Ho Chi Minh for a negotiated settlement to the war. Then Johnson dropped his own bombshell: "I have decided that I shall not seek and I will not accept the nomination of my party for another term as your president."

Unable to build a Great Society at home and wage a war at the same time, Johnson got out of the race. He later confided to his biographer Doris Kearns the reasons why:

*O*n one side, the American people were *stampeding me to do something about Vietnam. On the other side, the inflationary economy was booming out of control. Up ahead*
*were dozens of dangerous signs pointing to another summer of riots in the cities. . . . And then the final straw. The thing I feared from the first day of my presidency was actually coming true. Robert Kennedy had openly announced his intention to reclaim the throne in the memory of his brother. . . . The whole situation was unbearable to me.*[2]

Doris Kearns,
*Lyndon Johnson and the American Dream*, 1976

Two days later, McCarthy swept the Wisconsin Democratic primary.

## Tragedy and Turmoil

According to Vietnamese tradition, the first guest through the door during the Tet holiday serves as a sign of the year to come. The Vietcong commandos who burst into the U.S. embassy in the early morning hours of Tet ushered in a troubled year for Americans, a year of turmoil, frustrated hopes, and shattered dreams.

Tensions over the war in Vietnam and the civil rights struggle at home had been building up for years. Now they exploded. The troubling events of 1968 would lead many Americans to reject the liberalism of the 1960s and embrace a new conservatism in hopes of bringing an end to the war and restoring peace at home.

**King's Assassination**  A nation still reeling from the shock of Tet and Johnson's refusal to run for reelection suffered another blow in April—the assassination of Martin Luther King, Jr., the civil rights leader. One of the earliest critics of U.S. involvement in Vietnam, King had linked the struggle for racial equality and economic justice to the struggle for peace. "The black revolution is much more than a struggle for the rights of Negroes," he declared. "It is forcing America to face all its interrelated flaws—racism, poverty, militarism, and materialism."

The news of King's murder stunned the nation. Thousands of his admirers took part in peaceful marches and memorial services, but the shock and grief soon turned to rage. Within hours, many

**Analyzing Decisions**
The war in Vietnam was not the only reason Johnson decided not to run for reelection in 1968. His health was another factor. Violence in the nation's cities was still another. Johnson feared he might be put in the position of having to decide whether or not to use federal troops against citizen rioters.

2 What other political event during the month of March contributed to Johnson's decision not to run for reelection?

African Americans stormed through the streets of cities around the country. Their anger and frustration exploded in rioting, looting, and burning. In Chicago, fires raged through a 20-block area of the city's heavily black West Side. In Washington, D.C., soldiers armed with rifles and machine guns stood guard outside the White House and the Capitol as blacks looted and burned.

**The Democratic Primaries**   While the nation agonized over unrest at home and war abroad, the presidential race picked up speed. Three candidates now scrambled for the Democratic nomination: Eugene McCarthy, Robert Kennedy, and Vice President Hubert Humphrey.

Although Humphrey championed civil rights and social reform, his tie to Johnson's Vietnam policies repelled the antiwar liberals. To line up convention support, Humphrey avoided the primaries and courted the Democratic party bosses, who in some states chose the delegates.

McCarthy waged a spirited crusade against the war and social injustice, but his low-key, intellectual style appealed mainly to educated middle-class liberals. "He has wit, charm, and grace," columnist I. F. Stone observed, "but he seems to lack heart and guts."

Robert Kennedy on the other hand, made passionate appeals on behalf of the have-nots of American society. Campaigning against poverty, racism, and the war, Kennedy reached out to African Americans, Native Americans, Hispanic Americans, and young protestors. With Johnson out of the race, Kennedy quickly became the front-runner.

Kennedy won early primary victories in Indiana and Nebraska, but McCarthy rebounded and scored a victory in the Oregon primary. California, the nation's most populous state, was next. Both candidates campaigned energetically, but when the polls closed on June 4, Kennedy had won 46 percent of the popular vote and McCarthy just 41 percent. California was a winner-take-all state, so Kennedy claimed all the convention delegates.

**Kennedy's Assassination**   That evening, moments after the victorious Kennedy spoke to cheering supporters at a Los Angeles hotel, he lay dying, the victim of an assassin's bullet. The nation reeled in

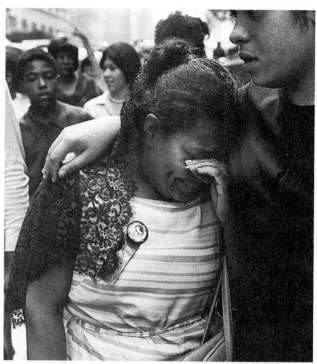

© COSTA MANOS, MAGNUM PHOTOS, INC.

**Thousands of mourners lined the route as a special funeral train carrying the body of Robert Kennedy wended its way from New York to Washington. Kennedy was buried in Arlington National Cemetery, a short distance away from his brother.**

shock. Within two months, two liberal leaders—both critics of the war and advocates of civil rights—had been killed. The deaths of King and Kennedy shattered the hopes of antiwar and civil rights activists who had sought to work within the political system. Many despaired that politics would ever be an effective way to enact change. "I won't vote," one young African American from New York declared. "Every good man we get they kill."

## The Election of 1968

The simmering anger and frustration felt by many Americans over the deaths of King and Kennedy would boil over in the August heat, as Democrats met in Chicago to nominate a candidate for president. The resulting convention turmoil would shock the nation and splinter the Democratic party. In the process, it

### Comparing and Contrasting

One was white; the other was black. One was an attorney from the Northeast; the other was a minister from the South. One came from the Establishment, the political and social elite; the other came from the disenfranchised, the politically and socially oppressed. Despite these differences, Robert Kennedy and Martin Luther King, Jr., were both widely regarded as leaders who could bridge chasms in the social order. King was able to appeal to both blacks and whites. Kennedy appealed to the young and the old, the poor and the rich.

would help pave the way for a new conservative era in presidential politics.

**The Democratic Convention**   With Kennedy dead and McCarthy unable to rally more than a few convention delegates, Hubert Humphrey looked like a sure winner of the Democratic nomination. Humphrey's support for Johnson's Vietnam policies,

UPI/BETTMAN NEWSPHOTOS

**Antiwar demonstrators clash with Chicago police on Michigan Avenue as Democrats select Humphrey as their presidential candidate. Americans all over the country watched the drama unfold on television.**
*What effect did the violence in Chicago have on Humphrey's chances in the coming election?*

however, angered many antiwar activists. Nearly 10,000 of them flocked to Chicago to protest, if they could not prevent, Humphrey's nomination.

Most of the demonstrators had come to pressure delegates to adopt an antiwar platform. Some, however, hoped to provoke violence that would discredit the Democrats. With memories of the riots after King's death still fresh, Chicago Mayor Richard Daley mobilized 12,000 Chicago police officers and put 5,000 National Guardsmen on call. "As long as I am mayor," he vowed, "there will be law and order."

Daley forces ringed the convention hall with barbed wire. On August 28, as convention delegates cast their ballots for Hubert Humphrey, helmeted police savagely clubbed demonstrators and bystanders in downtown Chicago. The protestors chanted, "The whole world is watching." Indeed, as television cameras broadcast the brutal scene to homes across the nation, the image of the Democrats as the party of disorder was etched in the minds of millions of Americans.

**Nixon and the Republicans**   The Republicans took advantage of the Democrats' disarray to present themselves as the party of stability. According to writer Norman Mailer, the Republican convention in Miami was a "convention of the clean, the brisk, the orderly, the efficient"—a marked contrast to the Democrats. Republican delegates quickly picked former Vice President Richard Nixon to once again be their candidate for president.

Just six years earlier, Nixon's political career seemed dead. In 1962, after losing the race for governor of California, Nixon had announced that he was retiring from politics, telling reporters, "You won't have Nixon to kick around anymore." But Richard Nixon was a fighter, not a quitter. Now he was making a comeback.

A shrewd politician, Richard Nixon saw that many Americans were frightened by the disorder and violence of the 1960s. They were impatient with urban violence and campus unrest, and they resented the counterculture's challenge to traditional values. Nixon would try to appeal to those who, as one reporter put it, yearned for "a kind of Eisenhowerian calm, after the pains and shocks and tragedies of the Democratic years."

In his acceptance speech at the Republican convention, Nixon echoed that deep yearning:

> *As we look at America, we see cities enveloped in smoke and flame. We hear sirens in the night. We see Americans hating each other; killing each other at home. And as we see and hear these things millions of Americans cry out in anger: Did we come all this way for this?*
>
> Richard M. Nixon,
> Republican Convention, 1968

Nixon promised to end the turmoil and to protect the "first civil right of every American . . . to be free from domestic violence." He attacked Johnson's Great Society, declaring that it was "time to quit pouring billions of dollars into programs that have failed." To Americans weary of the Vietnam War, he promised "peace with honor."

**The Wallace Campaign**   The only threat to Nixon's presidential campaign came from further right. The conservative governor of Alabama, George Wallace, was running as the candidate of the American Independent Party. In his campaign for the presidency, Wallace was attempting to capture the same conservative voters that Nixon sought—those who feared school integration, resented the Great Society's antipoverty programs, and despised antiwar protestors.

As governor of Alabama, Wallace had once pledged to enforce "segregation now . . . segregation tomorrow . . . segregation forever." As a presidential candidate, he tried to appeal to the fears and prejudices of blue-collar workers around the country by lashing out at the "briefcase-totin' bureaucrats, ivory-tower guideline writers, bearded anarchists, smart-aleck editorial writers, and pointy-headed professors looking down their noses at us."

Wallace called for victory in Vietnam, and he denounced the antiwar protestors. "If any demonstrator ever lays down in front of my car," he pledged to his supporters, "it will be the last car he will ever lay down in front of."

Wallace's popularity climbed as his attacks grew more shrill. By mid-September, polls showed that he had won the support of 21 percent of the voters. His campaign suffered a setback, however, when he picked Curtis LeMay, a retired air force general, as his running mate. LeMay frightened even devoted Wallace supporters when he argued that the United States should "drop nukes on Vietnam."

**The Election**   By the end of September, polls showed Humphrey trailing Nixon by 15 percentage points and leading Wallace by only 7 points. Crippled by his loyalty to Johnson's Vietnam policy, Humphrey was falling further and further behind. In mid-October he tried to salvage his campaign by calling for a halt to the bombing of North Vietnam. Johnson tried to help by ordering a complete halt to the bombing on October 31.

Humphrey managed to close in on Nixon, but it was too late. On election day Nixon won 43.4 percent of the popular vote, edging out Humphrey by less than 1 percent. Nearly 14 percent of the voters rejected both the Republican and Democratic parties and cast their votes for Wallace.

The 57 percent of voters who supported Nixon or Wallace signaled the rise of a new conservative majority. Since the election of 1964, the Democrats had lost nearly 12 million voters, including many in the once solidly Democratic South. The New Deal **coalition,**

© CHARLES BONWAY, BLACK STAR

**Sensing victory as election day draws near, Nixon supporters are jubilant as their candidate arrives to speak at a campaign rally. The slogan on the hats reads, "Nixon's the One."**

## STUDY GUIDE

### Recognizing Propaganda

The portion of Nixon's acceptance speech on page 669 is an example of propaganda. The word *we* is used six times, establishing an emotional rhythm between Nixon and his audience.

Names of specific cities and specific acts of violence are replaced with poetic and moralistic generalities: "cities enveloped in flames . . . Americans hating each other." The sentence "Did we come all

this way for this?" adds the metaphor of a journey to the speech, inviting Americans to rise up against the present immorality to recapture their destiny.

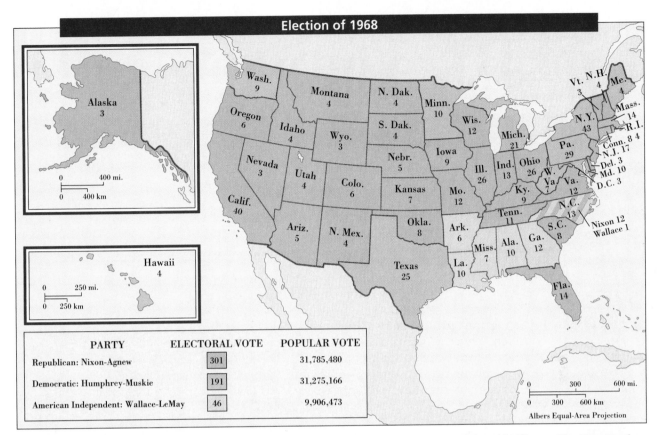

## Election of 1968

| PARTY | ELECTORAL VOTE | POPULAR VOTE |
|---|---|---|
| Republican: Nixon-Agnew | 301 | 31,785,480 |
| Democratic: Humphrey-Muskie | 191 | 31,275,166 |
| American Independent: Wallace-LeMay | 46 | 9,906,473 |

**Nixon beat Humphrey by half a million votes, ushering in a new era of conservative presidential politics. "In city after city," one observer noted, "racial** **conflicts had destroyed the old alliance. The New Deal had unraveled block by block."** *Where did Nixon garner most of his support? Where was Wallace particularly strong?*

or alliance, of liberals, blacks, and southern whites was finally shattered over two divisive issues—civil rights and the war in Vietnam. Many of those who abandoned the Democrats felt that the party's social reforms—particularly the push for civil rights—had gone too far and that the Democrats had failed in Vietnam.

Some observers interpreted the election as a sign that the American political system was still alive and healthy. One British journalist noted, "The enormous power of the presidency passed peacefully from one man to another [despite] the fear that the country was coming apart."

Others, however, were disheartened by the outcome of the 1968 election. For them, Nixon's election signaled more than just the end of a liberal era. It marked a defeat for those who had tried to work within the American political system to bring about racial equality, economic justice, and an end to the war in Southeast Asia.

## SECTION REVIEW

### Checking Facts

1. Why was the Tet offensive a turning point in the war in Vietnam?

2. What did Lyndon Johnson mean when he said, "If I've lost Walter, then it's all over"?

3. How did the Republicans take advantage of the violence and disorder associated with the Democratic convention?

4. Briefly describe Richard Nixon's political career up to 1968. How did Nixon position himself as a presidential candidate in 1968?

### Thinking Critically

5. **Analyzing Decisions** Why did Johnson deny the request by General Westmoreland for an additional 206,000 troops?

6. **Comparing and Contrasting** Compare and contrast George Wallace's campaign for president with Richard Nixon's.

### Linking Across Time

7. In 1968, a liberal era ended and a conservative era began. Since your birth, has the United States tended to have conservative or liberal presidents? Do you predict a change in the political orientation of the country in your lifetime? Why or why not?

# Case Study

# LBJ, Vietnam, and the Troop Request

## MARCH 1968

Memorandum for the Secretary of Defense
Subject:The Infeasibility of Military Victory in Vietnam

   As a contribution to current deliberations and your own ongoing review of the situation, this memorandum argues the case that the idea of military victory in Vietnam is a dangerous illusion at any price that would be compatible with the U.S. interests, the interests of the people of South Vietnam, or the cause of world peace. . . .

                 Townsend Hoopes
                 Under Secretary of the Air Force
                 March 14, 1968

## The Case

On February 28, 1968, General Earle G. Wheeler arrived at Andrews Air Force Base, Maryland, from Vietnam and went directly to the White House. Wheeler, the chairman of the Joint Chiefs of Staff, carried a report that he and General Westmoreland had prepared in Vietnam. At the White House, Wheeler met with President Johnson and his senior advisers to present a summary of the report. Wheeler and Westmoreland asked the president for 206,000 more troops to counteract the recent Tet offensive.

The magnitude of the request shocked some, including the president. In a grim outline of the situation, Wheeler focused on the political and military weakness of the South Vietnamese and stressed that the Tet offensive had not yet run its course.

The choices open to the president were not attractive ones, especially in an election year. Meeting the troop request would require calling up reserves, an unpopular act that would put the country in a state of wartime readiness. Funding such an escalation would require new taxes as well as cuts in domestic programs vital to the Great Society. On the other hand, denying the request, or supplying only a fraction of the troops requested, would signal to the enemy that the American war effort had limits.

## The Background

The Tet offensive was a watershed for American policy in Vietnam. Both those who supported the war and those who opposed it saw in Tet an opportunity—and a need—to change the American war effort radically. Neither group believed any longer in the strategy of a limited war won by wearing down the North Vietnamese. For hawks, Tet was the act of a desperate enemy, a last-ditch effort to strike a crippling blow. The hawks hoped for a change in U.S. strategy that would support new offensives against a much weakened enemy. For many in the military, Tet presented the United States with an opportunity to win the war quickly and go home.

For doves, the days of Tet were watched as a nightly television horror show. Coverage of the offensive revealed that the distinctions between civilians and combatants, fighting and murder, purpose and senselessness were blurred beyond recognition. A negotiated end to the war seemed the only sensible, humane solution.

After General Wheeler's briefing, President Johnson assigned his incoming secretary of defense, Clark Clifford, to study the implications of granting the troop request. Clifford was one of Johnson's oldest and most trusted supporters. He had served as special counsel for President Truman, left government to establish a private law practice, and later advised President Kennedy. Until his appointment as secretary of defense, Clifford had not been a formal member of the Johnson administration, but he was thought to be hawkish.

The Clifford Task Force, as it came to be known, started to work that weekend. The president had given them four days.

## The Opinions

Of the four men shown at the right, only one, General Wheeler, was an official member of the nine-person task force. But each of the four had direct access to the task force, and their diverse opinions were all represented and argued before the group.

Taken together, the opinions of Wheeler and Westmoreland epitomize the military view of the war. Both generals were eager to shed the political constraints that kept the war limited. Both saw the conflict as a war of wills. Winning the war, in their view, was only as far away as finding the necessary political and moral resolve. In the past these views had been supported by the White House, especially by President Johnson.

Enthoven was one of a number of junior officials who had almost daily contact with Clifford

UPI/BETTMANN NEWSPHOTOS

*"The single most important factor in prolonging the war is Hanoi's calculation that there is a reasonable possibility of change in U.S. policy. . . . We are winning the war in Vietnam, but Hanoi is still not ready to give up."*

—General Earle G. Wheeler, Chairman, Joint Chiefs of Staff

THE BETTMANN ARCHIVE

*"I do not see how the enemy can long sustain [his] heavy losses. . . . Adequate reinforcement should allow me to . . . capitalize on his losses by seizing the initiative in other areas. Exploiting this opportunity could materially shorten the war."*

—General William C. Westmoreland, Commander of U.S. Troops in South Vietnam

AP/WIDE WORLD PHOTOS

*"We know that despite a massive influx of 500,000 U.S. troops . . . our control of the countryside and the defense of the urban areas is now essentially at pre-August 1965 levels. A new strategy must be sought."*

—Alain Enthoven, Assistant Secretary of Defense

AP/WIDE WORLD PHOTOS

*"Like everyone else who had been deeply involved in explaining the policies of the war and trying to understand them and render some judgement, I was fed up with the `light at the end of the tunnel' stuff. I was fed up with the optimism that seemed to flow without stopping from Saigon."*

—Harry C. McPherson, White House speech writer

and the other task force members. The brutal honesty of these officials had a tremendous impact on the working of the task force and on Clark Clifford himself.

McPherson was a speech writer for the president. In just a few weeks, McPherson, President Johnson, Clifford, Wheeler, and a few others would collaborate on a speech about Vietnam that Johnson would deliver to the entire country.

## The Options

The Johnson administration was far from unified in regard to the troop request, and to the war in general. Tet had called into question issues of both strategy—how the war was being fought—and policy—why the war was being fought. The Clifford Task Force, initially formed to analyze the single issue of the troop request, soon found itself asking fundamental questions about the basic motives and aims of the war effort. The options that were open to Johnson were varied and complex:

1. Maintain the war effort. Give Westmoreland some additional troops to meet needs caused by the Tet offensive.
2. Widen the war effort. Give Westmoreland the 206,000 troops, and try to win the war.
3. Expand and improve the South Vietnamese army as the first priority in a continuing war effort.
4. Get out of the war.
5. Some combination of the above.

Of course, not *any* combination of the above would work. For example, option 4 is not compatible with options 1 and 2. It is possible, however, for option 3 to work with option 4. For example, South Vietnamese troops could be used to replace American troops as a peace settlement was being negotiated. In addition, some variation of option 3 could be integrated with option 1 or 2.

## The Decision

On Sunday evening, March 31, 1968, President Johnson addressed the country about Vietnam. Half an hour before the address, Clark Clifford was invited to the family quarters at the White House. Clifford was so unsure of Johnson's position on the war that he had composed a letter of resignation to deliver if Johnson's address announced an escalation of the war.

It had been a difficult month for the two men. The Clifford Task Force reported to Johnson on March 4. The report simply recommended that the president send a small number of additional troops to Vietnam. Johnson delayed any immediate decision and continued to meet with his top advisers. As the month wore on, Clifford came increasingly to doubt the direction of the war effort. As his doubts grew, so did the strain on his relationship with Johnson. Clifford finally suggested that Johnson convene the so-called Wise Men, a small group of influential business and military leaders that Johnson occasionally called together to advise him on policy.

The 14 Wise Men—among them Dean Acheson, secretary of state under President Truman; General Omar Bradley, World War II commander; Henry Cabot Lodge, former senator and twice ambassador to South Vietnam; and Arthur Goldberg, ambassador to the United Nations and former secretary of labor and Supreme Court justice—met at the White House on March 25. After briefings by Johnson's advisers, the group reported to the president after lunch the next day. The views of each man were heard in turn.

Johnson was deeply impressed by what he heard. Except for a small minority that supported the current policies, the group agreed that the United States should find a way to reduce the American commitment in Vietnam as a prelude to getting out of the war altogether. The Wise Men said what the newspapers and protesters in the street had been saying for weeks.

Now, five days later, Johnson and Clifford stood together for a moment before Johnson motioned Clifford into a White House bedroom and showed him the final two paragraphs of the address. The address would end with a call for peace in Vietnam and the announcement that Johnson would not seek reelection. Clark Clifford was stunned.

Johnson also announced that he would make only a small increase in the number of troops in Vietnam, and he would stop the bombing of large portions of North Vietnam. Johnson also called for the South Vietnamese to take a greater role in the war and pledged support for that effort from the United States.

AP/WIDE WORLD PHOTOS

THE LYNDON BAINES JOHNSON LIBRARY, AUSTIN

**President Johnson meets with General West-moreland, Clark Clifford, and Dean Rusk, left. Weary, he agonizes over his decision, above.**

## The Interpretations

The routine matter of a troop request changed the nature of American involvement in Vietnam. When the month of March began, it seemed possible that the war might escalate and the number of troops in Vietnam rise by 206,000. When the month ended, President Johnson had announced his intention to retire from public life, and the United States had halted the bombing of North Vietnam as the first step in a peace initiative designed to end the war. It was a decisive moment. For the first time, the United States sought to de-escalate the war. For the first time, the United States served notice that American resources were limited. How and why such a dramatic change in policy occurred is subject to a variety of interpretations.

Some historians maintain that the important decision-making process in this case took place among the American public. These historians argue that after Tet, the public consensus against the war forced Johnson to change direction. The decisive role of the Wise Men in Johnson's decision supports this argument.

Other historians place more importance on the governmental decision-making process. These historians focus on the role played by Johnson's advisers—notably Clark Clifford—in influencing Johnson's decision. For these historians, Clifford forced Johnson to question assumptions about the war effort that had never been challenged before. According to this view, Johnson was reeducated about the war by his own top advisers. During the process, he came to understand how little public support there was for the war effort.

The war would last another five years. The main objective—to keep South Vietnam from falling to communism—did not change. Johnson's address did, however, change how that objective was to be met. First, the United States would pursue a political rather than military settlement to the war. The United States would negotiate. Next, while the fighting continued, the United States would make sure that the South Vietnamese were doing a full share of the fighting. These two new strategies guided the war effort, with a few exceptions, until the war ended.

## Think About It

1. How did the Tet offensive influence the decision-making process of Johnson and his administration?

2. Analyze how the decision-making process regarding the troop request was influenced by the fact that it was an election year. How might the process have been different had it not been an election year?

3. Some historians credit Clark Clifford for the turnabout in Johnson's policies. Give reasons for and against this argument.

4. Some historians argue that while the North Vietnamese and Vietcong lost the battles of the Tet offensive, the offensive caused Americans to lose confidence in their government and military. Give several facts that support this argument.

5. American presidents are often accused of being isolated from the people. In this case, how was President Johnson exposed to the opinions of the American public?

# The War at Home

## Fall 1964: Berkeley Students Demand Right to Free Speech

MARIO SAVIO, A 21-YEAR-OLD STUDENT AT THE BERKELEY CAMPUS OF THE UNIVERSITY OF CALIFORNIA, SENT A LETTER TO A FRIEND IN AUGUST OF 1964. "I'M TIRED of reading about history," he wrote. "I want to make it." Savio got his chance that fall when he returned to Berkeley. Uneasy about student activism, university officials had banned on-campus recruitment for off-campus political activities. Led by Savio, a group of students founded the Berkeley Free Speech Movement (FSM) to protest the ban.

On December 2, nearly 6,000 students rallied on the steps of Sproul Hall, the administration building of the university. Folk singer Joan Baez joined the throng, singing the civil rights anthem, "We Shall Overcome." Savio stirred the students to action with a fiery speech. Universities, he claimed, had become vast knowledge factories serving only the interests of U.S. corporations. Students were treated not as human beings but as products rolling off an assembly line, diploma in hand. He called on his fellow students to resist:

AP/WIDE WORLD PHOTOS

> *There is a time when the operation of the machine becomes so odious, makes you so sick to heart, that . . . you've got to put your bodies upon the gears and upon the wheels . . . and you've got to make it stop.*
>
> Mario Savio,
> December 2, 1964

Inspired by Savio's speech, more than 1,000 students marched into Sproul Hall and staged a sit-in. This was the first but by no means the last time students would use civil disobedience to press their demands on campus. Just after 3:00 A.M., police began clearing the building, arresting nearly 800 demonstrators.

In the days following the arrests, nearly 70 percent of Berkeley students protested. They picketed administration buildings, brandishing signs that read "Shut This Factory Down" and "I Am a U.C. Student: Do Not Fold, Bend, or Mutilate."

University officials eventually backed down. In early 1965, they lifted the ban on campus political activity. By 1965, however, student protests had spread like wildfire across the nation's campuses. Unlike the "Silent Generation" of the 1950s, the rebellious students of the 1960s became outspoken critics of American society. At first, their protests focused on students' rights. Soon, however, a new issue would arise to fuel student passions—the war in Vietnam.

## The Birth of the Student Movement

The students who protested at Berkeley were children of the post-World War II baby boom. Growing up in the 1950s, they were now attending college in unprecedented numbers. In 1950 only one million young Americans attended college. By 1960 that number had jumped to four million. By the end of the decade, nearly eight million students flooded the nation's campuses.

Raised in the prosperity of the postwar years, the college students of the 1960s had grown up in economic security, free of the worries that had troubled their Depression-era parents. Seventy-five percent of them came from families with incomes above the national average. Mostly white and middle class, student activists could afford to be idealistic and rebellious.

Their idealism was stirred by a youthful President Kennedy, who appealed to young Americans in 1961 to "ask not what your country can do for you—ask what you can do for your country." Thousands responded, joining the Peace Corps and VISTA, its domestic counterpart.

Others, like Mario Savio, joined in the civil rights movement. Inspired by blacks who risked their lives in the struggle for racial equality, nearly 1,000 northern white students volunteered for SNCC's Mississippi Freedom Summer Project in 1964. As the white volunteers journeyed south, they got a firsthand look at racism and poverty in the United States. They returned to their northern campuses that fall schooled in the techniques of nonviolent civil disobedience and determined to fight injustice.

Only a minority of American college students joined the protest movement. At the height of campus unrest in 1970, a bare 12 percent identified themselves as part of the radical New Left. The majority of students joined fraternities and sororities, cheered at football games, and majored in subjects that they hoped would help them earn a good living after college. Although they rejected radical politics, many of these students still shared the activists' concerns about students' rights, civil rights, and the war in Vietnam.

Although the student rebels were a minority, they were vocal and attended some of the nation's top universities. Their protests would draw increasing attention as the decade progressed.

**Students for a Democratic Society**   One of the earliest radical student groups was the Students for a Democratic Society (SDS). Formed by a small group of students at the University of Michigan in 1960, SDS formed the core of the New Left, a rebirth of radical American politics. Disillusioned with liberalism, members of the New Left believed that problems such as racism and war could only be solved through sweeping changes in American society.

In June 1962, 60 members of SDS from a dozen campuses met at Port Huron, Michigan, to draft what they called "an agenda for a generation." It began: "We are people of this generation, bred in at least modest comfort, housed now in universities, looking uncomfortably to the world we inherit."

Written for the most part by Tom Hayden, a 22-year-old student from the University of Michigan, the document went on to spell out the ills afflicting the United States. The United States, Hayden argued, was controlled by massive government, corporate, and educational bureaucracies that left individuals powerless. As a cure, SDS envisioned a radical movement to bring about "participatory democracy," in which citizens would seize control over decisions affecting their lives.

The Port Huron Statement signaled the political awakening of a generation of students and the beginning of an era of student activism. As SDS member Sharon Jeffrey recalled, "It was exalting. We felt that we were different, and that we were going to do things differently. . . . It felt like the dawn of a new age."

**Protesting the War**   At first, SDS tackled domestic issues. In the summer of 1964, SDS volunteers moved into poor urban neighborhoods and organized residents to fight for jobs, better housing, schools, and community services.

By the fall of 1964, SDS had organized chapters on nearly 50 campuses around the country. Now a new issue loomed—the war in Vietnam. At its December 1964 national convention, SDS members voted to protest the war by organizing a march on Washington for the following April. Since U.S. involvement in Vietnam was still limited to military advisers and aid, opposition to the war remained muted. No one expected more than a few thousand marchers. Then President Johnson began to escalate the United States commitment to South Vietnam.

When Johnson ordered the large-scale bombing of North Vietnam in 1965 and sent in the first combat troops, the **antiwar movement** mushroomed. Some Americans felt betrayed by Johnson, whom they had considered a peace candidate in 1964. SDS now led a

STUDY GUIDE

**Evaluating Sources**

Evaluating sources helps you to assess the usefulness of a historical document. The idealism of the 1960s is no better expressed than in the 50-page Port Huron Statement. With a stated aim of providing "an agenda for a generation," the document opens with the quietly self-conscious words, "We are people of this generation." The emphasis on *this generation* shows that the students who drafted the document were determined from the beginning to make the New Left a youth movement.

crusade to end the war in Vietnam. Within a single year, the ranks of the SDS had swollen to more than 150 chapters with 10,000 members.

On April 17 more than 20,000 people crowded around the Washington Monument for the SDS anti-war march—the first of increasingly massive, and eventually more militant, protests. Folksinger Judy Collins sang "The Times They Are A-Changin'." The words seemed prophetic:

*C*ome *senators, congressmen*
    *Please heed the call*
*Don't stand in the doorway*
*Don't block up the hall.*
*For he that gets hurt*
*Will be he who has stalled.*
*There's a battle*
*Outside and it's ragin'*
*It'll soon shake your windows*
*And rattle your walls*
*For the times they are a-changin'.*

Bob Dylan,
"The Times They
Are A-Changin'," 1963

That spring SDS also helped organize several university "teach-ins." The first teach-ins took place at the University of Michigan at Ann Arbor. On March 24, 1965, shortly after the first U.S. ground combat troops landed in South Vietnam, over 3,500 students and professors jammed into four lecture halls. They sang folk songs, analyzed U.S. foreign policy, and debated the war until dawn. In the following weeks, similar teach-ins sprouted up at campuses across the nation.

**Resisting the Draft**    Opposition to the war led some students to resist the **draft,** a system of selecting individuals for military service. Since the early 1950s, all 18-year-old men had been required to register for the draft. In theory, all those who registered were eligible to serve in the armed forces if needed. However, individuals could be given **deferments,** or postponements of military service, because of their health or occupation. College students were among those who received deferments in large numbers during the Vietnam War.

Critics of the draft pointed out that partly because of college deferments, the burden of the war fell unfairly on the poor, the working class, and minorities. In fact, poor and working-class men were twice as likely to be drafted, and if drafted, twice as likely

AP/WIDE WORLD PHOTOS

AP/WIDE WORLD PHOTOS

**Students organized antiwar demonstrations at the University of Wisconsin, above, in October 1967, and at the University of Washington, right, in November. Dave Wyatt burned his draft card at the University of Washington demonstration in protest against Dow Chemical, a high-profile company that manufactured napalm for the military.**

to fight as men from the middle class. African Americans made up 18 percent of those drafted to fight in Vietnam, although they were only 10 percent of the nation's population.

During the Vietnam War, thousands of defiant young men challenged the idea that citizens have a military obligation to their country. "The war in Vietnam is criminal and we must act together, at great individual risk, to stop it," the resisters declared. They argued that without a draft, the government could not continue to wage the war.

Some became **conscientious objectors,** claiming that their moral or religious beliefs prevented them from fighting in the war. Others, in defiance of federal law, refused to register for the draft or burned their draft cards. Protesters harassed campus recruiters for the military and disrupted campus ROTC (Reserve Officers' Training Corps) classes. Some went to jail for refusing to be drafted. Thousands more fled the country.

As the number of young men called up by the draft increased from 5,000 per month in 1965 to 50,000 per month in 1967, the ranks of draft resisters swelled. By the fall of 1966, more than three dozen draft resistance groups had sprung up on college campuses around the country.[1]

## Growing Opposition to the War

Along with the increasing number of U.S. troops in Vietnam, the antiwar movement also grew. Religious groups, peace groups, antinuclear groups, civil rights groups, and women's groups joined the students in protesting the war.

In February 1967, over 2,500 members of Women Strike for Peace, most of them middle-class housewives, stormed the Pentagon demanding to see "the generals who send our sons to Vietnam." When refused entrance, the women began pounding on the doors with their shoes. Secretary of Defense Robert McNamara eventually ordered that the women be allowed to enter and present their petition to an aide.

Huge antiwar rallies in the spring of 1967 drew hundreds of thousands of protesters to New York City and San Francisco. Marching alongside the students were Americans from all walks of life: priests, business people, mothers pushing children in strollers.

Antiwar protests grew as more and more Americans demonstrated a willingness to risk arrest in acts of civil disobedience protesting the war. The SDS rallying cry became "From Protest to Resistance." Thousands responded in what organizers billed as a dramatic confrontation between the "people" and the "warmakers"—the March on the Pentagon. On October 21, 1967, more than 50,000 protesters crowded onto the Pentagon steps where armed troops awaited. Scores of young men burned their draft cards as supporters chanted, "Burn cards, not people." Some protesters, pleading with the troops to join them, placed flowers in the barrels of the rifles. Hundreds of protesters were arrested, and many were beaten.

Key leaders, too, began to criticize the war in 1967. Senator William Fulbright, once a supporter of the war, held a series of televised hearings in which critics of the war analyzed U.S. policy. Martin Luther King, Jr., pointed out that each dollar spent in Vietnam was one dollar less for social reform at home. By early 1966 the federal government was pouring nearly $2 billion a month into Vietnam—more than the Johnson administration ever spent in a single year on the war on poverty.

**War Divides the Nation**   By 1967 the United States was deeply divided over the war. Hawks, those who supported the war, urged stepping up the war effort to win a military victory. Doves, those who supported the withdrawal of U.S. troops and a negotiated end to the war, questioned both the cost and the morality of the war.

Many Americans were neither hawks nor doves but were disturbed both by the war and the protests against it. A December 1967 poll showed that 70 percent of Americans believed the protests were "acts of disloyalty" to the soldiers fighting the war. As the war raged on, however, many became convinced that the United States was hopelessly bogged down in an unwinnable war. Their frustration echoed in the words of one Iowa housewife: "I want to get out, but I don't want to give up."

## STUDY GUIDE

### Recognizing Bias

Ironically, the draft was biased in favor of its greatest detractors, middle-class college students. Under the system, most students were shielded from induction by staying in school. In addition, draft counseling was available to students but not to other groups.

**1** What were some of the avenues open to students who wanted to evade the draft?

FLIP SCHULKE, LIFE MAGAZINE © TIME WARNER INC.

**Members of the Silent Majority were not always silent during the 1960s. These demonstrators in Cocoa Beach, Florida, are on their way to a rally in** support of the war. Like many Americans of the time, they believed that if the country was at war, they had a duty to support it, and if drafted, to fight.

**Bringing the War Home** In the aftermath of the Tet offensive, public opinion on the war shifted dramatically. In early January 1968, hawks outnumbered doves by 62 to 22 percent. By March the number of hawks had fallen to 41 percent, while the number of doves had climbed to 42 percent.

Antiwar protests increasingly stirred the nation's campuses. From January to June 1968, nearly 40,000 students at more than 100 colleges staged protests. Though most protests were peaceful, violence occasionally erupted.

The most violent uprising took place that spring at Columbia University in New York City and reflected the growing militancy of the SDS. The protest at Columbia linked two potent issues—civil rights and the Vietnam War. At noon on Tuesday, April 23, more than 600 students rallied to protest university ties to military research. They also objected to a university plan to build a gym on public parkland in a nearby Harlem neighborhood.

When university officials refused to listen to student demands, the protest escalated. Led by SDS and the Students' Afro-American Society, the protesters took over five university buildings, including the office of the university president. "We are fighting to recapture a school from business and war," wrote student James Kunen, "and rededicate it to learning and life." A week later, New York City police officers stormed the buildings to arrest the students and drag them off to waiting police vans. One Day in History on pages 684 and 685 contains a map showing the layout of the Columbia campus and the site of the proposed gym.

## The Media and the War

The antiwar protesters gained a powerful ally as the war drew on—the mass media. Television, especially, played an important role in molding public opinion. Satellite technology meant that the war could be broadcast at home almost as it happened. The scenes of brutal fighting, desperate refugees, and dying U.S. soldiers shocked the more than 60 million Americans who tuned in to the nightly news.

In contrast to earlier wars, the military did not censor the press in Vietnam. Reporters and photographers easily got press passes and tramped through the muddy jungle, side by side with American patrols. In 1968, at the height of U.S. involvement, 800 reporters covered the Vietnam War.

**Early Reporting on the War**  During the early years of the war, most reporters agreed that the United States was fighting the spread of communism and that South Vietnam deserved and needed American support. They applauded South Vietnamese leader Diem. In June 1960 *Newsweek* called him "one of Asia's ablest leaders."

**A More Critical Press**  After the Tet offensive in early 1968, however, respected reporters like Walter Cronkite began to raise serious questions about the war. After a trip to Saigon in 1968, Cronkite told viewers, "To say we are closer to victory today is to believe, in the face of the evidence, the optimists who have been wrong in the past." Such reports undercut official optimism and eroded public support for the war.

Reporters not only questioned official reports that the war could be won but raised more fundamental questions: Should the United States be in Vietnam? Was Vietnam worth the cost? In the wake of Tet, James Reston, a columnist for the *New York Times*, asked: "What is the end that justified this slaughter? How will we save Vietnam if we destroy it in the battle?"

The media also brought home the immense tragedy of the war—its cost in human lives. In June 1969 *Life* magazine published the photos of 242 Americans who had been killed in one week in Vietnam. Their young faces served as a reminder that the nightly casualty figures were real people—the sons, brothers, husbands, and fathers of those at home.

**The My Lai Massacre**  One of the most shocking incidents of the war surfaced in November 1969. Journalist Seymour Hersh discovered that in March 1968, U.S. forces under the command of Lieutenant William Calley had massacred nearly 350 Vietnamese civilians in the village of My Lai. Americans read the account of 22-year-old Private Paul Meadlo: "We huddled them up. We made them squat down. . . . I poured about four clips into the group. . . . The mothers was hugging their children. . . . Well, we kept right on firing."

Lieutenant Calley was court-martialed and sentenced to life imprisonment. Though the actions of the U.S. forces shocked Americans everywhere, some felt a certain amount of sympathy for Calley, who claimed he was "following a direct order." The military eventually reduced Calley's sentence.

## Nixon and the Antiwar Movement

Public pressure had made the Vietnam War a key issue during the 1968 election. President Johnson had been forced out of the race for his failed Vietnam policies. Johnson realized that the unpopularity of the war overshadowed his other accomplishments.

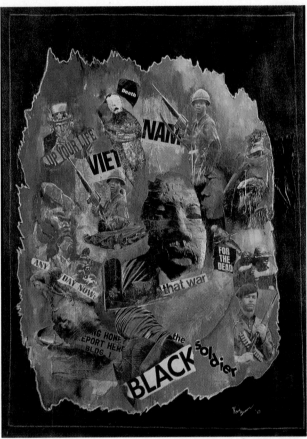

COURTESY KAY BROWN

**This collage by Kay Brown is a tribute to the courage and patriotism of African Americans who fought in Vietnam and a lament for those who died in battle.**

Richard Nixon had been elected president in part because he promised an end to the unpopular war.

The Vietnam War    681

In June 1969 President Nixon announced that he would start bringing U.S. troops home as part of his plan to "Vietnamize" the war. The fighting continued, however, and so did the protests. On October 1 nearly two million Americans across the nation demonstrated for peace in Vietnam. One month later over 300,000 protesters flooded Washington, D.C., taking their plea for peace to the White House. By the end of the year, doves outnumbered hawks on college campuses across the nation by three to one.

To rally support for his policies, President Nixon appealed to what he called the Silent Majority. In a November 3 speech, Nixon declared that a minority was threatening America's security "by mounting demonstrations in the streets. . . . North Vietnam cannot defeat or humiliate the United States," the president insisted. "Only Americans can do that." To fend off this enemy at home, Nixon appealed "to you, the great silent majority of my fellow Americans—I ask for your support."

Conflict over the war would come to a head the following spring. A new wave of demonstrations and violence would rock the country and cause many on both sides of the issue to fear for the nation's future.

**The War Comes Home**   On April 30, 1970, President Nixon announced that he had ordered U.S. troops to invade Vietnam's neutral neighbor, Cambodia, to clean out communist bases there. His expansion of the war soon led to massive protests across the country.[2]

Students at Ohio's Kent State University were outraged by the Cambodian invasion. Two days after the president's announcement, they surrounded the campus ROTC building, pelting it with firecrackers and rocks. Then they burned it to the ground. In response, Ohio Governor James Rhodes called National Guardsmen to Kent State on May 3.

The next day at noon, about 600 students held a peaceful protest on the Kent State campus commons. A campus police officer bellowed through a bullhorn: "This assembly is unlawful! This is an order—disperse immediately!"

The students refused to leave. Some lobbed stones and sticks at the soldiers, shouting, "Pigs off campus!" In reply the troops hurled tear gas at the students. Then their commander ordered, "Prepare to move out and disperse this mob."

The National Guardsmen, many as young and nervous as the students they confronted, pointed their bayonets at the demonstrators and marched toward them. Choking and weeping from the tear gas, dozens of students fled. A group of guardsmen retreated to the top of a nearby hill. Suddenly they turned, raised their rifles, and fired into the crowd.

"My God," a girl screamed, "they're killing us!" Seconds later, 9 students had been wounded, and 4 students were dead. None of them were radical activists. One was an ROTC student, and two had simply been crossing the campus on their way to lunch.

The guardsmen claimed they had fired in self-defense. A later investigation found otherwise, declaring the action of the National Guardsmen "unwarranted and inexcusable."

UPI/BETTMAN NEWSPHOTOS

**Startled and angry, Kent State students try to evade exploding tear gas canisters.**

**Assessing Outcomes**

Nixon's Silent Majority speech in November 1969 divided the American public. By finding an enemy within the borders of the country—the antiwar movement—Nixon set the nation against itself. The speech did not contain any new policies and was designed only to rally support for the existing war effort.

2  Why did the invasion of Cambodia lead to massive protests in the United States?

Public reaction following the shootings revealed just how deeply divided the country was during the 1960s. Some Americans blamed the students for the violence at Kent State. They resented the college students for their privileges, their countercultural values, and their rebelliousness. Other people condemned the government. The grief-stricken father of Allison Krause, one of the slain students, asked, "Is this dissent a crime? Is this a reason for killing her?"

**Jackson State** Violence flared again a week later at the nearly all-black college of Jackson State in Mississippi. An outbreak of vandalism in downtown Jackson prompted local officials to call in 500 National Guard troops to back up 80 state highway patrol officers and 125 city police.

On the evening of May 14, rocks and bottles began to fly in downtown Jackson, and a city truck was set on fire. At 10:30 P.M., police, highway patrol officers, and National Guard troops approached the nearby campus where students had gathered. Suddenly a bottle crashed near an officer. Without warning, police and highway patrol officers opened fire. The hail of bullets lasted nearly 30 seconds. Twelve students were wounded, and two were killed, both innocent bystanders.

**The End of a Decade** The protests after the Cambodian invasion marked the climax of a decade of student protest. Although some protests would continue until the war ended in 1973, the massive demonstrations of the 1960s were over. Many students were frustrated by their failure to end the war. The pioneers of the student movement, the SDS, splintered into smaller extremist groups like the militant Weathermen. Other students gave up political action altogether.

Government harassment of the New Left also took a toll. Although prohibited by law from spying on American citizens, the CIA collected files on 7,200 Americans. FBI agents secretly joined leftist groups and triggered feuds between members or instigated violent encounters with the police. Racked by internal dissent and weakened by government crackdowns, the New Left fell apart as the war in Vietnam wound down and U.S. troops returned home.

Although the student movement failed in its goal of radically transforming U.S. society, it did succeed in effecting change. The antiwar protests helped to force a shift in U.S. policy. The campus demonstrations brought about reforms in how universities were governed and enlarged students' role in campus life.

The radicalism of students during the 1960s alarmed many Americans and fueled growing conservatism. Along with the inner-city riots, assassinations, and the war in Vietnam, widespread campus unrest seemed to be a sign that something was deeply wrong with the country.

AP/WIDE WORLD PHOTOS

**This photograph shows a room in Alexander Hall, a woman's dormitory at Jackson State College, the morning after the shooting. Investigators counted 230 bullet holes in the building.**

## SECTION REVIEW

### Checking Facts

1. What does SDS stand for? What were the goals of the group?

2. Why was the Vietnam War a "living room war?" How was media coverage different than in earlier wars?

3. How did Richard Nixon rally support for his Vietnam policies?

4. Describe the student movement at the end of the 1960s. How was campus unrest viewed by many Americans?

### Thinking Critically

5. **Evaluating Sources** How did the lyrics of "The Times They Are A-Changin'" reflect the goals of New Left groups like the SDS?

6. **Recognizing Bias** Describe the role of the media in changing American opinion about the war in Vietnam.

### Linking Across Time

7. Describe your generation. Do you identify with your generation as much as students did during the 1960s? Explain why or why not.

## Columbia University Erupts

*NEW YORK—With the brashness of a victorious bananarepublic revolutionary, the mustachioed undergraduate sat in the chair of the president of New York's Columbia University and puffed on an expropriated cigar. He and his cohorts . . . had seized the command center of one of the world's greatest centers of learning.*
— Life, May 9, 1968

### Campus Siege

Over 600 Columbia students rallied to protest the war and to express outrage over a university plan to build a gymnasium on public land in nearby Harlem. As the rally started to break up, Mark Rudd, the 20-year-old chairman of the Columbia SDS, yelled, "Hamilton Hall is right over there. Let's go!" The students took over five buildings in all. Eventually their numbers swelled to 1,000.

Dr. Logan Wilson, President of the National Council on Education, called the uprising "the result of premeditated and organized activity involving outsiders."

© B. FREER, BLACK STAR. INSET, AP/WIDE WORLD PHOTOS

## Elsewhere in the News

### Vietnam Casualties

WASHINGTON—The Defense Department today identified 13 servicemen from the New York area as having been killed in Vietnam recently.

### Year of Human Rights

TEHRAN—Iran's capital was the site for the International Conference on Human Rights. U.N. Secretary General U Thant used the meeting to call for an end to apartheid in South Africa.

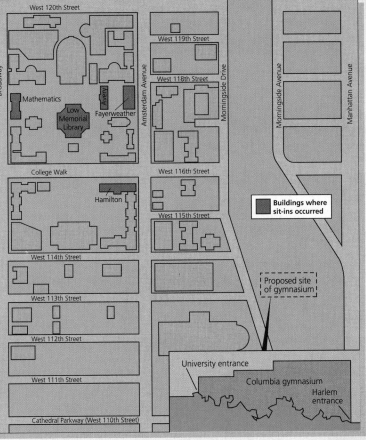

Map labels: West 120th Street, West 119th Street, West 118th Street, West 116th Street, West 115th Street, West 114th Street, West 113th Street, West 112th Street, West 111th Street, Cathedral Parkway (West 110th Street), Broadway, Amsterdam Avenue, Morningside Drive, Morningside Avenue, Manhattan Avenue, Mathematics, Low Memorial Library, Avery, Fayerweather, College Walk, Hamilton

Buildings where sit-ins occurred

Proposed site of gymnasium

University entrance, Columbia gymnasium, Harlem entrance

## Related Stories
- Harlem Blacks Deplore Jim Crow Gym
- College Protests This Year—200 and Rising
- Students Plan Nationwide Boycott
- Students Rock Mexico City, Prague, Tokyo, and Paris

© TED COWELL, BLACK STAR

## Violence Strikes Columbia

In the early morning hours of April 30, exactly one week after the siege began, over 1,000 New York police officers swept onto the campus to empty the five student-held buildings. There were 722 arrests; 148 people were injured, including 20 New York police officers.

## Psychedelic Ship Sails

NEW YORK—The cruise ship *Independence* was launched today. The ship sports an exterior mural of an orange, yellow, and raspberry sun-burst with eyes.

# Chapter 20 Review

**1954**
Eisenhower applies "domino theory" to Vietnam struggle.

| 1944 | 1946 | 1948 | 1950 | 1952 | 1954 | 1956 |

**September 1945**
The Vietminh, composed principally of communists, declare Vietnam independent.

**May 1950**
Truman supports French against Vietminh.

**May 1954**
French lose control in Vietnam; U.S. involvement grows.

## Summary

Use the following outline as a tool for reviewing and summarizing the chapter. Copy the outline on your own paper, leaving spaces between headings to jot down notes about key events and concepts.

**I. War in Southeast Asia**
  A. The French War in Indochina
  B. The United States Enters the War
  C. Johnson's War
  D. Fighting the War

**II. 1968: A Year of Crises**
  A. Tet: A Turning Point
  B. Tragedy and Turmoil
  C. The Election of 1968

**III. The War at Home**
  A. The Birth of the Student Movement
  B. Growing Opposition to the War
  C. The Media and the War
  D. Nixon and the Antiwar Movement

## Ideas, Events, and People

1. Identify Ho Chi Minh, his goals, and his role in the Vietnam War.
2. What modern nations comprise Indochina, and what natural resources make this area strategically important?
3. What was the significance of the fall of Dien Bien Phu?
4. Identify Ngo Dinh Diem, and tell how he adversely affected the position of the United States in Vietnam.
5. Why did the Vietminh and later the Vietcong view a unified Vietnam as an absolute necessity?
6. Why do you think many Americans felt betrayed by President Lyndon B. Johnson when he escalated the Vietnam War?
7. Describe the inequity of deferments that allowed some men to avoid military service during the Vietnam War.
8. What was the Ho Chi Minh trail? Why did bombings fail to stop the flow of supplies?
9. List four disadvantages experienced by U.S. troops in Vietnam.
10. How did Martin Luther King, Jr., link the civil rights movement to his opposition of U.S. policy in Vietnam?
11. Identify General William C. Westmoreland and Clark Clifford. Discuss their opposing views.
12. Describe Richard Nixon's strategy for winning the presidency in 1968.
13. What groups made up the New Deal coalition? Why did supporters leave the coalition in 1968, and how did they realign?

## Social Studies Skills

**Recognizing Stereotypes**
Write a description of an antiwar student protester of the 1960s. Exchange papers with another class member. Read for possible stereotypes and evaluate in writing the reliability of the profile you receive.

## Critical Thinking

1. **Recognizing Assumptions**
What assumptions did Johnson make when he sent troops to Vietnam? Later, what did he assume when anchorman Walter Cronkite questioned U.S. policy in Vietnam?

2. **Analyzing Behavior**
Congress had not declared war when Johnson sent U.S. troops to Vietnam in 1965. Explain Johnson's actions in gaining authority to do this. What information came to light years later?

**November 1963**
President Kennedy is assassinated.

**March 1965**
Johnson sends first U.S. troops to Vietnam.

**April 1968**
King's assassination triggers riots.

**1963**
Kennedy continues to increase aid and advisers to Vietnam.

**April 1965**
SDS leads first massive anti–war march in Washington.

**June 1968**
Robert Kennedy is assassinated.

**November 1968**
Nixon wins presidential election.

### 3. Identifying Cause and Effect

What effect did the communist takeover in China have on U.S. policy in Vietnam?

### 4. Comparing and Contrasting

Compare and contrast the containment policies of presidents Dwight D. Eisenhower and John F. Kennedy.

## Extension and Application

### 1. Citizenship

Use books, periodicals, and newspapers to learn about the plight of American POWs (Prisoners of War) and MIAs (Missing in Action) in Vietnam. Make a timeline to show what has been done by both the government and private citizens on their behalf. The more than 3,500 members of the National League of Families of American Prisoners and Missing in Southeast Asia still believe some U.S. servicemen are imprisoned in the almost impenetrable mountain range that runs the length of Vietnam. In writing, explain types of social action that might be taken to further the League's cause of verifying that prisoners are in Vietnam, and promoting their return.

### 2. Community Connection

Contact friends, neighbors, or veterans' groups to locate two Vietnam veterans who would be willing to visit your class. Interview them regarding their Vietnam experiences and their adjustment after the war. Write a personal response to information imparted in each interview. Preface your theme with short biographical sketches of each interviewee.

### 3. Global Connection

Research the various forms of government in the countries of Southeast Asia today. In a brief paragraph, compare each with the government that held power in the 1960s.

## Geography

1. What part did the countries on the map below play in President Eisenhower's "domino theory"?
2. How different might U.S. involvement in Vietnam have been if the two countries were neighbors rather than thousands of miles apart?
3. What difficulties did U.S. troops face because almost the entire country of South Vietnam was a guerrilla war zone?
4. Why did North Vietnam choose the location shown on the map for the Ho Chi Minh Trail? How did its location and terrain affect how each side fought the war?
5. Look at the map on page 671. Third-party presidential candidates have won very few states in this century. In 1968, what factors enabled George Wallace to win in the South?

CHAPTER 21

# The Nixon Years

## August 8, 1974: The President Decides

After a week of sleepless nights, an exhausted, pale President Nixon walked into the Oval Office of the White House and sat down behind his desk. He was alone except for a couple of television technicians and the White House photographer, Ollie Atkins. His voice cracked as he joked nervously with the television cameraman.

At 9 P.M. the television crew signaled Nixon to begin. The president cleared his throat and gazed into the camera: "Good evening. This is the thirty-seventh time I have spoken to you from this office in which so many decisions have been made that shape the history of this nation." Then came the moment that so many people

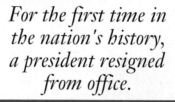

*For the first time in the nation's history, a president resigned from office.*

had anticipated. For the first time in the nation's history, a president resigned from office.

Less than two years before, a beaming, triumphant President Nixon had addressed the nation, fresh from a landslide reelection victory. He had forged a new conservative coalition and was widely hailed for his bold foreign policy moves.

Yet he had overstepped the limits of the presidency and had broken the laws he had sworn to uphold. Richard Nixon had defied the American constitutional system, and now that system had taught him that no one is above the law, not even the President of the United States.

THE NATIONAL ARCHIVES/NIXON PROJECT

*President Nixon hugs his daughter Julie shortly before his resignation speech.*

*President Nixon boards a helicopter on the first leg of his journey back to California. By the time his plane lands, Gerald Ford will have been inaugurated as the new president and Nixon will be a private citizen.*

# A New Majority

## May 8, 1970: Workers Battle Antiwar Protesters

WHEN YOU WERE STILL UP ON BROADWAY YOU COULD HEAR THE RUCKUS, THE HOLLERING. THE PEACE DEMONSTRATORS TRYING TO OUT-SHOUT THE construction workers. The construction workers hollering, 'U.S.A., all the way' and 'We're Number One.' And the peace demonstrators screaming up there that the war was unjust and everything else."

Thirty-one-year-old Joe Kelly, construction worker and family man, was one of several hundred workers who battled peace demonstrators in New York City that day. Wearing a yellow construction helmet bearing the message "For God and Country," Kelly joined in, hurling insults and throwing punches.

The violent noon-hour rampage marked the beginning of two weeks of flag-waving marches in support of the Nixon administration and its Southeast Asia policies. The marchers were fed up with what they called the "flag-burning radicals" who opposed the war.

Although other workers joined in, the construction workers led the way. Their hard hats soon became a symbol of traditional American values. Many, like Joe Kelly, were demonstrating for the first time in their lives.

Their message found a sympathetic ear at the White House. A few days after the Wall Street riots President Nixon himself was awarded his own hard hat inscribed "Commander-in-Chief."

AP/WIDE WORLD PHOTOS

## The War Within

Like the workers and demonstrators who came to blows on Wall Street, American society by the end of the 1960s was divided into hostile camps. A decade of war and social change had ripped the nation apart. Not since the Civil War had the country seemed so divided—with conservatives pitted against liberals, workers against students, whites against blacks, the old against the young.

As the 1960s drew to a close, the United States seemed to be at war with itself. Riots rocked 125 American cities following the assassination of Martin Luther King, Jr., in April 1968. In August of that year, police battled protesters at the Democratic National Convention in Chicago. Then, in October 1969, nearly 300 members of the Weather Underground, a militant wing of the Students for a Democratic Society (SDS), swept through the streets of Chicago smashing windows and shouting, "Long live the victory of the people's war." Scenes of these so-called days of rage filled the television news, fueling the fears of millions of Americans.

**The Conservative Backlash**   Like construction worker Joe Kelly, a growing number of Americans became fed up with the social protests of the 1960s. The

---

result was a conservative **backlash,** a sudden reaction against the liberalism of the 1960s. Mostly white working-class and middle-class Americans, these people saw the protests as an unprincipled attack on traditional values: hard work, family, religion, patriotism, and respect for law and order. They feared that unchecked violence and social disorder would destroy the country.

In part, they blamed the liberal policies of the Johnson years for the unrest of the decade. They resented the Warren Court for "meddling" in social issues and for "coddling" criminals. According to one poll, by 1968 three out of five Americans disagreed with the Warren Court's decisions.

**It is ironic that the hard hat became a symbol of conservatism.**

They also resented paying taxes to support federal programs that they believed benefited only the poor and minorities. As one middle-class Chicagoan put it, "We are the forgotten men. We don't get one cent from the government." The cost of living rose steadily during the 1960s (by more than 7 percent in 1969), and income failed to keep pace. Many Americans saw the good life slipping away from them, and they resented it. They yearned for a return to traditional values and an end to the turmoil.

**Nixon and the "Silent Majority"**   In his 1968 campaign for president, Richard Nixon shrewdly tapped the deep well of discontent felt by these Americans, whom he called the "silent majority." He promised to listen to "the great majority of Americans, the forgotten Americans, the non-shouters, the non-demonstrators."

Raised in a hard-working middle-class family, Nixon seemed to share the silent majority's values. He campaigned against the Great Society's "welfare mess" and pledged to "quit pouring billions of dollars into programs that have failed." He railed against Supreme Court decisions that he claimed had "tipped the balance against the peace forces in this country

and strengthened the criminal forces." He promised to end the Vietnam War honorably and to restore law and order.

His appeal to what one writer called "the unblack, the unyoung, and the unpoor" paid off. In his victory speech after defeating Hubert Humphrey, Nixon promised to end the years of turmoil and unite the country: "We want to bridge the generation gap. We want to bridge the gap between the races. We want to bring America together."

But despite his promises of unity, Nixon would divide Americans even further. Intent on holding onto power, he took to heart the advice of one of his aides who claimed that the art of politics was the art of discovering who hated whom. Nixon would play on the anger and fears of the silent majority as he set about building a new conservative coalition.

## Nixon's New Conservatism

Once in office, Nixon sought to address the two major concerns of the silent majority—resentment of the federal government and fear of social disorder. However, a powerful civil rights movement, a broad antiwar coalition, and a Congress controlled by Democrats would limit his attempts to advance conservative legislation. A practical man as well as a fighter, President Nixon would compromise where necessary and pursue his conservative agenda where possible.

© 1970 RANAN LURIE, CARTOON NEWS

**This cartoon shows President Nixon driving backward—in effect reversing progress made in civil rights during the 1960s.**

**Recognizing Points of View**

From reading about a few incidents only, you might think that the labor movement generally supported Nixon. In fact, labor's view of Nixon was generally negative. Nixon and labor had been at odds since the Red Scare of the late 1940s, when Nixon was making a political reputation by investigating communists in government. In the 1968 campaign, labor fought bitterly against Nixon. Only a few highly conservative unions—such as the construction unions—supported Nixon.

Thus, in his first term, Nixon accepted many liberal programs and signed bills to boost social security benefits, to expand the Job Corps, and to build low-cost housing. He approved Democrat-sponsored legislation to lower the voting age to 18 and established the Environmental Protection Agency (EPA) and the Occupational Safety and Health Administration (OSHA).

**Nixon's New Federalism**   Even as he signed these liberal bills, Nixon began to steer a more conservative course. He introduced what he called the **New Federalism**—a series of programs that would "reverse the flow of power and resources from the states and communities to Washington and start power and resources flowing back . . . to the people."

To shift power back to the states, Nixon established a program of revenue sharing through which the federal government returned some of its tax money to local governments. He and his supporters hoped that more conservative state and local governments would use the money for law enforcement and civic projects instead of liberal programs that would create jobs for the unemployed.

In one of his most controversial moves, Nixon sought to reduce the federal government's role in the nation's welfare system. In August 1969 the president introduced the Family Assistance Plan (FAP), an attempt to streamline the massive federal welfare bureaucracy and reduce welfare cheating. Instead of piecemeal handouts and a maze of federal agencies, regulations, and caseworkers, the FAP was a simple plan designed to give poor families a minimum annual income and then let them take responsibility for themselves. The FAP proposed a guaranteed minimum yearly income of $1,600 for a family of four. To qualify for aid, heads of households had to sign up for job training.

The FAP quickly came under fire from both conservative and liberal camps. Conservative critics rejected the idea of a guaranteed annual income and insisted that the new program would only increase the number of people on the welfare rolls. Liberals denounced the plan, claiming that the payments were inadequate and that the job training program prepared trainees for low-paying jobs that held little chance for advancement. Although the plan passed in the House, it died in the Senate.

Despite his failure to overhaul the welfare system, Nixon successfully chipped away at the Great Society's base by cutting off federal grants for urban renewal, job training, and education. In 1973 he abolished the Office of Economic Opportunity, a cornerstone of Johnson's antipoverty program.

When the Democratic majority in Congress opposed his bids to reduce funding for certain programs, Nixon defied them by impounding, or refusing to spend, the funds. By 1973 Nixon had impounded nearly $15 billion in funds, crippling more than 100 federal programs. Programs in the areas of health, housing, education, and the environment were the hardest hit.

The courts eventually ruled that impoundment was illegal because it gave the president a veto power not granted in the Constitution. Only Congress, they ruled, had the authority to decide how federal funds should be spent.

**Law and Order**   To combat crime and social unrest, Nixon appointed his former law partner, John Mitchell, attorney general. A steely-eyed veteran of backroom politics, Mitchell was an archconservative. He boasted, "This country is going so far right you won't recognize it."

As head of the Justice Department, Mitchell promoted measures to strengthen police powers—

even at the cost of civil liberties. For example, he supported the use of wiretaps without a court order and the detention of criminal suspects without bail.

To silence antiwar and civil rights protesters and other critics, Nixon and Mitchell marshaled the forces of several federal agencies. The president used the Internal Revenue Service (IRS) to harass enemies by auditing their tax returns. The Federal Bureau of Investigation (FBI) illegally tapped their phones and broke into their homes and offices, searching for information to embarrass and discredit them.

In addition, undercover FBI agents joined the ranks of the SDS and black militant groups like the

AP/WIDE WORLD PHOTOS

**Scenes like this one were common in many cities during the early 1970s. Bolstered by the Nixon administration's conservative policies on law enforcement and civil liberties, police and the FBI broke up many radical and militant groups that had formed during the 1960s.**

Black Panthers. In some cases the agents deliberately set up violent clashes between these groups and the police. In 1969, for example, when the FBI targeted the Black Panther Party, an estimated 28 Panthers were killed by police. Hundreds more were arrested.

## Building a New Majority

While shifting the national agenda toward more conservative programs, Nixon was also looking ahead to the elections of 1972. He had been elected in 1968 by a slim plurality—less that 1 percent of the popular vote. Congress remained in Democratic hands. The president realized that to regain Republican control of Congress and to be reelected himself he would need to forge a new majority. [1]

Shortly after the 1968 election, Nixon adopted a strategy that would guide his policies for the remainder of his presidency. In a report entitled "The Emergence of a Republican Majority," Kevin Phillips, a Nixon campaign aide, analyzed the results of the 1968 election. He claimed that conservative Democrats—primarily white ethnic voters, southern whites, suburbanites, and blue-collar workers—were tired of the liberals who had come to control the Democratic party. He argued that these voters were ready to leave the Democrats and join the Republicans to form a new conservative majority under Nixon's leadership.

**An Appeal to the South** According to Phillips's report, a growing number of conservative Americans lived in the Sun Belt—the southern states, plus Texas, California, New Mexico, Oklahoma, and Arizona. Since the end of World War II, these states had more than doubled in population.

The South had long been a Democratic stronghold, but many white southern Democrats believed that the party had become too liberal. As a result, some of them had left the party and supported the conservative segregationist George Wallace in the 1968 presidential election. These conservative Democrats had helped Wallace—the former governor of Alabama—win 13.5 percent of the popular vote and carry five southern states. Nixon planned to lure these voters away from Wallace with his conservative agenda. By adding the Wallace voters and other discontented Democrats to the 43.4 percent of Americans who had voted for Nixon in 1968, the Republicans hoped to build a powerful new majority that would help them recapture the Congress and hold on to the White House.

© ROGER MALLOCH, MAGNUM PHOTOS, INC.

**Nixon's southern strategy was designed to lure voters like this one away from George Wallace.** *What does the slogan on the woman's button tell you about Wallace's political platform?*

Nixon adopted a "southern strategy" to appeal directly to southern white conservatives. To bring these voters into the Republican camp, the president would appeal to their discontent with racial integration, a liberal Supreme Court, and eastern liberals.

**Attacks on Civil Rights**   In the 1968 election, Nixon won barely 13 percent of the black vote, and he knew he was unlikely to attract more black voters in 1972. To gain votes in the South, Nixon believed he could afford to alienate blacks on civil rights issues.[2] His position was made clear in a September 1968 press conference when he stated: "There are those who want instant integration and those who want segregation forever. I believe we need to have a middle course between those two extremes." In effect, Nixon was siding with those who wanted to delay desegregation and was telling African Americans seeking their rights that they were extremists.

Once in office, Nixon used the Department of Health, Education and Welfare (HEW) to carry out his strategy. In 1969 HEW stepped in to delay desegregation plans for school districts in South Carolina and Mississippi, despite a Supreme Court ruling that school desegregation begin at once. Shocked by the turnaround in federal policy, the NAACP responded, "For the first time since Woodrow Wilson we have a national administration that can be rightly characterized as anti-Negro."

Two years later the Supreme Court ruled that courts could order the desegregation of school systems by busing if necessary. Nixon went on television to denounce the ruling and to urge Congress to prohibit forced busing. Although Congress did not heed his call, southern segregationists got the message—President Nixon was on their side. The message also reached those in northern cities—including many Democrats—who opposed busing.

Nixon further angered civil rights supporters by opposing the extension of the Voting Rights Act of 1965. This act had added one million African Americans to the voting rolls, greatly increasing black political power. Despite the president's opposition, Congress voted to extend the act.

## STUDY·GUIDE

**Analyzing Decisions**
The Voting Rights Act of 1965 outlawed the use of literacy tests in many southern states. Such tests were used to deprive blacks of their voting rights.

Nixon's decision to oppose extension of the bill had the effect of both angering civil rights supporters and appealing to conservative white southerners.

**2** Why did Nixon believe he could afford to alienate African Americans on civil rights issues?

**The Nixon Court**   Many conservatives also resented the liberalism of the Warren Court. In their eyes, recent Supreme Court rulings on questions such as integration and school prayer were an attack on traditional values.

To reverse the liberal decisions of the Warren Court, Nixon sought to fill vacancies on the Court with conservative judges. When Chief Justice Earl Warren resigned in 1969, Nixon nominated conservative federal judge Warren Burger to head the court. Later that year Nixon selected a conservative southerner, South Carolina federal circuit judge Clement Haynsworth, to fill another opening. He hoped this appointment would help solidify his support among white southerners.

Haynsworth, however, quickly came under fire for his record of antilabor and anti–civil rights rulings, and the Senate rejected his appointment. Furious at the defeat, Nixon chose another conservative southern judge, though one much less qualified than Haynsworth—Florida federal appeals court judge G. Harrold Carswell. Civil rights groups were outraged. During a state election campaign in 1948, Carswell had affirmed his belief in white supremacy. Even more damaging was his poor record as a federal judge; many of his rulings had been overturned by higher courts. Even Carswell's promoters were half-hearted in their support.

When the Senate rejected Carswell's nomination, Nixon claimed the votes against Haynsworth and Carswell reflected the Democratic Senate's prejudice against the South. He used the defeat to further align himself with southern conservatives. "I understand the bitter feelings of millions of Americans who live in the South," Nixon declared.

Nixon's subsequent choices to fill seats on the Supreme Court—Harry Blackmun, Lewis F. Powell, and William Rehnquist—were all well qualified and conservative. The Senate confirmed these nominations with little opposition.

Although Nixon appointed four conservative justices to the court, the Nixon Court did not always rule conservatively. In fact, on issues such as abortion, desegregation, and the death penalty, the court took a liberal stance. However, on other issues, such as civil liberties, police power, and censorship, the court's rulings reflected a shift to the right.

**Attacks on Liberals**   In his bid to capture the Wallace vote, Nixon launched shrill attacks on his liberal opponents—the press, the liberal Democrats, and the student protesters. To carry out the broadsides he enlisted the aid of his outspoken vice president, Spiro Agnew. In speeches across the country, Agnew used his license from the administration and a knack for colorful language to characterize the administration's opponents. He called liberal Democrats "sniveling hand-wringers." The television news media drew Agnew's scorn for what he saw as a liberal bias. The Nixon administration also had a fear of what they saw as the Eastern establishment. As a result, Agnew called media executives "curled-lip boys in eastern ivory towers." While Nixon insisted his goal was to bring Americans together, Agnew revealed a different strategy: "If in challenging, we polarize the American people, I say it is time . . . to rip away the rhetoric and to divide on authentic lines."

Nixon's southern strategy failed to yield major Republican victories in the 1970 state and congressional elections. The southern strategy did, however, lay the groundwork for Nixon's own reelection campaign in 1972. Coupled with the policy of New Federalism, the southern strategy also helped shift the national agenda to the right. While the policies of Johnson's Great Society had promised to protect the rights of the poor and minorities, Nixon's new conservatism promised to look out for the middle class. Yet even as Nixon was reshaping the political landscape at home, a far more pressing issue demanded his attention abroad—the Vietnam War.

## SECTION REVIEW

### Checking Facts

1. Explain why by the end of the 1960s American society was becoming divided into hostile camps.
2. Describe the silent majority. What were some of the major concerns of this group?
3. How did Nixon attack the civil rights movement? What was his strategy in doing so?
4. Explain the southern strategy. What were the effects of the strategy?

### Thinking Critically

5. **Recognizing Points of View** Evaluate the Nixon law and order campaign from Nixon's perspective. What kinds of laws did he hope to enforce, and what kind of order did he envision?
6. **Analyzing Decisions** Why did Nixon use the Department of Health, Education and Welfare to delay desegregation plans in South Carolina and Mississippi? What were some of the effects of this decision?

### Linking Across Time

7. Do you think there is a "New Silent Majority" today? What kinds of people comprise this group? Give several examples of political and social action by this group.

# From War to Détente

## November 13–15, 1969: Protesters Demand an End to War

DURING THE EVENING OF THURSDAY, NOVEMBER 13, THOUSANDS OF PEOPLE ASSEMBLED OUTSIDE THE GATES OF VIRGINIA'S ARLINGTON NATIONAL CEMETERY. Across the Potomac River lay Washington, D.C. The lights of the capital twinkled in the distance as the group stood in the darkness and biting cold.

In single file the protesters set off to walk the four miles across the river to the White House. Each marcher carried a lighted candle and a placard bearing the name of a U.S. soldier killed in Vietnam or a Vietnamese village destroyed by the war. Six drummers beating out a funeral march led the way. Just outside the gates of the White House, each marcher paused for a moment and spoke aloud the name on the placard.

The first marcher was Judy Droz, a 23-year-old widow and the mother of a ten-month-old child. Softly she spoke the name of her husband, Lieutenant Donald G. Droz, who had been killed in Vietnam the previous April. Behind her, in turn, another woman angrily shouted out her dead brother's name. Hour by hour, one by one, they came. Forty-five thousand marchers, forty-five thousand names—through two nights and days, the March against Death continued.

On Saturday, November 15, two hours after the last marcher filed past the White House, nearly 300,000 Americans swarmed around the Washington Monument. From all over the nation, they had journeyed to Washington to protest U.S. involvement in the Vietnam War. The largest demonstration in the nation's history, the November mobilization reflected the mushrooming opposition to the war. The

© BONNIE FREER

protesters were no longer just long-haired student radicals but ordinary Americans like Judy Droz.

## Ending the War in Vietnam

Vietnam by the end of the 1960s had become, in the words of one Nixon aide, "a bone in the nation's throat." By 1969, about fifteen years after U.S. advisers were first sent to Vietnam, more than 36,000 Americans had come home in flag-draped coffins.

Nixon knew he had to end this unpopular war. During the 1968 campaign, he had claimed to have a secret plan for ending the war quickly and achieving peace with honor in Vietnam. In fact, however, the war would drag on for four years. In the end, the settlement would bring neither peace to Vietnam nor honor to the United States.

**Vietnamization** Despite pressure to end the war quickly, Nixon was determined to keep an independent pro–United States government in South Vietnam and preserve America's prestige as the leader of the free world.

But even the most optimistic military advisers estimated that it would take eight more years for the United States to win the war in Vietnam. The president knew the American people would never accept eight more years of war. Increasingly, they wanted American troops to come home—now.

In May 1969 Nixon unveiled his secret plan: South Vietnamese soldiers would be trained and equipped to take the place of American troops, a process that came to be known as Vietnamization. As the South Vietnamese took over more of the fighting, U.S. troops would start coming home.

Vietnamization was part of a larger shift in foreign policy, known as the Nixon Doctrine. On an Asian tour in 1969, Nixon redefined America's role in Southeast Asia and the rest of the third world. The United States would no longer step in militarily to protect its Asian allies from communist threats. The United States would continue to provide weapons and financial aid, but in the future Asian nations would have to fight their own wars.

In November 1969 Nixon announced the withdrawal of 60,000 troops from Vietnam. Over the next three years, the number of American troops in Vietnam dropped from more than 500,000 to less than 25,000. The troop withdrawals, Nixon believed, would help silence antiwar protesters and buy him time to pursue a more favorable settlement on the battlefield and in the Paris peace talks.

### The Paris Peace Talks

Peace talks had begun in Paris in 1968 but had yielded few results. Around the table sat representatives of the United States; its ally, the Thieu government of South Vietnam; North Vietnam; and its ally, the South Vietnamese communists known as the Vietcong. Each side had interests to protect; neither side was willing to compromise.

The United States and South Vietnam insisted that all North Vietnamese forces withdraw from South Vietnam and that the Thieu regime remain in power. The North Vietnamese and the Vietcong demanded that U.S. troops withdraw from South Vietnam and that the Thieu government be replaced by a coalition government that would include the Vietcong.

Nixon sought to reopen the peace talks by sending his national security adviser, Henry Kissinger, to negotiate secretly with North Vietnam's foreign minister, Le Duc Tho. Kissinger, a Jewish refugee who had escaped Nazi Germany, was a respected professor of international relations at Harvard University when Nixon tapped him for government service. Kissinger, a skilled negotiator, was also ambitious. "What interests me," he once said in an interview, "is what you can do with power."

Nixon shared that interest. Over the years he relied more and more on Kissinger alone to help him carry out foreign policy, eventually appointing him

Secretary of State. Convinced that debate would weaken their ability to negotiate, Kissinger and Nixon kept their foreign policy moves hidden from the American press, the public, and even from Nixon's own cabinet.

### The Secret War

One such hidden policy lay at the core of Nixon's strategy for winning the war in Vietnam. To force the North Vietnamese to negotiate as American forces withdrew, Nixon ordered the secret bombing of enemy supply routes and bases in Cambodia, Laos, and North Vietnam in March 1969. As Nixon confided to aide H. R. Haldeman:

> *I* call it the madman theory, Bob. I want the North Vietnamese to believe I've reached the point where I might do anything to stop the war. We'll just slip the word to them that "for God's sake, you know Nixon is obsessed about communism. We can't restrain him when he's angry—and he has his hand on the nuclear button"—and Ho Chi Minh himself will be in Paris in two days begging for peace.
>
> H. R. Haldeman,
> *The Ends of Power,* 1978

The bombing raids failed to completely cut the supply lines or bring the North Vietnamese to the bargaining table. Instead, the attacks spread the war to Cambodia and Laos. Despite the failure of the air attacks, Nixon and Kissinger believed that eventually their strategy would work. For the next four years the United States would pursue the same carrot-and-stick policy, tempting North Vietnam with the carrot of negotiations, then threatening them with the stick of escalating war.

### A Bigger Stick

More than 3,600 secret bombing missions and 110,000 tons of bombs had failed to wipe out communist bases in Cambodia. Nixon decided he needed a bigger stick. On April 30, 1970, he went on television to announce that he was sending U.S. troops across the border into Cambodia to attack North Vietnamese bases.

Nixon's Secretary of Defense Melvin Laird and Secretary of State William Rogers opposed the move. Both men feared the reaction of the American public.

STUDY GUIDE

**Analyzing Decisions**
The policy of Vietnamization was based on Nixon's belief that Americans would not support the war without a committed ally. The policy appealed to both liberals and conservatives. For liberals, it meant American troops would be coming home. For conservatives, it meant that the United States was not abandoning its allies. The effect of this decision was to buy time for the administration to seek a negotiated peace.

Yet Nixon insisted, convinced that his bold move would stun the North Vietnamese and force them to negotiate.

**Growing Opposition at Home**   Nixon hoped to rally support for his policy by making it public. Instead, the news provoked widespread protests. College campuses exploded in demonstrations and violence as the National Guard opened fire on and killed antiwar protesters at Kent State and local police did the same at Jackson State.

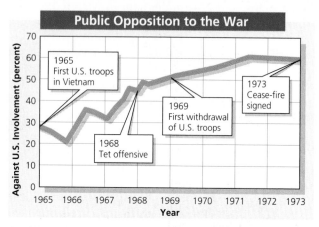

**Opposition to the war in Vietnam grew as the war dragged on.** *In what year was the opposition the highest?*

Despite the public outcry, Nixon and Kissinger insisted that their strategy would bring the war to an honorable end. Others disagreed. An editorial in a respected Midwest newspaper argued:

> *In asking the American people to support the expansion of the Vietnam war to Cambodia, as he has already expanded it to Laos, [Nixon] asks them to believe the same false promises which have repeatedly betrayed them against their will into ever deeper involvement on the mainland of Asia.*
>
> *They are asked to seek peace by making war; to seek withdrawal of our troops by enlarging the arena of combat; to diminish American casualties by sending more young men to their death.*
>
> St. Louis Post-Dispatch, May 3, 1970

Further damage to the government's credibility came in June 1971, when the *New York Times* published the "Pentagon Papers," a secret Defense Department study of U.S. involvement in Vietnam prepared during the Johnson administration. Leaked to the press by a former Defense Department analyst, Daniel Ellsberg, the report offered evidence that in the past the government had lied to the public about the war. Publicly, American presidents had insisted that the United States was fighting to keep South Vietnam free from communism. According to the "Pentagon Papers," the real reason for pouring troops into Vietnam was to "avoid a humiliating defeat." Although there was nothing in the work damaging to the Nixon administration, the White House tried to block publication of the report. The Supreme Court upheld the right of the *Times* to print it.

**The Final Years of War**   Despite U.S. training and billions of dollars in military aid, the South Vietnamese troops proved unable to defeat the communist forces. In a disastrous test of Vietnamization in February 1971, South Vietnamese troops invaded neighboring Laos to cut off the flow of supplies from North Vietnam to South Vietnam. Alerted to South Vietnamese battle plans by Vietcong agents, the North Vietnamese troops crushed the South Vietnamese forces in just six weeks.

Finally, in October 1972, talks reopened in Paris. For the first time in nearly ten years of war, peace seemed within reach. The North Vietnamese agreed to drop their demand that South Vietnam's President Thieu be replaced by a coalition government. Kissinger, too, offered critical concessions. The United States would allow North Vietnamese troops to remain in South Vietnam. Furthermore, the United States would agree to let the Vietcong play a role in a final political settlement. A cease-fire agreement was negotiated that called for the withdrawal of all remaining American troops and the return of all American prisoners of war.

With the 1972 election approaching, the White House was eager to reach a firm agreement of peace. A settlement of the festering war in Vietnam would assure Nixon's reelection. In fact, just days before the November election, a beaming Kissinger announced, "Peace is at hand."

The settlement fell apart, however, when South Vietnamese President Thieu refused to sign the treaty. He knew he was doomed if North Vietnamese troops were allowed to remain in the South.

Again Nixon used the military to force Hanoi to negotiate. On December 18, he ordered the bombing of North Vietnam's major cities, Hanoi and Haiphong. For 12 days bombers hammered away. The "Christmas" bombings—the most massive bombings of the war—laid waste to homes, hospitals, and factories. Thousands of civilians were killed. The *New York Times* called it "diplomacy through terror."

In January 1973, the North Vietnamese agreed to return to the bargaining table. It took just one week to negotiate an agreement nearly identical to the one hammered out the previous October. What broke the stale-

mate? The bombing had taken its toll, but even more important was U.S. pressure on Thieu. Nixon promised that the United States would "respond with full force should the settlement be violated by North Vietnam" and sent $1 billion in military equipment to the South Vietnamese. Reassured, Thieu signed the cease-fire.

Although Nixon claimed he had achieved peace with honor, many Americans believed that the agreement

**U.S. Troops in Vietnam, 1965–1973**

**Even as U.S. troops were being withdrawn from Vietnam, bombing operations against North Vietnam continued.** *For each year on the graph, identify events that led to an increase or decrease in the number of U.S. troops in Vietnam.*

brought neither. These critics pointed out that the same peace agreement could have been reached four years earlier. In those four years about 107,000 South Vietnamese, 500,000 North Vietnamese, and 21,000 more American troops had been killed.

**The Fall of Saigon**
The peace accords failed to bring peace to Vietnam. Issues unresolved by the treaty would be settled by soldiers on the battlefield not politicians in Paris.

Shortly after the last American troops left in March 1973, the cease-fire collapsed. Fighting

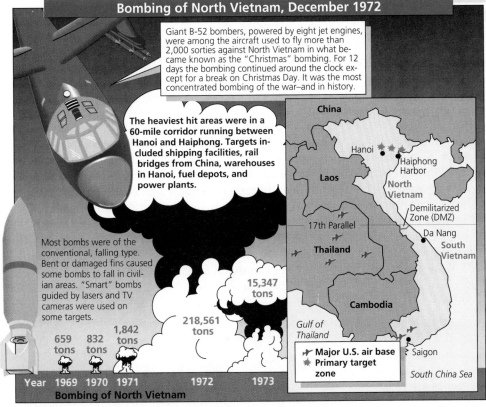

**Bombing of North Vietnam, December 1972**

Giant B-52 bombers, powered by eight jet engines, were among the aircraft used to fly more than 2,000 sorties against North Vietnam in what became known as the "Christmas" bombing. For 12 days the bombing continued around the clock except for a break on Christmas Day. It was the most concentrated bombing of the war–and in history.

The heaviest hit areas were in a 60-mile corridor running between Hanoi and Haiphong. Targets included shipping facilities, rail bridges from China, warehouses in Hanoi, fuel depots, and power plants.

Most bombs were of the conventional, falling type. Bent or damaged fins caused some bombs to fall in civilian areas. "Smart" bombs guided by lasers and TV cameras were used on some targets.

| Year | 1969 | 1970 | 1971 | 1972 | 1973 |
|---|---|---|---|---|---|
| | 659 tons | 832 tons | 1,842 tons | 218,561 tons / 15,347 tons | |

**Bombing of North Vietnam**

China
Hanoi
Haiphong Harbor
Laos
North Vietnam
Demilitarized Zone (DMZ)
17th Parallel
Da Nang
Thailand
South Vietnam
Cambodia
Gulf of Thailand
Saigon
South China Sea

✈ Major U.S. air base
✳ Primary target zone

broke out not only in Vietnam but also in Laos and Cambodia. In March 1975 North Vietnam launched an offensive against the weakened forces of South Vietnam. Thieu turned to Washington for aid; Congress refused to grant it.

In April 1975 communist troops marched into Saigon. American television audiences watched as desperate South Vietnamese, many of whom had supported the Americans, scrambled to escape. A U.S. Army medic described the turmoil on an aircraft carrier offshore:

© PETER GRIDLEY, FPG INTERNATIONAL; © J.L. ATLAN, SYGMA

**Vietnam veterans themselves sponsored the Vietnam Veterans Memorial in Washington, D.C. Black granite panels carry the names of 58,000 Americans who died in Vietnam. Visitors to the wall touch the names they know, and some take home rubbings of a friend's name. The monument was designed by Maya Lin, then a 21-year-old senior at Yale.**

*There were people coming out in boats, half-sinking boats. . . . There were all these choppers we had left there; they were using these to fly out, the Vietnamese. This flight deck was so full of choppers that we had to push them overboard because there was no room, we couldn't get our own choppers in. . . . It was total chaos.*

Al Santoli,
*Everything We Had,* 1981

In the dawn hours of April 30, 1975, Saigon fell to the communists; soon after, South Vietnam surrendered to North Vietnam.

**The Costs of the War**  The nation paid a high price to end the war in Vietnam. More than 58,000 Americans were dead; 300,000 were wounded, many of them permanently disabled. More than $150 billion had been poured into the war, while social programs at home went underfunded.

For the first time in history America had lost a war. The extreme optimism and self-confidence felt by Americans following World War II had been shattered. Despite every advantage in wealth and technology the United States had been unable to defeat a third world nationalist movement.

The people of Southeast Asia also paid a great price for the war in Vietnam. In the course of the war, more than eight million tons of bombs—the equivalent of 640 Hiroshimas—had been dropped on Southeast Asia. Two million Vietnamese and uncounted Cambodians and Laotians were dead. Their land lay in ruins, their villages—to the Vietnamese the heart of their ancient culture—destroyed.

## U.S. Intervention in Vietnam

**1956**
South Vietnam cancels elections promised in Geneva Accords.

**1960**
National Liberation Front is formed to overthrow U.S.-backed government in South Vietnam.

**February–March 1965**
Johnson orders bombing of North Vietnam and sends first U.S. combat troops to South Vietnam.

**June 1969**
Nixon announces first withdrawal of American troops from Vietnam.

**January 1973**
The United States, South Vietnam, the Vietcong, and North Vietnam sign cease-fire agreement.

1954  1957  1960  1963  1966  1969  1972  1975

**1954**
French are defeated by Vietnamese at Dien Bien Phu; Geneva Accords divide Vietnam into North and South Vietnam, pending national elections in1956; the United States assumes support of South Vietnamese government.

**August 1964**
U.S. Congress passes Gulf of Tonkin Resolution, giving president power to "prevent further aggression" against U.S. forces in Vietnam.

**1968**
Communists launch Tet offensive. Johnson rejects Westmoreland's request for more U.S. troops.

**April 1970**
American and South Vietnamese forces invade Cambodia; protests occur at home.

# Détente

Although President Nixon's Vietnam policy provoked fierce criticism, he was widely hailed for a series of bold moves elsewhere. Envisioning a new world order, Nixon abandoned the cold war policy of confrontation and initiated a policy of **détente,** an attempt to repair strained relations between the United States and the communist powers. In a dramatic reversal of nearly 25 years of cold war politics, Nixon sought better relations with both China and the Soviet Union.

**A New World View** The world in 1970 little resembled the world of the 1950s, when the cold war policy of containment was forged. The two superpowers, the United States and the Soviet Union, had been replaced by five economic superpowers—the United States, the Soviet Union, Japan, China, and the European Economic Community—the nations of western Europe. President Nixon believed that economic power was the key to political power and that these five superpowers would determine the political future.

Nor was the communist world united in 1970. Tensions between the Soviet Union and China had erupted in the 1960s, resulting in armed clashes between the two former allies in 1969. By playing one communist power against the other, Nixon and Kissinger hoped to gain concessions from both.

Nixon and Kissinger shared a belief in *realpolitik,* practical politics.[1] According to this view, a nation should pursue policies and make alliances based on its national interests, rather than on any particular view of the world. Thus, if improved relations with China

UPI/BETTMANN NEWSPHOTOS

**President Nixon showed a great deal of cultural sensitivity on his trip to China, making toasts to Chinese leaders, eating with chopsticks, and in general going out of his way to have pleasant casual contact with the Chinese people.**

and the Soviet Union would benefit the United States, then the United States should set aside its bias against communism and pursue those relations.

Kissinger and Nixon promoted a foreign policy based on a **balance of power** among nations. "It will be a safer world and a better world," the president declared in 1971, "if we have a strong, healthy United States, Europe, Soviet Union, China, Japan—each balancing the other."

Nixon and Kissinger believed that détente was the key to this balance. Détente would limit communist expansion and curb the nuclear arms race through negotiation rather than armed conflict.

Détente made sense economically, too. The United States was not eager to pour billions of dollars into another regional conflict like Vietnam. In addition, trade with the Soviet Union and China would open up new markets for American products.

Nixon was able to undertake this bold shift in foreign policy in part because of his reputation as a cold warrior. Elected to Congress in 1946 on an anticommunist platform, he gained fame in the 1940s as a member of the House Un-American Activities Committee. Certainly no one could question Nixon's genuine commitment to anticommunism.

**China** Since the communist takeover of China in 1949, the United States had refused to recognize the People's Republic of China, the most populous nation on earth. Diplomatic relations between the two nations had been cut off. Instead, the United States recognized the anticommunist Chinese government in exile on the island of Taiwan.

The United States had treated the People's Republic as an outlaw nation; it had cut off trade and vetoed the country's admission to the United Nations.

---

To the cold war policy-makers, the People's Republic was a "red menace" threatening to gobble up its Asian neighbors.

The winds of change, however, began to blow in the fall of 1970 when Nixon confided to a *Time* magazine reporter that he wanted to go to China. Then in April 1971, a ping-pong ball made headline news when the Chinese hosted an American table tennis team—the first official contact between the two nations in more than two decades. Only one week later the United States announced the end of the trade embargo against China.

The Chinese were eager for friendship with the United States as security against the Soviet Union.[2] In July 1971 Nixon sent Kissinger on a secret mission to Beijing. Soon afterwards Nixon stunned the world with the announcement that he would travel to China to normalize relations between the two countries. That fall, after the United States abandoned its opposition, China was admitted to the United Nations.

In February 1972 Nixon arrived in China for a week-long visit. Accompanied by reporters and televi-

© J.P. LAFFONT, SYGMA

**Soviet leader Leonid Brezhnev and President Nixon share a lighter moment during Nixon's trip to Russia in 1972. As well as better relations with the Soviet Union, Nixon hoped the Soviets might put pressure on the North Vietnamese to end the war in Vietnam.**

sion camera crews, the president visited the Great Wall and met with Chinese leaders Mao Zedong and Zhou Enlai. Friendly gestures abounded. Chinese musicians played "America the Beautiful," and Nixon quoted lines from Mao's poetry.

The United States and China agreed to allow greater scientific and cultural exchange and to resume trade. Although formal diplomatic relations were not established until 1979, Nixon's trip marked the first formal contact with China in more than 25 years.

**The Soviet Union**   In a second dramatic foreign policy move, Nixon visited Moscow only three months after his trip to China.

The Soviets eagerly welcomed the thaw in cold war politics. They wanted to prevent a Chinese-American alliance and to slow the costly arms race. They also hoped to gain access to U.S. technology and to buy badly needed American grain.

During his visit Nixon met with Soviet leader Leonid Brezhnev and signed agreements on trade and technological exchange. Even more important, Nixon signed a landmark arms agreement, the result of negotiations known as the Strategic Arms Limitation Talks (SALT). The agreement did not end the arms race. However, by limiting the number of certain types of nuclear weapons, it eased tensions between the two nations.

## The Election of 1972

Nixon's trips to China and the Soviet Union boosted his popularity at home. In the summer of 1971, following the invasion of Laos, only 31 percent of the American public supported Nixon's policies. By the summer of 1972, however, after his well-publicized visits abroad, his approval rating soared to nearly 62 percent. As election day neared, a Republican victory seemed certain.

**The Divided Democrats**   The Democratic party was hopelessly split. Four major candidates competed for the presidential nomination: former vice president Hubert Humphrey, Maine senator Edmund Muskie, South Dakota senator George McGovern, and Alabama ex-governor George Wallace.

STUDY GUIDE

**Predicting Consequences**
Following the invasion of Laos, Nixon's approval rating was only 31 percent. Following trips to China and the Soviet Union, Nixon's popularity soared to 62 percent. To the extent that one recognizes the American public's dissatisfaction with the war in Vietnam and its desire to renew peaceful relations abroad, Nixon's rise in popularity was predictable.

2 Why were the Chinese eager for friendship with the United States?

Humphrey, who had lost to Nixon in 1968, was unable to muster support for a rematch. The moderate Muskie started strong but was soon overtaken by the liberal McGovern. McGovern's opposition to the Vietnam War gave voters a clear alternative to Nixon's war policies.

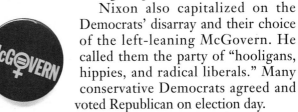

Wallace posed the greatest threat to Nixon. Wallace had galvanized many conservative voters with his attacks on busing, criminals, protesters, and "pointy-headed intellectuals." As a Democratic nominee or a third-party candidate, Wallace could pull these voters away from Nixon. Wallace won a string of southern primaries and came in a close second in some northern states. His campaign was cut short in May 1972 by a would-be assassin's bullet. The attack left Wallace paralyzed for life and forced him to withdraw from the campaign.

An early opponent of the Vietnam War and a social reformer, McGovern won a number of key primaries. Recent reforms in Democratic party rules had increased the number of women, minorities, and young delegates at the convention, assuring McGovern's nomination. McGovern was not a middle-of-the-road candidate. He called for a $30 billion cut in defense spending, immediate withdrawal from Vietnam, and pardons for Vietnam draft resisters.

Many traditional Democratic supporters were unhappy with the party's drift to the left. Denied a seat at the convention, AFL-CIO president George Meany ordered union members—traditionally staunch Democrats—to withhold support from McGovern.

**The Republican Campaign**   Nixon's campaign suffered no setbacks. His trips to China and the Soviet Union and his withdrawal of U.S. troops from Vietnam helped silence his foreign policy critics. An upturn in the economy further bolstered his popularity. He easily won over voters who had previously

supported Wallace with promises to fight busing and end "the age of permissiveness."

Nixon also capitalized on the Democrats' disarray and their choice of the left-leaning McGovern. He called them the party of "hooligans, hippies, and radical liberals." Many conservative Democrats agreed and voted Republican on election day.

Nixon won the 1972 election in a landslide, carrying every state but Massachusetts. He won 60.8 percent of the popular vote. The electoral vote margin was even greater, 520 to 17. The southern strategy had paid off.

Yet a shadow loomed over Nixon's victory. He had authorized a "dirty tricks" campaign against the Democrats. Shortly before the election, burglars hired by the Committee to Re-Elect the President had been caught breaking into Democratic national headquarters in Washington. Nixon and his aides denied any involvement in the break-in, and for the time, at least, the public believed them. As Nixon began his second term, however, the tangled story behind the burglary began to unravel.

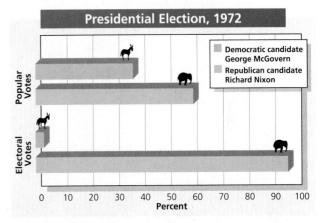

**Nixon won the 1972 election with more than 90 percent of the electoral votes.** *What factors contributed to his victory?*

## SECTION REVIEW

### Checking Facts

1. Explain how the policy of Vietnamization fit in with the Nixon Doctrine.

2. Explain the costs of the war in Vietnam from the perspective of the United States and from that of the people of Southeast Asia.

3. Why were both the Soviet Union and China receptive to visits by President Nixon?

4. Why was Nixon's popularity so high just before the election in 1972?

### Thinking Critically

5. **Analyzing Decisions**  Why was Vietnamization an attractive policy for Nixon? What were the effects of Vietnamization?

6. **Predicting Consequences**  Why was the Thieu government unwilling to sign a peace treaty that

allowed North Vietnamese troops to remain in South Vietnam? What were some of the consequences for South Vietnam of agreeing to the cease-fire in 1973?

### Linking Across Time

7. United States involvement in Vietnam officially ended in 1973. What effects of the war are still part of American life?

# Crisis in the Presidency

## June 17, 1972: Burglars Break into Democratic Party Headquarters

SHORTLY AFTER MIDNIGHT ON JUNE 17, 1972, SECURITY GUARD FRANK WILLS WAS MAKING HIS ROUNDS OF THE WATERGATE BUILDING, A VAST OFFICE-APARTMENT COMPLEX IN Washington, D.C. As he checked the doors connecting the building to an underground parking garage, the 24-year-old Wills noticed something odd. The locks on the doors had been taped to keep them from locking. "I took the tape off, but I didn't think anything of it," he said later. "I thought maybe the building engineer had done it." Wills finished his rounds and then strolled across the street to a diner for a cheeseburger, french fries, and a shake.

An hour later Wills was back at work. Once again he checked the garage doors. They had been re-taped! This time Wills called the police.

The police found more taped doors on the building's sixth floor, headquarters of the Democratic National Committee (DNC). They cautiously began to search the DNC offices one by one.

Suddenly, behind a glass and wood partition, one of the police officers spotted an arm. "Hold it!" he shouted. "Come out!" A moment later, not two but ten hands shot up. Five men dressed in business suits emerged. On the floor lay lock picks, 40 rolls of film, two cameras, two "bugs"—tiny electronic devices for listening—and $1,754 in cash.

When police returned the next day they found more electronic equipment, several suitcases, and $3,566.58 in cash. They also found a tiny

UPI/BETTMANN NEWSPHOTOS

black address book. In it, next to the name Howard Hunt, was a telephone number and a note: W. House.

It would take 22 months and the combined efforts of the Congress, the press, and the courts to bring the Watergate story to light. What emerged was not just the story of a burglary but a tale of crimes committed by the man sworn to uphold the Constitution and the nation's laws—the president of the United States.

## The Nixon White House

By the time Richard Nixon first took office in 1969 the White House was already the seat of considerable power. Since the outbreak of World War II, American presidents had gradually assumed powers in foreign policy making that the Constitution seemed to reserve for Congress. During the war President Roosevelt had, in effect, made treaties with foreign nations without the advice or consent of the Senate. Both Truman and Johnson had sent troops into combat without a congressional declaration of war. When national security was at stake, they argued, the president had to be able to respond quickly—even if that meant Congress was not consulted.

Nixon, however, outdid his predecessors in ignoring constitutional checks on presidential powers. He impounded funds for federal programs he opposed, defying the constitutional mandate that Congress control spending. He ordered U.S.

---

### STUDY GUIDE

**As You Read**
Identify the events that led the House Judiciary Committee to draft articles of impeachment against President Nixon. Also, think about the following concept and skills.

**Central Concept**
• understanding how the constitutional system of checks and balances, including the powers of **impeachment**, curbed abuses of power by the executive branch

**Thinking Skills**
• evaluating sources
• analyzing behavior
• recognizing propaganda

troops to invade Cambodia without seeking congressional approval. As the executive branch flexed its muscles, the legislative branch weakened, and the balance of powers set forth in the Constitution tipped in favor of a more powerful presidency. By the 1970s the constitutional presidency had become what some critics called the imperial presidency.

**President Nixon**   Richard Nixon reached the White House after nearly 25 years in politics. A skilled lawyer and a shrewd politician, Nixon loved public life and hoped to be remembered as a great statesman. He greatly admired former presidents Woodrow Wilson and Teddy Roosevelt.

Yet Nixon had a darker side. At times mean-spirited and suspicious, he made his reputation in the late 1940s by hounding alleged communists in the U.S. government. This was the Nixon who thrived on the power of the imperial presidency and whom his critics dubbed King Richard.

**The Inner Circle**   Nixon surrounded himself with a small group of trusted and loyal aides. At the head of what some critics called the palace guard stood Harry Robins "H. R." Haldeman, the president's chief of staff, and John Ehrlichman.

Haldeman was Nixon's closest aide. A former advertising executive, Haldeman first worked for Nixon in his 1956 campaign for vice president. The uncomplaining Haldeman described his role: "I get done what he wants done, and I take the heat for it."

Ehrlichman, a former Seattle lawyer, handled domestic policies. Together with Henry Kissinger, Haldeman and Ehrlichman formed an inner circle that wielded more power than the president's cabinet.

**The Enemies List**   By surrounding himself with aides who almost always agreed with him, Nixon created his own house of mirrors, where all opinions reflected his own. Protected from criticism, Nixon grew increasingly isolated.

One Nixon aide recalled: "You were either for us or against us, and if you were against us we were against you." In 1971 Nixon ordered his special counsel, Chuck Colson, to put together an enemies list. Colson, who described himself as a "flag-waving . . . anti-press, anti-liberal, Nixon fanatic" eagerly set about his task.

Colson drew up a list of more than 200 individuals and 18 organizations that the administration regarded as enemies. The list included many notable liberal Americans. Among them were politicians such as Senators Edward Kennedy and George McGovern, Representatives Bella Abzug and Shirley Chisholm, and the entire black leadership of the House; college presidents, such as Kingman Brewster of Yale University; Hollywood stars, such as Steve McQueen, Paul Newman, and Jane Fonda; and 57 members of the media.

Once the list was complete, Nixon asked the FBI to spy on these individuals and try to discredit them. He also ordered the IRS to harass them with tax audits.

**The Huston Plan**   Nixon's fears were fed by a concern that the antiwar movement might undo him as it had toppled Johnson in 1968. The massive public outcry following the announcement of the Cambodian invasion in April 1970 had shaken the president. He believed he had to silence his critics or face defeat at the polls in 1972.[1]

In June 1970 White House aide Tom Huston submitted a plan for a secret police operation to combat the antiwar movement. The Huston plan would expand and unify the work of the FBI, the CIA, the National Security Agency, and the Defense Intelligence Agency. The entire operation would be run out of the White House. To defend what the White House considered to be national security, agents would infiltrate antiwar groups, open people's mail, and tap their telephones. They would break into homes and offices, in search of information that could be used to discredit or even blackmail Nixon's critics.

Although Huston admitted that much of the plan was illegal and would violate the rights of U.S. citizens, President Nixon approved it. FBI chief J. Edgar Hoover, however, feared that the plan would reduce the FBI's power and blocked it.

**CREEP**   As the 1972 presidential election neared, Nixon's worries mounted. The Republican party had failed to regain control of either the House or the Senate in the congressional elections of 1970. Past campaign losses, to John F. Kennedy for president in 1960 and to Pat Brown for governor of California in 1962, haunted Nixon. He wanted four more years in the White House.

In early 1971, however, Nixon looked like a loser. A poll in February showed Democratic presidential hopeful Edmund Muskie out in front of Nixon by 43 to 40 percent. By March Muskie's lead had grown to 44 to 39, and by May he led Nixon by a margin of 47 to 39 percent.

Taking no chances with his reelection campaign, the president put his trusted friend John Mitchell in charge. In March 1971 Mitchell resigned as attorney general and set up the Committee to Re-Elect the President (CREEP). The burly, pipe-smoking Mitchell soon launched a massive illegal fund-raising campaign. Of the nearly $60 million collected, over $350,000 was squirreled away in a special fund to pay for "dirty tricks" operations against Nixon's Democratic foes.

**The Plumbers** Nixon feared that the press might expose his illegal campaign activities. Those fears deepened that summer when the *New York Times* published the "Pentagon Papers." Although the report dealt with Vietnam policy prior to the Nixon administration, Nixon feared their publication would lead to leaks of classified documents damaging to his administration. To prevent such a disaster, CREEP created a special investigations unit, nicknamed "the plumbers," to stop security leaks.

**The protective wings of the American Eagle are shown here as giant ears—symbolic of domestic spying by the Nixon Administration.**

© MEL FURUKAWA/NEW YORK TIMES

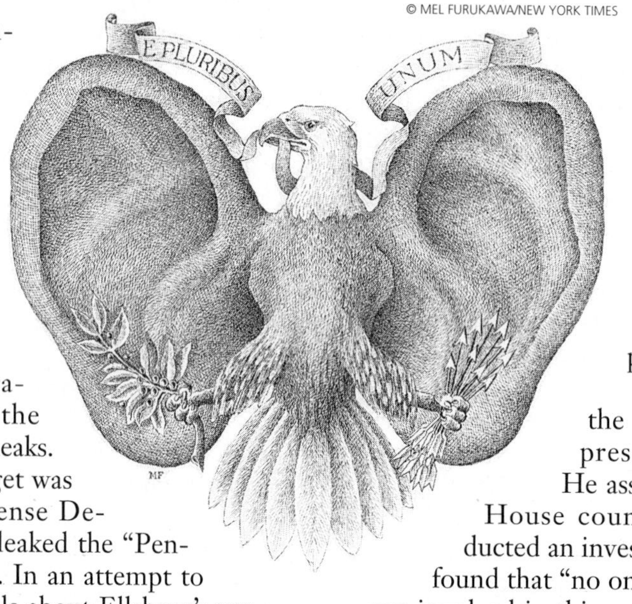

The plumbers' first target was Daniel Ellsberg, the Defense Department analyst who had leaked the "Pentagon Papers" to the press. In an attempt to uncover embarrassing details about Ellsberg's personal life, the plumbers broke into the office of Ellsberg's psychiatrist. However, they found nothing they could use against Ellsberg.

Then, in January 1972, CREEP plumber G. Gordon Liddy came up with a daring plan. A team of plumbers would break into Democratic National Committee headquarters, copy documents, and wiretap the phones. By doing so the White House could keep tabs on Democratic election strategies. Okayed by John Mitchell, the plan was set in motion in the early morning hours of June 17, 1972, at the Democratic Party's offices in the Watergate complex.

## *Unraveling Watergate*

Later on the morning of June 17, Bob Woodward and Carl Bernstein, two reporters for the *Washington Post*, got a call about the Watergate break-in. Woodward, a 29-year-old Yale graduate, and Bernstein, a 28-year-old college dropout, were an unlikely team. Inexperienced but ambitious, the two young reporters worked tirelessly to uncover the entire story.

Their investigations soon revealed that two of the Watergate conspirators—G. Gordon Liddy and E. Howard Hunt—were employees of CREEP. They also learned that the burglars had been paid from a CREEP fund controlled by the White House staff. The deeper the two reporters dug, the more evidence they found that the Watergate break-in was one of many illegal activities planned and paid for by the president's advisers.

Eager to put a lid on the investigation, Nixon held a press conference that August. He assured the public that White House counsel John Dean had conducted an investigation of the incident and found that "no one on the White House staff was involved in this very bizarre incident." At the same time Nixon secretly authorized the payment of more than $460,000 in CREEP funds to keep the Watergate burglars quiet about White House involvement.[2]

Woodward and Bernstein kept digging. In a front-page story on October 10, the two reporters pulled together the evidence they had unearthed that summer.

STUDY GUIDE

**Analyzing Behavior**

When J. Edgar Hoover blocked the Huston plan, Nixon decided to use the resources of his reelection committee to combat the antiwar movement and his personal critics. The committee raised millions of dollars for Nixon, much of it in cash, in violation of new laws that required stricter reporting of campaign contributions.

2 Why was it so important to Nixon that the link between the Watergate burglars and CREEP remain secret?

*FBI agents have established that the Watergate bugging incident stemmed from a massive campaign of political spying and sabotage conducted on behalf of President Nixon's re-election and directed by officials of the White House and the Committee for the Re-election of the President.*

Bob Woodward and Carl Bernstein,
*Washington Post,* October 10, 1972

It was sensational news. The White House fought back, calling the *Post*'s story "a senseless pack of lies" put together by the liberal paper to discredit the administration. As the 1972 election neared, Nixon worked to bury the Watergate story.

For a time the president's strategy seemed to work. Few other journalists picked up the story. Just before the 1972 election, polls showed that only 48 percent of Americans had even heard of Watergate.

**The Watergate Trial**   The Watergate story might have remained just a bizarre incident, but in early 1973, shortly after Nixon began his second term, the Watergate burglars went on trial before federal judge John J. Sirica. Nicknamed Maximum John because of his reputation for handing out long prison terms, Sirica was a no-nonsense judge who warned the Watergate defendants, "Don't pull any punches—you give me straight

answers." Angered by the Watergate scandal, Sirica was determined to use his courtroom to search for the real story behind the Watergate break-in.

Afraid of a lengthy prison sentence, one of the Watergate burglars, James W. McCord, agreed to cooperate. In a letter to Judge Sirica, McCord alleged that White House officials had lied about their involvement in the affair and had pressured the defendants "to plead guilty and remain silent." McCord's letter blew the lid off the case.

**The Senate Hearings**   While Judge Sirica pursued the case in a Washington courtroom, the Senate began its own investigation of Watergate. From May to November 1973, the Senate Select Committee on Presidential Campaign Practices heard testimony from a parade of White House officials.

Sam J. Ervin, the 76-year-old senator from North Carolina, chaired the committee. Ervin was a Harvard Law School graduate who had earned the respect of his colleagues during his 18-year Senate career.

Ervin was known to be a staunch defender of First Amendment rights. He called the Constitution "the finest thing to come out of the mind of man." Ervin steered the hearings with a commanding wit and down-to-earth common sense.

On April 30, 1973, Nixon made another attempt to shield the White House from the gathering storm by

**By the spring of 1973, Watergate was big news and the byline of Woodward and Bernstein was familiar** to readers following the story. *What role did the press play in bringing the scandal to light?*

© THE WASHINGTON POST

**Analyzing Behavior**

Many legal experts were critical of how Judge Sirica handled the case of the Watergate burglars. The critics argued that Sirica had put himself in the role of prosecutor during the trial. Some argued that Sirica sought the truth with the same ends-justifying-means tactics that Nixon used to hide it. Sirica's behavior can also be analyzed as a search for the truth in its broader context.

The Watergate committee, above, was chaired by Sam J. Ervin, at right. H. R. Haldeman, center, and John Ehrlichman, lower right, were among those questioned.

AP/WIDE WORLD PHOTOS

UPI/BETTMANN NEWSPHOTOS

UPI/BETTMANN NEWSPHOTOS

UPI/BETTMANN NEWSPHOTOS

announcing the resignations of Dean, Haldeman, and Ehrlichman. All three men had been involved in Watergate. Speaking on television, the president denied any attempt at a cover-up and vowed: "There can be no whitewash at the White House." However, polls showed that half of those watching believed the president had taken part in a cover-up.

Under pressure from Congress and the public, Nixon ordered Attorney General Elliot Richardson to appoint a special prosecutor to investigate Watergate. Richardson chose Harvard law professor Archibald Cox and promised the Senate that Cox would have complete independence from the White House and broad powers of investigation.

Public interest in the case grew that summer as the Senate committee began televised hearings. Each day millions of Americans watched—fascinated—as the story unfolded.

The most damaging testimony came from John Dean, the White House counsel. Dean testified for nearly 30 hours. He claimed that there *had* been a cover-up and charged that the president himself had directed it.

Then, in July, another bombshell exploded. White House aide Alexander Butterfield told the Senate Committee that in early 1971 Nixon had installed a tape recording system in the White House. The news that the president had bugged his own office was electrifying. Here was proof of Nixon's guilt or innocence.

By August, the hearings were the top-rated daytime television show. Democrat Sam Ervin became a national hero as he grilled Mitchell, Haldeman, Ehrlichman, and other White House figures about Watergate.

Republican senator Howard Baker asked each witness the question all Americans wanted the answer to: "What did the President know and when did he know it?"

**The Tapes** Both the Senate committee and special prosecutor Cox called on Nixon to surrender tapes of conversations that might pertain to the Watergate break-in. Nixon refused and claimed executive privilege, insisting that the release of the tapes would endanger national security. Cox and Ervin persisted. Cox declared, "There is no exception for the president from the guiding principle that the public, in the pursuit of justice, has a right to every man's evidence." He sought a court order to force Nixon to hand over the tapes.

Nixon again tried to shift attention away from the scandal. On August 15 he urged Americans to put Watergate behind them. He felt that after 12 weeks and 2 million words of televised testimony, it was time to get on with the "urgent business of our nation." Few Americans agreed.

Finally, Nixon ordered Attorney General Richardson to fire Cox. Richardson, remembering his promise to the Senate, refused and resigned. When Richardson resigned, Nixon ordered the deputy attorney general, William Ruckelshaus, to fire Cox. Ruckelshaus refused and was himself fired. Finally, Solicitor General Robert

Bork fired Cox. Public outcry over what came to be known as the Saturday Night Massacre forced Nixon to appoint another special prosecutor, attorney Leon Jaworski. Jaworski renewed the demand for the tapes. Nixon balked and Jaworski took the case to court.

The crisis was deepening. Already nearly 50 Nixon administration officials, including Mitchell, Haldeman, and Ehrlichman, faced criminal charges.

That fall Nixon's troubles multiplied. In October 1973, Vice President Spiro Agnew pleaded no contest to charges of income tax evasion and accepting bribes while governor of Maryland and resigned. Nixon nominated Gerald R. Ford, a popular conservative congressman from Michigan, to fill the post. Congress quickly confirmed the nomination.

Then, in December, Nixon's own finances came under fire. Federal investigators reported that in 1970 and 1971 the president had paid only about $800 a year in federal taxes on an annual salary of $200,000. Since 1969 he had paid no state income tax even though he was still a legal resident of California.

Pressure for the tapes was also mounting. In April 1974, the president released edited transcripts of some of the tapes in question. Although his aides had cut the most incriminating comments, many people were shocked by the profanity, pettiness, and ethnic insults that peppered the president's conversations.

Even more revealing was what was missing from the tapes. Gaps in the tapes indicated the president was not telling the public the whole truth. When Nixon again refused to release the unedited tapes, Jaworski took the case to the Supreme Court. On July 24, in *U.S. v. Nixon*, the Supreme Court unanimously ruled that President Nixon had to release the tapes.

**The Move for Impeachment**   Also in July the House Judiciary Committee began to draft articles of **impeachment**, or charges, against the president. The impeachment process allows Congress to check the power of officials in the executive and judicial branches. Impeachable offenses include criminal activity, but are not limited to acts that are illegal.

Under the Constitution the House of Representatives determines whether impeachment charges are justified. If so, the Senate then serves as the jury for the trial. Only one president, Andrew Johnson, had ever been impeached.

On July 30, following several days of televised debate, the House committee voted to recommend impeachment of President Nixon on three counts: obstructing justice by trying to cover up the role of the White House in the Watergate burglary; violating the rights of U.S. citizens by using the FBI, CIA, and IRS to harass critics; and defying congressional authority by refusing to turn over the tapes. The articles of impeachment would now go to the House of Representatives for a vote.

Nixon was trapped. On August 5 he handed over the tapes, confessing that they were "at variance with some of my earlier statements." The tapes revealed that just days after the Watergate break-in, the president had ordered the CIA to halt the FBI investigation of the case: "Don't go any further into this case, period." Impeachment charges seemed certain.

**The Final Days**   For three days Nixon paced, brooded, and conferred with his few remaining friends in Congress. No matter how he counted the votes in the House and Senate, they added up to certain impeachment and probable conviction in the Senate.

By Wednesday, August 7, key Republican leaders had joined the chorus demanding the president's

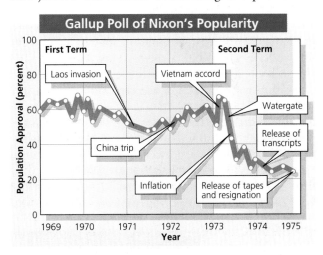

**Like a roller coaster, Nixon's popularity rose and fell with events.** *How popular was he when he resigned?*

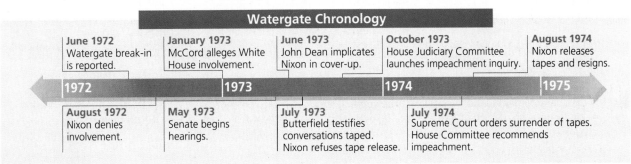

**Watergate Chronology**

**June 1972**
Watergate break-in is reported.

**August 1972**
Nixon denies involvement.

**January 1973**
McCord alleges White House involvement.

**May 1973**
Senate begins hearings.

**June 1973**
John Dean implicates Nixon in cover-up.

**July 1973**
Butterfield testifies conversations taped. Nixon refuses tape release.

**October 1973**
House Judiciary Committee launches impeachment inquiry.

**July 1974**
Supreme Court orders surrender of tapes. House Committee recommends impeachment.

**August 1974**
Nixon releases tapes and resigns.

1972   1973   1974   1975

The casual, offhand dialogue in this cartoon suggests a White House where cover-ups and lies are routine.

Thirty-one Nixon administration officials were sent to prison for Watergate-related offenses.

resignation. Nixon made his decision. That evening Nixon met with a group of 46 loyal Congressional leaders. In a long rambling speech, he thanked them for their years of support. Twenty minutes later he would address the nation—the first American president ever to resign from office.

The following day Nixon and his family flew back to California, and Gerald Ford was sworn in as president. At last, President Ford declared, "Our long national nightmare is over." A president had fallen, but the American political system had survived.

**The Aftermath**  A month later President Ford pardoned Nixon for any crimes he may have committed while in the White House. Many Americans felt Nixon had escaped justice. Others, however, believed it was time to put Watergate to rest and to look to the future.

To counter the trend toward greater presidential power and curb future abuses, Congress enacted a series of laws. The War Powers Act of 1973 required the president to consult with Congress before sending American troops into prolonged action. In 1974 Congress passed the Congressional Budget and

Impoundment Control Act which prohibited the impounding of federal money by the president.

Also in 1974 Congress strengthened the Federal Election Campaign Act of 1972, setting limits on campaign contributions. Finally, Congress extended the Freedom of Information Act by passing the Privacy Act, allowing citizens to have access to the files that the government may have gathered on them.

The Nixon White House had threatened the foundation of American democracy—constitutional law. Yet, as many pointed out, the system worked. The legislative and judicial branches reasserted their powers to rein in the executive branch. Congress investigated the charges, and the independent judiciary forced the president to release evidence. Eventually 31 Nixon administration officials were convicted and went to prison for Watergate-related offenses.

At the same time, Watergate was deeply disquieting. The nation's leaders had committed serious crimes. Then the new president had pardoned the most important offender. Had a deal been made? How could Americans continue to trust their government? Coming on the heels of the war in Vietnam, Watergate further undermined the nation's self-confidence.

## SECTION REVIEW

**Checking Facts**

1. Explain why in the 1970s the presidency was called the imperial presidency.
2. Describe the Huston plan. What were its goals? What about the plan was illegal?
3. What were the three impeachment charges against Nixon? Give evidence to support each of the charges.

4. List several laws that Congress passed after Watergate in an attempt to curb presidential power and the potential for presidential abuses.

**Thinking Critically**

5. **Evaluating Sources** How did the Supreme Court rule in *U.S. v. Nixon*? What were some of the practical and theoretical effects of the decision?

6. **Analyzing Behavior** President Ford described Watergate as "our long national nightmare." What reasons did Ford have for pardoning Nixon? Explain your answer.

**Linking Across Time**

7. What are some of the effects of Watergate on Americans' trust of their government?

For over two hundred years, American newspapers and magazines have published political cartoons. Reading political cartoons from the past can help you appreciate how people of other times felt about issues that were important then. Interpreting current political cartoons can increase your awareness of differing views on today's important issues.

## Learning the Skill

A cartoon is meant to entertain readers, usually by using a play on words or by creating amusing visual images. A political cartoon is a type of cartoon that not only entertains in one of these ways but also makes a comment on a current political issue by using caricatures, symbols, and analogies. Political cartoons often attempt to influence readers to agree with the cartoonist's point of view.

To interpret a political cartoon, study the use of each of the visual techniques described below. Then combine the individual messages to determine what impression the cartoonist wants to leave with the reader.

### Caricature

A caricature is an exaggerated picture. By deliberately exaggerating one or more unusual or distinctive features of a well-known subject, the cartoonist produces a comic image and at the same time helps the reader to recognize the subject. The cartoon on this page, for example, exaggerates two of President Nixon's most recognizable facial features—the size of his nose and the dark circles around his eyes.

### Symbol

A symbol is an idea, image, or object that stands for or suggests something else. Some symbols are widely used and need no explanation. For example, a crown as a symbol of royalty and a dove as a symbol of peace are recognized almost anywhere. In the cartoon at the right, the person labeled Congress symbolizes the father figure in the story of George Washington and the cherry tree. The ax behind Nixon's back is a symbol of his guilt. The cartoonist in this case expects the reader to be familiar with the cherry tree story and to recognize these symbols.

### Analogy

An analogy is the comparing of two relationships by using one as a reference for illustrating the other. For example, an analogy might be drawn between the benefits of walking and the benefits of reading, as follows: reading is to the mind as walking is to the body.

In the cartoon on this page, evidence of President Nixon's actions is compared to George Washington's ax. The analogy is that the evidence in the Watergate affair was to Congress as the ax

*I claim executive privilege.*

BILL MAULDIN, ©1973 CHICAGO SUN TIMES

was to George Washington's father—definite proof of his involvement. In this unfavorable comparison, Nixon does not admit his offense as young Washington did. Instead he uses his privilege as the nation's chief executive to try to hide the evidence of his actions.

## Practicing the Skill

1. What symbol in the cartoon on page 706 stands for the United States?
2. In the same cartoon, what message does the cartoonist give by replacing the eagle's wings with huge ears?
3. Find a cartoon in a current newspaper or magazine. Explain the use of caricatures, symbols, and analogies. What is the cartoon's message?

# Television

## John Dean Live: The Watergate Testimony

*T*elevision is only 50 years old, an infant when compared with other sources of historical evidence. Television, however, can show and tell a historian what few other sources can: how someone looked while he walked, the sound of his voice, or the details of his gestures. The television record is a combination of pictures, sound, and motion that allows a historian to witness events with the same immediacy as someone living at the time.

### The Evidence

On June 25, 1973, John Dean, former legal counsel to President Nixon, began testifying before the Senate Watergate investigating committee. All three of the major networks carried the event live.

In the 30 hours of televised testimony and questioning that followed, Dean provided the first evidence of direct presidential involvement in the Watergate cover-up. The excerpts below are taken from Dean's account of two meetings with President Nixon at the White House. What can you tell about Dean's attitude toward

*March 13, 1973*

*T*oward the end of the conversation, we got into a discussion of Watergate matters specifically. I told the President about the fact that there were money demands being made by the seven convicted defendants, and that the sentencing of these individuals was not far off. It was during this conversation that [White House staff chief H. R.] Haldeman came into the office. After this brief interruption by Haldeman's coming in, but while he was still there, I told the President about the fact that there was no money to pay these individuals to meet their demands. He asked me how much it would cost. I told him that I could only make an estimate that it might be as high as $1 million or more. He told me that that was no problem, and he also looked over at Haldeman and repeated the same statement. He then asked me who was demanding this money and I told him it was principally coming from Hunt through his attorney. The president then referred to the fact that Hunt had been promised Executive clemency.

*March 21, 1973*

As I have indicated, my purpose in requesting this meeting particularly with the President was that I felt it necessary that I give him a full report of all the facts that I knew and explain to him what I believed to be the implication of those facts. It

was my particular concern with the fact that the President did not seem to understand the implications of what was going on. For example, when I had earlier told him that I thought I was involved in an obstruction of justice situation he had argued with me to the contrary after I had explained it to him. Also, when the matter of money demands had come up previously he had very nonchalantly told me that that was no problem and I did not know if he realized that he himself could be getting involved in an obstruction of justice by having promised clemency to Hunt.

• • • • • • • • • • • • • • • • • •

I then proceeded to tell him that perjury had been committed, and for this cover-up to continue it would require more perjury and more money. I told him that the demands of the convicted individuals were continually increasing and that with sentencing imminent, the demands had become specific.

• • • • • • • • • • • • • • • • • •

After I finished, I realized that I had not really made the President understand because after he asked a few questions, he suggested that it would be an excellent idea if I gave some sort of briefing to the Cabinet and that he was very impressed with my knowledge of the circumstances but he did not seem particularly concerned with their implications.

the events that he describes? Does he seem apologetic for anything he did?

## The Interpretation

An estimated 47 million homes watched the first day of hearings as Dean read quietly into a microphone from a 245-page manuscript. Poised and calm, Dean accused the president of crimes and wrongdoings, including bribery and obstruction of justice.

A historian looking at the televised coverage of the Dean testimony would have to contend with several issues. First, the historian would recognize that the testimony was self-serving: Dean was cooperating with the committee in an effort to keep himself out of jail. Furthermore, the language Dean used was circumspect, cautious, and unaffected. He presented only facts and made no attempt to characterize those facts as good or bad, right or wrong. For example, during the meeting of March 13, most people would recognize that Dean is describing the crimes of bribery and obstruction of justice when he discusses the plan to pay money to the seven convicted defendants. Dean, however, never uses those words.

The historian would also note how Dean's testimony is constructed to portray Nixon as an informed, active participant in the cover-up. Instead of making a simple accusation, Dean describes many conversations where Nixon could have responded to the legality or morality of the cover-up. The absence of any such response is more condemning than anything Dean could have said about Nixon.

UPI BETTMANN NEWSPHOTOS

UPI BETTMANN NEWSPHOTOS

AP/WIDE WORLD PHOTOS

**With the support of his wife, Maureen, John Dean begins his first day of testimony.**

After Dean finished reading his statement, he was questioned by members of the committee. This body of evidence—the bulk of the testimony—would allow the historian to make firsthand observations of Dean responding to the often hostile committee. Television captures all the nuances of body language: postures, tone of voice, facial expressions, and gestures.

Televised testimony offers the historian a rare opportunity to watch a political crisis unfold "live." Ironically, it is this same immediacy that makes the television record difficult to interpret. Background information is often absent. Casual references to names, events, and dates that make sense to a contemporary viewer may be baffling to the historian. Visual clues meaningful to one generation may mean nothing to the next. In the almost 20 years since Dean's testimony, it is easy to forget who Hunt was, for example, or how much older Dean looked on television than in the boyish photos supplied by the White House.

Television always assumes that the viewer and events are contemporaries. This is its biggest virtue—and chief shortcoming—as a reliable source of historical evidence.

## Further Evidence

Dean's testimony was only part of over 300 hours of televised Watergate hearings. Since then television has become an even greater part of political life in the United States. Use your library to find out about televised political meetings or hearings in your area. You may be able to watch congressional hearings on a cable or public television station. School board and city council meetings in some cities are also televised. Watch a broadcast that interests you, and evaluate how the broadcast might be useful to a historian in the future. For example, what kind of information can you gather by listening to the broadcast? What can you tell about what people say by observing their tone of voice, demeanor, and facial expressions?

# Chapter 21 Review

## Summary

Use the following outline as a tool for reviewing and summarizing the chapter. Copy the outline on your own paper, leaving spaces between headings to jot down notes about key events and concepts.

**I. A New Majority**
  A. The War Within
  B. Nixon's New Conservatism
  C. Building a New Majority

**II. From War to Détente**
  A. Ending the War in Vietnam
  B. Détente
  C. The Election of 1972

**III. A Crisis in the Presidency**
  A. The Nixon White House
  B. Unraveling Watergate

## Ideas, Events, and People

1. Describe some of the events and political policies that helped bring about the conservative backlash of the late 1960s.
2. Give two examples of conservative policies implemented by President Nixon.
3. Why did conservatives criticize the Family Assistance Plan? Why did liberals denounce it?
4. What events led the NAACP to label the Nixon administration "anti-Negro"?
5. Identify Henry Kissinger. Describe his various roles in the Nixon administration.
6. Why were many Americans critical of the bombing of enemy supply lines in Cambodia?
7. Why did many Americans disagree with the U.S. invasion of Cambodia?
8. Explain why President Nixon was eager to implement a policy of détente with the People's Republic of China and the Soviet Union.
9. How did better relations between the United States and the People's Republic of China affect the balance of power in the world?
10. What happened in South Vietnam after U.S. forces left in 1973?
11. Why didn't American anticommunists criticize President Nixon for his friendly overtures to the People's Republic of China and the Soviet Union?
12. Briefly explain how the impeachment process works in the United States.
13. Identify John Dean, H. R. Haldeman, and John Erlichman. Describe the role of each in the Watergate scandal.

## Social Studies Skills

**Reading Political Cartoons**

Thomas Curtis has a national reputation as the author of cartoons with a conservative viewpoint. He penned the cartoon below in 1973 while working for the *Milwaukee Sentinel*. Identify the symbols the author uses to convey his message. How do you interpret the cartoon?

"Do I smell blood?"

©1973 CURTIS CARTOONS

February 1972
Nixon reopens communication with People's Republic of China.

January 1973
Cease–fire agreement ends Vietnam War.

August 1974
Nixon becomes first president to resign.

1972    1973    1974    1975

May 1972
Nixon visits the Soviet Union.

June 1972
Democratic National Committee headquarters in Watergate complex is burglarized.

July 1974
House Judiciary Committee recommends impeachment of Nixon.

April 1975
Communist forces march into Saigon.

# Critical Thinking

### 1. Making Generalizations
President Nixon impounded funds that were to be used for federal programs, supported wiretapping without a court order, and authorized secret bombings. What generalization can you make about his methods for accomplishing goals?

### 2. Recognizing Values
Two segments of society with different values disagreed over the Vietnam War. Explain how the silent majority and social protesters differed on the issues of patriotism and law and order.

### 3. Identifying Cause and Effect
What were two effects of President Nixon's trip to the People's Republic of China?

### 4. Analyzing Decisions
How did Nixon's belief in *realpolitik* influence decisions he made about the Soviet Union and the People's Republic of China?

### 5. Recognizing Assumptions
What assumptions did President Nixon make when he designed his Vietnamization policy, replacing U.S. troops with South Vietnamese combatants?

### 6. Identifying Cause and Effect
What actions of the Nixon administration caused Congress to enact the War Powers Act and the Congressional Budget and Impoundment Act?

# Extension and Application

### 1. Citizenship
List five personal qualities you think a president should possess. Suppose you were able to vote tomorrow, what three domestic issues would concern you most? What three global issues would concern you? If no candidate held your views on all issues, write an essay to explain how you would determine your choice.

### 2. Global Connections
Research and prepare an oral or written report on events in the Middle East that saddled President Nixon and the nation with a severe energy crisis in 1973.

### 3. Linking Across Time
The Vietnam War polarized the U.S. public. Identify a social or political issue today that drastically divides people. Research the issue; then present in writing arguments for both sides of the question. Be sure to give each side equal conviction.

### 4. Evidence of the Past
Forty-four states permit television cameras in certain courtrooms. (Indiana, Mississippi, Missouri, South Carolina, South Dakota, and Texas prohibit the practice.) Discuss what future historians might learn from these televised records. Do you consider it fair to defendants that their trial is televised? Write a paragraph telling why or why not.

# Geography

1. What region of the country did Nixon target to be the base of a new Republican majority? What issues were important to voters in this region?
2. Based on the map on page 699, why do you think more U.S. air bases were located in Thailand than in South Vietnam?
3. What effects did the Vietnam War have on the countries in the region of Southeast Asia?
4. Suppose you were drawing two maps, the first showing the countries that were superpowers in 1950 and the second showing the countries that were superpowers in 1970. How would the maps differ?

# Hemispheric Relations

## December 20, 1989: Western Hemisphere Nations React to Panama Invasion

President George Bush listened intently as his aides outlined the plan to invade Panama. Casualties could not be avoided. Yet the conduct of General Manuel Noriega—dictator, accused drug trafficker, double agent—angered Bush more and more each day.

The president's order was simple and direct. "Let's do it," he declared.

His words sent a 24,000-troop task force on its way to seize the Panama Canal and the capital, Panama City. Through a series of phone calls, foreign leaders were advised of the president's decision.

The Organization of American States (OAS) expressed its "regret," though it did not condemn the invasion. Member nations were more outspoken. Cuba "condemned" and Venezuela "deplored" the operation. Peru recalled its ambassador. Mexico was outraged. The prime minister of Canada was sympathetic, but other Canadians worried that his position associated them "with America's aggressive actions."

Western Hemisphere countries were sensitive to the U.S. action because of its history of intervention in the affairs of its neighbors. They would no longer be satisfied to let their "big brother" take control of their destinies.

*His words set into motion a marathon of telephone calls, informing foreign leaders of the decision.*

© STEPHEN FERRY/GAMMA-LIASON

*Within days of the invasion, U.S. troops controlled most of Panama.*

*Above is one of many crossing points along the more-than-2,000-mile border between Mexico and the United States. Each day thousands of people cross in both directions to visit relatives, to vacation, to shop, or to work.*

# Latin America

## July 28, 1985: Peru Limits Payments on Its Foreign Debt

NEWLY ELECTED PRESIDENT OF PERU, ALÁN GARCÍA PÉREZ, DID MORE THAN PROMISE HIS NATION A BRIGHTER FUTURE. IN HIS INAUGURAL SPEECH ON JULY 28, THE handsome 36-year-old García dropped a bombshell on the international banking community. He vowed that Peru would limit the payments on its staggering $13.7 billion foreign debt to no more than 10 percent of the nation's annual export earnings. Since the expected value of Peru's 1985 exports totaled only $3 billion, 10 percent of that amount would pay less than one-third of the $1.1 billion the country owed for 1985.

Faced with economic woes and social unrest at home, García had little choice but to attack the debt. As he declared during his inaugural: "Let the peoples of the world hear me. President Alán García knows that Peru has a great and first creditor: its own people." Indeed Peru's fragile five-year-old democracy faced tough domestic challenges: armed rebels and a critically ill economy. In 1985 Peru's annual inflation rate soared to 250 percent, and two-thirds of Peru's workers were either unemployed or working only part time.

García's announcement sent shock waves through the U.S. banking community. By 1985 the Latin American debt totaled more than $350 billion—more than three times the region's annual income. Much of it was owed to U.S. banks. What if the other Latin American nations followed García's example? The leading debtor nations, Mexico, Brazil, and Argentina, together owed more than $200 billion. If

© M. ROGERS, FPG INTERNATIONAL

they were to limit debt payments to a fraction of export earnings, U.S. banks, and ultimately the U.S. economy, would soon feel the pinch.

The debt crisis of the 1980s laid bare the links between the U.S. and Latin American economies. It opened a new chapter in the often troubled relations between Latin America and its northern neighbor.

## A History of Underdevelopment

Latin America stretches southward 7,000 miles from the southern border of the United States to Cape Horn. It includes Mexico and the nations in Central America, the Caribbean, and South America. Latin America covers nearly eight million square miles, an area two-and-a-half times the size of the United States. Within that immense region lie diverse landforms—from the towering peaks of the Andes to the steamy tropical forests of the Amazon, from the dry plains of northern Mexico to the rich grasslands of Argentina.

The people of Latin America are just as diverse. They include native Indians, Europeans, black Africans brought over as slaves to labor in the colonial plantations, and people of mixed descent resulting from years of intermarriage. Asian immigrants, too, have flocked to these shores. Because most of Latin America was colonized in the 1500s by the Spanish and the Portuguese, most Latin Americans speak either Spanish or Portuguese or both.

Latin America's population of more than 432 million is growing at a rate of about 2 percent a year, making it one of the fastest growing regions in the world. In 1980, 61 percent of Latin Americans lived in cities of 2,000 or more. The remaining 39 percent lived in rural areas. Most of them are poor farmers, or *campesinos*, who toil on huge plantations or eke out a living on their own small plots of land.

The economies of Latin America range from the rapidly industrializing giant Brazil to Haiti, the poorest nation in the Western Hemisphere. Although most countries have experienced economic growth recently, they still face serious social and economic problems, especially poverty, hunger, and illiteracy. In 1985 two-thirds of Latin Americans were undernourished. In the poorest countries, such as Honduras and Haiti, half the children die before their fifth birthday.

Like the United States, most Latin American nations were former colonies. Despite this common heritage, the development of the two regions has been strikingly different. While the United States grew into a prosperous, industrialized democracy, most Latin American nations have suffered from a lack of industrial development, as well as from widespread poverty and political instability.

**The Economics of Dependency** For much of their history, Latin American nations have depended primarily on the export of agricultural products such as coffee, sugar, or bananas, and natural resources such as tin, copper, and oil.[1] As U.S. industries expanded, they came to rely more and more on the resources of Latin America. Latin American oil fueled

**Latin America includes Mexico and the nations of South America, the Caribbean, and Central America, which consists of the countries between Mexico and Colombia.** *Use the map to name the Central American countries.*

**Comparing and Contrasting**
The United States started out as 13 British colonies that declared their independence in 1776. Most countries in Latin America started out as colonies, too, but the historical parallels end there. The United States grew into an industrial powerhouse in the latter half of the 1800s. Latin America saw little industrial development during this same period.

**1** What were the major Latin American exports during this period?

© ROBERT HOLMES, FPG INTERNATIONAL

© HALLINAN, FPG INTERNATIONAL

© MARTIN ROGERS, FPG

© DON COWAN, FPG INTERNATIONAL

© SUZANNE L. MURPHY, FPG INTERNATIONAL

© HAROLD & FLAVIA DE FARIA CASTRO, FPG INTERNATIONAL

**Latin America's populations include descendants of Indians, Africans, and Spanish colonists, as well as Asian immigrants. They live in large cities such as Sao Paulo, Brazil, and on isolated farms, as in Peru.**

U.S. factories and cars. Latin American sugar sweetened U.S. soft drinks. U.S. corporations, confident of the reliability of the market in the United States, invested heavily in plantations, mines, and sugar mills. Soon profits as well as resources were exported to the United States.

With few other outlets for their products, Latin American nations developed a **dependency** on the U.S. market. If the U.S. market were to dry up, they would face serious economic problems. This dependency was in part due to the lack of industrialization. Although the industrial revolution swept the United States in the post–Civil War era, the shift from an agricultural base to an industrial one did not occur in Latin America until after World War II.

**Unshared Wealth**   In most Latin American countries, wealth is concentrated in the hands of a few. Throughout Latin America the top 10 percent of the population earn 40 percent, or more, of the nation's income. In the United States, by contrast, the top 20 percent earn that much of the country's income. As a result, Latin America has a vast gap between the wealthy few and the multitudes who live in grinding poverty. The desire of the poor to share in their nation's wealth has helped to fuel reform movements.

**The Struggle for Democracy**   The same wealthy few also often control the government, aided by their allies, the military. Unlike the U.S. military, most Latin American militaries have little respect for democracy and civilian rule when their interests and the interests of the ruling class are threatened. Time and again military leaders have stepped in to take over the government. The frequent violent shifts from democracy to dictatorship have created a climate of political instability throughout the region.

## Latin America Since 1945

The years following World War II brought sweeping changes to Latin America. Economies grew rapidly, and democracy flourished throughout the region. Yet, by the 1970s two shadows loomed over Latin America—deepening economic crises and the rise of military dictatorships.

**Economic Growth**   In the postwar prosperity of the 1950s, the rapidly growing economies of the industrialized nations of North America and western Europe clamored for Latin American resources. Factories needed Latin America's oil and mineral resources. A growing number of consumers hungered for Latin America's bananas, coffee, and sugar. As the world economy grew, Latin America prospered.

Export income and loans helped fund Latin America's own industrial development. In 1950 Latin America produced just $11 billion worth of manufactured goods. By 1974 that total had climbed to $66 billion.

Foreign investment mounted too. By the mid-1960s, U.S. investment reached $9 billion, and in 1980 it topped $35 billion—nearly 80 percent of all private American investment in the third world. Increased investment gave foreign companies control over a huge share of the industries in Latin American nations. Of the 55 largest companies in Brazil during the 1960s, 31 of them were in foreign hands. Thus, despite spectacular growth, Latin America continued to rely heavily on foreign capital, technology, and markets.

In addition, economic growth did not benefit rich and poor alike. Often the nation's wealth, agricultural or industrial, remained in the hands of a few, thus widening the gap between rich and poor. In Brazil, for example, the percentage of the national income going to the top 10 percent of the population rose from 40 percent in 1960 to 51 percent in 1980. The poorest half of the population claimed only 17 percent of the national income in 1960. Their share had fallen to 13 percent by 1980.

**The Growing Debt**   As industrial production grew, Latin American nations began borrowing from banks in the United States and western Europe to finance their economic growth. Bigger factories demanded more electric power, more raw materials, and improved transportation systems. Bankers, eager to cash in on the economic boom, flocked to Latin America. Brazil, a rapidly industrializing nation, increased its public foreign borrowing from nearly $4 billion in 1968 to over $8 billion by 1972.

Latin American countries sank even deeper in debt when the oil-producing nations of OPEC raised oil prices in 1974 and 1979. Oil-poor nations, such as Argentina and Brazil, needed more money to buy oil to power their factories and run their cars, trucks, and buses. Oil-rich nations, such as Mexico and Venezuela, borrowed money to finance the search for more oil and to boost industrial production.

The banks, flooded with oil profits, willingly loaned these nations more money. Both oil-poor and oil-rich nations hoped that increased export earnings from industrial production would help them pay back the loans. However, the ability of the borrowers to repay their loans depended on two factors: an expanding international market for products from Latin American countries and stable interest rates. In the 1980s, after nearly 30 years of growth, the industrial countries of North America and western Europe suffered a short but fairly severe recession. As production in these countries declined, unemployment rose, and the demand for Latin American exports fell.

**Notice how rapidly Brazil's public and private debts rose in comparison with its debt payments.** *How did the devaluation of the cruzeiro and the nation's deficit trade balance affect Brazil's ability to pay back its debt?*

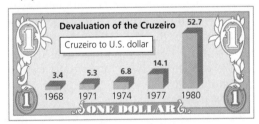

As their export earnings declined, Latin American nations were also hit by rising interest rates, which soared from about 9 percent in 1978 to above 20 percent in early 1981. The results were disastrous. For example, the yearly interest on a $10 billion loan in 1978 totaled less than a billion dollars. By 1981 that yearly interest mushroomed to over $1.8 billion, while the debtor found it harder and harder to earn the export dollars needed to pay the debt. From 1978 to 1981, Brazil's interest payments on its foreign debt swelled from $2.7 billion to $9.2 billion.

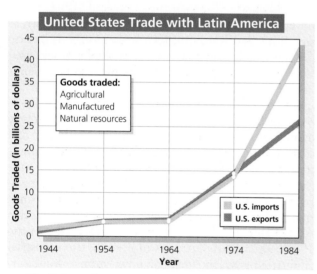

**The U.S. market continues to rely on Latin America for many import needs.** *How do you account for the split between imports and exports after 1974?*

The debt consumed more and more of Latin America's export earnings. In 1977 Latin America's debt payments were less than a third of its exports; by 1982 they were 59 percent. Once-eager bankers closed their doors to the struggling debtors, refusing to loan them more money. One despairing financial manager of the Mexican national oil company Pemex lamented in September 1982, "Six months ago, there were so many bankers in [my office] you couldn't walk across the room. Now they don't even answer my telephone calls."

**The Rise of Democracy** The victory of democracy over dictatorship during World War II led many Latin Americans to demand democracy at home. A group of Brazilians opposed to the dictator ruling their country in the 1940s declared, "If we fight against fascism at the side of the United Nations so that liberty and democracy may be restored to all people, certainly we are not asking too much in demanding for ourselves such rights and guarantees."

Postwar prosperity also kindled the desire for democracy. The emerging industrial middle class believed that in the postwar world its interests would be better served by democracy than dictatorship. By the end of 1945, dictators had been forced out of seven countries—Cuba, El Salvador, Guatemala, Colombia, Peru, Venezuela, and Brazil. A wave of free elections swept across Latin America. New political parties sprouted, and women gained the right to vote. By 1959 only four military governments remained in power—an all-time low for Latin America.

The new democracies faced serious challenges—poverty, illiteracy, and hunger. Often their attempts at economic change, such as land reform, disturbed the upper classes, who feared the loss of their wealth and power. The elite turned to their traditional allies, the military, to halt the reforms. From 1962 to 1964, democratic governments in eight countries fell to military dictatorships.[2]

**Voices for Change** The failure of Latin American democracies and the rise of repressive military governments led some Latin Americans to choose a more radical means of bringing about change. During the 1960s, left-wing revolutionary guerilla movements sprang up throughout Latin America. Many Latin Americans were inspired by the success of Castro's 1959 revolution in Cuba and the gains made there in health care, housing, literacy, and other social reforms. Revolutionaries were willing to postpone democratic reforms such as free elections and a free press until basic social reforms had been achieved.

During the 1960s the Roman Catholic church added its voice to those clamoring for reform in Latin America. The church had long been an ally of the rich and powerful. In the 1960s, however, thousands of young priests and nuns began to speak out against the social injustices that kept millions of Latin Americans poor. In a region where 80 percent of the population was Roman Catholic, the church became a powerful force for social change.

**STUDY·GUIDE**

**Identifying Cause and Effect**
One must be cautious in assessing blame for the tremendous debt burden Latin American countries incurred during the 1970s and 1980s. The countries overextended themselves by borrowing heavily during a period of prosperity, and U.S. banks were eager to accommodate them. Both must share the responsibility. Then came the worldwide recession in the early 1980s.

**2** Why did upper class Latin Americans conspire to overthrow democratically elected governments during the 1960s?

The belief that the church must side with the poor in the struggle for social justice became known as **liberation theology.** This belief led many religious leaders to call for socialist reforms. As Mexican Bishop Sergio Mendes declared in 1970, "Only socialism can give Latin America a true development. . . . I believe that a socialist system best conforms to Christian principles of true brotherhood, justice, and peace."

Because of their calls for sweeping change, left-leaning clergy were often the targets of government repression. In March 1980 Salvadoran Archbishop Oscar Arnulfo Romero, an outspoken critic of his government's violent abuses of human rights, was murdered by a right-wing assassin as he said mass.

**A Troubled Era**   By 1970 the military ruled in most of Latin America. Only Costa Rica, Uruguay, Chile, Mexico, Colombia, and Venezuela enjoyed democracies. Chile and Uruguay fell to dictators during the 1970s.

To maintain their power, many of these military dictatorships tortured and killed their opponents. The military in Argentina murdered nearly 15,000 Argentinians in its "dirty war" during the 1970s. In Guatemala, 15,000 Guatemalans, many of them Indian peasants, were killed between 1970 and 1974.

The economic crises of the 1970s and massive opposition to the repression, however, ultimately led to the fall of many of these military governments during the 1980s. Even Guatemala and Argentina, for decades in the grip of military rulers, returned to civilian rule. Yet these fragile new democracies face serious challenges—a still powerful military, astronomical debts, and soaring unemployment.

## U.S.–Latin American Relations

After World War II, American politicians and investors continued to look on Latin America as a backward area in need of protection and available for economic exploitation. The United States wanted democratic governments and the free-enterprise system to flourish in Latin America so that these nations would be good allies and trading partners. However, it also wanted to protect U.S. investments in Latin America and to stop the spread of communism in the Western Hemisphere. On occasion these foreign policy goals conflicted with each other.

Many Latin Americans wanted to develop their own industries rather than just supply raw materials and cheap labor for U.S.-owned businesses. Some reform-minded Latin American politicians also wanted to break up large plantations and redistribute land to small farmers. Some wanted to **nationalize** certain industries, to take them from private owners and run them as national government businesses. Such programs were popular with lower classes but opposed by major landowners and business people.

The U.S. government also opposed these movements because they contained socialistic elements, the same as communism to many Americans. Also, U.S. investors would lose if these reforms succeeded.

**A Policy of Intervention**   To protect U.S. business interests and prevent communist-style politicians from achieving successes in Latin America, the United States government often supported right-wing dictators who oppressed and victimized Latin American citizens. A policy of **interventionism,** government interference in the political or economic affairs of another country, had been practiced by the United States in Latin America for nearly 100 years. Since World War II, intervention came to mean anything from providing weapons and training for Latin American armies to economic sanctions and invasions by U.S. troops.

In the late 1940s and early 1950s, the socialist government in Guatemala began to redistribute land and to nationalize foreign-owned properties, including those of a major U.S. firm, the United Fruit Company. The Eisenhower administration supplied military aid for a 1954 invasion that overthrew the Guatemalan government and installed a new leader friendly to U.S. interests. Pro-United States strongmen ruled Guatemala until the mid-1980s, and the military remained the power behind the government through 1990.

This pattern of intervention in Latin America was repeated many times from the 1950s to 1990, in Cuba, the Dominican Republic, Chile, El Salvador, Nicaragua, Grenada, and Panama. The policy cut across partisan lines and was carried out under both Republican and Democratic administrations.

**Recognizing Points of View**
The United States and Latin America have always looked at the issue of intervention from different perspectives. The Eisenhower-backed invasion that overthrew the Arbenz government in Guatemala in 1954 is a case in point. Latin Americans were glad to see Arbenz go. Nevertheless, they insisted that his socialist government was a Guatemalan problem, and it was up to Guatemalans to solve it. The United States had no right to intervene.

© RAYMOND DEPARDON, MAGNUM
PHOTOS, INC.

© NAYTHONS, GAMMA-LIAISON

**U.S. intervention in the internal affairs of Latin American countries has at various times been economic, political, direct, or indirect. At the left, a farm laborer in Chile registers his protest by carrying a sign that reads, "We say no to exploitation." U.S. soldiers, above right, rest after having invaded and secured the small island-nation of Grenada off the coast of Venezuela in 1983.**

In 1970, when socialist Salvador Allende was elected president of Chile, the Nixon administration objected to the takeover of American businesses. It also feared that a Marxist regime would develop strong ties to Cuba and the Soviet Union. The United States began a program designed to help Allende's enemies force him from office. American actions included denying loans to Chile, providing money to opposition organizations, even supporting plots to assassinate Allende. Finally, in 1973 a military force headed by General Augusto Pinochet seized the government, and Allende was killed in the fighting. Even though Pinochet's government abolished civil liberties, executed thousands, and ended economic reforms, the United States quickly resumed trade and economic relations with Chile. Strongman Pinochet remained in power until 1989, when a civilian president was installed, although Pinochet retained control of the armed forces.

A more recent example was President Bush's dispatch of military troops to Panama in December 1989. After other attempts failed, President Bush used force to topple a cruel dictator and drug smuggler, not to combat a communist threat. The troops arrested General Manuel Noriega, Panama's military strongman, and flew him back to Florida to stand trial on numerous drug-trafficking and money-laundering charges.

**The Alliance for Progress**   Not all of U.S. relations with Latin America since 1945 involved the use of force or coercion. Many efforts were made to help Latin American nations economically. In 1961 the Kennedy administration introduced a multimillion dollar program called the Alliance for Progress. This plan was in response to Castro's success in Cuba and was designed to help Latin Americans combat their economic and social problems, as well as to strengthen their democratic institutions. The program provided more than $10 billion over the next nine years to aid health care, industrial development, housing construction, agricultural productivity, and military training. However, the Alliance for Progress died during the Johnson administration, when United States attention and resources were diverted to the Vietnam War.

President Carter tried to develop in Latin America a more favorable image of the United States. His administration cut back on military aid to South and Central American dictators and negotiated an agreement to give control of the Panama Canal to that nation by the year 2000. President Reagan, while moving forcefully to combat what were seen as communist

JOHN F. KENNEDY LIBRARY, BOSTON, MA

threats, introduced the Caribbean Basin Initiative of 1981, which provided economic assistance, incentives for investment in Latin America, and easier access to U.S. markets.

Most Latin Americans, however, continued to resent U.S. interference in their affairs. They saw the United States as a neighborhood bully, willing to do anything to get its way with its weaker neighbors, even to the point of arming and encouraging military dictators who violated human rights. Mexican writer Octavio Paz described their attitude this way:

> *T*he . . . *[people of the United States] are always among us, even when they ignore us or turn their back on us. Their shadow covers the whole hemisphere. It is the shadow of a giant. And the idea we have of that giant is the same that can be found in fairy tales and legends: a great fellow of kind disposition, a bit simple, an innocent who ignores his own strength and who we can fool most of the time, but whose wrath can destroy us.*

Octavio Paz, 1981

## Future Challenges

Latin America no longer wants to be merely a supplier of food and raw materials to the United States. It wants to compete in manufacturing and high technology as well. In 1990 efforts began to eliminate trade barriers and establish a better climate for interdependent investment in North and Latin America.

The increasingly serious debt crisis also affects the hemispheric relationship. If Latin American debtor nations do not control their economies and repay U.S. banks, many American financial institutions may fail, and American citizens will pay the price. This interdependence encourages U.S. and Latin American interests to cooperate. One rather controversial plan, for example, involves "debt for nature" swaps, in which debts would be cancelled if Latin American nations use the money for debt repayment to protect their environment and wildlife.

Immigration problems also demand cooperative solutions. By the mid-1980s, an estimated six million illegal immigrants were living in the United States, and the vast majority of them came from Latin America. In 1980 alone, according to one estimate, some 500,000 Latin Americans entered the United States illegally.

Illegal drugs represent yet another problem for hemispheric relations. Latin America is the major source of drugs consumed in the United States. Colombia and other countries are cooperating in efforts to decrease drug production and smuggling, but so far the results have been disappointing.

All these growing problems demand increased attention and cooperation. These joint efforts hinge on the recognition that the United States and Latin America now depend on each other and that only equal partners can solve mutual problems.

**Dock workers load Brazilian coffee onto a ship destined for the United States. Latin American nations also strive to increase the amount of manufactured and industrial goods they export.**

© EDUARDO SIMOES/F4, 1986, PICTURE GROUP

## SECTION REVIEW

### Checking Facts

1. How did Latin Americans finance their economic development in the 1960s? How did the oil crisis bring development to a halt?

2. What positive steps did Presidents Kennedy and Carter take to improve U.S.–Latin American relations?

3. What are the major unresolved issues facing the United States and Latin America today?

### Thinking Critically

4. **Comparing and Contrasting** How did Latin America and U.S. leaders differ on the issue of nationalization of industries?

5. **Identifying Cause and Effect** What effect did Castro's reforms in Cuba have on other Latin American nations?

6. **Recognizing Points of View** Why has the United States felt a need to intervene in the internal affairs of various Latin American countries? How do Latin Americans feel about this?

### Linking Across Time

7. President Theodore Roosevelt made the decision to build the Panama Canal back in 1903. How do you think he would have reacted to President Carter's decision to turn over control of the canal to Panama?

People need to understand current events in order to make decisions about election issues, causes, and career choices. To stay informed, people use a variety of news sources, from broadcast media (television and radio) to print media (newspapers and newsmagazines).

As the pictograph shows, over the past 25 years Americans have turned from dependence upon print media to broadcast media for their news. Think about the medium that supplies your news. How much information do you really get? How do you know the information is accurate? Is the medium you choose the most efficient for you? As a news consumer, you need to evaluate the strengths and limitations of each news medium available to you.

have captured your attention in the newspaper. News events that are immediate and dramatic, such as crashes, arrests, and storms, make an especially strong

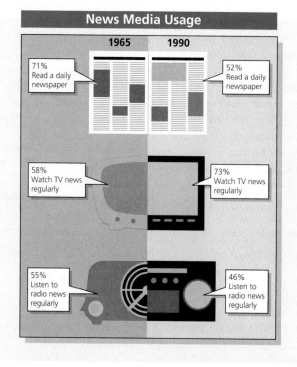

**News Media Usage**

**1965**

71% Read a daily newspaper

58% Watch TV news regularly

55% Listen to radio news regularly

**1990**

52% Read a daily newspaper

73% Watch TV news regularly

46% Listen to radio news regularly

**During the period 1965 through 1990, many Americans switched from newspapers to TV for their news.** *How do you account for these changes?*

and radio replace individual reading with an oral presentation of news stories. Both have the advantages of being up-to-the-minute. Stories can be edited and updated almost until airtime. Reporters can even interrupt their prepared broadcasts while they are on the air to include new information.

Radio and TV are also similar in offering a wide spectrum of broadcasts, ranging from headlines to in-depth discussion or talk shows. On both commercial radio and television stations, news reports tend to be short, touching only on major points and not allowing for sufficient background and development of complex stories.

Educational radio stations can provide in-depth news coverage. Television news also provides formats that allow more thorough treatment: longer news and interview programs such as the "MacNeil/Lehrer News Hour," "Meet the Press," "Nightline," and live cable coverage of proceedings of the U.S. House and Senate.

News presentations on radio and television also differ in some important ways. Radio news coverage is often continuous, so news stories can reach the public almost immediately. Hence, radio is often the best source for late-breaking local news. Radio sets are so portable that reporters can transmit news broadcasts from almost anywhere at any time.

## *Learning the Skill*

Whatever your primary source of news, you will need to ask yourself the same basic questions a good reporter asks: Are the facts complete and accurate? Is it the truth? Then you will need to think critically about news reports by evaluating your sources of information, testing interpretations, and watching out for bias.

### Broadcast Media

Think of a news story you heard on radio or saw on television that probably would not

impression on television because TV allows the viewer to witness the event while it is actually happening.

Visual impact and immediacy are television's main strengths. Events you have read about in this chapter, such as the overthrow of Allende in Chile and the invasion of Panama, were seen by many Americans on television as the dramas unfolded.

The strong visual images that set TV news apart from radio are a large part of its presentation, but these two broadcast media have basic similarities. Both TV

Radio stations typically have lower news budgets than television, however, which limits radio's independent news-gathering capability. What kind of news does your favorite radio station deliver?

## Print Media

Print media have more time and space to carry a greater variety of news stories, as well as columns and editorials, than broadcast media do. Reader comment and opinion sections offer interaction with subscribers. You can pick and choose your news by reading the menu of headlines or the first few paragraphs of a story.

Many big-city dailies such as the *Los Angeles Times* specialize in comprehensive national coverage. National newspapers such as *USA Today* have shorter pieces, more flashy and entertaining. Local newspapers tend to combine the two approaches with a larger focus on community news.

Print news is less immediate than broadcast news and becomes out-of-date more quickly. The typical newspaper story is written only hours before it reaches the reader, while newsmagazines have deadlines as much as a week before printing. Reporters can correct or add to stories no sooner than their next issue.

Newsmagazines can carry longer articles and more elaborate photographs and illustrations than newspapers. The booklike format of newsmagazines allows in-depth treatment of topics, so often their stories are more analytical than those in some daily newspapers.

**Iraq's invasion of Kuwait in August 1990 immediately dominated news in the United States.** *How do the headlines in the newspaper and the newsmagazine shown here emphasize different aspects of the event?*

## Sources and Interpretations

To get the most accurate profile of current events, you must think critically about the news you hear or read. First, think about the source of the news story: those that reveal their sources of information are more reliable because they allow you to evaluate the source.

Second, many news stories don't just provide the facts; they also analyze and interpret them. Stories can easily have a political slant because of the perceived bias of subscribers or listeners. When you choose an analytical source, you get more complete coverage as well as a journalist's assistance in interpreting the significance of events and actions. At the same time, such analyses may interpret events in a way that reflects the reporters' own biases or the biases of their target audience.

Ask yourself whether the news you hear or read is even-handed. Is news involving other nations reported on the scene, or is it a news service version received second-hand? Does the viewpoint show any ethnocentric or nationalistic bias? Think about

the difference between fact and opinion when you digest a news item. Can the facts be verified? Is the writer's personal opinion expressed? Think carefully, too, about the journalist's argument. Is it logical?

## *Practicing the Skill*

1. Find two articles in current newspapers and in newsmagazines on a topic involving Latin America. Which provided more in-depth coverage, the newspaper or newsmagazine? Decide what points the articles were trying to make. Were they successful?

2. Read newspaper articles reporting on trade with Latin America. Did the articles you read reflect any bias on the part of the journalists who wrote them? List any unsupported statements.

3. Listen to a news program on a radio or television station. Write a short report summarizing the information and ideas that were presented. Explain how the format of the program influenced the way the news was presented.

# Mexico

## 1975: Workers in Tijuana, Mexico, Assemble U.S. Products

**T**ERESA AND HER TWO SISTERS LEAVE THEIR SCRAP-LUMBER AND CARDBOARD HOUSE ON THE OUTSKIRTS OF TIJUANA. DUST SWIRLS ABOUT THEIR FEET AS THEY TRUDGE down the road that leads into the Mexico–United States border town.

At the factory they join another dozen young women waiting for the siren's blast that signals the next shift. The factory is a large, two-story building made of corrugated steel. It is one of several hundred U.S.-owned assembly plants located just south of the border. This one produces electronic circuit boards.

Teresa describes her work in the factory:

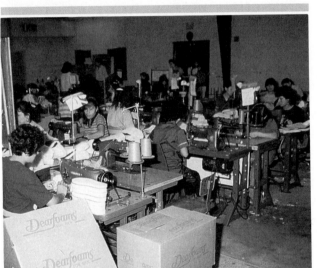

LAREDO DEVELOPMENT FOUNDATION

*E*veryone [goes] to their work place, their booth, and we begin work at exactly 8:00. They give ten minutes for the latecomers, but after that they send us home. . . . I work on the large circuits. There are many numbers and a map which show where all the wires and parts go. You find the parts and place them in as fast as you can. . . . We have to put out the work for nine-and-a-half hours, not talk, but sometimes we do anyway when the manager isn't looking.

Peter Baird and Ed McCaughan,
*Beyond the Border,* 1979

The factory in which Teresa works was established under Mexico's Border Industrialization Program (BIP). Mexico provides tax breaks and other incentives to encourage foreign investors to set up factories just south of the border. The electric circuits, garments, and toys move north across the border for final assembly. When the products move back north, U.S. manufacturers pay only a "value added" U.S. customs duty for the work that has been done. This is low because they pay to Mexican laborers only a fraction of the labor costs they would pay in their home country.

Most of the workers are unmarried women, 18–22 years old. Eyestrain forces many of them to quit after only a year or two. The young women put up with the tedious, boring work and the long hours because their pay enables them to contribute to their families' income and buy goods they could otherwise not afford.

## An Overview of Mexico

**M**exico is the northernmost Latin American country and the southern neighbor of the United States, joined by a 2,000-mile border. The journey south across the border, one U.S. observer has noted, is a dizzying study in contrasts. In the space of a few hundred yards, the traveler goes from a land of plenty to a land of want.

Octavio Paz, one of Mexico's greatest living poets, compared the two countries in a magazine article primarily intended for U.S. readership.

## STUDY GUIDE

**As You Read**
Identify factors that have strained friendly relations between the United States and Mexico during the past 50 years. Also, think about the following concepts and skills.

**Central Concepts**
- recognizing the importance of **self-determination** to Mexico
- recognizing the **interdependency** of the United States and Mexico

**Thinking Skills**
- comparing and contrasting
- recognizing points of view

© JUERGEN SCHMITT, THE IMAGE BANK, CHICAGO

**Mexico's cityscapes vary from the modern giant skyscrapers of Mexico City, right, to the outdoor markets of Guadalajara, top, where Indians sell their crafts under the shade of a tree. Note the Spanish-style plaza in the middle of the city.** *What does the plaza tell you about Mexico's heritage?*

*O ur countries are neighbors, condemned to live alongside each other; they are separated, however, more by profound social, economic, and psychic differences than by physical and political frontiers. . . . The really fundamental difference is an invisible one. . . . We are two distinct versions of Western civilization.*

Octavio Paz,
*The New Yorker,* 1979

Sixty percent of today's Mexicans are *mestizos,* mixed-blood descendants of the Indians who lived there when the Spanish arrived and of their Spanish conquerors. Another 29 percent are pure Indian, and the rest are of European, African, or Asian ancestry.

When the Spanish arrived in Mexico in 1519, the Indian population had already settled in large villages. Tenochtitlan, the great capital of the Aztec empire, numbered about 100,000 people and was larger than any city in Spain at that time.

The Spanish, aided by an outbreak of smallpox that devastated the Aztecs on the eve of battle, quickly conquered the Indians. The gold and silver of the Aztec empire was shipped to Europe where eventually it helped pay for the Industrial Revolution. The Spanish imposed on the Indians a language and the Roman Catholic religion. They also reinforced the social stratification that already existed, in which the very rich ruled the very poor.

Spanish colonists in Mexico gained independence in 1821. Twenty-seven years later the new nation lost a war with the United States and was forced to give up half its land to its North American neighbor. Modern Mexico dates from 1910, when revolutionary forces overthrew the dictatorship of Porfirio Diaz.

Today Mexico is a republic of more than 88 million people who live in a nation three times the size of Texas. The six major geographic regions contain a large variety of landscapes and climates, including high mountains, dry deserts, fertile valleys, and tropical forests. As in the United States, increasing mechanization of farms has pushed farmers and peasants off the land and into the cities. Today 72 percent of Mexicans live in cities. Mexico City, with a population of nearly 20.2 million, is the world's second-largest city.

Although Mexico has a growing middle class, which has given it some political stability, it continues to be a nation of the very rich and very poor. For example, the top 10 percent of the population receives over half the national income. The poor are very poor. The per capita income in 1984 averaged $2,082, compared to a U.S. per capita income the same year of $10,328. Unemployment is widespread.[1]

**STUDY GUIDE**

**Comparing and Contrasting**
The differences between U.S. and Mexican social traditions are deep-rooted. The U.S. tradition of democratic representation and majority rule stretches back through colonial times and beyond, all the way to the Magna Carta. The Mexican tradition of social stratification, with political power firmly in the hands of the rich, goes back through the Spaniards all the way to the Aztecs.

1 What is the major economic problem that Mexico faces today?

Hemispheric Relations

## The United States and Mexico

Following the Mexican Revolution a pattern developed in the relations between Mexico and the United States that continued for decades. During the previous Diaz dictatorship, American companies had invested heavily in Mexico, particularly in railroads, utilities, petroleum, and mining. But Mexico in 1910 was intent on **self-determination,** on assuming full control of its own destiny.

In the 1930s President Franklin Roosevelt initiated the policy of "the good neighbor." He discarded the threat of force used by earlier presidents in favor of offering economic incentives such as loans in exchange for political control. Mexico put the Good Neighbor Policy to the test in 1938, when it nationalized its oil holdings. Although unable to block nationalization, the U.S. government negotiated some compensation for American oil companies.

Mexico and the United States share two major river systems, the Colorado and the Rio Grande. Irrigation waters from these two systems have transformed thousands of arid acres in the American Southwest and, to a much lesser degree, in northern Mexico into profitable farmland. Division of the waters from these two rivers has been a source of conflict for more than 100 years. Should allocation be made according to whose land abuts the river or according to who first receives the water? A 1944 treaty took both into account to determine the annual amount of water to be allocated to Mexico.

Water was not the only resource to flow between the two countries. Years of political turmoil in Mexico combined with lack of economic opportunity there resulted in major population shifts, from the countryside to the big cities and from southern Mexico to the border region. This large border pool of unskilled labor often became an issue between the two nations. During the Depression, the United States saw the pool as a threat to unemployed Americans. But during World War II, when the United States faced a labor shortage, it persuaded Mexico to send *braceros,* temporary workers, north.

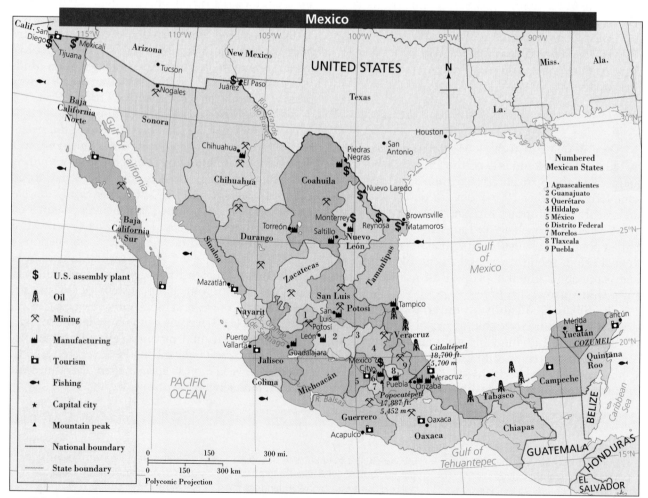

**This political and economic map shows the locations of many of the U.S.-owned assembly plants in the border region.** *Can you think of a reason why so many Mexican cities have a "twin" city just across the border in the United States?*

**Economic Issues**   When the *bracero* program ended in 1965, Mexico's border provinces suffered from a high unemployment rate. Mexico's BIP encouraged U.S. manufacturers to open assembly plants in the 12.5 mile strip immediately south of the border. Most of these assembly plants, called "runaway shops" or *maquiladoras*, produced electronics, garments, and toys. By 1986, 800 such foreign-owned assembly plants employed some 250,000 people. Their location along the border prompted a population explosion in the border towns. Tijuana's population, for example, grew nine times its size in a 30-year period, from 62,000 in 1950 to 566,000 in 1980.

The plants continue to be attractive to American and multinational owners. Labor costs are cheap, the plants are located near their U.S. counterparts, and Mexican politics are more stable than in East Asia or Caribbean nations where cheap labor is also available. From the Mexican point of view, a segment of the population otherwise unemployed now has work. However, the workers are not receiving the technical training once hoped for. Working conditions, though acceptable by Mexican standards, do not always compare favorably to the working conditions prescribed by law in the United States.

Mexico has a saying, "When the U.S. sneezes, Mexico catches pneumonia," meaning that the Mexican economy is so closely tied to the U.S. economy through debt, investments, and trade, that change in one nation's economy quickly affects the other. For example, when in the 1960s U.S. inflation approached 10 percent a year, Mexico's inflation shot up to 20 or 30 percent. When in the 1970s the U.S. economy slowed down with recession, Mexico's economy plunged.

This link to the U.S. economy, and through it to the world's, was nowhere more apparent than during the days of Mexico's oil boom and its subsequent collapse. When large reserves of oil were first found along Mexico's east coast in the 1970s, hopes were high that this would solve many of Mexico's economic and social problems. Anticipating the new oil revenues and needing capital to finance development of the oil industry, Mexico borrowed heavily. Then rising interest rates caused a crisis, and in 1982 Mexico devalued the peso. By 1985 Mexico's debt payment was equal to 60 percent of the value of its exports. Finally, in 1986 the price of oil declined, and the bubble burst. Many industries were forced to shut down, resulting in even more unemployment, and the gross domestic product fell by 4 percent.

U.S. and other tourists, however, found the frequent devaluation of the peso attractive. Mexico's beautiful and varied landscape, its rich archaeological heritage, and its warm climate has resulted in a promising tourist industry. Yet the number of U.S. tourist dollars spent in Mexico just barely tops the amount spent by Mexican tourists at Disneyland and at other U.S. tourist centers. Overall, more than 90 percent of the foreign travel by Mexicans is to the United States, and Mexican tourism relies heavily on Americans.

**Political Issues**   Central to the political issues between the two nations is the issue of **interdependency,** the mutual support they provide one another. To summarize their economic interdependencies: immigrants, natural resources, agricultural products, and profits flow from south to north into the United States, while runaway shops and massive bank loans move from north to south into Mexico. The old perception of United States as the northern giant who can crush the impoverished southern peasant still haunts both partners. Paz's description of the conflict, written in 1972, still holds true today:

> *T*he United States, smiling or angry, its hand open or clenched, neither sees nor hears us but keeps striding on, and as it does so, enters our lands and crushes us. It is impossible to hold back a giant; it is possible, though far from easy, to make him listen to others; if he listens, that opens the possibility of coexistence.
>
> Octavio Paz,
> *The Other Mexico,* 1972

To Mexico, coexistence includes the possibility of disagreement. President Luis Echeverria (1970-1976) attempted to position his country as champion of the third world. Echeverria and his successors sided with Fidel Castro in Cuba and with Salvador Allende in Chile, both of whom the U.S. government strongly opposed. Mexico argued against U.S. intervention in Central America.

---

### STUDY GUIDE

**Recognizing Points of View**

One has to consider all points of view when trying to evaluate the merits of the Border Industrialization Program. The Mexican government approves of the program, with some reservations, because it provides a boost to a depressed area. Multinational corporations benefit from cheaper labor costs, and consumers benefit from lower prices. American unions, however, have voiced some concern that the long-term effects on the U.S. labor force will be negative.

**Cultural Issues** The recent communications revolution affects Mexico no less strongly than other parts of the world. Radio and TV airwaves bombard Mexico with the latest popular music, sitcoms, and sport broadcasts from the United States. Spanish soundtracks are added to American films so they can be screened throughout Latin America. Yet Mexico not only manages to hold its own against this cultural onslaught, it also sends something back in exchange.

The increase in the number of Hispanic Americans means there is now a large audience in the United States for Spanish language films, radio, and television. Most large American cities have a Spanish TV channel that broadcasts programs produced in Mexico. Music with a Latin beat attracts fans who far exceed the Spanish-speaking audience. Many soccer and other sports fans prefer to listen to Mexican broadcasts of games because they are uninterrupted by commercials.

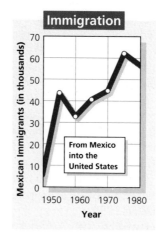

**Immigration**

Mexican Immigrants (in thousands)

From Mexico into the United States

Year

United States Border Inspection Station

AP/WIDE WORLD PHOTOS

**The San Ysidro, California, border crossing is the world's busiest. Mexican immigrants add to the traffic.**

## The Shared Border

The traffic that daily crosses the U.S.-Mexican border symbolizes many of the issues between the two nations. A busload of tourists from Phoenix pauses briefly on its way to a folk art exhibit in Guadalajara. A domestic worker who lives in Nogales, Mexico, walks across the border to Nogales, Arizona, and shows her immigration "green card" on the way. A manager of a garment factory rides his bicycle from the plant headquarters in El Paso, Texas, to the factory across the Rio Grande in Ciudad Juarez. Truckloads of freshly harvested vegetables wait in line to move through the border crossing.

Although the supporters of the 1986 Simpson-Rodino bill expected it to curb illegal immigration, the flow continues. The bill required American employers to determine that all their workers were in this country legally. The bill also granted amnesty to

almost 2 million Mexican immigrants who had lived in the United States since 1982. Still, the pursuit of better living conditions and the possibility of crossing a largely unguarded border undoubtedly will prove to be a continual lure to Mexico's poor.

The 1944 treaty allocating the waters of the Rio Grande and Colorado river systems did not discuss the quality of the water supplied. Industrial pollutants and salts washed out of North American soils have long affected the water that reaches the border regions. In the 1960s the two governments amended the 1944 treaty to "guarantee" the quality of the water to reach Mexico. The United States agreed to pay damages for past excess salinity of waters.

Analysts say that by the year 2000 the demands of southern California alone will cause a water shortage. Underground reserves of water that lie on either side of the border have never been covered in any treaty. Undoubtedly, the quality and quantity of water that reaches Mexico from the shared rivers will be an issue between the two nations for many years to come.

**Checking Facts**

1. How did the Border Industrialization Program help bring the United States and Mexico closer?

2. How did the worldwide collapse of oil prices in 1986 affect the U.S. and Mexican economies?

3. Why is self-determination a crucial issue in the thinking of Mexicans today?

**Thinking Critically**

4. **Comparing and Contrasting** Many countries have become defensive in the face of American cultural dominance around the world. Has this ever been a problem for Mexico?

5. **Recognizing Points of View** Octavio Paz says that the United States and Mexico are "two distinct versions of Western

civilization." What does he mean? Why has this sometimes caused misunderstanding between the two countries?

**Linking Across Time**

6. What was the major cause of friction between the United States and Mexico 150 years ago? What are the major issues dividing the two countries today?

# Canada

## August 1979: National Border Divides U.S.–Canadian Family

B ETWEEN THE UNITED STATES AND CANADA AT THE NORTHERN EDGE OF VERMONT, THE INTERNATIONAL BOUNDARY CUTS THROUGH A SMALL TOWN. ON THE AMERICAN SIDE OF the border, the town is called Derby Line, Vermont; on the Canadian side, it is Rock Island, Quebec.

The imaginary line separating the two countries wanders through the rows of Derby Line's backyard vegetable gardens and divides shelves of books at the Binational Library. It splits in two a tool factory built across a narrow section of the Tomifobia River. The strangest stretch of border, however, is the one that cuts through the home of Irene Bolduc and her family.

"This is the border," says Irene Bolduc, pointing to the edge of a door-frame. "See, over in the living room, you are in the United States. Step into the kitchen, *et voilà*, you are in Canada."

Irene Bolduc is a Canadian citizen, as is her son Michel. When he lived at home, Michel was careful to keep his bed on the Canadian side of the bedroom. His sister Arlette, however, is an American, since the hospital where she was born is in Newport, Vermont. When Michel moved away from home, Arlette took over his bedroom. She carefully moved the bed to the American side of the room so that officials could not challenge her American citizenship.

As in the Bolduc home, the 5,535-mile-long border between the United States and Canada is undefended. The frequency and ease with which Americans and Canadians travel back and forth across the boundary to work, to shop, and to play demonstrates the special **interdependency** between the two countries. Former Canadian Prime Minister Pierre Elliott Trudeau calls the friendship between the two nations "a lesson of peace to all nations."

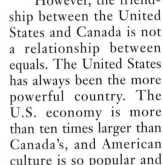
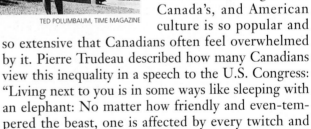

TED POLUMBAUM, TIME MAGAZINE

## *The Special Relationship*

The long-standing, peaceful friendship between the United States and Canada is based on mutual respect between neighbors who share a common language and a common heritage. Although Canada is home to a large French-speaking minority, English is the predominant language in both countries. Many Americans as well as many Canadians trace their roots to ancestors in Great Britain.

However, the friendship between the United States and Canada is not a relationship between equals. The United States has always been the more powerful country. The U.S. economy is more than ten times larger than Canada's, and American culture is so popular and so extensive that Canadians often feel overwhelmed by it. Pierre Trudeau described how many Canadians view this inequality in a speech to the U.S. Congress: "Living next to you is in some ways like sleeping with an elephant: No matter how friendly and even-tempered the beast, one is affected by every twitch and grunt."

**Economic Ties That Bind**  Nowhere are the twitches and grunts of the American elephant more troublesome to Canadians than in matters relating to

---

### STUDY GUIDE

**As You Read**
Analyze the special relationship that exists between the United States and Canada. Also, think about the following concept and skills.

**Central Concept**
• recognizing **interdependency** and how it affects relations between the United States and Canada in political and economic affairs

**Thinking Skills**
• recognizing points of view
• identifying cause and effect
• making inferences

their country's economy. The uneasy feeling that Trudeau and other Canadians share about the United States is based in part on the way American companies dominate Canadian business and industry. In 1976, for example, U.S. companies controlled 36 percent of Canada's paper and wood pulp industry, 43 percent of its mining industry, 45 percent of its manufacturing plants, and 58 percent of its oil and natural gas refineries. Of the 100 largest companies in Canada at that time, 40 were American owned.

Some Canadians claim that American ownership of Canadian companies has turned their country into a branch of the U.S. economy. However, others believe that the economic ties between Canada and the United States have benefited Canada in many ways. Hugh G. Aitken, a Canadian university professor, has explained the mixed feelings many Canadians have over this issue:

*N*o one doubts that American investment has accelerated the pace of economic development in Canada . . . but it seems also likely to convert Canada into a hinterland of United States industry. . . . To each spurt of

*expansion there is a corresponding shrinkage in Canada's freedom of action, in its self-reliance, and in its ability to chart its own course for the future.*

Hugh G. Aitken, 1970

The enormous Autoplex complex in Oshawa, Ontario, is a case in point. Built by a subsidiary of General Motors, the plant is an ultramodern facility, in which industrial robots weld car bodies. Canadian auto workers at the plant earn at least $17.50 an hour ($15 in U.S. money). Many of them are grateful for the opportunity to hold well-paying jobs and to gain experience with state-of-the-art manufacturing technology. However, a decline in car sales in the United States can lead to layoffs at the Canadian plant, and some workers resent that their jobs are vulnerable to economic ups and downs in another country.

Economic conditions in the United States also affect Canadians who invest in American firms, as you can see from the chart on the next page. Although more Americans control companies in Canada than the reverse, some Canadians do own businesses in the United States. In recent years Canadian investors

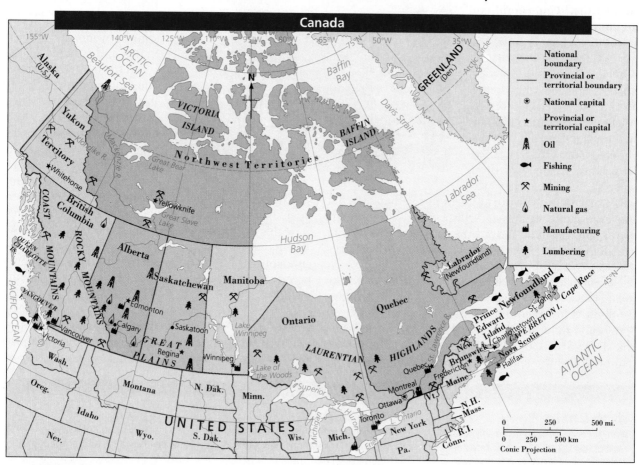

**The U.S.–Canada border has two parts. Many of the same resources are located on both sides of the border.**

*Where would you expect the population of Canada to be most dense? Why?*

have crossed to the U.S. side of the border to buy oil and refining industries, manufacturing plants, land, and other real estate. Near Bellingham, Washington, for example, investors from Vancouver, British Columbia, built seven major housing developments in the mid-1970s. Canadians also own office buildings, shopping centers, and movie theaters in New York and other U.S. cities.[1]

**Exporting American Culture**   As is the case with business ownership, the exchange of cultures between Canadians and Americans also favors the United States. Some Canadians feel they must struggle to maintain their national identity in the face of the American films, music, radio, and television programs that flood their country. American cultural imports are everywhere. Country singer Johnny Cash, for instance, posed recently for advertisements to sell automatic teller services for a Toronto bank.

What irritates many Canadians is that they seem to know everything about the United States, while Americans know little or nothing about Canada. Peter Gzowski, the host of a Canadian radio talk show, expresses it this way: "I can talk American politics. . . . But if we start talking about Ottawa politics, there's no conversation. Because I have to explain everything to you. That's a nuisance."

In recent years Canadians have become more conscious of the cultural differences between themselves and their American neighbors. A newspaper columnist in Calgary, Alberta, once published a list of 85 things he disliked about the United States. Among his dislikes were cruise missiles, the FBI, and Frank Sinatra. The columnist also mentioned a few things he liked about American culture, such as hot dogs and New England farms. Like this columnist, many Canadians are clear about their views of American culture but are less sure of what they think about their own.

GM CANADA, LTD.

**Robots weld and paint car bodies in the giant Autoplex plant in Oshawa, Ontario. The plant, built by a subsidiary of General Motors, is one of the largest automotive complexes in North America. The chart at left compares American and Canadian investments in the other's country.** *What are the advantages and disadvantages of foreign investment?*

**U.S. and Canadian Investments**

Investments (in billions of dollars)

■ United States investments in Canada
■ Canadian investments in the United States

Year: 1980 1981 1982 1983 1984 1985 1986 1987

Pierre Berton, a Canadian historian, sums up the confusion many Canadians feel about their country's cultural identity: "We know who we are not, even if we aren't quite sure who we are. We are not Americans."

## Give and Take Between Neighbors

The Canadian struggle to establish a separate national identity has sometimes led to policy disputes with the United States. Historically, the two countries have been able to settle these disputes peacefully. However, there have been times over the past 30 years when disagreements have strained the special relationship between the two countries. These disagreements—over foreign policy, environment, and trade—show that even the warmest friendship can become frosty when the national interests of two countries collide.

**STUDY GUIDE**

**Recognizing Points of View**
Americans and Canadians look at the world from different points of view. The United States is a superpower, with all the responsibilities that go with superpower status. Canada, on the other hand, has preserved its historic ties with Great Britain. It continues its allegiance to the British Crown and maintains close relations with other countries that were once British colonies.

1  Why do Canadians sometimes feel overwhelmed by the special relationship between the United States and Canada? What do they fear most?

**Conflicts over Defense and Foreign Policy** In matters of defense and foreign policy, Canada has historically been the junior partner of the United States. In 1961 John Diefenbaker, then prime minister of Canada, insisted that "Canadians wish to make their own decisions in international affairs." Despite this assertion, Diefenbaker approved of Canada's participation in NORAD, a radar system based in Colorado Springs designed to detect and respond to a nuclear attack against North America. Diefenbaker's approval meant that American electronic equipment and bombers capable of carrying nuclear weapons could be positioned on Canadian soil.

By joining the American air defense network, the Canadian government in effect gave up control of its own defense policy. During the Cuban missile crisis of October 1962, for example, President John Kennedy ordered North American air defense systems to go on full alert. For 48 hours following the order, the Diefenbaker government refused to authorize the alert of air defense bases in Canada. However, Royal Canadian Air Force installations linked to

His successor, Lester Pearson, did not share Diefenbaker's reluctance. After taking office, Pearson sealed his close friendship with President Kennedy by agreeing to keep Canada in NORAD and to equip Canadian bombers with American-built nuclear weapons.

This harmonious joining of the defense systems of Canada and the United States was short-lived, however. When Lyndon Johnson became president following Kennedy's assassination and the war in Vietnam heated up, a period of mistrust began between Ottawa and Washington. In April 1965 Pearson urged a suspension of American air strikes against North Vietnam to pave the way for a negotiated settlement of the war.

Pearson's suggestion provoked an angry outburst from President Johnson. The day after Pearson's speech Johnson invited him to a meeting at the presidential retreat at Camp David, Maryland. In a heated exchange, Johnson protested that Pearson had joined the ranks of the "know-nothing" "do-gooders" who opposed his Vietnam policy. Furthermore, he complained, he was getting tired of receiving advice from foreign visitors. This sharp difference of opinion between the two leaders over American involvement in Vietnam led to a period of icy tension between the two governments. Relations between Canada and the United States were further strained by the flight to Canada of more than 20,000 young Americans, who chose to leave the country rather than fight in Vietnam.

When Pierre Elliott Trudeau became Canada's prime minister in 1968, he continued to underscore the differences between Canadian and U.S. foreign policy. While in office, Trudeau made official visits to Moscow, Beijing, and East Germany, visits which were viewed with

KUCH IN WINNEPEG FREE PRESS

**A Canadian newspaper cartoonist shows Prime Minister John Diefenbaker unable to walk a straight line, for or against nuclear weapons.**

NORAD went on full alert anyway, responding automatically to orders from Colorado Springs, despite lack of approval from their own government.

Diefenbaker's wavering about Canada's defense link with the United States led to the defeat of his government in the Canadian election of April 1963.

suspicion by President Richard Nixon. On his visit to the Soviet Union in May 1971, Trudeau signed a friendship agreement between his government and Moscow. Under this agreement, Canada and the Soviet Union promised they would talk to each other about mutual problems at regular intervals. Improved

---

**STUDY GUIDE**

### Identifying Cause and Effect

As part of its strategy to maintain a separate identity, Canada charts an independent course in foreign policy whenever possible. Thus, Diefenbaker refused to follow the United States'

lead during the Cuban missile crisis. He insisted that Canada had the right, and the duty, to make its own decisions. Similarly, Pearson refused to follow the United States into Vietnam. Trudeau

signed a friendship agreement between Canada and the USSR, and his country continued to trade with Cuba during all the years of the U.S. embargo.

relations with the Soviet Union helped to shift Canada further from under the umbrella of American foreign policy.

### Charting a Course in Latin America

The Canadian shift away from dependence on American foreign policy has also affected Canada's relations with Latin America. Unlike the United States, Canada traditionally held itself aloof from involvement in the region. At the same time, Canadians have occasionally viewed Latin America as a place where they could assert their independence from the United States. For instance, Canada continued to trade with Cuba after Fidel Castro overthrew the dictatorship of Fulgencio Batista and established close ties with the USSR. The United States, on the other hand, ended all trade with Cuba and tried to convince its allies to isolate the island economically. Despite U.S. pressure, Canada stood firm.

Canada has also asserted itself by seeking membership in the Organization of American States (OAS), a forum where representatives of countries in the Western Hemisphere discuss trade and other policy questions. As early as 1968, Prime Minister Trudeau expressed interest in joining the OAS, as long as Canada could act independently of the United States. Four years later Canada joined the organization as a nonvoting Permanent Observer, a post created by the OAS expressly for Canada.

Canada continued in that position until October 1989, when Brian Mulroney requested full membership. This was swiftly approved by OAS member nations. By this action Mulroney demonstrated that he intends Canada to play a more active and independent role in hemispheric affairs.

At the same time, Mulroney also moved to strengthen Canada's ties with the United States. He enjoyed close and friendly relations with presidents Ronald Reagan and George Bush. In 1987 Reagan and Mulroney successfully negotiated a path-breaking U.S.–Canadian trade agreement. In many ways this agreement has restored the special relationship between the two countries.

### Restrictions or Free Trade

Trade between Canada and the United States is critical to the economic health of both countries. Canada has historically been the major trading partner of the United States. In 1975, 66 percent of Canada's $32 billion in exports of meat, metals, minerals, and other goods went to the United States. Of the $34.6 billion worth of cars and trucks, machine tools, coal, and other products imported into Canada, 68 percent came from the United States. Trade between the United States and the province of Ontario alone exceeds all American trade with Japan.

Despite the importance of this trade, economic relations between the countries have not always been smooth. In August 1971 President Nixon created a breach between Canada and the United States by announcing a new set of U.S. trade restrictions. He raised by 10 percent taxes on items imported into the United States. In addition he reduced taxes on goods imported from foreign factories owned by U.S. companies. Together these changes gave U.S. companies a trade advantage over their foreign-owned competitors. Canadians doing business with the United States were angered when Nixon refused to grant Canada an exception to this policy. Although trade continued, the new regulations caused many in the Canadian business community to question the special nature of their economic ties to the United States.

The Free Trade Agreement, signed by President Reagan and Prime Minister Mulroney in 1988, largely removed those doubts. Under the agreement, all taxes and other trade restrictions between Canada and the United States will end by the year 2000. The agreement also ends controls on trade in energy products, such as oil, natural gas, coal, uranium, and electricity, and encourages joint Canadian-American business ventures.[2]

Although most Canadian business owners applaud the Free Trade Agreement, some Canadian workers oppose it. They fear that Canadian businesses will not be able to compete successfully with larger American firms, and that they will lose their jobs if Canadian companies are forced out of business. Other Canadians argue that the agreement will mean the end of Canada's ability to control its own resources. However, its supporters insist that the Free Trade Agreement will strengthen the Canadian economy by opening American markets to Canadian-produced goods, thus creating more jobs for Canadian workers.

Heated debate over the Free Trade Agreement was

a major issue in Canada's 1988 election. Although voters returned Mulroney to office, arguments over the merits of the agreement continue to divide Canadians. Whether or not the agreement will lead to a merging of the Canadian and American economies, as some Canadians fear, it clearly signals the beginning of a new era in U.S.–Canadian relations.

**Sharing the Environment**  As with foreign policy and trade, disputes over environmental issues often begin with Canada at a disadvantage. Airborne pollutants that cause acid rain, for example, cross the U.S.–Canadian border in both directions. However, Canada receives more than twice the amount of air pollution from the United States as the United States gets from Canada. Coal-fired electrical power plants in the Ohio Valley spew sulfur oxides into the atmosphere, while automobile exhaust systems in northern U.S. cities add nitrogen oxides. When these chemicals return to earth as rain, they damage forests and kill the fish in lakes and rivers. As a result of acid rain, more than 14,000 Canadian lakes are nearly fishless.

Although the United States and Canada have been discussing how to deal with acid rain since July 1979, agreements have been slow in coming. Power companies in the United States have balked at the cost of installing scrubbers, machines that remove sulfur from smoke before it goes up power plant chimneys. The most encouraging sign of progress came in June 1989, when President Bush promised to cut nearly half of U.S. output of emissions that cause acid rain by the year 2000.[3]

The management of natural resources, such as the Great Lakes, has also been a sticky question for the United States and Canada to resolve. Some 20 million Americans and one third of all Canadians get their drinking water from this shared resource. Agreements between the United States and Canada have improved water quality in the lakes over the past 20 years. However, disagreements remain over how lake water should be used. For example, when the level of the Mississippi River sank low enough to strand barges in 1988, Illinois Governor James Thompson proposed that water from Lake Michigan be diverted through existing canals and rivers from Chicago to the Mississippi. The suggestion set off alarm bells for Canadian environmentalists like Don Gamble.

> *W*ater is to the Canadians as the Alps are to the Swiss—something that transcends the resource. It's so much a part of how Canadians see themselves. . . . So when someone comes along and says, "Look, we got a problem in the lower Mississippi, give us some water," Canadians say, "Not on your life."
>
> Don Gamble,
> in *National Geographic*, 1990

How Canada and the United States resolve disputes over shared resources such as the Great Lakes and common problems like acid rain will partly determine the quality of life in both countries in the coming years. Environmental issues are likely to stay high on the agenda for discussion between the two countries in the future.

## Acid Pollution

1 Air pollution from factories and automobiles contains sulfur dioxides and nitrogen oxides.

2 These oxides can attack and corrode metals and stone. They also combine with fog and dust to form smog.

3 The oxides react with air moisture (clouds) to form sulfuric acid, which falls as acid rain.

The wind carries acid pollution thousands of miles.

4 Nitrogen oxides contribute to the formation of ozone. This artificial ozone is a major part of acid pollution, causing respiratory problems in people and animals and damaging crops.

5 Acid rain strips plants and soil of vital nutrients.

6 Acid rain runoff contains poisons that kill aquatic species.

**Studies completed in 1988 indicated that the buildup of acid in lakes can be reversed once the pollution is stopped. However, a lake may not fully recover for 100 years or more.**

## Canada at a Crossroads

Relations between Canada and the United States in the coming years also hinge on how Canada resolves key questions about its own future as a nation. Since the 1960s, a long-simmering constitutional crisis has created tension between the French-speaking province of Quebec and the rest of Canada, which speaks English. Although the United States can be a sympathetic observer to these struggles, this problem is one that Canada must grapple with alone.

The history of Canada's current crisis can be traced to the way in which Canada was settled. French traders and explorers, such as Samuel de Champlain, founded settlements in what is now Quebec as early as 1608. French settlers in Quebec City and other towns clung to their native language and created a French-Canadian culture distinct from the English-speaking, British-based culture found in the rest of Canada.

Although politically part of Canada, Quebec has long sought independence from economic and cultural control by English-speaking Canadians. Laws protect the rights of French-speaking Canadians to preserve their own language and culture. Even so, some citizens of Quebec have demanded that Quebec become an independent country.

The clashes between French and English speakers in Canada have been less violent in recent years. However, the issue of independence for Quebec has

SYGMA

**Quebec separatists demonstrate their support for an independent Quebec nation by waving provincial flags.**

not gone away. In 1980 Prime Minister Trudeau, himself a native of Quebec, launched a drive to unify Canada by revising the Canadian constitution. After becoming prime minister in 1984, Brian Mulroney continued the search for compromise. Although many plans for changing the constitution have been proposed, none has been acceptable to both Quebec and Canada's nine other provinces.

The most recent compromise, hammered out after months of intense negotiations between Mulroney, Quebec Premier Robert Bourassa, and representatives of the other provinces, was called the Meech Lake Accord. Announced on April 30, 1987, the accord granted Quebec recognition as a "distinct society" with the right "to preserve and promote" its identity. The agreement spelled out the rights of Quebec and the other provinces to control immigration, suggest appointments to the Supreme Court of Canada, and veto possible future changes in the Canadian constitution.

Although many in Canada hoped the Meech Lake Accord would end Canada's constitutional crisis, it did not do so. The agreement called for unanimous approval of the accord within three years, by June 23, 1990. The deadline came and went, with two provinces, Manitoba and Newfoundland, unwilling to ratify the agreement.

With the death of the Meech Lake Accord, Canada must begin again the process of shaping its national union. In coming years, the United States may need to establish relations with two countries north of its border, rather than the current one.

## SECTION REVIEW

**Checking Facts**

1. Describe the major foreign policy disagreements between the United States and Canada since 1960.
2. Explain why the Free Trade Agreement of 1988 marks the beginning of a new era in U.S.–Canadian relations.
3. What are the major environmental issues the United States and Canada have yet to solve?

**Thinking Critically**

4. **Identifying Cause and Effect** Why did Canada lose a certain amount of control over its foreign policy once it relinquished control of its defense policy?
5. **Identifying Cause and Effect** How have the close economic ties between the United States and Canada benefited both countries?
6. **Recognizing Points of View** Why do Canadians have mixed

feelings about the close economic ties between the United States and Canada? Why hasn't this been a problem for the United States?

**Linking Across Time**

7. How is the constitutional crisis that Canada faces over the status of Quebec similar to the crisis the United States faced over secession during the nineteenth century? How is it different?

# Border South, Border North

High along the Continental Divide in southwest Colorado, a small stream rises. As it snakes southeastward through the Rocky Mountains, the waters widen and deepen to become the legendary Rio Grande.

The Rio Grande courses south through the state of New Mexico, neatly dividing the state in half. At El Paso, Texas, it takes on special significance. No longer just a turbid river, the Rio Grande, from El Paso to the Gulf of Mexico, defines about two-thirds —nearly 1,240 miles—of the U.S.–Mexican border.

## Defining Borders

Borders like the Rio Grande define the geographic extent of a nation's territory. They are politically sensitive places where people from different cultures come together for every purpose from commerce to warfare.

The United States has borders on the south and the north. These are defined by both natural features and surveyors' lines, mutually agreed upon by the United States and its border nations.

The 2,076-mile border between Mexico and the United States follows the southern limits of California, Arizona, New Mexico, and Texas. The southern limit of Texas is defined by the contours of the Rio Grande.

The border between Canada and the United States is in two parts. The primary part runs in a nearly straight line along the 49th parallel from the Pacific Ocean to the Great Lakes. The border then cuts through Lakes Superior, Huron, Erie, and Ontario.

Between Lakes Erie and Ontario, it runs across Niagara Falls, with the American Falls on the U.S. side and Horseshoe Falls on the Canadian side. From the Great Lakes, the border follows the St. Lawrence Seaway and along the northern limits of New York, Vermont, New Hampshire, and Maine, ending at the Atlantic Ocean.

The second part of the northern border separates Alaska from the Yukon Territory and the province of British Columbia.

Besides being defined by natural features and lines drawn on a map, U.S. borders share other similarities. Both borders are largely unguarded, except for immigration personnel. In fact, the U.S.–Canadian border is the longest undefended border in the world. Because the borders are open, they are boundaries rather

---

**Border disputes with our southern and northern neighbors have always been resolved through diplomacy.**

---

than barriers. Much of the northern border along the 49th parallel is marked only by a 20-foot-wide strip of land cut through the forest. During dry seasons along the U.S.–Mexican border, the Rio Grande is often reduced to a trickle, and people can easily walk across the river bed.

The nature of our country's borders has periodically led to disputes with our neighbors. These disputes, which have occurred

over fishing rights, territorial claims, and concerns about pollution, have been settled for almost 150 years solely by peaceful negotiation.

## An Unruly River

In 1970 the United States and Mexico signed a treaty that helped resolve nearly a century of argument about the position of the U.S.–Mexican border. The dispute arose because of the unstable nature of the Rio Grande.

The river goes through an arid region of the Americas. Arid-region rivers generally have unstable banks due to a lack of moisture and vegetation. When large volumes of water surge through such rivers, they tend to meander; that is, over long periods of time, they shift direction in looping, winding patterns.

Since the mid-1800s, the Rio Grande has shifted slowly around El Paso, Texas, and Ciudad Juárez in the Mexican state of Chihuahua. By 1905 the river had shifted direction so much that El Chamizal, a 600-acre parcel of land that once was part of Ciudad Juárez, was now on the U.S. side of the river. The ownership of El Chamizal was settled diplomatically by making the land part of El Paso, and its residents, formerly Mexican nationals, U.S. citizens.

The river continued shifting, however. Between 1905 and 1970, there have been 247 border changes, involving the transfer of nearly 1,000 acres of land.

## Fish and Acid Rain

The U.S.–Canadian borders have also been disputed. That

part of the border separating Alaska from the Yukon includes a border line drawn into the Pacific Ocean just south of Prince of Wales Island. Canadians recognize a 1903 boundary known as the Alaska–British Columbia Line. The United States insists that the border should be drawn 25 miles farther south.

At stake in this dispute are the fishing grounds in the Dixon Entrance to the Hecate Strait. If the 1903 border prevails, the Alaskan fishing industry will be deprived of a rich source of income. Should the border be redrawn, Canada's fishers will have to share their bountiful catch.

Along the U.S.–Canadian border in the northeastern United States, the dispute centers on acid rain. Prevailing winds drive this toxic mist across the border in both directions, leading to serious environmental damage. Canada receives twice as much acid rain from the United States as does the United States from Canada.

No border, defended or wide open, can stop airborne pollutants. So the solution requires as much science as diplomacy. President Bush unveiled a clean-air program in 1989, designed to attack acid rain at its source. Combined with Canadian efforts, the Bush proposal will help to address a border issue that has strained U.S.–Canadian relations since the late 1970s.

**THINK ABOUT IT:** Unlike the United States, some nations have tightly controlled closed borders. Aside from pollution, what else can move across closed borders?

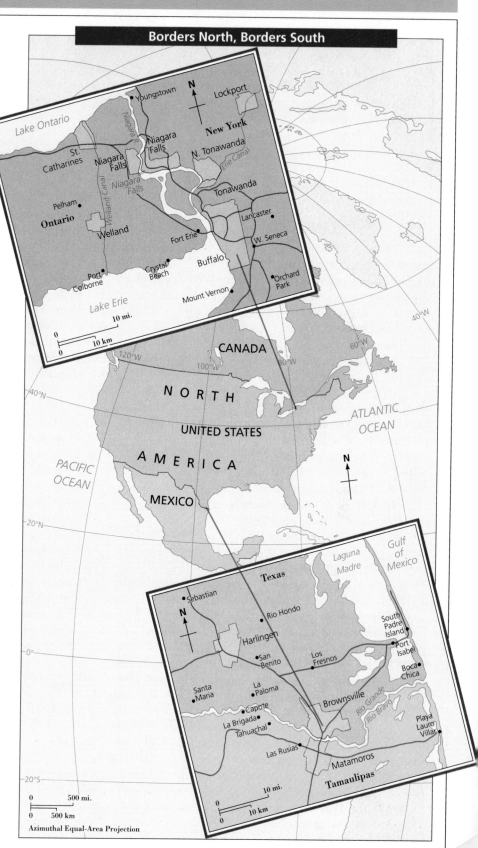

Borders North, Borders South

# Chapter 22 Review

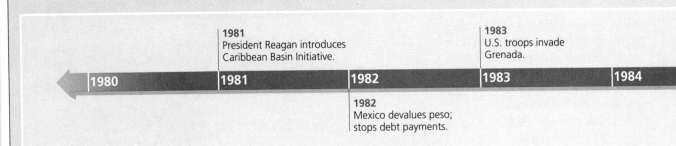

1981
President Reagan introduces Caribbean Basin Initiative.

1983
U.S. troops invade Grenada.

1980 | 1981 | 1982 | 1983 | 1984

1982
Mexico devalues peso; stops debt payments.

## Summary

Use the following outline as a tool for reviewing and summarizing the chapter. Copy the outline on your own paper, leaving spaces between headings to jot down notes about key events and concepts.

**I. Latin America**
A. A History of Underdevelopment
B. Latin America Since 1945
C. U.S.–Latin American Relations
D. Future Challenges

**II. Mexico**
A. An Overview of Mexico
B. The United States and Mexico
C. The Shared Border

**III. Canada**
A. The Special Relationship
B. Give and Take Between Neighbors
C. Canada at a Crossroads

## Ideas, Events, and People

1. How did Latin America come to be economically dependent on the United States? How did that dependency change after World War II?
2. What caused the rapid economic growth in Latin America following World War II?
3. By far the greatest number of people in the United States belong to a vast middle class. How is Latin America different from the United States in that respect?
4. Explain the U.S. policy of intervention in Latin America. How did that policy result in U.S. support of military dictators?
5. Why have many Mexicans moved from the countryside to the city?
6. What makes tourism an important and successful industry in Mexico?
7. Explain this Mexican saying: "When the United States sneezes, Mexico catches pneumonia." What are some examples?
8. Why have some U.S. industries located their assembly plants in Mexico near the U.S. border? Who benefits, and in what ways?
9. What natural feature of the Rio Grande resulted in a longstanding dispute between the United States and Mexico?
10. Describe and account for the unusual relationship that the United States and Canada have enjoyed over the years.
11. How do the borders between the United States and Canada reflect their unusual relationship?
12. How did Canada give up control of its own defense policy?
13. How did the war in Vietnam call attention to differences between the United States and Canada over foreign policy?
14. Explain the importance of the Free Trade Agreement signed in 1988 by President Reagan and Canadian Prime Minister Mulroney.
15. Why do acid rain and the Great Lakes involve special cooperation between Canada and the United States?
16. How does Quebec's history help to explain the constitutional crisis in the 1990s between Quebec and the rest of Canada?

## Social Studies Skills

### Analyzing News Media

Read or listen to a news story about events in Canada or a Latin American nation. Choose a medium that is not your customary source of news. Evaluate the new medium, comparing it with your usual choice. Spanish-speaking students might compare the coverage of Latin American issues by English-language and Spanish-language media.

**July 1985**
Peru limits debt payments.

**1985**

**1986**

**1986**
Congress passes Simpson–Rodino immigration bill.

**1987**

**1988**

**1988**
United States and Canada sign Free Trade Agreement.

**1989**
U.S. forces enter Panama, arrest General Noriega.

**1989**

**October 1989**
Canada asks to join Organization of American States.

# Critical Thinking

**1. Identifying Cause and Effect**
Why have Latin American economies historically been dependent on the United States? What problems has dependency created?

**2. Identifying Cause and Effect**
How did the rise of military dictatorships lead to revolutionary guerrilla movements in some Latin American countries?

**3. Analyzing Decisions**
Below is a photo of an American Chrysler factory in Toluca, a town near Mexico City. Compare this photo with the one on page 728. What does each suggest about Mexico's economy? How does each type of industry benefit Mexico at this time?

# Extension and Application

**1. Cooperative Learning**
In general, Canadians are right in saying that they know far more about the United States than Americans know about Canada. Work with a small group to explore one aspect of life in Canada today:

for example, movies, politics, schools, sports, the arts, or environmental issues. If possible, read a Canadian newspaper or listen to a Canadian radio station as part of your research. Finally, have each group present its findings to the rest of the class.

**2. Community Connection**
Investigate resources in or near your community that reflect the cultural heritage of Mexico. Use your findings to prepare an annotated list with information about museums, restaurants, newspapers, paintings and other works of art, and music or dance groups.

**3. Global Connection**
Use a current world almanac to discover the most recent population figures of the world's 10 to 15 largest cities, noting which cities are in the Western Hemisphere. Present your findings in a bar graph.

**4. Citizenship**
Investigate the role of an informed citizenry in shaping future immigration policy. Using the *Readers' Guide to Periodical Literature*, find and read one article on the topic. Report to your class by writing a one-paragraph summary of what you have learned.

# Geography

1. According to the map on page 719, which city is farther west: Lima, Peru or Miami? Describe the location of South America in relation to the United States.
2. How is industrial growth in the United States related to the strength of Latin American exports?
3. What reasons does the United States give to justify supporting repressive dictatorships in Latin America?
4. Why do Canadians have mixed feelings about their country's ties to the United States?

© S. DORANTES, SYGMA

# Unit 8 Review

*I*t is only in the last 20 years or so that presidents appear to have thrown caution and even constitutional scruples to the wind, as it were, and ventured, on their own authority, into military operations that were in fact acts of war, that were on a large scale, that were in distant parts of the globe, and that constituted 'commitments' whose vindication threatened the integrity of our political and constitutional system.

Professor Henry Steele Commager,
March 8, 1971

## Concepts and Themes

Intervention played a major role in U.S. foreign policy after World War II. The United States intervened in both Vietnam and Latin American countries in attempts to keep communist governments out. This intervention ranged from economic sanctions to sending troops. President Nixon also employed the policy of détente to keep communism contained. The post-World War II years were marked, too, by changing economic relations with Latin America and Canada, as well as crises over the extent of presidential power.

1. How does the above quote apply to the actions of presidents Lyndon Johnson and Richard Nixon in the Vietnam War?
2. Give two reasons why U.S. administrations intervened in Latin American affairs. Apply your answers to Guatemala and Chile.
3. Which do you think would best promote democracy in third world countries: military assistance; technical assistance in such areas as agriculture, small industry, and health care; a combination of these? Explain your answer.
4. Tell how the United States' economic dominance helps and how it hinders Canada.

## History Projects

1. **Evidence of the Past**

   Imagine the year is 2100, and you are a historian. You have just viewed three TV tapes. The tapes record President Nixon on his China tour, Nixon in the Soviet Union, and John Dean testifying about Watergate. From these sources alone, write a capsule evaluation of Richard Nixon's presidency.

2. **Geography**

   In groups, learn about acid rain, including the inability to contain it within borders, the extent of worldwide damage, and the individual's role in combating the problem. In groups, write a feature for the school newspaper. Submit all articles.

3. **One Day in History**

   Work in small groups to create the front page of a daily newspaper for one day in April 1968. Research actual events in newspaper microfiches and reference books listing historical chronologies.

4. **Case History**

   The hawks and doves took opposing positions on the Vietnam War. Consult newspapers, periodicals, and library books to obtain quotes representing both sides of the question. Write a brief conclusion giving your own viewpoint and your reasons.

## Writing Activities

1. Research Agent Orange, a U.S. herbicide used in Vietnam. Write a report that explains why this defoliant was used and what long-term effects resulted from its use. (See the Writer's Guide on pages 825–827.)
2. Read further about workers in Mexico in the 1960s and 1970s. Write a narrative telling about an hour in the life of a vendor pictured on page 729.

## The Arts

- *Carrying the Darkness*, edited by W. D. Ehrhart; an anthology of Vietnam poetry.
- *The Kandy-Kolored Tangerine-flake Streamline Baby* by Tom Wolfe; a look at the offbeat culture of the 1960s.
- *All the President's Men* by Bob Woodward and Carl Bernstein; two reporters' account of unraveling Watergate. This book was also made into a film.
- *Born on the Fourth of July*, a film about a disillusioned Vietnam veteran.

# UNIT NINE

# The New Conservatism

Cathie Bleck

**Chapter 23: New Challenges**
**Chapter 24: A Changing Nation in a Changing World**

# "Double Face"

*The United States is a nation of immigrants who came to this land in search of new opportunities. Throughout history these immigrants have been faced with the same dilemma: how to preserve their native language and culture in the face of pressure to change and adapt to a new society. The narrator in the following selection explores the ways her Chinese culture conflicts with that of her new country.*

## from *The Joy Luck Club*

### by Amy Tan

My daughter wanted to go to China for her second honeymoon, but now she is afraid.

"What if I blend in so well they think I'm one of them?" Waverly asked me. "What if they don't let me come back to the United States?"

"When you go to China," I told her, "you don't even need to open your mouth. They already know you are an outsider."

"What are you talking about?" she asked. My daughter likes to speak back. She likes to question what I say.

"Aii-ya," I said. "Even if you put on their clothes, even if you take off your makeup and hide your fancy jewelry, they know. They know just watching the way you walk, the way you carry your face. They know you do not belong."

My daughter did not look pleased when I told her this, that she didn't look Chinese. She had a sour American look on her face. Oh, maybe ten years ago, she would have clapped her hands—hurray!—as if this were good news. But now she wants to be Chinese, it is so fashionable. And I know it is too late. All those years I tried to teach her! She followed my Chinese ways only until she learned how to walk out the door by herself and go to school. So now the only Chinese words she can say are *sh-sh, houche, chr fan,* and *gwan deng shweijyau.* How can she talk to people in China with these words? Pee-pee, choo-choo train, eat, close light sleep. How can she think she can blend in? Only her skin and her hair are Chinese. Inside—she is all American-made.

It's my fault she is this way. I wanted my children to have the best combination: American circumstances and Chinese character. How could I know these two things do not mix?

I taught her how American circumstances work. If you are born poor here, it's no lasting shame. You are first in line for a scholarship. If the roof crashes on your head, no need to cry over this bad luck. You can sue anybody, make the landlord fix it. You do not have to sit like a Buddha under a tree letting pigeons drop their dirty business on your head. You can buy an umbrella. Or go inside a Catholic church. In America, nobody says you have to keep the circumstances somebody else gives you.

She learned these things, but I couldn't teach her about Chinese character. How to obey parents and listen to your mother's mind. How not to show your own thoughts, to put your feelings behind your face so you can take advantage of hidden opportunities. Why easy things are not worth pursuing. How to know your own worth and polish it, never flashing it around like a cheap ring. Why Chinese thinking is best.

No, this kind of thinking didn't stick to her. She was too busy chewing gum, blowing bubbles bigger than her cheeks. Only that kind of thinking stuck.

**David Hockney created this collage from photographs in 1985.** *What impression does the fragmentation of the woman's face give you? How does this image mirror the narrator's U.S. experience?*

"Finish your coffee," I told her yesterday. "Don't throw your blessings away."

"Don't be so old-fashioned, Ma," she told me, finishing her coffee down the sink. "I'm my own person."

And I think, How can she be her own person? When did I give her up?

My daughter is getting married a second time. So she asked me to go to her beauty parlor, her famous Mr. Rory. I know her meaning. She is ashamed of my looks.

What will her husband's parents and his important lawyer friends think of this backward old Chinese woman?

"Auntie An-mei can cut me," I say.

"Rory is famous," says my daughter, as if she had no ears. "He does fabulous work."

So I sit in Mr. Rory's chair. He pumps me up and down until I am the right height. Then my daughter criticizes me as if I were not there. "See how it's flat on one side," she accuses my head. "She needs a cut and a perm. And this purple tint in her hair, she's been doing it at home. She's never had anything professionally done."

She is looking at Mr. Rory in the mirror. He is looking at me in the mirror. I have seen this professional look before. Americans don't really look at one another when talking. They talk to their reflections. They look at others or themselves only when they think nobody is watching. So they never see how they really look. They see themselves smiling without their mouth open, or turned to the side where they cannot see their faults.

"How does she want it?" asked Mr. Rory. He thinks I do not understand English. He is floating his fingers through my hair. He is showing how his magic can make my hair thicker and longer.

"Ma, how do you want it?" Why does my daughter think she is translating English for me? Before I can even speak, she explains my thoughts: "She wants a soft wave. We probably shouldn't cut it too short. Otherwise it'll be too tight for the wedding. She doesn't want it to look kinky or weird."

And now she says to me in a loud voice, as if I had lost my hearing, "Isn't that right, Ma? Not too tight?"

I smile. I use my American face. That's the face Americans think is Chinese, the one they cannot understand. But inside I am becoming ashamed. I am ashamed she is ashamed. Because she is my daughter and I am proud of her, and I am her mother but she is not proud of me.

Mr. Rory pats my hair more. He looks at me. He looks at my daughter. Then he says something to my daughter that really displeases her: "It's uncanny how much you two look alike!"

I smile, this time with my Chinese face. But my daughter's eyes and her smile become very narrow, the way a cat pulls itself small just before it bites. Now Mr. Rory goes away so we can think about this. I hear him snap his fingers, "Wash! Mrs. Jong is next!"

So my daughter and I are alone in this crowded beauty parlor. She is frowning at herself in the mirror. She sees me looking at her.

"The same cheeks," she says. She points to mine and then pokes her cheeks. She sucks them outside in to look like a starved person. She puts her face next to mine, side by side, and we look at each other in the mirror.

"You can see your character in your face," I say to my daughter without thinking. "You can see your future."

"What do you mean?" she says.

And now I have to fight back my feelings. These two faces, I think, so much the same! The same happiness, the same sadness, the same good fortune, the same faults.

I am seeing myself and my mother, back in China, when I was a young girl.

My mother—your grandmother—once told me my fortune, how my character could lead to good and bad circumstances. She was sitting at her table with the big mirror. I was standing behind her, my chin resting on her shoulder. The next day was the start of the new year. I would be ten years by my Chinese age, so it was an important birthday for me. For this reason maybe she did not criticize me too much. She was looking at my face.

She touched my ear. "You are lucky," she said. "You have my ears, a big thick lobe, lots of meat at the bottom, full of blessings. Some people are born so poor. Their ears are so thin, so close to their head, they can never hear luck calling to them. You have the right ears, but you must listen to your opportunities."

She ran her thin finger down my nose. "You have my nose. The hole is not too big, so your money will

not be running out. The nose is straight and smooth, a good sign. A girl with a crooked nose is bound for misfortune. She is always following the wrong things, the wrong people, the worst luck."

She tapped my chin and then hers. "Not too short, not too long. Our longevity will be adequate, not cut off too soon, not so long we become a burden."

She pushed my hair away from my forehead. "We are the same," concluded my mother. "Perhaps your forehead is wider, so you will be even more clever. And your hair is thick, the hairline is low on your forehead. This means you will have some hardships in your early life. This happened to me. But look at my hairline now. High! Such a blessing for my old age. Later you will learn to worry and lose your hair, too."

She took my chin in her hand. She turned my face toward her, eyes facing eyes. She moved my face to one side, then the other. "The eyes are honest, eager," she said. "They follow me and show respect. They do not look down in shame. They do not resist and turn the opposite way. You will be a good wife, mother, and daughter-in-law."

When my mother told me these things, I was still so young. And even though she said we looked the same, I wanted to look more the same. If her eye went up and looked surprised, I wanted my eye to do the same. If her mouth fell down and was unhappy, I too wanted to feel unhappy.

I was so much like my mother. This was before our circumstances separated us: a flood that caused my family to leave me behind, my first marriage to a family that did not want me, a war from all sides, and later, an ocean that took me to a new country. She did not see how my face changed over the years. How my mouth began to droop. How I began to worry but still did not lose my hair. How my eyes began to follow the American way. She did not see that I twisted my nose bouncing forward on a crowded bus in San Francisco. Your father and I, we were on our way to church to give many thanks to God for all our blessings, but I had to subtract some for my nose.

It's hard to keep your Chinese face in America. At the beginning, before I even arrived, I had to hide my true self. I paid an American-raised Chinese girl in Peking to show me how.

"In America," she said, "you cannot say you want to live there forever. If you are Chinese, you must say you admire their schools, their ways of thinking. You must say you want to be a scholar and come back to teach Chinese people what you have learned."

"What should I say I want to learn?" I asked. "If they ask me questions, if I cannot answer . . ."

"Religion, you must say you want to study religion," said this smart girl. "Americans all have different ideas about religion, so there are no right and wrong answers. Say to them, I'm going for God's sake, and they will respect you."

For another sum of money, this girl gave me a form filled out with English words. I had to copy these words over and over again as if they were English words formed from my own head. Next to the word NAME, I wrote *Lindo Sun*. Next to the word BIRTHDATE, I wrote *May 11, 1918*, which this girl insisted was the same as three months after the Chinese lunar new year. Next to the word BIRTHPLACE, I put down *Taiyuan, China*. And next to the word OCCUPATION, I wrote *student of theology*.

I gave the girl even more money for a list of addresses in San Francisco, people with big connections. And finally, this girl gave me, free of charge, instructions for changing my circumstances. "First," she said, "you must find a husband. An American citizen is best."

She saw my surprise and quickly added, "Chinese! Of course, he must be Chinese. 'Citizen' does not mean Caucasian. But if he is not a citizen, you should immediately do number two. See here, you should have a baby. Boy or girl, it doesn't matter in the United States. Neither will take care of you in your old age, isn't that true?" And we both laughed.

"Be careful, though," she said. "The authorities there will ask you if you have children now or if you are thinking of having some. You must say no. You should look sincere and say you are not married, you are religious, you know it is wrong to have a baby."

I must have looked puzzled, because she explained further: "Look here now, how can an unborn baby know what it is not supposed to do? And once it has arrived, it is an American citizen and can do anything it wants. It can ask its mother to stay. Isn't that true?"

But that is not the reason I was puzzled. I wondered why she said I should look sincere. How could I look any other way when telling the truth?

See how truthful my face still looks. Why didn't I give this look to you? Why do you always tell your friends that I arrived in the United States on a slow boat from China? This is not true. I was not that poor. I took a plane. I had saved the money my first husband's family gave me when they sent me away. And I had saved money from my twelve years' work as a telephone operator. But it is true I did not take the fastest plane. The plane took three weeks. It stopped everywhere: Hong Kong, Vietnam, the Philippines, Hawaii. So by the time I arrived, I did not look sincerely glad to be here.

Why do you always tell people that I met your father in the Cathay House, that I broke open a fortune cookie and it said I would marry a dark, handsome stranger, and that when I looked up, there he was, the waiter, your father. Why do you make this joke? This is not sincere. This was not true! Your father was not a waiter, I never ate in that restaurant. The Cathay House had a sign that said "Chinese Food," so only Americans went there before it was torn down. Now it is a McDonald's restaurant with a big Chinese sign that says *mai dong lou*—"wheat," "east," "building." All nonsense. Why are you attracted only to Chinese nonsense? You must understand my real circumstances, how I arrived, how I married, how I lost my Chinese face, why you are the way you are.

When I arrived, nobody asked me questions. The authorities looked at my papers and stamped me in. I decided to go first to a San Francisco address given to me by this girl in Peking. The bus put me down on a wide street with cable cars. This was California Street. I walked up this hill and then I saw a tall building. This was Old St. Mary's. Under the church sign, in handwritten Chinese characters, someone had added: "A Chinese Ceremony to Save Ghosts from Spiritual Unrest 7 A.M. and 8:30 A.M." I memorized this information in case the authorities asked me where I worshipped my religion. And then I saw another sign across the street. It was painted on the outside of a short building: "Save Today for Tomorrow, at Bank of America." And I thought to myself, This is where American people worship. See, even then I was not so dumb! Today that church is the same size, but where that short bank used to be, now there is a tall building, fifty stories high, where you and your husband-to-be work and look down on everybody.

My daughter laughed when I said this. Her mother can make a good joke.

---

## Responding to Literature

1. Why was Lindo Jong unable to teach her daughter to have "Chinese character"?

2. Explain why this passage from Amy Tan's book is called "Double Face."

*For Further Reading*
Erdrich, Louise: *Love Medicine*
Helprin, Mark: *Winter's Tale*
Wilson, August: *Fences*

CHAPTER 23

# New Challenges

## January 20, 1981: Ronald Reagan Takes Office

On a balmy, overcast morning in Washington, D.C., Ronald Reagan awoke in Blair House, the U.S. government's official guest quarters. The date was January 20, 1981, the day Reagan would be sworn in as the 40th president of the United States.

The nation was changing more than its president on that January morning. It was leaving behind a frustrating decade and entering a new one that the president-elect hoped would become "a time of renewal." Left behind were the turmoil of a reeling economy and the discouragement of seeing the nation's power and influence decline throughout the world. Ahead, he hoped, were a renewed optimism and a more conservative approach to solving problems, which would restore the nation's prosperity.

Although the nation was hopeful as Ronald Reagan took the oath of office, in many ways the 1980s would be no less difficult than the preceding decade. The United States would continue its struggle to redefine its place in a new and rapidly changing world.

> *America was changing more than its president that January morning.*

© D. GOLDBERG, SYGMA

*The President and Mrs. Reagan accept congratulations at a gala inaugural ball.*

*Finally free after 444 days of captivity at the hands of anti-American Iranians, the hostages are treated to the traditional American celebration of courage and heroism--a ticker-tape parade through New York City.*

# Ford and Carter

## Winter 1973: Oil Embargo Fuels Gas Panic

DURING THE WINTER OF 1973–74, AN UNFA-MILIAR DRAMA WAS ENACTED AT GAS STA-TIONS ALL ACROSS THE UNITED STATES. FROM DAWN TO DUSK, CARS QUEUED UP AT the gas pumps, forming lines that often snaked down the street for blocks. Panicky motorists rushed to any gas station that had a supply, and they often had to wait for two hours or more. When they finally did reach the pump, they were often limited to buying only a few gallons of gas—and at a higher price! Even after the oil embargo was over, gas prices continued to rise. Another round of sharp increases occurred during the energy crisis of 1979. By the end of the decade, the price of gasoline was over one dollar a gallon, more than twice the 1973 price.

The competition for fuel frayed people's nerves and rattled their tempers. Drivers fought with one another, waved guns at harried service station employees, and sometimes even smashed gas pumps in rage and frustration. "These people are like animals foraging for food," said the owner of a station in Miami. "If you can't sell them gas, they'll threaten to beat you up, wreck your station, run over you with a car."

TED LAU, TIME MAGAZINE

A feeling of powerlessness intensified the motorists' anger. Political and trade decisions made halfway around the globe hindered their freedom to drive to work or the shopping center. The forces at work at the gas pumps would continue to overshadow American life throughout most of the 1970s: religious fervor and political unrest in the Middle East, the unstable politics that governed the international flow of oil, and a runaway U.S. economy.

## Ford Follows Nixon

When Richard Nixon resigned the presidency in disgrace, he left to his successor, Vice President Gerald R. Ford, a nation in crisis. American prestige had been battered by a humiliating defeat in Vietnam, and the American people were deeply shaken by the Watergate scandal.

Ford tried to pull the country together. On September 8, 1974, in an effort to consign the Watergate scandal to history, Gerald Ford pardoned Richard Nixon for any federal crimes he might have committed as part of the Watergate break-in and cover-up. The pardon outraged many Americans who strongly believed that all citizens, even the president, must be accountable to the Constitution and the laws of the land. Despite Ford's best intentions, the United States remained a troubled and divided nation.

### The Stagflation Dilemma

Perhaps the greatest obstacle to President Ford's effort to restore public faith in government was his inability to control the economy. Since the end of World War II in 1945, most Americans had become used to a rising standard of living. Now, however, two economic conditions that rarely occur at the same time shattered American prosperity: slowing productivity and rising inflation.

Industry had begun stagnating, or slowing down. During the 1970s industrial productivity—the rate of goods produced per hour— had slowed, causing the

---

cost of producing goods to rise. At the same time, foreign firms, especially those in Japan and West Germany, were able to manufacture high-quality goods quickly and inexpensively and to market them successfully in the United States. American consumers spent more on these high-quality, less expensive products, causing U.S. productivity to slow down even more.

The second cause of the American economic dilemma was the rise of **inflation**. As a result, the dollar fell in value against foreign currencies, and its purchasing power at home and abroad fell dramatically. A pair of gloves that once sold for $5 might now sell for $10. The annual inflation rate, which had been 3.3 percent in 1972, soared to 11 percent by 1974.

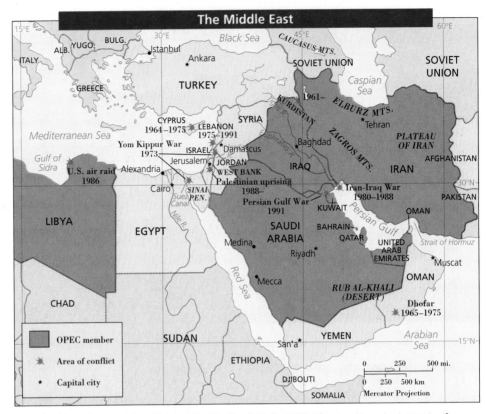

**The Middle East**

When the members of OPEC raised oil prices in 1973, they sent a message to the United States and the Soviet Union: third world countries would no longer cater to the needs of the superpowers. About 17 years later, Iraq's threat to oil supplies resulted in a massive U.S. military buildup in Saudi Arabia. *What Middle Eastern nations belong to OPEC?*

Economists referred to this combination of *stag*nating growth and spiraling in*flation* as **stagflation.**

**An Energy Crisis Is Born**  The major cause of the United States' inflationary spiral was an international oil crisis with roots in the turbulent politics of the Middle East. The U.S. economic machine demanded huge amounts of oil. Nearly one-third of that demand was being met by foreign suppliers—principally Arab nations.

Since 1960, many oil-rich nations in Africa, the Middle East, and South America had sold their oil as part of the Organization of Petroleum Exporting Countries (OPEC). OPEC countries set common prices and regulated production quotas and ceilings. This allowed them to control both the price and availability of oil throughout the world.

During the Yom Kippur War in 1973, between Israel and Syria and Egypt, Saudi Arabia imposed an **embargo,** or a restriction of trade, on oil shipped to Israel's allies, including the United States. At the same time, other OPEC countries nearly quadrupled their prices. Although the embargo was lifted in 1974, its economic effects continued through the end of the decade.[1]

**Wheels and Steel**  The oil embargo had a profound effect on the U.S. auto and steel industries. The big, gleaming cars produced in Detroit had long represented American know-how around the world. Now, more than any other product, they symbolized the United States' industrial decline.

When the Arab oil embargo and OPEC price increases hit the U.S. economy in 1973, most American

STUDY GUIDE

**Identifying Cause and Effect**
As foreign goods increased their market share in the United States, sales of domestic goods dropped. This resulted in decreased U.S. production and layoffs of American workers, which in turn meant increased unemployment. High unemployment meant American workers had less money to spend on consumer goods, which further slowed the economy and hastened the onset of recession.

1 Why was the United States' oil supply restricted?

TED THAI, TIME MAGAZINE

**Angry at the rapidly rising levels of imported cars in the United States, unemployed steelworkers in Fairfield, Alabama, vented their frustration by bashing this Toyota.**

*Why were Americans buying so many Japanese cars during the 1970s?*

Again, foreign steel manufacturers presented stiff competition. Because of their computerized and automated production facilities, they were able to keep production costs down. U.S. steel companies, whose plants were old-fashioned by foreign standards, saw their costs rise 10 percent a year, forcing them to raise the price of American steel. As a result, American manufacturers began buying nearly one-fifth of their steel from foreign producers. The steel industry appealed to Congress to use stiff quotas, tariffs, and other international agreements to set limits on imports.

car buyers wanted nothing to do with Detroit's oversized "gas-guzzlers." Many consumers switched to foreign cars, especially those manufactured in Japan. Imported autos, which held only a 17 percent share of the U.S. market in 1970, captured a whopping 37 percent by 1980. By that year, a dozen American auto plants had closed down and 300,000 auto workers had lost their jobs.

The steel industry came close to a complete collapse. In 1946 the United States provided 60 percent of the world's steel. By 1980 that figure had fallen to 14 percent, and steel executives questioned whether their industry could survive.

Congress refused, fearing retaliation by foreign governments against American trade.

**The President Responds**   President Ford decided that the economy could best be revived by attacking inflation. At press conferences, he wore a red and white lapel button emblazoned with the letters WIN, the acronym for "Whip Inflation Now." In addition he supported high interest rates, which made money more expensive for everyone to borrow, including the government. By tightening credit Ford hoped to reduce spending, which would result in an oversupply of goods and thus lower prices. Ford also clamped

---

★ ★ ★   **PRESIDENT'S GALLERY**   ★ ★ ★

*"I have not sought this enormous responsibility, but I will not shirk it. Those who nominated me and confirmed me as Vice President were my friends. . . . They were of both parties, elected by all the people and acting under the Constitution in their name. It is only fitting then that I should pledge to them and to you that I will be the President of all the people."*

*On Taking the Oath of Office, August 9, 1974*

COURTESY, GERALD R. FORD LIBRARY

*Gerald R. Ford*

Gerald R. Ford, 1974–1977

**Background:**
• Born 1913
• Republican, Michigan
• Served in the Navy 1942–1946
• Elected to House of Representatives 1948
• Succeeded to presidency 1974

**Achievements in Office:**
• Amnesty program for Vietnam War draft dodgers
• Council on Wage and Price Stability (1974)

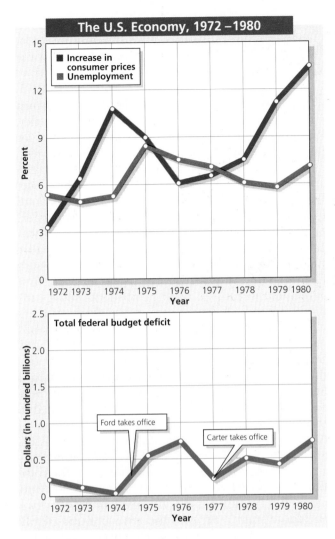

## The U.S. Economy, 1972–1980

- ■ Increase in consumer prices
- ■ Unemployment

*(Top chart: Percent vs. Year, 1972–1980)*

**Total federal budget deficit**

*(Bottom chart: Dollars in hundred billions vs. Year, 1972–1980)*

Ford takes office

Carter takes office

**Economic stagflation had begun when Nixon took power. Between 1974 and 1980, presidents Ford and Carter tried short-term methods of curing the economy's woes.** *According to the charts, what effect did these methods have on the U.S. economy?*

down on government spending by vetoing new health, housing, and education legislation.

The measures Ford took helped to cool inflation, which fell to 6 percent by 1976. However, as a result of Ford's restrictions, industrial production plummeted and unemployment rose. Before long, almost one out of every ten people was out of work. During 1974 and 1975, the country plunged into its worst **recession,** or economic slowdown, since the Great Depression.

## Carter Takes Charge

The struggling economy was the key issue as Americans went to the polls in 1976 to elect a president. Although Americans liked Gerald Ford well enough as a person, they rejected his leadership, especially his economic policies. James Earl Carter, a peanut farmer and former governor of Georgia, was elected the nation's 39th president.

Jimmy Carter knew that he had to cure the economic ills that were draining the nation's vitality. He tried to jolt the economy out of recession by increasing government spending and cutting taxes. Both measures were meant to stimulate economic growth. Unemployment came down, but inflation took off. For two years the annual inflation rate hovered above 10 percent.

Further fueling inflation was a dramatic OPEC price increase in 1979. The cost of a barrel of OPEC oil zoomed to $30, and another oil shortage ensued. Businesses, industries, and homeowners faced energy shortages, and once again motorists lined up at gas stations to buy expensive fuel.

Carter asked Americans to turn down their thermostats to 68 degrees in the winter, switch off unnecessary lights, and go "gasless" on Sundays. Businesses reduced their operating hours and schools extended vacations, all in an effort to conserve energy. As a result of these dramatic life style changes, Carter's approval rating fell to 26 percent, lower than President Nixon's had been at the darkest moments of his presidency. Americans were weary of want and sacrifice, and they directed their anger and frustration at Washington.[2]

## Human Rights and Foreign Policy

Standing up for **human rights** at home and abroad was the cornerstone of Jimmy Carter's foreign policy. A devout man, Carter tried to apply the religious principles that governed his private life to the conduct of public affairs. Like Woodrow Wilson early in the 20th century, Carter crafted a foreign policy based on the defense of basic rights and freedoms he believed should be available to all people throughout the world: the right to choose leaders in fair and honest elections, the right to a

and other nations refused to participate in the 1980 Olympic Games in Moscow, and, in addition, the U.S. government imposed a grain embargo on the Soviet Union.

**Playing the Peacemaker**   Carter's stand on human rights was reflected in other areas of his foreign policy. His primary goals were to foster peace and respect for other nations' sovereignty.

For example, Carter sought to slow down the arms race between the United States and the Soviet Union. American and Soviet negotiators worked hard to draft a treaty limiting the number of missiles, bombers, and nuclear warheads each side could stockpile. Finally, in June 1979 Carter and Soviet leader Leonid Brezhnev signed the second Strategic Arms Limitation Treaty (SALT II), expanding the first agreement negotiated during President Nixon's administration.

Continuing Nixon's policy of détente, Carter hoped to reduce the "balance of terror" between the United States and the Soviet Union. However, strong opposition to the SALT II agreement surfaced in the United States. Congress did not believe the limits set forth by the treaty could be verified. The treaty languished in the Senate. In response to the Soviet invasion of Afghanistan, Carter asked the Senate to delay consideration of the pact. In the end SALT II was never ratified.

Two other foreign policy initiatives illustrate Carter's approach to world affairs. Despite strong conservative opposition, the U.S. Senate ratified two Panama Canal treaties. One gave control of the Panama Canal to the Panamanian government by the year 1999. The second gave the United States the right to defend the neutrality of the canal.

Continuing President Nixon's efforts, Carter established normal diplomatic relations with communist China. In doing so, he cleared the way for valuable technical and commercial exchanges between the two formerly hostile nations.

**The Camp David Accord**   President Carter's most successful foreign policy initiative was to assist in forging a peace treaty between Israel and Egypt, two age-old enemies. In 1973 the fourth Arab-Israeli war broke out since the creation of Israel in 1948. When the hostilities finally ceased, a tense, bitter diplomatic

© ARTHUR GRACE, STOCK BOSTON

**Jimmy Carter's commitment to human rights included efforts to help disabled Americans, who fought for equal access in American society.**

fair trial, the right to worship and travel freely, the right to free expression.

When Carter thought a nation had violated the human rights of its citizens or those of another country, he spoke out strongly. This was particularly true of the Soviet Union. The Kremlin often punished **dissidents,** those who openly criticized Soviet policies. When Carter offered imprisoned or exiled dissidents his moral support, Soviet leaders accused him of meddling in their internal affairs.

In 1979 the Soviet Union invaded Afghanistan. Outraged at what he considered to be interference in the affairs of a sovereign nation, Carter ordered sanctions against the Soviet Union. The United States

---

STUDY·GUIDE

**Predicting Consequences**

Carter's firm stand on human rights meant harsh words and actions toward U.S. enemies. Given his tough standards, how would Carter treat the friends of the United States? The same, as two leaders found out. Both the Shah of Iran and President Somoza of Nicaragua enjoyed U.S. support, but both denied their own people basic human rights. During Carter's presidency both the Shah and Somoza were threatened by violent revolutions. Carter could have intervened. Instead he chose a hands-off policy, and both leaders were toppled.

stand-off ensued between the victorious Israelis and the defeated Egyptians.

In 1978 President Anwar al-Sadat of Egypt told American news reporter Walter Cronkite that he would do whatever he could to make peace with Israel. Carter then seized what he knew was a unique opportunity. In September of that year, Carter invited Israeli Prime Minister Menachem Begin and President Sadat to Camp David. For two weeks, Carter, Secretary of State Cyrus Vance, and others patiently talked the two leaders through their differences and tried to reconcile them. Finally Carter was able to make the historic announcement that the two leaders had constructed a "Framework for Peace." In March 1979, Begin and Sadat flew to Washington to sign the formal accord in the White House.

**The Iranian Hostage Crisis**   In February 1979 Shah Mohammad Reza Pahlavi, the absolute ruler of Iran and a close ally of the United States, was deposed in a revolution sparked by extreme liberal and conservative Iranians. Iran's new leader, Muslim cleric Ayatollah Ruhollah Khomeini, despised the United States for its political, financial, and military support of the shah.

On November 4, an armed mob stormed the U.S. embassy in Tehran, the capital of Iran, and seized diplomats and military personnel. Angry and frustrated, Americans stared helplessly at their television screens while an angry, chanting Iranian mob set up a giant poster that defiantly proclaimed in English, "U.S. Can Not Do Anything."

For many months, it seemed that the message on the Iranian poster told the truth. Finally, in April 1980, President Carter authorized a daring commando raid to rescue the hostages. The raid was a disaster for the United States. Encountering a violent dust storm over southern Iran, several of the helicopters ferrying the commandos to Tehran suffered mechanical failures. The raiders landed to assess the situation, and decided to scrub the mission. As the commandos beat a hasty retreat from the Iranian desert, a helicopter collided with a cargo plane, killing eight men and wounding five.

Months later Carter agreed to release $8 billion in Iranian assets he had ordered "frozen" in the United States at the start of the crisis. But it was not until January 20, 1981, President Ronald Reagan's inauguration day, that the hostages were freed.

## A New Sense of Limits

The United States' troubled economy and apparent weakening of power and influence in foreign affairs left many Americans troubled and pessimistic about the future. Throughout the 1970s, Americans faced change in nearly every facet of their lives. The nation that had sent men to the moon, the nation where everything had seemed attainable, was developing an unfamiliar sense of limits.

**The Polluting of America**   This sense was typified by a newly urgent concern for the environment. Environmentalists warned that the United States' natural resources were being abused and destroyed by two forces. The first was governmental reluctance to curb unrestricted industrial growth and commercial development. The second was the greed and unscrupulous actions of businesses that placed profit before responsibility. Environmental horror stories became front-page news. Birds hatched chicks deformed by severe genetic abnormalities. Commercial fishing crews returned from the deep oceans with

**★ ★ ★  PRESIDENT'S GALLERY  ★ ★ ★**

"Let us learn together and laugh together and work together and pray together, confident that in the end we will triumph together in the right. The American dream endures. We must once again have full faith in our country—and in one another. I believe America can be better. We can be even stronger than before."

*Inaugural Address,*
*January 20, 1977*

JIMMY CARTER LIBRARY

James Earl Carter, Jr., 1977–1981

**Background:**
- Born 1924
- Democrat, Georgia
- Graduated from the United States Naval Academy 1946
- Served in the Navy 1946–1953
- Elected state senator 1962
- Elected governor 1970

**Achievements in Office:**
- Negotiation of Israel-Egypt peace treaty (1978)
- Negotiation of SALT II treaty (1979)

catches contaminated by mercury and a wide variety of industrial chemicals. Oil spills fouled stretches of coastline with heavy crude that destroyed scenic beauty and sometimes killed the local wildlife.

Then in 1978 the problem hit home. The soil and groundwater of Love Canal, New York, a community near Niagara Falls, was found to be so polluted by poisonous chemicals from nearby industries that the Environmental Protection Agency (EPA) declared the entire town unfit for human habitation. The residents of Love Canal were evacuated, their homes boarded up, and the community sealed off by a tall, chain-link fence. The United States had its first toxic–waste ghost town.

Throughout the 1970s legislation was proposed to protect the environment. Congress toughened air pollution standards and imposed strict regulations on the logging industry. In 1972 the government told business and industry that the release of toxic waste into U.S. waterways must stop by 1985. To further improve water quality, the EPA distributed $19 million to local governments for the construction of waste treatment plants. In 1978 Interior Secretary Cecil Andrus extended for two decades restrictions against development on 40 million acres of federal lands in Alaska. In addition President Carter placed more than 100 million acres of Alaskan land under the federal government's protection as national parks, national forests, and wildlife refuges.

**The Nuclear Power Dilemma**  Environmentalists also objected to the spread of nuclear power plants throughout the United States. Well-organized protesters appeared in every part of the country to condemn the construction and operation of nuclear power plants. Although the protesters filed legal challenges, waged spirited public information campaigns, and sometimes resorted to civil disobedience, their concerns went largely unheeded—that is, until one fateful day in March 1979.

On that day a series of human and mechanical errors in the number two reactor of the Three Mile Island nuclear power station near Harrisburg, Pennsylvania, combined to produce the worst nuclear power accident in U.S. history. A nuclear reactor core overheated and released a wave of radioactive water and steam. Fearing a massive release of radiation, officials evacuated 100,000 nearby residents. The disaster never came, but the reactor, littered with radioactive debris, had to be shut down for six years.

The nuclear dilemma typified the difficult 1970s, a decade in which every advance harbored a setback and every promise included a threat. Looking back, some observers believe the decade forced a fundamental change in the American outlook, described by economist Robert Lekachman as "a shift from the easy politics of growth to the era of limits."

© DIRCK HALSTEAD, TIME MAGAZINE

**Jimmy Carter, a nuclear engineer himself, is briefed at Three Mile Island following a nearly catastrophic accident.**

## SECTION REVIEW

### Checking Facts
1. What is stagflation? What two conditions combine to cause it?
2. Explain the primary cause of inflation during the 1970s.
3. How did President Jimmy Carter respond to the Soviet invasion of Afghanistan?
4. How did the issues of the environment and nuclear power suggest some limitations of the American dream?

### Thinking Critically
5. **Identifying Cause and Effect** How did the Iranian hostage crisis and the failure of the rescue mission probably doom President Jimmy Carter's bid for a second term as president in 1980?
6. **Analyzing Decisions** Why might Gerald Ford have thought that pardoning Richard Nixon would have a positive effect on the American spirit?

### Linking Across Time
7. In 1936, President Franklin Roosevelt addressed an audience at Temple University. In his speech, F.D.R. said, "The truth is found when men are free to pursue it." How does this statement help to explain the fundamental basis for President Jimmy Carter's foreign policy some 40 years later?

# The Reagan Revolution

## October 1980: Reagan Campaigns in Illinois

THE GYMNASIUM OF EUREKA COLLEGE IN ILLINOIS WAS PACKED WITH STUDENTS EXCITEDLY WAVING BANNERS, CHEERING, AND SINGING. THE OCCASION ON THIS CRISP October evening in 1980 was an old-fashioned pep rally—and more. For there, joining the crowd in a chorus of "Neath the Elms," was Ronald Reagan. Reagan had graduated from Eureka nearly 50 years before. Now he was making a sentimental visit to his alma mater while campaigning for the presidency.

To enthusiastic applause, Reagan rose to address the throng. In his speech the candidate harked back to his youth in the small farm communities around Eureka. He told the crowd, "Everything good that has happened to me—everything—started here."

Reagan always presented himself as a man rooted in the wholesome values of an earlier time and place. Life was better back then, he suggested. People were good. They believed in family and trusted in God. They stood on their own two feet and wouldn't have the government meddling in their lives. People might have been poor, as Reagan had been, but they had faith and courage to see them through, and good neighbors to look after them if they needed help. With hard work and a bit of luck, a person could still improve his life and achieve the American dream, just as Reagan had.

EUREKA COLLEGE

Such a simple, sturdy United States existed only in myth. Nevertheless, the future president's poignant picture of it touched a deep longing in many Americans.

The sentimental feeling he evoked became more important than any single issue in Reagan's campaign. Here was a man with a vision of a good, simple past that could also be the future. He believed, and promised his audience that chilly night in Eureka, that it could be "morning in America" again.

## A Broad New Coalition

Reagan's race for the presidency came at a time when the country's mood was beginning to change. Many Americans were rejecting the strident protest movements and boisterous freedoms of the 1960s and the expensive government social programs of the 1970s. A powerful conservative groundswell had been building momentum for years.

The changing mood of the country found its voice in Ronald Reagan. He received support from nearly all

---

**As You Read**
Identify the political and religious coalition that supported the Reagan presidency and the domestic policies that shaped it. Also, think about the following concepts and skills.

**Central Concepts**
- recognizing that a **neoconservative** agenda marked the Reagan presidency
- understanding how **Reaganomics** affected the economy

**Thinking Skills**
- recognizing bias
- drawing conclusions
- predicting consequences

segments of American society: Democrats and Republicans, the rich and the poor, insiders as well as outsiders. This broad-based support swept Reagan into office with a mandate—an emphatic, clear order from the voters—to make changes in the way the nation was run. The people were eager for Reagan to deliver on his promise to "get the government off people's backs" and restore the old-fashioned virtues of the heartland.

**A New Conservatism**  As the 1980s began, many conservative Americans believed that equality had been carried too far in the 1960s and 1970s. They challenged the central beliefs of liberalism: that a fair and equal society can be achieved and that government ought to play a major role in guaranteeing and regulating it. These conservatives believed that the government had spent too much of the taxpayer's money; created bloated, inefficient bureaucracies; and kept the economy from flourishing on its own.

Those Americans most attracted by Reagan's appeal were also convinced that some problems just couldn't be solved, especially by the government, and must simply be accepted. Government, they believed, should withdraw from most areas of American life. People should behave with more restraint and discipline. Business and industry, in particular, should be freed from government restraint so they could become more profitable and thus strengthen the country. This was **neoconservatism**, a new type of conservatism. It signaled a return to the type of conservative thinking that was popular in the early years of the twentieth century.

**The Religious Right**  Neoconservatism was not the only new doctrine to gain favor during the 1970s. When President Jimmy Carter proudly proclaimed himself "born again," he spotlighted a major trend in American culture—the re-emergence of evangelical Christianity as a powerful religious and political force.

The most recent wave of evangelism began in the 1950s with the spiritual crusades of the Reverend Billy Graham. The movement grew rapidly in the 1960s and 1970s with the advent of television ministers—dubbed televangelists—who preached to huge home audiences via Christian television networks. By the middle of the 1970s, as many as 70 million Americans identified themselves as "born again."

© JOHN BRYSON, SYGMA

**Ronald Reagan appears with televangelist Jerry Falwell, top center, at a moral majority rally.**

In contrast to Jimmy Carter, a moderate political liberal, many evangelicals saw their religious zeal reflected in political conservatism. Like conservatives, they were morally opposed to drugs, pornography, abortion, and equality for homosexuals. They firmly rejected liberal social policies and strongly favored free enterprise and a foreign policy backed up by a strong military.

During the 1980 presidential campaign, a California-based group called Christian Voice flooded the Midwest and South with political literature. The group's candidate was Ronald Reagan. In fact, Reagan benefited more than Carter from religious political activism. Through Reagan, the evangelicals believed, Biblical principles could become law.

One of the most effective political organizations of the religious right was the moral majority, founded in 1979 by another televangelist, the Reverend Jerry Falwell. In a little over a year, the moral majority registered between 2 and 3 million new

STUDY·GUIDE

**Recognizing Bias**

Many of Reagan's domestic and foreign policies were inspired by the beliefs of the religious right. He opposed the Equal Rights Amendment for women. He desired a constitutional amendment banning abortion. He refused to address the AIDS epidemic. These decisions were supported by conservative Christians who believed in traditional Christian roles for women and who favored discrimination against homosexuals. Points of view other than those embraced by the religious right had little influence on Reagan's legislative agenda.

voters. Falwell and his associates enjoyed the confidence of President Reagan and exerted powerful political influence—that is, until the organization was disbanded in 1989. This followed a series of sex scandals and financial wrongdoings within other groups of the religious right that, in the minds of many Americans, had discredited the moral force of the entire movement.

**Shifting Political Allegiance**    Ronald Reagan's election triumph over President Carter was much more than a victory for neoconservatism and the religious right. It also represented a reshuffling of many historic voting patterns in the United States.

Reagan captured 44 of the 50 states, giving him 489 electoral votes to Carter's 49. The Republicans also captured the Senate. This landslide was primarily due to the force of Reagan's personality. Many voters simply liked him as a person, and they had enormous confidence in Reagan's ability to cure the nation's ills.

Reagan ran strongly in his own part of the country, the West and Southwest, where Republicans usually do well. However, he also captured the industrial states around the Great Lakes and in the Northeast, which had become Democratic strongholds. In those states, large numbers of voters became "Reagan Democrats." They were mostly blue-collar and ethnic voters who responded to his pledges to revive the economy, fight communism, and oppose abortion. The South was another Democratic stronghold, as well as being Jimmy Carter's native region. Yet Reagan, boosted by his support from the religious right, won every southern state except Carter's home state of Georgia. The aging of the American population also worked in Reagan's favor. Many older voters viewed the 69-year-old Reagan as a politician who would be sensitive to their needs.

## Reagan+Economics=Reaganomics

Ever since the 1930s, most American presidents had subscribed to the ideas of British economist John Maynard Keynes. Keynes believed that the key to stimulating an economy was government spending, which often required higher taxes.

Reagan and his advisors replaced this approach with what was called supply-side economics. The new theory argued that the key to economic vitality was reducing taxes, especially those on wealthy individuals and corporations. Lower taxes would encourage more saving and investment, which would lead to business expansion and more jobs. The result would be a larger supply of goods for consumers who, thanks to tax cuts, now had more money to spend.

Within months of taking office, Reagan got Congress to approve one of his biggest campaign promises: a major reduction of income taxes that favored, above all, the wealthiest Americans. That raised a tough question. Lower taxes meant less money flowing into the Treasury, but Reagan was also sharply increasing military spending. How was he going to balance the budget, as he had also promised voters?

His answer was to chip away at domestic programs. Welfare benefits and food stamp allocations were cut back. A million recipients of food stamps were removed from the government rolls. Fewer government grants and programs were available to revitalize big cities and pay for children's meals in the nation's public schools. Medicare benefits were slashed, requiring the elderly to pay more for health care. Many public service jobs disappeared. Unemployment compensation was reduced.

Most of the scaled-down programs had grown out of the liberal social agenda that had dominated

★ ★ ★  **PRESIDENT'S GALLERY**  ★ ★ ★

*"We are a nation that has a government—not the other way around. And this makes us special among the nations of the Earth. Our government has no power except that granted it by the people. It is time to check and reverse the growth of government which shows signs of having grown beyond the consent of the governed."*

*Inaugural Address,
January 20, 1981*

AP/WIDE WORLD PHOTOS

Ronald Reagan, 1981–1989

**Background:**
• Born 1911
• Republican, California
• Governor of California 1967–1975

**Achievements in Office:**
• Economic Recovery Tax Act (1981)
• Proposal for SDI (1983)
• INF Treaty with the Soviet Union (1987)
• Three appointments to Supreme Court

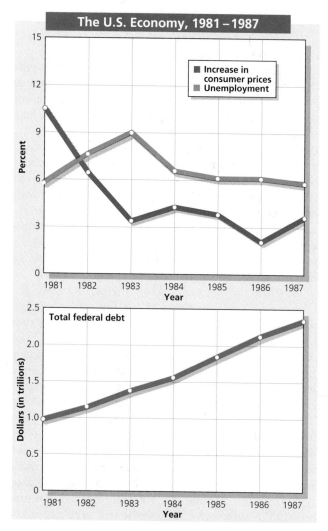

### The U.S. Economy, 1981–1987

**Total federal debt**

Reagan's economic policies halted runaway inflation and unemployment. At the same time, government spending—mostly on defense—outpaced revenues. The resulting deficit made people wonder if the prosperity of the Reagan years was built on borrowed money. *When did consumers see the benefits of Reaganomics?*

---

controlling the double-digit inflation of the Carter years. However, interest rates remained so high that many Americans could not afford to borrow money to make major purchases or expand businesses.

The nation slumped into another severe two-year-long recession as productivity declined. A third of the nation's factories and mines stood idle. Detroit's auto sales plunged to their lowest levels in two decades. By late 1982 unemployment had risen to nearly 10 percent of the labor force, or about 11 million people, the greatest number of unemployed since 1940.

Many farmers and businesspeople were caught in a bind. They had taken out loans at high interest rates during the 1970s, when prices were high. Now, with farm income down they could not make their payments. Many farmers lost their farms, sometimes after generations of family ownership. Business bankruptcies skyrocketed. During a single week in August 1982, a record 572 businesses failed, the highest weekly total since the Great Depression.

By the end of 1982, the tide turned. Interest rates dropped to about half of the all-time high of 21.5 percent it had hit in 1981. With interest rates falling, companies could afford to invest again. With inflation edging down, people could keep more of their tax cuts and buy houses, cars, and smaller consumer items like VCRs.

Unemployment was still above 9 percent in 1983, but increased business activity did create more jobs. Productivity turned upward. A cycle of growth was restored. In 1984 the gross national product increased by over 9 percent, the biggest one-year gain since 1951.

**The Drive to Deregulate** In Ronald Reagan's view, business and industry were hamstrung by government red tape. He believed this kept companies less profitable than they might otherwise be and accounted for some of the weaknesses in the American economy.

Reagan signaled that his administration would give companies more leeway to operate freely. He set up a President's Task Force on Regulatory Relief to advise him on how rules could be eased. He chose officials who shared his outlook to fill openings in the federal agencies that watched over various industries.

Soon the new approach took effect. The National Highway Traffic Safety Administration slowed its demands for air bags and tighter fuel-efficiency standards

---

presidential and congressional politics for decades. Cutting them back fit Reagan's conservative view that the government should be less involved in the lives of its people, even those people who needed help.[1]

**Recession and Recovery** Reagan's economic politics, dubbed **Reaganomics,** sparked a radical change in government fiscal policy. The policies succeeded in

---

for cars, requirements the auto industry had protested were too expensive. The Federal Communications Commission took a hands-off attitude toward cable television, allowing almost unrestricted growth in that new field.

At the direction of President Carter, Congress had begun to free the airline industry of regulations controlling its fares and routes. The Reagan administration strongly encouraged the process. Passengers reaped a bonanza of additional flights and cheaper fares as the airlines cut into one another's territory and waged bruising price wars. Away from the big cities, however, the effect was sometimes the opposite. Some small communities lost service altogether.

**The Environmental Rearguard** The restrictions that Reagan lifted from American industry were not all just red tape. Many regulations were aimed at preventing companies from polluting the air or water or dumping dangerous wastes. Thus Reagan's policy of deregulation ran smack up against the environmental movement that had made major gains in the 1970s.

To the environmentalists' dismay, Reagan often sided with business. He suggested that some risk or

damage to the environment was the price the country had to pay if it wanted companies to provide jobs, build up profits, and strengthen the economy.

Reagan's first Secretary of the Interior, the controversial James Watt, sharply increased the amount of public land that corporations could use for oil drilling, mining, and logging. The EPA eased the safety checks required on new chemicals and pesticides and relaxed its rules on the expensive pollution-control equipment that companies had to use.

The environment was one issue about which Reagan's economic philosophy seemed to put him out of step with most Americans. In a 1985 public opinion poll, two-thirds of the public rejected Reagan's approach, saying they would be willing to pay higher prices and even sacrifice some jobs in return for tighter limits on pollution.[2]

## Steadying the Conservative Course

In many ways Reagan's leadership and popularity unified the nation. But his policies increased long-standing divisions as well. Strains were soon showing between different economic and racial groups as well as between conservatives and liberals.

**Shortcomings of the Revolution** Reagan's tax cuts benefited everybody, but they benefited the rich most of all. At the same time, his cuts in social programs drove those at the bottom of the economy deeper into poverty, creating what social scientists

**EPA Budget**

Total U.S. Budget (percent)

1.0 0.9 0.8 0.7 0.6 0.5 0.4 0.3 0.2 0.1 0

1981 1983 1985 1987

Year

Although air and water pollution continued during the Reagan era—partly due to government deregulation of industry— the EPA budget dropped sharply during Reagan's first three years.

## STUDY GUIDE

**Predicting Consequences**
Government deregulation boosted business profits, but how would it affect business ethics? Most businesses continued to act responsibly. Some, such as the savings and loan industry, abused

their new freedom. By the late 1980s, thousands of S & Ls went bankrupt because of irregular and illegal business practices. The predicted cost to the taxpayers exceeded half a trillion dollars.

2 Describe Ronald Reagan's environmental policies.

called a new urban underclass. Reagan's critics charged that he was splitting the nation into a society of "haves" and "have-nots."

Many women voters had first been drawn to Reagan by his pro-family philosophy. Increasingly, however, they were put off by his lack of concern for women's issues. In 1983 the *New York Times* identified

© JOE TRAVER, GAMMA LIAISON

**In 1981 Arizona judge Sandra Day O'Connor became the first woman to serve on the Supreme Court. Reagan nominated her in part because of her conservative views.**

a "gender gap" in attitudes toward Reagan, as more women opposed his re-election.

Reagan's supporters and opponents alike worried about one spectacular failure of Reaganomics: its inability to produce a balanced budget. During the 1980 campaign, Reagan attacked Carter for spending $73.8 billion more than the government took in that year. By 1985, however, the deficit had zoomed to more than $212 billion. By the following year, Reagan had run up a greater total deficit than all the presidents in American history combined.

## A New Orientation on the Supreme Court

Reagan's conservative philosophy included passionate opposition to two major Supreme Court decisions—that prayer in public schools is unconstitutional and that women have a constitutional right to abortion. On both of these deeply emotional issues, Reagan sought Constitutional amendments that would reverse the court's decisions. Meanwhile, he waited for his chance to appoint justices who favored judicial restraint, and thus would leave policy making to the legislative and executive branches of government.

Reagan's first Supreme Court appointment was a historic one. In 1981 he named Sandra Day O'Connor the first woman justice in the Court's history. Later he appointed more justices, thus solidifying what appeared to be a conservative bloc.

The Supreme Court began to hand down some conservative decisions that pleased the president. For example, the Court modified and curtailed affirmative action hiring programs that had benefited minorities. It limited the rights of criminal suspects. It upheld the right of states to prohibit private homosexual sex between consenting adults.

Nevertheless, the court's new direction proved to be a slow drift toward conservatism, not a sharp turn. Moreover, at the conclusion of Reagan's presidency in 1989, the original school prayer and abortion decisions were still the law of the land.

## SECTION REVIEW

**Checking Facts**

1. What is neoconservatism?
2. How did Reagan's election reshuffle traditional U.S. political patterns?
3. How does Reaganomics differ from Keynesian economic theory?
4. How did deregulation affect the airline industry?

**Thinking Critically**

5. **Predicting Consequences** How might Reagan's environmental policies affect Americans and people around the world in the future?
6. **Drawing Conclusions** What were the effects on different groups of Americans of Reagan's economic policies? Of his social programs?

**Linking Across Time**

7. As U.S. businesses grew into large corporations in the late 1800s, the government helped them succeed by maintaining liberal immigration policies, by passing protective tariffs, and by granting land for railroads. Most leaders at that time regarded corporate and national interests as closely related. How did Ronald Reagan's economic philosophy reflect this view?

# The Cold War Reheats

## 1983: United States Invades Caribbean Island Nation

HAROLD HARVEY WAS JOLTED AWAKE AROUND 6:00 A.M. THE COMMOTION OUTSIDE SOUNDED LIKE SHOOTING AND EXPLOSIONS—BUT HOW COULD THAT BE? This was Grenada, a sleepy little tourist haven in the Caribbean. The last thing Harvey and the other American medical students at St. George's University expected to wake up to was gunfire.

Yet from their dormitory they could see jet fighters strafing the nearby airport. Artillery on the ground fired back. "Then I saw the paratroopers jumping," Harvey said. "It was really thrilling to see, kind of like an old John Wayne movie, but I knew people were going to get killed."

Suddenly, live bullets began crashing through the windows and walls of the dormitory rooms. Some students rolled under their beds; others took cover in bathtubs. "The worst thing," recalled student Stephen Renae, "was not knowing where the planes were from."

In fact, the planes were American. At dawn that day, a largely American attack force, launched from Navy ships off the Grenada coast, had invaded the island. Later, after the students had been safely evacuated, they learned the reasons for the fighting. President Reagan had been growing uneasy over an increasing Cuban and Soviet influence in Grenada, which he saw as a danger to American security in the

Caribbean. This extraordinary attack showed how far he was willing to go to demonstrate the United States' heightened hostility toward its cold war rivals.

## Challenging the Soviets

When Ronald Reagan was a young film actor in Hollywood, he played the part of a wild West hero in such films as *Santa Fe Trail* (1940) and *Law and Order* (1953). When he arrived in Washington in 1981, he brought with him some of the swagger and steely resolve of the western heroes he had portrayed on the screen.

Ever since his days as president of the Screen Actors' Guild, from 1947 to 1952 and again in 1959, Reagan had been a fervent anticommunist. During Congressional investigations into communist activity in the movie industry in the late 1940s and early 1950s, Reagan worked to expose suspected communists.

In 1982 Reagan told an audience that the Soviet Union was "an evil empire." It was, he said, "the focus of evil in the modern world." The president served notice on the Soviets that he intended to confront them whenever possible.

© MATTHEW NAYTHONS, GAMMA-LIAISON

© RANDY TAYLOR, SYGMA

---

**STUDY GUIDE**

### As You Read
Identify the foreign-policy trouble spots and triumphs that defined Ronald Reagan's presidency. Also, think about the following concept and skills.

### Central Concept
- understanding the **arms race** and how it changed during the Reagan presidency

### Thinking Skills
- predicting consequences
- drawing conclusions
- assessing outcomes
- recognizing points of view

**The Arms Buildup**   Reagan did not intend to craft a foreign policy that was all bluster with no backup. Although he preached economy in government and cut many domestic programs, he proposed the biggest arms buildup in American history. Reagan wanted to develop new weapons systems and enlarge the fleet. He said that military power would make the nation feel good again about itself and its place in the world. "America is back, standing tall," he said. The cost was a breathtaking $1.5 trillion over a five-year period.

While Reagan pressed for more planes, missiles, and ships, Soviet foreign policy strengthened his hand. The Soviet war in Afghanistan raged on. Soviet support for communist guerilla activity in Central America, Africa, and the Philippines remained active.

Two incidents in 1983 confirmed Reagan's worst fears about the Soviet Union. The first occurred in Poland, where a popular democratic revolution had been simmering for several years. The Polish government, near collapse from nationwide strikes, made dramatic concessions to workers, further emboldening them to reject communism and press for freedom. The Soviets, alarmed at the possibility of losing an important eastern European satellite, engineered the installation of a new, repressive government in Poland. Many leaders of the pro-democracy movement were jailed or lost their jobs. Some analysts think only the intervention of Pope John Paul II, himself a Pole, prevented Soviet military intervention.

In a second incident, the Soviets earned worldwide condemnation in 1983 for shooting down a Korean Airlines passenger jet that had accidentally entered Soviet airspace. The jet, attacked by a MIG fighter, plunged into the Pacific, killing all 269 passengers and crew.

**Negotiation Through Strength**   While building up America's military strength, Reagan offered the Soviets numerous proposals for controlling or reducing nuclear and conventional arms. The president believed that by making the United States strong and taking a hard line, he could intimidate the Soviets into concessions at the bargaining table.

For example, Reagan made a blunt offer to the Soviets. If they would agree to destroy some of their missiles aimed at western Europe, then the United States would call off the placement in western Europe of additional U.S. missiles targeted at the USSR. Talks on this question began in 1981. Dissatisfied with their progress, Reagan ordered the installation of more U.S. missiles in 1983. The talks collapsed, and it became clear to the Soviets that they were dealing with a tough negotiator.

Reagan's refusal to consider any unilateral, or one-sided, reduction of the American nuclear stockpile prompted an intense debate throughout the country during 1982 and 1983. Politicians, scientists, and church leaders formed a nuclear freeze movement, calling for a halt to the production and placement of nuclear weapons. In June 1982 one million Americans marched in support of the movement. The march was the largest peacetime protest ever staged by Americans.

**Star Wars**   Since the dawn of the nuclear age, the United States and Soviet Union had maintained a nuclear balance called mutual deterrence. The theory held that as long as both countries were targeted by accurate missiles capable of complete destruction, neither nation would ever start a nuclear war.

In 1983, however, President Reagan made a proposal that threatened to destroy the foundation of mutual deterrence by rendering Soviet missiles impotent. He urged a system of orbiting satellites that could fire laser beams to shoot down any Soviet missiles launched toward the United States. Reagan called the system the Strategic Defense Initiative (SDI). The press quickly dubbed it "Star Wars."

**This cartoon by Mark Alan Stamaty satirizes Reagan's defense buildup, especially his desire to expand U.S. nuclear forces.** *What does the middle panel suggest about nuclear strength and deterrence?*

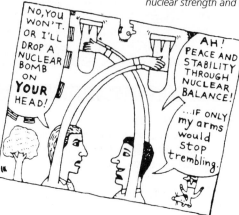

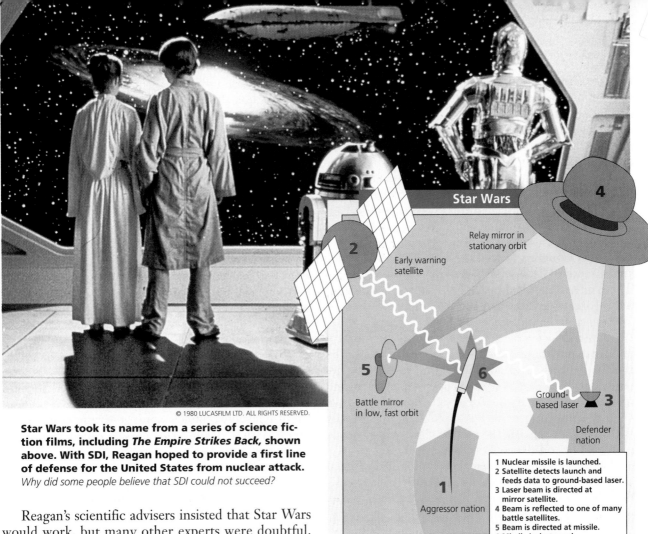

**Star Wars took its name from a series of science fiction films, including *The Empire Strikes Back*, shown above. With SDI, Reagan hoped to provide a first line of defense for the United States from nuclear attack.**
*Why did some people believe that SDI could not succeed?*

**Star Wars**

Relay mirror in
stationary orbit

2
Early warning
satellite

4

5
Battle mirror
in low, fast orbit

6

Ground-
based laser 3

Defender
nation

1
Aggressor nation

1 Nuclear missile is launched.
2 Satellite detects launch and
  feeds data to ground-based laser.
3 Laser beam is directed at
  mirror satellite.
4 Beam is reflected to one of many
  battle satellites.
5 Beam is directed at missile.
6 Missile is destroyed.

Reagan's scientific advisers insisted that Star Wars would work, but many other experts were doubtful. They maintained that such a technologically complex system could never be completely effective. In addition, the critics pointed out, the satellites would be vulnerable to attack themselves. Soviet leader Yuri Andropov argued that the Star Wars defense system would only speed up the **arms race,** opening the floodgates to "all types of strategic arms, both offensive and defensive." Despite such criticism, SDI found support and funding in Congress. **1**

## *Crises in Central America*

While the United States and the Soviet Union argued over nuclear arms, the cold war was heating up quickly in the United States' backyard. For many decades the United States had treated the nations of Central America with casual disdain. When the United States thought that invading or occupying a Central American country was in its interest, there was little these nations could do except protest. The United States encouraged democracy in Central America but was also willing to support corrupt dictators there who served U.S. interests.

Partly in response to U.S. support for repressive Central American governments, communist movements accompanied by armed guerilla resistance flourished throughout the region. Pointing to Soviet and Cuban involvement in these rebel movements, President Reagan made Central America a priority in his war against communism. "The national security of all the Americas is at stake in Central America," Reagan told a joint session of Congress in 1983. "If we cannot defend ourselves there, we cannot expect to prevail elsewhere."

---

**STUDY GUIDE**

**Predicting Consequences**
Reagan believed that the establishment of a communist government in any Central American nation would have dire consequences for the hemisphere. Such a nation might attempt to export its revolution to other nations. Further, a communist nation could be used as a conduit for arms shipments to leftist guerilas attempting to topple other governments.

**1** What risks did President Reagan take in pursuing SDI?

**El Salvador**   Soon after taking office, Reagan became concerned about the instability of the government in El Salvador, a country about the size of Massachusetts. The right-wing government, controlled by military officers and a small group of landowners, had come to power in a coup two years earlier. Now this government was shaky. Leftist guerillas were attacking government forces in the countryside, where peasant people had struggled in poverty for decades.

Fearing that another Central American country would go the way of communist Cuba, Reagan persuaded Congress to send military aid to El Salvador and American "advisers" to train Salvadoran soldiers. The United States had to act, he reasoned, because the Salvadoran guerillas had the backing of Cuba and Nicaragua, and ultimately of the Soviet Union.

Opponents of Reagan's policy claimed that poverty and government oppression were the real causes of the rebellion. The Reagan administration pressed the government of El Salvador to speed up its land reform and to outlaw the military "death squads" that roamed the country killing anyone they suspected of sympathizing with the guerillas. In 1982 these right-wing squads murdered up to 100 people a week.

With U.S. encouragement El Salvador held national elections in 1984 and elected a moderate civilian president, José Napoleón Duarte. Despite Duarte's attempts to further democratize that nation, the guerillas pressed their attacks, and the death squads continued to terrorize the people. American military and humanitarian aid continued but at reduced levels. Congressional leaders in the United States began to doubt that a solution imposed from the outside would ever solve El Salvador's internal political struggles.

**Grenada**   Located some 90 miles off the coast of Venezuela, the nutmeg-rich island of Grenada seemed an unlikely place for the cold war to get hot. Events began simmering when Maurice Bishop overthrew the government, installed his own leftist dictatorship, and aligned Grenada with Cuba and the Soviet Union. U.S. intelligence learned that Cuban troops were on the island building an airstrip capable of handling long-range jets. The Grenadan government claimed the airstrip was needed to handle increased tourism, but Reagan denounced the project as "the Soviet-Cuban militarization of Grenada."

In October 1983 Grenadan leftists, dissatisfied with Bishop's less-than-complete dedication to Marxism, staged an uprising on the island. Perhaps fearing trouble in their own countries, six neighboring Caribbean states asked the United States to intervene. On October 25 Reagan dispatched an invasion force to Grenada to oust the leftists and install a pro-democracy government.

Many nations were greatly disturbed by Reagan's decision to unleash American firepower against the tiny island nation. Some Latin American nations were especially outraged by what they perceived as yet another U.S. assault on their territorial integrity. In addition, American and foreign observers alike were bothered by what they saw as the apparent U.S. decision to use force instead of diplomacy in Latin America.

**Nicaragua**   Grenada wasn't the only Latin American nation where the United States looked to a military rather than a diplomatic solution. In Nicaragua, as in El Salvador, Ronald Reagan decided to fight communism with American military aid.

In Nicaragua the left-wing government was made up of Marxist revolutionaries who called themselves Sandinistas. In 1979 the Sandinistas, after years of guerilla warfare, had finally overthrown the brutal Nicaraguan dictator Anastasio Somoza. The Somoza family had ruled the country with iron fists and U.S. support since the 1930s.

Now the Sandinistas found themselves opposed by right-wing guerillas, including some former officers of Somoza's despised paramilitary National Guard. Not unexpectedly, President Reagan backed the right-wing guerillas, called contras, after the Spanish word *contra*, meaning "against." As part of a covert operation, the CIA trained and armed approximately 10,000 contras at bases in Honduras and Costa Rica.[2]

Reagan justified these actions by portraying Nicaragua as "a Soviet ally on the American mainland only two hours' flying time from our own borders." The Sandinistas were being aided by Cuban military advisers, medical experts, and teachers. In addition the Soviet Union was also sending aid, including such sophisticated weapons as fighter planes and attack helicopters. Intelligence reports also indicated that the Sandinistas were sending military aid to the leftist rebels in El Salvador.

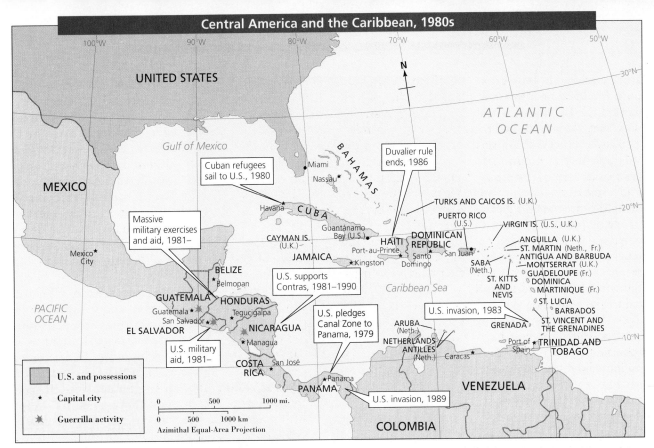

## Central America and the Caribbean, 1980s

UNITED STATES

ATLANTIC OCEAN

Gulf of Mexico

MEXICO

Mexico City

Cuban refugees sail to U.S., 1980

Duvalier rule ends, 1986

Miami

Nassau

BAHAMAS

Havana

CUBA

TURKS AND CAICOS IS. (U.K.)

PUERTO RICO (U.S.)

VIRGIN IS. (U.S., U.K.)

Massive military exercises and aid, 1981–

CAYMAN IS. (U.K.)

Guantánamo Bay (U.S.)

HAITI

DOMINICAN REPUBLIC

ANGUILLA (U.K.)

ST. MARTIN (Neth., Fr.)

ANTIGUA AND BARBUDA

JAMAICA

Port-au-Prince

Santo Domingo

San Juan

SABA (Neth.)

MONTSERRAT (U.K.)

GUADELOUPE (Fr.)

BELIZE

Belmopan

Kingston

U.S. supports Contras, 1981–1990

Caribbean Sea

ST. KITTS AND NEVIS

DOMINICA

MARTINIQUE (Fr.)

ST. LUCIA

GUATEMALA

HONDURAS

Tegucigalpa

U.S. pledges Canal Zone to Panama, 1979

U.S. invasion, 1983

BARBADOS

Guatemala

San Salvador

NICARAGUA

ARUBA (Neth.)

GRENADA

ST. VINCENT AND THE GRENADINES

EL SALVADOR

Managua

NETHERLANDS ANTILLES (Neth.)

Port of Spain

TRINIDAD AND TOBAGO

U.S. military aid, 1981–

COSTA RICA

San José

Caracas

PACIFIC OCEAN

PANAMA

Panama

U.S. invasion, 1989

VENEZUELA

COLOMBIA

- U.S. and possessions
- ★ Capital city
- ✳ Guerrilla activity

0     500     1000 mi.

0     500     1000 km

Azimithal Equal-Area Projection

**The central role that communist Cuba played in the Caribbean and in Central America made political instability in that region a major concern of President Reagan. He feared the domino effect—one nation after another falling to communism—in the Americas.** *Use this map to describe the U.S. role in Central America.*

As the CIA role in Nicaragua became more widely known, heated debate erupted in the United States. News emerged early in 1984 that the CIA had placed mines in the harbors of Nicaraguan ports and trained the contras to incite mob violence and to murder their political opponents. An angry Congress forbade any more military aid to Nicaragua. Congress relaxed its ban in 1986. By that time, however, Reagan's Nicaraguan policy was being undermined by allegations that the President and his aides had broken the law in their efforts to support the contra resistance.

## The Iran-contra Scandal

Throughout the summer of 1987, millions of Americans sat riveted to their TV screens, following one of those rare Congressional hearings that achieve major importance and high drama. The hearings reminded many viewers of another televised proceeding 14 years earlier, when the nation followed the unfolding events of the Watergate scandal.

Once again, as with Watergate, Congress was looking into wrongdoing by officials in the administration, including some close to the president. Once again, the abuses concerned officials taking the law into their own hands. Once again, the key question was: Who authorized the illegal activities? Specifically, was the president involved?

According to Hawaii Senator Daniel K. Inouye, co-chairman of the Congressional committee, the Iran-contra scandal was "much more serious than Watergate, not because of who was (or was not) involved but because of what was involved: the formulation and conduct of American foreign policy."

**Guns for Hostages**    The details of the Iran-contra scandal were complicated and murky. In essence, U.S. officials privately arranged arms sales to Iran, presumably with the hope that Iran would use its influence to

STUDY GUIDE

**Drawing Conclusions**
Some people thought that Iran-contra was more serious than Watergate because an important constitutional question was at stake. The separation-of-powers doctrine gives the president sole authority to make foreign policy. If the president's advisers operated without his knowledge or authority, then they, in effect, were making important foreign policy decisions. That was a clear and dangerous violation of the Constitution that could have had serious consequences for the United States.

free American hostages being held by pro-Iranian groups in Lebanon. This was at a time—the mid-1980s—when Washington was publicly condemning Iran as a terrorist nation and insisting that the United States would make no deals for the hostages' release. To make matters worse, profits from the arms sales were secretly funneled to the Nicaraguan contras to help finance their guerilla war against the Sandinistas. Congress had specifically forbidden any military aid to the contras.

These activities were carried out by the President's National Security Council (NSC), which was supposed to be a research and advisory body. An NSC aide, Marine Colonel Oliver North, and his boss, Admiral John Poindexter, ran the secret operation.

© JASON BLEIBTREU, SYGMA

**Like some latter-day cowboy, a Nicaraguan contra hoists his high-tech assault rifle. Such weaponry figured in the Iran-contra scandal.**

shredded evidence and altered crucial documents.

North was later tried and convicted of some of these offenses. So was Poindexter, who had made similar admissions. North was sentenced to community service, but later his sentence was set aside on appeal. Poindexter received a six-month jail term.

**Reagan's Role**   The report of the Congressional committees stopped short of accusing the president of wrongdoing, but it took a dim view of his hands-off management style. Reagan was portrayed as being "fuzzy" on specific details and out of touch with important activities within his administration.

The scandal made the president look bad either way. If he did not know what Poindexter and North were doing in his name, then, his critics contended, he must be incompetent. If he did know, then he was guilty of breaking the law forbidding military aid to the contras—a law which he himself had signed.

**North Steals the Show**   After initial denials, President Reagan finally admitted that arms had been sold to Iran, saying the purpose was to establish good relations with political moderates in that country. However, he denied any knowledge of money flowing to the contras. When Congress held hearings, Admiral Poindexter confirmed Reagan's account. Poindexter testified that he kept the President ignorant of the Iran-contra connection in order to protect him.

Despite Admiral Poindexter's sensational admissions, his aide, Colonel North, was unquestionably the star of the televised hearings. North portrayed himself as a simple patriot who, if he had erred, had done so out of his zeal to serve the nation and help the "freedom fighters" in Nicaragua. He admitted he had previously lied to Congress in order to mask his illegal activities. He further testified that he had

## Summitry Thaws the Cold War

A remarkable transformation in Soviet-American relations began to take shape at the beginning of Ronald Reagan's second term as president. The agent of change was Mikhail Gorbachev, a dynamic leader committed to reforming his country's collapsing economy and establishing productive ties with the West. The setting for this transformation was a series of summit meetings between President Reagan and General Secretary Gorbachev.

STUDY GUIDE

**Assessing Outcomes**

Did the sentences handed down to North and Poindexter send the wrong signals to future presidential advisers? Some people argued that the relatively light sentences handed out implied that

politically desirable ends justify whatever means were necessary to achieve them. Had the sentences been harsher, future presidential staffs might be less likely to engage in similar covert and

illegal operations. Given the nature of the sentences, the message appeared to be that such operations will be tolerated, despite the important constitutional questions involved.

**Ice Breaking**   Ronald Reagan and Mikhail Gorbachev first met on a cold morning in November 1985, in Geneva, Switzerland. Publicly, their manner was friendly. Privately, their exchanges were direct, at times even undiplomatic. Their two days of talks produced no breakthroughs. Gorbachev held to his view that outer space should be weapon-free. Reagan stood firm, reserving the right of the United States to implement SDI as protection against Soviet missiles. Yet, the meeting in Geneva was a success. It initiated a thaw in the cold war. The meeting gave the world hope that although each of the two superpowers possessed the ability to destroy the world, neither had the will to do so.

In October 1986 the two leaders met again, this time in Reykjavik, Iceland. At this meeting, Gorbachev unveiled a broad range of new arms control proposals covering topics such as long and medium-range missiles and SDI. Reagan and his advisers were stunned by the sweep of Gorbachev's proposals. In an attempt to capture an historic opportunity, both sides worked long beyond the scheduled close of the meetings. Neither Reagan nor Gorbachev, however, would compromise on the issue of weapons in space. In the end this second meeting produced no agreement.

**Arms Cuts**   Reagan and Gorbachev met twice more to discuss arms control. In December 1987, Gorbachev and his wife Raisa visited Washington. In late spring 1988, the Soviets hosted the Reagans. At both meetings, style overshadowed substance. Americans caught "Gorbymania"; Soviets marvelled at Ron and Nancy in Red Square.

Yet, in the midst of the social activities the Intermediate-range Nuclear Forces (INF) treaty went into effect in June 1988. The treaty was the first agreement of its kind; it aimed to reduce the number of nuclear missiles in each superpower's arsenal. Although covering only one type of missile, the treaty cleared the way for later arms pacts. The meetings had other outcomes as well, for Reagan and Gorbachev laid a foundation for further discussions between the two powers concerning cultural and scientific cooperation.

The INF treaty was perhaps the greatest foreign policy triumph of Ronald Reagan's presidency.

Ironically, his victory sprang from what may have been Reagan's most obsessive fear—Soviet communism. After escalating the arms race and increasing tensions between the superpowers, Reagan concluded his tenure as president on much friendlier terms with the Soviets. Reagan had gone further than any previous president in stabilizing Soviet-American relations.

**The 1988 Election**   As Reagan's second term drew to a close, the election campaign for his successor heated up. The Republicans' clear choice to follow him was his vice president, George Bush. In the Democratic Party, several candidates vied for the nomination. Among the candidates who made a strong showing in primary elections was Jesse Jackson. During the 1960s Jackson had worked in the civil rights movement with Martin Luther King, Jr. Along with the support of many African Americans, Jackson attracted a "rainbow coalition" of supporters from various ethnic groups. Jackson's supporters believed his candidacy addressed problems such as homelessness, unemployment, and inequality generally avoided by the other major-party candidates.

Although Jackson won several primaries, he did not gain enough support to clinch the nomination. Ultimately the Democrats nominated Michael

© DIRCK HALSTEAD, TIME MAGAZINE

**During the 1988 primaries, Jesse Jackson visited a soup kitchen in Middletown, Connecticut, promising help for the poor and unemployed.**

## STUDY GUIDE

### Recognizing Points of View

Why was Reagan so intent on developing SDI? Why was Gorbachev so intent on seeing it stopped? Reagan believed SDI was the most important bargaining chip he had in dealing with the Soviets. Without the threat of SDI, the Soviets might be less willing to negotiate. For his part, Gorbachev knew the Soviet economy would collapse if he had to devote huge sums of money to developing a military response to SDI. Without SDI to worry about, the Soviets could spend less on weapons and more on rescuing their faltering economy.

Dukakis, governor of Massachusetts. One reason for choosing Dukakis was his reputation for having brought about the so-called "Massachusetts Miracle" of economic recovery from the deep economic recession of the early 1980s.

**The Presidential Race** Dukakis faced an uphill battle because he was not widely known and his positions on domestic and foreign policies had to be presented and clarified.

Bush was well known but entered the race with advantages and disadvantages. The country was at peace and generally prosperous. Bush had been a part of a popular administration, and it was to his advantage to continue most of Reagan's policies. Bush, however, faced a number of problems that had begun to emerge during Reagan's second term. Many Republicans had been defeated in the congressional elections of 1986, a sign that many voters were wearying of a conservative government. Confidence in the ongoing prosperity of the country was shaken on October 19, 1987, when the stock market fell an astounding 508 points—about 22 percent. And, like Watergate more than a decade earlier, the Iran-contra scandal had suggested that illegal activity was no stranger to the Oval Office. Bush would have to disassociate himself from these difficulties and make voters see him as an independent leader.

**Electronic Campaigning** In 1988 both candidates made extensive use of **electronic campaigning,** a campaign strategy that uses television, video, and satellite technology to sway voters. Electronic campaigning had its roots in the 1960 Kennedy-Nixon

WORLD WIDE PHOTOS

**In 1992 George Bush won the votes of most Reagan supporters.**

debates. These debates made it clear that once candidates began to campaign on television, the impression they made onscreen could influence voters as much as—or perhaps even more than—their positions on issues. Both Bush and Dukakis relied heavily on expert consultants to produce expensive, carefully scripted television commercials and promotional materials for their campaigns. The candidates were packaged and promoted as if they were consumer products —laundry detergent or breakfast cereal. The campaign did little to bring the candidates into focus for the electorate. Instead of concentrating on the issues, TV ads often became personal attacks on the opposing candidate. As a result, 1988 has been called "the year of the negative ad campaign."

Although Dukakis led Bush by 17 percent in an opinion poll taken in July 1988, the Bush campaign fought back. The Republicans ran ads with the message that Dukakis would be ineffective at dealing with crime. The ads featured an African American named Willie Horton, who was furloughed from prison by Dukakis and soon after committed a rape. Bush won an election victory almost as big as Reagan's two earlier triumphs. Bush carried 40 states, giving him 426 electoral votes to 112 for Dukakis. The polling results showed that 85 percent of those who had supported Reagan also voted for Bush. George Bush, who claimed Texas as his home, won in the South, as had Reagan. Bush also attracted enough "Reagan Democrats" to capture northern industrial states like Michigan and Ohio. The voters seemed to be saying that they not only wanted Bush for president, but also that they wanted him to continue Reagan's policies.

## SECTION REVIEW

**Checking Facts**

1. What incidents in 1983 convinced Americans that the Soviet Union had hostile intentions toward the rest of the world?
2. What is SDI ?
3. Why did Congress reduce aid to El Salvador?
4. Who were the contras?
5. Describe the Iran-contra guns-for-hostages deal.

**Thinking Critically**

6. **Drawing Conclusions** How free and autonomous were the governments of Central American and Caribbean nations during the Reagan administration? How heavily did U.S. policies influence their actions?
7. **Assessing Outcomes** How did the summits between Reagan and

Gorbachev begin a new chapter in Soviet-American relations?

**Linking Across Time**

8. Gorbachev took Reagan by surprise at the Reykjavík summit with his sweeping proposals. How was Gorbachev different from previous Soviet leaders such as Nikita Khrushchev?

The election of Ronald Reagan proved the accuracy of predictions that his personality and brand of politics were what Americans wanted in 1980. Candidates for public office and the political leaders who help select them make many decisions based on how they think voters will respond. Predicting the responses of individuals and communities can be useful in other situations, too.

## Learning the Skill

Many people like to imagine what the future will bring. However, accurate predictions of the future depend on gathering reliable facts and observing past behavior patterns in similar situations.

In the following exercise, you will predict the outcome of the 1980 presidential election using information available at that time. The chart at the right presents some of the events that politicians in 1980 used to make their predictions. Use the following steps to make realistic predictions:

1. Review what you already know. Making a list of facts and events like the one on this page can help you understand some of the important events of the 1970s and how they affected people.
2. Define and analyze patterns. Try to determine what the facts tell you about the 1970s. Notice that this series of events left Americans feeling angry, frustrated, and helpless about the economy, their leaders, and the nation's identity
3. Incorporate your knowledge and observations of similar

situations. Republican party leaders knew from other experiences that voters suffering through hard times often responded to patriotic messages. After a decade of political disappointments, Republicans knew that a call for a stronger government would play well with many voters.
4. Make a prediction. In 1980 Republican leaders correctly predicted that a candidate who promised to "restore America's strength and pride"—namely Ronald Reagan—would attract a majority of voters.

## Practicing the Skill

Now apply the steps described above to another situation. A major issue during Reagan's term was the U.S. role in the conflict between the Sandinistas and the contras in Nicaragua. Explain how you might have predicted Congress's decision on this matter.

For steps 1 and 2, review materials on pages 768–769. For step 3, incorporate information about a situation similar to Nicaragua, the U.S. position in Vietnam.

© JOHN NEUBAUER, FPG INTERNATIONAL

| Making Predictions | |
|---|---|
| **Facts** | **Observations** |
| The OPEC oil embargo caused inflation and a shortage of fuel. | Americans felt helpless and angry. |
| President Ford vetoed programs in health, housing, and education to reduce government spending and fight inflation. | Many people lost jobs; Americans suffered the worst recession in 40 years. |
| President Carter increased government spending and cut taxes, ending the recession and reducing unemployment. | Americans lost spending power as inflation rose. |
| Carter called on Americans to conserve energy and work toward energy self-sufficiency. | Americans felt frustrated at being asked to bear such a great burden. |
| To conserve energy, Americans bought smaller, imported cars. U.S. automakers lost sales to Japanese and German makes. | American workers suffered unemployment as several automobile plants closed and their materials suppliers lost business. |
| Americans were taken hostage by Iranians. A rescue attempt 5 months later failed. The hostages were released after 14 months only when Carter unfroze Iranian assets. | Americans saw their leaders forced to give in to terrorist demands. |

# The Rap on the Eighties

*During the eighties, Americans focused on their own comfort and appearance, trying to live well and look good. Images in magazines, television commercials, and billboard advertisements everywhere reflected the ideal life style and appearance. People tried to attain these ideals by working harder, adopting more healthful habits, sporting the newest fashions, and buying the latest electronic gadgets.*

Although the provocative political and social messages in **rap music** alienated many people, those it did appeal to were from a variety of social and economic backgrounds. Most rap fans enjoyed the image of power, independence, and arrogance projected by flamboyant rappers.

**Shopping malls** gave people immediate and easy access to a variety of consumer goods and services. As a result, malls often replaced downtown areas as both shopping and social centers.

Musicians from South Africa to Australia staged concerts to finance the fight against environmental problems and world hunger. **"Live Aid"** was the first hugely successful concert of this kind.

The abuse of cocaine, especially crack, soared as people took comfort from the illusion of control that it offered them. In response to the problem, people all across the nation told American youths to **"just say no,"** a phrase coined by then First Lady Nancy Reagan.

In addition to **spiking, dyeing, or bleaching their hair,** some people paid as much as $30 to have the hair on the sides of their heads shaved into designs or words. A haircut like this one typically took about one hour to create.

**Competition to** get into the most prestigious universities increased as an increasing number of employers required their employees to have college educations.

# Chapter 23 Review

| 1973 Supreme Court legalizes abortion. | August 1974 Nixon resigns. Gerald Ford assumes presidency. | | November 1979 Americans are taken hostage in Iran. | April 1980 U.S. raid to free hostages fails. |

**1973** | **1974** | **1975** | **1976** | **1977** | **1978** | **1979** | **1980** | **1981**

1973
Saudi Arabia imposes oil embargo on U.S.

November 1976
Jimmy Carter is elected 39th president.

March 1979
100,000 flee nuclear accident at Three Mile Island, Pennsylvania.

January 1981
Ronald Reagan is sworn in as 40th president.

## Summary

Use the following outline as a tool for reviewing and summarizing the chapter. Copy the outline on your own paper, leaving spaces between headings to jot down notes about key events and concepts.

**I. Ford and Carter**
  A. Ford Follows Nixon
  B. Carter Takes Charge
  C. Human Rights and Foreign Policy
  D. A New Sense of Limits
**II. The Reagan Revolution**
  A. A Broad New Coalition
  B. Reagan + Economics = Reaganomics
  C. Steadying the Conservative Course
**III. The Cold War Reheats**
  A. Challenging the Soviets
  B. Crises in Central America
  C. The Iran–contra Scandal
  D. Summitry Thaws the Cold War
  E. The 1988 Election

## Ideas, Events, and People

1. Explain stagflation and its effect on the economy during the Ford administration.
2. Why did Gerald Ford pardon Richard Nixon? How did the pardon affect the American people?
3. How did Jimmy Carter respond to the Soviet invasion of Afghanistan?
4. Why was the Senate reluctant to ratify the SALT II treaty?
5. During the 1970s, what environmental problems most concerned the American people? How did the government respond to these environmental concerns?
6. How did Reaganomics differ from Keynesian economic theories?
7. How did President Reagan's deregulation policies affect the environment?
8. What was the Strategic Defense Initiative? Why did U.S. critics oppose it?
9. How did Ronald Reagan's foreign policies address communism in El Salvador? In Nicaragua? In Grenada?
10. How did the Iran–contra scandal affect Ronald Reagan's presidency?

## Social Studies Skills

### Making Predictions

How do you think future historians will rate Gerald Ford, Jimmy Carter, and Ronald Reagan as presidents? After carefully considering the material in sections 1, 2, and 3, which president do you think will be rated the most successful politically? Who do you think will be most admired as a person? Which president will be judged as having best represented American values and ideals? Be sure to back up your predictions with solid evidence from the text.

## Critical Thinking

### 1. Comparing and Contrasting

Compare and contrast the foreign policies of Presidents Jimmy Carter and Ronald Reagan. What was the cornerstone of each president's foreign policy? In what ways did each president succeed? How did each fail? Looking back, which president's foreign policies seem to have been more effective?

### 2. Analyzing Behavior

In the 1980 presidential election, Ronald Reagan surprised political analysts by capturing the votes of many Democrats. Why did so many Democrats vote for a Republican presidential candidate in 1980?

**June 1982**
One million Americans march for nuclear freeze.

**November 1984**
Reagan is reelected to second term.

**Summer 1987**
Iran–contra hearings begin on Capitol Hill.

**November 1988**
Bush defeats Dukakis in presidential election.

| 1982 | 1983 | 1984 | 1985 | 1986 | 1987 | 1988 | 1989 | 1990 |

**October 1983**
U.S. invades Grenada; installs pro–U.S. government.

**November 1985**
First Reagan–Gorbachev summit takes place in Geneva, Switzerland.

**October 1987**
Stock market plunges 508 points in one day.

# Extension and Application

### 1. Citizenship

Two critical issues that spanned the Ford, Carter, and Reagan presidencies still affect the United States today: energy conservation and the protection of the environment. As a class prepare a pamphlet titled *Conserving America's Future*. The pamphlet should be divided into two sections. In the first section, explain the importance of energy conservation and list the ways each citizen can conserve energy. This section might also discuss several alternative energy sources, such as solar and geothermal power. The second section should summarize the most important environmental issues facing the nation in the 1990s. The pamphlet should conclude with a list of suggestions for conservation at the local and national levels and general rules for responsible care of the United States' environment.

### 2. Global Connection

During the 1970s, 1980s, and 1990s, citizens of the United States were frequent targets of international terrorism abroad because of U.S. foreign policies. Many other countries, however, were also plagued by attacks from dozens of terrorist groups—each fighting for its own cause. Conduct research on the rise of international terrorism during these two decades. Use your research to prepare a brief report explaining how terrorist activities around the globe affected people and their governments. Be sure to discuss how the affected nations attempted to combat terrorism.

### 3. Linking Across Time

On December 29, 1940, with the German army on the march throughout Europe, President Franklin Roosevelt told the American people, "We must be the great arsenal of democracy." Discuss this statement in class. What do you think Roosevelt meant at the time he made this statement? Is the United States still the great arsenal of democracy today? In what ways? Does the word "arsenal" refer only to military might, or does it have another meaning?

### 4. Cooperative Learning

Hold a mock debate in class between former presidents Gerald Ford, Jimmy Carter, and Ronald Reagan. The subject of the debate will be the U.S. economy. Select three students to play the parts of the presidents. Then organize the rest of the class into research and debate-preparation teams—one for each of the three presidents. The researchers must locate as much information as possible on the economic policies of the president to whom they've been assigned. Then the debate-preparation teams should organize information on 3-by-5-inch note cards for their president to use as a reference during the debate. During the discussion, each president should address the following issues: my economic policies; how these economic policies affected the American people; why the policies failed or succeeded.

# Geography

1. Why were the Middle East nation's able to create an energy crisis in the United States?
2. To which countries in Central America did the United States send troops during the 1980s? What were the objectives of these military maneuvers?
3. What larger concerns about Central and South America motivated Reagan's support for the Nicaraguan contras?
4. How did the sale of arms to the Middle East contradict Reagan's stated Middle East policy?

CHAPTER 24

# A Changing Nation in a Changing World

## Summer 1992: Athletes Meet in Barcelona

An arrow arced across the night sky to light the torch that opened the Games of the 25th Olympiad. Almost 11,000 athletes from a record 172 countries met in Barcelona, Spain, to compete for coveted Olympic medals. From start to finish, the games reflected the historic changes that had taken place in the world in recent years. At the opening ceremony, one of the first teams to enter was from South Africa, a country not represented in 32 years. The Soviet Union, which ceased to exist in 1991, was represented by the Unified Team of athletes from now independent republics.

Athletes from other countries also mirrored the cataclysmic changes around the world since the 1988 Olympics. For the first time since 1936, Germans from the east and west competed for the same country. Germany, divided for almost 45 years, was unified in October 1990.

The winning team in the 102.8K cycling event was made up of two "Ossis," former East Germans, and two "Wessis," West Germans. All four men—Uwe Peschel, Michael Rich, Christian Meyer, and Bernd Dittert—were excited to be gold medalists. Willi Daume, president of the German National Olympic Committee, however, saw more than an athletic victory when he said: "This gold medal is the most important of all those we could win. This achievement is proof that East and West can work together harmoniously as one team."

> *"This achievement is proof that East and West can work together."*

LIONEL CIRONNEAU, AP/WIDE WORLD PHOTOS, INC.

*Two former East Germans and two West Germans cycled to victory as a team in the 1992 Olympics.*

© R. BOSSU, SYGMA

*At midnight on November 9, 1989, East German officials opened the hated Berlin Wall that divided East and West Berlin for 28 years. As East Berliners streamed freely into West Berlin, it seemed that a new world was being born.*

# After the Cold War

## May 6, 1992: Gorbachev Comes to Fulton, Missouri

THE SPRING SUN SHONE DOWN ON THE CAMPUS OF WESTMINSTER COLLEGE IN FULTON, MISSOURI, ON THE MORE THAN 10,000 PEOPLE GATHERED THERE. THEY had come to hear a speech by Mikhail Gorbachev, former president of the Soviet Union.

One student, Carolyn O'Donley, basked in the thrill of seeing a major historical figure on her campus of just 750 students. "Gorbachev and his wife, Raisa, walked through the crowd shaking people's hands," she said. "Everyone was very excited—it was a very positive feeling to have them here." She added, "I think there were reporters from every country in the world, too."

The reporters were there to cover more than a speech, for Gorbachev was in fact the second major historical figure to visit the school. In 1946—before any of today's students were born—Winston Churchill, prime minister of Great Britain during World War II, had spoken at Westminster. In a famous speech, Churchill warned of the onset of the cold war and of Soviet oppression in Europe. "From Stettin in the Baltic to Trieste in the Adriatic an iron curtain has descended across the continent," Churchill said.

Now Gorbachev—who did more than any other person to end the cold war and lift the iron curtain from Europe—looked out on the sea of faces assembled. He picked up on Churchill's theme when he said that the world was no longer divided between East and West, but "between the rich and the poor countries, between the North and the South." People in the crowd applauded enthusiastically, as they did

SPENCER TIREY, AP/WIDE WORLD PHOTOS, INC.

throughout his speech. Some had camped overnight on the college's lawn to get a good seat for the event.

A statue of Churchill and a slab of the former Berlin Wall also stood onstage. The eight sections of the wall, with their riot of colors, graffiti, and shapes, contrasted with Gorbachev's calm voice. Like Churchill before him, Gorbachev warned the world about imminent dangers. "We live today in a watershed era," he cautioned about the end of the cold war. "One epoch has ended and a second is commencing. No one yet knows how concrete it will be—no one." He called for strict controls on nuclear and chemical weapons and for protection of human rights.

Gorbachev blamed both his own country and the United States for the hostilities of the cold war. He looked to the future when he added a warning for all: "It is quite clear that the enhanced integration and interdependence of the world at the same time creates new tensions."

## Arms Reductions

In speaking of new tensions, Gorbachev alluded to the old tensions between the two superpowers, which had neared their peak in the early 1980s. Ronald Reagan and his chief aides believed passionately that Soviet imperialism must be resisted by keeping American military forces in high gear. George Bush, Reagan's successor, also continued to press the merits of democratic capitalism around the globe and to speak out vigorously against communism. Bush, too, believed in bargaining from a position of military strength.

---

### STUDY GUIDE

**As You Read**

Identify the key events and trends in world politics in the late 1980s and early 1990s. Also, think about the following concepts and skills.

**Central Concepts**

- recognizing the effects of Gorbachev's policies of **glasnost** and **perestroika** on the Soviet Union and elsewhere
- recognizing how the cold war's end changed U.S. foreign policy

**Thinking Skills**

- analyzing behavior
- predicting consequences
- recognizing points of view

By late 1989 the Reagan and Bush strategy produced results. Presidents Bush and Gorbachev met aboard a ship in the Mediterranean Sea near the island of Malta to discuss ending the arms race. Less than a year later, the superpowers agreed to limit their troops and conventional forces in Europe, reduce stockpiles of nuclear weapons, and dismantle 30 percent of their long-range nuclear missiles.

As American fears of Soviet expansionism lessened, the United States withdrew all land- and sea-based tactical nuclear weapons in Europe and Asia. Bush also ordered the Air Force's Strategic Air Command to relax its 24-hour-a-day combat-ready status. Gorbachev called Bush's order a "great event," then raised the stakes: he ordered the destruction of all Soviet short-range nuclear missiles and halted nuclear testing for one year. In October 1991 NATO leaders responded by cutting their nuclear forces in Europe by 80 percent. Such cutbacks offered relief to both sides after a decade of unprecedented military buildups in peacetime.

## The Downfall of Communism

When the Soviet Union, which considered itself the beacon of the world communist movement, began to falter in the late 1980s and then collapsed in 1991, the repercussions were enormous. As Soviet leader, Mikhail Gorbachev launched policies of **glasnost,** and **perestroika**—openness and restructuring—that lodged deeply in citizens' minds. Anti-communist revolutions swept Eastern Europe after 1989. Western aid to these emerging democracies, pegged at $24 billion in 1992, seemed too much to some Westerners but far too little to those suffering hardship in struggling new democracies.

© SHONE, GAMMA-LIAISON

**Soviet citizens could vote for non-communists for the first time in 1989, breaking down the USSR's one-party system (right). Two years later, crowds toppled statues of Lenin and other ex-leaders in disgust (above).**

© A. NOGUES, SYGMA

**Breakup of the Soviet Union** When he took office in March 1985, Gorbachev confronted a faltering Soviet economy. He hoped to improve everyday life for Soviet citizens and get more consumer goods into the shops by easing the central government's near-total control over the economy. Communist Party loyalists, however, feared for their jobs and special privileges. It was this faction—the Soviet Union's political elite—that plotted a coup against Gorbachev in August 1991.

★ ★ ★  **PRESIDENT'S GALLERY**  ★ ★ ★

*"Some see leadership as high drama, and the sound of trumpets calling, and sometimes it is that. But I see history as a book with many pages, and each day we fill a page with acts of hopefulness and meaning. The new breeze blows, a page turns, and the story unfolds. And so today a chapter begins, a . . . story of unity, diversity, and generosity—shared, and written, together."*

*Inaugural Address,*
*January 20, 1989*

WIDE WORLD PHOTOS, INC.

George Bush, 1989–1993

**Background:**
• Born 1924
• Republican, Texas
• Elected to the House of Representatives 1966
• Elected vice president 1980, 1984

**Achievements in Office:**
• Americans with Disabilities Act (1990)
• Clean Air Act (1990)
• Negotiation of the START treaty (1991)

For three days coup leaders in Moscow, trying to overthrow Gorbachev, placed themselves in power. They struck while Gorbachev and his family vacationed in the Crimea, 800 miles to the south, confining him in his villa. The coup attempt was met with immediate condemnation not only from world leaders but also from Soviet citizens. Defiantly opposing the coup was Boris Yeltsin, president of the Russian Federation, the largest republic in the USSR. From his office in Moscow Yeltsin rallied a fearful but growing crowd to oppose the coup, at times speaking from the balcony to thousands gathered in the streets.

As the coup failed and its leaders surrendered, Gorbachev seized the moment. He resigned as Communist Party leader and banned any party involvement in government affairs. With these moves, the party's 73-year-old monopoly on political power came to an end. Millions of ordinary Soviet citizens had stopped paying their party dues over the previous year, and now most of the rest also cut their ties.

With centralized control now seen as the greatest threat to *glasnost* and *perestroika*, the Soviet Union began to break up. People living in many of the USSR's 15 republics and belonging to more than 100 ethnic groups agitated for autonomy. The first to break from the union were the Baltic peoples of Lithuania, Latvia, and Estonia. They had voted to secede in February and March 1991. Ukraine,

breadbasket of the Soviet Union, declared its independence just days after the August coup, as did nine other republics.

Although Gorbachev survived the coup attempt in August 1991, his presidency was doomed. Soviet citizens heralded Yeltsin as the most popular figure among them. The United States and other major nations also acknowledged the shift. When Gorbachev recognized this fact, he resigned.

**A New Germany** The USSR's declining influence in the late 1980s set off a political chain reaction. Unification of the two Germanies, divided since 1949, came swiftly on the heels of Gorbachev's sweeping reforms.

Months of street protests in East Germany, for 40 years a Soviet ally, led to the ouster of aging communist leader Erich Honecker in October 1989. East Germans had been fleeing their country all summer through Hungary, and now the trickle became a flood. On November 9, 1989, the government acknowledged reality and said it would issue an exit visa to anyone who asked. Hordes of citizens immediately began to break through the Berlin Wall, a symbol of Germany's division built on Soviet orders in 1961.

Tearful reunions of divided families and friends filled the streets. Strangers hugged one another, and the crowds brought traffic to a halt. One reporter called it "the greatest street-party in the history of the

**A dizzying series of political and economic changes swept the former Soviet Union and its allies in Eastern Europe after 1989. By the early 1990s the region had fragmented into many independent nations.** *Which of the countries shown here used to be part of the Soviet Union?*

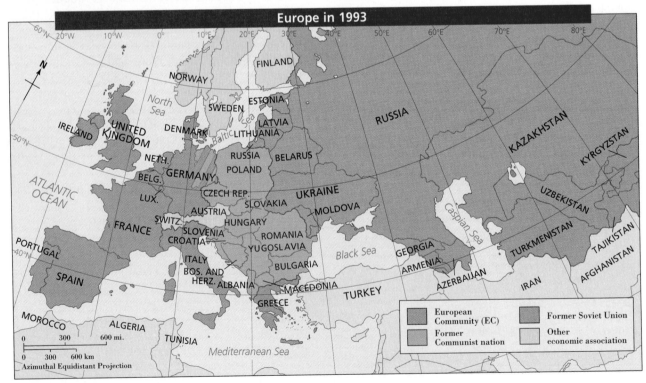

Europe in 1993

European Community (EC)

Former Communist nation

Former Soviet Union

Other economic association

Azimuthal Equidistant Projection

world." All day and night people chopped away pieces of the Berlin Wall as music played from windows. An East German carried a poster that read, "Only today is the war really over." In a single weekend about two million East Germans surged into West Berlin, buying simple goods—such as bananas, blue jeans, and uncensored newspapers—unavailable in their country. Others merely strolled. Thousands never returned east.

Plans immediately began for unifying the two countries. On October 3, 1990, far sooner than anyone had predicted, the two nations joined as the Federal Republic of Germany. Overnight the 62 million West Germans and 16 million East Germans became a European powerhouse, their combined economy worth $1 trillion a year.

The hastiness of the move, however, brought problems. Goods from the eastern region's deteriorating factories could not compete in the west. Unemployed youths and others, some affiliated with neo-Nazi groups, made unprovoked attacks on refugees and immigrant workers. Despite the difficulties of merging two dissimilar nations, Germany moved forward in the early 1990s as private owners and the government began to rebuild the decaying eastern region

**From the Baltic to the Adriatic**  By 1989 no communist leader in Eastern Europe could count on Soviet tanks to suppress his opponents. The first country to loosen communism's grip was Poland. Lech Walesa, a shipyard worker in the Baltic port of Gdansk, led the labor union Solidarity in the 1980s as it won concessions from the government. Even after Solidarity was banned, Walesa's character inspired the anti-government movement. Pope John Paul II, a Pole, also lent inspiration from afar to these forces. Under growing public protest, the communist president was obliged to step aside. Walesa was elected president of Poland in a December 1990 landslide.

Czechoslovakia's relatively smooth passage to democracy resulted in the election in 1989 of playwright Vaclav Havel as president. Slovaks in the eastern portion of the country, however, wanted a separate nation, and Czechs in the western portion were obliged to concede. Havel, a Czech, lost office in 1992 in a democratic vote mainly because few Slovaks would vote for him. He reluctantly agreed that the nation should be split by 1993.

© R. RAJTIC-ZOJA PICTURES

**Young gunmen prowl the streets of Sarajevo, in the former country of Yugoslavia, in 1992. U.S. and European forces did not intervene in the civil war.**

Europe's worst violence since World War II began in June 1991 in Yugoslavia. People in the republics of Slovenia and Croatia, hating the Serbians who controlled the Yugoslavian government, declared their independence. Serb militias entered, and fighting spread to the ethnically mixed republic of Bosnia-Herzegovina. Yugoslavia erupted into full-scale civil war by early 1992. Ancient cities such as Mostar, Sarajevo, and Dubrovnik became smoking ruins.

The bloodbath was so fierce that UN Secretary-General Boutros Boutros-Ghali admitted little hope of halting it. He termed the situation "tragic, dangerous, violent, and confused." European and U.S. forces shied away from trying to intervene in the raging chaos. Instead, the UN in September 1992 expelled what was left of Yugoslavia from the world forum.

## New Military Priorities

As communist governments in Eastern Europe fell, the United States reevaluated its diplomatic and military goals. The public consensus, to reduce both military forces and the defense budget, nevertheless touched off arguments about how much and how fast. In early 1992 the Pentagon ordered personnel and other cuts that would save $103 billion over five years. Ironically, these cutbacks were announced just weeks after the fighting men and women had

**Analyzing Behavior**

One of the main concessions Polish workers won was the right to form labor unions independent of the Communist Party. The union Solidarity, however, quickly grew into a broad-based anti-communist movement with millions of members. The Polish government declared martial law and banned Solidarity, but anti-communist activists pursued their cause, operating underground. They published newspapers, spoke out in churches, and eventually demonstrated in public again for more freedoms. Within a decade they achieved their goal—overthrowing the communist leadership.

A Changing Nation in a Changing World    783

© J.T. ALTMAN, SYGMA

**President George Bush visited U.S. troops in Saudi Arabia as they prepared to expel Iraqi forces from Kuwait. Bush said Iraq's invasion "will not stand."**

proved their effectiveness by winning a war in a Middle East battleground.

### The Persian Gulf War

Iraqi dictator Saddam Hussein, who coveted the oil reserves of his neighbors, overran and annexed the emirate of Kuwait in August 1990. The invasion proved to be only the first of many ill-conceived decisions. Hussein touched off the largest world confrontation since the Vietnam War and saddled his country with one of the worst defeats in military history.

Hussein wrongly gambled that nearby Saudi Arabia, a U.S. ally, would stay out of the squabble. Just days after the invasion Saudi Ambassador Bandar bin Sultan met with President Bush, who decided to commit American military forces. "I give my word of honor," Bush told him in the private meeting. "I will see this through with you."

Bush and his secretary of state, James Baker, devoted themselves to knitting together a coalition of countries to fight Iraq. Twenty-eight nations joined the effort, including several Arab states. The most personnel came from U.S.—a half million troops—Saudi, British, Egyptian, Syrian, and French ranks.

On January 17, 1991, the U.S.-led military force launched air strikes against Iraqi military targets in Baghdad, the capital, and other cities. For five weeks Allied aircraft flew more than 40,000 sorties, demolishing Iraqi industrial and military sites, and draining the fighting spirit of Iraqi troops. Many Iraqi civilians were also killed. The ground war began on February 24, 1991, when Allied tanks and personnel advanced against Iraqi troops in Kuwait.

Hussein had tried to draw Israel into the war in a desperate ploy to detach the Arab members from the coalition. Here too his efforts failed. Israel, although hit by numerous Scud missiles launched from Iraq, stayed out of the war at the urging of the American government.

The Allies pressed forward to a quick victory. When the 1,000-hour air battle and 100-hour ground blitz ended, about 100,000 Iraqi soldiers lay dead and Kuwait was liberated. Fewer than 300 Allied troops died as a result of the war. When it ended, more than 90 percent of

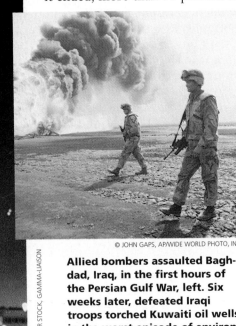

© JOHN GAPS, AP/WIDE WORLD PHOTO, INC.

**Allied bombers assaulted Baghdad, Iraq, in the first hours of the Persian Gulf War, left. Six weeks later, defeated Iraqi troops torched Kuwaiti oil wells in the worst episode of environmental sabotage ever, above.**

© L. VAN DER STOCK, GAMMA-LIAISON

the American public approved of how President Bush had handled the war.

While fleeing Kuwait, Hussein's forces set fire to Kuwait's oil fields, filling the skies with thick black smoke and coating both sea and land with oily sludge. Scientists could not gauge the long-term effects of the environmental sabotage.

**The Role of the United Nations**    Despite its cost in lives and dollars, the Persian Gulf War helped the United States regain the military prestige it had lost in Vietnam. More important, U.S. leadership boosted American influence in the Arab world and set the stage for new Middle East peace talks. These held out the most promise yet that Israel and its Arab neighbors would come to terms. The war also brought new respect to the United Nations, which had unanimously condemned Iraqi aggression and sponsored the Allied military effort.

The Gulf War solidified the UN's changing role in world affairs. Created in 1945, the UN was often ignored by the superpowers or their allies. Yet it contributed to world peace, as UN negotiators arranged cease-fire agreements in dozens of conflicts. These ranged from the 1949 Arab-Israeli war to the end of hostilities in 1988 between Morocco and the Polisario Front in a battle over the Western Sahara.

When Iraq invaded Kuwait, the UN took on new importance in battling aggression. For the first time U.S. and Soviet leaders, cooperating with the UN, worked together to end a world crisis. UN forces, wearing blue helmets or berets, continued to police the world's hotspots and attempted to bring order to troubled lands. About 14,000 UN troops protected food shipments to embattled Yugoslavia in 1992, while other UN forces remained on patrol in Cambodia, Mozambique, Somalia, the Western Sahara, Lebanon, Angola, El Salvador, and the Golan Heights. The annual cost of the peace patrols for 1992 was estimated at more than $3 billion.

## Old Problems, New Hope

With the end of the cold war came both new hope and new challenges to maintain a peaceful world. After Gorbachev's landmark steps to open Soviet society to democracy and a free-market economy, optimism blossomed worldwide. Cooperation extended even to Antarctica, as 24 leading nations signed an accord in October 1991 to protect the frozen continent's environment from exploitation.

China proved an exception in at least one important way. Although its aging leaders allowed some free enterprise to take root, they generally clamped down on political freedoms. China's rulers ordered troops in June 1989 to crush a democracy movement in Beijing. Twenty months later they sentenced two youthful leaders of the movement to 13 years in prison, while others had to remain in hiding.[1]

**Change in South Africa**    In March 1992 white South Africans, in the last whites-only election slated to be held there, voted to share political power and economic opportunity with the nation's black majority. Nevertheless, problems continued at the southernmost edge of the African continent.

President Pieter Botha, who supported the **apartheid** form of government that denied most rights to blacks, resigned under growing pressure in August 1989. Frederik W. de Klerk succeeded him and instituted a number of reforms designed to end racial separatism and give black South Africans more political and social rights. Most dramatically, in early 1990 de Klerk released Nelson Mandela, who as leader of the anti-apartheid African National Congress (ANC) had

© PATRICK ZACHMANN, MAGNUM PHOTOS, INC.

**Nelson Mandela's tour of the United States in February 1991 took him to New York City, where mayor David Dinkins (right) hosted the South African.**

**STUDY GUIDE**

**Predicting Consequences**
Crushing the democracy movement in 1989 had many consequences for China's rulers. Some of the movement's leaders escaped to the United States and other countries, where they carried on their struggle. In addition, free-market reforms allowed some Chinese to prosper, and world opinion turned against communist regimes.

**1** How did China's communist rulers combat the democracy movement?

been imprisoned more than 27 years. De Klerk's government also recognized the ANC, a guerrilla movement that had been banned.

De Klerk's changes led to immediate results. The ANC ended its 29-year guerrilla campaign against the government in August 1990 and suspended all military action. In response, President Bush sought to lift American economic sanctions against South Africa. World athletes also applauded South Africa's change of heart, and in July 1991 the International Olympic Committee allowed South Africa to take part again in the Olympic Games.

Yet whites did not give up political control, and bloodshed continued in 1992. Some of the fighting flared among Africans of different ancestry. Violence also raged between black activists and whites who opposed the efforts to dismantle apartheid.[2]

**Democracy in Latin America**   The winds of political change that swept Eastern Europe, Africa, and Asia in the 1980s and early 1990s touched the Americas as well. Military governments in Chile, Brazil, and Argentina stepped down or were voted out. Nicaraguan president Daniel Ortega Saavedra, head

© JOHN HOPPER, AP/WIDE WORLD PHOTOS, INC.

**The election of Violeta Barrios de Chamorro as president of Nicaragua brought an end to 10 years of civil war. Daniel Ortega Saavedra, ousted from office, stood by at her inauguration.** *Why did U.S. Vice President Dan Quayle (rear) attend the ceremony?*

of the leftist Sandinista Party, lost an election in February 1990 to Violeta Barrios de Chamorro, the conservative candidate backed by the United States. The Sandinistas' defeat marked the end of a civil war that had pitted U.S.-backed "contras" against Ortega's Sandinista troops. A precarious peace also came to war-torn El Salvador, where a treaty signed in January 1992 ended a 12-year civil war that had claimed 75,000 lives.

Nearby Panama also had a dramatic change of government, but here the U.S. military forced the change. In February 1988 a U.S. federal grand jury indicted Panamanian leader Manuel Antonio Noriega on drug-dealing charges. U.S. troops stormed the Central American nation in December 1989 to overthrow Noriega and bring him to trial. After hiding for ten days in a Vatican diplomatic mission, Noriega surrendered. The United States alleged that he had turned Panama into a depot to launder illicit money and channel drugs between Colombian drug cartels and U.S. dealers. In April 1992 a jury in Florida convicted him of these crimes. Although Noriega claimed he was a prisoner of war, the judge sentenced him to 40 years in prison.

In nearby Haiti political instability and extreme poverty drove thousands to flee their homeland. Jean-Bertrand Aristide, the country's first freely elected president, was overthrown by the military in September 1991 just months after taking office. Thousands of Haitians tried to flee the political persecution and economic chaos that followed. Using makeshift boats, these desperate Haitians set out over 600 miles of ocean in an attempt to reach Florida. American officials refused to admit the immigrants as political refugees, and in early 1992 the Supreme Court ordered that the Haitian refugees be returned to their home country. The ruling, however, did not stop more Haitians from trying to reach Florida.

**Middle East Peace Talks**   The Persian Gulf War prodded many Arabs and Israelis to try again to bury their ancient hostilities and live in peace. Using diplomatic influence gained in the war, Secretary of State James Baker brought together negotiators from many countries and factions in late 1991.

The massive changes Gorbachev unleashed also had a ripple effect in Israel. Almost 400,000 Soviet Jews were allowed to immigrate to Israel in the late

## STUDY·GUIDE

**Recognizing Points of View**

Whites make up about 13 percent of South Africa's population, while blacks make up most of the rest. Most blacks believe that as a majority they have a

right to rule the country. Whites, who own most farms and businesses, fear that under majority rule they would lose many rights.

**2** What changes have occurred in South Africa since early 1990?

1980s and early 1990s. Israel asked for a $10 billion loan from the United States to help resettle the immigrants. In return, Israeli leaders agreed to come to the negotiating table in Washington, D.C. The talks held out the most promise in years for a resolution of the Arab-Israeli conflict.

**Battles for Markets**   Although the cold war had ended, competition and even conflict over trade continued. Through the 1980s and early 1990s, the United States almost always led the world in exporting goods to other nations. In 1991 the United States exported goods valued at $422 billion and services valued at $145 billion. Yet beginning in the early 1980s Americans imported more than they exported each year, creating a costly **trade deficit.** The country was losing ground to its main competitors, including the European Community (EC), a 12-nation trade bloc, and the Asian nations of Japan, Taiwan, South Korea, and China.

One response to global economic competition was to form a U.S.-led trade bloc, a tactic Presidents Reagan and Bush pursued. In 1988 the United States signed an agreement with Canada—by far its largest trading partner—to gradually remove tariffs and other obstacles to their cross-border trade, on everything from lumber to cassettes to cars. Then, in a momentous event, the two nations joined with Mexico to sign the North American Free Trade Agreement (NAFTA) in August 1992.

The pact offered two main benefits. It would end most cross-border tariffs and quotas on goods and services by the year 2000, and it would give the NAFTA members greater leverage in negotiating with the EC and the Asian powers. With this leverage, businesses could nurture potential new markets while maintaining old ones. U.S. and Canadian labor unions and some corporate leaders opposed NAFTA. Their main fear was that manufacturing jobs would move to lower-wage plants in Mexico and thus hurt American and Canadian workers. Environmentalists also worried about pollution controls.

The trade pact promised to lower consumer prices on thousands of items. In addition, as the EC model showed, a trade pact promised to lower political tensions by making economies more interdependent. Through 45 years of cold war the United States and most other nations had focused their energies on military and political competition. In the 1990s the world's horizons brightened with the hope that economic cooperation among former enemies would replace military blocs.

© REUTERS/BETTMAN ARCHIVE

**McDonald's Corporation opened a restaurant in Beijing, China, in 1992 as part of its worldwide expansion. In an increasingly global economy, all nations face pressure to allow more foreign investment.**

## SECTION REVIEW

**Checking Facts**

1. In what ways did George Bush carry on the foreign policy of his predecessor, Ronald Reagan?

2. What effect did Gorbachev's policies have on the Soviet Union's 15 separate republics?

3. Why could Germany unite its two parts as communism faltered?

4. What actions by Iraq triggered the Persian Gulf War? How did U.S. and UN forces respond?

**Thinking Critically**

5. **Predicting Consequences**
How is global economic competition changing relations between the United States and neighboring Canada and Mexico?

6. **Recognizing Points of View**
U.S. intervention in Nicaragua and Panama forced out governments that U.S. leaders viewed as bad or counterproductive. How might residents of those countries react to military or political intervention by a foreign power?

**Linking Across Time**

7. During most of the 19th century the United States had to import machinery from Europe just as we now import oil from the Middle East. How does this new dependence influence U.S. relations with Middle Eastern countries?

## Mikhail Gorbachev Resigns

MOSCOW—"Mikhail S. Gorbachev, the trailblazer of the Soviet Union's retreat from the cold war and the spark for the democratic reforms that ended 70 years of communist tyranny, told a weary, anxious nation tonight that he was resigning as president and closing out the union."

—*New York Times*, 1991

© REUTERS/BETTMAN ARCHIVE

### Soviet Flag Comes Down

At 7:32 P.M., shortly after Gorbachev resigned, the Soviet flag with hammer and sickle was lowered from atop the Kremlin. Russians raised the white, blue, and red flag of their republic. Chimes rang out for several minutes from the Spassky Tower clock nearby.

© REUTERS/BETTMAN ARCHIVE

## Elsewhere in the News

### Hemophiliacs and AIDS

NEW YORK— Because of tainted U.S. blood supplies, the virus that causes AIDS has infected almost every hemophiliac born before 1985.

### Funding Foreign Studies

WASHINGTON—Government grants of $150 million will improve universities' international programs and fund students who learn foreign languages.

© GENE BERMAN, AP/WIDE WORLD PHOTOS, INC.

## Increasingly Free Press

The newspaper *Izvestia*, formerly controlled by the Soviet government, reports Gorbachev's resignation and announces that most world leaders have recognized Boris Yeltsin as Russian leader. Shortages of newsprint, however, restrict its circulation.

## Related Stories

- Morale in Soviet Military Plummets
- Fighting Continues in Republic of Georgia
- Soviet Olympic Committee Ponders What Flags and Anthems to Use
- Cities Debate Name Changes—Leningrad to Saint Petersburg?
- Breakup of Union Keeps Mapmakers Busy

## Bread Lines in Moscow

In Moscow, as well as in other ex-Soviet cities home to millions, long lines of people snaked through the streets waiting to buy bread. U.S. planes delivered food left from the Persian Gulf War to many cities, earmarking it for hospitals, orphanages, and homes for the elderly.

© LIU HEUNG SHING, AP/WIDE WORLD PHOTOS, INC.

## Shifting Job Market

HAVERHILL, MASS.—After a printing plant closed in this old industrial city, workers used federal funds to retrain, some as lawyers' assistants.

## Euro Disney Dress Code

PARIS—Euro Disneyland, scheduled to open in spring 1992, will require its employees to sport the same clean-cut look as employees in other Disney parks.

# Domestic Turmoil

## June 10, 1991: Gulf War Vets Welcomed Home

**Y**ELLOW RIBBONS, THE NATION'S SIGN OF RE-MEMBRANCE, FLUTTERED FROM TREE TRUNKS. YELLOW RIBBONS WERE WOUND AROUND STOP SIGNS AND STREET LIGHTS. Painted yellow ribbons smiled up from the pavement. After weeks of being glued to their televisions, the nation was glad to see the Gulf War come to a conclusion. New York City had gone all out for for the nation's official "welcome home" parade. Thousands of cheering admirers lined Broadway as artillery Captain Jeffery Davis and 24,000 other Gulf War veterans marched by.

This was Captain Davis's second parade. A month after participating in the ground assault in Kuwait, Davis had been honored in a triumphal parade in his Pennsylvania hometown. As the echoes of the marching bands faded, however, so did Captain Davis's hopes for the future. Like many of his fellow soldiers, Captain Davis had planned to make the military a lifetime career. After serving seven years, Captain Davis was squeezed out of the army by budget cuts. "I served well," the 29-year-old officer told *TIME*, "Now I hope I can compete in the real world." Many of the men and women leaving the military had marketable skills. The military helped with information on job search and job interviewing techniques. Nevertheless, many would find it tough to make the adjustment to civilian life in a troubled economy. "Driving a tank in combat isn't exactly the greatest preparation for civilian life," one Gulf War veteran said.

© DONOVAN REESE, TONY STONE WORLDWIDE

## Recession and Readjustment

**T**he end of the cold war, not the end of the Gulf War, was at the root of the military cutbacks. As the cold war drew to an end, immense defense budgets could no longer be justified as necessary to combat the communist threat. By 1989, U.S. defense spending had increased to $282 billion, nearly one-third of the nation's budget. Less than a year later, the U.S. military began to implement spending cuts that resounded throughout the economy. The cuts began as the economy plodded through a period of slow growth after the booming 1980s. By early 1991 the economy was fraught with problems: economic growth had halted; unemployment was rising; and the after-tax income for most workers was falling. Defense spending, still the single largest budget item, had been drastically cut. The economy, and the nation, needed to readjust.

**The Arms Build-Down** Americans realized the economy was in serious trouble as the effects of military budget cuts spread across the country. The terms of treaties signed with the Soviet Union in the late 1980s called for major troop reductions. The Pentagon moved to eliminate 500,000 active-duty U.S. military personnel by 1997. Army, navy, marine, and air force reserve units throughout the country also felt the budget cutters' axe. The axe even reached overseas as the Pentagon ended operations or cut staff levels at 150 facilities, trimming civilian as well as military payrolls. The 1990 cuts, affecting

---

**As You Read**
Identify the effects the changing economy exerted on the way Americans lived and worked in the 1980s and 1990s. Also, think about the following concepts and skills.

**Central Concepts**
- recognizing how defense spending, a **global economy**, and a **budget deficit** all affect communities
- understanding the growth of the national debt

**Thinking Skills**
- identifying cause and effect
- analyzing data

about one-fourth of the U.S. military facilities in Europe, touched air fields, barracks, and even remote weather stations. Some of these had been under U.S. control since the end of World War II. These first cuts set the pace for those to follow. "General Motors is eliminating 74,000 employees over three years," said General Colin Powell, chairman of the Joint Chiefs of Staff. "We're doing that many alone from January to September [of 1992]."

The defense cuts also affected U.S. civilians. An estimated 1.35 million defense industry workers would lose their jobs by 1997. Demand was dropping for everything from soldiers' socks to billion-dollar B-2 bombers. Areas surrounding defense industry giants were particularly hard-hit. Following cancellation of the Seawolf nuclear submarine program, General Dynamics, Connecticut's second largest employer, planned to lay off nearly a quarter of its 17,000 workers. In Dallas-Forth Worth, half the manufacturing jobs lost were defense-related. In San Diego the same defense-related job losses totaled one-third of all lost jobs. Across the country, two-thirds of the 190,000 manufacturing jobs lost in 1990 were in military-related industries.[1]

Military contracts from foreign governments saved some defense-related jobs. Workers at the Mc-Donnell-Douglas complex in St. Louis, for example, prepared to supply Saudi Arabia with 72 new F-15 fighters. Nevertheless, the U.S. military was the primary customer for the defense industry, and cuts in U.S. defense spending cost defense contractors a major portion of their business. Defense contractors scrambled, often unsuccessfully, to find civilian uses for military technology. However, the recession limited the industry's ability to retool factories and retrain employees for other high-tech uses such as high-speed trains, power-generating plants, or environmental safeguards. Companies and workers began looking to the government to help pay for transforming the factories. "Priming the pump is the way to go," said John O'Brien, chairman of Grumman Corporation, a leading defense contractor.

© RICHARD HOWARD

**Many defense-related manufacturing facilities, like this shipyard in Bath, Maine, once employed thousands of people at a single location.**

**The Stubborn Recession** Defense was not the only industry caught in a changing world. Automobile makers, typical of many manufacturers, found themselves losing out to worldwide competition. In 1988 U.S. automakers earned a record $11 billion in profits. Three years later they lost a record $7.5 billion. Falling revenue was only a symptom of their economic ills: the U.S. share of worldwide automobile sales fell from 75 percent in 1950 to just 19 percent in 1991. American industry had come face-to-face with the realities of a **global economy.** This new system of worldwide trade was evident in the variety of inexpensive, foreign-made goods that American consumers found in local stores. The popularity of those foreign products upset the balance of trade between the United States and other countries. By the 1990s, Americans bought more goods from foreign nations—about $100 billion more—than they sold to other countries. This trade deficit, or gap between the value of imports and exports, weakened the nation's economy. This hurt the nation's ability to compete with foreign companies.

The nation's inability to compete hit home in the nation's industrial towns and cities. In the video documentary *Roger and Me*, filmmaker Michael Moore recorded what happened to his hometown of Flint, Michigan, as General Motors closed its facilities there. Once a thriving middle-class community, Flint began to resemble a ghost town. Unemployed autoworkers left town to seek jobs elsewhere, and local businesses quickly lost most of their customers. Deputies evicted people from their homes because they could not pay their rent or meet their mortgages. Along Flint's main street, boards covered the windows and doors of stores, restaurants, movie theaters, and offices.

Meanwhile in Washington, D.C., the Bush administration and Congress struggled to find ways to jumpstart the economy. Bush proposed a cut in the capital gains tax that he said would stimulate new investment. Calling the proposal a tax break for the rich, the Democrats in Congress defeated it. Faced with an ever-growing deficit, Bush broke his "no new taxes" campaign pledge. After a series of budget summits with congressional leaders, Bush agreed to a tax increase that fell mostly on those with low and middle incomes. The Federal Reserve Bank carried out another recession-fighting strategy, cutting interest rates 18 times from 1989 to the end of 1992. Lower interest rates had spurred the economy out of every recession since 1948 by fueling consumer spending and increasing demand for manufactured goods. The recession of the early 1990s, however, proved unyielding. Interest rates on savings accounts went down as well, driving investors to the stock market where they hoped for greater returns. For retirees who depended on the interest income from their savings accounts, lower interest rates often meant real hardships.

The recession persisted, and by late 1992 the U.S. economy stood trapped in the longest stagnant period since World War II. Sales at major corporations and neighborhood shops alike kept declining, forcing more layoffs—blue collar and white collar as well. Government, businesses, and consumers found themselves with little cash to promote economic growth.

**Ballooning Debt**   Many economists believed that the recession's stubbornness was due in part to the nation's enormous debt. For years the federal government had operated with a **budget deficit,** spending more money each year than it collected in taxes and revenues. In 1992 the deficit reached $333 billion. Some economists estimated that the deficit could soar to $500 billion, 5 percent of the nation's income, by the year 2002. The government financed the deficit by selling billions of dollars worth of bonds each month, often to overseas investors. Paying the interest on those bonds reduced the government's resources for combatting the recession. In addition, interest payments diverted spending away from programs to improve

**As the 1990s began, American consumers purchased imported products, like the Korean automobile shown below, rather than American-made goods. The resulting trade deficit, shown in the chart, injured the U.S. economy.** *Why are the trade figures for the years 1980 and 1990 alarming to economists?*

© J. P. LAFFONT, SYGMA

### U.S. Imports and Exports, 1960–1990

| Year | Imports | Exports |
|------|---------|---------|
| 1960 | 15.0 | 19.6 |
| 1970 | 40.0 | 42.7 |
| 1980 | 244.9 | 220.6 |
| 1990 | 495.0 | 394.0 |

Dollars (in billions)

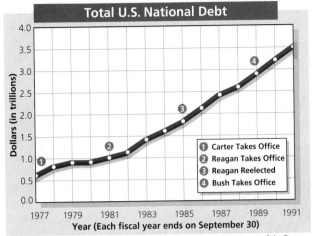

**Total U.S. National Debt**

① Carter Takes Office
② Reagan Takes Office
③ Reagan Reelected
④ Bush Takes Office

*Year (Each fiscal year ends on September 30)*

Source: Department of the Treasury

**The large national debt led some economists to say that the nation had mortgaged its children's future.** *If the debt decreases at the same rate it increased, how long will it be before the nation owes less than a trillion dollars?*

education, end drug abuse, rebuild the nation's roads and railways, and fight urban decay. Government economists kept predicting that the economy would rebound by mid-1992, but high levels of personal and corporate debt worked against recovery. Like the government, individuals and corporations were paying interest on their own debts.[2]

## *Wealth and Poverty*

The severe recession and the economic policies that grew from it touched people at all income levels. However, the effects on the wealthy, the middle class, and the poor were vastly different. In 1989, the richest 1 percent of U.S. households owned 36 percent of the country's total

**Cartoonist Tom Toles implies that the budget deficit, which adds to the national debt each year, imperils the country as much as a foreign enemy.** *Why is the deficit threatening the White House?*

private wealth. This represented a 5-percent increase in the wealthy elite's share since 1983. At the same time, the number of people living in poverty rose from about 11 percent of the population in the 1970s to about 15 percent in 1991.

**The Income Gap** The rich got richer for a number of reasons. Top corporate executives commanded ever-higher salaries. Even during the layoffs and plant closings of the late 1980s and early 1990s, pay for top executives continued to rise, soaring to 160 times the pay of an average worker. High salaries were not the only avenue to wealth. Many well-off people benefited from tax-law changes. The Reagan administration argued that giving the wealthy more capital to invest would expand business. The effects would "trickle down" to the middle and lower classes. In 1986, tax reform decreased taxes on the wealthy from 70 percent to 30 percent of their taxable income, but the "trickle down" effect never occurred.

Others became rich through elaborate and sometimes illegal business deals. In the 1980s, a wave of corporate takeovers swept the country. One of the largest was Chevron's takeover of Gulf Oil at a cost of $13.4 billion dollars. The two brokerage houses

© TOM TOLES, THE BUFFALO NEWS

**STUDY GUIDE**

**Analyzing Data**
The graph on this page shows that the national debt began to rise soon after Reagan took office. The debt continued to rise during Reagan's second term and Bush's presidency. Nevertheless, it wasn't until the presidential campaign of 1992 that the debt became a major topic of discussion.

**2** What problems prevented the economy from recovering its strength in the early 1990s?

A Changing Nation in a Changing World     793

involved in the merger together received $45 million. Corporate mergers offered great profits to some merger specialists while extracting a high price from the nation's economy. Corporations that might be takeover targets often sacrificed long-term performance in favor of short-term profits. This practice weakened the economy.

The deregulation of the banking industry opened another avenue for enrichment. Officers in institutions such as Lincoln Savings and Loan in California made large loans to businesses that had little or no chance of succeeding. Often, the bankers knew—or even chose from their own circle of friends and relatives—the business's top executives. The borrowers paid themselves huge salaries; the banking executives pocketed fat commissions. When the borrowers' businesses failed, the bank often failed as well. There was no money available to repay the investors or to cover the deposits of the customers. Taxpayers got the bill for more than a thousand bank or savings and loan failures, at an estimated cost of $500 billion.

Greed became glamorous in the 1980s. While money moguls played for real on Wall Street, the average person could experience vicarious thrills offered by Hollywood.

early 1990s also barreled through suburban America. Forty percent of the jobs lost in the recession of the early 1990s were white collar jobs. Hard-working members of the middle class, like Ben D'Cruz, saw the American dream evaporate before their eyes. D'Cruz, now a U.S. citizen, immigrated from Malaysia in the early 1970s. In 1991, he was laid off from a $48,000-a-year job at Norden Systems in New York. He looked in vain for a comparable position; he applied for jobs paying as little as $19,000 without success. After spending most of his retirement savings, D'Cruz relied on unemployment and his wife's earnings to make ends meet. "It's very tough out there," he said. "Even if you go out of Long Island, it's happening all over." Many of the white collar layoffs were probably permanent, as global competition forced companies to cut costs aggressively.

Otherwise encouraging economic developments failed to make a difference for hard-pressed middle-class Americans in the early 1990s. Home mortgage rates fell to the lowest rate in two decades, while prices dropped for numerous consumer goods such as television sets and personal computers. Nevertheless, consumer purchases did not increase because consumers found that their incomes had not kept pace with rising costs. In 1991 an automobile cost an average family 25 weeks of gross wages, up from 19 weeks in 1980. The increased taxes on the middle class had left them with less money to spend than they had a decade earlier.

**Pressures on the Middle Class**   With the sharp reduction in taxes paid by the wealthy, America's middle class carried the bulk of the tax burden for the failed savings and loans.[3] In the late 1980s and early 1990s, working people coped with stagnant incomes and a declining quality of life. More and more businesses were moving factories and jobs to cheaper, less regulated foreign labor markets; and changing technologies were making many blue collar jobs obsolete. For Americans in the middle and the lower ranks, affordable health care became increasingly difficult to find. Many retirees learned that their union pension plans had been mismanaged. Most of all, they watched their children's opportunities for a better future dwindle.

Unlike previous downturns, the recession of the

**The Frayed Safety Net**   As the recession deepened, the people with the least money to spend lost the most economic ground. Half the adults living in poverty, 14 million people, were classified as **working poor.** These adults earned less than $12,195, too little to pull a family of four out of poverty. The nation's

**Identifying Cause and Effect**
Sometimes an action can have unpredicted effects. The Reagan administration thought that relaxing or removing some controls on business would strengthen the economy. This policy did boost the economy, but it also allowed some stockbrokers, corporate raiders, and savings and loan executives to bend rules and use unethical practices that damaged the economy.

**3** Who had to pay for the illegal practices that damaged the economy?

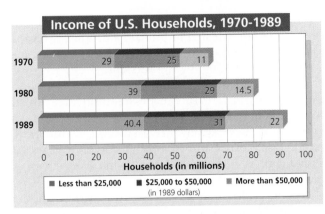

## Income of U.S. Households, 1970-1989

| Year | Less than $25,000 | $25,000 to $50,000 | More than $50,000 |
|------|------|------|------|
| 1970 | 29 | 25 | 11 |
| 1980 | 39 | 29 | 14.5 |
| 1989 | 40.4 | 31 | 22 |

Households (in millions)

■ Less than $25,000　　■ $25,000 to $50,000　　■ More than $50,000
(in 1989 dollars)

**As the 1990s began, the numbers of working poor, poor, and homeless Americans continued to increase. Here, volunteers pitch in to feed the homeless.** *Which groups of earners grew fastest between 1970 and 1990?*

© A. TANNENBAUM, SYGMA

poorest people had been left out of the business boom of the 1980s. Like the middle class, the working poor lost jobs to foreign labor and automation. In addition, job prospects for workers with limited education remained bleak. Workers fortunate enough to hold on to basic jobs watched their earning power plummet.

These circumstances affected some Americans more than others. Between 1983 and 1989 the net worth of white families fell about 8 percent. During the same period, however, the net worth of African American and Hispanic families fell 42 percent. Women and children were now the poorest of the poor; the number of poor single-parent families increased. By 1989, nearly 1 out of every 5 children was living in poverty; 14 percent of these children were white, 35 percent were Hispanic, and 43 percent were African American.

The economic losses of African Americans and Hispanic Americans were mainly felt in the cities. In the early 1980s, city dwellers earned about 10 percent less than suburban dwellers; the gap widened to 41 percent by 1987. City revenues fell, and urban dwellers began to see the effects of neglected infrastructure, including crumbling streets, leaking sewers, and broken bridges. Many cities needed to close or consolidate schools and eliminate educational programs due to decreased revenues for education. While unemployment and need for aid to the poor and homeless rose, cities found that their share of federal dollars fell. Federal aid to cities in 1992 was 64 percent less than it had been in 1980.[4]

## The 1992 Election

Hard hit by recession, American voters approached the 1992 presidential election with one chief concern: the economy. The Democratic and Republican parties brought their fundamental disagreement concerning how to invigorate the economy into the heart of the presidential campaign. Republicans favored increasing the incentives available to big and small businesses in order to help them expand and create more jobs. Democrats preferred higher taxes on the wealthy, more funds for job retraining, and investment by both the private sector and government in the infrastructure and education.

The weak economy overshadowed the fact that, for the first time in over 40 years, the country was free from the threat of nuclear confrontation with the Soviets. Yet candidates also had to address concerns about skyrocketing health care costs, drugs and violence in the nation's cities, and the need for improved education to prepare America's workers for global competition.

**Three-Way Race** After besting a number of opponents in Democratic primaries, 45-year-old Arkansas Governor Bill Clinton received his party's nomination for president. Clinton challenged the Republican candidate, President George Bush, by focusing on the faltering economy. Clinton chose Tennessee Senator Albert Gore, Jr., a well-known environmentalist, as his running mate. Bush retained Vice President Dan Quayle to run for a second term.

## STUDY GUIDE

**Assessing Outcomes**
The move of the affluent and the middle class from cities to suburbs began in the 1950s and 1960s and continued through the 1970s and 1980s. This

movement, often described as "white flight," caused the racial and economic composition of cities to change.

4 Besides their own low salaries, what problems did the working poor confront in many cities?

Bill Clinton, shown here campaigning in New York City, toured the country in a bus to deliver his "time for a change" message.

© IRA WYMAN/SYGMA

A record number of legislators either chose not to run again or were defeated in primary elections. A record 164 women stepped forward to run for Congress; another 8 women sought governorships.

**Voter Appeals**  In the presidential race, Bush offered a long career of government service and his first-term successes in foreign affairs. Democratic challenger Bill Clinton brought twelve years of experience as governor of Arkansas and a reputation as a reformer. With no government experience, Ross Perot ran on his business success. To a large extent, the campaign centered on voters' convictions about which candidate could lead the nation out of economic decline. Bush painted Clinton as a "tax-and-spend" Democrat. Clinton attacked Bush's concentration on foreign policy and his neglect of domestic concerns, especially the economy, health care, education, and crime. Bush cast shadows on Clinton's character, citing his avoidance of military service and his participation as a young man in antiwar demonstrations overseas. Democrats attempted to capitalize on reports that Bush took part in secret, illegal arms shipments to Iran in the 1980s. The campaign grew more complicated with Perot's witty participation in the presidential debates and his 30-minute commercials. Relying almost exclusively on electronic campaigning, Perot purchased his own television time at a cost of $60 million. Perot used the time to loosely define his programs for solving economic problems and political stalemate in Washington.

The presidential campaign changed abruptly when a third candidate entered the contest. Enthusiastic volunteers formed a grass-roots movement to place Texas billionaire H. Ross Perot on the ballot in all 50 states. Perot financed his campaign with his own money, supplemented with small donations. Capitalizing on voter discontent with gridlock between the Republican president and a Democratic-controlled Congress, Perot outlined a program to cut the federal budget deficit in five years. His plan asked all Americans to "share the pain" of fixing the problems in the nation's economy. Running as a Washington outsider, Perot insisted that politicians had forgotten that they were working for the American people.

The voters' discontent with elected officials also changed the complexion of many congressional races.

Deep voter concerns about the country's economic future moved Clinton into the White House, ousting President Bush after a single term. Clinton became the first Democrat elected to the White House since Jimmy Carter in 1976.

The electoral vote outcome gave 370 electoral votes to Clinton, 168 to Bush, and none to Perot. But

---

### ★ ★ ★  PRESIDENT'S GALLERY  ★ ★ ★

*"America has called upon me to be our next president. But our forebears call on all of us at this moment to honor their efforts, their sacrifices, their ideals, and their lives, by working hard and working together to improve this good and great nation as much for our children, and our children's children, as those who preceded us did for us. They call on us to take our dreams and our hopes, and make them real. Thank you, and God bless America."*

Address to the Media
November 4, 1992

© M. REINSTEIN, FPG INTERNATIONAL

William J. Clinton, 1993–

**Background:**
- Born 1946
- Rhodes Scholar, Oxford University 1968–1970
- Democrat, Arkansas
- Democratic nominee for House of Representatives 1974
- Elected attorney general of Arkansas 1976
- Elected governor of Arkansas 1978, 1982, 1984, 1986, 1990

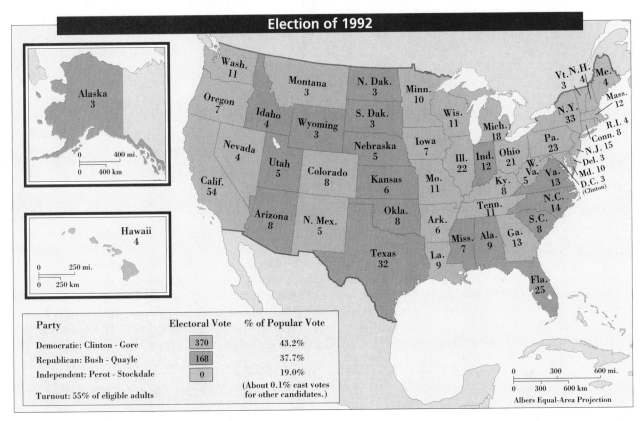

## Election of 1992

### Alaska
3

### Hawaii
4

| State | Electoral Votes |
|-------|-----------------|
| Wash. | 11 |
| Oregon | 7 |
| Idaho | 4 |
| Montana | 3 |
| N. Dak. | 3 |
| Minn. | 10 |
| Vt. | 3 |
| N.H. | 4 |
| Me. | 4 |
| Mass. | 12 |
| Nevada | 4 |
| Wyoming | 3 |
| S. Dak. | 3 |
| Wis. | 11 |
| Mich. | 18 |
| N.Y. | 33 |
| R.I. | 4 |
| Conn. | 8 |
| Calif. | 54 |
| Utah | 5 |
| Colorado | 8 |
| Nebraska | 5 |
| Iowa | 7 |
| Ill. | 22 |
| Ind. | 12 |
| Ohio | 21 |
| Pa. | 23 |
| N.J. | 15 |
| Del. | 3 |
| Md. | 10 |
| D.C. | 3 (Clinton) |
| Arizona | 8 |
| N. Mex. | 5 |
| Kansas | 6 |
| Mo. | 11 |
| Ky. | 8 |
| W. Va. | 5 |
| Va. | 13 |
| N.C. | 14 |
| Texas | 32 |
| Okla. | 8 |
| Ark. | 6 |
| Tenn. | 11 |
| S.C. | 8 |
| La. | 9 |
| Miss. | 7 |
| Ala. | 9 |
| Ga. | 13 |
| Fla. | 25 |

| Party | Electoral Vote | % of Popular Vote |
|-------|----------------|-------------------|
| Democratic: Clinton - Gore | 370 | 43.2% |
| Republican: Bush - Quayle | 168 | 37.7% |
| Independent: Perot - Stockdale | 0 | 19.0% |
| Turnout: 55% of eligible adults | | (About 0.1% cast votes for other candidates.) |

Albers Equal-Area Projection

**In 1988, electors in 40 states cast their votes for George Bush. In 1992, Bush's reelection bid garnered electoral votes in only 18 states, many of them small.**

*In what areas of the country was Bush's support the strongest? Why do you think this was so?*

the 1992 election results were significant in several other areas. Although Clinton's margin in electoral votes was 2 to 1, his margin in popular votes was only 5 percent. Clinton garnered 43 percent of the popular vote, compared to Bush's 38 percent. Perot's support gave him an astounding 19 percent of the vote, more than any independent candidate had received in 80 years. The voters' desire for change rippled through the nation. In California, voters sent two women to the U.S. Senate. Voters in that state also elected Jay C. Kim, a naturalized Korean immigrant, as the first person of Korean heritage to serve in Congress. In Colorado, Ben Nighthorse Campbell, a member of the Northern Cheyenne, moved from the House to the Senate, becoming the first Native American elected to that chamber. In Illinois, Carol Moseley Braun became the first African American woman to hold a U.S. Senate seat. Across the country, 14 more African Americans, 9 more Hispanics, and 23 more women won seats in Congress. These historic changes made Congress a more representative body than ever before.

## SECTION REVIEW

### Checking Facts

1. What is meant by the term *budget deficit*?
2. What effects did defense budget cutbacks have on the nation's economy?
3. Name three ways the wealthy increased their share of the nation's personal wealth in the late 1980s.
4. Who are the "working poor"? About how many Americans are classified as "working poor"?

### Thinking Critically

5. **Analyzing Data**
   What effect did the $333 billion deficit in 1992 have on the nation's ability to maintain and repair its infrastructure?
6. **Identifying Cause and Effect**
   George Bush won the 1988 election while unemployment was near its lowest in 14 years, about 5.3 percent. He lost in 1992 when unemployment was up to 7.5 percent. Besides this shift, what effects of his administration contributed to voters' dissatisfaction with the economy?

### Linking Across Time

7. What similarities exist between America of the 1930s and America of the early 1990s?

## The Congressional Record: Day Care

The Congressional Record *is the official transcript of the proceedings of the U.S. House of Representatives and the Senate. It contains budgets, bills, testimonies, articles, and other items introduced for the record in Congress. It is one of the primary public documents historians use to learn about politics and legislation in the nation since 1873. The nation's earlier legislative history is documented in similar records published between 1789 and 1873.*

### The Evidence

In response to the growing need for day care, Senators Christopher Dodd and Orrin Hatch introduced the 1989 Act for Better Child Care (ABC), just one of many proposals submitted by members of Congress in an attempt to solve the problems related to child care. The following excerpts are from arguments made regarding the passage of the ABC bill that appear in the *Congressional Record*. Mr. Coats and Mr. Adams are senators. The president they address is the Senate's presiding officer.

*June 16, 1989*

**Mr. COATS.** Mr. President, I rise today in opposition to S. 5, the Act for Better Child Care or ABC bill. . . .

There are two very different approaches to child care. One is a commonsense approach which gives tax relief to the working poor so that they can make these important child care decisions for themselves. The other is a $2.5 billion boondoggle that will primarily benefit bureaucracies, not individuals. . . .

We must always remember that the child care needs of employed parents are diverse. . . . A truly profamily policy must not neglect the needs or overlook the contributions of working families that sacrifice the benefits of a second income to have a parent stay at home. . . .

The fact of the matter is, that more than one-third of all families with preschool age children are "Ozzie and Harriets," homemaker mothers married to breadwinner fathers. . . . These families sacrifice on the average of $13,000 a year to have mom at home raising the children. They are paying in effect, $13,000 a year for child care. Yet under the ABC bill, these families would get nothing. I do not know about you, but I do not think that is fair, and I can assure you that these hardworking families will not think it fair either if we pass this discriminatory bill. . . .

**Mr. ADAMS.** Mr. President, I rise in support of the majority leader's substitute to S. 5, the Act for Better Child Care, the so-called ABC bill. . . . Let me emphasize that a great portion of the people we are trying to help do not deal very well with tax credits. They do not understand them very well. They have a very difficult time with the complexity of vouchers. . . .

I am pleased, as the Senator stated, that there are still one-third of the families that are the Ozzie and Harriet families, so called. . . . Hurrah for that. But that is not where our problem is.

It is in the other two-thirds, Mr. President, where we have created the latchkey kids. The latchkey kid must come home to no one because both are working, and often he or she has to take care of younger siblings. We cannot be confident of our nation's future if we do not take better care of our nation's children. . . .

This bill. . . . deals with the following statistics: 63 percent of the mothers with children under age 18 are working. These are the two-thirds who are not the Ozzie and Harriet families staying at home. Two-thirds of those mothers are either the sole supporter of their family or have husbands who earn less than $15,000 a year. And only 2 percent of all the preschool children with working mothers can be accommodated in the licensed day-care centers we have today.

## The Interpretation

Because the *Congressional Record* is essentially a word-for-word transcript of the official proceedings in Congress, historians primarily refer to it to discover specific legislators' arguments. However, they also use it to assess the prevailing attitudes and concerns of the American people. From these excerpts, you can learn about two lawmakers' attitudes towards day care and something about American culture. You can infer that many people believe that an ideal American family is one that is headed by a homemaker mother and a breadwinner father. You might also infer that many young children take care of themselves after school from the fact that Americans have developed the term *latchkey kids*.

Like any single document, the *Congressional Record* is a limited resource. It contains information only about issues lawmakers have decided to discuss. Furthermore, since politicians know their comments will be recorded, it tends to contain statements that are more diplomatic than candid.

The *Congressional Record* is also a cumbersome document. Since the entries are catalogued by day and indexed by month, historians need to have a general idea of when an event occurred to be able to find it quickly.

Finally the *Congressional Record* has a hidden limitation. According to Senate Document 100-1 and House Document 100-248, members of Congress can revise and extend their remarks up to five months after they have made them. This enables them to regulate the impressions they give the American public. These laws do not technically entitle congresspersons to change the content of their remarks. Yet, since only another congress-person can challenge the remarks made by a colleague, some content changes could remain unchecked.

## Further Exploration

Like the *Congressional Record,* many public documents—such as the minutes from PTA meetings—are word-for-word transcripts of official proceedings. Pretend that you are a historian studying your community. Review the minutes of a PTA or a student council meeting. What can you learn from the minutes about your community or school? What types of things would be difficult to learn? In other words, what are the limitations of this type of evidence?

**All of the proceedings of Congress, including speeches before special sessions of the House and Senate, are recorded in the pages of the *Congressional Record* (shown below). Members of Congress are allowed to edit their remarks and to insert items in the *Record,* such as speeches or articles, that were not read on the House or Senate floors.**

# America Faces a New Century

## June 3, 1992: 100 World Leaders Meet at Earth Summit

PRESIDENT GEORGE BUSH FACED A DILEMMA AS HE PREPARED TO ATTEND THE EARTH SUMMIT IN RIO DE JANEIRO. MORE THAN 100 LEADERS FROM AROUND THE globe were meeting in Rio to plan cooperative efforts for protecting the environment. Representatives from several European nations had drafted a treaty to stabilize at 1990 levels the emissions of gases that contribute to a dangerous warming of the earth's climate. The deadline for the stabilization was the year 2000. The President's dilemma was whether or not to sign the treaty. Either decision would unleash a storm of criticism. If the President signed the treaty, employees and companies in the U.S. auto industry would be angry about the economic hardships that adopting the new standards would cause during a recession. If Bush refused to sign the treaty, he would be scorned by most environmentalists at the summit. His solution was a threat to boycott the summit unless the deadline was eliminated. The President insisted that American automakers needed more time to adapt their cars to the new standards in order to stay competitive with foreign companies.

When President Bush's stand on the climate treaty became known, a Brazilian newsweekly ridiculed him, calling him "Mr. Smoke" and "Uncle Grubby." Summit leaders accused Bush of sabotaging the conference, since a major treaty could not be implemented without U.S. involvement. However, other nations agreed to Bush's demands, and deadlines were

© ALLAN TANNENBAUM, SYGMA

THE FUTURE IS IN YOUR HANDS

eliminated from the treaty. When the President signed the treaty at the Rio conference, he testily defended his actions: "America's record on environmental protection is second to none, so I did not come here to apologize."

For President Bush, an even less favorable trade-off at the Earth Summit was a treaty to protect rare and endangered plants and animals. According to Bush, "That proposed agreement threatens to retard biotechnology and undermine the protection of ideas." The president did not sign this treaty. He objected both to language specifying how the preservation would be financed and to measures that he claimed would hurt U.S. industry by infringing on patent rights. The president, however, agreed with leaders of other industrialized countries to help provide money and technology to developing countries so they could meet the commitments of the Rio treaty.

## Probing the Limits

In the 1990s trade-offs like those at the Earth Summit are likely to multiply for U.S. leaders and citizens. The United States, like other countries, faces global economic competition and a need to set priorities for a host of domestic concerns. Americans must decide what compromises they are willing to make. They also need to decide how much they want to spend in such areas as the environment, health care,

---

### STUDY GUIDE

**As You Read**
Identify the areas in which Americans will be making trade-offs in the 1990s and in the next century. Also, think about the following concepts and skills.

**Central Concepts**
- recognizing that Americans will have to decide what values are important
- understanding how **biotechnology** could revolutionize the way many people live

**Thinking Skills**
- recognizing points of view
- recognizing bias
- recognizing propaganda
- identifying cause and effect
- making inferences

education, improved communication and transportation, and urban renewal.

## Environmental Debate

Environmental issues often spur bitter and passionate disagreement between conservationists and business people. Conservationists criticize government for doing too little to protect the environment. Businesses complain they cannot make a profit or compete with foreign firms if forced to meet strict pollution or waste disposal standards.

© J. P. FORDEN, SYGMA

**Pollution of the environment can be countered through community clean-ups, above. Destruction of the habitats of endangered species, such as the spotted owl, right, is harder to reverse.**

SYGMA

Most environmental programs try to compromise between these competing interests. One such example is air pollution control.

For many decades, automobiles and factories spewed pollutants into the air. In 1990 the Environmental Protection Agency reported that nearly 150 million Americans lived in areas where the air was considered unhealthy. After much debate, Congress finally passed the Clean Air Act in 1990. The bill set standards and deadlines for factories, oil refiners, and automakers.

The Clean Air Act did not deliver clean air as soon as environmentalists had hoped it would. Partly this was because Representative John D. Dingell from Detroit, chairman of the House Energy and Commerce Committee, won concessions for automakers. They had asserted that the costs of some requirements exceeded the benefits and that some changes were unrealistic. The new law also delayed both tougher standards for diesel buses and rules for mandating use of alternate fuels for fleets of cars, buses, vans, and trucks. President Bush supported the compromise Clean Air Act for some of the same reasons he signed the final Rio agreement: it balanced environmental protection with protection of people's jobs and businesses.

Another recent environmental trade-off pitted the logging industry against environmentalists. A committee chaired by Secretary of the Interior Manuel Lujan, Jr., sided with the timber industry in voting to exempt from the Endangered Species Act timber sales on some federal lands in Oregon. Lujan ignored biologists' warnings that cutting down these forests would destroy the northern spotted owl's habitat. Lujan claimed that preventing the timber sales would cost 32,000 jobs. The Sierra Club and other environmental groups challenged the decision in federal appeals court.

**Affordable Health Care**    Perhaps no issue has proved more controversial than health care insurance. After years of increases exceeding the rate of inflation, the cost of health care skyrocketed to $800 billion in 1991. One debate centers on how to control the costs of Medicaid for the poor and Medicare for the elderly. Another controversy concerns how to provide care for the 36 million Americans who have no medical insurance. People generally agree that a way must be found to make medical care available to all. However, disagreement abounds over who is to administer the medical care, how much care is to be provided, and who is to pay the resulting costs.

Because Medicaid benefits are primarily paid for by each state, several states have attempted to make

A Changing Nation in a Changing World    801

© P. F. GERO, SYGMA

© REUTERS/BETTMANN

**As aging Americans, left, spoke out for afford-able health care, young Americans faced re-lated concerns. Basketball star Magic Johnson, above, who tested positive for the AIDS-causing virus, became a crusader for safe sex practices and increased medical research.**

the system more fair and cost-effective. In Oregon, legislators spent five years creating a plan based on the controlled spending of limited resources. Their plan prioritized 709 medical treatments on the basis of medical effectiveness and their value to society. When projections showed that state funds ran out at item 587, officials determined that procedures 588 through 709 would not be covered that year. Critics charged that the Oregon plan rationed health care unfairly. Before the plan could be implemented, the federal government declared that it violated the Americans with Disabilities Act.[1]

A more successful health care system was imple-mented by Hawaii through its Prepaid Health Care Act, passed in 1974. The act requires employers to provide health insurance coverage for all full-time workers. Employers and workers share in the insur-ance cost. Unemployed and part-time workers are covered by the state.

States with large urban populations will most likely be unable to afford a comprehensive program such as Hawaii's. Such states often have many people who are poor, unemployed, or need special or long-term care. Even so, these states cannot restrict health care as Oregon attempted to do, according to a deci-sion of the federal government.

**Women's Concerns**   Affordable health care ranks high among the issues galvanizing women in the last decade of the century. In their continuing quest for equality, women won new political victories in the

early 1990s but also suffered defeats. Among the vic-tories was the large number of women who ran in primary elections. In 1992 voters nominated 11 women for Senate seats and 108 for House seats, both record numbers. So many were successful—4 in the Senate, 48 in the House— that the news media called 1992 "Year of the Woman."

**Women in the Labor Force, 1920–1990**

Median male income: $6,670
Median female income: $2,237
66% less than males in 1970

Median male income: $17,752
Median female income: $8,101
54% less than males in 1987

U.S. Workers (percent)

Year

**In the early 1990s women made up about half the work force, but two big issues remained. One was a need for quality day care for children. The other was salary, some of which paid for day care.** *Why was pay still an issue for most working women?*

***STUDY GUIDE***

**Recognizing Bias**
Working women often encounter an invisible barrier, called the "glass ceil-ing," on their climb to the executive of-fice. What bias does this show toward women? Barely one half of one percent of top executives are women. Even the few who make it into top positions of vice president or higher are paid 42 percent less than their male counterparts.

**1**  In what way did Oregon legislators try to make their state's health care plan cost-effective?

Despite political gains, women did not reach the summit in their long climb to equality. As the 1990s began, 60 percent of American women worked outside the home but earned just 71 cents for every $1 earned by full-time male workers. Three of every five working women still held low-paying "pink-collar" jobs such as secretary, waitress, sales clerk, and hairdresser. Women who earned yearly salaries of $30,000 or more made up just 13 percent of working women, versus 40 percent of working men at that salary level. African American, Hispanic, and Native American women lagged even farther behind the national average. For example, African American women with college degrees earned 10 percent less than their white counterparts. The average Hispanic woman earned almost 20 percent less than the average white American woman.

In the 1990s abortion remained one of the most controversial issues. On one side of the argument were people who believed that every woman had the right to choose for herself whether to have an abortion. On the other side of the argument were people who held a pro-life position and who wanted to overturn *Roe* v. *Wade*, which in 1973 legalized abortion. Since 1989, when the U.S. Supreme Court, in *Webster* v. *Reproductive Health Services*, upheld a state's right to restrict abortions, anti-abortion supporters chipped away at legalized abortion through increasingly restrictive state laws.

## *The New Pluralism*

Like women, ethnic groups are seeking a greater voice and power in the 1990s. The increasing ethnic diversity of the United States dates back to 1965. At that time President Johnson and Congress reopened the gates to immigrants and ended the bias against Asian and Hispanic immigrants. The Immigration Act of 1965, wrote one observer, created "a stampede, almost an invasion" of people "who hungered to enter."

The surge of immigrants arriving in the 1980s did not match the waves that had come in the early 1900s. Still, 750,000 immigrants each year are having a significant impact on the nation. Statistics show that the native-born white population is not growing as fast as other racial and ethnic populations of the United

States. This led *TIME* to predict that white Americans may be a minority group in less than 70 years.[2]

**Unity and Diversity**    During the 1970s and 1980s poverty and political conflicts in several parts of the world drove people toward the United States. Devastating wars in Southeast Asia created waves of political refugees, and the United States accepted more than 500,000 Asian refugees between 1975 and 1990. Even more entered the United States from the Philippines, China, Taiwan, South Korea, India, and Pakistan.

The chance for economic success that attracted legal immigrants also attracted millions of undocumented immigrants—people living in the United States without proper visas. In 1986 Congress passed the Immigration Reform and Control Act. The law offered undocumented immigrants who had lived in the United States since 1981 the chance to become legal residents. More than one million immigrants

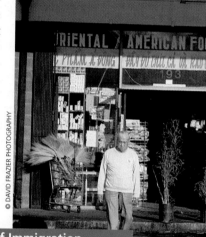

© DAVID FRAZIER PHOTOGRAPHY

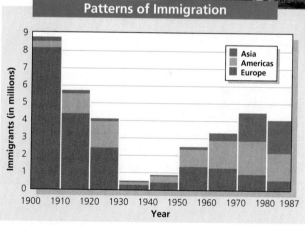

**Patterns of Immigration**

Immigrants (in millions) — Year

Asia
Americas
Europe

**About 11 million immigrants entered the United States between 1965 and 1990. Many, like the Vietnamese man above, sought and found better jobs here.** *According to the chart, how did immigration change after 1960?*

**Recognizing Bias**
The immigration laws of the 1920s were biased in favor of people from Western Europe. The number of people allowed to immigrate each year from any one country was based on the number of people of that nationality already living in the United States. The 1965 Immigration Act was also biased in favor of relatives of U.S. citizens rather than of people from a certain region.

**2** How will the ethnic makeup of the United States population probably change in the 1990s because of immigration?

took advantage of the law during the first year it was in effect. As one Mexican-born housekeeper said:

*I* *am so happy. I prayed and prayed the INS [Immigration and Naturalization Service] wouldn't find me. I never knew what the next month would bring. Now I'll be able to make plans for the future. I already feel like it's my country.*

Yolanda Perez
in "Out of the Shadows," *TIME*, May 4, 1987

The effects of such extensive immigration concerned many Americans. Some state governors complained that immigrants were competing with unemployed U.S. citizens for the limited number of available jobs. In 1981, however, a congressional committee reported that immigrants "work hard, save and invest, and create more jobs than they take." Other critics, forgetting America's immigrant past, wondered how so many new people, with their different customs, foods, and languages, would fit into American culture.

Despite these concerns, many experts predict that the United States will be as enriched and stimulated by its modern immigrants as it has been throughout its history. Cultural and ethnic differences conceived as problems in earlier times came to be treasured for adding richness and diversity to American culture.

**Political Shifts**   With changes in population came attempts to make political changes. Using 1990 census information, state lawmakers and their legislative mapmakers began readjusting congressional, state, and local legislative district lines to conform to growth and shifts in population. This redistricting would have wide effects, including government contract awards and election of those who were not white to local, state, and national offices.

Gerrymandering—redrawing congressional districts to give one ethnic group or political party an electoral majority—went on as usual. For many Democrats the goal was to create districts in which African American and Hispanic American candidates would win elections. For many Republicans the goal was to pack minorities into compact districts and leave white majorities in surrounding districts. This type of redistricting raised the likelihood that increased numbers of white Republicans would offset any black and Hispanic gains.

**As this map shows, many Americans moved south and west during the 1980s in search of good jobs and new homes in warmer climates.** *Which states had the greatest percentage increases in population? Which states lost population?*

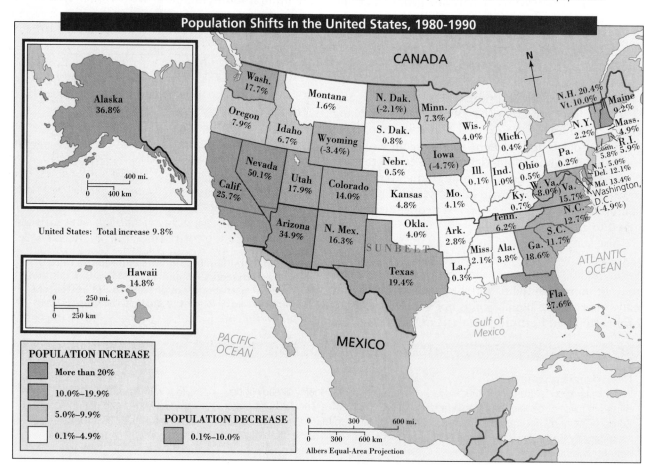

Opponents of gerrymandering complain that it removes the need to negotiate compromises and form coalitions, the normal work of politics. Critics point out that Asian Americans in California have substantial political power, which they got the old-fashioned way—by winning the votes of other groups rather than forming districts composed almost exclusively of a single group.

Even without gerrymandering, the 1990 census led to the creation of new electoral districts that increased the number of African Americans in the House of Representatives from 26 to 35 and the number of Hispanic legislators from 10 to 17. Still, ethnic minority groups remained underrepresented because so many of them were not yet citizens, failed to vote, or lived in predominantly white areas.

© PETER TURNLEY, BLACK STAR

**After the rioting in Los Angeles in May 1992, people pitched in to help rebuild their neighborhoods. This crew helped a store owner clean up his property.**

Racial Issues   At the beginning of the 1990s, African Americans found they had gained scant political power, and their lives had changed little during the preceding 10 years. Many African Americans lived in middle-class areas, but far more continued to live in inner city areas, where they remained trapped by drugs, crime, gangs, high unemployment, widespread poverty, and poor schools.

**During the 1980s, more than 1.8 million African Americans became managers and professionals.** *How many African American households reached the middle class?*

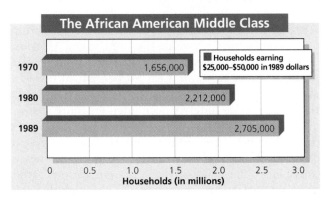

### The African American Middle Class

| | Households earning $25,000–$50,000 in 1989 dollars |
|---|---|
| 1970 | 1,656,000 |
| 1980 | 2,212,000 |
| 1989 | 2,705,000 |

Households (in millions)

One such area erupted in riots in the summer of 1992 when residents of depressed south central Los Angeles took to the streets to vent their anger. The riot began in reaction to a not-guilty verdict in the widely publicized trial of four white police officers who were videotaped savagely beating an African American motorist. African Americans had focused on the trial of the officers as a way to redress the police brutality that many blacks believe plagues their community.[3]

When a jury acquitted the police officers, some African Americans reacted by burning and looting stores and businesses. Thousands of people of all colors joined in. The loss of stores and businesses in Los Angeles was devastating to owners as well as to those who earned their wages there. Once order returned to the area, community residents, people from other neighborhoods, and business owners came together to clear the rubble. People of all ethnic groups, businesses, and the federal government began to rebuild the community and improve the conditions that led to the riot. In rebuilding, African Americans took an active part in addressing issues

## STUDY GUIDE

### Recognizing Propaganda
In the 1980s and early 1990s, racist groups surfaced on many college campuses, spreading racially slanted messages through graffiti and pamphlets.

In a nation where free speech is guaranteed to all citizens, it is important to recognize the intent of such expression.

**3** How was racism evident in American cities in the 1990s?

that have a long history: getting a fair share of building contracts and access to loan money and property insurance.

While many African Americans live in ghettos like south central Los Angeles, many have escaped poverty. Almost 1 million moved up to the middle class during the 1980s, as the number of black managers, professionals, technical workers, and government officials grew by 52 percent. Though African Americans still encounter discrimination in the labor market, many now earn substantial incomes, live in middle-class suburbs, and enjoy the benefits of comfortable life styles.

Some Hispanics also made gains, but most struggled for a foothold on the ladder of upward mobility. Recently arrived immigrants from Mexico, Puerto Rico, and Central and South America were often held back by the language barrier and limited education. They typically held jobs in restaurants or worked in other low-paying service industries. Those who had gotten a college education, however, expected to earn the same wages as their white counterparts.

On the other hand, the condition of Native Americans improved little during the past decade. The reservations remain among the most poverty-stricken areas in the country. Unemployment there runs as high as 70 percent, and alcoholism is common. There is a new spirit of activism, however, among Native Americans that has led to court victories requiring the return of land or payment for land taken by force.

© JIM PICKERELL, FPG INTERNATIONAL

**The Americans with Disabilities Act of 1990, signed by President Bush, safeguarded workers like this telephone operator from discrimination. Even before the law was passed, millions of disabled persons held jobs.**

---

## Educating Tomorrow's Workers

Technological advances and changes in the global economy during the past decade dramatically changed the nature of work and the composition of the work force in the United States. Factories made use of new technologies to lower costs and improve production. Computers and industrial robots helped streamline manufacturing methods. In some factories computers regulated every step of the manufacturing process—from the selection of raw materials to processing, packaging, and inventory control. Fewer factory workers were needed in automated plants, and those employees who remained required

specialized skills. Many jobs requiring specialized skills could be held by disabled persons.

Farming continues to change as much as manufacturing. Many farmers now run their farms like corporations, or agribusinesses, with high-tech equipment to help them oversee large operations. One Illinois farmer uses a computer to keep track of how much corn each of his 5,000 steers eats. Computers and new types of farm machinery allow fewer farmers to produce more food, reducing the number of jobs in agriculture and speeding the movement of people from rural areas to cities and suburbs. In 1990, less than 2 percent of all Americans lived on farms.

**The Changing Job Market**   As jobs in agriculture and manufacturing have disappeared, many American workers have found work in the service industry. Service positions accounted for 90 percent of the 42.6 million new jobs created between 1950 and 1984. By 1990 the service industry accounted for more than 75 percent of all nongovernment, nonfarm jobs in the United States. That number represents an increase of more than 15 percent since 1960. These businesses serve customers and service their possessions rather than manufacturing new goods. They include retail

---

stores, restaurants, hotels, banks, computer software companies, insurance companies, stock brokerages, and accounting firms. One reason for the growth in service businesses is a shift in consumer spending patterns. As income grew for many Americans in the 1970s and 1980s, they were able to fulfill their basic needs with a smaller proportion of their income. They then began to spend more on services such as home maintenance, investment advice, health care, recreation, and travel.

The small number of jobs in the service industry that pay handsome salaries generally require specialized skills and training. But most service jobs pay far less than manufacturing jobs, which are fast disappearing because of corporate downsizing and relocation of plants to foreign countries. New immigrants and workers from inner cities are often unskilled and qualified only for such low-paying service positions as fast-food worker, data-entry clerk, or gas station attendant.

The early 1990s brought improvements for one group of workers because of the passage of the Americans with Disabilities Act (ADA). The act bans discrimination in hiring, promotion, and firing of handicapped persons. This group includes those who are hearing or visually impaired, mentally handicapped, HIV positive, physically impaired, or stricken with cancer or epilepsy.

**Challenges for the Schools** As jobs in all fields become more "high-tech" and demanding, workers need to be better prepared and educated. In 1983 a presidential commission warned that American students lagged behind students in other industrialized nations. In a report entitled *A Nation at Risk*, the commission recommended more homework, longer school days and a longer school year, higher salaries for teachers, and emphasis on such basic subjects as English, math, science, social studies,

and computer science. That the goals set in 1983 had not been met was evident in the "education summit" called by President Bush in 1989. He and the nation's governors agreed on six broad, national goals. These include making sure all children are healthy and intellectually stimulated enough to start school, and raising the level of American students from near the bottom among industrialized nations to the top in math and science achievement. These goals would raise the high school graduation rate from about 75 percent to 90 percent, erase illiteracy, and make schools safe and drug free.

Education reformers, however, cannot agree on how to achieve these goals. Some believe more federal, state, and local funds are needed. Others point out that unless parents and communities encourage academic excellence, merely increasing spending will not be enough.

**Prospects for School Reform** During the 1980s and early 1990s, school districts throughout the nation tried many programs to improve their educational systems. Some yielded encouraging results, while the outcome of others is still unknown. The school of education at Boston University began managing all the public schools in Chelsea, Massachusetts, in 1990. Milwaukee has given some poor students vouchers to attend private schools if they choose. Iowa, Arkansas, Utah, Ohio, and several other states are experimenting with various forms of school choice.

None of these plans tackles the controversial issue of school funding. All American schools are not created equal. Each community funds its schools by levying property taxes on homeowners. As a result, affluent communities generally spend far more

**New types of computers—from those that read and draw building plans (above) to those that help high school students learn math (left)—transformed education and work. Many jobs in the 1990s will require more skills than ever before.**

A Changing Nation in a Changing World     807

to educate their children than inner city and working-class communities. The federal government and states have tried to equalize educational systems by distributing more tax money to poorer districts, but with little success. State legislatures in the early 1990s are using the courts to determine whether they can equalize funding for schools through an increase in state taxes or sales taxes rather than property taxes.[4]

The cry for school reform has grown weaker in the early 1990s as Americans, suffering from a recession, use their limited resources to satisfy other priorities. California, Massachusetts, New York, Connecticut, and other states, hit hard by the recession, have all cut school budgets. Many districts have cut or reduced programs such as foreign languages, music classes, and sports. Class sizes are expanding and the school year is getting shorter.

In contrast to these negative trends, an innovative experiment called Microsociety shows promising results. For the program's five elementary schools—two in Massachusetts and three in New York—the school day is split in half. In the morning students attend traditional classes in history, science, English, and math. In the afternoon they put their lessons to work by simulating real-life experiences such as holding jobs, paying taxes, and owning businesses. Results have been dramatic. After six years, the mostly African American students at City Magnet School in Lowell, Massachusetts, tested an average of two years above the national norms in both reading and math.

## Panorama of the 1990s

As the last decade of the twentieth century comes to a close, Americans can expect technology to continue altering both their work and their leisure dramatically. Advances in computer hardware and software will probably transform people of all kinds —recreational users as well as professionals—into computer enthusiasts. **Biotechnology,** technology applied to biology, is revolutionizing such fields as medicine and food production. Engineers and designers around the globe work on new ways of representing and manipulating enormous amounts of multimedia information.

**High-Tech Recreation**   San Francisco holiday shoppers in 1991 got a taste of the new technology that is likely to become commonplace in the next century. They waited in line for up to 90 minutes and paid $4 for four minutes to play a virtual reality (VR) game. Players donned a stereoscopic helmet with screens that filled the player's field of vision with a moving picture of a different world. As they moved their heads, the scene around them changed as it would in the physical world. Images in VR are not pretaped but are instead generated by computer graphics as the players move their heads.

Virtual reality is more than an arcade game. Architects use virtual reality as a communications tool that lets them put their clients "inside" a planned building and helps verify the correctness of computer models of the building. In a Tokyo department store, customers

© NASA, PETER ARNOLD, INC.

**A pilot in training uses virtual reality equipment to simulate flight. The new technology harnesses computer and video systems to create stunning imaginary scenes for recreation or for work.** *What other practical uses could virtual reality have?*

**Making Inferences**
For the 1988–1989 school year, per student spending in the Chicago area varied from $5,265 in the city of Chicago to $9,000 in some wealthy suburbs. In communities with large school expenditures, students scored much higher on achievement tests than children in most Chicago schools. As a result, one can infer that the amount of money spent per student significantly affects student success.

**4** What causes the growing gap in school spending between city and suburban schools?

can put on virtual reality goggles and a glove to design their own kitchen.

Computers also have entered the world of sports science, becoming an indispensable training aid for competitors. In swimming, for example, computers measure and analyze the oxygen intake of athletes stroking against a pump-generated current. Swimmers' blood can be tested for chemicals such as lactic acid to determine the rate of energy production. Pennsylvania State University researcher John Shea developed the "Leaper Beeper" in which sensors connected to a laptop computer measure a diver's performance. During practice, coded beeping noises tell the divers in the air how high they jumped and how far down they pushed the diving board.

**New Movement, New Power**  In the area of transportation, magnetic levitation (maglev) trains may carry passengers at speeds up to 300 miles per hour. Maglev trains ride suspended by magnetic fields above a single guideway similar to a monorail. The federal government has authorized the expenditure of $725 million by 1997 for development and production of the nation's first maglev prototype.

However, before maglev trains can revolutionize ground transportation, some problems need to be solved. Engineers contend that some proposed systems will require more than 40 times the electricity consumed by Japan's bullet trains that go half as fast. Also, as these trains rush through the air, they generate the sound of hurricane-force winds.

Biotechnology also promises to revolutionize the way we live. After the discovery of recombinant DNA principles, scientists predicted that genetic engineering would soon produce a host of new and improved natural products, such as skim milk right from the cow and radishes as big as yams. Reduction of government regulations on genetically engineered products in 1992 spurred research and development. One product being developed is a tomato that can ripen on the vine and be

SYGMA

**Futuristic automobiles hold the promise of revolutionizing travel as well as burning less fuel. The cost of developing them, however, is very high.**

shipped without rotting. This new variety of tomato should have improved flavor over those now picked green and ripened artificially with gas. The Food and Drug Administration is evaluating the tomato to be sure it is safe for consumption.

Development of new drugs through biotechnology and genetic engineering gives hope to Americans suffering from illnesses. Biotechnology firms have already produced synthetic insulin, growth hormones, and drugs that stimulate the production of red and white blood cells. New drugs may give immunity to people who are likely to get diseases like malaria.

New developments raise new concerns about regulation and testing. Critics question the wisdom of excessive tampering with nature. Should parents be allowed to choose the gender and physical characteristics of their children, for example? Those who benefit from a new product may push for quick approval by government regulators. Experts warn, however, that only careful testing can guard against harmful long-term effects and prove the usefulness of a product.

## SECTION REVIEW

**Checking Facts**

1. How did the compromise Clean Air Act of 1990 affect businesses and workers?

2. Why did the federal government refuse to approve the Oregon plan for medical insurance?

3. What effects did immigrants have on the nation's economy, according to a 1981 congressional report?

4. How might redistricting affect government?

5. Besides public anger with the legal system, what factors contributed to the eruption of the 1992 riot in Los Angeles?

**Thinking Critically**

6. **Recognizing Bias**
Some education reformers believe that many problems in education could be solved if more money were spent on schools. How is this point of view biased?

7. **Recognizing Values**
Some people argue that as a democracy and a nation of immigrants, the United States has an obligation to keep its borders open to new immigrants. Evaluate this argument.

**Linking Across Time**

8. What technological advances may radically alter the way Americans live in the next century?

A Changing Nation in a Changing World      809

# Case Study

# The Future of Walden Woods

## SUMMER 1990

> *Of all the characters I have known, perhaps Walden wears best, and best deserves its purity. Many men have been likened to it, but few deserve the honor. Though the woodchoppers have laid bare first this shore and then that, and the Irish have built their sties by it, and the railroad has infringed on its border, and the ice-men have skimmed it once, it is itself unchanged, the same water which my youthful eyes fell on; all the change is in me.*
>
> —Henry David Thoreau, *Walden, or Life in the Woods,* 1854

### The Case

On December 1, 1986, the development firm of Boston Properties submitted a building proposal to the town of Concord, Massachusetts, to construct a 147,000-square-foot office park and a 518-space parking structure in an area known as Brister's Hill, 700 yards from Walden Pond. At about the same time, another developer submitted a proposal to build Concord Commons, a 251-unit condominium complex on Bear Garden Hill, 1,400 yards west of Walden Pond. The board accepted the office park proposal without hesitation and, after some negotiations, eventually reached a compromise agreement with the Concord Commons developer as well. Upon hearing of the acceptance of both of these proposals, members of historical preservation organizations such as the Thoreau Country Conservation Alliance (TCCA) mobilized their resources to fight the two construction projects. A battle between those people in favor of building development and those

people in favor of historical preservation then ensued for control of Walden Woods.

### The Background

The intense debate over the development projects stems from the history of Walden Pond and Walden Woods. From 1845 to 1847, Henry David Thoreau composed his masterwork, *Walden, or Life in the Woods,* while living in a one-room house on the shores of Walden Pond. In this extended essay, Thoreau promoted the values of solitude and the idea that nature can renew your energy and sense of well-being. In writing Walden and other works, he was inspired by Walden Pond and also by the surrounding woods and hillsides. Today Thoreau is considered the father of the conservationist movement, and Walden Woods its birthplace.

Walden Woods at present looks very little like it did during Thoreau's time, when only farmland and railroad tracks interrupted it. Now a four-lane highway slices through the woods to the northeast of the pond. An average of 42,000 cars per day travel this congested commuter highway.

© OWEN FRANKEN, STOCK BOSTON

**Scenes such as this inspired Thoreau to write, "You must converse much with the field and woods, if you would imbibe such health into your mind and spirit as you covet for your body."**

Thousands of people visit Walden Pond each summer, leaving their cars in a parking lot across the road from the pond. Located next to the pond is Concord's town landfill, which the state will eliminate by the year 2000. Also nearby is Walden Breezes trailer park, which the state owns and is currently attempting to eliminate. Finally, approximately 35 homes are located throughout the Walden Woods area.

With so many human beings congesting the area, Concord has had to develop zoning laws to regulate commercial and residential development. These zoning laws restrict the size of construction projects. State Law Chapter 774 offers the only way to get around such size restrictions. However, it applies only to building projects in towns such as Concord where affordable housing makes up less than 10 percent of the total housing available. Under this law a developer can be exempted from zoning restrictions as long as the developer reserves 30 percent of the project for low- or middle-income housing. This is exactly what the Concord Commons developer did.

## The Arguments

Historical preservationists fear that the construction of condominiums will eventually lead to the destruction of a site that is of historic value. Historians such as Thomas Blanding, head of the TCCA, find it disturbingly ironic that the place where one man wrote so compellingly about the virtues of solitude could become a crowded suburb.

Preservationists note an additional irony. Thoreau is revered by many as the father of the conservationist movement—a movement that seeks to protect natural beauty and wildlife. A portion of the woods that inspired the conservationist movement has already been deforested, but the proposed building projects would alter the area even further.

On the other hand, those in favor of the building projects note that Walden Woods is hardly a pristine environment. Over the last 100 years, the increasing amount of human traffic to Walden Woods has already changed the area greatly. Therefore, they continue, the developments will really have very little impact on the area. They note that the developers have agreed to prevent tourists from parking in the office complex lot on weekends, which could otherwise increase the number of visitors to the area. In addition, they claim that the proposed condominium site does not detract from the beauty of Walden Pond. In fact, the condominiums will be built a good 1,400 yards from the pond.

Furthermore, supporters of the development projects argue that the areas scheduled for development in Walden Woods do not share the historical significance of Walden Pond. The town of Concord hired a lawyer to prove that Bear Garden Hill and Brister's Hill were never actually part of Thoreau's stomping grounds. This lawyer found only one reference to Bear Garden Hill in the 1906 index to Thoreau's Journal and used this fact to refute the TCCA's claim that the hill is of historic importance.

Kevin Convey, a journalist for *Boston Magazine,* responded to the Concord lawyer's argument by pointing out that the 1906 index is an incomplete guide to Thoreau's Journal. In fact, according to Convey and the TCCA, Thoreau's Journal does actually contain a great many references to Bear Garden Hill.

Advocates of the residential development offer a final argument. They believe that State Law Chapter 774 should guarantee completion of the project because the plans include the construction of affordable housing in a town where less than 10 percent of the housing is considered to be affordable. The developer of Concord Commons claims that 42 of the 135 intended units will qualify as low- to moderate-income housing and claims that opponents really just want to prevent affordable housing from being built in the area because such housing might lower area residents' property values. According to developers, opponents of the projects are attempting to mask their true economic concerns with historical and environmental concerns.

The TCCA has responded to this charge by accusing the Bear Garden Hill developers of incorporating affordable housing into their construction proposal just to get past zoning restrictions. In fact, the TCCA notes that only 7 of the 135 units Concord approved qualify as truly low-income housing. In addition, the TCCA points out that five of the six founding members of the TCCA don't even own property in Concord and five would actually qualify for low- or middle-income housing themselves.

## The Outcome

Eighteen days after the town approved the site plan for Boston Properties, Susan Dean, chair of the Concord Historical Commission, appealed the decision in a superior court. Newspapers as far away as Great Britain picked up the story. Three years later, former Eagles' vocalist Don Henley became involved in the issue and organized the Concert for Walden Woods. His purpose was to raise enough money to purchase the two building sites and convert them into wildlife sanctuaries—an ex-

pensive proposition since Boston Properties set the price for Brister's Hill at somewhere between $7 and $10 million. Henley also announced that he intended to look for alternative sites at which to build affordable housing.

In August 1990, Henley, the state, and the developers came to an agreement over Concord Commons. Henley bought the land for $3.5 million and agreed to find an alternate site for the planned housing units. This willingness encouraged advocates of housing. "It's easy to say 'no' to a project," said a spokesman for the state, "but the people who were opposed to it have taken on the responsibility of finding an alternative. That's unusual."

Henley continued his fight to preserve Walden Woods, negotiating with Boston Properties for the site of their office project. To help raise the money, environmentalists—including pop stars, politicians, and actors—wrote a book of essays on the environment.

## The Significance

The outcome of the debate over Walden Woods may have a lasting impact on other areas slated for residential development in Massachusetts by determining how broadly the Chapter 774 zoning act may be interpreted. And the fact that Henley and the historical preservationists were successful in getting developers to relocate the housing development project may signal a shift in American attitudes away from residential and commercial development—or at least toward historical preservation.

## Think About It

1. Organize in chronological order the events involved in the debate over Walden Woods. When you are finished, make a list of causes and effects that appear on your list. Then link the causes to the corresponding effects.
2. Make two columns on a sheet of paper. On one side, list the arguments made by advocates of the developments. On the other side, list the arguments of their opponents. Draw lines to connect related arguments. Are there any arguments that stand alone? If so, is that significant? Explain your answer.

"While I bask in the sun on the shores of Walden Pond, by this heat and this rustle, I am absolved from all obligation to the past. The council of na- tions may reconsider their votes; the grating of a peb- ble annuls them." In this passage, Thoreau describes the regenerative power of nature.

3. Would you consider Walden Woods, including Bear Garden Hill and Brister's Hill, a historic site? Why or why not? Do you think that all historic sites should be protected from com- mercial development? Why or why not?

4. In small groups, meet to discuss the most re- cent agreement reached to settle the Walden Woods debate. Do you think that the agree- ment is fair to both sides in this debate? Brain- storm to come up with other solutions to the debate that all parties concerned might find to be satisfactory.

5. Now that Don Henley and his organization have managed to obtain permission to purchase the properties, what issues has this resolved? What issues has it failed to address? What effect might the solution have on debates between other historical/environmental preservationists and residential and commercial developers?

6. Who do you think should be able to make de- cisions about land use: the people who live in the area, the federal government, or con- cerned citizens from other parts of the country or even the world? Why?

# Chapter 24 Review

**June 1989**
Chinese troops massacre students in Beijing.

**December 1989**
Bush and Gorbachev hold first arms talk.

**July 1990**
Bush signs the Americans with Disabilities Act.

**August 1990**
Iraq invades Kuwait

1989

1990

**July 1989**
Supreme Court upholds a state's right to restrict abortion.

**December 1989**
U.S. troops invade Panama, seize General Noriega.

**February 1990**
Nelson Mandela is freed in South Africa.

**October 1990**
Two Germanies unite as one country.

## Summary

Use the following outline as a tool for reviewing and summarizing the chapter. Copy the outline on your own paper, leaving spaces between headings to jot down notes about key events and concepts.

**I. After the Cold War**
  A.  Arms Reductions
  B.  The Downfall of Communism
  C.  New Military Priorities
  D.  Old Problems, New Hope

**II. Domestic Turmoil**
  A.  Recession and Readjustment
  B.  Wealth and Poverty
  C.  The 1992 Election

**III. America Faces a New Century**
  A.  Probing the Limits
  B.  The New Pluralism
  C.  Educating Tomorrow's Workers
  D.  Panorama of the 1990s

## Ideas, Events, and People

1. What forces led to communism's collapse in the Soviet Union? Which did Gorbachev himself unleash?
2. How did the focus of U.S. foreign policy shift after the end of the cold war?
3. Why did President Bush and Secretary of State Baker seek to involve a large number of nations in the coalition against Iraq in the Persian Gulf War?
4. What benefits might NAFTA give U.S. workers and businesses? What drawbacks might it have?
5. What prompted the U.S. military cutbacks of the early 1990s?
6. How did the workings of a global economy affect American cities and towns in the early 1990s?
7. How did Reagan and Bush tax policies affect wealthy Americans? Poor Americans?
8. In what different ways did the recession of the early 1990s change suburban and urban America?
9. Why was the Endangered Species Act not effective in protecting the habitat of the northern spotted owl in Oregon?
10. Why will health care continue to be an important issue in the 1990s?
11. According to the 1983 report *A Nation at Risk*, what should be done to improve the educational system in the United States?
12. What scientific breakthrough allowed work in genetic engineering to progress in the 1980s?

## Social Studies Skills

**Reading Political Cartoons**

In recent years, environmental concerns have caused most communities to change methods of waste management, or garbage disposal. Create an original cartoon focusing on the problem of waste disposal in your community. Share your cartoon with classmates. Find out whether they interpreted its message correctly.

## Critical Thinking

**1. Drawing Conclusions**
In 1990 many people predicted that a reunited Germany would become Europe's greatest economic power. Draw your own conclusion using information in the text and in current news accounts.

**2. Recognizing Assumptions**
Some critics of NAFTA argue that free trade will drive down Americans' wages to Mexican levels. What assumptions does this argument make?

**3. Comparing and Contrasting**
How was the recession of the early 1990s similar to the Great Depression of the 1930s? How were the two eras different?

| January–February 1991<br>U.S.-led forces oust<br>Iraq from Kuwait. | August 1991<br>Coup fails in Soviet Union;<br>union crumbles. | | June 1992<br>Earth Summit is held<br>in Rio de Janeiro. | November 1992<br>Bill Clinton is elected<br>42nd president. |

**1991**       **1992**       **1993**

| November 1990<br>Bush signs the 1990<br>Clean Air Act. | December 1991<br>Gorbachev resigns; Yeltsin<br>becomes Russian leader. | May 1992<br>Riots flare in Los<br>Angeles, other cities. | August 1992<br>Three nations agree to<br>North American Free Trade Act. |

**4. Recognizing Cause and Effect**

In the early 1990s home mortgage rates were lower than they had been in 20 years, yet sales of new homes rose slowly. What caused the slow sales?

**5. Making Generalizations**

From which regions did most immigrants in the United States arrive between 1965 and 1990? Did people from each region have similar reasons for emigrating?

**6. Recognizing Point of View**

What are the two sides of the argument concerning abortion? Why do you think emotions run so high on this issue?

## Extension and Application

**1. Global Connection**

Work with classmates to make a timeline titled "Freedom Explosion." Begin with March 1985 when Gorbachev became leader of the Soviet Union. Include events from this chapter and events from late 1992 to the present. Divide the work if you wish, with each student researching one country. Illustrate your timeline with photos, drawings, and small maps.

**2. Citizenship**

Research the process by which an immigrant becomes a United States citizen. Your local library would have this information. If possible, interview a person who became a citizen as an adult or one who is preparing for U.S. citizenship. Report your findings and compare them in class.

## Geography

**1.** According to the map below, how many former communist nations share a border with western European nations? How might a shared border affect their economic modernization?

**2.** If the nations colored yellow on this map become members of the European Community, what would be the total number of countries in the EC?

**3.** The Baltic nations of Lithuania, Latvia, and Estonia were the first to break from the USSR. Does their location suggest a possible reason?

**4.** According to the map on page 797, in which region or regions of the country did Bill Clinton win large numbers of electoral votes?

**5.** Study the map on page 719 and locate Brazil and Rio de Janeiro. Why do you think Rio was a good choice for the site of the Earth Summit in 1992?

# Unit 9 Review

> By 1989 four major processes of change were at work reshaping what had come to be called East-West relations: liberalization and reform inside the Soviet Union; the democratization of Eastern Europe; the determined move toward economic integration in Western Europe; and a new, apparently irresistible drive toward unification of East and West Germany. The conjunction and the cumulative impact of these ongoing changes promised to transform Europe—and the U.S. role in Europe. . . .
>
> It is, above all, Mikhail Gorbachev who is changing the world. . . . All this activity and diversity, all this openness and restructuring, are transforming the Soviet Union, Europe and East-West relations. . . .
>
> [The United States] will need to learn to be a power, not a superpower. We should prepare psychologically and economically for reversion to the status of a normal nation, still seeking to encourage democratic institutions, strengthen the rule of law and advance American interests.
>
> Jeane J. Kirkpatrick,
> Georgetown University, 1989

## Concepts and Themes

The cold war ended at the end of the 1980s. Since Kirkpatrick made the remarks above, the two Germanys have reunited, and the other changes she mentioned are still, as she said, ongoing. The United States and the former Soviet Union are discovering what it means to be a power, not a superpower. The recent past has brought changes —breathtaking transformations—in the world and in the United States.

1. What changes in U.S. immigration patterns resulted from the Immigration Act of 1965? What population shifts have happened within the United States?
2. What was the Soviet economy like when Gorbachev took office? What changes took place under his policy of *perestroika?* What were some of the results?
3. How might democratization in Eastern Europe affect global markets in the 1990s?
4. What do you think Kirkpatrick meant when she said that the United States must learn to be "a power, not a superpower"? What practical differences could it make to be a "normal nation"?

## History Projects

1. **One Day in History**
   Create a timeline tracing the current democracy movement in Europe. Use an almanac or the *Readers' Guide to Periodical Literature* to help you identify the significant dates and events.
2. **Evidence of the Past**
   Examine the journal *Vital Speeches* for 1990 or later. Find a speech that reflects one or more of the changes Kirkpatrick lists. Write a summary.
3. **Culture of the Time**
   Work with a small group to plan and present a comic skit about some aspect of popular or teenage culture of the 1980s or 1990s. For example, create a skit about clothing styles, hair styles, shopping malls, or Walkmans.

## Writing Activities

1. Write a short biography about a prominent person of the 1980s. Begin your research with the *Readers' Guide*. Possible subjects are Sally Ride, the first woman in space; Jesse Jackson, the civil rights leader; and Mikhail Gorbachev. (See the Writer's Guide, page 826, for guidelines on expository writing.)
2. Choose a recent invention that changed the way people live: for example, camcorders, rock videos, robots, electronic artificial limbs. Describe it, and tell how it has changed lives, including yours. (See the Writer's Guide, page 825, for guidelines on descriptive writing.)

## The Arts

- *A Yellow Raft in Blue Water* by Michael Dorris; a novel of women with a shared past and future.
- *Do the Right Thing;* Spike Lee's movie portraying racial tension in a Brooklyn neighborhood.
- *Riding the Iron Rooster* by Paul Theroux; the writer's railroad trip across modern China.

# A Century of Changes

As your study of *American Odyssey* has revealed, the twentieth century has been a transforming period for the United States. At the beginning of the century, the United States was just beginning to play an international role, but by mid-century the nation had emerged as the world's preeminent economic and political power. And now as we approach the end of the century, the United States finds itself still powerful but ever more linked to and affected by the other nations of our increasingly interdependent world.

On the homefront, technology and economic prosperity have dramatically changed the way Americans live. During this century technology has brought us new ways of getting around and of exchanging information—automobiles and radio, airplanes and television, space shuttles and FAX machines. These new networks of transportation and communication have linked us together as a people and increased our mobility. New agricultural technologies have dramatically increased farm productivity while drastically decreasing the percentage of our population involved in farming. Medical technology has eliminated the threat of many diseases, enabling us to live longer lives. And computers have changed the ways we do just about everything, from grocery shopping to conducting scientific research.

Even the ethnic makeup of American society has changed during this century of transformation. Waves of immigration have increased our ethnic diversity, bringing especially dramatic growth in the Hispanic and Asian populations. And in the final decades of the century, older people are becoming a larger percentage of the population as Americans live longer, thanks to modern medical technology as well as higher standards of living.

As Americans become a more diverse people, the challenge to extend the promises of the Constitution to the full spectrum of the population goes on. The courageous efforts of many African Americans, Native Americans, women, and others have won great expansion of legal and civil rights, but many concerns remain to be addressed.

Despite all these changes, as adults you will face many of the same issues that Americans have always faced. For example, each generation must grapple with balancing individual rights and the power of the state, with protecting the interests of the minority while upholding our system of majority rule. However, the changing world in which you live will also confront you with new challenges. The examples on the next two pages will give you a sense of what some of these challenges may be. As informed and active citizens, you will play a crucial role in addressing these future challenges and in preserving our democratic system.

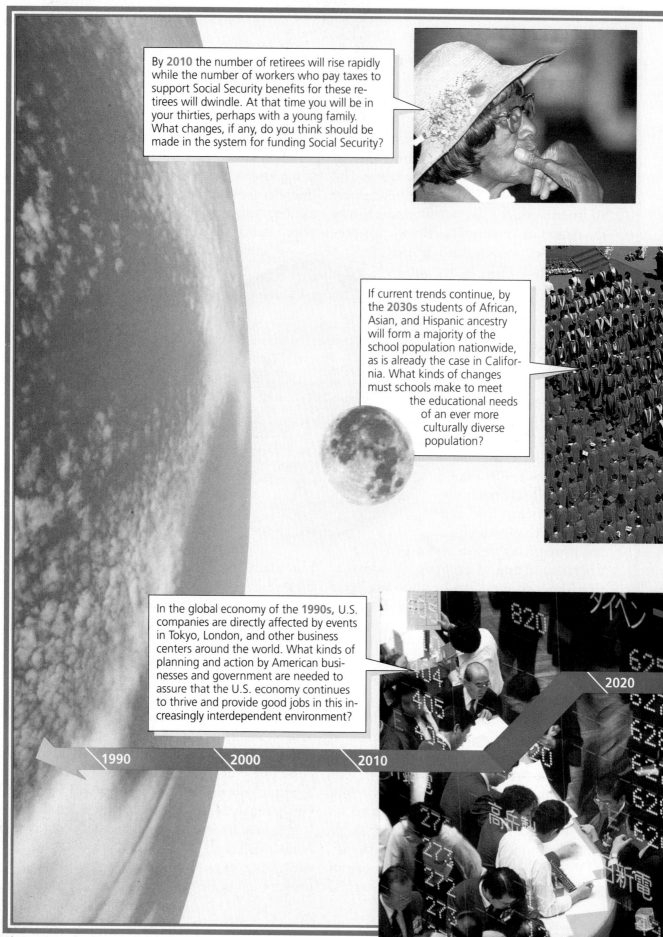

By **2010** the number of retirees will rise rapidly while the number of workers who pay taxes to support Social Security benefits for these retirees will dwindle. At that time you will be in your thirties, perhaps with a young family. What changes, if any, do you think should be made in the system for funding Social Security?

If current trends continue, by the **2030s** students of African, Asian, and Hispanic ancestry will form a majority of the school population nationwide, as is already the case in California. What kinds of changes must schools make to meet the educational needs of an ever more culturally diverse population?

In the global economy of the **1990s,** U.S. companies are directly affected by events in Tokyo, London, and other business centers around the world. What kinds of planning and action by American businesses and government are needed to assure that the U.S. economy continues to thrive and provide good jobs in this increasingly interdependent environment?

1990      2000      2010      2020

By **2020** genetic engineering techniques may make it possible to prevent genetic defects such as hemophilia or sickle cell anemia. Should such technology be used to allow parents to choose the physical characteristics of their children? To what extent, if any, should society regulate the use of biotechnology?

Computer models predict that by **2050** average temperatures worldwide will have risen between 3 and 8 degrees Fahrenheit because of the build-up of carbon dioxide and other gases in the atmosphere. Such changes would severely disrupt world agriculture and perhaps cause sea levels to rise as the polar ice caps melt. What responsibilities do we as citizens today have to minimize these changes?

2030

2040

2050

2060

2070

# *Activities*

1. Americans have a wide range of opinions about each of the questions posed on the previous two pages. Choose one of these questions to research. Based on your study, prepare a presentation that includes a range of points of view about the issue as well as your own opinions.

2. Dealing with issues like the ones you have just read about will require a vigorous political system for formulating public policy. However, the rate of citizen participation in the United States as measured by the percentage of eligible adults who actually vote has been declining for years. In fact, it is among the lowest of any democratic nation. After using library resources to research this trend, prepare a list of proposals you think might help to increase the rate of voter participation.

3. One much-discussed impact of technology is the effect of television on the political process. Some critics claim that TV has converted politics into entertainment. They point out that the 10-second "sound bites" favored in TV news do not allow the time needed to present complex issues or unconventional points of view that require explanation. For one week, follow the way a current political story is reported on TV and in newspapers. In a written report, compare the two forms of coverage. Do you think the criticisms of TV coverage are valid?

# Sourcebook

# A Writer's Guide

## Part 1
## Composing Paragraphs

When you write, you group related sentences to create paragraphs. The following steps can help you write paragraphs that effectively convey your ideas.

1. **Identify your purpose and audience.** More than anything else, your purpose and audience will determine what and how you write. A paragraph you write to explain a series of events to a friend, for example, will be far different from a paragraph you write to persuade your neighbors to support a new youth organization. Look at the model paragraph in the table below. The writer's purpose was to give teachers and students an understanding of the range of effects the settlement of the coal strike might have. For more information on writing for different purposes, refer to Part 4 of this Writer's Guide, on pages 825–827.

2. **Write a topic sentence.** State your main idea in a sentence. You may find it useful to draft several versions of this topic sentence. However, since not every paragraph needs a topic sentence, you might not include one in the finished paragraph. Notice how the topic sentence in the model below changes during the revising process.

3. **Develop your main idea.** Make a list of any related ideas and supporting details that come to mind. Write them as sentences. Then review the sentences to decide whether they contribute to your purpose. You can follow the development of ideas into sentences in the model below.

4. **Organize your sentences.** The purpose for your paragraph generally determines the best way to organize your ideas. For example, if you are writing to tell the story of an event, you will want to present your information in chronological order. Your purpose for writing social studies paragraphs will most often be to tell the story of an event or a series of events, to convey an experience, to clarify information, and/or to persuade. Refer to Part 4 of this Writer's Guide, on pages 825–827, for help in choosing the most appropriate purpose for your paragraph. Once you have chosen your purpose, arrange your sentences according to the pattern best suited to achieving that purpose. Notice that a comparison pattern is used in the model paragraph below.

5. **Connect your sentences.** Write your sentences in order, adding transitions and cue words to show relationships between ideas. To see how cues can clarify a writer's purpose, examine the chart in the skill lesson on page 283.

6. **Edit your paragraph.** Expand and improve your sentences, varying their structure and length, adding modifiers, and revising word choices. Cut sentences that don't contribute to the main idea or that disrupt the flow of your paragraph.

### Composing Paragraphs

| Topic Sentence / Supporting Details | First Draft | Revised Paragraph |
|---|---|---|
| **Topic Sentence**<br>Settlement of the coal strike was a partial success for everyone.<br><br>**Supporting Details**<br>Roosevelt was praised for settling the strike.<br>Roosevelt didn't send federal troops.<br>Mine owners didn't have to recognize the mine workers' union.<br>Mine workers won 10 percent pay increase and nine-hour work day.<br>The public could stop worrying about lack of fuel in the coming cold winter.<br>Big business won because public resentment against business stopped growing.<br>Everyone got a square deal. | Settlement of the coal strike was a partial success for everyone. Mine workers won 10 percent pay increase and nine-hour work day. Mine owners didn't have to recognize a mine worker's union. Roosevelt was praised for settling the strike without sending in troops. Big business won because public resentment against business stopped growing. The public could stop worrying about lack of fuel for the coming cold winter. Everyone got a square deal. | The coal-strike settlement could be described as a "square deal for everyone." Mine workers won a 10 percent pay increase and a nine-hour work day, but not the recognition of their union. Mine owners won because they were not forced to recognize the mine workers' union. Big businesses also won because the settlement successfully stopped the rising tide of public resentment against them. In addition, President Roosevelt earned praise for his part in settling the strike without sending in troops. Even the public benefited, because it could at last stop worrying about a possible fuel shortage in the coming cold winter. |

## Part 2
## *Taking Notes*

Throughout the school year, you will take notes to keep track of important ideas and facts. Taking notes is an important step in getting ready to write; it is a way to make sense of and remember what you read and hear. Whatever your reason for taking notes, a clear, easy-to-follow system will make your notes easier to refer to and more useful as references.

The sample note cards on this page illustrate three different types of notes: summary, fact, and quotation. All four cards reflect the following note-taking procedure:

1. **Card #**  Give each card a separate number.

2. **Outline Section**  Identify the question being answered or the section of your working outline addressed by each note card.

3. **Type of Note**  Write what you wish to record.

   a. **Summary Note**  Summarize from memory, if possible. Identify the main ideas, paraphrasing important ideas in your own words. Include only those details necessary for recall or for understanding. Use key words. If necessary, refer to Part 3 on page 824 of this Writer's Guide for additional help.

   b. **Fact Note**  Write succinctly, including only key words and important facts. Shortcut by using abbreviations and symbols.

   c. **Quotation Note**  Use quotation marks to set off the quote from your own words. Be sure to identify the speaker if different from the author of your source.

4. **Comment**  Write down any thoughts that might be helpful when you refer to the card later.

5. **Source Identification**  Prepare a numbered bibliography card for each source. Use these bibliography card numbers to quickly and easily identify the source of each note card.

6. **Source Page Number**  Include the correct page numbers from which you took the information in case you need to find this information again.

Now turn to page 270 in Chapter 8 to find the source material used to create the cards below.

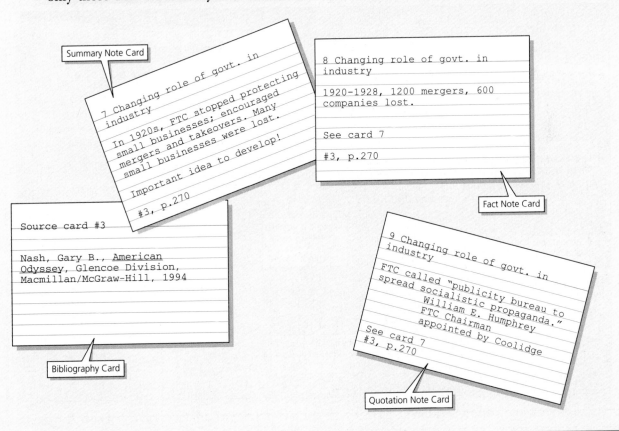

Summary Note Card

7 Changing role of govt. in industry

In 1920s, FTC stopped protecting small businesses; encouraged mergers and takeovers. Many small businesses were lost.

Important idea to develop!

#3, p.270

Fact Note Card

8 Changing role of govt. in industry

1920-1928, 1200 mergers, 600 companies lost.

See card 7

#3, p.270

Bibliography Card

Source card #3

Nash, Gary B., <u>American Odyssey</u>, Glencoe Division, Macmillan/McGraw-Hill, 1994

Quotation Note Card

9 Changing role of govt. in industry

FTC called "publicity bureau to spread socialistic propaganda." William E. Humphrey FTC Chairman appointed by Coolidge

See card 7

#3, p.270

## Part 3
# *Summarizing What You Read*

To be sure you understand and remember what you read, you can summarize important ideas. Following these guidelines will help:

1. **Read the whole paragraph or section.** Do not try to begin summarizing before you have read an entire passage.

2. **Identify the main ideas.** Read the passage again, this time noting the main ideas. Look at the example at the bottom of this page. The marginal notes alongside the sample passage are examples of such main idea notes.

3. **Note key words.** Write down or highlight key words and phrases that will help you remember the main ideas. Examine the highlighted words and phrases in the passage below.

4. **Be concise.** Write down or highlight only sentences that convey main ideas. Do not include any details that do not affect the meaning of the sentence and that do not help clarify the main ideas.

5. **Paraphrase.** Write your summary in your own words. Do not copy sentences exactly as they are written. Writing down the ideas in your own words will ensure that you understand what you have read. Use key words and phrases as they appear in what you read, but choose your own words to connect the ideas. Note that the summary paragraph at the bottom of the page contains key words from the passage it summarizes, but some sentences have been combined and others have been changed by varying the phrases connecting the ideas.

6. **Review.** Use this checklist as you read through your summary:

   - Are the facts accurate?
   - Does the summary include adequate information to ensure that you will remember and understand the main ideas expressed in the material you read?
   - Are all details related to the main idea?

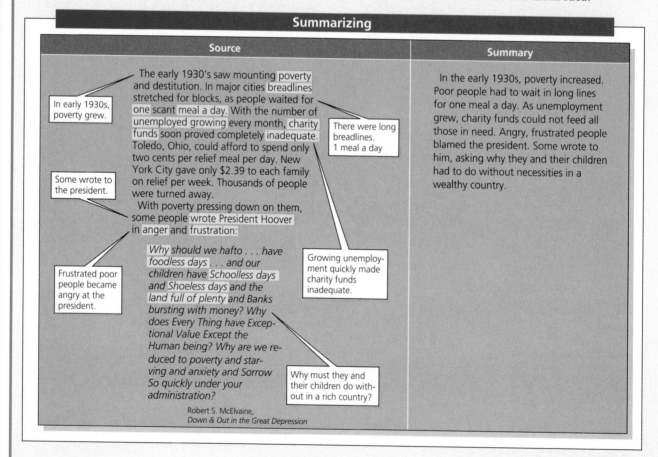

### Summarizing

**Source**

In early 1930s, poverty grew.

The early 1930's saw mounting poverty and destitution. In major cities breadlines stretched for blocks, as people waited for one scant meal a day. With the number of unemployed growing every month, charity funds soon proved completely inadequate. Toledo, Ohio, could afford to spend only two cents per relief meal per day. New York City gave only $2.39 to each family on relief per week. Thousands of people were turned away.

There were long breadlines. 1 meal a day

With poverty pressing down on them, some people wrote President Hoover in anger and frustration:

Some wrote to the president.

Frustrated poor people became angry at the president.

*Why should we hafto . . . have foodless days . . . and our children have Schoolless days and Shoeless days and the land full of plenty and Banks bursting with money? Why does Every Thing have Exceptional Value Except the Human being? Why are we reduced to poverty and starving and anxiety and Sorrow So quickly under your administration?*

Growing unemployment quickly made charity funds inadequate.

Why must they and their children do without in a rich country?

Robert S. McElvaine,
*Down & Out in the Great Depression*

**Summary**

In the early 1930s, poverty increased. Poor people had to wait in long lines for one meal a day. As unemployment grew, charity funds could not feed all those in need. Angry, frustrated people blamed the president. Some wrote to him, asking why they and their children had to do without necessities in a wealthy country.

## Part 4
# Writing for Different Purposes

The purpose for your writing largely determines how and what you write. In social studies, your purpose in writing will most often be to tell what happened, to explain why or how it happened, and/or to persuade. Narrative, descriptive, comparative, expository, and persuasive writing will help you to achieve these goals.

### Narrative Writing

To tell the story of an event or a series of events, you will often use narrative writing. In this type of writing, events are usually arranged in chronological order. In addition, transitional words and phrases are used to help clarify the relationships between events. The following paragraph is a good example of narrative writing. However, note that it also contains elements of good descriptive writing—sensory details and figurative language. These enhance the narrative in that they help you to better envision what happened.

> No one who saw the explosion of the first H-bomb ever forgot it. Out of a blast of white heat, five times hotter than the center of the sun, billowed a monstrous mushroom cloud. Purple, gray, and yellow and nearly 100 miles wide, it climbed 25 miles into the sky. The blast carved a mile-long crater in the bottom of the ocean and spilled radioactive dust over thousands of square miles. Nuclear scientists had let a terrible genie out of the bottle, and now there was no way to put it back.

### Descriptive Writing

To convey an experience as vividly as possible, you will want to use descriptive writing—writing that incorporates sensory details and/or figures of speech. Sensory details appeal to the senses, enabling the reader to see what you have seen, hear what you have heard, feel what you have felt, and so on. Figures of speech, such as simile and metaphor, compare unfamiliar objects or events to familiar objects or events so that the reader can envision these less familiar objects and events more easily.

The following two paragraphs show you how you can expand sentences to more vividly convey an experience. Think about all of the senses to which these words and phrases appeal. Also look for the similes and metaphors and notice how they help you to "see" and "feel" what it was like to be in a dust storm.

### Basic Paragraph

> On Sunday, April 14, 1935, people on the Great Plains of the United States experienced a dust storm. The blowing dust formed clouds that extended over 1,000 feet into the air and several miles wide. Birds flew to escape the choking dust. Rain brought some dust to the ground as mud. Motorists had to stop because they were unable to see through the dust. The dust piled up on railroad lines, where it stayed until snow plows cleared it away. The removal of the dust from the railroad lines took the plows several days.

### Expanded Paragraph

> On Sunday, April 14, 1935, one of the biggest dust storms of this century swept over the Great Plains of the United States. Huge black clouds of dust, more than 1,000 feet high, formed a wall miles wide. Birds flew frantically trying to escape suffocation in the roiling storm. Motorists were stranded for hours along the highway, totally blinded by the impenetrable cloud. The rain sent mud balls splattering to the ground. Dust from the "black blizzard" piled up on railroad lines, and it took snow plows several days to clear off the tracks.

### Comparative Writing

If your aim is to help clarify how two or more things are alike or different, you will be using comparative writing. In comparative writing, you point out similarities and/or differences and usually arrange your material point by point from the least important or significant point to the most important point.

The following paragraphs compare the progressive reformers of the early 1900s with the Populists of the 1880s and 1890s. As you read these paragraphs, think about how these comparisons help you to better understand the progressive reformers.

> Like the populists of the 1880s and 1890s, progressives feared the concentration of power in the hands of the wealthy few. While hard-working immigrants could not afford to provide for their hungry and ill children, financiers like J. P. Morgan became millionaires by manipulating ownership of the companies for which these immigrants toiled. Through campaign contributions and bribes, trusts bought influence with lawmakers. Progressives wanted reforms to protect the public interest.
>
> Unlike the populists, who usually lived in

rural areas, the progressives generally lived in cities. By the 1890s, cities faced crippling problems: housing shortages, political corruption, and spiraling crime rates. In the chaotic cities, progressives wanted to reestablish order and stability.

Progressives were also unlike populists in their greater faith in experts. While populists emphasized the wisdom of average people, progressives focused on the ability of knowledgeable experts to analyze and solve problems. Just as Thomas Edison had conquered technological problems in developing the light bulb, progressives believed that trained experts could analyze and conquer crime, alcoholism, and political corruption. Many progressives praised business owners for their expertise in solving the problems of producing and distributing goods and in running a store or a factory smoothly. Though fearing the power of big businesses, progressives often respected the efficient methods used by businesses.

Now read about how the Union and the Confederacy compared in terms of their military preparedness during the American Civil War. How does the writer of this passage arrange the comparisons between the two armies?

The Union could draw its fighting force from a population of 22 million that included foreign-born immigrants, free African Americans, and escaped slaves. With this size population, the North was able to raise a much larger army than the South. The eleven Confederate states had a population of only nine million, nearly three million of whom the Confederacy refused to let fight because they were slaves.

What the South lacked in numbers, it made up for in military skill and experience. The Confederacy could draw from a talented pool of military minds that included many officers from West Point and veterans of the Mexican American War. It was a seasoned West Point general, Robert E. Lee of Virginia, who assumed command of the Confederate army. Also, many white southerners were members of local militia units and were skilled marksmen.

This superior military training might have given the South a clear advantage over the North were it not for the fact that almost all resources for waging war—steel mills and iron mines, important industries, and transportation facilities—were located in the North. Over 70 percent of the nation's railroads ran through the North.

Most naval facilities and ships were in the North as well. By comparison, the Confederacy possessed inferior natural resources, industry, and transportation. Furthermore, the South lacked the financial resources to manufacture or acquire these necessities of war.

The South tried to make up for its disadvantages by fighting a defensive war. Southerners fortified their cities and waited for the Union to invade. If the Union forces invaded, Confederate strategists reasoned that southerners would at least be fighting on familiar terrain, amid supporters, and close to supplies.

*Expository Writing*

When you write to explain something—a process, the relationship between a cause and an effect, how to do something—you engage in expository writing. This type of writing is similar to narrative writing in that it tells what happened. However, expository writing goes a step further than narrative writing in that it also explains why or how something happened.

Most often you will want to arrange your information chronologically, from least important to most important, or by point-by-point comparisons. You may also want to use transitions such as *then*, *while*, and *before*, as well as dates to help keep the order clear.

The following expository paragraphs explain some of the events that led to U.S. involvement in the Vietnam War. Look for transitions and dates that help keep the order of events clear.

In 1950, just before the outbreak of the Korean War, Truman agreed to send $20 million in direct military aid to the French. Over the next four years, the United States paid for most of the French war effort, pumping more than $2.6 billion into the French effort to "save" Vietnam from communism.

Despite U.S. aid, France was losing the war. When in May 1954 the Vietminh overran Dien Bien Phu, a French outpost in northwestern Vietnam, it signaled the end of French control of Vietnam.

The day after the French surrendered at Dien Bien Phu, representatives of the United States, Great Britain, France, the Soviet Union, China, Laos, Cambodia, and the Vietminh met in Geneva to hammer out a peace agreement. According to its terms, Vietnam would be temporarily divided along the 17th parallel. The Vietminh *would withdraw to the north of that line, and the French would withdraw to the south. Vietnam would be reunified in 1956 after national elections. The Vietminh signed, confident that they would win the promised elections.*

The following expository writing details some of the effects of the post–Civil War policy of Reconstruction on the nation. Pay attention to the way this passage goes beyond narrative writing by explaining why legislation benefiting African Americans passed during Reconstruction.

*In 1866 northerners fought Johnson's policies by electing a Radical Republican majority to Congress. The Radical Republicans quickly enacted legislation designed to punish the former Confederate states, to increase Republican power in the South, and to create conditions that would promote economic development and racial equality in the South. The ten years during which the Radical Republicans were in power became known as Reconstruction.*

*Much of the legislation passed during Reconstruction increased the rights and freedoms of African Americans. This benefited the Republicans in two ways: it made the Republicans popular with a large new pool of voters, and it diminished white southerners' ability to dominate the South politically and economically. In 1866 Congress passed a Civil Rights Act that granted citizenship to African Americans and prohibited states from diminishing the rights accompanying this citizenship. In addition, ratification of the Fourteenth Amendment in 1868 prevented states from denying rights and privileges to any U.S. citizen. The Fifteenth Amendment of 1870 guaranteed that no citizen could be denied the right to vote based on race, color, or former servitude. The Enforcement Act of 1870 empowered federal authorities to prosecute anyone who violated the Fourteenth or Fifteenth amendments.*

*New state governments were established under the Reconstruction acts. White southerners who protested the acts refused to vote in the elections that set up these governments. Their protest had two results: Republicans, who had little support in the South before the Civil War, won control of every new state government; and African Americans began to exert influence at the polls.*

*Persuasive Writing*

Still another type of writing common in social studies is persuasive writing. The goal of this type is to persuade, or convince, someone to accept your point of view. To best achieve this, follow these tips:

- State your position clearly.
- Choose the strongest arguments possible to support your position. These arguments should explain why this particular position is more valid than other positions.
- Include relevant facts and statistics to support your position.
- Organize your reasons in order of importance, from least important to most important.
- Use words and phrases that will appeal to the reader's emotions.

The Cherokee County Central Labor Body wrote the following to President Roosevelt in 1938 to alert him to the problems in their district. Notice how this group implemented the points above.

*This letter comes to you from the . . . lead and zinc field of southeastern Kansas. Thirty-eight percent of the entire world supply of lead and zinc ore is produced in this district. We have here health hazards known as "lead poisoning" in the smelters and silicosis, the most dreaded industrial disease known to medical science. . . . These health hazards can be eliminated if the mining trusts will install air cleaning devices. This, of course, costs money and the greedy, grasping employers apparently haven't any extra. . . . Why [doesn't] the labor department make a health and hygiene survey of this district? Will you add your voice to ours in requesting this be done[?]*

On the day of his inauguration—January 20, 1961—John F. Kennedy gave the persuasive speech excerpted below. Try to figure out as you read what Kennedy was trying to persuade the thousands of people gathered before him to believe. Make a list of the words and phrases Kennedy used that might appeal to the emotions of the people who heard him.

*Let the word go forth . . . that the torch has been passed to a new generation of Americans—born in this century, tempered by war, disciplined by a hard and bitter peace. . . . Let every nation know, whether it wishes us well or ill, that we shall pay any price, bear any burden, meet any hardship, support any friend, oppose any foe to assure the survival and the success of liberty. . . . All this will not be finished in the first 100 days. Nor will it be finished in the first 1,000*

## Part 5
# *Answering Essay Questions*

An essay question actually provides clues as to how it should be answered. Key words in the essay question—*compare, contrast, describe*—tell you what kind of action you are expected to perform. Other words tell you what you should focus on, helping you to limit your topic. In fact, you can usually just rearrange an essay question to form the topic sentence for your answer to it. Look at the chart below to learn how to do this.

Once you know what kind of action you will be expected to perform and have written a topic sentence, begin selecting supporting information. Start by listing all the details related to your topic that come to mind. Write each as a complete sentence.

Then check each sentence to see if it supports your main idea. Eliminate any that do not strengthen or clarify your topic sentence and any that may be inaccurate. Next arrange details in the order that will best accomplish your purpose. For help, refer to page 822 of this Writer's Guide. Finally, read your answer, asking yourself these questions:

- Have I stated clearly in a topic sentence what the essay will be about?
- Are all of the details accurate?
- Does each sentence support the main idea?
- Are these supporting sentences arranged in a way that makes sense?
- Have I made the relationships between ideas clear enough? Or could I add dates and transitions to better clarify these relationships?

### Creating Topic Sentences

| Essay Question | Word Clues | Action Expected | Topic Sentence (revised question) |
|---|---|---|---|
| Compare the culture of the Depression decade with today's culture. | Compare | Point out similarities and differences | The culture of the Depression decade was like our culture today in some ways. It was, however, different in several other ways. |
| Contrast immigrants to the United States at the turn of the century with those who came before 1890. | Contrast | Point out differences | Immigrants to the United States at the turn of the century differed in several ways from those who came before. |
| Describe the role of the media in changing American public opinion about the war in Vietnam. | Describe | Tell about features, using details to create a vivid impression | The media played a major role in changing American public opinion about the war in Vietnam. |
| Explain the popularity of both escapist fiction and realistic fiction during the thirties. | Explain | Tell in what way or for what reason | Both escapist fiction and realistic fiction were popular during the thirties for several reasons. |
| How did the Republicans take advantage of the violence and disorder associated with the Democratic Convention in 1968? | How | Tell by what means or in what way | Republicans took advantage of the violence and disorder associated with the Democratic Convention in 1968. |
| Summarize Ronald Reagan's environmental policies. | Summarize | Briefly state main ideas, including only important details necessary for accuracy and clarity | The major aspects of Ronald Reagan's environmental policies include the following consequences. |
| What are some possible consequences of an alliance between industry and the military? | What | Name events, objects, ideas, or features that meet certain criteria | An alliance between industry and the military might have the following consequences. |
| Why might it have been possible to regulate the hours of women and children in the early 1900's but not the hours of men? | Why | Give reasons that justify | It might have been possible to regulate the hours of women and children in the early 1900s because . . . . |

## Part 6

# *Writing a Research Report*

The job of preparing a research report can be divided into four stages: planning, researching, writing, and improving. Read the following steps and guidelines for completing each stage to help ensure the success of your research projects.

*Stage One:*
*Planning a Research Report*

1. **Choose a topic.** Usually you will be given a list of topics from which to choose or an overall category within which your topic must fit. Within these limits, let your own interest determine your selection. It is much easier to research a topic that interests you. If necessary, ask a friend or classmate to brainstorm with you for topic ideas.

2. **Narrow your topic.** Focus on a single aspect of the topic, making sure it is narrow enough to be researched in the available time and to be covered in the length allowed for your research paper. For example, if the topic is the Great Depression, you might narrow your focus to the New Deal. You might further narrow your focus to the Tennessee Valley Authority or to the Emergency Relief Act. What topics might be too narrow for a report of the length you were allowed?

*Stage Two:*
*Researching Your Topic*

1. **Write focus questions.** Make a list of questions that you want your research to answer. This will help you focus your research. Use these questions to create a working outline.

2. **Locate information.** The resource books you select will vary depending on your topic. In many cases, you can start with an encyclopedia. Refer to the skill lesson on page 237 for information on selecting appropriate reference materials. In addition, you will need to consult the card catalog for books specifically related to your topic.

3. **Read and take notes.** Let your working outline be your guide. Refer to it often to determine the usefulness of what you read. Take notes on information that helps answer any outline questions or that adds interesting details about any of the

questions. When you find information that meets neither of these criteria, you may need to change your outline to include it. Parts 2 and 3 of this Writer's Guide, on pages 823 and 824, provide guidelines on taking notes and summarizing.

4. **Organize your notes.** Group your note cards according to sections of your outline. Revise your outline as necessary, adding or removing items based on the notes you took.

*Stage Three:*
*Writing a Draft*

1. **Fill out your outline.** Write sentences that provide answers to your revised outline questions. Incorporate various kinds of information, including quotes from primary and secondary sources and charts and graphs. Add details, including all information you wish to present in your report.

2. **Connect your ideas in paragraphs.** Use Parts 1 and 4 of this Writer's Guide to complete this step.

*Stage Four:*
*Improving Your Research Paper*

1. **Review your work.** Reread your research paper. Use a checklist like the following to evaluate it.

   - Is my position clear and persuasive?
   - Does the paper follow my outline?
   - Does it make each point clearly?
   - Does it achieve my purpose for writing?
   - Are comparisons appropriate and useful?
   - Is the sequence correct and clear?
   - Are descriptions vivid?
   - Is it appropriate for my audience?

2. **Hold a revising conference.** Work with a friend or classmate. Ask your partner to use your checklist and to make suggestions for improvement.

3. **Revise and edit.** Use your own evaluation and suggestions from your conference partner to make improvements in your paper. Then proofread carefully to find any spelling or grammatical errors. Mark corrections on your draft.

4. **Make a final copy.** Type or write neatly. Be careful to make all the corrections you marked on your draft.

# The Changing World

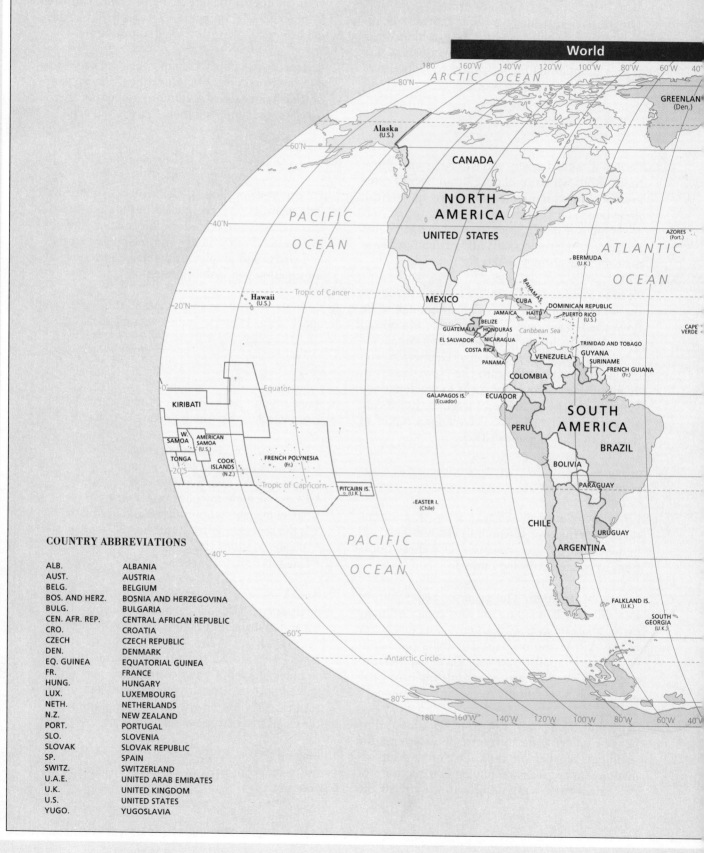

World

ARCTIC OCEAN

GREENLAND (Den.)

Alaska (U.S.)

CANADA

NORTH AMERICA

UNITED STATES

ATLANTIC

OCEAN

AZORES (Port.)

BERMUDA (U.K.)

PACIFIC

OCEAN

Tropic of Cancer

Hawaii (U.S.)

MEXICO

BAHAMAS

CUBA

DOMINICAN REPUBLIC

JAMAICA    HAITI    PUERTO RICO (U.S.)

CAPE VERDE

BELIZE

GUATEMALA    HONDURAS    Caribbean Sea

EL SALVADOR    NICARAGUA

COSTA RICA

PANAMA

TRINIDAD AND TOBAGO

VENEZUELA    GUYANA

SURINAME

FRENCH GUIANA (Fr.)

Equator

KIRIBATI

COLOMBIA

GALAPAGOS IS. (Ecuador)

ECUADOR

SOUTH AMERICA

PERU

BRAZIL

W. SAMOA    AMERICAN SAMOA (U.S.)

TONGA    COOK ISLANDS (N.Z.)

FRENCH POLYNESIA (Fr.)

BOLIVIA

PARAGUAY

Tropic of Capricorn

PITCAIRN IS. (U.K.)

EASTER I. (Chile)

CHILE

URUGUAY

ARGENTINA

PACIFIC

OCEAN

FALKLAND IS. (U.K.)

SOUTH GEORGIA (U.K.)

Antarctic Circle

## COUNTRY ABBREVIATIONS

| | |
|---|---|
| ALB. | ALBANIA |
| AUST. | AUSTRIA |
| BELG. | BELGIUM |
| BOS. AND HERZ. | BOSNIA AND HERZEGOVINA |
| BULG. | BULGARIA |
| CEN. AFR. REP. | CENTRAL AFRICAN REPUBLIC |
| CRO. | CROATIA |
| CZECH | CZECH REPUBLIC |
| DEN. | DENMARK |
| EQ. GUINEA | EQUATORIAL GUINEA |
| FR. | FRANCE |
| HUNG. | HUNGARY |
| LUX. | LUXEMBOURG |
| NETH. | NETHERLANDS |
| N.Z. | NEW ZEALAND |
| PORT. | PORTUGAL |
| SLO. | SLOVENIA |
| SLOVAK | SLOVAK REPUBLIC |
| SP. | SPAIN |
| SWITZ. | SWITZERLAND |
| U.A.E. | UNITED ARAB EMIRATES |
| U.K. | UNITED KINGDOM |
| U.S. | UNITED STATES |
| YUGO. | YUGOSLAVIA |

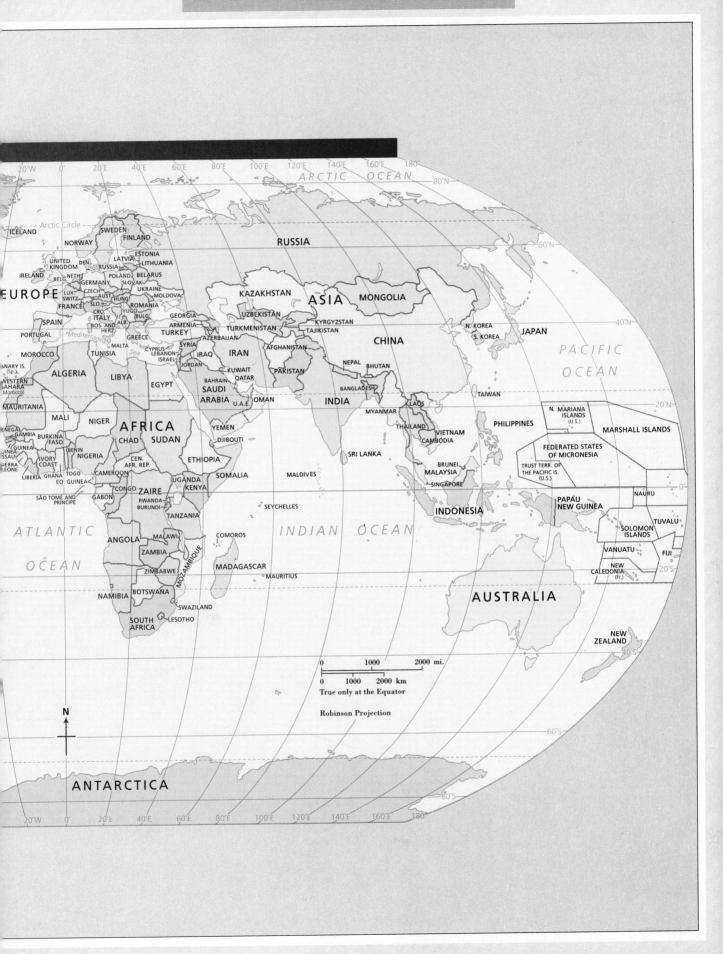

## United States: Political

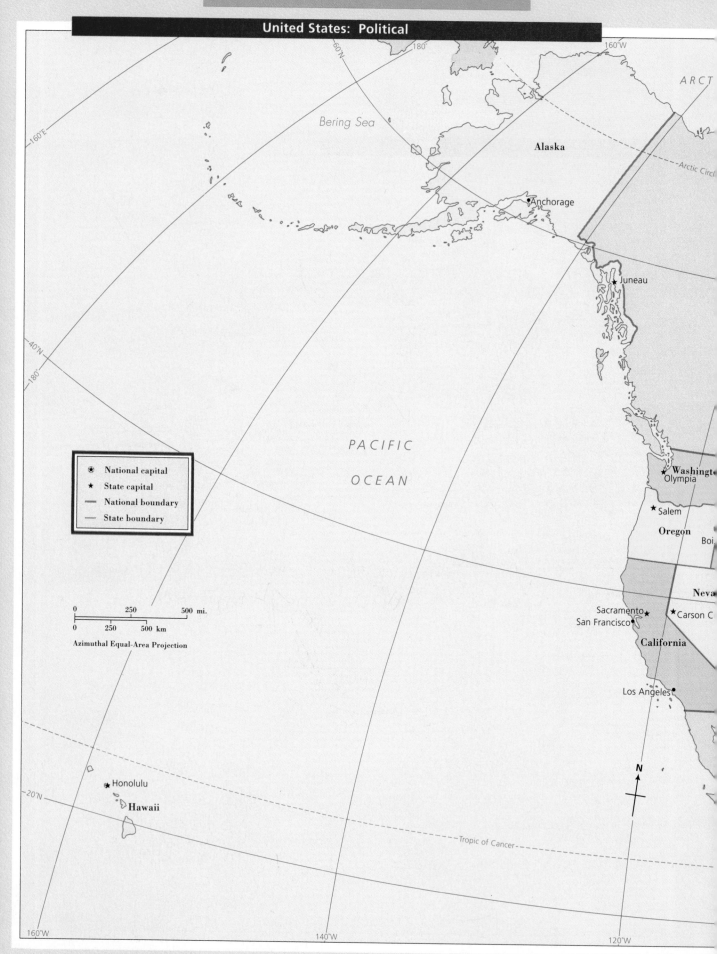

ARCT

Bering Sea

Alaska

•Anchorage

Arctic Circle

★ Juneau

PACIFIC

OCEAN

★ Washingt
Olympia

★ Salem

Oregon

Boi

Neva

Sacramento•★   ★ Carson C
San Francisco•

California

Los Angeles•

N

| | |
|---|---|
| ✹ | National capital |
| ★ | State capital |
| — | National boundary |
| — | State boundary |

| 0 | 250 | 500 mi. |
|---|---|---|
| 0 | 250 | 500 km |

Azimuthal Equal-Area Projection

★ Honolulu

Hawaii

Tropic of Cancer

160°E

40°N

180

20°N

160°W

140°W

120°W

60°N

180

160°W

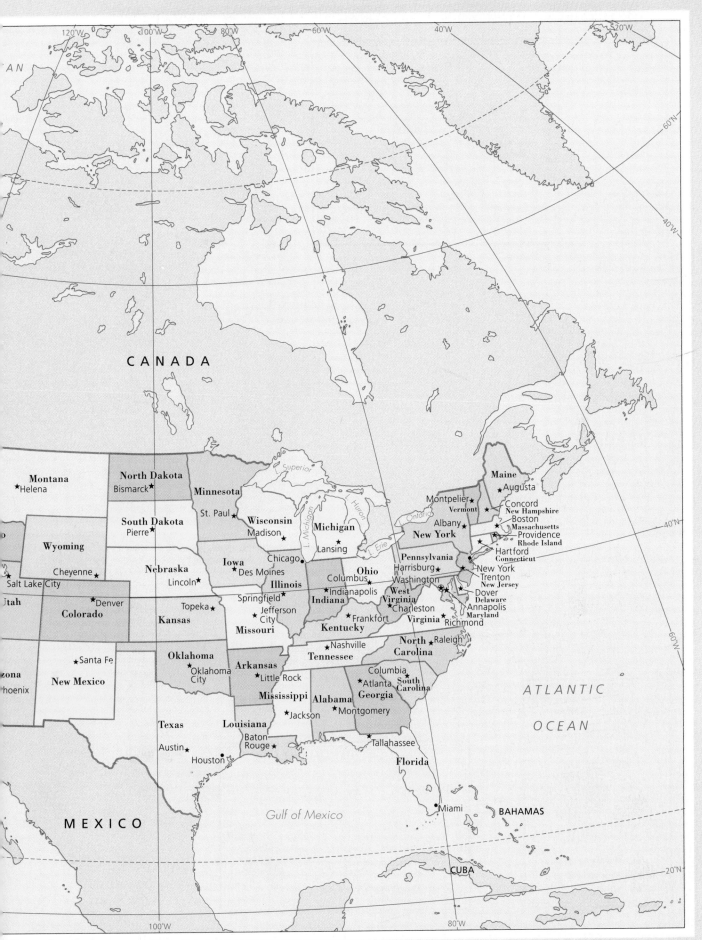

CANADA

Montana
★Helena

North Dakota
Bismarck★

Minnesota
St. Paul★

L. Superior

Maine
★Augusta

Montpelier★     Concord
Vermont    New Hampshire
Boston

South Dakota
Pierre★

Wisconsin
Madison★

Michigan
★Lansing

L. Huron

L. Ontario

Albany★    Massachusetts
New York    Providence
Rhode Island
Hartford
Connecticut

Wyoming

Cheyenne★

Salt Lake City★

Nebraska
Lincoln★

Iowa
★Des Moines

Chicago

Illinois
Springfield★

Ohio
Columbus

Indianapolis★
Indiana

L. Michigan

L. Erie

Pennsylvania
Harrisburg★

Washington

New York
Trenton
New Jersey
Dover
Delaware
Annapolis
Maryland

Utah

Colorado
★Denver

Kansas
Topeka★

Jefferson
City★
Missouri

Kentucky
Frankfort★

West
Virginia
Charleston★

Virginia
Richmond★

Santa Fe★

New Mexico

zona

hoenix

Oklahoma
★Oklahoma
City

Arkansas
★Little Rock

Tennessee
Nashville★

North
Carolina
Raleigh★

Columbia★
Atlanta★
Georgia
South
Carolina

Texas

Mississippi
★Jackson

Alabama
Montgomery★

Austin★

Louisiana
Baton
Rouge★

Houston

Florida

Tallahassee★

ATLANTIC

OCEAN

MEXICO

Gulf of Mexico

Miami    BAHAMAS

CUBA

## United States: Physical

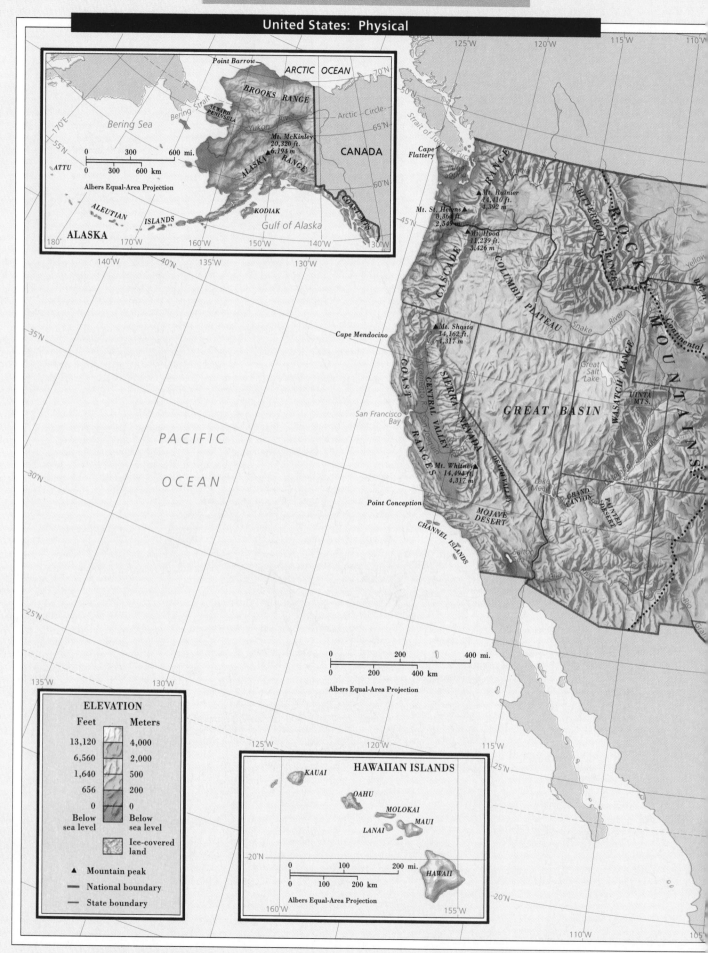

ARCTIC OCEAN

Point Barrow

BROOKS RANGE

SEWARD PENINSULA

Yukon River

Arctic Circle

70°N

65°N

60°N

CANADA

Mt. McKinley
20,320 ft.
6,194 m

ALASKA RANGE

Bering Strait

Bering Sea

ATTU

ALEUTIAN ISLANDS

KODIAK

Gulf of Alaska

COAST MTS.

300    600 mi.

300    600 km

Albers Equal-Area Projection

**ALASKA**

55°N

180°    170°W    160°W    150°W    140°W    130°W

170°E

135°W

40°W

Cape Flattery

Strait of Juan de Fuca

Puget Sound

Mt. Rainier
14,410 ft.
4,392 m

Mt. St. Helens
8,364 ft.
2,549 m

Mt. Hood
11,239 ft.
3,426 m

CASCADE RANGE

COLUMBIA PLATEAU

Snake River

BITTERROOT RANGE

ROCKY MOUNTAINS

Continental

Mt. Shasta
14,162 ft.
4,317 m

Cape Mendocino

Great Salt Lake

WASATCH RANGE

UINTA MTS.

COAST RANGE

SIERRA NEVADA

CENTRAL VALLEY

Sacramento R.

San Joaquin R.

San Francisco Bay

GREAT BASIN

Mt. Whitney
14,494 ft.
4,317 m

DEATH VALLEY

Lake Mead

GRAND CANYON

PAINTED DESERT

Point Conception

MOJAVE DESERT

CHANNEL ISLANDS

Salton Sea

Gila River

**PACIFIC**

**OCEAN**

35°N

30°N

25°N

135°W    130°W    125°W    120°W    115°W

125°W    120°W    115°W    110°W

50°N

45°N

200    400 mi.

200    400 km

Albers Equal-Area Projection

### ELEVATION

| Feet | | Meters |
|---|---|---|
| 13,120 | | 4,000 |
| 6,560 | | 2,000 |
| 1,640 | | 500 |
| 656 | | 200 |
| 0 | | 0 |
| Below sea level | | Below sea level |

Ice-covered land

▲ Mountain peak

— National boundary

— State boundary

### HAWAIIAN ISLANDS

KAUAI

OAHU

MOLOKAI

LANAI    MAUI

HAWAII

25°N

20°N

100    200 mi.

100    200 km

Albers Equal-Area Projection

160°W    155°W

CANADA

GREAT PLAINS

BLACK HILLS

BADLANDS

SAND HILLS

Peak ft. n

Lake of the Woods

MESABI RANGE

Red River

Missouri River

Lake Superior

Lake Huron

Lake Michigan

Des Moines River

Platte River

CENTRAL PLAINS

OZARK PLATEAU

Wabash River

Ohio River

Lake Ontario

Lake Erie

ADIRONDACK MTS.

CATSKILL MTS.

Susquehanna River

ALLEGHENY PLATEAU

APPALACHIAN MOUNTAINS

CUMBERLAND PLATEAU

BLUE RIDGE MTS.

St. Lawrence River

Lake Champlain

WHITE MTS.
▲ Mt. Washington
6,288 ft.
1,917 m

Cape Cod

NANTUCKET
MARTHA'S VINEYARD

LONG ISLAND

Cape May
Delaware Bay

Chesapeake Bay

Cape Hatteras

ATLANTIC
OCEAN

OUACHITA MTS.

Arkansas River

Mississippi River

Red River

Tennessee River

▲ Mt. Mitchell
6,684 ft.
2,037 m

Fall Line

ATLANTIC COASTAL PLAIN

Savannah R.

Altamaha R.

EDWARDS
PLATEAU

Colorado River

Brazos River

Sabine River

Red River

Pearl River

Tombigbee River

Alabama River

Chattahoochee River

GULF COASTAL PLAIN

Galveston Bay

Mobile Bay

Pensacola Bay

Cape Canaveral

Tampa Bay

Lake Okeechobee

BAHAMAS

EVERGLADES

Cape Sable

FLORIDA KEYS

Tropic of Cancer

MEXICO

Gulf of Mexico

CUBA

## Territorial Expansion of the United States

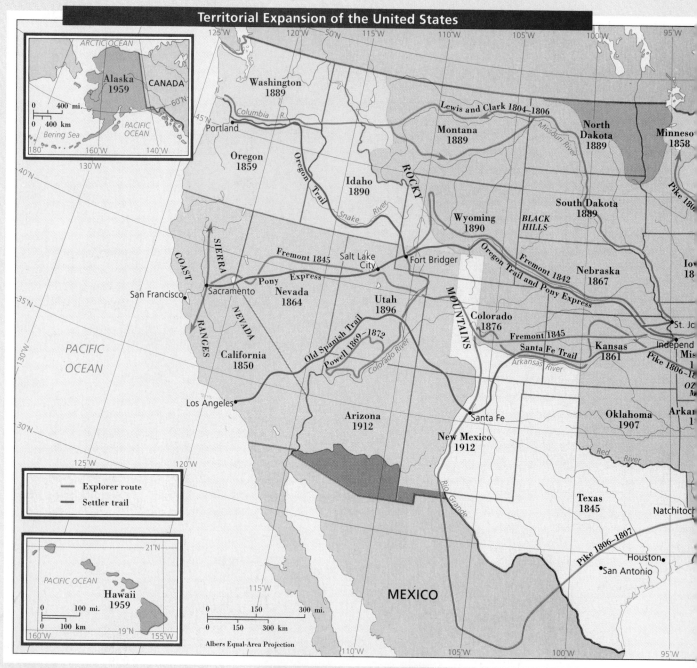

Alaska 1959
CANADA
ARCTIC OCEAN
PACIFIC OCEAN
Bering Sea

0    400 mi.
0    400 km

Washington 1889
Portland
Columbia R.
Oregon 1859
Oregon Trail
Idaho 1890
Snake River
Montana 1889
Lewis and Clark 1804–1806
Missouri River
ROCKY
North Dakota 1889
Minneso 1858
Pike 180

SIERRA NEVADA
Fremont 1845
Salt Lake City
Fort Bridger
Oregon Trail and Pony Express
Wyoming 1890
BLACK HILLS
South Dakota 1889
Fremont 1842
Nebraska 1867
Iow 18

San Francisco
Sacramento
Pony Express
Nevada 1864
Utah 1896
MOUNTAINS
Colorado 1876
Fremont 1845
Santa Fe Trail
Kansas 1861
St. Jo
Independ
Pike 1806–18
OZ
M
Mis

COAST RANGES
PACIFIC OCEAN
California 1850
Old Spanish Trail
Powell 1869–1872
Colorado River
Arkansas River

Los Angeles
Arizona 1912
Santa Fe
New Mexico 1912
Oklahoma 1907
Arkar

Rio Grande
Red River
Texas 1845
Natchitoch

MEXICO
Pike 1806–1807
Houston
San Antonio

### Legend
— Explorer route
— Settler trail

Hawaii 1959
PACIFIC OCEAN

0    100 mi.
0    100 km

0    150    300 mi.
0    150    300 km
Albers Equal-Area Projection

### Lewis and Clark 1804–1806
William Clark and Meriwether Lewis, guided by the Shoshone princess Sacagawea and the slave York, crossed the Rockies and reached the mouth of the Columbia River.

LEWIS AND CLARK EXPEDITION
1804    1954
UNITED STATES POSTAGE    3¢

### Zebulon Pike 1806–1807
Pike not only explored the Arkansas and Red rivers of the Southwest but also entered Spanish territory. His reports on the rich overland trade with Mexico and Spanish military weakness helped stimulate American expansion into Texas.

### John Charles Fremont 1842–1844
Fremont's love of the wilderness inspired him to undertake expeditions to Wyoming, the Northwest, and California. His surveys charted America's westward expansion.

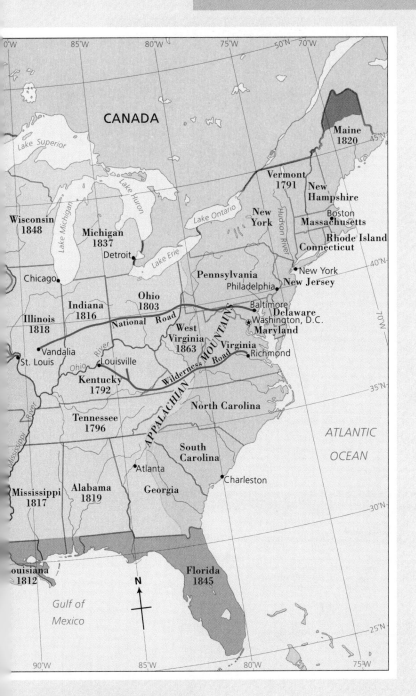

CANADA

Maine 1820

Vermont 1791
New Hampshire
New York
Massachusetts
Boston
Rhode Island
Connecticut

Wisconsin 1848
Michigan 1837
Detroit
Chicago

Pennsylvania
Philadelphia
New York
New Jersey

Ohio 1803
Indiana 1816
Illinois 1818
National Road
West Virginia 1863
Baltimore
Delaware
Washington, D.C.
Maryland

Vandalia
St. Louis
Ohio River
Louisville
Kentucky 1792
Wilderness Road
APPALACHIAN MOUNTAINS
Virginia
Richmond

Tennessee 1796
North Carolina

South Carolina
Atlanta
Charleston

Mississippi 1817
Alabama 1819
Georgia

ATLANTIC OCEAN

Louisiana 1812
Florida 1845

N

Gulf of Mexico

Mississippi River

## Territorial Expansion of the U.S.

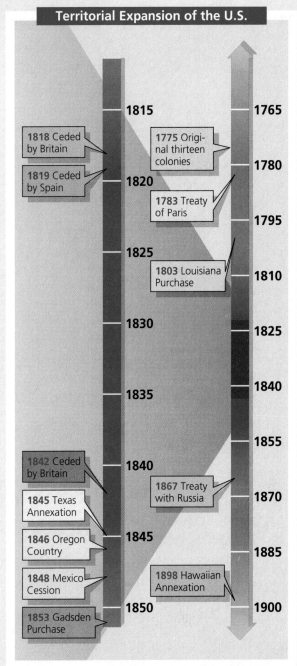

1815
1818 Ceded by Britain
1819 Ceded by Spain
1820
1825
1830
1835
1840
1842 Ceded by Britain
1845 Texas Annexation
1846 Oregon Country
1848 Mexico Cession
1850
1853 Gadsden Purchase

1765
1775 Original thirteen colonies
1780
1783 Treaty of Paris
1795
1803 Louisiana Purchase
1810
1825
1840
1855
1867 Treaty with Russia
1870
1898 Hawaiian Annexation
1885
1900

**John Wesley Powell 1869** The Spanish explorer Coronado first discovered the Grand Canyon in 1540, but a party led by geologist and American Indian scholar John Wesley Powell first saw the canyon from the Colorado River. The canyon extends in a winding course for about 280 miles and ranges in width from 4 to 18 miles.

**Oregon Trail 1840s** Fur traders and missionaries opened this route stretching 2,000 miles to Oregon. Pioneers undertook the difficult six months' journey in Conestoga wagons.

Crossing a River

**Promontory Point, Utah Territory, 1869** A golden spike marked the completion of the first transcontinental railroad linking the West Coast with the rest of the nation. The frontier steadily grew smaller as Americans settled in the vast empty spaces.

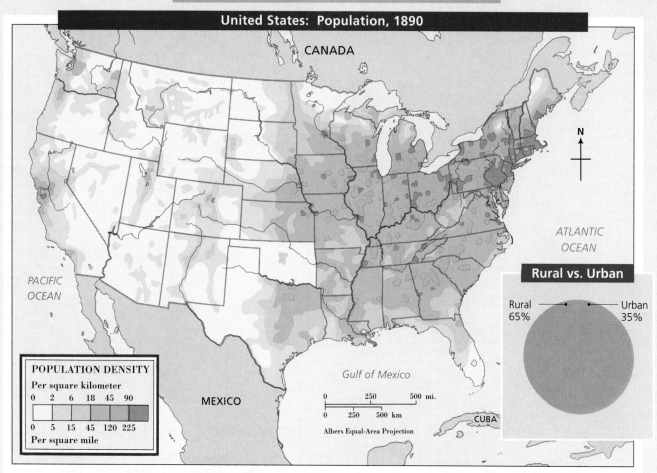

## United States: Population, 1890

CANADA

ATLANTIC OCEAN

PACIFIC OCEAN

N

### Rural vs. Urban

Rural 65%　Urban 35%

Gulf of Mexico

MEXICO

CUBA

0　250　500 mi.
0　250　500 km
Albers Equal-Area Projection

**POPULATION DENSITY**
Per square kilometer
0　2　6　18　45　90
0　5　15　45　120　225
Per square mile

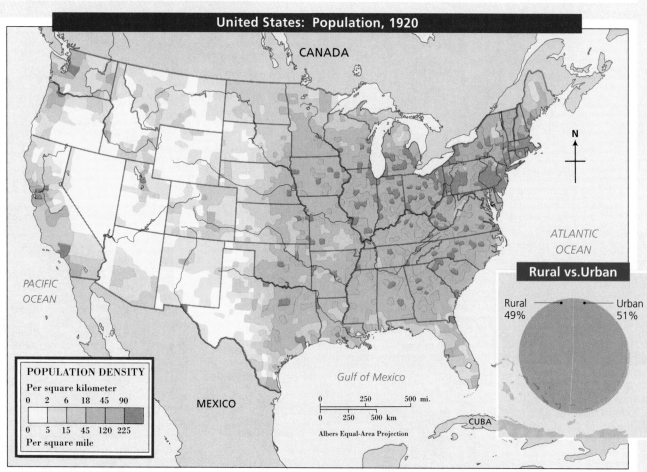

## United States: Population, 1920

CANADA

ATLANTIC OCEAN

PACIFIC OCEAN

N

### Rural vs. Urban

Rural 49%　Urban 51%

Gulf of Mexico

MEXICO

CUBA

0　250　500 mi.
0　250　500 km
Albers Equal-Area Projection

**POPULATION DENSITY**
Per square kilometer
0　2　6　18　45　90
0　5　15　45　120　225
Per square mile

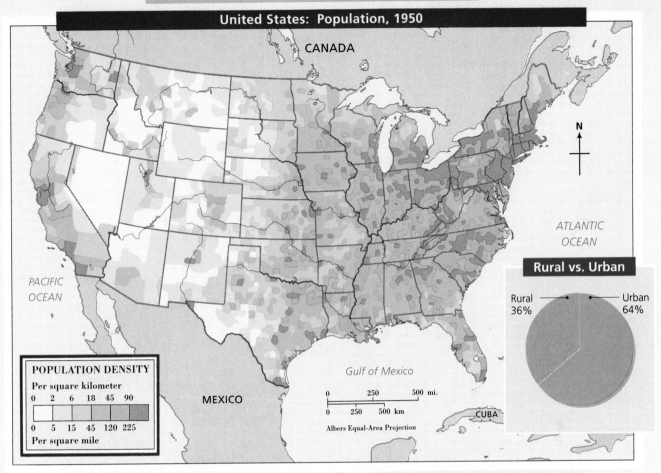

## United States: Population, 1950

CANADA

N

PACIFIC OCEAN

ATLANTIC OCEAN

### Rural vs. Urban

Rural 36%

Urban 64%

Gulf of Mexico

MEXICO

CUBA

**POPULATION DENSITY**

Per square kilometer

0   2   6   18   45   90

0   5   15   45   120   225

Per square mile

0   250   500 mi.

0   250   500 km

Albers Equal-Area Projection

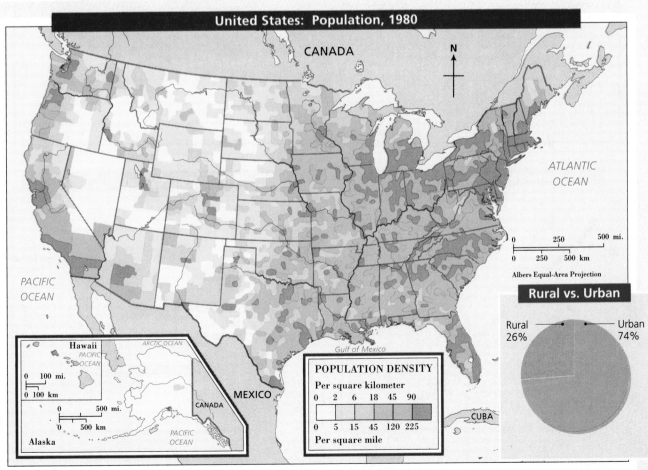

## United States: Population, 1980

CANADA

N

PACIFIC OCEAN

ATLANTIC OCEAN

0   250   500 mi.

0   250   500 km

Albers Equal-Area Projection

### Rural vs. Urban

Rural 26%

Urban 74%

Gulf of Mexico

MEXICO

CUBA

**Hawaii**

PACIFIC OCEAN

ARCTIC OCEAN

0   100 mi.

0   100 km

0   500 mi.

0   500 km

CANADA

**Alaska**

PACIFIC OCEAN

**POPULATION DENSITY**

Per square kilometer

0   2   6   18   45   90

0   5   15   45   120   225

Per square mile

Census Bureau county population estimates for 1988 do not indicate significant changes in population density per square mile from those shown for 1980.

839

## United States: Agriculture and Industry

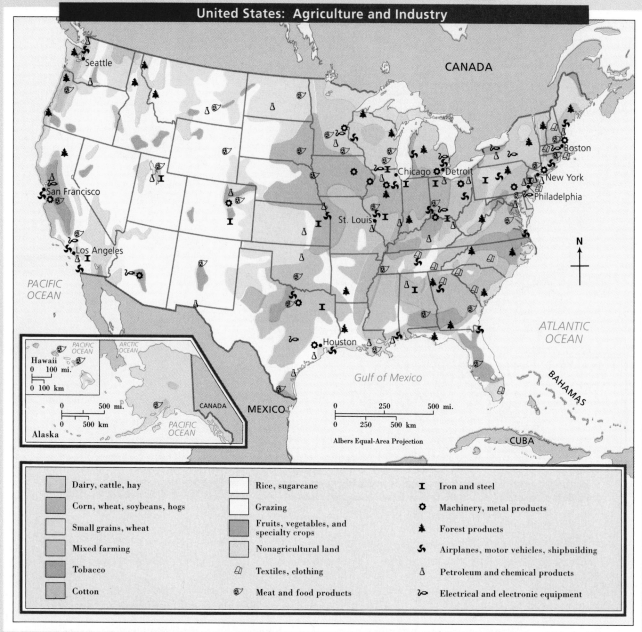

CANADA

Seattle

San Francisco

PACIFIC
OCEAN

Los Angeles

Houston

Chicago • Detroit

St. Louis

Boston

New York

Philadelphia

N

ATLANTIC
OCEAN

Gulf of Mexico

BAHAMAS

CUBA

MEXICO

Hawaii
0    100 mi.
0    100 km

PACIFIC
OCEAN

ARCTIC
OCEAN

CANADA

Alaska

PACIFIC
OCEAN

0         500 mi.
0    500 km

0        250        500 mi.
0    250    500 km

Albers Equal-Area Projection

**Legend:**

- Dairy, cattle, hay
- Corn, wheat, soybeans, hogs
- Small grains, wheat
- Mixed farming
- Tobacco
- Cotton
- Rice, sugarcane
- Grazing
- Fruits, vegetables, and specialty crops
- Nonagricultural land
- Textiles, clothing
- Meat and food products
- **I** Iron and steel
- Machinery, metal products
- Forest products
- Airplanes, motor vehicles, shipbuilding
- Petroleum and chemical products
- Electrical and electronic equipment

## Farmers in the Labor Force

Farmers (percent)

40
35
30
25
20
15
10
5
0

1900 1910 1920 1930 1940 1950 1960 1970 1980 1990
Year

## Employment by Industry, 1987

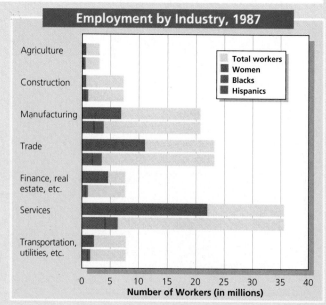

Agriculture

Construction

Manufacturing

Trade

Finance, real estate, etc.

Services

Transportation, utilities, etc.

Total workers
Women
Blacks
Hispanics

0    5    10    15    20    25    30    35    40
Number of Workers (in millions)

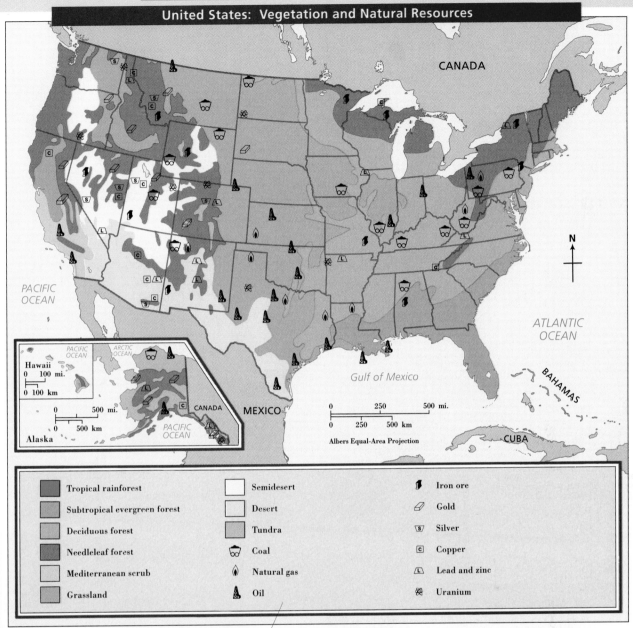

# United States: Vegetation and Natural Resources

CANADA

PACIFIC OCEAN

ATLANTIC OCEAN

N

PACIFIC OCEAN

ARCTIC OCEAN

Hawaii
0        100 mi.
0        100 km

0        500 mi.
0        500 km

Alaska

CANADA

PACIFIC OCEAN

MEXICO

Gulf of Mexico

BAHAMAS

0        250        500 mi.
0        250        500 km

Albers Equal-Area Projection

CUBA

| | | | | | | |
|---|---|---|---|---|---|---|
| | Tropical rainforest | | Semidesert | | | Iron ore |
| | Subtropical evergreen forest | | Desert | | | Gold |
| | Deciduous forest | | Tundra | | S | Silver |
| | Needleleaf forest | | Coal | | C | Copper |
| | Mediterranean scrub | | Natural gas | | L | Lead and zinc |
| | Grassland | | Oil | | | Uranium |

## U.S. Forestland, 1987

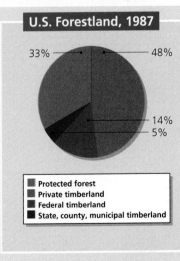

33% — 48%

14%
5%

- Protected forest
- Private timberland
- Federal timberland
- State, county, municipal timberland

# World Trade Power

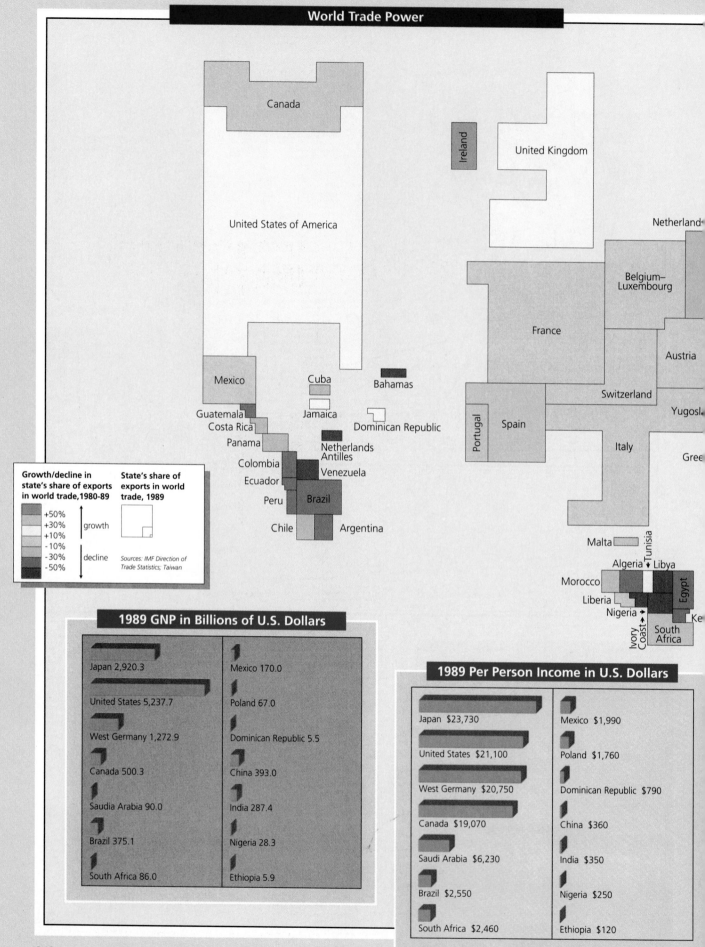

**Growth/decline in state's share of exports in world trade, 1980-89**

| | |
|---|---|
| +50% | |
| +30% | growth |
| +10% | |
| -10% | |
| -30% | decline |
| -50% | |

**State's share of exports in world trade, 1989**

Sources: IMF Direction of Trade Statistics; Taiwan

Canada

Ireland

United Kingdom

Netherland

United States of America

Belgium–Luxembourg

France

Austria

Switzerland

Mexico

Cuba

Bahamas

Jamaica

Dominican Republic

Portugal

Spain

Yugosl.

Guatemala

Costa Rica

Panama

Netherlands Antilles

Italy

Gree

Colombia

Venezuela

Ecuador

Peru

Brazil

Chile

Argentina

Malta

Tunisia

Algeria

Libya

Morocco

Egypt

Liberia

Nigeria

Ivory Coast

South Africa

Ke

## 1989 GNP in Billions of U.S. Dollars

Japan 2,920.3

Mexico 170.0

United States 5,237.7

Poland 67.0

West Germany 1,272.9

Dominican Republic 5.5

Canada 500.3

China 393.0

Saudia Arabia 90.0

India 287.4

Brazil 375.1

Nigeria 28.3

South Africa 86.0

Ethiopia 5.9

## 1989 Per Person Income in U.S. Dollars

Japan $23,730

Mexico $1,990

United States $21,100

Poland $1,760

West Germany $20,750

Dominican Republic $790

Canada $19,070

China $360

Saudi Arabia $6,230

India $350

Brazil $2,550

Nigeria $250

South Africa $2,460

Ethiopia $120

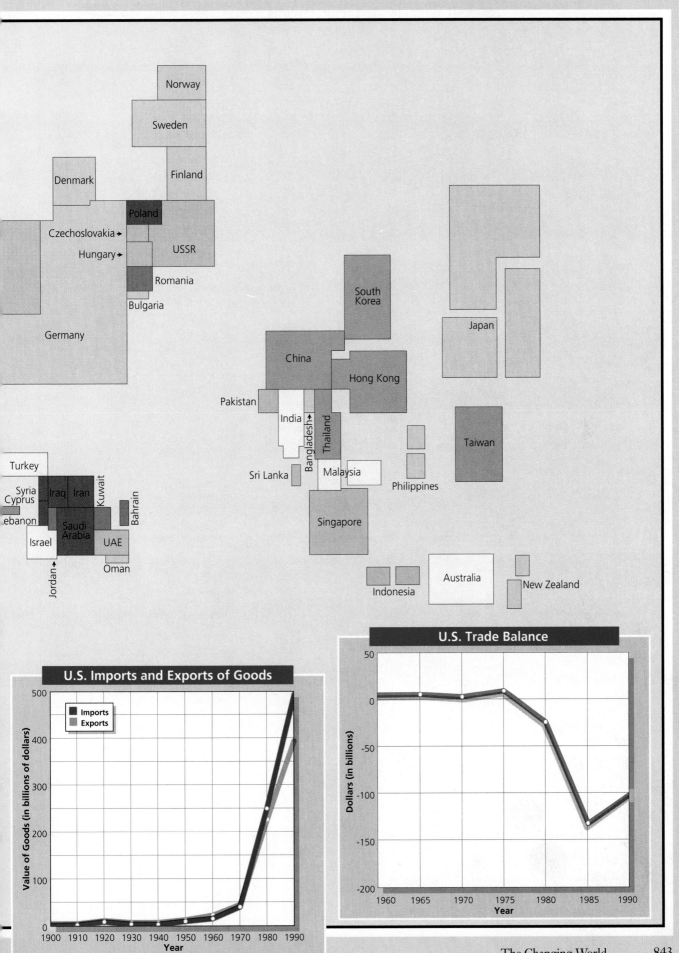

Norway
Sweden
Denmark
Finland
Poland
Czechoslovakia →
Hungary →
USSR
Romania
Bulgaria
Germany

South Korea
Japan
China
Hong Kong
Pakistan
India
Bangladesh →
Thailand
Taiwan
Sri Lanka
Malaysia
Philippines

Turkey
Syria
Cyprus
Iraq
Iran
Kuwait
Bahrain
Lebanon
Saudi Arabia
Israel
UAE
Oman
Jordan →

Singapore

Indonesia
Australia
New Zealand

## U.S. Imports and Exports of Goods

Imports
Exports

Value of Goods (in billions of dollars)

500

400

300

200

100

0

1900 1910 1920 1930 1940 1950 1960 1970 1980 1990

Year

## U.S. Trade Balance

Dollars (in billions)

50

0

-50

-100

-150

-200

1960 1965 1970 1975 1980 1985 1990

Year

## Nationalism in Southeastern Asia

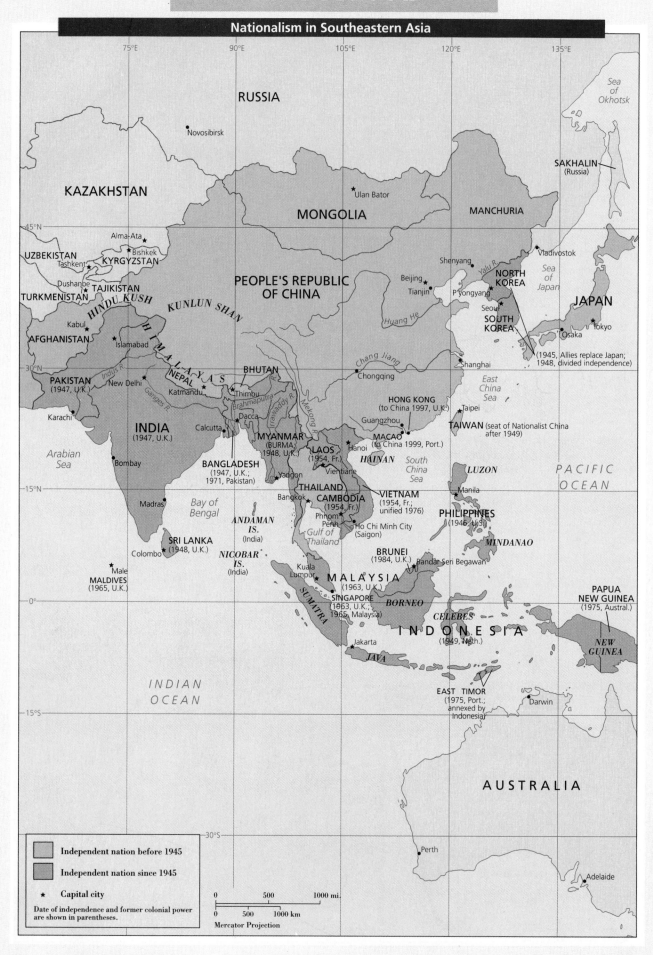

RUSSIA

Novosibirsk

KAZAKHSTAN

MONGOLIA

Ulan Bator

MANCHURIA

Vladivostok

Alma-Ata

Sea of Okhotsk

SAKHALIN (Russia)

UZBEKISTAN    Bishkek
Tashkent    KYRGYZSTAN
Dushanbe    TAJIKISTAN
TURKMENISTAN

Shenyang

NORTH KOREA

Sea of Japan

JAPAN

HINDU KUSH    KUNLUN SHAN

PEOPLE'S REPUBLIC OF CHINA

Beijing
Tianjin    P'yongyang

Seoul    Tokyo
SOUTH KOREA    Osaka

Kabul
AFGHANISTAN
Islamabad

Huang He

Chang Jiang

Shanghai

(1945, Allies replace Japan; 1948, divided independence)

HIMALAYAS    Chongqing

East China Sea

PAKISTAN (1947, U.K.)    Indus R.    New Delhi
NEPAL    BHUTAN    Thimbu
Katmandu

HONG KONG (to China 1997, U.K.)    Taipei

Karachi    Ganges R.    Dacca    Brahmaputra    MACAO (to China 1999, Port.)
Guangzhou

TAIWAN (seat of Nationalist China after 1949)

INDIA (1947, U.K.)    Calcutta    MYANMAR (BURMA; 1948, U.K.)    Hanoi    HAINAN    South China Sea    LUZON
LAOS (1954, Fr.)

Arabian Sea    Bombay    BANGLADESH (1947, U.K.; 1971, Pakistan)    Yangon    Vientiane

Manila    PACIFIC OCEAN

Madras    Bay of Bengal    ANDAMAN IS. (India)    THAILAND    Bangkok    CAMBODIA (1954, Fr.)    VIETNAM (1954, Fr.; unified 1976)    PHILIPPINES (1946, U.S.)

SRI LANKA (1948, U.K.)    Phnom Penh
Colombo    NICOBAR IS. (India)    Gulf of Thailand    Ho Chi Minh City (Saigon)    MINDANAO

Male    BRUNEI (1984, U.K.)    Bandar Seri Begawan
MALDIVES (1965, U.K.)    Kuala Lumpur    MALAYSIA (1963, U.K.)

PAPUA NEW GUINEA (1975, Austral.)

SUMATRA    SINGAPORE (1963, U.K.; 1965, Malaysia)    BORNEO    CELEBES    NEW GUINEA

INDONESIA (1949, Neth.)

Jakarta    JAVA

INDIAN OCEAN    EAST TIMOR (1975, Port.; annexed by Indonesia)    Darwin

AUSTRALIA

Perth

Adelaide

**Legend:**
- Independent nation before 1945
- Independent nation since 1945
- ★ Capital city

Date of independence and former colonial power are shown in parentheses.

0    500    1000 mi.
0    500    1000 km
Mercator Projection

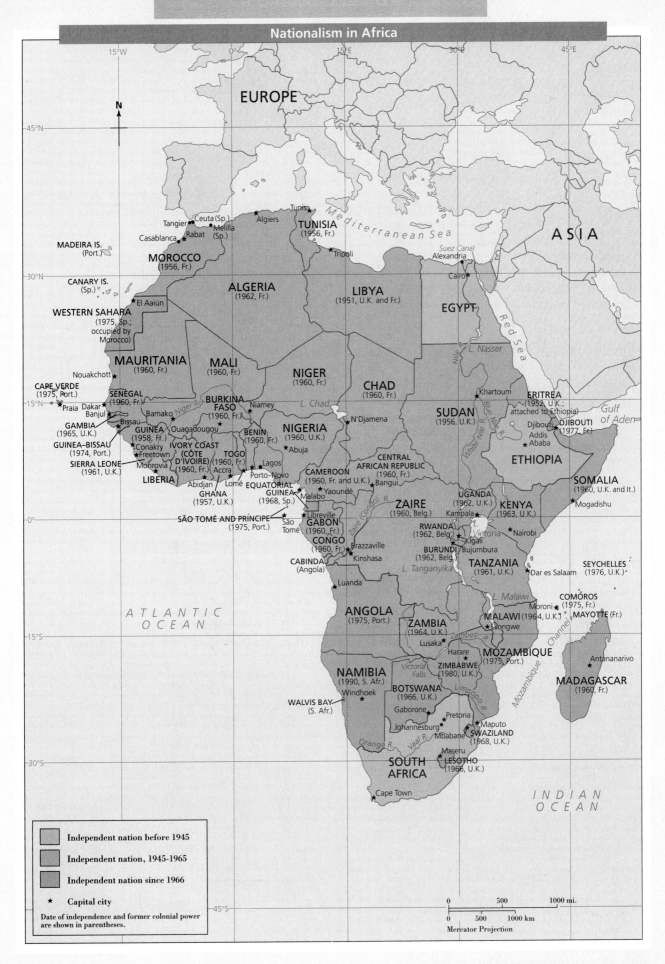

EUROPE

ASIA

Mediterranean Sea

Tunis
Algiers
TUNISIA
(1956, Fr.)
Tangier
Ceuta (Sp.)
Melilla
(Sp.)
Casablanca
Rabat
MADEIRA IS.
(Port.)
MOROCCO
(1956, Fr.)
Tripoli
Suez Canal
Alexandria
Cairo
CANARY IS.
(Sp.)
ALGERIA
(1962, Fr.)
LIBYA
(1951, U.K. and Fr.)
EGYPT
El Aaiún
WESTERN SAHARA
(1975, Sp.;
occupied by
Morocco)
Red Sea
L. Nasser
MAURITANIA
(1960, Fr.)
MALI
(1960, Fr.)
NIGER
(1960, Fr.)
CHAD
(1960, Fr.)
Khartoum
ERITREA
(1952, U.K.;
attached to Ethiopia)
Gulf
of Aden
Nouakchott
CAPE VERDE
(1975, Port.)
SENEGAL
(1960, Fr.)
Niamey
L. Chad
SUDAN
(1956, U.K.)
Djibouti
DJIBOUTI
(1977, Fr.)
Praia
Dakar
Bamako
BURKINA
FASO
(1960, Fr.)
N'Djamena
Blue Nile R.
Addis
Ababa
Banjul
GAMBIA
(1965, U.K.)
Bissau
GUINEA
(1958, Fr.)
Ouagadougou
NIGERIA
(1960, U.K.)
BENIN
(1960, Fr.)
CENTRAL
AFRICAN REPUBLIC
(1960, Fr.)
ETHIOPIA
GUINEA–BISSAU
(1974, Port.)
Conakry
Freetown
IVORY COAST
(CÔTE
D'IVOIRE)
(1960, Fr.)
TOGO
(1960, Fr.)
Abuja
White Nile R.
SIERRA LEONE
(1961, U.K.)
Monrovia
Accra
Lagos
CAMEROON
(1960, Fr. and U.K.)
Bangui
SOMALIA
(1960, U.K. and It.)
LIBERIA
Abidjan
Lomé
Porto-Novo
EQUATORIAL
GUINEA
(1968, Sp.)
Malabo
Yaoundé
UGANDA
(1962, U.K.)
KENYA
(1963, U.K.)
Mogadishu
GHANA
(1957, U.K.)
SÃO TOMÉ AND PRÍNCIPE
(1975, Port.)
São
Tomé
GABON
(1960, Fr.)
Libreville
CONGO
(1960, Fr.)
Brazzaville
ZAIRE
(1960, Belg.)
Zaire (Congo) R.
RWANDA
(1962, Belg.)
Kigali
Kampala
L.
Victoria
Nairobi
CABINDA
(Angola)
Kinshasa
BURUNDI
(1962, Belg.)
Bujumbura
TANZANIA
(1961, U.K.)
Dar es Salaam
SEYCHELLES
(1976, U.K.)
Luanda
L. Tanganyika
ATLANTIC
OCEAN
ANGOLA
(1975, Port.)
ZAMBIA
(1964, U.K.)
Lusaka
L. Malawi
Zambezi R.
COMÓROS
(1975, Fr.)
Moroni
MALAWI (1964, U.K.)
MAYOTTE (Fr.)
Lilongwe
Harare
MOZAMBIQUE
(1975, Port.)
Antananarivo
NAMIBIA
(1990, S. Afr.)
Victoria
Falls
ZIMBABWE
(1980, U.K.)
Mozambique Channel
MADAGASCAR
(1960, Fr.)
WALVIS BAY
(S. Afr.)
Windhoek
BOTSWANA
(1966, U.K.)
Limpopo R.
Gaborone
Pretoria
Maputo
Johannesburg
Mbabane
SWAZILAND
(1968, U.K.)
Orange R.
Vaal R.
Maseru
LESOTHO
(1966, U.K.)
SOUTH
AFRICA
Cape Town
INDIAN
OCEAN

Independent nation before 1945

Independent nation, 1945-1965

Independent nation since 1966

★ Capital city

Date of independence and former colonial power
are shown in parentheses.

0        500        1000 mi.

0    500   1000 km

Mercator Projection

# The Declaration of Independence

*In Congress, July 4, 1776*

## Introduction

When, in the course of human events, it becomes necessary for one people to dissolve the political bands which have connected them with another, and to assume, among the powers of the earth, the separate and equal station to which the laws of nature and nature's God entitle them, a decent respect to the opinions of mankind requires that they should declare the causes which impel them to the separation.

## Basic Rights

We hold these truths to be self-evident: that all men are created equal, that they are endowed by their Creator with certain unalienable rights; that among these are life, liberty, and the pursuit of happiness; that to secure these rights, governments are instituted among men, deriving their just powers from the consent of the governed; that whenever any form of government becomes destructive of these ends, it is the right of the people to alter or to abolish it, and to institute new government, laying its foundation on such principles, and organizing its powers in such form, as to them shall seem most likely to effect their safety and happiness. Prudence, indeed, will dictate that governments long established should not be changed for light and transient causes; and accordingly all experience hath shown that mankind are more disposed to suffer, while evils are sufferable, than to right themselves by abolishing the forms to which they are accustomed. But when a long train of abuses and usurpations, pursuing invariably the same object, evinces a design to reduce them under absolute despotism, it is their right, it is their duty, to throw off such government, and to provide new guards for their future security.

Such has been the patient sufferance of these colonies; and such is now the necessity which constrains them to alter their former systems of government. The history of the present King of Great Britain is a history of repeated injuries and usurpations, all having in direct object the establishment of an absolute tyranny over these states. To prove this, let facts be submitted to a candid world.

## Charges Against the King

He has refused his assent to laws, the most wholesome and necessary for the public good.

He has forbidden his governors to pass laws of immediate and pressing importance, unless suspended in their operation till his assent should be obtained; and when so suspended, he has utterly neglected to attend to them.

He has refused to pass other laws for the accommodation of large districts of people, unless those people would relinquish the right of representation in the legislature, a right inestimable to them, and formidable to tyrants only.

He has called together legislative bodies at places unusual, uncomfortable, and distant from the depository of their public records, for the sole purpose of fatiguing them into compliance with his measures.

He has dissolved representative houses repeatedly, for opposing, with manly firmness, his invasions on the rights of the people.

He has refused, for a long time after such dissolutions, to cause others to be elected; whereby the legislative powers, incapable of annihilation, have returned to the people at large for their exercise; the state remaining, in the meantime, exposed to all the dangers of invasion from without and convulsions within.

He has endeavored to prevent the population of these states; for that purpose obstructing the laws for the naturalization of foreigners, refusing to pass others to encourage their migrations hither, and raising the conditions of new appropriations of lands.

He has obstructed the administration of justice, by refusing his assent to laws for establishing judiciary powers.

He has made judges dependent on his will alone for the tenure of their offices, and the amount of payment of their salaries.

He has erected a multitude of new offices, and sent hither swarms of officers to harass our people and eat out their substance.

He has kept among us, in times of peace, standing armies, without the consent of our legislatures.

He has affected to render military independent of, and superior to, the civil power.

He has combined with others to subject us to a jurisdiction foreign to our constitution and unacknowledged by our laws, giving his assent to their acts of pretended legislation:

For quartering large bodies of armed troops among us;

For protecting them, by a mock trial, from punishment for any murders which they should commit on the inhabitants of these states;

For cutting off our trade with all parts of the world;

For imposing taxes on us without our consent;

For depriving us, in many cases, of the benefits of trial by jury;

For transporting us beyond seas, to be tried for pretended offenses;

For abolishing the free system of English laws in a neighboring province, establishing therein an arbitrary government, and enlarging its boundaries, so as to render it at once an example and fit instrument for introducing the same absolute rule into these colonies;

For taking away our charters, abolishing our most valuable laws, and altering fundamentally the forms of our governments;

For suspending our own legislatures, and declaring themselves invested with power to legislate for us in all cases whatsoever.

He has abdicated government here, by declaring us out of his protection and waging war against us.

He has plundered our seas, ravaged our coasts, burned our towns, and destroyed the lives of our people.

He is at this time transporting large armies of foreign mercenaries to complete the works of death, desolation, and tyranny already begun with circumstances of cruelty and perfidy scarcely paralleled in the most barbarous ages, and totally unworthy the head of a civilized nation.

He has constrained our fellow-citizens, taken captive on the high seas, to bear arms against their country, to become the executioners of their friends and brethren, or to fall themselves by their hands.

He has excited domestic insurrection among us, and has endeavored to bring on the inhabitants of our frontiers, the merciless Indian savages, whose known rule of warfare is an undistinguished destruction of all ages, sexes, and conditions.

## Response to the King

In every stage of these oppressions we have petitioned for redress in the most humble terms; our repeated petitions have been answered only by repeated injury. A prince whose character is thus marked by every act which may define a tyrant is unfit to be ruler of a free people.

Nor have we been wanting in our attentions to our British brethren. We have warned them, from time to time, of attempts by their legislature to extend an unwarrantable jurisdiction over us. We have reminded them of the circumstances of our emigration and settlement here. We have appealed to their native justice and magnanimity; and we have conjured them, by the ties of our common kindred, to disavow these usurpations, which would inevitably interrupt our connections and correspondence. They, too, have been deaf to the voice of justice and consanguinity. We must, therefore, acquiesce in the necessity which denounces our separation, and hold them, as we hold the rest of mankind, enemies in war, in peace, friends.

## Independence

We, therefore, the representatives of the United States of America, in General Congress assembled, appealing to the Supreme Judge of the world for the rectitude of our intentions, do, in the name and by the authority of the good people of these colonies, solemnly publish and declare that these United Colonies are, and of right ought to be, free and independent states; that they are absolved from all allegiance to the British crown, and that all political connection between them and the state of Great Britain is, and ought to be, totally dissolved; and that, as free and independent states, they have full power to levy war, conclude peace, contract alliances, establish commerce, and do all other acts and things which independent states may of right do. And for the support of this declaration, with a firm reliance on the protection of Divine Providence, we mutually pledge to each other our lives, our fortunes, and our sacred honor.

# The Constitution
## of the United States

### Preamble*

We the people of the United States, in order to form a more perfect union, establish justice, insure domestic tranquility, provide for the common defense, promote the general welfare, and secure the blessings of liberty to ourselves and our posterity, do ordain and establish this Constitution for the United States of America.

## Article 1
## The Legislature

### Section 1. Congress

All legislative powers herein granted shall be vested in a Congress of the United States, which shall consist of a Senate and House of Representatives.

### Section 2. House of Representatives

1. **Election and Term of Members** The House of Representatives shall be composed of members chosen every second year by the people of the several States, and the electors in each State shall have the qualifications requisite for electors of the most numerous branch of the State legislature.
2. **Qualifications** No person shall be a representative who shall not have attained to the age of twenty-five years, and been seven years a citizen of the United States, and who shall not, when elected, be an inhabitant of that State in which he shall be chosen.
3. **Representation per State** Representatives *and direct taxes* shall be apportioned among the several States which may be included within this Union, according to their respective numbers, *which shall be determined by adding to the whole number of free persons, including those bound to service for a term of years, and excluding Indians not taxed, three-fifths of all other persons.* The actual enumeration shall be made within three years after the first meeting of the Congress of the United States, and within every subsequent term of ten years, in such manner as they shall by law direct. The number of representatives shall not exceed one for every thirty thousand, but each State shall have at least one representative; *and until such enumeration shall be made, the State of New Hampshire shall be entitled to choose three, Massachusetts eight, Rhode Island and Providence Plantations one, Connecticut five, New York six, New Jersey four, Pennsylvania eight, Delaware one, Maryland six, Virginia ten, North Carolina five, South Carolina five, and Georgia three.*
4. **Vacancies** When vacancies happen in the representation from any State, the executive authority thereof shall issue writs of election to fill such vacancies.
5. **Impeachment and Other Powers** The House of Representatives shall choose their speaker and other officers, and shall have the sole power of impeachment.

### Section 3. Senate

1. **Number and Election** The Senate of the United States shall be composed of two senators from each State, *chosen by the legislature thereof,* for six years; and each senator shall have one vote.
2. **Overlapping Terms and Filling Vacancies** Immediately after they shall be assembled in consequence of the first election, they shall be divided as equally as may be into three classes. *The seats of the senators of the first class shall be vacated at the expiration of the second year; of the second class at the expiration of the fourth year; and of the third class at the expiration of the sixth year, so* that one-third may be chosen every second year; *and if vacancies happen by resignation, or oth-*

---

* Parts of the Constitution in italics are no longer in force or no longer apply. Headings have been added as a guide to reading the Constitution.

*erwise, during the recess of the legislature of any State, the executive thereof may make temporary appointments until the next meeting of the legislature, which shall then fill such vacancies.*

3. **Qualifications** No person shall be a senator who shall not have attained to the age of thirty years, and been nine years a citizen of the United States, and who shall not, when elected, be an inhabitant of that State for which he shall be chosen.

4. **Leader of the Senate** The Vice President of the United States shall be President of the Senate, but shall have no vote, unless they be equally divided.

5. **Other Officers** The Senate shall choose their other officers, and also a President pro tempore, in the absence of the Vice President, or when he shall exercise the office of President of the United States.

6. **Impeachment Power** The Senate shall have the sole power to try all impeachments. When sitting for that purpose, they shall be on oath or affirmation. When the President of the United States is tried, the Chief Justice shall preside: and no person shall be convicted without the concurrence of two-thirds of the members present.

7. **Penalties** Judgment in cases of impeachment shall not extend further than to removal from office, and disqualification to hold and enjoy any office of honor, trust or profit under the United States: but the party convicted shall nevertheless be liable and subject to indictment, trial, judgment and punishment, according to law.

## Section 4. Elections and Meetings

1. **Election of Congress** The times, places and manner of holding elections for senators and representatives shall be prescribed in each State by the legislature thereof; but the Congress may at any time by law make or alter such regulations, except as to the places of choosing senators.

2. **Required Sessions** The Congress shall assemble at least once in every year, *and such meeting shall be on the first Monday in December, unless they shall by law appoint a different day.*

## Section 5. Rules and Procedures

1. **Organization** Each house shall be the judge of the elections, returns and qualifications of its own members, and a majority of each shall constitute a quorum to do business; but a smaller number may adjourn from day to day, and may be authorized to compel the attendance of absent members, in such manner, and under such penalties as each house may provide.

2. **Rules of Conduct** Each house may determine the rules of its proceedings, punish its members for disorderly behavior, and, with the concurrence of two-thirds, expel a member.

3. **Record of Proceedings** Each house shall keep a journal of its proceedings, and from time to time publish the same, excepting such parts as may in their judgment require secrecy; and the yeas and nays of the members of either house on any question shall, at the desire of one-fifth of those present, be entered on the journal.

4. **Adjournment** Neither house, during the session of Congress, shall, without the consent of the other, adjourn for more than three days, nor to any other place than that in which the two houses shall be sitting.

## Section 6. Privileges and Restrictions

1. **Compensation and Immunity** The senators and representatives shall receive a compensation for their services, to be ascertained by law, and paid out of the treasury of the United States. They shall in all cases, except treason, felony and breach of the peace, be privileged from arrest during their attendance at the session of their respective houses, and in going to and returning from the same; and for any speech or debate in either house, they shall not be questioned in any other place.

2. **Restrictions** No senator or representative shall, during the time for which he was elected, be appointed to any civil office under the authority of the United States, which shall have been created, or the emoluments thereof shall have been increased during such time; and no person holding any office under the United States shall be a member of either house during his continuance in office.

## Section 7. Establishing Laws

1. **Tax Bills** All bills for raising revenue shall originate in the House of Representatives; but the Senate may propose or concur with amendments as on other bills.

2. **Procedure** Every bill which shall have passed the House of Representatives and the Senate, shall, before it becomes a law, be presented to the President of the United States; if he approve he shall sign it, but if not he shall re-

turn it, with his objections to that house in which it shall have originated, who shall enter the objections at large on their journal, and proceed to reconsider it. If after such reconsideration two-thirds of that house shall agree to pass the bill, it shall be sent, together with the objections, to the other house, by which it shall likewise be reconsidered, and if approved by two-thirds of that house, it shall become a law. But in all such cases the votes of both houses shall be determined by yeas and nays, and the names of the persons voting for and against the bill shall be entered on the journal of each house respectively. If any bill shall not be returned by the President within ten days (Sundays excepted) after it shall have been presented to him, the same shall be a law, in like manner as if he had signed it, unless the Congress by their adjournment prevent its return, in which case it shall not be a law.

3. **Role of the President** Every order, resolution, or vote to which the concurrence of the Senate and House of Representatives may be necessary (except on a question of adjournment) shall be presented to the President of the United States; and before the same shall take effect, shall be approved by him, or being disapproved by him, shall be repassed by two-thirds of the Senate and House of Representatives, according to the rules and limitations prescribed in the case of a bill.

## Section 8. Powers Delegated to Congress

1. **Taxation** The Congress shall have power to lay and collect taxes, duties, imposts, and excises, to pay the debts and provide for the common defense and general welfare of the United States; but all duties, imposts and excises shall be uniform throughout the United States;

2. **Credit** To borrow money on the credit of the United States;

3. **Commerce** To regulate commerce with foreign nations, and among the several States, and with the Indian tribes;

4. **Naturalization and Bankruptcy** To establish a uniform rule of naturalization, and uniform laws on the subject of bankruptcies throughout the United States;

5. **Money and Weights** To coin money, regulate the value thereof, and of foreign coin, and fix the standard of weights and measures;

6. **Counterfeiting** To provide for the punishment of counterfeiting the securities and current coin of the United States;

7. **Post Offices** To establish post offices and post roads;

8. **Copyrights and Patents** To promote the progress of science and useful arts by securing for limited times to authors and inventors the exclusive right to their respective writings and discoveries;

9. **Federal Courts** To constitute tribunals inferior to the Supreme Court;

10. **International Law** To define and punish piracies and felonies committed on the high seas, and offenses against the law of nations;

11. **War** To declare war, *grant letters of marque and reprisal*, and make rules concerning captures on land and water;

12. **Army** To raise and support armies, but no appropriation of money to that use shall be for a longer term than two years;

13. **Navy** To provide and maintain a navy;

14. **Military Regulations** To make rules for the government and regulation of the land and naval forces;

15. **Militia** To provide for calling forth the militia to execute the laws of the Union, suppress insurrections and repel invasions;

16. **Militia Regulations** To provide for organizing, arming, and disciplining the militia, and for governing such part of them as may be employed in the service of the United States, reserving to the States respectively the appointment of the officers, and the authority of training the militia according to the discipline prescribed by Congress;

17. **National Capital** To exercise exclusive legislation in all cases whatsoever, over such district (not exceeding ten miles square) as may, by cession of particular States and the acceptance of Congress, become the seat of the government of the United States, and to exercise like authority over all places purchased by the consent of the legislature of the State in which the same shall be, for the erection of forts, magazines, arsenals, dockyards, and other needful buildings; and

18. **Elastic Clause** To make all laws which shall be necessary and proper for carrying into execution the foregoing powers, and all other powers vested by this Constitution in the government of the United States, or in any department or officer thereof.

## Section 9. Powers Denied to Congress

1. **Slave Trade** *The migration or importation of such persons as any of the States now existing*

shall think proper to admit, shall not be prohibited by the Congress prior to the year one thousand eight hundred and eight, but a tax or duty may be imposed on such importation, not exceeding ten dollars for each person.

2. **Habeas Corpus** The privilege of the writ of habeas corpus shall not be suspended, unless when in cases of rebellion or invasion the public safety may require it.

3. **Unfair Punishments** No bill of attainder or ex post facto law shall be passed.

4. **Direct Taxes** *No capitation, or other direct, tax shall be laid, unless in proportion to the census or enumeration herein before directed to be taken.*

5. **Export Taxes** No tax or duty shall be laid on articles exported from any State.

6. **Ports** No preference shall be given by any regulation of commerce or revenue to the ports of one State over those of another; nor shall vessels bound to, or from, one State be obliged to enter, clear, or pay duties in another.

7. **Public Money** No money shall be drawn from the treasury, but in consequence of appropriations made by law; and a regular statement and account of the receipts and expenditures of all public money shall be published from time to time.

8. **Titles of Nobility** No title of nobility shall be granted by the United States: and no person holding any office of profit or trust under them, shall, without the consent of the Congress, accept of any present, emolument, office, or title, of any kind whatever, from any king, prince, or foreign State.

## Section 10. Powers Denied to the States

1. **Absolute Restrictions** No State shall enter into any treaty, alliance, or confederation; grant letters of marque and reprisal; coin money; emit bills of credit; make anything but gold and silver coin a tender in payment of debts; pass any bill of attainder, ex post facto law, or law impairing the obligation of contracts, or grant any title of nobility.

2. **Conditional Restrictions** No State shall, without the consent of the Congress, lay any imposts or duties on imports or exports, except what may be absolutely necessary for executing its inspection laws: and the net produce of all duties and imposts laid by any State on imports or exports, shall be for the use of the treasury of the United States; and all such laws shall be subject to the revision and control of the Congress.

3. **Additional Restrictions on States** No State shall, without the consent of Congress, lay any duty of tonnage, keep troops, or ships of war in time of peace, enter into any agreement or compact with another State, or with a foreign power, or engage in war, unless actually invaded, or in such imminent danger as will not admit of delay.

# Article II
# The Executive Branch

## Section 1. President and Vice President

1. **Term of Office** The executive power shall be vested in a President of the United States of America. He shall hold his office during the term of four years, and, together with the Vice President, chosen for the same term, be elected as follows:

2. **Electoral College** Each State shall appoint, in such manner as the legislature thereof may direct, a number of electors, equal to the whole number of senators and representatives to which the State may be entitled in the Congress; but no senator or representative, or person holding an office of trust or profit under the United States, shall be appointed an elector.

3. **Election Process** *The electors shall meet in their respective States, and vote by ballot for two persons, of whom one at least shall not be an inhabitant of the same State with themselves. And they shall make a list of all the persons voted for, and of the number of votes for each; which list they shall sign and certify, and transmit sealed to the seat of the government of the United States, directed to the President of the Senate. The President of the Senate shall, in the presence of the Senate and House of Representatives, open all the certificates, and the votes shall then be counted. The person having the greatest number of votes shall be the President, if such number be a majority of the whole number of electors appointed, and if there be more than one who have such majority, and have an equal number of votes, then the House of Representatives shall immediately choose by ballot one of them for President; and if no person have a majority, then from the five highest on the list the said house shall in like manner choose the President. But in choosing the President, the votes shall be taken by States, the representation from each State having one vote; a quorum for this purpose shall consist of a member or members from two-thirds of the*

*States, and a majority of all the States shall be necessary to a choice. In every case, after the choice of the President, the person having the greatest number of votes of the electors shall be the Vice President. But if there should remain two or more who have equal votes, the Senate shall choose from them by ballot the Vice President.*

4. **Date of Elections** The Congress may determine the time of choosing the electors, and the day on which they shall give their votes; which day shall be the same throughout the United States.

5. **Qualifications** No person except a natural-born citizen, *or a citizen of the United States at the time of the adoption of this Constitution,* shall be eligible to the office of President; neither shall any person be eligible to that office who shall not have attained to the age of thirty-five years, and been fourteen years a resident within the United States.

6. **Succession** In case of the removal of the President from office, or of his death, resignation, or inability to discharge the powers and duties of the said office, the same shall devolve on the Vice President, and the Congress may by law provide for the case of removal, death, resignation, or inability, both of the President and Vice President, declaring what officer shall then act as President, and such officer shall act accordingly, until the disability be removed, or a President shall be elected.

7. **Salary** The President shall, at stated times, receive for his services a compensation, which shall neither be increased nor diminished during the period for which he shall have been elected, and he shall not receive within that period any other emolument from the United States, or any of them.

8. **Oath** Before he enter on the execution of his office, he shall take the following oath or affirmation:—"I do solemnly swear (or affirm) that I will faithfully execute the office of President of the United States, and will to the best of my ability, preserve, protect and defend the Constitution of the United States."

### Section 2. Powers

1. **Military Powers** The President shall be commander in chief of the army and navy of the United States, and of the militia of the several States, when called into the actual service of the United States; he may require the opinion, in writing, of the principal officer in each of the executive departments, upon any subject relating to the duties of their respective offices, and he shall have power to grant reprieves and pardons for offenses against the United States, except in cases of impeachment.

2. **Treaties and Appointments** He shall have power, by and with the advice and consent of the Senate, to make treaties, provided two-thirds of the senators present concur; and he shall nominate, and by and with the advice and consent of the Senate, shall appoint ambassadors, other public ministers and consuls, judges of the Supreme Court, and all other officers of the United States, whose appointments are not herein otherwise provided for, and which shall be established by law: but the Congress may by law vest the appointment of such inferior officers, as they think proper, in the President alone, in the courts of law, or in the heads of departments.

3. **Vacancies** The President shall have power to fill up all vacancies that may happen during the recess of the Senate, by granting commissions which shall expire at the end of their next session.

### Section 3. Duties

He shall from time to time give to the Congress information of the State of the Union, and recommend to their consideration such measures as he shall judge necessary and expedient; he may on extraordinary occasions, convene both houses, or either of them, and in case of disagreement between them with respect to the time of adjournment, he may adjourn them to such time as he shall think proper; he shall receive ambassadors and other public ministers; he shall take care that the laws be faithfully executed, and shall commission all the officers of the United States.

### Section 4. Impeachment

The President, Vice President and all civil officers of the United States, shall be removed from office on impeachment for, and conviction of, treason, bribery, or other high crimes and misdemeanors.

## Article III
## The Judiciary

### Section 1. Federal Courts

The judicial power of the United States shall be vested in one Supreme Court, and in such inferior courts as the Congress may from time to time ordain and establish. The judges, both of the Supreme and inferior courts, shall hold their offices during good behavior, and shall, at stated times, receive for their services, a compensation which shall not be diminished during their continuance in office.

## Section 2. Authority

1. **General Jurisdiction** The judicial power shall extend to all cases, in law and equity, arising under this Constitution, the laws of the United States, and treaties made, or which shall be made, under their authority;—to all cases affecting ambassadors, other public ministers and consuls;—to all cases of admiralty and maritime jurisdiction;—to controversies to which the United States shall be a party;—to controversies between two or more States;—*between a State and citizens of another State;* between citizens of different States; —between citizens of the same State claiming lands under grants of different States, and between a State, or the citizens thereof, and foreign states, citizens or subjects.

2. **Supreme Court** In all cases affecting ambassadors, other public ministers and consuls, and those in which a State shall be party, the Supreme Court shall have original jurisdiction. In all the other cases before mentioned, the Supreme Court shall have appellate jurisdiction, both as to law and fact, with such exceptions, and under such regulations as the Congress shall make.

3. **Jury Trials** The trial of all crimes, except in cases of impeachment, shall be by jury; and such trial shall be held in the State where the said crimes shall have been committed; but when not committed within any State, the trial shall be at such place or places as the Congress may by law have directed.

## Section 3. Treason

1. **Definition** Treason against the United States shall consist only in levying war against them, or in adhering to their enemies, giving them aid and comfort. No person shall be convicted of treason unless on the testimony of two witnesses to the same overt act, or on confession in open court.

2. **Punishment** The Congress shall have power to declare the punishment of treason, but no attainder of treason shall work corruption of blood, or forfeiture except during the life of the person attainted.

# Article IV
# Relations Among States

## Section 1. State Records

Full faith and credit shall be given in each State to the public acts, records, and judicial proceedings of every other State. And the Congress may by general laws prescribe the manner in which such acts, records, and proceedings shall be proved, and the effect thereof.

## Section 2. Citizen Privileges

1. **Equal Treatment** The citizens of each State shall be entitled to all privileges and immunities of citizens in the several States.

2. **Extradition** A person charged in any State with treason, felony, or other crime, who shall flee from justice, and be found in another State, shall on demand of the executive authority of the State from which he fled, be delivered up, to be removed to the State having jurisdiction of the crime.

3. **Fugitive Slaves** *No person held to service or labor in one State, under the laws thereof, escaping into another, shall, in consequence of any law or regulation therein, be discharged from such service or labor, but shall be delivered up on claim of the party to whom such service or labor may be due.*

## Section 3. New States and Territories

1. **Admission Policy** New States may be admitted by the Congress into this Union; but no new State shall be formed or erected within the jurisdiction of any other State; nor any State be formed by the junction of two or more States or parts of States, without the consent of the legislatures of the States concerned as well as of the Congress.

2. **Congressional Authority** The Congress shall have power to dispose of and make all needful rules and regulations respecting the territory or other property belonging to the United States; and nothing in this Constitution shall be so construed as to prejudice any claims of the United States, or of any particular State.

## Section 4. Guarantees to the States

The United States shall guarantee to every State in this Union a republican form of government, and shall protect each of them against invasion; and on application of the legislature, or of the executive (when the legislature cannot be convened) against domestic violence.

## Article V
## Amending the Constitution

The Congress, whenever two-thirds of both houses shall deem it necessary, shall propose amendments to this Constitution, or, on the application of the legislatures of two-thirds of the several States, shall call a convention for proposing amendments, which, in either case, shall be valid to all intents and purposes, as part of this Constitution, when ratified by the legislatures of three-fourths of the several States, or by conventions in three-fourths thereof, as the one or the other mode of ratification may be proposed by the Congress; provided *that no amendments which may be made prior to the year one thousand eight hundred and eight shall in any manner affect the first and fourth clauses in the ninth section of the first article, and* that no State, without its consent, shall be deprived of its equal suffrage in the Senate.

## Article VI
## General Provisions

1. **Government Debt** All debts contracted and engagements entered into, before the adoption of this Constitution, shall be as valid against the United States under this Constitution, as under the Confederation.
2. **Supremacy** This Constitution, and the laws of the United States which shall be made in pursuance thereof; and all treaties made, or which shall be made, under the authority of the United States, shall be the supreme law of the land; and the judges in every State shall be bound thereby, anything in the constitution or laws of any State to the contrary notwithstanding.
3. **Loyalty to the Constitution** The senators and representatives before mentioned, and the members of the several State legislatures, and all executive and judicial officers, both of the United States, and of the several States, shall be bound by oath or affirmation to support this Constitution; but no religious test shall ever be required as a qualification to any office or public trust under the United States.

## Article VII
## Ratification

The ratification of the conventions of nine States shall be sufficient for the establishment of this Constitution between the States so ratifying the same.

Done in Convention by the unanimous consent of the States present the seventeenth day of September in the year of our Lord one thousand seven hundred and eighty-seven and of the independence of the United States of America the twelfth. In witness whereof we have hereunto subscribed our names.

[Signed by George Washington, president and deputy from Virginia, and representatives of twelve of the thirteen states.]

## First Amendment (1791)
## Speech and Religion

Congress shall make no law respecting an establishment of religion, or prohibiting the free exercise thereof; or abridging the freedom of speech, or of the press; or the right of the people peaceably to assemble, and to petition the government for a redress of grievances.

## Second Amendment (1791)
## Weapons and the Militia

A well-regulated militia being necessary to the security of a free State, the right of the people to keep and bear arms shall not be infringed.

## Third Amendment (1791)
## Quartering Troops

No soldier shall, in time of peace, be quartered in any house, without the consent of the owner, nor in time of war, but in a manner to be prescribed by law.

## Fourth Amendment (1791)
## Search and Seizure

The right of the people to be secure in their persons, houses, papers, and effects, against unreasonable searches and seizures, shall not be violated, and no warrants shall issue, but upon probable cause, supported by oath or affirmation, and particularly describing the place to be searched, and the persons or things to be seized.

## Fifth Amendment (1791)
### Rights of Accused Persons

No person shall be held to answer for a capital or otherwise infamous crime, unless on a presentment or indictment of a grand jury, except in cases arising in the land or naval forces, or in the militia, when in actual service in time of war or public danger; nor shall any person be subject for the same offense to be twice put in jeopardy of life or limb; nor shall be compelled in any criminal case to be a witness against himself, nor be deprived of life, liberty, or property, without due process of law; nor shall private property be taken for public use without just compensation.

## Sixth Amendment (1791)
### Right to a Fair Trial

In all criminal prosecutions, the accused shall enjoy the right to a speedy and public trial, by an impartial jury of the State and district wherein the crime shall have been committed, which district shall have been previously ascertained by law, and to be informed of the nature and cause of the accusation; to be confronted with the witnesses against him; to have compulsory process for obtaining witnesses in his favor, and to have the assistance of counsel for his defense.

## Seventh Amendment (1791)
### Jury Trial in Civil Cases

In suits at common law, where the value in controversy shall exceed twenty dollars, the right of trial by jury shall be preserved, and no fact tried by a jury shall be otherwise reexamined in any court of the United States, than according to the rules of the common law.

## Eighth Amendment (1791)
### Limits on Punishment

Excessive bail shall not be required, nor excessive fines imposed, nor cruel and unusual punishments inflicted.

## Ninth Amendment (1791)
### Powers of the People

The enumeration in the Constitution of certain rights shall not be construed to deny or disparage others retained by the people.

## Tenth Amendment (1791)
### Reserved Powers

The powers not delegated to the United States by the Constitution, nor prohibited by it to the States are reserved to the States respectively, or to the people.

## Eleventh Amendment (1795)
### Suits Against States

The judicial power of the United States shall not be construed to extend to any suit in law or equity, commenced or prosecuted against one of the United States by citizens of another State, or by citizens or subjects of any foreign State.

## Twelfth Amendment (1804)
### Election of the President and Vice President

The electors shall meet in their respective States, and vote by ballot for President and Vice President, one of whom, at least, shall not be an inhabitant of the same State with themselves; they shall name in their ballots the person voted for as President, and in distinct ballots the person voted for as Vice President, and they shall make distinct lists of all persons voted for as President, and of all persons voted for as Vice President, and of the number of votes for each, which lists they shall sign and certify, and transmit sealed to the seat of government of the United States, directed to the President of the Senate;—The President of the Senate shall, in the presence of the Senate and House of Representatives, open all the certificates and the votes shall then be counted;— The person having the greatest number of votes for President shall be the President, if such number be a majority of the whole number of electors appointed; and if no person have such majority, then from the persons having the highest numbers not exceeding three on the list of those voted for as President, the House of Representatives shall choose immediately, by ballot, the President. But in choosing the President, the votes shall be taken by States, the representation from each State having one vote; a quorum for this purpose shall consist of a member or members from two-thirds of the States, and a majority of all the States shall be necessary to a choice. And if the House of Representatives shall not choose a President whenever the right of choice shall devolve upon them, *before the fourth day of March next following*, then the Vice President shall act as President, as in the case of the death or other constitutional disability of the President. The person having the greatest number of votes as Vice President shall be the Vice President, if such number be a majority of the whole number of electors appointed, and if no person have a majority, then from the two highest numbers on the list, the Senate shall choose the Vice President; a quorum for the purpose shall consist of two-thirds of the whole number of senators, and a majority of the whole number shall be necessary to a choice. But no person constitutionally ineligible to the office of President shall be eligible to that of Vice President of the United States.

# Thirteenth Amendment (1865) Abolition

## Section 1. End of Slavery

Neither slavery nor involuntary servitude, except as a punishment for crime whereof the party shall have been duly convicted, shall exist within the United States, or any place subject to their jurisdiction.

## Section 2. Enforcement

Congress shall have power to enforce this article by appropriate legislation.

# Fourteenth Amendment (1868) Rights of Citizens

## Section 1. Dual Citizenship

All persons born or naturalized in the United States, and subject to the jurisdiction thereof, are citizens of the United States and of the State wherein they reside. No State shall make or enforce any law which shall abridge the privileges or immunities of citizens of the United States; nor shall any State deprive any person of life, liberty, or property, without due process of law; nor deny to any person within its jurisdiction the equal protection of the laws.

## Section 2. Number of Representatives

Representatives shall be apportioned among the several States according to their respective numbers, counting the whole number of persons in each State, excluding Indians not taxed. But when the right to vote at any election for the choice of electors for President and Vice President of the United States, representatives in Congress, the executive and judicial officers of a State, or the members of the legislature thereof, is denied to any of the male inhabitants of such State, being twenty-one years of age, and citizens of the United States, or in any way abridged, except for participation in rebellion, or other crime, the basis of representation therein shall be reduced in the proportion which the number of such male citizens shall bear to the whole number of male citizens twenty-one years of age in such State.

## Section 3. Penalty for Rebellion

No person shall be a senator or representative in Congress, or elector of President and Vice President, or hold any office, civil or military, under the United States, or under any State, who, having previously taken an oath, as a member of Congress, or as an officer of the United States, or as a member of any State legislature, or as an executive or judicial officer of any State, to support the Constitution of the United States, shall have engaged in insurrection or rebellion against the same, or given aid or comfort to the enemies thereof. But Congress may by a vote of two-thirds of each house, remove such disability.

## Section 4. Public Debt

The validity of the public debt of the United States, authorized by law, including debts incurred for payment of pensions and bounties for services in suppressing insurrection or rebellion, shall not be questioned. But neither the United States nor any State shall assume or pay any debt or obligation incurred in aid of insurrection or rebellion against the United States, or any claim for the loss or emancipation of any slave; but all such debts, obligations, and claims shall be held illegal and void.

## Section 5. Enforcement

The Congress shall have power to enforce, by appropriate legislation, the provisions of this article.

# Fifteenth Amendment (1870)
## Voting Rights

### Section 1. Right to Vote

The right of citizens of the United States to vote shall not be denied or abridged by the United States or by any State on account of race, color, or previous condition of servitude.

### Section 2. Enforcement

The Congress shall have power to enforce this article by appropriate legislation.

# Sixteenth Amendment (1913)
## Income Tax

The Congress shall have power to lay and collect taxes on incomes, from whatever source derived, without apportionment among the several States, and without regard to any census or enumeration.

# Seventeenth Amendment (1913)
## Direct Election of Senators

### Section 1. Method

The Senate of the United States shall be composed of two senators from each State, elected by the people thereof, for six years; and each senator shall have one vote. The electors in each State shall have the qualifications requisite for electors of the most numerous branch of the State legislatures.

### Section 2. Vacancies

When vacancies happen in the representation of any State in the Senate, the executive authority of such State shall issue writs of election to fill such vacancies: Provided, that the legislature of any State may empower the executive thereof to make temporary appointments until the people fill the vacancies by election as the legislature may direct.

### Section 3. Exception

*This amendment shall not be so construed as to affect the election or term of any Senator chosen before it becomes valid as part of the Constitution.*

# Eighteenth Amendment (1919)
## Ban on Alcoholic Drinks

### Section 1. Prohibition

*After one year from the ratification of this article the manufacture, sale, or transportation of intoxicating liquors within, the importation thereof into, or the exportation thereof from the United States and all territory subject to the jurisdiction thereof for beverage purposes is hereby prohibited.*

### Section 2. Enforcement

*The Congress and the several States shall have concurrent power to enforce this article by appropriate legislation.*

### Section 3. Ratification

*This article shall be inoperative unless it shall have been ratified as an amendment to the Constitution by the legislatures of the several States, as provided in the Constitution, within seven years from the date of the submission hereof to the States by the Congress.*

# Nineteenth Amendment (1920)
## Women's Suffrage

### Section 1. Voting Rights

The right of citizens of the United States to vote shall not be denied or abridged by the United States or by any State on account of sex.

### Section 2. Enforcement

The Congress shall have power to enforce this article by appropriate legislation.

# Twentieth Amendment (1933)
## Terms of Office

### Section 1. Beginning of Terms

The terms of the President and Vice President shall end at noon on the twentieth day of January, and the terms of senators and representatives at noon on the third day of January, of the years in which such terms would have ended if this article had not been ratified; and the terms of their successors shall then begin.

### Section 2. Congressional Sessions

The Congress shall assemble at least once in every year, and such meeting shall begin at noon on the third day of January, unless they shall by law appoint a different day.

### Section 3. Presidential Succession

If, at the time fixed for the beginning of the term of the President, the President-elect shall have died, the Vice President-elect shall become President. If a President shall not have been chosen before the time fixed for the beginning of his term, or if the President-elect shall have failed to qualify, then the Vice President-elect shall act as President until a President shall have qualified; and the Congress may by law provide for the case wherein neither a President-elect nor a Vice President-elect shall have qualified, declaring who shall then act as President, or the manner in which one who is to act shall be selected, and such persons shall act accordingly until a President or Vice President shall have qualified.

### Section 4. Special Cases

The Congress may by law provide for the case of the death of any of the persons from whom the House of Representatives may choose a President whenever the right of choice shall have devolved upon them, and for the case of the death of any of the persons from whom the Senate may choose a Vice President whenever the right of choice shall have devolved upon them.

### Section 5. Effective Date

*Sections 1 and 2 shall take effect on the fifteenth day of October following the ratification of this article.*

### Section 6. Ratification

*This article shall be inoperative unless it shall have been ratified as an amendment to the Constitution by the legislatures of three-fourths of the several States within seven years from the date of its submission.*

## Twenty-First Amendment (1933) End of Prohibition

### Section 1. Repeal

The eighteenth article of amendment to the Constitution of the United States is hereby repealed.

### Section 2. Upholding State Laws

The transportation or importation into any State, territory, or possession of the United States for delivery or use therein of intoxicating liquors, in violation of the laws thereof, is hereby prohibited.

### Section 3. Ratification

*This article shall be inoperative unless it shall have been ratified as an amendment to the Constitution by conventions in the several States, as provided in the Constitution, within seven years from the date of submission hereof to the States by the Congress.*

## Twenty-Second Amendment (1951) Limit on Presidential Terms

### Section 1. Two-term Limit

No person shall be elected to the office of the President more than twice, and no person who has held the office of President, or acted as President, for more than two years of a term to which some other person was elected President shall be elected to the office of the President more than once. *But this article shall not apply to any person holding the office of President when this article was proposed by the Congress, and shall not prevent any person who may be holding the office of President, or acting as President, during the term within which this article becomes operative from holding the office of President or acting as President during the remainder of such term.*

### Section 2. Ratification

*This article shall be inoperative unless it shall have been ratified as an amendment to the Constitution by the legislatures of three-fourths of the several States within seven years from the date of its submission to the States by Congress.*

## Twenty-Third Amendment (1961) Voting in the District of Columbia

### Section 1. Number of Electors

The District constituting the seat of government of the United States shall appoint in such manner as the Congress may direct:

A number of electors of President and Vice President equal to the whole number of senators and representatives in Congress to which the District would be entitled if it were a State, but in no event more than the least populous State; they shall be in addition to those appointed by the States, but they shall be considered, for the purposes of the election of President and Vice President, to be electors appointed by a State; and they shall meet in the District and perform such duties as provided by the twelfth article of amendment.

### Section 2. Enforcement

The Congress shall have power to enforce this article by appropriate legislation.

## Twenty-Fourth Amendment (1964) Ban on Poll Taxes

### Section 1. Voting Rights

The right of citizens of the United States to vote in any primary or other election for President or Vice President, for electors for President or Vice President, or for senator or representative in Congress, shall not be denied or abridged by the United States or any State by reason of failure to pay any poll tax or other tax.

### Section 2. Enforcement

The Congress shall have power to enforce this article by appropriate legislation.

## Twenty-Fifth Amendment (1967) Presidential Succession

### Section 1. Vacancy in the Presidency

In case of the removal of the President from office or of his death or resignation, the Vice President shall become President.

### Section 2. Vacancy in the Vice Presidency

Whenever there is a vacancy in the office of the Vice President, the President shall nominate a Vice President who shall take office upon confirmation by a majority vote of both houses of Congress.

### Section 3. Disability

Whenever the President transmits to the President pro tempore of the Senate and the speaker of the House of Representatives his written declaration that he is unable to discharge the powers and duties of his office, and until he transmits to them a written declaration to the contrary, such powers and duties shall be discharged by the Vice President as Acting President.

### Section 4. Determining Disability

Whenever the Vice President and a majority of either the principal officers of the executive departments or of such other body as Congress may by law provide, transmit to the President pro tempore of the Senate and the speaker of the House of Representatives their written declaration that the President is unable to discharge the powers and duties of his office, the Vice President shall immediately assume the powers and duties of the office as Acting President.

Thereafter, when the President transmits to the President pro tempore of the Senate and the speaker of the House of Representatives his written declaration that no inability exists, he shall resume the powers and duties of his office unless the Vice President and a majority of either the principal officers of the executive departments or of such other body as Congress may by law provide, transmit within four days to the President pro tempore of the Senate and the speaker of the House of Representatives their written declaration that the President is unable to discharge the powers and duties of his office. Thereupon Congress shall decide the issue, assembling within 48 hours for that purpose if not in session. If the Congress, within 21 days after receipt of the latter written declaration, or, if Congress is not in session, within 21 days after Congress is required to assemble, determines by two-thirds vote of both houses that the President is unable to discharge the powers and duties of his office, the Vice President shall continue to discharge the same as Acting President; otherwise, the President shall resume the powers and duties of his office.

## Twenty-Sixth Amendment (1971) Eighteen-year-old Vote

### Section 1. Right to Vote

The right of citizens of the United States, who are eighteen years of age or older, to vote shall not be denied or abridged by the United States or by any State on account of age.

### Section 2. Enforcement

The Congress shall have power to enforce this article by appropriate legislation.

## Twenty-Seventh Amendment (1992) Congressional Pay Raises

No law, varying the compensation for the services of the Senators and Representatives, shall take effect, until an election of Representatives shall have intervened.

# United States Presidents

| President | Born | Birthplace | Occupation or Profession | Political party | Served | Died |
|---|---|---|---|---|---|---|
| George Washington | Feb. 22, 1732 | Westmoreland County, VA | Planter | None | 1789–1797 | Dec. 14, 1799 |
| John Adams | Oct. 30, 1735 | Braintree, MA | Lawyer | Federalist | 1797–1801 | July 4, 1826 |
| Thomas Jefferson | Apr. 13, 1743 | Albermarle County, VA | Planter, Lawyer | Democratic-Republican | 1801–1809 | July 4, 1826 |
| James Madison | Mar. 16, 1751 | Port Conway, VA | Lawyer | Democratic-Republican | 1809–1817 | June 28, 1836 |
| James Monroe | Apr. 28, 1758 | Westmoreland County, VA | Lawyer | Democratic-Republican | 1817–1825 | July 4, 1831 |
| John Quincy Adams | July 11, 1767 | Braintree, MA | Lawyer | Democratic-Republican | 1825–1829 | Feb. 23, 1848 |
| Andrew Jackson | Mar. 15, 1767 | Waxhaw settlement, SC (?) | Lawyer | Democratic | 1829–1837 | June 8, 1845 |
| Martin Van Buren | Dec. 5, 1782 | Kinderhook, NY | Lawyer | Democratic | 1837–1841 | July 24, 1862 |
| William H. Harrison | Feb. 9, 1773 | Berkeley, VA | Soldier | Whig | 1841 | Apr. 4, 1841 |
| John Tyler | Mar. 29, 1790 | Greenway, VA | Lawyer | Whig | 1841–1845 | Jan. 18, 1862 |
| James K. Polk | Nov. 2, 1795 | near Pineville, NC | Lawyer | Democratic | 1845–1849 | June 15, 1849 |
| Zachary Taylor | Nov. 24, 1784 | Orange County, VA | Soldier | Whig | 1849–1850 | July 9, 1850 |
| Millard Fillmore | Jan. 7, 1800 | Locke, NY | Lawyer | Whig | 1850–1853 | Mar. 8, 1874 |
| Franklin Pierce | Nov. 23, 1804 | Hillsboro, NH | Lawyer | Democratic | 1853–1857 | Oct. 8, 1869 |
| James Buchanan | Apr. 23, 1791 | near Mercersburg, PA | Lawyer | Democratic | 1857–1861 | June 1, 1868 |
| Abraham Lincoln | Feb. 12, 1809 | near Hodgenville, KY | Lawyer | Republican | 1861–1865 | April 15, 1865 |
| Andrew Johnson | Dec. 29, 1808 | Raleigh, NC | Tailor | National Union | 1865–1869 | July 31, 1875 |
| Ulysses S. Grant | Apr. 27, 1822 | Point Pleasant, OH | Soldier | Republican | 1869–1877 | July 23, 1885 |

| President | Born | Birthplace | Occupation or Profession | Political party | Served | Died |
|---|---|---|---|---|---|---|
| Rutherford B. Hayes | Oct. 4, 1822 | Delaware, OH | Lawyer | Republican | 1877–1881 | Jan. 17, 1893 |
| James A. Garfield | Nov. 19, 1831 | Orange, OH | Lawyer | Republican | 1881 | Sep. 19, 1881 |
| Chester A. Arthur | Oct. 5, 1829 | Fairfield, VT | Lawyer | Republican | 1881–1885 | Nov. 18, 1886 |
| Grover Cleveland | Mar. 18, 1837 | Caldwell, NJ | Lawyer | Democratic | 1885–1889 | June 24, 1908 |
| Benjamin Harrison | Aug. 20, 1833 | North Bend, OH | Lawyer | Republican | 1889–1893 | Mar. 13, 1901 |
| Grover Cleveland | Mar. 18, 1837 | Caldwell, NJ | Lawyer | Democratic | 1893–1897 | June 24, 1908 |
| William McKinley | Jan. 29, 1843 | Niles, OH | Lawyer | Republican | 1897–1901 | Sep. 14, 1901 |
| Theodore Roosevelt | Oct. 27, 1858 | New York, NY | Author | Republican | 1901–1909 | Jan. 6, 1919 |
| William H. Taft | Sept. 15, 1857 | Cincinnati, OH | Lawyer | Republican | 1909–1913 | Mar. 8, 1930 |
| Woodrow Wilson | Dec. 29, 1856 | Staunton, VA | Educator | Democratic | 1913–1921 | Feb. 3, 1924 |
| Warren G. Harding | Nov. 2, 1865 | near Blooming Grove, OH | Editor | Republican | 1921–1923 | Aug. 2, 1923 |
| Calvin Coolidge | July 4, 1872 | Plymouth Notch, VT | Lawyer | Republican | 1923–1929 | Jan. 5, 1933 |
| Herbert C. Hoover | Aug. 10, 1874 | West Branch, IA | Engineer | Republican | 1929–1933 | Oct. 20, 1964 |
| Franklin D. Roosevelt | Jan. 30, 1882 | Hyde Park, NY | Lawyer | Democratic | 1933–1945 | Apr. 12, 1945 |
| Harry S. Truman | May 8, 1884 | Lamar, MO | Businessman | Democratic | 1945–1953 | Dec. 26, 1972 |
| Dwight D. Eisenhower | Oct. 14, 1890 | Denison, TX | Soldier | Republican | 1953–1961 | Mar. 28, 1969 |
| John F. Kennedy | May 29, 1917 | Brookline, MA | Author | Democratic | 1961–1963 | Nov. 22, 1963 |
| Lyndon B. Johnson | Aug. 27, 1908 | near Stonewall, TX | Teacher | Democratic | 1963–1969 | Jan. 22, 1973 |
| Richard M. Nixon | Jan. 9, 1913 | Yorba Linda, CA | Lawyer | Republican | 1969–1974 | |
| Gerald R. Ford | July 14, 1913 | Omaha, NB | Lawyer | Republican | 1974–1977 | |
| James E. Carter, Jr. | Oct. 1, 1924 | Plains, GA | Businessman | Democratic | 1977–1981 | |
| Ronald W. Reagan | Feb. 6, 1911 | Tampico, IL | Actor | Republican | 1981–1989 | |
| George H. W. Bush | June 12, 1924 | Milton, MA | Businessman | Republican | 1989–1993 | |
| William J. Clinton | Aug. 19, 1946 | Hope, AK | Lawyer | Democratic | 1993– | |

# A Chronology of Events

## POLITICS AND ECONOMICS

**1900** ILGWU aims to shorten 70-hour work week

**1901** Oil discovered in Texas

**1901** U.S. citizenship granted to Cherokees, Chickasaws, Choctaws, Creeks, Seminoles

**1904** Panama Canal begun

**1904** Northern Securities Company prosecuted for antitrust violation

**1905** Eugene Debs helps found International Workers of the World

**1906** Congress passes Pure Food and Drug Act and Meat Inspection Act

**1909** W.E.B. Du Bois helps form NAACP

**1912** Roosevelt forms Progressive party

**1913** 16th Amendment institutes income tax

**1914** Congress establishes FTC to stop unfair business practices

**1914** Panama Canal completed

**1914** World War I begins

**1916** Louis Brandeis is first Jewish Supreme Court justice

**1917** Immigrants required to pass literacy tests

**1917** U.S. enters World War I

**1918** World War I ends

**1919** American Communist party founded

**1920** 19th Amendment extends vote to women

**1922** Supreme Court rules Child Labor Law unconstitutional

**1924** National Origins Act restricts immigration

## ARTS AND LITERATURE

**1900** L. Frank Baum publishes *The Wonderful Wizard of Oz*

**1900** Theodore Dreiser's *Sister Carrie* appears

**1901** Scott Joplin composes "The Easy Winners"

**1902** Frank Lloyd Wright completes first "prairie style" home

**1904** George M. Cohan writes Broadway show *Little Johnny Jones*

**1904** Ida Tarbell publishes *The History of the Standard Oil Company*

**1906** Upton Sinclair's *The Jungle* appears

**1912** James Weldon Johnson publishes *Autobiography of an Ex-Colored Man*

**1920** Sinclair Lewis's *Main Street* becomes best-seller

**1922** Sinclair Lewis publishes *Babbitt*

**1922** Louis Armstrong joins King Oliver's Creole Jazz Band

## SCIENCE AND TECHNOLOGY

**1903** Orville and Wilbur Wright launch motorized airplane at Kitty Hawk, NC

**1913** Ford Motor Company begins operation of the world's first moving assembly line

**1915** First transcontinental telephone call

**1916** Electric clocks introduced

**1921** Albert Hull invents vacuum tube that produces microwaves

**1923** Coolidge gives first presidential message ever broadcast

**1923** DuPont manufactures first Cellophane

## DAILY LIFE

**1890–1920** Major period of immigration from southern and eastern Europe

**1907** Rauschenbusch publishes *Christianity and the Social Crisis*

**1908** Jack Johnson becomes first African American heavyweight boxing champion

**1909** Robert Peary and Matthew Henson are first to reach the North Pole

**1910** Boy Scouts and Camp Fire Girls established

**1912** Albert Louis makes first parachute jump from airplane in U.S.

**1917** Pulitzer Prize Awards instituted

**1918** U.S. begins Daylight Savings Time

**1919** RCA established

**1920** KDKA, first U.S. commercial radio station, begins broadcasting

**1922** First mechanical telephone switchboard installed in New York City

**1905**     **1910**     **1915**     **1920**

# 1900

**1928** U.S. signs Kellogg-Briand Pact outlawing war

**1929** Stock market crash begins Great Depression

**1932** First woman senator elected

**1933** Franklin Roosevelt becomes president; gives first fireside chat

**1933** New Deal begins

**1933** Frances Perkins becomes first woman cabinet member

**1935** CIO founded

**1935** Social Security Act passed

**1938** House Un-American Activities Committee established

**1938** Fair Labor Standards Act sets 40-hour work week

**1939** World War II begins

**1940** First peacetime military draft instituted

**1941** Japanese bomb Pearl Harbor; U.S. enters World War II

**1942** Congress creates Women's Auxiliary corps of army, navy, marines, air force, coast guard

**1942–1945** Japanese interned in U.S.

**1944** Roosevelt reelected to record 4th term

**1945** World War II ends

**1946** Cold war begins

**1948** Truman ends segregation in armed forces

**1949** Soviets get atomic bomb

---

**1925** F. Scott Fitzgerald publishes *The Great Gatsby*

**1925** *New Yorker* magazine first published

**1926** Dorothy Parker publishes her first book of verse, *Enough Rope*

**1927** *The Jazz Singer* becomes first talking motion picture

**1928** Walt Disney releases Mickey Mouse cartoon, first animated film with sound

**1930** Grant Wood exhibits *American Gothic*

**1931** Chester Gould introduces "Dick Tracy"

**1932** Jay Gorney and "Yip" Harburg introduce "Brother, Can You Spare a Dime?"

**1934** Benny Goodman organizes swing band

**1935** George and Ira Gershwin create opera *Porgy and Bess*

**1936** Teddy Wilson and Lionel Hampton integrate Benny Goodman's band

**1936** Margaret Mitchell publishes *Gone with the Wind*

**1937** *Snow White and the Seven Dwarfs* is first feature-length cartoon

**1939** Lillian Hellman's play *The Little Foxes* appears

**1941** Orson Welles directs and stars in *Citizen Kane*

**1942** James Cagney wins Oscar for his role in *Yankee Doodle Dandy*

**1943** Rodgers and Hammerstein produce *Oklahoma*

**1945** Dizzy Gillespie orchestra features bebop

**1945** Richard Wright publishes *Black Boy*

**1947** Williams publishes *A Streetcar Named Desire*

**1949** Miller publishes *Death of a Salesman*

---

**1926** Richard Byrd and Floyd Bennett make first successful airplane flight over North Pole

**1927** First TV signal transmitted

**1927** Charles Lindbergh flies nonstop across Atlantic

**1929** Kodak introduces 16-mm color movie film

**1930** Clyde W. Tombaugh discovers planet Pluto

**1930** Hans Zinsser develops effective immunization against typhus

**1930** Ernest O. Lawrence invents cyclotron, a particle accelerator known as atom smasher

**1932** First technicolor film developed

**1936** Boulder Dam completed, creating largest U.S. reservoir

**1938** National Cancer Institute established

**1939** Color television first demonstrated

**1939** Leo Szilard proves that chain reaction occurs during nuclear fission

**1942** Leo Szilard and Enrico Fermi produce first nuclear reaction and split atom

**1943** Salman A. Waksman discovers streptomycin; uses to cure tuberculosis

**1945** Atomic bombs dropped on Hiroshima and Nagasaki

**1946** John P. Eckert and John Mauchly develop electronic digital computer

**1948** Transistor invented

**1948** Research begun on peaceful uses for atomic energy

---

**1925** Charleston becomes popular dance step

**1925** Scopes tried

**1926** Gertrude Ederle swims English Channel

**1927** Babe Ruth hits 60 home runs in a season

**1929** Large-scale marketing of frozen foods

**1931** "Star-Spangled Banner" becomes official U.S. national anthem

**1933** 21st Amendment ends prohibition

**1935** Second New Deal begins

**1936** TVA brings rural electrification

**1941** Vitamins and minerals added to milk, bread, other common foods

**1942** U.S. rations food, fuel oil, gasoline

**1943** Jitterbug becomes most popular dance

**1946** Richard Byrd leads expedition to South Pole

**1947** Jackie Robinson becomes first African-American to play major league baseball in the 20th century

---

**1925**   **1930**   **1935**   **1940**   **1945**

# 1950

## POLITICS AND ECONOMICS

**1950** Korean War starts

**1950–1954** Red Scare grips U.S.

**1952** Puerto Rico becomes a commonwealth

**1954** Supreme Court rules segregated schools unconstitutional

**1955** King leads Montgomery bus boycott

**1955** U.S. begins economic aid to South Vietnam, Laos, Cambodia

**1959** Castro overthrows Batista in Cuba

**1960** First lunch counter sit-ins to force desegregation

**1960** Nixon-Kennedy campaign debates televised

**1961** 23rd Amendment gives vote to District of Columbia residents

**1962** César Chávez founds National Farm Workers Association

**1965** Immigration Act opens doors of U.S.

**1965** First U.S. combat troops to Vietnam

**1966** Congress passes truth-in-packaging law

**1966** NOW founded

**1968** King assassinated; riots in over 100 cities

**1968** AIM founded

**1971** 26th Amendment lowers voting age to 18

**1972** Watergate burglars arrested

**1973** Military draft ends

**1973** Cease-fire agreement ends Vietnam War

**1973** OPEC oil embargo

**1973** Supreme Court legalizes abortion

## ARTS AND LITERATURE

**1952** Ralph Ellison publishes *Invisible Man*

**1952** John Steinbeck publishes *East of Eden*

**1954** Marlon Brando and Eva Marie Saint star in *On the Waterfront*

**1955** Arthur Mitchell is first African American in major dance company

**1955** Jim Henson creates first Muppet, Kermit

**1956** Elvis Presley is most popular singer

**1958** Leon Uris publishes *Exodus*

**1960** Chubby Checker records "The Twist"

**1960** William Shirer publishes *The Rise and Fall of the Third Reich*

**1961** Joseph Heller publishes *Catch-22*

**1962** Bob Dylan records "Blowin' in the Wind"

**1964** Beatles begin performing in U.S.

**1966** Truman Capote publishes *In Cold Blood*

**1968** Stanley Kubrick wins Oscar for special effects in *2001: A Space Odyssey*

**1970** Donald Sutherland and Elliott Gould star in *M\*A\*S\*H*

**1973** Linda Blair stars in *The Exorcist*

**1974** Chicago's Sears Tower replaces New York's World Trade Center as world's tallest building

## SCIENCE AND TECHNOLOGY

**1951** Fluoride shown to reduce tooth decay

**1951** Rachel Carson publishes *The Sea Around Us*

**1951** Video camera developed for recording pictures and sound together

**1952** U.S. tests H-bomb

**1953** Jonas Salk develops polio vaccine

**1955** Severo Ochoa synthesizes RNA

**1955** Nuclear power produces electricity for public use

**1957** Soviets launch *Sputnik*

**1958** NASA established

**1958** Xerox Corporation produces first commercial photocopying machine

**1961** Alan Shepard becomes the first American in space

**1962** John Glenn becomes first American to orbit the Earth

**1963** Measles vaccine developed

**1964** Surgeon general links cigarette smoking with cancer

**1969** Neil Armstrong becomes first man on moon

**1970** EPA established

**1970** First Earth Day celebrated

**1971** C. H. Li synthesizes human growth hormone

**1971** Underground nuclear test explosion causes earthquakes in Alaska

**1972** DDT banned

**1974** Scientists suspect fluorocarbons to harm ozone layer

## DAILY LIFE

**1950s** Americans build bomb shelters

**1951** First commercial color TV broadcast takes place

**1956** Movies and movie stars first appear on TV

**1958** Jet planes used for commercial flights

**1959** St. Lawrence Seaway opens

**1960** Birth control pills become available to public

**1962** Johnny Carson begins hosting "The Tonight Show"

**1965** Riots erupt in Los Angeles, Chicago, and Cleveland

**1966** Uniform Time Act sets beginning and end of daylight-saving time

**1968** Movie ratings G, PG, R, X established

**1969** 3-day Woodstock Music and Art Fair held

**1971** Cigarette ads banned from TV

**1974** Hank Aaron breaks Babe Ruth's lifetime home run record of 714

| 1955 | 1960 | 1965 | 1970 |

# 1950

**1977** Carter pardons draft evaders of Vietnam War period

**1978** Carter assists in peace talks between Egyptian President Sadat and Israeli Prime Minister Begin

**1979** Iran holds U.S. citizens hostage

**1979** U.S. establishes diplomatic relations with People's Republic of China

**1981** Sandra Day O'Connor becomes first female Supreme Court justice

**1982** One million march for nuclear freeze

**1983** U.S. invades Grenada

**1986** Congress passes Immigration Reform and Control Act

**1987** Iran-Contra hearings begin

**1987** Stock market falls 508 points in one day

**1989** Berlin Wall falls

**1991** Multinational force liberates Kuwait after Iraqi invasion

**1991** Russian President Boris Yeltsin declares the formation of a Commonwealth of Independent States, saying the Soviet Union has ceased to exist. Mikhail Gorbachev, the last president of the Soviet Union, resigns

**1992** Multinational forces intervene in Somalia and the former Yugoslavia

WOMEN MAKE POLICY *NOT* COFFEE

---

**1975** Vincent Bugliosi publishes *Helter Skelter*

**1977** Alex Haley's *Roots: The Saga of an American Family* dramatized for TV

**1977** George Lucas directs *Star Wars*

**1978** Marilyn French publishes *The Women's Room*

**1980** 6th edition of *Grove's Dictionary of Music and Musicians* published

**1983** Alice Walker receives Pulitzer Prize for *The Color Purple*

---

**1977** Astronomers discover rings around Uranus

**1977** Fluorocarbon use banned

**1977** Saccharin consumption linked to cancer

**1978** AMA study links cigarette smoking to heart disease and lung cancer

**1979** Black hole discovered at center of Milky Way Galaxy

**1980** *Voyager 1* photographs Saturn's 13th and 14th moons and Jupiter's 15th and 16th moons

**1988** First patent granted on a form of animal life, for a genetically engineered mouse

**1990** Ellen Ochoa is first Hispanic woman to enter astronaut training

**1992** World leaders attend Earth Summit in Rio de Janeiro to forge multinational initiatives for protecting the environment

---

**1977** Energy crisis strikes U.S.

**1978** Gasoline is sold on odd-even days because of oil shortage

**1979** Nuclear accident at Three Mile Island; residents within 10–20 miles evacuated

**1980** Max and Kris Anderson make first nonstop balloon flight across North America

**1980** U.S. Olympics team boycotts summer games in Moscow to protest Soviet invasion of Afghanistan

**1980** Mt. St. Helens erupts several times

**1988** U.S. suffers worst drought in 50 years

**1988** Commission puts total U.S. AIDS cases at 61,000

**1989** *Exxon Valdez* oil spill damages Alaska shoreline

**1990** Twentieth anniversary of Earth Day celebrated

**1992** Hurricane Andrew devastates southern Florida

---

**1975**      **1980**      **1985**      **1990**      **1995**

2000

# Glossary

## A

**ABC powers** Argentina, Brazil, and Chile; in Woodrow Wilson's presidency, the ABC powers agreed to mediate between the United States and Mexico (p. 212)

**abolitionism** In the 1800s, the movement to put an end to slavery in the United States (p. 77)

**accommodation** The policy under which certain African Americans accepted the results of white racism in order to achieve economic success (p. 192)

**alien** A person who resides in a country but is not a citizen (p. 45)

**alliance** A pact or association of nations joined in a common cause (p. 214)

**Americanization** The adoption and absorption of the dominant culture of the United States, beginning with its language, its laws, and its government (p. 193)

**anarchism** Opposition to any form of government; the theory that all governments should be abolished (p. 248)

**amnesty** An act by which the government grants pardon for crimes to a large group of individuals, usually in response to the group's acts of consolation (p. 102)

**annex** To add or attach a new territory to an existing country (p. 204)

**antiwar movement** A movement led by college students to oppose U.S. involvement in the Vietnam War, using such methods as marches and "teach-ins" (p. 677)

**apartheid** In South Africa, an official policy of racial segregation (p. 785)

**appeasement** The policy of compromising or giving in to the demands of a hostile nation in the hope of maintaining the peace (p. 399)

**arbitration** A method of settling a dispute by agreeing in advance to accept the decision of an impartial outsider (p. 183)

**arms race** During the cold war, U.S. and Soviet competition in building up a supply of military hardware, especially nuclear weapons (pp. 478, 767)

**assimilation** The absorption of minority group members into the main culture of U.S. society; a process of taking in and absorbing, as nutrients into the body, or ideas into the mind (p. 631)

**Axis powers** In World War II, the alliance of Germany and Italy, and later Japan (p. 398)

## B

**baby boom** The unusually rapid population growth of the post-World War II period in the United States, lasting through the mid-1960s (p. 507)

**backlash** A strong, sudden reaction against an idea or policy (pp. 526, 691)

**balance of power** A condition in which the major powers are equal enough in strength to prevent the aggression of any and maintain the safety of all (p. 701)

**barrio** In a U.S. city, a mostly Hispanic neighborhood; in Spanish-speaking countries, a district of a town or city (p. 628)

**Big Stick** The U.S. policy of influencing hemispheric affairs through power, not words; from Theodore Roosevelt: "Speak softly, but carry a big stick" (p. 206)

**bilingualism** The use of two languages; the ability to use two languages with equal fluency (p. 631)

**biotechnology** The application of technology and engineering to biology, resulting in new developments in fields such as medicine and food processing (p. 808)

**black codes** Laws adopted in the South that severely restricted the rights of newly freed slaves (p. 103)

**black power** In the 1960s, a movement of African Americans that had as its goal to work for the economic, political, and social goals of blacks using black leadership and organization, without the help of whites (p. 586)

**black pride** Pride in being African American: pride in one's African ancestry and one's American nationality (p. 585)

**blacklisting** Efforts to brand people as communists and prevent them from holding certain jobs: from lists of people suspected of communist affiliation (p. 539)

**blitz** An intensive attack, often combining air and land forces, from the German *blitzkrieg*, or "lightning war"; in World War II, the German bombing raids on England (p. 405)

**bolshevism** A radical socialist ideology; from Bolshevik, the name of V.I. Lenin's left-wing majority party during the Russian Revolution (p. 230)

**boycott** An organized agreement not to buy or use a certain product or deal with a certain company, in order to exert pressure for change (pp. 132, 566)

**brinksmanship** Practice of attempting to keep the peace among nations by letting it be known that one will never back down and is prepared to cross the brink of war (p. 476)

**budget deficit** The situation that results when a government spends more money each year than it collects in taxes and revenues (p. 792)

## C

**cabinet** A body of persons appointed by the president to lead the various departments of government and to serve as the president's official advisors (p. 41)

**capital** Accumulated money or other material wealth that is devoted to the production of more wealth; material wealth acquired in business by an individual or company (p. 270)

**capitalism** An economic system based on open competition in a free market, in which individuals and companies own the means of production and operate for profit (p. 187)

**carpetbaggers** Northern opportunists who moved to the South and took advantage of unsettled post-Civil War conditions; scornfully dubbed *carpetbaggers*, after a kind of homemade luggage, because they had only what they carried (p. 108)

**Central Powers** In World War I, Germany and Austria-Hungary and their allies, Turkey and Bulgaria; opposed to the Allies (p. 213)

**charismatic** Possessing an unusual ability to win people's devotion and allegiance (p. 635)

**checks and balances** The system by which each of the three branches of government prevents the others from gaining excessive power (p. 37)

**Chicano** A Mexican-American (p. 435)

**CIA** Central Intelligence Agency; the agency of the federal government charged with matters of espionage; under President Harry Truman, the CIA's duties came to include certain covert operations that were deemed necessary to maintain national security (p. 484)

**circuit rider** In colonial America, a minister who traveled from church to church, following a regular route (p. 75)

**civil disobedience** A strategy for causing social change by means of nonviolent resistance to unfair laws (pp. 442, 571)

**civil liberties** Freedom to enjoy the rights guaranteed by the constitution of the state or nation (pp. 224, 444)

**civil rights** The political, economic, and social rights of a citizen; particularly, those guaranteed under the U.S. Constitution, such as the right to vote and the right to equal treatment under the law (p. 561)

**coalition** A temporary alliance (of nations, parties, etc.) formed for a specific action or purpose (pp. 599, 670)

**cold war** The U.S.-Soviet conflict that followed World War II in which the two powers avoided military confrontation but opposed each other's political and economic goals (pp. 465, 467)

**commune** A group of people who live communally, with collective ownership and use of property, often having shared goals, philosophies, and ways of life (p. 637)

**Conestoga** A large wooden wagon used by pioneers in moving west (p. 56)

**conscientious objector** A person who refuses military service because of moral or religious principles (p. 679)

**conscription** Compulsory enrollment in military service; the draft (p. 221)

**consensus decision-making** A management style, such as that of President Dwight Eisenhower, based on general agreement (p. 545)

**constitution** The basic and supreme laws of a nation, state, or society; a plan of government (p. 34)

**consumer price index** A measure of the change in the cost of goods and services as compared with their cost in a fixed time period; also called the cost-of-living index (p. 429)

**containment** After World War II, the U.S. policy of securing the peace by trying to contain communism, or keep it from expanding beyond its current borders (pp. 465, 655)

**corollary** A proposition added to another as a natural consequence or effect, such as Teddy Roosevelt's corollary to the Monroe Doctrine (p. 207)

**corporation** A group of individuals authorized by law to act as a single entity; a business owned by many investors (p. 270)

**corruption** Evil or morally unsound behavior, such as taking bribes (p. 168)

**covert operations** Secret or undercover government missions (p. 484)

**credit** A delayed payment plan in which a purchaser puts money down and pays the balance in installments; time allowed for payment of something sold on trust (p. 294)

**cultural diffusion** The spread from one cultural group to another of customs, ways of life, and other products of human thought and work (p. 638)

**culture of poverty** After World War II, the hungry, homeless, largely invisible members of a generally affluent American society (p. 514)

## D

**D-Day** June 6, 1944, the day the Allied forces landed on the beaches of Normandy, in France, leading to the defeat of Germany (p. 412)

**deferment** The postponement of a person's induction into military service for reasons such as health or occupation (p. 678)

**deficit spending** A government policy of borrowing money in order to spend more than is received in taxes (p. 437)

**demagogue** A leader who gains power by appealing to people's emotions and prejudices (p. 372)

**demobilization** The postwar process of dismissing the troops from military service and shifting citizens and businesses back to peacetime pursuits (p. 496)

**dependency** The condition of relying on (another nation) for support or aid (p. 720)

**depression** A period of extended and severe decline in a nation's economy, marked by low production and high unemployment (p. 328)

**détente** During the cold war, an attempt to lessen the tension between the United States and the communist powers (p. 701)

**direct primary** An election open to all voters in a party; in a direct primary, candidates are chosen by the voters rather than by the party leaders (p. 169)

**disarmament** The act or policy of reducing or destroying military weapons (p. 265)

**discrimination** The denial of rights because of someone's race, religion, age, sex, or other quality (p. 379)

**dissident** One who disagrees with established beliefs and policies; before Gorbachev's presidency, a citizen of the USSR who spoke out against Soviet policies (p. 756)

**dole** Money or goods given as charity; during the Great Depression, government relief payments; to be "on the dole" was to receive such payments regularly (p. 363)

**Dollar Diplomacy** During the William Howard Taft presidency, the government policy of encouraging the investment of U.S. capital in China (p. 207)

**doughboys** Nickname for the U.S. infantrymen in World War I (p. 221)

**draft** The selection of persons for a particular compulsory assignment; a system of selecting persons to serve in the military (p. 678)

**due process** The legal procedures that safeguard an individual's rights (p. 606)

## E

**electronic campaigning** A political campaign strategy in which a candidate attempts to influence voters through television ads (p. 772)

**electronic media** Forms of communication transmitted electronically and reaching the general public; primarily, radio and television (p. 548)

**emancipation** Freedom from bondage; particularly, freedom of African Americans from slavery (p. 77)

**Emancipation Proclamation** President Lincoln's official statement of January 1, 1863, declaring that all slaves in the states that were under Confederate control would be freed (p. 96)

**embargo** A restriction or stoppage of trade (pp. 46, 753)

**enfranchisement** Attainment of the rights of citizenship, especially the right to vote (p. 574)

**eugenics** In the early 1900s, a movement advocating an attempt to improve the human race by controlling hereditary factors in mating (p. 194)

**expansionism** The policy or process of increasing a nation's land area by acquiring new territory (p. 137)

**extended family** A family unit making up one household and including parents and children along with other relatives such as grandparents, aunts, uncles, and cousins (p. 628)

**external tax** A tax levied on goods coming into an area, such as the tax the British Parliament imposed on sugar entering the American colonies (p. 26)

## F

**fad** A sudden, short-lived enthusiasm for a style, product, idea, or activity (p. 295)

**Fair Deal** President Harry S. Truman's plan for the postwar United States, including greater involvement of the federal government in such aspects of life as health care and education (p. 532)

**fascism** A strongly nationalistic ideology, named for the Fascist Party of Italy; a government characterized by racism and militarism; a repressive one-party dictatorship (p. 397)

**federal regulation** Control by the Federal government rather than private interests (p. 382)

**Federalists** In the 1790s, followers of Alexander Hamilton; those who favored a strong federal government (p. 39)

**feminist** Activist who works for political, economic, and social rights for women equal to those of men (p. 615)

**filibuster** The tactic of making extended speeches to delay or prevent a vote on a piece of legislation (p. 577)

**foreclosure** The legal procedure for reclaiming a piece of property when the buyer is unable to keep up the mortgage payments (p. 336)

**frontier** In American history, the line where the settled area met the wilderness; the zone where land controlled by colonists met land controlled by Native Americans (p. 54)

**fundamentalism** In the United States, a Protestant movement characterized by the belief that the words of the Bible were inspired by God and should be interpreted literally and followed strictly (p. 307)

## G

**generation gap** The differences in values, tastes, and attitudes between members of different age groups, especially adolescents and their parents (p. 635)

**gerrymandering** Dividing the voting districts in a way that increases or decreases representation by a certain group or party (pp. 108, 605)

**GI Bill of Rights** Legislation passed by Congress in 1944 to provide World War II veterans with education and housing benefits (p. 496)

*glasnost* A Russian word for the policy of openness begun by Soviet President Gorbachev, encouraging free expression and an end to party censorship (p. 781)

**global economy** System of worldwide trade (p. 791)

**Good Neighbor policy** During the Franklin Roosevelt presidency, the U.S. policy of not interfering in the internal affairs of hemispheric neighbors (p. 396)

**Great Compromise** During the Constitutional Convention, the agreement by which both small and large states got part of what they wanted: two senators for every state and representatives based on the population (p. 38)

**gross national product** (GNP) The total value of all goods and services produced in a nation in a given year (p. 428)

**guerilla warfare** Fighting by small, independent bands, using such tactics as sabotage and sudden ambushes (p. 660)

**guru** In Hinduism, a person's spiritual teacher; any recognized leader or guide (p. 635)

## H

**hard money** Currency consisting of gold or silver coins as opposed to paper (p. 35)

**holding company** A company that "holds" other companies by owning controlling shares of stock in them (p. 181)

**holocaust** The slaughter of about 6 million Jews by the Nazis during World War II (p. 414)

**homestead** Land awarded by the U.S. government to settlers who would live on it and farm it for five years, under the Homestead Act of 1862 (p. 116)

**horizontal integration** The merger of competing companies involved in a strategic stage of an industry, such as oil refining, in order to dominate that industry (p. 125)

**human rights** Basic rights and freedoms assumed to belong to all people everywhere (p. 755)

## I

**immigrant** Person who enters a country to live there (p. 154)

**impeachment** Charges of misconduct brought against a public official (pp. 604, 709)

**impressment** The practice of forcing people into public service, as American sailors forced to serve on British vessels in the late 1700s (p. 44)

**industrialism** Replacement of agriculture with manufacturing as the main source of economic growth (p. 121)

**industrial productivity** The amount of goods produced in one hour of labor (p. 268)

**Industrial Revolution** The rapid shift from hand manufacturing at home to machine manufacturing in factories, including the economic and social changes that resulted (p. 65)

**inflation** A sharp, continuing rise in prices caused by too much money and credit relative to the available goods (pp. 428, 753)

**initiative** A reform that allowed citizens to introduce a bill to a legislature or to bypass the legislature and propose a new law by petition (p. 169)

**injunction** A court order requiring an individual or company to do something, such as end a strike (p. 133)

**interdependency** The condition of being dependent on, and supportive of, each other, as the United States and Latin America (pp. 731, 733)

**internal tax**  A tax levied on goods produced and consumed within an area, such as the stamp tax imposed by the British Parliament on the American colonies (p. 26)

**interventionism**  The policy of intervening, or interfering, in the affairs of another nation; in World War II, the position of those who opposed isolationism and believed the United States should give all possible support to the Allied forces short of war (pp. 406, 723)

**irreconcilables**  During World War I, a group of senators who opposed the idea of a League of Nations and could not be reconciled to voting for it (p. 235)

**isolationism**  Avoidance of conflicts and alliances with other nations; indifference to affairs outside the United States; at the beginning of World War II, a policy of forming no alliances and taking no sides (pp. 46, 406)

**Issei**  A first-generation Japanese American (p. 444)

## J

**judicial branch**  The part of the government that includes the court system (p. 37)

## L

**League of Nations**  An international association established to maintain world peace; started in 1920 during the Woodrow Wilson presidency (p. 232)

**legal repression**  The official restriction of dissent, often taking the form of punishment of those who openly express unpopular political opinions (p. 224)

**Lend-Lease Act**  The program by which the United States provided arms and supplies to the Allies in World War II before joining the fighting (p. 406)

**liberation theology**  The philosophy of a movement of Christian activists working for social justice, especially in Latin America (p. 723)

**limited war**  Beginning in the Truman presidency, the policy of avoiding global war by confining the fighting to one area and using conventional weapons, not nuclear power (p. 472)

**lynching**  A mob action in which a person is executed without a trial, often by hanging (p. 165)

## M

**machine**  A well-organized political organization that controls election results by awarding jobs and other favors in exchange for votes (p. 155)

**mandate**  A clear expression of the wishes of the voters, expressed in election results (p. 595)

**Manifest Destiny**  The idea popular in the mid-1800s that the United States had the right and duty to invade and occupy the entire continent of North America (p. 137)

**martyr**  A person who voluntarily suffers death rather than renounce religious principles; any person who chooses to die or endure great suffering for a cause (p. 584)

**mass media**  The methods by which information and entertainment are transmitted to large numbers of people; includes newspapers, television, and radio (pp. 295, 350)

**massive retaliation**  The cold war policy of the United States by which aggression against any ally would be met with an immediate all-out strike using nuclear weapons (p. 476)

**materialism**  Philosophy that places regard for money and material possessions over intellectual, spiritual, and artistic values (p. 304)

**McCarthyism**  In the mid-1900s, the use of intimidation and accusation in the name of anticommunism; later, labeling anyone who dissents from approved ideas as a traitor (p. 538)

**melting pot**  A society in which a number of racial, ethnic, and cultural groups are absorbed and blended together; from a literal vessel used for melting metals (p. 193)

**merger**  Combination of competing firms in a particular industry into a single larger company; any combination of several companies into one larger firm (p. 124)

**migration**  The movement of people from one country or region to another (p. 432)

**militant**  A person who is aggressive in promoting a cause (p. 574)

**Missouri Compromise**  A series of legislative agreements that allowed Missouri to be admitted to the Union as a slave state (p. 84)

**mobilization**  Preparation for war, including the efforts of both military and civilian personnel (p. 220)

**moratorium**  An official authorization to suspend payments, as of a debt; an officially authorized period of waiting (p. 362)

**muckraker**  A writer whose investigative articles or books attacked abuses such as child labor and corruption in high places (p. 162)

## N

**national debt**  In the late 1700s, the amount of money owed to Americans and to other countries after the American Revolution; the total amount of money owed by the federal government (p. 42)

**national liberation**  Freeing a nation from control by another nation (p. 654)

**national market**  The nationwide economic system made possible by the U.S. transportation network (p. 122)

**nationalize**  To turn the ownership or control of a property or industry over to the federal government (p. 723)

**nationalization**  The process of changing a property or industry from private to government ownership; after World War II, Iran's declaration that its oil fields, with their British-owned factories, were the property of the Iranian government (p. 485)

**nativism**  A preference for native-born Americans over immigrants (p. 194)

**nazism**  The fascist ideology of Adolph Hitler's Nazi Party, including strong nationalism, racism, and aggression (p. 397)

**neoconservative**  The conservative philosophy of the Reagan presidency that opposed excessive bureaucracy, federal spending, and government intervention in people's private lives (p. 760)

**neutrality**  The policy of remaining impartial in a dispute, including not taking sides in a war; the policy of remaining unallied (pp. 44, 213)

**New Deal** In the 1930s, President Franklin Roosevelt's program designed to bring about economic recovery and reform (p. 362)

**New Federalism** In the Nixon presidency, a series of programs designed to reduce the role of the federal government in people's lives and to return power and resources to state and local governments (p. 692)

**New Freedom** In the Wilson presidency, a program that sought to restore competition by breaking up the trusts (p. 188)

**Nisei** Second-generation Japanese Americans; the children of immigrants, the Issei (pp. 411, 444)

**nonviolent resistance** The act of demonstrating for a change in policy while refusing to fight authorities (p. 569)

**nullification** Before the Civil War, the right that some states claimed to reject, or render null and void, any federal law it believed violated the Constitution (p. 74)

## O

**oligopoly** The control of an entire industry, such as meat packing, by a few major producers (p. 270)

**Open Door** In the early 1900s, the policy of allowing all nations equal opportunity to trade with other nations, particularly China (p. 209)

## P

**perestroika** A Russian word for restructuring; Soviet President Gorbachev's name for his economic policy, which favors less government intervention and more private initiative (p. 781)

**Populist Party** A "people's party" made up of farmers who advocated certain reforms; the Populists ran a presidential candidate in 1892 (p. 128)

**pragmatist** A person who is concerned with practical solutions to problems rather than with ideas and theories (p. 596)

**progressives** Reformers of the early 1900s who worked to solve certain problems caused by industrialization and urbanization (p. 160)

**propaganda** A form of public information used to mold public opinion by employing techniques such as the use of emotionally charged language, name–calling, appeals to peer pressure, and the bandwagon approach (p. 223)

## R

**racism** The idea that one race is superior to others, and that race determines a person's character or ability; prejudice and discrimination toward members of one racial group, usually a minority (p 440)

**rank and file** Ordinary people as opposed to leaders (p. 224)

**ratification** Formal approval and acceptance (p. 35)

**rationing** A policy of limiting the use of certain essential goods in times of scarcity, such as war (p. 429)

**Reaganomics** The economic policies of the Ronald Reagan administration, based on supply-side economic theory and involving the reduction of taxes and federal spending (p. 762)

**reapportionment** A change in the number of legislative seats assigned to each district (p. 605)

**recall** A procedure that allows citizens to remove an elected official from office before the person's term ends (p. 169)

**recession** A period of declining productivity and reduced economic activity (p. 755)

**recharter** Allows (banks) to continue operating by an official act of the government (p. 76)

**Reconstruction** The years of rebuilding the nation after the Civil War; the southern states reorganized their governments and were restored to the Union (p. 102)

**referendum** A process by which citizens vote directly for or against a political proposal or bill (p. 169)

**reform** To change for the better by removing defects or malpractices (p. 168)

**repatriation** Return to a person's country of birth or citizenship (p. 339)

**representation** The right to be represented by delegates chosen in a free election; the election of officials who represent the views of a particular group (pp. 37, 629)

**reservationists** A group in Congress who approved the idea of the League of Nations with reservations; they would support it if certain modifications were made to the proposal (p. 235)

**resource management** The scientific management of natural resources (p. 180)

**revolution** The violent struggle to throw off the rule of a government; any sudden change (p. 29)

## S

**scientific management** A management theory using efficiency experts to examine each work operation and find ways to minimize the time needed to complete it (p. 278)

**scorched earth policy** Policy of breaking the enemy's will by destroying food, shelter, and supplies (p. 98)

**secede** To withdraw formally from the Union (p. 74)

**secession** The act of withdrawing formally from an organization or nation; in 1860 and 1861, the effort of southern states to withdraw from the Union (p. 92)

**Second Great Awakening** A revival in religious interest that swept the western frontier in the 1790s (p. 75)

**Second New Deal** The second stage of Franklin Roosevelt's economic recovery and reform program, which was launched in his annual message to Congress on January 4, 1935 (p. 373)

**sectionalism** Strong allegiance to local interests over those of the whole nation (p. 85)

**segregation** The enforced separation of racial groups in schooling, housing, and other public areas (p. 560)

**self-determination** The right of all people to decide what form of government they will live under (pp. 211, 631, 730)

**separatism** Position of groups like the Black Muslims, who opposed integration and called for separation of the races by having blacks return to Africa or live on separate land in the United States (p. 586)

**settlement house** A neighborhood center providing educational and social services to needy people, established between 1889 and 1910 (p. 165)

**sharecropping** A system in which landowners provide farmers with land, seed, and supplies in exchange for a share in the crop (p. 106)

**slave labor force** A group of people owned by a master and made to work without pay (p. 85)

**Social Darwinism** The application of Darwin's theory of evolution to human society (p. 126)

**social gospel movement** A movement emphasizing the application of Christian principles to social problems (p. 163)

**socialism** An economic theory advocating collective or government ownership of factories and other businesses instead of private ownership (p. 187)

**speculation** A risky business venture involving buying or selling a property in the hope of making a large, quick profit; making investments in the stock market (p. 327)

**speculator** A person who buys property, such as land or bonds, in the hope that its value will go up (p. 42)

**spoils system** An arrangement by which victorious parties or candidates reward their supporters with jobs, contracts, etc. (p. 74)

**stagflation** An unusual economic condition that combines a stagnant economy with rising prices (p. 753)

**standard of living** The material well-being of the individuals or groups in a society (p. 290)

**status symbol** A possession thought to reflect a person's wealth, prestige, or superior position in society (p. 347)

**strike** An organized work stoppage used to force an employer to meet certain demands, such as for better wages, hours, and conditions (p. 131)

**subsidy** A government grant of money to an individual or company for a purpose thought to benefit society (p. 364)

**suburb** A community at the edge of a large city (p. 152)

**suburbia** The suburbs of a city; the suburban culture (p. 504)

**suffrage** The right to vote (p. 170)

**syndicate** A chain of newspapers under central ownership; an agency that provides articles or features to a number of newspapers or magazines (p. 304)

## T

**tariff** A tax or fee on imported goods (p. 68)

**Teapot Dome Affair** In the Warren Harding presidency, a bribery scandal; famous ever since as an example of executive corruption (p. 261)

**temperance** Moderation in, or total abstinence from, the use of alcoholic beverages (p. 77)

**tenement** A city apartment building, often a crowded, run-down apartment building in the slums (p. 152)

**territorial integrity** Protection of a nation from the infringement on its land of another nation (p. 209)

**textile** Fabric, especially woven or knitted; cloth (p. 64)

**third world** The newly independent, developing nations in Asia, Latin America, Africa, and the Middle East (p. 483)

**totalitarian** (A government) controlled by a single person or party; suppressing freedom and controlling every aspect of life (p. 397)

**trade deficit** A gap in value between a country's imports and exports, in which the country buys more than it sells, creating an unfavorable balance of trade (p. 787)

**Triple Entente alliance** Before World War I, one of the two great European alliances, consisting of Britain, France, and Russia; also called the Allies (p. 214)

**Truman Doctrine** The belief of President Truman that communism was a worldwide threat, and the United States should meet it by helping all people whose freedom was threatened by communism (p. 466)

**trust** A consolidation of companies dominating an industry, controlling production and prices, usually formed for the purpose of reducing competition (pp. 157, 181)

**turnpike** A road on which travelers must pay tolls (p. 67)

## U

**unconstitutional** In violation of the Constitution (p. 46)

**undocumented immigrant** A person who lacks the legal papers necessary for residence in the United States (p. 628)

**unemployment** The condition of being out of work; the number of unemployed persons relative to the potential labor force (p. 339)

**union** Also **labor union** or **trade union**: a group of workers who are organized for the purpose of gaining better wages, hours, and other benefits (p. 131)

**unionization** The organization of the workers in a particular industry into unions (p. 371)

**urbanization** The growth of cities; the assumption of an urban way of life (p. 153)

**utopia** Perfect or ideal society (p. 76)

## V

**vertical integration** The effort of a firm to reduce costs by controlling all aspects of production in an industry, eliminating payment of independent suppliers (p. 125)

## W

**wages** Payment for work or services, usually on an hourly, daily, or piecework basis (p. 65)

**welfare capitalism** Programs adopted by employers in order to convince workers that they did not need unions; for example, providing employees with doctors and nurses and organizing employee athletic teams (p. 272)

**women's liberation** A movement by women to gain economic, legal, political, and social rights equal to those of men (p. 614)

**working poor** Members of the U.S. work force with earnings too low for them to rise above poverty (p. 795)

# Index

# D

McCarthy and, 538
Native Americans and, 520
*quoted* on bombing of Japan, 419
*quoted* on religion, 506
*quoted* on Sputnik, 481
Vietnam and, 655–656
Eisenhower Doctrine, 487
El Alamein, 412
Elbe River, 460
El Chamizal, 740
elderly, poverty among, 516–517
election laws, 168, 186
Electoral Commission, 109
electoral votes, vs. popular, 73, 92, 98, 797
electricity, 122, 268, 291, 348
    during New Deal, 359
    to rural areas, 374, 384, 385
    after World War II, 498
Elementary and Secondary Education Act, 600
Ellington, Duke, 303
Ellis, Clyde T., 348
"Ellis Island" (Bruchac), 21
Ellis Island, 580
Ellison, Ralph, 560
Ellsberg, Daniel, 698, 706
El Paso, 740
El Salvador, 629, 722, 723, 768, 785
    peace in, 786
emancipation, 77, 96–97
Emancipation Proclamation, 96, 198
embargo
    grain, 756
    oil, 752–755
    in World War II, 408
Embargo Act, 46, 65
"Emergence of a Republican Majority, The" (Phillips), 693
Emergency Relief Act, 332
Emerson, Ralph Waldo, 91
Emlen, Anne, 31
*Emperor Jones* (O'Neill), 305
Empire State Building, 270
*Empire Strikes Back, The*, 767
employment
    under Bush, 791–795
    in 1920s, 276–282
    in 1990s, 806–807
    statistics, 127
    of women. *See* working women
    during World War II, 428–429, 432–433, 437
    after World War II, 497, 499
    *See also* Equal Employment Opportunity Commission (EEOC); unemployment
Endangered Species Act, 801
*Ends of Power, The* (Haldeman), 697
energy crisis, 752–755
Enforcement Act, 104, 109
*Engel v. Vitale*, 604, 606
England, 11, 15
    colonists and settlers from, 7, 9, 10, 14
    explorers from, 6
    indentured servants from, 14
    New Amsterdam and, 12
    Spanish-American War and, 137
    *See also* Great Britain
English Channel, swimming the, 302
*Enola Gay*, 416
Enthoven, Alain, 673–674
environment
    acid rain and, 738, 740–741
    Bush and, 800–801
    Canada and, 738
    Carter and, 757–758
    Civilian Conservation Corps (CCC) and, 376–377
    Gore, Albert, and, 796
    Native Americans and the, 3, 4

prediction for future, 819
Reagan and, 763
Roosevelt, Theodore, and, 180–181
    during World War II, 434
Environmental Protection Agency (EPA), 692, 758, 763, 801
EPA. *See* Environmental Protection Agency (EPA)
Equal Employment Opportunity Commission (EEOC), 617, 622–625
Equal Pay Act, 616
Equal Rights Amendment (ERA), 620–621
ERA. *See* Equal rights Amendment (ERA)
Erie Canal, 52, 67, 70–71
Eriksson, Leif, 6
Erlichman, John, 705, 708, 709
Ervin, Sam J., 707, 708
*Escobedo v. Illinois*, 604, 606
Espionage Act, 219, 224, 225, 236
Estonia, 782
Ethiopia, Italian invasion of, 397
eugenics movement, 194
Euro Disneyland, 789
Europe
    Embargo Act and, 46
    Hitler and, 404–405
    immigrants from, 66, 116, 154, 193–195
    Monroe Doctrine and, 136–137
    trade with American colonists by, 7
    and United States, in early twentieth century, 210, 396–397
    Wilson, Woodrow, and, 211–213
    World War I and, 211–217, 234 *(map)*
    World War II and, 413–415 *(maps)*, 463, 466
    Yalta agreements and, 462
European Community (EC), 787
Europeans, 1, 6–9
Evans, Hiram Wesley, 310
Evans, Mari, 554
Everett, Edward, 61, 62
Evers, Medgar, 577
*Everything We Had*, 661, 700
evictions, 339–340
evolution, 307–308
Exodusters, 102
expansionism, 137–139, 204–205
    justified, 209
    *map*, 136
*Explorer I*, 546
explorers, 6–9, 54–56
Exports, Embargo Act and, 46

# F

factories, 64–69, 114
    assembly line in. *See* assembly line
    child labor in, 150, 164
    in 1800s, 122–126
    decline in employment in some, 291
    during Great Depression, 339–340
    in Mexico, 728
    New Deal and, 364–365
    in 1920s, 276–279
    in 1990s, 806
    during Progressive era, 167
    urbanization and, 153–154
    Wilson, Woodrow, and, 190
    worker safety in, 171
    in World War I, 223
    after World War II, 417, 497
fads, 295, 304
    in 1950s, 512–513
    in 1960s, 643
Fair Deal, 532
Fair Employment Practices Committee (FEPC), 442, 443–444
Fair Labor Standards Act, 375

Fall, Albert, 262
Falwell, Jerry, 760–761
families
    during Great Depression, 341–342
    in 1950s, 507
    during World War II, 429, 436
Family Assistance Plan (FAP), 692
Far East, trade with, 138
Farm Board, 330
Farmer, James, 574
Farmers' Alliances, 129
Farmers' Almanac *(photo)*, 12
farms and farmers
    African American, 9, 106, 108, 191
    American Revolution and, 28, 30
    change in, to manufacturing, 64–69
    in Civil War, 98
    in colonial America, 10, 13, 14
    as Democrats, 75
    Dust Bowl, 336, 351
    in 1800s, 128–131
    factories and, 64–65
    frontier, 57, *(graph)* 57
    during Great Depression, 329, 330, 336–339
    liquor tax and, 43
    machinery on, 122, 153, 291
    migrant, 519
    migration from Great Plains to California by, 336–337
    Native American, 4
    in 1920s, 291
    in 1950s, 500
    in 1990s, 806
    New Deal and, 370
    *painting* of, 382
    plantations and, 9. *See also* plantations
    poverty among, 517
    Reagan and, 762
    rebellion led by Daniel Shays, 36
    Second New Deal and, 374
    subsidies for, 374
    tenant. *See* tenant farmers
    TVA and, 365
    World War II and, 428, 432
    *See also* agriculture
Farragut, David, 96
fascists, 397
fashion
    in automobiles, 293
    in clothes, 291, 295
    fads, 295
    in 1950s, 512
    in 1960s, 638
Faubus, Orval, 564
Faulk, John Henry, 539
Faulkner, William, 305
Federal Bureau of Investigation (FBI)
    New Left and, 683
    Nixon and, 693, 705
"Federal city," 42
Federal Civil Defense Administration (FCDA), 473–474
Federal Communications Commission (FCC), 763, 808
Federal Deposit Insurance Corporation (FDIC), 366, 794
Federal Election Campaign Act, 710
Federal Emergency Relief Administration (FERA), 363, 380
Federal Employee Loyalty Program, 536
Federalists, 39–40, 41, 44, 45
    Marshall, John, and, 45–46
    as Whigs, 75
federal regulation. *See* regulation, business
Federal Reserve Bank, 792
Federal Reserve Board, 190
Federal Trade Commission (FTC), 190, 262, 270
Feis, Herbert, 264

Johnson, Andrew, and, 105
*See also* Congress
House Un-American Activities Committee
    (HUAC), 534–543
housing
    under Eisenhower, 547
    under Fair Deal of Truman, 532
    GI Bill and, 498
    under Johnson, Lyndon, 600, 601
    in 1950s, 498, 502–503, 517
    during World War II, 433–434
Housing Act, 532
Housing and Urban Development (HUD),
    Department of, 601
Houston, 270, 501
Hovenden, Thomas, 82
Howard, O. O. *(photo)*, 107
Howard University, 305
    Law School, 562
*How the Other Half Lives* (Riis), 152
HUD. *See* Housing and Urban Develop-
    ment (HUD), Department of
Hudson, Henry, 7
Hudson River, 7, 67
Hue, 657
Huerta, Dolores, 612
Huerta, Victoriano, 212
Hughes, Charles E., 216, 261, 265
Hughes, Langston, 245, 305–306, 587
Hugo, Victor, 578
Hull, Cordell, 408
Hull House, 160, 164, 165
human rights, 755–756
Humphrey, Hubert, 585, 668–671
    Nixon vs., 702, 703
Humphrey, William E., 270
Hundred Days, 362–366
Hungary, 249, 462, 478
hunger, in Civil War, 97
hunger strikes, 255
Hunt, E. Howard, 706
hunter-gatherers, 1, 2–3
hunting, 2–3, 4, 5, 57. *See also* trapping
Huron Native Americans, 5, 7
Hurston, Zora Neale, 306
Hussein, Saddam, 784–785
Huston, Tom, 705
Hyde Park, New York, 606

## I

"I Am a Veteran of Vietnam" (Halpern), 651
IBM, 499
Ice Age, 2
ice fishing, 5
Ickes, Harold, 380
"If We Must Die" (McKay), 306
*Il Duce*, 397
Illinois, 56, 217
*Illinois*, 217
Illinois River, 70
Illiteracy, 172
"I Love Lucy," 521
"Immigrant Experience, The" (Olivas), 555
immigrants
    African Americans and, 191
    as Democrats, 75
    Ford, Henry, and, 277
    Ku Klux Klan and, 310
    and melting pot, 193–194
    in 1990s, 803–804
    Palmer raids and, 250–251
    political reform and, 168
    during Progressive era, 193–195
    progressives and, 191, 197
    rural America and, 311–312
    undocumented, 628, 629, 630, 803

after World War I, 248
immigration
    effects of, 608–609
    illegal, 519
    Johnson, Lyndon, and, 601
    Latin America and, 725
    Populist Party and, 128
    restrictions on, 193–195, 312, 313
    to U.S. cities, 154
Immigration Act of 1965, 608–609, 803
Immigration and Naturalization Service
    (INS), 629–630
Immigration Reform and Control Act, 803
impeachment, 105, 709
imperialism, 205
implied powers, 42
impoundment, 692, 710
impressment, 44, 45
indentured servants, 9, 12, 13, 14
India, 469
Indiana, 58, 310
Indian Bureau, 382
Indian Claims Commission (ICC), 632, 633
Indian Removal Act, 61–63
Indian Reorganization Act, 381–382
indigo, 8, 11, 14
Indochina, 408, 654–655
Indonesia, 469
"industrial democracy," 273
Industrial Revolution, 65–69, 197
Industrial Workers of the World (IWW),
    197, 224–225, 257
industry
    automobiles and, 291–292
    baby boom and, 507
    deregulation of, 762–763
    under Ford, 752–755
    Great Depression and, 329
    horizontal and vertical integration of, 125
    in late 1800s, 121–126, 157
    New Deal and, 364–365
    in 1920s, 268–273, 290–293
    in World War II, 412, 428
    after World War II, 417, 497–501
    *See also* business
inflation
    under Ford, 753, 754–755
    under Reagan, 762
    in World War II, 428–429
    after World War II, 527
initiative, 169, 187
Innes, William T., 653
Inouye, Daniel K., 769
INS. *See* Immigration and Naturalization
    Service (INS)
insurance, 272
interdependency, 731
interest rates
    under Bush, 792
    under Reagan, 762
Interim Committee, 419, 420
Internal Revenue Service (IRS), Nixon and,
    693, 705
Interstate Commerce Commission, 262
    segregation and, 574
interstate highway system, 500, 546–547
interventionism, 406, 426, 723–724
Inuit, 632
inventions, 122
*Invisible Man* (Ellison), 560
*Invisible Scar, The* (Bird), 340
Iran
    Eisenhower and, 483
    hostage crisis, 757, 769–770
Iran-contra scandal, 769–770
Iraq, 784–785
Ireland, immigrants from, 14, 45, 66, 154, 193
Ireland, Sam, 178
iron, 11, 121, 122, 125
iron curtain, 460–462, 465

Iroquois Confederacy, 5
irreconcilables, 235
irrigation, by Native Americans, 4
isolationism, 46, 235, 236
    World War II and, 406, 426
Israel, 756–757, 785
Issei, 444
Italy
    immigrants from, 154
    Treaty of Versailles and, 233–234
    World War I and, 213
    World War II and, 397, 412
    *See also* Mussolini, Benito
Iwo Jima, 415
IWW. *See* Industrial Workers of the World
    (IWW)

## J

Jackson, Andrew, 46, 72–75
    Cherokee and, 61, 62, 63
    election of, as president, 73–74
    Second Bank of the United States, 189
    veto by, 69
Jackson, Mahalia, 577
Jackson, William, 38
Jackson State University, 683
jails, in colonial America, 10
Jamaica, African Americans from, 253, 306
Jamestown, 7
Japan
    automobiles from, 754
    China and, 209, 470
    immigrants from, 194, 210, 310
    Pearl Harbor attack by, 409, 410, 426–427
    Russia and, 209–210
    trade with, 138, 408, 411
    Treaty of Versailles and, 234–235
    Vietnam and, 654
    World War II and, 394, 400–401, 415–417
Japanese Americans
    internment of, 444–446, 448–449
    in World War II, 411, 444–446, 448–449
Jaworski, Leon, 709
Jay, John, 30
    French Revolution and, 44–45
Jazz Age, 284–285, 300–306
*Jazz Singer, The*, 300
Jefferson, Thomas, 29, 34, 40, 42–45
    Lewis and Clark expedition and, 54
    New Orleans and, 55
    as president, 41, 45, 48, 49
    *quoted*, 41, 44
Jesus, 267, 269
Jews
    and anti-Semitism during 1930s, 372
    concentration camps and, 414
    Hitler and, 397, 414
    holocaust involving, 414
    immigration of, 154, 194
    Ku Klux Klan and, 310
    Nazis and, 402, 403, 414
    *poem* regarding feelings of, 393
    Star of David and, 403
Jiang Jieshi, 400, 469–470
"Jim Crow" laws, 191–192, 193
jitterbuggers, 438
*Job, The* (Lewis), 282
Job Corps, 692
John, Jasper, 649
Johnson, Andrew, 102–107
Johnson, Charles S. *(photo)*, 306
Johnson, Hiram, 235
Johnson, Lyndon B., 599–601
    Canada and, 736
    civil rights and, 577–579, 585, 588
    Great Society of, 589–601

## S

# Credits